BLACK LITERATURE
CRITICISM

BLACK LITERATURE

CRITICISM

Excerpts from Criticism of the Most Significant Works
of Black Authors over the Past 200 Years

VOLUME 3: Marshall-Young

INDEXES

James P. Draper, Editor

Gale Research Inc. • DETROIT • LONDON

STAFF

James P. Draper, *Editor*

Andrea M. Gacki, Kyung-Sun Lim, *Assistant Editors, Black Literature Criticism*

Robyn Young, *Contributing Editor*

Cathy Falk, Marie Lazzari, Sean R. Pollock, David Segal, Bridget Travers,
Contributing Associate Editors

Jennifer Brostrom, John P. Daniel, Judy Galens, Tina Grant, Alan Hedblad, Elizabeth P. Henry,
Andrew M. Kalasky, Christopher K. King, Susan M. Peters, James Poniewozik, Johannah Rodgers,
Mark Swartz, Janet M. Witalec, *Contributing Assistant Editors*

Jeanne A. Gough, *Permissions & Production Manager*

Linda M. Pugliese, *Production Supervisor*
Maureen Puhl, Jennifer VanSickle, *Editorial Associates*
Donna Craft, Paul Lewon, Lorna Mabunda, Camille Robinson, Sheila Walencewicz, *Editorial Assistants*

Maureen Richards, *Research Supervisor*
Paula Cutcher-Jackson, Judy L. Gale, Robin Lupa, Mary Beth McElmeel, *Editorial Associates*
Tamara C. Nott, *Editorial Assistant*

Sandra C. Davis, *Permissions Supervisor (Text)*
Josephine M. Keene, Denise M. Singleton, Kimberly F. Smilay, *Permissions Associates*
Maria L. Franklin, Michele Lonoconus, Shelly Rakoczy (Co-op), Shalice Shah, Nancy K. Sheridan,
Rebecca A. Stanko, *Permissions Assistants*

Margaret A. Chamberlain, *Permissions Supervisor (Pictures)*
Pamela A. Hayes, *Permissions Associate*
Nancy M. Rattenbury, Keith Reed, *Permissions Assistants*

Mary Beth Trimper, *Production Manager*
Mary Winterhalter, *Production Assistant*

Arthur Chartow, *Art Director*
C. J. Jonik, *Keyliner*
Kathleen A. Mouzakis, *Graphic Designer*

The paper used in this publication meets the minimum requirements
of American National Standard for Information Sciences—Permanence Paper for Printed Library Materials, ANSI Z39.48-1984. ∞™

Copyright © 1992
Gale Research Inc.
835 Penobscot Building
Detroit, MI 48226-4094

ISBN 0-8103-7929-5 (3-volume set)
ISBN 0-8103-7932-5 (Volume 3)
A CIP catalogue record for this book is available from the British Library

Printed in the United States of America

Published simultaneously in the United Kingdom
by Gale Research International Limited
(An affiliated company of Gale Research Inc.)

Contents of Volume 3

Introduction ix

List of Authors Included xiii

Acknowledgments xvii

Paule Marshall 1929-
In her first work, *Brown Girl, Brownstones*, American novelist Marshall depicted
a young black girl's increasing sexual awareness and search for identity 1363

Claude McKay 1889-1948
Jamaican-born American poet McKay was a forerunner of the militant spirit
behind the Harlem Renaissance and the civil rights movement, evidenced in his
poem "If We Must Die": "If we must die, O let us nobly die. . ./ Like men we'll
face the murderous, cowardly pack,/ Pressed to the wall, dying, but fighting
back!" 1375

Ron Milner 1938-
American dramatist Milner affirmed family values in the play *What the Wine
Sellers Buy*, in which Rico—a pimp and hustler—tempts those around him to
trade morality for material gain 1402

Thomas Mofolo 1876-1948
The first great figure of modern African literature, Lesothan novelist Mofolo
wrote about the legendary Zulu warrior Chaka in *Chaka*, an epic tragedy of
paramount literary and historical significance 1410

Toni Morrison 1931-
One of the most important American novelists of the twentieth century,
Morrison won the Pulitzer Prize for *Beloved*, the story of a former slave's
daughter who returns from the grave to seek revenge for her brutal death 1422

Ezekiel Mphahlele 1919-
While in self-imposed exile in Nigeria, South African writer Mphahlele published
Down Second Avenue, which has been called "the autobiography of most
Africans" 1446

S. E. K. Mqhayi 1875-1945
Regarded as perhaps the last great tribal bard, South African writer Mqhayi was
deemed *imbongi yesizwe*—poet laureate of his people—for his *izibongo*, or
traditional African lyric poetry composed in the Xhosa language 1459

Walter Dean Myers 1937-
Although he grew up with the idea that "writing had no practical value for a black
child," American author Myers went on to publish several award-winning novels
for black teens, including *Fast Sam, Cool Clyde, and Stuff* and *It Ain't All for
Nothin'* 1469

Gloria Naylor 1950-
Focusing on seven black female residents of Brewster Place—a dilapidated ghetto
neighborhood—Naylor immortalized the spirit she admired in her mother, aunt,
and grandmother in the novel *The Women of Brewster Place* 1482

Ngugi wa Thiong'o 1938-

Author of *Weep Not, Child*, the first English-language novel to be published by an East African, Ngugi later rejected Western influences and insisted on writing in indigenous African languages 1495

Lewis Nkosi 1936-

In *Mating Birds*—a novel that has been viewed as an indictment of apartheid in the author's native South Africa—Nkosi wrote about a young Zulu student who is about to be hanged for allegedly raping a white woman 1515

Christopher Okigbo 1932-1967

Often called Africa's finest poet, Okigbo was committed to social justice in writing and in deed: at the outbreak of the Nigerian Civil War in 1967, he was killed in action as a member of the Biafran Army 1522

Sembène Ousmane 1923-

When he realized that his fiction reached only a limited audience in his native Senegal, Ousmane became a filmmaker; he wrote and directed *Mandabi*, the first African movie to reach an international audience 1531

Gordon Parks 1912-

Regarded as a modern Renaissance man for his pioneering accomplishments in several fields, Parks wrote, directed, produced, and composed the musical score for the film *The Learning Tree*, a work based on his autobiographical novel of the same title 1551

Okot p'Bitek 1931-1982

Ugandan writer p'Bitek pleaded for the preservation of the cultural tradition of his native Acholi people in his prose poem *Song of Lawino* 1559

Adam Clayton Powell, Jr. 1908-1972

A flamboyant and controversial U.S. Congressman from New York, Powell made enormous political gains for black Americans, documenting his views on American race relations in *Marching Blacks* and *Keep the Faith, Baby!* 1581

Dudley Randall 1914-

Called Detroit's First Poet Laureate, Randall founded Broadside Press, a Michigan-based publishing company that helped launch the careers of many black poets. A renowned poet himself, he is the author of *Cities Burning* and *After the Killing* 1592

Ishmael Reed 1938-

Proponent of Neo-HooDooism—a concept that incorporates aspects of voodoo and other cultural traditions into literature—novelist and poet Reed satirized American political and social systems in *Yellow Back Radio Broke-Down*, *Mumbo Jumbo*, and *Reckless Eyeballing* 1608

Jacques Roumain 1907-1944

With the poetry collection *Ebony Wood* and the novel *Masters of the Dew*, Haitian writer Roumain introduced to literature the distinctive psychological viewpoint of the Afro-Haitian 1627

Sonia Sanchez 1934-

Sanchez rocketed to literary fame with her first works *Homecoming* and *We a BaddDDD People*—two volumes of poetry that use urban black dialect to reach a wide audience 1647

Léopold Sédar Senghor 1906-

Former president of the Republic of Senegal, Senghor was instrumental—along with Aimé Césaire—in formulating the concept of negritude. He wrote: "But if I must choose at the moment of ordeal/ I would choose the verse of the rivers, of the winds and of the forests. . ./ I would choose my weary black people, my peasant people." 1671

Ntozake Shange 1948-

Shange's best-known play—*for colored girls who have considered suicide/ when the rainbow is enuf*—combines poetry, prose, music, and dance to portray the sufferings and joys of seven African-American women 1688

Wole Soyinka 1934-
Nobel Prize-winner Soyinka is one of Africa's finest writers. He incorporates traditional Yoruban folk-drama with European dramatic forms to create works that are considered rewarding, if demanding, reading 1703

Wallace Thurman 1902-1934
A self-described "erotic bohemian" during the Harlem Renaissance, American writer Thurman attacked the favoring of light-skinned over dark-skinned blacks in *The Blacker the Berry*, a work whose title comes from the African-American saying "the blacker the berry, the sweeter the juice." 1725

Melvin B. Tolson 1898?-1966
A Gallery of Harlem Portraits celebrates the cultural diversity of Harlem during the 1920s and delineates poet Tolson's hope for interracial unity 1734

Jean Toomer 1894-1967
Cane—an innovative volume of avant-garde poetry, short stories, drama, and prose vignettes—explores African-American culture and spirituality in the rural South and the urban North and is considered Toomer's greatest contribution to literature 1748

Desmond Tutu 1931-
World-famous South African archbishop Tutu is one of the foremost critics of his country's system of apartheid. In his speech collections *Crying in the Wilderness* and *Hope and Suffering*, he called for the end of apartheid in South Africa and freedom for blacks worldwide: "You are either for or against apartheid. . . . You are either on the side of the oppressed or on the side of the oppressor. You can't be neutral." 1769

Amos Tutuola 1920-
Hailed as the founder of Nigerian literature, novelist Tutuola is best known for *The Palm-Wine Drinkard*, a work noted for its blend of traditional Yoruban folktales and unconventional use of the English language 1776

Derek Walcott 1930-
West Indian poet Walcott delineated his struggle between opposing African and European values in the poem "A Far Cry from Africa": "I who am poisoned with the blood of both,/ Where shall I turn divided to the vein?/ I who have cursed/ The drunken officer of British rule, how choose/ Between this Africa and the English tongue I love?" 1790

Alice Walker 1944-
In the Pulitzer Prize-winning novel *The Color Purple*, Walker portrayed the life of Celie, a poor Southern black woman who is victimized physically and emotionally by men for thirty years. While attacked for its unflattering view of black men, *The Color Purple* is one of the most popular books in America today ..1808

Margaret Walker 1915-
Since the publication of her first poem, "I Want to Write," when she was nineteen years old, American author Walker has devoted nearly fifty years to celebrating black American culture 1830

Booker T. Washington 1856-1915
Chastised by his opponents as a fawning accommodationist but embraced by his followers as a misunderstood pioneer in the early struggle for black rights, American writer Washington urged racial cooperation in his 1895 Atlanta Compromise speech: "To those of my race who . . . underestimate the importance of cultivating friendly relations with the southern white man, . . . I would say cast down your bucket where you are, cast it down in making friends in every manly way of the people of all races by whom we are surrounded." 1851

Phillis Wheatley 1753?-1784
Commonly referred to as America's first black author, Wheatley was the first African-American to have published a collection of poems in the United States. (Jupiter Hammmon published a single broadside poem in 1761.) While popular during her day, *Poems on Various Subjects, Religious and Moral* is now of more historical than literary interest 1879

vii

Walter White 1893-1955
A blond, blue-eyed African-American, Harlem Renaissance writer White infiltrated lynching organizations and reported his findings on mob violence in *Rope and Faggot: A Biography of Judge Lynch* 1903

John Edgar Wideman 1941-
Blending European and black literary traditions, Wideman focused on the lives of families living in Homewood—a black ghetto district in Pittsburgh where Wideman himself was raised—in *Damballah* and *Sent for You Yesterday* 1917

John A. Williams 1925-
Williams is best known for *The Man Who Cried I Am*, a novel about a plan to round up 22 million African-Americans when they become too "unruly." 1932

Sherley Anne Williams 1944-
American writer Williams hoped to "heal some wounds" made by racism in the wake of slavery in *Dessa Rose*, a novel about a whip-scarred, pregnant slave in jail for killing white men 1950

August Wilson 1945-
Heralded as a major new voice in American theater, playwright Wilson is in the process of examining each decade of the twentieth century through the medium of drama. So far, *Ma Rainey*, *Joe Turner's Come and Gone*, and *The Piano Lesson* have garnered enthusiastic reviews 1962

Harriet Wilson 1827?-?
Considered the first novel in English published by a black American woman, *Our Nig* tells the tragic story of Frado, an indentured mulatto servant who is beaten by her white mistress and deserted by her traveling husband 1975

Charles Wright 1932-
Wright—a "black black humorist"—depicted the difficulties black men face in their quest for the American dream in *The Wig*, the story about a fair-skinned black man who bleaches his hair "silky smooth blond." 1984

Richard Wright 1908-1960
Wright's acclaimed *Native Son* is one of the first works to portray—often in graphic, brutal accounts—the dehumanizing effects of racism on blacks. Focusing on Bigger Thomas, a young black chauffeur who accidently kills a white woman, Wright attacked racial injustice in America, as he continued to do in *Black Boy* 1994

Frank Yerby 1916-
Dubbed by one critic "the prince of the pulpsters," American novelist Yerby is one of the most popular writers in the United States. Typical of his books, the blockbuster *The Foxes of Harrow* is a lush Southern romance about a dashing young man's adventures 2022

Al Young 1939-
Inventor of the genre "musical memoirs"—a hybrid of autobiography, criticism, mysticism, music, and poetry—American author Young created such memorable characters as O. O. Gabugah, MC, and Shakes—a young black man who speaks in Shakespearean English 2032

BLC Author Index 2051

BLC Nationality Index 2055

BLC Title Index 2057

Introduction

A Comprehensive Information Source on Black Literature

*B*lack Literature Criticism (*BLC*) presents a broad selection of the best criticism of works by major black writers of the past two hundred years. Among the authors included in *BLC* are eighteenth-century memoirist Olaudah Equiano, poet Jupiter Hammon, and poet Phillis Wheatley; nineteenth-century autobiographer Frederick Douglass, poet Paul Laurence Dunbar, diarist Charlotte Forten, and essayist Booker T. Washington; such twentieth-century masters as novelist Chinua Achebe, novelist James Baldwin, poet Gwendolyn Brooks, poet Countee Cullen, novelist Ralph Ellison, dramatist Lorraine Hansberry, poet Langston Hughes, fiction writer Zora Neale Hurston, novelist Toni Morrison, novelist Ngugi wa Thiong'o, dramatist Wole Soyinka, and novelist Richard Wright; and emerging writers Andrea Lee, Charles Johnson, Lewis Nkosi, and August Wilson. The scope of *BLC* is wide: one hundred twenty-five writers representing the United States, Nigeria, South Africa, Jamaica, and over a dozen other nations are covered in comprehensive author entries.

Coverage

This three-volume set is designed for high school, college, and university students, as well as for the general reader who wants to learn more about black literature. *BLC* was developed in response to strong demand by students, librarians, and other readers for a one-stop, authoritative guide to the whole spectrum of black literature. No other compendium like it exists in the marketplace. About half of the entries in *BLC* were selected from Gale's acclaimed Literary Criticism Series and completely updated for publication here. Typically, the revisions are extensive, ranging from completely rewritten author introductions to wide changes in the selection of criticism. Other entries were prepared especially for *BLC* in order to furnish the most comprehensive coverage possible. Authors were selected for inclusion based on the range and amount of critical material available as well as on the advice of leading experts on black literature. A special effort was made to identify important new writers and to give the greatest coverage to the most studied authors.

Each author entry in *BLC* attempts to present a historical survey of critical response to the author's works. Typically, early criticism is offered to indicate initial responses, later selections document any rise or decline in literary reputations, and retrospective analyses provide modern views. Every endeavor has been made to include the seminal essays on each author's work along with recent commentary providing current perspectives. Interviews and author statements are also included in many entries. Thus, *BLC* is both timely and comprehensive.

Organization of Author Entries

Information about authors and their works is presented through eight key access points:

■ The **Author Heading** cites the name under which the author most commonly wrote, followed by birth and death dates. Uncertain birth or death dates are indicated by question marks. Name variations, including full birth names when available, are given in parentheses on the first line of the **Biographical and Critical Introduction**.

■ The **Biographical and Critical Introduction** contains background information about the life and works of the author. Emphasis is given to four main areas: 1) biographical details that help reveal the life, character, and personality of the author; 2) overviews of the major literary interests of the author—for example, novel writing, autobiography, social reform, documentary, etc.; 3) descriptions and summaries of the author's best-known works; and 4) critical commentary about the author's achievement, stature, and importance. The concluding paragraph of the **Biographical and Critical Introduction** directs readers to other Gale series containing information about the author.

■ Most *BLC* entries include an **Author Portrait**. Most also contain **Illustrations** documenting the author's career, including holographs, title pages of works, letters, or pictures of important people, places, and events in the author's life.

■ The **List of Principal Works** is chronological by date of first book publication and identifies the genre of each work. For non-English-language authors whose works have been translated into English, the title and date of the first English-language edition are given in brackets beneath the foreign-language listing. Unless otherwise indicated, dramas are dated by first performance rather than first publication.

■ **Criticism** is arranged chronologically in each author entry to provide a useful perspective on changes in critical evaluation over the years. Most entries contain a detailed, comprehensive study of the author's career as well as book reviews, studies of individual works, and comparative examinations. To ensure timeliness, current views are most often presented, but never to the exclusion of important early pieces. For the purpose of easy identification, the critic's name and the date of the critical work are given at the beginning of each piece of criticism. Unsigned criticism is preceded by the title of the source in which it appeared. Within the criticism, titles of works by the author are printed in boldface type. Publication information (such as publisher names and book prices) and certain numerical references (such as footnotes or page and line references to specific editions of works) have been deleted at the editor's discretion to provide smoother reading of the text.

■ Critical essays are prefaced by **Explanatory Notes** as an additional aid to readers of *BLC*. These notes may provide several types of valuable information, including: 1) the reputation of the critic; 2) the perceived importance of the work of criticism; 3) the commentator's approach to the author's work; 4) the apparent purpose of the criticism; and 5) changes in critical trends regarding the author. In some cases, **Explanatory Notes** cross-reference the work of critics within the entry who agree or disagree with each other.

■ A complete **Bibliographical Citation** of the original essay or book follows each piece of criticism.

■ An annotated **Further Reading List** appears at the end of each entry and suggests resources for additional study.

Other Features

BLC contains three distinct indexes to help readers find information quickly and easily:

■ The **Author Index** lists all the authors appearing in *BLC*. To ensure easy access, name variations and name changes are fully cross-indexed.

■ The **Nationality Index** lists all authors featured in *BLC* by nationality. For expatriate authors and authors identified with more than one nation, multiple listings are offered.

■ The **Title Index** lists in alphabetical order all individual works by the authors appearing in *BLC*. English-language translations of original foreign-language titles are cross-referenced to the foreign titles so that all references to a work are combined in one listing.

Citing *Black Literature Criticism*

When writing papers, students who quote directly from *BLC* may use the following general forms to footnote reprinted criticism. The first example is for material drawn from periodicals, the second for material reprinted from books.

Robert B. Stepto, "Storytelling in Early Afro-American Fiction: Frederick Douglass' 'The Heroic Slave'," *The Georgia Review*, XXXVI (Summer 1982), 355-68; excerpted and reprinted in *Black Literature Criticism*, ed. James P. Draper (Detroit: Gale Research, 1992), pp. 585-88.

Edward Margolies, *Native Sons: A Critical Study of Twentieth-Century Negro American Authors* (J. B. Lippincott, 1968); excerpted and reprinted in *Black Literature Criticism*, ed. James P. Draper (Detroit: Gale Research, 1992), pp. 59-64.

Acknowledgments

The editor wishes to acknowledge the valuable contributions of the many librarians, authors, and scholars who assisted in the compilation of *BLC* with their responses to telephone and mail inquiries. Special thanks are offered to *BLC*'s two chief advisors: Clarence Chisholm, Chairman of the Afro-American Studies Section of the Association of College and Research Libraries, and Arnold Rampersad, Woodrow Wilson Professor of English and Director of American Studies at Princeton University.

Comments Are Welcome

The editor hopes that readers will find *BLC* to be a useful reference tool and welcomes comments about the work. Send comments and suggestions to: Editor, *Black Literature Criticism*, Gale Research Inc., Penobscot Building, Detroit, MI 48226-4094.

Authors Included
in *Black Literature Criticism*

Chinua Achebe   1930-

Jamil Abdullah Al-Amin (H. Rap Brown)   1943-

Maya Angelou   1928-

Ayi Kwei Armah   1939-

William Attaway   1911?-1986

James Baldwin   1924-1987

Toni Cade Bambara   1939-

Amiri Baraka (LeRoi Jones)   1934-

Barry Beckham   1944-

James Madison Bell   1826-1902

Louise Bennett   1919-

Mongo Beti (Alexandre Biyidi)   1932-

Arna Bontemps   1902-1973

David Bradley   1950-

William Stanley Braithwaite   1878-1962

Gwendolyn Brooks   1917-

Claude Brown   1937-

Sterling Brown   1901-1989

William Wells Brown   1816?-1884

Dennis Brutus   1924-

Ed Bullins   1935-

J. E. Casely-Hayford   1866-1930

Aimé Césaire   1913-

Charles W. Chesnutt   1858-1932

Alice Childress   1920-

John Pepper Clark   1935-

Austin Clarke   1934-

Eldridge Cleaver   1935-

Lucille Clifton   1936-

Joseph Seamon Cotter, Sr.   1861-1949

Countee Cullen   1903-1946

Frank Marshall Davis   1905-1987

Samuel R. Delany   1942-

William Demby   1922-

Owen Dodson   1914-1983

Frederick Douglass   1817?-1895

W. E. B. Du Bois   1868-1963

Paul Laurence Dunbar   1872-1906

Cyprian Ekwensi   1921-

Lonne Elder III   1931-

Ralph Ellison   1914-

Buchi Emecheta   1944-

Olaudah Equiano   1745?-1797

Frantz Fanon   1925-1961

Nuruddin Farah   1945-

Jessie Redmon Fauset   1882-1961

Rudolph Fisher   1897-1934

Charlotte L. Forten   1837?-1914

Charles Fuller   1939-

Ernest Gaines   1933-

Marcus Garvey   1887-1940

Nikki Giovanni   1943-

Donald Goines   1937?-1974

Nicolás Guillén   1902-1989

Alex Haley   1921-

Jupiter Hammon   1711?-1800?

Lorraine Hansberry   1930-1965

Frances Ellen Watkins
  Harper   1825-1911

Robert Hayden   1913-1980

Bessie Head   1937-1986

Chester Himes   1909-1984

Pauline Elizabeth Hopkins   1859-
  1930

Langston Hughes   1902-1967

Zora Neale Hurston   1901?-1960

Charles Johnson   1948-

Fenton Johnson   1888-1958

James Weldon Johnson   1871-
  1938

Gayl Jones   1949-

Adrienne Kennedy   1931-

Jamaica Kincaid   1949-

Martin Luther King, Jr.   1929-
  1968

Etheridge Knight   1931-1991

George Lamming   1927-

Nella Larsen   1891-1964

Camara Laye   1928-1980

Andrea Lee   1953-

George Washington Lee   1894-
  1976

Audre Lorde   1934-

Joaquim Maria Machado de
  Assis   1839-1908

Haki R. Madhubuti (Don L.
  Lee)   1942-

Clarence Major   1936-

Malcolm X (Malcolm Little; El-
  Hajj Malik El-Shabazz)
  1925-1965

Paule Marshall   1929-

Claude McKay   1889-1948

Ron Milner   1938-

Thomas Mofolo   1876-1948

Toni Morrison   1931-

Ezekiel Mphahlele   1919-

S. E. K. Mqhayi   1875-1945

Walter Dean Myers   1937-

Gloria Naylor   1950-

Ngugi wa Thiong'o   1938-

Lewis Nkosi   1936-

Christopher Okigbo   1932-1967

Sembène Ousmane   1923-

Gordon Parks   1912-

Okot p'Bitek   1931-1982

Adam Clayton Powell, Jr.   1908-
  1972

Dudley Randall   1914-

Ishmael Reed 1938-

Jacques Roumain 1907-1944

Sonia Sanchez 1934-

Léopold Sédar Senghor 1906-

Ntozake Shange 1948-

Wole Soyinka 1934-

Wallace Thurman 1902-1934

Melvin B. Tolson 1898?-1966

Jean Toomer 1894-1967

Desmond Tutu 1931-

Amos Tutuola 1920-

Derek Walcott 1930-

Alice Walker 1944-

Margaret Walker 1915-

Booker T. Washington 1856-1915

Phillis Wheatley 1753?-1784

Walter White 1893-1955

John Edgar Wideman 1941-

John A. Williams 1925-

Sherley Anne Williams 1944-

August Wilson 1945-

Harriet Wilson 1827?-?

Charles Wright 1932-

Richard Wright 1908-1960

Frank Yerby 1916-

Al Young 1939-

ACKNOWLEDGMENTS

The editor wishes to thank the copyright holders of the excerpted criticism included in this volume, the permissions managers of many book and magazine publishing companies for assisting in securing reprint rights, and Anthony Bogucki for assistance with copyright research. The editor is also grateful to the staffs of the Detroit Public Library, Wayne State University Purdy/Kresge Library Complex, and the University of Michigan Libraries for making their resources available. Following is a list of the copyright holders who have granted permission to reprint material in this volume of *BLC*. Every effort has been made to trace copyright, but if omissions have been made, please let the editor know.

COPYRIGHTED EXCERPTS IN *BLC*, VOLUME 3, WERE REPRINTED FROM THE FOLLOWING PERIODICALS:

African Arts, v. 5, Spring, 1972 for "Ousmane Sembène and the Cinema of Decolonization" by Robert A. Mortimer. (c) 1972 by the Regents of the University of California. Reprinted by permission of the publisher and the author.—*African Literature Today,* n. 12, 1982. Copyright 1982 by Heinemann Educational Books Ltd. All rights reserved. Reprinted by permission of Africana Publishing Corporation, New York, NY. In Canada by Heinemann Educational Books Ltd.—*African Today,* v. 18, October, 1971; v. 29, third quarter, 1982. (c) Africa Today Associates. Both reprinted by permission of *Africa Today,* Graduate School of International Studies, University of Denver, Denver, CO 80208.—*America,* v. 152, April 27, 1985. (c) 1985. All rights reserved. Reprinted with permission of America Press, Inc. 106 West 56th St., New York, NY 10019.—*The American Book Review,* v. 4, July-August, 1982. (c) 1982 by *The American Book Review.* Reprinted by permission of the publisher.—*American Mercury,* v. XVIII, July, 1929 for "Sport in the Bible Country" by H. L. Mencken. Copyright 1929, renewed 1956 by American Mercury Magazine, Inc. Reprinted by permission of the Literary Estate of H. L. Mencken.—*The Antioch Review,* v. 3, Summer, 1945 for "Richard Wright's Blues" by Ralph Ellison. Copyright 1945, renewed 1972 by Ralph Ellison. Reprinted by permission of the William Morris Agency, Inc. on behalf of the author.—*Ariel: A Review of International English Literature,* v. 12, July, 1981 for "Begging Questions in Wole Soyinka's 'Opera Wonyosi' " by Bernth Lindfors. Copyright (c) 1981 The Board of Governors, The University of Calgary. Reprinted by permission of the publisher and the author.—*Arizona Quarterly,* v. 39, Autumn, 1983 for "Jean Toomer's 'Cane': The Search for Identity through Form" by Alan Golding. Copyright (c) 1983 by Arizona Board of Regents. Reprinted by permission of the publisher and the author.—*The Atlantic Monthly,* v. 225, March, 1970 for "Richard Wright Reappraised" by Stanley Edgar Hyman. Copyright 1970 by The Atlantic Monthly Company, Boston, MA. Reprinted by permission of the Literary Estate of Stanley Edgar Hyman.—*Belles Lettres: A Review of Books by Women,* v. 4, Winter, 1989. Reprinted by permission of the publisher.—*Best Sellers,* v. 42, November, 1982. Copyright (c) 1982 Helen Dwight Reid Educational Foundation. Reprinted by permission of the publisher.—*Black American Literature Forum,* v. 18, Winter, 1984 for "On 'The Color Purple', Stereotypes, and Silence" by Trudier Harris; v. 20, Fall, 1986 for a review of "Dessa Rose" by Doris Davenport; v. 21, Spring-Summer, 1987 for "Paule Marshall's Women on Quest" by Missy Dehn Kubitschek; v. 21, Fall, 1987 for "Jean Toomer as Poet: A Phenomenology of the Spirit" by Robert Jones; v. 22, Winter, 1988 for "Two Worlds: Influence on the Poetry of Wole Soyinka" by Tanure Ojaide; Copyright (c) 1984, 1986, 1987, 1988, Indiana State University. All reprinted by permission of Indiana State University and the respective authors./ v. 22, Winter, 1988 for an interview with Wole Soyinka by Anthony Appiah. Copyright (c) 1988 Indiana State University. Reprinted by permission of Indiana State University, Wole Soyinka and Anthony Appiah.—*The Bloomsbury Review,* v. 11, March, 1991 for "Mourning the Loss of a Generation" by Mark Hummel. Copyright (c) by Owaissa Communications Company, Inc. 1991. Reprinted by permission of the author.—*Book World—The Washington Post,* July 3, 1983; November 15, 1987; February 28, 1988; May 7, 1989; October 7, 1990. (c) 1983, 1987, 1988, 1989, 1990, *The Washington Post.* All reprinted with permission of the publisher.—*Books Abroad,* v. 41, Autumn, 1967. Copyright 1967 by the University of Oklahoma Press. Reprinted by permission of the publisher.—*Callaloo,* v. 7, Spring-Summer, 1984 for "Seven Women and a Wall" by Judith V. Branzburg. Copyright (c) 1984 by Charles H. Rowell. All rights reserved. Reprinted by permission of the author./ v. 9, Spring, 1986; v. 11, Spring, 1988; v. 12, Summer, 1989. Copyright (c) 1984, 1986, 1988, 1989, by Charles H. Rowell. All rights reserved. All reprinted by permission of the publisher.—*Canadian Review of African Studies,* v. 18, 1984. Reprinted by permission of the publisher.—*CLA Journal,* v. XIV, March, 1971; v. XV, September, 1971; v. XVI, September, 1972; v. XXXII, March, 1989; v. XXXIII, September, 1989. Copyright (c) 1971, 1972, 1989, by The College Language Association. All used by permission of the College Language Association.—*Commonweal,* v. CXII, September 6, 1985. Copyright (c) 1985 Commonweal Foundation.

Literary Realism, 1865-1920," in **Slavery and the Literary Imagination,** new series. Edited by Deborah E. McDowell and Arnold Rampersad. The John Hopkins University Press, 1989. (c) 1989 The Johns Hopkins University Press. All rights reserved. Reprinted by permission of the publisher.—Anozie, Sunday O. From **Christopher Okigbo: Creative Rhetoric.** Evans Brothers Limited, 1972. (c) Sunday O. Anozie 1972. Reprinted by permission of Evans Brothers Limited of HarperCollins Publishers, Ltd.—Bâ, Sylvia Washington. From **The Concept of Negritude in the Poetry of Léopold Sédar Senghor.** Princeton University Press, 1973. Copyright (c) 1973 by Princeton University Press. All rights reserved. Reprinted by permission of the publisher.—Baker, Houston A., Jr. From **Long Black Song: Essays in Black American Literature and Culture.** The University Press of Virginia, 1972. Copyright (c) 1972 by The Rector and Visitors of the University of Virginia. Reprinted by permission of the publisher.—Bell, Bernard W. From **The Afro-American Novel and Its Tradition.** The University of Massachusetts Press, 1987. Copyright (c) 1987 by The University of Massachusetts Press. All rights reserved. Reprinted by permission of the publisher.—Berrian, Brenda F. From "Through Her Prism of Social and Political Contexts: Sembène's Female Characters in 'Tribal Scars'," in **Ngambika: Studies of Women in African Literature.** Edited by Carole Boyce Davies and Anne Adams Graves. Africa World Press, Inc., 1986. (c) Africa World Press, 1986. All rights reserved. Reprinted by permission of the publisher.—Bishop, Rudine Sims. From **Presenting Walter Dean Myers.** Twayne, 1990. Copyright 1991 by Twayne Publishers. Reprinted with the permission of Twayne Publishers, a division of G. K. Hall & Co., Boston.—Bone, Robert. From **Down Home: Origins of the Afro-American Short Story.** Columbia University Press, 1988. Copyright (c) 1975 by Robert Bone. All rights reserved. Used by permission of the publisher.—Bone, Robert. From **The Negro Novel in America.** Revised edition. Yale University Press, 1965. Copyright (c) 1965 by Robert Bone. All rights reserved. Reprinted by permission of the author.—Bunche, Ralph J. From a foreward to **How Far the Promised Land?** By Walter White. The Viking Press, 1955. Copyright (c) 1955 by Poppy Cannon White. Renewed (c) 1983 by Jane White Viazzi. Used by permission of Viking Penguin, a division of Penguin Books USA Inc.—Christ, Carol P. From **Diving Deep and Surfacing: Women Writers on Spiritual Quest.** Beacon Press, 1980. Copyright (c) 1980 by Carol P. Christ. Used by permission of Beacon Press.—Collier, Eugenia. From "Fields Watered with Blood: Myth and Ritual in the Poetry of Margaret Walker," in **Black Women Writers (1950-1980): A Critical Evaluation.** Edited by Mari Evans. Anchor Press/Doubleday, 1984. Copyright (c) 1984 by Mari Evans. All rights reserved. Used by permission of Doubleday, a division of Bantam Doubleday Dell Publishing Group, Inc.—Curb, Rosemary K. From "Pre-Feminism in the Black Revolutionary Drama of Sonia Sanchez," in **The Many Forms of Drama, Vol. V.** Edited by Karelisa V. Hartigan. University Press of America, 1987. Copyright (c) 1987 by University Press of America, Inc. All rights reserved. Reprinted by permission of the publisher.—Dixon, Melvin. From "Rivers Remembering Their Sources," in **Afro-American Literature: The Reconstruction of Instruction.** Edited by Dexter Fisher and Robert B. Stepto, The Modern Language Association of America, 1979. Reprinted by permission of the Modern Language Association of America.—Fabre, Genevieve. From "Genealogical Archaeology or the Quest for Legacy in Toni Morrison's 'Song of Solomon'," in **Critical Essays on Toni Morrison.** Edited by Nellie Y. McKay. Hall, 1988. Copyright 1988 by G. K. Hall & Co. All rights reserved. Reprinted by permission of the author.—Fowler, Carolyn. From **A Knot in the Thread: The Life and Work of Jacques Roumain.** Howard University Press, 1980. Copyright (c) 1972, 1980 by Carolyn Fowler. All rights reserved. Reprinted by permission of Howard University Press.—Frank, Waldo. From a foreward to **Cane.** By Jean Toomer. Boni and Liveright, 1923. Copyright 1923 by Boni & Liveright. Copyright renewed 1951 by Jean Toomer. Reprinted by permission of Liveright Publishing Corporation.—Garvey, Marcus. From **Philosophy and Opinions of Marcus Garvey; or, Africa for the Africans.** Edited by Amy Jacques Garvey. Second edition. Frank Cass & Co. Ltd., 1967. Reprinted by permission of Frank Cass & Co. Ltd.—Gates, Henry Louis, Jr. From **Figures in Black: Words, Signs, and the "Racial" Self.** Oxford University Press, Inc., 1987. Copyright (c) 1987 by Henry Louis Gates, Jr. All rights reserved. Reprinted by permission of Oxford University Press, Inc.—Geis, Deborah R. From "Distraught Laughter: Monologue in Ntozake Shange's Theater Pieces," in **Feminine Focus: The New Women Playwrights.** Edited by Enoch Brater. Oxford University Press, 1989. Copyright (c) 1989 by Oxford University Press, Inc. Reprinted by permission of the publisher.—Gérard, Albert S. **From Four African Literatures: Xhosa, Sotho, Zulu, Amharic.** University of California Press, 1971. Copyright (c) 1971 The Regents of the University of California. All rights reserved. Reprinted by permission of the publisher.—Gloster, Hugh M. From **Negro Voices in American Fiction.** University of North Carolina Press, 1948. Copyright (c) 1948, by The University of North Carolina Press. Renewed 1975 by Hugh M. Gloster. Reprinted by permission of the publisher and author.—Goba, Bonganjalo. From "A Theological Tribute to Archbishop Tutu," in **Hammering Swords into Ploughshares: Essays in Honor of Archbishop Mpilo Desmond Tutu.** Edited by Buti Tlhagale and Itumeleng Mosala. Skotaville Publishers, 1986. Copyright (c) 1986 The Desmond Tutu Theology Series Committee. All rights reserved. Reprinted by permission of the publisher.—Gross, Theodore L. From **The Heroic Ideal in American Literature.** The Free Press, 1971. Copyright (c) 1971 by Theodore L. Gross. Reprinted with permission of The Free Press, a division of Macmillan Publishing Company.—Guillaume, Alfred J., Jr. From "Negritude and Humanism: Senghor's Vision of a Universal Civilization," in **The Harlem Renaissance: Revaluations.** Amritjit Singh, William S. Shiver, Stanley Brodwin, eds. Garland-Publishing, Inc., 1989. (c) 1989 Amritjit Singh, William S. Shiver, and Stanley Brodwin. All rights reserved. Reprinted by permission of the publisher.—Hackett, Francis. From **On Judging Books: In General and in Particular.** The John Day Company, 1947. Copyright 1947 by Francis Hackett. Renewed 1975 by Signe Toksvig Hackett. Reprinted by permission of HarperCollins Publishers, Inc.—Harlan, Louis R. From **Booker T. Washington:**

PHOTOGRAPHS AND ILLUSTRATIONS APPEARING IN *BLC*, VOLUME 3, WERE RECEIVED FROM THE FOLLOWING SOURCES:

BLACK LITERATURE
CRITICISM

Paule Marshall

1929-

American novelist and short story writer.

Marshall is recognized as a prominent and innovative voice in contemporary American literature. A passionate champion of the individual's search for personal identity, she has been praised by critics as one of the first authors to explore the psychological trials and concerns of black American women. Drawing upon her experiences as an African-American woman of Barbadian heritage, she embodies the cultural dichotomy that provides the major tensions in her work. Although her writing deals primarily with black and feminist issues, critics note that the power and importance of Marshall's work transcends color and sexual barriers and speaks to all individuals.

Marshall was born in Brooklyn, New York, to Barbadian parents in 1929. In several essays and interviews she commented on her childhood reluctance to acknowledge her West Indian heritage and spoke of the discrimination she felt growing up in Brooklyn's Stuyvesant Heights. Marshall was profoundly influenced by the conversations she overheard between her mother and other women from their community. The power these women wielded with their words, their sharp character analyses, and the poetic rhythms of their Barbadian dialect instilled in Marshall a desire to capture some of their "magic" on paper. In an interview with Alexis De Veux in *Essence* she stated: "Perhaps the most important influence in my becoming a writer is due to those fantastic women, my mother and her friends, who would gather every afternoon after work—they did day's work—and talk.... In that kitchen I was in the presence of art of a very high order because those women, in their talk, knew what literature was all about."

In addition to listening to her mother in what she called "the wordshop of the kitchen," Marshall spent much time at the public library, where she encountered the works of William Thackeray, Henry Fielding, and Charles Dickens. Her subsequent discovery of a volume of Paul Laurence Dunbar's poetry filled a gap she had sensed in her reading. Unlike the other books she knew, this work was written in black vernacular and conveyed images familiar to Marshall from her own life. Dunbar's poetry, Marshall later said, "validated the black experience" for her, and she continued to seek out other writings by African-Americans. The works of Zora Neale Hurston and Gwendolyn Brooks, and especially Ralph Ellison's collection of critical essays *Shadow and Act,* were of particular importance in shaping Marshall's ideas.

After receiving her B.A. from Brooklyn College in 1953, Marshall began working as a researcher for a small magazine, *Our World.* She was soon promoted to staff writer and sent to Brazil and the Caribbean on assignments; she would later draw upon these experiences in her fiction. While working for *Our World* and attending Hunter College she began writing *Brown Girl, Brownstones* (1959). Despite the novel's commercial failure, it received critical praise and prompted Marshall to pursue a literary career. Since then, Marshall has earned her living almost solely by writing. She has received several prestigious awards, including a Guggenheim Fellowship and a National Endowment for the Arts Fellowship. In addition, she has taught creative writing courses at Yale University, Columbia University, the University of Iowa, and the University of California at Berkeley.

Marshall's first novel, *Brown Girl, Brownstones,* is a frank depiction of a young black girl's search for identity and increasing sexual awareness. Autobiographical in tone, the story is about Brooklyn-born Selina, the daughter of Barbadian immigrants Silla and Deighton. Selina's ambitious mother, Silla, wants most of all to save enough money to purchase the family's rented brownstone. Yet father Deighton is a charming spendthrift who simply wants to return to his homeland. When Deighton unexpectedly inherits some island land, he makes plans to return there and build a home. Silla meanwhile schemes to sell his inheritance and fulfill her own dream. Selina is deeply affected by this marital conflict but "emerges from it self-assured, in spite of her scars," wrote Susan McHenry in *Ms.* magazine. Selina eventually leaves Brooklyn to attend college; later, realizing her need to become acquainted with her parent's homeland, she resolves to go to Barbados. McHenry commented: "*Brown Girl, Brownstones* is meticulously crafted and peopled with an array of characters, and the writing combines authority with grace.... Paule Marshall...should be more widely read and celebrated." Carol Field added in the *New York Herald Tribune Book Review*: "[*Brown Girl, Brownstones*] is an unforgettable novel written with pride and anger, with rebellion and tears. Rich in content and in cadences of the King's and 'Bajun' English, it is the work of a highly gifted writer."

Since the publication of *Brown Girl, Brownstones,* Marshall has developed her fiction around her belief that one's past must be known and accepted before personal integrity may be achieved. Critics often refer to *Brown Girl, Brownstones* as a *bildungsroman* and have praised Marshall's exploration of psychological struggle and enlightenment in her short story collection *Soul Clap Hands and Sing* (1961). The stories here deal with aging men who are forced to come to terms with their emotional and spiritual decline. In her other works of short fiction, particularly the stories "The Valley Between" and "Reena," she examined women's attempts to overcome sexual and racial discrimination and focused on the difficulties women face in personal relationships.

Marshall's most widely reviewed work to date is *Praisesong for the Widow* (1983), winner of the Before Columbus American Book Award. This novel, like *Brown Girl, Brownstones,* involves a black woman's search for identity. The narrative concerns an affluent widow in her sixties, Avatar (Avey) Johnson, who, in her struggle to make her way in a white world, has lost touch with her West Indian-African-American roots. Novelist Anne Tyler remarked in the *New York Times Book Review*: "Secure in her middle class life, her civil service job, her house full of crystal and silver, Avey has become sealed away from her true self." While on her annual luxury cruise through the West Indies, however, Avey has disturbing dreams about her father's great aunt whom she visited every summer on a South Carolina island. She remembers the spot on the island where Ibo slaves, upon landing in America, supposedly took one look at their new life and walked across the water back to Africa. Avey decides to try to escape the uneasiness she is experiencing by flying back to the security of her home. While on Grenada awaiting the next flight to New York, she reminisces about the early years of her marriage, when she and her husband Jay

used to dance to jazz records in their living room and, on Sundays, listen to gospel music and recite poetry. Gradually though, in their drive for success, the couple lost "the little private rituals and pleasures, the playfulness and wit of those early years, the host of feelings and passions that had defined them in a special way back then, and the music which had been their nourishment," wrote Marshall in the novel. In the morning, Avey meets a shopkeeper who urges her to accompany him and the other islanders on an excursion to Carriacou, the island of their ancestors. Still confused from the past day's events, she agrees. During the island celebration, Avey undergoes a spiritual rebirth and resolves to tell others about her experience. Jonathan Yardley concluded of Avey and her story: "*Praisesong for the Widow*... is a work of quiet passion—a book all the more powerful precisely because it is so quiet. It is also a work of exceptional wisdom, maturity and generosity, one in which the palpable humanity of its characters transcends any considerations of race or sex; that Avey Johnson is black and a woman is certainly important, but Paule Marshall understands that what really counts is the universality of her predicament."

"My work asks that you become involved, that you think," Marshall once commented in the *Los Angeles Times*. "On the other hand,... I'm first trying to tell a story, because I'm always about telling a good story." In her novels and short stories Marshall has celebrated her cultural heritage and explored the psychological battles fought by black American women. "One of the reasons it takes me such a long time to get a book done," she explained, "is that I'm not only struggling with my sense of reality, but I'm also struggling to find the style, the language, the tone that is in keeping with the material. It's in the process of writing that things get illuminated." Wrote critic Barbara T. Christian: "[Marshall's works] form a unique contribution to Afro-American literature because they capture in a lyrical, powerful language a culturally distinct and expansive world."

(For further information about Marshall's life and works, see *Black Writers; Contemporary Authors,* Vols. 77-80; *Contemporary Authors New Revision Series,* Vol. 25; *Contemporary Literary Criticism,* Vol. 27; *Dictionary of Literary Biography,* Vol. 33: *Afro-American Fiction Writers after 1955;* and *Short Story Criticism,* Vol. 3.)

PRINCIPAL WORKS

Brown Girl, Brownstones (novel) 1959
Soul Clap Hands and Sing (short stories) 1961
The Chosen Place, The Timeless People (novel) 1969
Praisesong for the Widow (novel) 1983
Reena and Other Stories (short stories) 1983; also
    published as *Merle: A Novella and Other Stories,*
    1984
Daughters (novel) 1991

Carol Field (essay date 1959)

[*In the excerpt below, Field warmly reviews* Brown Girl, Brownstones, *describing it as a poignant and fresh work.*]

Rarely has a first novel come to hand which has the poignant appeal and the fresh, fierce emotion of ***Brown Girl, Brownstones.* . . .**

Racial conflict and the anger and frustration it nurtures are part of this tale, but equally, if not more, important are the personal conflicts of men and women making roots in a new land, of men and women caught in duels of love and hate, of ambition, envy and failure.

While Selina is the heroine of this novel, it is her parents who give it and her its depth and color. Through them, through their passions, their clashes, their hopes, the girl assumes shape and meaning.

To Silla, gaunt and strong, the brownstone house in Brooklyn which she leased represented a giant step from the slavish toil she had known in Barbados. To own the once elegant building, to cut up its enormous chambers, to have a houseful of well-paying roomers was her dream. Other "Bajuns" were doing it, making money, getting ahead in the new world. With a little help from her husband she could swing it, she knew, but Deighton was no man to depend on. . . .

He was handsome; he loved good clothes; he had ambitions for getting on in the world but they were woven of the stuff of dreams. Starting correspondence courses, he saw himself successful as a radio mechanic, an accountant, a trumpeter in a jazz band and then, realizing his limitations, he dropped them. How he willfully and wantonly checkmates Silla in her illegal efforts to capitalize on Barbados land he unexpectedly inherited makes the heart-stirring climax of the book.

Wonderfully, in incidents and scenes that hold the nuances of character as well as language rich with Barbados locution, Mrs. Marshall puts the quickness of life into these two. The tortured Silla, remembering her wretched childhood, spells out its details in anguished words for Selina, seeking to explain her ambition and hardness. But it is the dream-bemused Deighton, with his charm, his good clothes, his fancy woman, his rosy-hued tales, who is closest to the girl's heart. While she inherits some of her mother's iron, she is, in her love of poetry and fantasy, of people and adventure, the daughter of Deighton. . . .

[***Brown Girl, Brownstones***] is an unforgettable novel written with pride and anger, with rebellion and tears. Rich in content and in cadences of the King's and "Bajun" English, it is the work of a highly gifted writer.

Carol Field, "Fresh, Fierce and 'First'," in New York Herald Tribune Book Review, *August 16, 1959, p. 5.*

Leela Kapai (essay date 1972)

[*In the following excerpt, Kapai discusses theme, characterization, and technique in* Brown Girl, Brownstones, Soul Clap Hands and Sing, *and* The Chosen Place, The Timeless People.]

Paule Marshall is the author of ***Brown Girl, Brownstones; Soul Clap Hands and Sing; The Chosen Place, The Timeless People;*** and a few short stories and articles. With a remarkable maturity in her work, she displays a subtle understanding of human problems and a mastery of the art of fiction. Some of the major themes in her works concern the identity crisis, the race problem, the importance of tradition for the black American, and the need for sharing to achieve meaningful relationships. In her technique she blends judiciously the best of the past tradition with the innovations of recent years. (p. 49)

Quest for identity is a perennial theme in literature. There is no age when a sensitive soul has not been troubled by questions about the meaning of his very own existence and his relation to the world around. The identity crisis assumes even more gravity for the minority groups who were either brought to this land or who came of their own accord in search of greener pastures. Lost in a new cultural environment, such people need more than ordinary effort to recognize and keep their identity alive. However, such self-questionings are not the prerogative of only the members of a particular group based on race, sex, or age; therefore, Miss Marshall concerns herself with people of all ages, of all races, and of all strata.

Miss Marshall's first book, ***Brown Girl*** . . ., is a *Bildungs-roman,* in which the trials and tribulations of growing up are complicated by the fact that Selina, the protagonist, is the daughter of Barbadian immigrants. Selina is caught between the conflicting attitudes of her parents, though she sympathises clearly with her father. . . . Selina shows her defiance and anger by her affair with an unsuccessful artist in her community. Since an inevitable part of growing up in America is coming to terms with racial conflict, Selina cannot escape it either. Her moment of revelation comes through Mrs. Benton, a typical "liberal" Northerner. To show her broad-mindedness, Mrs. Benton showers Selina with tales of her generosity to her "girl," who was "so honest too." She compliments Selina for her poise and speech, adding "it's just wonderful how you've taken your race's natural talent for dancing and music and developed it . . ." . . . So Selina realizes that she is, after all, set for the stereotype role of an entertainer. And as if to confirm it, Mrs. Benton requests her to say something "in that delightful West Indian accent." This first exposure to racist attitudes forces Selina to see the life around her in a new light.

In the moment of her need, Clive fails her too, and Selina has to fall back upon her inner strength. She realizes then that despite her differences with her mother, she is very much like her. She also learns to value her people; "they no longer puzzled or offended her." She admits, "they had bequeathed her a small strength. She had only this to sustain her all the years." ... (pp. 49-50)

[The next book, *Soul Clap Hands and Sing,*] is, as a critic put it, held together not by mere alliteration but by theme. In contrast to the first novel, these novellas deal with old men who, approaching their end, realize that they have failed to live. (pp. 50-1)

In both **"Barbados"** and **"Brooklyn,"** the protagonists learn the truth about themselves through two young girls. In the former, the aging farmer Watford, who returns to his home rich after fifty years of toil in Boston, keeps himself aloof, disdaining others and assuming the superiority of his masters. When at last he turns to a young woman for affection, he is spurned mercilessly.... In **"Brooklyn"** Max Berman, a teacher of French literature, not only fails in his attempt to seduce a fair Negro girl and sees the futility of his life, but also enables her to see where she belongs. All her life Miss Williams had been sheltered by her parents from the white people as well as from the darker members of her race. She had thus grown up belonging to no world. Max's behavior makes her accept her blackness with pride.

The old men of the next two novellas are Gerald Motley in **"British Guiana"** and Heitor Baptista Guimares in **"Brazil."** A descendant of Hindu, Chinese, and Negro ancestors, Motley does not know who he really is. He tolerates Sidney's arrogance and contempt because he serves as a constant reminder of what he could have been. Seeing Sidney's pain he feels glad that "he is old and would never know pain again." Death is perhaps the only merciful end of his state. In **"Brazil"** Guimares, the night-club entertainer, known by his assumed name O Grand Caliban, finds himself "lost in the myth he has created." On the eve of his retirement, he realizes that his white partner has robbed him not only of his years of glory, but even deprived him of his very name. He too perhaps has no chance to retrieve his lost identity.

Thus in all the four novellas, the old men finally come to see the truth, but their time is gone. Out of the ashes of the old, a new phoenix arises, and it seems that the nameless young girl of **"Barbados"** with her politically aware boyfriend, Miss Williams of **"Brooklyn,"** Sidney Parrish of **"British Guiana,"** and the madonna-like wife of Caliban bearing his child in **"Brazil"** are the heralds of a new future.

The question of identity is brought to the fore again in *The Chosen Place....* Merle Kinbona is an enigmatic woman who, in the words of Allen, "somehow is Bournehills." Merle's traumatic experience in childhood when her mother was shot by her white father's lawful wife haunted her all her life. Even though her father never acknowledged her, he arranged for her schooling; however, material comforts have never compensated for love and understanding. Merle is now in her hometown after a long stay in London where she had a nervous collapse after her marriage with a young African broke

on his learning of her past relationship with a white woman. At Bournehills, she is trying to forget her hurt and misery behind the facade of endless chatter and assumed indifference. By the end of the novel, she has learnt she must go back to Africa to pick up whatever broken pieces of her life remain. (pp. 51-2)

The search for identity of all educated black women seems to be Miss Marshall's concern in **"Reena** [a short story published in *American Negro Short Stories,* edited by J. H. Clark]. Reena, obviously the writer's alter-ego, is an intelligent girl who gradually grows aware of the acute injustice of the society. After her struggle at college and two abortive affairs with young men who use her for their own ends, she faces the problem of finding a suitable mate. The educated black men are either settled or they prefer white women. Her marriage to an aspiring photographer does not last too long, for he resents Reena's success. Reena resolves to bring up her children fully aware of their own personalities and race and plans to take them to Africa to show them black men living with pride in their heritage.

Closely connected with the question of identity is the race issue. In *Brown Girl...* the racist attitude of White America looms large in the background. Selina's cry of anguish voices the feelings of all people of all minorities. Her desire for violence, "to grab the cane and rush into some store on Fulton Street and avenge that wrong by bringing it smashing across the white face behind the counter"... is not uncommon too. In **"Brooklyn"** the life of Miss Williams is an evidence of the ambiguous identity experienced by many blacks. She succeeds, however, in accepting herself as a proud member of her race and thwarts the centuries old pattern of seduction and exploitation. Motley and Caliban in **"British Guiana"** and **"Brazil"** respectively suffer on account of the white power structure that encouraged no individualism.

The Chosen Place... weaves in the race issue subtly in the entire story. Harriet represents the spirit of the white world. She is only a step ahead of the Bentons of this world. When she fails to comprehend why a woman would sell the eggs to someone else rather than feed her own family, she takes it to be another backward streak of the incorrigibles. Her impotent anger and frustration come out vividly in the carnival scene where she realizes that the reign of people like her is over and a new generation is emerging. Her death seems to be a symbolic end of all that white America stands for and the ever-mourning waves of the ocean perform the ablution of the old sins of the past. Perhaps a new race of active men like Saul and sympathetic ones like Allen will create better understanding between the races.

This new world, Miss Marshall feels, will be created only through an acute awareness of the past.... Since Miss Marshall believes that without tradition one has no real existence, she has all her major characters go back to their ancient heritage. (pp. 53-4)

Miss Marshall says, "My concern has always been not only with content, what is being said, but also the way it is being said, the style." This concern shows in her craftsmanship. She uses a judicious mixture of the old and the new in fictional tradition. The plots of her novels are unambiguous and interesting containing conflict and suspense to keep the reader engrossed. But she uses liberally symbolic language to heighten the meaning; thus her stories are very often capable of being taken on different levels of meaning. At one level, *Brown Girl*... is the story of Selina's growing up, but on another level, it is also the story of "any people undergoing fundamental change and disruption." ... *Soul Clap*... deals with the identity crisis of the protagonists, but it also represents the passing away of the old order and the time for the new. *The Chosen Place*... at one level deals with the problems of its characters, but on the other level traces the history of black-white relationships. (pp. 55-6)

Paule Marshall excels in her character portrayals, but one must confess that she is partial to her women. They receive more careful attention, but that too is for a certain end, for she believes that the Negro woman has been neglected in literature. (p. 56)

Her women are complex characters but with hidden reservoirs of strength, which they need in order to survive. The mother in *Brown Girl*... is presented sympathetically despite her harshness; it is because the writer sees her as a product of her environment. If she is ruthless, it is understandable, if not excusable. Merle also is strong; her suffering has neither bent nor broken her. With her incessant chatter she may seem out of her mind at times to some, but that is her way of letting off her steam and diverting others from her sorrows.

In her attempt to battle with the old stereotype of the strong mother portraiture, Miss Marshall becomes unduly harsh with all mothers. Silla destroys her man and alienates her children by her very strength; Clive's mother keeps him tied to her apron-strings. In **"Brooklyn"** the mother of Miss Williams shares the responsibility in creating the ambiguity in her life. Similarly, in *The Chosen Place*... the mothers or the mother-figures, black or white, fail miserably. Harriet's obsession with meaningful life grew out of her mother's passivity; Leesy, the mother-substitute for Vere, cannot understand the new politically conscious modernized young man. In short, there is no mother who is depicted favorably.

Among men, Selina's father is portrayed well enough though he loses our sympathy eventually. The character studies of the men in *Soul Clap*... also succeed in capturing their despondent states of mind. Saul, however, is the best creation of her fictional world. He is strong, yet has his weaknesses too and is very much aware of the common bond that unites all human beings. Thus he is a very human character.

Even though the writer does not use Joycean style of stream of consciousness technique, she frequently fo-cuses on the subconscious mind of the characters. Combined with the editorial omniscience, her method succeeds in giving us an insight into the characters. In her first novel, the problem of the point of view is somewhat simplified, for we see the action mostly through the protagonist's eyes. But we do see the events from Silla's angle and also from Deighton's perspective. In her novellas most of the narrative is seen through the consciousness of the protagonists. Her last novel shows an adept handling of the point of view. She makes use of the mystical quality of the island where in the solitude each of the major characters faces his past and the flashbacks assist us in understanding his motivation.

Like Ralph Ellison Paule Marshall believes that the "Negro American writer is also an heir of the human experience which is literature...." From Eliot and Joyce she has learned the value of tradition. And then she does not forget the value of folk material. She tells us that she learned the first lessons of the narrative art from listening to her mother and her friends. After their hard day of scrubbing floors, they had to talk out their hurts and humiliations. Their acute observations about the people they worked for and their vivid portrayals filled their young listener with awe and admiration. Miss Marshall sees their gift as a part of the great oral tradition.... She feels that the mysterious element that held her spellbound has its source in the archetypal African memory. She uses it time and again, but it is at its best in *The Chosen Place*....

Through Miss Marshall's comments and, best of all, through her works, one can attempt to formulate her aesthetic beliefs. She seems to be quite in agreement with some of the tenets of the much discussed black aesthetics, and yet she differs too. Miss Marshall also stresses the need for identity. She too believes in understanding of one's past, both individual and historical. She too stands for reviving the African cultural heritage which gives supremacy to man over the machine. She too believes that the black writer owes a great responsibility to himself and to his world, to express his views to the world through his art. But here she diverges. Her works show that she does not believe that the art of the black writer should serve only one end. Like several other writers, she knows that the American writer cannot deny his Western heritage. She is equally proud of her black heritage but believes that her art should be devoted to showing the relationship of an individual to the other inhabitants of this world, no matter what their color, race, or geographic location is. She writes of blacks, very often of West Indians, simply because a writer writes best when he makes use of what he knows best. Her characters are, therefore, human beings first; their racial identity is secondary so far as the art is concerned. This fact does not make her any less believer in black pride; in fact, her pride stems out of her deep confidence. (pp. 57-9)

Leela Kapai, "Dominant Themes and Technique in Paule Marshall's Fiction," in CLA

Journal, *Vol. XVI, No. 1, September, 1972, pp. 49-59.*

Anne Tyler (essay date 1983)

[*An American novelist and critic, Tyler is the author of* The Accidental Tourist *and* Breathing Lessons. *In the following excerpt, she lauds the universal appeal of* Praisesong for the Widow.]

[*Praisesong for the Widow*] rings with the same music and some of the same lilting Barbadian speech [as *Brown Girl, Brownstones*], but it is a firmer book, obviously the product of a more experienced writer. It lacks the soft spots of the earlier work. From the first paragraph, it moves purposefully and knowledgeably toward its final realization.

The widow of the title is Avey Johnson, black and middle aged, decorous to a fault in her tasteful dress, her long-line girdle and her underarm shields. The praise-song is performed by a group of dancing natives on the tiny island of Carriacou, and how Avey Johnson comes to be there—how she leaves her luxurious cruise ship and her two staid women friends—is a story that's both convincing and eerily dreamlike . . . .

The reader knows before Avey what her trouble is. Secure in her middle class life, her civil service job, her house full of crystal and silver, Avey has become sealed away from her true self. Her dreamy intimations of something gone wrong will have to become near night-mares—with Avey stumbling disheveled down a burning stretch of sand, then succumbing to a mortifying siege of illness in front of strangers—before she fully comprehends.

There are times when her ordeal makes us slightly uneasy. She seems consciously set up for some of her embarrassment, uncharacteristically willing to prolong it, as, for instance, when she submits to a sponge bath even after she is well enough to take herself in hand again. For the most part, though, we are borne along by Avey's story without question—first, because of the subtle, intriguing aura of mystery, with scenes proceeding unexplained and strangers appearing to know and welcome her, and, second—much more important—because that true self of Avey's is described by means of breathtakingly vivid glimpses of her first years with her husband.

If there is a clearer evocation of early marriage anywhere else in literature, I can't think what it would be. Avey recalls her young husband, Jay, in the finest detail—that startling kind of detail that comes only when a buried memory is unexpectedly recovered . . . .

What is touching is not that Avey's husband is now dead but that he died long before his physical death. He was done in by poverty and racism and the constant pressure to succeed. By the time his family had "arrived," Avey's husband was another person entirely. (p. 7)

Jay Johnson became the more somber Jerome, endlessly pushing ahead. At his funeral everyone "congratulated her on how well she had held up in the face of her great loss."

Will black Americans, reading of Avey Johnson's rebellion against her homogenization, sympathize with it? Will they willingly accompany her on her journey backward to find her own "tribe"? I can't answer that. All I'm sure of is that her other journey—her wistful journey to her younger self—is universal, and it is astonishingly moving. (pp. 7, 34)

Anne Tyler, "A Widow's Tale," in The New York Times Book Review, *February 20, 1983, pp. 7, 34.*

Darryl Pinckney (essay date 1983)

[*In the following excerpt, Pinckney offers a somewhat negative review of* Praisesong for the Widow, *suggesting that Marshall has a one-dimensional approach to her characters.*]

Paule Marshall does not let the black women in her fiction lose. While they lose friends, lovers, husbands, homes, or jobs, they always find themselves. The precocious heroine of *Brown Girl, Brownstones* . . . comes of age and rejects the class aspirations of her tightly knit Barbadian community in Brooklyn. The willful teacher of *The Chosen Place, The Timeless People* . . . is middle-aged and heading toward a sharp turn in her rocky road, one that will take her into battle with developers on her Caribbean island, and then to the unknown in Africa. The well-heeled woman approaching old age in *Praisesong for the Widow* finds spiritual renewal on a remote island in the Caribbean.

In exploring the stages of black women's lives, Marshall insists that the woman with enough nerve can win even when the deck is stacked and the other players are hostile. Nerve, here, means making radical choices, and though the liberating destinies Marshall gives to her heroines are often unconvincing, the attraction of her work lies in a deep saturation in the consciousness of her characters and the ability to evoke the urban or tropical settings in which they toil. (p. 26)

The journey into the past, moving closer to one's cultural background, is a recurring theme in Paule Marshall's fiction. Discovering the Caribbean or Africa has, for her, the properties of psychic healing. In her latest novel, *Praisesong for the Widow,* this pilgrimage serves an almost exorcistic function. It is a quest for purity and release. (p. 27)

The renewal that Avey Johnson, the widow of the title, finds in the Caribbean may be ambiguous because of the awkward construction of the novel. It is an interior monologue told in the third person. The narration wanders from the inside of Avey Johnson's dreams to speculations more proper to an omniscient voice. Moreover, much is told in internal flashbacks, and this makes for a cumbersome reliance on the past perfect to keep chronology straight. The curious monotone in the writing is a disappointment, considering the animation Marshall is capable of giving exotic settings, as she did in a collection of short stories, **Soul Clap Hands and Sing** . . . . **Praisesong for the Widow** hasn't much substance, though we review with Avey Johnson her steep climb of years, and we get a sense of endless procrastination waiting for her to get to wherever she is going. (pp. 27-8)

Avey cannot explain to her friends or even to herself why she wants to leave the cruise . . . .

Avey is, one assumes, on the verge of a nervous breakdown. She has the withdrawn tendencies of someone in a paranoid state. She is repelled by people and things, anxious to keep her mental balance. But Marshall cannot make very vivid or menacing Avey's nightmares involving the old woman from her childhood. She spends paragraphs describing the ship, the meals, the routine, the pointless consumption and idle luxury in solemn detail that becomes both tedious and laughable.

Avey's panic does not abate once she is ashore. There are no taxis in sight and Avey spends several paranoid pages wondering why there is such a huge crowd on the Grenada wharf and why they were all speaking a strange language and why they were well dressed but ferrying in decrepit craft and where they were going. She is told by a sneering taxi driver that it is the season of the annual "Excursion." People from the out-island of Carriacou prepare all year for the festive return home . . . .

Carriacou is the island where Avey undergoes her transformation—but not until we are given the story of her life, a story of working for and getting everything she wanted only to wonder about the cost. (p. 28)

The outline of Avey's story is familiar. But instead of blaming the years for Avey's disappointments, Marshall leaves us with the impression that it was somehow Jay's fault. Unlike Deighton [in **Brown Girl, Brownstones**] who, by his temperament, was the architect of his own ruin, Jay completed his night courses. He worked overtime and remained faithful to his wife. Yet there is a faint note of condescension toward his ambition to get his family from the five-floor walk-up to the house and garden in North White Plains. This seems to be a favorite notion of Marshall's: the price of pulling up one's bootstraps is the soul, and men are more likely than women to sell theirs. The trade-off is particularly damaging to blacks since they can never belong to the white world, but that world forces them to give up the culture that is their only possibility of redemption.

Avey's trip to Carriacou is occasioned by an improbable meeting with an old man, Lebert Joseph, in a rum shop down the beach from the hotel where she is staying until she can get a flight out. She confides her unease immediately, and this is peculiar, given the code of propriety by which she has lived for so long. But

Marshall means to present a woman who is desperate, although we never get more than the sense of a bored, somewhat frightened tourist. Joseph invites Avey to make the Excursion with him. He has known many who suffer from her ailment: "People who can't call their nation. For one reason or another they just don't know. Is a hard thing. I don' even like to think about it. But you comes across them all the time here in Grenada. You ask people in this place what nation they is and they look at you like you's a madman."

Slavery always seemed a fairly reasonable explanation of why most black people cannot name their tribe, but Lebert Joseph is a creation of unforgivable sentimentality . . . . The odd notion that south of the border, in the Caribbean or Africa, the elderly among the people will come forward to lead their lost brethren back to their roots can only result in sentimentality.

Avey is taken ill during the crossing—strange that the description of vomiting in this novel is as off-putting as the descriptions of sex—and this makes her more vulnerable. She is open to the ministrations of Joseph's large family who welcome her as one restored to them.

Dust jacket for Marshall's 1983 novel.

Avey participates in the rituals of the homecoming, which climax in a dance and a prayer addressed to the ancestors and called the "Beg Pardon." . . . The ceremony stirs in Avey memories of the church services she attended with her old aunt in South Carolina and helps her to make sense of her recent dreams. She returns to New York resolved to "spread the word" about her discovery of the "Beg Pardon."

Such romanticizing of black culture in no way honors it. Romanticization has been constantly debated among black artists, its practitioners claiming that one must know the past in order to shape the future. The question is, what value has the past when it is so reduced? It is, at best, a kind of overcompensation. Paule Marshall has throughout her work pitted a mystical, lyrical African past against the evils of the West. Such an easily conceived idea of the cultural past does not increase our understanding of it. (p. 29)

Virginia Woolf observed that when women come to write novels, they probably find themselves wanting to alter established values, to make important what is insignificant to men and to make trivial what men think essential. Marshall shares this subversive inclination and sometimes it brings satisfying results. But Woolf also warned against a distorting element that can enter the fiction of those who are painfully aware of their "disability," and in Marshall's case the distorting element is not only a simplistic view of culture but also a simplistic idea of strength. The women in her novels are meant to seem courageous but they have more of the manic certitude of religious fanatics. They have an almost narcissistic appreciation of their own states of mind but little is revealed about the complicated forces against which they claim to struggle. This limited picture of the world is what sets Marshall's women apart from those of Zora Neale Hurston, whose women are more tolerant, forgiving, and, one might say, truly experienced.

Perhaps this one-dimensional approach comes from current strains in black feminism. To counter the image of the black woman as victim, a different picture is deemed necessary, one that inadvertently makes such words as "nurturing," "positive," and "supportive" unbearable. One is constantly aware of a manipulation of reality at work in Marshall's fiction and this causes us too distrust it. (pp. 29-30)

> *Darryl Pinckney, "Roots," in* The New York Review of Books, *Vol. XXX, No. 7, April 28, 1983, pp. 26-30.*

Linda Pannill (essay date 1985)

[*In the following excerpt, Pannill comments on the force and influence of Marshall's female characters in* Reena and Other Stories.]

As critics have recognized, each [of the four novellas in *Soul Clap Hands and Sing*] is about spiritual decay and the sadness of age without wisdom. Marshall chose to include only two—"**Brooklyn**" and "**Barbados**"—in the recent *Reena, and Other Stories*. Because the other fictions in *Reena, and Other Stories* have female protagonists, "**Brooklyn**" and "**Barbados**" are now placed in a context which invites an interpretation that focuses on the women characters. The woman in each is, it is true, a minor character, a background figure seen through the distorting eye of a man, but she does effect the recognition on his part of his limitations. Also, the woman is the one who changes, and she articulates the theme, speaking for the author. In a commentary in [the work], Marshall says "**Brooklyn**" was based on an incident of sexual harassment she experienced in the 1950s. The protagonist, Dr. Berman, a white professor of literature, tried to pressure Miss Williams, a young Black woman, into a liaison. He propositions her (with a promise of help with her writing) as they stand at the top of a flight of plunging stairs. Although she is shocked, nearly toppling, Miss Williams learns from the experience, overcoming the fear of white people she has been taught; later she refuses Dr. Berman, saying, "In a way you did me a favor. You let me know how you and most of the people like you—see me . . . . Look how I came all the way up here to tell you this to your face. Because how could you harm me? You're so old you're like a cup I could break in my hand." Though the novella appears to be about the old man's wish to be saved from his failed life by a young woman he thinks of as a Gauguin painting, the reader is liable to agree with Miss Williams that "What matters is what it meant to [her]."

The protagonist of "**Barbados**," the other novella reprinted in *Reena, and Other Stories* from *Soul Clap Hands and Sing,* is Mr. Watford, who has retired from a job in the United States to the island he came from, where he no longer feels at home. In a large white house on a plantation of dwarf coconut trees, he sets himself above his neighbors and ignores the young servant girl (nameless in the story) who lives in the house with him—until he is stirred by seeing her dancing with a young man. Then it is too late to approach her, of course, and when he does she finally speaks out, saying, "You ain't people, Mr. Watford, you ain't people!" The political button she wears, "The Old Order Shall Pass," underlines the message of this "Cassandra watching the future wheel before her eyes."

Paule Marshall says the women characters in *Soul Clap Hands and Sing* are "bringers of the truth," but this motif is less evident in the two novellas not collected in *Reena, and Other Stories.* Possibly they were omitted because they are less effective, "**British Guiana**" being a bit unclear in its symbolism and "**Brazil**" a bit obvious. Another reason might be that in both, the women are more passive and less important as characters—although Sybil in "**British Guiana**" is unusually interesting, with a dancer's grace and the perceptiveness her name implies. Maybe "**Brooklyn**" and "**Barbados**" are the better-written fictions in part *because* of the relative prominence of the female characters! A lot of the imagination in these stories is invested in the women, the revelations coming from them; in **"Brooklyn,"** for example, it seems the author is speaking back to the professor who harassed her years before; it seems that she had to write this story to do it.

Also collected in *Reena, and Other Stories* are three short stories.... **"The Valley Between,"** Marshall's first published story, is notable because the heroine, Cassie, is white. A young wife and mother, she is pressured into giving up college classes to stay at home with her daughter. In a commentary, the author says the character was white "to camouflage my own predicament." That **"The Valley Between"** was her first published story says something about the primacy in Paule Marshall's writing of women's concerns, and that she would reprint apprenticeship work to make this point says something about her self-confidence—and her integrity. The title story of the collection, **"Reena,"** was written for a special women's issue of *Harper's* in 1962 and was reprinted by Toni Cade Bambara in the important anthology *The Black Woman* (1970). A *tour de force*, **"Reena"** is, as the author says, a "story-essay" made up almost entirely of monologue, Reena speaking about her life as an educated and ambitious Black woman. Her listener is the narrator, her *alter ego,* a woman writer. The story's power comes from the convincingness of the speaking voice and the telling details, so that Reena is both an individual and a representative of women like her, women who have been left out of literature. The finest short story in the collection is **"To Da-duh, In Memoriam,"** an autobiographical work in which the narrator recalls a childhood visit to her grandmother in Barbados. "Da-duh" tries to make her granddaughter see what is valuable in the island but is abashed by the little girl's tales of skyscrapers ("building the city out of words"), her Tin Pan Alley songs and jitterbug dancing. The child's dancing fails to help them understand one another. Years after the grandmother's death the narrator is still trying to understand her background, painting her memories of the island in a loft above a noisy factory in New York. Though the paintings, we are told, fail, the story, with its complete understanding of the older and the younger women, succeeds.

For the reader familiar with Paule Marshall's work the most interesting part of *Reena, and Other Stories* is the one-hundred-page novella, **"Merle,"** abstracted from the 1969 novel *The Chosen Place, The Timeless People,* four-hundred-and-seventy-two-pages long. **"Merle"** is not lifted from one section of the novel but from passages throughout, rewritten. The alteration she has made in her work signals Marshall's recognition that Merle, one of a large cast of characters in the original, is her important creation:

> Merle remains the most alive of my characters. Indeed, it seems to me she has escaped the pages of the novel altogether and is abroad in the world. I envision her striding restlessly up and down the hemisphere from Argentina to Canada, and back and forth across the Atlantic between here and Africa, all the while speaking her mind in the same forthright way as in the book.

Merle is a colossal figure, almost always in motion, first seen trying to drive across the fictional Caribbean island of Bourne while the roads seem to twitch under her. Merle is voluble, difficult, generous, weary. A complete believable character (capable, like E. M. Forster's "round characters," of surprising us), she is also a symbolic one. A "bourne" is a boundary, of course, and Bourne Island, a former British Colony, has many such divisions; Merle embodies them all, in conflict. This is evident in her appearance, a mixture of European and African clothing, the silver bracelets worn by the island women and long earrings in the shape of saints, sad-faced but always dancing with her movements. Merle is the unacknowledged daughter of an island aristocrat, himself the descendant of an English planter and a slave. As a young woman she spent many years in England, where she was kept by the wealthy white woman who gave her the earrings. The relationship, presented as an exploitative one, broke up Merle's marriage to an African student, who left her, taking their daughter to Africa. Following a breakdown, Merle returned to the island, where she has just been fired from her teaching job for teaching the history of the island instead of the history of England. Now she runs a hotel on the Atlantic coast, in the house inherited from her father. Though apparently a broken woman, Merle has the power to speak uncomfortable truths. Periodically, however, she falls silent and locks herself in a room which is the analogue to her depressed mind. This room, the creation of a failed artist, is filled with white ancestors' heavy furniture, half-unpacked trunks brought from England, and many pictures: old prints of planters and slaves, a slave ship, her daughter's photograph. Not surprisingly, Merle admits to fascination with King Lear; like him, she is a half-mad monarch without a country, but she is not a father cast out by his daughters: she is a daughter cast out by her fathers.

In *The Chosen Place, The Timeless People* Merle is only one of the characters, Black and white, female and male, in a novel of epic ambitions. Among the others are Vere, a young man who has just returned to the island jobless, and his Great Aunt Leesy; Allen and Saul, social scientists who have come from the United States to do yet one more study of poverty on the island, and Saul's wealthy wife Harriet; Stinger and Gwen, who work in the cane fields; and many others. While there is a great deal of significant detail and telling incident (and, I think, too much dialogue and description), these characters don't come to life as Merle does, especially the white characters.... [By] foregrounding Merle in the novella Marshall is able to place the other characters in the background, where they belong. In the process, some memorable scenes are lost: Vere beating his faithless mistress with one of her own white dolls; Saul fleeing the hot cane fields and the sight of Gwen's turned-up eyes under a load of cane, eyes "that you find upon drawing back the lids of someone asleep or dead"; the palpable hunger Harriet sees among children whose parents are in the fields all day, hunger that "prowled angrily up and down, its footsteps shaking the weak floorboards, its fists pounding the walls, demanding to be appeased";

the carnival parade with its re-enactment of an island slave rebellion and its dancing. But what is gained is the excavation of the novel's best story, Merle's. The author's decision to turn the novel into a novella (a choice for which I know no precedent) may also reveal a new confidence in allowing her heroine to carry the burden of the novel's theme, the unforgivable damage done by racism and the exploitation of Third World peoples. A prominent motif in the novel, Cuffee Ned's slave rebellion, part of the fictional island's history, is omitted in the novella, but Cuffee Ned is, in a sense, subsumed into Merle, who is, after all, a rebel too.

Besides the condensing and tightening of structure involved in making the novella, there were changes to make the style more succinct. Comparison with the original shows adjectives and adverbs deleted and redundancies and entire passages of description omitted, changes indicating not only greater assurance on the author's part and greater confidence in her readers but a skillful writer's ability to continue to perfect her prose.

The literary criticism concerned with Paule Marshall's work has typically overlooked her artistry and emphasized nonliterary matters, focusing only on her themes and discussing her characters as though they are people. For example, John Cook chooses to discuss what he sees as the growth of the author's political consciousness, praising *The Chosen Place, The Timeless People* over the earlier work on political grounds, for its "unambiguous political perspective" and Pan-Africanism. He censures Marshall for "a temperamental difficulty...her predilection for personal as opposed to political subjects" and for her interest in "sexual conflict," as though these were not what novels are made of. By positing a false dichotomy between the personal and the political and by overlooking the dynamics of fiction writing, he misses part of the meaning of the work: not only is Marshall concerned in her books with the need to speak out, but her writing fictions, taking on, as a Black woman, the powerful role of shaper, is itself a political act. (Yet essays on Paule Marshall are still appearing which do not attempt to take into account the implications of the author's being a Black *woman* writer.) (pp. 65-70)

> *Linda Pannill, "From the 'Wordshop': The Fiction of Paule Marshall," in* MELUS, *Vol. 12, No. 2, Summer, 1985, pp. 63-73.*

Missy Dehn Kubitschek (essay date 1987)

[*In the excerpt below, Kubitschek examines the protagonist's quest for identity in* Brown Girl, Brownstones, Soul Clap Hands and Sing, *and* Praisesong for the Widow.]

Marshall's depictions of the quest [for identity] change dramatically from novel to novel. Deborah Schneider locates the reason for these changes in the climate of the times during which the novels were written. *Brown Girl, Brownstones* indicates its '50s origin, for example,

through its accent on art and individualism, Selina's distaste for community action, and her unconsciousness of the effect of sex roles on her parents' lives; *The Chosen Place, The Timeless People,* on the other hand, reflects the political activism and community focus of the '60s. The changing times undoubtedly affected Marshall's artistic concerns, but another reason for the shift may be as important, particularly with *Praisesong for the Widow* as an additional piece of evidence. The questers in these three novels are of radically different ages. *Brown Girl* covers six years of Selina Boyce's adolescence; *The Chosen Place,* a year of Merle Kinbona's middle age; *Praisesong,* several days in Avatara Johnson's sixty-fourth year. The forces which motivate and affect the questers naturally differ because of their ages. A typical adolescent, Selina must discover both her identity and her community. Merle has no doubts about her community, her experiences in England having confirmed her commitment to Bournehills, but she must reconcile the paradoxes of that community and heritage into a unified self. The most alienated of the three, Avey must discard both a false self and a false definition of community to rediscover her identity.

The key experiences and significant influences differ for each quest not simply because of the questers' unique temperaments but because the sums of their past experiences vary so widely. Thus, the adolescent Selina's parents figure prominently in her development, while Avey remembers hers only intermittently. In order to become an adult, Selina must battle with and become reconciled to her mother; Avey, on the other hand, contends with the apparition of her dead husband. Because at eighteen she has had time for only a few independent actions, Selina must come to terms with only one of her own deeds (her intended fleecing of the Association), and the novel focuses on her potential. Merle and Avatara must accept, on the other hand, many years' worth of their own and others' excruciatingly painful, self-betraying or self-evading actions.

Though each quester seeks a place within a community as opposed to a privately defined role, each must journey outward from that community. *Brown Girl* and *The Chosen Place* end with the beginnings of that journey, Selina's embarking for the Caribbean and Merle's setting off for Kampala. *Praisesong,* on the other hand, details Avey's travels. Avatara's age precludes the open-endedness of the first two novels; the practice of her rediscovered integrity must be immediate if she is to contribute to her society, and *Praisesong*'s ending shows her on the journey home. The sense of identity also changes from novel to novel: Merle and even Selina have to create a good part of their identities while Avatara, in claiming her whole and original name rather than the diminutive Avey, essentially rediscovers hers. The more static nature of identity in *Praisesong* accords with the whole texture of the novel, which is the closest of the three to the classical pattern of the quest as articulated by [Joseph] Campbell. As Campbell notes, the classical quester undertakes the journey to renew his society rather than to find himself.

In discussing the relationship of these two issues, political responsibility and self-acceptance, Marshall makes a signal contribution to the modern quest: In both *Brown Girl, Brownstones* and *The Chosen Place, The Timeless People,* political commitment precedes the solidification or unification of the quester's individual personality. When Selina casts one of her two silver bracelets into the graveyard of her neighborhood and keeps the other on her wrist, her action, like the exchange of wedding rings, testifies to her political commitment. Likewise, Merle supports "the little fella" of Bournehills in the midst of her personal fragmentation. These characters show an alternative to the tradition of *Invisible Man,* in which the protagonist remains in hibernation until he has assimilated his experience and is ready to emerge as a unified (and therefore less vulnerable) personality. To some extent, this variation may be characteristic of gender, women traditionally having performed the roles of nurturing which cannot be postponed, no matter what difficulties assail. Gabriel and Elizabeth in Baldwin's *Go Tell It on the Mountain* might represent these two opposing approaches in their favorite Biblical passages: Gabriel favors "Put thine house in order," while Elizabeth inclines toward "Everything works together for them that love the Lord." *Brown Girl, Brownstones* and *The Chosen Place, The Timeless People* recognize that, because society and the individual are mutually creative, the unification of self cannot take precedence over political commitment to change: If personal identity is privileged, the warped culture will continually subvert the individual's gropings toward internal coherence, and the individual will never move into the second phase, commitment.

In order to be useful, this commitment must find a suitable voice, a problem for all three of Marshall's questers. Overcoming a multitude of different silences—of the individual, of the women missing from the literary canon, of the politicians purportedly representing women—has become a touchstone of the women's movement and of women's studies (to name only a few examples, Carol Gilligan's study of women's cognitive and moral development *In a Different Voice,* Tillie Olsen's book on working-class and female writers *Silences,* Adrienne Rich's collection of essays *On Lies, Secrets, and Silence*). Selina, Merle, and Avatara confront different problems in discovering authoritative voices for their insights.

Selina initially envies her mother's eloquence and only gradually develops her own abilities. Desirous of the easy yet powerful flow of Bajan dialect of the women seated around her mother's kitchen table, Selina resists if also, for it cannot describe her own experience—to use Robert Stepto's terms, Selina's parents and community urge her into a journey of ascent into the literacy of the dominant culture, which must affect her voice. When she learns to manipulate her community with the language of domination, the experience does not help her to locate a true identity; in addition, it amounts to a political betrayal. Selina comes into painful maturity as an honest member of the Bajan community through her

speech respectfully refusing the Association's scholarship. She cannot explain herself or her motivations fully, for the Association's members cannot understand her emotional vocabulary; nevertheless, they understand her apology and respect for them.

Selina's story concentrates on development; Avatara's, on discovery. In order to focus her energies on the economic struggle, Avey has censored her own voice. While settled in this pattern, she uses silence as a weapon, hiding her bad faith by indicating that others are simply impolite for bringing up difficult topics. When her daughter Marion calls after the Poor People's March on Washington, for example, she nearly hangs up; on many topics, she simply refuses to speak. The authority of the ancestor who in a dream issues her call to adventure, great-aunt Cuney, insists that Avatara narrate the Ibos' story. Avatara thus speaks with the tribal authority of the griot.

Unlike the others, Merle has no difficulty in learning to articulate. Literate in both the tribe's and the dominant culture's worlds, she must instead learn to control her expression. Recognized as the spokesperson for Bournehills, Merle already has the authoritative social voice which Avatara discovers. Unable to fulfill that role without exhausting herself, however, she alternates between compulsive speech and catatonia. Merle's experience exemplifies the first two stages in the cycle of nothingness/empowerment/naming anew which [Carol] Christ identifies as the female quest. In order to make her path a spiral rather than an endlessly repeating circle, Merle must rename herself; that is, find a self-image which permits her to speak when she is not representing the community, a personal voice. Her decision to travel to Kampala, confront her husband, and contact their child suggests a possible breakthrough. Although the Tiv epithet notes the unbreakable continuity of destructive cycles, individuals seem able to advance: Recognizing that she has made the same mistakes in her relationships with Andrew and Saul, Harriet kills herself; having realized his true sexual nature, Allen will no longer unwittingly hurt himself and others by trying to establish sexual relationships with women; satisfied that he knows what travel and exploration can tell him, Saul decides to abandon field work and stay in the United States. Thus, every major character in *The Chosen Place, The Timeless People* changes through self-recognition and accompanying self-rejection or self-acceptance, and the survivors progress to some degree. Merle too will come more fully into her own.

Paule Marshall's female questers, then, achieve energized, articulate identities, with each quester resolving the problems of her particular stage of life. An adolescent, Selina separates from her parents without rejecting them, acknowledges her community while denying its right to determine her personality. The middle-aged Merle recovers from her disappointments in her own character and her husband's personal rejection. Revitalized, she journeys to Africa to establish a relationship with their child; her renewed self-respect and consequent interest in her personal life does not signal a retreat from her political commitment, however. For Merle, Bournehills is home, and she intends to return to her political commitments there. As an older woman, Avatara must throw off the psychological bondage of many years' loyalty to a false ideal which had seemed the only means of survival. Instead of being handicaps, her age and family position grant her the authority to educate the youngest part of her immediate community, her grandsons. Marshall has thus expanded the nature and duration of the classical quest pattern. The quest is no longer an isolated if perhaps lengthy incident in the quester's life but a lifelong commitment and, in her first two novels, a continuous modification of identity. While speaking in her own voice of her own experience, each quester addresses a wider community, until, in the final scene of *Praisesong,* the empowered woman quester becomes a griot speaking in tribal language of universal concerns. (pp. 55-9)

> *Missy Dehn Kubitschek, "Paule Marshall's Women on Quest," in* Black American Literature Forum, *Vol. 21, Nos. 1-2, Spring-Summer, 1987, pp. 43-60.*

FURTHER READING

De Veux, Alexis. "Paule Marshall: In Celebration of Our Triumph." *Essence* 10, No. 1 (May 1979): 70-1, 96-8, 123-35.
    Detailed interview in which Marshall comments on her personal goals as a writer.

Marshall, Paule. 'The Negro Woman in American Literature: Paule Marshall." *Freedomways* 6, No. 1 (Winter 1966): 20-5.
    Text of a speech given by Marshall at a three-day conference on "The Negro Writer's Vision of America." Marshall was one of four women writers who discussed the role of black writers; she focuses her comments on the myths that she believes have halted honest depictions of black characters in literature.

————. "Shaping the World of My Art." *New Letters* 40, No. 1 (Autumn 1973): 97-112.
    Marshall discusses childhood experiences that helped shape her thinking, writing, and beliefs.

————. "Shadow and Act." *Mademoiselle* 79, No. 2 (June 1974): 82-3.
    Review of Ralph Ellison's *Shadow and Act.* Marshall examines the theme of the work and comments on its influence on her fiction.

————. "The Making of a Writer: From the Poets in the Kitchen." *New York Times Book Review* (9 January 1983): 3, 34-5.
    Highly acclaimed commentary on the foundations and elements of Marshall's personal and artistic beliefs. Marshall recounts the distinctive poetic art of her mother's Barbadian dialect and its impact on her writing.

McCluskey, John, Jr. "And Called Every Generation Blessed: Theme, Setting, and Ritual in the Works of Paule Marshall." In *Black Women Writers (1950-1980): A Critical Evaluation,* edited by Mari Evans, pp. 317-36. New York: Anchor Press/Doubleday, 1984.
    Explores themes in Marshall's major works.

Waniek, Marilyn Nelson. "Paltry Things: Immigrants and Marginal Men in Paule Marshall's Fiction." *Callaloo* 6, No. 2 (Spring-Summer 1983): 46-56.
    Examines the alienation motif in *Soul Clap Hands and Sing.*

Washington, Mary Helen. "I Sign My Mother's Name: Alice Walker, Dorothy West, Paule Marshall." In *Mothering the Mind: Twelve Studies of Writers and Their Silent Partners,* edited by Ruth Perry and Martine Watson Brownley, pp. 155-63. New York: Holmes & Meier Publishers, 1984.
    Contains revealing commentary from Marshall about her relationship with her mother. Washington examines the dynamics of the mother-daughter relationship and discusses its effects on Marshall's fiction.

Claude McKay

1889-1948

(Born Festus Claudius McKay; also wrote under pseudonym Eli Edwards) Jamaican-born American poet, novelist, short story writer, journalist, essayist, and autobiographer.

McKay was a major writer of the Harlem Renaissance, a period during the 1920s and early 1930s of unprecedented artistic and intellectual achievement among black Americans. His work includes dialect verse celebrating peasant life in Jamaica, militant poems challenging white authority in the United States, fictional works realistically depicting black life in both Jamaica and America, and philosophically ambitious novels about the efforts of blacks to cope in Western society. Perhaps more than any other black writer of his time, McKay managed to convert anger and social protest into poems of lasting value. The publication in 1919 of his most popular poem, "If We Must Die," was at once a shout of defiance and a proclamation of the unbreakable spirit and courage of the oppressed black individual; thus the work is considered a major impetus behind the Harlem Renaissance and the civil rights movement in the decade following World War I. In all his works, McKay searched among the common folk for a distinctive black identity, hoping to find a way to preserve the African spirit and creativity in an alienating world.

McKay was born in the hills of Jamaica to peasant farmers whose sense of racial pride greatly affected the young McKay. His father was instrumental in reinforcing this pride, telling his son folktales about Africa as well as stories about McKay's African grandfather's enslavement. From accounts of his grandfather's experiences with white men, McKay acquired an early distrust for whites. Under the tutelage of his brother, a schoolteacher and avowed agnostic, McKay was imbued with freethinking ideas and philosophies. In 1907 he left his rural home to apprentice as a woodworker in Brown's Town, where he met Walter Jekyll, an English linguist and specialist in Jamaican folklore. Jekyll helped further McKay's developing interest in English poetry, introducing him to such British masters as John Milton, Alexander Pope, and Percy Bysshe Shelley. He also encouraged McKay to write verse in his native dialect. In 1909 McKay moved to Kingston, Jamaica's capital, where he later served as a constable. His native town, Sunny Ville, was predominantly black, but in substantially white Kingston the caste society, which placed blacks below whites and mulattoes, revealed to McKay alienating and degrading aspects of city life and racism. His exposure to overt racism in Kingston soon led him to identify strongly with the plight of blacks, who, he saw to his alarm, there lived under the near-total control of whites.

In 1912, with Jekyll's assistance, McKay published his first volumes of poetry, *Songs of Jamaica* and *Constab Ballads.* Both works are collections of lyrical verse written in Jamaican vernacular; the former celebrates nature and the peasant's bond to the soil, while the latter decries injustices of city life. In the same year, 1912, McKay traveled to the United States to study agriculture. After attending Tuskegee Institute in Alabama and Kansas State College, he decided to quit his studies in 1914 and move to New York City. By 1917, because of his associations with two prominent men of letters—Frank Harris, editor of *Pearson's Magazine,* in which McKay's militant poem "To The White Fiends" appeared, and Max Eastman, editor of the Communist magazine *The Liberator,* in which the poem "If We Must Die" was first published—McKay established literary and political ties with left-wing thinkers in Greenwich Village. After the publication of "If We Must Die," McKay began two years of travel and work abroad. In London he worked on the socialist periodical *Workers' Dreadnought;* he published his third collection, *Spring in New Hampshire, and Other Poems,* in 1920. McKay returned to the United States in 1921 and took up various social causes. His most highly acclaimed poetry volume, *Harlem Shadows,* appeared the following year. Shortly thereafter, McKay left America for twelve years, traveling first to Moscow to attend the Fourth Congress of the Communist Party.

McKay was extolled in the Soviet Union as a great American poet, but he grew disenchanted with the Communist party when it became apparent he would have to subjugate his art to political propaganda. By 1923 McKay had moved to Paris; later, he journeyed to the south of France, Germany, North Africa, and Spain. From 1923 until his return to the United States in 1934, he concentrated on writing fiction, completing his novels *Home to Harlem* (1928); *Banjo: A Story without a Plot* (1929), and *Banana Bottom* (1933), as well as a collection of short stories, *Gingertown* (1932). All but *Home to Harlem,* which became one of the first bestsellers by a black writer, were almost wholly neglected by critics and the reading public. Once back in Harlem, he wrote his autobiography, *A Long Way from Home* (1937), in an attempt to bolster his financial and literary status. Following the publication of this work, McKay developed an interest in Roman Catholicism and became active in Harlem's Friendship House, a Catholic community center. His work there led to the writing of *Harlem: Negro Metropolis* (1940), an historical essay collection that sold poorly. By the mid-1940s McKay's health had deteriorated and, after enduring several illnesses, the author died of heart failure in Chicago.

McKay reached his zenith as a poet with the publication of *Harlem Shadows,* a collection that "clearly pointed to the incipient Renaissance," according to George E. Kent. Comprised of new works in addition to works previously published in periodicals and in the volume *Spring in New Hampshire, Harlem Shadows* contains poems based on conventional forms, most notably the sonnet. Evident in these poems is the chief conflict McKay faced as an author: he was a black poet writing within a tradition espoused by whites. McKay expressed this conflict when he wrote: "A Negro writer feeling the urge to write faithfully about the people he knows from real experiences and impartial observation is caught in a dilemma ... between this group and his own artistic conscientiousness." While maintaining a sense of universality that denied judgement of merit based on race, McKay sought a vital identity for the black individual.

Harlem Shadows contains McKay's most militant and race-conscious poems, including his best-known work, "If We Must Die," a sonnet he had excluded from *Spring in New Hampshire* to avoid reference to "color." This piece, composed in response to racial violence that occurred throughout America during the summer of 1919, was interpreted by some commentators as a warlike cry by black radicals. According to Stephen H. Bronz, however, "If We Must Die" was written "to apply to an extreme situation; such desperate fighting need be resorted to only when 'the mad and hungry

dogs' are at one's very heels, as McKay felt was the case in 1919." The poem is considered to have a universal message; indeed, British Prime Minister Winston Churchill recited it before the House of Commons in an emotional response to Nazi Germany's threat of invasion during World War II. McKay's militancy has been variously interpreted. Jean Wagner, for example, saw hatred as a significant theme in McKay's poetry and asserted that "among all black poets, [McKay] is *par excellence* the poet of hate." Yet hatred is employed not in the service of destructive aims, but rather as a vehicle of change, as in the sonnet "The White City," which calls upon hatred to vitalize oppressed spirits.

McKay also wrote important novels and short stories, expressing in them the energy and spontaneity of the common folk. His third novel, *Banana Bottom,* is recognized as his greatest achievement in fiction. Therein, as in *Home to Harlem, Banjo,* and several short stories, McKay depicted the black individual in white Western culture and juxtaposed the opposing value systems of these two societies. *Banana Bottom* recounts the experiences of a Jamaican peasant girl, Bita Plant, who is rescued by white missionaries after being raped. Bita's new providers try to impose their cultural values on her by introducing her to organized Christianity and the British educational system. Their actions culminate in a bungled attempt to arrange Bita's marriage to an aspiring minister. The prospective groom is exposed as a sexual aberrant, whereupon Bita flees white society, eventually finding happiness and fulfillment among the black peasants. In his previous novels, McKay presented the theme of cultural dualism through two protagonists—one exemplifying the primitive black individual, the other typifying the educated black. Bita, however, embodies both characteristics and merges instinct and intellect. Commenting on the resolution of *Banana Bottom,* Michael B. Stoff noted that "of peasant origin and possessing a cultivated intellect, Bita Plant represents McKay's first successful synthesis of two cultures."

McKay's reputation as an author was never greater than during his period of fame in the 1920s. Despite his apparent decline in later years, his literary accomplishments are acclaimed as pioneering efforts by a black artist, and his influence on later writers is unquestioned. His work not only inspired such Francophone poets as Aimé Césaire and Léopold Senghor—authors whose verse espoused tenets of negritude, a movement begun in the 1930s that sought to reclaim African cultural heritage—but also writers of the Black Arts Movement, which flourished during the 1960s through such acclaimed poets as Amiri Baraka (LeRoi Jones) and Haki R. Madhubuti (Don L. Lee). McKay's poetic forms were once thought by some to be too conventional and limiting for the density of his themes; however, he has recently been praised for the intensity and ardor of his poetry. *Banana Bottom* is recognized as McKay's most skillful delineation of the black individual's predicament in white society and as the culmination of the author's efforts to articulate the tension and unease he experienced as a black man in white society. Two other works by McKay, *Harlem: Negro Metropolis* and the essay *The Negroes in America,* have not been closely studied by critics, but most commentators concur that these works show McKay acting in the role of social critic, enhancing his reputation as one who devoted his art and life to social protest.

(For further information about McKay's life and works, see *Black Writers; Contemporary Authors,* Vol. 104; *Dictionary of Literary Biography,* Vols. 4, 45, 51; *Poetry Criticism,* Vol. 2; and *Twentieth-Century Literary Criticism,* Vols. 7, 41. For related criticism, see the entry on the Harlem Renaissance in *Twentieth-Century Literary Criticism,* Vol. 26.)

PRINCIPAL WORKS

Constab Ballads (poetry) 1912
Songs of Jamaica (poetry) 1912
Spring in New Hampshire, and Other Poems (poetry) 1920
Harlem Shadows (poetry) 1922
Home to Harlem (novel) 1928
Banjo: A Story without a Plot (novel) 1929
Gingertown (short stories) 1932
Banana Bottom (novel) 1933
A Long Way from Home (autobiography) 1937
Harlem: Negro Metropolis (nonfiction) 1940
Selected Poems (poetry) 1953
The Dialect Poetry of Claude McKay (poetry) 1972
The Passion of Claude McKay: Selected Poetry and Prose, 1912-1948 (poetry, fiction, and nonfiction) 1973
Trial by Lynching (short stories) 1977
My Green Hills of Jamaica (essays and short stories) 1979
*The Negroes in America (nonfiction) 1979

* This work was originally published in Russian in 1923.

William Stanley Braithwaite (essay date 1919)

[*Braithwaite was a black American poet, critic, and anthologist who was instrumental in the American poetry revival of the early twentieth century. He consciously avoided racial themes in his own writing, demanding instead that poetry, as an art form, should be written for its own sake. In the following excerpt from a discussion of McKay's sonnet "The Harlem Dancer," he presents McKay as "the keystone of the new movement in racial poetic achievement."*]

The most significant accomplishment among . . . recent poems are two sonnets signed by "Eli Edwards" which appeared in *The Seven Arts* for last October. "Eli Edwards," I understand, is the pseudonym of Claude McKay, who lives in New York City, choosing to conceal his identity as a poet from the associates among

whom he works for his daily bread. His story as it is . . . is full of alluring interest, and may one day be vividly featured as a topic of historic literary importance. For he may well be the keystone of the new movement in racial poetic achievement. (p. 277)

Here [in **"The Harlem Dancer"**], indeed, is the genuine gift—a vision that evokes from the confusing details of experience and brings into the picture the image in all its completeness of outline and its gradation of color, and rendered with that precise surety of form possessed by the resourceful artist. The power in this poet is, I think, his ability to reproduce a hectic scene of reality with all the solid accessories, as in **"The Harlem Dancer,"** and yet make it float as it were upon a background of illusion through which comes piercing the glowing sense of a spiritual mystery. Note the exalted close of Mr. Edward's riotous picture of the dancer when

> . . . . looking at her falsely-smiling face,
> I knew herself was not in that strange place—

he translates the significance of the intoxicated figure with its sensuous contagion into something ultimate behind the "falsely-smiling face," where "herself"—be it the innocent memory of childhood, perhaps of some pursuing dream of a brief happiness in love, or a far-away country home which her corybantic earnings secures in peace and comfort for the aged days of her parents—is inviolably wrapped in the innocence and beauty of her dreams. This sonnet differs in both visionary and artistic power from anything so far produced by the poets of the race. The visual quality here possessed is extraordinary; not only does Mr. Edwards evoke his images with a clear and decisive imagination, but he throws at the same time upon the object the rich and warm colors of his emotional sympathies. (p. 278)

> *William Stanley Braithwaite, "Some Contemporary Poets of the Negro Race," in* The Crisis, *Vol. 17, No. 6, April, 1919, pp. 275-80.*

Walter F. White (essay date 1922)

[*White was an American essayist, novelist, nonfiction writer, and autobiographer. His Harlem Renaissance novels* The Fire in the Flint *(1924) and* Flight *(1926) depict middle-class African-Americans and the effects of racism on their lives. White was also a civil rights activist and a prominent member of the National Association for the Advancement of Colored People (NAACP). His nonfiction work* Rope and Faggot: A Biography of Judge Lynch *(1929) examines such issues as the roots of mob violence and racial discrimination. In the following excerpt, he offers a favorable review of McKay's poetry collection* Harlem Shadows.*]

With the publication of **Harlem Shadows** by Claude McKay we are introduced to the work of a man who shows very genuine poetical promise. His work proves

him to be a craftsman with keen perception of emotions, a lover of the colorful and dramatic, strongly sensuous yet never sensual, and an adept in the handling of his phrases to give the subtle variations of thought he seeks. He has mastered the forms of the lyric and the sonnet—in fact, there is in this volume perhaps too much sameness of form. Yet one can have no quarrel with a man who works in that medium in which he is most at home, and I do not quarrel with Mr. McKay for sticking to these modes of expression.

I wish that I had the ability to convey the sheer delight which this book of verse gives me. Keenly sensitive to color and beauty and tragedy and mirth, he does, as Max Eastman says in his introduction, cause us to "find our literature vividly enriched by a voice from this most alien race among us." Mr. McKay is most compelling when he voices his protest against the wrongs inflicted on his people, yet in his love lyrics there is a beauty and a charm that reveal the true poetic gift. (pp. 694-95)

Walter F. White, "Negro Poets," in The Nation, *New York, Vol. CXIV, No. 2970, June 7, 1922, pp. 694-95.*

Burton Rascoe (essay date 1928)

[*Rascoe was an American literary critic. In the following excerpt from a review of McKay's novel* Home to Harlem, *he lauds the author's tragic portrayal of the "serving class" Harlemite.*]

Home to Harlem is a book to invoke pity and terror, which is the function of tragedy, and to that extent—that very great extent—it is beautiful. It is hard to convey to the reader the impression this novel leaves upon the mind, just as it is hard to convey the impression that a blues-song leaves upon the mind. One reads, one hears and the heart is touched.

Out of his individual pain, Claude McKay, the poet, has fashioned his lyrics; and out of his impersonal sorrow he has written a fine novel. **Home to Harlem** is a story involving the lives led by the lost generation of colored folk in the teeming Negro metropolis north of One Hundred and Tenth Street, New York. It is a story not of the successful Negroes who have done well in the trades and professions and have built themselves homes, sent their children to school, and engaged in civil and social pursuits of a sober and respectable nature: it is the story of the serving class—longshoremen and roustabouts, house-maids and Pullman porters, waiters and wash-room attendants, cooks and scullery maids, "dime-snatchers", and all those who compensate for defeat in life in a white man's world by a savage intensity among themselves at night.

Most of the scenes of **Home to Harlem** are in the cabarets and gin-mills where jazz bands stir the blood to lust in an atmosphere as orgiastic as a pagan Saturnalia. But there are scenes, too, on railroads dining-cars where cooks and waiters have scant respect for Pullman porters and feuds are carried on between chef and pantry-man. And there are scenes in buffet flats and in the barrack quarters for railroad employees in Pittsburgh and in the small rooms for which a steep rent is paid in over-congested Harlem.

Home to Harlem is not a novel in the conventional sense. The only conflict in the mind of Jake, the hero, is as to whether he will keep on working at whatever insecure, underpaid drudgery he can find to do on the docks, in the stoke-hole of a steamer and in dining-cars or turn his handsome body and good looks into the shameful asset of a "sweet-man", kept in luxury on the earnings of a woman. The only conflict of wills engaged in by the hero is when he takes a girl away from his former buddy, and anger and hate flare into being, with drawn gun and open razor. When the book closes and he is going away to Chicago with the girl to start life anew, he is the same wondering, indecisive being he was in the beginning, who "preferred the white folks' hatred to their friendly contempt" and found a sinister satisfaction in the fact that the white man is too effete to know the sensual pleasures of the blacks. (p. 183)

The language of **Home to Harlem,** whether Mr. McKay is setting forth dialogue in a perfect transcription of Negro slang and dialect or is telling his story in the Negro idiom, is a constant joy. A big black buck "lazied" down the street; another chap is "sissified"; Aunt Hattie remarks concerning some imported liquor offered her, "Ef youse always so eye-filling drinking it, it might ginger up mah bones some", and a sadistic yellow-brown girl inciting her new lover to attack her former lover cries "Hit him, Obadiah! Hit him I tell you. Beat his mug up foh him, beat his mug and bleed his mouf! Bleed his mouf! Two-faced yaller nigger, you does ebery low-down thing, but you nevah done a lick of work in you lifetime. Show him, Obadiah. Beat his face and bleed his mouf"

Mr. McKay is not at all solicitous toward his reader. He makes no case, he pleads no cause, he asks no extenuation, and he doesn't explain his idiomatic phrases. There is no glossary at the end of the book as there was to Carl Van Venchten's *Nigger Heaven;* and the unsophisticated happily will read whole pages of this novel depicting the utmost moral degradation without ever knowing what it is about. And this is just as well. (p. 184)

Burton Rascoe, "The Seamy Side," in The Bookman, *New York, Vol. LXVII, No. 2, April, 1928, pp. 183-85.*

W. E. B. Du Bois (essay date 1928)

[*An American educator and man of letters, Du Bois is an outstanding figure in twentieth-century American history. He was a founder of the NAACP and edited that organization's periodical,* The Crisis, *from 1910 to 1934. Du Bois deplored the movement in black literature toward exploiting sordid aspects of African-*

American culture, believing instead that black writers should depict exemplary characters who would counterbalance past stereotypes. In the following excerpt from a review of Home to Harlem, *he vehemently disapproves of McKay's passionate and unrestrained characterizations of black Harlemites.*]

[Claude McKay's novel *Home to Harlem*] for the most part nauseates me, and after the dirtier parts of its filth I feel distinctly like taking a bath. This does not mean that the book is wholly bad. McKay is too great a poet to make any complete failure in writing. There are bits of *Home to Harlem,* beautiful and fascinating: the continued changes upon the theme of the beauty of colored skins; the portrayal of the fascination of their new yearnings for each other which Negroes are developing. The chief character, Jake, has something appealing, and the glimpses of the Haitian, Ray, have all the materials of a great piece of fiction.

But it looks as though, despite this, McKay has set out to cater for that prurient demand on the part of white folk for a portrayal in Negroes of that utter licentiousness which conventional civilization holds white folk back from enjoying—if enjoyment it can be called. That which a certain decadent section of the white American world, centered particularly in New York, longs for with fierce and unrestrained passions, it wants to see written out in black and white, and saddled on black Harlem. This demand, as voiced by a number of New York publishers, McKay has certainly satisfied, and added much for good measure. He has used every art and emphasis to paint drunkenness, fighting, lascivious sexual promiscuity and utter absence of restraint in as bold and as bright colors as he can.

If this had been done in the course of a well-conceived plot or with any artistic unity, it might have been understood if not excused. But *Home to Harlem* is padded. Whole chapters here and there are inserted with no connection to the main plot, except that they are on the same dirty subject. As a picture of Harlem life or of Negro life anywhere, it is, of course, nonsense. Untrue, not so much as on account of its facts, but on account of its emphasis and glaring colors. I am sorry that the author of *Harlem Shadows* stooped to this. I sincerely hope that he will some day rise above it and give us in fiction the strong, well-knit as well as beautiful theme, that it seems to me he might do.

> *W. E. B. Du Bois, in a review of "Home to Harlem," in* The Crisis, *Vol. 35, No. 6, June, 1928, p. 202.*

Claude McKay (essay date 1932)

[*In the following excerpt from an essay first published in the* New York Herald-Tribune Books *in 1932, McKay responds to black critics who faulted him for his forthright portrayals of lower-class blacks in his fiction.*]

When the work of a Negro writer wins recognition it creates two widely separate bodies of opinion, one easily recognizable by the average reader as general and the other limited to Negroes and therefore racial.

Although this racial opinion may seem negligible to the general reader, it is a formidable thing to the Negro writer. He may pretend to ignore it without really succeeding or being able to escape its influence, for very likely he has his social contacts with the class of Negroes who create and express this opinion in their conversation and through the hundreds of weekly Negro newspapers and the monthly magazines.

This peculiar racial opinion constitutes a kind of censorship of what is printed about the Negro. No doubt it had its origin in the laudable efforts of intelligent Negro groups to protect their race from the slander of its detractors after Emancipation, and grew until it crystallized into racial consciousness. The pity is that these leaders of racial opinion should also be in the position of sole arbiters of intellectual and artistic things within the Negro world. For although they may be excellent persons worthy of all respect and eminently right in their purpose, they often do not distinguish between the task of propaganda and the work of art.

I myself have lived a great deal in the atmosphere of this opinion in America, in sympathy with and in contact with leaders and groups expressing it and am aware of their limitations.

A Negro writer feeling the urge to write faithfully about the people he knows from real experience and impartial observation is caught in a dilemma (unless he possesses a very strong sense of esthetic values) between the opinion of this group and his own artistic conscientiousness. I have read pages upon pages of denunciation of young Negro poets and story-tellers who were trying to grasp and render the significance of the background, the fundamental rhythm of Aframerican life. But not a line of critical encouragement for the artistic exploitation of the homely things—of Maudy's wash tub, Aunt Jemima's white folks, Miss Ann's old clothes for work-and-wages, George's Yessah-boss, dining car and Pullman services, barber and shoe shine shop, chittling and corn-pone joints—all the lowly things that go to the formation of the Aframerican soil in which the best, the most pretentious of Aframerican society still has its roots.

My own experience has been amazing. Before I published *Home to Harlem* I was known to the Negro public as the writer of the hortatory poem **"If We Must Die."** This poem was written during the time of the Chicago race riots. I was then a train waiter in the service of the Pennsylvania Railroad. Our dining car was running between New York, Philadelphia and Pittsburgh, Harrisburg and Washington and I remember we waiters and cooks carried revolvers in secret and always kept together going from our quarters to the railroad yards, as a precaution against sudden attack.

The poem was an outgrowth of the intense emotional experience I was living through (no doubt with thousands of other Negroes) in those days. It appeared in the radical magazine the *Liberator,* and was widely reprinted in the Negro press. Later it was included in my book of poetry ***Harlem Shadows.*** At the time I was writing a great deal of lyric poetry and none of my colleagues on the *Liberator* considered me a propaganda poet who could reel off revolutionary poetry like an automatic machine cutting fixed patterns. If we were a rebel group because we had faith that human life might be richer, by the same token we believed in the highest standards of creative work.

"If We Must Die" immediately won popularity among Aframericans, but the tone of the Negro critics was apologetic. To them a poem that voiced the deep-rooted instinct of self-preservation seemed merely a daring piece of impertinence. The dean of Negro critics [William S. Braithwaite] denounced me as a "violent and angry propagandist, using his natural poetic gifts to clothe [arrogant] and defiant thoughts." A young disciple characterized me as "rebellious and vituperative."

Thus it seems that respectable Negro opinion and criticism are not ready for artistic or other iconoclasm in Negroes. Between them they would emasculate the colored literary aspirant. Because Aframerican group life is possible only on a neutral and negative level our critics are apparently under the delusion that an Aframerican literature and art may be created out of evasion and insincerity.

They seem afraid of the revelation of bitterness in Negro life. But it may as well be owned, and frankly by those who know the inside and heart of Negro life, that the Negro, and especially the Aframerican, has bitterness in him in spite of his joyous exterior. And the more educated he is in these times the more he is likely to have.

The spirituals and the blues were not created out of sweet deceit. There is as much sublimated bitterness in them as there is humility, pathos and bewilderment. And if the Negro is a little bitter, the white man should be the last person in the world to accuse him of bitterness. For the feeling of bitterness is a natural part of the black man's birthright as the feeling of superiority is of the white man's. It matters not so much that one has had an experience of bitterness, but rather how one has developed out of it. To ask the Negro to render up his bitterness is asking him to part with his soul. For out of his bitterness he has bloomed and created his spirituals and blues and conserved his racial attributes—his humor and ripe laughter and particular rhythm of life.

However, with the publication of ***Home to Harlem*** the Aframerican elite realized that there was another side to me and changed their tune accordingly. If my poetry had been too daring, my prose was too dirty. The first had alarmed, the second had gassed them. And as soon as they recovered from the last shock, they did not bite

their tongues in damning me as a hog rooting in Harlem, a buzzard hovering over the Black Belt scouting for carcasses and altogether a filthy beast.

If my brethren had taken the trouble to look a little into my obscure life they would have discovered that years before I had recaptured the spirit of the Jamaican peasants in verse, rendering their primitive joys, their loves and hates, their work and play, their dialect. And what I did in prose for Harlem was very similar to what I had done for Jamaica in verse. (pp. 132-35)

On the "broader" side (literally at least) my work has been approached by some discriminating critics as if I were a primitive savage and altogether a stranger to civilization. Perhaps I myself unconsciously gave that impression. However, I should not think it was unnatural for a man to have a predilection for a civilization or culture other than that he was born unto. Whatever may be the criticism implied in my writing of Western Civilization I do not regard myself as a stranger but as a child of it, even though I may have become so by the comparatively recent process of grafting. I am as conscious of my new-world birthright as of my African origin, being aware of the one and its significance in my development as much as I feel the other emotionally. (p. 137)

A sincere artist can represent characters only as they seem to him. And he *will* see characters through his predilections and prejudices, unless he sets himself deliberately to present those cinema-type figures that are produced to offend no unit of persons whose protest may involve financial loss. The time when a writer will stick only to the safe old ground of his own class of people is undoubtedly passing. Especially in America, where all the peoples of the world are scrambling side by side and modern machines and the ramifications of international commerce are steadily breaking down the ethnological barriers that separate the peoples of the world. (p. 139)

> *Claude McKay, "A Negro Writer to His Critics," in his* The Passion of Claude McKay: Selected Poetry and Prose, 1912-1948, *edited by Wayne F. Cooper, Schocken Books, 1973, pp. 132-39.*

M. B. Tolson (essay date 1954)

[*Tolson was an American poet, journalist, and dramatist. In his best-known collection of verse,* Harlem Gallery *(1965), he used both standard and black English to depict the lives of African-Americans and to examine the role of the black artist in mainstream society. In the following excerpt from a review of* Selected Poems, *he lauds the universality of McKay's poems.*]

Professor Dewey, in his preface to [***Selected Poems***], singles out a line from the lyric, **"North and South"**: "A wonder to life's common places clings." The quotation revitalizes Yeats' observation that poets of the new idiom were "full of the unsatisfied hunger for the commonplace," since no manna fell, supposedly, from either the Temple or the Capitol. In this tradition, then, and out of a heterogeneity of experiences with an underlying unity, Claude McKay, as wheelwright, constable, agriculturist, porter, longshoreman, waiter, vagabond, rebel, and penitent, created his best poems.

Contrived seemingly as the plot of the Hardyesque is the triangle of a poet mythicized by Harlem, feted by Moscow, and haloed by Rome. His sensibility quick with image and idea, McKay explores the plurality of his world, inward and outward. He can etch, with a Dantean simplicity terrifying in detail, a picture of himself as surgeon in the grotto of the self.

> I plucked my soul out of its secret place,
> And held it to the mirror of my eye,
> To see it like a star against the sky,
> A twitching body quivering in space....

McKay likes to explore the axis of day and night when he holds the looking glass to his ego, his race, his moment, his milieu; and sometimes what he sees shocks him, as in the case of his beloved Africa, bereft of her ancient honor and arrogance and glory, and he cries: "Thou art the harlot, now thy time is done, / Of all the mighty nations of the sun."

Although his odyssey took him into Temple and Capitol, his poems are without ideological vestiges. McKay's verse has interludes during which his "memory bears engraved the high-walled Kremlin" or his soul tingles in Tetuan from "Filigree marvels from Koranic lines." Often he cannot stay till dawn in a caravansary; some bedeviling urge drives him toward the rain of fluid rock. He is aware that his passions are "saturated with brine," and, leaving the crystal glass of lyricism, he can only cry, "O tender word! O melody so slender!"

McKay, like his contemporaries of the Negro Renaissance, was unaffected by the New Poetry and Criticism. The logic of facts proves Mr. Tate's observation that this literary ghetto-ism "too often limited the Negro poet to a provincial mediocrity," from which he is just now escaping. Thus, in that era of ethnic mutation, McKay's radicalism was in content—not in form: The grammar of *The Souls of Black Folk* demanded the seven league boots of the "huge Moor."

The Negro poet of the 20's and 30's broke the mold of the Dialect School and the Booker T. Washington Compromise. For the first time he stood upon a peak in Darien, but he was not silent. Like the Greeks of Professor Gilbert Murray, he had stumbled upon "the invention of habit breaking." It is aphoristic that he gave the "huge Moor" and Desdemona a shotgun wedding, minus the ceremony "Traditional, with all its symbols / Ancient as the metaphors in dreams" for the poet-rebel, whether in content or form, travels *his* hypotenuse and not the right angle, toward *his* reality.

In his most famous poem ["**If We Must Die**"], Claude McKay's "if" reaches beyond this time and that place.

> If we must die, let us not die like hogs
> Hunted and penned in an inglorious spot,
> While round us bark the mad and hungry dogs,
> Making their mock at our accursed lot.
> If we must die, O let us nobly die,
> So that our precious blood may not be shed
> In vain; then even the monsters we defy
> Shall be constrained to honor us though dead!
> O kinsmen! we must meet the common foe!
> Though far outnumbered let us show us brave,
> And for their thousand blows deal one deathblow!
> What though before us lies the open grave?
> Like men we'll face the murderous, cowardly
>   pack,
> Pressed to the wall, dying, but fighting back!

The mood of McKay's "must" is grammatical, psychological, and philosophical. The simile, "like hogs," packs both rhetorical and dialectical implication, as foreshadowed in the words "let us not die." The theme, ignobleness versus nobleness in man's tragedy, escapes, in this poem, from the abstract and the didactic into the reality of the imagination. McKay insures the catholicity of his theme in two ways: he does not reveal the ethnic identity of his protagonist, nor does he hog-tie the free will of the attacked by the imposition of an affirmative decision. This, then, is the poem, above all others in the *Selected Poems*, which, in the holocaustal year 1919, signalized Claude McKay as the symbol of the New Negro and the Harlem Renaissance. The poem is a pillar of fire by night in many lands. (pp. 287-90)

> *M. B. Tolson, "Claude McKay's Art," in Poetry, Vol. LXXXIII, No. 4, January, 1954, pp. 287-90.*

Jean Wagner (essay date 1962)

[*Wagner, a French author and critic, is an authority on American slang and dialects. His* Les poètes nègres des États-Unis *(1962;* Black Poets of the United States, *1973) is recognized as one of the most innovative sources available for the study of African-American poets. In the following excerpt from this work, he presents an extensive overview of McKay's poetry, focusing on stylistic and thematic devices.*]

The two collections [of poetry] published in Jamaica in 1912 constitute a diptych of McKay's experience in his native island. The first, *Songs of Jamaica,* is a sort of highly colored epitome of the years of childhood and young manhood spent in the mountains, where he listened to Nature's great voice and shared the life of the black peasantry. Often in direct opposition to these first poems are those of *Constab Ballads,* which reveal the disillusionment and pessimism the poet felt when plunged into the life of the capital. These first two volumes are already marked by a sharpness of vision, an inborn realism, and a freshness which provide a pleasing contrast with the conventionality which, at this same time, prevails among the black poets of the United States.

Not the least original aspect of these seventy-eight poems is the rough but picturesque Jamaican dialect in which most of them are written, and of which they constitute the earliest poetic use. Thus we are far removed from the dialect of the Dunbar school, which was taken over from the whites who had concocted it in order to maintain the stereotype of black inferiority and to limit blacks more surely to the role of buffoons under orders to entertain the master race. An instrument of oppression when handled by white writers, the dialect became an avowal of subservience in its use by Dunbar, most of whose readers were whites. Furthermore, the themes treated in it had also been exploited by the former oppressors before Dunbar's arrival on the scene. None of these afterthoughts need be entertained in the case of McKay's dialect. Here everything is entirely and authentically Negro. It all comes directly from the people and is rooted in the soil, alike the phonology, often flavored with a delightful exoticism, and the rather summary morphology; the typically fantastic placing of the tonic accent and the somewhat rudimentary syntax, seldom in accord with the Queen's English; and, finally, the often unexpectedly roughhewn words and images, which originate in the hard-working folk's immediate contact with a soil reluctant to part with its riches.

As long as he lived, McKay's own speech kept the stamp of this rustic accent, as the recordings that have been preserved bear witness. As for the whimsicalities of the Jamaican tonic accent, they often preclude any certain solution to the problem of scanning many of his lines, whether in dialect or standard English.

Every bit as much as their language, it is the poetic quality of these works that links them genuinely to the people for whom they were written. It was no mere rhetorical flourish when McKay entitled his first collection *Songs of Jamaica.* For six poems, he adds in an appendix melodies which he composed. The songs and ballads he did not set to music are so rhythmical that a musical accompaniment could easily be provided. (pp. 204-05)

How close the bond of sympathy was between McKay and the people is manifested also by the realism with which he characterizes the black Jamaican peasant. Here, too, the contrast with Dunbar is embarrassingly evident. McKay's portraits at once transcend the limits which, in James Weldon Johnson's view, inevitably weighed on American Negro dialect and forced it to sound only the registers of humor and pathos. In any case, there is no humor to be found here, nor will it play any part in the later work. These peasants are not the ignorant, lazy, thieving clowns all too often held up for ridicule by Dunbar's school, stereotypes designed to amuse the members of a superior race. "Our Negroes were proud though poor," McKay will later declare. "They would not sing clowning songs for white men and

allow themselves to be kicked around by them." Unlike the character portraits usually associated with American Negro dialect, these portraits are the actual incarnation of a whole people's racial pride.

All in all, McKay's characterization of the Jamaican peasant is substantially that of the peasant anywhere in the world: deeply attached to his plot of land, over which he labors with an atavistic skill; and unsparing of himself, yet seemingly condemned to unalleviated poverty, since there is always someone to snatch the fruits of his labor. He owes his pride to the sense of work well done, and has no feeling of inferiority vis-à-vis the whites whom, when the occasion arises, he will address in the bluntest terms. (p. 206)

[McKay's critique of society becomes urgent in poems] where the responsibilities of the whites are categorically stated. They have organized the economic life of the island so as to profit from the resources that nature had destined for the blacks. That is the force of the following lines, in which the poet apostrophizes his native island:

> You hab all t'ings fe mek life bles',
> But buccra 'poil de whole
> Wid gove'mint an'all de res'
> Fe worry naygur soul.

(pp. 207-08)

[All of the poems in *Songs of Jamaica*], nevertheless, end on a note of faith in the future. In **"Two-an'-Six,"** Sun's discouragement is dispelled by the loving, consoling words uttered by his wife:

> An' de shadow lef' him face,
> An' him felt an inward peace
> As he blessed his better part
> For her sweet an' gentle heart.

In **"Hard Times,"** it is faith in Providence that resounds in the last stanza:

> I won't gib up, I won't say die,
>   For all de time is hard;
> Aldough de wul' soon en', I'll try
> My wutless best as time goes by,
>   An' trust on in me Gahd.

All in all, health, vigor, and self-assurance make up the impression left by this portrait of the black Jamaican peasant, whose age-old practical virtues and wisdom have not been sapped by his material poverty. Thus the optimism that McKay discovers in this rural milieu is derived, in the first place, from extant moral values. But there are racial reasons also. For it is highly significant that all these country folks are blacks, excluding the mulattoes whom McKay implicitly rejects as all too eager to see in their white ancestry a justification for disdaining the blacks. Finally, the real values that constitute the superiority of the black peasant reside in his closeness to the soil of Jamaica. One can scarcely overstress the importance of this element in McKay's trinitarian symbolism, which associates the good with the black race and the soil. (pp. 210-11)

[McKay's] roots in the soil of his native island are amazingly deep and lasting. These roots make him one with the soil. Through them he draws in his nourishment; the island's enchanting scenes call forth his earliest verses, and no one will ever rival him in praise for the mildness of its climate, the vividness of its colors, the luxuriance of its vegetation, or the coolness of its streams. (p. 211)

But uniting the black man and the earth is a more intimate, subtle relationship, a secret harmony as it were, and simply to name the familiar scenes is enough to arouse in the poet's sensibilities a physical resonance, to send a tremor through his frame:

> Loved Clarendon hills,
> Dear Clarendon hills,
> Oh! I feel de chills,
> Yes, I feel de chills
> Coursin' t'rough me frame
> When I call your name.

Thus the union of the poet and his land is consummated in a romantic ecstasy. This correspondence between Nature and the poet is indeed "the organic exaltation produced by physical agents" or the recollection of them, "the joy of all the senses in contact with the world" which Cazamian analyzed, many years ago, in the English Romantics. Like them, McKay felt constantly drawn to nature and sensed the need to become totally merged in it. The emotion it aroused in him transcended by far the exclusively aesthetic plane. For Nature is an ever renewed source of strength, and instinctively he returned to commune with it. (pp. 212-13)

McKay, for whom the earth was at the origin of everything, would certainly have signed his name to the exclamation of Shelley's Prometheus: "O, Mother Earth!" The earth is the whole man. He had already proclaimed this before he had turned twenty, and he realized it all the more clearly after he had left it and experienced enormous disillusionment in contact with the city, whose inhabitants he looked on as rootless, in the most concrete sense of the word:

> Fool! I hated my precious birthright,
> Scorning what had made my father a man.

He attributed to his native soil, the nurturer, all the strength of his character and his poetic vigor .... (p. 214)

Between the black man and the earth there is a total identification. When, vexed by the city, he returns to his mountains, he will see in this return not only a reunion with the earth, but with his people also .... Thus the racial values he associates with the soil also help to tinge his feeling for nature, and in his mind he conceives nature and the city as mutually exclusive forces. (pp. 214-15)

Hatred of the city is one of the principal motifs in McKay's Jamaican poems, and the American poems will offer variations on the same theme. In Dunbar's work one could already note some aversion toward urban civilization, but this was only sporadic, and the motivation behind it was entirely different. Dunbar was sensitive, above all, to the ravages wrought by industrialization which, as it spread ever wider, made men's lives ugly and polluted the air they breathed. His reaction might even be interpreted, in part, as the tuberculosis victim's struggle for the pure air he knew he needed.

But with McKay the theme is not merely more amply treated; it acquires in the racial context a symbolic importance not found in Dunbar. The city, presented as the antithesis of the land, is consequently the enemy of the black man also. (p. 215)

[In McKay's **Constab Ballads,** the] city symbolizes an evil that is multiple. In part it finds expression in the traditional ways but also, and especially, it adopts other forms that are significant in the racial context.

We will not linger long over the former, which for the most part illustrate the corrupting power of the city, on which McKay superimposes his keen awareness of the corruption rampant among the police. (p. 217)

The police are also reputed to be a tool in the hands of the whites for oppressing the blacks. This is the lament of the apple woman in **"The Apple Woman's Complaint,"** when the police forbid her to sell her wares in the street. If she is not allowed to ply her modest trade honestly, she will have to live by stealing, and in either case she will be at odds with the police, who in any event live at her expense. From this poem we cite only those passages that present the attitude of the police as having originated in hatred of the blacks:

> Black nigger wukin' laka cow
> An' wipin' sweat-drops from his brow,
> Dough him is dyin' sake o' need,
> P'lice an' dem headman boun' fe feed.
> . . . .
> De headman fe de town police
> Mind neber know a little peace,
> 'Cep' when him an' him heartless ban'
> Hab sufferin' nigger in dem han'.
> . . . .
> We hab fe barter out we soul
> To lib' t'rough dis ungodly wul';—
> O massa Jesus! don't you see
> How police is oppressin' we?

The vehemence of this protest against oppression, here placed in the mouth of the apple woman, and the boundless despair of the last stanza, are in violent contrast with the cold objectivity of the social critique voiced in the rural poems of *Songs of Jamaica.* It heralds what will be McKay's stance in his American poems. Of all the Jamaican poems, **"The Apple Woman's Complaint"** is the most bitter, violent, and militant. Thus it serves to make entirely plain the changes that city residence brought about in McKay. (pp. 217-18)

[McKay's] American poems give vent to his racial pride with a forcefulness he had never exhibited before. This outburst is so authentic, and so much in keeping with his own fiery, passionate temperament, that little influence need be attributed to the stimulus he could have found elsewhere in the paeans to race that were being sounded by his compatriot Garvey. Furthermore, as he faced the onslaught of white insolence, his pride grew in militancy without losing any of its nobility:

> Your door is shut against my tightened face,
> And I am sharp as steel with discontent;
> But I possess the courage and the grace
> To bear my anger *proudly* and unbent.

His pride is like that of a tree deeply rooted and prepared to withstand the hostile elements:

> Like a strong tree that in the virgin earth
> Sends far its roots through rock and loam and clay
> And *proudly* thrives in rain or time of dearth . . .

As this pride is strengthened and tested by adversity, he raises racial consciousness to the aesthetic plane. One would almost be tempted to affirm that the poet is inaugurating a hedonism of color, when one beholds how with a supremely refined sensuality he savors the heady joy of his blackness, gaining awareness of it amidst a community that tortures him, but to which he feels superior in every fiber of his being . . . . (p. 223)

No one ever expressed with such a wealth of nuances the opposing eddies that swirl in a mind in search of equilibrium amid stupidly hostile surroundings. This attempt at introspective insight clearly demonstrates how racial pride can act as a redemptive force.

Yet it must meet a rude challenge when, gloriously garbed, the poet's sworn enemy, the White City, displays the whole spectrum of her seductive wiles in order to win him over and ruin him . . . . (p. 224)

To no lesser degree than the intoxication of being black, Claude McKay learned in America how intoxicating it is to hate. He vents his joy in **"The White City"**:

> I will not toy with it nor bend an inch.
> Deep in the secret chambers of my heart
> I muse my life-long hate, and without flinch
> I bear it nobly as I live my part.
> My being would be a skeleton, a shell,
> If this dark passion that fills my every mood,
> And makes my heaven in the white world's hell,
> Did not forever feed me vital blood.
> I see the mighty city through a mist—
> The strident trains that speed the goaded mass,
> The poles and spires and towers vapor-kissed,
> The fortressed port through which the great ships
>   pass,
> The tides, the wharves, the dens I contemplate,
> Are sweet like wanton loves because I hate.

Hatred has acquired quite a power of transfiguration. It becomes the favored theme of the poet's song, for it alone can make his surroundings bearable.

It was once declared that hatred is not a poetic emotion. If this act of exclusion were to be acquiesced in, it would oblige us to find no poetic merit whatever in Claude McKay's most striking poems since he, among all black poets, is *par excellence* the poet of hate. This, when situated in its racial context, has a very special characteristic. As **"The White City"** so clearly shows, it is the actual prerequisite for his survival, since it transmutes into a paradise the base inferno of the white world. It is a sort of antidote secreted throughout his being and which prevents the White City from emptying him of his substance—were it not for this fostering flood of hatred, which constantly provides him with fresh energies, he would be reduced by the city to the level of a skeleton, of a sea creature's abandoned shell. Hatred is the compensatory factor that assures the equilibrium of his personality, allowing him to adapt himself adequately to his environment. (pp. 225-26)

With the publication of **"If We Must Die,"** the incarnation of the new spirit and the spokesman for a whole people at last resolved to witness no longer, in resignation and submissiveness, the massacre of its own brothers at the hands of the enraged white mob, but to return blow for blow and, if necessary, to die. With the possible exception of James Weldon Johnson's "Negro National Hymn," no poem by any black poet has been so frequently cited and extolled. (p. 229)

The welcome accorded this sonnet is also due, in part, to its being one of those poems in which McKay's poetic gift reaches beyond the circumstances of the day to attain the universal. Along with the will to resistance of black Americans that it expresses, it voices also the will of oppressed peoples of every age who, whatever their race and wherever their region, are fighting with their backs against the wall to win their freedom . . . .

It is important, at this juncture in our examination of McKay's hatred, to try to determine against what,

McKay speaking at the Fourth Congress of the Communist party in Moscow, 1922.

exactly, his hatred was directed. One might, indeed, choose to regard him as a last-ditch defender of Negro culture, filled with a global detestation of America and the Western culture for which, in his eyes, it stood. This interpretation of his cultural attitude has actually found supporters. (p. 230)

McKay appears to have expressed all the complexity of his real feelings about America in the sonnet entitled **"America"**:

> Although she feeds me bread of bitterness,
> And sinks into my throat her tiger's tooth,
> Stealing my breath of life, I will confess
> I love this cultured hell that tests my youth!
> Her vigor flows like tides into my blood,
> Giving my strength erect against her hate,
> Her bigness sweeps my being like a flood.

What is predominant here, and basic also, is his love for America, whose strength acts on the poet like a stimulant. The other half of the picture, the hatred that America has for blacks, does not obliterate the poet's love for it. McKay's hatred does not mean a rejection of America; it is a reproach directed against the country's inability to reconcile discriminatory practices with egalitarian democratic doctrines. In the last analysis, what he hates is not America, but evil. An unpublished sonnet makes this explicit:

> I stripped down harshly to the naked core
> Of hatred based on the essential wrong.

We know that the essential evil is the division between man and man, the white man's hatred and contempt for his fellow man, and the exploitation of black by white. In the "civilized hell" of America, evil adopts the most varied guises. But a natural defense reaction leads McKay to note those in particular which deny the black man's humanity. The metaphors often depict America as a kind of vampire seeking to deprive the victim of his substance and to leave him a mere shell or skeleton. America becomes, for instance, a tiger, his striped coat representing the stripes of the American flag, who seizes his prey by the throat and nourishes himself on the blood.... (pp. 231-32)

In another poem, **"Birds of Prey,"** whites are depicted as birds darkening the sky with their wings, then swooping down on their victims to gorge themselves on the hearts.... (p. 232)

Blood and heart quite assuredly have a symbolic value in these poems, which denounce the depersonalization of the black man and his exploitation by society's rulers, who glut themselves on his financial and artistic substance. But this carnage also requires a more literal interpretation, so that the poems may be understood as a condemnation of lynching, like the sonnet **"The Lynching,"** where McKay speaks more openly.

At times, too, McKay succeeds in utilizing a less violent mode to chant the horrors of racial discrimination. **"The Barrier"** is a delightful poem which, in a manner that is partly light and partly serious, considers the interdict prohibiting any love between a black man and a white woman. It is reminiscent of those trials that judged a man's intentions when, in the Deep South, blacks used to be convicted of the "visual rape" of a southern white beauty.... (pp. 232-33)

Though McKay may justifiably be called the poet of hatred and rebellion, his real personality would be seriously misrepresented if one were to treat him as an out-and-out rebel. Without meaning to do so, Richard Wright undoubtedly slights McKay in his nobility by asserting of him: "To state that Claude McKay is a rebel is to understate it; his rebellion is a way of life." To adopt this point of view is to overlook the remarkable self-mastery that McKay could summon up, and to neglect the personal purification and, when all is considered, the moral elevation that McKay believed he could derive from his hate.

It is, indeed, admirable that in his case hatred and rebellion did not become, as they might have, a vehicle lurching onward without reins or brakes. Even when he revels in his hate, he does not wallow in it, and in the midst of the hurricane he retains his control:

> Peace, O my rebel heart!...

However passionate his rebellious flights of rhetoric, they are always lucid and dominated by an unflagging will to self-transcendence:

> Oh, I must search for wisdom every hour
> Deep in my wrathful bosom sore and raw.

He simply does not look on hatred as an end in itself. It is but a stage on the path that ends in the divine charity, for which its purifying action prepares the way. Understood thus, McKay's hatred is a holy anger the manifestation of which occurs only in entire clarity of mind, as did the divine anger directed against the deleterious hypocrisy of the Pharisees, or against the merchants who had made of the temple a "den of thieves." Ultimately, what sets a limit to hatred is the spiritual. Such is the message of the sonnet **"To the White Fiends,"** in which God compels hatred to stop on the brink of murder, directing it to a higher goal:

> Think you I am not fiend and savage too?
> Think you I could not arm me with a gun
> And shoot down ten of you for every one
> Of my black brothers murdered, burnt by you?
> Be not deceived, for every deed you do
> I could match—out-match: am I not Afric's son,
> Black of that black land where black deeds are done?
> But the Almighty from the darkness drew
> My soul and said: Even thou shalt be a light
> Awhile to burn on the benighted earth,
> Thy dusky face I set among the white
> For thee to prove thyself of higher worth;
> Before the world is swallowed up in night,
> To show thy little lamp: go forth, go forth!

Thus, far from being a "way of life," McKay's hatred undergoes a sublimation that induces it to consume itself. In its place comes a tranquillity that is not indifference, but a deepening and internalization of racial feeling. (pp. 235-36)

In McKay's work, the feeling for nature occupies almost as important a place as racial feeling.... Unlike Countee Cullen or Langston Hughes, who never vibrated in unison with nature (which usually remains a mere concept for them), McKay brings to it the understanding and sympathy of a person who grew up in it and whose rare sensitivity brought him to an authentic integration with it. In *Harlem Shadows,* the nature poems make up nearly one-third of the volume. The languorous sweetness of their lyricism is like a cool breeze from the Isles, introducing a note of most welcome tranquillity into the militant fierceness of the poems of rebellion. (p. 236)

It can be seen that McKay's feeling for nature has no autonomous existence. Since it is linked with the racial symbolism of the earth and remains closely subordinated to it, seen from this point of view it most often amounts to the enunciation of a sense of belonging.

Its expressive value, because of this role, falls together with that of the African theme as treated by many poets of the Negro Renaissance. For them, Africa is the land still unpolluted by the inhuman machine outlook of the white man, hungry to enslave his fellow men. But for them—those who are unable to identify with America, the land that treats them inhumanely—Africa is the substitute land where they can seek their roots; Africa is the mother with whom, in the place of stepmotherly America which has rejected them, they try to form an *a posteriori* bond of relationship.

McKay is totally unconcerned with these substitute values. For he comes from a land where blacks are in the majority, where he struck roots both tenacious and extraordinarily deep, a land with which his identification was perfect, if one allows for the extraterritorial status he imposed on the city of Kingston. He has no need to go all the way to Africa to find the palm trees to which he can compare the black girls. Jamaica is his Africa, and its exoticism is a genuine exoticism, not a dream escape to some substitute fatherland the need for which springs from a feeling of frustration.

It is not surprising, therefore, that he keeps the African theme within much more modest limits than the other Renaissance poets, whose feeling of unqualified admiration for Africa he does not share. The whole body of his work contains scarcely more than half a dozen poems devoted to Africa, and not one of them can be considered an apologia. (pp. 238-39)

In **"Outcast,"** it is again the sense of being captive in the white man's empire that occupies the poet's mind, rather than any feeling of solidarity with Africa. Nevertheless, this second factor emerges with greater clarity here than in any other poem by McKay. But he is less

intent on affirming his link with Africa than in regretting that the elements forming this link have been lost or forgotten.... He must be taken to express his kinship with the blacks of the United States, whose spokesman he has become, and to state the truth, as suggested by the poem's title, that he himself has been rejected by the white American majority. These two ingredients are more obvious than any putative avowal of genuine solidarity with Africa. (p. 242)

Thus if McKay is a forerunner of the Negro Renaissance, this is not due to his vision of Africa. The genuine quality of his Jamaican exoticism had immunized him against the heady African mirage, and his ability to stand resolute against its seductions attests, in the last resort, the cohesiveness and equilibrium of his personality.

McKay has left us only a few poems dealing with Harlem, the "Mecca of the Negro Renaissance." His 1922 volume, though entitled *Harlem Shadows,* has but two poems on the theme, the title poem and **"The Harlem Dancer."** (p. 243)

Yet, though for these reasons he can scarcely be called the poet of Harlem, at least he has the merit of being the first to introduce Harlem into Negro poetry. For in December, 1917, **"The Harlem Dancer"** appeared in *The Seven Arts,* and **"Harlem Shadows"** was included in *Spring in New Hampshire* (1920). Earlier than Langston Hughes, it is Claude McKay who provided the first annotations on the frivolous night life that, until the 1929 crash, would enable Harlem to prosper. These poems might also be said to constitute the first poetic documents on the reactions of the black man borne to the urban centers by the tide of the Great Migration. There is nothing astonishing in the fact that McKay, as a shrewd observer of every aspect of city life, paid particularly close attention to this phenomenon.

"Harlem Shadows" is a poem in a minor key on the prostitutes that urban civilization, with its lack of humanity, had thrown onto the Harlem sidewalks. The poem is reminiscent of those that McKay, in the 1912 volumes, had devoted to the moral debacle of two country girls as a result of their going to live in Kingston. But **"Harlem Shadows"** is an innovation in the sense that McKay attributes a primordial importance to the prostitutes' color (blackening them further by referring to them as shadows) and makes their downfall symbolic of the whole race's. In each case, the blame is implicitly allotted to racial oppression. This biased suggestion deviates significantly from McKay's usually realistic, objective manner, and one would have expected him to treat these prostitutes as victims of the city rather than as slaves of the master race. This deference to racial propaganda spoils the end of the poem, which otherwise would have been very much to the point.... (p. 244)

"The Harlem Dancer" plunges us into the atmosphere of one of the countless night spots that sprang up in Harlem after World War I. This sonnet raises the problem of another sort of prostitution, that of Negro art to popular (mainly white) demands. White people appear in the sonnet as drunken spectators who gobble up with their eyes the form of a naked black dancer. Between the young whites, in search of venal pleasures, and the nobility of the black beauty, the comparison is to the advantage of the latter. She appears before us in all the pride of a tall palm tree swaying majestically in the wind, yet she is an uprooted palm tree, torn from a kindlier country where she has left her soul. Her natural grace and beauty contrast with the artificial setting into which she has been transplanted, and her forced smile cannot hide her longing for her native land. Underneath the exoticism of detail, we once again come upon a thesis greatly favored by McKay and the Negro Renaissance, maintaining that the white world, more often than was generally believed, was a setting unfit to receive all that blacks have to offer it. (pp. 244-45)

Poets have often been attracted by the theme of black dancers. Dunbar . . . has left us entertaining portrayals of evenings spent dancing the quadrille with, in his day, the added savor of forbidden fruit. Jazz, in its turn, will soon find its true poet in Langston Hughes. Thus it need not surprise us that McKay also should have chosen to see in the liberation of the dance, as in the spontaneity and the subtle rhythms of the dancers, an especially revealing manifestation of the "immortal spirit" of his race, since here one could note the urge to expand, to express oneself, to free oneself, instincts that in daily life had to be kept in check at every instant.

But whereas Dunbar and Hughes let themselves be swept away by the vortex of the dance, McKay remained the detached observer, though sensing the emotion that radiated from the dancers to him. His view is an external one; a space remains between him and the crowd of dancers and allows him no identification with them . . . . It can be sensed that McKay experiences a measure of despair vis-à-vis the tragedy of this superficial response of a whole race to the oppression and contempt by which it is victimized.

This is, we believe, another manifestation of McKay's reserved attitude when confronted by the folk temperament, with which he never felt entirely at ease. Other elements that lead us to the same conclusion are the total absence of humor throughout his poetry and his preference for such classical poetic forms as the sonnet. Spirituals, blues, and jazz, whose popular forms were taken over by Langston Hughes, Sterling Brown, and many other poets, have no place in McKay's poetic work. In this connection, it is necessary to correct the mistaken view propounded by Henry Lüdeke (no doubt on the basis of uncertain information) that in **Harlem Shadows** the rhythms were "strongly influenced by popular poetry, above all the spirituals." Quite the contrary, McKay must have had a background awareness that the popular forms and outlook could become, as has in reality often occurred, an excuse for avoiding personal reflection, and so would have been only another sort of escapism for the poet. Thus, while he

defends Negro art against the deformations that whites inflicted on it, he defended it no less vigorously against those Negroes who were tempted to ask of it something that it could not provide: a soul . . . . [In] Harlem he could now see to what a degree this culture was emptied of substance the moment it lost contact with the soil, which alone could give it life, and was transported to the city, which in McKay's eyes had ever been a corrupting influence. In a word, he judged Negro popular culture, as he had encountered it in America, to be incapable of fulfilling his need for an authentic spiritual life. (pp. 246-47)

[McKay], with his nonconformist temperament, was repelled by the idea of adhering to traditions that took the place of individual reflection. His religious poetry is the expression of an inner growth, and his discovery of God the result of his individual search for truth. From a more general vantage-point, his poetic opus may be considered as the account of a vast attempt at a synthesis between the antagonistic elements of the black world and the Western world warring within him. There can be no denying that McKay, like every black exiled in a white milieu, was for a long time a divided man, so that it is possible to speak of his cultural dualism. But he never acquiesced in being torn apart by this dichotomy. His whole being urged him to find unity. The critique to which he subjected the antinomies deprived them, little by little, of their contingencies and laid bare their authentic values. In Jamaica, he affirmed the primacy of the soil and contrasted it with the inanity of the dream, cherished by the mulattoes, of a heightened social status. He rejected the mirage of Africa as a source of racial pride, looking on it as merely pathetic. He shunned the nationalism of a Garvey, whom he regarded as a charlatan, and while he defended Negro folklore against whites, who would have denatured it, he nevertheless could not find spiritual sustenance in it. On the other hand, it was his natural instinct to evaluate the possibilities of spiritual advancement offered by Western, Christian culture, but there too he perceived the corroding evil that sowed hatred between men. In his dialogue with the West, conducted through the medium of his hatred, this emotion was slowly filtered of its dross as he came to grasp the necessity of raising himself above it. Unless the individual is engaged in a ceaseless effort to transcend himself, no victory over hatred will ever be possible. Neither rationalism nor Communism could provide the higher principle capable of reconciling the conflicting theses of his cultural eclecticism. At long last he discovered this principle within himself, and at the same time he discovered God. Thus his spiritual itinerary is an account of the internalization of his racial feeling.

"I was always religious-minded as some of my pagan poems attest. But I never had any faith in revealed religion." (pp. 248-49)

[McKay's] skepticism, which was aroused by rationalist influences, signifies an estrangement from the church rather than from God. It would seem equally likely that this estrangement was motivated by certain practices or pastoral attitudes on the part of the Anglican clergy....

Be that as it may, the poet's critique of what we shall call the official faith soon led him to become his own spiritual advisor. This imbues him with a taste for that upward movement of the soul that a victory over his passions represents, and it accustoms him to view progress as a continual upgrading of the individual through self-transcendence, which alone makes existence worthwhile "in an empty world." These are the qualities of soul that McKay brings to the spiritual enrichment of black poetry, as his voice blends in with those of the American black poets. (p. 251)

His fundamental expectation in turning to God, and the object of the prayers he addresses to Him, is the light of truth.... That this is the ultimate objective of his spiritual quest is confirmed by the sonnet **"Truth,"** written shortly before he died:

> Lord, shall I find it in Thy Holy Church,
> Or must I give it up as something dead,
> Forever lost, no matter where I search,
> Like dinosaurs within their ancient bed?
> I found it not in years of Unbelief,
> In science stirring life like budding trees,
> In Revolution like a dazzling thief—
> Oh, shall I find it on my bended knees?
> But what is Truth? So Pilate asked Thee, Lord,
> So long ago when Thou wert manifest,
> As the Eternal and Incarnate Word,
> Chosen of God and by Him singly blest;
> In this vast world of lies and hate and greed,
> Upon my knees, Oh Lord, for Truth I plead.

His prayer will be granted, and divine illumination will bring him to recognize at last that the "essential evil" he had spent his life hunting down and fighting is not outside, but within him. To track down injustice and oppression by hating America is to fight against shadows. The basic evil is hate itself, and that is what he must hate. It is hate that wrecks unity, setting men one against the other, and the individual against himself. But it is the farthest point to which the pagan doctrines can lead one. God alone can lead a man further on and conquer hate itself:

> Around me roar and crash the pagan isms
> To which most of my life was consecrate,
> Betrayed by evil men and torn by schisms
> For they were built on nothing more than hate!
> I cannot live my life without the faith
> Where new sensations like a fawn will leap,
> But old enthusiasms like a wraith
> Haunt me awake and haunt me when I sleep.
> And so to God I go to make my peace.

(pp. 256-57)

Jean Wagner, "Claude McKay," in his Black Poets of the United States: From Paul Laurence Dunbar to Langston Hughes, *translated by Kenneth Douglas, University of Illinois Press, 1973, pp. 197-257.*

Michael B. Stoff (essay date 1972)

[*In the following excerpt, Stoff examines McKay's work within the context of 1920s primitivism, analyzing thematic and structural elements in* Home to Harlem, Banjo, *and* Banana Bottom.]

The cult of primitivism which gripped many American intellectuals during the 1920s manifested itself in a number of ways. The rising interest in jazz, the study of African art forms, and the examination of tribal cultures were all variations on the theme of the primitive. The Negro as the uncorrupted remnant of preindustrial man became the central metaphor in this cult. Against the background of a tawdry culture stood the instinctive, sensual black man whose "dark laughter" represented a fundamental challenge to the effete civilization of white America.

The primitivism in Claude McKay's art manifests itself even in his earliest efforts. As a Jamaican youth, McKay composed a series of dialect poems later published in two volumes: *Songs of Jamaica* (1912) and *Constab Ballads* (1912). Both thematically, through their emphasis on everyday peasant life, and stylistically, through their use of native dialect, these poems reveal McKay's fascination with Jamaican folk culture. They capture the exotic and earthy qualities of the black peasantry with a lyrical sensitivity reminiscent of Robert Burns. (p. 127)

McKay's depiction of the Jamaican peasant is integrally related to a stereotyped image of the world's peasantry. His peasants have a universality of condition and reaction which allows them to be exchanged with peasants of any nationality. This conception is consistent with McKay's later claim: "As a child, I was never interested in different kinds of races or tribes. People were just people to me." In describing McKay's image of the Jamaican peasant, the French literary critic Jean Wagner has written:

> All things being equal, McKay's portrait of the Jamaican peasant is in substance that of the peasant the world over. Profoundly attached to the earth, he works the soil with a knowledge gained from age long habit; although a hard worker, the Jamaican, like his counterpart the world over, is condemned to exploitation.

This perception of common qualities among the world's masses later furnished McKay with a theoretical basis for his own peculiar vision of the ideal political state. At this early point in his life, the concept of a "universal peasantry" heightened his sensitivity to folk-art traditions of other cultures. That interest supplied him with a foundation for much of his work.

McKay emigrated from Jamaica in 1912 at the age of twenty-two. He carried with him not only a deep regard for the Jamaican peasantry but also a special vision of the island itself. He retained that vision until his death in 1948. The image of Jamaica as paradise permeates all his recollections of the island. In McKay's first American poems and in his later autobiographical material,

Jamaica becomes the metaphorical equivalent of Eden. Its simplicity and freshness offered refuge from the complexities of a modern, industrialized world. (pp. 128-29)

McKay did not lose the vision of Jamaica as an undefiled Eden where instinct and sensation reigned supreme. Although he never returned to his island home, he was forever swept back thematically to his preindustrial, peasant origins. (p. 130)

McKay was also obsessed with describing the social role to be played by the intellectual. His membership in a visible and oppressed minority further complicated matters. In essence, the entire body of his art can be seen as a mechanism through which he sought to transform these personal problems into public issues. Such a transformation entailed an insistent reference to a recurring pattern of images. That pattern was the juxtapositioning of the instinctive black man and the educated Negro. These images defined, with increasing precision, McKay's own concepts and made them salient within a broader cultural context.

McKay's earliest use of this construction came in the first of his three novels, **Home to Harlem.** The book was published in 1928, the sixth year of McKay's expatriation from America. Its appearance initiated a violent debate among the black literati over the propriety of its theme and subject matter. Many of McKay's peers agreed with Langston Hughes's evaluation. Hughes argued that because it was so "vividly alive," **Home to Harlem** could legitimately be labeled, as "the first real flower of the Harlem Renaissance."

The elder black literary figures and much of the established Negro press were revolted by what they believed to be overtly crude allusions in McKay's book. Claiming the book was not representative of Negro life, this Old Guard expressed its shock and indignation at the lasciviousness of the novel. Its very existence, they suggested, was a calculated affront to the black community. W. E. B. Du Bois's reaction was typical of the initial reviews:

> **Home to Harlem** for the most part nauseates me, and after the dirtier parts of its filth I feel distinctly like taking a bath . . . . It looks as though McKay has set out to cater to that prurient demand on the part of white folk for a portrayal in Negroes of that utter licentiousness which convention holds white folk back from enjoying—if enjoyment it can be labeled [see Du Bois excerpt dated 1928].

The controversy enveloping **Home to Harlem** was merely the surfacing of an underlying tension engendered by conflicting visions of the Harlem Renaissance. The Old Guard saw the Renaissance as a vehicle for social amelioration. The Renaissance would not only demonstrate the intellectual achievements of the black man, but would also uplift the masses to some arbitrary level of social acceptability.

It was precisely this view of the Harlem Renaissance, this venture in cultural pretension, that McKay's work fundamentally challenged. His notion of a renaissance was an aggregation of " . . . talented persons of an ethnic or national group working individually or collectively in a common purpose and creating things that would be typical of their group." In 1929, McKay defined the problems one faced when speaking of a "racial renaissance." He delineated the tactics and sources to be employed in creating such a movement [in his novel **Banjo**]:

> We educated Negroes are talking a lot about a racial renaissance. And I wonder how we're going to get it. On one side we're up against the world's arrogance— a mighty cold hard white stone thing. On the other the great sweating army—our race. It's the common people, you know, who furnish the bone and sinew and salt of any race or nation. In the modern race of life we're merely beginners. If this renaissance is going to be more than a sporadic scabby thing, we'll have to get down to our racial roots to create it . . . . Getting down to our native roots and building up from our people is . . . culture.

For McKay, this meant the conscious and studied illumination of black folk-art tradition whose central themes would be the indestructible vitality of the primitive black man and the inextricable dilemma of the educated Negro.

Home to Harlem is a vivid glimpse of the lower depths of black life in urban America. Its peripatetic plot and dialect-oriented style are consistent with its thematic emphasis on the black man as the unrestrained child of civilization. Set in New York's black ghetto, the novel establishes Harlem as a carnal jungle. Our senses are subjected to a barrage of erotic images: "Brown girls rouged and painted like dark pansies. Brown flesh draped in colorful clothes. Brown lips full and pouted for sweet kissing. Brown breasts throbbing with love." At the core of this physical world lies the cabaret Congo, "a real little Africa in New York." Forbidden to whites, the Congo is a distillation of Harlem life. Its atmosphere is filled with the "tenacious odors of service and the warm indigenous smells of Harlem." Its allusions to the unrepressed African culture provide an apt setting for the return of the novel's hero, Jake Brown.

Jake, an Army deserter, is introduced as the natural man whose actions are guided by intuition. He is the instinctive primitive, deeply rooted in the exotic mystique of Africa. As he walks down Lenox Avenue, he is overcome by the pulsations of Harlem life. "His flesh tingled," the narrator tells us, and "he felt as if his whole body was a flaming wave." Jake and Harlem are inexorably bound by a "contagious fever . . . burning everywhere," but burning most fervently in "Jake's sweet blood." That primitive passion sustains Jake and represents a profound threat to the cultural rigidity of modern society.

In contrast to Jake, McKay inserts himself as the Haitian immigrant Ray. Ray represents the cultivated intellect, the civilized black whose education has sensitized his mind but paralyzed his body. Intellectually, Ray can comprehend the cluster of sensations and emotions about him, yet he lacks the naturalness of action and spontaneity of response that are the hallmarks of a Jake Brown. Although envious of Jake, Ray harbors the obsessive fear that "someday the urge of the flesh ... might chase his high dreams out of him and deflate him to the contented animal that was the Harlem nigger strutting his stuff."

The result is a vision of the intellectual, and especially the black intellectual, as social misfit. Ray is capable of sensing and recording life, but he is unable to live it. "He drank in more of life," writes McKay, "than he could distill into active animal living." There is no outlet for his immense store of emotional energy. Robbed by his "white" education of the ability to act freely and impulsively, Ray remains little more than a "slave of the civilized tradition." Caught between two cultures, he is immobilized. "The fact is," he tells Jake as he flees to Europe,

> ... I don't know what I'll do with my little education. I wonder sometimes if I could get rid of it and lose myself in some savage culture in the jungles of Africa. I am a misfit—as the doctors who dole out newspaper advice to the well-fit might say—a misfit with my little education and constant dreaming, when I should be getting the nightmare habit to hog in a lot of dough like everybody else in this country.... The more I learn the less I understand and love life.

The implications of Ray's final statement are not only applicable to McKay's personal problems but related to a broader cultural phenomenon. Notions of escape, alienation, and crude commercialism were by no means uniquely black images. They were embraced by intellectuals of varying hues in the twenties. McKay's use of these themes places the black experience into a larger cultural context. Blackness only added a further convolution to the already complex problem of the intellectual's social adaptability.

Ray's expatriation leaves the fundamental questions raised by the novel unresolved. The continuing focus on Jake, and his reunion with the "tantalizing brown" girl Felice, imply that only the instinctive primitive can survive happily in white civilization, its dehumanizing tendencies are irrelevant to his innately free existence. The intellectual, defiled by the process of civilization, is doomed to wander in search of that potency of action he has irrevocably lost.

McKay's second novel, *Banjo,* published in 1929, pursues the issues raised in *Home to Harlem.* Although the scene has shifted to Marseille's harbor district, the structural dualism characterizing *Home to Harlem* is present once more. Lincoln Agrippa Daily, familiarly known as Banjo, replaces Jake Brown while McKay again enters as Ray. The dichotomy is now expanded and more lucidly articulated.

In *Banjo* there is a sharpening of figurative focus and a widening of thematic scope. With the character Banjo, McKay adds a new dimension to the earthy black and provides a more concise definition of his own racial conceptions. At the same time, Ray's disposition has progressed from a confused uneasiness with American life to a coherent denunciation of western civilization. This increased clarity of imagery allows McKay to move toward a resolution to the quandary of the black intellectual.

The primitive black is given additional depth in *Banjo.* The loose plot, an account of the lives of a group of beach boys in the port city of Marseille, provides a background for the development of the protagonist, Banjo. He is the same intuitive vagabond originally described in *Home to Harlem*—with one significant difference. While Jake is nebulously characterized as a laborer, Banjo is depicted as an artist. He is a jazzman whose life is the embodiment of his art. Like the songs he plays, Banjo is unrestrained, free-spirited, and vibrantly alive. McKay immediately establishes the intimate relationships between Banjo and his music: "I never part with this instrument," Banjo says in the opening pages of the novel. "It is moh than a gal, moh than a pal; it's mahself." (pp. 130-35)

[The banjo] is the cultural expression of American Negro folk-art, and Banjo represents the prototype black folk-artist lustily proclaiming the vitality of his race. His music, "the sharp, noisy notes of the banjo," is not derived from a pretentious adaptation of European culture. Drawing inspiration from the "common people," Banjo's art represents the truest expression of black culture.

Again juxtaposed to this earthy, intuitive black man is the intellectual Ray. Recently expatriated from America, Ray comes to Marseille in search of an artistic haven where he could "exist *en pension* prolitarian of a sort and try to create around him the necessary solitude to work with pencil and scraps of paper." Ray has not given up his earlier passion for writing, and although he is occasionally forced to work as a laborer, he never renounces his "dream of self-expression." Once in the Vieux Port, he finds, instead of solitude, a band of beach boys whose free and undisciplined lifestyle is particularly appealing to Ray's vagabond sensibilities. As a result, he immediately establishes an intimate relationship with the members of the group and especially with their leader, Banjo. At this point, the linear progression of the plot becomes of secondary importance, and the novel is reduced to a vehicle for the delineation of Ray's (*i.e.,* McKay's) brief against civilization and the formulation of a solution to his intellectual quandary.

McKay's condemnation of Western civilization in *Banjo* is inexorably tied to the psychological problems arising from his blackness. In 1937 he wrote, "What, then, was my main psychological problem? It was the problem of color. Color-consciousness was the fundamental of my restlessness." And it is color-consciousness which is the fundamental of Ray's hatred for civilization. "Civilization is rotten," Ray proclaims, and in the following passage, McKay defines the sociological basis of Ray's sentiments:

> He hated civilization because its general attitude toward the colored man was such as to rob him of his warm human instincts and make him inhuman. Under it the thinking colored man could not function normally like his white brother, responsive and reacting spontaneously to the emotions of pleasure or pain, joy or sorrow, kindness or hardness, charity, anger, and forgiveness . . . . So soon as he entered the great white world, where of necessity he must work and roam and breathe the larger air to live, that entire world, high, low, middle, unclassed, all conspired to make him painfully conscious of color and race . . . . It was not easy for a Negro with an intellect standing watch over his native instincts to take his own way in this white man's civilization. But of one thing he was resolved: civilization would not take the love of color, joy, beauty, vitality and nobility out of *his* life and make him like one of the poor masses of its pale creatures.

Although the imagery utilized in the preceding passage is applied to the peculiar condition of the black man, this vision of a devitalizing, dehumanizing civilization is part of the larger, biracial indictment of American culture. While McKay's attack is rooted in color-consciousness, its targets remain remarkably similar to those of the general assault. McKay finds the fraudulence and duplicity of Western civilization in a multitude of situations beyond its psychological effect on individual black men. The arduous but profitable exercise of lifting the "white man's burden" was, for McKay, a particularly noxious undertaking of the civilized world. Under the guise of Judeo-Christian morality, Western civilization succeeded in its drive to commercialize and exploit the "uncivilized" masses of the earth. Furthermore, McKay saw the trend toward cultural standardization as effectively robbing the world of its "greatest charm"—ethnic diversity. The result was the creation of a sterile, monolithic culture in which "the grand mechanical march of civilization had leveled the world down to the point where it seemed treasonable for an advanced thinker to doubt that what was good for one nation or people was also good for another." Yet Ray does commit the "treasonous" act of disputing this conceptualization. And it is in his dissent that he arrives at an uneasy resolution of the problem which has plagued him through two novels.

In the closing pages of the novel, Ray explains that he has always wanted "to hold on to his intellectual acquirements without losing his instincts. The black gifts of laughter and melody and simple sensuous feelings and responses." It is in this rather untenable position that his problem lies. Given a world in which the terms intellect and instinct have been assigned opposing definitions, it seems improbable that one figure can plausibly synthesize both qualities. Ray's attempt at such a synthesis is achieved through his decision to join Banjo in the vagabond life. Thematically, this decision represents a rejection of the standard-

ized white civilization and an affirmation of the cultural diversity of the beach boys' existence.

Nevertheless, we are uneasy with the solution Ray has developed, and in his closing monologue, he unwittingly defines the source of our dissatisfaction. Although he hopes to learn from Banjo how to "exist as a black boy in a white world and rid his conscience of the used-up hussy of white morality," Ray realized that "whether the educated man be white or brown or black, he cannot, if he has more than animal desires, be irresponsibly happy like the ignorant man who lives simply by his instincts and appetites." However, "irresponsible happiness" is the essence of a Jake or a Banjo. Ray's inability to adopt this posture precludes the possibility of his successfully embracing their lifestyle or their method of survival in the white world. Despite his delusions, Ray remains the same "misfit" at the conclusion of *Banjo* that he was when he expatriated from America in *Home to Harlem.*

In *Banana Bottom,* the third and last of his novels, McKay achieves an aesthetic structure which permits the formulation of a viable resolution to the predicament of the educated black man. This resolution is viable in that it does not contradict any of the definitions set forth in the novel, and it is consistent with McKay's affirmation of the primitive elements of black life. This new form is attained by abandoning the structural dualism of his earlier works in favor of a single protagonist. In this way, McKay frees himself from the limitations imposed by the rigid polarizations of instinct and intellect in separate characters. No longer constricted by Ray's inability to reject even a part of his cerebral existence, or Jake's (and by extension, Banjo's) static, unattainable sensuality, McKay now produces a novel in which the main character can credibly embody both instinct and intellect.

The plot of *Banana Bottom* is relatively simple. Set in the West Indies, the story commences with the rape of a young Jamaican peasant girl, Bita Plant. Following the incident, Bita becomes the ward of the Craigs, a white missionary couple who, with an air of condescension, take pity on the girl. In the best Anglo-Saxon missionary tradition, they see in her the golden opportunity for demonstrating to their peasant flock "what one such girl might become by careful training [and] . . . by God's help." As a result, they send her to a finishing school in England with the hope of "redeeming her from her past by a long period of education." After a six-year absence, Bita returns to Jamaica only to find that, for all her education, she is irrepressibly attracted to the island's peasant life. Despite the Craigs' insistence on her marriage to a black divinity student and on the devotion of her life to missionary work, Bita rejects their civilized world in favor of the simplicity of peasant life.

The novel derives its power from the dynamic tension established between the conflicting value systems of Anglo-Saxon civilization and the Jamaican folk culture. This thematic dichotomy first manifests itself in the contrasting reactions to Bita's rape. Priscilla Craig expresses her shock and indignation with an unveiled sanctimony. The "oversexed" natives, she comments, are "apparently incapable of comprehending the opprobrium of breeding bastards in a Christian community." On the other hand, the village gossip, a peasant woman named Sister Phibby, reacts with a knowing smile indicating her "primitive satisfaction as in a good thing done early."

McKay expands and sustains the tension of contrary value systems through the ever-present antagonism between the civilized Christ-God of retribution and puritanical repression, and the African Obeah-God of freedom and primeval sensuality. Throughout the novel, the white missionaries and native ministers are constantly troubled with the problem of wandering flocks which "worship the Christian God-of-Good-and-Evil on Sunday and in the shadow of the night ... invoke the power of the African God of Evil by the magic of the sorcerer. Obi [is] resorted to in sickness and feuds, love and elemental disasters." And although the missionaries struggle desperately to win the native populace, it is the Obeah-God who rules Jamaica, and it is the primitive African value system which is at the core of the peasant culture.

Portrait of McKay.

Of peasant origin and possessing a cultivated intellect, Bita Plant represents McKay's first successful synthesis of two cultures. When she finds it necessary to choose a lifestyle, it is a relatively easy decision. As opposed to Ray, she is not fraught with the vague uncertainties and questioning doubts over her ability to survive in either culture. Bita has readily internalized the concept of her blackness and willingly accepted her racial origins. Bearing no warping hatred for white civilization, she is characterized by an assertive self-confidence derived from a sense of her own innate worth .... (pp. 136-41)

In Bita Plant, McKay at last succeeds in framing an aesthetic solution to the black intellectual's problem of social incongruence. By rejecting not intellect nor education but rather the "civilized" value system in favor of the primitive values of a black folk culture, the intellectual can ultimately escape the stigma of "misfit." On the surface, this solution does not seem to differ from the one developed in **Banjo.** Yet in **Banana Bottom,** McKay makes an important distinction not present in his earlier work. For the first time, McKay distinguishes between education, or the cultivation of the intellect, and the necessary acceptance of the value system implied by that education. Ray's failure to make this distinction is the source of his problem. Believing, on the one hand, that a rejection of civilization implies a rejection of intellect, and at the same time, desiring desperately to hold his intellectual acquirements, Ray is immobilized. He can neither remain in a white world which denies his humanity, nor move into a black world which denies his intellect. However, once the distinction is made, the element of conflict between instinct and intellect is removed. Bita, who rejects the civilized value system but not her intellect, can move easily from one world to another without impairing either instinct or intellect. Unfortunately, it is one of McKay's personal tragedies that although he is capable of making this distinction in his art, he is unable to make it in his life. "My damned white education," he wrote in his autobiography, "has robbed me of much of the primitive vitality, the pure stamina, the simple unswaggering strength of the Jakes of the Negro race." (pp. 141-42)

Claude McKay was an integral part of the American literary movement of the 1920s. Responsive to metaphors embodied in the cult of the primitive, McKay's art served to reinforce the image of the Negro as the simple, liberated, uncorrupt man. At the same time, his work provided the means by which McKay made his personal problem of social incongruence part of the larger cultural phenomenon expressing itself in the white expatriate movement. His life represented a less successful effort. Forever seeking fulfillment of his desires to escape color-consciousness and recapture lost innocence, McKay was doomed to an existence directly opposed to the life he apotheosized in his art. It is McKay's special and tragic irony that although he clung tenaciously to the conception of himself as a "free spirit," his obsessions condemned him to a life of slavery. (p. 146)

Michael B. Stoff, "Claude McKay and the Cult of Primitivism," in The Harlem Renaissance Remembered, *edited by Arna Bontemps, Dodd, Mead & Company, 1972, pp. 126-46.*

Robert Bone (essay date 1975)

[*Bone, an American critic and educator, is the author of* The Negro Novel in America *(1958; rev. ed., 1965; see Further Reading) and* Down Home: A History of Afro-American Short Fiction from Its Beginnings to the End of the Harlem Renaissance *(1975). A student of African-American, English, and American literature, Bone has said of himself: "A white man and critic of black literature, I try to demonstrate by the quality of my work that scholarship is not the same thing as identity." In the following excerpt from* Down Home, *he divides McKay's literary career into four phases—provincial, picaresque, pastoral, and retrospective—concluding that the Jamaican pastoral tales represent the author's most pronounced rejection of Western society.*]

The Afro-American short story entered an authentic local-color phase in the 1920's. There had been a false dawn in the 1890's, when [Paul Laurence] Dunbar and [Charles Waddell] Chesnutt more or less reluctantly adopted the conventions of the local-color school. But their brand of local color was less ethnic than regional in character....

It was not until the Harlem Renaissance that Negro writers were able to embrace the local-color concept with genuine enthusiasm. (p. 139)

The new emphasis on Negritude found its formal embodiment in local color. Thriving on the exotic and the picturesque, local-color fiction was based on the exploitation of distinctiveness for its own sake....

From a strictly literary standpoint, the glorification of blackness yielded mixed results. On the positive side, it brought a new subject matter within the purview of the black writer. Since whatever was distinctive was probably of folk origin, the lives of the black masses were accepted as a legitimate subject for the first time. Still more importantly, their speech was perceived as a powerful expression of ethnicity. Heretofore the distinctive qualities of Negro speech had been viewed as a badge of social inferiority....

On the negative side, the superficialities of local color took their toll. The appeal of this genre is primarily to the reader's *curiosity:* his anthropological interest, so to speak, in the quaint customs of the natives. Many authors of the Harlem Renaissance, quick to perceive the commercial possibilities inherent in the form, indulged the white man's appetite for the bizarre at the expense of a profounder art. (p. 140)

The local-color movement, however, is not devoid of formal implications. Latent in its focus on the region or the parish or the neighborhood are the devices and resources of the pastoral tradition. The best of local-color fiction strives to transcend the merely picturesque, and when it succeeds, it moves in the direction of pastoral. (p. 141)

[The] myth of separation and reunion, which is central to the art of D. H. Lawrence, captivated the imagination of Claude McKay. For McKay shared with Lawrence, the great primitivist of twentieth-century letters, a fascination with "the world before the Flood, before the mental-spiritual world came into being." Throughout his career, McKay yearns for that state of Perfect Oneness before the Flood.... (pp. 159-60)

Claude McKay's spiritual journey carries him from oneness to multiplicity and back again. The quest for experience is the basis of his personal peregrinations (recorded in *A Long Way from Home*), his poems of vagabondage, and his picaresque novels, *Home to Harlem* and *Banjo.* Experience, however, leads to chaos and division in the soul, caused not only by the white man's contumely, but the curse of intellect, which sunders men and women from their primitive emotions. Recoiling from racial insult and abuse, and the complexities of consciousness as well, McKay turns for solace to the simple and harmonious strains of pastoral. The fruits of his revulsion from occidental civilization are the novel, *Banana Bottom,* and the book of stories, *Gingertown.* (p. 160)

McKay's characteristic stance as a writer is that of a wanderer or vagabond. His constant theme is the isolation of modern man, cut off from his emotional roots and deprived of love by the artificial barriers of race or class or nationality. (p. 161)

McKay's literary career may be divided into four phases. The first, or provincial phase, encompasses his first two books of verse, *Songs of Jamaica* (1912) and *Constab Ballads* (1912). The second, or picaresque phase, includes a book of poems, *Harlem Shadows* (1922), and two novels, *Home to Harlem* (1928) and *Banjo* (1929). The third, or pastoral phase, consists of a book of stories, *Gingertown* (1932) and a novel, *Banana Bottom* (1933). The fourth, or retrospective phase, includes an autobiography, *A Long Way from Home* (1937), and a sociological study, *Harlem: Negro Metropolis* (1940).

The stories of *Gingertown* mark a transition from the picaresque to the pastoral phase. The first six tales are concerned with Harlem life. They express McKay's ambivalent feelings toward the black metropolis which, despite its glamor and excitement, he comes to regard as a whited sepulcher. The last six represent the recoil of McKay's imagination from the polluted centers of occidental civilization. Four are set in Jamaica, one on the Marseilles waterfront, and one in North Africa. Their esthetic mode is pastoral; they celebrate the values of simplicity, community, harmony with nature, reconciliation with one's fellow man, and freedom from political or sexual repression.

The two halves of the book were written at different times and under strikingly different circumstances. The Harlem tales were written in France between 1923 and 1926. (pp. 162-63)

The second half of the collection was written in North Africa in 1930-1931. McKay had left Europe to escape "the white hound of Civilization." He had gone completely native in Morocco, whose landscape, people, and exotic customs reminded him of his Jamaican homeland. In the spring of 1931 he settled in Tangier to work on *Gingertown.* He was joined by an Afro-American woman of bohemian inclinations who was in flight from the stuffiness of bourgeois Harlem. After an idyllic "honeymoon" they quarreled, and she returned to Paris and her white lover. Wounded and resentful, McKay retreated to the mountains of Spanish Morocco, where he completed *Gingertown* and *Banana Bottom.*

This disastrous love affair compounded McKay's bitterness and increased his alienation from occidental values. The figure of his paramour, torn between her black and white lovers, became in his imagination an emblem of the Negro soul, torn between two hostile cultures and antagonistic ways of life. At the same time, his withdrawal to the mountains awakened memories of his Jamaican childhood. In surroundings reminiscent of his native village he made a valiant effort to repossess his peasant heritage. The pastoral impulse which inspired his early poems now became the source of McKay's most enduring fiction.

The Harlem tales of *Gingertown* are concerned with the cultural dilemma of blacks who are compelled to function in a white man's world. These tales reflect McKay's experience as an immigrant to the United States from the West Indies. They express his shock and dismay at being transplanted from a country which is 90 percent black to one where the opposite ratio obtains. The tension that results between the self and its environment, leading in turn to a divisiveness within the self, is McKay's essential theme. He is concerned not so much with the humiliations and inconveniences of segregation as with the breach they open in the black man's soul. (pp. 163-64)

The protagonists of McKay's Harlem stories are men or women divided against themselves. Trying to escape their blackness, and the penalties imposed upon it by the white world, they expose themselves to psychological disaster. They may experience a brief moment of happiness while in pursuit of white ideals, but invariably it proves to be illusory. Sooner or later some racial trauma intervenes to remind them that the barriers of caste are insurmountable. What holds these tales together is the fantasy of playing white. McKay is trying to exorcise a certain kind of psychological infatuation.

The dangers and temptations of "white fever" are the focal point of these tales.... The first half of *Gingertown,* in short, is part of a now familiar literature of extrication, whose aim is to liberate the blacks from psychological enslavement to a false cultural ideal.

Unfortunately the literary quality of McKay's Harlem stories is not high. These early tales, after all, were his first experiments with prose fiction. Their awkwardness of style, which is especially pronounced in the dialogue, suggests that the former poet, in shifting his major emphasis to prose, has not yet mastered his new medium. The widely anthologized **"Truant"** is hardly free of this defect, but by virtue of its summary position it merits more extensive treatment than the rest. This story, which concludes the Harlem section of *Gingertown,* illustrates McKay's dilemma as he tries to dramatize his disenchantment with the urban scene through the inappropriate conventions of the picaresque.

As the story opens, the hero and his wife are watching a vaudeville show from the "Nigger Heaven" of a Broadway theater. The curtain discloses a domestic scene in which a troupe of Irish actors personifies the happy family of American popular culture. The initial impact of the scene is idyllic, but its ultimate effect is ironic, for the Merry Mulligans possess the warmth, cohesiveness, and cultural integrity conspicuously lacking in the life of the black protagonist. The note of harmony on which the story opens thus serves as an ironic commentary on the disintegrating marriage of the two main characters.

Barclay Oram is an autobiographical creation closely related to the figure of Ray in *Home to Harlem* and *Banjo.* In a long flashback we learn that he has emigrated from the West Indies in pursuit of his dream of attending a Negro university. At Howard he meets and marries Rhoda, an Afro-American girl of middle-class background and assimilationist outlook. As the tale unfolds, Rhoda emerges as a kind of enchantress who holds her man in thrall to the false values of an artificial civilization. Nor does fatherhood relieve Barclay's feeling of entrapment, for he envisions his daughter marrying a railroad waiter like himself and raising children "to carry on the great tradition of black servitude."

As the present action of the tale begins, Barclay is rousted out of bed at an early hour, in order to report for work on the Pennsylvania Railroad. It is a disastrous trip, and during the layover in Washington he gets drunk, thereby missing the return run. Savoring his truancy, he is not at all disturbed when he is laid off for ten days. Rhoda, however, reproaches him for irresponsibility, and her rebuke precipitates a crisis which is resolved by Barclay's desertion of his wife and child. Through the metaphor of truancy, McKay depicts the black man as a dropout from the Western world, a *pícaro* who is condemned to a life of eternal wandering.

The trouble with **"Truant"** is a radical divergency of form and content. In his expansionist phase (Jamaica to New York), McKay gravitates instinctively toward the devices and conventions of the picaresque. The phase of recoil, however (New York to Jamaica), cannot be expressed through the same medium. The picaresque is a suitable instrument for the *celebration* of Harlem life (as in *Home to Harlem*), but it cannot be adapted to the theme of urban disenchantment. Pastoral is the appropriate vehicle for the expression of anti-urban sentiments. At this point in his career, McKay has made the emotional transition from expansion to recoil, but has not yet grasped its formal implications. He will do so in his stories of Jamaican peasant life.

Structurally speaking, **"Truant"** is the hinge of *Gingertown.* The last of the Harlem tales, it provides a logical transition to the counterstatement. For if **"Truant"** is a myth of disaffiliation, the Jamaican tales are parables of pastoral refreshment and renewal. As McKay's imagination turns from Harlem to Jamaica, a corresponding shift in tone occurs. Feelings of revulsion for the Western world are replaced by a vast affection for the Caribbean island and its people. (pp. 164-67)

To describe the latter half of *Gingertown* as McKay's "Jamaican tales" is only an approximation. Two of the weaker stories, **"Nigger Lover"** and **"Little Sheik,"** have Mediterranean rather than Caribbean settings. A third, **"When I Pounded the Pavement,"** is not in fact a story, but an autobiographical account of McKay's experience in the Kingston constabulary. The three remaining tales, which constitute the core of *Gingertown,* are set in the Jamaican highlands. **"Crazy Mary"** is an undistinguished piece, but **"The Agricultural Show"** and **"The Strange Burial of Sue"** are McKay's best stories.

"The Agricultural Show" is a pure specimen of Renaissance pastoral. The central characters are Bennie, an impressionable schoolboy, and his brother Matthew, the village pharmacist. Matthew, who is something of a local booster, undertakes to organize a country fair.... The fair is a communal ritual in which all segments of society participate, and during which all petty barriers of caste or class are momentarily surmounted.

Matthew plays the role of mediator, who orchestrates and harmonizes the great event. Under his direction, lowlander and highlander mingle for a day; Baptist, Methodist, and Anglican rub elbows; village, town, and city folk are represented; black, white, and all shades in between take part. United in a common venture, the peasantry, gentry, and aristocracy transcend their traditional roles. Among the surging throngs, artificial distinctions of rank and status give way to a natural camaraderie, while on the speakers' platform a symbolic reconciliation of the classes and races is effected. (pp. 167-68)

To a modern sensibility, unacquainted with the pastoral tradition, **"The Agricultural Show"** will seem a sentimental fantasy. When the lion lies down with the lamb, our cynical century believes, only the lion gets up. We will mistake the author's purpose, however, if we read the story as a realistic social commentary. It is rather a poetic vision, an expression of an inner need. McKay's Jamaican pastoral, with its images of racial harmony and social peace, is an objective correlative of the inner harmony that he so desperately seeks. Split and shredded by his contact with the Western world, he returns in his imagination to Jamaica in order to reconstitute his soul.

What follows is a process of reduction. Tormented by his doubleness, McKay endeavors to achieve a psychic unity by exorcising his Western self. From the complexities of Negro experience in America, he turns to the simplicities of Jamaican peasant life. Intellectuality, which he has come to regard as a burden, is renounced in favor of instinct and emotion. The oneness of spirit that he craves necessitates a stripping away of the false veneer of white civilization and a closer accommodation to his primitive sources. The alien culture must be repudiated, and especially in its oppressive sexual forms. Such are the themes of McKay's most impressive story, **"The Strange Burial of Sue."**

The plot turns on a sexual triangle involving the title character, her husband, and an adolescent boy. Sue Turner is a peasant woman of free-loving ways, who is nonetheless universally respected and admired in her community. A hardworking field hand, volunteer nurse, and befriender of pregnant village girls, she conducts her private life in such a way as to threaten neither Turner nor the village wives. Her husband is a steady man, amiable, phlegmatic, and totally lacking the proprietary attitude toward sex.... (pp. 168-69)

Burskin is a shy and awkward youth, still a virgin at the outset of his liaison with Sue. After a passionate affair of several months' duration, she jilts him for a glamorous adventurer recently returned from Panama. Jealous and importunate, Burskin makes a scene at the local grogshop which precipitates a public scandal. Turner, who has thus far been a model of patience and forbearance, now feels compelled to undertake a legal action against the youth who has abused his generosity. Before the case can come to trial, however it is rendered moot by the sudden death of Sue, perhaps brought on (the facts are never clear) by an unsuccessful effort to abort Burskin's child.

The story gains a new dimension with the introduction of the brown-skinned village parson. A self-righteous busybody, he sees fit at one point to protect the public morals by expelling Sue from church. He represents, in short, the intrusion of Anglo-Saxon values on a world more African than European. Two rival codes of conduct, or concepts of goodness, are thus at issue in the tale. The permissive sexual code of the black peasantry, inherited from slavery times if not from Africa, is weighed against the missionary morals of the Baptist seminarian. As in *Banana Bottom,* McKay employs the metaphor of sexuality to dramatize the sharp divergencies of culture, lifestyle, and moral outlook that separate the colonizer from the colonized.

In **"The Strange Burial of Sue,"** the folk community rallies in defense of its immemorial customs. On the occasion of Sue's funeral, the whole mountain range turns out in tribute to her popularity. The parson makes the error, in his graveside sermon, of denouncing Sue as a backslider and a sinner. Outraged, Turner drives him off and invites the people to bear witness to his wife's goodness. In effect the folk community defrocks the village parson, rejecting him as the emissary of an alien culture. In defiant tribute to her passion—a value cherished by the black peasants—Turner plants two flaming dragon's bloods on his wife's grave.

Claude McKay's Jamaican pastorals, written in North Africa from 1930 to 1933, mark the outer limits of his flight from the West. The flight was doomed, as we can see in retrospect, because the fugitive was fleeing from himself. Within a year or two of the publication of **Gingertown** and **Banana Bottom,** McKay was back in the United States. In 1940 his last book appeared, a sympathetic portrait of urban life entitled **Harlem: Negro Metropolis.** His pastoral phase therefore must be seen as one polarity in a larger pattern of vacillation and ambivalence. It was a passing phase, expressive of a deep revulsion from the Western world, but incapable of sustaining an integrated moral vision. (pp. 169-70)

> *Robert Bone, "Three Versions of Pastoral," in his* Down Home: Origins of the Afro-American Short Story, *Columbia University Press, 1988, pp. 139-70.*

Geta J. LeSeur (essay date 1989)

[*In the following essay, LeSeur discusses McKay's poetry and comments on aspects of his romanticism.*]

Jamaica gave to English and American literature a great poet in Claude McKay. As a Negro writer writing at a time when it was popular to use modern forms, he chose to combine the lilting melody and warm human emotion of the earlier romantics in his writing. He wrote poems of exuberance, sorrow, faithful affection, patriotism, and sturdy independence. In such poems as **"The Tropics in New York," "Flame-Heart," "The Spanish Needle," "The Snow Fairy," "Spring in New Hampshire,"** and **"Home-Thoughts,"** these attitudes are poignantly expressed with allegiance to the native and foreign—Jamaica and the United States—the real and the romantic. McKay never saw any of these as being in conflict; they were always two "natures" completely independent of each other. This, however, was a personal and literary philosophy. His poetry is one which says yes to life—rich, free, passionate, and concerned.

McKay has been referred to from time to time as "Jamaica's Bobbie Burns," which in itself is an interesting but valid comparison. Those who knew him personally and those who only know his poetry constantly made this reference. McKay himself made this statement more precise in his autobiography, **A Long Way From Home,** and in the short article **"On Becoming a Catholic":**

> I had always thought of myself as a pagan. I chose Burns as my model, as he was so strong, sweet and amorous of abundant life, and I was writing in the Jamaican dialect.

The comparison is by no means an accident and seems even more relevant when it is noted that Robert Burns was supposed to visit Jamaica after an unlucky love affair with his Scottish sweetheart. The trip never came to fruition, however. Burns' poetry was only one aspect of British literature that all Jamaicans and British colonials were expected to master. Every school boy and girl was expected to memorize several British lyrics, ballads, and narratives or be whipped for not doing so. It is no accident, therefore, that McKay and his schoolmates knew and admired poets like Burns, Keats, Shelley, and Wordsworth. When McKay says that he used Burns as a model, he is also suggesting a silent rebellion on the part of a West Indian youth. When he wrote poetry in the Jamaican Scottish dialect, he used Burns' Scottish dialect as a model. His first poems published in the dialect were **Songs of Jamaica** (1912) and **Constab Ballads** (1912). This was only the beginning of the sturdy independence and faithful affection he was to exercise throughout his life and writing career.

Allegiances and coalitions were goals visualized by Claude McKay. They are present in his autobiography, as a specific statement of purpose, and in his verse. Although a radical, he was a conservative poet, for his verse forms were traditional. The sonnet was his favorite, and he actually wrote most of his poems on the time-honored subjects of love and nature. Regardless of the fact that the writing tradition adopted by McKay was that of the romantic "movement" from his school days in Jamaica, it was not until he came to the United States in 1912 at age twenty-three that his best poetry-writing began. Max Eastman, his lifelong friend and editor of the *Liberator,* which he coedited, later said this of him:

> It was not until he came to the United States that Claude McKay began to confront the deepest feelings in his heart and realize that a delicate syllabic music could not alone express them. Here his imagination awoke, and the colored imagery that is the language of all deep passion began to appear in his poetry.

And about the poetry written in America, Eastman goes on to say:

> The quality is here in them all—the pure, clear arrow-like transference of his emotion into our breast, without any but the inexitable words—the quality that reminds us of Burns and Villon and Catullus, and all the poets that we call lyric because we love them so much. It is the quality that Keats sought to cherish when he said that "Poetry should be great and unobtrusive, a thing which enters into the soul, and does not startle or amaze with itself, but with its subject . . . It is the poetry of life and not the poet's chamber. It is the poetry which looks upon a thing and sings."

McKay has said that, of the English models and schools of writing he has been associated with, it is the classicists and romantics that he admires, but he owes "allegiance to no master." He adds that he has used only that which he considered to be the best of the poets of all ages. The language used in his poetry was that derived from the Jamaican dialect, archaic words, and figures of speech, which are then reshaped to suit his specific purposes. The introductory pages ("Author's Word") to

Harlem Shadows has been cited repeatedly by scholars, critics, and McKay's readers to justify or support theories regarding his poetry. The important information given in that short essay is that McKay thinks the traditional should work best on "lawless and revolutionary passions and words," so as to give the feeling of the "highest degree of spontaneity and freedom." "For me," he says, "there is more quiet delight in 'The golden moon of heaven' than in 'the terra-cotta disc of cloud land'." The last quoted line here is ironically from a poem by one of the best-known Harlem Renaissance poets, Langston Hughes.

It is no accident that Claude McKay felt uncomfortable with the poetry and lifestyle of the New Negro Movement of the 1920s. He was never really a part of that whole milieu. He disagreed with their involvement with "art for art's sake" and with their being self-appointed messiahs to uplift the privileged few. Theirs was a tightly knit circle which excluded many. Because McKay's tendencies were more akin to the European tradition and experience, he was a misfit at a time when blackness was being celebrated. First, McKay's reading was Byron, Shelley, Keats, and the late Victorians. Secondly, his friends, personal and literary, were the whites in New York's suburbs and its downtown Greenwich Village. Thirdly, he was older than most of the Renaissance writers—Hughes, Cullen, Toomer, and others. And fourthly, he lived in Europe during most of the key Renaissance years. Consequently, for these reasons and more, he was, as Frank Harris of *Pearson's Magazine* noted, "an oddity, . . . a noble black poet with romantic intentions."

McKay felt a great tension between black content and traditional white form, and this, for him, was perhaps the hardest problem to solve. He grappled with the two as to where the thrust of his writing should be. He had been praised for producing poems which gave no hint of color. James Weldon Johnson, one of the few close black poet friends he had, advised him to do so; and, from the collection *Spring in New Hampshire*, "**If We Must Die**," perhaps his best-known poem, was left out to retain the "no color" identity. The poem begins:

> If we must die, let it not be like hogs,
> Hunted and penned in an inglorious spot,
> While round us bark the mad and hungry dogs,
> Making their mock at our accursed lot.

The problem became a personal one of how to keep his allegiance to the British models—whose poetry he truly felt and knew well—and be a black poet emotionally. Writing poetry was not difficult for him, but what was difficult was the personae in conflict, the paradox of self which mars some of the poems.

Consequently, while McKay constantly preferred to keep the West Indian identity and the British training, he was conscious that nothing could change the fact that he was a writer who also happened to be a Negro. When told to mask his identity, and when in his novel *Banana Bottom* (1933) certain words were changed into "British-isms," he became extremely angry and replied to his publishers and friends in this way:

> Of all the poets I admire, major and minor, Byron, Shelley, Keats, Blake, Burns, Whitman, Heine, Baudelaire, Verlaine and Rimbaud and the rest—it seemed to me that when I read them—in their poetry I could feel their race, their class, their roots in the soil, growing into plants, spreading and forming the background against which they were silhouetted. I could not feel the reality of them without that. So likewise I could not realize myself writing without that conviction.

Again, the problem of allegiance and coalition were surfaced to deal with these constant attempts to subjugate color to content. The natural and the creative became problematic also. McKay, regardless of all the places to which he traveled, realized that the artist's faith had to be in his origins, a patriotism as one might find in Whitman's America and in Yeats' Ireland. Furthermore, McKay's best poetry and prose were about Jamaica; as for him, the artist being inseparable from his roots would be an alien thought.

The title of his autobiography, *A Long Way from Home,* is from a Negro spiritual, the opening line of which is, "Sometimes I feel like a motherless child, a long way from home." The title, however, is not coincidental, and even though McKay never returned to Jamaica but chose American citizenship instead, the title is a misnomer because Jamaican memories permeate his best later writings. The poetry looks romantically to Jamaica and prophetically to blackness. His prophecy for Jamaica as an independent, Third World nation, for example, was fulfilled in the last two decades. *Spring in New Hampshire* (1920) and *The Selected Poems* (1953) have in them mostly nostalgic lyrics about Jamaica and songs celebrating nature, and they reflect those themes found in the nineteenth-century Romantics.

McKay's romanticism exhibits itself in several ways but primarily in his writing and lifestyle. His literary heroes were writers of conventional works, the sonnet his favorite mode of expression, but some of his poems are done in freer style. An example of the combination of Jamaican remembrance and celebration of nature in the less conventional style is "**Flame-Heart**."

> So much I have forgotten in ten years,
> So much in ten brief years! I have forgot
> What time the purple apples come to juice,
> And what month brings the shy forget-me-not.
> I have forgot the special, startling season
> Of the pimento's flowering and fruiting;
> What time of year the ground doves drown the
> fields
> And fill the noonday with their curious fluting.
> I have forgotten much, but still remember
> The poinsetta's red, blood-red, in warm December.

Many critics have lingered over the meaning of the last line, which also closes stanza II, but the intention here is only to show the poems as examples of the different aspects of McKay's romanticism. He has forgotten the cycles of the seasons, but the emotion of the poem is rich in West Indian images.

In **"The Spanish Needle"** McKay uses a more conventional pattern to write about a very common and wild weed in Jamaica by the same name. It is a plant much like a dandelion in America, but the language and tone which he uses in the poem make the Spanish needle become a regal plant; thus the common and everyday in the hands of a romantic like McKay becomes uncommon. The following verses of that poem show the endearment which he feels for the ordinary:

> Lovely dainty Spanish needle
> With your yellow flower and white,
> Dew bedecked and softly sweeping,
> Do you think of me to-night?
>
> Shadowed by the spreading mango,
> Nodding o'er the rippling stream,
> Tell me, dear plant of my childhood,
> Do you of the exile dream?
>
> Do you see me by the brook's side
> Catching crayfish 'neath the stone,
> As you did the day you whispered:
> Leave the harmless dears alone?
> ....
> Lovely dainty Spanish needle,
> Source to me of sweet delight,
> In your far-off sunny southland
> Do you dream of me to-night?

This poem is very much in the romantic tradition of Shelley and Keats and is probably one of the few poems by McKay that every Jamaican schoolchild must recite "by heart." **"Home-Thoughts"** is one of his better poems with the homeland theme:

> Oh something just now must be happening there!
> That suddenly and quiveringly here,
> Amid the city's noises, I must think
> Of mangoes leaning o'er the river's brink,
> And dexterous Davie climbing high above,
> The gold fruits ebon-speckled to remove,
> And toss them quickly in the tangled mass
> Of wis-wis twisted round the guinea grass;
> And Cyril coming through the bramble-track
> A Prize bunch of bananas on his back;
> ....
> This is no daytime dream, there's something in it,
> Oh something's happening there this very minute!

The use of local words like *mango, wis-wis, guinea grass, bramble track, purple apple, ground dove, pimento, pingwing, rose apple, poinsetta,* and *banana* in **"Flame-Heart," "The Spanish Needle,"** and **"Home-Thoughts"** are entire images in themselves, and even without notes to explain their meanings and connotations, the mood, tone and theme of the poems are obvious. These poems all go back to the West Indian scene, and in them are found the similar conflicts and opposing attractions which plagued McKay throughout his lifetime. In them, also, joy and sorrow are accepted with the stoic indifference which was part of the romantic passion.

"The Snow Fairy," "Spring in New Hampshire," and **"After the Winter"** use the same American seasonal landscape as their background. They too are good, have a simplicity of diction and tone, and are full of longing and passion, but they by no means compare with the lilting, spontaneous yet deep emotion of **"Tropics in New York."** In comparing a few lines from **"Spring in New Hampshire"** with **"The Tropics in New York,"** one can see that the differences are very obvious, not only because of the subject, but because of McKay's involvement with the places closest to his heart:

> Too green the springing April grass,
> Too blue the silver-speckled sky,
> For me to linger here, alas,
> While happy winds go laughing by,
> Wasting the golden hours indoors,
> Washing windows and scrubbing floors.

The weariness and tedium of scrubbing floors in spring is felt, while outdoors the enjoyment of nature passes. Rather than being happy in nature, there is sorrow because the speaker is physically removed from it but is mentally aware of its presence. He is a prisoner of circumstance. **"The Tropics in New York"** finds the speaker a prisoner also in a foreign country, but the nostalgia, though sorrowful, is much more lyrical, and he seems closer to this subject, and the poem is richer:

> Bananas ripe and green, and ginger-root,
> Cocoa in pods and alligator pears,
> And tangerines and Mangoes and grape fruit,
> Fit for the highest prize at parish fairs,
>
> Set in the window, bringing memories
> Of fruit-trees laden by low-singing rills,
> And dewy dawns, and mystical blue skies
> In benediction over nun-like hills.
>
> My eyes grew dim, and I could no more gaze;
> A wave of longing through my body swept,
> And, hungry for the old, familiar ways,
> I turned aside and bowed my head and wept.

McKay obviously is the speaker in this poem, although he speaks for the hundreds of West Indians who became exiles away from their homeland primarily because of economic and diplomatic reasons. The poem, therefore, does have a oneness of feeling about it. The alienation felt is one of time and distance, and the consequence and helplessness is clearly felt in the last three lines. The progression is from glorious song to despair. It is one of his most moving poems on this theme, and the experience, as in **"If We Must Die,"** is the universal black experience.

It is not in the poems only that Claude McKay's romantic nature is exhibited, but in his lifestyle and relationship with people and the world. He traveled to Russia, England, Spain, Germany, and Morocco, and he had romances singularly with each of them. The flirting with Communism was short-lived, and in England he was just another West Indian. Both experiences were disappointing because of the romantic notions he held about them. Burns, Keats, Wordsworth, and Shelley were dead, and prejudice was alive. Learning from those two short "romances," he tried to savor the best in all of the other countries which he visited and in which he lived. In Spain it was the romanticism of the bullfight and the world of Hemingway; in Germany and France it was the beautiful art and architecture. The despairing moments were overshadowed by the glorious experiences of the people he met and the new countrysides to sing about. Again, some of McKay's better writings were done in Europe. His best works were not about the New York, Jamaica, or American scenes while he was living in these places but when he was away from them. In Tangiers, Morocco, he felt at home more than at any other time in his life. In a letter to Max Eastman . . . he wrote, "There are things in the life of the natives, their customs and superstitions reminiscent of Jamaica." And in another letter (1 September 1932) he stated, "My attachment to Tangiers is sort of a spiritual looking backwards."

McKay, therefore, seemed to have done his best work when he maintained a distance between himself and his subject. This in itself was not true of all romantic writers, but it is true of the romantic spirit for nostalgia, mysticism and fascination. About life McKay wrote to Eastman (28 July 1919):

> . . . life fascinates me in its passions. It may survive when everything else is dead and fused into it. I revere all those spirits who in their little (bit?) way are helping the life force to attain its wonderful and beautiful communication.

In the same letter he says, "I love your life more than your poetry, more than your personality. This is my attitude toward all artists."

It is apparent that McKay believes strongly in the nationality, personal identity, and uniqueness that each writer brings to his art. It is that special uniqueness which makes each one different and reinforces the sturdy independence of each human's nature. It was in Europe and elsewhere that he missed America most and in America that he reminisced about Jamaica consistently.

All poetry, McKay thought, should be judged by its own merits, not by categories of race and nationality. The double standard was something which he opposed, and this too was carried over into his lifestyle. Because he was a "foreign" Negro with white friends, the reality of racial prejudice and the embarrassing moments he experienced from whites and blacks left him torn. He wanted to be accepted, but the pain which nonacceptance brought others plagued him. He was not accepted by the blacks of the Harlem Renaissance group, and his friends were the white literati, not the black "Niggerati," as he called them. It is no wonder, then, that the romantic modes and distances worked best for McKay. Some of the most personal poems are about those experiences such as **"To the White Fiends"** and **"The White House."** The militancy and anger are there and very uncompromising. Regardless of this, it was the realm of "literary truth" with which McKay was most preoccupied. He spoke of and "defined" it in a letter to Eastman:

> I think that if the intellectual idea of literary truth were analyzed, it would prove at bottom to be nothing more than "a wise saying" or a "beautiful phrase" delivered in a unique and startling manner— an addition to the sum of the universal wisdom of mankind. Such a wisdom exists telling of the passions, the folly and the sagacity, success and failure, pain and joy of life. It existed long before modern science and I believe it will continue to exist as vigorous and independent as ever as long as humanity retains the facilities of feeling, thinking—the inexhaustible source of which great and authentic literature springs whether it is cerebral or sentimental, realistic or romantic.

The essence of McKay's romanticism was not only in his poetry, but in the life he lived, the places he visited, and the people and ideas he encountered. His daily vocabulary was very interestingly sprinkled with romantic asides, as was his autobiography, *A Long Way from Home,* and his letters to Max Eastman of *The Liberator.* In *A Long Way from Home,* the Pankhurst secretary is a "romantic middle class woman"; his radical days on *The Liberator* were "rosy with romance"; "The Wonder-vogel had lost their romantic flavor"; he mentions "D. H. Lawrence's psychic and romantic groping for a way out"; and he comments on the fact that "it was grand and romantic to have a grant to write." It is obvious that McKay was completely immersed in a romantic style of life very similar to that of some of his British models and contemporaries. A vocabulary interspersed with words carrying the romantic notion means that he consciously draws attention to where his allegiances to nature, life, and self lie. All of these coalesced to create poetry which said yes to life by its explicit philosophy.

Claude McKay has been called "Jamaica's Bobbie Burns," although he gave up that citizenship some twenty-eight years later. The land of his birth, Jamaica, about which he wrote his best prose, verse, and lyrics, still claims him as its citizen. The comparison with the Scottish Burns is by no means superficial, however, as there are many similarities in their writing and points-of-view. The romantics—Keats, Shelley, Wordsworth, Whitman, and Yeats—were also his literary heroes, because of the content of their works and the lifestyles which they led. It was, and still is, unusual to have a black man writing in the mode of the romantics, using their themes, subject matter, and meter. The two natures of self and art, of allegiance and coalition, were things for which McKay worked throughout his life and career. Regardless of his thoroughly British orientation, emotionally and literarily he never forgot his blackness. For a modern poet, the sonnet was his favorite form, and he wrote most of his poems on the time-honored subjects of love and nature. The universality of his romanticism and poetry surpasses color or time lines. (pp. 296-308)

Geta J. LeSeur, "Claude McKay's Romanticism," in CLA Journal, Vol. XXXII, No. 3, March, 1989, pp. 296-308.

FURTHER READING

Bone, Robert. "The Harlem School." In his *The Negro Novel in America,* rev. ed., pp. 65-94. New Haven, Conn.: Yale University Press, 1965.
    Examines the impact of Expressionism on McKay's three novels.

Brawley, Benjamin. "The New Realists." In his *The Negro Genius: A New Appraisal of the Achievement of the American Negro in Literature and the Fine Arts,* pp. 231-68. New York: Dodd, Mead & Co., 1937.
    Brief overview of McKay's poetry and fiction. Brawley favors McKay's "exquisite and dynamic verse" over the author's novels "of a baser hue."

Bronz, Stephen H. "Claude McKay." In his *Roots of Negro Racial Consciousness, The 1920s: Three Harlem Renaissance Authors,* pp. 66-89. New York: Libra Publishers, 1964.
    Biographical and critical appraisal of McKay's poetry, fiction, and nonfiction.

Condit, John Hillyer. "An Urge Toward Wholeness: Claude McKay and His Sonnets." *CLA Journal* XXII, No. 4 (June 1979): 350-64.
    Explores the apparent imbalance between McKay's movement toward universalism and his strong individualism.

Cooper, Wayne F. *Claude McKay: Rebel Sojourner in the Harlem Renaissance.* Baton Rouge: Louisiana State University Press, 1987, 441 p.
    Comprehensive biography.

————, ed. *The Passion of Claude McKay: Selected Poetry and Prose, 1912-1948.* New York: Schocken Books, 1973, 363 p.
    Important collection of McKay's poems, short stories, articles, essays, and letters from all phases of the author's literary career. In the introduction, Cooper presents a biographical and thematic survey, stressing McKay's preoccupation with the black individual's search for identity in the modern world.

Giles, James R. *Claude McKay.* Boston: Twayne Publishers, 1976, 170 p.
    Critical biography.

Greenberg, Robert M. "Idealism and Realism in the Fiction of Claude McKay." *CLA Journal* XXIV, No. 3 (March 1981): 237-61.
    Explores McKay's sense of idealism as expressed in his realistic novels.

Hansell, William H. "Jamaica in the Poems of Claude McKay." *Studies in Black Literature* 7, No. 3 (Autumn 1976): 6-9.
    Examines McKay's Jamaican poems, focusing on such elements as love, innocence, beauty, and a sense of community as reflections of the poet's idealized vision of his homeland. Hansell posits that the island is to McKay "an inspirational symbol for all Negroes of a place and condition where life could be different from what they typically experienced."

————. "Some Themes in the Jamaican Poetry of Claude McKay." *PHYLON* XL, No. 2 (June 1979): 123-39.
    Analyzes the poems in *Songs of Jamaica* and *Constab Ballads,* discerning four thematic categories that became lifelong concerns in McKay's works: "poems on commonplace settings and activities, love poems, poems portraying the peasant mind, and poems with racial or social themes."

Kent, George E. "The Soulful Way of Claude McKay." In his *Blackness and the Adventure of Western Culture,* pp. 36-52. Chicago: Third World Press, 1972.
    Explores McKay's efforts to develop a group consciousness among blacks in Western culture.

————. "Claude McKay's *Banana Bottom* Reappraised." *CLA Journal* XVIII, No. 2 (December 1974): 222-34.
    Studies McKay's *Banana Bottom* within the context of other Harlem Renaissance identity novels, faulting the work for oversimplified characterizations and plot contrivances.

McLeod, A. L. "Memory and the Edenic Myth: Claude McKay's *Green Hills of Jamaica.*" *World Literature Written in English* 18, No. 1 (April 1979): 245-54.
    Evaluation of McKay's *My Green Hills of Jamaica* as flawed nostalgia.

McLeod, Marian B. "Claude McKay's Russian Interpretation: *The Negroes in America.*" *CLA Journal* XXIII, No. 3 (March 1980): 336-51.
    Views McKay's 1923 essay *The Negroes in America* as a major disclosure of the author's political and literary philosophy.

Nicholl, Louise Townsend. "A Negro Poet." *The Measure: A Journal of Poetry,* No. 17 (July 1922): 16-18.
    Appreciative review of McKay's poetry collection *Harlem Shadows,* commending the poet's lyricism, detached perspective, and delineation of conflict.

Pyne-Timothy, Helen. "Perceptions of the Black Woman in the Work of Claude McKay." *CLA Journal* XIX, No. 2 (December 1975): 152-64.
    Studies the female characters in McKay's literary works, noting that they typically provide psychological and economic support for the male characters. Pyne-Timothy further contends that McKay portrays two kinds of female characters: survivors and victims.

Ramchand, Kenneth. "The Road to *Banana Bottom.*" In his *The West Indian Novel and Its Background,* 2d ed., pp. 239-73. London: Heinemann, 1983.
    Examines McKay's treatment of cultural dualism in his three novels. Ramchand labels *Banana Bottom*

"the first classic of West Indian prose" and praises the protagonist Bita Plant as "the first achieved West Indian heroine."

Redding, J. Saunders. "Emergence of the New Negro." In his *To Make a Poet Black,* pp. 93-125. College Park, Md.: McGrath Publishing Co., 1939.
    Historical study of African-American writers during the Harlem Renaissance, characterizing McKay as a seminal author whose poems demonstrate "the proud defiance and independence that were the very heart of the new Negro movement."

Story, Ralph D. "Patronage and the Harlem Renaissance: You Get What You Pay For." *CLA Journal* XXXII, No. 3 (March 1989): 284-95.

Explores white patronage of Harlem Renaissance writers, depicting McKay's associations with radical leftist patrons as, in some ways, atypical of the movement.

Van Mol, Kay R. "Primitivism and Intellect in Toomer's *Cane* and McKay's *Banana Bottom:* The Need for an Integrated Black Consciousness." *Negro American Literature Forum* 10, No. 2 (Summer 1976): 48-52.
    Contrasts McKay's treatment of cultural dualism in *Banana Bottom* with that of Jean Toomer in *Cane.* In both works the authors present a successful integration of Western intellect and African primitivism as essential components of black consciousness.

Ron Milner

1938-

American dramatist.

Milner is acknowledged as one of the leading black dramatists of the late 1960s and 1970s. Along with such playwrights and directors as Ed Bullins, Lonnie Elder III, and Woodie King, Jr., Milner sought to reaffirm the importance of traditional family values and self-determination. He stated: "We're at the end of a catharsis.... We're no longer dealing with 'I am somebody' but more of who that 'somebody' really is." Many of Milner's dramas involve individuals struggling to maintain their moral beliefs while confronted by crime, drugs, and racism. Because his protagonists are often forced to choose between two opposing values, Milner is labeled a moralist. While some reviewers consider his work melodramatic and contrived, Milner has garnered praise for the stark realism of his settings and authentic recreation of urban dialogue and idioms.

Milner was born in Detroit, Michigan, and grew up on Hastings Street, also known as "'The Valley'—with the Muslims on one corner, hustlers and pimps on another, winos on one, and Aretha Franklin singing from her father's church on the other," according to Geneva Smitherman. Milner decided to become a writer after realizing that people on Hastings Street had a story to tell: "The more I read in high school, the more I realized that some tremendous, phenomenal things were happening around me. What happened in a Faulkner novel happened four times a day on Hastings Street. I thought why should these crazy people Faulkner writes about seem more important than my mother or my father or the dude down the street. Only because they had someone to write about them. So I became a writer." He attended Northeastern High School and, later, Highland Park Junior College and Detroit Institute of Technology. In a 1975 interview with *Detroit Free Press* writer Betty DeRamus, Milner joked, "I've taught at college more than I've attended." While teaching at Lincoln University in Pennsylvania in 1966, he met Langston Hughes, who helped shape him as a playwright. Milner recalled: "It was a brilliant experience to know Langston.... Langston taught me about simplicity and how to reach the people you're talking to. He made me understand that your style is simply your personality. If you don't get your personality into your work, you don't have signature, any flavor, any uniqueness. You must have the kind of warmth that invites people into your work. Part of it is natural talent, but a lot is just understanding how to talk *to* people instead of *at* them."

In 1966 Milner produced his first play, *Who's Got His Own*. Indicative of the work to come, *Who's Got His Own* focuses on a black family and the theme of black manhood. The play centers on Tim, his sister Clara, and his mother Mrs. Bronson. After a four-year absence,

Tim returns home to attend the funeral of his father, a man he has hated all his life. In a dramatic confrontation with his mother and sister, he learns for the first time his father's tragic past: when his father was a little boy, he witnessed the rape of his mother and his father's murder by a white mob. Tim and Clara come to see their abusive father as a human being who, unable to fight racial oppression, turned his anger on himself and on his family. "What is primarily at issue in the play," critic Beunyce Rayford Cunningham summarized, "is the question of black manhood, the expression of which has historically been thwarted."

Who's Got His Own was quickly followed by *The Monster* (1969), *The Warning—A Theme for Linda* (1969), and *(M)ego and the Green Ball of Freedom* (1971). Milner is best known, however, for *What the Wine Sellers Buy* (1973). The work centers on the tempting of seventeen-year-old Detroit youth Steve Carlton by Rico, a black pimp and hustler. Rico—a dynamic, slick personification of the devil—entices those around him to trade morality for material gain. When Steve's family desperately needs money, Rico suggests that Steve use his girlfriend, Mae, as a prostitute. Steve struggles to resist with the help of his mother and the deacon of the local church. The deacon advises Steve: "Wanna know what a man is, don't look at his car, his clothes, his bank account, look at his woman. Whatever he is will be right there in her. If she's a whore, then he is a whore too . . . ." Another character asks, "What the wine sellers [hustlers] buy, is it half so precious, half so sweet as what they sell?" Steve answers no: "If I sell you Mae, what am I gon buy?" Critics had mixed reactions to *What the Wine Sellers Buy*. While some noted stylistic flaws and predictable scenes in the play, others lauded Milner's strong characterizations and authentic dialogue. "As in all morality plays, good and the power of love triumph," DeRamus noted, but "what makes *Wine Sellers* different is that the villain, Rico, is no cardboard figure who is easily knocked down. He is, in fact, so persuasive and logical that he seduces audiences as well as Steve." *What the Wine Sellers Buy* received the harshest criticism from black reviewers. Some called the play "not Black enough," "commercial," and "overly sensational." As Smitherman noted, however, "the full impact of *Wine Sellers* was not missed on the people for whom it was intended—[the] 'young folks'."

Milner's work of the 1980s focuses on the black middle class. *Don't Get God Started* (1987), which features gospel music composed by Marvin Winans, contains sketches that depict affluent blacks who, plagued by drug addiction and marital infidelity, find solace by turning to God. The comedy *Checkmates* (1987) contrasts a well-to-do, young, urban couple with their happily married landlords. Milner also produced several musicals, including: *Season's Reasons: Just a Natural Change* (1976), *Jazz-set* (1980), and *Crack Steppin'* (1981). Today Milner continues to write and often teaches or leads playwriting workshops in the Detroit area.

Unlike many dramatists of the 1960s who wrote confrontational protest plays, Milner focused on quieter dramas that stress family ties and individual integrity. "Milner's dramatic work [is] an eloquent and incisive witness to the heroic efforts of the black family to combat the increasing spiritual blight of contemporary urban life," observed Cunningham. "Intense expression and psychological probing joined with a deep regard for the urban family," she concluded, "have made playwright Ron Milner a pioneering force in the contemporary Afro-American theater."

(For further information about Milner's life and works, see *Black Writers; Contemporary Authors,* Vols. 73-76; *Contemporary Authors New Revision Series,* Vol. 24; *Contemporary Literary Criticism,* Vol. 56; and *Dictionary of Literary Biography,* Vol. 38: *Afro-American Writers after 1955: Dramatists and Prose Writers.*)

PRINCIPAL WORKS

Who's Got His Own (drama) 1966
The Monster (drama) 1969
The Warning—A Theme for Linda (drama) 1969
(M)ego and the Green Ball of Freedom (drama) 1971
What the Wine Sellers Buy (drama) 1973
These Three (drama) 1974
Season's Reasons: Just a Natural Change (drama) 1976
Work (drama) 1978
Jazz-set (drama) 1980
Crack Steppin' (drama) 1981
Checkmates (drama) 1987
Don't Get God Started (drama) 1987

Larry Neal (essay date 1968)

[*In the following excerpt from an essay originally published in* The Drama Review *in 1968, Neal examines characterization in* Who's Got His Own.]

Ron Milner's **Who's Got His Own** is of particular importance. It strips bare the clashing attitudes of a contemporary Afro-American family. Milner's concern is with legitimate manhood and morality. The family in **Who's Got His Own** is in search of its conscience, or more precisely its own definition of life. On the day of his father's death, Tim and his family are forced to examine the inner fabric of their lives: the lies, self-deceits, and sense of powerlessness in a white world. The basic conflict, however, is internal. It is rooted in the historical search for black manhood. Tim's mother is representative of a generation of Christian Black women who have implicitly understood the brooding violence lurking in their men. And with this understanding, they have interposed themselves between their men and the object of that violence—the white man. Thus unable to direct his violence against the oppressor, the Black man becomes more frustrated and the sense of powerlessness deepens. Lacking the strength to be a man in the white world, he turns against his family. So the oppressed, as Fanon explains, constantly dreams violence against his oppressor, while killing his brother on fast weekends.

Tim's sister represents the Negro woman's attempt to acquire what Eldridge Cleaver calls "ultrafemininity." That is, the attributes of her white upper-class counterpart. Involved here is a rejection of the body-oriented life of the working class Black man, symbolized by the mother's traditional religion. The sister has an affair with a white upper-class liberal, ending in abortion. There are hints of lesbianism, i.e. a further rejection of the body. The sister's life is a pivotal factor in the play. Much of the stripping away of falsehood initiated by Tim is directed at her life, which they have carefully kept hidden from the mother.

Tim is the product of the new Afro-American sensibility, informed by the psychological revolution now operative within Black America. He is a combination ghetto soul brother and militant intellectual, very hip and slightly flawed himself. He would change the world, but without comprehending the particular history that produced his "tyrannical" father. And he cannot be the man his father was—not until he truly understands his father. He must understand why his father allowed himself to be insulted daily by the "honky" types on the job; why he took a demeaning job in the "shit-house"; and why he spent on his family the violence that he should have directed against the white man. In short, Tim must confront the history of his family. And that is exactly what happens. Each character tells his story, exposing his falsehood to the other until a balance is reached.

Who's Got His Own is not the work of an alienated mind. Milner's main thrust is directed toward unifying the family around basic moral principles, toward bridging the "generation gap." (pp. 199-200)

> Larry Neal, "The Black Arts Movement," in
> The Black American Writer: Poetry and
> Drama, Vol. II, *edited by C. W. E. Bigsby,*
> *1969. Reprint by Penguin Books Inc., 1971,*
> *pp. 187-202.*

Edwin Wilson (essay date 1974)

[*In the following excerpt, Wilson examines* What the Wine Sellers Buy *as a morality play.*]

More and more, black theater appears to be a movement which has found its own voice and is here to stay. The latest evidence is *What the Wine-Sellers Buy* .... Written by Ron Milner, it reiterates themes and forms which have become the hallmarks of black theater and which confirm its authenticity.

What the Wine-Sellers Buy is first and foremost a morality play. Steve, a young high school student whose father died when he was a small child, is being corrupted by Rico, a pimp. Rico is a modern Mephistopheles who argues that the only way a black man can get ahead is to have money and the only way to get money is through illegal means—dope, prostitution, etc.... Opposed to Rico in the struggle for Steve's soul is Steve's mother and her friend, Jim Aaron. The latter is a contractor and like Steve's mother, a churchgoer.

As in all good morality plays there is a physical confrontation between the opposing forces, in this case between Rico and Jim, and in the showdown Jim proves to be more than Rico's equal. Steve's mother enters the struggle as well, explaining to Steve that his father, though a hustler, held some things in his life pure, which is not the case with Rico. In the end, after a tempestuous internal battle, Steve rejects Rico's way. The title of [*What the Wine-Sellers Buy*] comes from the Rubaiyat of Omar Khayyam: "I wonder often what the vintners

buy one half so precious as the stuff they sell." Rico wanted Steve to sell his soul and turn his girlfriend—a basically decent person—into a prostitute. The moral of the play is that if you sell your total person, no matter what you receive, it is not "half so precious" as what you sold.

But Steve does not accept the acquiescent course of his mother and Jim either. He determines to be his own man, neither subservient to whites nor a prey to corrupting forces in his own group. This moving toward a new direction, rejecting white models on the one hand and black extremism on the other, is characteristic of the note struck again and again in today's black theater. So, too, is the positive, moral tone. The latter is all the more remarkable because of the violent, profane picture painted of the urban ghetto; the plays pull no punches and it is out of a raw, ruthless environment that the moral emerges.

The concern with a young man coming of age is another feature of black theater. As in last season's *The River Niger,* to which [*What the Wine-Sellers Buy*] bears a strong affinity, the emphasis is not on past grievances and injustices, but on the future—on the problems and perils young people face growing up in broken homes and a hostile environment, and their determination to overcome these forces. Hand in hand with this attitude goes an enormous vitality in the work itself both in the writing and the playing....

What the Wine-Sellers Buy is a sprawling play, and like others of its type, overwritten at times but the play gives further evidence that black playwrights today, like its hero, Steve, are determined to find their own way, in this case, a way to speak out in the theater.

> Edwin Wilson, "A Black Morality Tale," in
> The Wall Street Journal, *February 21, 1974,*
> *p. 12.*

Walter Kerr (essay date 1974)

[*In the following excerpt, Kerr offers a generally negative review of* What the Wine Sellers Buy, *noting: "As Mr. Milner goes on with his work, he will do well to let ... people speak for themselves instead of steadily saluting the evening's cause."*]

If you have ever gone to any of the summertime festivals of street plays—exceedingly simple moralities in which Virtue and Vice contend for the souls of ghetto youngsters ... you will recognize Ron Milner's *What the Wine-Sellers Buy* right off. Its bones are the bones of all such exhortations to "stay clean," its neighborhood pieties the same neighborhood pieties, its warnings the very same warnings. At the end of the evening a lad who has *almost* been seduced by a Mephisto-like figure into pimping his thoroughly nice girl reaches out to the girl, clutches her tight, and firmly announces "We ain't goin'" his way, it costs too much." The homily has simply been moved indoors ..., opulently mounted, opened up by its author to cram just as much lifelike detail—and perhaps as much dramatic truth—into its elementary design as possible.

How much? At what point does a slogan stop being a slogan and begin to dissolve into the ambiguity and abrupt candor and restless complexity we're willing to call art? There are three or four suddenly hushed moments in Mr. Milner's play when we can very nearly hear the metamorphosis taking place, the evening gliding upward into felt personal truths that are not necessarily suitable for placards.

[Mae], the girl trapped between her love for a boy and the boy's mistaken notion of what will best secure their futures, is taking a severe dressing-down from her mother. The piece, like all such pieces, is full of scoldings: there must be spokesmen for the Right. But, halfway through the older woman's entirely conventional tirade, the girl cuts her off with a cry. The cry is not what we expect. The girl is begging her mother to hit her, hit her hard. Not to wake her up, to drum some sense into her. She scarcely needs that. She simply wants her mother to touch her, to put a hand to her, never mind how fiercely or what for. "When you stopped whipping, you just took your hands away," [Mae] says.... Something over and above the rhetoric has crept in, and its presence has an authority that no amount of righteous finger-wagging will ever equal.

[Mae] is given another such opportunity to escape the strict programming of Our Lesson for Today (Mr. Milner seems to write best for this reluctant, defiant changeling). Under too much pressure from the boy, who is now daydreaming that prostitution will earn them enough money to buy a service truck and turn legitimate, she tries flight. Phoning her father in another city, she asks if she can come to him.

The scene itself is resolutely sentimental, unabashedly stock. The girl fondles a teddy bear as she listens to the refusal we know is certain, a faltering "Oh?" trickling out of her as she absorbs a father's lame excuses. But the conversation goes on a bit longer, grows lighter, and she has pretty well swallowed her disappointment by the time talk turns to Christmas. What would she like for a present this year? The answer pops out of her, eyes glinting maliciously. "A truck," she says.

Of course she knows that the request is absurd. She has suddenly seen herself as absurd, her situation as absurd; she is laughing at her own pain, and the flash of bold humor cuts through everything that is saccharine about the sequence like an honest-to-God breadknife.

As Mr. Milner goes on with his work, he will do well to let impulse interrupt him oftener, let people speak for themselves instead of steadily saluting the evening's cause. He has a certain gift for decoration, even when it is being applied to the all-too-obvious. His Mephisto, for instance, emerges as a spider-legged, flair-skirted, sombrero-crowned cock of the roost who cannot discuss the prospects of chicken farming without turning his throat into a barnyard pianoforte....

[The panderer Rico] is often mesmerizing to watch as he sidles through what seem to be no more than cracks in the hall doorway, dressed in everything from zebra-stripes to tapestried red-and-golds that would look well on the backs of playing cards. If he resembles anything at all it is a Fifth Musketeer, recently cashiered from the King's service for good cause.

Mephisto, however, is still Mephisto, and what he has in mind for his prey is Hell. As soon as one of the Virtues—in this case a bourgeois contractor—begins an impassioned speech that may persuade our young hero to think twice, we know that the devil in the back room will slink instantly from his lair, ready to tug the other way. While the boy propositions his girl, [Rico] stands above them in a pale blue spot-light, dictating the boy's ploys, sometimes reciting them with him....

A debating-society regularity haunts the play: a high school coach speaks sharply on the subject of sex; the boy traps the girl immediately afterward. The first act lights fade away on the boy's first taste of marijuana. The second act lights fade away on the *girl's* first taste. Motivations stand in the corner, waiting, until they are needed: if the boy requires new prompting along a wrong path, his mother becomes ill and there is no money for medicine. This done, we lose the mother for up to an hour afterward.

And the slogans keep on raining. "If you don't respect us, we got to respect ourselves," the girl declaims, as likely as not to automatic applause. "If I sell you, then what am I gonna buy, huh?" the boy finally asks, repenting his plans. It's very much an "I'm gonna tell you somethin'" play, with the speaker promptly making good his word.

Graham Greene once remarked that it was no more than a single step from the medieval morality play—with, perhaps, a central figure named Ambition—to *Macbeth*. But it is the step that makes all the difference, so great a difference that by the time we get to *Macbeth* it is no longer possible to say precisely where the most urgent ambition lies. **What the Wine-Sellers Buy** hasn't yet made the stop. Though it comes teasingly close a few times..., the formula locks it in as tightly as though Mephisto's claws *were* inescapable. In the service of virtue, a theatrical vice wins. The characters haven't freedom enough to act for themselves.

> *Walter Kerr, in a review of "What the Wine-Sellers Buy," in* The New York Times, *Section II, February 24, 1974, p. 1.*

Ron Milner with David Richards (interview date 1975)

[*In the following 1975* Washington Star—News *interview, Milner and Richards discuss the play* What the

Wine Sellers Buy *and comment on the role of black theater in American society.*]

[Richards]: *Is* **What the Wine Sellers Buy** *an autobiographical play?*

[Milner]: A similar incident happened to me when I was young. But I think I would have just passed over it, except that I saw the same thing happening to other guys as well—young guys who were clear-headed and intelligent, and able to achieve, suddenly using all their energies to turn over dope. They'd bought a system of values that says anything you do to get a car or money or clothes is all right.

When you live in a city that has the highest murder rate in the world, you begin to ask yourself why. You trace it back to the same type of incident again and again: Someone embracing the street. It's always been my belief that you can't say the ghetto is hip, because it is very dangerous. You can love it and learn from it, as long as you can perceive the good AND the bad of it.

I've actually seen a 10-year-old boy sniffing salt—not cocaine; he didn't have any concept of what cocaine was—but salt, because he wanted to look like Superfly. You see enough cases of this and it suddenly becomes important enough to write about. The big thing I ask in

Herbert Rice and Loretta Green as Steve and Mae in Milner's What The Wine Sellers Buy.

the play is, what do you care more about: People or things? How much of yourself are you willing to sell?

In your play, though, the hero resists the temptation to sell his soul. This ending was regarded not only as unusual, but actually surprising, by a lot of people. Why?

A lot of people were disappointed by it, too. You know the idea that you can't have a drama, especially a black drama, unless it ends in some kind of tragedy. This is related to the Western concept of drama as despair—what O'Neill called "impending doom."

It's hard for me to say I've written a happy ending when the kid is still faced with the same temptations. He's merely said no in one instance. But I think there has to be some kind of belief that you can do something about your life—and not just suffer what's imposed upon you. For a long time, black writers dwelled on our negative history. They could never see any real victory. For them, the only victory lay in the ability to endure defeat. I was consciously trying to break that.

I function a great deal on what I intuitively feel are the needs of the time. And the needs of the time are for the positive. I don't think black people, people in a crisis, can afford a theater that is merely artifact or entertainment. It has to have a functional effect. Like the African artist: He carves a stool you can sit on, or a spoon you can use.

You don't believe in the theater for its own sake?

Theater for theater's sake is incest. It gets thinner and thinner each time and drifts off into abstraction. But when it's directly involved in life, even when it's badly done, it can cause people to argue, discuss, grow, or at least clarify where they stand. It's true, the aesthetic side can do something for you spiritually. But you can't let that prevent you from communicating on a basic level.

Several critics referred to **Wine Sellers** *as a morality play. Do you object to that description?*

To me, it is directly, obviously and consciously a morality play. The only thing that bothered me was the way the term was used—as a put-down. What kind of a person would consider a morality play unreal at the same time Watergate was going on? By and large, the critics are white, 50 and suburban, and they feel they've had their morality plays. I happen to think they're wrong. I also know that the young, black audience I'm writing for needs this morality play.

You mentioned Superfly. Was that a direct influence on your writing the play?

I could have written it five years earlier or five years later; it was always sitting there in the backlog of my memories and ideas. Superfly gave me a sense of urgency to get it out. But the hustler has been in the ghetto all along. A big mistake that many black writers made was thinking that because they had escaped his kind of philosophy, the problem had actually gone away.

We all jumped directly into the political arena. And one day, we looked up and the character was still there, magnified 20 times on the movie screen and doing his thing on a grander level than ever before. I believe the artist and the people walk side by side—maybe the artist is one-half step ahead sometimes, and sometimes it's the people who are leading. But this is an instance in which the black writer was out of touch with the people. We should have dealt with this problem of values years ago.

Much of the black theater of the 1960s was a vilification of whitey and his values. Is this still an important strain?

Well, it's still there, but much more in the background. In the 1960s, even though we were developing a black audience, there was a strong consciousness of the white audience. We felt we had to strike out at it, explain ourselves to it, relate to it somehow, even though there may not have been any actual whites in the theater some nights. I think we've cut down on that negative white influence, worked out our own aesthetic, and developed our own criteria. Now our plays are aimed at a totally black audience, which makes for a completely different tone and effect. You have to have something to say to your brothers or else shut up. What shape are we in? Where do we go from here? It's like the difference between the way you talk to your family when you're alone, and the way you talk when there are other people in the room.

Did you always want to be a writer?

Every neighborhood has a dude who tells stories, makes up the characters, and does all the sound effects as he goes along. I was doing that when I was five or six. I never thought of it as writing until I got to high school, although that's what it was.

I grew up on Hastings Street, which was pretty infamous and supposedly criminal. I guess it was. But it had other sides, too. The more I read in high school, the more I realized that some tremendous, phenomenal things were happening around me. What happened in a Faulkner novel happened four times a day on Hastings Street. I thought why should these crazy people Faulkner writes about seem more important than my mother or my father or the dude down the street. Only because they had someone to write about them. So I became a writer. Ultimately, I got a John Hay Whitney Fellowship and a Rockefeller Fellowship for a novel I was doing, "Life With Father Brown." I met Langston Hughes and we became friends. That's when things really began to get clear in my mind.

Is there any special reason why you've chosen to live in Detroit?

People always ask me why I've continued to live in Detroit. I've had chances to move on. But it seemed to me they were saying, "you're something, but the rest of the people there are nothing." How can something come from nothing? I'm an extension of the place and people I come from. So I've never wanted to leave. The neigh-borhood grows with you if you grow, and it doesn't grow if you don't grow. But basically, it's always with you, wherever you go.

Ron Milner and David Richards, in an interview in Authors in the News, *Vol. I, edited by Barbara Nykoruk, Gale Research Company, 1976, pp. 349-50.*

Frank Rich (essay date 1982)

[*In the following excerpt, Rich presents a brief, negative review of* Jazz-set.]

Ron Milner's *Jazz Set* looks like a play that has been re-thought so many times that the author finally forgot what he was thinking about in the first place. It's full of half-baked ideas, blurry characters and fractured narrative lines that lead nowhere....

Mr. Milner, best known for *What the Wine-Sellers Buy,* has tried to construct this work like a jazz composition. The characters are identified only by the instruments they play in a sextet; the free-form writing contains repeated rhetorical phrases, rhythmic group chants and incoherent poetry that one assumes to be scat-dialogue. While there's nothing wrong with this stylistic ground plan, Mr. Milner executes it sloppily, using it as a license to commit all manner of self-indulgent theatrical sins.

The content that lies beneath the obfuscatory words is soap opera. As we gradually learn through some embarrassingly bathetic flashbacks, the musicians have been variously victimized by drug addiction, jail sentences, homosexual rape, familial betrayals and wartime horrors. After three acts, these interchangeable people finally realize that "the music is what's important"— and that it can lead them all to "harmony and peace," not to mention future club bookings.

The play gets better as it goes along only because each act—or "set"—is briefer than the one before....

Jazz Set ain't got that swing and don't mean a thing.

Frank Rich, "In Free-Form," in The New York Times, *July 21, 1982, p. C17.*

Clive Barnes (essay date 1987)

[*In the following excerpt, Barnes describes* Don't Get God Started *as a morality play about the rising black middle class.*]

There is a kinship between the theater and three quite diverse human activities—a court trial, a political meeting and a religious service. And the more intense, more overtly dramatic any of these theatrical kin become, the more they take on the trappings of a performance.

The actual ritual of any religious observance is extraordinarily close to a theatrical experience, and not only did the medieval world, with its miracle and mystery plays, see the link between religion and religious drama, but the connection has never been lost on the more modern gospel revivalists.

Most gospel revival shows on Broadway—perhaps the best was *Your Arms Too Short to Box With God*—have been, in effect, staged cantatas.

In a purely dramatic sense the new gospel musical *Don't Get God Started* . . ., is more ambitious, although not necessarily better. . . .

What makes *Don't Get God Started* a different kind of gospel show is the contribution of black playwright Ron Milner, best known for his play, *What the Wine-Sellers Buy.*

Amidst the gospel imprecations and admonitions to mend our ways and find God, Milner has inserted five dramatic vignettes, all intended to show the decadence of the world in general and the rising black middle class—who it seems are not all like that nice, wise old Mr. Cosby—in particular.

The sins of the younger generation—much to the disdain and disgust of their elders—are demonstrated by three troubled couples and two sex perverts.

In one couple, the wife, a snobbish doctor's daughter, deserts her honest, hardworking, blue collar husband, and becomes a cold-slabbed victim of adultery, booze and pills.

In another the husband, before his redemption by the Church, sacrifices his life, family and honor to demon cocaine, while with a third, a good-natured but badly duped hairdresser puts her boyfriend through law school only to have him leave her for a rich white girl.

Other God-steppers are a comic sex addict, Silk, who cannot get enough of his habit, and a parishioner, Sister Needlove, who confuses Christian love with earthly love and gets the hots for the hot gospel.

All these vignettes are as naive and simplistic as the comic episodes in a medieval miracle play—but, as staged by Milner himself—they make their point . . . .

The preview audience I saw [*Don't Get God Started*] with was very free with its cries of assent and obviously heartfelt "Amens!," and individual feeling about the show will unquestionably depend upon one's feeling toward gospel teaching and singing.

Because if you yourself don't get started, from a pure entertainment point of view (if such a viewpoint is not irreverent or even sinful), whether God gets started or not is fundamentally irrelevant.

> *Clive Barnes, "Gospel Fills 'Don't Get God Started'," in* New York Post, *October 30, 1987.*

Howard Kissel (essay date 1988)

[*In the following excerpt, Kissel contends that* Checkmates *is a mediocre play, adding that perhaps it should not have been produced.*]

Let's be blunt. If *Checkmates,* a play about two black couples, one elderly and nostalgic, the other young and aggressive, were about whites, it probably wouldn't have been done.

Yes, there should be black plays on Broadway, but let's not accept the mediocre just to make A Statement.

This play never goes anywhere. The young couple either argue or dance off to the bedroom. He takes umbrage at her career independence, at her gay friends. (There is something unsettling about the virulence with which one minority attacks another.) She, in turn, is unsympathetic to his job problems. Even when something real happens—she gets an abortion without telling him she's pregnant—it seems too pat.

When the older couple are not dashing to the bedroom, they reminisce about World War II, a key turning point for American blacks.

The playwright, Ron Milner, is more interested in scoring points than telling stories. At times he's successful, as when the young husband throws a stack of women's magazines to the floor, derisively reading the titles of articles all focusing on The Self. Some of the older man's reminiscences are vivid and his wife's ironic remarks are sharp.

But Milner is a bit too reverential of the old folks, too contemptuous of the young. Nothing seems thought through, and often scenes fade out feebly, a suitable prelude to a commercial but not theatrically effective. . . .

Checkmates reflects an almost cynical economic awareness of a new black audience eager to come to Broadway. It has been shrewdly cast, handsomely mounted and well-directed. If only this effort had been expended on a real play.

> *Howard Kissel, "'Checkmates' Really Fails to Check Out," in* Daily News, *New York, August 5, 1988.*

FURTHER READING

Jeanpierre, Wendell A. Review of *Who's Got His Own,* by Ron Milner. *The Crisis* 74, No. 8 (October 1967): 423. Favorable review of *Who's Got His Own.* The critic writes: "Ron Milner's *Who's Got His Own* is a highly-charged, well-structured and thoroughly absorbing play that sharply delineates the psychological degeneration of a small Negro family subjected to the corrosive effects of racism."

King, Woodie, Jr. "Log of a Theater Hit: Directing *Winesellers.*" *Black World* XXV, No. 6 (April 1976): 20-26.
  Describes his experiences as director and co-producer of *What the Wine Sellers Buy.*

Mitchell, Loften. "The Season is Now: A Review of Two Plays." *The Crisis* 74, No. 1 (January–February 1967): 31-4.
  Criticizes the "White Establishment" for not allowing full expression of the "black experience" in *Who's Got His Own.*

Nicholas, Xavier. Review of *What the Wine-Sellers Buy*, by Ron Milner. *Black World* XXV, No. 6 (April 1976): 95-7.
  Negatively assesses *What the Wine-Sellers Buy* as a narrow, one-dimensional play with "no imagination."

Smitherman, Geneva. "'We are the Music': Ron Milner, People's Playwright." *Black World* XXV, No. 6 (April 1976): 4-19.
  Brief biography of Milner, review of *Season's Reasons,* and interview with the playwright.

Thomas Mofolo

1876-1948

(Full name Thomas Mokopu Mofolo; also Thomas Mopoku Mofolo) Lesothan novelist.

Mofolo is considered the first great author of modern African literature. Written in the Sesotho language, his three novels concern the radical effects of Christian teachings on traditional African society. *Chaka* (1925; *Chaka: An Historical Romance*, 1931), Mofolo's most highly regarded work, focuses on the great Zulu warrior Chaka. Mofolo completed the work in 1912, but his missionary publishers withheld the manuscript for fear of sparking an interest in traditional—and thus non-Christian—African customs. After revision, *Chaka* was published in 1925 and translated into English in 1931. Today the novel is considered an epic tragedy of literary and historical significance and has served as the model for numerous subsequent works about Chaka, one of the most celebrated legendary figures in African literature.

Mofolo was born in Kojane, Basutoland (now Lesotho), a small country surrounded by the Republic of South Africa. The third son of Christian parents, he was educated at local religious schools and then sent to Morija to work as a houseboy for the Reverend Alfred Casalis, who headed the Bible School, printing press, and Book Depot there. In 1894 Casalis enrolled Mofolo in the Bible School, and two years later Mofolo entered the Teacher Training College, earning a certificate in 1899. He then began work as an interpreter at the printing press, but the operation was suspended during the South African War (also known as the Boer War or Anglo-Boer War), which began in October 1899 and continued until 1902. Mofolo studied carpentry for two years and taught at various schools until 1904, when he returned to Morija as secretary to Casalis and proofreader for the press.

Exposed to a variety of books at the Morija Book Depot, Mofolo read religious works, African and European histories, and novels by such writers as H. Rider Haggard and Marie Corelli. Several missionaries encouraged him to write works of his own, and his Christian allegory *Moeti oa bochabela* (1907; *The Traveller to the East*, 1934) became the first novel written in Sesotho. His next novel, *Pitseng,* the story of two boys and their gradual understanding of Christianity under an African teacher, was published in 1910. During this period Mofolo also began research for a novel based on the life of the Zulu warrior-king Chaka. Traveling to Pietermaritzburg—the former Zulu capital Mgungundluvu—Mofolo visited Chaka's gravesite and collected historical data, recollections, and legends that had persisted in oral literature. The manuscript of *Chaka* was submitted to the Morija printers around 1912. Despite acknowledgement of the novel's extraordinary qualities, the missionaries were deeply divided over whether to publish the work, with those who opposed it citing their fear that the novel's depiction of traditional Africa would entice the indigenous reader to return to a non-Christian way of life. After a campaign by supporters and the excision of some material, *Chaka* was published in 1925. Mofolo, however, had left the Morija press after the novel was rejected. Disillusioned and feeling betrayed, he gave up writing.

He afterward held various jobs, including recruiter and labor agent for diamond mines, sugar plantations, and large farms, manager of a postal route, and trade store owner. In 1933 Mofolo returned to his home district, where he purchased a large farm from a white landowner; however, the farm was later confiscated by the government. Mofolo spent several years and much money in an unsuccessful court fight to regain his land. In 1940, impoverished and ill, he retired to live on a pension until his death in 1948.

Mofolo's *Chaka* has been called by many critics a masterpiece of world literature. Regarded by contemporary reviewers as an "Africanized" Christian tract, the novel has more recently been assessed as a sophisticated fusion of Christian philosophy, African praise-poetry and myth, and elements from Western literatures. Although it is a fictionalized historical biography, *Chaka* retains much that is factual. The story depicts the rise and decline of the early nineteenth-century Zulu monarch Chaka, who systematically conquered Natal and by 1824 ruled over 50,000 subjects. The illegitimate son of chief Senzangakona and Nandi, a woman from a neighboring tribe, Chaka is ostracized by his father and physically brutalized by his peers. In retaliation, he resolves to lead a life of vengeful aggression. He becomes an innovative chief and then a warrior-king whose egoism and bloodlust give rise to a reign of terror that ends when he is murdered by his half brothers.

Mofolo used several diverse stylistic elements in *Chaka*, including the rhythm and narrative devices of African praise-poems, which were performed to honor Bantu monarchs; the didactic elements of African oral narratives, which traditionally served as vehicles for moral instruction; and Biblical terminology, which reflected his missionary schooling. Because the novel form is not intrinsically African, Mofolo also used some of the conventions of the Western novel. He combined these various stylistic forms throughout *Chaka*, shifting from one to another when appropriate for dramatic or thematic emphasis. Mofolo's use of witch doctors in the novel exemplifies his skillful synthesis of these various traditions. The role of the witch doctor has been interpreted as: a literal commentary on good and bad witch doctors in the tribal community; a symbolic revelation of Chaka's personality traits and true desires reminiscent of the witches in *MacBeth;* and an allegorical rendering of a Mephistophelean devil with whom the Faustian Chaka makes a pact.

Mofolo's *Chaka* demonstrates the author's respect for Chaka and traditional African ways of life, unlike the negative depictions of these subjects by white historians. For this reason, Mofolo has profoundly influenced such African authors as Léopold Sédar Senghor, Abdou Anta Ka, and Djibril Tamsir Niane, whose works celebrate Chaka's military and political genius. Translated into English, French, German, and several African languages, *Chaka* remains one of the great works of African literature.

(For further information about Mofolo's life and works, see *Contemporary Authors,* Vol. 121 and *Twentieth-Century Literary Criticism,* Vol. 22.)

PRINCIPAL WORKS

Moeti oa bochabela (novel) 1907
    [*The Traveller to the East,* 1934]
Pitseng (novel) 1910
*Chaka (novel) 1925
    [*Chaka: An Historical Romance,* 1931]

*This novel was written between 1909 and 1912.

The Times Literary Supplement (essay date 1931)

[*In the following excerpt, an anonymous critic offers a brief, positive review of* Chaka.]

Those who believe that the negro races are incapable of great achievements should read **Chaka: An Historical Romance,** by Thomas Mofolo, which paints a partly accurate and partly imaginary picture of the rise of the Zulu power in old South Africa, and combines it with a realistic study of a noble character consciously ruining itself by deliberately cultivating the quality of ferocity. From every point of view it is a striking work and well deserves the tributes which Sir Henry Newbolt pays in his introduction . . . .

The development and ruin of the central character are traced in a way that recalls the Nemesis of the Greeks. We watch with growing sympathy the cruel trials and extraordinary prowess of Chaka's boyhood, his first dealings with witch-doctors and his first romance. We watch his successive temptations by the supreme witch-doctor with alarm and soon with horror; for a trail of death and cruelty is the price of each advance towards Chaka's ultimate ambition—the lordship of all South Africa. When indeed the tempter offers him "such a chieftainship that if a man were to leave the place where thou now art, in his youth, on foot, and go to the bounds of thy territory, he would be an old man before he returned," at the price of murdering "the one thou dost love more than any other on earth," we first catch a real glimpse of the terrible path on which Chaka has entered. Gradually, as he grasps after greater and greater chieftainships and the terror of the Zulu arms penetrates across mountain and desert to the remote tribes of the North, Chaka paying each time the witch-doctor's price of greater and greater cruelty, murdering his own mother, whole tribes and peoples, whole regiments of his own armies, all our sympathy flies; but we read on, fascinated, until the final scene of Chaka's own murder by his brothers comes with a feeling almost of relief. It is a grim story, but it is not mere realism. Again and again the reader feels that he is obtaining, even amid the greatest horrors, a genuine insight into the mind and traditions of the African peoples as they were before the coming of the white man.

> A review of "Chaka: An Historical Romance," in The Times Literary Supplement, No. 1539, July 30, 1931, p. 596.

Henry Newbolt (essay date 1931)

[*Newbolt, one of the most popular English poets of the early twentieth century, is best known for his poems on naval and patriotic subjects. In the following excerpt from his introduction to* Chaka, *he discusses the novel's literary, historical, and cultural value.*]

Rome had her African colonies, and there were born in them writers who are still remembered. But there is a wide gulf between cultivated quasi-Romans such as Apuleius or Augustine, and the life of the primitive

African world of the veld and forest. Mofolo takes us little more than a century back in time, but the society whose secrets he reveals to us [in *Chaka*] is literally and in the deepest sense a prehistoric, or even a timeless society. In it we may see our own origins and the magnified image of our own spiritual conflicts.

It is unfortunate that we cannot read his work in the language in which it was written. Translation is here more than usually thwarting, because the book is not a mere record of events, or a historian's analysis of motives, but a piece of imaginative literature. It has the persuasive charm, we are told, of a fine language finely written, and this naturally cannot be reproduced adequately in English. (p. x)

It is right I think to speak of Mofolo's book as an imaginative work, but there can be no doubt that in the author's own view it is a serious contribution to history. His first four pages are enough to prove this, and his intention is further shown by the fact that he has made more than one journey into Natal to ascertain dates and other details for his narrative. The result is certainly an interesting and convincing record, probably a valuable one. If it is put side by side with accounts of the same events in such books as Miss Gollock's *Lives of Eminent Africans,* Sir Godfrey Lagden's *The Basutos,* and the Rev. A. T. Bryant's *Olden Times in Zululand and Natal,* it will be found to differ from them very seldom on points of fact, while it shows, as might be expected, more intimate knowledge of native life and thought, and a more serious attitude towards the character and motives of the African peoples and their chiefs. In Mofolo's pages not only Chaka himself, but all the persons in the drama (except the witch-doctors) are treated as inheritors of human feelings and an ancient culture: they are shown in turn as kindly or cruel, faithful or faithless, single-minded or ambitious, but they are never judged from a political standpoint, and still less are they ever portrayed as beings of an inferior race, childish or ridiculous even in their most violent and criminal moments. From any such misrepresentation Mofolo is saved as well by his moral sense as by his artistic instinct. He is a soul by nature Christian, and sees in every crisis the clash of good and evil, of gentleness and militarism, of chivalry and brutality. For him Chaka's irresistible career is the perfect and unanswerable example of the ruin of human life by the rule of force, deliberately adopted and consistently followed. Dingiswayo is chosen to heighten the effect by contrast. He is not on the same scale as Chaka, and in battle he was probably no less whole-heartedly a fighting man; but his principal characteristic is skillfully brought out. In Chapter X, after the capture of his enemy Zwide, we are told that "Dingiswayo detained his prisoner a few days and then released him, and sent him to his home in peace, as if he had paid a friendly visit and was never a prisoner." In Chapter XXV we find Chaka on the last night of his life dreaming the last of his terrible dreams. Among them, "he saw his chief Dingiswayo, and the noble acts he did when he tried to instill a spirit of humanity into the tribe: and he saw himself bringing to naught those high endeavors." By his conquest of the whole African world he had raised himself to almost superhuman rank: "he had become the originator of all that was evil."

But this is not the whole account of the matter: it is only the vision of the sinner, agonized by remorse. Mofolo looks more deeply into it: he looks behind the crimes to the source of them. Chaka's guilt is the working out of a Nemesis: as the son of Nandi and Senzangakona he was "a sin incarnate, damned from birth." The tragedy falls naturally into five Acts. In the first we see the trials and triumphs of the boy, hated and ill-used by his more legitimate half-brothers. In the second he flies from home, in danger of death, and on the open veld he meets the witch-doctor Isanusi, the tempter from nowhere, the visible symbol of his own hardening ambition. In the face of this mysterious stranger Chaka sees at one moment unbounded malice and cruelty, at the next compassion and the truest love. In a sweet voice which is not the voice of a deceiver he offers Chaka deliverance from his oppressors, and a chieftainship greater than that of his father. But the gaining of this will demands great sacrifices. Chaka accepts the bargain without hesitation.

In the third Act Chaka comes to the capital of Dingiswayo, falls in love with his new chief's sister Noliwe, and distinguishes himself in war. Isanusi's promises are all coming true: Senzangakona dies, and Chaka is appointed by Dingiswayo, as overlord, to succeed him. In the fourth Act Dingiswayo is murdered by Zwide, the enemy whom he had spared. Chaka steps into his place as overlord, and is tempted by Isanusi to aim at a still wider lordship, to make himself the supreme chief of the African world. The sacrifice for this must be the life of his betrothed, Noliwe. Again he accepts without hesitation, and kills the victim with his own hand, in a scene which could not be surpassed for tenderness and horror. Nor could any hand better the art with which Isanusi persuades him to this final and fatal decision.

The fifth and last Act traces with great power the change which now comes upon Chaka and his world. The tragedy is no longer concerned merely with the fated fall of an ambitious chieftain: it becomes the apocalyptic vision of a monstrous beast, consumed by an all-destroying blood-lust. To quench this unquenchable thirst Chaka's own child, his own mother, his own faithful warriors in thousands must all be sacrificed: and at last he cannot sleep till he has slaughtered with his own hand. His deliverance can only come by death: his own brothers drive their spears into his heart, and as he falls dying his evil genius Isanusi is suddenly present to demand his reward. He is gone again as suddenly; we hear no more of him. Being but a symbol, an attribute, the evil part of the man's nature, he inevitably passes away with him. (pp. xi–xiv)

I have drawn only the essential outlines of the drama, the mere bones of it: and this can give no idea of the richness and vitality of the whole work. It has many characters in it, and none of them are more curious than the two servants, Ndlebe and Malunga, whom Isanusi gave to Chaka for his attendants and guardians. They are gifted with sub-human faculties—animal cunning and acute animal senses—and they are clearly intended, like Isanusi himself, to symbolize faculties or instincts of Chaka's own nature. The whole business of the witch-doctor's profession is thus raised from the contempt which commonly attends it among our own writers, its real origin is hinted at, and its effects at least partly accounted for. At any rate it has become a fit subject for serious art. It is only upon these terms that magic can find an entrance into our Western scheme of thought. What we have hardly yet realized is that feelings or beliefs or practices which cannot claim any sanction from our religion, our science, or our philosophy may yet have a traceable origin and a psychological value: but not until they have been studied in their native environment. Some of our explorers have discovered this.... Isanusi in his striking appeal to Chaka...to act according to his true nature, tells him that there is another life, and that "all that a man does here the Sun when it sets takes with it to that great city of the living, the city of those who, *ye* say, have died and are dead: and his acts await him there." Yet this does not in Mofolo's mind clash with that other passage on a later page: when Noliwe dies we are told that her spirit fled and went to Dingiswayo "to the place of glory above." So Mofolo...belongs not only to the Africa of the future, but to the Africa of the past: he can write of both with perfect sincerity, because his feeling is identical with both. This double sympathy is no small part of his claim on our attention—he belongs to an intermediate age which may be quickly passing. It would be well if we could ensure that his successors shall not be tempted to gain a more advanced civilization at the cost of becoming less characteristic Africans. (pp. xiv-xv)

> *Henry Newbolt, in an introduction to* Chaka: An Historical Romance, *by Thomas Mofolo, translated by F. H. Dutton, 1931. Reprint by Oxford University Press, London, 1967, pp. vii-xv.*

Ezekiel Mphahlele (essay date 1962)

[*Mphahlele, an expatriate South African critic, novelist, and short story writer, is considered one of Africa's leading literary figures and a significant contributor to the development of African writing in English. In the following excerpt, he examines the witch doctor Isanusi in* Chaka *as a symbol of the protagonist's deepening moral depravity.*]

Mofolo's first novel, **Moeti oa bochabela (The Pilgrim of the East)** gives an account of African life in ancient days. It is about a boy who wanders away from his home in search of "the unknown Creator." He believes that the Creator does not like the brute behaviour of his people, disgust in whose drunkenness, hatred and other moral lapses has caused him to leave home.

His next novel, **Pitseng,** also in Sotho, is set in a village that is built in a hollow (*Pitseng*—at the pot). It is a love story telling of the education and courtship of a modern African. It is a classic in its language and idiom.

In his introduction to **Chaka,** Sir Henry Newbolt says Mofolo's first novel is something like a mixture of *Pilgrim's Progress* and Olive Schreiner's *Story of an African Farm*. Although it is not likely that Mofolo was acquainted with Christopher Marlowe, **Chaka** is an interesting mixture of Tamburlaine and Dr. Faustus. (p. 170)

Chaka is in a sense a religious king. He might not feel that he is the scourge of the ancestors, but he believes that his witch-doctor, Isanusi, is an efficient intercessor between his people, epitomized by himself, and his ancestors; inasmuch as the witch-doctor in traditional African society is not a mere dealer in charms and potions, but is the moral conscience of his people. It is to him that the people appeal when they want to know what to do so that they do not offend the community and thereby the spirits of the ancestors.

Mofolo's king commits tyrannical acts in alarming succession. But he has his moments of "psychic conflict." His career began as a compensatory response to people's despise of him which arose from the fact that he was a chief's illegitimate child. It was also a response to his brother's lust for his own blood, and to his father's ill-treatment of his mother (she was expelled from the royal house). After the last attempt by his brothers to take his life, "he resolved that from that time on he would do as he liked: whether a man was guilty or not he would kill him if he wished, for that was the law of man. Chaka was always a man of fixed purpose.... But until now his purposes had been good. Henceforth he had only one purpose—to do as he liked, even if it was wrong, and to take the most complete vengeance that he alone would imagine." We can almost hear Edmund in *King Lear* or Richard III speaking.

This is where the Faustian element comes in. Chaka meets Isanusi, the witch-doctor, who is to "work on him," so that he conquer the chieftainship which he believes rightly belongs to him. Isanusi tempts him further and confronts him with the "moral problem of choice." Chaka can procure another kind of medicine which will make him king of a much bigger empire than he ever dreamed of. "It is very evil, but of great power," says the witch-doctor. "Choose." He asks Chaka to give this serious thought first, because he will have to murder and shed much blood in the process of becoming the desired monarch. Isanusi provides Chaka with two attendants: Ndlebe (ear) with long ears that could catch the faintest whisper from miles away and report back to the king; Malunga, whose work was to doctor the regiments so that they are brave and obedient.

Chaka succeeds to the stool. He has been to the river and seen a serpent which came out of the water, coiled itself round him, licked his body, and receded, staring at him. This is the messenger of the ancestors, which is to assure Chaka that his career deserves their watchfulness and assistance.

Isanusi comes up again with that suggestion of a potent medicine. The king must give the blood of one he loves most, to be mixed with the medicine.

"I Chaka had no need of deep thought. I have decided upon the chieftainship of which thou hast spoken. But I have no children and I do not know if the blood of my mother or my brothers would be sufficient. But if it is, I will give it you that ye may compound your medicines of it."

"But among those whom thou has promised there is not included the one thou dost love with the love of which I spoke. *Her* thou hast passed over. Think of *her* and tell us thy decision."

"Apart from these, the one I love is Noliwe."

"So be it. Think well which thou dost desire. The chieftainship without Noliwe.... But thou wilt not win it unless thou kill Noliwe, thou thyself, with thy own hand. [Isanusi smiles and continues.] Today, Chaka, we are teaching thee the highest kind of witchcraft when men kill their children or their parents so that the spirits may receive them and prosper them."

Isanusi is a symbol of Chaka's other self. Whenever he is in a tricky situation he need only shout, "Isanusi," and the witch-doctor will be there to assist. The decision is confirmed, and Noliwe, who has already delivered Chaka's child (unknown to him) is killed by his own hand in a scene that is full of pathos.

Chaka makes several reforms and gathers a number of small tribes under him and they become part of the Zulu nation, protected against the plundering expeditions of men like Zwide and Matiwane. Chaka's military genius creates the most formidable army in Africa at the time.

At the peak of his power and manhood, Chaka begins to be plagued by nightmares. He leaves his homestead in order to be "alone" outside the city. Even then he continues in lust for blood and sends one division of his army to destroy another. Bodies continue to feed a very large pit just outside the city. But he feels the approach of death. (pp. 170-72)

Chaka knows death is near and he cannot flee. In his... dream he sees Noliwe, the woman he loved; Dingiswayo, now dead, who was against unnecessary bloodshed and forgave those he conquered; the trusted soldier of whose popularity he was so jealous that he sent him to distant lands to fetch a stone from which metal is made so that he perish, and who dragged his living corpse back to his king.

Isanusi does come to claim his price in cattle. Chaka's attendants, Ndlebe and Malunga, simply disappear without a word of explanation. Chaka must pay the supreme price. His brothers murder him. The hyenas do not touch him; they merely circle round his body.

Indeed Chaka's life story stripped of all the romance still reads like a romance, as can be seen in E. A. Ritter's magnificent biographical epic, *Shaka Zulu,* which was published in 1955. Mofolo tells his story as a Christian, who is concerned with the battle between Evil and Good in Chaka. The manner of telling it is in the tradition of African oral literature—interspersed with songs and snatches of moralizing. (p. 173)

> *Ezekiel Mphahlele, "The Black Man's Literary Image of Himself," in his* The African Image, *Faber & Faber, 1962, pp. 166-203.*

O. R. Dathorne (essay date 1966)

[*In the following excerpt, Dathorne appraises Mofolo's* The Traveller to the East, Pitseng, *and* Chaka, *focusing on the last-named work.*]

Thomas Mofolo..., the greatest Sotho writer, was a product of Morija and even worked for the Paris Evangelical Mission there at one time. Perhaps Mofolo's work more than any of his contemporaries, shows what Jahn [see Further Reading] has called "the synthesis of Sotho tradition and Christianity." The New Testament had been rendered into Southern Sotho as far back as 1868, a Southern Sotho-English dictionary had been produced at Morija in 1876, and an anonymous collection of folklore had been published at nearby Platberg in 1850. It is therefore no cause of surprise that Mofolo published *Moeti oa bochabela (The Traveller to the East)* in 1907.

In the story Fekisi is disgusted with the life round him. He begins to ask certain questions about the source of cloud and rain, the origin of the sun, the nature of God. He finds that the world of nature seems by contrast to be happy and more pleasant. An old man, Ntsoanatsatsi, tells him that men formerly originated from the place where the sun rises every morning, and in a vision he sees a man rising out of a pool, brighter than the sun. It is this he decides to seek.

Mofolo's form is the familiar hero-quest story found in the tale. But the impetus for the hero's departure is never the disgust that Fekisi feels; this alienation is a direct result of the Christian presence which had driven a wedge in tribal society and divided kinsmen on the question of ideology. It is interesting that to seek the Christian ideal Fekisi has to leave the familiar haunts of his tribe and his gods and to travel far away across open fields and deserted lands. It is as if the thoughtful, honest Mofolo were telling the reader that Christianity was far removed from the African plane of realism and was an elusive, insubstantial phantom which had to be sought. But his hero up to the time of setting out remains very much a Mosotho; appropriately he sings a praise-song to his father's cattle before he finally departs.

The first stages of his journey are disappointing; the people he encounters are no better than those he has left behind. It is with relief that he leaves all human company and treks across desert until he reaches the sea. There he meets three white elephant hunters who convert him and incidentally return to him some of the happiness he had lost. Mofolo adds that his hero "accepted all they told him, he believed them." On the occasion of receiving the first sacrament he sees Christ at the altar and rushes forward. He is found dead.

Mofolo had altered the hero-quest tale in an important way; not only was there little link with nature but, as has been shown, there was an abomination of man. In addition the whole allegorical interpretation was centred on the protagonist; it was *his* search, for *his* needs, for *his* boon. Nothing like this had existed in traditional oral literature and perhaps Mofolo was really visualising this as the only possibility for the new emerging individual consciousness, that it should bear the consequences of egocentricity. The burden of the responsibility of the tribe could be carried by one man in the oral tales, because behind him and ahead of him there was the *wholeness* of the tribe. It was from where he had come and it was the place to which he was returning. His adventures only made him more loyal, more readily able to appreciate what he had left behind; they confirmed the superiority of the tribe. But Mofolo's hero is alienated because he has lost the ability to pivot within the consciousness of the tribe which is itself disintegrating. His death confirms his pointless vacillations and the illogicality of alienation.

By contrast **Pitseng** is a disappointment. All his life Mofolo had to choose between the amiable offerings of Christian cameraderie and the set diet of an uncompromising art. The difficulties of the situation were made even more emphatic especially as he was an employee of Morija. It is only by taking this into consideration that one can accept the second novel at all; it was an attempt to pacify his teachers, employers and publishers. For the third, **Chaka,** the world had to wait until 1925, owing to its outright rejection by the missionaries. Another, *Masaroa,* still remains unpublished.

The second novel is named after the village of Pitseng in which it is set. Mr. Katse has brought Christianity to the village and soon has a very large following, including Alfred Phakoe and Aria Sebaka. Katse, rather arbitrarily, dispenses the benefits of the good life and he decides that the two children should in time marry. Alfred goes off to a training school and Aria becomes an assistant at the school. Alfred withstands all temptations and returns to marry Aria. This is the bare bones of the highly moral story and it is not really possible that the author of **Moeti oa bochabela** was capable of seeing the world in such unequivocal and obvious terms.

What however seems to deserve some mention in the book is the relationship that the hero has with nature. It is a relationship that is to become more evident in **Chaka.** The rejection of nature that had been noticed in the first novel, as well as in the work of Mangoela, Segoete and Motsamai was part of the rejection of their

tradition. In the oral literature there is rapport between man and nature and therefore nature is never rhapsodised nor objectified. It is intrinsic, whole and consummatory. After the initial rejection, Mofolo's return to nature is to do with its rediscovery through Europe; it is now seen with European eyes. For instance as Alfred journeys to Aria's home:

> The finches again flew up in a swarm and passed by quite close to them, but a little distance away they wheeled and rushed past them and settled in the reeds. It was as through they were trying to greet him in this manner.

The hesitation "as though" is important: in the world of oral literature they would have greeted him. Mofolo hesitates because, like his hero of the first novel, he had journeyed away from his people's ethos on a voyage of repudiation.

This is the key to an understanding of **Chaka.** It is no simple debunking of legend, but in Noni Jabavu's words "it becomes the apocalyptic vision of a monstrous beast, consumed by an all-destroying blood-lust." The historical Chaka is only the impetus for Mofolo's psychological study of the nature of repudiation. Mofolo reverts to the theme of the first novel—and this was his testament—the individual could not survive. Both Christian and pagan needed the props of tribal security. It is no accident that both Fekisi who saw Christ, and Shaka who connived with the devil, had to die.

Chaka is forced into individuality; he is the illegitimate son of Senzangakona, chief of the Ifenilenja tribe, and Nandi. Hated by his jealous brothers he is forced to flee from home. He grows up quite alone but brave and his mother wants to ensure that her son inherits the chieftainship. She has him anointed by the great serpent of the deep and he is put in the care of the evil Isanusi. His brothers never let up against him and finally his own father orders that he should be killed. This marks the turning point in Chaka's alienation.... **Chaka** has suffered from being too closely regarded as historical reconstruction and too little as a great novel, apart from its melodrama. A *Times Literary Supplement* review in 1931 [see excerpt dated 1931] thought it was a partly accurate and partly imaginary account and Mphahlele sees Chaka as a king given the moral problem of choice [see excerpt dated 1962]. But **Chaka** is neither pure history nor ethics; it is part of the tradition of the praise-poem and the hero monomyth but both of these have undergone a startling blend and a unique transformation. The catalytic effect of the missionaries had caused a renewal of concepts; a new melancholy has entered the African soul and no longer can the natural world, gods and man be accepted *in toto,* without question.

To say that Mofolo's two great novels belong to the *genre* of **Pitseng** and are mere exercises in the complacency of missionary teaching is to misunderstand them and Mofolo. They are above all the quests of befuddled individuals, catapulted from the security of tribal consciousness into the personal uncertainty of metaphysical speculation. What should concern the reader of today is not the individual enquiry but the tragic necessity for it. (pp. 152-53)

O. R. Dathorne, "Thomas Mofolo and the Sotho Hero," in The New African, Cape Town, Vol. 5, No. 7, September, 1966, pp. 152-53.

Albert S. Gérard (essay date 1971)

[*In the following excerpt, Gérard notes the importance of Mofolo's novels in African and world literature and discusses their embodiment of Christian philosophy, African culture, and Western literary conventions.*]

[The] foundation of the novel in Southern Sotho must be ascribed to a man of remarkable genius, who belonged to the same generation as Mqhayi among the Xhosa: Thomas Mofolo. (p. 108)

[In] 1905-1906 he composed the first Sotho novel. His sponsors were fully aware of the novelty of the thing. One of them said that it was "an absolutely original work of imagination," and F. H. Dutton, one-time director of education in Basutoland was later to describe it as a "surprise": "it was a new product—not a history, but a novel describing native life in ancient days." The book was *Moeti oa bochabela* (*The Traveller to the East*), which was first serialized in *Leselinyana* in 1906, and appeared in book form in 1907.

Actually, it is more than a mere ethnographical novel. It is a quest story set in Lesotho before the coming of the white man. The hero, Fekesi, is an idealistic young man who is prompted by two impulses. One is of a moral nature: he is horrified at the evil ways of the village people, who live in drunkenness, quarrels, and sexual promiscuity; the other is intellectual, and has to do with the mystery of the origins of the universe. (p. 109)

Moeti oa bochabela is, of course, a Christian tract, ostensibly based on the antithesis of Africa—"clothed in great darkness," "a fearful darkness," Africa is the place "in which all the things of darkness were done,"—and the radiant light of the white man and of his religion, "the light that has come." This somewhat obvious symbolism involves a measure of suppression, perhaps of insincerity. By the beginning of this century, the Sotho people had been in touch with Europeans far less commendable than their devoted French missionaries, and Mofolo certainly knew that the white man's society was no faithful materialization of the City of God. Although the overall symbolism is simple and rather inadequate, Mofolo is by no means insensitive to the more subtle relations between Christianity and African culture. His highly unfavorable presentation of allegedly actual African mores may have prompted, as a reaction, the glorification of old-time Lesotho in Segoete's *Raphepheng*, which was to appear in 1913. But the fact remains that underneath the disparaging depiction of the minor characters of the novel, there is—illustrated by the elder's speeches, the mythical story of Kgodumo-

dumo, and the motivations of Fekesi himself—the memory of and the aspiration to a life of orderliness and virtue that are presented as independent of any Christian teaching. So that the hero's discovery of Christianity is, as much as a conversion to a new faith, a return to beliefs and manners that had antedated both the introduction of Christianity and the degradation of morality exemplified in the early chapters of the book. Mofolo's ideal, then, may be said to be less one of rejection of traditional values in favor of Christian standards, than one of syncretism. Christianity is the new way toward the restoration of ancient purity. Mofolo has his white characters themselves point to the similarity between the legend of Kgodumodumo and the story of Jesus Christ. As Miss P. D. Beuchat has written, "*Moeti oa bochabela* is interesting in that it shows the merging of Sotho beliefs and Christian thought."

Sotho readers can enjoy the outstanding style of that first novel. But everyone can appreciate its careful two-part structure of search and discovery, hankering and fulfillment, evil and good. Moreover, the writer makes skillful use of the allegorical vision. Miss Beuchat goes on to claim that "the novel ends with a highly mystical scene, a dream or revelation which little resembles anything that Mofolo might have been taught by the rather austere Protestant faith in which he was brought up."

Yet, he could have drawn his inspiration from the Bible and/or from Bunyan. Jack Halpern has wondered "just what the Basuto of the 1860s made of *Pilgrim's Progress*, the first work to be translated and published." The reply seems to be that they found it congenial to their own mode of thought, as did countless African readers in about three dozens of languages. And there is little doubt that Mofolo's example encouraged his former teacher Segoete to make use of the same technique—albeit with less skill—in *Monono ke moholi, ke mouoane*, which was to be printed three years later.

It is in character depiction that the book—like so many African novels—is defective. In tribal societies, little attention is paid to individual inwardness. A person's awareness of self is primarily as a member of the group, and not—as is the case in Western society—as an autonomous individual whose chief legitimate preoccupations are with his own personal identity, rights, and privileges. This fundamental culture trait has many literary implications. Not only are African writers notoriously clumsy in the expression of strictly personal emotions such as love but also, more generally, their interests are ethical rather than psychological, and they are seldom able to present convincing individual characters. Their societal outlook drives them to turn character into type, so that the reader's response is one of moral edification rather than imaginative empathy.... This particular cultural trait makes it very difficult even for Europeans versed in the African languages to provide a balanced appraisal taking into account both the conscious purposes of the writer and his society's notion of the function of literature. To illustrate the kind of patronizing ethnocentricity to which white readers are liable, I cannot resist quoting a pronouncement made on *Moeti oa bochabela* by Professor W. A. Norton of the University of Cape Town in 1921. He called the book "a charming odyssey...which, with a little more bloodshed, might have been saga, or, in verse, an embryo epic"!

Mofolo next embarked on a second novel, which was to have been entitled *The Fallen Angel* (Sotho title unknown). According to the *Livre d'Or,* the purpose of the book was to disprove some unspecified theory of Marie Corelli's; whether this was actually so or not is open to doubt. As we have seen in connection with *Moeti oa bochabela,* and as we shall see again when dealing with *Chaka,* at least some of the missionaries displayed complete lack of understanding in their interpretation of Mofolo's intentions. Anyhow, the author showed his manuscript to a missionary who disapproved of it; the work never reached print, and its whereabouts are unknown, if in fact it still exists.

Mofolo's second published novel was *Pitseng,* which was serialized in *Leselinyana* before it appeared in book form in 1910. The title refers to a village in the Leribe district. One of the chief characters in the book is the Reverend Katse, preacher and schoolteacher in Pitseng. He is a portrait of Mofolo's former teacher, Segoete, and the writer insists on his selfless dedication to the task of converting the pagans and educating the young. There is, however, little connection between Katse's career and the love plot on which the book is flimsily built, except that a considerable amount of Katse's preaching has to do with love and marriage. (pp. 110-13)

The many disquisitions on courtship and marriage in the book illustrate the confusion that, in Lesotho as in many parts of Africa, resulted from the intrusions of Christian ethics. The new ideal of genuine feeling, sexual restraint, and monogamy is extensively described in Katse's sermons and is enacted in the story of Alfred and Aria. These two, however, can hardly be said ever to come to life, so that there is a wide gap between the edifying purpose of the book and the realistic description of actual mores as observed by Alfred. Whereas Mofolo's earlier volume was marked by the unquestioning identification of European mores with the Christian ideal, *Pitseng* strongly emphasizes the contrast between this ideal and actual behavior among Christians, both black and white. In Pitseng and in the Cape Colony, he notices that native Christians do "like most white people who put God last in everything," and indulge in aimless flirtations and desultory promiscuity. And he comes to the unpalatable conclusion that "the heathens are telling the truth when they say that the evil influences come from the Whites and come into Lesotho with the Christian converts, because this habit whereby a young man decides independently upon marriage, consulting only with his girl friend, started with the converts. This attitude has completely destroyed the youth of Lesotho."

Noting that proper respect for the sacredness of courtship and marriage is more often found among heathens than among Christians, Mofolo extols the time-honored ways of the Sotho.... But traditional marriage customs have other aspects than this restraint and this symbolic indirection in conveying personal desires.... [Two] elements in traditional marriage, the bride-price and polygamy, are precisely those to which Mofolo takes exception, dutifully following the teaching of the missionaries, like so many of the early writers. His objection to polygamy is of course consonant with the overall Christian and Western concept of marriage. But his criticism of the bride-price seems to be more specifically an echo of French Protestant policy in Lesotho.... (pp. 113-15)

The main source of African puzzlement in this matter is of course the fact that "objectionable" traits cannot be separated from "approved" features in either of the two main conceptions that Christianization brought face to face. This appears clearly—although, no doubt, unintentionally—in the development of the love plot in *Pitseng.* Although Alfred and Aria avoid the "reprehensible" aspects of African courtship practice, that is, the bride-price and polygamy, and although they refrain from the promiscuity so widely spread, according to Mofolo, among the Christian village youth, yet they do not conform to the aspect of custom that the writer explicitly extols, namely, the total submission to parental will. Alfred and Aria select each other from the depth of their personal feelings, without previously seeking their parents' approval. Nor could it have been otherwise: the Christian insistence upon inner feeling and personal responsibility, and therefore upon personal freedom, was bound to disrupt the traditional morality. It is noteworthy that a similar critique was to be raised by Jolobe in *Thuthula* and, much later, in a Rhodesian novel, *Nhorvondo dzokuwanana* (*The Way to Get Married* [1958]) by a Shona author, Paul Chidyausiku.

While it is quite true, as Daniel Kunene points out that the two young people "are, for most of the time, portrayed as statues of virtue, sitting upon their high pedestals and looking with disapproval and even dismay at the goings-on of ordinary mortals," *Pitseng* contains all the data of the dilemma that the new view of marriage raised in most African societies. And although Mofolo fails, as he was bound to do, to provide a convincing picture of the ideal syncretism he advocates, this novel has more realistic subtlety than the previous one, because it is based on something that was fast becoming fundamental in the African mind: a clear perception of the antinomy between Christian theory and Christian practice. "Christianity," Mofolo writes, "is very good, it is better than anything on earth, if only all Christians would behave as this man [Katse] does."

While he was composing *Pitseng,* presumably in 1909, Mofolo was journeying through Natal on a bicycle, gathering historical background information for a new novel, to be based on the life of the early nineteenth-century Zulu conqueror, Chaka.... The result was

Chaka, a genuine masterpiece of insight and composition, and perhaps the first major African contribution to world literature. (pp. 115-16)

It is . . . not surprising that Mofolo, as an African and as a Sotho, should have been interested in the momentous career of that Zulu Napoleon. What is less expected, however, in view of the strictures legitimately leveled at the deficiencies of most modern African fiction both with regard to character depiction and plot organization, is that Mofolo's research and mediation and genius should have produced a work that is remarkable for the clarity of its structure, the sharpness of its psychological insight, and the depth of its ethical approach. Although *Chaka* has been variously described as "an historical romance" and "a Bantu epic," it is really a tragedy, both in terms of construction and significance. Peter Sulzer perceptively observed that "while it has the rhythm of an epic, its inner structure and tragic content bring it near the sphere of the dramatic." *Chaka* can be defined as a narrative tragedy in prose, built along the simple curve of growth and decline which defines the structure of classic tragedy at its best. (pp. 116-17)

With great psychological acumen, Mofolo, in the first four chapters of the novel, goes to the very roots of his hero's fate. As Ezekiel Mphahlele rightly observed, "His career began as a compensatory response to people's despise of him which arose from the fact that he was a chief's illegitimate child. It was also a response to his brother's lust for his own blood and to his father's ill-treatment of his mother" [see excerpt dated 1962]. In tribal societies, estrangement from the group is the worst fate that can befall an individual. The numerous outlaw stories in the Icelandic sagas are cases in point. Chaka's suffering at being rejected by the tribe is the primary conditioning factor of his later development. His sense of alienation and frustration kindles an unquenchable thirst for revenge and domination, which he will be able to gratify as a result of the bravery and resilience he has acquired in resisting the most cruel persecutions.

Chaka's boyhood comes to an end when he decides to seek redress at the court of his father's overlord, Dingiswayo, head of the Mthethwa. Historically, this took place in the early years of the nineteenth century. On his way through the forest, "he reviewed all his life since his childhood, and he found that it was evil, terrifying, fearsome." . . . The philosophy experience has taught him is that "on earth the wise man, the strong man, the man who is admired and respected is the man who knows how to wield his spear, who, when people try to hinder him, settles the matter with his club." . . . The realization leads him to the ethics of unlimited self-assertion which accounts for all his subsequent behavior. "He resolved that from that time on he would do as he liked: whether a man was guilty or not he would kill him if he wished, for that was the law of man . . . . Until now his purposes had been good. Henceforth he had only one purpose—to do as he liked, even if it was wrong, and to take the most complete vengeance that he

alone could imagine." . . . From a reluctant victim, Chaka deliberately turns himself into an unscrupled revenger. It is at that moment he has his first meeting with one Isanusi, whose name means "witch doctor" in Zulu.

The status of this supernatural character in the novel was bound to cause considerable attention among the critics, not least because the beliefs of Africans are usually supposed to be just crude superstitions. (pp. 117-18)

[Early] critics appraised the book against the backdrop of the traditional image of Chaka as a bloodthirsty monster of motiveless malignity. They were struck by the fact that Mofolo's interpretation seemed to turn him not only into a human being with definable and intelligible human motivation, but almost into a victim of his malignant fate. Hence, presumably, they show a proclivity to overemphasize the role of Isanusi and to load him with full responsibility for Chaka's evil deeds. As late as 1947, we find M. Leenhardt still claiming that "les magiciens exigent la maturation du projet criminel" ["the witch doctors demand the fulfillment of the criminal designs"]. But in 1948, Luc Decaunes, in what was at the time the best discussion of *Chaka,* hardly mentioned this supernatural element, but analyzed the book in terms of fate and freedom . . . . (p. 119)

[We] still find the notion that Isanusi is a genuine supernatural being and the decisive casual agent in Chaka's career. In 1953, without discussing the witch doctor himself, Sulzer stated that the two envoys whom Isanusi places at the disposal of the Zulu warrior "are personifications of the bestial features which take ever greater hold of Chaka." Nevertheless, as late as 1963, Miss Beuchat wrote that in the person of the witch doctor "we are presented with a supernatural explanation for Chaka's succumbing to evil," because "at the most crucial moments, when subsidiary crises occur, the power is there to challenge Chaka's decisions and remind him of his previous undertakings." And in the same year the Soviet critic L. B. Saratovskaya claimed that "Mofolo's book is permeated with the concept of fate, of a mysterious higher force which controls Chaka's actions." Other recent commentators, however, have preferred to work along lines that had been suggested by Sir Henry Newbolt when he wrote that Isanusi is "the visible symbol of [Chaka's] own hardening ambition" [see excerpt dated 1931]. "The witch doctor," said Mphahlele, "is a symbol of Chaka's other self," and Claude Wauthier viewed him as a "personification of paganism." More recently, Kunene has shrewdly noticed that "if we compare the thoughts of Chaka at the time he hears the wailing in the village while he is hiding in the forest, with Isanusi's words during his first meeting with Chaka, we see identical sentiments, almost identical words."

It is as irrelevant to ask whether Mofolo actually conceived of Isanusi as a real supernatural being within the Chaka-world, as it is to discuss whether Shakespeare believed in witches. The point is that the Sotho sorcerer fulfills exactly the same function as do the witches in *Macbeth:* he helps crystallize the hero's impulses; he coaxes him into articulate awareness of his own desires and of their implications. When Isanusi, speaking of Chaka's ancestor, says, "If thou dost not spill blood he will take no pleasure in thee"..., he simply confirms the philosophy of status through strength to which the young man had come unaided during his earlier meditation. And when the sorcerer adds, "The medicine with which I inoculated thee is a medicine of blood. If thou dost not spill much blood it will turn its potency against thee and compass thy death. Thy work is to kill without mercy, fashioning thyself a road to thy glorious chieftainship," he merely makes Chaka fully conscious of the logic and of the dangers inherent in the course he has already decided to take.

At that point, we must observe, Isanusi assumes that the young man merely wants to be reinstalled into his birthright as the eldest son and successor of Senzangakona. Chaka's ambition so far has nothing that could be called illegitimate. It is Chaka himself who makes Isanusi understand that his aspirations are of wider scope.... (pp. 119-21)

At Dingiswayo's court, Chaka's story branches off into three narrative trends: his bravery against the chief's enemy, Zwide, earns him the honor of being placed at the head of Dingiswayo's army; he falls in love with the king's sister, Noliwe, who loves him too; at the death of Senzangakona (which actually occurred in 1816), Chaka is made chief in his father's stead, much to the fury of his half brothers. In each case, his success is facilitated by the intervention of Isanusi's mysterious delegates— Malunga, who represents bravery and strength, and Ndlebe, who represents intelligence and cunning. Thus far, however, Chaka's overt purposes have been legitimate. Nor has any actual evil been involved in their materialization, devious and uncommon though the devices of Isanusi's envoys may be. (pp. 121-22)

When Dingiswayo dies (this was in 1817), Chaka is not aware that Isanusi's henchmen have made arrangements for the king to be conveniently killed so that the young chief can succeed him at the head of the Mthethwa. In a sense, this is a climax in Chaka's career. Although he has acquiesced in evil, he himself bears no actual guilt for the murderous treachery that has brought him to the throne.

The point of no return is reached when Isanusi reappears after Dingiswayo's death as he had reappeared at the grave of Senzangakona. He explains to Chaka that further progress in power entails a new dedication to evil.... "It is a difficult matter, for it is thou who must provide the right medicine, and not I." ... This medicine, it soon turns out, is the blood of Noliwe, which must be mixed with the food of the warriors. And although Chaka is willing to sacrifice his beloved instantly, the witch doctor insists that he wait for a period of nine months, "in which to confirm his

decision so that he might not wish to turn back too late when the work had begun." ... The true nature of Chaka's longing is made clear when he changes the name of his tribe from Mthethwa to Zulu (which means "People of Heaven"), "because I am great, I am even as this cloud that has thundered, that is irresistible. I, too, look upon the tribes and they tremble"—and Mofolo, for once, intervenes in the story to comment: "we...must wonder at the arrogance and ambition of this Kafir who could compare his greatness to that of the Gods,"...adding, "Then it was that he sacrificed his conscience for his chieftainship."...(pp. 122-23)

It is important to understand the peculiar significance with which the murder of Noliwe is endowed in the total symbolism of the work, for the character of the girl and everything that is connected with her seem to be of Mofolo's own invention.

Describing Chaka's reform of the army, Mofolo mentions that he forebade his soldiers to marry at the usual early age:

> He said that the married man ... thought of his wife and children, so that he ran away and disgraced himself. But the unmarried man fought to kill instead of being killed, and to conquer, so that he might enjoy the praises of the maidens. All the same, Chaka did not forbid them absolutely. He promised that the troops that surpassed the others in war would be released first from this bondage of celibacy, even if they had not remained long in that state: more, they would be given wives by the chief himself....

And the writer adds the following, highly meaningful, generalizations:

> The reader must remember that above all else on the earth the Black Races love to marry. Often in speaking of the good things of life people do not mention marriage, because *marriage is life*. Therefore we can understand well how hard the warriors of Chaka worked to gain this reward. To set his regiments an example, Chaka remained a bachelor till the end of his life. (... italics mine)

Mofolo provides another reason for Chaka's rejection of marriage. Marriage, Isanusi had advised him, "is a hindrance to a chief, and brings dissension in his house." ... Indeed, it was sometimes the custom in Africa for a newly enthroned monarch to kill, or otherwise dispose of, all potential pretenders. Chaka's bachelorhood and his enforcement of celibacy on his warriors are part of a pattern that culminates in the murder of Noliwe and signals the victory of the values of war and death symbolized by Isanusi over the values of love and life. (p. 123)

Self-imposed sterility, as in the case of Chaka, is viewed as so unnatural an attitude in the African culture context that it can only stir puzzlement and awe. But Mofolo turns it into an image of evil, the symbolism of which is clinched by the murder of Noliwe. As Chaka's beloved, as a woman, the instrument of human perpetuation, Noliwe is truly the embodiment of the forces of love and life in Chaka. His falling in love with her was the sign that, at that early stage in his evolution, he was still capable of redemption; it stood on a par with his devotion to Dingiswayo. On the level of Chaka's psychology, her murder illustrates his complete surrender to the evil impulses of self-assertion. In the wider symbolism of the work, it brings to its highest intensity the antinomy of fame and love, of power and life. It is the most repellent aspect of the overall destruction that is the only way to worldly glory and might.

In the introduction to his French translation of the work, Victor Ellenberg writes that *Chaka* is "the story of a human passion, ambition, first uncontrolled, then uncontrollable, which fatally grows and develops, as if fanned by some implacable Nemesis, and consumes everything until it ruins the moral personality and leads to the unescapable punishment." The Nemesis, however, is no outward power. It is the very same immanent logic of crime and punishment which was at work in *Macbeth.* The murder of Noliwe marks the moment of Chaka's rupture with human nature, as does the murder of Banquo of Macbeth. From that point on, bloodshed becomes an addiction. The tyrant's downfall is linked to his rise by an inexorable chain of cause and effect. The growing extent of his power also increases the number of his enemies and compels him to impose ever sterner control upon his warriors. He is, therefore, threatened from two sides: by those who resent his ruthless authority, and by those who want a larger share of its benefits—until his two half brothers, from whom he had wrenched the chieftainship at the death of their father, pluck up enough courage to kill him. (pp. 124-25)

It is obvious that Mofolo had fully assimilated the Christian view of man as a free agent, totally responsible for his acts. Among Chaka's deeds, he makes a perfectly clear distinction between those that are prompted by legitimate justice, and those that result from a fiendish lust for power. At every decisive point, the meaning and consequences of contemplated actions are fully described by Isanusi, and Chaka always makes up his mind in complete awareness of what he is doing. Few African works exhibit such a profoundly integrated sense of the meaning of freedom and guilt in Christian ethics. (p. 125)

[While] the central idea of *Chaka* is coherently and impressively Christian, it would be an over simplification to suggest that any other types of outlook were altogether foreign to Mofolo. Indeed, the last page of the novel is unobtrusively marked by the emergence of two other standards of valuation.

It is all too often forgotten that as a Sotho, Mofolo participated in the vivid legacy of bloody memories that his nation had inherited from the times of the Wars of Calamity. The Sotho people had suffered grievously as a result of Chaka's imperialism, and national feeling may well have played its part, side by side with Christian inspiration, in Mofolo's choice of this particular evil hero. Some patriotic satisfaction, one presumes, was involved in illustrating the workings of immanent

justice, not only on Chaka, but also on the Zulu nation as a whole. Before dying, Chaka prophesies for the benefit of his half brothers: "It is your hope that by killing me ye will become chiefs when I am dead. But ye are deluded; it will not be so, for Umlungu (the White Man) will come and it is he who will rule, and ye will be his boundmen." ... Writing those words, Mofolo may have felt some complacency at this reversal of fortune for the enemies of his people, particularly in view of the fact that Zulu resistance to white occupation had finally been put down in 1906.

But Mofolo was not only a Christian and a Sotho. He was also an African, whose native continent was being increasingly and irresistibly incorporated into the white man's sphere. Awareness of their identity and of the need to overcome tribal definitions and differences was spreading fast among African intellectuals in those early years of the century.... Owing to its privileged status as a British protectorate, Lesotho's active part in this movement was negligible. The feeling was there, however, and we catch a fugitive echo of it in the subdued pathos of the last paragraph of *Chaka:*

> Even today the Mazulu remember how that they were men once, in the time of Chaka, and how the tribes in fear and trembling came to them for protection. And when they think of their lost empire the tears pour down their cheeks and they say: "Kingdoms wax and wane. Springs that once were mighty dry away." ...

It is difficult to escape the impression that at this final stage the Christian and the Sotho in Mofolo have made room for the African, who renounces, for a brief while, his tribal rancors and his new definition of good and evil to ponder on the past greatness of his race and on its present subjugation, finding some undivulged hope, perhaps, in the notion that the white man's empire, too, will wane some day.

It may have been this final impression that, in later times, was to enable Senegal's Léopold Sédar Senghor and Mali's Seydou Badian to extol Chaka, in poetry and on the stage, as the heroic, self-denying ruler, who does not hesitate to sacrifice the tenderest passion of the heart in order to ensure the greatness and to defend the freedom of his people. Mofolo's conception of Chaka is entirely different and, as far as can be ascertained, much closer to historical fact. The Sotho author is by no means blind to his hero's inherent greatness, but he judges him and indicts him in the name of an essentially ethical view of life. Besides the technical skill and the depth of outlook which it evinces, Mofolo's novel is unique in its successful combination of traditional African and modern Christian elements.

But it is considerably more than a novel. Apart from the wider, universal ethical significance of the curve in Chaka's career—from innocence to evil, and from crime to punishment—the story also has that mysterious quality in which all myths partake. In his *Nachwort,* which is easily the most perceptive analysis of *Chaka* to date, Sulzer points out that the Zulu monarch is, in some respects, an inverted image of Christ, while exhibiting, in other respects, fundamentally Faustian elements. Ever since its inception in sixteenth-century Spain, the modern European novel has been essentially realistic. Yet, literary realism ignores the realities of mystery that are basic to human experience. However extensively the certainties of science and logic have grown, the fundamental questions—the whence, the why, and the whither—of human existence and behavior still remain unanswered. It is with these that myth deals, and the level of myth can only be reached through nonrealistic, nonrational channels. The mystery in *Moby Dick,* the madness in *Don Quixote* and *Hamlet,* the magic in *Macbeth* and *Faust,* these are the elements that raise such works to the higher levels of myth. If they are so undefinably satisfying, it is because they beckon to the dim reluctant awareness within us that in all important matters uncertainty is still our lot. Whether Mofolo's **Chaka** can be claimed to rank with them is a matter for cultured Sotho readers and critics to decide. The mere fact that the question can be raised is in itself significant. (pp. 125-27)

> *Albert S. Gérard, "Literature in Southern Sotho," in his* Four African Literatures: Xhosa, Sotho, Zulu, Amharic, *University of California Press, 1971, pp. 101-80.*

FURTHER READING

Armah, Ayi Kwei. Review of *Chaka,* by Thomas Mofolo. *Black World* XXVI, No. 4 (February 1975): 51-2.
    Discusses characterization in *Chaka.*

Burness, Donald. "Thomas Mofolo's *'Chaka'.*" In his *Shaka, King of the Zulus, in African Literature,* pp. 1-24. Washington, D.C.: Three Continents Press, 1976.
    Examines elements from African and Western literary traditions and Christian philosophy in *Chaka.*

Franz, G. H. "The Literature of Lesotho." *Bantu Studies* IV (1930): 145-80.
    Bibliographical information, plot summaries, and criticism of Lesothan literature, including Mofolo's novels.

Jahn, Janheinz. "The Tragedy of Southern Bantu Literature." In his *Neo-African Literature: A History of Black Writing,* pp. 100-20. New York: Grove Press, 1968.
    Studies the effects of Christian missionary education on the works of Bantu writers. Jahn includes a discussion of Mofolo's changing attitude toward Western Christianity.

Spronk, Johannes M. "Chaka and the Problem of Power in the French Theater of Black Africa." *The French Review* LVII, No. 5 (April 1984): 634-40.
    Details the influence of Mofolo's *Chaka* on other works about the Zulu chieftain written by dramatists of Africa's French theater.

Werner, A. "A Mosuto Novelist." *The International Review of Missions* 14, No. 6 (April 1925): 428-36.
    Plot summary of *The Traveller to the East,* which Werner compares with John Bunyan's *Pilgrim's Progress.*

Toni Morrison

1931-

(Born Chloe Anthony Wofford) American novelist, dramatist, and editor.

The author of five critically acclaimed novels, Morrison has been called the high priestess of village literature. Her award-winning works chronicle small-town black American life, employing "an artistic vision that encompasses both a private and a national heritage," according to Angela Wigan. Through such works as *The Bluest Eye* (1969), *Song of Solomon* (1977), and *Beloved* (1987), Morrison has earned a reputation as a gifted storyteller whose troubled characters seek to find themselves and their cultural riches in a society that warps or impedes such discovery. As stated by Charles Larson, each of Morrison's novels "is as original as anything that has appeared in our literature in the last 20 years. The contemporaneity that unites them—the troubling persistence of racism in America—is infused with an urgency that only a black writer can have about our society." Morrison herself has stated that she willingly accepts critical classification as a "black woman writer" because the label does not limit her writing. She maintained: "I really think the range of emotions and perceptions I have had access to as a black person and a female person are greater than those of people who are neither.... My world did not shrink because I was a black female writer. It just got bigger."

Morrison was born Chloe Anthony Wofford in Lorain, Ohio, to Ramah Willis Wofford and George Wofford, a shipyard welder. As an adolescent, she read classic Russian novels, Gustave Flaubert's *Madame Bovary,* and the works of Jane Austen. She later commented: "These books were not written for a little black girl in Lorain, Ohio, but they were so magnificently done that I got them anyway—they spoke directly to me out of their own specificity. I wasn't thinking of writing then ... but when I wrote my first novel years later, I wanted to capture that same specificity about the nature and feeling of the culture *I* grew up in." Morrison attended Howard University—where she changed her name to Toni because Chloe was hard to pronounce—and in 1955 received a master's degree from Cornell University. In 1957 she returned to Howard to teach English and there met Harold Morrison, a Jamaican architect; she married Morrison and had two sons. After their divorce in 1964, she worked as an editor for a textbook subsidiary of Random House, where she is currently a senior editor. During this time she wrote her first novel, *The Bluest Eye,* which was published in 1969.

The Bluest Eye is a novel of initiation set in Lorain, Ohio. Pecola Breedlove, a young black girl, desperately wants blue eyes, thinking that they will make her beautiful. She drinks several quarts of milk at the home of her friends Claudia and Frieda McTeer just to use

their Shirley Temple mug and gaze at young Temple's blue eyes. One day Pecola is raped by her father; when the child she conceives dies, Pecola goes mad. She comes to believe that she has the bluest eyes of anyone. Morrison began *The Bluest Eye* with the following lines: "Here is the house. It is green and white. It has a red door. It is very pretty." This passage, reminiscent of the "Dick and Jane" reading primer, is repeated twice. The second version closely resembles the first but is written without standard capitalization or punctuation. The third version is run together without spaces or distinction between words. Each version of the passage represents a type of family: The first version represents a white family; the second, a struggling yet happy black family; and the third, which has been labeled the "distorted run-on" version, represents Pecola's family. *The Bluest Eye* has been praised as an excellent study of black girlhood in America. Reviewing the work, Ruby Dee wrote that Morrison "digs up for viewing secret thoughts, terrible yearnings and little-understood frustrations common to many of us. She says these are the gnawings we keep pushed back into the subconscious, unadmitted, but they must be worked on, ferreted up and out so we can breathe deeply, say loud and truly believe 'Black is beautiful.'"

Sula Peace, the heroine of Morrison's next work, *Sula* (1973), is an embodiment of paradox and ambiguity. In the course of the story she drops a young boy, Chicken Little, to his death; watches with interest as her own mother dies by fire; and seduces Jude, her best friend's husband. Despite her moral ambiguity, Sula is an inspiring symbol of freedom in her community. Critics were struck by the bizarre characters in *Sula*—among them Eva Peace, Sula's despotic, crippled grandmother, and Shadrack, a World War I veteran and founder of National Suicide Day. While they lauded Morrison's powerful prose, some commentators found the violent deaths and apparent amorality in the novel disturbing; Jerry H. Bryant found "something ominous" in "the chilling detachment" with which Morrison drew her characters. *Sula* was nominated for a National Book Award in 1974. *Song of Solomon*, Morrison's third novel, won the National Book Critics Circle Award the year of its publication, 1977. *Song of Solomon* is the story of Milkman Dead, who acquires his first name when his mother is spotted breast-feeding him when he is four years old. His surname, however, is the result of a mistake: a drunken Yankee soldier incorrectly registered his grandfather with the Freedmen's Bureau. *Song of Solomon* portrays Milkman's quest for identity and search for his ancestry. In a review of *Song of Solomon,* Anne Tyler commented: "I would call the book poetry, but that would seem to be denying its considerable power as a story. Whatever name you give it, it's full of magnificent people, each of them complex and multilayered, even the narrowest of them narrow in extravagant ways." Morrison followed *Song of Solomon* with *Tar Baby* (1981), a novel critics generally found less impressive than Morrison's earlier works. Jadine Childs, a black Sorbonne-educated model, is the "tar baby" who entraps the "rabbit" represented by William Green, called Son. This "novel of ideas" has been called an allegory of colonization. For example, the "white imperialist" candy-maker Valerian Street, who paid for Jadine's schooling and employs her aunt and uncle as domestics, "colonizes" an isolated French West Indian island, Isle des Chevaliers, by building an estate there. Morrison explained that she used this setting for the novel because she wanted the characters to have "no access to any of the escape routes that people have in a large city." Although *Tar Baby* was praised for its provocative themes and beautiful language, some critics found the work obscure and claimed that its characters lack motivation for their behavior. With the publication of this novel, however, Darwin T. Turner called Morrison a major American novelist and "an artful creator of grotesques destined to live in worlds where seeds of love seldom blossom."

Morrison published her next novel, *Beloved,* in 1987. A central incident in the work involves a fugitive slave who murders her infant daughter to spare her a life in bondage. Morrison based this scenario on an article she read in a nineteenth-century magazine while editing *The Black Book* (1974), an unconventional history of blacks in America, for Random House. Like Sethe, the protagonist of *Beloved,* Margaret Garner was a runaway slave who was tracked by her owner to Cincinnati, where she sought refuge with her freed mother-in-law. Faced with imminent capture, Garner attempted to murder her four children, succeeding in killing one. "I just imagined the life of a dead girl which was the girl that Margaret Garner killed," Morrison explained. "And I call her Beloved so that I can filter all these confrontations and questions that she has . . . and then to extend her life . . . her search, her quest." In *Beloved,* Sethe's daughter returns from the grave after twenty years and becomes enmeshed in the lives of Sethe and Denver, Beloved's sister.

This highly acclaimed novel became a source of controversy several months after publication. When *Beloved* failed to win the 1987 National Book Award or the National Book Critics Circle Award, forty-eight prominent black writers and critics signed a tribute to Morrison's career and published it in the January 24, 1988, edition of the *New York Times Book Review.* The document suggested that despite the international acclaim Morrison has garnered for her works, she has yet to receive sufficient national recognition. The writers' statement prompted heated debate within the New York literary community, and some critics charged Morrison's supporters with racist manipulation. When *Beloved* was awarded the 1988 Pulitzer Prize for fiction, Robert Christopher, the secretary of the Pulitzer board, stated: "[It] would be unfortunate if anyone diluted the value of Toni Morrison's achievement by suggesting that her prize rested on anything but merit."

Morrison is recognized as an important and highly original writer, and her depiction and understanding of black American heritage have drawn a wide readership. Morrison, who is presently teaching at Princeton University and at work on another novel, strives to make her works distinctly African-American and thereby locate a common element in black literature. In the essay "Rootedness: The Ancestor as Foundation," she wrote: "I don't regard Black literature as simply books written *by* Black people, or simply as literature written *about* Black people, or simply as literature that uses a certain mode of language in which you just sort of drop g's. There is something very special and very identifiable about it and it is my struggle to *find* that elusive but identifiable style in the books."

(For further information about Morrison's life and works, see *Authors and Artists for Young Adults,* Vol. 1; *Black Writers; Concise Dictionary of American Literary Biography, 1968-1987; Contemporary Authors,* Vols. 29-32; *Contemporary Authors New Revision Series,* Vol. 27; *Contemporary Literary Criticism,* Vols. 4, 10, 22, 55; *Dictionary of Literary Biography,* Vols. 6, 33; *Dictionary of Literary Biography Yearbook, 1981;* and *Something about the Author,* Vol. 57.)

PRINCIPAL WORKS

The Bluest Eye (novel) 1969
Sula (novel) 1973
The Black Book [editor] (history) 1974
Song of Solomon (novel) 1977
Tar Baby (novel) 1981
Dreaming Emmett (drama) 1986
Beloved (novel) 1987

Eleanor W. Traylor (essay date 1983)

[*In the following excerpt from an essay first published in 1983, Traylor analyzes Morrison's portrayal of African-American culture in* Tar Baby.]

Like the rain of color drenching the patchwork collages of Romare Bearden, the crystalline images governing the brilliant fiction of Toni Morrison invite us to absorb experience with multitextured vision. Both the writer and the painter reschedule our imagination and alter the way we see by contracting the distance between the familiar and the strange, finding the point of juncture. What is apparent on the canvases of Bearden is certainly obvious in the novels of Toni Morrison. For instance, "the evocations and associations in Bearden's works are indeed so strong, and so deliberately and specifically and idiomatically either downhome rural or up-north urban, that his preoccupation with imagery from Afro-American experience . . . appears to be surpassed only by his commitment to the esthetic process." That process for Bearden is one that "gives his painting the quality of a flat surface painted by hand." That process for Morrison is one that gives her novels the quality of the signifyin' oral tale of Afro-American folk tradition. A flat surface painted by hand is, of course, a wall, much like the historical and mythological walls that Aeneas saw everywhere in the ancient-modern city of Carthage or like the wall painted in 1967 by the OBACHI painters of Chicago or like the walls of our grandparents' houses in south Georgia decorated in newsprint. Bearden's story-murals are made for homes whose walls, no longer restrictors of rooms, could open outward upon the history of the world. Likewise, a tale recounted from mouth to mouth personalizes experience, making it not the possession of any teller but the possession of the whole wide community whose tale it is, much as the blues singer's task invites the world to dance.

The fate of Brer Rabbit, the imported wise scamp of the Afro-American bestiary, and the evocation of the title *Tar Baby,* is not quite the fate of the poor hapless river on Isle des Chevaliers. That island, the primary setting of the story told in *Tar Baby,* "three hundred years ago, had struck slaves blind the moment they saw it." On that island, signifying a virgin world, civilization by forced labor had disturbed the balance of nature and "the land, clouds and fish were convinced that the world was over, that the sea-green green of the sea and sky-blue of the sky were no longer permanent." This perception is precisely what had blinded the first one hundred slaves who looked upon the land. "A rain forest already two thousand years old and scheduled for eternity" had been felled to accommodate "magnificent winter houses on Isle des Chevaliers." But the forest had shielded the river and equalized the rain, and now with the earth "hollowed . . . where there had been no hollow," the poor river had "crested, then lost its course, and finally its head. Evicted from the place where it had lived, and forced into unknown turf, it could not form its pools or waterfalls, and ran every which way."

The tale of the hapless river, crashing "headlong into the haunches of hills with no notion of where it was going, until exhausted, ill and grieving, it slowed to a stop just twenty leagues short of the sea: becoming "a swamp . . . a shriveled fogbound oval seeping with a black substance that even mosquitoes could not live near," foreshadows one half of the story of *Tar Baby.* A variant of the "tar baby" tales featuring the fabulous escapades of Brer Rabbit, by turns a practical joker, a braggart, a wit, a glutton, a ladies' man, and a trickster whose essential ability to outwit eviction and flourish in unknown turf prefigures the other half. Thus, a new fable, the tale of the river, and an old one, the fable of Brer Rabbit and the tar baby, play point counterpoint, and weave, like fine patchwork, threads of a multitude of stories, legends, and tales into the fabulous collage. *Tar Baby* is a modern fable of society in which humanity, like the faces on a Bearden scape, is Black.

A man standing on the deck of a ship is the image opening Toni Morrison's *Tar Baby;* the scene calls to mind a similar one from a book written 194 years ago. The man, whose name we learn to be Son, about to jump ship in *Tar Baby,* is reminiscent of a man called Equiano in *The Life Of Olaudah Equiano* or *Gustavas Vassa, the African* (1789). Equiano's tale is a slave narrative recounting the historical and mythical, the terrifying and mighty passage of the African from the oldest world to the newest. Standing on the deck of a slave ship, the young Equiano recalls his beloved homeland, contemplates means of escape from the dreadful ship, and concludes that he will learn to "navigate" circumstances that would otherwise destroy him. In *Tar Baby,* Son, a refugee, jumps ship and swims to Isle des Chevaliers, the highly symbolic setting (a virgin world raped by the machinations of man) in which the primary action of the story told in *Tar Baby* takes place. Son arrives on the island, climbs aboard a docked houseboat, searches for food, finds too little, spies a great house not far from the houseboat, and enters it. Thus, the quick brushstroke that opens *Tar Baby* introduces Son, the Brer Rabbit of the story, and outlines, by suggestion, the details of the earlier tale in which the rabbit, foraging for food, enters the fenced-in garden-world of Farmer Brown, the self-appointed keeper of the bounty of the world. Having been introduced in the first six pages, a prologue to the novel, Son, though we are ever conscious of his presence, does not reappear for eighty more pages, during which we learn the ways of Farmer Brown.

This re-created Farmer Brown of Toni Morrison's *Tar Baby* is called Valerian Street. His name is interesting; it derives from the Latin proper noun Valerius, the name of a Roman clan, a number of families connected by a common descent and the use of the same name. One relative of the noun Valerius is *valeo* meaning "to be vigorous," "to have force," "to be strong," "to be worth." Yet another meaning of the same word is "to bid farewell"; it may also be an expression of scorn. According to *Cassell's New Latin Dictionary*, the expression from Cicero *"si talis est deus, valeat"* means "let me have nothing to do with him" and *"quare valeant ista"* means "away with them"! Moreover, Valerian, a farmer, was Roman emperor from A.D. 253 to 260. In *Tar Baby*, Valerian Street is a retired, resigned, no longer vigorous or forceful industrialist, a former candy manufacturer who has inherited and brought to corporate success his family's candy business. Now he has "bought an island in the Caribbean for almost nothing; built a house on a hill away from the mosquitoes and vacationed there when he could and when his wife did not throw a fit to go elsewhere. Over the years, he sold off parts of it, provided the parcels were large and the buyers discreet." Of Valerian Street, we learn that "his claims to decency were human: he had never cheated anybody. Had done the better thing whenever he had a choice and sometimes when he did not." In his prime, "he married Miss Maine," a beauty queen whose name is Margaret and who, he discovers, after years of marriage, has never been and has no possibility of becoming a woman.

In her own mind, Margaret, Miss Maine, wife of Valerian Street, fancies herself an envied beauty as in the fairy tale "Beauty and the Beast," or as Cinderella rescued by a slightly aging (for Valerian is almost twenty years older than she) wealthy prince, or as the uneasy queen of "Snow White and the Seven Dwarfs" who keeps asking the mirror, "Who is the fairest of them all?" For Margaret, though it has not been her intention, is a failed wife and mother. Although her beauty, during her childhood, was a source of pain to her as it made her victim of the begrudgeful, yet her beauty has been her sole claim to personhood since her parents, scared a little by her beauty, "stepped back and let her be. They gave her care, but they withdrew attention. Their strength they gave to the others [of their children] who were not beautiful; their knowledge, what information they had they did not give to this single beautiful one. They saved it, distributed it instead to those whose characters had to be built. The rest of their energies they used on the problems of surviving in a country that did not want them there."

Thus Margaret, when she met Valerian, was completely won by him when the first thing he said to her was "You really *are* beautiful," and she asked him, "Is that enough?" and he replied, "Beauty is never enough...but you are." Thinking that at last she is loved for *herself*—a *self* that has never developed—she is disabused when married to the elegant, worldly businessman, Valerian Street, and expected to supervise a great house in Philadelphia (so unlike in many ways, but in certain others very like, the trailer home that she was born into), command the respect of servants sophisticated and capable beyond her comprehension though not much older than she, and be the mother of a baby boy. The task is beyond her capability; she expected to be Valerian's valentine, a constant sweetheart: "Margaret lived for the concerts Valerian took her to, and the dinners for two at restaurants and even alone at home." Nevertheless, when Ondine, the wife of Sydney—they are "the colored couple" who efficiently manage the Street household—explains to Margaret the characters in *Search for Tomorrow*, Margaret makes the only real friend that she has ever known. But "Valerian put a stop to it saying that she should guide the servants, not consort with them." Yet, "Valerian was never rude to Ondine or Sydney, in fact he pampered them. No, the point was not consorting with Negroes, the point was her ignorance and origins. It was a nasty quarrel...It frightened Margaret—the possibility of losing him." So it was that when Margaret's first and only child is born, a son, Michael, she loves him, of course; she knows that his birth binds the adoring Valerian to his family. But Margaret, the beautiful child-lady, is resentful of the attention that now she must share with the beautiful baby and cannot resist pricking him, from time to time, with pins or burning him with cigarettes or cutting his flesh, ever so gently, with knives. Valerian learns of this, as we do, years after it has happened. He learns of it on Isle des Chevaliers at Christmas dinner when Ondine can no longer suppress her rage at Margaret and at the circumstances in the Street household and shouts, "You baby killer! I saw you! I saw you!...I used to hold him and pet him. He was so scared...All the time scared. And he wanted her to stop...so bad. And every time she'd stop for a while, but then I'd see him curled up on his side, staring off. After a while...he didn't even cry...A little boy who she hurt so much he can't even cry."

The servants of Margaret and Valerian Street, Ondine and Sydney Childs, are like members of the family. They have nourished and made stable the Street residences for over thirty years. Indeed, they are so immersed in the ways of the Street family, that, except for their accomplished science and style, unremarkable in either Valerian or Margaret, and except for their link with Jadine, their niece, they appear to have had no other nascence. Jadine, the daughter of Sydney's dead sister, has been raised by Ondine and Sydney since she was twelve. Even earlier, Jadine would live with them "at Valerian's house" in the summer. When they had sent her away to school, "they had gotten Valerian to pay her tuition while they sent her the rest." Ondine and Sydney are "good as gold" people whose distinction in life has become their servanthood. They live in a suite of their own within the Street's magnificent house on Isle des Chevaliers; they are both guardians of the family and the extension of the family ways. They know

Margaret and Valerian so well that they not only anticipate their needs and wants but prescribe them. Their own personal rituals—ablutions, eating habits, little ways of being and doing—are in perfect rapport with the Streets'. They even respond to the other two servants, residents of the island, as the Streets do. Gideon and Therese, natives of Isle des Chevaliers, do the menial chores of the Street household while Ondine is the cook and Sydney is valet-butler. The Streets and the Childses call Therese and Gideon "Mary" and "Yardman"; they do not know their names—they do not inquire. To Ondine and Sydney Childs, Mary and Yardman are shiftless, trifling "niggers" to be dealt with accordingly, for they are proper Philadelphia Negroes in the terms of Dr. Dubois. Indeed, Ondine and Sydney, as they are, are more *valeo* than Valerian: they are stronger than he, who now spends his days sitting in a greenhouse on a tropical island listening to the radio, for agile industriousness has kept them vigorous except for Ondine's arthritic knees and feet; they are more than worthy of their hire and the Streets have rewarded them; they are assured of better than social security as long as they are with and in the family. Like Pauline Breedlove of Morrison's *The Bluest Eye,* Ondine and Sydney work hard, are reliable, aim to please and do. Unlike Pauline, they do not shoo away their niece, Jadine, as Pauline shoos away her daughter, Pecola, in order to lavish attention upon the blue-eyed child of the family she serves, yet Ondine and Sydney give Jadine over to Valerian and Margaret, who guide her choices and mold her ways and steer her thinking in the manner in which they wish to guide and mold and steer their own son, Michael, who rejects them.

Jadine, a "copper Venus," has grown up to become a high-fashion model who is also a "graduate of the Sorbonne...an accomplished student of art history...an expert on cloisonne...An American now living in Paris and Rome, where she had a small but brilliantly executed role in a film." At twenty-five, Jadine is confident of her conclusions concerning the nature of things: "Picasso," she tells Valerian, "*is* better than an Itumba mask. The fact that he was intrigued by them is proof of *his* genius, not the mask makers'." But, after all, she has been taught in the schools what *real* culture is. Assured and confident of the fruits of her assumptions, her choices, her way of life, and her successes, Jadine's self-confidence has been deeply wounded only once. In Paris, at a "Supra Market," shopping for a party celebrating her having been "chosen for the cover of *Elle*" magazine, having received "a letter from a charming old man saying your orals were satisfactory to the committee," and being wooed by "three gorgeous and raucous men...in Yugoslavian touring cars," Jadine sees a woman,

> a woman much too tall. Under her long canary yellow dress Jadine knew there was too much hip, too much bust. The agency would laugh her out of the lobby, so why was she and everybody else in the store transfixed? The height? The skin like tar against the canary yellow dress? The woman walked down the aisle as though her many-colored sandals were press-
>
> ing gold tracks on the floor. Two upside-down V's were scored into each of her cheeks, her hair was wrapped in a gelee as yellow as her dress... She had no arm basket or cart. Just her many-colored sandals and her yellow robe... The woman leaned into the dairy section and opened a carton from which she selected three eggs. Then she put her right elbow into the palm of her left hand and held the eggs aloft between earlobe and shoulder. She looked up then and they saw something in her eyes so powerful it had burnt away the eyelashes.

> She strolled along the aisle, eggs on high, to the cashier, who tried to tell her that eggs were sold by the dozen or half-dozen—not one or two or three or four—but she had to look up into those eyes too beautiful for lashes to say it... The woman reached into the pocket of her yellow dress and put a ten-louis piece on the counter and walked away, away, gold tracking the floor and leaving them all behind.

In this woman, Jadine catches a glimpse of an essence, a beauty, an assurance, a womanliness, an indwelling elegance, a nurture, an authenticity that she had never known before and certainly not achieved. Jadine follows the woman with her eyes, unable to mask her admiration and even awe, but just as the woman disappears, "she turned her head sharply around to the left and looked right at Jadine. Turned those eyes too beautiful for eyelashes on Jadine and, with a small parting of her lips, shot an arrow of saliva between her teeth down to the pavement...below." Hence on Isle des Chevaliers, visiting her "Nanadine" and Uncle Sydney for Christmas at L'Arbe de la Croix, the house of Valerian and Margaret Street, Jadine still ponders the splendid woman holding three eggs aloft in a market in Paris. She sought the woman's approval with her eyes, but the woman spat a rejection that shook Jadine's self-assurance for the first time in her life until she meets Son, the Brer Rabbit whom she, as tar baby of Toni Morrison's modern fable, ensnares.

In a scene recalling Richard Wright's *Native Son,* Morrison's Son, hiding in Margaret Street's walk-in closet, is discovered. Son's entry into the Street household, his reentry into the action of the fable, dissolves all pretensions. Attitudes, buried deep, emerge; hidden fears erupt; Margaret, the aged beauty, is convinced that Son has come to rape her; Ondine and Sydney are outraged at the invasion of "niggerdom"; Valerian, managing style, topples under pressure; and Jadine, embarrassed, contemptuous, and insulted, is now Beauty both terrified by and interested in the Beast. Son has entered the house looking for nourishment. Wet, filthy, and hungry from his sea-change, Son, like the rabbit, has inadvertently entered the bounteous garden-world of Farmer Brown, emperor of abundance. The collision-encounter between Son and the inhabitants of L'Arbe de la Croix and the outgrowth of that form the heart of the tale told in *Tar Baby.*

Tar Baby is a fable, and a fable, for one thing, is a story in which values are juxtaposed and exposed. In the world that a fable creates, persons, places and things assume strange contours bearing large, small, or no resemblance to persons, places, and things in the world we call reality. Wit, humor, subtlety, irony, and verbal color—exquisite finesse—are the materials that shape the fabulous, which, on canvas or in story, presents an image of a world. The world painted by the opulent palette of Toni Morrison, grand fabulist of our time, is a world as much afflicted by bad ideas as blessed by good ones. Yet the fabulous genius of Morrison does not accuse her world so much as it exposes and defines its moral, emotional, and spiritual quagmire and points to its source of renewal and regeneration. The people who inhabit the world created in *The Bluest Eye* (1970), *Sula* (1973), *Song of Solomon* (1977), and *Tar Baby* (1981) represent the ideas that daily bombard them, for these are solidly twentieth-century people. And what that means, in one sense, is that they receive ideas, good or bad, more rapidly than any other people in human history ever have. They are the inheritors of the industrial age, where by means of stupendous technology, ideas, like medicines, are unleashed, many times insufficiently tested, upon the populace and found only later to be fatal.

The people of this fable-world imbibe toxic ideas like Pauline Breedlove of *The Bluest Eye* swallowing whole the nineteen-twenties extravaganzas of movieland and hating herself, her husband, and her child by comparison. Or like Sula of the novel by that name or First Corinthians of *Song of Solomon* or Jadine of *Tar Baby,* they ar miseducated by cant; by historical, cultural, and political bias or ignorance of schoolish books; by insidious daily-diet propaganda sponsored by money-mongers; by the pretensions of those who live in the valleys and islands of abundance in this world; by the surrender to pretensions of those who could but do not call upon mother wit and an ancestry endowing them with extraordinary sensibility to double-sight and pierce the core of bad ideas; by foolish slogans rampant in this world convincing many that "if you White, you right; if you Black, stand back or catch up"; by the perennial lusts of a world where "every / body / wants / to be / boozie woozie." An affliction of bad ideas, like a rain of bile, pours down upon the natural landscape and the people of the story-world of Toni Morrison. The deluge makes "the daisy trees marshal for war . . . winds do not trade . . . bees have no sting . . . no honey" and "the avocado tree . . . folds its leaves tightly over its fruit." People caught in the storm of bad ideas lose their direction and become bemused like Shadrack of *Sula* or become dangerous to the life of their neighborhoods like Soaphead Church or Geraldine, who scorn little Pecola of *The Bluest Eye,* or unhinged like Hagar of *Song of Solomon,* or disconnected from their life-engendering source like Jadine, or bedazzled like Son of *Tar Baby.* Still worse, others, like Valerian Street, whom many wish to become, are beyond the hope of life at its urgent sources—joy, pain, love, struggle . . . . (pp. 136-43)

Unlike Valerian, Son is not guilty of the crime of unseasonal innocence—a state of spiritual ignorance and vacuity, self-barricaded willfulness, allowing only what one desires to pass for what is. Son, born and raised in Eloe, Florida, knows both the briar patch and the fruit of life. In Eloe, more a neighborhood than a town, people know that life is a nourishing root, sometimes gall and sometimes sweeter than coolest well water at a dogday noon. Such people are the source of nourishment and of renewal in the fable-land of Toni Morrison. They are shelters from the storm of bad ideas that afflict that world; they are not self-righteous, nor are they free from error; they think neither too little of themselves nor too much; they know both anguish and joy—neither overwhelms them; they can hear and taste and touch and see a lie two hours before it manifests, yet they themselves may lie; but they never call it truth. They do not separate character from ability or industry from fraternity or individuality from communality. To them, a person is more than what he or she does; a person is not merely the sum of his or her work or achievement or talents—those are expected of any human being according to his gifts. No, the people who are sources of nourishment and clear vision in this world measure a person in a different way. They measure a man in a certain way: a man is a good man, over all he says and does, if he understands something crucial to his *man-ness*—his own and that of his tribe—and understanding that acts or does not act, knows or can be instantly reminded of the boundaries of his *can-ness*. Understanding makes him deft, on beat, in time, graphing arcs of movement—soul, mind, body—more arduous and adroit than "grace under pressure" or "purity of line." No, the motion of such a man is more like the invisible ripple of still wings in high flight. The men who teach Milkman in *Song of Solomon* are such men; Gideon of *Tar Baby* is such a man; and in Sydney reside those qualities and their opposite. Guitar of *Song of Solomon* and Son, the journeymen of *Tar Baby,* have the makings of such men.

The people who are sources of nourishment in this fable-world also measure women in a certain way; a woman is a good woman, over all she says or does, if she knows something crucial to her *woman-ness*—her own and that of her tribe. Knowing that, she moves or does not move; if perplexed, she can instantly be reminded of the inscape of her *is-ness*. Knowing makes her easy, still resilient, alchemic, salient, protogenic. The motion of a woman who *knows* is very like the sea: tidal, undulating, mirroring the sun or cloud, whichever sustains life at any moment. The people who are guides and measures of moral probity in a world as much afflicted by bad ideas as blessed by good ones are the progenitors of and heirs to the fundamental ethos of African American sensibility untainted by pretension, unpolluted by the storm of bilious thought that pummels the world in which they live.

Son issues from such people; he knows them on sight. Even in the midst of his own transgression, he is able to purify his spirit in the storm. But for eight years, he has traveled far from Eloe. He has fought in Vietnam and seen his world from different shores. He has worked at sea and mingled with all manner of men, but mainly he has been a refugee from transgression caused by transgression. . . . Son, arriving on Isle des Chevaliers at Christmastime, is a starving man in search of nourishment. He is offered the bounty of Christmas food at the table of Valerian Street; he is not nourished by it. Rather, it is Son, the man in search, who brings a nourishment to the house that it has, heretofore, not known. He unlocks the mental dungeon of Sydney and Ondine; he reveals to Valerian Margaret, who is forced to crack her mirror; he offers Valerian the gift of introspection. Son, in turn, finds his meal, his potion and his portion, at the island home of Gideon and Therese, menial servants in the House of Street. But Son finds something else. In the household of the Streets, Son, a man benumbed by a deluge of experience, rediscovers feeling. He discovers desire—intense and delicious. This, he feels, is love inspired by the "copper Venus" of the house. Son is not an ignorant man; he is, like Guitar of *Song of Solomon,* a bedazzled man. Bedazzlement in a world of storm is a common malady afflicting the best of men. The "big white fog" hanging curtainlike over such a world creates illusions that pass for reality. Guitar of *Song of Solomon,* like Bigger Thomas of Richard Wright's *Native Son,* enraged by the deluge of bad ideas that afflicts his world, attempts to murder the deluded. But to rid the land of the deluded is itself an illusion—a bedazzlement. For the fog that is ubiquitous can be cleared only within the mind, the spirit of those who inhabit the stormridden world. And the way to that clearing is through the guides, the sources of nourishment in this world. Son, the Brer Rabbit of *Tar Baby,* sees in Jadine the appearance of something real. He is bedazzled.

If the fable wrought in *Song of Solomon* is about a man, Milkman, overweaned but potentially vivifying, who must make a "journey home" to find his bearings in his world, and if the fable wrought in *The Bluest Eye* is about a community whose greatness is its ability to send forth children of the light, of little Claudia, but whose blight, by surrender to pretension, makes possible its derangement of a lovely child—Pecola—and if the fable wrought in *Sula* is about the offspring of that same community who somehow do not fully comprehend its glory and range askew, then *Tar Baby* is about a woman, Jadine, who, disconnected from the life potential of her origins, has lost the crucial is-ness of her tribe. "She has forgotten her ancient properties." That loss has cast her adrift as in a wide world alone, and even when she meets the issue of the tribe, now lost to her, though she feels the authenticity of its is-ness and though it awakens in her what has slept before, she cannot manage the motion—tidal, undulating, protogenic—of the knowing women of her tribe.

The communion, the sweet and bitter wine, that Son and Jadine taste together is contained in the very cup of trembling. Those who have tasted from that cup know its baptism. That communion and its affliction are the deep pulse of the heart of *Tar Baby.* The beat of that pulse must be experienced in the blood. On the page, we have not seen its like since the story of Teacake and Janie in Zora Hurston's *Their Eyes Were Watching God.*

But in that story, Janie and Teacake are both deep within their shared ancestral source. The distance between Son and Jadine is an immensity not of the flesh, not even of the heart, but of the soul of things. Son is a man whose journey far from home, has undernourished him; he sees in Jadine the *look* of home absent of its is-ness. Despite his effort, his diluted strength cannot endow it. In Son, Jadine has found the source from which she is disconnected; the woman in the yellow dress has seen the disconnection and forsworn it. The women of Eloe, for Son, honoring custom and his heart, have brought her to them, have seen the disconnection and rebuked it. These women, like those of *The Bluest Eye, Sula,* and *Song of Solomon,* young, middle-aged, and old (among them the mother of Claudia, the Maginot Line; Nell, Eva; Pilate, Circe, the woman whose is-ness revitalizes Milkman; also Therese and, in her way, Ondine) despite any flaw, know the crucial thing Jadine does not. She has seen it in the woman in the yellow dress, and she has drunk of it from Son. She cannot find it in herself. She is, perhaps, an unwilling Delilah sucking at the Samson strength of Son. But more and more terribly, Jadine is the embodiment in language of the carcinogenic disease eating away at the ancestral spirit of the race at the present time. It is that disease at which the pen-knife of Toni Morrison cuts.

Jadinese is the disease of disconnection, whose malignancy causes a slaughter of reality. The disease has a long history, and, in America, has manifested itself often and variously in the life, in the government, and in the literature of the country. Disconnection is the disease from which all who live in the land suffer. Some admit their malady; they may, if they wish, become whole. Others are deluded and call their illness health, for they live invincibly in a slaughter of reality. From time to time, some experience a shock from which, if they recover, they gain recognition and seek wholeness. All American writers have been tortured by the national disease. Some have been victims of the malady of disconnection and have themselves been carriers. Others have been diagnosticians, anatomists, or surgeons. And some have achieved, through the practice of letters, epiphany—a vision of wholeness. Thus, from the birth date of the literature of the country, American writers may be fully understood and finally judged by the record that they have left either of their own affliction or of their perception of the anatomy, symptoms, and effects of the national disease—a slaughter of reality— or by their vision of wholeness and by the implicit audience that their efforts have specifically addressed: those who acknowledge their malady; those who are invincibly deluded (in which case, the writer is representative); or those who may from time to time experience a shock from which, if they recover, they gain recognition and seek and may achieve, like the writer, wholeness. (pp. 143-46)

The Afro-American novelist has consistently attempted connection. Posing at least two cultural traditions and offering a third dimension of synthesis, novelists from William Wells Brown to Ralph Ellison have offered paradigms of wholeness. That offering is a phase of literary history awaiting the critic's full report. Within the wake of the consummation that is Ellison's *Invisible Man* (1952), another phase begins. And from the publication of James Baldwin's *Go Tell It on the Mountain* (1953) to the present time, the history of the Afro-American novel demands a scholarship that must teach itself its duties. Toni Morrison and her contemporaries, exposing the present awful and crucial effects of disconnection, and simultaneously working at possibilities of wholeness in new forms born of old traditions that they and they alone fully possess, await the most serious and fully conscious—whole—investigation that the soul of the critic can mount.

Exquisitely told, *Tar Baby* is a story about nourishment—the devastation caused by its lack and the regenerative power of its presence. It is the story of a man in search of nourishment and of a woman whose nourishing power, cut off from its source, has been defused. It is the story of a world where pretension wars with authenticity and where people who live in that world must choose, for there are guides. And those guides, throughout the fabulous fiction of Toni Morrison, are legion. They are, for instance, women who, like those to whom *Tar Baby* is dedicated, are representative of a culture, of a time, of a magnificence perpetually present in human history.... The women of the dedication are the grandmother, mother, aunts, and sister of the writer; these, then, are the guides to whom the narrative voice of the writer is accountable. Thus, it is not the narrative voice alone that measures sensibility in the story told in *Tar Baby*. Neither is it the narrator who makes crucial judgments, for, after all, what is judged in the world of the story is the behavior of a woman—of women. That judgment implies a definition exceeding the grasp of any narrator alone. Only the cultural integrity from which the storyteller draws is able to adjudicate, much less to authenticate, crucial aesthetic and moral judgments. So the women of the dedication join, as guides, the woman of the "burnt eyelashes" and Therese and the women of Eloe, as well as, by implication, the chorus of women of the Morrison canon. These women, by allusion, figure the warrior women, the market women, the calabash-carrying women, the queen women, the life-bearing, culture-bearing women of their own ancient origins. In their songs, their tales, their reference, these women acknowledge women of other cultures whose paradigms they either approve or reject. Just so, the adroit brush of the narrator shades a faint outline of the Clytemnestras, Cassandras, Penelopes, Helens, Hekubas, Andromaches, Medeas, Sapphos, Salomes, Judiths, Deborahs, Esthers, Cinderellas, Goldilockses, or latter-day Revlon girls: women who sink a culture or save it, who delude it or provide it clarity. *Tar Baby* is a sublime story of a people whose experience, ancestral and present, has prepared them to circumnavigate deluge, and their humanity, the source of nourishment in the world in which they live, like the faces on a Bearden scape is Black. (pp. 148-49)

Eleanor W. Traylor, "The Fabulous World of Toni Morrison: 'Tar Baby'," in Critical Essays on Toni Morrison, *edited by Nellie Y. McKay, G. K. Hall & Co., 1989, pp. 135-50.*

Toni Morrison (lecture date 1988)

[*The following excerpt is from a lecture entitled "Unspeakable Things Unspoken: The Afro-American Presence in American Literature" delivered by Morrison at the University of Michigan in 1988. Here, she shows her works to be distinctly African-American by evaluating the first sentences of her five novels.*]

The question of what constitutes the art of a black writer, for whom that modifier is more search than fact, has some urgency. In other words, other than melanin and subject matter, what, in fact, may make me a black writer? Other than my own ethnicity—what is going on in my work that makes me believe it is demonstrably inseparable from a cultural specificity that is Afro-American? (p. 19)

Let me suggest some of the ways in which I activate language and ways in which that language activates me. I will limit this perusal by calling attention only to the first sentences of the books I've written.... (p. 20)

● ● ● ● ●

The Bluest Eye begins "Quiet as it's kept, there were no marigolds in the fall of 1941." That sentence, like the ones that open each succeeding book, is simple, uncomplicated. Of all the sentences that begin all the books, only two of them have dependent clauses; the other three are simple sentences and two are stripped down to virtually subject, verb, modifier. Nothing fancy here. No words need looking up; they are ordinary, everyday words. Yet I hoped the simplicity was not simpleminded, but devious, even loaded. And that the process of selecting each word, for itself and its relationship to the others in the sentence, along with the rejection of others for their echoes, for what is determined and what is not determined, what is almost there and what must be gleaned, would not theatricalize itself, would not erect a proscenium—at least not a noticeable one. So important to me was this unstaging, that in this first novel I summarized the whole of the book on the first page. (In the first edition, it was printed in its entirety on the jacket).

The opening phrase of this sentence, "Quiet as it's kept," had several attractions for me. First, it was a familiar phrase familiar to me as a child listening to adults; to black women conversing with one another; telling a story, an anecdote, gossip about some one or event within the circle, the family, the neighborhood. The words are conspiratorial. "Shh, don't tell anyone else," and "No one is allowed to know this." It is a secret between us and a secret that is being kept from us. The conspiracy is both held and withheld, exposed and sustained. In some sense it was precisely what the act of writing the book was: the public exposure of a private confidence. In order fully to comprehend the duality of that position, one needs to think of the immediate political climate in which the writing took place, 1965-1969, during great social upheaval in the life of black people. The publication (as opposed to the writing) involved the exposure; the writing was the disclosure of secrets, secrets "we" shared and those withheld from us by ourselves and by the world outside the community.

"Quiet as it's kept," is also a figure of speech that is written, in this instance, but clearly chosen for how speakerly it is, how it speaks and bespeaks a particular world and its ambience. Further, in addition to its "back fence" connotation, its suggestion of illicit gossip, of thrilling revelation, there is also, in the "whisper," the assumption (on the part of the reader) that the teller is on the inside, knows something others do not, and is going to be generous with this privileged information. The intimacy I was aiming for, the intimacy between the reader and the page, could start up immediately because the secret is being shared, at best, and eavesdropped upon, at the least. Sudden familiarity or instant intimacy seemed crucial to me then, writing my first novel. I did not want the reader to have time to wonder "What do I have to do, to give up, in order to read this? What defense do I need, what distance maintain?" Because I know (and the reader does not—he or she has to wait for the second sentence) that this is a terrible story about things one would rather not know anything about.

What, then, is the Big Secret about to be shared? The thing we (reader and I) are "in" on? A botanical aberration. Pollution, perhaps. A skip, perhaps, in the natural order of things: a September, an autumn, a fall without marigolds. Bright common, strong and sturdy marigolds. When? In 1941, and since that is a momentous year (the beginning of World War II for the United States), the "fall" of 1941, just before the declaration of war, has a "closet" innuendo. In the temperate zone where there is a season known as "fall" during which one expects marigolds to be at their peak, in the months before the beginning of U.S. participation in World War II, something grim is about to be divulged. The next sentence will make it clear that the sayer, the one who knows, is a child speaking, mimicking the adult black women on the porch or in the back yard. The opening phrase is an effort to be grown-up about this shocking information. The point of view of a child alters the priority an adult would assign the information. "We thought it was because Pecola was having her father's baby that the marigolds did not grow" foregrounds the flowers, backgrounds illicit, traumatic, incomprehensible sex coming to its dreaded fruition. This foregrounding of "trivial" information and backgrounding of shocking knowledge secures the point of view but gives the reader pause about whether the voice of children can be trusted at all or is more trustworthy than an adult's. The reader is thereby protected from a confrontation too soon with the painful details, while simultaneously provoked into a desire to know them. The novelty, I thought, would be in having this story of female

violation revealed from the vantage point of the victims or could-be victims of rape—the persons no one inquired of (certainly not in 1965)—the girls themselves. And since the victim does not have the vocabulary to understand the violence or its context, gullible, vulnerable girl friends, looking back as the knowing adults they pretended to be in the beginning, would have to do that for her, and would have to fill those silences with their own reflective lives. Thus, the opening provides the stroke that announces something more than a secret shared, but a silence broken, a void filled, an unspeakable thing spoken at last. And they draw the connection between a minor destabilization in seasonal flora with the insignificant destruction of a black girl. Of course "minor" and "insignificant" represent the outside world's view—for the girls both phenomena are earth-shaking depositories of information they spend that whole year of childhood (and afterwards) trying to fathom, and cannot. If they have any success, it will be in transferring the problem of fathoming to the presumably adult reader, to the inner circle of listeners. At the least they have distributed the weight of these problematical questions to a larger constituency, and justified the public exposure of a privacy. If the conspiracy that the opening words announce is entered into by the reader, then the book can be seen to open with its close: a speculation on the disruption of "nature," as being a social disruption with tragic individual consequences in which the reader, as part of the population of the text, is implicated.

However a problem, unsolved, lies in the central chamber of the novel. The shattered world I built (to complement what is happening to Pecola), its pieces held together by seasons in childtime and commenting at every turn on the incompatible and barren white-family primer, does not in its present form handle effectively the silence at its center. The void that is Pecola's "unbeing." It should have had a shape—like the emptiness left by a boom or a cry. It required a sophistication unavailable to me, and some deft manipulation of the voices around her. She is not *seen* by herself until she hallucinates a self. And the fact of her hallucination becomes a point of outside-the-book conversation, but does not work in the reading process.

Also, although I was pressing for a female expressiveness (a challenge that re-surfaced in *Sula*), it eluded me for the most part, and I had to content myself with female personae because I was not able to secure throughout the work the feminine subtext that is present in the opening sentence (the women gossiping, eager and aghast in "Quiet as it's kept"). The shambles this struggle became is most evident in the section on Pauline Breedlove where I resorted to two voices, hers and the urging narrator's, both of which are extremely unsatisfactory to me. It is interesting to me now that where I thought I would have the most difficulty subverting the language to a feminine mode, I had the least: connecting Cholly's "rape" by the whitemen to his own of his daughter. This most masculine act of aggression becomes feminized in my language, "passive," and, I think, more accurately repellent when deprived of the male "glamor of shame" rape is (or once was) routinely given.

The points I have tried to illustrate are that my choices of languages (speakerly, aural, colloquial), my reliance for full comprehension on codes embedded in black culture, my effort to effect immediate co-conspiracy and intimacy (without any distancing, explanatory fabric), as well as my (failed) attempt to shape a silence while breaking it are attempts (many unsatisfactory) to transfigure the complexity and wealth of Afro-American culture into a language worthy of the culture.

• • • • •

In *Sula,* it's necessary to concentrate on *two* first sentences because what survives in print is not the one I had intended to be the first. Originally the book opened with "Except for World War II nothing ever interfered with National Suicide Day." With some encouragement, I recognized that it was a false beginning. *"In medias res"* with a vengeance, because there was no *res* to be in the middle of—no implied world in which to locate the specificity and the resonances in the sentence. More to the point, I knew I was writing a second novel, and that it too would be about people in a black community not just foregrounded but totally dominant; and that it was about black women—also foregrounded and dominant. In 1988, certainly, I would not need (or feel the need for) the sentence—the short section—that now opens *Sula.* The threshold between the reader and the black-topic text need not be the safe, welcoming lobby I persuaded myself it needed at that time. My preference was the demolition of the lobby altogether. As can be seen from *The Bluest Eye,* and in every other book I have written, only *Sula* has this "entrance." The others refuse the "presentation"; refuse the seductive safe harbor; the line of demarcation between the sacred and the obscene, public and private, them and us. Refuse, in effect, to cater to the diminished expectations of the reader, or his or her alarm heightened by the emotional luggage one carries into the black-topic text. (I should remind you that *Sula* was begun in 1969, while my first book was in proof, in a period of extraordinary political activity.)

Since I had become convinced that the effectiveness of the original beginning was only in my head, the job at hand became how to construct an alternate beginning that would not force the work to genuflect and would complement the outlaw quality in it. The problem presented itself this way: to fashion a door. Instead of having the text open wide the moment the cover is opened (or, as in *The Bluest Eye,* to have the book stand exposed before the cover is even touched, much less opened, by placing the complete "plot" on the first page—and finally on the cover of the first edition), here I was to posit a door, turn its knob and beckon for some four or five pages. I had determined not to mention any characters in those pages, there would be no people in the lobby—but I did, rather heavy-handedly in my view, end the welcome aboard with the mention of Shadrack and Sula. It was a craven (to me, still) surrender to a worn-out technique of novel writing: the overt announcement to the reader whom to pay attention to. Yet the bulk of the opening I finally wrote is about the community, a view of it, and the view is not from within (this is a door, after all) but from the point of view of a stranger—the "valley man" who might happen to be there on some errand, but who obviously does not live there and to and for whom all this is mightily strange, even exotic. You can see why I despise much of this beginning. Yet I tried to place in the opening sentence the signature terms of loss: "There used to be a neighborhood here; not any more." That may not be the world's worst sentence, but it doesn't "play," as they say in the theater.

My new first sentence became "In that place, where they tore the nightshade and blackberry patches from their roots to make room for the Medallion City Golf Course, there was once a neighborhood." Instead of my original plan, here I am introducing an outside-the-circle reader into the circle. I am translating the anonymous into the specific, a "place" into a "neighborhood," and letting a stranger in through whose eyes it can be viewed. In between "place" and "neighborhood" I now have to squeeze the specificity and the *difference;* the nostalgia, the history, and the nostalgia for the history; the violence done to it and the consequences of that violence. (It took three months, those four pages, a whole summer of nights.) The nostalgia is sounded by "once"; the history and a longing for it is implied in the connotation of "neighborhood." The violence lurks in having something torn out by its roots—it will not, cannot grow again. Its consequences are that what has been destroyed is considered weeds, refuse necessarily removed in urban "development" by the unspecified by no less known "they" who do not, cannot, afford to differentiate what is displaced, and would not care that this is "refuse" of a certain kind. Both plants have darkness in them: "black" and "night." One is unusual (nightshade) and has two darkness words: "night" and "shade." The other (blackberry) is common. A familiar plant and an exotic one. A harmless one and a dangerous one. One produces a nourishing berry; one delivers toxic ones. But they both thrived there together, *in that place when it was a neighborhood.* Both are gone now, and the description that follows is of the other specific things, in this black community, destroyed in the wake of the golf course. Golf course conveys what it is not, in this context: not houses, or factories, or even a public park, and certainly not residents. It is a manicured place where the likelihood of the former residents showing up is almost nil.

I want to get back to those berries for a moment (to explain, perhaps, the length of time it took for the language of that section to arrive). I always thought of Sula as quintessentially black, metaphysically black, if you will, which is not melanin and certainly not unquestioning fidelity to the tribe. She is new world black and new world woman extracting choice from choicelessness, responding inventively to found things. Improvisational. Daring, disruptive, imaginative, modern, out-of-the-house, outlawed, unpolicing, uncontained and uncontainable. And dangerously female. In her final conversation with Nel she refers to herself as a special kind of black person woman, one with choices. Like a redwood, she says. (With all due respect to the dream landscape of Freud, trees have always seemed feminine to me.) In any case, my perception of Sula's double-dose of *chosen* blackness and *biological* blackness is in the presence of those two words of darkness in "nightshade" as well as in the uncommon quality of the vine itself. One variety is called "enchanter," and the other "bittersweet" because the berries taste bitter at first and then sweet. Also nightshade was thought to counteract witchcraft. All of this seemed a wonderful constellation of signs for Sula. And "blackberry patch" seemed equally appropriate for Nel: nourishing, never needing to be tended or cultivated, once rooted and bearing. Reliably sweet but thorn-bound. Her process of becoming, heralded by the explosive dissolving of her fragilely-held-together ball of string and fur (when the thorns of her self-protection are removed by Eva), puts her back in touch with the complex, contradictory, evasive, independent, liquid modernity Sula insisted upon. A modernity which overturns pre-war definitions, ushers in the Jazz Age (an age *defined* by Afro-American art and culture), and requires new kinds of intelligences to define oneself.

The stage-setting of the first four pages is embarrassing to me now, but the pains I have taken to explain it may be helpful in identifying the strategies one can be forced to resort to in trying to accommodate the mere fact of writing about, for and out of black culture while accommodating and responding to mainstream "white" culture. The "valley man's" guidance into the territory was my compromise. Perhaps it "worked," but it was not the work I wanted to do.

Had I begun with Shadrack, I would have ignored the smiling welcome and put the reader into immediate confrontation with his wound and his scar. The difference my preferred (original) beginning would have made would be calling greater attention to the traumatic displacement this most wasteful capitalist war had on black people in particular, and throwing into relief the creative, if outlawed, determination to survive it whole. Sula as (feminine) solubility and Shadrack's (male) fixative are two extreme ways of dealing with displacement—a prevalent theme in the narrative of black people. In the final opening I replicated the demiurge of discriminatory, prosecutorial racial oppression in the loss to commercial "progress" of the village, but the references to the community's stability and creativeness (music, dancing, craft, religion, irony, wit all referred to in the "valley man's" presence) refract and subsume their pain while they are in the thick of it. It is a softer embrace than Shadrack's organized, public madness—his disruptive remembering presence which helps (for a while) to cement the community, until Sula challenges them.

• • • • •

"The North Carolina Mutual Life Insurance agent promised to fly from Mercy to the other side of Lake Superior at 3:00."

This declarative sentence is designed to mock a journalistic style; with a minor alteration it could be the opening of an item in a smalltown newspaper. It has the tone of an everyday event of minimal local interest. Yet I wanted it to contain (as does the scene that takes place when the agent fulfills his promise) the information that **Song of Solomon** both centers on and radiates from.

The name of the insurance company is real, a well known blackowned company dependent on black clients, and in its corporate name are "life" and "mutual;" *agent* being the necessary ingredient of what enables the relationship between them. The sentence also moves from North Carolina to Lake Superior—geographical locations, but with a sly implication that the move from North Carolina (the south) to Lake Superior (the north) might not actually involve progress to some "superior state"—which, of course it does not. The two other significant words are "fly," upon which the novel centers and "Mercy," the name of the place from which he is to fly. Both constitute the heartbeat of the narrative. Where is the insurance man flying to? The other side of Lake Superior is Canada, of course, the historic terminus of the escape route for black people looking for asylum. "Mercy," the other significant term, is the grace note; the earnest though, with one exception, unspoken wish of the narrative's population. Some grant it; some never find it; one, at least, makes it the text and cry of her extemporaneous sermon upon the death of her granddaughter. It touches, turns and returns to Guitar at the end of the book—he who is least deserving of it—and moves him to make it his own final gift. It is what one wishes for Hagar; what is unavailable to and unsought by Macon Dead, senior; what his wife learns to demand from him, and what can never come from the white world as is signified by the inversion of the name of the hospital from Mercy to "no-Mercy." It is only available from within. The center of the narrative is flight; the springboard is mercy.

But the sentence turns, as all sentences do, on the verb: promised. The insurance agent does not declare, announce, or threaten his act. He promises, as though a contract is being executed—faithfully—between himself and others. Promises broken, or kept; the difficulty of ferreting out loyalties and ties that bind or bruise wend their way throughout the action and the shifting relationships. So the agent's flight, like that of the Solomon in the title, although toward asylum (Canada, or freedom, or home, or the company of the welcoming dead), and although it carries the possibility of failure and the certainty of danger, is toward change, an alternative way, a cessation of things-as-they-are. It should not be understood as a simple desperate act, the end of a fruitless life, a life without gesture, without examination, but as obedience to a deeper contract with his people. It is his commitment to them, regardless of whether, in all its details, they understand it. There is, however, in their response to his action, a tenderness, some contrition, and mounting respect ("They didn't know he had it in him.") and an awareness that the gesture enclosed rather than repudiated themselves. The note he leaves asks for forgiveness. It is tacked on his door as a mild invitation to whomever might pass by, but it is not an advertisement. It is an almost Christian declaration of love as well as humility of one who was not able to do more.

There are several other flights in the work and they are motivationally different. Solomon's the most magical, the most theatrical and, for Milkman, the most satisfying. It is also the most problematic—to those he left behind. Milkman's flight binds these two elements of loyalty (Mr. Smith's) and abandon and self-interest (Solomon's) into a third thing: a merging of fealty and risk that suggests the "agency" for "mutual" "life," which he offers at the end and which is echoed in the hills behind him, and is the marriage of surrender and domination, acceptance and rule, commitment to a group *through* ultimate isolation. Guitar recognizes this marriage and recalls enough of how lost he himself is to put his weapon down.

The journalistic style at the beginning, its rhythm of a familiar, hand-me-down dignity is pulled along by an accretion of detail displayed in a meandering unremarkableness. Simple words, uncomplex sentence structures, persistent understatement, highly aural syntax—but the ordinariness of the language, its colloquial, vernacular, humorous and, upon occasion, parabolic quality sabotage expectations and mask judgments when it can no longer defer them. The composition of red, white and blue in the opening scene provides the national canvas/flag upon which the narrative works and against which the lives of these black people must be seen, but which must not overwhelm the enterprise the novel is engaged in. It is a composition of color that heralds Milkman's birth, protects his youth, hides its purpose and through which he must burst (through blue Buicks, red tulips in his waking dream, and his sisters' white stockings, ribbons and gloves) before discovering that the gold of his search is really Pilate's yellow orange and the glittering metal of the box in her ear.

These spaces, which I am filling in, and can fill in because they were planned, can conceivably be filled in with other significances. That is planned as well. The point is that into these spaces should fall the ruminations of the reader and his or her invented or recollected or misunderstood knowingness. The reader as narrator asks the questions the community asks, and both reader and "voice" stand among the crowd, within it, with privileged intimacy and contact, but without any more privileged information than the crowd has. That egalitarianism which places us all (reader, the novel's population, the narrator's voice) on the same footing reflected for me the force of flight and mercy, and the precious, imaginative yet realistic gaze of black people who (at one time, anyway) did not mythologize what or whom it mythologized. The "song" itself contains this unblinking evaluation of the miraculous and heroic flight of the legendary Solomon, an unblinking gaze which is lurking in the tender but amused choral-community response to the agent's flight. Sotto (but not completely) is my own giggle (in Afro-American terms) of the proto-myth of the journey to manhood. Whenever characters are cloaked in Western fable, they are in deep trouble; but the African myth is also contaminated. Unprogressive, unreconstructed, self-born Pilate is unimpressed by Solomon's flight and knocks Milkman down when, made new by his appropriation of his own family's fable, he returns to educate her with it. Upon hearing all he has to say, her only interest is filial. "Papa?... I've been carryin' Papa?" And her longing to hear the song, finally, is a longing for balm to die by, not a submissive obedience to history—anybody's.

● ● ● ● ●

The opening sentence of *Tar Baby,* "He believed he was safe," is the second version of itself. The first, "He thought he was safe," was discarded because "thought" did not contain the doubt I wanted to plant in the reader's mind about whether or not he really was—safe. "Thought" came to me at once because it was the verb my parents and grandparents used when describing what they had dreamed the night before. Not "I dream," or "It seemed"or even "I saw or did" this or that—but "I thought." It gave the dream narrative distance (a dream is not "real") and power (the control implied in *thinking* rather than *dreaming.*) But to use "thought" seemed to undercut the faith of the character and the distrust I wanted to suggest to the reader. "Believe" was chosen to do the work properly. And the person who does the believing is, in a way, about to enter a dream world, and convinces himself, eventually, that he is in control of it. He believed; was convinced. And although the word suggests his conviction, it does not reassure the reader. If I had wanted the reader to trust this person's point of view I would have written "He was safe." Or, "Finally, he was safe." The unease about this view of safety is important because safety itself is the desire of each person in the novel. Locating it, creating it, losing it.

You may recall that I was interested in working out the mystery of a piece of lore, a folk tale, which is also about safety and danger and the skills needed to secure the one and recognize and avoid the other. I was not, of course, interested in re-telling the tale; I suppose that is an idea to pursue, but it is certainly not interesting enough to engage me for four years. I have said, elsewhere, that the exploration of the Tar Baby tale was like stroking a pet to see what the anatomy was like but not to disturb or distort its mystery. Folk lore may have begun as allegory for natural or social phenomena; it may have been employed as a retreat from contemporary issues in art, but folk lore can also contain myths that re-activate themselves endlessly through providers—the people who repeat, reshape, reconstitute and reinterpret them. The Tar Baby tale seemed to me to be about masks. Not masks as covering what is to be hidden, but how masks come to life, take life over, exercise the tensions between itself and what it covers. For Son, the most effective mask is none. For the others the construction is careful and delicately borne, but the masks they make have a life of their own and collide with those they come in contact with. The texture of the novel seemed to want leanness, architecture that was worn and ancient like a piece of mask sculpture: exaggerated, breathing, just athwart the representational life it displaced. Thus, the first and last sentences had to match, as the exterior planes match the interior, concave ones inside the mask. Therefore "He believed he was safe" would be the twin of "Lickety split, lickety split, lickety lickety split." This close is 1) the last sentence of the folk tale. 2) the action of the character. 3) the indeterminate ending that follows from the untrustworthy beginning. 4) the complimentary meter of its twin sister [uu / uu / with uuu / uuu /], and 5) the wide and marvelous space between the contradiction of those two images: from a dream of safety to the sound of running feet. The whole mediated world in between. This masked and unmasked; enchanted, disenchanted; wounded and wounding world is played out on and by the varieties of interpretation (Western and Afro-American) the Tar Baby myth has been (and continues to be) subjected to. Winging one's way through the vise and expulsion of history becomes possible in creative encounters with that history. Nothing, in those encounters, is safe, or should be. Safety is the foetus of power as well as protection from it, as the uses to which masks and myths are put in Afro-American culture remind us.

● ● ● ● ●

"124 was spiteful. Full of a baby's venom."

Beginning *Beloved* with numerals rather than spelled out numbers, it was my intention to give the house an identity separate from the street or even the city; to name it the way "Sweet Home" was named; the way plantations were named, but not with nouns or "proper" names—with numbers instead because numbers have no adjectives, no posture of coziness or grandeur or the haughty yearning of arrivistes and estate builders for the parallel beautifications of the nation they left behind, laying claim to instant history and legend. Numbers here constitute an address, a thrilling enough prospect for slaves who had owned nothing, least of all an address. And although the numbers, unlike words, can have no modifiers, I give these an adjective—spiteful (There are three others). The address is therefore personalized, but personalized by its own activity, not the pasted on desire for personality.

Also there is something about numerals that makes them spoken, heard, in this context, because one expects words to read in a book, not numbers to say, or hear. And the sound of the novel, sometimes cacaphonous, sometimes harmonious, must be an inner ear sound or a sound just beyond hearing, infusing the text with a musical emphasis that words can do sometimes even better than music can. Thus the second sentence is not

one: it is a phrase that properly, grammatically, belongs as a dependent clause with the first. Had I done that, however, (124 was spiteful, comma, full of a baby's venom, or 124 was full of a baby's venom) I could not have had the accent on *full* [/ uu / u / u pause / uuuu / u].

Whatever the risks of confronting the reader with what must be immediately incomprehensible in that simple, declarative authoritative sentence, the risk of unsettling him or her, I determined to take. Because the *in medias res* opening that I am so committed to is here excessively demanding. It is abrupt, and should appear so. No native informant here. The reader is snatched, yanked, thrown into an environment completely foreign, and I want it as the first stroke of the shared experience that might be possible between the reader and the novel's population. Snatched just as the slaves were from one place to another, from any place to another, without preparation and without defense. No lobby, no door, no entrance—a gangplank, perhaps (but a very short one). And the house into which this snatching—this kidnapping—propels one, changes from spiteful to loud to quiet, as the sounds in the body of the ship itself may have changed. A few words have to be read before it is clear that 124 refers to a house (in most of the early drafts "The women *in the house* knew it" was simply "The women knew it." "House" was not mentioned for seventeen lines), and a few more have to be read to discover why it is spiteful, or rather the source of the spite. By then it is clear, if not at once, that something is beyond control, but is not beyond understanding since it is not beyond accommodation by both the "women" and the "children." The fully realized presence of the haunting is both a major incumbent of the narrative and sleight of hand. One of its purposes is to keep the reader preoccupied with the nature of the incredible spirit world while being supplied a controlled diet of the incredible political world.

The subliminal, the underground life of a novel is the area most likely to link arms with the reader and facilitate making it one's own. Because one must, to get from the first sentence to the next, and the next and the next. The friendly observation post I was content to build and man in *Sula* (with the stranger in the midst), or the down-home journalism of *Song of Solomon* or the calculated mistrust of the point of view in *Tar Baby* would not serve here. Here I wanted the compelling confusion of being there as they (the characters) are; suddenly, without comfort or succor from the "author," with only imagination, intelligence, and necessity available for the journey. The painterly language of *Song of Solomon* was not useful to me in *Beloved*. There is practically no color whatsoever in its pages, and when there is, it is so stark and remarked upon, it is virtually raw. Color seen for the first time, without its history. No built architecture as in *Tar Baby*, no play with Western chronology as in *Sula*; no exchange between book life and "real" life discourse—with printed text units rubbing up against seasonal black childtime units as in *The Bluest Eye*. No compound of houses, no neighborhood, no sculpture, no paint, no time, especially no time because memory, pre-historic memory, has no time. There is just a little music, each other and the urgency of what is at stake. Which is all they had. For that work, the work of language is to get out of the way.

I hope you understand that in this explication of how I practice language is a search for and deliberate posture of vulnerability to those aspects of Afro-American culture that can inform and position my work. I sometimes know when the work works, when *nommo* has effectively summoned, by reading and listening to those who have entered the text. I learn nothing from those who resist it, except, of course, the sometimes fascinating display of their struggle. My expectations of and my gratitude to the critics who enter, are great. To those who talk about how as well as what; who identify the workings as well as the work; for whom the study of Afro-American literature is neither a crash course in neighborliness and tolerance, nor an infant to be carried, instructed or chastised or even whipped like a child, but the serious study of art forms that have much work to do, but are already legitimatized by their own cultural sources and predecessors—in or out of the canon—I owe much. (pp. 20-33)

Toni Morrison, "Unspeakable Things Unspoken: The Afro-American Presence in American Literature," in Michigan Quarterly Review, *Vol. XXVIII, No. 1, Winter, 1989, pp. 1-34.*

Genevieve Fabre (essay date 1988)

[*In the following excerpt from a 1988 revision of a lecture originally delivered at the Salzburg Seminar in American Studies in June 1985, Fabre evaluates* Song of Solomon, *a work she believes upholds a legacy bestowed by African-American ancestors.*]

The early struggle of black women to achieve literacy (an authorial voice), closely associated with the quest for freedom, has paved the way for the present battles and empowerment. As Toni Morrison says: "their strategies of survival became our maneuvers for power." This continuity between past and present is crucial and must be maintained. It creates bonds, kinship, mutual obligations, and a shared communal history of struggle for artistic expression that is a form of power. Contemporary black women writers are calling for a revision (an inversion of concepts, myths, images) and reexamination of important issues concerning their situation in American society and culture. As persons who have experienced life not only as blacks but also as women artists who have inherited the gift to "speak in tongues," they feel they can illuminate and authenticate parts of the black experience that have been ignored or misrepresented. Recorded from their perspectives with daring honesty and uncompromising outspokenness, the "souls of black folks" can be framed into new words and songs, shaped into new configurations; "coming" as Morrison says "from the rim of the world" and "rustling with

life," to become "the touchstones by which all that is human can be measured."

Black women writers call attention to the distinctiveness of their experiences and vision that differs as broadly from that of some black male writers as it does from that of whites, and which has never been adequately recognized. They claim the Afro-American tradition but "insist on their own name and central place." They do not strive for separatism but for the recognition of the singularity of their identity and of their expressive gifts. They wish to free themselves from the prescriptive tenets of a black aesthetic whose canons have been defined mostly by male critics. They also set themselves apart from white feminists who argue that sexism is more important than racism, who have ignored the particular fate or concerns of their black sisters and often used them as mere tokens for their cause. As blacks, women, and artists, their components are indissociable. None can be discarded without impairing the total vision which determines their artistic strategies, shapes their stylistic tone and profile, the pitch of their voices, and their symbolic imagination. Finally black women writers expose the inadequacies and the "signs of omission" of mainstream ideological discourse. They lay down a number of challenges to the purveyors of literary history, and questioning their monolithic and absolutist pronouncements, they call for an honest, sustained, and more perceptive analysis of their work. Their writings, deliberately disruptive and disturbing in their bold investigations, are part of a struggle against all forms of authority. In the process of interaction with a hostile environment their discourse takes shape, and their artistic consciousness evolves as a rejoinder. "Their gaze so lovingly unforgiving, stills, agitates, stills again." Triumphing over interdiction, they reveal the limits and the constraints of a system that has excluded their voices, and that should take greater heed of the problems of alterity and acknowledge the essential significance of *difference*. In a culture, a country that has always looked for a unifying language, for myths to express its national mind and ethos, but one that is also aware of its pluralistic nature, the chorus of black-women voices joined by many other minority or "third world" women—Chicanas, Hispanics, Asiatics, American Indians—forces a new dialogue. This dialogue, which points at tensions, at inexhaustible wealth and contradictory multiplicity, orchestrates different degrees of otherness and creates a potential for an artistic experience and the development of a new national literary consciousness, no longer indifferent to difference. One is struck, in reading/hearing black women, by their insistence on the exploration of the legacy. Throughout their writings and talks, these women are expressing in eloquent and pressing ways their claims to a legacy that is distinctively theirs, and affirming their authority as participants, interpreters, and perpetuators. As witnesses for the future, they insist on their responsibility to build a heritage to be passed on to the new generations. The search for the legacy often presented as a ceremonial appropriation that follows a ritualistic pattern, dealt with in remarkably different ways by Alice

Walker (*In Search of Our Mother's Gardens*) or Audre Lorde (*Sister Outsider*), who set the principles for an inquiry into the dialectics of black womanhood in the essay, or in a fictional work by Toni Morrison (*Song of Solomon*), celebrates narrative and parable that dramatize an archetypal journey across ancestral territory.

The main call in Walker's book is the "daughters" in an attempt to build intricate emotional and *artistic* bonds and a definite lineage: "we must know our mothers's names,...[their] words,...[their] actions,...[their] lives." Her own impulse is more to recollect and reconstruct forgotten lives, if necessary "bone by bone" (an image we find also in *Song of Solomon*), to retrieve them from oblivion and neglect. Walker's spirited visit to her mother's gardens—the concept of garden, an organizing metaphor, has replaced Virginia Woolf's idea of a room of one's own—is itself a pilgrimage pursued with filial piety and care, with a sense of will and direction: "in search of my mother's garden, I found my own." Embracing her maiden name in tribute to one of her ancestors who "walked" through the continent, Walker reenters the garden of the past with a sense of reverence and wonder for places, she reinvents the lives of the women who call her from history. She creates her own garden, a blend of symbolic properties, peopled with ancient spirits, studded with images that capture the unique quality of her heritage as artist, as black, as woman, and as southerner.

In her reevaluation of black womanhood, Walker is anxious to set some guidelines for those who will record the legacy. Their writings should move away from sociology—from a discourse that emphasized the image of black women as victims—to a greater concern for the ambiguities, the dilemmas, and contradictions. "It must be away from the writing of explanation and further into mystery, poetry and prophecy."

Song of Solomon is precisely one of these incursions into "mystery, poetry and prophecy." The experience of legacy is treated with many ironic overtones that point to certain paradoxes, and to the fundamental complexities of the quest. Other novels have done this—*Invisible Man,* for instance, through the numerous adventures of a nameless hero, examines the intricate legacy of the past and of history. Yet, *Song of Solomon* strikes a different and perplexing note, perhaps because it deliberately avoids chronological development and linear structure. Its drifting and uninformed hero is caught in the ambiguities of a quest that presents itself as a succession of riddles; each recorded incident, act, or word is a new adventure that further complicates the overall puzzle. And the legacy—an ever elusive reality—takes on many serious or trivial forms: a name, a birthmark, a bag of bones, or a song. Each is presented as a possible clue or a new mystery. The deciphering of the enigma is seen as a game in which the character and reader are jostled from one puzzle to the next. Answers are presented piece by piece through hints that create further suspense, and this accounts for the structure of this enigmatic narrative: a pattern of revelation and deception, of recognition and denial.

The legacy is spelled out through stories that are often fables, or jokes, *lies* as Zora Neale Hurston would call them. Each story re-creates a particular patch of the past, but also reveals a new mystery and then calls for another story. In different places, by different characters, the same story is picked up, retold, expanded into further complexity and mystery. It is as though there is a crucial deficiency in each telling, so each generates the other, as though the assertion each makes raised new questions. And all queries converge toward Pilate the depository: "She who heard the voice and sang the song." The accumulation of stories, the call and response pattern, their gradual emerging into the single story of the hero's ancestry, create an interesting structure. The legacy is that of voices to be listened to, voices that replace that of the narrator, each offering its own fragmented perception of the truth, while the author dramatizes the gap between the telling and what is being told.

Morrison's protagonist is entrusted with the task of putting bits and pieces together, of de/re/constructing chronology and genealogy. The use of Milkman is ironic; this male hero is unimaginative and uncommitted, a reluctant confidant, a poor listener who does not pay attention to words, asks the wrong questions, and offers erroneous interpretations. He is ill equipped for the quest: an imperfect inquirer into a heritage that is cumbersome to him. Pressed as he is by many questions set by those who entrust him with the secrets of their lives, his blunders paradoxically enrich the message. Revelations about the past bear no clear meaning to him at the time when they are uttered. Yet each becomes a part of his own history and must be put together in quilt fashion, like scraps to be seized before the wind carries them away, or to be stored like the mysterious stones his aunt has collected throughout her life.

By entrusting her own narrative to many voices (and basing its structure on many stories), Morrison acknowledges the debt that any black writer has to the oral tradition, the true legacy of black people. She reminds us that the storytelling tradition, so strong in black culture, is still alive. In homes, on street corners, in barbershops, stories are devised and told as statements, familiar historical realities, or as forms of entertainment, a thing to be created and enjoyed. Stories bear witness to the past, to the struggle of black people to survive in their triumphs and the familiar, reality and fantasy; creating both history and myth. The stories in *Song of Solomon* are about naming and misnaming, and about birth and death. Names are an essential part of the legacy, and names have stories which, incongruous, preposterous as they are, must be cared for.

Morrison calls attention to the importance of naming as a ritual in black people's lives. Blacks received dead patronyms from whites—through a trick illiteracy played on them, allowing the literate to mess up their names. In the Dead family—thus misnamed as a result of some white official's ignorance—first names were given by illiterate fathers who took a fancy to the shape for a letter or to a sound. Thus, people and places receive their names—names are "disguises, jokes or brand names"—from yearnings, gestures, flaws, events, mistakes, weaknesses. Names endure like marks or have secrets they do not easily yield. Only when the whole story is told, the mystery unveiled, can the full meaning be grasped. *Song of Solomon* is strewn with such words, offered as riddles or as clues to the legacy: Song, Solomon, Shalimar, Sugarman... Part of Milkman's task is to trace the history of each name and to search for the one name that is real, the ancestor's name.

Milkman's name itself is a joke, but it is also his fate. The child who was breast-fed too long is doomed to become the subject of other people's fantasies: his mother's, Hagar's, Guitar's. His rechristening (by a man who is an important community figure in the book, a newsbreaker who cannot be entrusted with any secret) is the first of a series of baptisms. Interestingly, this ludicrous nickname makes Milkman an improbable perpetuator of his father's legacy. It unexpectedly sets him free from the legacy of the "Dead" house, from the dead side of his family. It estranges him from a father outraged to see his son renamed for reasons unknown to him, one that brings a tinge of shame on his reputation. Macon Dead himself fights against the odds of his own name—Dead—and tries to retrieve Milkman as his rightful heir. In his manly world where women exist only in the shadow or in the margin of life, his son belongs to that centrality where power and property can help build the legacy to be handed down from one male generation to the next.

The history of his name places Milkman in an ambiguous situation. The legacy—the true legacy that Milkman will acknowledge only late in his life—is sharply contrasted with the heritage his father has shaped for him. Significantly, while the latter is controlled by the authority of the men, the former is placed under the care of an unconventional feminine world. Milkman will waver in his quest between the world his father wants him to build—urging him on a straight path that ultimately will prove a dead end—and the sinuous line that the women, mostly his aunt, invite him to follow, a path that will take him on "the journey *back,*" the journey *home.* Pilate, Macon Dead's sister, who "has been given the worst possible name, that of "Christ killing Pilate," is nevertheless the one who knows that the sanctity and magic of names is not to be disregarded. Her name is her sole legacy and must be saved from oblivion. That name, because it is the only word her father ever wrote, will go from the family Bible to a little box that she hangs from her ear. The box belonged to her mother who died before she was born. Pilate's unusual name therefore becomes appropriate for this woman who had an unusual childbirth "inching her way into life out of a still silent indifferent cave of flesh," without a navel, the strangest woman in town, recon-

structing in the margin of the city a communal world rooted in ancestral lore.

With her reverence for the legacy, her secrecy and defiance, she becomes Milkman's pilot, the guiding force, the pedagogue who introduces him to the mysteries of life and death, and of blackness ("You think dark is just one color, but it ain't.... There are five or six kinds of black. Some silky, some woolly...."); with her pebbly voice, she spells for him the secrets of the world. This woman with no navel has to be taken seriously. She also has literally to invent herself. Her many gifts as natural healer, skilled wine maker, singer, conjure woman and soothsayer, truth giver, bear witness to the extent of the legacy of black womankind. She initiates Milkman into the wisdom and beliefs and souls of his people, and challenges his indifference and ignorance.

Thanks to Pilate, the uncomfortable boy foresees a future, is given a sense of purpose. His first visit to Pilate's house initiates his journey into the legacy: "in the winehouse of this lady who had one earring, no navel and looked like a tall black tree," amid the pervading odor of fermenting fruit and pine, Milkman is reborn. Pilate and her house, in sharp contrast to his father's house of death, bring a promise, suggest the possibility of flight. It is the seedbed of cultural activity. Symbolically it is for Milkman the threshold, both margin and *limen,* which represents the liminal phase of his rites of passage, the precursor of a real and permanent change that will involve a long and exacting pilgrimage.

"Black women can fly." This statement is emphatically made by black women in their writings. Pilate is the embodiment of that image. But the flying is in Morrison's text not just a metaphorical expression of black women's spirituality, it is rooted in ancient belief and folklore. Pilate has inherited the gift to fly—which, according to certain legends, was only given to those who knew the secret word. The absence of a navel isolates her, ensuring both fear and respect, but it also brings her close to the flying ancestor. It sets her free from conventional relationships, free to define the values according to which she will live, to design a life of her own, and to interpret on her own terms and unequivocally the particular legacy of her people. It also designates her as a mythical outsider, a sort of messiah. It is through her that the oracle will speak. Stories of names are thus inextricably woven into life stories. Significantly, many stories in *Song of Solomon* are also about birth and death, these essential rites of passage, about difficult and improbable beginnings and premature and violent endings; and they all share the same weird, uncanny, and awesome character. Birth is the one ritual that is closest to death and as "unnatural." There is the story of Milkman's birth after he has been saved from his father's scheme of destruction, "his father trying to stop him dead before he was born," of Pilate's incredible birth after her mother's death, a birth that gives her a unique body. There are the cruel and violent deaths of fathers: Pilate and Macon's, shot off a fence;

Guitar's father sliced in two by a sawmill. And in the background we have the endless accounts of many other deaths that occur daily in front of churches or in the streets. These stories of unnatural birth and deaths can be read as variations on the fate of a family whose name is Dead, but also as metaphors on the black condition, on an existence where nothing is to be taken for granted or *granted*. In a world where whites wish to see black people dead, where blacks "ain't supposed to die a natural death," it is not surprising that any birth looks like a miracle, that death is the subject of so much talk, predictions, threats or jokes, and of ritualized care. The dead bodies appearing and disappearing among the living, wait to receive the proper burial. And the living can become either wholly dedicated to the dead—as Ruth or Pilate are to their fathers—or to some death game. In their fight for survival blacks cannot escape the white man's strokes or the murderous fantasies of their brothers and sisters. They can either play the numbers game—with Guitar and his Brotherhood, The Seven Days Friends—and make even the number of deaths among whites and among blacks, or they can try to conjure death through some old trick, by playing

humorously or imaginatively with it. No wonder so many stories are ones of craziness. Put together, they create a crazy quilt with a sense of pattern. The craziness is more on the women's side, whose voices echo Ryna's ancestral scream, all plead for the dead to return, "Sugarman don't leave me no more." The community watches silently, and with no surprise, these familiar scenes of madness. They record these sounds in children's rhymes. And the craziness of the black world is only matched by the insanity of the white world's devices.

Milkman discovers how much of the legacy revolves around this uncertain balance between life and death, how much wisdom and craziness are drawn from the familiarity with death. In Morrison's story everyone seems to be preying upon the other, each character is both a predator and a potential prey. Milkman's relation to Guitar develops into this sort of game. Guitar, the initiator (who first brought him to Pilate's house), the interpreter of his dreams, fears and wishes, is also the experienced trickster cunning and violent: the avenger. This double of Milkman is both friend and adversary.

Morrison in 1989.

"Could you save my life or would you take it?" Morrison tells us that all human relationships boil down to these two fundamental questions. In her story, Guitar, the master of ambiguity, is the only exceptional person who could answer yes to both. The alternative, one is told, is either destruction or salvation. In the end, in his final leap, Milkman wheels into his friend's arms, surrendering to or freeing himself from Guitar's obsessive pursuit. *Song of Solomon* thus unfolds between two leaps. Characters are left on the edges from which they can either lose their balance and fall, or "surrender to the air and ride it."

Between Mr. Smith's fateful leap and Milkman's flight in the air, the protagonist's awkward yet persistent exploration of the legacy is in many ways archetypal. The journey, as in many other quests in American literature, must be redemptive of past flaws and weaknesses, and retributive. It must do justice to the dead and to the living. Milkman's journey is a succession of leaps and falls, of attempted deaths and incomplete rebirths, of blunders and triumphs, of moments of vulnerability or exhilaration. The real goal of his journey is disguised even to himself. He leaves the Dead house to free himself from "the wings of other people's nightmares." He leaves, cursed by one of his sisters who exposes his ignorance, vacuous and indifferent to other people's feelings. He sets off to find the gold that will buy his freedom—faithful both to the mercantile spirit of his father, and to the historical heritage of slaves, striving to buy their freedom.

Morrison deftly underlines the ambivalent character of each of Milkman's decisions or steps, which are at the same time an escape from and a recognition of the legacy. As he progresses into his journey, however, his resistance and estrangement weaken. Committed to paying his dues, he finds himself immersed in a heritage he can no longer deny. As he is acknowledged as one of the tribe by those who have known his ancestors, he rises in fuller recognition of the meaning of kinship, of the rich filiation of several generations. He travels back in space and time to the woodlife of Pennsylvania and the wilder backwoods of Virginia, to the days of slavery when blacks moved in wagons toward the promised land. He gets closer to home, to the South, and to Africa wherefrom the Flying Ancestor, the one with the real name, came.

The journey, however, is full of pitfalls and trials. It takes him, the city bred, farther away from civilization, into close connection with the asocial powers of life and death, with the cosmos or chaos. Milkman's errand into the wilderness becomes a mock story of survival, a joke. Through the last stages of the quest, he feels alternately aloof, unconcerned, off center or, on the contrary, involved and caring. During moments of vacuity the very question "is it important for you to find your own people?" becomes itself aimless, and Guitar's vengefulness and suspicion deprive him of the only person he could trust. But when, on the other hand, moments of revelation occur, they are like new baptisms: as when in

the heart of nature he "walks the earth," or when he watches the skinning of a bobcat, or again when he falls into the arms of the only person who does not threaten his life, a woman called Sweet.

In the deceptive creeks and woods or among country people where his presence—a black man with a white heart—is first an offense, the tests and trials become necessary rites of passage. They further purify him and initiate him back into the tribe. The spatial distance that he has to cover gives a measure of his original estrangement and disconnectedness. Morrison, who follows the conventional pattern of lyric epic adventure quest story, combines motifs from that tradition with those that belong specifically to Afro-American history and myth. Her narrative that makes the movements through time and space so artistically visible and responsive to each other is not just another version of a prototypical story: it is immersed in the Afro-American experience, informed by the sensibility, and the imagination of black people. In spite of Milkman's inadequacy and bewilderment, and of the ambiguities, and the wrong speculations, the quest must be pursued and completed. Sounds, words, upon which Milkman stumbles, will be his guides: a moan like a woman's voice, a children's song, names of people, his people, names of places named after his people, offer him the final clues he needs to reconstruct the whole message, to resurrect dead lives and fading memories.

Deciphering the song that the children are singing, thus keeping the story alive, Milkman finds new meanings for old words. The Byrd's house with its appropriate name delivers the last clue to the riddle, and this revelation must be shared with Pilate to whom it had initially been entrusted. She must be told about her mother's name, her father's wish to be buried where he belongs: at Solomon's leap where his own father "sailed off into the sky like an eagle." The wish, if fulfilled, will create history and complete the myth.

In the last swift scene, each gesture and act, unreal as they are, assume perfection and finality. They are the reenactment of familiar rites and rituals, and Milkman's leap, the fulfillment of a dream, is an act of faith in the legacy, an act of communion with Pilate, and with his flying ancestor. Milkman's and Pilate's names can enter the legend, for a new story to be written, a new song invented, that will record the story and secrecy of their lives and deaths. Thus, deeds generate songs, songs generate deeds in an uninterrupted act of creation. The long voyage in the land of the ancestors, exploring their dreams and frustrations, their failures and triumphs is also the story of the genesis of a culture and of a people who, living on the edge of life and death, have managed to create that culture and to keep it alive. *Song of Solomon* is a beautiful statement on the survival of the legacy and on the legacy of survival; on the power of memory, collective memories kept alive through names, stories, words, and songs; on the power of music that accompanies all the rituals of life, from birth to death, and through which feelings and the totality of experience are expressed. Transmitted orally from mouth to mouth and ear to ear, the legacy endures. Its secret is revealed but its secrecy remains. The song that weaves its way through the book is the sacred text: a proclamation available to all, and the repository of secrets. In its way of encoding messages as spirituals did, of yielding and keeping its secrecy, it becomes also the epitome of all narrative.

The strength and richness of that oral tradition is the legacy that black writers have inherited. Armed with pen and paper, and a long fight for literacy, they can now write. But they should do so with the same respect for the word and the devotion that Old Macon Dead showed when he wrote the only word he ever did, or that Pilate showed when she stored that word in her little box. From Zora Neale Hurston to Morrison, black women writers have felt a sense of responsibility toward the heritage—a legacy of beliefs, creeds, customs, and rituals—but also of endurance and humiliation, bereavements and victories—that must now endure through their writing. The leap into the air is a fit metaphor for the secret and hazardous act of writing, an act of faith and communion, the fulfillment of a promise and a pledge. (pp. 105-14)

> *Genevieve Fabre, "Genealogical Archaeology or the Quest for Legacy in Toni Morrison's 'Song of Solomon',"* in *Critical Essays on Toni Morrison, edited by Nellie Y. McKay, G. K. Hall & Co., 1988, pp. 105-14.*

Deborah Horvitz (essay date 1989)

[*In the following essay, Horvitz examines the ghost Beloved and comments on what she symbolizes.*]

Toni Morrison's fifth novel, *Beloved* (1987), explores the insidious degradation imposed upon all slaves, even when they were owned by, in Harriet Beecher Stowe's term, "a man of humanity." The novel is also about matrilineal ancestry and the relationships among enslaved, freed, alive, and dead mothers and daughters. Equally it is about the meaning of time and memory and how remembering either destroys or saves a future. Written in an anti-minimalist, lyrical style in which biblical myths, folklore, and literary realism overlap, the text is so grounded in historical reality that it could be used to teach American history classes. Indeed, as a simultaneously accessible and yet extremely difficult book, *Beloved* operates so complexly that as soon as one layer of understanding is reached, another, equally as richly textured, emerges to be unravelled. Morrison has referred to her novel as a "ghost story" and begins and ends with Beloved, whose name envelopes the text.

The powerful corporeal ghost who creates matrilineal connection between Africa and America, Beloved stands for every African woman whose story will never be told. She is the haunting symbol of the many Beloveds—generations of mothers and daughters—hunted down and stolen from Africa; as such, she is, unlike mortals, invulnerable to barriers of time, space, and place. She moves with the freedom of an omnipresent and omnipotent spirit who weaves in and out of different generations within the matrilineal chain. Yet, Morrison is cautious not to use Beloved as a symbol in a way that either traps the reader in polemics or detaches one from the character who is at different times a caring mother and a lonely girl. Nor is Beloved so universalized that her many meanings lose specificity. She is rooted in a particular story and is the embodiment of specific members of Sethe's family. At the same time she represents the spirit of all the women dragged onto slave ships in Africa and also all Black women in America trying to trace their ancestry back to the mother on the ship attached to them. Beloved is the haunting presence who becomes the spirit of the women from "the other side." As Sethe's mother she comes from the geographic other side of the world, Africa; as Sethe's daughter, she comes from the physical other side of life, death. There is a relationship, too, between Beloved's arrival and the blossoming of Sethe's memory. Only after Beloved comes to Sethe's house as a young woman does Sethe's repression of countless painful memories begin to lift. Beloved generates a metamorphosis in Sethe that allows her to speak what she had thought to be the unspeakable.

In *Beloved* the ghost-child who comes back to life is not only Sethe's two-year-old daughter, whom she murdered eighteen years ago; she is also Sethe's African mother. This inter-generational, inter-continental, female ghost-child teaches Sethe that memories and stories about her matrilineal ancestry are life-giving. Moreover, Beloved stimulates Sethe to remember her own mother because, in fact, the murdered daughter and the slave mother are a conflated or combined identity represented by the ghost-child Beloved.

Mother-daughter bonding and bondage suffuses Morrison's text. Sethe's nameless mother is among the African slaves who experienced the Middle Passage and, late in the text, she relates that ordeal through a coded message from the ship revealing that she too is a Beloved who, like Sethe, has been cruelly separated from her own mother. This cycle of mother-daughter loss, perceived abandonment, betrayal, and recovery is inherent in and characterizes each mother-daughter relationship in the novel. But in the present tense of the novel—Ohio in 1873—Sethe barely remembers, from so long ago,

> her own mother, who was pointed out to her by the eight-year-old child who watched over the young ones—pointed out as the one among many backs turned away from her, stooping in a watery field. Patiently Sethe waited for this particular back to gain the row's end and stand. What she saw was a cloth hat as opposed to a straw one, singularity enough in that world of cooing women each of whom was called Ma'am.

This is mainly how she remembers her mother, simply as an image, a woman in a field with a stooped back in a cloth hat.

Sethe does, however, have one other quite specific memory of this obscure mother, of what may have been their only interaction following the two weeks the nameless Ma'am was allowed to nurse her. She remembers that Ma'am

> picked me up and carried me behind the smoke-house. Back there she opened up her dress front and lifted her breast and pointed under it. Right on her rib was a circle and a cross burnt right in the skin. She said, "This is your ma'am. This," and she pointed. "I am the only one got this mark now. The rest dead. If something happens to me and you can't tell me by my face, you can know me by this mark." Scared me so. All I could think of was how important this was and how I needed to have something important to say back, but I couldn't think of anything so I just said what I thought. "Yes, Ma'am," I said. "But how will you know me? How will you know me? Mark me, too," I said. "Mark the mark on me too."

Because Sethe is not marked, she thinks she has no link with her mother. In fact, before Beloved helps Sethe's memory unfold, Sethe firmly believes that because Ma'am is physically dead, they are not emotionally tied. When her mother was hanged, Sethe did not know why. Probably Ma'am was caught trying to escape from the plantation, but the daughter born in bondage refuses to believe her mother could have run. It would mean that she left Sethe behind, emphasizing in this generation the continuous pattern of severed mother-daughter relationships. In other words, her memories of Ma'am are buried not only because their relationship was vague and their contact prohibited but also because those recollections are inextricably woven with feelings of painful abandonment. If Sethe remembers her mother, she must also remember that she believes her mother deserted her.

As Sethe tells this story to Denver and Beloved, she becomes frightened: "She was remembering something [Ma'am's language] she had forgotten she knew." Murky pictures and vague words begin to creep into her mind and she knows that they come from that place inside her—the place Paul D. refers to as the locked and rusted tobacco tin—that stores, but can never lose, forgotten memories. Ma'am's language erupts into her conscious mind signaling the beginning of Sethe's slow metamorphosis. "Something privately shameful...had seeped into a slit in her mind right behind the...circled cross," and she remembers that she does or did have a link with her mother that transcends the cross in the circle. She is afraid to remember but ashamed not to. Recollections of "the language her ma'am spoke...which would never come back" creep into her consciousness. She remembers one-armed Nan, the slave who was in charge of Sethe and the other children on the plantation where Sethe grew up. Nan "used different words," words that expressed her mother's native African, and these words link Sethe back both to her mother and to her mother's land, the place where women gathered flowers in freedom and played in the long grass before the white men came:

Words Sethe understood then but could neither recall nor repeat now. She believed that must be why she remembered so little before Sweet Home except singing and dancing and how crowded it was. What Nan told her she had forgotten, along with the language she told it in. But the message—that was and had been there all along. Holding the damp white sheets against her chest, she was picking meaning out of a code she no longer understood. Nighttime.

Although Sethe has forgotten the words of her mother's language, they continue to exist inside her as feelings and images that repeatedly emerge as a code that she relies on without realizing it. This code holds animated, vital memories, such as the one of her mother dancing juba, as well as the most painful act of Sethe's life: her mother's absence.

Sethe is shocked as she continues to find meaning in a code she thought she no longer understood. She remembers that she felt the dancing feet of her dead mother as she was about to give birth in Denver. Pregnant and thinking she is going to die because her swollen feet cannot take another step, she wants to stop walking; every time she does so, the movement of her unborn child causes her such pain that she feels she is being rammed by an antelope. Although Sethe wonders why an antelope, since she cannot remember having ever seen one, it is because the image of the antelope is really an image of Ma'am dancing. Sethe's antelope kicking baby and her antelope dancing mother are one and the same:

> Oh but when they sang. And oh but when they danced and sometimes they danced the antelope. The men as well as the ma'ams, one of whom was certainly her own. They shifted shapes and became something other. Some unchained demanding other whose feet knew her pulse better than she did. Just like this one in her stomach.

Stored in childhood but only now unlocked, the link between the unborn Denver's kicks and the dead ma'ams kicks as she danced the antelope erupts in Sethe's memory. As she bears the next generation in her matrilineal line, Sethe keeps her mother's African antelope dancing alive: she links the pulses of her unchained, vigorously moving mother and her energetic, womb-kicking daughter forever.

A second and perhaps the most crucial part of this story from her past is that Sethe, as Nan tells her, is the only child her mother did not kill:

> She told Sethe that her mother and Nan were together from the sea. Both were taken up many times by the crew. "She threw them all away but you. The one from the crew she threw away on the island. The others from more whites she also threw away. Without name she threw them. You she gave the name of the black man. She put her arms around him. The others she did not put her arms around. Never. Never. Telling you. I am telling you, small girl Sethe."

Conceived with a Black man in love, rather than with a white master through rape, Sethe, named after her father, is the only child her mother allowed to survive.

Significantly, she is flooded with these memories in response to questions from her own daughter, Beloved, who wants to know everything in Sethe's memory and actually feeds and fattens on these stories. What Beloved demands is that Sethe reveal memory and story about her life before Sweet Home, memory about her African speaking, branded mother and her life right after Sweet Home when she cut Beloved's throat. In other words, because they share identities, the ghost-child's fascination lies in the "joined" union between Sethe's mother and herself. Sethe's memory is being pried wide open by Beloved's presence. She forces Sethe to listen to her own voice and to remember her own mother, her ma'am with the special mark on her body, along with her mother's native language, songs, and dances.

This cycle of mother-daughter fusion, loss, betrayal, and recovery between Sethe and her mother plays itself out again in the present relationship between Sethe and Beloved. Beloved transforms from a lonely affectionate girl into a possessive, demanding tyrant, and her ruthlessness almost kills Sethe. There is even a connection between this ruling Beloved and the slave-driver. Because any attempt to possess another human being is reminiscent of the slave-master relationship, Denver links Sethe and the slave-drivers when she warns Beloved that Sethe, like "the men without skin" from the ship, "chews and swallows." Beloved is furious and ferocious. When she first comes to the farmhouse where Sethe and Denver live, she appears because the other side is lonely—devoid of love and memory. She yearns for Sethe and cannot take her eyes off her. "Sethe was licked, tasted, eaten by Beloved's eyes." But what starts out as a child's love and hunger for a mother from whom she has long been separated turns into a wish to own Sethe, to possess her, to merge with her and be her. Beloved gets rid of Paul D. and eventually excludes Denver from their play. Just as the disembodied baby ghost Beloved hauntingly possessed Sethe, so the flesh-and-blood adolescent Beloved tries to own and dominate her. Sethe is as haunted by the girl's presence as she was by her absence because possession of any kind involving human beings is destructive.

These "possessive" attachments raise the important moral dilemma underlying Sethe's act; either Sethe must be held accountable for Beloved's death or the institution of slavery alone killed the child. If Morrison wants to humanize and individualize the "great lump called slaves," then perhaps she is suggesting that Sethe, like any individual, is answerable and responsible for her own actions. The namesake for Beloved's Sethe is the biblical Seth, born to replace his brother, the murdered Abel. Perhaps Morrison's Sethe, too, is a "replacement" for her brothers and sisters murdered by the system of slavery and lost to her nameless ma'am. If so, then the inevitable confrontation between Sethe, the replacement

child saved by her ma'am, and Beloved, the protected child murdered by hers, represented the impossible choice available to the enslaved mother.

Certainly one reason Beloved comes back is to pass judgment on Sethe. When Sethe first realizes that Beloved is the ghost of her third child, she wants desperately for the girl to understand that she tried to kill her babies so that they would be protected from captivity forever. Sethe assumes Beloved will forgive her. She does not. For Beloved, her mother's protection became the act of possession that led to her own death, which was murder. Beloved becomes mean-spirited and exploits her mother's pain. Sethe gives Beloved story after story of her love and devotion to her. She tells her how nothing was more important than getting her milk to her, how she waved flies away from her in the grape arbor, how it pained her to see her baby bitten by a mosquito, and how she would trade her own life for Beloved's. Sethe tries to impress upon her how slavery made it impossible for her to be the mother she wanted to be.

For Sethe her children are her "best thing," yet they have all been ruined. The murdered Beloved torments Sethe, Howard and Buglar have left home, and Denver is so afraid of the world that it is only starvation that forces her off the front porch. Sethe begs the ruling Beloved not only for forgiveness for the obvious but also for the return of her "self." But Beloved does not care:

> She said when she cried there was no one. That dead men lay on top of her. That she had nothing to eat. Ghosts without skin stuck their fingers in her and said beloved in the dark and bitch in the light. Sethe never came to her, never said a word to her, never smiled and worst of all never waved goodbye or even looked her way before running away from her.

What is most striking here is that Beloved responds to Sethe's entreaties not only in the language of the murdered daughter but also in the tortured language of the "woman from the sea." Death and the Middle Passage evoke the same language. They are the same existence; both were experienced by the multiple-identified Beloved.

To appreciate fully Beloved's attack on her mother, it is important to look back to Morrison's previous pages, written without punctuation, composed of some lines written in complete sentences with spaces after them, while others are not. The writing is fluid, open, created in the first person with no names and no reference to time or place. This rhetoric communicates what may at first appear to be an unintelligible experience, a story of images which the reader must grope and finally fail to figure out. In fact, breaking the barriers of form, this key passage, much like Morrison's ghost moving beyond human barriers, communicates the death-like Middle Passage suffered by Sethe's mother. She, Sethe's mother, is the woman "from the sea."

In the remembered ghost story, a woman is crouching on a ship where there is not enough room; there is bread that she is too hungry to eat and so little water that she cannot even make tears. Prisoner on a rat infested ship where she is urinated on by the "men without skin," which is how the clothed white men look to her, she uses words almost identical to the ones Beloved shouts at Sethe: Beloved says "dead men lay on top of [me]"; the speaker "from the sea" says "the man on my face is dead." Beloved tells Sethe that "ghosts without skin stuck their fingers in [me]"; the woman from the ship says that "he puts his finger there; Beloved blames Sethe for not coming to her, not smiling and not waving goodbye before she left her; the woman on the ship says "she was going to smile at me she was going to a hot thing." The point is that "Beloved" exists in several places and has more than one voice. While in the pages of unpunctuated writing she is the voice of the woman on the ship, thirty pages later she uses almost the same words as Sethe's daughter, and each voice shouts to a Sethe. At the end of this section, the collective voice screams: "I am not dead Sethe's is the face that left me Sethe sees me see her now we can join a hot thing." The "hot thing," referred to repeatedly by both voices, expresses the passion that permeates the text, the fantasy that it is possible to join with and possess the lost Beloved. It expresses the desperately writhing and thwarted wish to be both "self" and "other" so as to regain the lost Beloved by becoming her. This is what each means when she says "her face is my own," or "the woman is there with the face I want the face that is mine." The "hot thing" expresses the wish to join, merge, and fuse with the lost mother.

Referring to the dead slaves being dumped overboard, the voice of the woman from the sea says "the men without skin push them through with poles," and then the speaker, Sethe's mother, enraged and mournful, protests: "The woman is there with the face I want they fall into the sea if I had the teeth of the man who died on my face I would bite the circle around her neck bite it away." Terrified and outraged by the iron collar placed on the slaves, she wants to "bite the circle around her neck bite it away" because she knows the woman hates its being there. The "woman with the face I want" is never definitively identified, but at the very end of the novel, Morrison, referring to the African women whose stories are lost, writes, "they never knew . . . whose was the underwater face she needed like that." Perhaps she, "the woman with the face I want," the lost underwater, drowned face, is someone on the ship with Sethe's mother. Most likely, given that she sees her own face reflected in the "underwater face," she is her own mother, Sethe's grandmother. If so, there is another generation in the line of tortured, invisible women, all of them Beloveds, who have been cruelly severed from their mothers and daughters. The loss of "the underwater face" represents not only the death of a woman, but the death of a mother and therefore the rupture of the mother-daughter bond, probably the strongest, most important relationship women can have. In this novel grief is not only for one deceased woman but for the empty space that she leaves inside all her daughters.

The two voices, Sethe's ma'am's and her daughter's, both of them Beloved's, merge. Yet within the fused voice, each describes her own, individual experience of horrific loss:

> I am Beloved and she is mine. [Sethe] was about to smile at me when the men without skin came and took us up into the sunlight with the dead and shoved them into the sea. Sethe went into the sea . . . . They did not push her . . . . She was getting ready to smile at me . . . . All I want to know is why did she go in the water in the place where we crouched? Why did she do that when she was about to smile at me? I wanted to join her in the sea but I could not move.

From the "place where we crouched," the slave ship, Sethe's mother has lost someone who jumped in the water—the woman Morrison says will never be known, but surely it is Sethe's grandmother. The author creates a fluidity of identity among Sethe's mother, Sethe's grandmother, and the murdered two-year-old, so that Beloved is both an individual and a collective being. They are the primary losses to Sethe, more so, even, than her husband, Halle. Beloved is the crucial link that connects Africa and America for the enslaved women. She is Sethe's mother; she is Sethe herself; she is her daughter.

Although at different times Sethe, her mother, and her daughter all live with the agonizing feeling that they have been betrayed by their mothers, perhaps most heart-breaking is the image of mother-daughter separation evoked when Beloved insists that a "Sethe," voluntarily and without being pushed, went into the sea. The agony stems from the child's assumption that she is being deliberately abandoned by her ma'am. A little girl stands on an enormous ship not understanding why her mother jumps overboard. Beloved lost her mother when she "went into the sea instead of smiling at [her]." And Sethe's mother wants an unidentified, lost woman on the ship, probably her ma'am, to know how urgently she tries "to help her but the clouds are in the way." This Beloved, Sethe's mother, wants desperately either to save her own mother or die with her, but she loses her again "because of the noisy clouds of smoke." (Beloved also says she lost "Sethe" again "because of the noisy clouds of smoke.") There was a riot on the ship and the noisy clouds of smoke were caused by guards' gunfire, which prevented the daughter from reaching her mother. Perhaps the sick slaves were forced overboard; maybe it was a mass suicide or an attempt to escape through the water. Or the gunfire could have occurred in Africa, before the ships were boarded, when the white traders were hunting down and capturing native Blacks. What is clear is that a woman on the ship went into the sea leaving a girl-child alone, bereft; and each was to the other a Beloved. What is also clear is that the novel is structured by a series of flashbacks, which succeed in bridging the shattered generations by repeating meaningful and multi-layered images. That is, contained in the narrative strategy of the novel itself are both the wrenching, inter-generational separations and the healing process.

The American and African Beloveds join forever in the last two pages of the novel as symbols of the past—exploding, swallowing, and chewing—and fuse with these same images in the present. The sickening fear of her body exploding, dissolving, or being chewed up and spit out links each enslaved Beloved with her sister in captivity. Africa is "the place where long grass opens," the slave ship is the crouching place, and the ghost-child is the girl seen "that day on the porch." The Beloved from each place is another's matrilineal heritage and future; and each Beloved merges with her other "selves" in the shared and horrific fear of losing her body. The gap is bridged between America and Africa, the past and the present, the dead and the living, the flesh and the spirit. But they are joined in a specific shared, secret horror, perhaps the most devastating effect of the violence heaped upon them by "the men without skin." Each lives in terror that her body will disintegrate or, quite literally, explode. Earlier in the text the ghost-child loses a tooth and

> Beloved looked at the tooth and thought, This is it. Next would be her arm, her hand, a toe. Pieces of her would drop maybe one at a time, maybe all at once. Or on one of those mornings before Denver woke and after Sethe left she would fly apart. It is difficult keeping her head on her neck, her legs attached to her hips when she is by herself. Among the things she could not remember was when she first knew that she could wake up any day and find herself in pieces. She had two dreams: exploding and being swallowed. When her tooth came out—an odd fragment, last in the row—she thought it was starting.

She cannot remember when she first knew "she could wake up any day and find herself in pieces," not simply because she was only two when her mother cut her throat, but because the fear predates her birth; it comes from the Beloveds in Africa and the ship: "In the place where long grass opens, the girl who waited to be loved and cry shame erupts into her separate parts, to make it easy for the chewing laughter to swallow her all away." The voice on the ship repeatedly hears "chewing and swallowing and laughter." The point is that enslaved women, not in possession of their own bodies, survived barbaric beatings, rapes, and being "swallowed" without total decompensation by emotionally dissociating themselves from their bodies. The price they paid was, of course, an enormous one; those that survived often did so with no shred of basic integrity or dignity regarding their bodies. The imagery emphasizes, too, those African women who did not survive the Middle Passage—those who were chewed up, spit out, and swallowed by the sea—those whose bodies and stories were never recovered. Morrison, speaking of the women whose stories are lost, says they are "disremembered," meaning not only that they are forgotten, but also that they are dismembered, cut up and off, and not re-membered.

The very end of the novel paradoxically appears to belie the crucial theme of the book, that it is imperative to preserve continuity through story, language, and culture between generations of Black women. The authorial voice says repeatedly "this is not a story to pass on," although it seems in this text that not to repeat is to lose stories crucial to Black heritage and American history and to the personal lives of Black women.

The paradox is the one posed by memory and history themselves when past memories hurt so much they feel as though they must be forgotten. Sethe could not pass on her mother's story for the same reason that, before Beloved came, she could not talk about the murder: "Every mention of her past life hurt. The hurt was always there—like a tender place in the corner of her mouth that the bit left." Remembering horrors of such enormous magnitude can cause a despair so profound that the memories cancel out the possibility of resolution or pleasure in the present and future. For example, the happiness that seemed possible between Sethe and Paul D. at the carnival was obliterated by the past, in the form of Beloved's arrival that very day. However, Morrison implies, even though memory of the past can prevent living in the present, to pursue a future without remembering the past has its own and even deeper despair for it denies the reality and sacrifice of those who died. Assuming individual and collective responsibility is a crucial concern of *Beloved,* and it is a responsibility to remember.

Like Sethe, Beloved herself is trapped by painful memories of the past at the end of her narrative. When white Mr. Bodwin comes to pick up Denver, Sethe becomes terrified because she associates Bodwin's hat with Schoolteacher's. She temporarily forgets where she is and who he is, and she tries to kill him. Sethe runs from Beloved into the crowd of women outside her house. The ghost-child, left "Alone Again," watches Sethe run "away from her to the pile of people out there. They make a hill. A hill of black people, falling." What Beloved sees is the "little hill of dead people" from the slave ship; she sees "those able to die . . . in a pile." She sees "rising from his place with a whip in his hand, the man without skin, looking. He is looking at her." While Sethe sees Bodwin as Schoolteacher, Beloved sees him as a slave-driver from the slave ship looking at her, suggesting again that Beloved, the daughter, is also the woman "from the sea," Sethe's mother. She runs away, naked and pregnant with stories from the past, back to the water from which she emerged, where the narrator says she will be forgotten.

The paradox of how to live in the present without cancelling out an excruciatingly painful past remains unresolved at the end of the novel. At the same time, something healing has happened. Sethe's narrative ends with her considering the possibility that she could be her own "best thing." Denver has left the front porch feeling less afraid and more sure of herself. Now that Beloved is gone there is the feeling that perhaps Sethe can find some happiness with Paul D., who "wants to put his story next to hers." As the embodiment of Sethe's memories, the ghost Beloved enabled her to remember and tell the story of her past, and in so doing shows that between women words used to make and share a story have the power to heal. Although Toni Morrison states that "it was not a story to pass on," she herself has put words to Beloved's tale. Though the ghost-child-mother-sister returns, unnamed, to the water, her story is passed on. (pp. 157-66)

> *Deborah Horvitz, "Nameless Ghosts: Posses-*
> *sion and Dispossession in 'Beloved'," in*
> *Studies in American Fiction, Vol. 17, No. 2,*
> *Autumn, 1989, pp. 157-67.*

FURTHER READING

Alexander, Harriet S. "Toni Morrison: An Annotated Bibliography of Critical Articles and Essays, 1975-1984." *CLA Journal* XXXIII, No. 1 (September 1989): 81-93.
Bibliography of essays about Morrison's novels and of interviews with the author.

Angelo, Bonnie. "The Pain of Being Black." *Time* 133, No. 21 (22 May 1989): 120-22.
Probes Morrison's views on contemporary issues concerning blacks.

Dickerson, Vanessa D. "The Naked Father in Toni Morrison's *The Bluest Eye.*" In *Refiguring the Father: New Feminist Readings of Patriarchy,* edited by Patricia Yaeger and Beth Kowaleski-Wallace, pp. 108-27. Carbondale: Southern Illinois University Press, 1989.
Investigates the image of a naked father as demonstrated by Cholly Breedlove in *The Bluest Eye.*

Fick, Thomas H. "Toni Morrison's 'Allegory of the Cave': Movies, Consumption, and Platonic Realism in *The Bluest Eye.*" *Journal of the Midwest Modern Language Association* 22, No. 1 (Spring 1989): 10-22.
Argues that T.S. Eliot's *The Waste Land* and Plato's "Allegory of the Cave" inform *The Bluest Eye,* for "they suggest Morrison's belief in the close relationship between intellectual traditions and particular economic and social conditions."

Lee, Dorothy H. "The Quest for Self: Triumph and Failure in the Works of Toni Morrison." In *Black Women Writers (1950-1980): A Critical Evaluation,* edited by Mari Evans, pp. 346-60. Garden City, NY.: Anchor Press/Doubleday, 1984.
Traces a common theme in Morrison's first four novels—a "motivating and organizing device" in the form of a "quest ... underscored by ironic insights and intensely evocative imagery."

Magness, Patricia. "The Knight and the Princess: The Structure of Courtly Love in Toni Morrison's *Tar Baby.*" *South Atlantic Review* 54, No. 4 (November 1989): 85-100.

Examines the theme of courtly love in *Tar Baby,* specifically comparing the work to *Le chevalier de la charrete* by Chrétien de Troyes.

McKay, Nellie. "An Interview with Toni Morrison." *Contemporary Literature* 24, No. 4 (Winter 1983): 413-29.
Morrison discusses the characters in her first four novels and the influence of black women on her writing.

————, ed. *Critical Essays on Toni Morrison.* Boston: G. K. Hall & Co., 1988, 219 p.
Anthology of critical essays, including reviews of Morrison's first four novels and interviews with the author.

Naylor, Gloria, and Morrison, Toni. "A Conversation." *The Southern Review* 21, No. 3 (July 1985): 567-93.
Naylor, author of *The Women of Brewster Place* (1982), and Morrison discuss their careers as women writers.

Otten, Terry. *The Crime of Innocence in the Fiction of Toni Morrison.* Columbia: University of Missouri Press, 1989, 101 p.
Locates the theme of a "fall"—a "necessary and potentially redemptive passage from a garden state of debilitating innocence to painful self-knowledge and its consequences"—in Morrison's five novels.

Story, Ralph. "An Excursion into the Black World: The 'Seven Days' in Toni Morrison's *Song of Solomon.*" *Black American Literature Forum* 23, No. 1 (Spring 1989): 149-58.
Examines the revolutionary group Seven Days in *Song of Solomon* as "a key element in the work's literary development and as a microcosm of the two primary ideological streams"—those of, for example, Malcolm X and Martin Luther King, Jr.—"which have characterized Afro-American political thought in the twentieth century."

Turner, Darwin T. "Theme, Characterization, and Style in the Works of Toni Morrison." In *Black Women Writers (1950-1980): A Critical Evaluation,* edited by Mari Evans, pp. 361-69. Garden City, NY.: Anchor Press/Doubleday, 1984.
Analyzes Morrison's writing techniques in her first four novels, contending that she "commands the storyteller's skill to persuade a reader to suspend disbelief by discovering credibility in the magic of the tale."

Wagner, Linda W. "Mastery of Narrative." In *Contemporary American Women Writers: Narrative Strategies,* edited by Catherine Rainwater and William J. Scheik, pp. 191-205. Lexington: University Press of Kentucky, 1985.
Explores the narrative structures of Morrison's first four novels.

Ezekiel Mphahlele

1919-

(Also writes as Es'kia Mphahlele and under pseudonym Bruno Eseki) South African novelist, autobiographer, short story writer, essayist, editor, poet, and critic.

A major African author and a provocative social critic, Mphahlele is especially known for his autobiography *Down Second Avenue* (1959) and the novel *The Wanderers* (1971). His writing has been marked by the alienation and pain he experienced during three distinct periods of his life: 1) living in South Africa from birth through early middle age; 2) a self-imposed twenty-year exile from South Africa; and 3) his ultimate return to that nation in 1977. A number of critics have labeled Mphahlele's fiction autobiographical or journalistic, suggesting that he, like many other South African writers, seeks to change the oppressive racial policies of the nation through fact-based fiction, thereby rejecting traditional novel and short story forms. Nevertheless, Gerald Moore noted of Mphahlele: "If he cannot give us the great black South African novel which has been so long awaited, it seems probable that no one at present can."

Mphahlele was born in Marabastad Township, a separate area for blacks in Pretoria, South Africa. His father Moses was a messenger and his mother Eva was a domestic. According to Moore, "Mphahlele was not yet fifteen when he suffered his first assault from a white constable. He learnt the full humiliation of his position as he cycled about the city, collecting the dirty washing of hostile and moody white customers. But somehow, at the sacrifice of any real life with her own children, his mother managed to put him through primary school." Although Mphahlele continued to collect laundry and perform domestic chores throughout his school days, his education progressed rapidly, and he was eventually trained as a teacher at Adams Teachers Training College and at the University of South Africa. Yet he was banned from the classroom in 1952 for protesting the segregationist Bantu Education Act. Mphahlele left South Africa in 1957 and began writing newspaper articles, criticism, fiction, and essays.

While he lived in self-imposed exile in Nigeria, Mphahlele published *Down Second Avenue,* which has been termed "the autobiography of most Africans." Although Mphahlele relates his experiences from age five until his departure from South Africa, some critics have called *Down Second Avenue* a fictional autobiography. Ursula A. Barnett wrote in response: "It is doubtless a true account in spirit of Mphahlele's life and that of the people around him. Even in his avowed fiction Mphahlele never compromises with the truth for the sake of dramatic effect or sentiment, as others are often tempted to do in their autobiographical writing." Mphahlele also published *The Living and the Dead, and Other*

Stories (1961), a collection of short stories including "The Suitcase." In this story a man sees a lucky chance in taking a suitcase that a woman left on a bus. He is arrested, and the police, after listening to the man insist that the suitcase is his, open it and find a dead baby inside. In the story "We'll Have Dinner at Eight," a white woman attempts to befriend her black employee by inviting him to dinner. The employee, thinking that she works for the police, kills her. Critics appraised this collection of short stories as a successful if uneven effort. In 1971 Mphahlele published *The Wanderers,* his acclaimed novel about South African blacks and whites in their country and in exile. John Updike remarked that the novel "shows the English-speaking whites (but not the Afrikaners) as people who, like the blacks, are unequally matched against the vast, murderous inertia that is Africa." James R. Frakes further commented: "If anger, first-hand experience, outrage, compassion, and topicality were the sole requirements for great literature, *The Wanderers* might well be one of the masterpieces of this declining part of the twentieth century." Several critics termed *The Wanderers* not a novel but an autobiography. In a 1971 interview, however, Mphahlele called *The Wanderers* "more fiction than autobiography," contending: "It's difficult to find a dividing line in one's mind between fiction and autobiography. All I can say is one's own experiences have a lot to do with any kind of fiction—much more to do than you probably would be aware of."

During his exile Mphahlele spent much time in the United States, earning his doctorate at the University of Denver and teaching at major universities. After living outside of South Africa for twenty years he returned to his home in 1977. He explained: "I want to be part of the renaissance that is happening in the thinking of the people. I see education as playing a vital role in personal growth and in institutionalizing a way of life that a people chooses as its highest ideal.... Another reason for returning, connected with the first, is that this is my ancestral home. An African cares very much where he dies and is buried. But I have not come to die. I want to reconnect with my ancestors while I am still active. I am also a captive of place, of setting. As long as I was abroad I continued to write on the South African scene. There is a force I call the tyranny of place; the kind of unrelenting hold a place has on a person that gives him the motivation to write and a style. The American setting in which I lived for nine years was too fragmented to give me these." Upon his return Mphahlele published the novel *Chirundu* (1981). In this work Chimba Chirundu rises through the ranks to become minister of transport and public works in an imaginary African country, but he is arrested when his first wife refuses to recognize their tribal divorce and accuses Chirundu of bigamy. Martin Tucker wrote: "With this situation Mphahlele comes to grips with issues of modernism and tribalism, of new and old Africa, of individualism and communal responsibilities." Mphahlele also wrote another autobiography, *Afrika My Music: An Autobiography, 1957-83* (1984), which details his life in exile.

Renewal Time (1988), a collection of short stories and essays, is Mphahlele's most recent work. In it Mphahlele reaffirms the tie with South Africa that has been characteristic of both his fiction and nonfiction. Having established himself as one of the most important critics of South African society, Mphahlele intends to keep writing about the nation's problems. "Race relations are a major experience and concern for the writer [in South Africa]," he said. "They are his constant beat. It is unfortunate no one can ever think it is healthy both mentally and physically to keep hacking at the social structure in overcharged language. A language that burns and brands, scorches and scalds. Language that is a machete with a double edge—the one sharp, the other blunt, the one cutting, the other breaking. And yet there are levels of specifically black drama in the ghettoes that I cannot afford to ignore. I have got to stay with it. I bleed inside. My people bleed. But I must stay with it."

(For further information about Mphahlele's life and works, see *Black Writers; Contemporary Authors*, Vols. 81-84; *Contemporary Authors New Revision Series*, Vol. 26; and *Contemporary Literary Criticism*, Vol. 25.)

PRINCIPAL WORKS

Man Must Live, and Other Stories (short stories) 1947
Down Second Avenue (autobiography) 1959
The Living and the Dead, and Other Stories (short stories) 1961
The African Image (essays) 1962; revised edition, 1974
The Role of Education and Culture in Developing African Countries (nonfiction) 1965
A Guide to Creative Writing (nonfiction) 1966
In Corner B, and Other Stories (short stories) 1967
The Wanderers (novel) 1971
Voices in the Whirlwind, and Other Essays (essays) 1972
Chirundu [as Es'kia Mphahlele] (novel) 1981
The Unbroken Song: Selected Writings of Es'kia Mphahlele [as Es'kia Mphahlele] (poetry and short stories) 1981
Afrika My Music: An Autobiography, 1957-83 [as Es'kia Mphahlele] (autobiography) 1984
Bury Me at the Marketplace: Selected Letters of Es'kia Mphahlele [as Es'kia Mphahlele] (letters) 1984
Father Come Home (children's book) 1984
Let's Talk Writing: Poetry (nonfiction) 1985
Let's Talk Writing: Prose (nonfiction) 1985
Renewal Time [as Es'kia Mphahlele] (short stories and essays) 1988

Saunders Redding (essay date 1971)

[*Redding was a distinguished critic, historian, novelist, and autobiographer. His first book,* To Make a Poet Black *(1939), is a scholarly appraisal of black poetry and is considered a landmark in criticism of black writers. In the following excerpt, he addresses the banning of* Down Second Avenue *and* The Wanderers *in South Africa.*]

Reading **Down Second Avenue** and **The Wanderers,** one finds it easy to understand why the author, Ezekiel Mphahlele, and his books are banned in his native South Africa. **Down Second Avenue** is autobiography which covers Mphahlele's life down to his flight into exile in 1957....

From the pen of another, less talented, less sensitive writer, **Down Second Avenue** could easily have become a sociological analysis of apartheid and/or a psychological explication of the effects of this "political" system upon its victims, black, white, colored and Indian. It is neither. One is made sharply aware of the operating sociological and psychological phenomena, not by the explication of them, but by the development of real life situations and especially by the presentation of striking real life characters . . . . (p. 78)

But it is impossible to do critical justice to a book that, while it meets the universally recognized literary canons, is at the same time meant primarily to serve a social function . . . . No work out of Africa since *Tell Freedom* by Peter Abrahams, which was published in 1954, has said so clearly that life for all people in South Africa is lived under social circumstances and in a spiritual temper so degrading as to destroy the hopes even of those who have been taught to believe—and do believe—that their salvation lies in the perpetuation of the "political" system called apartheid. This is the unstated thesis and the unspoken preachment: the world must save South Africa in spite of itself. Perception of this comes through the superb artistry of Mphahlele's storytelling, and the story itself, personal as it is, affirms man's common humanity and bridges the gap between one culture and another.

Though *The Wanderers* is presented as a work of fiction, the reader coming to it directly from *Down Second Avenue* suspects that many of the experiences it relates were the author's own . . . . But the similarity, which, anyway, is more apparent than real, does not erode the interest that the first page of *The Wanderers* arouses. Indeed, the interest grows and grows, though not because of the central story line, which works itself out in simple and dramatically logical ways.

The Wanderers takes its title from a group of rootless people, black and white, who, alienated by the social realities of South Africa, are forced into exile . . . . They seek more than refuge; they seek life—in Nigeria, in Kenya, in Tanzania. Recounting the wanderings of his characters provides an opportunity for the author to explore the milieu of these African countries, and what, among other things, you get is a panoramic view of almost the whole of the "dark continent."

If this makes it sound as if *The Wanderers* is some sort of travelogue, forget it. It is a carefully constructed work of fiction that brilliantly and imaginatively dramatizes man's irremediable alienation from the family of man and incidentally supplies insights into political, social and economic problems to which Africa is presently seeking solutions.

Ezekiel Mphahlele is one of a half dozen living South African writers, including Nadine Gordimer, Peter Abrahams, Bloke Modisane and Alan Paton, the value of whose work is vouched for by its rejection at home. (pp. 78-9)

Saunders Redding, "Out from Second Avenue," in Africa Today, Vol. 18, No. 4, October, 1971, pp. 78-9.

Ezekiel Mphahlele with Bernth Lindfors and others (interview date 1971)

[*Bernth Lindfors, Ian Munro, Richard Priebe, and Reinhard Sander edited* Palaver: Interviews with Five African Writers in Texas *(1972). They recorded and transcribed public dialogues with each author at the University of Texas at Austin, sometimes meeting individually with the author to "probe more deeply." The African authors themselves edited the interviews before publishing. In the following excerpt from an interview conducted in April 1971 and published in* Palaver, *Mphahlele discusses his development as a writer.*]

[Interviewer]: *In the first book you published,* **Man Must Live,** *it seems that the problems of racism weren't dealt with as strongly as in some of your later works. What do you think was the reason for this?*

[Mphahlele]: When I wrote those stories in **Man Must Live,** it was a kind of adventure into the literary field. I wrote things without the intention of having them published, and when I got them together, I sent them to a small publishing house just as a matter of interest, to see what their attitude would be towards them. When they read them, they decided to publish them. It was about 1941 when I started to write them, and things were pretty confused in my mind. I was twenty and was living in a town on the reef—the gold reef, about twelve miles out of Johannesburg—and it was a very secluded place. So I had a good deal of the natural setting around me; I wasn't living in a ghetto.

I was interested in people, in their own ghetto life and their own little dramas and tragedies, which would not necessarily have to do with the racial issue. That was my first entry into literature—my interest in people as people and not as political victims. It was when I became a teacher and came into contact with people and felt the political pressures around me that I began to wake up and became very sensitive to the political situation. Later, I wrote a number of things that I still have manuscripts of and which have never been published in book form. They appeared in *Drum* magazine, and in them I put the ghetto people aside, by themselves, acting out their dramas but at the same time implying the political pressure over them.

In the mid-fifties it was reported that you were working on a novel while in South Africa. What was this about, and what became of it?

It was really a novel that had been turning around in my mind which later became **Down Second Avenue.** I decided to chuck the novel altogether and simply write an autobiography. I did part of it in South Africa in

1956, did much of it in 1957. From about January to June I did about half of it and did the other half as soon as I got to Nigeria.

What was your method of composing **Down Second Avenue**? *I know you wrote it on the run. Did you go back and write the interludes later?*

No, I did the interludes at the same time. I would write about my people and the events they were caught up in, and then literally come to a stop and try to think about what these things were doing to me, and found I could not express it in the strict order of biography. So I decided on the method of the interlude.

Do you think that in **Down Second Avenue** *more attention is paid to the development of events than to people? For instance, though Dinku Dikae seems to be a hero, the focus is less on the character than on the event.*

Yes, I think you are right. Because I found myself involved in events, events stick out in my mind throughout the period I talk about in *Down Second Avenue.* And yet I wouldn't say people had escaped my attention even then because the people themselves were part of these events. This is what happens in ghetto life. When anything happens down a street it becomes a big event and it really becomes memorable. I never forget the fights; I never forget the police rushing down on horseback. These events really stick out in my mind, and the people I would be interested in were those very close to my life.

In **Down Second Avenue** *the chapter "Church Shillings" seems to be a rather crucial one, for you say you had come to feel that Christianity was an integral part of the system of oppression in South Africa. Do you still feel that way? Do you feel Christianity has a place in Africa today?*

When the black man tries to use Christianity for a political problem such as in southern Africa he finds it doesn't take him anywhere. It ends up in contentment and thoughts about the future world, not about the present. Even when people try to use it so that it has relevance they come to a dead end somewhere because it has a theology that does not necessarily fit in with the political tempo of any particular time. Those who have tried to use it have always failed because they were using an impossible tool on impossible terms—a tool that is not gcared for political resistance. The theology of the Christian world is against any kind of political overthrow or political agitation. It is the gospel of kindness, of humility, of nonviolence. It instills a sense of authority to the extreme extent that you do nothing about it. LeRoi Jones would argue that Islam is the other preference. I don't see that there is any choice between the two. When we have pushed all these foreign religions into the background or flushed them out of our minds, do you know what we are left with? We are left with ourselves to depend on—no props, no visions of the world to come, no guardian angels—only our naked selves with our ancestors to think of. Who are our ancestors? They are those who fell by the white man's

gun. Those are the ones we think of, and those are our moral props if we need any at all. When we have eventually divested ourselves completely of the Christian myth we will know we have won a battle.

Do you feel that there is a clear distinction between fiction and autobiography or that there is really just a continuum?

It's difficult to find a dividing line in one's mind between fiction and autobiography. All I can say is one's own experiences have a lot to do with any kind of fiction—much more to do than you probably would be aware of. It depends very much on one's attitude towards the people he meets at different times. It's unlikely that a man would create a character just out of the air. It would have to have a basis in fact and he might build up composite characters. He might even pick up one particular character that he knows very much about. As far as events are concerned, one has to invent a lot of them. I think one could say something is more autobiography than fiction and something is more fiction than autobiography, but the two are never completely separate in the novelist.

Where do you put **The Wanderers** *in that scheme?*

I would say *The Wanderers* is more fiction than autobiography. It has an autobiographical framework and it has real-life people in it, but it is still more fiction than autobiography. I plotted it that way—in the sense that I wanted to bring out the life of exile and put myself as the central character at different points. I then said to myself I want to find out in my own life what exile has led to. It has led to a disorientation in the children. It has led to a disorientation in my own self and it has led to discoveries in other territories and a realization of myself. Then I said I don't want to leave it as an open-ended thing in terms of a father-son relationship. Something has to happen to the son and that is a fictional plot. In that way I have a beginning and an ending, as distinct from *Down Second Avenue.* To that extent it is more fiction than autobiography.

Could one regard your work as a whole, including . . . **The Wanderers**, *as that of a journalist-novelist, in the sense that you're mostly relying on your own experience? In* **The Wanderers**, *for instance, the reporter is the main figure.*

I have relied very much on personal experiences, particularly after leaving South Africa, in the impressions I have of people and the countries I went to. I relied on my experience very much in the relationship between father and son in *The Wanderers;* although a great deal of it again is still fictionalized, much of the dialogue is what did take place. In my short stories I rely for the main dramatic incidents on news items I read in the newspapers and what other people recount as anecdotes. Literally not a single central event in my short stories is my own invention.

Was your experience working for the magazine Drum *in South Africa, then, more influential on your development than your reading of novels?*

No, my reading of novels did a lot—reading Dickens, reading Richard Wright, reading some of the short fiction by black Americans, reading Russian novels and short stories—much more than *Drum* because I hated that job. But what I did get out of the experience at *Drum* were things which I would not otherwise have seen—going into other ghettos besides my own and getting into political events and other situations as a political correspondent.

In a recent interview, you said that you saw no hope for a great literature emerging from South Africa in its present political state—either black or white literature. Do you think it's possible for writers to produce more mature or better works from a position outside? Are there crippling problems for the writer in exile, too?

That is something I really haven't made up my mind about. In both situations there are crippling factors, but those in exile are still less excruciating than those inside the country. In the country we are looking at life, as it were, through a keyhole; we see only that part which affects our lives directly. It would be almost impossible to write an all-inclusive novel, but at the same time, in exile you have this kind of spiritual, mental ghetto you live in. It's crippling in the sense that you just want a place to lay your eggs on and you don't find it easily. But you still have the freedom of vision which you would not have had in South Africa, and your experiences in exile have also contributed to your growth.

Does the writer in exile feel that he is getting out of touch with the situation back home?

I don't think that is important because the writer absorbs and accumulates experience in himself and he can go somewhere and make use of that experience because it is an experience which has left an imprint on his personality over a period. It is not something which can be cleaned out of his system. Being out of touch with the situation doesn't matter so much because you are aware of the historical events. You are aware of that so you don't need that physical closeness any more. In the beginning you thought you did. I've become thoroughly exasperated by the feeling that I was trying to reach out and then I felt I was quite at home. I didn't need that physical presence.

Most of your own work could be called protest writing. Though you write mainly in prose, do you feel that poetry should be protest poetry?

It seems to me a permanent human condition for poetry to be protest poetry of one kind or another. It will reflect a sense of urgency at one time which it doesn't at another time in history. There will always be people who will be writing poetry that does not have any kind of social relevance but is a kind of music box. It replays a human experience and that is that. But there will also be

poets who simply are committed to some ideal, whose poetry makes a frontal attack on social or political matters of one kind or another. Today, or say twenty years from now, it may not be the same kind of protest, but it will always be protest for the simple reason that whenever you write prose or poetry or drama you are writing a social criticism of one kind or another. If you don't, you are completely irrelevant—you don't count. (pp. 39-43)

Ezekiel Mphahlele and others, in an interview in Palaver: Interviews with Five African Writers in Texas, *edited by Bernth Lindfors and others, African and Afro-American Research Institute, The University of Texas at Austin, 1972, pp. 39-44.*

Samuel Omo Asein (essay date 1980)

[*In the following excerpt, Asein assesses Mphahlele's "humanism" and "universalist vision" as revealed in* Man Must Live *and* The Wanderers.]

There are a few African writers who have contributed much to the development of modern African literature and have had little written about them. Of the few, the black South African writer, Ezekiel Mphahlele, stands out rather pathetically as a much neglected, generally underestimated and often misjudged writer. (p. 38)

The reasons for the neglect which Mphahlele has suffered in the last decade seem obvious. I believe he is not 'popular', especially among the younger generation, because of his views, more often than not misinterpreted, on sensitive issues of race, inter-personal relationships and the destiny of the black man in the contemporary world. For well over thirty years, his integrationist attitudes as a person and as a writer have been progressively moulded into more definable shapes by a distinctly humanist vision which has its roots in Mphahlele's firm belief in the eternal value of a brotherhood that does not compromise man's essential humanity. It is that vision too which serves as the pivotal element in his artistic creations as well as the formative factor of his personality as an individual. Such indeed has been the close relationship between his two personalities as an artist and as individual that he could assert unequivocally the essential Mphahlele: "As for what I really am, and my place in the South African revolution, I shall let my writings speak for me." Mphahlele's writings do provide us with just that testimony. (p. 39)

When he wrote his earliest short stories which subsequently appeared in the collection **Man Must Live,** his one absorbing interest was in "people as people rather than as political victims," and he sought to focus on ordinary South African blacks and coloureds "in their own ghetto life and their own little dramas and tragedies." His style and perspective followed in the humanist tradition which his mentors [Richard Wright and Langston Hughes] represented. In the last few years, Mphahlele has become visibly absorbed in the quest for a new sociopolitical order which would accommodate his vision and whose very foundation would rest on what he defines as a "more genuine cross-cultural nationalism."

Thus in his short stories his first interest usually centres on the human condition which they help him to illustrate. In these stories there is more often than not an articulate statement of what constitutes the reality of that condition and how it has in turn moulded the quality of life and fortunes of his protagonists. His characters, even when they appear to us as escapists, evoke a sympathetic response from us because we are aware of the fact that they are mere victims of situations in which we ourselves could be trapped irrespective of our background and racial or cultural affiliations. (p. 42)

The details of [the] . . . stories in *Man Must Live* exemplify the major features of the early Mphahlele: a ponderous style and somewhat apolitical humanism which borders on escapism; but there is nevertheless a concentration of sensibility in his consuming interest in the predicament of the individuals who inhabit his fictional world. In his later stories Mphahlele provides further illuminations of that world through both direct and implicit commentaries on the socio-political background of events and experiences. The political implications of these events and experiences emerge from the stories without his having to force into our hands a political banner.

Even when Mphahlele presents situations that are obviously political in nature he constantly strives to draw from the experiences yet another illustration of the frustrations and indignities which the black man is subjected to in South Africa. Thus his attention shifts inevitably from the event as a socio-political phenomenon to the human condition which it is meant to illustrate. **"The Suitcase"** is one of such stories; so also is **"Dinner at Eight."** . . . (p. 44)

Nowhere in Mphahlele's writings is his universalist vision or his humanism better illustrated than in his absorbing novel, *The Wanderers,* in which he provides a fictional framework for his socio-political ideal of harmonious co-existence of the various racial groups in South Africa. (pp. 45-6)

The main story itself focuses on Timi who is the central character, his wife, Karabo, their son, Felang, and the intermingling relationship between the Timi household on the one hand and other characters drawn from the racial communities in South Africa. (p. 46)

The Wanderers begins with reflections on Felang's death and ends with an account of how he met his death. Between the glimpses of that enigmatic character we are led through several landscapes and we are made to share in the anxieties and ordeals of the characters whose consciousnesses centre around a single problem of existence under the shadow of apartheid. It is their communal search for self-realisation which universalizes the central experience in the novel. The final act of

commitment of Felang reflects Mphahlele's own modified views and his efforts to reconcile his humanist ideal with the socio-political imperatives of our time. (pp. 46-7)

Timi has completed the cycle of his growth. If we accept the reading that Timi is to a large extent a fictional projection of Mphahlele himself, it is easy to follow the pattern of his growth from the escapist and liberal humanist of his early writings through the period of vacillations trying to identify with a communal purpose to the pragmatist who, in seeking to reinforce the old foundations of his humanist ethos, now sees ultimate self-realisation in commitment to his land and the destiny of his people. This final resolution is evident in Mphahlele's almost mystical veneration of the harmony of a land and its people. To that extent his confessed longing for his lost homeland and his wish, in spite of the situation in South Africa, to return home and face death when it does come, is indicative of the same kind of attachment that he has sanctioned in the fictional world of *The Wanderers* . . . . (p. 47)

The question that does arise ultimately is: wherein lies the value of Mphahlele's humanism in the context of the South African situation and the contemporary experience in Africa as a whole? Where does Mphahlele stand in the on-going struggle in Southern Africa? He has directed us to his works for some of the answers, and our quest for those answers has yielded specific affirmatives. Mphahlele proposes an integrationist resolution, but it is a solution that must be based strictly on a firm guarantee of the humanity of the constituent groups in that society. (pp. 47-8)

[Mphahlele's] commitment is to the macrocosm; and the political realities in South Africa are a fragment of the totality of the human condition that is central to his thought. His vision encompasses a wider world and community of races. (p. 48)

A noticeable shortcoming of Mphahlele's formulations is the almost total neglect of a clearly defined strategy for realising the ideal framework, be it social, economic or political, within which his humanism will not be seen to be a mere intellectual indulgence. There can be no doubt that he believes in the value of his own vision of the South African reality and of the alternatives that his humanism has guided him to propose. This reservation notwithstanding, it is difficult to contest Mphahlele's claim to more serious attention in our study of African literature in the contemporary idiom. His significance is defined by the consistency of his thematic focus in his writings and utterances on the black-white issue, and as much by the complementarity of resonances both of his theories and of his practice as a writer. His persistent articulation of a humanist ideal which he sublimates from even the most overtly dated sketch cannot but be seen as a significant contribution to the heritage of ideas in contemporary African writing of which he is a distinguished pioneer. (pp. 48-9)

Samuel Omo Asein, "The Humanism of Ezekiel Mphahlele," in Journal of Commonwealth Literature, *Vol. XV, No. 1, August, 1980, pp. 38-49.*

Gerald Moore (essay date 1980)

[*Moore is the author of* Twelve African Writers *(1980). In the following excerpt from this work, he surveys Mphahlele's literary career. Moore's essay was originally published in a different form in his 1962 study* Seven African Writers.]

The advent of Ezekiel Mphahlele's first book, **Down Second Avenue** (1959), at the same moment that West African writing was beginning to assert itself, was a challenge to the understanding both of Western readers and of African readers themselves. There is hardly a single generalization which could be made about the predominantly peasant culture of West, East or Central Africa which would be equally applicable to the urban, industrialized Africa for which Mphahlele spoke. This Africa of vast segregated modern cities, mine-dumps, skyscrapers and jazz-clubs was as alien and remote to the Nigerian or Senegalese reader of that time as Dallas or Harlem might have been. But the challenge to South African understanding by the new West African writers was equally great, for there was an almost insuperable temptation for them to lump together the tropical cultures of Africa as 'backward' (and perhaps backward-looking), because of certain characteristics which they shared with the rural and tribal remnants of South Africa itself—remnants often dismissed as 'blanket-Africans' by the city-dweller.

In truth, the black man in urban South Africa had then more in common with the North American blacks than with his neighbours in tropical Africa. Like the black American, he inhabits a society which is dominated by whites in a far grimmer and more universal sense than any tropical colony has ever been. And this domination is expressed not merely in the colonial ritual and pantomime satirized during that same decade by Mongo Beti, Ferdinand Oyono and Chinua Achebe, but in every department of his daily life. His residence, his movements, his place and grade of work, his education, his sexual and family life are all subject to intense regulation, all governed by an alien mythology about the black man's place in the natural scheme of things. He cannot even walk down a street at certain hours without breaking the law. An outcast in his own country, he has to scrutinize every doorway, every bench, every counter, to make sure that he has segregated himself correctly. He is permanently on the run. (pp. 41-2)

Partly as a result of his very exclusion, partly as a result of the far greater urbanization and industrialization of the South, and partly as a result of the impoverishment of the overcrowded 'Homelands', the black South African is oriented more and more towards a way of life which hysterically denies him admittance. A member of the most educated, Westernized and (patchily) prosper-

ous black community in Africa, he asks only that he be accepted as such. No amount of official mystification about 'the Bantu' will induce him to look back to the tribe and the Bantustan as offering an adequate way of life. He is drawn irresistibly towards the cities, which need his labour but deny his civil existence. But in the cities he can exist only on sufferance and in circumstances which emphasize his helot status. (p. 42)

This is the supreme irony of the South African situation and the irony which, without specifically dwelling on it, Mphahlele makes manifest. His whole life has been an unrelenting struggle to achieve the way of life for which his urban upbringing and liberal education had prepared him. But to achieve that life, he had to become an exile. The logic of events drove him, through Nigeria, Paris, Kenya and Zambia to that urban black America whose similarity he had always recognized. But at the root of the dissatisfaction he felt for all these places lay a certain perverse nostalgia, and it must have been this very nostalgia which finally induced him to return to Vorster's South Africa. (p. 43)

Mphahlele was not yet fifteen when he suffered his first assault from a white constable. He learnt the full humiliation of his position as he cycled about the city, collecting the dirty washing of hostile and moody white customers. But somehow, at the sacrifice of any real life with her own children, his mother managed to save enough to put him through primary school. Though he rose daily at four to do the domestic chores or the washing round . . . he passed out in the first grade. So his mother strained an extra inch and sent him to St. Peter's Secondary School in Johannesburg.

Mphahlele's fierce prose evokes all the strain of those years of adolescence. Both structure and style in **Down Second Avenue** show the attempt to enlarge the normal limits of autobiography, so that the book will be both a record of events, more or less chronological, in the author's life, *and* an immediate, impressionistic evocation of certain typical moods and moments which don't belong at any special place within it, but must be allowed to spill their fear and anguish over the book as a whole. These are evoked in the sections called Interludes, which contain some of Mphahlele's most angry and electric writing in the book. The search for immediacy has muted the common tendency for the writer (especially the exile) to see even the painful events of youth and childhood through a certain softening haze. In the Interludes we actually hear the steely clang of police boots in the yard, the thunder of hard knuckles on the door at dawn, the sirens, the cries and the sickening blows which authority rains upon the unprotected. . . . (p. 46)

In 1957 [Mphahlele left South Africa] for Nigeria, where he was to teach until 1961. (p. 51)

It was during those four years in Nigeria that Mphahlele achieved his greatest period of fertility as a writer. **Down Second Avenue,** presumably completed by 1958, was published in the following year. In 1961 the newly established Mbari Publishing House in Nigeria brought out a volume of his short stories entitled *The Living and Dead.* (p. 52)

[*The Living and Dead* contains the majority of Mphahlele's] best work in fiction. When I first wrote of these seven stories, in the first edition of the present work, I formed a strong impression that the title story and **"He and the Cat"** must be considerably later in composition than the others, and must represent a movement towards [the]... 'reconciliation of protest and acceptance' for which he was striving. However, the researches of Professor Bernth Lindfors have made it clear that **"He and the Cat"** was published as early as 1953. It nevertheless stands out from the stories which surround it by reason of its economy of means and its introspective quality, as the narrator, obsessed with his own problems, focuses slowly and with difficulty on what is around him.

It is a deceptively simple story. The narrator goes to a lawyer's office to seek help with a problem that is consuming him. He takes his place in the waiting-room with about twenty others. The clients gossip in snatches, the clerk comes to summon them one by one. At a table a little apart sits a man sealing envelopes, with the picture of a black cat on the wall behind him. Gradually this withdrawn figure becomes more and more important, until he dominates the whole room, the whole mood of the scene.... (pp. 53-4)

Whatever the chronology of its composition, this story shows a technical assurance not always evident in the rest of the collection. Here Mphahlele is content to write directly out of experience, without looking for the conventional type of 'plot'. The narrator's egocentric obsession with his legal anxieties is gently displaced by his slow awareness of the quiet presence of another man, more completely locked within the dark walls of his own experience than the narrator can ever be.

Several other stories in the collection show characters who, whether black or white, are borne helplessly along in a stream of events which they cannot master or understand. They seldom act, and when they do, like Mzondi in **"We'll Have Dinner at Eight"** or Timi in **"The Suitcase"**, they act disastrously. In the first-mentioned story there is a somewhat inadequately prepared murder: Mzondi kills the sentimental white employer who has invited him to dinner, because he mistakenly believes that she is pumping him on behalf of the police. In the second, a desperate man steals a suitcase which a girl has left beside him in a bus. He is taken to a police station on suspicion of theft and is there found to be carrying a dead baby around with him. Although the story of **"The Suitcase"** is apparently based on an actual event, these plots are rather too obtrusive in the neat way events are unfolded, and the stories suffer from a thinness of fictional texture.

"The Master of Doornvlei", first published in 1957 and reprinted in the same collection, is a more substantial story. The incident with the bull and the stallion which finally brings about the confrontation between Mfukeri and his master is convincing and appropriate, for this kind of projected conflict is precisely what we expect to find between two men who have no love for each other but have been held together by a certain mutuality of interest. The story is made all the stronger by the fact that the old, black foreman is not in himself at all a sympathetic character, though he comes to stand in sympathetic opposition to the Boer farmer.

But the other outstanding story in this collection is **"The Living and Dead"**. Unlike most of Mphahlele's stories, this one is not unidirectional, and its greater length gives it that degree of amplitude which is almost essential to real achievement in this form. The structure is daringly unorthodox for a story of only a few thousand words. Mphahlele begins with the thoughts and experience of two apparently unconnected people on a day in urban South Africa. Lebona, a railway sweeper, has just seen a man pushed backwards down the train steps and trampled to death by the rush-hour crowd. He has also picked up a letter which he found lying on the track. Thoughts of the letter and the casually abrupt death of the unknown man obsess him. Meanwhile Stoffel Visser, a middle-class white resident, has just completed a report to the Government urging that 'kaffir' servants should all be moved out of the white areas into their own locations. His obsession, very different from Lebona's, is the fear that white civilization will be swamped in a rising sea of black labour. But because his own servant, Jackson, has not returned in time from leave, Stoffel has overslept and has failed to send the report in time to the responsible Minister. A man comes to the door with a letter addressed to Jackson, saying that he found it on the railway line. He spills out a confused story of seeing a poor man killed at the station. Stoffel lends him half an ear, while impatiently longing for his departure. A moment later, Jackson's wife Virginia appears on the doorstep which Lebona has just vacated. She knows nothing of Jackson's whereabouts and is highly agitated by his disappearance. Stoffel fails to hand her the letter. Instead, he dismisses her and reports matters to the police, after which he guiltily opens the letter himself. By this time the reader has concluded that the dead man at the station is probably Jackson, and this suspicion is reinforced when the letter proves to be a desperate summons to Jackson from his dying father in Vendaland. He sends his son some photographs of his family for safe keeping and begs him to come and look after the farm. But the strength of the story is that the dead man turns out not to be Jackson and remains as unknown at the end of the story as at its beginning. (pp. 54-6)

It would have been easy to make this story the preparation for a reforming of Stoffel Visser, the breaking of a new light into his bleak corridor of bigotry. Mphahlele's ending is truer and, as we come to see it, inevitable. This is how things happen in a society dominated by racial mythologies. And the way in which Mphahlele draws his apparently random, anonymous threads together into a significant pattern of unacknowledged human relationship, unaccepted human responsibility, shows an altogether new power in his imaginative resources. (p. 57)

Critics and scholars have theorized for some years about the dearth of full-length fiction from black South Africans; on the face of it, this dearth is the more surprising in that South Africa made an early start with the novels of Mofolo, Phatje, Dhlomo and others, in the first thirty years of the century. Since then the considerable achievements in poetry, short fiction and autobiography have not been matched by any novel of major scale. To insist that writers like Peter Abrahams and Alex LaGuma are 'coloured' rather than black may seem like participating in the racial obsessions of the authorities, but it remains true that the world of experience tapped in a work like La Guma's *A Walk in the Night* (which is in any case a short novel rather than a novel) is not the same as that revealed in the journalism and short stories of the black writers. To the voluntary segregation practised by most coloureds has been added the enforced segregation which puts them in different townships, different schools, different universities and a different range of jobs. Hence La Guma's work is centred upon the world he knows intimately, that of coloured slum-life in and around Cape Town. Although we may discern at a deep, unrealized level a phenomenon we can call 'South African literature', the absence of common experience, common education and common communication in a country so deeply and bitterly divided does force us to admit that a novel by a white, or Indian or coloured writer, however sensitive and perceptive, cannot be regarded as cancelling the expectations which attend upon a new black South African fiction.

It was into this atmosphere of expectancy that Mphahlele, certainly the best established black South African writer today, launched his novel *The Wanderers* in 1971. The first thing that must be said about this book is that it is simply not a novel. Rather, it is a thinly disguised autobiography, which extends the story of *Down Second Avenue* to cover the author's last couple of years in South Africa . . . and his subsequent wanderings in Africa and Europe. Comparison with the earlier book, however, can only damage *The Wanderers* as much as any insistence that it is a novel. As a novel it totally lacks shape and relevance; for the form of the novel demands rather more than an arbitrarily sawn-off section of the author's own experience. Incidents should be included only because they are important to the action, and not simply because they happened; events should be presented with some sense of their moral complexity, rather than in self-justification. The motive of self-justification is dangerously prominent in much of *The Wanderers* . . . .

The range of experience presented in this book has faced Mphahlele with real problems of style. The prose of *Down Second Avenue* was angry and often abrupt, but, unlike the writing of many of *Drum*'s contributors, it never struck a note of wishful Americanism or a

breathless striving for toughness of effect. Such a note does occasionally obtrude in *The Wanderers*. (pp. 59-60)

The Wanderers comes nearest to having a life of its own in the earlier chapters, and particularly in the section dealing with the author's visit to a Boer potato farm in the effort to trace a girl's missing husband, who has been sent there for forced labour by the police. This lacks the immediacy of the late Harry Nxumalo's celebrated *Drum* articles on the potato farms of Bethel, but Mphahlele's dialogue is at its most successful when he is rendering Bantu speech . . . . The effect of such reporting is to give a certain human weight to even the most simple speech. Mphahlele, however, appears to have no ear for the mannerisms or accentuation of educated black South African talk. Everyone in this reach of society 'talks like a book', and there is an unintended effect of condescension when such characters are confronted by Indian or coloured speakers, whose mannerisms Mphahlele seems much more anxious to observe. (pp. 61-2)

The weaknesses of *The Wanderers* show as much in these kinds of detail as in its overall lack of fictional organization and authorial 'distance'. The disappointment is the greater in that this is the mature work of a good writer, the writer who above all might be expected to produce a black South African novel of real substance and achievement. Stories like **"Mrs. Plum"** and **"The Living and Dead"** give us room to hope that Mphahlele will one day write a full-length work of fiction that displays a comparable power to organize and to project and develops more fully the style manifest in some of the short stories, now that the story of his wanderings has been told. (p. 63)

Mphahlele earns his place in this book because he is the most important black South African writer of the present age, by virtue of his all-round achievement and his lifelong commitment to literature. Others may have equalled or excelled him in autobiography, or in criticism, or in the short story. But Mphahlele's contributions in all three of these fields add up to a career of major distinction. If he cannot give us the great black South African novel which has been so long awaited, it seems probable that no one at present can. The fragmentation of creative achievement into the poems and short stories in which black South Africa has been so prolific must be seen as the obverse of those conditions which make major fiction so difficult of achievement there. The corpus of Mphahlele's work remains rich enough, however, in qualities of insight, compassion and intelligence. (pp. 65-6)

Gerald Moore, "Ezekiel Mphahlele: The Urban Outcast," in his Twelve African Writers, *Indiana University Press, 1980, Hutchinson, 1980, pp. 41-68.*

Ogunjimi 'Bayo (essay date 1985)

[*In the following essay, 'Bayo views Mphahlele as a forerunner in connecting South Africa's oppressive racial policies with its economy.*]

If Alex La Guma represents the psycho-social crisis of apartheid, Ezekiel Mphahlele, in **The Wanderers,** explores the economic facet of the system. Our study of Mphahlele also establishes the intimacy between literature and journalism in South Africa. More than in any other part of the continent, the development of the prose form is closely related to journalism. In South African literary development, journalism and literature are the victims of the pernicious censorship regulations. Makhudu Rammopo asserts that it was journalism (allied to the new nationalism) which, up to the thirties, played alone the important rôle of publicizing the black man's dilemma.

But the actual crisis of the profession is depicted by Kane-Berman:

> *Apart from the editor of* The World, *at least 18 black journalists spent periods in detention in 1976, 1977 and 1978. Most were on the staff of* The World *but other publications were also involved, among them* Drum, Post, *the* Rand Daily Mail, *the* Daily Dispatch, Muslim News, *the* Daily News, *the* Sunday Times *and* The Voice. *The Union of Black Journalists was one of the black consciousness organizations banned in October 1977 and its President, Joe Thloloe, spent more than a year in detention.*

There is thus the need to establish this critical and social reality in order to negate Nkosi's aesthetic view that "*what we do get from South Africa (. . .) is the journalistic fact parading outrageously as imaginative literature*". Literary aestheticism as far as that country is concerned is a dream for the future and fiction writers should devise possible plots and methods to combat apartheid. The journalistic approach is a medium for effective creative imagination in Mphahlele.

Thus, in **The Wanderers,** the social conscience embodied in the character of the journalist is dramatically involved in the search for Rampa, Naledi's husband. Mphahlele creatively employs his journalistic experiences to create his fictional form. The encounters of Timi Tabane are analogous to those of Mbeki, the journalist, involved in [Allen] Cook's research on prison-farms in South Africa. Although this was published in 1982, Mphahlele had earlier produced a testimony to the relationship between racism and labour economy in that country. Economy creates a force for the intensification of racism and racism becomes a complementary *sine qua non* for a capitalist-oriented economy. Whatever the economic factors that motivate apartheid, the 19th century theories of racism are actively at work. The politics of farm and prison labour and the economies of labour acquisition make Mphahlele's book vital in the sphere of ideology and racism. Researches by various bodies have authenticated the fact that the consolidation of a heinous and inhuman doctrine is more

prominent in the area of labour control and this forms the central link between apartheid and international monopoly capital. While South African novelists expose the gangrene of the system in relationship to the impoverishment of the oppressed, there is no deep exploration of the grotesqueness of racism in relationship to the economy of labour. Mphahlele exposes this hidden and unexplored facet of the culture of alienation and capitalism and his setting and theme are quite uncommon. This facet needs to be given a more coherent artistic expression in the African novel.

Many South African novelists describe the ordeal of their major characters from the point of view of the migrant labour force. When individuals move freely to the city, they are choked immediately as in the case of Xuma in Abraham's *Mine Boy* and Stephen Kumalo in Paton's *Cry The Beloved Country.* The Pass Law is the central core for legalizing illegality and the security, legal and judicial systems of that country. Novels from other regional settings describe the crisis of rural-urban contradictions but racism is absent.

• • • • •

Mphahlele exposes the various dysfunctional social patterns in the Republic by using the journey motif. Through this artistic medium, his reader encounters the various strands of apartheid culture and structure. The novel starts with Rampa's move to the city to seek employment. He is soon missing and Timi and Naledi are involved in looking for him. The symbolism in this ordeal is not far-fetched. Rampa is a socio-cultural and political phenomenon in the system; he is not an individual but the "*Everyman of his race*". In the novel, Timi plays the crucial rôle of beating the censorship laws and restrictions.

While capitalism organizes various strategies to exploit the working class, prison-farms have rarely existed in other regions of Africa, even during the colonial period. The Republic is a sort of client-State but has different degrees of economic independence and dependence. Cook describes the complex structure of racism and the economy and the link with international capitalist forces:

> *In 1953, the United Nations' International Labour Organization's Ad Hoc Committee on Forced Labour found that there existed in South Africa* 'a legislative system applied only to the indigenous population (. . .) to channel the bulk of the indigenous inhabitants into agricultural and manual work and thus create a permanent, abundant and cheap labour force' *and that in this sense* 'a system of forced labour of significance to the national economy appears to exist in the Union of South Africa'.

• • • • •

The "deruralization" process as depicted in **The Wanderers** is a cumulative move towards creating such a cheap labour force. The process paradoxically produces a form of ruralization based on racial segregation rather than on any viable political or economic development.

This social ostracism is represented by Glendale Farm. Forced labour (as described by the I.L.O. in 1953) is the basis of the Bantustan Programme aimed at making Africans a rootless "foreign" work-force, directed and manipulated through an all-embracing apparatus of influx control and labour bureaux.

Harriman has observed that Bantustanization is not only immoral but illogical since it can relegate over 18 million Africans to "*cocoons, living in destitution and poverty and (...) a state of perpetual deprivation*".

Such illegal settlements make it impossible for the working class to mobilize coherently as the nature of class structure becomes less rigid and defined. Thus, in **The Wanderers,** an attempt to organize a force to destabilize the Bantustanization scheme at Goshen Farm is thwarted because, as observed by the South African Council of Churches, "*the words 'Farm Labourer', stamped into a black man's pass, are the stamp of doom. He cannot change his job to that of an industrial worker and thus he starts a life-cycle of poverty and, often, ill-treatment*".

At the beginning of the novel, several Blacks have been forced on to trucks while "*white farmers raided labour bureaux and police stations to collect their human cargo for their farms*". Youths arrested for not being in possession of identity pass-books constitute the lion's share of this "human cargo". This is the outcome of the Bantu Education Act of 1945. In the words of the narrator: "*The white Government of South Africa has laid down that Negroes shall be taught only those things that would make them willing followers of the white man's instructions*". One can thus see that such a system provokes an ideological crisis since humanism is not coterminous with apartheid.

The mutilating hegemonic structures in South Africa are akin to the moral hollowness of Eliot's "wasteland". Timi's journey in search of Rampa is a study of a land corroded by power which is more directed to the sphere of psycho-social patterns in the process of hegemony reaffirmation:

> *It was a land corroded by power, power that one felt directly through its various tentacles. At the point and time one felt the clutch, or its menace; the limbs of power were right there holding Stenguns, driving tanks that spat fire to keep a riot under control. The limbs of power were right there, operating the instruments of torture in the prison cells. In town, in the townships, one felt the menacing presence.*

> *It was a land corroded by power. When you saw the outlying fields eroded, you knew that they had been abandoned because the young men had gone to the mines. When you saw the village people scratch the surface of the soil for a living, you knew this was so. When you saw the squatters near the cities, where the black people lived, you knew the claws of power were right here (...) But power is an image in the mind. You need to feel, taste, smell it at the point at which you are subject to its control. You need to be face to face with the man who possesses it, personifies it.*

The topography is the subject of a pathological study. The physical beauty of the land hides the corrosiveness which leads to the anarchy of the soul, spirit and mind. To Dennis Brutus, it is a land scarred by terror, "*rendered unlovely and unlovable*". Like their fellow-poets, South African novelists evoke an image of "miles of arid earth" which illuminates comprehensively the complexity of apartheid.

Mphahlele exposes the violence existing in Glendale Farm. Makatona, the monstrous bully, has the various characteristics of inhumanity that Cook attributes to farm-owners who employ forced labour. The evidence that comes to light during Timi's search provides an incontrovertible proof of this. Their diabolical actions include sadistic assaults, murder, arson and partial mutilation of their labourers. Children are also involved in this emasculation.

As in La Guma's novels, the cycle of aggression is visible. Though the victims of Glendale Farm occasionally answer back with the language of violence, this is not strong enough to liberate them but Timi's journey is symbolic as an ideological action to rescue the oppressed. On the other hand, oppression boomerangs as usual. The farmers and their victims are psycho-pathological specimens as witnessed by the brutalization of Makotona, the guards and overseers.

● ● ● ● ●

The bestiality as described by Mphahlele is not an isolated phenomenon: it is a part of the policy to grease the wheels of the apartheid system. Cook contends that "*not only do farmers have little to fear from the police and the machinery of South African justice; they sometimes harness this machinery to carry out assaults and torture on their behalf*". Thus the rationalization and protestations of the Government that labour farms are ways of decongesting the prisons are irrelevant cogitations.

Despite the fact that mankind has advanced in the spheres of socio-economic and political development, little has been achieved in terms of moral obligation and spiritual relationships. This facet is more predominant in apartheid literature and that of the Caribbean and America which develops into the ideology of liberalism. Nkosi assesses the relevance or otherwise of the latter in South African fiction:

> *Among white authors, those denounced most frequently—Gordimer, Paton, Jacobson, Breytenbach—are also the ones who remind the white public more frequently of the many things to which the white public has closed its mind. It is for this reason that, despite a massive propaganda campaign which proclaims them to be new leaders of the South African avant-garde, the group of Afrikaans writers known as the* Sestigers *have remained, on the whole, curiously irrelevant, even faintly comic.*

Liberalism collapses into the politics of racism that gives birth to it. Jacobson, in *A Dance In the Sun,* fails to articulate creatively his dream of harmonious existence.

Paton can only produce a picture of an emasculated protagonist. In **The Wanderers,** the characterization of Steve Cartwright shows that the crisis of liberalism is like the abortion of culture, giving birth to generic miscegenation and possibly the miscegenation of thought. Liberalism as evidenced in Cartwright produces the psychology of class and status differentiation. The love between him and Naledi is more Platonic than passionate or humanistic. It is an aborted love that does not enhance the mind and society at large—spiritually or morally. The love between Ignatius Louw and Joseph's sister in *A Dance In the Sun* is meant to satisfy the sexual lust of the former. To the latter, it is the power of the master over his servant. The relationship between Naledi and Cartwright cannot be more successful than this. Initially, she denies his advances by arguing: *"You're a white man, Mr. Cartwright, I am a country girl"*. Thus the Immorality Act can only produce the psychology of "apart-hood".

Apartheid is a doctrinal offshoot of Gobineau and Grant's race theories that abhor miscegenation but, in South Africa today, such a theory is unrealistic. As far back as 1941, Dhlomo foresaw the possibility of racial discrimination being discredited and eliminated by an increase in sexual relations between Blacks and Whites (and a consequent breakdown of social sanctions) or the sheer increase in the number of Mulattos who would naturally blur racial lines. However, it is undeniable that liberalism borrows from 19th century intellectualism. The shadow that bourgeois ideology casts on liberalism is represented in the antagonistic personality of Cartwright himself. His confessions testify that liberalism is a dangerous heresy:

> Several times I've tried to dissociate myself from it all
> (...) Sometimes I say to myself, 'Steve Cartwright,
> you're white; you live in a segregated white area, you
> eat, sleep, breathe and mate white, you're privileged,
> you're doomed with the rest of your race'. At other
> times I've said to myself, 'What the hell! I'm not
> responsible for the sins of my fathers and of my tribe;
> why should Steve Cartwright be made responsible for
> the wickedness unleashed by a government of white
> thugs, of Nazi-headed hoodlums who hate Blacks,
> Indians, Jews and Mulattos? And what are you doing
> about it, Steven Cartwright?'.

Mphahlele writes on the meaninglessness of liberalism as an ideology of development and co-operation:

> Moderate; liberal. Bad words in a situation of conflict.
> In any situation that requires less than militancy to
> redress wrongs done to any section of a people. To be a
> liberal you have to be white. Which is why liberals in
> South Africa, both as an informal group and later as a
> political party (now defunct), looked ridiculous when
> they canvassed African support and membership. A
> black liberal is a kind of chimera.

To Ngugi (like Mphahlele), liberalism is a moderating force against a revolutionary ideology. Of course, liberalism is assuming the posture of "a scapegoat" for its inability to achieve its objectives.

● ● ● ● ●

The last section of **The Wanderers** explores the themes of exile, neo-colonialism and the general crisis of an ideologue like Timi Tabare. The end of the road for the South African artist is inevitably exile in all its ramifications. Physical exile is undertaken by Timi and there is a regional shift in the movement of the plot to a West African country called "Iboyoru" (this is identified in Mphahlele's autobiography, **Down Second Avenue,** as Nigeria).

Initially, Timi feels a sense of relief where an abundance of freedom, rather than tyranny, prevails but exile seems to be no consolation. In Iboyoru, his psychological crisis is replaced by a new form of anguish provoked by the chaos of both the social and physical milieu of the country: *"alienation, aloneness, nostalgia, the longing to be back in fire, just so long as he would be suffering along with others of his kind."* Exile means moving from *"preventive detention to preventive detention"*. The ideologue's sense of commitment throws him into a nostalgic panic and the aberration of the social environment makes him perceive power as a universal gadget of oppression.

The novelist's South African environment produces an aggressive psychology in his characters. The historical developments and militant psychology that culminated in a massive genocidal onslaught during the Soweto upheavals, the incarceration of nationalists like Mandela and Steve Biko, the crisis of exile that confronts the artist, are all imperatives to choose between the culture of slavery and revolutionary commitment. Our case-study is Felang, Timi's son, who, in exile, is just fifteen. He is undoubtedly reflecting on his South African background when he develops hostility against the Whites in Iboyoru.

He should therefore be dealt with as a social phenomenon, a symbolism for the children weighed down by the wrath of apartheid. Bishop Desmond Tutu once observed that

> (...) young children learn hatred and bitterness when
> they sit at night and listen to their mothers telling
> about the indignities they suffered during the day
> because they are black.

Felang's assertive psychology radiates from the frustration-aggression hypothesis. The "latent revolt" emerging in him is psycho-pathological:

> When he was four, Felang would stand and look at the
> long line of men and teenagers being led to the police
> station. 'Ntate, why are all those men arrested?'.
> 'Because they don't have passes', his father would
> reply.
> 'What is a pass?'.
> 'You'll understand when you're bigger. Just now, only
> understand that the police are people we don't like.
> We spit when we see them. Let me see you spit!'.

On moving to Lao-Kiku in East Africa, Felang's aggressiveness grows stronger and he runs away to join the freedom fighters. He is killed in action and his death reveals the infanticide committed against children forced by the system to defend themselves. Mphahlele uses Felang as an indirect example of the anti-apartheid campaign in exile and Dennis Brutus, in *A Simple Lust*, sees this as a strategic rôle for the exiled artist.

Towards the end of the novel, Mphahlele seems to value more the essence of the budding generation in the revolutionary struggle. For him, educational mobilization is vital. At a philosophical level, he endeavours to inculcate in the children a more logical perception of the Universe. In a series of rhetorical questions, he sets an ideological goal for his own and the budding generation:

> *How can I do more than launch the children upon the route to self-discovery? Different times make, and demand, different heroes. How can I make my children understand we have all wandered away from something—all of us Blacks? That we are not in close contact with the spirit of Nature, although we may be with its forces, that growing up for us is no more that integrated process it was for our forebears, but that this is also a universal problem? (. . .) How can I make these children understand that the cruelty of the times demands that I recognize the limitations of my traditional humanism, that, if the white world reminds me that I'm black, I must reserve my humanism for those of my colour and fight power with the instruments of its enthronement? How can they understand that the basic truths I'm teaching them only amount to a state of mind that becomes of little immediate import in the face of economic and political power?*

• • • • •

Mphahlele's humanism is his ideology but while that humanism pragmatically embraces all the living forces in Nature and his race, it does not represent the prodigality of Négritude. Apparently referring to the coiner of the word (Aimé Césaire), he warns: "*Sing and dance and laugh but don't tell me you're proud of having invented nothing*". As reflected in this novel and other writings, his humanism and ideology have a dialectical formation. (pp. 120-28)

Ogunjimi 'Bayo, "Mphahlele: The Aesthetics and Ideology of Alienation," in Présence Africaine, *No. 135, third quarter 1985, pp. 120-28.*

FURTHER READING

Albert, Richard N. Review of *Renewal Time*, by Es'kia Mphahlele. *Small Press* 7, No. 3 (June 1989): 40.
> Maintains that *Renewal Time* is "required reading for those who would better understand what living under apartheid is like."

French, Howard W. Review of *Renewal Time*, by Es'kia Mphahlele. *The New York Times Book Review* (30 April 1989): 38.
> Praises *Renewal Time*, commenting: "Mr. Mphahlele collects haunting scenes from [his] childhood, steeps them in the alienation of his lengthy exile, which lasted from 1957 to 1977, and illustrates the bitter estrangement upon his return."

Jarrett-Kerr, Martin. "Exile, Alienation and Literature: The Case of E'skia Mphahlele." *Africa Today* 33, No. 1 (First Quarter 1986): 27-35.
> Explores Mphahlele's exile and its manifestation in his works.

Obuke, Okpurc O. "South African History, Politics and Literature: Mphahlele's *Down Second Avenue,* and Rive's *Emergency.*" *African Literature Today: Retrospect and Prospect* 10 (1979): 191-201.
> Compares *Down Second Avenue* with Richard Rive's *Emergency*, two autobiographies that, while not fiction, contain carefully selected incidents that reflect a specific "purpose."

S. E. K. Mqhayi

1875-1945

(Full name Samuel Edward Krune Mqhayi) South African poet, biographer, novelist, short story writer, lyricist, autobiographer, and translator.

Mqhayi is recognized as a leading Xhosa-language poet and prose writer. He is remembered primarily for his *izibongo,* traditional African lyric poems that gained him the title *imbongi yesizwe,* equivalent to poet laureate of his people. Hailed by Albert S. Gérard as "perhaps the last of the great tribal bards" for his contributions to Xhosa poetry, Mqhayi is also credited with introducing the Western genre of prose fiction into Xhosa literature in the early twentieth century. According to R. H. W. Shepherd: "His contributions to Xhosa literature...were outstanding in quality, and by them and in other ways he helped in no small measure to stabilize and purify the Xhosa language."

Mqhayi was born in Gqumahashe (or Gqamahashe) in the Victoria East District of Cape Province. He attended school in Evergreen from 1882 to 1885, when his family moved to Centane in the Transkei, where Mqhayi's great-uncle Ngonzana (or Nzazana) was a local chieftain. Mqhayi took great interest in the official activities he witnessed at his uncle's judicial court, the "Great Place," and later wrote: "I thank my father for taking me to Centane, for it was the means of my getting an insight into the national life of my people." After completing a teaching course, Mqhayi worked as an educator and journalist for several years. During that time he contributed to influential Xhosa newspapers and periodicals, including *Izwi labantu* and *Iimvo zabantsundu,* which he edited from 1920 to 1922. He retired from education in 1922 to assist in programs designed to standardize Xhosa grammar and syntax and the Xhosa-language Bible. In 1925 Mqhayi settled near King William's Town in a hilltop retreat named Ntab'ozuko, or "Mount of Glory." From there he traveled widely among the Xhosa-speaking peoples, who acknowledged him as the "poet of the race." He died in 1945.

One of Mqhayi's earliest prose works, the novel *U-Samson* (1907), presents an adaptation of the biblical story of Samson, imaginatively rendered to critique South African society in the era following the Anglo-Boer War. However, another biblically inspired work, the novella *Ityala lamawele* (1914), has received considerably more critical attention. Published in 1914, though written several years earlier, *Ityala lamawele* is based on the biblical story of Tamar's sons in Genesis 38:27-29 as well as on Mqhayi's memories of Ngonzana's law court at the "Great Place" in Centane. The novella relates the tale of twins whose dispute over their birth order—and thus, inheritance rights—is decided through the native justice system. According to Gérard,

"it was Mqhayi's aim [in *Ityala lamawele*] to vindicate traditional native justice threatened by the colonial administration." Another major prose work is the utopian novel *U-Don Jadu* (1929), which describes a culturally and racially integrated Christian society in twentieth-century South Africa that combines the best of European and African cultures.

While Mqhayi's prose works are highly regarded by critics, it is as a poet that he is chiefly remembered. Working in the oral tradition of tribal court bards, he composed many *izibongo,* traditional praise poems that proclaim the accomplishments of chiefs and other public figures, celebrate cultural holidays, or comment on current events. These poems are not purely laudatory; A. C. Jordan has explained that tribal bards "had not only to praise the chief but also to criticize him." Mqhayi has been noted for treating modern themes in this ancient traditional form: some of his *izibongo* discuss British colonialism in Africa, and several are addressed to British royalty and administrators, albeit often ironically. Late in his career, Mqhayi experimented with European forms unfamiliar in Xhosa poetry, such as the sonnet and the heroic couplet, but most critics have expressed disappointment with these attempts to force Xhosa into foreign forms, especially noting the flatness of his rhymes. Most critics concur with Wandile Kuse that "Mqhayi was at his best when he wrote or recited poetry in the oral tradition."

While a lack of translations has hampered Mqhayi's international reputation, his work is beloved and renowned among Xhosa-speaking peoples and has received high praise from other South African writers. Jordan attested to Mqhayi's literary achievement when, in an obituary tribute, he wrote: "Mqhayi takes the highest place in Xhosa literature. He has done more than any other writer to enrich Xhosa. In his hands it receives a fresh impress, and he has revealed all its possibilities as a powerful medium of expression of human emotion."

(For further information about Mqhayi's life and works, see *Twentieth-Century Literary Criticism,* Vol. 25.)

PRINCIPAL WORKS

U-Samson (novel) 1907
Ityala lamawele (novella and short stories) 1914; also published as *Ityala lamawele* [enlarged edition] (novella, short stories, and poetry) 1931
U-Sogqumahashe (biography) 1921
I-Bandla laBantu (poetry) 1923
U-bomi bom-fundisi uJohn Knox Bokwe (biography) 1925
Isikumbuzo zomPolofiti u-Ntsikana (biography) 1926

Imihobe nemibongo yokufundwa ezikolweni (poetry)
    1927
*"Nkosi sikelel' iAfrika" (lyric) 1927; published in
    journal *Umteteli waBantu*
U-Don Jadu (novel) 1929
U-Mhlekazi u-Hintsa (poetry) 1937
U-Mqhayi wase-Ntab'ozuko (autobiography) 1939
I-nzuzo (poetry) 1943
Mqhayi in Translation (abridged autobiography and
    novel) 1976

*Comprises seven stanzas of the African National Anthem.
    The first stanza was composed earlier by Enoch Sontonga.

A. C. Jordan (essay date 1945)

[*Jordan is a South African novelist, short story writer,
educator, and critic. His novel* Inggoumbo yeminyanya *(1940) is considered a classic of Xhosa literature. In
the following excerpt from a memorial tribute written
soon after Mqhayi's death, he discusses* Ityala lamawele, U-Don Jadu, *and Mqhayi's poetry.*]

Mqhayi was born on the banks of the Tyhume on the 1st
of December, 1875. He attended school at Evergreen, in
the Tyhume Valley, at the age of seven. During the three
years at this school he met three of the men who were
destined to influence his whole life and career. These
were the Rev. E. Makhiwane, the Rev. P.J. Mzimba and
Mr. J. Tengo Jabavu. In 1885 he accompanied his father
to his new home in Centane (Kentani) and remained
there for six years. Then he came to attend school at
Lovedale where he received some training as a teacher
before he went into the world. His literary career began
in East London, when, with the encouragement of Dr.
Rubusana, and Messrs N. C. Mhala, A. K. Soga, and G.
Tyhamzashe—all of them distinguished leaders of the
time—he began to contribute *izibongo* (praise poems)
and historical information to the periodical *IZwi labaN-
tu* (The Voice of the Bantu). Later on he became sub-
editor of this paper, but circumstances compelled him to
return to teaching, and for many years he served as a
teacher among the Ndlambe people. Then he became
editor of the *IimVo zabaNtsundu,* but even this he had
to give up after some time and go back to teaching. This
time he was offered a post at his *Alma Mater,* Lovedale,
but during the few years in the world Mqhayi's views on
South African history and how it should be taught in
African Schools had undergone such modification that
he found himself compelled either to be false to his own
convictions and teach history as the authorities would
have him teach it, or to give up teaching altogether. He
decided on the latter. On leaving Lovedale he went to
make his home on the "summit" of Ntab'ozuko—a
Mount Helicon whence he descended in his impressive
kaross on great tribal or state occasions to sing the
praises of important personalities. (pp. 105-06)

We owe a great deal to the six years in Centane. For it
was during this time that Mqhayi began to understand
the culture and history of his people. It was there that he
saw *imidudo, iintlombe, intonjane, imiyeyezelo, amadi-
ni,* etc. As he relates, he used to sit spell-bound, listening
to *inkundla* orations. It was there that he first listened to
izibongo and himself began to "lisp in numbers,"
praising favourite oxen, other boys or himself. It was
there that he began to appreciate the beauty, dignity and
subtleties of Xhosa, and to acquire the amazingly wide
vocabulary that even Tiyo Soga would have envied. (p.
106)

Because [Mqhayi] was nurtured in Christian culture and
in the primitive culture of his own people at the same
time, Christianity was for him not an "escape from the
City of Destruction," but a mode of life abundant that
was not irreconcilable with his native culture. Small
wonder then that Tiyo Soga's translation of *The Pilgrim's Progress* should have had such an appeal for him
that at the age of thirteen he was able to recite its first
chapter with such feeling and expression that many who
listened to him at an elocution competition at the
Station School at Lovedale feared that "much learning
hath made him truly mad."

To discuss all his writings is impossible. We shall
therefore refer to his masterpiece, *ITyala lamaWele,* to
his prose work *UDon Jadu,* and lastly to his poetry in
general. *ITyala lamaWele* includes fiction, history and
poetry. The book owes its title to the novelette that
covers its first half—the lawsuit of the twins. The plot of
this novelette is suggested by Verses 28-29 of the 38th
Chapter of the Book of Genesis. As the author states in
the preface, the purpose of the story is to give a picture
of legal procedure among the Xhosa people, and to show
the democratic spirit in which it is carried out. A civil
dispute has arisen between Babini and Wele, twin-sons
of Vuyisile, born under circumstances similar to those
described in Genesis, Chapter 38. Having lived at a
headman's kraal for six years as a boy in Centane,
Mqhayi is conversant with legal procedure. The stating
of the case by the plaintiff, his cross-questioning by the
councillors, the calling-in of witnesses, the *hlonipha*
language used by the mid-wives in submitting evidence,
the declamation of the bard at the end of each session,
the reaction of the men to *izibongo,* the unassuming
manner of the sage Khulile as he makes an exposition of
the principles underlying the law of primogeniture, the
pronouncement of the verdict and Chief Hintsa's sympathy with the senior twin in pronouncing it, the
humble but dignified manner in which Babini receives
the verdict given against him—all these give a beautiful
picture of social life among the Xhosa during the reign
of Hintsa. It is these and the beauty and dignity of the
language that give this novelette its fascinating power
and such a high place in Xhosa Literature. Mqhayi is
not a great creator of individual character. Hardly any
character stands out in this story, and consequently the
impression left in the reader's mind is the collective
dignity and refinement of the chief and his subjects.

In the latter half of the book, fiction and fictitious characters disappear, and we have true history. The "death" of Khulile synchronizes with the arrival of the Fingos from the east and of the news of a white race coming "from the sea." The relations between the Xhosa and these new-comers, the diplomacy exercised by the White men in driving a wedge between the Xhosa and the Fingos on the one hand and between the two rival sections of the Xhosa on the other, the mutual jealousies and the bitter rivalry that broke the unity of the Xhosa and contributed towards their downfall—all these are related with commendable restraint by Mqhayi. In beautiful style he traces the fortunes of the Xhosa people beyond the "emancipation" of the Fingos, beyond the death of Hintsa, beyond Sarili's exile, beyond Maqoma and Sir Harry Smith, right up to the acceptance of the new loyalties and to the disaster of the *Mendi,* by which time the subject is no longer the Xhosa alone, but the Bantu of South Africa in general. The book closes with short biographies of the new leaders of the "reaction to conquest." An interesting feature is the bard's own development. The poetry in this book punctuates the prose, each piece being appropriate to the incident under consideration. In the lawsuit as well as in the early chapters of the history, the versification, in keeping with the theme, is in the style of the traditional *izibongo,* but with the acceptance of the new loyalties by his people towards the close of the book, the bard himself begins to experiment in modern versification. Therefore, to be fully appreciated, *ITyala lamaW-ele,* though partly fact and partly fiction, partly verse and partly prose, must be viewed as a whole. Then it has the effect of a great epic drama in which the bard, like a Greek Chorus, comments upon, or predicts, the fortunes of his people.

Next to *ITyala lamaWele,* Mqhayi's most important prose work is *UDon Jadu.* Through the influence and guidance of Don Jadu, a highly educated African, the *amaRanuga* (detribalized Africans) of the Eastern Province acquire land of about the area of the Transkeian Territories. All kinds of industry begin to spring up in this new province of Mnandi (Sweetness). As a result, in a few years the population is double that of the Transkei. The Union Government becomes interested, and vote large sums of money to promote the scheme. Self-government is granted to the people of Mnandi and, the Union Government having disappeared from the scene, Great Britain assumes guardianship. Don Jadu is the first president.

There is neither racialism nor isolationism in Mnandi. Immigration is encouraged, and experts of all races and shades of colour come from the four corners of the earth to make a permanent home there. There is full social, economic and political equality. According to the constitution, women are free to go into parliament, but the sensible women of Mnandi decline this offer on the grounds that there is enough work for them to do at their homes! Mnandi is a Christian state, and Christ is the "President" of the Ancestral Spirits. Ministers of religion are officers of state, and their stipends come from the general revenue. Magistrates and ministers of religion work in close co-operation. In fact, Church and State are so closely knit together that there is no distinction between the police and deacons' courts. Education is compulsory. Xhosa is the first language, but English is such an important second language that no one who is not strictly bilingual may hold an office of state. Baby boys are baptized and circumcised in the Temple eight days after birth, and Holy Confirmation forms part of an initiation ceremony held in the Temple between the ages of fifteen and twenty. All these ceremonies are supervised by the magistrate and the minister of religion together. The marriage ceremony is conducted by the magistrate and subsequently blessed by the minister of religion. Divorce is prohibited by law. The importation or sale of liquor is prohibited by law. Home-brewing is allowed, but anyone found drunk in public places is locked up in a lunatic asylum, dressed in the uniform of the asylum and is for seven days subjected to the same treatment as the legitimate inmates of that institution. People who are sentenced to penal servitude receive wages for their labour. There are no prisons.

UDon Jadu makes very interesting and thought-provoking reading. It is true that in constructing a "bridge" between our present South Africa and his Utopia, the author idealizes away a few hard facts, but—

> its soul is right,
> He means right,—that, a child may understand.

If we turn to his poetry, we find that Mqhayi, though perhaps possessing more talent, is nevertheless more limited in scope, than some of the younger Nguni poets. Essentially a poet of the traditional type, for theme he is almost wholly confined to concrete subjects, usually human beings. He is confined to lyrical verse, chiefly odes and elegies. Even historical themes he was never able to put into narrative verse. If he had been able to write narrative poetry, we can almost be sure that the poem entitled "UmHlekazi uHintsa," instead of consisting of eight cantos disappointingly lacking in unity, should have been an epic. Again, it is a pity that in his later writings he decided to break entirely with the diction and artistic formlessness of *izibongo* in favour of modern versification. With his limited knowledge of prosody it was only natural that he should not be able to go much further than discover rhyme—of all the artificial ornaments of Western versification the most obvious, and yet to Bantu the least desirable. A sense of effort and strain is always with us when we read his rhymed verse, and very often we feel that in order to observe rhyme, the poet has sacrificed sense, virility and easy flow of language. His favourite rhyme scheme is the heroic couplet, and because he invariably writes end-stopped lines, his rhymed verse makes dull and monotonous reading.

But if we judge Mqhayi by what he has achieved instead of judging him by what he has failed to achieve, then there is no doubt that his best poetry is of a high order.

To understand him, let us remind ourselves that one of the essential qualities of *ubumbongi* was true patriotism, not blind loyalty to the person of the chief, but loyalty to the principles that the chieftainship does or ought to stand for. On public occasions *imbongi* had not only to praise the chief but also to criticise him by means of those epithets and metaphors that make such an interesting characteristic of *izibongo*. Obviously then only a man who took genuine interest in the social welfare of his people can be *imbongi*. Mqhayi possessed this quality, hence his being known as *ImBongi yesiZwe Jikelele,* which title was conferred upon him by a Zulu in Johannesburg. But Mqhayi had a double loyalty. As a Xhosa he was loyal to the Xhosa chiefs and their ancestors, and as a British subject he had to be loyal to the British king. A poem written during the Boer War in the *IZwi labaNtu* of March 13th, 1900, shows how very sincerely Mqhayi had accepted British guardianship. Each stanza has a refrain, *"SingamaBritani!"* (We are Britons!). Nurtured in Christianity and in the policy of the "Old Cape Liberals," he believed that the conquest of Southern Africa by the British was the working out of a Divine Purpose. After the defeat in 1879, he makes the Zulus say in the poem **"ISandlwana":**

> *Wozani, maBritani, sigezan'izingozi;*
> (Come, ye Britons, let's bathe one another's
>   wounds!)

Then the Zulus go on to tell the British that their own defeat was the working out of God's purpose, so that from the British, the Zulus might receive a new life, a new birth, a new learning, and see the Love of the Son of the Great-Great, and fight His battles.

But the Act of Union drove the "Old Cape Liberals" to the background, and representations to Britain did not receive the usual kind of reception. Britain was forgetting that she had "children" in Africa. So the poem written in praise of the Native Labour Contingency of 1916, **"umKhosi wemiDaka,"** opens with the significant lines:

> Awu! Ewe, kambe, siyabulela,
> Lakuth'ikokwethu lisicinge,
> . . . . . .
> Ngexesha lalo lokuxakeka.

> (O yes! We must feel honoured, I suppose, that
> our father has remembered us in his time of
> need.)

But Mqhayi has not quite lost faith in the British connection. In the elegy written on the disaster of the *Mendi,* though bemoaning the loss of the flower of Africa, he reminds his people that some such worthy sacrifice had to be made if they truly loved Britain; he reminds them how God sacrificed His own Son, the Messiah. Again the working-out of a Divine Purpose! If the ties with Britain are not to break, as they threaten to do, this sacrifice must be.

> Ngoko ke So-Tase! kwaqal' ukulunga!

> Le nqanaw' uMendi namhlanje yendisile,
> Naal' igazi lethu lisikhonzile.

The last word in the second line, *yendisile,* is very eloquent. *Ukwendisa* is to give one's daughter in marriage, and those who know the mutual obligations between the families involved in a marriage-contract as Mqhayi understands marriage, will understand how strong should have been the ties, according to him, between Britain and the Africans after the disaster of the *Mendi.* But the Victorian Days were gone, never to return, and, if anything, Post-Union South Africa was threatening to undo all the good that Mqhayi had seen in the Victorian Policy. It is therefore in true *imbongi* spirit, and as a patriot praising and criticising a chief in public, that in praising the Prince of Wales in 1925, Mqhayi, after a succession of metaphors and similes, in which he likens the prince to all the mighty fabulous animals of Bantu Folklore, should utter words which may be translated as follows:

> Ah, Britain! Great Britain!
> Great Britain of the endless sunshine!
> . . . .
> You gave us Truth: denied us Truth.
> You gave us *ubuntu:* denied us *ubuntu;*
> You gave us light: we live in darkness;
> Benighted at noon-day, we grope in the dark.

Mqhayi has written several religious poems, on Christmas, on the Gospel, and on kindred subjects. Perhaps the best illustration of his deep-seated religion is to be found in the closing lines of a poem entitled **"In Taba kaNdoda,"** written in praise of a little mountain peak near King William's Town. A poem of forty lines, it closes as follows:

> Would that I had tongues, O Mount of my home
> O footstool of the God of my fathers,
> Thou, whose brow, facing the setting-sun,
> Is smitten by the rays of the closing day.
> So would I, protected, sing thy praise;
> So would I, forsaken, fly to thee,
> And kneel in humble prayer by thee,
> Who art the stepping-stone between me and my
>   God.
> Still shall the aliens stare not understanding,
> While, praying, on this slope I build a ladder,
> And scale the vast fatiguing heights, to kiss
> The Feet of God the Father—Creator, Most High.

"Nature for Nature's sake" hardly has a place in *izibongo* of the old type, and Mqhayi's nature poems are on the whole disappointing. But this does not mean that he was blind to the beauties of nature. Scattered here and there are couplets that reveal not only his sensitiveness to the beauties of nature, but also his genius for the "precious word":

> Imizi yalo mlambo niyayibona na
> *Ukutyityimba* yakombelelwa yingxangxasi!
> (Lo, how the rushes on the waterside
> Thrill to the music of the cataract!)
> Kunqanqaza oonogqaza emathafeni,
> *Kukhenkceza* iinyenzane equndeni.
> (Grass-warblers clinking in the fields,

Cicadas shrilling in the meads)
Ndee *ntshoo-o!* ntshobololo-o-o!
Ndaxel' inkwenkwez' ingen' elifini.
(Sliding away, sliding away I go,
Like a meteor swimming into a cloud.)

If this article has shown that Mqhayi was the soul of his people, and that to understand him is to understand their hopes and aspirations, then it will have served its purpose. Mqhayi takes the highest place in Xhosa literature. He has done more than any other writer to enrich Xhosa. In his hands it receives a fresh impress, and he has revealed all its possibilities as a powerful medium of expression of human emotion. His prose as well as his poetry contains expressions that became proverbial long before his death. If much of his verse will soon be forgotten, and for many generations to come, his prose style will remain something for younger writers to emulate. (pp. 107-16)

> A. C. Jordan, "Appendix: Samuel Edward Krune Mqhayi," in his Towards an African Literature: The Emergence of Literary Form in Xhosa, *University of California Press, 1973, pp. 103-16.*

Albert S. Gérard (essay date 1971)

[*In the following excerpt from his* Four African Literatures: Xhosa, Sotho, Zulu, Amharic *(1971), Gérard examines Mqhayi's prose and poetry within the contexts of African literature and culture.*]

It was not until the beginning of the twentieth century that the Western genre of imaginative prose fiction was introduced into Xhosa literature, most prominently by a man who—somewhat paradoxically—was also perhaps the last of the great tribal bards.

Samuel Edward Krune Mqhayi was the great-grandson of Mqhayi, a one-time councillor of Chief Ngqika, who was killed by the English in 1835. (p. 53)

Mqhayi, while attending school intermittently, acquired a remarkable knowledge of his people, their history, and their language. "It was there," Jordan writes, "that he first listened to *izibongo* (praise-poems), and himself began to 'lisp in numbers,' praising favourite oxen, other boys or himself. It was there that he began to appreciate the beauty, dignity and subtleties of Xhosa, and to acquire the amazingly wide vocabulary that even Tiyo Soga would have envied" [see essay dated 1945]. He used to listen to the stories of the wars that the old men of the village told in the evenings. He learned how to extemporize praise songs in honor of his cows, his dogs, and his friends. And he also watched with fascination the judicial proceedings at the court of Chief Nzanzana. (p. 53)

After training as a teacher, he taught for a time in East London. But he was not really interested in teaching, and he soon left to become secretary of the congregation of the Reverend Rubusana, who fostered his growing concern with social and racial problems. He contributed...to Mhala's newspaper, *Izwi Labantu,* and later became one of its editors. After a new stay at Kentani, he resumed his work on *Izwi Labantu* but the journal had to stop publication for lack of funds and because of differences of opinion among the editors. Mqhayi again went to East London as a teacher, and assisted Jabavu in the editing of *Imvo Zabantsundu* from the turn of the century until Jabavu's death in 1921. His first poems were printed there.

Mqhayi's poetic talent soon caused him to be known as "the poet of the race." As a result of his linguistic abilities, he had been appointed in 1905 a member of the Xhosa Bible Revision Board. At that time, Dr. William Govan Bennie (1868-1942) was chief inspector for Native Education in the Cape. He sought Mqhayi's help in standardizing Xhosa spelling and in codifying Xhosa grammar. From then on, the young man devoted himself mainly to writing. His first published book was **U-Samson,** an adaptation of the Bible story of Samson.

Mqhayi's first original work was **Ityala lama-wele (The Lawsuit of the Twins),** which was printed in 1914, quite some time, he claims in his autobiography, after he had actually composed it. As a result of this publication, Z. K. Matthews writes, Mqhayi "sprang into fame at once as one of the best Xhosa writers, to be classed with men like Soga and Rubusana." The story takes place during the reign of Hintza, chief of the Gcaleka Xhosa, who was killed while attempting to escape from British imprisonment in 1835. The plot was suggested by the story of the birth of Thammar's twins in Genesis 38:27-29. It concerns a legal dispute between twins over who is the elder and therefore entitled to their father's inheritance. Mqhayi's memories of Nzanzana's court enabled him to provide, as Alice Werner pointed out, "a very illuminating picture of native judicial procedure." But Mqhayi's purpose was by no means merely ethnographic or antiquarian. The theme of justice is an important one in all literatures, as justice and law are the very foundation of the social order. A large portion of early narrative writing in Europe focuses on the theme of revenge. The trial of Ganelon in the *Chanson de Roland,* the *Njalssaga,* for example, illustrate the conflict between the primitive practice of private vengeance on the one hand, and the social and religious requirements of impartial and impersonal justice on the other hand. This was still a major theme in serious drama of the Renaissance and of the seventeenth century throughout Western Europe. Other aspects of justice preoccupied African writers during the early years of the twentieth century.... [It] is important to notice that there is considerable difference in approach between [Lesothan writer Azariele] Sekese and Mqhayi. The former, living in a British Protectorate where the native judicial system was not threatened by the European authorities, felt free to criticize its abuses from inside. The situation was by no means the same in South Africa. By the end of the nineteenth century, Xhosa chiefs in the Ciskei had seen their authority and their judicial privileges eroded by the setting up of district councils whose members were appointed by the Cape authorities. Whereas Sekese wanted to criticize the chiefs' courts in the hope of improving them, it was Mqhayi's aim to vindicate traditional native justice threatened by the colonial administration. He made this clear in the foreword to *Ityala lama-wele*: "Although I am no kind of expert on the legal affairs, I have, however, the conviction that the legal system of the Xhosas is not in the slightest degree different from that of the enlightened nations. When the white races came to this country, they found that the people of this country are virtually experts—all of them—in legal procedures." He even goes so far as to claim that "the white races took for themselves a considerable share of the customs and laws of the Xhosas." The chief virtue of Xhosa law, he says, is that it is based upon jurisprudence. Consequently, he goes on, "in this short tale I am endeavouring to show the efforts, the pains, and the time that the Xhosas take when they research into the origin of law, for they are trying to base it upon precedent." In the story itself those efforts, described in minute detail, come to nothing since the case appears to be one for which there is no precedent, even in the memory of the oldest man of the tribe. In his foreword, Mqhayi further claims that he is trying to show "that the king is not the final arbiter of affairs by himself, as foreigners believe is the case with us." Actually, in the tale it is the chief who makes the final decision, a highly subtle and ambiguous one, although he first has all the evidence gathered and listens to the advice of all the notables. At the end of the trial, the author describes the reactions of the people as follows:

> And concerning the judgement, some were mumbling, finding fault, and seeing many errors. But the majority did not forget a case that had proceeded with decorum and justice, and that had been spoken well, in which all aspects had been examined, and the judgement given with great skill.

The second part of the volume contains a historical account of the Xhosa nation through the nineteenth century and up to the famous *Mendi* episode, when a ship loaded with South African soldiers was sunk by a German submarine in the early months of World War I. By this time, as Jordan rightly observes, "the subject is no longer the Xhosa alone, but the Bantu of South Africa," one more interesting example of the growth of intertribal solidarity in the early decades of this century. (pp. 54-6)

In 1925 [Mqhayi] published *UBomi buka J. K. Bokwe (Life of J. K. Bokwe),* a biography of the Reverend Bokwe. This was followed in 1927 by a collection of poems for children,... *Imihobe nemibongo (Songs of Joy and Lullabies).*

In 1929 Mqhayi produced his second important work of prose fiction which is also the first Xhosa utopia, *U-Don Jadu.* This book, which provides the writer's picture of an ideal South African society, has been usefully summarized and discussed by Jordan in his article on Mqhayi [see essay dated 1945]. (p. 56)

It is interesting to compare Jordan's analysis with the harsh judgement passed upon *U-Don Jadu* by a European critic, John Riordan:

> In *UDon Jadu* the hero passes from town to town, solving all problems overnight, and leading raw tribesmen from a primitive state to an advanced civilization in a matter of weeks.... Thus does Mqhayi allow his imagination, fostered by a repulsive hunger for self-glorification, to run riot and escape into a world of pure fancy, where probability is grossly violated and logical development unknown. True, Mqhayi's imagination is colourful and productive, but it is not disciplined. His mastery of language is undoubted, but he blatantly tries to impress by playing with big words and archaisms. His glittering facade of words is unsupported by any real substance and so we go away unsatisfied [see Further Reading].

Obviously, Riordan had expected what Mqhayi never intended to give: a realistic, social, and psychological novel of the Western type. Jordan too recognizes that "Mqhayi is not a great creator of individual character," and that "hardly any character stands out in this story." This is a critique frequently leveled at the African novel in general, whose failure in character depiction must be ascribed to two main causes. First, concern with the individual personality is not a feature of traditional oral literature any more than it is of traditional tribal society. The individual apprehends himself first and foremost as part of the group, rather than as a separate personality endowed with its own rights and privileges. Literature is a public activity dealing with matters of public interest, and purely private experiences and emotions are seldom deemed worthy of literary treatment. Second, this particular trend in the native culture was further reinforced by the historical situation. In his autobiography, Mqhayi explains that the idea for *U-Don Jadu* can be traced back to his school years at Lovedale. He used to make frequent visits to his father in Grahamstown, and during those trips, he had to pass through the little town of Alice. There it was, he tells us, that he became aware for the first time of the antagonism between black and white. So far, he had lived a sheltered life at the court of his great-uncle and in the quiet multiracial seclusion of Lovedale. But in Alice, he witnessed how Xhosa cattle was requisitioned out of the common pastures to make room for the white people's cattle, and he realized the growing hostility between both racial groups. As cattle was the foundation of Xhosa economy, and therefore of Xhosa society, this was a problem of life and death for the Xhosa nation as a whole. *U-Don Jadu* grew out of these experiences and this realization. It was not meant as a realistic description of a situation that every one knew anyway. It was designed as a blueprint for the future coexistence of both races in South Africa. And it was conceived in a spirit of compromise and syncretism. There are only three things that Mqhayi forcefully rejects: the South African government, the prison system, and imported hard liquor as opposed to the native home-brewed beer. His ideal state is not a preliminary study in Bantustan. It is a multiracial society that places a high premium on education and progress, and it is a Christian society that has incorporated many of the beliefs and customs dear to African hearts. In the elaboration of this Bantu utopia, Mqhayi exhibits uncommonly powerful intellectual imagination. (pp. 57-9)

Mqhayi's next book was a biography of the Gold Coast scholar and advocate of Pan-Africanism, Dr. J.E.K. Aggrey, whose visit to South Africa in 1921 had initiated, if we are to believe Vilakazi, "a new spirit of co-operation and understanding between Africans and Europeans." (p. 59)

Mqhayi published a collection of eight cantos on Chief Hintza, *U-Mhlekazi U-Hintsa (Hintsa the Great . . .*). At the same time, he was writing his autobiography, which was first published in German, in Diederich Wester-mann's collection, *Afrikaner erzähler ihr Leben . . .*, before it appeared in Xhosa under the title *U-Mqhayi wase Ntab'ozuko (Mqhayi of the Mountain of Beauty . . .*). His last volume was one more collection of poems, entitled *I-nzuzo (Reward . . .*). In the late twenties, Mqhayi had settled on Tilana's Hill, near Berlin. He had renamed the place "Ntab'ozuko" (The Mountain of Beauty). This was on the territory of the Ndlambe clan, and at the same time that he established a model farm for the benefit of the Xhosa peasants, Mqhayi acted as poet laureate and secretary to the Ndlambe chieftain. (p. 59)

It was perhaps as a poet that Mqhayi was chiefly valued by the Xhosa audience, not least because he had completely mastered the form and the spirit of the traditional praise poem (*izibongo*) while adapting it to modern circumstances and topics. He was known as *imbongi yesizwe* ("Poet Laureate"), and Vilakazi calls him "the Father of Xhosa poetry," because "he is responsible for a transition from the primitive bards who sang the *izibongo*." The main function of the tribal bard (*imbongi*) was to strengthen the cohesion of the group, usually by celebrating the glorious figures of the past and extolling the authority of the reigning chief. Mqhayi's volume on Hintza is an example of this, as are the obituary eulogies of local figures in *I-nzuzo*. But since the central preoccupation of the izibongo in its purest form is to promote the prosperity and the greatness of the group, it does not deal solely with the chiefs, but also with any public events that may be significant in that respect. Hence Mqhayi's poetic treatment of topics that, to the European reader, sound hardly promising: *I-nzuzo* contains a poem written in appreciation of the bimonthly agricultural journal published at Umtata! Throughout the year, seasonal festivals offer opportunities to remind the tribe of its past achievements and to advise it for the future; therefore, the many New Year poems that Mqhayi composed. As Jabavu wrote, "the topic of the expiration of one year and the incoming of a new one is almost Mqhayi's annual exercise and monopoly, and he does it with gusto." But Mqhayi's inspiration also reached beyond the traditional tribal basis, and he wrote abundantly, in poetry and in prose, about prominent Africans of past and present. Further, his Christian beliefs merged into

the edifying and societal purposes of traditional poetry in moralizing pieces dealing with such abstract subjects as Truth, Hope, and Love. If we are to believe Vilakazi, Mqhayi's attempts at innovation were not always successful. His poems dealing with nature, the Zulu critic says, are "dull," and those on religious subjects are "mere oratorical exercises" when compared with those of his successor Jolobe. Mqhayi "excelled in heroic poetry of the traditional type, and showed great skill in weaving his people's customs, legends, and myths into his poems."

The imbongi's role was not simply to praise the chief. As his major concern was with the welfare of the nation, he often felt called upon to criticize any abuses by the powers that be. On this score, too, the tradition was modified and enlarged by Mqhayi in the light of a historical situation where actual authority was vested in European hands. When the Prince of Wales (later Edward VIII) visited South Africa in 1925, the poet was entrusted with the privilege of delivering an izibongo of his composition. Jordan informs us that the poem began in the usual fashion, with "a succession of metaphors and similes, in which he likens the prince to all the mighty fabulous animals of Bantu Folklore." Then comes a section that is here quoted in Jordan's translation:

> Ah, Britain! Great Britain!
> Great Britain of the endless sunshine!
>
> She hath conquered the oceans and laid them low;
> She hath drained the little rivers and lapped them
>   dry;
> She hath swept the little nations and wiped them
>   away;
> And now she is making for the open skies.
>
> She sent us the preacher: she sent us the bottle,
> She sent us the Bible, and barrels of brandy;
> She sent us the breechloader, she sent us cannon;
> O, Roaring Britain! Which must we embrace?
>
> You sent us the truth, denied us the truth;
> You sent us the life, deprived us of life,
> You sent us the light, we sit in the dark,
> Shivering, benighted in the bright noonday sun.

Jordan quotes this passage to show "that the idiom, style and technique of the traditional praise-poem can be applied most effectively to modern themes." But in its own right, it is a little masterpiece of irony and conscious artistry. It may be pure coincidence that the translation appears as a sort of inverted Elizabethan sonnet, with the couplet at the beginning instead of the end. But the structure of the poem is as carefully devised as that of a sonnet. It falls into two main parts, each of which is announced by an apostrophe ("Ah, Britain!" "O, Roaring Britain!"), and each of the three quatrains is a clearly distinguishable step in a continuous process of heightening tension. The first quatrain, describing Britain's universal power, is in the third person, objective and impersonal in tone, although a note of subdued irony creeps in as Britain's victories over nature (oceans, rivers) appear as an icon of her conquest of men (nations), and as the effects of her might are couched in increasingly destructive terms (oceans laid low, rivers lapped dry, nations wiped away). The last line is probably designed as ambivalent, referring both to the physical skies conquered by air power, and to the way the British manipulate the heavenly Gospel for purposes of their own. This, at any rate, is suggested by the mention of "the preacher" at the beginning of the second quatrain.

This third stanza has a more direct personal character ("She sent *us* the preacher") and refers to the particular experience that Mqhayi and his people have gained of British power. This experience is tersely described in its fundamental ambivalence: while England sent the Africans the light of Christianity, she also introduced them to liquor and firearms, both of them agents of destruction. The modulation in the second apostrophe ("Roaring Britain" instead of "Great Britain") contains an ominous, although hidden and implicit, answer to the question in the quatrain's last line. The main attribute of England, the source of her political greatness and power, is not the "sunshine" of Christian civilization, but the roaring, destructive might of artillery. It is not likely that Mqhayi, a devout member of the Presbyterian church, wanted to invite his people to use violence as a response to violence. The interrogative form of the line suggests the pathetic perplexity of the African in general, and intimates how tempting it is for him to conclude that only armed power, not the Christian faith, can redeem the African from the quandary where Britain herself placed him.

The gradual heightening of emotion reaches its climax in the last stanza, where Britain is now directly and aggressively apostrophized: the "you-us" relation replaces the "she-us" of the second quatrain and the impersonal "she" of the first. At the same time, the poet relinquishes metaphorical language and indicts Britain in straightforward terms, for bringing the truth of religion in theory and ignoring it in practice, and for bringing the light of progress and civilization while depriving the black population of its livelihood. The last two lines of the poem revert with deadly irony, to the light imagery of the beginning. Although Britain, the land where the sun of Christianity and modern civilization shines endlessly, sent the light to Africa, the African remains in the cold and the darkness of oppression, with only his native, physical "bright noonday sun" to console him. The translation can only preserve the bare bones of the poem's structure. There is little doubt that a study of the musical and connotational values of the Xhosa original would enhance our appreciation of this brief masterpiece, the quality of which certainly suggests that more of Mqhayi's work should be made available to an international audience. (pp. 59-62)

Albert S. Gérard, "Xhosa Literature," in his Four African Literatures: Xhosa, Sotho, Zulu, Amharic, *University of California Press, 1971, pp. 21-100.*

Wandile Kuse (essay date 1975)

[*In the following excerpt, Kuse offers a brief survey of Mqhayi's principal works.*]

When Mqhayi wrote his first two poems for *Izwi LabaNtu* (The Voice of the People) in 1897, he was immediately acclaimed as *Imbongi yakwaGompo neyeSizwe Jikelele*. In these two poems the two main themes of Mqhayi's life's work are delineated, viz:

(a) In **"Izwe IakwaNdlambe" ("The Domain of the Ndlambe People"),** he declared his unshakeable loyalty and fidelity to the polity and traditions of his people.

(b) In **"UNtsikane"** he portrayed his quest to transcend local and ethnic considerations by heroising the first notable Xhosa convert to Christianity. Christianity and the values of Western European civilization had become the vehicles of "progress" in the eyes of Mqhayi's generation of writers. They were, however, not uncritical of proselytizers to the new ways of the alien civilization. (p. 183)

The evolutionary development of Mqhayi's attitudes is reflected in his contributions to two publications in particular: *Izwi labaNtu* and *Imvo zabaNtsundu.* He became editor of the former within the first year of its existence, but funding dried up and the journal collapsed in 1910. Mqhayi then became editor of *Imvo zabaNtsundu* which was being produced in King William's Town. The various columns to which he contributed included "Abantu" ("People"), "E ZaKomkhulu" ("News from the Court") and "Incoko" ("Conversation")....

During the Anglo-Boer War (1899-1902) and World War I (1914-1918), Mqhayi wrote poetry which alluded to the hostilities between the Europeans in South Africa and in Europe. The significance of these wars of the "natives," his countrymen, is elaborated upon in the body of the poems. His ideas were further elaborated in his prose fiction. His first novel, an adaptation of the Biblical story of "Samson and Delilah" entitled *USamson* . . . , offered a critique of South African society in the years following the Anglo-Boer War. He conceived of the "natives" as the impotent "sleeping giant" who, in the words of Shakespeare's Mercutio, willed and wished "a plague on both your houses." The image was sustained by the Titan's act which brought to ruin the edifice constructed by the collusion of liberal white men and reactionary racists at the expense of the indigenous peoples of South Africa. Mqhayi was always aware that the intrusion of Europeans into the patterns of behaviour and politics of Africans was not always gentle and altruistic.

Mqhayi's name is, of course, pre-eminently associated with his epoch-making classic *Ityala Lamawele (The Lawsuit of the Twins). Imvo* . . . quotes Professor Z. K. Matthews as saying that Mqhayi "sprang into fame at once as one of the best Xhosa writers, to be classed with men like Soga and Rubusana." The negative posture of

USamson led Mqhayi, in dialectical fashion, to the positive assertion of indigenous values in **Ityala Lamawele.** This book is a compendium of various styles: the opening is dramatic and thereafter the prose is punctuated by heroic poetry, historical and biographical sketches as well as legend and mythology. Here Mqhayi projected his image of men and women of culture who propagated the best ideas of their time. His heroes and heroines encompassed the representatives of tradition as well as men and women educated in the ways of the West. The first part of the work is an exciting portrayal of the ways of tradition while the latter part is a series of biographical sketches and historical situations.

Mqhayi's next work of fiction, **uDon Jadu** appeared in 1929. This book is both a utopia and an allegory. Its themes are parallel to two other books by Mqhayi and demonstrate the dynamic relationship between fiction and social reality. The *persona* (the narrative is in the first person singular) is an amalgam of the hero of the autobiography, **UMqhayi waseNtabozuko** and the author's free translation of C. Kingsley Williams' *Aggrey of Africa—uAggrey umAfrika,* a work inspired by the visit to South Africa of Aggrey, the Ghanaian as a member of the Phelps-Stokes Commission on Education in Africa. Excepting the autobiography, Mqhayi's last two books underline the fact that he was pre-eminently a poet—a veritable traditional oral bard whose awareness and sensitivity to the great issues of his times as well as his responsiveness to the creative impulse led him to experiment often with European modes of rhyme and rhythm—not altogether successfully. In 1937, Mqhayi wrote **"UMhlekazi uHintsa,"** (a poem in eight cantos). On the hundredth anniversary of the assassination of the Paramount Chief of the Xhosa, he felt the urge to reassert his credentials as the royal bard of old times. His composition won the May Esther Bedford Competition First Prize. It is a poem that sustains the viability of the oral techniques of praise poetry in the written format. Mqhayi's last book of poems, **Inzuzo,** suggests that he was both an oral and literate poet who was socially aware and was well steeped in the techniques and content of the oral culture of his people while experimenting with English Romantic forms.

Mqhayi was at his best when he wrote or recited poetry in the oral tradition. My favorite poem by Mqhayi is his praise of a Ndlambe chief entitled **"Aa! Silimela!"** It is not included in any volume of Mqhayi's corpus of written works. The music of his poetry communicates even if one does not understand the words. However, there is a translation of the first paragraph of the poem Mqhayi wrote on the occasion of the recruitment of the "Black Brigade," a black South African contingent in the First World War. If one has seen the film *Patton* one can sympathize with Mqhayi's sentiments in response as it were to Patton's saying, "When your grandchildren expectantly ask you what you did in the great world war, you would not like to have to say 'you were shovelling shit in Louisiana'." Mqhayi introduces the poem **"Umkhosi WemiDaka"** in this manner:

Awu! Ewe kambe siyabulela
Lakuth' ikokwethu lisicinge
Ngokuya kusebenz' emazibukweni
Ngexesha lalo lokuxakeka.
Be singobani na thina boomthina?
Ukuba singanced' ukumkani weBritain
Ingangalale' engatshonelwa langa
Int' elawul' umhlaba nolwandle!
Kungoku nesibhakabhak' isingxamele!

Niyeva ke, madodana, niphakamile
Isizwe senu sisemqulwini wezizwe.
Ze niguye, ze niqambe;
Nenje nje, nenje nje! Nenje nje, nenje nje!
Nenje nje, nenje nje! Nenje nje, nenje njeya.

We are indeed grateful and impressed
That His Britannic Majesty
Should think of asking us to come
And work as stevedores
At a time when he is under pressure.
Who were we?
To even think of lending a hand
To the King of Britain
On whose empire the sun never sets.
His dominions extend over land and sea
As things now stand
He is ready to colonize the heavens.

Listen now fellows!
Your people now belong to the Commonwealth of
    Nations.
You should celebrate and dance
And act like this and this and that!

This bitterly satirical poem goes on to say that some good is bound to come out of the sacrifice by Africans for others. (pp. 183-84)

> *Wandile Kuse, "Mqhayi: Oral Bard and Author," in* The South African Outlook, *Vol. 105, December, 1975, pp. 183-84.*

FURTHER READING

Review of *U-Mqhayi wase-Ntab'ozuko,* by S.E.K. Mqhayi. *Bantu Studies* XIV (1940): 203-04.
>   Favorable appraisal of Mqhayi's autobiography. According to the critic: "The language of the book is clear and pleasing, colloquial but dignified, forming a model on which young writers of Xhosa might well mould their own style."

Kuse, Wandile. "Mqhayi through the Eyes of His Contemporaries." *South African Outlook* 105 (1975): 185-88.
>   Discusses poetic tributes to Mqhayi by J.J.R. Jolobe, Yale-Manisi, Adolphus Z. T. Mbebe and St. J. Page Yako, and Lettie G. N. Tayedzerhwa.

Opland, Jeff. "Praise Poems as Historical Sources." In *Beyond the Cape Frontier: Studies in the History of the Transkei and Ciskei,* edited by Christopher Saunders and Robin Derricourt, pp. 1-37. London: Longman, 1974.

Surveys the works of *imbongi* (praise poets), including Mqhayi.

————. "Two Unpublished Poems by S.E.K. Mqhayi." *Research in African Literatures* 8, No. 1 (Spring 1977): 27-53.

Xhosa transcriptions and English translations of a recording of the poems "Ah Velile" and "A! Silimela!" made by Mqhayi in the 1930s. Opland includes critical comment on the texts.

Riordan, John. "The Wrath of the Ancestral Spirits." *African Studies* 20, No. 1 (1961): 53-60.

Includes a brief negative assessment of *U-Don Jadu* in an appreciative review of A. C. Jordan's novel *Inggoumbo yeminyanya* (1940). According to Riordan: "Mqhayi's imagination is colorful and productive, but it is not disciplined. His mastery of language is undoubted, but he blatantly tries to impress by playing with big words and archaisms. His glittering facade of words is unsupported by any real substance and so we go away unsatisfied."

Scott, Patricia E. *Samuel Edward Krune Mqhayi, 1875-1945: Bibliographic Survey.* Grahamstown, S. A.: Rhodes University, 1976, 31 p.

Includes comprehensive bibliographies of Mqhayi's journalism, anthologized works, translated poetry, unpublished manuscripts, and works about Mqhayi.

Shepherd, R.H.W. "S.E.K. Mqhayi: His Life." *South African Outlook* 105 (1975): 191.

A brief, appreciative biography. According to Shepherd: "Few men have been more honored among African people than was S.E.K. Mqhayi.... His contributions to Xhosa literature as poet, historian, biographer, and translator were abundant and outstanding in quality, and by them and in other ways he helped in no small measure to stabilize and purify the Xhosa language."

Walter Dean Myers

1937-

(Also has written as Walter M. Myers) American novelist, short story writer, nonfiction writer, and author of children's books.

Myers is one of modern literature's premier authors of fiction for young adults. Two of his novels for teens, *The Young Landlords* (1979) and *Motown and Didi: A Love Story* (1984), have won the prestigious Coretta Scott King Award, and his text for the picture book *Where Does the Day Go?* (1969) received the Council on Interracial Books for Children Award in 1969. As Carmen Subryan has noted, "Whether he is writing about the ghettos of New York, the remote countries of Africa, or social institutions, Myers captures the essence of the developing experiences of youth."

One possibility Myers never foresaw as a youth was that of supporting himself as a writer. He was born into an impoverished family in Martinsburg, West Virginia, and at age three was adopted by Herbert and Florence Dean, who settled in New York City's Harlem district. Although he wrote poems and stories from his early teens onward and won awards for them, his parents did not encourage his literary talents. "I was from a family of laborers," he remembers in an autobiographical essay in *Something about the Author Autobiography Series,* "and the idea of writing stories or essays was far removed from their experience. Writing had no practical value for a Black child. These minor victories [and prizes] did not bolster my ego. Instead, they convinced me that even though I was bright, even though I might have some talent, I was still defined by factors other than my ability." The dawning realization that his possibilities were limited by race and economic status embittered Myers as a teen. "A youngster is not trained to want to be a gasoline station attendant or a clerk in some obscure office," he states. "We are taught to want to be lawyers and doctors and accountants—these professions that are given value. When the compromise comes, as it does early in Harlem to many children, it comes hard."

Myers admits he was not ready to accept that compromise. Through high school and a three-year enlistment in the army, he read avidly and wrote short stories. After his discharge from the service, he worked in a variety of positions, including mail clerk at the post office, inter-office messenger, and interviewer in a factory. None of these tasks pleased him, and when he began to publish poetry, stories, and articles in magazines, he cautiously started to consider a writing profession. "When I entered a contest for picture book writers," he claims, "it was more because I wanted to write *anything* than because I wanted to write a picture book."

Myers won the contest, sponsored by the Council on Interracial Books for Children, for his text of *Where Does the Day Go?* In that story, a group of children from several ethnic backgrounds discuss their ideas about night and day with a sensitive and wise black father during a long walk. Inspired by the success of his first attempt to write for young people, Myers turned his attention to producing more picture books. During the early 1970s he published three: *The Dancers* (1972), *The Dragon Takes a Wife* (1972), and *Fly, Jimmy, Fly!* (1974). Though in more recent years he has concentrated on longer works for older children, Myers continues to write texts for picture books occasionally. In 1980 he released a fable set in India, *The Golden Serpent,* and in 1984 an animal adventure, *Mr. Monkey and the Gotcha Bird.*

Myers accepted an editorial position with the Bobbs-Merrill publishing company in 1970 and worked there until 1977. His seven-year tenure taught him "the book business from another viewpoint," as he puts it in his autobiographical essay. "Publishing is a business," he writes. "It is not a cultural institution.... It is *talked* about as if it were a large cultural organization with several branches. One hears pronouncements like 'anything worthwhile will eventually be published.' Nonsense, of course. Books are published for many reasons, the chief of which is profit." In retrospect, however, Myers feels that he has benefitted from his experiences in Bobbs-Merrill, even though he was laid off during a restructuring program. "After the initial disillusionment about the artistic aspects of the job, I realized how foolish I had been in not learning, as a writer, more about the business aspects of my craft," he concludes. Armed with the pragmatic knowledge of how the publishing industry works, Myers has supported himself by his writing alone since 1977.

By the time he left Bobbs-Merrill, Myers had already established a reputation as an able author of fiction for black children, based largely upon his highly successful novels for teens such as *Fast Sam, Cool Clyde, and Stuff* (1975) and *Mojo and the Russians* (1977). Both tales feature, in Subryan's words, adventures depicting "the learning experiences of most youths growing up in a big city where negative influences abound." Central to the stories is the concept of close friendships, portrayed as a positive, nurturing influence. Subryan stated: "Because of the bonding which occurs among the members of the group, the reader realizes that each individual's potential for survival has increased." Myers followed the two upbeat novels with a serious one, *It Ain't All for Nothin'* (1978), that Subryan claimed "reflects much of the pain and anguish of ghetto life." The account of a boy caught in a web of parental abuse, conflicting values, and solitary self-assessment, *It Ain't All for Nothin'* "pretties up nothing; not the language, not the circumstances, not the despair," according to Jane Pennington. The story has a positive resolution, however, based on the care and support the central character receives from fellow community members.

In the *Interracial Books for Children Bulletin,* Myers described his priorities as an author. He tries, he says, to provide good literature for black children, "literature that includes them and the way they live" and that "celebrates their life and their person. It upholds and gives special place to their humanity." Myers strives to present characters for whom urban life is an uplifting experience despite the potentially dangerous influences. In his first Coretta Scott King Award-winner, *The Young Landlords,* several teens learn responsibility when they are given a ghetto apartment building to manage. Lonnie Jackson, the protagonist of *Hoops* (1981), profits from the example of an older friend who has become involved with gamblers. Concerned with stereotyping of a sexual as well as a racial sort, Myers creates plausible female characters and features platonic friendships between the sexes in his works. "The love in *Fast Sam, Cool Clyde, and Stuff* is not between any one couple," wrote Alleen Pace Nilsen. "Instead it is a sort of general feeling of good will and concern that exists among a group of inner city kids." Nilsen, among

others, also noted that Myers's fiction can appeal to readers of any race. She concluded that he "makes the reader feel so close to the characters that ethnic group identification is secondary." Subryan expressed a similar opinion: "By appealing to the consciousness of young adults, Myers is touching perhaps the most important element of our society. Myers's books demonstrate that writers can not only challenge the minds of black youth but also emphasize the black experience in a nonracist way that benefits all young readers."

Myers wrote in *Something about the Author Autobiography Series* that the reception of his novels gave him a new role as an author. "As my books for teenagers gained in popularity I sensed that my soul-searching for my place in the artistic world was taking on added dimension. As a Black writer I had not only the personal desire to find myself, but the obligation to use my abilities to fill a void." Children and adults, he suggests, "must have role models with which they can identify," and he feels he must "deliver images upon which [they] could build and expand their own worlds." Noting that in his own life he has "acquired the strengths to turn away from disaster," Myers concludes: "As a Black writer, I want to talk about my people.... The books come. They pour from me at a great rate. I can't see how any writer can ever stop. There is always one more story to tell, one more person whose life needs to be held up to the sun."

(For further information about Myers's life and works, see *Authors and Artists for Young Adults,* Vol. 2; *Black Writers; Children's Literature Review,* Vols. 4, 16; *Contemporary Authors,* Vols. 33-36; *Contemporary Authors New Revision Series,* Vol. 20; *Contemporary Literary Criticism,* Vol. 35; *Dictionary of Literary Biography,* Vol. 33: *Afro-American Fiction Writers after 1955; Something about the Author,* Vols. 27, 41; and *Something about the Author Autobiography Series,* Vol. 2.)

PRINCIPAL WORKS

Where Does the Day Go? [as Walter M. Myers] (juvenile fiction) 1969
The Dancers (juvenile fiction) 1972
The Dragon Takes a Wife (juvenile fiction) 1972
Fly, Jimmy, Fly! (juvenile fiction) 1974
Fast Sam, Cool Clyde, and Stuff (juvenile fiction) 1975
The World of Work: A Guide to Choosing a Career (handbook) 1975
Social Welfare (essay) 1976
Brainstorm (juvenile fiction) 1977
Mojo and the Russians (juvenile fiction) 1977
Victory for Jamie (juvenile fiction) 1977
It Ain't All for Nothin' (juvenile fiction) 1978
The Young Landlords (juvenile fiction) 1979
The Black Pearl and the Ghost; or, One Mystery after Another (juvenile fiction) 1980
The Golden Serpent (juvenile fiction) 1980
Hoops (juvenile fiction) 1981

The Legend of Tarik (juvenile fiction) 1981
Won't Know Till I Get There (juvenile fiction) 1982
The Nicholas Factor (juvenile fiction) 1983
Tales of a Dead King (juvenile fiction) 1983
Mr. Monkey and the Gotcha Bird: An Original Tale (juvenile fiction) 1984
Motown and Didi: A Love Story (juvenile fiction) 1984
The Outside Shot (juvenile fiction) 1984
*Adventure in Granada (juvenile fiction) 1985
*The Hidden Shrine (juvenile fiction) 1985
*Ambush in the Amazon (juvenile fiction) 1986
*Duel in the Desert (juvenile fiction) 1986
Sweet Illusions (juvenile workbook) 1986
Crystal (juvenile fiction) 1987
Shadow of the Red Moon (juvenile fiction) 1987
Fallen Angels (juvenile fiction) 1988
Me, Mop, and the Moondance Kid (juvenile fiction) 1988
Scorpions (juvenile fiction) 1988
The Mouse Rap (juvenile fiction) 1990

*These works are part of the "Arrow" series of juveniles.

Walter Myers (essay date 1979)

[*The following excerpt is from an article that was first published in 1979 as part of a "From the Author" series sponsored by* Interracial Books for Children Bulletin. *Here, Myers attempts to answer the question "Is it time to say 'enough' about racism in children's literature?"*]

I was at a conference at a small school in Michigan. The focus of the conference was on literature for children. My talk had gone reasonably well, touching upon my own publications and my seven-year career as an editor. The question and answer period was divided into two sections, interrupted by a more than welcome coffee break. At the beginning of the second session a young man in the front of the auditorium raised his hand. He hadn't participated in the earlier session although I had noticed him taking careful notes.

"Mr. Myers, apart from your personal interest in multi-ethnic literature," he asked, "don't you think we've been harping on the issue of racism in children's books for some time now?"

The inference, of course, was that the "some time" had been too long a time. I asked him to elaborate on his question and, rather uncomfortably it seemed, he expressed the view that the push against racism in children's books, while commendable in itself, had become anachronistic in these enlightened times. What's more, the issue was being greatly overplayed by some people and some groups.

The response from the rest of the assembly was immediate. What buzzing there had been ceased. This was clearly a question that had been on more than one mind—and indeed I had heard similar questions from librarians and educators in Michigan, Kansas, New Jersey, New York and Texas, mostly within the last two years.

This essay is an attempt to answer, from my own viewpoint, this question: Is it time to say "enough" about racism in children's literature? I think I can express my viewpoint best by sharing my experiences as a Black writer.

I first became involved in writing for children some ten years ago by entering the CIBC's first contest for unpublished Third World writers. Before that I had been writing short fiction primarily, with only a dim awareness of the crying need for children's books reflecting the Third World experience. It became clear upon examination of the materials then available that books did not do for Black or other Third World children what they did for white children—they did not deliver images upon which Black children could build and expand their own worlds. But this was in 1969 and publishers and librarians alike were voicing similar concerns about the lack of suitable materials for Blacks and other Third World children. It was just, I felt, a matter of time before the situation would be rectified.

But I soon discovered that there was a lot of resistance, even resentment, to this idea. I visited my daughter's grade school in Brooklyn at the request of the school librarian. After speaking to a bright group of seven-year-olds I was introduced to the principal. I showed him my first book—*Where Does the Day Go?* (1969)—and he thumbed through it quickly, looking at the pictures. I fully expected him to say something tactfully complimentary. Instead, he said that he didn't feel that the book belonged in his school's library. There were no white children in the book! There were several Black children, a Japanese girl and a Puerto Rican boy, but no white child. I began to wonder if my work would be ignored—or remain unpublished—if I did not include white children. Would I be unable to write about all-Black neighborhoods?

My next book, *The Dancers* (1972), was published some two years later. I need not have been worried about not having white children in this book. The publisher introduced a white character for me. He's not in the story, but he appears in as many pictures as possible and seems to be in the story. This being a Black writer was not going to be an easy task.

The Dancers and *The Dragon Takes a Wife* (1972) inspired some of the most virulent hate mail imaginable. I've received hate mail in response to my magazine articles—an article about interracial adoption drew a lot of angry letters from whites, for instance—but the mail about these children's books represented a different beast altogether. The letters were primarily from parents, people who could keep my work from school shelves and from local libraries. Many correspondents were furious that I—a Black author—had "invaded" the white world of fairy tales; "obscene" was one of their milder labels for *The Dragon Takes a Wife.*

But, despite these minor annoyances, I still felt that the time was soon coming when literature for Black children would really blossom and that all children's literature would be truly humanistic. The accusations that Black writers wouldn't or couldn't write well was being mocked by the CIBC contest, which had attracted a host of good Third World writers, excited by the opportunity to chronicle their own experiences. Such writers as Sharon Bell Mathis, Ray Sheppard, Virginia Driving Hawk Sneve, Margaret Musgrove and Mildred Taylor were demonstrating that not only were they excellent writers but that their work did have viable markets.

By the mid-seventies, however, the promise of the late sixties and early seventies seemed suddenly hollow. The number of Black writers being published decreased as Black political activity decreased. The reasons for this were clear. Publishing companies had never tried to develop markets for Third World literature. Instead, they had relied upon purchases made through Great Society government funds, and when these were phased out the publishers began to phase out Third World books. Books were spaced so that their publication would not coincide with other Black books because sales representatives complained that they couldn't represent too many at one time. A look at the most recent catalogs shows that there are fewer books being published for Black children now than a decade ago. (pp. 14-15)

I have had good experiences in my writing career as well as bad. But while I am hopeful for my own efforts I am not hopeful for the body of literature that still needs to be produced. I am not hopeful for the writers who are being turned away because "Black books aren't selling." I am not hopeful for the librarian who claims to love children and children's literature and yet can tell me that American children who are white do not need to learn of the Black experience, or that the Black experience need no longer be chronicled with truth and compassion. But most of all I am not hopeful for the millions of Third World children who will be forced to grow up under the same handicaps that I thought, a decade ago, that we were beginning to overcome. I'm afraid that the time has not yet come to say "enough" about racism in children's books. (p. 15)

> *Walter Myers, "The Black Experience in Children's Books: One Step Forward, Two Steps Back," in* Interracial Books for Children Bulletin, *Vol. 10, No. 6, 1979, pp. 14-15.*

Patricia Lee Gauch (essay date 1980)

[*In the following excerpt, Gauch examines plot and characterization in* The Young Landlords.]

[*The Young Landlords* is] about four black teen-agers, the Action Group, who in a spontaneous act of commu-

nity service, get tricked into becoming slum landlords of a deteriorating apartment house in their Harlem neighborhood. The plot—kids running a slum building, The Joint, and catching a stereo thief—stretches the imagination at more than one point.

It works as a convenient vehicle, however, for introducing such great characters as the Captain, a cool, pig-eyed numbers man; Mrs. Brown, a tenant whose "companion," the great boxer Jack Johnson, periodically dies and is reborn; "slap slap" Kelly, whose slick street talk is pure music, and best of all, Askia Ben Kenobi, the wild black mystic whose karate dance threatens everything from bannisters to petty thieves.

There are other incidents in the plot—a mild love interest between Gloria and the narrator, for one—but they pale beside such scenes as the rollicking rent party which a caped Kenobi turns into a sandwich-throwing brawl, or the scene where landlords Gloria and Paul get marooned in a lightless bathroom.

There are ideas, too, about the conflict between tenants and slumlords. About the hot-goods industry, police lethargy, newspapers' predilection for story over facts. Important ideas, particularly for the reader who doesn't live next to The Joint.

Mr. Myers's story starts slowly; tightening would have helped. But there are funny lines and scenes, the dialogue is real, and as the narrator says: "Mostly the whole experience was an up kind of thing."

> *Patricia Lee Gauch, in a review of "The Young Landlords," in* The New York Times Book Review, *January 6, 1980, p. 20.*

Malcolm Bosse (essay date 1981)

[*In the following excerpt, Bosse offers a generally favorable review of* The Legend of Tarik.]

"It came to pass" are the opening words in [*The Legend of Tarik*], suggesting we are in for magic and adventure, heroes and villains, with a final showdown between good and evil. Mr. Myers doesn't disappoint us. He has written what is nearly a compendium of devices used in such fiction.

Tarik has seen his father murdered by a sadistic brute who terrorizes the African countryside (historical time unspecified). Befriended by two old men, who also have scores to settle with this same El Muerte, the boy undergoes a long period of systematic training that will prepare him to take his revenge.

The old men teach him the skills of a warrior, but more important they help him to see, hear and feel with uncommon facility, for without extraordinary qualities, as much spiritual as physical, he cannot hope to overcome an opponent who is the embodiment of evil. Tarik is given tasks to perform, and their successful completion brings him closer to manhood. While on these quests, encountering the magical and the terrifying, he learns to look at evil, to accept the truth and to use his intelligence with confidence.

Equipped with a magic sword, a powerful horse and the Crystal of Truth, Tarik sets out in the company of Stria, a girl whose passion for revenge far exceeds his own and whose portrayal is one of the book's strengths. Adventures come thick and fast. Comic relief is provided by a garrulous baker, who proves loyal in spite of his professed cowardice. The three companions move inexorably toward the final confrontation with El Muerte. The climax is, of course, predictable, as it should be in a tale of vengeance.

And as it should be in a legend, omens and prophetic dreams abound. Also conforming to the tradition of allegory, the characters are broadly drawn, some of them standing for a single quality: Faithfulness, obsession, wisdom, etc. Even so, the story does have a contemporary feeling, because moral questions of conduct are given a skeptical treatment, with a resultant ambiguity about their solutions.

In spite of a thinness of detail, particularly in descriptions of the physical setting, and a few unfortunate metaphors ("El Muerte's smile was like a white wound in the belly of a whale"), in balance it is an admirably paced novel, with plenty of action and enough about loyalty and courage to satisfy young readers who can find in parables and legends a clue to their own lives.

> *Malcolm Bosse, in a review of "The Legend of Tarik," in* The New York Times Book Review, *July 12, 1981, p. 30.*

Publishers Weekly (essay date 1983)

[*In the following review, a critic labels* The Nicholas Factor *a "disturbing, powerful work."*]

[Myers] explores an intriguing idea [in ***The Nicholas Factor***]: does an elite group have the right to impose its views on society, even if it believes its vision is right? Gerald is a college student who's asked to join the Crusade Society, a snobby campus organization. He's approached by a government agent who wants him to keep an eye on the group, heightening his already aroused suspicions about Crusader activities. After a few meetings, he's off to a Peruvian jungle with them on a do-gooder mission with an Inca tribe.... Suddenly, the project is called off and the Crusaders are being hustled out of Peru, but Gerald and Jennifer discover a village filled with sick and dying Indians, caused by a Crusader "inducement" meant to accomplish their mission. The chase is on, as the leaders of the Crusaders realize what the two have found out. The reference to the Crusaders of yore is telling, for they were religious zealots who felt a holy obligation to impose their will. Myers probes and makes one think about the notion of right and wrong as it applies to implementing one's vision of the world. A disturbing, powerful work.

> *A review of "The Nicholas Factor," in* Publishers Weekly, *Vol. 223, No. 11, March 18, 1983, p. 70.*

Beth Nelms, Ben Nelms, and Linda Horton (essay date 1985)

[*In the following excerpt, Beth Nelms, Ben Nelms, and Linda Horton briefly identify the main themes and concerns of Myers's young adult fiction.*]

Walter Dean Myers writes about ordinary situations—but with concern and a sense of drama. His stories are realistic and low-key but optimistic. His ***Fast Sam, Cool Clyde and Stuff,*** for example, is one of the best teenage problem novels, not nearly as widely recognized as it should be.

Lonnie Jackson, who first appeared in ***Hoops,*** a basketball story set in Harlem, is not one of his strongest characters. Often he seems to go with the flow, letting things happen to him rather than making things happen. But in this latest book, Lonnie leaves Harlem and learns a lot about himself—and about the day-to-day problems of the college athlete and of a black youth in a predominantly white midwestern school.

Young readers who identify with the cool, resourceful but sometimes confused rookie will learn a lot, too. Sherry, the track star, teaches Lonnie to respect a woman as an equal. Eddie, the emotionally disturbed child he helps, brings out the best in Lonnie and shows him something about his own potential. Colin, his white roommate, and his family show him that there are hardships and warm family relationship outside of Harlem. Even Dr. Weiser, the sarcastic history professor who is prejudiced against all athletes, makes a point about the importance of academic regimen. And in Ray, the former college player he meets, he sees the disillusionment of the has-been athlete who doesn't make it in the pros.

The Outside Shot is more than a basketball story, but there is enough action on the court to satisfy the young reader who thinks he's going to make it to the big time with athletic skills. When Lonnie says, "I told myself that I wasn't ever going to give up.... If I had an outside shot I was going to take it," he's talking about more than basketball. (p. 95)

> *Beth Nelms, Ben Nelms, and Linda Horton, "A Brief but Troubled Season: Problems in YA Fiction," in* English Journal, *Vol. 74, No. 1, January, 1985, pp. 92-5.*

Walter Dean Myers (essay date 1986)

[*In the following excerpt, Myers examines the role of the American book publishing industry in promoting readership of books by and about blacks. He argues: "It is the urgent task of the black community to reinvest value in education and, specifically, in read-*

ing skills. If the market is created the books will come.... [If] we continue to make black children nonpersons by excluding them from books and by degrading the black experience, and if we continue to neglect white children by not exposing them to any aspect of other racial and ethnic experience in a meaningful way, we will have a next racial crisis."]

I write books for children, filled with the images I've accumulated over the years, with stories I've heard from my father and my grandfather. Many take place in the Harlem of my youth. The names of boyhood friends, Binky, Light Billy, Clyde, creep into the stories, and memories of them and of summer days playing endless games of stoopball next to the Church of the Master on Morningside Avenue keep the stories ever alive for me. I'm drawn to the eternal promise of childhood, and the flair of the young for capturing the essence of life.

When I began writing for young people I was only vaguely aware of the problems with children's books as far as blacks were concerned. My own encounters with black symbols and black characters were no less painful than those of the generations that followed me. There was the first mention of blacks in history. There were "slaves" being led from ships. Not captives, slaves. In truth, I don't remember Little Black Sambo, the large red lips pouting from the page, the wide eyes, the kinky hair going off in all directions, as being particularly bothersome. I'm not sure if it was the awe in which I held the tiger, or if I had just separated myself from this image. But later I do remember suffering through the Tom Swift books, and the demeaning portrait of Eradicate, the major black character in the series.

The pain was not so much that the images of my people were poor, but that the poor images were being made public. There they were in books for all of my white classmates to see. I had already internalized the negative images, had taken them for truth. No matter that my mother said that I was as good as anyone. She had also told me, in words and in her obvious pride in my reading, that books were important, and yet it was in books that I found Eradicate Sampson and the other blacks who were lazy, dirty and, above all, comical.

When the images of Dinah, the black maid in the Bobbsey Twins, Friday in "Robinson Crusoe," Eradicate in Tom Swift and the overwhelming *absence* of blacks in most books were telling the children of my generation that being black was not to be taken seriously, they were delivering the same message to white children. I knew that no homage to racial equality delivered by my teachers could, for me, offset even one snicker when Friday was depicted as a "savage," or when Dinah or Eradicate Sampson said something stupid.

I once worked in a personnel office in lower Manhattan where we hired both administrative and technical workers. I soon discovered that the hiring process was not so much a careful analysis of the applicant's abilities as it was a matching of appearance and behavior with the image of the successful candidate. When my otherwise liberal co-worker chose white males over women and black applicants, he was simply responding to what had been his cultural experience, that blacks and women were not the kinds of people who filled certain positions. I wonder how many many books he had read—how many images of blacks—had led him to believe that a black man would not be a successful chemist or sales manager. Had he ever seen a black person in a book who was not an athlete or a service worker?

The 1960's promised a new way of seeing black people. First, and by far most important, we were in the public consciousness. Angry black faces stared out from our television sets, commanded the front pages of our tabloids. We were news, and what is news is marketable. To underscore the market the Federal Government was pumping money into schools and libraries under various poverty titles. By the end of the 60's the publishing industry was talking seriously about the need for books for blacks.

Publishers quickly signed up books on Africa, city living and black herpes. Most were written by white writers. In 1966 a group of concerned writers, teachers, editors, illustrators and parents formed what was to be called the Council on Interracial Books for Children. The council demanded that the publishing industry publish more material by black authors. The industry claimed that there were simply no black authors interested in writing for children. To counter this claim the council sponsored a contest, offering a prize of $500, for black writers. The response was overwhelming. It was the first time I had actually been solicited to write something about my own experience. That first year Kristin Hunter, a fine writer from Philadelphia, won the prize in the older children's category and I won in the picture book category for my book ***Where Does the Day Go?*** Subsequently, the winners of the contest, authors such as Sharon Bell Mathis, Ray Sheppard and Mildred Taylor, have gone on to produce books that not only have won national recognition but, not incidentally, have made nice profits for their publishers. The industry proudly announced that it had seen the error of its ways and fully intended to correct the situation.

I felt proud to be part of this new beginning. Langston Hughes, the brilliant black poet and novelist, had lived a scant half mile from me in Harlem. He had written for young people and I fancied myself following in his footsteps. I had learned from Hughes that being a black writer meant more than simply having one's characters brown-skinned, or having them live in what publishers insist on describing on book jackets as a "ghetto." It meant understanding the nuances of value, of religion, of dreams. It meant capturing the subtle rhythms of language and movement and weaving it all, the sound and the gesture, the sweat and the prayers, into the recognizable fabric of black life....

I understood, and I know the others did too, that it was not only for black children that we wrote. We were

Walter Dean Myers, about age six.

was cut in half. For every 100 books published this year there will be one published on the black experience. Walking through the aisles at this year's American Library Association meeting in New York City was, for me, a sobering and disheartening experience. Were black writers suddenly incapable of writing well? Of course not, but we were perceived as no longer being able to sell well.

The talk in publishing circles has switched to book packaging, books for the preschool offspring of Yuppie parents, and the hoped-for upswing in retail stores. In the 70's black people called on publishers to exercise what then seemed to me the industry's responsibility. We demanded that the industry publish multicultural literature that reflected the society we live in.

I have changed my notion of the obligation of the book publishing industry. While it does have the responsibility to avoid the publishing of negative images of any people, I no longer feel that the industry has any more obligation to me, to my people, to my children, than does, say, a fast-food chain. It's clear to me that if any race, any religious or social group, elects to place its cultural needs in the hands of the profit makers then it had better be prepared for the inevitable disappointments.

What is there to be done? We must first acknowledge that in much of the black community reading as both a skill and as recreation is seriously undervalued. It is the urgent task of the black community to reinvest value in education and, specifically, in reading skills. If the market is created the books will come. Blacks are, arguably, the largest homogenous group in the country. We should be able to command a great share of the market and fulfill much of our needs ourselves.

If this seems unnecessarily harsh, or just not feasible, then we will simply have to wait for the next round of race riots, or the next interracial conflict, and the subsequent markets thus created. We can be sure, however, of one thing: if we continue to make black children nonpersons by excluding them from books and by degrading the black experience, and if we continue to neglect white children by not exposing them to any aspect of other racial and ethnic experiences in a meaningful way, we will have a next racial crisis. It will work, but it's a hard price for a transient market.

In the meanwhile there will be black artists recording the stuff of our lives in rich and varied hues, and they will continue to do so. We will twist and smooth and turn our lines carefully to the sun and wait, as we have done before, to offer them to new travelers who pass this way.

Walter Dean Myers, "I Actually Thought We Would Revolutionize the Industry," in The New York Times Book Review, *November 9, 1986, p. 50.*

writing for the white child and the Asian child too. My books did well, and so did the books of other black writers . . . . Things were looking up. I believed that my children and their counterparts would not only escape the demeaning images I had experienced but would have strong, positive images as well. And, though I was not happy with all the titles being published, the quality of the books written by blacks in the 70's was so outstanding that I actually thought we would revolutionize the industry, bringing to it a quality and dimension that would raise the standard for all children's books. Wrong. Wrong. Wrong.

No sooner had all the pieces conducive to the publishing of more books on the black experience come together than they started falling apart. The programs financed by the Johnson Administration and his Great Society were being dismantled under President Nixon. By the time President Ford left office the "Days of Rage" had ended and the temper of the time was lukewarm. Blacks were no longer a hot political issue. The libraries were the major markets for black children's books, and when they began to suffer cutbacks it was books on the black experience that were affected most.

In 1974 there were more than 900 children's books in print on the black experience. This is a small number of books considering that more than 2,000 children's books are published annually. But by 1984 this number

Jeanne Betancourt (essay date 1987)

[*In the following review, Betancourt examines the method and message of Myers's* Crystal.]

Crystal Brown, a beautiful 16-year-old black girl, is a new hot property in the glamour business. Based solely on her looks, Crystal is being packaged as a model and actress for fame and big bucks.

Walter Dean Myers's neatly constructed story [*Crystal*] is packed with behind-the-scenes episodes that teen-age readers are likely to enjoy—going to a hot club with a famous movie star, having limos at your service, wearing fabulous furs, being made up, fussed over, photographed. In his cinematic and easy-to-read style, Mr. Myers, whose books include the popular *Motown and Didi,* brings us to the heart of Crystal's dilemma, showing both the fun and seamy sides of the young model's life.

As her star rises, Crystal's personal conflicts escalate. Will she give up her old friends in Brooklyn for new friends who can help her in the business? Will she take off all her clothes for a photo spread in the top men's magazine? Will she sleep with the director to insure a starring role in his new film?

When Crystal decides not to continue as a teen-age model-actress she is choosing to go back to being just another kid. She doesn't have a brilliant career on her horizon or a knight in shining armor waiting for her on Fulton Street. She returns to a world where her mother is still a disappointed, bitter woman, her neighborhood a slum and her high school a "zoo." But it's her life, peopled by wonderful friends who represent the values she has lived by and a childhood she is not ready to give up.

While some readers may feel that in Crystal's silver slippers they would have made a different choice, they may still respect Crystal for her courage. And the next time the reader looks in the mirror wishing for a "perfect" face and figure, perhaps she will remember Crystal's experiences and be able to live through her own childhood less vulnerable to daydreams generated by a commerce that glamorizes youth and physical perfection to sell products, and that stimulates fantasies about extreme wealth and fame as a reward for beauty that is only skin deep.

Walter Dean Myers has written another fine book that touches the conflicts of adolescent readers.

> *Jeanne Betancourt, in a review of "Crystal,"
> in* The New York Times Book Review,
> *September 13, 1987, p. 48.*

Nancy Vasilakis (essay date 1989)

[*In the following review, Vasilakis praises* Me, Mop, and the Moondance Kid *as an "entertaining story by a champion yarn-spinner."*]

The power of positive thinking as a philosophy of life, or at least of baseball, has its advantages and its limitations, as T.J. eventually discovers in this entertaining story [*Me, Mop, and the Moondance Kid*] by a champion yarn-spinner. The eleven-year-old hero and his younger brother, Moondance, have recently been adopted. They have retained ties to the orphanage where they were raised, particularly to Mop (Miss Olivia Parrish) and to the kindly, mishap-prone Sister Carmelita. In his typical waggish style Myers recounts the adventures of the three children as they attempt to defy history by turning their Little League team into winners and, at the same time, make the pugnacious Mop appealing enough to be adopted by the coach. Several minor plot threads involving an old derelict and a ferocious cat, among others, fill out the story. Myers takes this hodgepodge of a plot and characters and succeeds in making them believable; and he also manages to prevent the happy ending from seeming inevitable. What keeps the reader guessing are the beguiling and self-deceiving defenses of the narrator. T.J. calls himself the star of the team even as he misses ball after ball at bat or in the field. A less generous-spirited person would have resented a younger brother who was better at the sport than he. But T.J. and meanness are strangers. Whether he's fishing Moondance's teddy bear out of the toilet or helping to catch a local crook, his sunny disposition remains intact. As an old derelict tells him, when T.J. momentarily considers seeking revenge on a bully, "'Some of us are . . . good at fighting and scratching our way through life,'" and "'some of us is gentle and kind.'" In a book alive with both types and an attention-getting plot as well, this theme of love and acceptance dances with an energy all its own. (p. 73-4)

> *Nancy Vasilakis, in a review of "Me, Mop,
> and the Moondance Kid," in* The Horn Book
> Magazine, *Vol. LXV, No. 1, January-February, 1989, pp. 73-4.*

Rudine Sims Bishop (essay date 1990)

[*Bishop is an authority on African-American children's literature. In the following excerpt from her 1990 study* Presenting Walter Dean Myers, *she explores the range and variety of Myers's published writings.*]

One of Myers's major contributions has been his authentic and generally positive portrayal of Black life in urban United States. The significance of this contribution becomes clear when it is placed in its historical context. Myers's first book was published in 1969. Just four years earlier, Nancy Larrick had lamented in the pages of the *Saturday Review* the near-total absence of Blacks in books published by juvenile publishers between 1962 and 1964. Historically, when Blacks had been portrayed in books for young people, the images presented had been laughable and insulting stereotypes, such as the servants in series like Tom Swift and the Bobbsey Twins. The advent of the civil rights movement of the sixties and the war on poverty of the

Johnson administration, along with the generally liberal attitude in the country, stimulated a major increase in the numbers of books by and about Blacks and other so-called minorities.

During the early part of this period, books about Blacks were frequently written by white authors, and many suffered from a lack of authenticity. However, by 1975, when *Fast Sam* was published, Myers saw himself as a part of a new beginning. A number of young adult novels by Black authors had already been published. Kristin Hunter's *The Soul Brothers and Sister Lou* had won, in a different category, the same Council on Interracial Books for Children Minority Writers Contest that had given Myers his start. Other novels with urban settings were Sharon Bell Mathis's *Teacup Full of Roses* and *Listen for the Fig Tree;* June Jordan's *His Own Where;* Rosa Guy's *The Friends;* Eloise Greenfield's *Sister;* Alice Childress's *A Hero Ain't Nothin' but a Sandwich.* The year of *Fast Sam* was also the year that Virginia Hamilton became the first Black author to win the Newberry Medal, although it should be pointed out that *M. C. Higgins, the Great* was not an urban novel.

The urban novels of the late sixties and early seventies were part of the new realism in adolescent literature. They not only presented Black characters, but they included previously avoided topics such as drugs, sex, and street violence. The characters often lived in harsh circumstances, and the authors portrayed them realistically. Parents were not always positive role models, and endings were not always happy. Growing up Black in the city was shown to be a very difficult task.

Myers's contribution in his early books was to add a much needed touch of humor to the developing portrait of Black life in the city. Other Black authors were offering hope for overcoming adversity and focusing on the tradition of survival that is strong in the culture and an important theme in Afro-American novels. But Myers called attention to the laughter that is also a strong tradition and one of the tools for survival.

Although he is not unique in presenting authentic representations of Blacks and Black life, his is a unique voice. At this writing he is the only Black male currently and consistently publishing young adult novels. Although he shares certain aspects of his world view with Black women authors, his voice has been tuned by barbershops and street corners, bongo drums and fatherhood, basketball and military service. His brand of humor, his facile rendering of the rhetoric of Black teenage boys, his strong focus on fathers and sons, are all shaded by his experience as a Black male. A look at Myers's urban novels reveals not only two sides of Black urban life, but also two important threads woven through the books. One thread is an authentic picture of life within a cultural group. The other is a set of themes, an offering of wisdom and insights into what it means to grow up a member of the Black community. In one set of his books, the harshness of the urban setting is backdrop; the focus is young people and their escapades.

In the other, the urban setting is an integral part of the story itself. The portrayal of the Black experience and the insights he offers can be found in both.

The authenticity of Myers's portrayals of Black life is heightened by his weaving of important elements of Black culture into his stories. He is best known for his realistic representation of the rhetorical, grammatical, and semantic characteristics of Black English. Whenever his Black characters speak, they sound like real Black people. It should be noted that although his informal vernacular is most noticeable to critics, his characters reflect the full range of Black urban speech, both female and male, from street corner rapping to formal standard English.

Another cultural thread that Myers weaves through the urban novels is religion. Particularly in the novels that include older female characters (such as Grandma Carrie in *It Ain't All for Nothin'* and Sister Gibbs in *Crystal*) the language and the music of the Black church are used to build character and setting. On the other hand, particularly in *Mojo and the Russians,* Myers recognizes that non-Christian belief systems can still exist in the Black community side by side with Christianity.

Other aspects of Black culture are woven into the stories as a part of the setting, a reflection of the details of daily living of people who belong to a distinct cultural group. References to sacred and secular music and to musicians are sprinkled throughout the books. Aphorisms turn up frequently, often in the mouths of older women. Occasionally the names of a few Black heroes can be found. In one book, *The Legend of Tarik,* Myers offers to young Black readers an epic Black hero whose qualities—strength, determination, endurance, intelligence, compassion—represent a cultural ideal.

Myers himself identifies what he and the other Black novelists were doing:

> I had learned from [Langston] Hughes that being a Black writer meant more than simply having one's characters brown-skinned, or having them live in what publishers insist on describing on book jackets as a 'ghetto.' It meant understanding the nuances of value, of religion, of dreams. It meant capturing the subtle rhythms of language and movement and weaving it all, the sound and the gesture, the sweat and the prayers, into the recognizable fabric of black life.

Also woven into the tapestry of Black life that Myers offers his readers are insights that might help them understand what it means to grow up Black in the urban centers of this nation. Myers is clear about the obstacles and hardships that often must be faced in such a setting, especially by people who are poor. Drugs, gangs, and violence are a fact of life in many large cities. Social agencies cannot always be depended on to provide support, or if they do help, their support sometimes comes at the expense of a loss of pride, dignity, or control over one's own life. Racism is a given. Myers is also clear about the potential for overcoming the hardships. He writes of love and laughter and offers compassion and hope. He writes of the need to find strength within oneself and of the possibility of finding strength within the group, whether the group is the family, the peer group, or the community.

This notion of community support, of Blacks helping Blacks, is important to Myers. He notes that television programs and books by white authors often portray whites helping Blacks (as in "Different Strokes" or "Webster," in which white families adopt Black children), or they portray Blacks helping whites, whites helping whites, but not usually Blacks helping Blacks. Myers says, "I find that a very precious relationship, and it's being omitted, so when I write I thought I should write about that."

At the same time that his books offer insights about Black life, they also deal with themes that can be found in other young adult literature and in literature in general: friendships and peer relationships, family, individual and social responsibility, love, growing up, finding oneself. Myers succeeds, therefore, in embedding the universal inside the particulars of the reflected lives of people whose image, in the field of children's and young adult literature, had for too many years suffered neglect and abuse. Again, Myers speaks for himself:

> What I wanted to do was to portray this vital community as one that is very special to a lot of people. I wanted to show the people I knew as being as richly endowed with those universal traits of love, humor, ambition as any in the world. This, I hope, is what my books do. That space of earth was no ghetto, it was home. Those were not exotic stereotypes, those were my people. And I love them.

Myers is proud to be an Afro-American young adult novelist, but he is first of all a writer and can and does write about other people, in other genres, and about other topics. He has written short stories, nonfiction magazine pieces, nonfiction children's books, books for older elementary-age readers, mysteries, adventure stories, easy-to-read science fiction, picture books, and a new novel offering some blank space and invitations for the reader to add his or her own writing to the book.

The adult stories, published in the seventies, reveal some of Myers's versatility. The stories offer a different world view from that in his work for young people. There is some bitterness (**"How Long Is Forever?"**), tragedy (**"The Vision of Felipe"**), loneliness (**"The Going On"**), insanity (**"The Dark Side of the Moon"**). One or two may be precursors of the work to come. **"The Vision of Felipe,"** set in Peru, features a gentle, sensitive, and compassionate young boy, who when orphaned by his grandmother's death goes off to the city to seek his fortune. Felipe is in many ways similar to Tito, the Puerto Rican boy in **Scorpions.** Like Tito, Felipe has been greatly influenced by his beloved grandmother's teachings, and his relationship with his friend Daniel is in some ways similar to that between Jamal and Tito.

Other stories are related to Myers's young adult work only in that they explore similar topics. **"Juby"** includes a white person studying voodoo, though the story is in a much darker vein than **Mojo and the Russians.** The dialect used in the narrative has a Caribbean flavor similar to the one in **Mr. Monkey and the Gotcha Bird.** Both **"Juby"** and **"Gums,"** in which a grandfather and his young grandson are overcome by their fear of a personified Death, may have their roots in the scary stories Myers remembers his father telling. **"Bubba"** features a white soldier who is part of the military escort for the funeral of a Black soldier killed in Vietnam. He spends the night in the home of the deceased soldier's mother and has to confront the issue of racism as it sometimes operates in the military. The issue is one of those touched on in **Fallen Angels.**

Myers has also produced two nonfiction books for young people, **The World of Work** and **Social Welfare.** **The World of Work** draws on the knowledge Myers acquired when he was a vocational placement supervisor for the New York State Employment Service. It is a guide to selecting a career, including descriptions of numerous jobs, their requirements, the method of entry, possibilities for advancement. True to his storytelling self, Myers introduces **The World of Work** with an imaginative speculation about how a hungry cave man might have created for himself the first job.

Social Welfare is a brief history and explanation of the welfare system, how it operates, who it serves, its problems, and some possible solutions. Both are well written—clear and straightforward. Both are over ten years old and somewhat dated, although **Social Welfare** is not nearly as dated as its author might wish it to be, given his expressed desire for change in the system. The books are nonfiction that is accurate, clear, and interestingly written.

Myers is willing to take risks with format, genre, and style, and he does so with varying degrees of success. **Brainstorm** is a science fiction story written with a limited vocabulary and designed for reluctant or remedial readers in fifth through eighth grades. Although Myers says that he would like to "bring some good literature" to the easy reader form, the restrictions on length and vocabulary make that a difficult task. It *is* possible to do what he did with **Brainstorm**—present interesting but undeveloped characters in a fast-moving plot. **Brainstorm** appeals also because it uses black-and-white photographs of a diverse group of teenagers who are the crew of a space ship sent to an alien planet to investigate the cause of a spate of "brainstorms" that have been destroying humans on earth.

Brainstorm received reasonably good notices, but the reviews of **The Black Pearl and the Ghost** range from scathingly negative to a cheerful acceptance of the book as spoof and a recognition of its good points. *Kirkus* called it "clunkingly obvious . . . hollow, creaky." The *Children's Book Services* reviewer found it "static . . . neither well-written nor interesting . . . trivia." On

Jacket illustration by Diane de Groat for The Young Landlords *(1979).*

the other hand, *Booklist* saw "funny characters . . . sprightly pace," and *Horn Book* accepted it as "exaggerated in style and designed to meet the tastes of children."

A good reviewer must consider what the author was trying to do. *The Black Pearl and the Ghost; or One Mystery after Another* is a spoof meant for children somewhere between ages seven and ten. The humor starts with the subtitle (the book consists of two mysteries, one after another) and continues through the joke shared with the reader but not the ghost-busting detective. It is a profusely illustrated book, although not quite a picture book, and an important part of the story is told in Robert Quackenbush's amusing pictures.

Myers's books for elementary school readers, including his picture books, show a vivid imagination at work. His realistic stories, *Where Does the Day Go?* and *The Dancers,* are built on premises that were unusual at the time of their publication: a group of Black and Hispanic children speculating about a natural phenomenon and receiving answers from a Black father, and a Black boy from Harlem intrigued by ballet. *Fly, Jimmy, Fly* shows a young boy using his imagination to soar above the city. *The Golden Serpent,* set in India and illustrated by

the Provensens, sets up a mystery that it leaves unresolved. *The Dragon Takes a Wife* takes the traditional knight-fights-a-dragon tale and twists it to make the dragon the protagonist, as Kenneth Grahame did in *The Reluctant Dragon.* Then Myers adds a touch of Blackness in the form of Mabel Mae Jones and her hip, rhyming spells. Although *Kirkus* called it "intercultural hocus pocus," other reviewers found it amusing, even delightful. The imaginative humor works. *Mr. Monkey and the Gotcha Bird* dips into African and Caribbean folk traditions for its narrative voice and its trickster monkey who outsmarts the gotcha bird who would have him for supper.

Myers's novel for readers under twelve, *Me, Mop, and the Moondance Kid,* echoes some of the concerns and qualities of his young adult novels. The story is told by T.J., who, along with his younger brother, Moondance, has been recently adopted. Their task is to help their friend Mop (Miss Olivia Parrish), who is still at the orphanage, to be adopted too, preferably by the coach of their Little League team, which they are trying to turn into a winner. The style is typical Myers: T.J.'s narration is easygoing and humorous, characters are credible and likable, the plot moves along briskly, and the human relationships are warm.

Sweet Illusions is a young adult novel, published by the Teachers and Writers Collaborative, that experiments with format. It is an episodic novel focusing on teenage pregnancy. Not only is each chapter narrated by a different character, but at the end of each chapter the reader is invited to help create the story by writing a letter, a song, a list, a daydream. Lined pages are available for writing directly in the book (with a caution about not writing in library books). The characters are Black, white, and Hispanic, and all of them are learning of the difficulties and responsibilities involved in becoming parents. Both the young women and the fathers of their children tell their stories, which raise hard issues involved in teenage pregnancy: decisions about abortion and adoption, parental and community attitudes toward the mothers, irresponsibility on the part of the fathers, continuing their education, providing for the child. The book works. Myers has, in a brief space, managed to create believable characters with individual voices. Their stories are unique and at the same time recognizable to anyone who has thought about or grappled with the problems of teenage pregnancy. The purpose is to provoke thought, which happens as readers get caught up in the characters and their stories.

In spite of its workbook format, *Sweet Illusions* received some serious critical attention. *Booklist,* for example, gave it high praise, calling it "an astute, realistic consideration of some of the problems associated with teenage pregnancy, valuable for personal reading as well as classroom discussion." Further, the reviewer found that "Myers' profiles are quick and clever; his characters, stubborn, confused, and vulnerable, draw substance and individuality from tough, savvy dialogue and credible back-drops." It is an unusual book that succeeds because it draws on Myers's highly developed craftsmanship.

Myers has developed a number of strengths as a writer. Critics agree that he has a fine ear for dialogue, which becomes one of the major means he uses to develop characterization and authenticate settings. Partly because their speech seems real, his characters seem real, too. Myers approaches his characters with warmth and sensitivity; he understands the concerns of young people. His first-person narratives project an intimacy that invites readers immediately into the world of the protagonist. Once there, his flair for drama keeps the pages turning.

When he wants to write humor, he knows how to create it with characterization, with language play, and with situations. Even in his serious books, humor is sometimes interjected, as in the scene in which a Hari Krishna and a Black Muslim fight over saving Tippy's soul in the bus station in *It Ain't All for Nothin'.* When the focus of a Myers book is humor, as in *Mojo and the Russians,* a reader may often laugh out loud.

Critics have not paid much attention to Myers's ability to turn a phrase, to create sharp, clear images outside the context of dialogue, but some of his figurative language is particularly apt. In *Won't Know,* he describes the house the seniors live in as seeming to "squat in the middle of the block, . . . thinking of itself as slightly better than the rest. It gave you the feeling that if it had been human it would have been a fat old man who used to have a lot of money." *Fallen Angels* is replete with vivid figurative language that brings to life the experience of war . . . .

[Critics] are not unanimous in their praise of Myers's work. Reviewers who have found flaws in his craft have focused on three areas: credibility (e.g., *Mojo and the Russians, The Young Landlords, The Nicholas Factor*), unevenness in plot (e.g., *Won't Know Till I Get There, Crystal, Hoops, The Legend of Tarik*), and weak characterization (e.g., *The Nicholas Factor, The Legend of Tarik*). These assessments are not unanimous, however: for every reviewer who found one of those aspects flawed, another found it strong.

The charges of lack of credibility occur in his humorous novels and in the adventure stories and can be answered by examining Myers's style and the genre in which he is writing. In his humorous novels, some critics respond to the exaggeration that is a part of a Black rhetorical style by testing the escapades of the young people against reality and finding them unbelievable. The adventure stories, too, employ some exaggeration, which may displease some reviewers.

Some of the urban novels, such as *Won't Know Till I Get There* and *Hoops,* have been described as slow moving. This unevenness may also be attributed to an aspect of Black rhetorical style, narrative sequencing, in which there is a tendency to meander off the route to the point one is trying to make, to take the long way when the direct route would be quicker.

The accusation of weak characterization came in response to *The Nicolas Factor* and *The Legend of Tarik,* both of which incorporate enough of the elements of the romantic adventure novel to influence the character development in the direction of types. Ironically, Myers has also been praised for his ability to create credible, well-delineated characters.

Myers's strengths as a novelist far outweigh his occasional shortcomings. In the *Horn Book* review of *Fallen Angels,* Ethel Heins referred to Myers as "a writer of skill, judgment, and maturity." He has honed that skill on a set of books that have earned him a place as one of the most important writers of young adult literature in the country today.

Myers loves his work. He seems always to be juggling a number of different projects—a book on Black history, a fictional book about a singer who moves from the church to secular music, another book on the order of *Sweet Illusions,* another picture book, even a book of nursery rhymes.

> As a writer there are many issues I would like to tackle. I am interested in loneliness, in our attempts to escape reality through the use of drugs or through

our own psychological machinations. I am interested in how we deal with each other, both sexually and in other ways, and the reasons we so often reject each other.

He has achieved some status in the field and is eager to stretch, to explore any and all kinds of ideas, to break away from whatever restrictions seem to be imposed on him because he is a Black writer. At the same time, he will continue writing about the lives of ordinary Black people, "to tell Black children about their humanity and about their history and how to grease their legs so the ash won't show and how to braid their hair so it's easy to comb on frosty winter mornings." May he keep on keepin' on; it ain't all for nothin'. (pp. 93-103)

> *Rudine Sims Bishop, in her* Presenting Walter Dean Myers, *Twayne Publishers, 1990, 123 p.*

FURTHER READING

Boyd, Alex. Review of *The Legend of Tarik,* by Walter Dean Myers. *Voice of Youth Advocates* 4, No. 4 (October 1981): 36
  Negative assessment of *The Legend of Tarik.* Boyd concludes: "Actually, this is an awful book. There is so much predictability in the shallow characters and situations that the mean-spirited violence is almost welcome, but not quite. The number of beheadings, impalements and other vicious ways by which numerous individuals are dispatched could only be enjoyed by the most surfeited devotee of the current wave of horror flicks."

Review of *Tales of a Dead King,* by Walter Dean Myers. *Kirkus Reviews* LI, No. 21 (1 November 1983): J205.
  Mixed assessment of *Tales of a Dead King.*

Lipsyte, Robert. Review of *Fast Sam, Cool Clyde, and Stuff,* by Walter Dean Myers. *The New York Times Book Review* (4 May 1975): 28, 30.
  Summarizes the plot of *Fast Sam, Cool Clyde, and Stuff,* noting of the author: "Myers has a gentle and humorous touch, especially with dialogue. Stuff's emotional growth over a year binds together what is

essentially a series of stories, all told with the soft distance of nostalgia."

Review of *The Nicholas Factor,* by Walter Dean Myers. *Publishers Weekly* 223, No. 11 (18 March 1983): 70.
  Labels *The Nicholas Factor* "a disturbing, powerful work," noting that Myers "explores an intriguing idea here: does an elite group have the right to impose its views on society, even if it believes its vision is right?"

Rochman, Hazel. Review of *Won't Know Till I Get There,* by Walter Dean Myers. *School Library Journal* 28, No. 9 (May 1982): 72-3.
  Examines theme and dialogue in *Won't Know Till I Get There.* Rochman determines: "The overt didacticism is quite superfluous: excellent characterization clearly demonstrates Myers' theme that those whom we perceive in terms of labels and group stereotypes— old, Black, female, enemy, delinquent, deserting mother—turn out to be widely differing, surprising and interesting individuals when we allow ourselves to know them."

Sutherland, Zena. Review of *The Dancers,* by Walter Dean Myers. *Bulletin of the Center for Children's Books* 25, No. 11 (July-August 1972): 174.
  Brief review of *The Dancers,* noting: "A story with good potential and some humor doesn't quite come off, although it may appeal to many children because of the subject and its unusual setting."

———. Review of *The Legend of Tarik,* by Walter Dean Myers. *Bulletin of the Center for Children's Books* 35, No. 3 (November 1981): 52.
  Overview of plot and characterization in *The Legend of Tarik.* Sutherland writes: "In some ways this story of medieval Africa has appeal and strength: it provides a much-needed fantasy hero who is black, it follows the classic pattern of Good triumphing over Evil, it is not overcrowded with characters or symbols or arcane terminology. It is weakened, however, by the slow start and equally slow pace, caused in part by the intermittent heaviness of the writing style."

Zvirin, Stephanie. Review of *Hoops,* by Walter Dean Myers. *Booklist* 78, No. 2 (15 September 1981): 98.
  Highly favorable assessment of *Hoops,* concluding: "Dialogue rings with authenticity, on-court action is colorful and well integrated into the story, and the author's dramatic conclusion is handled with poignancy and power."

Gloria Naylor

1950-

American novelist, critic, and short story writer.

Naylor is best known as the author of *The Women of Brewster Place* (1982), for which she won the American Book Award in 1983. Born and raised in New York City, Naylor recalled: "Growing up in the North in integrated schools, I wasn't taught anything about Black history or literature.... When I discovered that there was this whole long literary tradition of Black folk in this country, I felt I had been cheated out of something. I wanted to sit down and write about something that I hadn't read about, and that was all about me—the Black woman in America." Discouraged by a dearth of books on black women by black women, Naylor endeavored to write one. Her first work, *The Women of Brewster Place*, focuses on seven black female residents of Brewster Place—a dilapidated ghetto housing project in an unidentified northern city—and their relationships with one another. As they cope with living in a racist and sexist society, they encounter further abuse from their own husbands, lovers, and children. "While *The Women of Brewster Place* is about the black woman's condition in America," Naylor explained, "I had to deal with the fact that one composite picture couldn't do justice to the complexity of the black female experience. So I tried to solve this problem by creating a microcosm on a dead-end street and devoting each chapter to a different woman's life. These women vary in age, personal background, political consciousness, and sexual preference. What they do share is a common oppression and, more importantly, a spiritual strength and sense of female communion that I believe all women have employed historically for their psychic health and survival."

The inspiration for *The Women of Brewster Place* came from several sources, according to Naylor: "The women [of Brewster Place] are women I never knew personally. But I have known that *spirit*, I have definitely known that *life*. That's how those characters were born. But they lived for me as characters with their own personalities and I let them have it. I wanted to immortalize the spirit I saw in my grandmother, my great aunt and my mom." *The Women of Brewster Place* was conceived as a short story, but Naylor expanded it into a novel, completing most of the manuscript while working as a hotel switchboard operator and studying at Brooklyn College. By the time she obtained her master's degree in African-American studies from Yale University in 1983, she was already recognized as an impressive new writer. Several years later, she published *Linden Hills* (1985) and *Mama Day* (1988) and secured her reputation as an author of formidable skill.

In *Linden Hills* Naylor abandoned the gritty realism of *The Women of Brewster Place* for an allegorical com-

mentary on the fallacies of black mobility and material success. Linden Hills, an exclusive suburb located near Brewster Place, is headed by Luther Nedeed, a real estate tycoon and mortician. The novel revolves around two young men, Willie and Lester, who meet Linden's residents while working odd jobs over the Christmas holidays. As Willie and Lester offer their services throughout the neighborhood, they witness Nedeed's malevolent control over the community and expose the idleness, hypocrisy, and bigotry of the townspeople. Critics have cited similarities between *Linden Hills* and Dante's *Inferno*. For example, Dante's hell consists of nine circles, with each descending layer populated by more repugnant sinners; in Naylor's novel, Linden Hills is composed of nine circular streets on a hill at the bottom of which reside the wealthiest and most decadent citizens. Michiko Kakutani observed: "Although the notion of using Dante's *Inferno* to illuminate the co-opting of black aspirations in contemporary America may strike the prospective reader as pretentious, one is quickly beguiled by the actual novel—so gracefully does

Miss Naylor fuse together the epic and the naturalistic, the magical and the real."

Mama Day, Naylor's most recent work, is set in an all-black rural community named Willow Springs, an island located off the coasts of South Carolina and Georgia. Willow Springs was founded by Sapphira Wade, an African slave and sorceress who married and later murdered her owner after forcing him to bequeath his land to his slaves and their offspring. The novel centers on two of Sapphira's descendants—Mama Day, the elderly leader and mystical healer of Willow Springs, who appeared briefly in *Linden Hills,* and Cocoa, Mama Day's strong-willed grandniece, who lives in New York City but returns to Willow Springs every summer. The book alternates between narratives about Mama Day and stories about Cocoa and her husband George, a young black man who lives by reason and ritual. Their lives collide when, visiting Mama Day on Willow Springs, Cocoa becomes deathly ill, and George is forced to put aside his rational thinking to save her. Ultimately, George saves Cocoa, but only by great personal sacrifice.

Despite the critical acclaim of *Linden Hills* and *Mama Day, The Women of Brewster Place* remains Naylor's most popular work. Adapted for television in a production starring Oprah Winfrey, Lynn Whitfield, and Cicely Tyson in 1989, the novel has enjoyed renewed interest. Naylor is currently at work on the fourth and final book in the loosely connected *The Women of Brewster Place-Linden Hills-Mama Day* series. Assessing Naylor's appeal, *Washington Post* reviewer Deirdre Donahue observed: "Naylor is not afraid to grapple with life's big subjects: sex, birth, love, death, grief. Her women feel deeply, and she unflinchingly transcribes their emotions.... Naylor's potency wells up from her language. With prose as rich as poetry, a passage will suddenly take off and sing like a spiritual.... Vibrating with undisguised emotion, *The Women of Brewster Place* springs from the same roots that produced the blues. Like them, her books sing of sorrows proudly borne by black women in America."

(For further information about Naylor's life and works, see *Black Writers; Contemporary Authors,* Vol. 107; *Contemporary Authors New Revision Series,* Vol. 27; and *Contemporary Literary Criticism,* Vols. 28, 52.)

PRINCIPAL WORKS

The Women of Brewster Place (novel) 1982
Linden Hills (novel) 1985
Mama Day (novel) 1988

Annie Gottlieb (essay date 1982)

[*In the following excerpt, Gottlieb reviews* The Women of Brewster Place, *concluding: "Miss Naylor bravely risks sentimentality and melodrama to write her compassion and outrage large, and she pulls it off triumphantly."*]

Ten or 12 years ago, the vanguard of the women's movement began exhorting the rest of us to pay attention to our relationships with other women: mothers, daughters, sisters, friends. How important those neglected bonds were, said representatives, how much of the actual substance of daily life they were. But it was hard, at first, for most women to *see* clearly the significance of those bonds; all our lives those relationships had been the backdrop, while the sexy, angry fireworks with men were the show.

Now, it seems, that particular lesson of feminism has been not only taken to heart, but deeply absorbed. Here are two first novels in which it feels perfectly natural that women are the foreground figures, primary both to the reader and to each other, regardless of whether they're involved with men. In Gloria Naylor's fierce, loving group portrait of seven black women in one housing development ..., the bonds between women are the abiding ones. Most men are incalculable hunters who come and go. They are attractive—but weak and/or dangerous—representatives of nature and of violence who both fertilize and threaten the female core.

Gloria Naylor's *The Women of Brewster Place* is set in one of those vintage urban-housing developments that black people (who are, in truth, "nutmeg," "ebony," "saffron," "cinnamon-red" or "gold") have inherited from a succession of other ethnic groups. The difference is that while the Irish and Italians used it as a jumping-off place for the suburbs, for most of its "colored daughters" Brewster Place is "the end of the line": "They came because they had no choice and would remain for the same reason." But the end of the line is not the end of life. With their backs literally to the wall—a brick barrier that has turned Brewster Place into a dead end—the women make their stand together, fighting a hostile world with love and humor.

There's Mattie Michael, dark as "rich, double cocoa," who defied her overprotective father to take a man who was pure temptation, almost a force of nature—a Pan. Pregnant and disowned, she made the instinctive matriarchal decision (I mean that word in the mythic, not the sociological, sense) to live without a man and invest all her love back into her child. Left in the lurch by the grown, spoiled son who results, she becomes the anchor for the other women of Brewster Place.

There's Etta Mae Johnson, survivor and good-time woman, who comes home to Mattie when her dream of redemption by marrying a "respectable" preacher is sordidly ended. There's Ciel Turner, whose husband, Eugene, ominously resents her fertility: "With two kids and you on my back, I ain't never gonna have nothin'...nothin'!" There's Kiswana (formerly Melanie) Browne, idealistic daughter of middle-class parents, who has moved to Brewster Place to be near "my people." Cora Lee, a welfare mother, likes men only because they provide babies, but she can't cope with children once they are older. She is *almost* lifted out of the inertia of her life by the power of art when Kiswana takes her to see a black production of Shakespeare in the park. And, finally, there are Theresa and Lorraine, lovers who embody the ultimate commitment of woman to woman and yet arouse uprise or loathing in most of the other women of Brewster Place.

Despite Gloria Naylor's shrewd and lyrical portrayal of many of the realities of black life (her scene of services in the Canaan Baptist Church is brilliant), *The Women of Brewster Place* isn't realistic fiction—it is mythic. Nothing supernatural happens in it, yet its vivid, earthy characters (especially Mattie) seem constantly on the verge of breaking out into magical powers. The book has two climaxes, one of healing and rebirth, one of destruction. In the first, Mattie magnificently wrestles Ciel, dying of grief, back to life. In the second, Lorraine, rejected by the others, is gang raped, a blood sacrifice brutally proving the sisterhood of all women. Miss Naylor bravely risks sentimentality and melodrama to write her compassion and outrage large, and she pulls it off triumphantly.

> *Annie Gottlieb, "Women Together," in* The New York Times Book Review, *August 22, 1982, pp. 11, 25.*

Loyle Hairston (essay date 1983)

[*In the following essay, Hairston favorably reviews* The Women of Brewster Place, *praising the book's rich and "well-drawn" characters.*]

The personal stories of several women whose lives intertwine by virtue of their residence on the same block comprise the subject matter of this award-winning first novel [*The Women of Brewster Place*]. Brewster Place, like so many urban areas, had more prosperous times as a lily-white community. Now, it has become what the media during the '60s christened a "ghetto"—that is, a black slum. But inhabiting this piece of urban real estate is a colorful cast of characters, who throb with vitality amid the shattering of their hopes and dreams.

We meet Mattie Michael first. Seduced and made pregnant in late adolescence by the local dandy in her native Tennessee town, Mattie is later beaten by her father for refusing to divulge the man's name and must leave home. With her son, Basil, she eventually finds her way to Brewster Place, where she develops quickly into a hard-working, resourceful woman bent on giving her son a good start in life. Indulged and doted upon, Basil grows into a trouble-prone teenager whose reckless ways lead to a manslaughter charge. Mattie mortgages her home to pay his bail only to be betrayed by her beloved son, who jumps bail and skips town, leaving his mother heartbroken and destitute.

In the course of her travails, Mattie has met Etta Mae Johnson, a confirmed hedonist whose dreams have been dissipated in her pursuit of "good times." For Etta, happiness is a man. Thus, attending church services with Mattie Michael one Sunday, she finds herself listening, not to the reverend's sermon, but to her old instincts telling her to lasso someone who can support her in the style "that complemented the type of woman she had fought all these years to become." The good reverend, however, proves to be as much a man of the world as of the cloth, experienced in exploiting the wiles of his congregation's female members.

We also meet Kiswana Browne, a naive, middle-class apostate given to revolutionary idealism. When Kiswana's mother visits her estranged daughter in her third-floor walkup on Brewster Place, readers are afforded an insightful look at the generation gap. Kiswana is a bright-eyed product of the '60s who received the dictum "black is beautiful" as political ideology. Mom, though upbraided for her "backwardness," proves to be more than a match for her militant daughter, who finally succumbs to a force more potent than her revolutionary zeal—a mother's love.

The saddest story in this collection is also the most amusing. It features young, overweight Cora Lee—a stereotypical "welfare mother." Cora has not given much thought to why she had her brood of children, nor has she considered what kind of future awaits them. Her more troubling concerns are the tragic lives of her favorite TV soap opera characters. Persuaded by Kiswana to take the children to an Afro-American cultural affair, she finds the event so stimulating that she goes home and jumps into bed with her current lover. Several stories later, we find her pregnant again.

For me the most penetrating of the stories is "The Two," with its well-drawn lesbian characters, Theresa and Lorraine. Sharp contrasts between the young lovers' personalities surface when Lorraine befriends Ben, the building superintendent and handy man. Although she doesn't see a rival in Ben, Theresa opposes the friendship for more complex reasons. The women's domestic conflict is exacerbated by their different reactions to the hostility directed at them by their neighbors, who are portrayed as harboring the bigoted social attitudes common to many Americans. The story ends in a spate of violence, with Ben being brutally murdered when he is mistaken for Lorraine's attacker.

Other characters are, for the most part, equally well-drawn, each with a strong individuality shaped out of the pathetic circumstances of their lives and all sharing a common fate—life has turned on them with a vengeance. Naylor's prose embraces them warmly, revealing in a vivid, fast-paced narrative their various levels of consciousness. While her subjects are Afro-American, these are not racial stories except in the context of U.S.

life. They are primarily stories about the human will to survive for as long as possible.

The world of Brewster Place is a familiar one in that it mirrors a real world of poverty and all of its attendant ills—humiliation, pain, powerlessness, loneliness, despair. As slice of life tales, however, Naylor's offerings leave unanswered the questions of social causality and how folk like those depicted are to overcome their degrading condition. Is individual initiative à la Horatio Alger the way out? Or is radical change in society required? In the flyfleaf of her book, Naylor quotes the Langston Hughes poem which asks, regarding "a dream deferred," "Does it dry up/like a raisin in the sun," or, as Hughes posed in the last line, "Does it explode!" Naylor's characters are unlikely to explode in the sense that Hughes meant. For even though most of them are shown as being vital, scrappy and endowed with the varieties of inner strength that spawns wisdom—the sagacity to attack their circumstances with a determination to alter the course of their lives—none, except for the young militant, envisions any hope of better times.

Understanding the dialectics of change would seem to be the moral task of the writer who quests for illuminating truths about people whose lives are under assault from an oppressive society. But perhaps Naylor, like most U.S. writers, is a kind of closet social Darwinist who does not see the U.S. as oppressive; who sees, rather, a nation with surmountable social problems that test the mettle of individual citizens. In any case, the narrative gives no hint that its author is in serious conflict with fundamental U.S. values. Consequently, questions arise about the moral and philosophical premises underlying her fiction. Whereas works like *Huckleberry Finn* and *Native Son* endure partly because they are critical of society, Naylor's first effort seems to fall in with most of the fiction being published today, which bypasses provocative social themes to play, instead, in the shallower waters of isolated personal relationships.

Indeed, in some recently published Afro-American fiction, the black man has eclipsed a hostile society as the archest villain in our midst, his image as brute and rapist having graduated from white supremacist myth to gospel truth. While *Brewster Place* does not suffer from this dreary perspective, it does confine its concerns to the warts and cankers of individual personality, neglecting to delineate the origins of those social conditions which so strongly affect personality and behavior.

I'm not suggesting that Naylor should have written a different book. I'm merely noting that what I look for in a story is absent—namely, some new insight into, some purposeful probing of, mundane reality. For a writer to achieve this requires, first and foremost, the courage to write from strong conviction, in addition to talent and knowledge—a stance that, to me, is especially incumbent upon Afro-Americans. Even though this may work against one's striving for recognition and success in the literary world, one might well ask whether recognition

by an establishment committed to maintaining a status quo that subjugates third world people at home and abroad is truly meritorious. In any case, the works of writers who lack conviction seldom survive as solid literature.

Notwithstanding the many questions it provokes about what is happening in contemporary Afro-American literature, *The Women of Brewster Place* is an enjoyable read. Naylor displays a fine talent as both story teller and prose stylist, armed as she is with a poetic feeling for the English language, folk speech and the contradictory nuances of personality. Here is a good beginning, rich in marvelous detail about characters with whom we can easily identify. Hopefully, her next offering will plumb further the depths of human experience. (pp. 282-85)

> *Loyle Hairston, in a review of "The Women of Brewster Place," in* Freedomways, *Vol. 23, No. 4, fourth quarter, 1983, pp. 282-85.*

Judith V. Branzburg (essay date 1984)

[*In the following excerpt, Branzburg examines characterization in* The Women of Brewster Place.]

Black writers often feel compelled to ask themselves in what ways and to what extent their art should serve the political-social needs of their race. The answer is not easy to find. Failure to write with a crusading mentality has often brought on accusations of betrayal of the race, while polemical writing had been criticized as dull and lacking in artistry or subtlety. For Afro-American women writers the perils of politics and art are more numerous than for the men. Not only must the women remain true to their race, they must also support racial unity by not being too hard on black men.

A number of contemporary women novelists, including Toni Morrison and Toni Cade Bambara, have succeeded in being faithful to art and their race while writing honestly about relationships between black men and women. Their writing has the power to move both through the situations of the characters and the beauty of the prose. Their novels also have a ring of truth because the women write with a black sensibility, with black rhythms, and in a black vernacular, exhibiting a type of imagination which takes its substance from the experience of being black, not non-white, in the United States.

This is the tradition in which Gloria Naylor has placed herself with *The Women of Brewster Place.* The success of her novel is in her rendering, in rich, sensuous, rhythmic language, a sense of the reality of Afro-American women's lives while including serious examination of racial and sexual politics. Without being overtly critical of the racism of America, Naylor manages to make the reader understand how the economic and social situation of black lives becomes one with personal lives, with the relationships between men and women,

women and women, and parents and children, without diminishing the humanity of the individuals involved. She makes it clear that the socio-economic reality of black lives creates black men's tendency to leave their lovers and children. She knows that black children need special training to survive in a society which holds blacks in disdain. But Naylor is also certain that black men are capable of taking more responsibility than they do, and that mothers of any color will try to do their best for their children. (p. 116)

Brewster Place is separated from the rest of the city by a brick wall erected to control traffic in the major part of the town. Disconnected from the business of the city by a wall, Brewster Place has become a dead end, literally and figuratively, for the black people who finally come to inhabit it. By setting Brewster Place off, Naylor is able to write of Afro-Americans untouched by whites in their daily, domestic lives.

The novel is organized around the lives of seven women, all of whom live on Brewster Place. Each chapter, or story, is devoted to detailing the circumstances of one of the women's lives. Naylor's intent is not to present all the different possible types or situations of Afro-American women, but to present a range that illustrates the difference in detail but the sameness in effect. Mattie Michael, the emotional center of the novel, is a middle aged woman who comes to Brewster Place from the South. Her story is the only one that does not take place entirely on Brewster Place. Before her coming, she has dedicated her life to raising her son, only to have him fail her. Etta Mae Johnson, an old friend of Mattie's southern childhood, comes to Brewster Place and Mattie to make a final attempt at finding a man who will stay with and support her. She is fearful that the charms which have stood her in good stead, allowing her to seduce men when she needed them, will now fail her. Kiswana Browne, a young political activist whose vision of her people was born in the Black Power movement, comes from the good side of the tracks, Linden Hills, to live and work with "the people" on Brewster Place. Another young woman, Lucielia Louise Turner, a kind of stepchild to Mattie, learns the pain of loving a man, Eugene, who cannot give her any kind of support, emotional or economic, and the anguish of the death of a child. Cora Lee, the welfare mother, seems a child herself. But she spends her life having babies, fascinated by them yet unable to deal with them once they are no longer infants. Finally, "The Two," is the story of the lesbians Lorraine and Theresa. They live isolated from the others on the street, separated because of their sexual love for each other. They become symbols both of women's pain and women's unity by the end of the novel.

Except in the "Kiswana" chapter, which is the least fully realized portrait, and "The Two" up until the point of Lorraine's rape, patterns of attraction to and abandonment by men, too much caring for children, and the realization of the solace, comfort and love that black women can give one another are repeated throughout the novel. But each retelling of the black women's tale is not simply a repetition. It is a building on the previous telling, gaining force and culminating in Lorraine's rape and its aftermath, Mattie's final vision. Both of these beautifully rendered last scenes address the question from Langston Hughes' poem, "What happens to a dream deferred?" which is posed on the prefatory pages of the novel. The rape is a male response, the tearing down the wall of Mattie's dream a female one. (pp. 117-18)

In each case, the women accept responsibility for their parts in their relationships with men, and can then continue their lives. By taking responsibility for mistakes, pain, and love, and in choosing each other, the women accept that they can, at least to some extent, control their lives. Such an acceptance means ceasing to be victims of others' wills or circumstances.... The men are finally incidental, good for pain and not much more. They come, do their dirty work, and go. The children fail too, for they are not strong enough to carry their parents' dreams. The women stay and support each other.

Naylor is as successful as she is at presenting the complexity of black lives without reducing the people to types simply because she is an accomplished writer. She is especially good at describing the sensuous and at evoking the sounds, smells, and feelings of any given situation. Her talent for creating rich, emotional characters makes her failings particularly disappointing. Kiswana, the Black Power activist and the two lesbians are flat characters, especially Kiswana. The only time Kiswana seems to come alive is in the few lines when she is thinking of her lover Abshu. The lesbians also fail because Naylor does not invest them with the sensuousness and fullness of feeling that characterizes the other women. The "Kiswana" chapter is also the only one in which Naylor fails to show the seamless intermingling of the political and the personal and resorts to a lecture from Kiswana's middle class and bourgeois, yet very proud mother. Naylor seems to have difficulty portraying women whose life choices or circumstances have separated them from the pain of financial struggle and heterosexual relations that mark all of Naylor's other women. But, taken as part of the whole, these are minor complaints. Naylor's ability to present the pain and love of her characters' lives carries her through.

So, although at the end of the novel the people leave a dying Brewster Place with their dreams still deferred, there is a sense of hope. The women have, at the very least, gained respect, the readers' and their own. (pp. 118-19)

Judith V. Branzburg, "Seven Women and a Wall," in Callaloo, *Vol. 7, No. 2, Spring-Summer, 1984, pp. 116-19.*

Jewelle Gomez (essay date 1985)

[*In the following excerpt, Gomez offers a negative review of* Linden Hills, *stating that the work leaves her "unsatisfied, somewhat like I've felt after my grandmother's* Reader's Digest *condensations."*]

It's hard for me to be overly critical of a young, black woman writer who has achieved national success, something so rarely offered to women of color in this country. It is doubly difficult when the work of that writer, Gloria Naylor, shows seriousness and intelligence, and, next to Toni Morrison, creates the most complex black women characters in modern literature. Still, Gloria Naylor's first novel, *The Women of Brewster Place* and now her second, *Linden Hills,* leave me unsatisfied, somewhat like I've felt after my grandmother's *Reader's Digest* condensations. I sense something important was happening but the abridgement left a bare skeleton, not a full experience. (p. 7)

Perhaps it is the sweeping scope of her story which makes Naylor believe she must wave characters and situations before us quickly rather than let us interact with them in an intimate way. But given her flair for lyrical narrative and pungent dialog there is no reason not to expect more from her. Too often, [*Linden Hills*] reads like a screenplay. Naylor gives us a visual effect or the rhythm of an event but we get no clear sense of either the impact on the characters or the emotional subtext. If there is no subtext, if this is merely the unfolding of a tapestry of diverse characters whose paths cross at random, then it is even more crucial for Naylor to attach her characters more firmly to the framework.

The Inferno motif shapes the narrative—which is fine, as the lives of black people are more than suitable for epic legends—but it often feels like a literary exercise rather than a groundbreaking adaptation. But having chosen a classical European tale to emulate, Naylor then does nothing to utilize the endless and rich African mythology to embellish the story and give it a more timeless significance. The first disappointment comes early and is woven throughout the book. Skin color has been a source of contention for Afro-Americans since we were forced onto these shores. Our color marked us as slaves and as inferior. We, as well as Europeans, have been taught that the fairer our skin the closer we are to human. Naylor uses that symbology liberally: the endless Nedeed men are coal black, squat, ugly and evil but Ruth, Willie's dream girl, has a face like "smokey caramel." All of the Nedeed wives have been fair-skinned and nearly invisible presences in the household. The current Mrs. Nedeed, somewhat darker, ironically delivers the first fair-skinned son; both are doomed from the beginning of the book. Given the complex and oppressive part that skin color has played in the economic, social and psychological lives of Afro-Americans I expected a more meaningful treatment of it. If "black" only symbolizes evil here, just as it does in most western literature, then why does neither the author nor her characters comment on that, either directly or obliquely? Perhaps Naylor feels she has done so by giving Willie the nickname "White," awarded to him because of his dark skin. But the reiteration of the symbolism here feels like simple acceptance of it.

Another weakness in the novel is the preponderance of mad people. This is, perhaps, where clinging to Dante has been most disadvantageous. On their descent Willie and Lester encounter their old friend Norman, a man who appears healthy most of the time until he is attacked by "the pinks." Then he claws madly at his skin, gouging and scraping to rid himself of imagined pink ooze which threatens to envelope him. His wife has reduced their household to the most harmless furnishings (paper plates, plastic flatware, only two chairs) in order to protect him when he is possessed. Laurel, the beautiful, "coffee-colored" heir to a house in Linden Hills, retreats into silence, classical music and endless swims in her backyard pool. She leaves her devoted grandmother bewildered and her "sketch" of a husband impatient. Laurel finally does a high dive into her empty pool on a snowy Christmas eve to escape the demons that haunt her—demons which, like "the pinks," are rather fantastic and ill-defined.

The Nedeed partriarchs pursue riches and power through their mortuary business and the conversion of Linden Hills into a desirable property. They shape the competition which drives others to scheme and connive to win a place in Linden Hills. The last Luther Nedeed loses control when his dark-skinned wife gives birth to a light-skinned son: he locks them both in the basement of their home. (And as if that were not enough, he has already been seen doing unsettling things with the corpses at the mortuary.) Then there are the Nedeed wives, most of whom have been chosen for their obsequiousness and malleability. The current Mrs. Nedeed (whose name, Willa, we learn only at the end of the book) seems to be in atypically good control of her faculties until her son dies in the basement and Luther refuses to let her out. Leafing through journals and photograph albums during her imprisonment, Willa sees a pattern of overbearance and abuse that has left the Nedeed women less than whole. And in one particularly chilling section she flips through a picture album that begins with the wedding of a vibrant girl named Priscilla to an antecedent Luther. As the pictures progress the shadow of Priscilla's son, yet another Luther, grows ominously until it covers her completely. Soon all traces of her once lively face appear to have been deliberately burned away from the photos. In another journal Willa watches the normal check list of groceries and recipes metamorphose into a grotesque catalogue of binging and purging.

Willa's explorations of the past prove to be the most engaging parts of the book, although so many people (good and evil) are crippled with neuroses it is hard to find one to hold on to. Perhaps that is part of the relentless descent into hell; but after a while I longed for one ordinary somebody who just goes home and watches television. Naylor sets a tone of relentless gothic horror but her bedlam is out of hand . . . . There are no innocents here except for Willie and Lester, and they are her weakest characters. Perhaps in light of the insanity around them their mundane concerns (where to find a job, what to do about being in love with a friend's wife) can only seem insignificant. Naylor does not give these concerns nearly as much attention as the more histrionic ones. A paragraph here and there touches on one boy's unease at the real intimacy he feels with his pal, or the other's bitterness toward his mother, but these are only passing moments on the way to the snake pit. Willie and Lester should be our link but they have neither wisdom or naiveté. They are young boys who have opted out of the system for no particular reason; they are not significantly oppressed by poverty nor inspired by genius; they have no driving vision of their own and so cannot compete dramatically with the really extraordinary characters.

I would have loved to see this trip through the eyes of Ruth, who does battle against her husband's "pinks" with a fierceness and love unmatched by any other character in the novel (a battle dropped half way through the book!). Or through the testimony of the alcoholic Reverend Hollis who is the only active adversary of Luther Nedeed. The telescope of Dr. Braithwaite, the town historian, would certainly have been revealing: he has killed the roots of the willow trees surrounding his home to provide an unobscured perspective from which to observe the life of most residents, including Luther, while he writes the definitive history of Linden Hills.

Time is another problem. As in *The Women of Brewster Place,* I am never secure in my sense of time. The history of Linden Hills is laid out from before the Civil War to the recent present but all events are set curiously adrift on the social and political sea that buffets Afro-Americans in this country. I don't need to know exactly where Willie and Lester are in relation to Brown vs. Board of Education, but even Dante worked within a specific sociopolitical milieu which shaped his vision. In Linden Hills some people behave like it is still the turn of the century while others talk about "disk cameras." For many of the issues Naylor touches upon, a clear sense of historical time is pivotal. For example, one character disavows a liaison with his male lover in order to marry the appropriate woman and inherit the coveted Linden Hills home, all at the direction of Luther Nedeed. This feudal machination is certainly not completely outdated (and never will be as long as there is greed), but who is the young man beset by this trauma? We receive so little personal information about him that his motivations are obscure. For a middle-class, educated gay man to be blind to alternative lifestyles in 1985 is not inconceivable but it's still hard to accept the melodrama of his arranged marriage without screaming "dump the girl and buy a ticket to Grand Rapids!" Naylor's earlier novel presented a similar limitation. While she admirably attempts to portray black gays as integral to the fabric of black life she seems incapable of imagining black gays functioning as healthy, average people. In her fiction, although they are not at fault, gays must still be

made to pay. This makes her books sound like a return to the forties, not a chronicle of the eighties. (pp. 7-8)

All of that said, the reason I have such high expectations is that Naylor is talented. Her writing can be lyrical and powerful, so I demand more than emulation....

I want Gloria Naylor to engage me, to intrigue, horrify and move me. She is eminently capable of that and more. But her writing jumps around from character to event as if it's not important how we feel about them. Naylor's work is important and intelligent. She takes black people and black women in particular more seriously than most writers do today. I want her craft to be equal to her vision. We know that we can master European forms. That's easy. I'm still looking for the evenly shaped work that I know will be crafted from Naylor's raw talent. A work that stands on its own in world literature. (p. 8)

Jewelle Gomez, "Naylor's Inferno," in The Women's Review of Books, *Vol. II, No. 11, August, 1985, pp. 7-8.*

Michiko Kakutani (essay date 1988)

[*In the following excerpt, Kakutani negatively appraises* Mama Day *and criticizes the novel's "pasteboard figures."*]

In her previous novel, **Linden Hills,** Gloria Naylor created an intimate portrait of a "perverted Eden," in which upper-middle-class blacks discover that they've achieved wealth and success at the expense of their own history and identity, that they've sold their souls and are now living in a kind of spiritual hell. **Mama Day,** her latest novel, similarly describes a hermetic black community, but this time, it's a pastoral world named Willow Springs—a small, paradisal island, situated off the southeast coast of the United States, somewhere off South Carolina and Georgia, but utterly sovereign in its history and traditions.

Legend has it that the island initially belonged to a Norwegian landowner named Bascombe Wade, and that one of his slaves—"a true conjure woman" by the name of Sapphira, who "could walk through a lightning storm without being touched"—married him, persuaded him to leave all his holdings to his slaves, then "poisoned him for his trouble." Before killing him, she bore him seven sons. The youngest of that generation also had seven sons, and the last of them fathered Miranda, or Mama Day. The great-nieces of Mama Day are Willa Prescott Nedeed, who readers of **Linden Hills** will recall came to an ugly and untimely end; and Ophelia, the heroine of this novel, who is likewise threatened with early and disfiguring death....

To set up the fast-paced events that conclude **Mama Day,** Ms. Naylor spends much of the first portion of the book giving us menacing hints and planting time bombs set to detonate later. We're told that Ophelia's the namesake of another Day, an unhappy woman who never recovered from one of the misfortunes that befell the family, and that her own hot temper is liable to get her into trouble. We're told that George [Ophelia's husband] suffers from a bad heart and that he shouldn't over-exert himself. We're told that Miss Ruby, a neighbor in Willow Springs, plans to use her magical powers against any woman who comes near her husband, and that her husband happens to be attracted to Ophelia. We're also told that Mama Day herself possesses potent conjuring powers, which she will use to defend her family.

One of the problems with this information is that it's force-fed into the story line, at the expense of character development and narrative flow. The plot is made to pivot around melodramatically withheld secrets (concerning the history of Willow Springs, the nature of Mama Day's second sight, the mysterious "hoodoo" rites practiced on the island); and we are constantly being reminded of the novel's themes by trite observations that are meant to pass as folk wisdom: "Home. You can move away from it, but you never leave it"; "they say every blessing hides a curse, and every curse a blessing" or "nothing would be real until the end."

To make matters worse, the island's residents, who are given to uttering such lines, come across as pasteboard figures, devoid of the carefully observed individuality that distinguished their counterparts in *Linden Hills.* Mama Day is just the sort of matriarchal figure that her name indicates—strong, wise and resolute; her neighbor, a "hoodoo" man known as Dr. Buzzard, is a folksy con man, who plays a crooked game of poker and makes moonshine on the side, and Ruby is the manipulative devil woman, absurdly possessive of her man. As for the visitors to Willow Springs, they're initially just as two-dimensional: Ophelia is a bigoted, demanding woman, who seems lucky to have found a husband at all, given her large mouth and even larger ego, while George appears to be a conscientious yuppie, neatly dividing his time between work, his wife and his passion for football.

Fortunately, as *Mama Day* progresses, Ms. Naylor's considerable storytelling powers begin to take over, and her central characters slowly take on the heat of felt emotion. The bantering exchanges between George and Ophelia demonstrate their affection, as well as their knowledge of each other's weaknesses, and George's gradual immersion in the world of Willow Springs serves to reveal much about both him and his wife.

Still, for all the narrative energy of the novel's second half, there's something contrived and forced about the story. Whereas Toni Morrison's recent novel *Beloved,* which dealt with many of the same themes of familial love and guilt, had a beautiful organic quality to it, weaving together the ordinary and the mythic in a frightening tapestry of fate, *Mama Day* remains a readable, but lumpy, amalgam of styles and allusions. The reader eventually becomes absorbed in George and Ophelia's story, but is never persuaded that the events, which overtake them, are plausible, much less inevitable or real.

> *Michiko Kakutani, in a review of "Mama Day," in* The New York Times, *February 10, 1988, p. C25.*

David Nicholson (essay date 1988)

[*In the following essay, Nicholson reviews* Mama Day, *concluding that the work is a "wonderful novel, full of spirit and sass."*]

In *Mama Day,* her third novel, Gloria Naylor manages a considerable feat: She bends black folk and spiritual lore to her uses, all the while scrupulously respecting the integrity of that lore. At the same time, she tells the moving modern-day story of love between two people who have every reason not to expect or get the happiness they eventually earn. It is a neat, and long overdue trick, for too much contemporary black writing retreats into games of language or form (the novels of Clarence Major or John Wideman) or into an imaginary, idealized past (Wideman, again, or Sherley Anne Williams). I do not mean to deny the obvious talents of these writers I have cited, but simply to say that black writing in the '80s seems to have failed to address many of the realities of black life in the '80s.

Here, Naylor manages to avoid both traps. While there are three narrators—the two lovers, George and Cocoa, tell their own stories and a third-person narrator relates the happenings on Willow Springs, a small sea island somewhere off the southeast coast—the effect is only a little confusing, and only at first. Eventually, we see that Naylor has told the story the way the story demanded to be told. Her writing, clear, precise and apt, is always a delight to read; it is often poetic, and yet the narrative thrust of the story is never made subordinate to the poetry.

It is true that Willow Springs, with New York City the setting of this novel, is a kind of never-never land. Off but part of neither South Carolina nor Georgia, it has belonged to its black inhabitants for nearly 200 years. The land has been passed down from Sapphira Wade, a full-blooded African who may have (or may not have) married her master, borne him seven sons and killed him after 1,000 days, then managed to "escape the hangman's noose, laughing in a burst of flames." Nonetheless, Naylor is less interested in escaping the present than in exploring its links with the past, and the landscape is less one of romanticized poverty than one where traditional values hold sway.

Some on Willow Island say Sapphira's sons (Naylor's inventive use of the name subverts images of black women inspired by the long gone, and deservedly so, *Amos 'n' Andy Show*) were by other men. Some say she smothered the slaveowner, or stabbed him, or poisoned him. She may even have actually loved him and he her. Whatever the truth, all who live on Willow Island agree

Cast for the made-for-TV movie version of The Women of Brewster Place *(clockwise from left): Jackée as the flamboyant Etta Mae, Paula Kelly and Lonette McKee as the lesbian lovers Theresa and Lorraine, Oprah Winfrey as Mattie, Lynn Whitfield as the troubled Ciel, Olivia Cole as the nosy Miss Sophie, Robin Givens as the militant Kiswana, Cicely Tyson as Kiswana's well-to-do mother, and Phyllis Yvonne Stickney as the child-like Cora Lee.*

that Sapphira Wade was a powerful woman: "a true conjure woman: satin, black biscuit cream, red as clay . . . She could walk through a lightning storm without being touched; grab a bolt of lightning in the palm of her hand; use the heat of lighting to start the kindling going under her medicine pot . . . " Her descendant, first daughter of the seventh son of a seventh son, is Miranda Day, Cocoa's great-aunt and the spiritual leader of Willow Springs.

The novel opens with Cocoa in New York, where, job-seeking, she is interviewed by George. Before they can become lovers and, eventually, marry, Cocoa must give up her preconceptions about New York and men. In a wonderful piece of business that manages to show women's anger towards men without being alienating, Cocoa thinks about George, the hierarchy of dating in New York, and the fact that she had had "two whole dates in the last month: one whole creep and a half creep. I could have gambled that my luck was getting progressively better and you'd only be a quarter creep."

For his part, George was raised in an orphanage where he "grew up with absolutely no illusions about yourself and the world." When he left, he tells us, "I had what I could see: my head and my two hands, and I had each day to do something with them." And so, he tells Cocoa and us, "until you walked into my office, everything I was . . . was owed to my living fully in the now." He is a man who operates by rote and ritual—there must always be five shirts in his closet, ready to wear at the beginning of the week. In order to become able to love Cocoa, he must begin to think in larger terms about the future and admit her into his world.

It is refreshing to read a book by a black woman in which black men are not objects of ridicule or instruments of torture. While Naylor gives us characters who are fools—vain, egocentric, given to making wrong choices or simply with too high an opinion of themselves and their abilities—these characters are always human, and their number equally divided between male and female.

George and Cocoa's story is in the foreground, but those parts that feature Mama Day, matriarch, healer and Willow Springs' vessel of wisdom, are not of lesser importance. In the chapters that alternate with George and Cocoa's story, we see Mama Day aiding a woman unable to bear children, quilting with her sister, Abigail, chiding the bootlegger and would-be conjure man, Dr. Buzzard. She is a woman of power, and it is on Willow Springs, where George accompanies Cocoa on her annual August return home for the first time in their four-year marriage, that her knowledge receives its ultimate test when Cocoa's life is threatened.

To tell more would be to spoil the novel for the reader. Naylor has made **Mama Day** suspenseful, but the suspense is of the best kind—the reader continues to read, not because something is being withheld, but because something is always being revealed. And what is revealed is not simply who is threatening Cocoa and why, but something infinitely more valuable: insights into the complex nature of people and matters of the heart such as the difficulty of accepting love.

Her characters are always themselves: foolish, irascible, wise. At one point, Miranda complains to Abigail that Cocoa has called her "overbearing and domineering" and said she "wasn't coming back to my funeral." Abigail replies, "Well, if you could manage that by next August, she won't have to explain why she's back home then."

Early in their visit to Willow Springs, George wins at poker with Dr. Buzzard, gets drunk and comes home to stand wrapped around a fence post, pondering his next move. The section ends:

> "Honey, ain't you coming up on the porch?" Miss Abigail asked me.
>
> "No, there's money in my pockets."
>
> "My answer was reasonable and I had concentrated carefully to avoid slurring my words, but after a moment of stillness, soft laughter encircled me before three pairs of even softer arms were guiding me up the steps."

This is a wonderful novel, full of spirit and sass and wisdom and completely realized.

David Nicholson, "Gloria Naylor's Island of Magic and Romance," in Book World—The Washington Post, *February 28, 1988, p. 5.*

Larry R. Andrews (essay date 1989)

[*In the following excerpt, Andrews discusses the concept of "black sisterhood" in* The Women of Brewster Place. *In an unexcerpted portion of the article, he also examines "female bonding" in* Linden Hills *and* Mama Day.]

A number of writers have portrayed strong friendships between black women (e.g., Morrison in *Sula,* Walker in *The Color Purple*), but these bonds are often broken or slackened by competitiveness, betrayal, and physical or socioeconomic separation, Gloria Naylor, in her first three novels—**The Women of Brewster Place** (1982), **Linden Hills** (1985), and **Mama Day** (1988)—devotes considerable attention to the special bond that can exist between women characters, including women of different generations. In the first two novels, this bond derives its power from the women's previous sense of isolation, from their mistreatment by men, and from their regenerative discovery, through suffering, of the saving grace of a shared experience. In **Mama Day** the power comes from folk tradition, from "foremothering," and from nature, as Naylor moves into the realm of matriarchal mythmaking. At its best this bond among women confers identity, purpose, and strength for survival. And the possibility of its achievement grows in the course of the three novels. But although it is dramatized in the novels as clearly desirable, the success of female friendship, of the black womanbond, remains limited and potential.

Naylor's exploration of black sisterhood is clearest in **The Women of Brewster Place,** where she focuses almost entirely on women. In the prologue ("Dawn"), she presents the female residents of the tenement as a vibrant community:

> Nutmeg arms leaned over windowsills, gnarled ebony legs carried groceries up double flights of steps, and saffron hands strung out wet laundry on back-yard lines. Their perspiration mingled with the steam from boiling pots of smoked pork and greens, and it curled on the edges of the aroma of vinegar douches and Evening in Paris cologne that drifted through the street where they stood together—hands on hips, straight-backed, round-bellied, high-behinded women who threw their heads back when they laughed and exposed strong teeth and dark gums. They cursed, badgered, worshiped, and shared their men . . . . They were hard-edged, soft-centered, brutally demanding, and easily pleased, these women of Brewster Place.

At the end of this "novel in seven stories," despite numerous conflicts, she unites the women in Mattie's dream of the block party (which may come true). They join in an act of protest against the power of men over women (the gang-rape of the lesbian Lorraine) and, more broadly, against the barriers of racist and class oppression (the bloodstained wall) that distort relations between the sexes. Even after Brewster Place has been condemned and abandoned in the epilogue ("Dusk"), the women carry on:

> But the colored daughters of Brewster, spread over the canvas of time, still wake up with their dreams misted on the edge of a yawn. They get up and pin those dreams to wet laundry hung out to dry, they're diapered around babies. They ebb and flow, ebb and flow, but never disappear.

The women are a collective repository of dreams, a resilient source of strength for continuing survival if not yet conquest.

In *Linden Hills,* which continues the fictional world of *Brewster Place* but moves up in social class to the black bourgeois housing development dominated by the mortician Luther Nedeed, Naylor places a more balanced emphasis on both men and women. At the same time, there seem to be far fewer possibilities of female community. Despite their college educations and, in some cases, professional careers, most of the women are isolated and vulnerable. Yet here, too, a sense of community comes to play an important role in the plot. When she is locked in the basement morgue with her dead child, Willa Nedeed's emerging discovery of the suffering of her female predecessors in the house gives her strength to survive, accept herself, and take revenge on her husband. Furthermore, the hope is more clearly developed in this novel that the sensitive black male, in the person of the poet Willie Mason, can begin to bridge the gap of understanding between men and women and to support women in their quest for identity.

In *Mama Day,* both the contemporary and the historical bonds between women are important, for connection to the past helps make possible a connection in the present. Naylor develops the three main characters (Mama Day, Ophelia, and George) much more fully than any of her previous characters as she explores a family related to Willa Nedeed from *Linden Hills.* Here female community becomes empowered by natural forces and religious tradition in the coastal island community of Willow Springs. The bond between women does not arise as a refuge from isolation, mistreatment by men, or loss of identity in the white and black bourgeois worlds. It predates and transcends these modern conditions. Most important is the historical connection that runs from the legendary free spirit who founded the community, Sapphira Wade, through Miranda (Mama Day) to Miranda's great-niece Ophelia. This connection among women is related to nature through Miranda's extraordinary powers of intuition, "magic," and fertility as well as through the cyclical sense of time that pervades the island community. At the climax of the novel, this form of sisterhood is affirmed and strengthened. At the same time, sisterhood can still be jeopardized by the seductions of modern America and the evil and divisive jealousy of someone like Ruby, who nearly succeeds in killing Ophelia with nightshade poison.

In all three novels Naylor uses a unified physical setting, a spirit of place—just as Gwendolyn Brook does in *In the Mecca* and Morrison in *Sula*—to provide a communal framework for the varied descriptions of the women who come to live in it. Like the Mecca tenement, Brewster Place offers close physical contact that makes the women's confrontation with each other inescapable and their mutual support compelling. In *Linden Hills,* however, the women are physically isolated in houses and separated by status distinctions. The possibilities for sisterhood here are less spatial and contemporary than temporal and historical. In *Mama Day* the rural South, alternating with New York scenes between George and Ophelia, offers a setting for a healing community with roots in female folk tradition and nature.

In *Brewster Place* a friendship based on the shared experience of black womanhood exists sometimes in the form of the mother-daughter relationship. One of the problems several women face is that in their isolation they come to focus all their needs on their children and define themselves exclusively as mothers, thus enacting a male-defined, exploitive role. This tendency has both negative and positive consequences. The book is dominated by Mattie Michael, whose presence is felt in all of the individual character studies. Given the weak model of her parents' marriage and her desire for Butch, she rejects the timid suitor her stern father favors and at the same time harbors no expectations that Butch will show responsibility for her or their baby. After the violent scene with her father and her ejection from home, she quickly converts from lover to mother. Miss Eva, with whom she later shares a household and whom she regards as a surrogate mother, finds Mattie's excessive mothering and sexual continence unnatural. Mattie sleeps with her son Basil and channels all her needs into mothering him. In fact, she renders him incapable of responsibility. When he skips bail and she loses her house, she faces a tragic awakening.

The positive effect of her mothering emerges later, however, in her influence over other women in Brewster Place, above all in the powerful healing scene in which she rocks and washes Ciel Turner from despair back to life:

> Like a black Brahman cow, desperate to protect her young, she surged into the room, pushing the neighbor woman and the others out of her way....
>
> She sat on the edge of the bed and enfolded the tissue-thin body in her huge ebony arms. And she rocked....
>
> ...Mattie rocked her out of that bed, out of that room, into a blue vastness just underneath the sun and above time. She rocked her Aegean seas so clean they shone like crystal, so clear and fresh blood of sacrificed babies torn from their mother's arms and given to Neptune could be seen like pink froth on the water. She rocked her on and on, past Dachau, where soul-gutted Jewish mothers swept their children's entrails off laboratory floors. They flew past the spilled brains of Senegalese infants whose mothers had dashed them on the wooden sides of slave ships. And she rocked on.
>
> She rocked her into her childhood and let her see murdered dreams. And she rocked her back, back into the womb,....

The female connection here participates in a whole history of mother-sorrow, black and white. But the bond is not just that of mother and daughter, even though Mattie had helped raise Ciel years earlier. It is woman-to-woman. Their similar suffering makes them equal. Lucielia had come to look on her own daughter Serena as "the only thing I have ever loved without pain." Just before Serena electrocutes herself, Ciel has detached herself emotionally from her unreliable man Eugene, who has too many problems of his own with "the Man." What Mattie and Ciel come to share in Mattie's act of primal mothering is their isolation, their burden of responsibility as mothers, and the loss of their children.

Another mother-daughter relationship that becomes sisterhood emerges not from suffering but from the daughter's discovery of her mother's sexuality. Kiswana Browne is "healed" in her conflict with her mother by coming to identify herself with her mother as a woman. Kiswana has allied herself with the only thoroughly positive male character in the novel, Abshu, and with the now moribund black militance of the sixties. Her mother, from middle-class Linden Hills, pulls her up short when Kiswana accuses her mother of being "a white man's nigger who's ashamed of being black!" Her mother reacquaints her with a tradition of pride and strong mothering in the example of her great-grandmother—a full-blooded Iroquois "who bore nine children and educated them all, who held off six white men with a shotgun when they tried to drag one of her sons to jail for 'not knowing his place'"—and in her own example as a mother toughening her children to meet the world. But despite this reestablished bond of women over generations, the clinching moment for Kiswana comes only when she notices for the first time her mothers' bright red toenail polish, like her own:

> I'll be damned, the young woman thought, feeling her whole face tingle. Daddy's into feet! And she looked at the blushing woman on her couch and suddenly realized that her mother had trod through the same universe that she herself was now traveling. Kiswana was breaking no new trails and would eventually end up just two feet away on that couch. She stared at the woman she had been and was to become.

From the moment of their parting laughter she begins a productive new life in organizing rent protest among the women of Brewster Place and returning to school.

Kiswana can also now bring sisterly nurture to Cora Lee, another woman unbalanced in her mothering. Strangely obsessed with doll babies as a child, Cora Lee bears numerous children by the many "shadow" men in her life who slip in and out of her bedroom at night. Much as she desires *babies,* she is bewildered when they start growing up and she simply cannot manage them. But the friendship of Kiswana Browne, through an invitation to Shakespeare in the park, rekindles her old dreams of education. The act of friendship and offer of help, once Kiswana gets beyond her own initial condescension, contributes to restoring Cora Lee's self-esteem both as a person and as a mother. Her new mothering energy will be directed toward her children's education, and she has found a sisterhood in Kiswana that lifts her out of her isolation.

The best example of sisterly friendship without the maternal connection is Etta Mae Johnson's relationship with Mattie. A woman weary but "still dripping with the juices of a full-fleshed life" in Preacher Woods' eyes, Etta returns to Mattie and Brewster Place as a homecoming herself:

> She breathed deeply on the freedom she found in Mattie's presence. Here she had no choice but to be herself. The carefully erected decoys she was constantly shuffling and changing to fit the situation were of no use here. Etta and Mattie went back, a singular term that claimed co-knowledge of all the important events in their lives and almost all of the unimportant ones. And by rights of this possession, it tolerated no secrets.

After Preacher Woods' one-night stand shatters her brief illusion that she might achieve her dream of quick respectability as a preacher's wife in the front pew, she returns again to Mattie as to a center: "She laughed softly to herself as she climbed the steps toward the light and the love and the comfort that awaited her." With no worthy object for her flamboyant spirit, Etta yet has the deep friendship, support, and even moral judgment of Mattie in warding off loneliness and despair.

The love between Etta and Mattie is described more pointedly in a key passage in the later chapter about the two lesbians, Lorraine and Theresa. But first a word must be said about this pair of lovers. This marriage of the timid and the tough is fraught with as much hostility as love. Alternating between fostering and fighting, these two young women are still struggling to find their identities. Lorraine hates the cynical gay bars that are Theresa's element and wants to feel at one with her neighbors in Brewster Place. Theresa resents Lorraine's vulnerability yet is uncomfortable when Lorraine acquires firm convictions. Each seeks a different community. When Lorraine discovers an accepting listener in the alcoholic janitor Ben, Theresa insists on their own mutual dependence as outcasts, and Lorraine rebels. After their first quarrel, when Theresa lets Lorraine go to the party by herself, there is no more opportunity for them to resolve their conflicts and reaffirm their love. Lorraine is physically and psychologically destroyed by C. C. Baker and his gang, and in her derangement she murders her only friend, Ben. Because of its unresolved tensions and concern over power, this relationship between two women, despite its seeming intimacy, remains less successful than that between Mattie and Etta, who generously accept and nurture each other.

That there is a connection between the two relationships is brought out significantly in the key passage referred to earlier. After a block association meeting where Mattie and Etta have defended the lesbians against the gossip Sophie and the others, Mattie feels uncomfortable about the lesbian relationhip and ponders with Etta the nature of female friendship . . . . What Mattie comes to realize, through the insight of her own experience, is that the deep bond she has felt with some women may have a wholeness and power (including the sensual) comparable to that of the lesbians and perhaps superior to any relationshp that seems possible with a man in the distorted world of black gender relations. This is surely the central expression of black sisterhood in the novel.

The strength of this sisterhood can be explained partly, but not entirely, by the men's failures in love. In a conversation with Toni Morrison (published in *The Southern Review*), Naylor speaks of her concern lest readers exaggerate her treatment of the male characters:

> I bent over backwards not to have a negative message come through about the men. My emotional energy was spent creating a woman's world, telling her side of it because I knew it hadn't been done enough in literature. But I worried about whether or not the problems that were being caused by the men in the women's lives would be interpreted as some bitter statement I had to make about black men.

Most of the men in the novel may indeed be so ego-crippled by racism as to be unable to love their women, but Naylor still holds them accountable: the irresponsible Butch, the enraged father who is ready to kick his pregnant daughter Mattie to death, the father who rejects his lesbian daughter Lorraine, the transient "shadows" in Cora Lee's bedroom, the hypocritical Preacher Woods, the insecure Eugene, who abandons Ciel, and, above all, C. C. Baker and his gang, whom Naylor describes with her most sardonic language. Only Abshu and Ben are capable of fruitful relationships with women, and Ben only out of guilt for his impotence in letting his wife sell their daughter into concubinage with a white man. Generally, therefore, the men abandon the women to double burdens of work and domestic life without support. Women become the victims of class, race, and sex, as Wade-Gayles points out. In this condition the friendship of other women is not only a saving grace but a political necessity. (pp. 1-10)

Larry R. Andrews, "Black Sisterhood in Gloria Naylor's Novels," in CLA Journal, Vol. XXXIII, No. 1, September, 1989, pp. 1-25.

FURTHER READING

Awkward, Michael. "Authorial Dreams of Wholeness: (Dis)Unity, (Literary) Parentage, and *The Women of Brewster Place*." In his *Inspiriting Influences: Tradition, Revision, and Afro-American Women's Novels*, pp. 97-134. New York: Columbia University Press, 1989.
> Discusses Naylor's *The Women of Brewster Place,* Toni Morrison's *The Bluest Eye,* and Zora Neale Hurston's *Their Eyes Were Watching God.* The critic focuses on "the unity of form and content" in Naylor's novel.

Brown, Rosellen. Review of *Mama Day,* by Gloria Naylor. *Ms.* XVI, No. 8 (February 1988): 74.
> Reviews *Mama Day,* a novel about "the healing power of women."

Eko, Ebele. "Beyond the Myth of Confrontation: A Comparative Study of African and African-American Female Protagonists." *Ariel* 17, No. 4 (October 1986): 139-52.
> Compares Kiswana Browne in Naylor's *The Women of Brewster Place* with Anowa in Ama Ata Aidoo's *Anowa,* Margaret Cadmore in Bessie Head's *Maru,* and Selina Boyce in Paule Marshall's *Browngirl, Brownstones.* The critic states that despite "obvious separations of time, space, and even genre," the characters reveal "many bonds and parallels."

Homans, Margaret. "The Woman in the Cave: Recent Feminist Fictions and the Classical Underworld." *Contemporary Literature* 29, No. 3 (Fall 1988): 369-402.
> Examines *Linden Hills* and Luce Irigaray's *Speculum of the Other Woman,* noting that "both Irigaray and Naylor are centrally preoccupied with their relation to a predominantly male literary and philosophical heritage...."

Ward, Catherine C. "Gloria Naylor's *Linden Hills:* A Modern *Inferno*." *Contemporary Literature* 28, No. 1 (Spring 1987): 67-81.
> Overview of *Linden Hills.* The critic writes: "[*Linden Hills*] is a modern version of Dante's *Inferno* in which souls are damned not because they have offended God or have violated a religious system but because they have offended themselves."

Ngugi wa Thiong'o

1938-

(Also has written as James Thiong'o Ngugi) Kenyan novelist, dramatist, essayist, short story writer, diarist, translator, journalist, critic, and author of children's books.

Ngugi, a pioneer in the literature of Africa and of his native country, Kenya, is widely regarded as the most significant writer of East Africa. His first novel, *Weep Not, Child* (1964), was the first English-language novel to be published by an East African, and his account of the Mau Mau Emergency in *A Grain of Wheat* (1967; revised edition, 1986) presented for the first time the African perspective on the Kenyan armed revolt against British colonial rule during the 1950s. Additionally, Ngugi's *Caitaani mutharaba-ini* (1980; *Devil on the Cross,* 1982) is the first modern novel in Gikuyu (or Kikuyu), a Kenyan language in which the author intends to continue writing his creative works. Ngugi explained that writing in Gikuyu enables him to communicate with the peasants and workers of Kenya. Hence he has been called, in the words of Shatto Arthur Gakwandi, "the novelist of the people."

Ngugi—born James Thiong'o Ngugi to Thiong'o wa Nduucu and Wanjika wa Ngugi—is the fifth child of the third of Thiong'o's four wives. He grew up in the city of Limuru in Kenya. He was one of the few students from Limuru to attend the elite Alliance High School, where "the emphasis in the education offered to us," commented Ngugi, "was on production of Africans who would later become efficient machines for running a colonial system." At Alliance he participated in a debate in which he contended that Western education was harmful. He recalled in a 1979 interview: "Although I was new in the school, I remember quite vividly standing up and trembling with anger, and saying that Western education could not be equated with the land taken from the peasants by the British. And I remember holding up a fountain pen and giving the example of someone who comes and takes away food from your mouth and then gives you a fountain pen instead. I asked the audience: Can you eat a fountain pen?" The headmaster subsequently counseled Ngugi against becoming a political agitator. Ngugi next attended Makerere University in Uganda and later the University of Leeds in Britain, where he was exposed to West-Indian born social theorist Frantz Fanon's *The Wretched of the Earth,* a highly controversial treatise in which the author maintained that political independence for oppressed peoples must be won—often violently—before genuine social and economic change may be achieved. Ngugi commented: "The political literature of Karl Marx and Friedrich Engels was important and soon overshadowed Fanon." Having become an ardent opponent of colonialism, Christianity, and other non-African influences in Kenya, Ngugi began writing plays and novels criticizing Kenyan society.

Ngugi wrote his first novel, *Weep Not, Child,* while he was a student at Makerere. The protagonist, Njoroge, desires an education, but the Mau Mau—Gikuyu militants who advocated violent resistance to British domination in Kenya—and the government repression of the rebels interrupt his plans and disrupt his family. In despair, Njoroge attempts suicide. According to G. D. Killam, "*Weep Not, Child* is a small book and in some respects a naive one. But in it, as in *The River Between,* Ngugi puts down a blueprint for the mature writing in *A Grain of Wheat* and *Petals of Blood.*" With his second novel, *The River Between* (1965), Ngugi attacked the tribal rite of female circumcision, in which the clitoris of a young girl is clipped in order to dampen "powerful" female sexuality. Ngugi opposed this tradition of "mutilation" as well as Christianity's condemnation of the rite; he believed that Christian missionaries only condemned female circumcision because it recognized female sexuality. Ngugi followed *The River Between* with *A Grain of Wheat.* The four main characters of this 1967 novel reflect upon the events of the Mau Mau Emergency and its consequences as they await "Uhuru Day," or the day of Kenyan independence. Angus Calder wrote that *A Grain of Wheat* "is arguably the best, and certainly the most underrated, novel to come from Black Africa."

In 1968 Ngugi—then an instructor at the University of Nairobi—and several colleagues mounted a successful campaign to transform the English Department of the university into the Department of African Languages and Literature; Ngugi would eventually become chairman of the newly created department. Thus Ngugi became a vocal proponent of African literature written in African languages, responding to a plea made by Obiajunwa Wali in his 1963 essay "The Dead End of African Literature?" Wali had written: "Until these writers"—specifically Chinua Achebe, Ezekiel Mphahlele, and especially Wole Soyinka—"and their western midwives accept the fact that any true African literature must be written in African languages, they would be merely pursuing a dead end, which can only lead to sterility, uncreativity, and frustration." After *A Grain of Wheat*, Ngugi rejected the Christian name of James and began writing under the name Ngugi wa Thiong'o. He also began translating his play *The Trial of Dedan Kimathi* (1976; *Mzalendo Kimathi*, 1978) into Gikuyu and with Ngugi wa Mirii wrote another play in Gikuyu, *Ngaahika Ndeenda* (1977; *I Will Marry When I Want*, 1982). Ngugi published his last English-language novel, *Petals of Blood*, in 1977; critics consider it his most ambitious work. An overtly political novel, *Petals of Blood* concerns four principal characters who are being held by the police on suspicion of murder: Karega, a teacher and labor organizer; Munira, headmaster of a public school in the town of Ilmorog; Abdulla, a half-Indian shopkeeper who was once a guerrilla fighter during the war for independence; and Wanja, a barmaid and former prostitute.

Charles Larson commented: "*Petals of Blood* is not so much about these four characters (as fascinating and as skillfully drawn as they are) as it is about political unrest in post-independence Kenya, and what Ngugi considers the failures of the new black elite (politicians and businessmen) to live up to the pre-independence expectations." Larson proved perceptive when he concluded: "In this sense, *Petals of Blood* is a bold venture—perhaps a risky one—since it is obvious that the author's criticisms of his country's new ruling class will not go unnoticed." In 1977 the Kenyan government arrested and detained Ngugi for one year.

"Ngugi's arrest on 31 December 1977," wrote Govind Narain Sharma, "detention for a year in the Maximum Security Prison at Kamiti, and being deprived of his prestigious position [as chair of the Department of Literature] at Nairobi University was, I think, a traumatic experience." In detention Ngugi wrote his memoirs—*Detained: A Writer's Prison Diary* (1981)—and vowed to write his creative works only in the Gikuyu language. He also began writing his first Gikuyu novel, *Caitaani mutharaba-ini* (1980), on sheets of toilet paper. Upon his release from detention, Ngugi lost his position at the University of Nairobi. Although he continued to write nonfiction in English, Ngugi wrote his novels and plays in Gikuyu and translated some of his works into other African languages. When his theater group was banned by Kenyan officials in 1982, Ngugi, fearing further reprisals, left his country for a self-imposed exile.

In 1986 Ngugi announced that he would bid a complete "farewell to English." Although the Kenyan government confiscated all copies of his most recent novel, *Matigari ma Njiruungi* (1986), in 1987, Ngugi persists in his aims to reach the African people through their native languages. "Language is a carrier of a people's culture," Ngugi explained, "culture is a carrier of a people's values; values are the basis of a people's self-definition—the basis of their consciousness. And when you destroy a people's language, you are destroying that very important aspect of their heritage . . . you are in fact destroying that which helps them to define themselves . . . that which embodies their collective memory as a people."

(For further information about Ngugi's life and works, see *Black Writers; Contemporary Authors*, Vols. 81-84; *Contemporary Authors New Revision Series*, Vol. 27; *Contemporary Literary Criticism*, Vols. 3, 7, 13, 36; and *Major 20th-Century Writers*.)

PRINCIPAL WORKS

The Black Hermit [as James T. Ngugi] (drama) 1962
Weep Not, Child [as James T. Ngugi] (novel) 1964
The River Between [as James T. Ngugi] (novel) 1965
This Time Tomorrow [as James T. Ngugi] (drama) 1966
A Grain of Wheat [as James T. Ngugi] (novel) 1967; revised edition, 1986
Homecoming: Essays on African and Caribbean Literature, Culture, and Politics (essays) 1972
Secret Lives, and Other Stories (short stories) 1976
The Trial of Dedan Kimathi [with Micere Githae Mugo] (drama) 1976
   [*Mzalendo Kimathi*, 1978]
Ngaahika Ndeenda [with Ngugi wa Mirii] (drama) 1977
   [*I Will Marry When I Want*, 1982]
Petals of Blood (novel) 1977
Caitaani mutharaba-ini (novel) 1980
   [*Devil on the Cross*, 1982]
Detained: A Writer's Prison Diary (diary) 1981
Writers in Politics: Essays (essays) 1981
Njamba Nene na mbaathi i mathagu (juvenile fiction) 1982
   [*Njamba Nene and the Flying Bus*, 1986]
Barrel of a Pen: Resistance to Repression in Neo-Colonial Kenya (nonfiction) 1983
Bathitoora ya Njamba Nene (juvenile fiction) 1984
Decolonising the Mind: The Politics of Language in African Literature (nonfiction) 1986
Matigari ma Njiruungi (novel) 1986
Njamba Nene na Chibu King'ang'i (juvenile fiction) 1986

Thomas R. Knipp (essay date 1967)

[*The following essay originally appeared in* Books Abroad *in 1967. Here, Knipp analyzes Ngugi's writ-*

ing technique in Weep Not, Child *and* The River Between.]

For the last decade and a half, a rich literature in metropolitan languages has been developing in West Africa. Foreigners have been reading in French the poetry of *negritude* and novels from Senegal and Cameroun. They have also read English speaking poets, novelists, and playwrights from Ghana and Nigeria. For a variety of reasons including poorly developed western school systems, political instability, and the priority of Swahili as a literary language, nothing of this kind was forthcoming from East Africa. In 1964, however, the first Kenya novel appeared. It was *Weep Not, Child* by James Ngugi, a talented young Makerere College graduate. Less than two years later, Ngugi had finished his second novel, *The River Between.* They were both received sympathetically by the critics. The *TLS* reviewer referred to *Weep Not, Child* as "a skillful work of art" and praised its "artistic success." The *Guardian* felt that *The River Between* "touches the grandeur of tap-root simplicity." No one would presume to predict on the basis of two short novels the future development of Ngugi's talent, much less the future direction of Kenyan literature. Nevertheless the birth of a literature is an auspicious occasion, and such things as technical and thematic analysis and comparative commentary seem not only warranted but useful.

Weep Not, Child is a story of a Kikuyu family living in the white highlands in the Fifties. Ngotho, a sharecropper on the lands of the black collaborator Jacobo, raises his sons and rules his wives in the benevolent traditions of a Kikuyu patriarchy and waits patiently for the gods to deliver the land from the white foreigners. The first part of the novel depicts traditional Kikuyu culture and also the forces of change that undermine it. While Ngotho waits patiently for the gods, one son, Boro, a World War II veteran, seeks his fortune in Nairobi where he drifts into politics. Another son, Kamua, is an apprentice carpenter, while the third son and central figure in the novel, Njoroge, is pursuing British liberal learning in the missionary school system. The arrest of the distant "black Moses," Jomo Kenyatta, signals a change in the tempo of these lives. Boro brings Mau Mau to the village, shoots the black collaborator, and finally kills a white highlander named Howlands. Ngotho is arrested after participating in an abortive strike. Beaten and castrated as a Mau Mau suspect by British noncommissioned officers, he dies, a victim of the unleashed forces of history. After an unsuccessful suicide attempt, Njoroge is left, fatherless and frightened, to face an unknown future.

Set in the highlands a generation or so earlier than *Weep Not, Child, The River Between* tells the story of Waiyaki, a Kikuyu boy who inherits intelligence, leadership, and a messianic complex from his father Chege. Sent to mission schools by his father to learn the white man's ways, Waiyaki returns convinced that knowledge is the only defense against encroachment; and he establishes a series of community schools. In the meantime the community, more remote from the white man than Ngotho's village in *Weep Not, Child,* becomes sharply divided between Christian converts and fanatical tribal purists. Waiyaki, who loves the Christian girl Nyambura, tries to find a path of compromise. When he refuses to renounce his beloved, both he and Nyambura are handed over to the *kiama* (tribal council), which has developed a passionate xenophobia. They face certain death.

The two novels are strikingly similar in both technique and theme. The strengths and weaknesses in them are so much of a piece as to suggest limits to the direction Ngugi's talent might take. One of the most successful devices he uses (although in excess it cloys a little) involves the quality of the prose itself. To communicate the characteristic thought of the African he employs short simple sentences free of idiom and, for the most part, of transition words. The vocabulary itself is simple and monosyllabic. The following is an example:

> Why should the white man have fought? Aaa! You could never tell what these people would do. In spite of the fact that they were all white, they killed one another with poison, fire and big bombs that destroyed the land. They had even called the people to help them in killing one another. It was puzzling. You could not really understand because although they said they fought Hitler (Ah! Hitler, that brave man, whom all the British feared, and he was never killed you know, just vanished like that), Hitler too was a white man. That did not take you very far. It was better to give up the attempt. (*Weep Not, Child*)

To communicate the quality of spoken Kikuyu he uses the devices and a kind of paraphrasis, especially on the exchange of commonplaces, as follows:

> "Why do you come home with darkness?" Chege at last asked, without raising his head. He spat on the floor.
> "We took the cattle to the plains."
> "The plains?"
> "Yes, Father."
> After a small silence—"That is far to go," he said.
> Waiyaki kept quiet. He was never at ease in front of his father.
> "Danger lurks in darkness."
> "Yes, Father."
> Again Waiyaki was uneasy. He darted a quick glance at the door. His father had not yet looked up.
> "Who showed you the way?"
> "I know all the ways in the ridges," he said proudly....
> "You have not eaten." There was softness in Chege's voice.
> "I have just come."
> "Go then and get your mother to give you something to put in your mouth." (*The River Between*)

This is a simplistic technique which enables Ngugi to achieve certain effects by reducing statements and situations to the elemental—the basic. Though it seems to communicate a kind of African mental process and while it has a certain charm, it tends to make Africans appear rather naive. Its effect is very different from that of Chinua Achebe's adaptation of Ibo proverbial patterns to communicate the *quality* and *complexity* of Ibo thought—especially in his portrait to Eseulu in *Arrow of God.*

In passages of dialogue and narrative action, this simplicity enables Ngugi to create fine pieces of restrained prose. He is especially good at depicting scenes of violence.

> "How old are you?"
> "I think 19 or thereabouts."
> "Sema affande!" one of the homeguards outside the small room shouted.
> "Affande."
> "Have you taken the oath?"
> "No!"
> "Sema affande!" barked the same homeguard.
> "No, Affande."
> "How many have you taken?"
> "I said none, Affande!"
> The blow was swift. It blinded him so that he saw darkness. He had not seen the gray eyes rise.
> "Have you taken Oath?"
> "I-am-a-school-boy-affande," he said, automatically lifting his hands to his face.
> "How many Oaths have you taken?"
> "None, sir."
> Another blow. Tears rolled down his checks in spite of himself....
> ":'Do you know Boro?"
> "He is my brother."
> "Where is he?"
> "I don't know."
>
> Njoroge lay on the dusty floor. The face of the gray eyes turned red. He never once spoke except to call him Bloody Mau Mau. A few seconds later Njoroge was taken out by the two homeguards at the door. He was senseless. He was covered with blood where the hob-nailed shoes of the gray eyes had done their work. (*Weep Not, Child*)

This simplicity which adds charm to the dialogue and power to certain narrative passages is much less clearly a virtue in the handling of character. The characters are not fully rounded and complex; rather they are representations of the author's attitudes. They are, in fact, almost allegorical. Thus Njoroge and his father and brothers are not intricately *human* persons caught in complex webs of interaction. They are representations of certain possible attitudes toward the forces of change let loose in Kenya. This is also true of characters like Kabonyi and Joshua, the tribal purist and the fanatic Christian in the second novel. The only difference that one can see in the characterization in the two novels is the almost super-human charisma of some of the characters—especially the hero—in *The River Between.*

> Waiyaki looked at the ground and felt small. Then he turned to the group and let his eyes fall upon them. His eyes were large and rather liquid; sad and contemplative. But whenever he looked at someone, they seemed to burn bright. A light came from them, a light that appeared to pierce your body, seeing something beyond you, into your heart. Not a man knew what language the eyes spoke. Only, if the boy gazed at you, you had to obey. That half-imploring, half-commanding look was insisting, demanding. Perhaps that was why the other boys obeyed him.

This whole tendency reminds one more of a folk tale than a novel, and this last technique is clearly a move away from the novel towards a form of stylized myth. Once, this is a tour de force—but only once. Such techniques of characterization will soon force Ngugi into an artistic *cul-de-sac.*

Characters thus simplified very easily acquire the quasi-symbolic function of representing the author's attitude toward some problem which, translated into the techniques of function, becomes the basis for conflict in the novel. The basis for conflict in both of these novels is the same—the force of history that holds Africa in so firm a grip today. In each novel Ngugi presents four basic responses to change. In *Weep Not, Child,* Ngotho relies almost completely on the old tribal gods to assert themselves and defend the traditional folkways. Chege does the same in *The River Between.* Isaac in the first novel, like Joshua in the second, puts his faith in the white man's ways—especially in Christianity. Boro and Kabonyi, who have both been exposed to the white man's world, reject its contents and values, but adopt its techniques of violence in order to drive the white man from the Kikuyu highlands. Finally, the heroes of the two novels, Njoroge and Waiyaki, the beneficiaries—like the author—of British liberal education, respond in truly syncretistic ways. They wish to select from both cultures that which is good, useful, and pertinent. In each case the author's sympathies are with the traditionalists and his convictions with the syncretists, but in each case the advocates of violence succeed in tearing asunder the walls of social stability.

Ngugi is also fond of putting his setting to symbolic use. We find the following passage in *Weep Not, Child:*

> Njoroge felt lonely.... Even the stars that later shone in the night gave him no comfort. He walked across the courtyard, not afraid of the darkness. He wished that Mwihaki was with him. Then he might have confided in her. In the distance the gleaming lights of the city where the call for the strike had been born beckoned to him. He did not respond.

The River Between opens with four short sentences:

> The two ridges lay side by side. One was Kameno, the other was Makuyu. Between them was a valley. It was called the valley of life.

One of these ridges is dominated by Christians, the other by pagans. The hero fears, "Perhaps there was no half-way house between Makuyu and Kameno." The young lovers, one pagan and the other Christian, meet secretly by the river. These last examples of geographic symbolism are part of an almost uncontrollable fondness for parallelism that Ngugi displays in his second novel. All characters and events seem to appear in twos. For instance, Christmas and initiation take place at the same time. This too seems to be a quality associated more with a folk mythmaker than a novelist.

These simplifying and myth-making propensities weaken Ngugi's art in still another way. By distilling his historical fable to its purest form and by reducing his elements of conflict to their lowest common denominator, he leaves himself with very little story to tell. He compensates for this, unfortunately, by reverting to melodrama and, occasionally, to sentimentality. The central story of *The River Between,* which is more dependent on these devices than its predecessor, concerns Waiyaki's love for Nyambura, the Christian girl. In what is really a sentimental retelling of *Romeo and Juliet,* the reader encounters divided loyalty, passionate speeches, selfless gestures, palpitating hearts, thwarted suitors, and a melodramatic climax in which the syncretistic union of the lovers is condemned by the enraged villagers who turn them over to the *kiama* for punishment. As the simplified characters move through the melodramatic action, they do not represent profound cultural conflict nor do they portray the subtle interaction of the personal and the cultural as is the case in Achebe's best fiction. Rather they reduce profound cultural rift to the level of melodramatic spite. Kabonyi, the leader of the forces of violent reaction, is pictured as merely hating Waiyaki, and his son and chief lieutenant is described as follows:

> Kaman had waited for him to go but Waiyaki had persisted in staying. Then he saw them embrace. And with intense pain he saw all he had half feared confirmed before his eyes. Waiyaki was his rival to the death.

Weep Not, Child is actually a better book than its successor because, while the sentimental love story grows in importance as the novel progresses, it is a more completely political book. And Ngugi's most obvious talent lies in portraying political conflict.

It is a better book also because of the presence of heroic old Ngotho, who, like Achebe's Okonkwo and Eseulu, is a moving and effective tragic African. We see him losing his sons to the schools and to the city. Then he is driven off the land. He stands powerless while his wife and son are arrested for violating the curfew. He is humiliated by history until he becomes a man who "no longer looked anybody straight in the face; not even his wives." His final arrest, torture, and castration are told with power and controlled indirection. Unfortunately his death is badly sentimentalized. But the ending of the book, while sentimental, is more effective than that of *The River Between.* Njoroge, his father dead, his brothers arrested, his dreams of education in ruins, turns for comfort to his black mothers as to the soul of Africa itself.

The two novels are not only similar in structure and technique, they are similar in theme—or themes. Both novels are concerned with the conflicts and changes generated by the white man. While it is true that, in *Weep Not, Child,* contact between black and white is more extensive and involved (in *The River Between* missionary contact is fairly recent and settler encroachment has not yet begun) and Ngotho's family has taken on many of the characteristics of the proletariat, racial conflict is not the primary theme of either work. The white man acts as a catalytic agent, and the changes

produced in Kikuyu society *because of his presence* are the chief concern of the novels. Both novels portray social conflict—Christian versus pagan, old versus young—within a community which, driven by forces of change, turns upon itself. Ngotho's anguish is illustrative.

> Whatever Ngotho had been prepared to do to redeem himself in the eyes of his children, he would not be ordered by a son to take oath. Not that he objected to it in principle. After all, oath-taking as a means of binding a person to a promise was a normal feature of tribal life. But to be given by a son! That would have violated against his standing as a father. A lead in that direction could only come from him, the head of the family. Not from a son; not even if he had been to many places and knew many things.

In *The River Between,* hostile elders fighting for tribal purity and troubled by Waiyaki's syncretism and enthusiasm for western education defy him with a simple "Young man, we are old."

Mau Mau, the most violent and poisonous form of intra-tribal conflict, is shown to be the result of the presence of the white man. In *Weep Not, Child* it is Boro and others like him who have gone to Nairobi and, during the war, even beyond into the white world itself where they have learned the politics of violence and the violence of politics that preach the philosophy and technique of resistance. And, ironically, it is they who, in the name of the tribe, confound their fathers. In the second novel Kabonyi, who turns the *kiama* into a Mau Mau-like kangaroo court to protect tribal purity through coercion, is a rebel Christian.

One theme that runs very clearly through both novels is the sacredness of the land. Unlike the characters in West African fiction, Ngugi's people are a people of the land. Their gods are gods of the land which they bestow on the Kikuyu.

> "Education is everything," Ngotho said. Yet he doubted this because he knew deep inside his heart that *the land was everything.* Education was good only because it would lead to the recovery of the lost lands. (italics mine)

The River Between is filled with references to men "crying for the soil" and of boys who are "a credit to the hills" and of teachers who "must build up the hills." Peace, prosperity, and joy are thought of as being in the land and from the land. Wise old Chege tells his son, "Salvation shall come from the hills."

Wherever this peace is rooted, however, Ngugi's conviction is clearly that it must be nurtured by education—western education.

> Whatever their differences, interest in knowledge and booklearning was the one meeting point between people such as Boro, Jacobo, and Ngotho. Somehow the Gikuyu people always saw their deliverance as embodied in education.

To Njoroge the opportunity to attend high school is "the realization of his dreams." In **The River Between,** Waiyaki expresses the same convictions.

> He increasingly saw himself as the one who would lead the tribe to the light. Education was the light of the country. That was what the people wanted. Education. Schools. Education . . . . He just wanted all the people to get learning.

One of the ironies that gives strength to both novels is that the author's and the reader's convictions are unequivocally on the side of education as represented by Njoroge and Waiyaki, who are brought low by the uncontrollable forces of change. Ngugi also quietly understates the irony that the presence of the white man is responsible for both the violently self-destructive conflicts within traditional society and the curative and purgative blessings of western education.

In these two short novels by James Ngugi fiction has made a most auspicious start in Kenya. In spite of their limitations they are compelling and impressive books. The negative notes are that one is simply a retelling of the other and that some of the techniques of which Ngugi seems so sure and so fond seem to lead away from rather than toward the density and complexity that one usually associates with the best fiction. However, he is a young man. He has told one story—twice. It is hoped that he has many other stories to tell. (pp. 161-69)

> *Thomas R. Knipp, "Two Novels from Kenya: J. Ngugi," in* Critical Perspectives on Ngugi wa Thiong'o, *revised, edited by G. K. Killam, Three Continents Press, 1984, pp. 161-69.*

Ngugi wa Thiong'o (essay date 1979)

[*The following excerpt is from a 1979 interview conducted with Ngugi by Katebalirwe Amoti wa Irumba and published in 1990 in Carol Sicherman's* Ngugi wa Thiong'o: The Making of a Rebel. *Sicherman edited her selection from an 85-page manuscript. Here, Ngugi—having recently been released from detention—discusses his childhood and development as a writer.*]

My parents lived partly on land, cultivating little stretches of land here and there, eking a living, and also working on other people's land for wages. My father and mother separated in 1946 or 1947, and thereafter my mother was the one who took care of us; that is, we three brothers and three sisters. She virtually shouldered *every* responsibility of our struggle for food, shelter, clothing, and education. It was my mother who initially suggested that I go to school. I remember those nights when I would come back home from school, and not knowing that she could not read or write, I would tell her everything that I had learnt in school or read to her something, and she would listen very keenly and give me a word of advice here and there.

My parents were not Christians. But at the same time they did not practice much of the Gikuyu forms of worship. My father was skeptical of religious and magical practices that went with rites of passages and rhythms of the seasons. He believed in land and hard work. The landlord on whose land we lived was an elder in the P.C.E.A. [Presbyterian Church of East Africa], then called the Church of Scotland Mission.

I remember one Christmas the wife of the landlord invited the children of the peasants to her house for a cup of tea and bread. The mountain of the slices of bread looked very alluring to us children, and we were eager to get on with the job of demolishing the mountain. But then she told us to pray. My brother and I opened our eyes and looked at one another, and we read the thoughts expressed in each other's face. We laughed in the midst of prayer, and we were heavily reprimanded by the lady of the house. She pointed out the differences between the religious Christian upbringing of her children, which made them possess good manners in God's presence, and that of peasants, which made us possess terrible manners even in Godly presence.

• • • • •

When I grew up I was very much aware of the physical confrontation between foreigners and Kenyans at Limuru. On one side of Limuru was the land controlled by the foreign settlers, and on the other side was the land controlled by peasants and Kenyan landlords. These two sides were divided by the famous railway line from Mombasa to Kampala. Now, the effects of European settlement were basically two. First was the forced removal of peasants from their land, which meant that now they were congested in very tiny dry areas, what the colonial government called the African reserves. Secondly, this same act of forced removal of peasants from their land, and hence their divorce from ownership and control of the means of production, created the beginning of a proletariat in Kenya. The buyers and hirers of this labour power of the people of Limuru were, of course, the settlers, to work their coffee, tea, and pyrethrum plantations. But around 1940, there was built a shoe manufacturing factory at Limuru owned by the foreign-owned East African Bata Shoe Company, and later a pig processing plant at Uplands, Uplands Bacon Factory. And so from around this time you began to get an industrial proletariat in Limuru employed by foreign capitalists. This pattern, I think, has continued to the present: a peasantry, a rural proletariat (many now working on farms of African settlers who replaced European settlers), and a growing industrial proletariat . . . .

In all my novels I have produced the foreign settlers and their class relationships in Kenya, from this historical experience of Kenya. Again in all my novels I have produced the 1948 general strike of Kenyan workers which at Limuru was carried out by workers at the Bata Shoe factory. So, right from the beginning I was groping towards some kind of class appreciation of our society in Limuru . . . . I grew up under the influence of Gikuyu peasant culture—songs, stories, proverbs, riddles around the fireside in the evenings—as well as those values that govern human relationships in a peasant community....

• • • • •

It was said that in the foreign missionary schools some things were deliberately held back from students to keep them ignorant about certain facts and aspects of life under colonists. But in the national [Gikuyu Karing'a] schools everything was deliberately given to the students to prepare them to face up to the harsh social conditions under colonialism.... In those national schools one was made aware of colonialism as an oppressive force, whereas in the foreign mission schools colonialism was seen as a good thing. National songs, poems, and dances played a very important role in national schools while in the foreign schools Christian hymns played the central role. In other words, in the national schools peasant cultures were at the center, they were glorified or upheld, developed and perpetuated. But in the missionary schools foreign culture and foreign cultural forms of expression were glorified and used to destroy all peasant cultures.

Alliance High School was, of course, very different from all my previous experiences of schools. For one thing, most of the teachers were foreigners; in fact, most of them were British. The emphasis in the education offered to us at Alliance was on production of Africans who would later become efficient machines for running a colonial system. Therefore in Alliance High School politics was frowned upon; Kenyan nationalists were castigated: they were seen as irresponsible agitators, hooligans, and undesirable specimens of human beings. So we were presented with two diametrically opposed images: the image of the Kenyan patriot as a negative human being and the image of the oppressor and his collaborator as positive human beings. Obviously the aim was to make us identify with the image of the collaborator, and to make us grow to admire and acquire all the values that go hand in hand with collaboration with imperialism.

One of my earliest experiences at that school, in 1955, was taking part in a debate on a motion that Western education had done more harm than good. Although I was new in the school, I remember quite vividly standing up and trembling with anger, and saying that Western education could not be equated with the land taken from the peasants by the British. And I remember holding up a fountain pen and giving the example of someone who comes and takes away food from your mouth and then gives you a fountain pen instead. I asked the audience: Can you eat a fountain pen? Can you clothe yourself with a fountain pen or shelter yourself with it? It was, in fact, my bold participation in that debate that made other students in later years elect me secretary of the Debating Society.... I remember the headmaster once calling me into his office and warning me never to become a political agitator, that all political agitators were scoundrels.... There was,

though, a period when I became rather too serious a Christian, waking up for prayers at five o'clock in the mornings. This may have cut the wings off my social concerns.

My interest in writing really goes back as far as my primary school days. That's when I read Stevenson, Dickens, and many other abridged versions of works by many European writers which were introduced to us by our then teacher of English, Samuel Kibicho. I remember in primary school arguing with a fellow student, Kenneth Bugwa. He told me that one could write a book and I told him, no, you cannot write a book; you might be arrested and imprisoned because you would not be qualified to do so. He was very adamant and argued quite correctly that one did not need to be highly educated, or to be licensed, in order to write a book. This argument had a strange consequence. When I went to high school, my friend went to a teacher training school. In his first year he started to write a book to prove to me that one could do so without being arrested. I can't remember now the fate of his novel, but he sent me excerpts in 1955 when I was in Form One at Alliance High School. I used to say to myself that when I grew up I would like to write the kind of stories people like Stevenson and Dickens had written.

At Alliance High School I was lucky, in that the library was quite adequate for a school like that. There were many novels, and I used to read them. I read Dickens, but also a lot of racist writing like Rider Haggard's *King Solomon's Mines* and the Biggles series by Captain W. E. Johns. Also, I read liberal writers like Alan Paton. I aslo remember reading many thrillers, and my first literary attempt was an imitation of the American thriller writer Edgar Wallace. I sent this story to *Baraza* [a government-sponsored magazine], which used to run a kind of literary page in Kenya—that was in 1956—but it was rejected. I remember once stumbling upon Tolstoy's *Childhood, Boyhood, Youth,* and one of my only two published efforts at Alliance was a short remembrance of my childhood influenced by my reading of Tolstoy. There were, of course, the texts used in our literature classes, like Shakespeare's *Macbeth* and *Julius Caesar;* Bernard Shaw's *Man and Superman;* Scott's *Ivanhoe;* and poems by Wordsworth, Longfellow, and Tennyson. Our headmaster was particularly fond of the arch-imperialist poet, Rudyard Kipling, and he always made us copy and recite his poems, in particular "If."

At Makerere University the course was based on the syllabus for English studies at the University of London. Thus it was a degree in the history of English literature, from the Celtic times to T. S. Eliot, as well as in the history of the English language. But the real importance of my studying at Makerere lay in this: that for the first time, I came into contact with African and West Indian writers. I remember three authors and books as being particularly important to me: Chinua Achebe's *Things Fall Apart,* George Lamming's *In the Castle of My Skin,* and Peter Abrahams' *Tell Freedom.* At Alliance I had seen *Tell Freedom* held by one of the teachers, and I can remember literally trembling when I saw the title. When I found the book in the library at Makerere, I was overjoyed. I read it avidly and later I read virtually all the books by Peter Abrahams—that was the beginning of my interest in South African literature. Achebe's *Things Fall Apart* started me on West African writers; from then on I followed closely the growth of West African literature. I used to go to the library and look up every item of fiction in West African journals and magazines, especially work by Cyprian Ekwensi (who, I came to learn, was also an admirer of Peter Abrahams). As for George Lamming, his work introduced me to West Indian writers, and this was the beginning of my interest in the literature of the African people in the Third World. Makerere was also important because of the central role of *Penpoint,* which had become the forum for writers in East and Central Africa.

So I would say that Makerere was very important for me because, side by side with the formal literary education, I had through the library access to the kind of literature that told me of another world, a world which was in many instances my own. But African literature and all Third World literature was *nowhere* in the syllabus. African writers were never mentioned in tutorials or in seminars. I discovered them for myself in the library. It was, in fact, a big surprise when I learnt through my own efforts that African and Third World people had, in fact, been writing for a long time—people like Aimé Césaire from the West Indies or other Negritude writers of Senghor's generation. There had been lot of writing going on in Africa by Africans, and in the rest of the Third World, for centuries. So just as at Alliance High School, I was once again confronted with two diametrically opposed images—the official or Eurocentric image as it emerged through the kind of curriculum I was exposed to in the English Department, and the image of a struggling world as it emerged through the kind of literature that I discovered for myself in the library.

● ● ● ● ●

At Leeds University there was at that time a radical intellectual tradition which had grown side by side with a conservative, formal tradition. And as was the case at Makerere, I once again identified with the unofficial, radical tradition. Leeds exposed me to a wider literary world; it made me aware of the radical literature that embraced the Third World as well as the socialist world.

I can remember very well the person who first introduced Frantz Fanon to Leeds. It was Grant Kamenju. He went to Paris, and in an obscure little bookshop he found Fanon's book *The Damned,* which was later published outside France under the title *The Wretched of the Earth.* And of course this book was a very important eye-opener for me and for other African students at Leeds. I think this was the only Fanon book I read at that time, but I read quite a lot of Caribbean literature, at the same time writing *A Grain of Wheat,* and arguing a lot about the problems of colonialism,

neo-colonialism, and imperialism, as well as travelling widely in Europe.

The political literature of Karl Marx and Friedrich Engels was important and soon overshadowed Fanon. Or rather, Marx and Engels began to reveal the serious weaknesses and limitations of Fanon, especially his own petit bourgeois idealism that led him into a mechanical overemphasis on psychology and violence, and his inability to see the significance of the rising and growing African proletariat. I avidly read Engels' *Socialism: Utopian and Scientific;* Marx's Preface to Engels' *A Contribution to the Critique of Political Economy;* some sections of *The German Ideology;* Engels' *Anti-Dühring;* and the first volume of Marx's *Capital* as well as his two studies on class struggles, *The Class Struggles in France* and *The Eighteenth Brumaire of Louis Bonaparte.* I was excited when I read in Engels' *Anti-Dühring* the notion that movement and hence change was fundamental in nature, human society, and thought, and that this motion was the result of the unity and struggle of opposites. I tried to use this notion in **A Grain of Wheat,** especially through the image of a grain which has to die in order to bear life. I would single out Lenin's work *Imperialism, the Highest Stage of Capitalism* as an eye-opener on the nature of imperialism in its colonial and neo-colonial stages. Even today I still think that this work ought to be compulsory reading for all students of African and Third World literatures. My first exposure to Marxist literature at Leeds University was also through many of the public lectures organized by the students outside the formal academic mainstream. Writers of progressive imaginative literature—people like Brecht and Gorky—were also important to me. Gorky's novel *Mother* should be read by all African patriots.

● ● ● ● ●

Those who produce should control the wealth; *he who produces should be able to control that which he produces.* We have a Gikuyu saying that *Muumbi arugagana icere,* literally meaning that the Creator or producer of pottery often cooks in broken pieces or in cracked pots. This describes aptly the nature of any class society, and more so, a class society under capitalism. Labour produces. Capital disposes. The maker or producer of pottery produces pots but he has no pot for his own use; the shoemaker makes shoes, but he walks barefoot; the builder builds magnificent houses, but he himself does not live in them—instead he continues to live in shacks; the mason builds wonderful cities but he himself has nowhere to live; the tailor makes super clothes, but he goes naked, or at best in tattered dress; the miner digs gold, coal, and other minerals and precious stones or extracts oil, but he himself has no decent clothes or shelter or food or cows; the soldier does the risky business of fighting, but glory and honour and salary increases go to the generals; peasants produce food, but they and their own go naked or badly dressed and hungry; the so-called underdeveloped world feeds and clothes and shelters the imperialist world, financing its luxury and arts and sciences and technology, but this underdeveloped world remains impoverished and an object of charity, like the hunting dog that ends up feeding on bones after the master has finished all the meat. The palace walls of a handful of capitalists are painted with the blood and sweat of a million hands. This handful has an army of intellectuals and artists, journalists, parliamentarians, etc., who rationalize and justify this exploitative relationship. But it is also true that all over the world the million hands are in revolt against that exploitative status quo.

• • • • •

I think that if the novel is to be meaningful it must reflect the totality of the forces affecting the lives of the people. And all the great novels, even in the bourgeois critical and literary tradition, have reflected this totality of forces at a particular moment of history. Take a novel like Tolstoy's *War and Peace* or his *Anna Karenina*—surely you will find that not much is left out of these novels. Most of the economic, political, cultural, and spiritual forces at work in Russian society of the nineteenth century are reflected there.... On the other side I find very disturbing the tendency by bourgeois and petit bourgeois critics to equate negative aspects of human beings with the true human condition; that is, if you show people as stupid, cowardly, vacillating, always terrified of death or life, sometimes wanting to commit suicide out of sheer despair, then you are said by those same critics to be depicting the true human condition. Why should we equate weakness with the true human condition? On the contrary, I would have thought that resistance to oppression and exploitation, the strong desire in human beings to overcome the negative aspects of nature and all the things that inhibit the free development of their lives—this is the most important of human qualities... We know that the transformations of the twentieth century have been the results of the struggles of peasants and workers. So how can we say that these two classes, whose labour has changed nature, are weak, naive, stupid, and cowardly?

• • • • •

Previously there was a tendency to have peasant and worker characters but give them the vacillating mentality and world outlook of the petite bourgeoisie. This is evident especially in my portrayal of peasant characters in *A Grain of Wheat*. What I have tried to do in *Petals of Blood* is to depict peasant and worker characters in their world outlook and also in their own view of classes and their relationships within their struggle, and especially as a people capable of freeing themselves from the clutches of their enemies, because this is historically true.

• • • • •

The African people must primarily rely on their own resources. To me this seems to be very, very crucial. We've got a saying in Gikuyu that *Ngemi Ciumaga na Mucii,* that is, "the strength of a people must come from themselves, or from the homestead." Only after this can

others find the basis for aiding them. You cannot go to war with your eyes on the strength of your friends. That way lies slavery and domination. (pp 18-25)

> *Carol Sicherman, in her* Ngugi wa Thiong'o: The Making of a Rebel, A Source Book in Kenyan Literature and Resistance, *Hans Zell Publishers, 1990, 486 p.*

Jennifer Evans (essay date 1987)

[In the following essay, Evans examines female characters in Devil on the Cross.]

While in the process of writing *Devil on the Cross* in detention, Ngugi explained in his prison diary the importance he attached to his heroine, Jacinta Wariinga:

> Because the women are the most oppressed and exploited section of the entire working class, I would create a picture of a strong determined woman with a will to resist and to struggle against the conditions of her present being. Had I not seen glimpses of this type in real life among the women of Kamiriithu Community Education and Cultural Centre? Isn't Kenyan history replete with this type of woman? Me Kitilili, Muraa wa Ngiti, Mary Muthoni Nyanjiru? Mau Mau women cadres? Wariinga will be the fictional reflection of this resistance heroine of Kenyan history. Wariinga heroine of toil...there she walks...

Ngugi evidently sees the image of Wariinga in an historical context, belonging to a feminine tradition of struggle and resistance found in both colonial and post-colonial Kenya. This concern with women is not new for Ngugi. All of his novels are sensitive to the burdens that Kenyan women have had to bear. Muthoni and Nyambura in *The River Between,* Njoroge's 'two mothers' in *Weep Not, Child* Mumbi and Wangari in *A Grain of Wheat.* Wanja and Nyakinyua in *Petals of Blood,* are all in their own ways 'resistance heroines' and the strongest symbols of cultural identity, community and continuity that these novels have to offer.

Ngugi has portrayed modern Kenya as ruthless, immoral and avidly materialistic. The complexities and inequalities of this new society are especially well illustrated by the fate of Wanja in *Petals of Blood. Devil on the Cross* focuses even more emphatically on the particular dilemma of women in a rapidly changing society and their exploitation in terms of class and sex, using women's position as a measure of the ills of contemporary Kenya.

Devil on the Cross is the story of Jacinta Wariinga, ostensibly narrated by the 'Gicaandi Player' or 'Prophet of Justice' at the request of Jacinta's mother, 'so that each may pass judgment only when he knows the whole truth. In many respects the pattern of Wariinga life resembles that of Wanja in *Petals of Blood.* Both approximate to the exemplary tale of Kareendi, told by Wariinga as the story of 'a girl like me...or...any other girl in Nairobi.' Sexual exploitation and discrimination are dominant factors in Kareendi's life. She is given few opportunities to develop her potential and is constantly at the mercy of men for her livelihood. She is very often reduced to the cursed 'cunt' Wanja protests about in *Petals of Blood*. For women like Kareendi there is no longer pride or joy in womanhood:

> To the Kareendis of modern Kenya, isn't each day exactly the same as all the others? For the day on which they are born is the very day on which every part of their body is buried except one—they are left with a single organ. So when will the Kareendis of modern Kenya wipe the tears from their faces? When will they ever discover laughter?

Even motherhood becomes a curse when the girl is young and unmarried and the man responsible will not admit it. While still at school, both Wanja and Wariinga become pregnant by wealthy older man who abandon them. Wanja kills her baby. Wariinga tries to kill herself, but is rescued. She is lucky enough to have a family who will take care of her child, and support her through secretarial college. She avoids Wanja's descent to the underworld of bars and prostitution, but must still face the disadvantages of her sex.

As a female office worker Wariinga suffers sexual harassment and intimidation. She is not expected to be blatantly for sale like the barmaid, but she is expected to be available for the boss. Wariinga comes to a fuller understanding of the nature of her dual exploitation as a worker and a woman in the course of the novel. Like Wanja, she realizes she must also choose her side: 'We who work as clerks, copy typists and secretaries, which side are we on? We who type and take dictation from Boss Kihara and his kind, whose side are we on in this dance? Are we on the side of the workers, or on the side of the rich? Who are we? Who are we?' Wariinga sees that in exchange for a miserable salary, female office workers must sacrifice their 'arms', 'brains', 'humanity' and 'thighs' to serve their bosses. Their exploitation is only a small part of the exploitation and expropriation which brings profits to the companies they work for. Wariinga is dismissed from the Champion Construction Company for refusing to be Kihara's 'sugar girl'. Muturi is dismissed from the same company for organizing a strike against low wages. At the end of the novel the same company is trying to take over the site of the garage co-operative to build a tourist hotel, or, as the garage workers call it, 'a factory for modern prostitution.'

Wariinga is a 'resistance heroine' because she rises to the challenge which confronts her. The experience at the Devil's Feast changes her from a spectator to a participant in the struggle. She gains a positive image and self-esteem by fighting back, and by refusing to accept the role ascribed to her. At the beginning of the novel Wariinga's hatred of herself and her blackness shows in her unbecoming appearance, spotted skin, singed hair, ill-fitting clothes, and awkward movement. In three successive unjust blows, men exert their power over her:

her boss sacks her, her boyfriend leaves her, and her landlord throws her out of her house. She is defeated, confused and lacking in confidence. 'Insistent self-doubt and crushing self-pity formed the burden that Wariinga was carrying that Saturday as she walked through the Nairobi streets....' The final section of the novel (Chapters 10, 11 and 12) commences two years after the Devil's Feast at Ilmorog, and is principally concerned with the new dynamic Wariinga. She has overcome daunting circumstances to deserve the title 'Wariinga, heroine of toil.' Once her potential is not masked or crushed, Wariinga becomes the beautiful woman she should be. By walking on Muturi's 'paths of resistance' she has gained a pride in her identity as a worker and as a black woman. She has achieved a personal wholeness and will no longer tolerate being treated as a 'single organ'. Wariinga's movement and appearance now have a unified perfection worthy of a true daughter of Mumbi:

> Today Wariinga strides along with energy and purpose, her dark eyes radiating the light of an inner courage, the courage and light of someone with firm aims in life—yes, the firmness and courage and faith of someone who has achieved something through self-reliance. What's the use of shuffling along timidly in one's own country? Wariinga, the black beauty! Wariinga of the mind and hands and body and heart, walking in rhythmic harmony on life's journey! Wariinga, the worker!

Wariinga works in a garage co-operative as a part-time car mechanic, while completing a course in mechanical engineering at the Polytechnic. She has dared to 'storm a man's citadel,' and, after some initial hostility and resistance, she has acquired respect and equality among fellow workers and students. She has also acquired physical and social confidence by learning karate and judo, and can adequately deal with any male intimidation. There is a touch of the invincibility of a comic-strip heroine about the new 'Wonder Woman' Wariinga, but Ngugi's portrayal of the karate-kicking car mechanic is obviously intended to carry a serious and important social meaning. Within the inequalities of the capitalist system, the novel as a whole lays heavy emphasis on the particular oppression of women in contemporary Kenya. Wariinga is above all important as a radical example of how a woman can resist being pushed, or tempted, into accepting subservient, degrading or decorative roles. Gaturia clearly explains Wariinga's social significance:

> We, the Kenyan youth, must be the light to light up new paths of progress for our country.
>   You for instance, are a very good example of what I am trying to say. Your training in mechanical engineering, fitting and turning and moulding, is a very important step. It is a kind of signal to indicate to other girls their abilities and potential.

Wariinga learns to cope with urban life and modern technology. She is a positive model for a new generation of Kenyan women. A positive image of her traditional inheritance is represented by the figure of Wangari. Much like Nyakinyua in *Petals of Blood*, Wangari is the archetypal strong peasant woman, 'the tiller,' the embodiment and symbol of Mother Kenya. Life on the land is extremely hard, but once she is dispossessed of her land Wangari finds her situation impossible. This woman, who has been a primary producer all her life, suddenly finds herself without useful employment. Her experiences in Nairobi highlight the problems of rapid social change and the particular difficulties faced by women in contemporary Kenyan society. Even an older woman like Wangari is insultingly treated as a sexual object. She explains that after she has told her troubles to one black shop manager, he laughs: 'He told me that the only job he could offer me was that of spreading my legs, that women with mature bodies were expert at that job.' Wangari's innocent and honest attempt to find work eventually leads to arrest and jail. She is charged with vagrancy and intending to steal. A woman who has in the past been at the centre of her rural community, apparently has no right or place in the capital city of her country, and is dealt with as a trespasser. Wangari may be unfamiliar with the ways of modern urban life, but she does understand truth and justice. Women like Wangari and Nyakinyua, who are old enough to have participated in Mau Mau, possess the wisdom of the people's history. They have an acute political consciousness and are more secure in their cultural identity than younger women like Wariinga and Wanja. A hardworking woman of the soil. Wangari stands in extreme contrast to the idle bourgeois wives and mistresses who lead the kind of frivolous lives once reserved for white colonial women. Contestants at the Devil's Feast are required to declare their cars and their women in order to identify their wealth and status. Kihaahu wa Gatheeca proudly boasts in his testimony that his second wife has nothing to do: 'she has no job other than decking herself out in expensive clothes and jewellery for *cocktail parties*.' Such personal indulgence and such a decorative passive role are completely alien to Wangari. She does not even have her ears pierced in the traditional fashion: '"Because, ours was not a time for adorning our bodies with flowers and necklaces. Ours was a time for decorating ourselves with bullets in the fight for Kenya's freedom!" Wangari said with pride, because she knew that the deeds of her youth had changed Kenya's history.' Wangari exemplifies the courage and spirit of the true Gikuyu woman, who has always participated in her people's struggles. It is in this image that the 'new' Wariinga is cast, and to this tradition that she belongs. Wangari is indeed a 'resistance heroine of Kenyan history' who can provide inspiration for the contemporary struggle, if she is acknowledged. Muturi, the politically conscious worker, recognizes her heroism and the fact that there are many women like her: 'Wangari, heroine of our country—all Wangaris, heroines of our land!' Gaturia, the intellectual, is also extremely impressed by Wangari's courageous behaviour when she brings the police to the cave, and they turn against her:

> Wangari raised her voice in song as they prodded at her and shoved her with clubs and batons and spat at her:

> If ever you hear drip, drip, drip, Don't think it's thundery rain.
> No, it'll be the blood of us peasants
> As we fight for our soil!

> And she was led out, still singing her defiance, her chained hands raised high above her head, the links gleaming like a necklace of courage.

Wangari does not need trinkets to decorate her body. Her beauty shines through her actions and transforms her chains. In his portrayal of Wangari, Ngugi acknowledges and pays tribute to the personal sacrifices and political contributions of peasant women. Within the task of historical retrieval and correction in which his novels are engaged this aspect is significant. Ngugi's fiction attempts to restore black men and black women to an active role in the making of their history.

While presenting the admirable qualities of the traditional rural woman, Ngugi does not seek to enshrine women in an irretrievable past. Coupled with his images of the traditional woman are images of 'new' women. Looking to the future, he points to paths of change and progress arising from his people's history. Wariinga and Wanja are heiresses to a proud female tradition. Their portrayal constitutes an eloquent plea that women have a right to respect and equality in the modern world. Women must struggle to attain this for themselves, but Ngugi also draws attention to the prejudiced and oppressive behaviour of men as a major obstacle which must be consciously tackled. In *Devil on the Cross* Gaturia complains of the exploitation of Kenyan women by the tourist industry, but Wariinga points out that the prejudices of Kenyan men are to blame, as well as the foreigners:

> Even you, the Kenyan men think that there is no job a woman can do other than cooking your food and massaging your bodies . . . . Why have people forgotten how Kenyan women used to make guns during the Mau Mau war against the British? Can't people recall the different tasks carried out by women in the villages once the men had been sent to detention camps? A song of praise begins at home. If you Kenyan men were not so scornful and oppressive, the foreigners you talk about so much would not be so contemptuous of us.

Ngugi portrays sexual confrontation between men and women as part of the destructive rivalry on which contemporary Kenyan capitalism thrives, and through which injustices and inequalities are perpetuated.

The ending of *Devil on the Cross* is optimistic in so far as it offers possibilities of new social orders in the future, but it is not conclusively 'happy'. Both Wariinga and Gaturia go through enlightenment and liberation in the process of finding themselves and each other but, like the ill-fated lovers of Ngugi's earlier novels, they are to find that the larger social forces impinge on their personal relationship. The fact that there is no simple 'happy' ending reinforces the point, made in *Petals of Blood,* that 'La Luta Continua!' As Ngugi has said: "The problem of men and women cannot be satisfactorily solved under the present system. Sexual relations are the reflection of an unequal economic system. Warĩĩnga refuses to settle down to marriage with Gaturia, because she discovers that her prospective father-in-law is her seducer, 'the Rich Old Man from Ngorika'. When Wangari delivers her condemnation of the thieves at the Devil's Feast 'her voice carried the power and authority of a people's judge.' Warĩĩnga also speaks with the voice of 'a people's judge' when she condemns the Rich Old Man to die. Warĩĩnga execution of her oppressor, like Wanja's execution of Kimeria in *Petals of Blood,* is more than personal revenge. It carries the force of communal retribution and justice.

Both Warĩĩnga and Wanja rise above the tale of Kareendi because they do not finally accept defeat and humiliation. Having come to the realization that there are more than the 'two worlds' of 'the eater' and 'the eaten', Warĩĩnga commits herself to the 'third world': 'the world of the revolutionary overthrow of the system of eating and being eaten.'

Ngugi has tailored the content, form and style of *Devil on the Cross* for his intended Gikuyu-speaking worker and peasant audience. His only concession to his foreign readers is to have made an English translation. Properly the work should be read aloud and communally in its original Gikuyu. An individual private reading of the English version can obviously not do justice to a work whose principal significance lies in its use of the Gikuyu language. But, in a novel which is so intimately concerned with Ngugi's individual and communual identity, it is also significant that images of women are such a prominent feature. Warĩĩnga the female protagonist of *Devil on the Cross,* is the successor to a line of heroines who have become increasingly central to the structure and meaning of Ngugi's novels.

The significant interplay of female images in Ngugi's life and literature is evident in *Detained.* He begins the first chapter of his prison diary with a direct reference to his fictional Gikuyu heroine: '*Warĩĩnga ngatha ya wĩra* . . . Warĩĩnga heroine of toil . . . there she walks haughtily carrying her freedom in her hands . . .' The second section of this chapter begins with Ngugi's contemplation of a photograph of his daughter Njooki, born to his wife Nyambura five months after his arrest, and the various names she has been given: 'Njooki, meaning she who comes back from the dead; or Aiyerubo, meaning she who defies heaven and hell; or Wamũingĩ, meaning she who belongs to the people.' Warĩĩnga and Njooki are both sources of inspiration and courage, of sanity and optimism, in the cruel and uncertain world of detention. In the third and concluding section of Chapter 1, Ngugi coalesces the images of Njooki and Warĩĩnga. As symbolic links with history and community, with the world beyond the prison walls, they give strength and meaning to Ngugi's resistance:

> Njooki, a picture sent through the post; and Warĩĩnga, a picture created on rationed toilet paper, have been more than a thousand trumpets silently breaking through the fortified walls of Kamĩtĩ Maxi-

mum Security Prison to assure me that I am not alone; Warĩĩnga by constantly making me conscious of my connection with history, and Njooki, by constantly making me aware that I am now in prison because of Kamĩrĩĩthũ and its people.

> But Warĩĩnga and Njooki also keep on reminding me that my detention is not a personal affair. It's part of the wider history of attempts to bring up the Kenyan people in a reactionary culture of silence and fear, and of the Kenyan people's fierce struggle against them to create a people's revolutionary culture of outspoken courage and patriotic heroism.

Considering the symbolic strength of the image of the pregnant woman and the possibilities for the future that she carries, which are finally represented by Mumbi in *A Grain of Wheat* and by Wanja in *Petals of Blood,* the dynamic relationship between Ngugi's life and his art is well illustrated by the fact that in detention he should himself be sustained by the images of a woman and a child. In the heroine of *Devil on the Cross* and his own daughter, he finds compelling symbolic value: 'Warĩĩnga . . . Njooki . . . my symbols of hope and defiance.' In the actual creation of human life through a woman, and the literary creation of the figure of a woman, Ngugi sees the essence of his own struggle and the communal struggle of the people of Kenya. (pp. 131-38)

> *Jennifer Evans, "Women and Resistance in Ngugi's 'Devil on the Cross'," in* Women in African Literature Today, *Vol. 15, 1987, pp. 131-39.*

Carol M. Sicherman (essay date 1989)

[*Sicherman is an authority on the history of Kenya. In the following excerpt, she examines Ngugi's treatment of Kenyan history in his fiction, focusing on* Petals of Blood.]

When Heinemann decided to reissue some of the most successful titles of its African Writers Series in a new format, Ngugi wa Thiong'o took advantage of the opportunity to revise certain details and to add significantly new passages in *A Grain of Wheat.* Two of the revisions, a change in political terminology and a correction of the historical detail, hint suggestively at my topic: the emergence of Ngugi's mature understanding of the role of history in African literature and of his own role in the rewriting of Kenyan history. Regarding a writer as the "conscience of the nation," Ngugi intends to make his compatriots see the history of Kenya for the last hundred years as the story of resistance to colonialism—and to neocolonialism. (p. 347)

In order to understand Ngugi's deploying of the history of Kenyan resistance, we need to know its political, cultural, and historiographical context. We need, further, to recognize that Ngugi blurs the lines between history and literature and that, perhaps as a consequence of this blurring of the two genres, the distinction between Ngugi and his narrators and certain characters also becomes blurred. This is certainly the case in the work on which I will focus, *Petals of Blood,* in which Ngugi's ideas are voiced by Karega and the lawyer (as well as by the collective "we" that at times assumes the narrative function). I will need first to sketch the evolution of Ngugi's handling of history and his emerging perceptions of the kind of history needed for Kenya, then to discuss his challenge to Kenyan historians (and to Ngugi himself as erstwhile historian), and finally to assess his critique of the first generation of Kenyan historians—who are, of course, Ngugi's age-mates. Having described this background, I can proceed to discuss interpretations of resistance, focusing first on Waiyaki, perceived as progenitor of the pre-presidential Kenyatta and of Mau Mau as well, and then on Mau Mau as the largest example. In both cases we will see an intermingling of history and legend—indeed, a transformation of legend into history—as well as fierce ideological disputes. A brief reflection on Ngugi's readership will bring this essay to an end if not a conclusion; no conclusion is possible, for the story continues.

• • • • •

The "ideal" African novel, Ngugi told an interviewer in 1969, would "embrace the pre-colonial past[,] . . . the colonial past, and the post-independence period with a pointer to the future"—a description of *Petals of Blood,* the novel that he started to write the following year. By then he knew that, like his character Munira, he "had to take a drastic step that would restore me to my usurped history, my usurped inheritance, that would reconnect me with my history" (*Petals of Blood*). Whereas Munira eventually retreats into religious fundamentalism, Ngugi has accomplished the reconnection.

Preoccupied with history from the start, Ngugi has gradually altered his view of the relationship of literature to history and the relationship of himself as creative writer to Kenyan historians. From the nationalist enthusiasm of a student writer living abroad, he has moved through the middle ground of *A Grain of Wheat* to the forthright evangelism of *The Trial of Dedan Kimathi, Petals of Blood,* and the later works—a writer tested by mature combat with the forces of neocolonialism at home. It must not be forgotten that *The River Between* and *Weep Not, Child* were both written while he was an undergraduate at Makerere College in Uganda and *A Grain of Wheat* while he was an MA student at Leeds University in England. The burgeoning of his political awareness during his years at Leeds (1964-67) certainly affected *Grain* but did not fully blossom until *Trial.*

Ngugi's first three novels, which look back in time, form a quasi trilogy in chronological progression that runs from *The River Between* (1965; drafted in 1960), *Weep Not, Child* (1964; drafted in 1962), and *A Grain of Wheat* (1967; completed in 1966)—running from the female circumcision controversy that came to a head in 1929 and led to the development of Gikuyu independent schools (*River*), through the Emergency (1952-56) declared to suppress Mau Mau (*Weep*), to the critical moment of Independence (*Grain*). The next novel picks up chronologically where *Grain* leaves off: set during the twelve years up to and including the very years when Ngugi was writing it (1970-75), *Petals* looks at the present in the light of the past. *Petals* contains not only many reminiscences of Mau Mau but also panoramic allusions to the more distant African past and to the black diaspora, going back through what Ngugi calls "a huge space of time" to show "three different phases of social formations: a long period of precapitalist, precolonialist, relations," then colonialism, and finally neocolonialism. The way in which past and present are viewed is reversed in the play *The Trial of Dedan Kimathi* (1976; written 1974-76), which looks at the past in the light of the present in an attempt to assess the enduring legacy of Mau Mau to independent Kenya. *I Will Marry When I Want*—the English title of Ngugi's first Gikuyu play, *Ngaahika Ndeenda*—looks squarely at the present, with an implied agenda for change. Finally, *Devil on the Cross,* his first Gikuyu novel (*Caitaani Mutharaba-ini*), looks at the present in the light of the future, setting a satiric critique of contemporary Kenya against a vision of a socialist Kenya purged of neocolonialism—the fulfillment of Ngugi's early requirement that the writer "be prepared to suggest" a future.

References to historical figures and events of earlier periods are nearly as important as the historical settings. Except for his apprentice plays and earlier short stories, Ngugi's works are dense with allusions to historical personages and events, the density becoming most marked in *Petals of Blood.* Even where the allusions are general rather than exact—"Siriana," for example, although modeled on Alliance High School, is founded some years before the actual founding of Alliance in 1926—the fiction is deeply imbued with history.

From the beginning Ngugi deliberately mixed fictional names with those of historical characters, hoping to heighten the illusion of fictional "reality"; as he says in the author's note to *Grain,* "fictitious" characters exist in a real "situation and [among] . . . problems [that] are real." Even so, he apparently felt some uneasiness about intermixing history and fiction; the author's note also explains that historical figures "like . . . Jomo Kenyatta and Waiyaki are unavoidably mentioned." In his subsequent works, there are no such apologies and certainly no avoidance; increasingly, the fictional characters intermingle with historical characters and events, functioning as illustrators of history.

In the earlier books, historical allusions are vague and inaccurate. The representation of the 1922 demonstration and massacre in the first version of *Grain,* faulty though it is, at least reduced the extraordinary understatement of *Weep:* "People were shot and three of them died." After *Grain,* it would seem, Ngugi read Kenyan history more attentively, unimpeded by the blinders of his colonial education. With Micere Mugo he conducted secondary research in English and primary research in Gikuyu while writing on *The Trial of Dedan Kimathi,* a work of the imagination that purports to contribute to the revision of Kenyan history that Ngugi regards as essential to his country's liberation from the colonial legacy. Perhaps doing historical research helped hone the awareness of history and of Kenyan historiography permeating his fourth novel.

Petals of Blood is thick with allusions to world black history and contains a number of pointed historiographical disquisitions. Indeed, the aesthetics of his fiction changes (for the worse, some critics argue), and there is often little difference between the writing in certain passages of the novel and in the closely related nonfiction written soon after (in particular, *Detained*). The scope of historical reference has widened in both time and space, ranging from the distant, legendary past "of Ndemi and the creators from Malindi to Songhai" to the nineteenth and twentieth centuries—"the past of L'Ouverture, Turner, Chaka, *Abdulla,* Koitalel, *Ole Masai,* Kimathi, Mathenge" (my italics indicate fictional characters). Against a backdrop of broadly sketched grandeur achieved long before by "the creators," the fictional characters take their place among not only the heroes of Kenyan resistance—from the early twentieth century (Koitalel arap Samoei) to Mau Mau (Dedan Kimathi, Stanley Mathenge)—but also among the heroes of resistance a century earlier elsewhere in Africa

Ngugi wa Thiong'o

(Chaka) and the New World (Toussaint L'Ouverture, Nat Turner). To contrast with the heroes, Ngugi lists a demonology, with three historical figures from the earlier twentieth century preceding their fictional analogues from the later twentieth century: "Kinyanjui, Mumia, Lenana, *Chui, Jerrod, Nderi wa Riera.*

The purpose of such collocations of historical and fictional characters is to make Kenyan readers reflect on their own place in the continuum of history. Sounding like a miniature Karega, the wise young hero of Ngugi's first children's book advises his classmates how to find their way out of the forest: "We must...find out where we are, in order to decide where we will go next. We cannot know where we are, without first finding out where we come from" (*Njamba Nene and the Flying Bus*). The Kenyan view of the past, Ngugi said in a 1978 interview, "up to now has been distorted by the cultural needs of imperialism"—needs that led historians to show "[first,] that Kenyan people had not struggled with nature and with other men to change their natural environment and create a positive social environment...[and second, that they] had not resisted foreign domination.

The first omission to which Ngugi calls attention concerns the history of common people, who were completely ignored by colonial and postcolonial historians despite the professed interest of the latter in "the history of the inarticulate." Ngugi's call for a history of the anonymous masses reacts to the commonplaces of his early education, when it was in the interest of colonial historians, "to stress what they claimed was the natural logic of Europeans in colonizing and dominating the Kenyan." (pp. 348-51)

The second element neglected by colonial historians— resistance to foreign incursions—divides into two parts: the history of mass movements and the history of heroes. A focus on certain heroes and on the creation of nation-states can help support the newly independent African states, led by heroes like Kenyatta, so that the postcolonial becomes, in Ngugi's terms, the neocolonial. Thus, the new historians, wittingly or not, become servants of the state: "...we are," William R. Ochieng' has rather pompously but correctly declared, "the founding fathers of the Kenya nation." Nation building necessarily involves myth building, and myths, as the Tanzanian historian Nelson Kasfir has said, may "decolonise African peoples by restoring their dignity." It is the choice of myth that is crucial. Many of the intellectual clashes in contemporary Kenya are between rival mythologies—very often between conflicting myths of Mau Mau but also between the historians' myth of a past splendid insofar as it rivaled white successes, and Ngugi's myth of the people's centuries-long "heroic resistance...their struggles to defend their land, their wealth, their lives."

● ● ● ● ●

Although Ngugi's conception of Kenyan history and his charges against the historians are open to some question, the call for action with which he concluded the interview quoted earlier has obvious relevance to his own practice as a novelist:

> Kenyan intellectuals must be able to tell these stories, or histories, or history of heroic resistance to foreign domination by Kenyan people ... looking at ourselves as ... as a people whose history shines with the grandeur, if you like, of heroic resistance and achievement of the Kenyan people.... I feel that Kenyan history, either pre-colonial or colonial[,] has not yet been written.

That history, he says in *Detained,* will show the "history of Kenyan people creating a ... fight-back, creative culture." Because of the deficiencies of professional historians, Ngugi argues, at the present time this story can be better told through literature.

Petals of Blood insists at some length on revising Kenyan historiography, first through the futile efforts of Karega to find suitable history texts for his pupils ... and then in Karega's appeal to the lawyer for help in his quest for "a vision of the future rooted in a critical awareness of the past," an awareness more specifically of economic history. The lawyer sends him "books and a list of other titles written by professors of learning at the University," the same university where Ngugi taught. But the books fail to answer his questions. (pp. 352-53)

Ngugi's understanding of his major theme, the history of resistance, has broadened since his undergraduate writing when his knowledge was limited to the Mau Mau rising and to a few major figures or episodes—Waiyaki's resistance and death in the early 1890s, Harry Thuku's campaign against colonial restrictions in 1921-22, the female circumcision controversy of 1929-31. In these works, legend carries equal weight with documentable history. Particularly in *The River Between* and *Weep Not, Child,* he emphasizes the prophecy of the seer Mugo wa Kibiro, with its dual message of the coming of the white man and the folly of resistance; there is an implication here, as Gitahi-Gititi has observed, that aside from Mau Mau and a few other episodes, "the Gikuyu people offered no resistance to colonial penetration"—an implication that Ngugi began to correct in *A Grain of Wheat* and wholeheartedly attacked in *The Trial of Dedan Kimathi* and *Petals of Blood.*

From 1976 on Ngugi has made plain his determination to participate in the decolonizing of Kenyan history. Indeed, in his later works he deliberately has dealt with periods and figures neglected by professional historians, as when he set his suppressed musical *Maitu Njugira* ("Mother Sing to Me"), in the 1930s, a period "almost totally ignored by Kenyan historians." *Maitu Njugira* dramatizes "actual history" based on Ngugi's research into "the actual laws and ordinances" of the 1930s. "These things of the past cement the present," said one of the actors; they create links to the future and at the same time implications too unpleasant for the government to countenance. "Writers are surgeons of the heart and souls of a community" (*Decolonising*), but official

Kenya declines the operation, retaining the old Kenyan history.

But what does the phrase "Kenyan history" mean? Karari Njama describes the pre-high school curriculum at Alliance High School in the 1940s, where Ngugi studied a decade later:

> In History we had been taught all the good the white man had brought us—the stopping of tribal wars, guaranteeing security ..., good clothings, education and religion, easy ways of communication and travel ... and, finally, better jobs that would make it easy to raise the standard of living above the uneducated Africans.... In teaching Kenya History, the question of land was cunningly omitted.

This is the background for the school strike in *Petals:* "We wanted to be taught African literature, African history, for we wanted to know ourselves better." Why should a student seeking an "education that will fit [him] in [his] own environment" be given instead "a lot about English Pirates and English Kings, and practically nothing of his local geography and history"—an education that makes him "a misfit in his own community?"

History was the field that offered the most scope of African intellectual initiatives in the 1940s and 1950s, but these had to take place outside of official confines because for an African to take "an interest in his people's past was unhealthy, ... a betrayal of the civilization to which he attached himself when he was educated and baptized a Christian." Well before Independence, however, nationalist stirrings provided unofficial alternative education at Alliance High School, where a secret political and educational organization taught "how the English people acquired their supremacy, how they came to our country, how they alienated our lands, and how hypocritical they are in their Christianity."

Although the official history of colonial times has gone, no comparably assured version has replaced it, for three main reasons: first, the particular historical bias imparted in the waning days of colonialism to the first post-Independence generation of African intellectuals, a bias incorporated in language; second, the absence of substantial written documentation for much of the precolonial past, which poses formidable problems of reconstruction from oral, linguistic, and archaeological sources; and, third and most important, the continued politicizing of intellectual discourse in the period following Independence.

The colonial view of history did not simply disappear at Independence, when European scholars of African history began to be replaced by their African pupils. "The history of East Africa," wrote Sir Reginald Coupland in 1938, "is only the history of its invaders"; it is thus the history of "the comings and goings of brown men and white men on the coast," behind which stretches the Conradian "inpenetrable darkness" of Black Africa. (pp. 354-55)

Deeply imbued with European values, the nationalist historians who emerged in the 1960s often took their mentors' history and produced "the older version turned upside down, with many of its faults intact." They took it for granted that progress was evolutionary and that "unity is the basis of progress," the latter assumption familiar in Kenyatta's theme-slogan, "We all fought for Uhuru." The carryover of European assumptions was, however, masked by an appearance of African nationalism. In the 1960s—the "golden age of consensus"—historians dwelt on three themes: "the bliss that was African life before the coming of the Europeans"; "the injustice of colonialism"; and "how gloriously the African fought his way to *Uhuru.*"

Ngugi himself, with his automatic adjective "glorious," seems to fall into this self-congratulatory pattern of thinking when he has his narrator reflect:

> [Ilmorog] had had its day of glory: thriving villages with a huge population of sturdy peasants who had tamed nature's forest.... And at harvest time...the aged would sip honey beer and tell the children, with voices taut with prideful authority and nostalgia, about the founding patriarch. (*Petals*)

Although the phrases roll out automatically in this passage, later Karega rejects such "worship" of the past in a passage that sounds like Ngugi's own recantation: "Maybe I used to [worship] it: but I don't want to continue worshipping in the temples of a past without tarmac roads, without electric cookers, a world dominated by slavery to nature"; the people who "tamed nature's forest," he feels, had become nature's slaves. Furthermore, Ngugi's sharp distinction between traitors and collaborators saves him from the tendency of historians as well as politicians to paint *all* colonial peoples as somehow resisters.

"Neocolonial" historians—Ngugi names "[Bethwell A.] Ogot, [Godfrey] Muriuki, [Gideon] Were and [William R.] Ochieng"—are merely "following on similar theories yarned out by defenders of imperialism" who "insist that we only arrived here yesterday." "Arrival" for such historians, Ngugi implies, means arrival of the "modern" (i.e., Western-style) nation—even though, as John Lonsdale has remarked, "the most distinctively African contribution to human history could be said to have been precisely the civilized art of living fairly peaceably together *not* in states." There are, consequently, "many questions about our history which remain unanswered," such as the history of international trade *before* the Portuguese "ushered in an era...that climaxed in the reign of imperialism over Kenya" and the resultant "heroic resistance."

An evaluation of Ngugi's charges against Kenyan historians should start with the correction implied in his own more recent work. *Detained,* indeed, stands in mild reproof to the author of *Petals of Blood,* for in the later book Ngugi demonstrates research in books like Ghai and MacAuslan's *Public Law and Political Change in Kenya* and, more significantly, in works by the very

historians he reviles in *Petals,* including Ogot and Ochieng'. A work by another of the supposed "neocolonial" historians, Gideon Were's *Western Kenya Historical Documents,* stands as an example of important research in oral history; Were's use of the word "documents" to describe the contents of his book implicitly challenges the notion that historians depend on *written* documents. Finally, the treatment by Godfrey Muriuki of the early colonial paramount chief Kinyanjui, in a widely respected study focusing on precolonial Gikuyu history, stands as a good example of precisely the kind of history that Ngugi calls for. Muriuki makes plain that Kinyanjui—one of the "traitors" who were "collaborators with the enemy" to whom Ngugi repeatedly refers—was typical of those chiefs created by the British out of "nonentities in the traditional society": men who, in gratitude for their masters' donation of power, were willing to support British interest "at all costs in order to bolster up their position and influence outside the traditional structure." Yet while Muriuki's own accomplishment as a historian is impressive, he himself acknowledges that historical studies in Kenya have accomplished little and, in fact, are in crisis, with student enrollment plummeting and research funds nonexistent.

Besides the ideological or political-prudential reason for the absence of consensus on Kenyan history, there is another and very practical cause: events and people lacking a connection with Europeans were also often lacking written documentation, and the historian must unravel oral history and analyze physical and linguistic evidence in order to assemble a coherent account of historical developments. Ngugi's narrator explains: "Just now we can only depend on legends passed from generation to generation by the poets and players...supplemented by the most recent archaeological and linguistic researches and also by what we can glean from between the lines of the records of the colonial adventurers." It remains to be seen whether this kind of history, necessarily local and tribal, can be incorporated in a truly "national" history, one that would achieve Ngugi's goal of unifying the country.

These problems of documentation, although imposing, pale before the third cause of historiographical difficulty: contemporary politics, which of course involves the dominant neocolonial ideology. What one of Ngugi's principal intellectual antagonists, William R. Ochieng', has said of *Detained*—"to Ngugi history is simply a propaganda instrument in the service of a chosen ideology"—could be said generally of historical writing, although in both genres the best writing rejects propaganda for legitimate and knowledgeable interpretation. A month before Kenyan Independence, Ali Mazrui observed (echoing Ernest Renan) "that one essential factor in the making of a nation is 'to get one's history wrong,'" to be "*selective* about what did happen" so as to build national unity. Characteristic of the 1960s and early 1970s, the vigorous tone of the statement, as well as its content, is a direct contradiction of the colonialist historians' claim that knowledge is neutral, a claim that deflected any challenge on ideological grounds.

There are no "pure facts"; everything "involve[s] interpretation." But writers must be conscious that they *are* interpreting. Writers on history must recognize that the basic terms of historical writing—"collaboration," "resistance," "nationalism"—still need definition, and Ngugi gives them a nudge in this direction. "The government says we should bury the past," the betrayer Mugo says in *A Grain of Wheat,* but Gikonyo cries: "I can't forget...I will never forget." It is therefore essential to "choose your side." This injunction marks a distinct change in Ngugi's fiction; the experience of detention and his more extensive reading in Kenyan history have helped him recognize that "an intellectual is not a neutral figure in society."

Interviewing Ngugi shortly after the publication of **Detained,** Emman Omari suggested provocatively that in his "extremity the objectivity is buried": "You have melodiously clapped hands for active resisters like the Kimathis; and...you have snapped at the Mumias" (Mumia, an early colonial chief patronized by the British, was their enthusiastic ally). Ngugi acknowledged Omari's implications: "When writing history for our children, which things do we want them to admire? Should they emulate traitors or heroes?" And Ngugi knows who is who, with Waiyaki foremost in the pantheon of heroes and Kinyanjui, Waiyaki's betrayer, prominent among the traitors. This either/or mentality unfortunately characterizes much of the intellectual and political discourse in Kenya today, despite appeals for finer discriminations.

The issue, as Ngugi sees it, is whether Kenya's rulers wish to lead a truly independent country, or whether they are—as he charges—merely lackeys for multinational businesses, the "thieves and robbers" of **Devil on the Cross.** Although historians have a particular responsibility to attempt clearheaded analysis, most remain partisan: like their own colonial teachers, they "delighted in abusing and denigrating the efforts of the people and their struggles in the past." Despite his bias, Ngugi's challenge makes *Petals of Blood* "compulsory reading" for African historians, while at the same time his own efforts have met with considerable criticism, partly for scholarly reasons and partly for political ones. Establishment critics accuse him of negativism in his earlier works and lack of artistry in his more recent, "committed" writing: as soon as he "seemed to have an axe to grind"—that is, after *A Grain of Wheat*—"he...ceased to be a creative writer" and wrote mere "propaganda."

● ● ● ● ●

Displaying their profession's common inability to accept literary interpretation of their field—rejecting that "blending of fact and fiction [that]...is precisely what makes it important"—historians object both to Ngugi's carelessness with details and to his promoting myth as history. Ngugi is conscious of this element in his writing: "This Harry Thuku [whose followers,' demonstrating

against his arrest, were massacred by police] has already moved into patriotic heroic legends and I have treated him as such in the early chapters of *A Grain of Wheat.*" But Ngugi also knows the historical Thuku, who fought against "forced labour, female and child slavery, high taxation without even a little representation, low wages, and against the oppressive *kipande* [pass] that the workers were obliged to carry with chains around their necks"—all except for the mention of "slavery," elements of Thuku's campaign frequently mentioned by historians. Literary treatments of history include legend as well as "facts" because writers seek to discover "not only what has happened"—the historians' task—"but the *ways* in which things are felt to happen in history." And the ways in which things are *felt* to happen may actually affect the way things *do* happen. Ngugi's Kenyan readers know full well how indistinguishable the exploits of Dedan Kimathi the historical figure (1920-57) are from those of Dedan Kimathi the legendary figure, and how the legend in turn inspired military action—facts—by Kimathi's followers.

Another major twentieth-century historical figure who became mythologized is Jomo Kenyatta, who is referred to a number of times in *A Grain of Wheat* and *Weep Not, Child*—often by his popular name, "The Burning Spear," a characteristic mythologizing appellation. Ngugi's treatment of Kenyatta was the subject of another paper by Ochieng' at the 1984 conference, a reproof for the mythologizing portrayal in the early novels and an attack on Ngugi's later analysis of Kenyatta as a failed hero, one who betrayed his country. Again controversy ensured, with Ochieng' defended by his colleague Henry Mwanzi through the same technique that Ochieng' had used in attacking Ngugi's depiction of the Mau Mau as a national liberation movement—bald assertion. It is difficult to write history about legends. Kenyatta may not have been the "fire-spitting nationalist that Ngugi imagined him to be," but Ngugi's imagination was not peculiar to himself, as Ochieng' acknowledges; he grew up with "myths" and "tribal gossip" about Kenyatta that then became part of history when people acted upon their beliefs.

A fascinating example of such mythologizing occurs in the history—or story—of Waiyaki, a Gikuyu leader of resistance against the British in the early 1890s. Whether Waiyaki was consistently such a leader is open to doubt, as are the circumstances of his death. But in *A Grain of Wheat,* doubts matter far less that what Ochieng' disparagingly calls "rumor" or "gossip"—the legend of "Waiyaki and other warrior-leaders [who] took arms" against the "long line of other red strangers who carried, not the Bible, but the sword." Defeated by the superior technology of "the whiteman with bamboo poles that vomited fire and smoke," Waiyaki was

arrested and taken to the coast, bound hands and feet. Later, *so it is said,* Waiyaki was buried alive at Kibwezi with his head facing to the centre of the earth.... Then nobody noticed it; but looking back we can see that Waiyaki's blood contained within it a seed, a grain, which gave birth to a political party. (emphasis added)

The weight Ngugi gives to what "is said," to "rumor" and "gossip" as agents in forming the imaginative life of his people, makes it clear that he knows that actual historical force of what "is said"—its role in politics. Myths made things happen during the Emergency.

The "facts" regarding Waiyaki are difficult to come by. He probably was not buried alive head downward. The most plausible hypothesis to account for the legend is that of T. C. Colchester, a colonial official, in an unpublished note. Colchester observes that until the 1930s the Gikuyu did not ordinarily bury their dead; Waiyaki's burial would have seemed so abnormal as to suggest that he had been "killed by burial," and, as Colchester adds, the coincidental death and burial at Kibwezi some years later of Waiyaki's antagonist, William J. Purkiss, might have fed the legend. As far as Waiyaki's character goes, Muriuki is no doubt historically correct: "He was neither the 'scheming rogue'— breathing treachery, fire and brimstone—of the company officials, nor was he the martyr" imagined by nationalists. But what is finally most important, where Ngugi is concerned, is not the evaluation of historians but Waiyaki's role in Gikuyu folklore—Waiyaki as martyr, "tortured . . . fighting for his country," an avatar of "the second disciple of God . . . Jomo Kenyatta."

Waiyaki—or his legend—caused future events: "When he died, he left a curse that we should never sell our land or let it be taken from us." The impossibility of confirming the deathbed curse is less important than the belief that people had in its truth, a belief that influenced events sixty years after Waiyaki's death. Waruhiu Itote (a leading Mau Mau general known as "General China") describes a Mau Mau reprisal modeled on Waiyaki's legendary martyrdom, a reprisal that particularly inflamed European opinion. Having been told by a witch doctor that to win the war the Mau Mau "must bury a European alive with a black goat," a Mau Mau did precisely that in 1954: "They buried him [Arundell Gray Leakey] with his face downwards, *as we hear* Waiyaki was buried by the Europeans at Kibwezi" (emphasis added). The phrase, *as we hear,* like Ngugi's *so it is said,* testifies both to the strong Gikuyu awareness of their own history in the Mau Mau period and to the power of myth to affect events.

The nearer to the present day the historians get, the more obviously embroiled in controversy their task becomes. The most immediate questions about the relationship of past to present have been provoked by the Mau Mau rising; among the most urgent is the question whether Mau Mau was merely a manifestation of local (Gikuyu) nationalism or, as Ngugi argues, a central and catalytic event in the struggle for Kenyan independence. Whereas Europeans spoke of Mau Mau as a barbaric and atavistic reversion and many educated Africans recognized intelligent and ruthless adaptation, the fighters themselves, agreeing with neither view, commonly saw a mainly laudable and certainly neces-

sary re-creation of the past—a mistake, in the opinion of Karari Njama, himself one of the few educated Mau Mau leaders. To counter that view, part of the job of first-generation historians was to develop comprehension of the past as not static (the view of illiterate Africans as well as of Europeans) but dynamic.

In their common enterprise of national interpretation historians and writers should support one another, carrying out what the American scholar St. Clair Drake told Ochieng' was the "sacred duty . . . to redeem our race through the written world." Such cooperation does exist; one testimony, indeed, to Ngugi's skill as a literary-historical artist has been citation of his novels by social scientists to illustrate their points. But too often the two professions manifest a kind of sibling rivalry evident during a 1984 conference of the Kenya Historical Association devoted to "The Historiography of Kenya: A Critique," which included analyses of literary treatments of history. The literary critics who attended the sessions were quick to point out their colleagues' deficiencies as literary analysts. The historians, said the critic Chris Wanjala, "showed lack of basic understanding about the way literature worked." In a riposte to Wanjala, the historian Henry Mwanzi dismissed "Ngugi's fans" for having "an emotional attachment to the man" that blinded them to "his falsification of our history." In fact some historians' political antipathy to Ngugi prevents rational discourse. Ochieng' roundly admits that he cannot bear to read Ngugi (his "style bores me to death"), but his aversion did not stop him from writing a review of *Detained* that concludes: "Ngugi is operating beyond the limits of his role as a writer. He is terrorising us." Ochieng's difficulty in reading Ngugi stems partly from the disabling effect of his animus and partly from too narrow a conception of "history," excluding the contribution of legend from its purviews.

The wars of the intellectuals and the post-Uhuru battle for recognition of the ex-freedom fighters were linked in February 1986 during the first commemorative meeting of ex-Mau Mau fighters. One purpose of the meeting was "to find ways to write the history of the Mau Mau movement" as a national phenomenon, refuting non-Gikuyu historians" allegations "that the Mau Mau was a tribal movement or a civil war." To the veterans their history seemed to have vanished. Ngugi's career-long emphasis on Mau Mau has to be seen as a form of resistance to this betrayal by oblivion, as a monument in words to the heroes of the forests.

Remembering for Ngugi requires the painful acknowledgement of imperfection. The heroic Mau Mau model, as readers of *A Grain of Wheat* know, fits few actual freedom fighters; for every Kimathi-style Kihika, there may be dozens or hundreds of Mugos. If the writing of history depends on the truth-telling of the survivors, how dependent are we on the Mugos who conceal the truth? There are records: even while in the forest, the freedom fighters kept "records [that] would form a book of history which would be read by our future generations," a leitmotif in Karari Njama's memoirs. These records showed an effort to place contemporary history in a wider context, although the ill-educated writers often knew little of that context. The writer of "A Book of Forest History"—a Mau Mau document captured by British forces—reported a meeting in the forest on 5 December 1953 during which he "learnt a lot of new things and ideas," chiefly concerning alleged English parallels to Mau Mau activities: from the Roman period through the seventeenth century, it seems, the British took oaths and entered the forest, staying "about 120 years" under the Romans. British resistance to Roman imperialism, by offering a precedent to Kenyan resistance, validated the later resistance to British imperialism.

But Kenyan historians have either avoided the Mau Mau records as political hot potatoes or have been so partisan and careless—as in Maina wa Kinyatti's *Kenya's Freedom Struggle,* which omits essential documentation—that they have not advanced our understanding. When previously secret official documents relating to Mau Mau became available in 1984 under the thirty-year rule, the *Standard,* a Nairobi daily, published reports of the "top-secret Mau Mau papers" that focused on British policy. Despite their fairly innocuous content—the first article, with front-page banner headlines, discussed British thinking behind the June 1953 banning of the Kenya African Union—the dispatches aroused such official ire that the *Standard* ceased its reports. Popular distrust of professional historians is consequently endemic. One speaker at the Mau Mau commemorative meeting urged "that the books and papers authored by Professor Ochieng be banned from Kenyan schools, a proposal that was thunderously supported," although hardly likely to take effect, especially since Ochieng' had just published the first textbook of Kenyan history and was shortly to assume the chair in history at Moi University. Furthermore, President Moi contributed to the 1986 controversy by declaring that the history of the Mau Mau should not be written.

In the same year, a time of sharply escalated repression of intellectuals, Moi made clear his choice of patriotic historian by naming Professor Ogot, who sees Mau Mau as a narrowly tribal rather than as a national struggle, to the position of chairman of the Posts and Telecommunications Corporation. There could be no better confirmation of Temu and Swai's assertions that the so-called "new history . . . has resulted in the production of history to serve a new class of exploiters." "Small wonder, then," add Temu and Swai, "that side by side with the development of postcolonial Africanist historiography has developed a crescendo of intellectual McCarthyism"—a remark particularly apt to Kenya in the period following Ngugi's necessary self-exile, imposed in 1982. One of the sad if understandable results of the repressive political climate in Kenya has been the drying up of creative writing, a theme of R. N. Ndegwa's reviews (or "laments," as she calls them) of the year's work, published in the *Journal of Commonwealth Literature.*

These are not merely professional but deeply personal matters. Ngugi's political ideas result from an effort to foster an organic connection between his past as the child of peasants steeped in tradition and his present as an international author, the kind of connection that Karega has maintained and that Munira has lost. A spectator of both public and his own private history, Munira suffers from an inability to feel an organic and constructive link to the past: "The repetition of past patterns had always frightened him. It was the tyranny of the past that he had always tried to escape."

Involvement in personal history seems to be a prerequisite for involvement in public history. Munira asks, "Could I resurrect the past and connect myself to it, graft myself on the stem of history even if it was only my family's history outside of which I had grown? And would the stem really grow, sprouting branches with me as part of the great resurgence of life?" But Munira hardly knows his siblings, feels both rejection and admiration of his father, is remote from his mother. Nonetheless, despite his claim to be disconnected from his past, he is overwhelmed by his discovery that Karega was the lover of his sister (the only sibling with whom he felt any connection) and that she killed herself soon after being told by her father to choose between Karega and her family. He also is distressed by the link between Karega's family and his own: Karega's mother was an *ahoi* on his father's land, and Karega's brother Ndung'iri was probably a member of the Mau Mau gang that cut off his father's ear. Only by working through these connections, by converting distress into understanding, could Munira become reintegrated; instead, he retreats into a crazed, ahistorical religiosity.

And there is a societal parallel to Munira's dislocation, in the transformation of the religious center of Ilmorog, "where Mwathi had once lived guarding the secrets of iron works and native medicine," into an archaeological museum, "a site for the curious about the past, long long before East Africa traded with China and the Indies." "The mythical Mwathi" in one sense does not exist and in another exists perenially, his traditional wisdom voiced, we deduce, by his spokesperson, Muturi; he thus stands for the continuity of past with present, which is broken by the earth-moving machines and the archaeologists' scientific labeling. It is the voice of Mwathi that Ngugi's later work strives to transmit.

• • • • •

The very density and casualness of Ngugi's allusions to Kenyan historical events and figures in his work published after 1975—as well as the proliferation of untranslated Gikuyu words and phrases—accords with the decision he made, upon completing **Petals of Blood** in October 1975, to write his creative work in Gikuyu. Further, he asserts that "the true beginning of my education" took place in "the six months between June and November of 1977" when, developing his first Gikuyu work in concert with Kamiriithu peasants, he "learnt [his] language anew" and "rediscovered the creative nature and power of collective work." With **Decolonising the Mind** in 1986, he said farewell to all writing in English (except, his practice has shown, journalism). Some months later, in September 1986, Heinemann Kenya published his second Gikuyu novel, **Matigari ma Njiruungi**, but readers of Gikuyu had little chance to buy it: in February 1987, in yet another act of intellectual supression, the Kenyan government confiscated all copies in bookshops.

Implicitly, the main audience for Ngugi's work now in both his languages is Kenyan—not just readers of Gikuyu but those Kenyans who must rely on English (there have, however, been some translations into Kiswahili, encouraged by Ngugi). With the switch to Gikuyu or Kiswahili, "I can directly have dialogue with peasants and workers," for he is now "not only writing *about* peasants and workers but...*for* peasants and workers." This change in audience clearly has had an effect on the intermixed genres of **Devil on the Cross.** Readers unacquainted with Gikuyu will increasingly depend not only upon translation but—in the case of nonKenyans at least—upon a more extensive cultural interpretation. The book is not closed on the interrelationships between literature and history; Ngugi has, however, turned a new leaf. (pp. 356-65)

> *Carol M. Sicherman, "Ngugi Wa Thiong'o and the Writing of Kenyan History," in* Research in African Literatures, *Vol. 20, No. 3, Fall, 1989, pp. 347-70.*

FURTHER READING

Balogun, F. Odun. "Ngugi's *Devil on the Cross:* The Novel as Hagiography of a Marxist." *Ufahamu* 16, No. 2 (1988): 76-92.

> Calls *Devil on the Cross* "not just another proletarian novel...but one most carefully crafted to achieve the author's ideological objectives, one of which is making the Christian religion undermine its believers" and serve "the interest of non-believers."

Kamenju, Grant. *"Petals of Blood* as a Mirror of the African Revolution." In *Marxism and African Literature,* edited by Georg M. Gugelberger, pp. 130-35. London: James Currey Ltd., 1985.

> Contends that *Petals of Blood* is a "demonstration of the truth and validity of Lenin's penetrating analysis" that the bourgeoisie talks of independence yet allies itself with the bourgeoisie of imperialistic nations. Kamenju adds that Ngugi's novel reveals Lenin's analysis in "the post-independence state, not only in Kenya but in Africa as a whole."

Levin, Tobe. "Women as Scapegoats of Culture and Cult: An Activist's View of Female Circumcision in Ngugi's *The River Between.*" In *Ngambika: Studies of Women in African Literature,* edited by Carole Boyce Davies and Anne Adams Graves, pp. 205-21. Trenton, N.J.: Africa World Press, Inc., 1986.

> Examines Ngugi's treatment of female circumcision in *The River Between.* Levin determines that Ngugi condemns (1) tribal tradition for continuing the "mutilation" of females and (2) Christianity for opposing circumcision because it acknowledges female sexuality.

Mamudu, Ayo. "Tracing a Winding Stair: Ngugi's Narrative Methods in *Petals of Blood.*" *World Literature Written in English* 28, No. 1 (Spring 1988): 16-25.

> Analyzes *Petals of Blood,* determining that it "demonstrates not a cleavage but an integration of form and content in many ways."

Neuhaus, M. E. K. "How Ngugi wa Thiongo Lost His Way: A Writer and the Politics of Disillusion in Africa." *Quadrant* 31, Nos. 1 and 2 (January/February 1987): 93-7.

> Overview of Ngugi's life, concluding: "The tragedy of Ngugi is that he lost his way in the search for social justice. With a keen sense of injustice, he naturally felt the injustices that remained in the post-colonial period. However he is naive in assuming that it was the system that brought injustice. This leads to the simple belief that changing the system will change injustice.... So with intellectual laziness Ngugi embraced the dogma of catchwords—'workers', 'peasants', 'revolution', 'exploited'—failing to see that this Western dogma has nothing more to offer than any other Western dogma."

Sharma, Govind Narain. "Socialism and Civilization: The Revolutionary Traditionalism of Ngugi wa Thiong'o." *Ariel* 19, No. 2 (April 1988): 21-30.

> Argues that Ngugi deviates from orthodox Marxism first by failing to consider the bourgeoisie as a kind of revolutionary force in society and then by regarding the peasantry as a primary force for bringing about Kenyan social change.

Sicherman, Carol. *Ngugi wa Thiong'o: A Bibliography of Primary and Secondary Sources 1957-1987.* London: Hans Zell Publishers, 1989, 249 p.

> Comprehensive bibliography of works by and about Ngugi.

Wamalwa, D. Salituma. "The Engaged Artist: The Social Vision of Ngugi wa Thiong'o." *Africa Today* 33, No. 1 (First Quarter 1986): 9-18.

> Traces the manner in which Ngugi "explicates the place of ideology, in particular the epistemological method of Marxian dialectical materialism and the concrete universal approach to concept development" in his critical works and through his plays and novels.

Lewis Nkosi

1936-

South African novelist, critic, dramatist, scriptwriter, librettist, and short story writer.

Known chiefly for his scholarly studies of contemporary African literature, Nkosi is the author of the novel *Mating Birds* (1986). In this work the author explored miscegenation under apartheid through the ordeal of Ndi Sibiya, a young Zulu student who is about to be hanged for allegedly raping a white woman. As Sibiya awaits his execution in a South African prison, he vividly details the events that led to his arrest and death sentence. Critics enthusiastically praised Nkosi's prose style and narrative structure in *Mating Birds,* and several have compared the work with Albert Camus's *The Stranger.*

Nkosi was born in Natal, South Africa, and attended local schools before enrolling at M. L. Sultan Technical College in Durban. In 1956 he joined the staff of *Drum* magazine, a publication founded in 1951 by and for African writers. In his *Home and Exile and Other Selections* (1965), Nkosi described *Drum*'s young writers as "the new African[s] cut adrift from the tribal reserve—urbanised, eager, fast-talking and brash." According to Neil Lazarus, the description fitted Nkosi as well. "Nkosi's whole bearing as a writer," he wrote, "was decisively shaped by the years in Johannesburg working for the magazine." In 1960 Nkosi left South Africa on a one-way "exit permit" after accepting a fellowship to study at Harvard University. Now living in England, he teaches and writes articles on African literature. In addition to the novel *Mating Birds,* he has also produced several plays and collections of essays, including *The Rhythm of Violence* (1963), *Malcolm* (1972), *The Transplanted Heart: Essays on South Africa* (1975), and *Tasks and Masks: Themes and Styles of African Literature* (1981).

Mating Birds tells the story of Sibiya, who spots a white woman across a fence on a segregated beach in Durban. Although the rules of apartheid keep them from speaking to each other, they begin a wordless flirtation across the fence. Soon Sibiya becomes obsessed with the woman and follows her everywhere. He learns that her name is Veronica and that she is a stripper at the local nightclub. One day Sibiya follows Veronica to her bungalow. Seeing him, she undresses in front of the open door and lies down on the bed. Sibiya enters her bedroom and has sex with her. Shortly after, they are discovered, and Veronica accuses Sibiya of rape. He is then beaten, arrested, and sentenced to death.

Many critics viewed *Mating Birds* as a commentary on South Africa's system of apartheid. George Packer, for example, observed: "*Mating Birds* feels like the work of a superb critic. Heavy with symbolism, analytical rather than dramatic, it attempts nothing less than an allegory of colonialism and apartheid, one that dares to linger in complexity." Other commentators, however, attacked the novel's ambiguous depiction of rape. "Nkosi's handling of the sexual themes complicates the distribution of our sympathies, which he means to be unequivocally with the accused man," noted Rob Nixon in the *Village Voice.* "For in rebutting the prevalent white South African fantasy of the black male as a sex-crazed rapist, Nkosi edges unnecessarily close to reinforcing the myth of the raped woman as someone who deep down was asking for it." For Henry Louis Gates, Jr., even the question of whether Sibiya raped at all remains unclear. This causes problems for the reader, as "we are never certain who did what to whom or why." Sibiya himself is unsure: "But how could I make the judges or anyone else believe me when I no longer *knew* what to believe myself?... Had I raped the girl or not?" Gates responded: "We cannot say. Accordingly, this novel's great literary achievement—its vivid depiction of obsession—leads inevitably to its great flaw." Sara Maitland further objected to Nkosi's portrayal of the white woman: "Surely there must be another way for Nkosi's commitment, passion and beautiful writing to describe the violence and injustice of how things are than this stock image of the pale evil seductress, the eternally corrupting female?"

Despite the novel's shortcomings, Michiko Kakutani concluded in the *New York Times, Mating Birds* "nonetheless attests to the emergence of...a writer whose vision of South Africa remains fiercely his own." Similarly, Sherman W. Smith lauded: "Lewis Nkosi certainly must be one of the best writers out of Africa in our time."

(For further information about Nkosi's life and works, see *Black Writers; Contemporary Authors,* Vols. 65-68; and *Contemporary Literary Criticism,* Vol. 45.)

PRINCIPAL WORKS

The Rhythm of Violence (drama) 1963
Home and Exile and Other Selections (essays) 1965
"The Prisoner" (short story) 1967; published in periodical *African Writing Today*
"The Chameleon and the Lizard" (libretto) 1971
Malcolm (drama) 1972
The Transplanted Heart: Essays on South Africa (essays) 1975
Tasks and Masks: Themes and Styles of African Literature (nonfiction) 1981; also published as *Tasks and Masks: An Introduction to African Literature,* 1982
Mating Birds (novel) 1986

The Times Literary Supplement (essay date 1966)

[*In the following excerpt, a reviewer praises Nkosi's keen understanding of the "American Negro dilemma" in* Home and Exile.]

There is no shrewder test of original intelligence nowadays than to write about race without either boring or repelling the reader. This test Mr. Nkosi passes triumphantly in his book of essays **Home and Exile.** Starting his journey with the strenuously multi-racial parties of the 1950s, held in the plush white suburbs of Johannesburg, he chronicles the gradual disillusionment of the South African intellectuals, their final withdrawal from a social and political position based on compromise and mediation, daily belied by a regime which permitted of neither. The old *Drum* of Anthony Sampson was a part of that world; its collapse cannot be better measured than by looking at the same magazine today. There is no one now to challenge the "pop" magazine stereotype as Can Themba, Bloke Modisane, Henry Nxumalo, Casey Motsisi, Ezekiel Mphahlele, Todd Matshikiza and Lewis Nkosi himself did, each in his different rhythm, so that the result became something unpredictable and alive, something far removed from the given formula of crime, sex and hair-straighteners. The first section of Mr. Nkosi's book shows the break-up of this whole group under the remorseless, steadily-tightening grip of apartheid. Of the writers just listed, four at least are now in exile and one is dead, murdered by the *tsotsis* a benevolent government forced him to dwell among. And yet the time of which Mr. Nkosi is writing is barely ten years ago.

Lewis Nkosi himself moved to Harvard and exile in 1961. The second section of his book offers a highly personal and inspiriting impression of New York and lays bare both the evident similarities and the fundamental differences between the situation of the urban industrialized Negro in South Africa and in America. Above all, he appreciates how much the American Negro, though condemned to be in a perpetual minority, has acted as a cultural peacemaker within the whole texture of society there:

> And I saw—and this is what seemed to set the younger generation apart—a young Negro walking down Lennox Avenue in a kind of rolling gait, which was later translated for me into a taunting, mischievously arrogant jazz phrasing by Miles Davis.... Miles and the younger jazz musicians seem to be expressing all the colour, subtleties, the mocking arrogance, and the defensive qualities of the life of a people who live on the fringe of a colour-bar society. There was a painful, though touching irony, when I saw the sons and daughters of white middle-class families desperately trying to appropriate this style, while the Negro was forever moving further "out"— way out—in order to evade definition.

It is this ability, rare among African writers, to enter with imagination and sympathy into the American Negro dilemma that enables Mr. Nkosi to observe that what happens in American society in the next few years is intimately involved with what happens in Africa itself. This interaction, which began to be significant after the war, has grown steadily more so with the mounting importance of Africa in international affairs and the answering intensification of the Civil Rights struggle. Experience has taught Mr. Nkosi to be wary of liberal white allies and to look to the black man, everywhere, for the resolution of his own problems. In the book's most challenging essay he argues that

> only when the black world is powerful enough to neutralize the camouflaged but hideously menacing power of the white nations of the West will it be possible for black and white men with a humanistic, conciliatory vision to share an identity of interests across the colour-line.

At first sight this reasoning summons up a dismal vision of African nations frenziedly amassing nuclear weapons and the other paraphernalia of "power", in the belief that this and only this will enable them to speak to East and West as equals, but perhaps Mr. Nkosi would not wish to push his case that far. Mexico, to cite only one example, has notably improved its international status in recent years without joining in the nuclear race. The development of a vigorous economy has more to do with it than power in the conventional sense. Too much reliance on foreign aid cannot fail to perpetuate a psychology of dependence, with all its attendant evils. The argument certainly has the merit of testing the easy liberal assumption that real human relationships can be established in total isolation from the surrounding social, political and economic arrangements. For, "when the chips are down in Harlem of Notting Hill Gate", the Negro intellectual will soon find that "none of his liberal white friends ... is likely to be out there in the streets with him".

> *"The Situation in Black and White," in* The Times Literary Supplement, *No. 3336, February 3, 1966, p. 85.*

Charlotte H. Bruner (essay date 1983)

[*In the following excerpt, Bruner favorably reviews* Tasks and Masks, *concluding: "*Tasks and Masks *is a landmark in African literary criticism, a must for any student in the field."*]

Tasks and Masks is an incisive and comprehensive critique of contemporary black African literature by Lewis Nkosi, one of its most astute and uncompromising critics. He posits the African writer's goal as twofold: his commitment to affect social change; and his task, as respectful heir, to continue what is worthy in the African tradition, as symbolized by the mask. In eight essays Nkosi defines this dichotomy. Treating the concomitant problems of language, history, Négritude and modernism, Nkosi relates these to the genres of the novel, poetry and drama.

Nkosi has long insisted that the African writer must not exploit exoticism but must compete on equal terms with writers of international stature. Himself an impeccable stylist and a dispassionate logician, he is severe, incisive, profound. For example, he locates Négritude in the context of the twentieth century, among the Marxists and socialists, in the absurdist movements of the 1920s and 30s: "Négritude is really a bastard child whose family tree includes, apart from the living African heritage, Freudianism, Marxism, Surrealism and Romanticism." (pp. 336-37)

Nkosi's own virtuosity is evident. Whenever available translation is inadequate, he provides his own for the Francophone poets. His study is thorough: he includes many writers and treats the work of each comprehensively. His fluent prose and admittedly personal judgments make his book interesting to the specialist and to the lay reader alike. *Tasks and Masks* is a landmark in African literary criticism, a must for any student in the field. (p. 337)

> *Charlotte H. Bruner, in a review of "Tasks and Masks: Themes and Styles of African Literature," in* World Literature Today *Vol. 57, No. 2, Spring, 1983, pp. 336-37.*

Henry Louis Gates, Jr. (essay date 1986)

[*Gates, an American critic and educator, is best known for his discovery of Harriet Wilson's 1859 narrative* Our Nig, *considered the first published novel by a black woman. In the following excerpt, he compares* Mating Birds *with other novels about interracial sex, particularly Amiri Baraka's* Dutchman *and Richard Wright's* Native Son.]

Mating Birds, [Lewis Nkosi's] first novel, confronts boldly and imaginatively, the strange interplay of bondage, desire and torture inherent in interracial sexual relationships within the South African prison house of apartheid. His play *The Rhythm of Violence* and his short story **"The Prisoner"** explored related themes. The treatment of miscegenation as a political indictment of a racist South Africa is not without its literary dangers and risks, however, and Mr. Nkosi's novel does not entirely escape them.

Black and white miscegenation has a long and curious history in literature, ranging in extremes from Shakespeare's representation of self-destructive jealousy in the figure of the noble blackamoor Othello to the pseudonymous American novelist Oliver Bolokitten's bizarre and perverse 1835 novel, *A Sojourn in the City of Amalgamation, in the Year of Our Lord 19–.* In Bolokitten's novel, white male and black female "amalgamation" is made possible only by the invention of an "ingenious" machine that protects "the husbands from those disagreeable evaporations exhaling from the odoriferous spouse . . . by fanning off the offensive air, and at the same time dispensing, by means of the vials, a delightful perfume." Perhaps Bolokitten was an Afrikaner.

We have come a long way from Bolokitten's racism to civil rights romance films starring Sidney Poitier (*A Patch of Blue, Guess Who's Coming to Dinner?*) and the cross-racial sexual encounters on prime-time television, from "Dynasty" and "Falcon Crest" to "The Jeffersons" and even "Kate and Allie." Miscegenation in these instances is a metaphor for social harmony and individual possibility.

More often than not, black authors write of interracial sex as a metaphor for self-destruction or in terms of the penalties exacted for violating a taboo. LeRoi Jones's allegorical play *The Dutchman* (1964) is a prime example of this genre. Clay, a middle-class black man, is stabbed to death by Lula, a white prostitute, after he flirts outrageously with her during a subway ride. Even where the sexual taboo is only implied, as in Richard Wright's *Native Son* (1940), the results are the same: Bigger Thomas, discovered alone with a drunken white girl in her bedroom, panics, smothers her while trying to stifle her drowsy voice and is sentenced to death. The white woman, in black literature, is bad news.

Mr. Nkosi's novel leaves this pattern undisturbed. Indeed, *Mating Birds* recalls in several ways both *The Dutchman* and *Native Son,* as well as Camus's *The Stranger, Othello* and Hegel's well-known essay "Of Lordship and Bondage," with a dash of Freud thrown in for flavor. It also brings to mind the persona of Eldridge Cleaver's *Soul on Ice,* obsessed with white women. These echoes seem intentional; indeed, this novel often reads as if Bigger Thomas had raped Mary Dalton before he killed her, then written a prison memoir from his cell on death row, discussing the social forces that made him do it and using Camus, Cleaver and Hegel as sources.

The novel, indeed, takes the form of a prison memoir, which 25-year-old Ndi Sibiya writes as he awaits execution by hanging, convicted of raping a white woman, Veronica Slater. Sibiya, expelled from his university for his political activities, is a sensitive, articulate and lyrical narrator. He tells of his irresistible and manic obsession with a woman he chances to see sunbathing on a beach in Durban—he on the nonwhite side and she in the border area between the two sides. Meeting on the beach almost daily, the two—according to Sibiya's not untroubled account—enter a dreamlike ritual replete with the subtle gestures of wordless flirtation and the silent exchanges of cues of desire . . . . This encounter unfolds under a stifling, "blazing" South African sunlight as blinding to reason as Camus's Algerian sunlight was in *The Stranger.*

Mr. Nkosi intentionally echoes the existential leap into the abyss of Camus's narrator with the one Sibiya is bound to make. First there is an explicit and erotic pantomime of sexual intercourse on the beach . . . . Then Sibiya follows Veronica home. With her door left ajar, she undresses and lies on her bed. Sibiya enters the bungalow and consummates his passion, only to be discovered, beaten, arrested and sentenced to death for rape.

This plot outline does not capture the book's lyrical intensity or its compelling narrative power. Mr. Nkosi has managed to re-create for his readers all the tortures of an illicit obsession, especially for ambiguities and indeterminacy of motivation and responsibility. While by the novel's end our sympathies are drawn to the black narrator, we are never certain who did what to whom or why: "But how could I make the judges or anyone else believe me when I no longer knew what to believe myself? . . . Had I raped the girl or not?" We cannot say. Accordingly, this novel's great literary achievement—its vivid depiction of obsession—leads inevitably to its great flaw.

Lewis Nkosi has created an allegory of the master and slave relationship that frequently echoes the language of Hegel's "Of Lordship and Bondage" in its description of the curious reversal of roles that concern between them. Phrases such as "the ultimate mirror in which she saw reflected the power of her sex and her race," "a horrible kind of duality within me" and "in the movement of the merest shadow she saw a subtler kind of power she could not yet acquire for herself" tip us off. (Sibiya's recollection of a racist university professor's lecture on African history even contains a reference to Hegel's *Philosophy of History*.) But Mr. Nkosi's novel never achieves Hegel's reversal of roles.

At the novel's end, the master remains the master, and the slave remains a slave and is doomed to die; never does Sibiya, the slave to his obsession, become the master even of his will. The ambiguities created by his own troubled story prevent the liberation that he and the reader eagerly seek from the novel's beginning. Unlike Bigger Thomas, then, who accepts that he is guilty of murder and walks eagerly to his fate, Sibiya in this tale leaves us far more perplexed and worried about the origin and nature of his obsession. As in *Native Son*, we are expected to identify an evil social environment as the ultimate cause of the protagonist's aberrant behavior. But by depicting Sibiya's obsession (rather than apartheid itself) so powerfully, perhaps Mr. Nkosi has created more ambivalence of motive than he wished or than is politically comfortable for blacks in a segregated South Africa.

The novel's very strength, perhaps, will make it a subject of heated debate, especially in a South Africa desperate to remain the last outpost of the West's fantasy of colonial subjugation.

> *Henry Louis Gates, Jr., "The Power of Her Sex, the Power of Her Race," in* The New York Times Book Review, *May 18, 1986, p. 3.*

Rob Nixon (essay date 1986)

[*In the following excerpt, Nixon praises the "bold psychological insight" in* Mating Birds *but criticizes the novel's "vexing sexual politics."*]

With *Mating Birds,* the exiled black South African Lewis Nkosi provides a rare perspective on miscegenation in a tale recounted entirely from the vantage point of a young black man charged with raping a white woman. In the ensuing court case, Sibiya, the novel's narrator and heroic victim, comes to feel the full weight of white paranoia, as he is abstracted from his humanity and tried as a cipher of "black brutality." The result is a book of bold psychological insight, but one marred by vexing sexual politics.

At its best, Nkosi's prose moves between an ascetic sensuality reminiscent of Camus and of Lawrence Durrell's more luxuriant eroticism. The novel turns on the relation of sensuality to violence—that is, of desire to the anger that prohibition stirs. However, Nkosi's handling of the sexual themes complicates the distribution of our sympathies, which he means to be unequivocally with the accused man. For in rebutting the prevalent white-South African fantasy of the black male as sex-crazed rapist, Nkosi edges unnecessarily close to reinforcing the myth of the raped woman as someone who deep down was asking for it.

Although set in South Africa, *Mating Birds* bears the melancholy mark of Nkosi's 25 years of exile. The sun, the sea, the sand of the Durban beach where Sibiya first encounters the white girl who becomes his obsession are described with a sensuality sharpened by nostalgia. Yet it is a very *literary* sensuality; it seems more indebted to Camus's writings about North Africa than to a full, deep memory of South Africa.

Camus is doubly to the point, since Nkosi models *Mating Birds* so closely on *L'Etranger.* The hero of each is defiantly indifferent to his imminent execution—Meursault for the unprovoked murder of an Arab, Sibiya for the alleged rape of a white stranger. Each disdains the charade of the court proceedings and refuses to kowtow to the moral pressures of his society. And each man's account of the fateful incident is blurred by amnesia.

Yet Sibiya's claim on our moral sympathies should be the more clear-cut of the two. Meursault is a French colonial, a *pied noir,* who randomly murders a member of a subject race; Sibiya belongs to a subject race. His trial is thick with racial slander, with "ethnopsychology" emitting an "odor of racial conspiracy," with the noxious rhetoric of a prosecutor intent on making "an example of him as a deterrent for other misguided natives." Quite clearly, he is to hang not only for rape but also for the "crime" of daring to sleep with a white woman.

But there are problems. By turning the whole narrative over to the accused man, Nkosi screens out the woman's perspective entirely. This would matter less were Nkosi's tale of miscegenation not impeded by an undertow of misogyny. Veronica, set apart on her whites-only beach, is a "monstrous provocation." She is "seductive bait," dismissed as "a high-class tart" replete with "sexual taunts," a "serene temptress" and "tormentor"; in short, says Sibiya, "the girl became a kind of sickness for me." His detailing how he came to commit an act that he himself sees as straddling rape and seduction is, from one perspective, the novel's source of strength. For we certainly gain insight into the power of one pathology to breed another: Veronica's extravagant, legislated remoteness unsexes and almost unhinges Sibiya. It is scarcely surprising, therefore, that when Sibiya determines to "smash the facade of propriety" he has in mind the white woman as (to misappropriate Reagan) the white man's window of vulnerability.

There is a redeeming honesty to Nkosi's portrait of a society so steeped in violence that it has throttled more innocent desires. But his preoccupation with the political corruption of sex also makes his sometimes unthinking treatment of sexuality all the more jarring: "I seized her then, seized her roughly with a long stoked-up violence that was a halfway house of love, murder, and rape. I even enjoyed the swift mobile look of fear that shot across her face, but there was also in the depths of her eyes a perverse excitement. She groaned, she moaned softly." If he hopes to capture our sympathies fully, surely Nkosi is obliged to create a character who would at least recognize a rape if he were perpetrating one?

Veronica's orgasm transforms her into an "abject animal," "a crushed animal." In another sexual episode, a woman becomes "a dumb suffering beast . . . still haughty but humbled by a seemingly seething lust." When Nkosi has exhausted his menagerie, he reaches for the military motif. Female flesh "surrenders" all over the place; Veronica's nylon stockings and lace panties hang "like a conqueror's flags on the rail above the shower tap."

Nkosi, like Sibiya, has evidently been afflicted with the Helen of Troy Syndrome, the perception of women primarily as loot for male wars. He has been taken to task in the past for ill-considered remarks like "the image of the white female beauty is the one that rings most frequently the cash register of the Negro psyche. In any case, we all know how notoriously alluring women of the ruling class have always proved to be for aspiring revolutionaries, black or white." This comment, among other offenses, wipes from the record the leading role of black women in striking back against the violence of apartheid.

Mating Birds leaves me with a strong, sad sense of Nkosi writing out of the frozen time of exile. Nkosi is a rare literary survivor of the late '50s, a time in South Africa that brought forth an extraordinary flurry of talented black writers. Their ability so alarmed the regime that it determined to silence them. Their options closed down rapidly and the majority fled abroad. . . .

In the wake of that ravaged generation, the tenor of black South African writing has altered radically. The obsessions of *Mating Birds,* in this context, appear somewhat anachronistic. Other writers have moved well beyond stories about the isolated anger of single victims of racism and have forged, instead, a formidable literature of retaliation deeply textured with the life of the black communities. I have in mind works like Alex La Guma's *In the Fog of the Season's End,* his *Time of the Butcherbird,* and above all Mongane Serote's *To Every Birth Its Blood,* one of the most astute and affecting novels ever to come out of South Africa. . . .

In the past 70 years, over 150 black South Africans have been hanged for raping or allegedly raping women, most of them white; no white man has *ever* been executed for raping a black woman, although, given the white man's political and economic supremacy, his is by far the commoner crime. *Mating Birds* provides a view from below of a baroque system of legal procedure in which justice isn't even an option, far less the probable outcome. For Nkosi is at his most convincing when he intuits the power of morally tone-deaf legislation to mangle both sexual fantasy and act.

> Rob Nixon, "Race Case," in The Village Voice, *Vol. XXXI, No. 30, July 29, 1986, p. 46.*

Sara Maitland (essay date 1986)

[*In the following excerpt, Maitland objects to Nkosi's portrayal of the white woman in* Mating Birds *as an "evil seductress."*]

I found [*Mating Birds*] a troubling and difficult novel—as I suspect Nkosi intended, though perhaps not in the way that he intended. The difficulty here is not a formal one: *Mating Birds* is a classic first-person account with a narrator assessing his life at its climax and end, written in moving, lucid prose with controlled flashbacks and a firmly located present. The problem is one of content. Nkosi's narrator is a South African awaiting execution at dawn for the rape of a white woman; the hero—coming from a rural childhood destroyed by apartheid land policy, a promising academic youth ruined by the racism of the university system and his own political involvement—faces up to his own sexual obsession with the woman, and indeed with white women more generally. He further acknowledges his sudden and impersonal sexual assault of her: his 'defence' is that she 'asked for it', that she was already promiscuous, cavorting naked at pornographic parties, that she blatantly 'led him on', 'wanted him to really'. And so forth: the classic defences of all rapists of all races under all regimes.

Nkosi is superficially ambiguous about his character's degree of guilt but the first person denies the woman her reality and experience, she remains pure fantasy object:

the narrator says she lied. And this is an overtly political book: at the very end the political prisoners in the gaol are singing freedom songs in the dawn as he goes out to die. Surely there must be another way for Nkosi's commitment, passion and beautiful writing to describe the violence and injustice of how things are rather than this stock image of the pale evil seductress, the eternally corrupting female? The polarisation of the choice between sexism and racism cannot be part of Nkosi's political or literary intention. (p. 25)

Sara Maitland, "Small Worlds," in New Statesman, Vol. 112, No. 2892, August 29, 1986, pp. 25-6.

George Packer (essay date 1986)

[In the following excerpt, Packer reviews Mating Birds, describing it as "an allegory of colonialism and apartheid."]

Mating Birds feels like the work of a superb critic. Heavy with symbolism, analytical rather than dramatic, it attempts nothing less than an allegory of colonialism and apartheid, one that dares to linger in complexity. Dr. Dufré, the Swiss criminal psychologist who pries Sibiya's story out of him "for the augmentation of scientific knowledge," wants to hear the Freudian family saga, the psychopathology of this one man. But Sibiya's tale eludes the doctor's formula; at heart this case history is political. "What in the end can we say to each other, this white man and I," thinks Sibiya, "that can break the shell of history and liberate us from the time capsule in which we are both enclosed?" For Sibiya, the crucial moment came after a fairly happy village childhood when his mother pushed him into the Lutheran seminary school: "The truth of the matter is, I am lost. To be more precise, I'm doubly lost. Unlike my father, I believe in nothing, neither in Christian immortality nor in the ultimate fellowship with the ancestral spirits."

His own experience appropriated, he turns to the temptation of his oppressors; when he is rejected intellectually, what remains is a terrible lust. The urge to "discover the sexual reasons for the white man's singular protectiveness toward his womenfolk" drains his autonomy and self-worth. The sexuality that feeds on a rotting soul is infected with oppression: it can consist only of voyeurism, the sense that life is elsewhere.

Until very near the end, Nkosi's story succeeds in powerful passages: the sudden disruption of village life that comes with [Sibiya's] father's death and the family's forced removal; the portrayal of his uneducated but ambitious mother, who slowly succumbs to the degradation of shebeen life in Durban; the desperate mood of young blacks "with a great deal of time on their hands and no idea of what to do with it." But the last pages can't meet the task that Nkosi has set himself.

The final scenes—the trial and the rape—present an almost insoluble problem. Nkosi has poignantly rendered a black's loss of self; but faced now with the harder task of finding a language for the white girl, the Other, he falls back on literary and political convention. Veronica turns out to be a stripper, a treacherous temptress—the "bait" Sibiya's old father had warned him about. Under the pressure of realism allegory turns into caricature, and Sibiya is just another victim. The language becomes stylized. At the bungalow doorway the narrator sounds like a highbrow pornographer.... And at the end of the book he resorts to the language of the pamphleteer.... (pp. 571-72)

The novel sets out to chart the hidden terrain of the oppressed, the link with the oppressor. But apartheid, dehumanizing oppressor and oppressed, is hardly available to the language of human complexity. Nearing its white-hot center, Mating Birds retreats. (p. 572)

George Packer, "Reports from the Inside," in The Nation, New York, Vol. 243, No. 17, November 22, 1986, pp. 570-74.

Neil Lazarus (essay date 1987)

[In the following excerpt, Lazarus negatively appraises Mating Birds as sexist. In an unexcerpted portion of the essay, he evaluates Nkosi as a critic.]

Once the worthiness and even the importance of Nkosi's project in Mating Birds has been duly credited... it becomes essential for us to recognize that the work is nevertheless deeply flawed. "Flawed," indeed, is perhaps too mild a term: for Mating Birds is, in fact, positively undermined by an insistent inner failure of vision, which takes the form of a virulent and structuring sexism. The problem here is not merely one of language or tone, although the specific terms of Nkosi's formulation do often appear to have been selected precisely because of their disturbing resonance: "How many times must I tell you the girl invited sexual attention? Don't you believe me when I say whatever else happened, that girl wanted it to happen? Right from the beginning I could tell she wanted it as much as I did," Sibiya tells Dufre, the Swiss criminologist who, with manifestly racist sensibilities, is "following" his case for an academic audience back in Europe. The point here is that in a comprehensively ironized text, there is nothing at all with respect to the presentation of women to separate Nkosi from his central protagonist. On another occasion, thus, we read of Veronica's "avid lust that transforms a woman at the moment of orgasm into an abject animal."

Such passages are supremely offensive and ubiquitous enough to make Mating Birds a difficult work to continue reading. Yet they do not determine the novel's androcentrism, but remain mere symptoms of it. The same can be said of countless casual references in the text: wherever women are introduced, they are not only routinely physicalized but also consistently reduced to a fetishized sexuality. Thus we read of "a blonde girl with green-blue eyes and a loose sexy mouth." And even Sibiya's mother is phrased in this vein, as "provocative" and "coquettish."

Mating Birds fails as a novel, however, because the central conceit upon which it is predicated is unsound and cannot sustain the burden that Nkosi places upon it. In *Tasks and Masks,* Nkosi praised South African novelist Enver Carim for "perceiv[ing] the ambiguous position of white women in a racist society. At times he sees the position of white women as lying between oppressor and oppressed." In *Mating Birds* Nkosi tries to emulate Carim in this perception. He wants Veronica to emerge simultaneously as the agent of Sibiya's destruction and, herself, as a pawn in the service of the over-arching racist order. She is to be puppeteer and puppet at the same time: on the one hand, orchestrating Sibiya's downfall; on the other, dancing to the tune of the dominant society's imperatives. As Sibiya concludes, in thinking about her "responsibility" for his plight:

> Veronica is responsible, of course, in a way, but only marginally, symbolically, responsible. The bearer of a white skin and the bearer of the flesh and blood of a gypsy, the bearer also, if I may so add, of a curse and a wound of which, not being very bright, she was not particularly aware, this English girl has simply been an instrument in whom is revealed in its most flagrant form the rot and corruption of a society that has cut itself off entirely from the rest of humanity, from any possibility for human growth.

Mating Birds seems to join, here, with Ayi Kwei Armah's *Why Are We So Blest?* in which a young African man, Modin, is drawn to his death through his attachment to a predatory white American woman, Aimee. In both novels, however, it is at the level of primary symbol that incoherence manifests itself. For neither Aimee nor Veronica is credible as the *subject* or active bearer of domination. In the case of *Mating Birds,* particularly, this lack of credibility is acute: for Nkosi so *naturalizes* culturally constructed gender relations, he so relentlessly sexualizes Veronica, that the reader is invited only to see her archetypally as Woman, the natural and fitting object of Man's lust. And such a perception, quite obviously, obliterates even the possibility of grasping Veronica's situation simultaneously, as oppressor and oppressed. A telling metaphor, early in the novel, speaks to this subject. Sibiya thinks back to a warning given to him by his father: "Never lust after a white woman, my child. With her painted lips and soft, shining skin, a white woman is a bait put there to destroy our men. Our ways are not the ways of white people, their speech is not ours. White people are as smooth as eels, but they devour us like sharks." White men, it seems, the architects and beneficiaries of the system, are like sharks. But what then are black men, drawn irresistibly to the "bait" cast before them? And

what are white women, bait to both black men and white, their whole reason for being consisting, apparently, in their attractiveness and seeming consumability? And above all, who casts the bait in the first place? For one cannot, surely, construct white men as both sharks and deep-sea fishermen.

Yet this is precisely what Nkosi seems to want to do. The result is a novel that collapses in on itself. And the implications of this are severe. For it is not only, as [James] Booth has correctly observed, that it is impossible to read Nkosi without wincing. Rather, or in addition, Nkosi's sexism returns to cast a grave shadow upon the humanism by which he sets such store. For, it would seem, the content of Nkosi's humanism does not transcend domination, but merely naturalizes and de-historicizes it in certain of its manifestations. Humanism emerges, in fact, as inhumane. One is reminded, ultimately, of Walter Benjamin's brilliant aphorism: "There is not document of culture which is not at the same time a document of barbarism." (pp. 116-18)

Neil Lazarus, "Measure and Unmeasure: The Antinomies of Lewis Nkosi," in The Southern Review, *Louisiana State University, Vol. 23, No. 1, January, 1987, pp. 106-18.*

FURTHER READING

Maja-Pearce, Adewale. "Compensatory Acts." *The Times Literary Supplement,* No. 4349 (8 August 1986): 863.
    Brief overview of *Mating Birds,* finding fault with the novel's characterization.

Ryan, Alan. "Passion in Black and White." *Book World— The Washington Post* (8 June 1986): 14.
    Praises *Mating Birds* as "possibly the finest novel by a South African, black or white, about the terrible distortion of love in South Africa...."

Thorpe, Michael. Review of *Home and Exile,* by Lewis Nkosi. *World Literature Today* 58, No. 3 (Summer 1984): 462.
    Generally favorable review of *Home and Exile.*

"Africa into England." *The Times Literary Supplement,* No. 3259 (13 August 1964): 723.
    Reviews *The Rhythm of Violence,* noting: "[It] is frankly programmatic and rather thin in texture."

Walder, Dennis. "Sophiatown Style." *The Times Literary Supplement,* No. 4153 (27 August 1982): 928.
    Evaluates *Tasks and Masks,* observing that in this work Nkosi "provides judicious, often stimulating, if not very original accounts of some...important issues."

Christopher Okigbo

1932-1967

(Full name Christopher Ifenayichukwu Okigbo) Nigerian poet.

An important transitional figure in contemporary African literature, Okigbo has been called Africa's finest poet. "For while other poets wrote good poems," Chinua Achebe observed, "Okigbo conjured up for us an amazing, haunting poetic firmament of a wild and violent beauty." In his poems, which have been described as highly musical, Okigbo combined traditional elements of African culture with non-African influences such as Christianity and Western poetic techniques. His work is complex, partly because of obscure allusions, but critics nevertheless acknowledge him as a master poet.

Not much is known about Okigbo's personal life. "I imagine him to have been the most mocking and mischievous child," Paul Theroux mused about the poet, "one of those high-spirited kids in shorts that screech and make the other children laugh. The sort of child who believes his village to be the centre of the world." Okigbo was born in Ojoto, Nigeria, in 1932. He was graduated from the University of Ibadan and worked as a teacher and librarian before thinking seriously about a literary career. "The turning point came in 1958," he explained when asked why he started writing poetry, "when I found myself wanting to know myself better." For Okigbo poetry would always remain a highly personal endeavor. He embraced African culture but rejected the literary concept of negritude, which, he felt, emphasized racial differences. He stated: "I think I am just a poet. A poet writes poetry and once a work is published it becomes public property. It's left to whoever reads it to decide whether it's African poetry or English. There isn't any such thing as a poet trying to express African-ness. Such a thing doesn't exist. A poet expresses himself." Okigbo's interest in social and political change in his own country, however, formed an inseparable part of his work. Okigbo maintained that it is impossible for a poet to examine his or her own identity in isolation—"any writer who attempts a type of inward exploration will in fact be exploring his own society indirectly," he stated. His concern for social justice was perhaps best expressed in his commitment to the Biafran secession. In July 1967, at the outbreak of the Nigerian Civil War, he enlisted in the Biafran Army. He was killed in action in August 1967.

During his lifetime Okigbo saw only two collections of his poetry published: *Heavensgate* (1962) and *Limits* (1964). Because he used myths, rituals, and dense, challenging symbolism in these works, critics were divided in their interpretations. Some argued that the collections are about humankind's quest for divinity; others viewed the poems as attacks on Christianity; and

Lee Hunt

a few commentators saw the works as projections of Okigbo's social and political views, especially those concerning the cultural and religious alienation Nigeria experienced during the colonial period. Wrote Romanus N. Egudu: "Christopher Okigbo's poetry is that of agonized and excruciating experiences. His historical and social insight has created a labyrinth of life, from which the process of extrication is not easy.... Okigbo's poetry is essentially a hodgepodge of many cryptic ingredients and this has naturally led to its tense obscurity—a quality by no means to its credit." In contrast, Okigbo's posthumous collection *Labyrinths, with Path of Thunder* (1971) is less "obscure" and easier to understand because "in it Okigbo makes, for the first time ever, a forthright and direct political statement," according to Sunday O. Anozie. Scholars consider this volume Okigbo's most mature work. Addressing complaints that Okigbo's poetry is extremely difficult to understand, a few commentators have suggested that Okigbo was more a craftsman than a poet with a message. "[In Okigbo's] poetry as a whole," Egudu explained, "the art seems to matter more than the thought that is communicated. This does not mean that his style is always successful: it simply means that his preoccupation in poetic activity is craftsmanship." Okigbo himself stated in an interview: "I don't think that I have ever set out to communicate a meaning. It is enough that I try to communicate experience which I consider significant."

Okigbo is perhaps best remembered today not so much for the content of his poems as for the distinct musical style and beauty of his verse. Theroux advised readers to *listen* to Okigbo's poetry in order to appreciate it fully: "Looking is confusion: what we see in the poem may be an impenetrable mystery, and there are words and phrases in Okigbo's poetry that are nearly impossible to figure out. Listening is simpler and more rewarding; there is music in [his] poetry . . . ." Okigbo's practice of infusing poetry with rhythm and song has been imitated by subsequent African writers. To some, Okigbo is an enduring muse; to others, he is a hero who, in the end, was more than "just" a poet. "Nothing can be more tragic to the world of African poetry in English than the death of Christopher Okigbo," Anozie wrote, "especially at a time when he was beginning to show maturity and coherence in his vision of art, life and society, and greater sophistication in poetic form and phraseology. Nevertheless his output, so rich and severe within so short a life, is sure to place him among the best and the greatest of our time."

(For further information about Okigbo's life and works, see *Black Writers; Contemporary Authors,* Vols. 77-80; and *Contemporary Literary Criticism,* Vol. 25.)

PRINCIPAL WORKS

Heavensgate (poetry) 1962
*Limits (poetry) 1964
†Poems: Four Canzones (poetry) 1968; published in periodical *Black Orpheus*
Labyrinths, with Path of Thunder (poetry) 1971
Collected Poems (poetry) 1986

* This work was first published in two parts in the periodical *Transition* in 1962.
† This work contains "Song of the Forest," "Debtor's Lane," "Lament of the Flutes," and "Lament of the Lavender Mist."

O. R. Dathorne (essay date 1968)

[*In the following excerpt, Dathorne describes* Heavensgate *as a work that "shows man in the process of striving towards a god."*]

[The] process of transformation is the key to all of Okigbo's verse—how can human beings grow again into gods, how are they to regain their pristine state of

spiritual innocence and yet retain their own sensuality? In order to deal with this problem Okigbo has forsaken the commonplace world and has chosen instead to reenact the entire cycle of birth, initiation and death. Because of the nature of his quest, his images tend to dwell on the disparity that exists between man's ambition and his puny attempts at becoming God.

Okigbo's verse shows man in the process of striving towards a god. The poet does not speak with an individual voice but with choral utterance, insisting on the infallibility of the statement and its divine nature. The five sections of *Heavensgate* demonstrate the technique. If Okigbo's poems are *about* anything, then *Heavensgate* attempts to work out the initiation into and the evolution of a religion. (pp. 82-3)

The five sections into which *Heavensgate* is divided clearly emphasize a striving—PASSAGE, INITIATION, WATERMAID, LUSTRA and NEWCOMER. . . . PASSAGE takes the reader to the childhood of the world and of the protagonist; it is both a time of 'dark waters of the beginning' and 'when we were great boys' . . . . The next section, INITIATION, rescues this vision of chaos 'in a symbolic interplay of geometric figures'. Here the angle, orthocentre, fourth angle, square, rhombus and quadrangle all suggest that a certain kind of order has been imposed; they form the series of intimations which the protagonist has had towards a complete harmony with himself and his world. The next section, WATERMAID, introduces the intercessor—a figure who is a mixture of a classical muse, the Virgin Mary, and a local priestess. She is described both as 'maid of the salt-emptiness, sophisti-creamy, native' and as 'wearing white light about her'. At the end of this section the protagonist finds himself in a state of cosmic aloneness; he is completely alienated from everything he knows . . . . (p. 83)

LUSTRA suggests with appropriate Christian as well as African pagan imagery that there is hope which comes through a redeemer who is neither Christian nor pagan . . . . But the dramatic quality of the poem is spoilt by the last four pieces called NEWCOMER which are irrelevant and do little for the continuity of the piece. They are verses for the poet's teacher-friend and his niece, and were all written in a single afternoon. They betray a weak side in Okigbo, his tendency at times to be so very personal that there seems little room for any universal message.

The method of *Heavensgate* is to combine traditional African and modern modes and to fuse them into a synthesized whole. Both traditional oral and western forms of verse are used. In addition the poet deploys imagery so that African and non-African elements build up into a whole. The result is the invention of a personal style and creed, personal because it is intensely subjective, although meaning accumulates from various references that belong to the common store of all mankind. Diagrammatically, Okigbo's way is the imagistic construction of an inverted pyramid; he works outwards from the apex towards a broad base.

Dramatic progression from the traditional to the 'modern' and to the fusing of the two is seen in the quality of the utterance. The voice is at first choral, concerned with communal issues; later the private voice marks the emergence of an individual sensibility. The initial invocation to mother Idoto, the goddess of the poet's community in Ijoto, is in fact a praise-song. References to water and to the oil-bean situate mother Idoto, for her shrine is near a river and the oil-bean is her sacred totem. But the praise-song to the goddess is to a Judaic Christian god as well, and echoes of the psalms make this point with force and ease.

That the poet is working out a personal religion becomes apparent later on in the references to Leidan, Anna, and Kepkanly which the poet has invented himself. Allusions to St Paul, John the Baptist, the Pope, angels, God, and Christ illustrate the subtlety of the fusion that is taking place.

Creation myths have a place in the poem; in one place there is the piety of 'dark waters of the beginning', in another there is the sensuality of rain falling on a beach, 'Over man with woman'. The creation that is taking place is not simply that of man but that of the individual, freeing himself from tribal rigours, so as to crystallize the experience of humankind into a succinct and enigmatic form.

This is not to suggest that *Heavensgate* follows a chronological progression from creation, through birth, the fall, sin, redemption, crucifixion and ascension, but what the poem certainly affirms is that all these elements are present. Okigbo's purpose is not to chart a religious history of mankind but to enact a theatrical demonstration of the significance of these matters for the individual now. This is why after the opening choral 'I', the individual does not exist in the poem and the closest personal note is struck by 'we'. (pp. 84-5)

[The ending of *Heavensgate*] indicates that the absence of the agents of darkness has made the way for a confrontation with a private and agonizing truth; the truth about tribeless man existing amidst a limbo of contradictions.... The last line states a temporary triumph over Christian and pagan madness that would seek to inhibit self. The protagonist's transition is still only a vacation from the disaster that awaits him in the world. (p. 87)

It is clear now that it is the protagonist who is aspiring towards the last glory of flesh, to be a living god, and the final triumph over death, to be resurrected. At the end of the poem when 'the cancelling out is complete', one can be sure that he has come nearer this concept of godhead.

Images made familiar from *Heavensgate* re-appear in *Limits.* The bird becomes 'weaverbird', the watermaid is 'queen of the damp half light', a deity is identifiable.

Flannagan and the Pope are once more mentioned and there are cryptic allusions to 'YUNICE at the passageway' and 'the twin-gods of IRKALLA.' Solitude is the dominant mood and the search for redemption does not end in a period of transition as in *Heavensgate,* but with complete oblivion. On the whole *Limits* works through a more tenuous medium, almost like a trance, towards an indefinable elusiveness. The protagonist possessed body and soul in *Heavensgate*; in *Limits* his absence emphasizes his insubstantiality.

Although Okigbo's verse is not as straightforward as it has been made to sound, its theme is the quest for ultimate wisdom. Okigbo has himself helped to obscure the real issues relevant to an appreciation of his poetry, by emphasizing that he does not strive in his poetry towards meaning in the accepted sense of the term. (p. 89)

But ... there is meaning in Okigbo's poetry even though it might be obscured by a too-ready desire to pun, or to exploit the more obvious devices of language for phonetic rather than semantic effects....

The protagonist in Okigbo's poetry had not yet come to a full understanding of all that life is; it is as if Okigbo feels that his protagonist must always be aspiring towards an elusive something which is afterlife and art and Heaven and ideals, and the drama of a realization of this need is his quest for fulfilment. (p. 90)

> *O. R. Dathorne, "African Literature IV: Ritual and Ceremony in Okigbo's Poetry," in* Journal of Commonwealth Literature, *No. 5, July, 1968, pp. 79-91.*

Paul Theroux (essay date 1971)

> [*Theroux is an expatriate American novelist, critic, and travel writer. He has traveled extensively in Africa, and several of his works are set in Kenya and Malawi. In the following excerpt, he proposes two methods for studying Okigbo's poetry: "one is to look at his poems, the other is to listen to his music."*]

There is no question about it: Okigbo is an obscure poet, possibly the most difficult poet in Africa. There are two ways of approaching him; one is to look at his poems, the other is to listen to his music.

By 'looking' I mean examining each word he uses, each echo from another poet (for there are many echoes; he was an extremely well-read person). To do this one would have to make a long list which would include such strange words as *kepkanly, anagnorisis, Yunice, Upandru, enki, Flannagan* and perhaps a hundred others. The meaning of these words would have to be found, and then it would be necessary to fit this meaning into the line, ignoring the word for the time being.

I tried this once and I was fortunate in having Okigbo a few feet away to correct my mistakes in interpretation. I was especially disturbed by 'Flannagan'; I could not find a reference to it. I asked Okigbo to tell me what it meant.

'Flannagan,' said Okigbo, 'was a priest that used to teach me in Primary School. He ran the Mission near my village.' (p. 135)

Many people have criticized Okigbo for writing as he did, and some of this criticism is well-founded. How can the average reader know that Flannagan is a priest?... A poet may present us with a mysterious little poem and teachers and critics may make a name for themselves by unravelling the mystery and showing us what exactly the poet meant to say or what he was getting at. It is possible that, in this exercise of interpretation, the critic may find more in the poem than the writer put in. This happens all the time, and it happens with Okigbo's critics more than others because there is often a smokescreen of obscurity thrown up which hides the meaning of the poem.

With Okigbo this must be accepted. There is not much use in saying that he is not obscure, because he certainly is, but once this has been accepted an approach to the poem can be made.

The approach can be made through the second method. That is, by listening. Looking is confusion: what we see in the poem may be an impenetrable mystery, and there are words and phrases in Okigbo's poetry that are nearly impossible to figure out. Listening is simpler and more rewarding; there is music in this poetry, and if we listen closely we hear three separate melodies: the music of youth, the clamour of passage (that is, growing up) and lastly, the sounds of thunder. (p. 136)

Okigbo was a careful craftsman; when he wanted someone to understand, when he considered something important enough to be made absolutely clear, he took pains to write with the utmost clarity. One could make too much of the obscurities, but as the poems stand—*Heavensgate, Limits,* 'Silences,' 'Distances'—there is plenty to digest without complicating the essential point: a man in search of purification, beset by visions and delays, fighting his way toward death. (p. 146)

Many biographies of Africans have been written, detailing the early rural life, the amazement at discovering education and political independence, the confusions and complexes wrought by urban life; and later the coups, the disappointment, the corrupt politics. In a much shorter space Okigbo has done all this; he has composed, in verse, an African autobiography, with all its pain and beauty, terror and mystery. At times it seems unfathomable, but the moment passes, and soon we are in familiar territory, the obscurity is like a cloud passing, it is brief but leaves an impression on us that we do not forget. Later, we may be able to piece this obscurity with something known and the result is often enlightenment.

'Path of Thunder' is a war poem; it is about the war that killed Okigbo himself. It is perhaps a testimony to his skill that even in this poem describing war's horrors, there is beauty. The end of this poem is also the end of the cycle of poems that began with *Heavensgate*. The last four lines describe what Okigbo stood for, constantly hoping that against chaos there could be beauty and order.... (p. 150)

> *Paul Theroux, "Christopher Okigbo," in* Introduction to Nigerian Literature, *edited by Bruce King, 1971. Reprint by Africana Publishing Corporation, 1972, pp. 135-51.*

Sunday O. Anozie (essay date 1972)

[*Founder of the Okigbo Friendship Society, Anozie is the author of* Christopher Okigbo: Creative Rhetoric *(1972). In the following excerpt from this work, he critically surveys Okigbo's poetry, including* Four Canzones.]

The four poems which Okigbo called *Canzones* and published in the journal *Black Orpheus*, No. 11, outline his earliest creative itinerary between 1957 and 1961. Considered as representative of the poet's *juvenilia*, two interesting observations can be made about *Four Canzones*. Firstly, these poems clearly indicate Okigbo's major physical displacements, all within the old Federation of Nigeria, since graduating from Ibadan University in 1956. Secondly, each of these physical displacements in time and space marks a new stage in Okigbo's poetic development and influence. (p. 24)

The central theme in Okigbo's *Four Canzones* is nostalgia. This is the result of successive impacts on a highly sensitive mind—hence the dual introspective and retrospective nature of these early poems. Okigbo's feeling of nostalgia is for the innocence of his childhood and for the peace and security of his birthplace. From both of these each successive growth or travel appears to him as a new physical as well as psychic displacement, in fact, a distancing into a form of alienation.

'Song of the Forest', the 1st Canzone, introduces into this central theme that of the *prodigal* or the *exile*, Okigbo's favourite protagonist. The poem itself is a bucolic *résumé* of an intensely introspective life.... Here the poet praises the pastoral ease and the security of village life in preference to the more complicated life in a modern city. Thus the poet insinuates (and here Okigbo is strongly partisan to the negritude tradition which he often criticizes) that the sole course open to the uprooted exile or prodigal is a return in humility and penitence to the original source of his being.... 'Debtors' Lane', the 2nd Canzone, was written in 1959 at Fiditi.... As a rural hideout apparently responding well to the poet's nostalgia, Fiditi was conducive to quiet creative reflections.... Within such a setting the first sub-theme in 'Debtors' Lane' emerges; the *rejection* of Lagos, its 'high societies' and 'mad generation', its sophisticated pleasures, its night clubs and cabarets....

The second sub-theme is that of personal *renunciation* of what the poet calls 'heavenly transports...of youthful passion' and the endless succession 'of tempers and moods'. This act of ascetic self-denial traces a ritualistic course throughout Okigbo's poetry and is invariably associated with cleansing and purification as a prelude to a new and creative life.... (pp. 25-7)

But 'rejection' and 'renunciation' simply are, within the present pale, themes within a still larger thematic structure: Okigbo's moralistic concern with the *individual* and the *society*.... His handling so early of the motif of individuals to whom 'repose is a dream unreal'—either because they are definite failures in life or just misfits in the urban context of it—clearly demonstrates Okigbo's didactic moral purpose as well as his awakening awareness of the consequences of social change in Nigeria. Thus the same themes which inform the city-based novels of Achebe, Ekwensi and Soyinka, the rise of individualism and moral liberalism with a concommitant increased range of preferential alternatives and a relaxation of traditional ties, are equally though implicitly present in Okigbo's poetry. (p. 27)

I have insisted rather heavily upon the social and moral thematic variations in the 2nd Canzone in order to emphasize the early encroachment of T. S. Eliot as a major poetic influence on Okigbo and to suggest that the two years spent at Fiditi mark a turning point in Okigbo's poetic career and thinking. From now on he is going to take poetry seriously as an art of creative self-expression embodying a personal vision of social reality.

The 3rd and 4th Canzones are forms of lament. The third, **'Lament of the Flutes'**, was written in 1960. The occasion was Okigbo's revisit to his birthplace, Ojoto, a little village near Onitsha in Eastern Nigeria. Brief though it was, this visit contained just the experience necessary to create a feeling of *reconciliation* in the poet.... [Reconciliation] (here, synonymous with initiation) is to be effected through a process of purification rites.... [This] is a concentric motif in Okigbo's poetry. (pp. 27-9)

Love, particularly a child's first love with its secret pains and its transience, is the last of Okigbo's variations on the theme of nostalgia in his *Four Canzones*. This theme is introduced into the 4th Canzone, entitled **'Lament of the Lavender Mist'**, where it is rescued from the usual banalities and romanticisms that surround poetic treatments of the Venus and Adonis motif by Okigbo's reticence and style of *griot* incantation. (pp. 29-30)

There are three levels to Okigbo's choice of images and symbols in *Four Canzones*.... There is, first of all, the *traditional* level, most noticeable in the 1st and 2nd Canzones which are strongly under the romantic and pastoral influence of the Roman poet, Virgil, or by logical extension the larger influence of the Greek poet, Theocritus of Syracuse, whose work in the same pastoral genre cannot have been unfamiliar to Okigbo. Then there is the *modern* level where Okigbo is concerned with modern actualities (**'Debtors' Lane'**) and also seeks

to integrate elements from his readings in modern and contemporary poetry. Finally comes the *private* level where a deep subjective layer of experience (**'Lament of the Lavender Mist'**) compels the poet to use new forms of synthesis or association of ideas in order to arrive at a verbal approximation of his feeling. (pp. 32-3)

The formal unity of Okigbo's *Four Canzones* derives from the fact that they are originally intended (or seemingly intended) to constitute a kind of syncretic musical pattern. Okigbo's bold ambition is latent in the chosen title—**'Canzones'**. He means to go back to the ancient Italian and, surely, the pre-Petrarchan habit of arranging lyrical bits in a group of stanzas so that the verses and the rhymes are disposed in a specially predetermined and uniform order throughout. The result is that usually each 'canzonette' becomes a little Provencal song filled with popular refrains, with sentiment and gaiety. (p. 34)

After this rather synoptic survey, two tentative conclusions may be drawn *vis-à-vis* the nature of Okigbo's creative itinerary between 1957 and 1961 as represented in his *Four Canzones.* First is that at the beginning of his poetic career, Okigbo was not unaware of—in fact, was haunted by—a certain 'devil' that required to be exorcised, or at least propitiated. This may be easily dismissed as one of the perennial concerns of poets— just one of those emotions often recollected in tranquility. But the truth is, that the 'devil' can sometimes assume flesh and blood and, as in the 4th Canzone, become the secret 'Lady of the Lavender Mist'. It seems more probable in fact that the 'devil' is Okigbo's sensuality, and the 'lady' is allied to his 'watermaid' and 'lioness' (*Heavensgate*), the bearer of the mystical vision he is always striving to recapture.... (p. 36)

The second is that Okigbo's poetic language at the same period is both unoriginal and diffident, vacillating between different, often conflicting traditions, and adapting whichever poetic forms and diction may have appealed to his curious and impressionable mind. It is evidence of Okigbo's genius and labour that he practically overcame in his later poetry most of these difficulties and succeeded in creating a poetic technique and an idiom purely his own. (pp. 36-7)

Heavensgate is one long sustained poem, not several poems. It has no one defensible theme in the sense of a 'basic idea', but it is throughout informed by a dynamic ritualistic rhythm which indicates at least two possible levels of analogical interpretation. At one level the poem may be seen as a ritualistic exploration of the process of creative intuition; at another as a mythical projection of a personal experience of the poet. But these two streams are constantly infusing and diffusing into each other because myth is essentially correlative to ritual: myth is the spoken part of ritual, the story which the ritual enacts. (p. 41)

The progression from **'Passage'** to **'Initiations'**, and to **'Watermaid'**, **'Lustra'** and finally to **'Newcomer'**—all areas of experience into which the poet-hero in *Heavens-*

gate moves—is itself, like the stations of the cross during the Easter season, sufficiently indicative of the ritualistic pattern of the poem. (pp. 41-2)

Okigbo's whole poetic output tends to fit into the Malinowskian definition of myth as 'a narrative resurrection of a primeval reality, told in satisfaction of deep religious wants, moral cravings, social submissions, assertions, even practical requirements', yet it would be wrong to assert categorically that Okigbo sets out to construct a myth. Okigbo's poetry is a poetry of strong tensions and conflicts. It is not a conscious myth-making. In *Limits* this tension between creative intuition and personal experience, certainly too between myth and ritual, is tightened up, and that in a way compelling one to seek its possible resolution only in terms of religious and spiritual conflict. In fact, Okigbo's poetic attitude on the whole reveals a crisis between a messianic and an apocalyptic conscience: that is, its emotional pendulum swings unsteadily between an expression of hope and a negation of it. Sometimes it moves spiritually round a belief in the restoration of a peaceful social and moral order, a new epoch; sometimes it affirms a disintegration of all existing social and moral codes in favour of a new and more sublime creative reality. (pp. 63-4)

As a general statement on the theme of Okigbo's second volume of poetry, it may be said, provisionally, that *Limits,* despite its two parts (the **'Siren Limits'** and **'Fragments out of the Deluge'**), is a poem of ten movements.... The central tension of **'Fragments'** is, in plain prose, the burning down of a pagan shrine, either imaginary or real, by the agents of Christian missionaries. In the poetic sensibility this act acquires a new figurative colour and idiom. It becomes the raping of the god and goddess of Irkalla by a warrior 'fleet of eagles' and the killing of the Sunbird which had forewarned their approach. By a prophetic intuition the poet sees the reappearance of the killed god 'outside at the window' followed by the resurrection of the Sunbird whose song he now hears 'from the Limits of the dream'.

'Siren Limits' is, on the contrary, concerned with a problem at the same time more universal and more particular. Universal, because in this part Okigbo discusses the problem common to young poets—that of articulation, the union of soul and voice, the expression of the essential one-self. In other words, he examines the pre-creative psychology or predicament of a poet. But it is also particular, because as a 'Siren' it acts as a particular poem in relation to a particular poet-hero within his particular set of involvements. Thus throughout **'Siren Limits'** the impression is that the poet-initiate is taking stock of his conscience, rigorously examining his state of mind before he finally and devoutly goes to the confessional box. Indeed our hero is enacting a prelude to his homecoming. (pp. 64-5)

[The] note on which *Limits* begins is characterized decidedly by a new structural strength such as is lacking in its predecessor *Heavensgate.* This strength is revealed

mostly in the tone or the voice that speaks in the poem. It is a tone which far from being reflective or sentimental . . . is neither conciliatory nor compromising. It is virile, almost sure of itself. This tonal strength which marks, we believe, a fresh advance in Okigbo's poetic technique, marks also the beginning of a clearer expression of his more genuine faith, an increasing commitment to a prophetic point of view—thus a new breadth of poetic intuition.

With 'Limits II' we move into an area of ritual cleansing which is expressed symbolically and significantly in terms of vital reconciliation with the essence of light. The idea is worked out on two image patterns; say, for instance, the botanical image or the principle of plants' phototropism, and also the Neoplatonic image of the soul. (p. 67)

Okigbo's commentary has the quality of an insidious art. As in every good work of art, including poetry, certain categories of plastic and fine art and music (particularly classic symphony and modern jazz), such commentaries can only be insinuated through tonal variations, images and rhythmical curves. These demand of the reader, spectator or audience a certain amount of healthy awareness and imaginative participation. Especially in poetry like Okigbo's, which is poor in visual symbols but built up almost exclusively on a jazz-like infra-structure of sound, what is expected of the reader is a painstaking disposition coupled with a good ear. (p. 71)

Okigbo may safely be called an artist who, like James Joyce, prefers not to be committed to a fixed position within his own works. Okigbo's position is generally nowhere fixed in his poetry: at one time he is in the centre of it, at another on the fringe; sometimes he may simply be jesting or complaining, at others just silent or paring his fingernails. This will make rather difficult, or quite nonsensical as biographical criticism, an attempt to pin the poet down to any particular point in his poetry. (pp. 72-3)

But just as Eliot was before him, Okigbo seems to be concerned with the more immediate problem of the poet and his personality in relation to his work and art. In other words, Okigbo is concerned with the artist's ego and with the nature of the experiences in which this is generally manifested . . . . [For] the poet of *Ash-Wednesday* and *The Waste Land,* as for the author of *Limits* and *Distances,* the acceptance of an intense personal experience lived in a pattern of symbolic death and rebirth is the central truth of both religious and creative intuition. This is the central ritualistic experience or message which informs Okigbo's poetic world, and one which he comments upon in 'Limits II.'

In that world, Eliot was Okigbo's favourite guide, as Dante had been Eliot's, as Virgil had been Dante's, as Homer had been Virgil's, and so on, since there are no frontiers to the continuity of human thought and artistic aspiration. Okigbo's is a world of dynamic relations and tensions. It is peopled, like Prospero's island, by strange echoes, solitudes, birds, beasts and silences—these for the poet may be various realities or aspects of one ideal mythical or symbolic reality. It is above all a world with two ends. At one end is the 'forest', meaning darkness, ignorance or the creative 'cloud of unknowing'; this is the world of debauched messianism. At the other is the 'sunlight', meaning knowledge, experience and 'the limits of the dream'; this is the world of triumphant apocalypse. In between these two ends there is a continuum, a 'passageway' only to be found through the ritual of purification and by the power of music, art and memory. For Okigbo the true artist or poet is one who is caught up in this primordial continuum. (pp. 77-8)

A sense of religious piety and the principle of ritual death and rebirth constitute the dynamics of the second part of *Limits*—'Fragments Out of the Deluge'. Underlying this is the poet's feeling of a personal tragedy. Besides a common sense of mythology and a certain prophetic range of imagery there is hardly any continuity between the first and the second parts of *Limits* and they should best be treated as two separate poems.... 'Siren Limits' is essentially expository in character whereas 'Fragments' is narrative and dramatic. The first is exploratory of the process of artistic expression— hence the symbolic role of the 'weaverbird'; the second is a prophetic discovery of the fountain-head of creative intuition, hence the use of the 'Sunbird' as a symbol. If the former introduces a thesis on the process of art and creativity which has to be worked out and somehow concluded..., the latter simply posits a tragic axiom, in fact a universal *status quo*. (p. 85)

By its theme and craft *Path of Thunder* differs from [Okigbo's earlier poetry].... This is so because in it Okigbo makes, for the first time ever, a forthright and direct political statement which itself undisguisedly defines the poet's own revolutionary option. But genetically speaking, *Path of Thunder* cannot be separated from the earlier poetry written by Okigbo, since it directly springs from the same parent stock or source of inspiration. (p. 174)

[In] Okigbo's poetic sensibility there seemed to exist a genetic struggle between a romantic pursuit of art for its own sake and a constantly intrusive awareness of the social relevance of art—its function, that is, as a means of embodying significant social comments....

[It is possible] that Okigbo in 1962 was afraid of the possible consequences of committing to his poetry statements that would have direct political connotations in the Nigerian scene. This may mean also that he had not at that time fully resolved within himself the problem of whether art should be separated from politics or a poet be free from ideological commitments. (p. 175)

It is precisely at this juncture that *Path of Thunder* comes in, not as the beginning of a prophecy but as the end of one. In parts, therefore, it is the celebration of the end of a long period of socio-political *attente* and indecision, both on an individual and a national level,

with all the hopes of renaissance and peace which this may imply. In this *Path of Thunder* does no more than reflect the contemporary mood of the Nigerian public.... Okigbo was one of the disenchanted but helpless 'John Citizens' but, unlike many, his own jubilation and hossanah cry, even as early as that time when it appeared a decisive turning-point had been made, was punctuated with sharp, sober warnings, reflective and suspicious. (p. 176)

Path of Thunder reflects the poet's own feeling of uncertainty about the political future of the country, a feeling which... amounts almost to a criticism of the new direction of events in Nigeria up to May 1966, when the poem itself was written. Nowhere is Okigbo's feeling of resentment more positively expressed than in the last of the poems written in May 1966, 'Elegy for Alto'. In this 'Elegy' the poet's repeated insistence on 'robbers', 'eagles' and 'politicians' (his hatred for these symbols of imperialism goes as far back as the poems of *Heavensgate* and 'Fragments out of the Deluge') amounts to an unequivocal suspicion as well as fear of a return of events to the *status quo ante*, with all the implications that this might contain.... (pp. 176-77)

Path of Thunder is, by its very theme and time of composition, a description of the general euphoria which marked the public mood between January and May 1966, after the first military coup in Nigeria. But it is also a poem of a characteristically individual and mature reflection, written by a man who had just turned thirty-three and who was filled more and more with the desire for commitment through positive action as an antidote to the boring insulation and anonymity through fear which art had hitherto provided him.... The discarding of the cloak of impersonality, with its corresponding desire for positive commitment, is even more clearly revealed by the poet's deliberate self-insertion (the possibility of sheer conceit and self-immolation on the poet's part cannot be ruled out) into two of the poems in *Path of Thunder*.... (p. 177)

Christopher's revolt was an essentially artistic one, expressed by means of his poetry. Prophetic, menacing, terrorist, violent, protesting—his poetry was all these and at the same time it was humane, modest and often sentimental. But in a society such as Okigbo lived and wrote in, where the few leaders, including ministers of culture, could hardly afford the cheap luxury of reading the works of their writers, Christopher's scarring message was naturally and safely insulated, by its shrewd and learned obscurity, from comprehension and possible censorship.

The problem of identity thus emerges effectively as one of the dominant themes in Okigbo's poetry. We have seen this variously treated—with the poet's own awareness of the intrusive world outside—in *Heavensgate, Limits* and *Distances,* in the form of man's perennial quest for self-discovery, both on the artistic and the psychic levels. Hence we can conclude that in these poems there exists a deep-seated consciousness of certain shifts in the personality structure of the main characters (who may not necessarily be the poet himself), with the corresponding desire for fulfilment and integration. This may also account for the generally archetypal pattern in Okigbo's poetry, shown in his preference for exiles, for the uprooted or the prodigal as protagonists, and also his use of myth and ritual to illustrate his ideal form of artistic experience. Thus a principle of creative intuition in art and poetry, by no means entirely original, is proposed for us and defined throughout Okigbo's poetry in terms of the individual artist's reconciliation of his first and second 'selves'. This refers to the capacity of every poet to rise above the inner contradictions of his personality and the existentialist *angst* imposed by his spiritual and physical worlds, in order to give forth an expression compatible with 'organic voice', the imprint, that is, of his own selfhood. The enactment of such a quest follows the well-known pattern of purification and initiation. It also outlines the course of true catharsis. (pp. 181-82)

The dilemma of Christopher Okigbo is that he never truly experienced this normal purgation of art. Every new artistic experience left, on the palate of his intuition, nothing but the sour taste of something raw and unfinished, a question mark and, therefore, a burning desire to start afresh. In other words, his poetic world is informed by a sense of the inscrutable absence of reconciliation of opposites. It is this that has shaped the puzzled syntax of his creative rhetoric. (p. 182)

> *Sunday O. Anozie, in his* Christopher Okigbo: Creative Rhetoric, *Evans Brothers Limited, 1972, 203 p.*

Chinua Achebe (essay date 1973)

[*Achebe is considered one of the most important figures in contemporary African literature. His novels, which chronicle the colonization and independence of Nigeria, are among the first works in English to present an intimate and authentic rendering of African culture. In the following excerpt from a 1973 essay, he briefly lauds Okigbo and his poetry.*]

The late Christopher Okigbo was perhaps a good example of an artist who sometimes had, and expressed, confusing ideas while producing immaculate poetry. He was, in the view of many, Africa's finest poet of our time. For while other poets wrote good poems, Okigbo conjured up for us an amazing, haunting poetic firmament of a wild and violent beauty. Well, Christopher Okigbo once said that he wrote his poems only for other poets: thus putting himself not just beyond the African pale but in a position that would have shocked the great English Romantic poet who defined himself as a man writing for men. On another occasion Okigbo said: "There is no African literature. There is good writing and bad writing—that's all." But quite quickly we are led to suspect that this was all bluff. For when Okigbo was asked why he turned to poetry, he said:

> The turning point came in 1958 when I found myself wanting to know myself better, and I had to turn and look at myself from inside.... And when I talk of looking inward to myself, I mean turning inward to examine myselves. This, of course, takes account of ancestors.... Because I do not exist apart from my ancestors.

And then, as though to spell it out clearly that ancestors does not mean some general psychological or genetic principle, Okigbo tells us specifically that he is the reincarnation of his maternal grandfather, a priest in the shrine of the Earth goddess. In fact, poetry becomes for him an anguished journey back from alienation to resumption of ritual and priestly functions. His voice becomes the voice of the sunbird of Igbo mythology, mysterious and ominous.

But it was not a simple choice or an easy return journey for Okigbo to make, for he never underrated his indebtedness to the rest of the world. He brought into his poetry all the heirlooms of his multiple heritage; he ranged with ease through Rome and Greece and Babylon, through the rites of Judaism and Catholicism, through European and Bengali literatures, through modern music and painting. But at least one perceptive Nigerian critic has argued that Okigbo's true voice only came to him in his last sequence of poems, **Path of Thunder,** when he had finally and decisively opted for an African inspiration. This opinion may be contested, though I think it has substantial merit. The trouble is that Okigbo is such a bewitching poet, able to cast such a powerful spell that, whatever he cares to say or sing, we stand breathless at the sheer beauty and grace of his sound and imagery. Yet there is that undeniable fire in his last poems which was something new. It was as though the goddess he sought in his poetic journey through so many alien landscapes, and ultimately found at home, had given him this new thunder. Unfortunately, when he was killed in 1967 he left us only that little, tantalizing hint of the new self he had found. But perhaps he will be reincarnated in other poets and sing for us again like his sunbird whose imperishable song survived the ravages of the eagles. (pp. 43-5)

> *Chinua Achebe, "Africa and Her Writers," in his* Morning Yet on Creation Day: Essays, *Anchor Press/Doubleday, 1975, pp. 29-46.*

FURTHER READING

Akporabara, Fred. "Christopher Okigbo: Emotional Tension, Recurrent Motifs, and Architectonic Sense in *Labyrinths*." *Nigeria* 53, No. 2 (April-June 1985): 6-13.
    Examines form, style, and theme in *Labyrinths*. The critic writes: "Unlike the poetry of J. P. Clark and Gabriel Okara, (his early poet companions), the poetry of Christopher Okigbo is not the poetry of statement but of tension and movement."

Anafulu, Joseph C. "Christopher Okigbo, 1932-1967: A Bio-Bibliography." *Research in African Literatures* 9, No. 1 (Spring 1978): 65-78.
   Brief biography and extensive bibliography of Okigbo.

Egudu, Romanus N. "Christopher Okigbo and the Growth of Poetry." In *European-Language Writing in Sub-Saharan Africa,* edited by Albert S. Gérard, pp. 740-54. Budapest: Akademiai Kiado, 1986.
   Overview of the development of Nigerian poetry, focusing on Okigbo as "the most significant poet" of the new generation.

Izevbaye, D. S. "Death and the Artist: An Appreciation of Okigbo's Poetry." *Research in African Literatures* 13, No. 1 (Spring 1982): 44-52.
   Explores the death motif in Okigbo's poetry, noting: "The subject of death produces two basic forms in his poetry: the lament for the dead, and the poem that has its setting in the land of the dead."

Ogundele, Wole. "From the Labyrinth to the Temple: The Structure of Okigbo's Religious Experience." *Okike,* No. 24 (June 1983): 57-69.
   Discusses the function of religion in Okigbo's poetry.

Theroux, Paul. "A Free Spirit." *West Africa,* No. 3590 (23 June 1986): 1322.
   Theroux recounts his meeting with Okigbo and provides personal insights into the poet.

Sembène Ousmane

1923-

(Also cited as Ousmane Sembène) Senegalese screenwriter, novelist, short story writer, and editor.

Ousmane is renowned for his films and novels that address social wrongs in his native Senegal. Based on Marxist-Leninist ideology, most of his works are about underprivileged groups or individuals facing opposition from a corrupt, bureaucratic system. In his films and books Ousmane typically denounces the burgeoning, westernized elite he sees in post-colonial Senegal. He also finds fault with traditional beliefs such as polygamy and superstition. Robert A. Mortimer observed: "Each [of Ousmane's films] has a dramatic integrity, using well-chosen visual images which move the viewer to a sense of injustice, to an awareness of the need to solve some basic problems. Ousmane does not seek to provide set answers to these social problems; never does he lapse into a cinema of slogans or revolutionary demonstrations. He recognizes that the film is a medium for shaping ideas and attitudes as the viewer reflects upon the story he has seen."

Ousmane was born in 1923 in the Casamance region of Senegal. He left school at the age of fourteen, after a fist fight with his school principal, and began work as a fisherman. After moving to Senegal's capital, Dakar, he found various jobs in manual labor. He worked in Dakar during the late 1930s, but when World War II began he was drafted by the colonial French into their armed forces, and he eventually participated in the Allied invasion of Italy. His later experiences as a longshoreman and union organizer in Marseilles, France, led to his first novel, *Le docker noir* (1956), about a black stevedore who writes a book but is robbed of the manuscript by a white woman. While not considered one of Ousmane's strongest novels, *Le docker noir* was the first of many works to depict Africans who fall victim to a corrupt social or political system. Most of Ousmane's fiction is based on historical events; for example, a newspaper article on the suicide of a black maid in France became the basis of *La noire de...* (1966; *Black Girl*, 1969), which won a Cannes Film Festival Special Prize; and *Les bouts de bois de Dieu* (1960; *God's Bits of Wood*, 1962) recounts the railworker strikes of 1947-1948 on the Dakar-Niger line, in which Ousmane participated. Critics praised *God's Bits of Wood* as a masterful portrayal of the dominant social and economic concerns of the union as well as of the individual sentiments of workers and their families. Meredith Tax commented: "In [Ousmane's] best-known book, *God's Bits of Wood* ..., modern history, tribal customs, ordinary lives, great scenes of mass battle, and several love stories are thrown together in a marvelous stew that simmers and boils with life."

Realizing that his novels were reaching only a limited, elite population in Senegal, where the majority of people are illiterate and speak the indigenous Wolof language, Ousmane turned to filmmaking. He saw film as a medium for mass communication and spent a year studying cinematography in the Soviet Union under the supervision of Marc Donskol. For his first short, *Borom Sarret* (1963), which details one tragic day in the life of a cart driver, Ousmane won the prize for best first work at the Tours Film Festival in 1963. Thereafter he began adapting his short stories and novels for the screen.

Ousmane's novel *Xala* (1973; *Xala*, 1976), adapted for film in 1974, treats two of his dominant themes: corruption of the African elite and the failings of polygamy. After appropriating government funds to finance his third marriage, the protagonist, El Hadji Abdou Kader Beye, is cursed with *xala*, or impotence, by a group of mendicants he has mistreated. Unable to consummate his new marriage, El Hadji loses the respect of his family and colleagues. To remove the *xala*, he ultimately gives in to the demands of the beggars, who spit on him while his first wife and her children watch. Ten scenes were cut from the film by Senegalese government censors, but Ousmane countered by distributing fliers to theater-goers describing the missing segments.

Although his works are often censored when shown in Senegal, Ousmane has gained a widespread viewership for his films in Africa and abroad, prompting Guy Hennebelle to dub him "the pope of African cinema." He is involved in all facets of filmmaking: writing, directing, producing, editing, casting, and collaborating on soundtracks. *Mandabi* (1968; *The Money Order*, 1969), which won prizes for best foreign film at the Venice Film Festival in 1968 and the Atlanta Film Festival in 1970, was the first film written and directed by an African to be commercially released in Senegal and is often considered the first African film to reach an international audience. Like many of Ousmane's works, *Mandabi* was released in both a French and a Wolof version. This film, based on Ousmane's novella *Le Mandat*, recounts the troubles experienced by Ibrahima, a poor, illiterate Senegalese man who attempts to cash a money order sent by his nephew in France. A bureaucratic banking system and greedy neighbors cheat Ibrahima of his money, leading him to assert that "honesty has become a crime in this day." Ousmane concludes many of his films on a similar note of despair; *Emitai* (1971; *Emitai*, 1973), for example, describes a heroic resistance against French rule by the small Diola population of Senegal but closes with a massacre of the villagers by the French.

Most critics contend that the collective movements portrayed in Ousmane's works—organizations of women, unions, and communities—offer a sense of hope for positive social change, yet others compare his works to Jean-Paul Sartre's existential play *No Exit*, which offers no promise of escaping existing social frameworks. In Ousmane's view, the bleakness of his works only mirrors that of the African world he observes. Artists, he maintains, "can neither invent anything or receive anything. We must see and know our society. We have to be within and without at the same time. Within in order to feel the heartbeat, and without to create the image that society gives to us. And it's from there that we take a position. But our role stops there because the artist alone cannot change society. He can, however, help to orient the society."

(For further information about Ousmane's life and works, see *Black Writers* and *Contemporary Authors,* Vols. 117, 125.)

PRINCIPAL WORKS

Le docker noir (novel) 1956
O Pays, mon beau peuple! (novel) 1957
Les bouts de bois de Dieu (novel) 1960
  [*God's Bits of Wood,* 1962]
Voltaïque (short stories) 1962
  [*Tribal Scars and Other Stories,* 1974]
Borom Sarret (screenplay) 1964
L'harmattan, Volume I: Référendum (fiction) 1964
Niaye (screenplay) 1964; adapted from his short story "Véhi-Ciosane"
Véhi-Ciosane; ou, Blanche-Genèse, suivi du Mandat (novellas) 1965
  [*The Money-Order; with White Genesis,* 1971]
La Noire de . . . (screenplay) 1966; adapted from his short story "La Noire de . . ."
  [*Black Girl,* 1969]
Mandabi (screenplay) 1968; adapted from his novella *Le Mandat*
  [*The Money Order,* 1969]
Tauw (screenplay) 1970
Emitai (screenplay) 1971
  [*Emitai,* 1973]
Xala (novel) 1973
  [*Xala,* 1976]
Xala (screenplay) 1974
  [*Xala,* 1975]
Ceddo (screenplay) 1977
  [*Ceddo,* 1978]
Dernier de l'empire (novel) 1981
  [*The Last of the Empire,* 1983]

Robert A. Mortimer (essay date 1972)

[*The following excerpt is from a 1972 revision of a paper originally presented at a symposium on "Black-*

World Film" at Rutgers University in May 1971. Here, Mortimer discusses Ousmane's transition from novelist to dramatist and examines several of his films.]

In the fall of 1969, a banner was unfurled across bustling Avenue William Ponty in Dakar to herald an unprecedented event. Emblazoned boldly upon the banner was MANDABI, the Wolofized version of the French "Le Mandat" or "the money order," the title of an award-winning film by the talented Senegalese filmmaker, Ousmane Sembene. The publicity celebrated a cultural and political event of considerable significance: for the first time, the work of a Senegalese director was being shown commercially in Senegal. West African filmmaking was moving beyond the select audience of international film festivals to reach a mass African audience. Therein stands a major landmark in the history of the black man and the film medium.

Film is obviously an attractive medium of expression for artists in countries with high rates of illiteracy. Indeed Sembene, the filmmaker, is the current *persona* of Sembene, the highly regarded novelist; his own personal itinerary from writer to cineast bears testimony to the relevance of the film as a vehicle of education and liberation in contemporary Africa. (p. 26)

Sembene's remarkable career is in itself a living document of the forces of social change in recent African history. Born in 1923 into a poor family in Ziguinchor, the main city of the Casamance region of southern Senegal, Sembene is an essentially self-educated man. He recalls having exercised thirty-five different trades from fisherman to mechanic to soldier on his way to becoming a cineast. Clearly the major experience of this formative period was the decade spent as a longshoreman on the docks of Marseille after World War II. Here he became a union organizer among the black workers, and he has continued to consider himself as a Marxist-Leninist. His profound concern and identification with the common man have been evident throughout his artistic career.

His first novel drew upon his life in Marseille. Published in 1956, **Le docker noir** ("The Black Dockworker") was, according to one critic, "very badly written." Each succeeding work, however, exhibited a polishing of style which soon established Sembene as one of the finest and most original writers in Africa. In 1957, he completed a second novel, **O Pays, mon beau peuple** ("The Country, My Beautiful People") which described the efforts of a Casamancais to create a modern, independent business in his own country against the pressures of the colonial merchants and the caste prejudices of the traditional peasant society. Peasants and workers came together in his third work, **Les bouts de bois de Dieu.** This major novel vividly recounts the story of the African laborers' strike on the Dakar-Bamako railway line in 1947-48, incorporating Sembene's concern with progressive social change into a work rich in its portrayal of the physical and social setting of West African semi-urban life.

Foreshadowing his artistic versatility, Sembene shifted effectively to the medium of the short story when he published *Voltaique* in 1962, a collection accalimed for the poetic tone and psychological insights in characterization that it revealed. One of these stories later became the subject of a film, as did the two novellas published a few years later as *Vehi-Ciosane* and *Le Mandat.* Although he published yet another novel in 1964 (*L'Harmattan,* an interpretation of the political events surrounding the 1958 referendum in which Senghor decided against voting for immediate independence), it seems that by the early 1960's, Sembene, the writer, was already thinking in terms of creations that might be carried to the screen.

Sembene has described his transition into filmmaking as follows: "I became aware of the fact that using the written word, I could reach only a limited number of people, especially in Africa where illiteracy is so deplorably widespread. I recognized that the film on the other hand was capable of reaching large masses of people. That is when I decided to submit applications to several embassies for a scholarship to pay for training in filmmaking. The first country to respond favorably was the Soviet Union. I spent a year at the Gorki Studio in Moscow, where I received a basically practical instruction under the direction of Marc Donskol." This decision to master the film medium, then, was prompted by Sembene's profound commitment to a socially relevant art. His literary subjects were the common people of Senegal struggling to cope with the oppression of colonialism and the disrupting forces of social change brought about by modernization. He was not content that the ideas and lessons contained in his art be limited to the African elite. As a socialist critical of the emerging post-colonial bureaucratic elite on the one hand, and a progressive critical of certain traditional practices on the other, Sembene had a message to convey. He concluded that movies offered a greater opportunity than books to "crystallize a new consciousness among the masses." The step into filmmaking was as much a political act as an artistic choice. The image was to teach a lesson of liberation, but at the same time Sembene was determined not to sacrifice his artistic integrity in taking that step toward a cinema of genuine decolonization.

Each of Sembene's films tells a movingly sad story. His protagonists are humble people exploited in one way or another by the disruption wrought upon their society by colonialism or its neocolonial vestiges. Each film has a dramatic integrity, using well-chosen visual images which move the viewer to a sense of injustice, to an awareness of the need to solve some basic problems. Sembene does not seek to provide set answers to these social problems; never does he lapse into a cinema of slogans or revolutionary demonstrations. He recognizes that the film is a medium for shaping ideas and attitudes as the viewer reflects upon the story he has seen.

Sembene's first production, *Borom Saret,* runs but nineteen minutes. Slowly paced and filmed in a semi-documentary style, Sembene uses these nineteen min-

utes to take us through the wearisome day of a *bonhomme charette* or cart-driver, who seeks to make a living from a horse and buggy taxi service. The driver transports a pregnant woman to the hospital, and then a father to the cemetery to bury his dead baby. The poverty of his passengers, his own rumpled old hat, the dusty street of the medina—all add up visually to a day in which no client is able to pay his fare. Finally a well-dressed young man persuades him to cart some of his belongings into a comfortable residential neighborhood in which horse and buggy wagons are prohibited. There a policeman appears, fines the driver, and confiscates his wagon. The victim returns sadly home without a franc, deprived of his means of livelihood. His wife leaves the children with him and goes out saying, "We must eat tonight . . . "

It is a tribute to the director's skill that in this rather short footage, Sembene is able to convey the heavy weight of poverty, the growing demoralization of an unproductive day, the frustration of the struggle to survive in a setting marked by the gap between the rich who make the law and the poor who suffer its inequities. The cart-driver tries his best to support his family only to have his wife thrown back upon her own resources at the end. The mood of the film is one of pathos, not of revolution, but the impact of the story is strong and troubling. For this film, the Tours Film Festival awarded Sembene its prize for the best first work in 1963.

In 1964, he transformed his short novel *Vehi-Ciosane* into a film entitled *Niaye,* a stark vision of the disintegration of traditional rural life under the dual pressure of out-moded authority relationships and colonial interference. As in the novel, the physical focus of the film is the central place of the village, the perfect visual image of rural Senegal, where the men gather beneath a tree to discuss village matters, or to gossip and listen to the *griot,* the traditional story-teller. The *griot* recounts a sordid tale of incest, suicide, murder, and corrupted power. The peaceful appearance of the countryside contrasts sharply with the underlying reality as the viewer learns that the village chief has impregnated his daughter to the despair of his humiliated wife who kills herself when she realizes that no one has the courage to avenge her by rebelling against the chief's authority. Their son later returns home traumatized by his military service in Indochina; the chief's cousin, covetous of his power, persuades the deranged young man to murder his father. The colonial administration legitimizes the conspiracy by naming the guilty cousin as the new chief with the approval of the village elders. At the end we see, however, that the *griot* and the daughter are overwhelmed by this corrupt hypocrisy, and decide to leave the village. The daughter momentarily considers abandoning her infant until she sees vultures circling overhead—a grim image summing up much of the film. She gathers up the baby, and much like the wife of the cart-driver, departs to an uncertain future.

Niaye is a strong dose of social criticism, perhaps too heavily administered to be convincing. The preface to the novel makes it clear that Sembene conceived the work as an attack upon uncritical glorifications of the past, a category within which he includes the doctrine of negritude. The film incorporates this same harsh message. Yet the novel, for all its violence, has a poetic quality—in its contrast between innocent victims and those corrupted by power, and in the dignity expressed by the *griot's* anguish at the disintegration of the ancestral legacy—which Sembene sought to capture on film. He passionately desired that *Niaye* be seen by its primary audience, the peasants of Senegal. As he had no commercial outlet for the work, he undertook the responsibility of distribution himself, touring the country to project and discuss the film personally. Thus he achieved the direct contact with his audience that had drawn him into filmmaking. He recalls with pleasure the long evenings spent discussing the problems raised by *Niaye* in the improvised "open-air theaters" of rural Senegal.

His third movie brought Sembene considerable international recognition as a cineast. *La Noire de...* won prizes at film festivals in France and Tunisia as well as at Dakar's special 1966 Festival of the Negro Arts. Adapted from one of the stories in *Voltaique,* this was Sembene's first direct cinematic treatment of the theme of black-white relations. The story is based in fact, drawn from an incident which Sembene read about in the French press. It portrays the tragic isolation and eventual suicide of an African girl taken to France as a maid. Two images in particular struck many viewers: the *marché aux bonnes* or "maid market" at which the French technical assistance family finds the maid—uncomfortably reminiscent of a slave market as filmed by Sembene—and the recurrent image of an African mask which the maid purchases as a toy for the European child and which comes to symbolize her cultural identity as she grows more despondent over her objectification by the French family.

Sembene himself was most struck by the expressiveness of the face of Thérèse Moissine Diop who plays the girl. In all of his cinema, Sembene has drawn remarkable performances from non-professional actors. As the illiterate and lonely maid rarely speaks to the family (her thoughts being expressed in background monologues), the camera must convey much of the inner turmoil she feels in this racist *huis-clos.*

La Noire de... is a moving portrait of racial exploitation. Sembene believes that the "maid trade", however, is a symbol of a larger issue: the neocolonial attitudes of the new African bureaucratic elite who condone such a relationship in return for European financial aid and technical assistance. In portraying poignantly the human consequences for one person caught up in this neocolonial system, Sembene sought to provoke thought upon the larger situation, and to raise questions about the content of genuine African independence.

Mandabi, the production of which was made possible by the artistic success of *La Noire de...,* takes up this same theme in a quite different story. It is the first work which Sembene produced in color (although he experimented with some color sequences which he eventually cut from *La Noire de...*) and he uses color to great advantage in presenting a visual panorama of life in modern Dakar. As anyone who has visited Senegal's capital will readily recall, the city is a palate of splendid colors. Sea, sky, flowers, open markets, and brilliant light provide the setting for the brightly colored fabrics of the women whose long *pagnes* and highly wound kerchiefs bob and wend their way through the busy downtown streets.

Sembene explodes this color in a visual assault upon the viewer as his hero Ibrahima Dieng goes upon his quest to cash a money order. In one of the striking early scenes, the viewer is overwhelmed by a sea of boubous as the men pour out of Dakar's impressive Grand Mosque. The long, flowing, often handsomely embroidered boubou of the traditional Senegalese man becomes a symbol of Ibrahima's traditional dignity; as he sets off upon a difficult errand or is rebuffed by an arrogant clerk, he majestically swishes his boubou into its proper stately fit to reassure himself of his worth and decency.

Mandabi is a political film lightly disguised as a farce. Mamadou Gueye, the Dakar office-worker whom Sembene turned into an international film-star in the lead role, renders an amusing Ibrahima. There are many comic sequences as Ibrahima and his wives Mety and Aram seek to capitalize upon the sudden "fortune" sent by their nephew in France. Yet the comedy and the color gradually fade in significance as the more somber shades of life in Dakar's shanty-town emerge. The tribulations of a simple man as he confronts the post-independence bureaucratic establishment (a visual carbon copy of the French administrative system) become painfully serious matters. Ibrahima encounters red tape at the post office, disdain at the city hall, cheating as he seeks the photograph required for his identity card, and finally venality from the young college-educated relative to whom he turns for assistance. At the same time, he becomes fair game for every neighbor who gets wind of the impending "wealth" out of which he is finally cheated. Humiliated by the nascent bourgeoisie of his country, Ibrahima cries out desperately in the film's closing scene that "honesty has become a crime in this day."

The impact of the film is strong. The characters are authentic, and the story is simple and convincing. From the first image of the nephew, a streetsweeper in Paris, dropping the money order into a mail box, to the closing image of Ibrahima's lamentation, one senses the concern with social and economic inequality that pervades Sembene's work. Once again the director does not give us a revolutionary figure, yet the film conveys its message of the need for change. Sembene's critique is implicit in the contrasting images of the shantytown and the well-to-do neighborhoods, or the honest but unemployed man and those who exploit the privileges of a seat behind a desk. The humor and the deft portrayal of ordinary family life allow Sembene to reach a large audience; without turning the movie into a manifesto, the director nevertheless employs his medium to teach a lesson. It is this effective combination plus its technical excellence that make *Mandabi* an artistic success as well as a landmark.

Sembene's most recent work is a short color film, commissioned by American churchmen to illustrate some of the profound dilemmas of modernization in contemporary Africa. Conceived essentially for western audiences, *Tauw* reiterates several themes already familiar from his earlier films. It focuses upon urban youth, faced by the dual problems of unemployment and changing values. The title character is a young man without prospects, engaging in petty thievery (snitching *croissants* from a carrier's tray) while wandering about Dakar in search of work, unable to purchase the ticket which would admit him to the docks for a possible job. He quarrels with his traditionalist father and breaks with his family; one senses as the film ends that Tauw stands on the verge of vagrancy or anomie. While this quasi-documentary short feature reflects issues to which Sembene has earlier drawn attention, he has further ideas for new work. He has already shot some footage in his native Casamance for a film treating the clash of temporal and spiritual authority. Another project calls for a major historical film on the nineteenth-century Malinke resistance leader, Samory Toure. These further themes suggest Sembene's conception of how the film can continue as a vehicle of growing African self-understanding. (pp. 26, 64-6)

> Robert A. Mortimer, "Ousmane Sembene and the Cinema of Decolonization," in African Arts, *Vol. 5, No. 3, Spring, 1972, pp. 26, 64-8, 84.*

John Updike (essay date 1977)

[*Updike is an American novelist, critic, short story writer, poet, and essayist. In the following excerpt, he reviews the novel* Xala.]

Xala, by Sembène Ousmane, describes itself, on the dust jacket, as "the basis for a highly acclaimed film of the same title which received accolades at the 1975 New York Film Festival." It is as short as a scenario (one hundred fourteen pages), flows in a succession of scenes without any chapter subdivisions, and contains bits of "business"—"Her tight-fitting dress split, a long, horizontal tear which exposed her behind"—that might be hilarious in a movie but fall rather flat in prose. The stills from the film bound into the book exist on the same continuum as the text, and help us to read it, rather than (as in most illustrated fiction) set up an irrelevant static of alternative visualization. Yet the novel is not thin. Its basic subject, the problems of polygamy in an urban society, resonates eerily in our own society of families extended by divorce and remarriage, of romantic renewals obtained at the price of multiplied obligations. The reality of magic in Mr.

Ousmane's interweave of erotic farce and stern social comment suggests, to a Westerner, what magically fragile constructs our personal pretensions are.

A *xala* (pronounced "hala") is a curse that produces impotence; one is laid upon the hero, a Senegalese businessman called El Hadji Abdou Kader Beye, on the night of his wedding to his third wife, the young and voluptuous N'Gone. El Hadji is "fifty-odd" and prosperous enough to keep his two other wives, Adja Awa Astou and Oumi N'Doye, in separate villas in the fashionable part of Dakar, and to provide a minibus for the transportation of his eleven children. Within the minibus, we are told, the children of each mother take a separate bench: "This segregation had not been the work of the parents but a spontaneous decision on the part of the children themselves." There are a number of such fascinating details of how polygamy works in urban Africa. "In the town, since the families are scattered, the children have little contact with their father. Because of his way of life the father must go from house to house, villa to villa, and is only there in the evenings, at bedtime. He is therefore primarily a source of finance..." The set time he spends with each wife is called a *moomé*; the first wife is given the title of *awa,* after the Arab word for "first woman on earth." "The first wife implied a conscious choice, she was an elect. The second wife was purely optional." El Hadji's second wife, the sharp-tongued, Frenchified Oumi, has the position of sexual favorite to lose to the third, so she is suspected as the source of the *xala.* When, after many futile trips to marabouts who cannot lift the curse, El Hadji finds one, deep in the bush, who succeeds, it is Oumi who has the benefit of his momentarily revived potency. The plot takes some pains to keep young N'Gone virginal, so that she can, without serious offense to sexual propriety, be discarded, as El Hadji's luxuriant world slips from him. His impotence poisons all his existence. "Day after day, night after night, his torment ate into his professional life. Like a waterlogged silk-cotton tree on the riverbank he sank deeper into the mud." The source of the *xala,* when finally revealed, is perhaps less surprising in the film, where the sound track has repeatedly placed the culprit before us; but the ritual exaction for the curse's removal, and the story's abrupt swerve into social protest, must surprise everyone not immersed in Africa's sense of communal responsibility or familiar with the moral indignation visited there upon elites busy aggrandizing themselves in the approved capitalist manner.

El Hadji's rise, overreaching, and fall are intelligible without magic. He is impotent with his third, much younger wife out of stagefright—the jocular chaffing at the wedding and the post-nuptial inspection of the bed linen lend intimacy an intimidating public dimension— and out of fright of his own hubris. His financial status collapses with his sexuality, because he is everywhere overextended. The pre-urban institution of polygamy, wherein the patriarch on the strength of his warrior potential alone ruled his docile compound of subsistence farmerettes, has been intolerably weighted by the

Western conceptions of husband, lover, and (of Western goods) provider. El Hadji's metropolitan attempt to combine status and gratification breaks his resources, which, we are reminded in a forceful parenthesis, are pathetically slender:

> (It is perhaps worth pointing out that all these men who had given themselves the pompous title of "businessmen" were nothing more than middlemen, a new kind of salesman. The old trading firms of the colonial period, adapting themselves to the new situation created by African Independence, supplied them with goods on a wholesale or semi-wholesale basis, which they then re-sold.)

El Hadji's vain tour of marabouts for cure is now recast as a vain search for credit; his cars and villas are repossessed. He stands finally before us naked, covered with spittle. Nakedness, Sembène Ousmane seems to say, is man's natural condition. The keen African body-sense supplies a rapture of precision to El Hadji's moment of relief from the *xala*:

> Hadji listened to the clicking of the beads as they fell at regular intervals onto one another. He looked up at the curved roof. Suddenly he felt as if he were on edge. A long-forgotten sensation make him break into bursts of shivering. It was as if sap was rising violently inside his body, running through its fibres and filling it right to his burning head. It went on coming in waves. Then he had the impression that he was being emptied. Slowly he relaxed and a liquid flowed through his veins toward his legs. All his being now became concentrated in the region of his loins.

Not all the writing is this vivid and fluent. The translator seems to have brought to the French some English awkwardnesses: words such as "fulsome" and "exhibitionism" are used in their root, rather than usual, meanings, and more than one word seems off in a passage like "Her eyes were lifeless, they had a deep inscrutability that seemed like a total absence of reaction. But there was the strength of controlled inertia burning in them." Such eyes have successfully defied description. Not so these: "The lack of sleep showed at the edge of his eyelids and bathed his eyes in a reddish lustre crossed by threads which according to the time of day or the place would take on the colour of stale palm-oil." Generally, the texture of Mr. Wake's translation answers well to Mr. Ousmane's tone—that light, level accent of French Africa's fiction, which voices its perceptions, however withering, with a certain pleasant dispassion, with a thinking man's articulations. (pp. 677-80)

> *John Updike, "The World Called Third," in his* Hugging the Shore: Essays and Criticism, *Alfred A. Knopf, Inc., 1983, pp. 676-86.*

Jonathan A. Peters (essay date 1982)

[*In the following excerpt, Peters compares Ousmane to a traditional African griot, or storyteller.*]

A Senegalese fable tells the story of three encounters by Fene-Falsehold and Deug-Truth who were companions on a journey. At the first village they are thrown out by a man whose wife is discourteous to both the strangers and her husband because Deug, when asked, suggests that she is the worst wife he has seen. An honest answer to the chief's enquiry in the second village similarly lands them in trouble: Deug tells him that the children are in charge in the village because they are the ones who share out the meat, reserving the choicest portions for themselves. But in the third, the king is forced to part with half of his wealth because Fene, now their spokesman, dupes him into believing that he can bring back to life not only his dead favourite, but his father and grandfather as well. The present king does not want to have to deal with the problems of three kings in a single kingdom, especially since his father had been a tyrannous king whom his son helped to put away. When they set out on their journey Fene had observed that God loved Deug-Truth more than him. But when he obtains half of the king's wealth as a result of his untruths he concludes that God may be on the side of truth but falsehood was the best way to succeed with men.

Sembène Ousmane, the internationally famous film-maker from the village of Ziguinchor, Senegal, has suffered much the same fate as Deug-Truth in terms of the reception of his fiction and his films. After more than two decades of artistic output he has so far received comparatively little critical attention deserving of his seven books of fiction and at least an equal number of films; for, if numbers do not provide a compelling reason for serious study, the issues he raises as well as the artistic quality of his fiction—to say nothing of his films which earn him first place among African film-makers—are sufficient to deserve more extensive analyses of the kind that some writers with certainly no greater contribution to African letters have received. One reason, perhaps, for his neglect among English-speaking writers and readers stems from the fact that some of his early works have never been translated into English while, among those translated, only his most widely praised novel, *Les Bouts de bois de Dieu* was almost immediately available in translation under the title *God's Bits of Wood.*

Another more significant reason may be that what he sees and expounds on repeatedly is the uncomfortable and even repelling 'truth' that black people are still undergoing a form of slavery in this, the latter portion of the twentieth century.... The intensely moral tone of many of [Sembène's] works is in keeping not only with the role of a truth-seeker, but also (more importantly) with the function of that truth-telling bard of old—the griot—who, in Sembène's own words, 'was not only the dynamic element in his tribe, clan or village but also the living witness of every occurrence ... placing before all at village gatherings the facts about each in full detail.' The story of truth and falsehood provides an excellent reference point for examining Sembène griot role as exemplified in his two novelettes, *Le Mandat* and *Véhi-*

Ciosane ou Blanche-Genèse, both of which have been made into films.

The major theme in both *The Money-Order* and *White Genesis* turns on the conflict between truth and falsehood in human affairs. The two stories in fact are studies on the value of morality. *White Genesis* is more tragic in its development but its end holds out the hope that truth, in bondage over a long period, will again be resurrected. *The Money-Order,* depicting somewhat humorously the misfortunes that surround its hero, ends on a note of pessimism. It is a structural parallel of the story of truth and falsehood in that its hero, Dieng, decides to give up his truthfulness and honesty in favour of deception and lies. The preference for falsehood evident in the society portrayed in *White Genesis* is constantly undermined by the griot-hero to the point where Sembène is able to suggest a new beginning through the illegitimate child of Khar Diob. In *The Money-Order,* after a series of misfortunes in which Dieng loses more than the value of the money-order sent by his nephew from Paris, he also loses his gullibility declaring: 'I am going to put on the skin of the hyena.... Why? Because it is only cheating and lies that are true. Honesty is a crime nowadays.'

White Genesis is a griot's story. Sembène himself remarks in the introduction that it is as old as the world itself. It is a story of incest set in the village of Santhiu-Niaye. Sembène introduces the story by describing the setting of the village close to the Atlantic Ocean in Senegal. The very monotony of this region which defies definition in terms of savannah or delta, steppe, grassland, etc., gives a parallel to the lack-lustre morality which permeates the village, threatening its life as much as the migration of its young men to the city in search of a better life.

The longest section of *White Genesis* gives us an extended view of Ngone War Thiandum, the mother of Khar Madiagua Diob. Before the story opens Khar had become pregnant and at first the responsibility of her pregnancy had been laid on the *navetanekat,* a migrant labourer called Atoumane. In spite of his denials the Diob family had wanted him killed on the strength of the accusation that he has violated their family honour. Since he is poor and perhaps of a low caste marriage with Khar would be undesirable; so the gravity of his offence in getting a girl pregnant whom he could not marry and who would forever be tainted by this episode in her life is quite obvious. Khar's brother, the mad Tanor who served time during the Second World War, destroys the labourer's groundnut crop and a crowd of villagers (which include Khar's uncle Medoune Diob) pursues and hunts the *navetanekat* for several days and nights. The identity of Khar's real violator is only gradually revealed. In fact, Ngone War Thiandum is one of the last people in the village to know. The scene in which she finds out that her husband is the father of the child their daughter, Khar, is expecting is depicted by means of a flashback. Gnagna Guisse, the wife of the shoemaker-griot, Dethye Law, can then no longer deny the truth when Ngone War Thiandum confronts her with it.

The whole story of *White Genesis* is overshadowed by events which have taken place long before the commencement of the story. By presenting these past occurrences through the mind of Ngone who is herself only just finding out the truth, Sembène is able to concentrate the action of the story into the few days when things reach a climax. The climax itself is the scene in which Khar delivers the baby, but already in this first major encounter with Ngone and her family we have the major outlines of the conflict.

In the opening portion of this episode we see Ngone in bed with her husband, Guibril, whom she is now forced by circumstances to despise. There is a delicate balance, however, between this sense of contempt and the genuine warmth of affection that contact with her husband's body conjures up in her through pleasant memories of their past relationship. The closing scene of this episode is the accouchement of Khar and it fittingly ends the long section, promising a resolution of one kind or another to this drama of incest.

The theme of incest in *White Genesis* is connected with themes of honour and nobility as well as morality and justice; it is also related to the theme of truth on which the Senegalese fable I referred to earlier is based. Sembène manages to interweave all these themes together to form a moral world not only as things are or as they used to be but, perhaps more important, as they should be. In accordance with this vision, Sembène makes a statement used first as an epigraph to the story and then recalled in the following reflection by Ngone War Thiandum at the end of our first encounter with her:

> The words of the sage came, luminous, into her mind: 'Sometimes a child is born into the most ordinary low caste family who grows up and glorifies his name, the name of his father, of his mother, of his whole family, of his community, of his tribe. More often, in a so-called high caste family which glories in its past, a child comes into the world who, by his actions, sullies his entire heritage, and even robs the individual diambur-diambur [freeborn] of his dignity.' She repeated these words to herself, but still she hesitated to act.

The whole purport of the passage reflects Sembène's belief that honour and nobility are not a typical characteristic of people of high birth, operating in a closed circuit. Rather, honour and dishonour are qualities that mark out individuals whether they are of humble or noble origin. The reference to 'so-called high caste' emphasizes Sembène's point.

Although Ngone is anxious to preserve the good name of her family, this duty and desire are not confined to those of her rank only. Indeed the most outspoken and uncompromising seeker after truth is not a member of a high caste, but one who acknowledges his lowly status. It is Dethye Law the griot-shoemaker who incorporates in his character the old virtues which had made their society great and which are now being trampled upon. The inherent truth behind the words of the sage is dramatized through the story. What Sembène is saying, in essence, is that Guibril Guedj Diob who was born into a family with a noble past, disgraces the reputation of not only his own high lineage but also the ordinary free-born citizen like Dethye Law. At the same time, we can say that someone like Dethye Law, born into an ordinary home, a low-caste griot home, can ennoble his community by his steadfast witness to the truth. It is this simple truth that *White Genesis* is designed to demonstrate.

Sembène Ousmane goes to great pains to document the inbreeding that takes place within a society where truth is seen as the prerogative of a particular class, one in which morality is a stylized process of maintaining dignity even if this means disguising or denying the truth. The crime of Guibril and his daughter Khar, an exception to this rule, is open for all to see. But the machinations of his brother, Medoune Diob, first of all instigating the invocation of the death penalty for Guibril Guedj Diob and his daughter and when this fails inciting the mad Tanor to kill his father are the kind of concern that the griot has. This concern with the truth is displayed throughout the story by Dethye Law as well as by others like Massar. Thus following the deaths of Guibril Diob at the hand of his son and the suicide of Ngone War Thiandum, Dethye Law makes an attempt at leaving which is designed to test the will of the villagers to uphold the truth.

Dethye has always spoken against those who have left the village because their desertion threatens the very survival of Santhiu-Niaye. But when the machinations of Medoune Diob go on unchallenged and even condoned by the present Imam, Dethye begins to be afraid that people like him who speak the truth will be threatened: the unscrupulous will not hesitate to eliminate those who speak against them once the moral will of the people is broken. His announcement that he is going to leave is followed by . . . exchanges which emphasize above all the fact that freedom and truth are not confined to the rich or those of noble ancestry . . . . At the time that the hero, Dethye Law, engages in this dialogue the climax of the story has already been reached. Khar has delivered her baby. Her mother, true to her guelewar upbringing and motto—'Rather die a thousand deaths in a thousand ways each more terrible than the other than endure an insult for a single day'—has already committed suicide. And Guibril Guedj Diob has been killed by his son Tanor, at the instigation of his uncle Medoune Diob. Tanor cannot succeed his father, not only because of his madness but also because of his patricide. Besides, the last we see of him is the scene where he is tied to a tree; the last we hear of him is Medoune's statement to the toubab-commandant that he has left for the city like many of the young men. Medoune Diob has not inherited everything. He has the chieftaincy, the pomp of receiving dignitaries like the white commandant on a tax-collecting mission—even Guibril Guedj's colourful parasol which Tanor, return-

ing home from the war in Indochina, had brought his father. In the light of these developments—especially the role of Medoune Diob in the liquidation of the incestuous Guibril—Dethye's decision that he can no longer live in Santhiu-Niaye is understandable.

Dethye Law is right on another point. The inhabitants of Santhiu-Niaye are not ready, in spite of their village's increasing desolation, to sacrifice the truth completely—yet. At the mosque where the faithful respond to the griot's intoning of the call to prayer five times a day, almost all the adherents desert the present conniving Imam in favour of Palla, his old rival for the position. The shifting of religious adherents also reflects the political scene, for Medoune Diob becomes ostracized in much the same way as Guibril was isolated when his incest became established. The changed situation also gives added significance to Dethye's comment that *in the past* the caste system made members of his family servants to the Ndiobene's. Thus, a society will prosper only if it dedicates itself to truth not as 'a gift, nor an inheritance' but as an ideal since 'the blood of truth is always noble, whatever its origin'. If we adopt this view, many of the roles in the story are immediately reversed. Dethye's unflagging efforts to preserve the truth make him a man of noble blood while the blood of the Ndiobene's has become tainted by the attempts to destroy the truth no less than by the sin of incest. This is the core of Sembène's message in the story.

For the cleansing to be complete, however, the new leadership has to banish Khar and her child from the village. Before her death, Ngone War Thiandum had hoped that this grandchild/stepchild would be a boy. But it is a girl that Khar brings into the world amid the injurious gossip that goes on about her. Unlike the gossip-mongers and even Ngone herself, Sembène is careful throughout to avoid making either father or daughter the seducer in their incestuous crime. Since the two of them say very little in *White Genesis,* we are forced to hold them equally guilty. Yet it is this act of banishment that holds out hope in any otherwise bleak ending. In a very short space of time Khar ceases to be a child and becomes a woman. She becomes even more precipitately an orphan caring for a new-born infant whose future, like hers, is unknown. Her attempt to abandon the child which would only handicap her bid to begin life afresh in a new environment, is merely a reflection on her dilemma. The instinctual maternal attachment of this child-mother-orphan to her daughter, Vehi-Ciosane Thiandum, restores the balance to the natural cycle. The child, then, becomes the symbol of hope, the nonracial 'white genesis' after a prolonged rule of dishonesty, corruption and evil.

The moralizing tone of the novelette is inevitable because of the virtual identity of subject and theme, and the signal role of Dethye Law as an exponent of these, a role of griot-moralist that echoes Sembène's own. All the same, a good portion of *White Genesis* concentrates on the lives of villagers outside the Ndiobene-Thiandum household. The favourite meeting spot for the men is under the shade of the beintan tree where the griot-shoemaker works. It is in its shade that intense contests take place between Badieye and Gornaru, two inveterate players of *yothe* (the local version of draughts complete with dry donkey droppings for counters) while the habitués discuss everything under the sun, from the moral dilemma that engulfs the village to bawdy dexterities.... Such episodes give body to the otherwise slim story of human calamity. It is essentially an internal conflict, for none of the strangers—the *navetanekat* or the white official and his retinue—change the dynamics of the village in any way. All the change comes from within. And the end of the story returns us to the sandy flats as Khar, unselfpityingly braces herself for the trip to a new life in Ndakaru with a child of infamous ancestry but who may well grow up to glorify an entire people.

The locale in *The Money-Order* shifts from a desolate rural setting to Dakar, capital of Senegal, for which Khar Madiagua Diob is headed at the end of *White Genesis*. There is a difference also in the central conflict between the two novelettes. The one in *White Genesis* is, as we have seen, primarily an internal village conflict, the nexus of which is the high caste family of the Ndiobene-Diob which is completely shattered at the end. By contrast, the inhabitants of the same quarters as Ibrahima Dieng, the central character of *The Money-Order,* are virtually indistinguishable in terms of birth and caste on account of their common misery. They help and hurt each other by lending or sharing small portions of the meagre foodstuffs and loans they manage to scrounge out of the over-priced store of Mbarka; by exchanging and spreading news and malicious gossip about the changing society and about each other; and by their jealous outrage against the petit bourgeois whose members include Mbarka and the new western educated elite. The central conflict is, however, a personal one. An external agent in the form of a money-order from Paris forces the jobless Dieng outside his familiar world into the unfamiliar world of the Dakar bureaucracy, leaving him disillusioned in the end.

Perhaps the most emphatic distinction between *White Genesis* and *The Money-Order* is one of tone. The intensely moralistic tone of the former is probably suited to the intention of Sembène to deal with a very serious issue affecting the health and welfare of a whole society. The tone is in fact not confined to the sermonizing hero, Dethye Law, but extends to others as well. Thus, Ngone War Thiandum tells her family griot, Gnagna Guisse (wife of Dethye Law): 'It is a sin to lie. It is unfriendly to lie to me.' And Gnagna Guisse defends to herself the prolonged cover-up of the truth by recalling the wisdom of the appropriate sage: 'Any truth that divides and brings discord among the members of the same family is false. The falsehood that weaves, unites and cements people together is truth.' In the middle of his frustrations over the money-order, Ibrahima Dieng's wife, Mety, spreads the rumour in the neighbourhood that their husband was robbed after he had cashed the money-order. Dieng rebukes her in this way: 'You must always speak the truth. However hard it is, you must always speak the truth.' But even as he says this, Dieng's faith in the truth is beginning to wear thin. He will soon change his mind about the truth when, ironically, he *is* robbed of the money not by pickpockets but by a relative of Mety who pretends to be a friendly and honest helper. It is this element of irony which most distinguishes *The Money-Order* from *White Genesis.* In *White Genesis* Sembène is involved with his hero. In *The Money-Order,* he is somewhat detached. (pp. 88-97)

[In] addition to his financial loss, Dieng also suffers from a broken nose at the hand of a practised apprentice of Ambrose, loses his credibility with many of those in his immediate circle and, above all, becomes cynical like the rest following his humiliation and his disillusionment with the truth.

What we have in *The Money-Order* is a crisis of faith. But it is not a crisis that is morbidly presented; rather we have a sequence in which Sembène places a good many characters, including Dieng himself, in ironic situations which point up the exploitative relationships that exist in the society at and between its successive levels. The role of protagonist fits Dieng because he remains one of those who have not yet become corrupted by the malaise and the indigence which permeate the quarter. Even his two wives are much wiser in the ways of the world than their husband whom they acknowledge as master in conformity with custom. In the face of the impatience that even his own wives show for his scruples and the vicious treatment he receives from the parasitic neighbours, the greatest plea for tolerance towards Dieng comes from Sembène himself in this comment about his hero:

> We must try and understand Ibrahima Dieng. Conditioned by years of blind, unconscious submissiveness, he fled from anything likely to cause him trouble, be it physical or moral. The blow of the fist he had received on his nose was an *atte Yallah*: the will of God. The money he had lost, too, it was ordained that it was not he who should spend it. If dishonesty seemed to have the upper hand, this was because the times were like that, not because Yallah wanted it so. These were times that refused to conform to the old tradition. In order to rid himself of his feeling of humiliation, Ibrahima Dieng invoked Yallah's omnipotence: for he was also a refuge, this Yallah. In the depths of his despair, and of the humiliation to which he had been subjected, the strength of his faith sustained him, releasing a subterranean stream of hope, but this stream also revealed vast areas of doubt. He did not, however, doubt the certainty that tomorrow would be better than today. Alas! Ibrahima Dieng did not know who would be the architect of this better tomorrow, this better tomorrow which he did not doubt.

The moral suasion of Dieng, when coupled with his simple approach to situations, stands in bold relief against a background of general cynicism, corruption and dishonesty. It is a major prop onto which much of the irony in the novelette is latched.

Ousmane directing the wedding party scene in Xala.

Although a good deal of the irony with which **White Genesis** is laced is verbal, this type of irony is often buttressed by irony of situation. We have already seen the ironic twist that the cashing of the money-order takes when Mbaye tells Dieng he has been robbed of his money. Mbaye uses the same story that Mety and Aram had invented to keep the neighbours from wheedling the money out of Dieng once it is cashed. In actual fact, Dieng has himself provided Mbaye with the story, after the dispute with Mbarka. Mbaye (a prototype for El Hadji Abdou Kader Beye, the hero of **Xala,** 1974) does not surprise us in his actions because we have been prepared for this outcome by Sembène's description of him as a member of the 'New Africa' generation, a breed of 'men who combined Cartesian logic with the influence of Islam and the atrophied energy of the Negro.' Since no difficulty is beyond him, it is easy to appreciate the enterprising solution he brings to bear when he disabuses Dieng of the bulk of the money.

Dieng has throughout the story a good deal of difficulty in establishing his identity, because at every turn the bureaucratic functionaries 'want a piece of paper to prove who I am.' This problem of identity is explored

on other levels. It is related to his 'fine clothes' which Mbarka tells him are 'just wind'. When he is mauled by Ambrose's apprentice, he returns home via the back alleys so that his neighbours will not see him in his present undignified state. But these very clothes provoke some derisive remarks and help create his identity crisis. Thus the prostitute tells him that he looks like a marabout; the letter-writer charges him with impersonating a marabout when he fails to pay fifty francs for having his letter read; Ambrose's apprentice calls him a 'fake marabout'; and in his reply to his nephew, Abdou, he himself promises to consult a 'real marabout' on Abdou's account. But the incident that tops all is the one in which he recites verses from the Koran as he thanks his Dakar nephew for the great assistance he has given him. Sembène comments thus:

> The distant cousin let him have his way. Out of the corner of his eye, he saw a policeman approaching them, feeling his chest pocket. When he reached them, the policeman looked at the two pairs of hands, at the man's face, then at the marabout (for he thought Dieng was one), and he joined his hands to theirs. Dieng took hold of one of his thumbs. He raised his forehead and his lips moved. Two passers-

by stopped and held out their hands. When he had finished murmuring, Dieng sprayed saliva all around. They all replied, 'Amine! Amine!' and rubbed their faces as they broke up.

Sembène's consistent depiction of Dieng and other characters in situations that are both ironical and laughable implies his conscious employment of satire. In a sense, it increases our sense of his detachment from the hero's predicament, in contrast to his apparent attachment to the moral stance of Dethye Law, the protagonist of *White Genesis.* The subtlety which characterizes the gently satiric tone of Sembène shows how painstaking and ingenious a craftsman he is. One will find *The Money-Order* full of structural irony only if one is ready to delve below the surface so as to discover the subterranean echoes and situational parallels that punctuate the narrative. Indeed, so replete is this work with satire and irony, that even the noble (if also humble) profession of griot is not left unscathed. Unlike Dieng's unintentional performance as a marabout, the unscrupulous Maissa, who is so determined to bilk Dieng of as much money as possible from whatever source without giving away any of his own, suddenly becomes a posturing griot 'extolling the nobel lineage of a young man dressed in European clothes: the beauty of the women, the boundless generosity and bravery of the men, the nobility of their conduct, all of it redounding on the young man, pure blood... from the purest of blood.' Although the young man is indifferent to traditional praises, he is embarrassed enough to slip Maissa a hundred-franc note in the middle of his intoning that he sings not for money but 'to keep the tradition alive.' And Dieng the 'marabout' who is at the police station trying to obtain an identity card admits that he knows 'nothing about life today', being 'overcome by Gorgui Maissa's lack of dignity in pretending to be a griot.'

Dieng's naïvety is crucial in achieving Sembène's goal of social criticism in *The Money-Order.* Yet, in spite of the exaggerations necessary to satire and such absurdities as the small amount of money which so completely dominated Dieng's world—25,000 francs CFA was the equivalent of approximately forty dollars in 1965— what Cameroonian writer Mbella Sonne Dipoko describes as 'dynamic realism' permeates this 'minor masterpiece'. This realism is even more poignant in the film. Indeed, Sembène has been widely praised and also widely upbraided, in the latter case for touches like the belching of Makhouredia Gueye (as Dieng) and an almost exclusive focus on the depressed areas of Dakar. Ironically, he has also been criticized for a lack of realism in his choice of costumes that are sometimes too colourful or dressy for the people portrayed in this and other films. The much wider audience that Sembène's films have received in both Senegal and elsewhere in Africa, justifies his badge of 'la meilleure école du soir' (the best night school) for the cinema in his country, where illiterates (like the bewildered Ibrahima Dieng) account for virtually eighty-five per cent of the population. His didactic purpose is better realized in the film than in the short novel, because the longer film is largely

in Wolof with occasional dialogue in French among the educated Senegalese. An example of his subtle touches shows Mbaye callously carrying on a telephone discussion in French with a prospective buyer for a house while its unwitting and fiercely possessive owner, Dieng, is trustingly sitting down waiting for Mbaye's help.

The use of Wolof in *Le Mandat,* Sembène's first colour film, also serves a political function. Sembène has declared himself in favour of 'un cinéma militant'. The bold use of a national language such as Wolof consequently represents a significant achievement in terms of breaking free from colonial domination, even though dependence on French came through in the process of making the film: the Wolof dialogue had to be written in French phrases that were literal translations of the as yet unwritten language of Wolof. (pp. 97-101)

Taken together, *The Money-Order* and *White Genesis,* the stories on which these two films are based, provide interesting, complementary and artistic case studies on justice, morality and honesty. Sembène is interested in a society where there will be social equality, not one in which women, as wives, will be lorded over by husbands or have to share their spouses with one or more co-wives; nor one in which people will be divided into high and low classes or professions by virtue of their birth. Still far short of this ideal, society is now encumbered by a resigned fatalism which accepts every misfortune as the will of Yallah. It is moreover, a morally and religiously bankrupt society where, according to an elder in *White Genesis*:

> The scriptures are a dead letter. For never in this village, nor in the whole of Senegal, where mosques nevertheless proliferate, not once have the penalties laid down by the holy scriptures been carried out. Go and see the authorities! We respect them and we cherish them; that seems to be all. That leaves us with the adda, the heritage of our fathers.

In *The Money-Order* it is not just that the scriptures are set aside, but that the very day-to-day communications constantly operate in a climate of mutual distrust. Mety, one of Dieng's two wives, observes at one point, 'Tell them the truth? They wouldn't believe it. It's simple: the truth isn't any use any more!' Dieng himself falls prey to the malaise when he implicitly affirms Mety's fabrication of the robbery: 'I have difficulty myself in believing it. Yet... well, honesty is a crime nowadays in this country.' The sponging Maissa tells his neighbour that 'people must help one another' and that 'man's remedy is man,' but he deserts Dieng at a time of need. The group solidarity shown by neighbours when they bring gifts to Dieng after the faked robbery is a fragile truce. The postman's assurances to Dieng that in concert they will change society is a wan hope, recalling us to Mety's observation at the outset that hope can kill. For the moment, all the dissimulation and lies help to preserve a society turned against itself, a society in which a small group of 'children'—young bureaucrats and insolent functionaries—is, in distributing the meat of prosperity reserving the choicest bits for itself and distributing the remnants unevenly among the masses. Sembène, as artist-griot, lays bare a society which subscribes to the moral of the fable that men (in spite of Gorgui Maissa) love falsehood rather than truth. (pp. 101-02)

> Jonathan A. Peters, "Sembène Ousmane as Griot: 'The Money-Order with White Genesis'," in African Literature Today, No. 12, 1982, pp. 88-103.

Harriet D. Lyons (essay date 1984)

[*In the excerpt below, Lyons examines West African folk traditions in* Xala.]

In this essay I wish to examine the film *Xala,* a work by a contemporary Senegalese novelist and film-maker, Ousmane Sembene, who has explicitly rejected the "atavistic" tendencies of the Négritude movement in favor of Marxist social realism. I hope to demonstrate not only that our understanding of the film can be increased by a knowledge of West African folk traditions but also that Dorson's notion of a "hidden" folk tradition is particularly useful in understanding an avowedly Marxist work. For Dorson believes that some of the themes and motifs of African folklore are not only pan-African but also international in distribution (in a context in which the values of the folklore-producing masses were always juxtaposed [and sometimes opposed] to those of an elite). Without this juxtaposition, Dorson believes there is no folklore; moreover, the cultural hegemony of the élite assures that all folklore is to some degree covert. Though this position may be extreme, Dorson has described a very important element of much folklore.

I shall argue that in Sembene's work the "covertness" of the folk material takes the form of suppression of detail combined with the retention of essential values. Sembene is thereby able to use folk elements in such a way as to give the work political implications that go well beyond the preservation and/or revival of a local tradition. One can, therefore, examine the folk elements of *Xala* without fear of consigning yet another expression of African creativity to the museum of primitive art. (p. 320)

At the end of Sembene's film *Xala,* the hero (or anti-hero), El Hadji Abdou Kader Beye, is forced to submit to a ritual of humiliation made all the more spectacular by its urban setting and the use of the trappings of upper-middle class life under neo-colonialism. El Hadji suffers from the *Xala,* a form of impotence caused by the curse of one who holds a grievance toward the victim. In an attempt to cure his *xala,* El Hadji has already travelled further and further from the comforts of elite, urban Dakar to seek out the services of ever more remote magical and religious practitioners. These have ranged from one who was a comic fraud, advising the middle-aged El Hadji to crawl toward the bed of his adolescent third wife carrying grotesque charms in his teeth, to Sereen Mada, a marabout, or Islamic hermit saint, renowned for his piety. The latter actually cures El Hadji's affliction, but his asceticism does not prevent him from restoring it when El Hadji's cheque bounces.

The denouement of this film and of the novel on which it is based raises a number of interesting questions, which commentators on the whole have been unable to answer and which might perhaps best be approached armed with a knowledge of certain prevalent themes in pre-colonial narratives and rituals of this region of West Africa.

One such question is why Sembene, a Marxist and a critic of some aspects of the Négritude movement's attachment to the irrational, should end a film with a ritual at all. It is apparently not the result of a sudden conversion; indeed, in the novel *Xala,* Sembene's comment on the prayers of El Hadji's pious first wife is an almost verbatim recapping of Marx's dictum on religion: "As others isolate themselves with drugs, she obtained her own daily dose from her religion."

One critic of the novel, Dorothy Blair, sees a disjunction between the bulk of the story and the ending. She suggests that Sembene, in his satirical portraits of El Hadji's circle, promises us comedy and instead "treats us to an emetic" in his sombre portrayal of El Hadji's downfall and the ritual designed to reverse it. In that ritual, El Hadji must submit to being spat upon by beggars, lepers, cripples, and assorted rejects of society. Blair sees the ritual as part of a particularly disquieting ending, in that there appears to be little hope that El Hadji will modify the corrupt ways which had led him (more than twenty years before) to cheat the beggar who leads the band out of his patrimony and, more recently, to sell rice intended for famine relief in order to finance his third marriage. Does the ritual serve any purpose, we may ask, once we rule out the possibilities that it represents either a testament to the author's religious faith or a genuine act of contrition on the part of the character?

In the program *Ousmane Sembene, Cinéaste and Novelist* broadcast by the Canadian Broadcasting Corporation (CBC) on 7 October 1980, the question was raised of a possible contradiction between Sembene's Marxism and his use of religious themes in his work. The question was answered by a reminder that, while Sembene himself is not religious, the lower-class African audience he desires to reach is religious. Themes from religion and folklore are vehicles which Sembene consciously employs to carry his message. Can we say anything, then, about Sembene's choice of ritual themes and the responses which they are likely to evoke in a West African audience? Do these themes provide a link between the social realist film and the surrealist, ritual ending? We may, perhaps, begin with the *xala* itself.

It is obvious that, as a literary conceit, the *xala* stands for the impotence of the Senegalese élite in the period which has followed independence. "What are we?" El Hadji asks the Chamber of Commerce, "Mere agents, less than petty traders. We merely redistribute. Redistribute the remains the big men deign to leave us."

The artifice by which impotence is made a secular symbol of political and economic conditions is a modern device which will almost certainly call forth in Sembene's audience associations belonging to an older system of ideas, a belief system appropriate to an enchanted universe but in certain crucial ways equivalent in its moral judgements to Sembene's own ideology. These ideas are not specific to the Wolof or to any other Senegalese group. Rather, they may be found in the mythology, folklore, and traditional exegeses of peoples throughout Francophone West Africa and perhaps other regions. In fact, much of my data is drawn from literature on the very similar traditions of the Dogon and the Bambara. The Bambara, according to A. Adu Boahen's Introduction to the English paperback edition of *God's Bits of Wood*, have retained more of non-Islamic religion than any of the other groups who commonly figure in Sembene's work; and they have brought some of those preserved items into the life of Sembene's urban milieu.

Throughout the region in question, myth and ritual draw connections between impotence, arrogance, and failure in self-control, particularly control over one's sexual impulses. Mythology and folklore are full of various sorts of tricksters who challenge God, are voracious in their lust for food and women, and are punished with actual or symbolic emasculation. One cycle of legends which draws heavily upon these themes concerns a mythic werewolf who can alternate between hyena and human form. (pp. 321-23)

Hyena-men are murderers, rapists, and thieves of food supplies. Significantly, however, they can be conquered by women or by men who use women's tools or women's wiles. Often, their insatiability is itself used by these feminine figures to lure them to their downfall. In one tale collected from a Bambara girl, a monster accosts a girl on her way home after having her hair done and threatens to eat her. She agrees to return with him to his cave, where he puts his head on her knee and demands that she search for lice (a service traditionally performed by spouses or lovers). She waits till he falls asleep and kills him with her spinning equipment.

In a hyena-man myth collected among the Bozo of Mali, impotence is attributed ironically to desire for all the trappings of powerful masculinity. In this story, a stranger arrives in a village which has been terrorized by a hyena-man who murders young husbands and then rapes and kills their wives. The stranger agrees to kill the hyena-man but only if the local chief will promise to give him his office and his wives if he succeeds. The stranger assumes female form to entrap the hyena-man and is about to kill the monster during the sexual act when the latter tells him that if he does so he must remain a woman until he dies. The two finally agree that the stranger may kill the hyena-man and resume male form if he consents to permanent impotence. He does so

and returns to the village, where he emasculates the chief in lieu of extracting the wives and title for which he no longer has any use. This, the widely known tale tells us, is the origin of impotence among men.

In this story about two characters who are in many ways spiritual cousins of El Hadji, the sacrifice of masculine prerogative is the price of power over the hyena-man, who himself knows no checks on his maleness. Ultimately, power over the hyena-man is power over both spiritual and physical decay. Hyena-men are followed by flies because they smell of excrement and are forbidden access to water, a medium which is not merely purifying but sacred in this region on the fringes of the Sahara.

It is interesting to see how many elements parallel to ones found in these tales crop up in the story of El Hadji and his ritual cure. The *xala* itself is impotence suffered as a result of greed and abuse of male sexual privilege. El Hadji has cheated the people of rice to take a third wife; he has cheated the beggar of his heritage to finance his early business ventures.

In other myths of this region, the act of incest is seen as a symbolic encapsulation of greed, arrogance, and unbridled lust. The most important Trickster of the Dogon and Bambara mythologies rapes his mother, the earth, attempts to rape his twin sister, vies for power with the creator God, and attempts to steal the seeds of all the plants meant to be food for men. He is punished by enforced circumcision, which traditional exegesis links to castration, and by permanent sterility, both of himself and of his crops. The theme of incest has been used by Sembene in *White Genesis* as a symbol for the total degeneration which has, in the case of some individuals, accompanied social change and the loss of rural values. The offender is a man of noble birth; his incestuous relationship with his daughter strips him of all mortal entitlement to his privileged position. In *White Genesis,* the community discusses killing the incestuous father, but his family griot (a person of low caste who acts as a combination praise singer and court jester to a noble) argues that, whatever the letter of the Koran may say, every man who marries a woman as young as his daughter—a category which includes a number of pillars of the community—is guilty of incest.

El Hadji, of course, does marry such a girl. El Hadji's marriage, which is of a type Sembene has elsewhere suggested may be essentially incestuous, precipitates his downward slide. It even involves him in the theft of food grains in the form of rice belonging to the National Grain Board.

It is interesting to compare the role of the griot in *White Genesis* and in *Xala,* since Sembene has been widely quoted (for example, on the CBC program mentioned earlier) as saying that the role of the filmmaker in contemporary West Africa is akin to that of the traditional griot. The griots sang the praises of their noble patrons and also attempted to defend them against accusations by others. Conversely, they had the right to speak out and rebuke their superiors for misdeeds. Their accusations could lead to purification from sin, particularly violations of sexual restrictions and abuses of privilege, though they were of a despised caste, forbidden to marry with the free-born. Purification could thus be attained through submitting to verbal abuse from the lowly. As "griot," Sembene the novelist and filmmaker is exposing his society's misdeeds in the hope of effecting purification. The actual griots in the film, unlike the admirable griots in *White Genesis,* have been reduced to mere cyphers and entertainers. Female griots wear money pinned to their dresses while greeting guests at El Hadji's wedding, an event which epitomizes the greed, lust, and addiction to power of El Hadji and his circle.

Speechmaking at ceremonies marking changes of status (for example, at weddings or funerals) was one of the griot's traditional functions. These speeches were often highly satirical. The use of satire links the griot with joking relatives who throughout Africa have assumed the function of purification from sin and who have the privilege of insulting and abusing each other when they meet. Insult, joking, and the license to tell the truth about another's character thus possess the power to remove sin and the afflictions caused by sin. We have already seen that in this region "sin" is largely equated with sexual lust, greed, and unmerited arrogance. The real griots in the film become greedy flatterers like the rest of society. Sembene, who aspires to the griot's role, constructs a new ritual of purification. This ritual employs a number of symbols very much in keeping with the ways prescribed for combatting pollution by traditional myth and ritual as well as with Sembene's view of social satire of the rest of the film. It is a restatement of that socially purifying satire in terms of a few widely recognizable visual symbolic images.

This is not to say that Sembene requires belief in a theology. Indeed, Sembene has said that his film is an attack on a "double fetishism," the traditional fetishism of the marabouts and the contemporary fetishism of western commodities. To an audience familiar with their context, certain items in Sembene's ritual are simply symbolic restatements of the message that purification comes from listening to the truths known by those your society despises, abandoning greed, and ceasing to use one's status and one's sex as means for assuming the privileges of the gods. Such traditional scholarly distinctions as that between "magic" and "religion" are irrelevant to Sembene; his quest is for elements of traditional belief and practice which articulate with his own moral vision. As various types of structural and semiotic analyses of film and literature have made clear, a carefully chosen symbolic item like a child's sled and the relationship of that item to other items, present or absent, can suggest, largely unconsciously, a whole chain of associations not actually spelled out on the page or screen, and thus deliver a complex message within the confines of a poem or a film, neither of which allows for much didactic commentary.

Thus, it does not matter whether El Hadji, Sembene, or the audience "believes" in El Hadji's cure; what matters is the associations which will be evoked by the symbols employed in effecting it, particularly upon persons of West African cultural background. Moreover, since some of the items, such as a special mystic virtue adhering to the lowly, are part of the European tradition as well, some of the messages will be decoded by non-African audiences. Indeed, many of these are among the messages which Dorson sees as embedded in folk traditions generally.

What, though, *are* the precise symbols and messages in Sembene's urban proletarian ritual? Here we must look at the specific images employed in the light of our mythic themes.

In the myths and legends we have mentioned, excessive maleness must be curbed if real power over evil is to be achieved. The stranger must accept impotence (or total femininity) to conquer the hyena-man. In the trickster myths, the sequel to the forced circumcision of the trickster, which simply deprives him of male power, is a voluntary castration on the part of a god, which paradoxically restores fertility to the world. To rid himself of his *xala*, El Hadji must, like some of the opponents of hyena-man, accept an appurtenance of femininity—one, moreover, belonging to a female he had hoped to conquer and had given to him in her stead. While the beggars spit on him, he must wear the crown from his third wife's wedding veil. Crowns on wedding veils are, in fact, a European symbol, which in this context may be associated with two different social ironies: the lowering of status, which Africans accept when they seek the tokens of prestige of their oppressors; and the subordination to a master, which women have traditionally accepted when they put on stately garments for their wedding ceremonies. In the traditional African context, the male acceptance of the feminine principle in order to acquire power over pollution was not intended to effect the emancipation of women; indeed, the statement made by males in such roles depends upon an equivalence between femininity and subordination. It takes, however, only a slight twist to add a new secular meaning to this symbolism. If the gods are not to step into the power vacuum left by men who acknowledge their limitations, as was traditionally the case, women may move into that gap. This would certainly be consistent with Sembene's generally intense concern and respect for African women, upon which many critics have remarked.

Not only does El Hadji wear a woman's wedding crown, but the pajama bottoms he clutches around his waist and his massive wristwatch adjacent to his naked chest accord him less dignity than the total nudity allowed him in the novel. They are pathetic trappings of former glory, their incongruousness a product of his harboring of toys of the colonizer and the dependency such harboring has brought about.

During the spitting, the foreground of the set is occupied by rows of empty bottles which once contained the soft drinks and mineral waters which El Hadji, at the height of his arrogance, employed to separate himself from even the waters of his native land. Hyena-men and other evil forces in myth are punished by being banned from the rivers and by the failure of rain to water their crops; the action of *Xala* takes place against a background of devastating drought. It is symbolic of the entire nature of El Hadji's "power" that he has been dependent upon bottled water from Europe even to wash his car; the car washing scene and the ritual scene are linked visually by the presence in both of a plastic pail, prominently placed on the right side of the screen. When El Hadji is finally forced to share his foreign waters with his countrymen, the fluid from the empty bottles is returned to him in the form of their spit.

Those who would assume high status in African societies, that is to say nobles and divine kings, are frequently forced to undergo abuse from those over whom they would elevate themselves. The griots' privilege of abusing their betters to remind them of their duties is one example of this type of social fact; in all cases, the spiritual well-being of the entire community depends on the abuse. A secular equivalent of this sort of practice is very evident in the ritual degradation of El Hadji. He is surrounded by a total cross-section of the lower orders of society, those over whom his kind have assumed superiority: beggars, cripples, his disinherited kinsman, and a peasant who has been robbed of his entire community's pathetic savings by the cowboy-hatted successor to El Hadji's seat in the Chamber of Commerce. There is even a student in jeans and workshirt. Like El Hadji, he has adopted European dress, but it is not the evening dress or business suit of El Hadji's cronies; rather it is the universal uniform which the international student community donned at a certain point in its history to demonstrate solidarity with the oppressed. This student, with his Wolof language newspaper, strikes a somewhat discordant note among the rags of the beggars. (Sembene's treatment of El Hadji's student activist daughter throughout the film has indicated that he appreciates both the good intentions and the limitations of children of the privileged classes who wish to lead revolutions.)

These are the people who strip El Hadji down to size, but in this case there is no noble role to which he may then return, suitably purified. He, too, has become one of the wretched of the earth, but the house and furniture which he has been prudent enough to put in his wife's name will insulate him from the full purifying effect of his wretchedness.

Traditional resolutions of the paradoxes of power depended upon the good will of gods whose existence Sembene does not recognize; a modern resolution to our ritual drama would require political good will which is equally nonexistent. Sembene can only use ritual trappings to define the terms of what Wole Soyinka has called his "aggressive, secular vision." Because he

cannot accept the false resolution of mystification, either traditional mystification or that revived by the Négritude movement, Sembene is left still awaiting a real solution to the paradoxes whose symbols he has forced us to observe. Meanwhile, he will attempt to use the cinema to restore a voice to those whose claims were heard in folklore and ritual but whom colonial and post-colonial discourse have silenced. (pp. 323-27)

> *Harriet D. Lyons, "The Uses of Ritual in Sembene's 'Xala',"* in Canadian Review of African Studies, *Vol. 18, No. 2, 1984, pp. 319-28.*

Brenda F. Berrian (essay date 1986)

[*In the following excerpt, Berrian examines the female characters in Ousmane's short story collection* Tribal Scars.]

If there is one enduring presentation in African literature it is the African mother. From the Soundiata epic to the epistolary novel, *Une si longue lettre* (1979) by the deceased Mariama Bâ, reverence for the African mother is expressed in various forms. In the past, the traditional African mother has been a Queen Mother, a trader, a soldier, an organizer of protest demonstrations, and the nurturer of future generations of children. Cognizant of the role that the mother plays in African societies is Ousmane Sembène, who prefers to set his female characters in their traditional settings as mothers and wives, in order to illustrate specific political and social points of view. Through the women, Sembène notes that in order for them to have new perceptions of themselves and to develop a more defined self-awareness, their men should no longer be the determining factor in their lives. Sembène is convinced that changes in social and political structures and attitudes in Africa are necessary if the African woman is to realize her full potential and importance in the future of her country.

A self-taught man, writer, and filmmaker from Senegal, Sembène is devoted to writing about African people and their aspirations. Most importantly, he is one of the first African writers to move his female characters from a secondary role, in which they compliment their men, to a primary one in which they express their feelings, hurts, joys, and think and react to pressing situations. For instance, in four selected short stories from *Voltaïque. Nouvelles* (1962) [*Tribal Scars*] Sembène introduces his mother who demands custody of her children at a divorce hearing; the mother who defies a tyrannical king in defense of her daughter; the mother who confronts her neglectful husband with his callousness, and finally, the mother who comes to terms with her marriage to a much older man.

In the short story, **"The Bilal's Fourth Wife,"** Sembène slips in modern ideas about marriage and divorce in a traditional village setting where he presents the couple, Suliman and Yacine. Suliman, a man past middle-age, takes great pains to present himself as a pious, devout

Moslem and family man before the public whereas, in private, he berates and beats his three wives unmercifully. His appetite for women younger than his daughters has not waned, and he takes advantage of his position as the bilal of the village mosque to make lecherous remarks and to fondle them. Because of his carefully preserved public image as a humble man and a guardian of polygamy, the young victimized women dare not complain expecting that their cries of outrage would not be believed. As the story progresses, Suliman is so consumed with his lust for young women that he fails to keep the mosque clean. Sympathetic male villagers take it upon themselves to find a fourth wife for Suliman in the person of the young, Yacine N'Doye.

Yacine, a 20-year old former "tomboy," is deemed to be a good candidate for Suliman's fourth wife for she has frightened the young men in the village with her outspokenness. Presumably, an older man like Suliman will be able to tame and mold her into a submissive wife, since it is assumed that she is naive and ignorant of her rights and sexual desires as a woman. Although Yacine would have liked to raise some objections, she follows her father's wishes and marries Suliman. Later, after three years of marriage and a son, the bored Yacine takes Suliman's nephew as her lover, as Suliman's sexual drive is diminishing. Her decision to take a lover is justifiable, for, in her mind, she is in her physical prime and married to a man she does not love. However, this triangle—wife, husband, and lover—becomes the main topic of village gossip when Yacine bears a son for her lover. In an attempt to salvage his tarnished image and manhood, Suliman vents his rage and jealousy upon his three wives and demands a divorce from Yacine. To his surprise, his demand receives a rebuttal from Yacine.

In **"The Bilal's Fourth Wife"** Sembène, with great humor, pokes fun at Senegalese attitudes toward divorce. He attacks the practice of double moral standards, which place women at a disadvantage. Sembène uses the character of Yacine to question and to disagree with the patriarchal Moslem marriage rules drawn up by males centuries ago. In spite of the rumors and intense external pressures, Yacine reveals a tremendous self-confidence. First, she refuses to be coerced by Suliman and her family into a divorce. Second, she is adamant about being treated on equal footing as a woman by the Cadi (special council of male elders called to review her case). Third, she questions why the woman is not free to take a lover when a man in a Moslem society can have four wives with the approval of the Koran and legal laws. These unyielding stances force the male elders to accept, with reluctance, the fact that there are two sides to every marital disagreement, and the woman's position is just as important as the man's.

As for Suliman, he has been made the laughing stock of the village by his inability to control his wife. His ego suffers a beating due to his physical limitations of not satisfying his young wife's sexual needs. What is at stake is Suliman's determination to humiliate Yacine publicly, for she has flaunted her relationship with his nephew with the birth of a child. Double standards, which govern the behavior of men and women in a Moslem polygamous marriage, are addressed again when Suliman asks for custody of his "son" and the return of the dowry.

Suliman does not regard Yacine as a human being who has feelings and rights, but as one of his possessions who is expected to boost his ego. A woman's place, he feels, is to obey her husband and to build her life around him. When his possession (Yacine) no longer brings him pleasure or bends to his needs, he must squash or beat it into submission as he has done with the other three wives. Since Yacine will not conform and retreat into the expected docility, Suliman tries to use psychological pressure and works within the traditional legal system to bring about her downfall. He becomes obsessed with the need to cause Yacine deep pain. Yacine's indiscretion must be exposed to draw attention away from his own inadequacies.

As mentioned before, through Yacine's protests and the divorce hearing, Sembène brings forth the argument that traditional Moslem marriage laws should be reevaluated and rewritten to protect the rights of women too. In support of Sembène's argument, Yacine demands that Suliman should return her virginity knowing full-well that virginity is highly prized and is linked to one's honor and esteem. With this brave announcement, she makes clear that something precious has been taken away from her—her honor and respectability.

Yacine's request to have her virginity returned is a clever tactic and approach in presenting her case in court. She knows that she was more valuable when she was chaste and that her value dropped with her affair with Suliman's nephew, making her second-hand merchandise. Suliman too cannot bear knowing that his wife has been handled by somebody else. His pride and respect have been challenged. He also fears Yacine's power over him—the power of informing the villagers of his sexual weakness.

Since Suliman cannot physically return Yacine's virginity and make her "pure as spring water" again, Yacine hopes that her request will enable the villagers to be more sympathetic toward her. The question then becomes why should women in Moslem marriages hand over the custody of their children to their former husbands. Fortunately, Froh-Toll, the head of the Cadi, is wise enough to debate the custody topic and rules in favor of Yacine with the statement:

> So by what right does Suliman demand custody of the child? There can always be doubt as to who is the father of a child. But never as to who is the mother.

With this pronouncement, Froh-Toll supports women's child rearing rights, which is an admirable step.

In Moslem societies, attitudes toward adultery are one-sided. Traditional customs tend to endorse the fact that married men engaged in extra-marital affairs cannot commit adultery, only women. The Senegalese society is built upon a patriarchal system with a Moslem/Christian/Animist religious foundation. As a consequence, the person who passes judgement on men and women is a man; the society, in which men and women operate, is male dominated. In the eyes of traditional Moslem law, the man's word is accepted as being truthful and binding, but the woman's word does not have the status and legitimacy. So while Suliman is not chastised for engaging in a sexual act with a young woman in the village, the villagers agree that Yacine should be punished for her affair. Yacine's actions upset the value system, which supports the idea that women must be faithful to their husbands. Consequently, her conscious revolt becomes a social act against the antiquated Moslem divorce laws and ingrained value systems.

Sembène's short story, **"The Mother"** is another example of the application of double moral standards in a Moslem society in Africa. This point is presented through the personage of the tyrannical king. The king, who has no intentions of cultivating the love and respect of his constituents, alienates himself and evokes the hatred and fear of his subjects to the point that they dream about seeing him burnt alive. Meanwhile, these same subjects are passive and obey the king's orders to murder men over fifty-years old. Thus, the king thinks that he owes no allegiance to anyone. He proceeds to pass a law that he will deflower every virgin before she is married. Over the years, only a few brave mothers succeed in saving their daughters from such a fate. When it is time for the king's daughter to marry, he repeals the law—separate rules for the poor and rich.

For the king, women represent danger, and he wishes to destroy them. By his actions, it appears that he harbours a deep hatred for women and cannot resist raping them. This psychological deviant is confused, insecure, and enjoys exerting his power through violent means. The king obviously likes inflicting pain upon women, because they are said to be the weaker sex.

Since nobody has the courage to defy the king's orders, the people's fears increase. It is only when the king travels that he encounters open resistance to his overtures from a young woman he fancies. In anger he has her locked up. The young woman's mother, a woman of "certain age," fights and pushes past the six feet tall servants to gain an audience with the king. The mother verbally battles and accuses him of outlandish and unfit behavior. Further, she courageously looks the king directly in his eyes and attacks him for not showing any respect for the mothers in the kingdom. She makes the point that without the love and tenderness of his mother he would not have been born. The king responds by slapping her face.

The subjects jump to the mother's defense after the king's display of anger and guilt. The mother's words had hit their target shaming the remaining males in the kingdom for their cowardice and failure to protect their women folk. The king's rule has been divisive and had led to the distrust of one another to the detriment of the society. This exhibition of internal strength and resilience by the mother topples the king's government. One conclusion is that anyone, male or female, who abuses power will not keep it.

Clearly, the king and the mother during their confrontation had struck each other in their most vulnerable spots, he on her face, and she at his ego. Yet a reversal of roles emerges for the so-called weak, defenseless mother becomes the stronger of the two. Without his bodyguards to shield him, the king, like most bullies, is defenseless. His deliberate attempt to limit the freedom of women ultimately results in the loss of his kingdom as a consequence of the words spoken by the African mother.

There is another interesting aspect in the Mother's depiction. One could say that Sembène has succumbed to one of the biased attitudes directed toward women when he describes the mother as ugly. However, it could also be said that Sembène deliberately calls the mother ugly, because of its common use in Senegalese society for strong-willed women. In African literature the good woman, who stays in her place, is always gentle, kind, and beautiful, but the woman, who possesses the courage to debate male prerogatives, is frequently labeled or pictured as a physically ugly person. Thus Sembène ends this story by singing praises in honor of mothers who rise up to protect their children.

This particular story argues that one's biological origin and sex do not alleviate one's responsibility to the collective community. Making the female character in **"The Mother"** bigger than life is characteristic of Sembène in both his films and literary works to convince and draw attention to the African woman's special place in contemporary African society. The men, in the story **"The Mother,"** were paralyzed with fear and failed to challenge the maniacal orders of the king. They also did nothing to overthrow the king-dictator. It was the woman, the mother, who came to the men's rescue. By magnifying the character of the mother Sembène scolds the men for their moral impotence and reproaches them for their lack of position action to oppose the king's oppressive policies.

The mother has done what is necessary to save and protect her daughter. She is, as [Anne] Lippert would say, "super human in her love." The mother may be ugly on the outside, but she is beautiful inside with her concern for her child's misfortune. She possesses spiritual qualities which allow her to look directly into the king's evil heart. This special power permits the mother to weave a hypnotic spell on the male listeners, causes them to grab the king, and renders them half-conscious of the fact that they have aided the mother in her triumph over the king.

Mores of another kind are explored in the short story, **"Her Three Days,"** where one meets Noumbé, the third wife of Mustapha. When the story opens Noumbé is preparing for her husband's visit during her allotted three days as dictated by the Koran. Drawing upon his filmmaking skills Sembène zooms in on Noumbé to show her haggard face, her weakened body after the bearing of five children in rapid succession, her anxieties and fears of being replaced by the fourth wife, and her fight to handle a heart condition. Although Noumbé is still young, she looks older because of her full financial duties of providing for her children.

In a sympathetic voice Sembène attacks the misuse of polygamy. If a man marries more than one wife, he is to treat them equally and not differentiate between them. This is a difficult task and even the best of men find that there is always one wife that he prefers among the group. For this reason, the remaining wives do not enjoy their husbands' companionship on an equal basis. In **"Her Three Days"** Mustapha prefers his fourth and youngest wife. It is his fourth wife's turn to be flattered and spoiled by him, and he casts aside his other three wives.

Relying upon a technique that worked successfully in *Les Bouts de bois de Dieu* (1960), Sembène delays Mustapha's entrance until the last pages of the short story. In this way, Mustapha is seen through Noumbé's eyes and thoughts. Hence, Mustapha is known before he actually appears in the text. Leaving Mustapha's entrance until the end of **"Her Three Days"** creates the necessary suspense and enables the sensitive reader to feel the internal struggles and pains that Noumbé undergoes during her long wait for Mustapha. With this combination of sympathy for Noumbé and tension it is not impossible to understand why she lashes out at Mustapha on the eve of his arrival on the third day.

During these three days of waiting Noumbé has cooked Mustapha's favorite dishes, beautified herself, dressed with extreme care, saved the meat, and borrowed money from her next-door neighbor to ensure Mustapha's comfort. When Mustapha does not show after two days and fails to send a message, Noumbé's physical pain is almost as great as her mental pain. While dosing herself with medicine to prevent a heart attack, Noumbé wonders why she and her three co-wives allow themselves to be Mustapha's playmates and wives of one man. She contemplates divorce, the hypocrisy of the co-wives in their pretense of happiness, and ponders how to escape from such an unsatisfying and demeaning relationship.

Apparently, these thoughts frighten Noumbé somewhat because they are in contradiction with her upbringing. She has been raised to be a submissive wife dependent upon her husband's whims, just as Mustapha's personality and behavior have been formed by years of indoctrination that the male is the dominant person in a male/female relationship. As his "right" and with the support of Moslem doctrines the acquisition of four wives is linked with his virility and manliness. As for Noumbé she has achieved status and esteem with her marriage and the births of her five children. Companionship, mutual respect, and sharing are not part of the bargain.

Mustapha has an exaggerated sense of his ego and masculinity. With an air of impatience he comes to see Noumbé at the end of the third day demanding that she serve him and his two male companions. No words of comfort or apologies pass across his lips. In response, Noumbé displays a sarcastic side of her personality in an attempt to preserve some shred of dignity. This small rebellious act brings on a mild heart attack, and Mustapha calmly leaves Noumbé to fend for herself while announcing his horror and disbelief that the Malian government has just passed a resolution condemning polygamy.

The collectivity of female support in the compound is demonstrated when the women rush to Noumbé's aid. It is characteristic of Sembène to show how the women come together and lend each other their strength and advice. On the first day of Noumbé's three days of waiting the women sing to share Noumbé's happiness and unconcealed joy. When Mustapha fails to show up, Aida, the next-door neighbor, kindly helps Noumbé and offers to keep her company. For fear of hurting her feelings the women stay away from Noumbé and avoid meeting her eyes so that she can save "face." However, they all run to her defense when she collapses from the strain of asserting herself before Mustapha. In short, the women come together because they know that their turn to be the displaced wife is coming. Still, Noumbé is resolved to be a mother and resigned to joining ranks with her abandoned co-wives. She once loved Mustapha, but she now rejects him. Her sense of self-worth is linked with common sense and necessity; therefore, she will not leave Mustapha for she is entrenched in Moslem traditions.

Without a doubt, Sembène wants his readers to note that Noumbé is a victim of circumstances. At the same time, he wants his readers to know that African women are also guilty of accepting rules imposed upon them and are responsible for some of the social evils. Noumbé's physical pain ties in with her timid knowledge that she is not pleased with her marriage. She submerges the thought that she is a playmate, since it is uncharacteristic for a devoted wife to question her plight. All of her life Noumbé has been groomed to be a good wife and mother, but not at the expense of her dignity. The waiting and the slow disintegration of hope cause her to mock Mustapha, who throws around his authority. Sembène's silent suggestion is that it is up to African men and women to solve their difficulties and take the initiative to improve their lot.

By lingering over Noumbé's suffering, jealousy, loneliness, and anger Sembène pleads the case against the African male's misuse of polygamy: their failure to treat each wife equally in all ways, including their failure to provide each with adequate financial, temporal and emotional support.

Like Noumbé, Nafi in **"Letters from France"** has been raised in a patriarchal society where man rules over woman, and one class over another. Viewed as a second-class citizen by her society and father, she is tricked into marrying a 73-year old man, who lives in Marseilles, France. The topic of love is not entertained for marriage is based on loneliness, a wish to live in France, and an old man's desire to retain his lost youth. Nafi, the young wife, will serve Demba, her husband, be an instrument for his pleasure, bear his children, greet his friends, and care for him in his old age. By selecting a young wife, like Suliman in **"The Bilal's Fourth Wife,"** Demba hopes that she will be easier to control and thereby gain much from the unbalanced relationship. Unfortunately, the carefully laid plan backfires when Demba succumbs to cancer.

Alone in a damp room with four walls in Marseilles, Nafi has plenty of time to reflect upon her situation and to examine, in a proper perspective, the social and moral values that are imposed upon Senegalese women. What she sees and comes to terms with (as Yacine and Noumbé did) is that she has to bear some of the blame for her marriage. She also must admit that she was initially pleased with the possibility of living in France, and smitten with the picture of a handsome young Senegalese man. The adjustment and the astonishment occur when Nafi arrives in Marseilles to learn that the young man in the photo is actually seventy-three years old.

In isolation for the first time in her life, cut off from sunshine, gaiety, and human warmth, Nafi rebels through the medium of letters to her girl friend in Senegal. She implores her anonymous girl friend, who is her link with the happy past, to believe in her. Nafi feels that she has touched "rock bottom" with her marriage to Demba. She is furious that she has married an old, unemployed man without a pension, cannot bear for him to touch her, and even wishes to contract a mysterious disease. As the story develops, Nafi is reduced to begging for a job for her husband with a shipping company, when she learns that she is pregnant. Divorce is contemplated, but she has no independent means and no friends to turn to for aid in Marseilles. Nafi's future brightens, however, when Demba is given a short-term job on a ship, sends money to her, and asks a young dock worker, Arona, to watch over her. Closed in with a crying baby, sad to find that Demba has cancer upon his return, but miserable enough not to play the role of a grieving wife, **"Letters from France"** reaches a melodramatic climax when Nafi tells Demba, on his death bed, that she is returning to Senegal.

Demba's elderly friends are greatly disappointed in Nafi for her failure to conform and exhibit some compassion for Demba. Nafi's explanation is that she is in an incompatible marriage locked in by loneliness. Her dreams to be independent and her own mistress haunt her. Nafi is not ashamed to confess to her girl friend that she had wished for Demba's death in order to be free. Nevertheless, her release does not come until the same elderly friends of Demba meet to decide her fate. Thanks to Arona's intervention she does not have to be hypocritical by mourning Demba for the required 40 days. The decision is that she will be sent back home.

With bitterness and relief, Nafi's past, present, and future have been monitored by male decisions. She is basically shy and innocent in Marseilles and finds it difficult to relate to the French and other Blacks. Nafi, who has some formal education, is a traditional young woman, who is not satisfied with her life. Although she protests loudly to her girl friend in her letters, she lacks the independence to rebel. Without recognizing it, Nafi is tied to her beliefs in the security of the clan and the extended family. There is an awareness that times are changing, but this does not lead her to disobey her father and husband. It is Demba's death that frees her from despair and makes it possible for her to return to Senegal.

Martin T. Bestman notes that: 'Sembène paints the image of Africa that is convulsive, a world that questions its norms and values." Indeed, Sembène does not hesitate to take to task such explosive topics as child paternity, adultery, arranged polygamous marriages, tyrannical men, divorce, child custody, and the imposition of double moral standards upon women. He identifies these issues and explores them in his fiction as a committed social critic. Sembène is committed to defending the rights of African women by insisting that they need to reclaim the economic, political, and social positions that they had held in the past. He is not afraid to expose the contradictions that control people's actions, and the collision with their menfolk that occurs when women assert themselves.

Sembène's female characters are not losers. In the four short stories each woman triumphs no matter how small the victory. By presenting such women Sembène opens up opportunities for African women to develop a more positive self-awareness and to draw upon capacities that have laid dormant within themselves. In order for Senegalese women to move forward, they must cast off outdated ideas and modes of behavior and view their plight realistically. In short, they must place themselves on the outside in order to look in. By doing so, they may begin to take steps to eliminate ignorance and mass illiteracy and improve their status in the twentieth-century. All four women—Yacine, the mother, Noumbé, and Nafi—challenge the traditional order, which condemned them to a secondary role. They, as mothers, are believable as characters. They, as mothers and women, through the prism of social and political contexts, will turn their faces to the future with hope for the future generation, their children. (pp. 195-204)

Brenda F. Berrian, "Through Her Prism of Social and Political Contexts: Sembène's Female Characters in 'Tribal Scars'," in Ngambika: Studies of Women in African Literature, *edited by Carole Boyce Davies and Anne Adams Graves, Africa World Press, Inc., 1986, pp. 195-204.*

FURTHER READING

Bayo, Ogunjimi. "Ritual Archetypes—Ousmane's Aesthetic Medium in *Xala." Ufahamu: Journal of the African Activist Association,* No. 3 (1985): 128-38.
Explores Ousmane's use of cultural motifs to express modern social structures.

Harrow, Kenneth. "Art and Ideology in *Les Bouts de bois de Dieu*: Realism's Artifices." *The French Review* 62, No. 3 (February 1989): 483-93.
Examines the structure of *Les bouts de bois de Dieu* as a realist technique.

McGilligan, Patrick, and Perry, G. M. "Ousmane Sembene: An Interview." *Film Quarterly* XXVI, No. 3 (Spring 1973): 36-42.
Interview with Ousmane, focusing on cinematography in Africa.

Ojo, S. Ade. "Revolt, Violence and Duty in Ousmane Sembene's *God's Bits of Wood." Nigeria* 53, No. 3 (July-September 1985): 58-68.
Discusses *God's Bits of Wood* as a Marxist-inspired protest novel.

Pfaff, Françoise. *The Cinema of Ousmane Sembene, A Pioneer of African Film.* Westport, Conn.: Greenwood Press, 1984, 207 p.
Study of Ousmane's career and influences, including detailed analyses of individual films.

Sevastakis, Michael. "Neither Gangsters Nor Dead Kings." *FLQ: Film Library Quarterly* 6, No. 3 (Summer 1973): 13-23, 40-48.
Examines Ousmane's films *La Noire de . . . , Borom Sarret, Mandabi, Tauw,* and *Emitai* as products of a "cautious revolutionary" who offers his characters no escape from their plights.

Gordon Parks

1912-

American autobiographer, poet, novelist, essayist, photographer, filmmaker, composer, and journalist.

Many critics consider Parks a modern Renaissance man. He is the author of four autobiographies, a novel, several volumes of poetry, and a collection of essays. He is also a noted musician, composer, film director, producer, and photographer. The wide scope of his expertise is all the more impressive when viewed in its historical context, for many of the fields in which he succeeded were once closed to blacks. Parks was the first black to work at *Life* magazine, *Vogue,* the Office of War Information, and the Farm Security Administration. He was also the first black to write, direct, produce, and score a film, "The Learning Tree," based on his 1963 autobiographical novel. Parks is modest about his achievements: "I did what I had to do. The first black this, the first black that. I don't appreciate that as much as people think I do. I have no doubt there were other blacks who could have done it just as well or a lot better. But through some misfortune, they didn't have the strength to withstand the racism, the intolerance or the pressures. I was fortunate enough to have come from a good family who gave me love and faith in myself."

The youngest of fifteen children, Parks grew up poor in Fort Scott, Kansas. He had a close relationship with his family, particularly his mother, who taught him to value honesty and equality. Even as a young boy, he was ambitious and vowed to make something of himself. When Parks was sixteen, his mother died. He went to live with his sister and her husband in Minnesota, but after an argument with his brother-in-law, he was thrown out of the house. Penniless and alone on the streets, he struggled to support himself with odd jobs—playing piano in a brothel and mopping floors at a slum hotel—and ate whatever he could find to keep from starving, even fighting a dog for a dead pigeon. In 1935 he found steady work as a dining car waiter on a train. While flipping through magazines left behind by passengers, he decided to become a photographer. Shortly thereafter he bought his first camera and began taking pictures of everyday life among blacks. Impressed by Parks's talents, an owner of an Eastman Kodak store helped the author's budding career by hosting a show of his photographs in Minneapolis. As his documentary work became increasingly known, Parks branched out to other areas and began photographing fashion models in Chicago. In 1942 he moved to Washington, D. C., to work for the Farm Security Administration photography department. His best-known FSA photograph is entitled "American Gothic, Washington, D.C."—a portrait of a black cleaning woman with a mop in one hand, a broom in the other, and an American flag behind her. When the FSA disbanded in 1943, Parks went to work for *Life* and

Vogue. During the 1950s he traveled extensively and completed over 300 assignments for *Life,* including reports on American ghettos, the Black Muslims, the Black Panthers, civil rights leaders, and world celebrities.

Parks found, however, that despite his love of and expertise in photography, he needed to express in words his intense feelings about his childhood. This need resulted in his first novel, *The Learning Tree* (1963). The novel concerns the Wingers, a black family living in a small town in Kansas during the 1920s, and focuses on Newt, the Wingers's adolescent son. "On one level, it is the story of a particular Negro family who manages to maintain its dignity and self-respect as citizens and decent human beings in a border Southern town," observed Jane Ball. "On another, it is a symbolic tale of the black man's struggle against social, economic, and natural forces, sometimes winning, sometimes losing." A *Time* reviewer commented: "[Parks's] unabashed nostalgia for what was good there, blended with sharp recollections of staggering violence and fear, makes an immensely readable, sometimes unsettling book."

Parks explored his life further in three other autobiographical volumes: *A Choice of Weapons* (1966), *To Smile in Autumn: A Memoir* (1979), and *Voices in the Mirror: An Autobiography* (1990). *A Choice of Weapons* begins when Parks is sixteen and describes how, after his mother's death, he found himself out on the street. He recounts his struggle to feed and clothe himself, all the while cultivating his ambition to be a photographer. The book's theme, according to *Washington Post* contributor Christopher Schemering, is that "one's choice of weapons must be dignity and hard work over the self-destructive, if perhaps understandable, emotions of hate and violence." Alluding to the unfortunate circumstances of his youth, Parks expressed a similar view in the *Detroit News:* "I have a right to be bitter, but I would not let bitterness destroy me. As I tell young black people, you can fight back, but do it in a way to help yourself and not destroy yourself."

To Smile in Autumn, Parks's third autobiographical volume, covers the years from 1943 to 1979. In this work Parks celebrates "the triumph of achievement, the abundance and glamour of a productive life," wrote *New York Times Book Review* contributor Mel Watkins. Parks also acknowledges, however, that his success was not without a price: "In escaping the mire, I had lost friends along the way.... In one world I was a social oddity. In the other world I was almost a stranger." Reviewing *To Smile in Autumn,* Ralph Tyler perceptively concluded: "Although this third memoir doesn't have the drama inherent in a fight for survival, it has a drama of its own: the conflict confronting a black American who succeeds in the white world."

Parks's fourth autobiographical book, *Voices in the Mirror,* reveals a more personal side of the author. Here Parks offers his impressions of the civil rights movement and the black power struggles of the 1960s and describes his encounters with Dwight D. Eisenhower, Winston Churchill, Malcolm X, Sugar Ray Robinson, and Ingrid Bergman, among others. In the book's epilogue, Parks writes: "I still have a passion for living, so this is no farewell, but rather the gathering in of observations I hope will make someone else's trials easier to bear.... What I give here is meant to show how I try to drum up courage to keep going."

In addition to his autobiographical writings and other literary publications, Parks has also produced several films: *The Learning Tree* (1968), *Shaft* (1971), *Shaft's Big Score* (1972), *The Super Cops* (1974), and *Leadbelly* (1976). His most recent project is *Martin* (1990), a ballet celebrating the life of Martin Luther King, Jr. He is currently at work on a biography of the eighteenth-century English painter J. M. W. Turner. Parks is a man with varied interests and talents; when asked why he is involved in so many different fields, he replied: "For a long time I passed it off as a sort of professional restlessness. But, in retrospect, I know that it was a

desperate search for security within a society that held me inferior simply because I was black. It was a constant inner rebellion against failure. I was a poor black boy who wanted to be somebody. So I created desires until I was drowning neck deep in them before I would attempt to swim my way out.... Perhaps if I had been fortunate enough to have gone on to college, to study medicine, engineering or whatever, I would not have become involved in so many other things. More than likely I would have given all my time to one chosen avocation. As it happened I tried several fields. In case one failed me I could turn to another one.... I was forced to rid myself of the insecurities that the lack of education brought me. But, in retrospect, I honestly say that I enjoyed the uncertainty of the broader and more precarious adventure." Parks continued, "...people often ask, given the choice of growing up a well-bred white boy bound for Yale and groomed to be a physician, wouldn't you rather have that? I say, in spite of the bruises, the scars, the brutality, I wouldn't have it any other way."

(For further information about Parks's life and works, see *Black Writers; Contemporary Authors,* Vols. 41-44; *Contemporary Authors New Revision Series,* Vol. 26; *Contemporary Literary Criticism,* Vols. 1, 16; *Dictionary of Literary Biography,* Vol. 33: *Afro-American Fiction Writers after 1955;* and *Something about the Author,* Vol. 8.)

PRINCIPAL WORKS

Flash Photography (nonfiction) 1947
The Learning Tree (autobiographical novel) 1963
A Choice of Weapons (autobiography) 1966
Gordon Parks: A Poet and His Camera (poetry) 1968
Born Black (essays) 1971
Gordon Parks: Whispers of Intimate Things (poetry) 1971
In Love (poetry) 1971
Moments without Proper Names (poetry) 1975
Flavio (essay) 1978
To Smile in Autumn: A Memoir (autobiography) 1979
Shannon (novel) 1981
†*Martin* (libretto) 1990
Voices in the Mirror: An Autobiography (autobiography) 1990

*These works include photographs by Parks.
†This work, a ballet in five acts, includes original music by Parks.

David Dempsey (essay date 1963)

[*In the following essay, Dempsey offers a generally negative review of* The Learning Tree, *describing it as a "rambling sort of novel held together by a string of melodramatic events."*]

The idea that nostalgia forms the basis for the novel of childhood is put to the test when the writer is a Negro. Just how much delight is there in growing up black? Richard Wright, in *Black Boy,* found very little. But in the character of young Newt Winger, in ***The Learning Tree*** Gordon Parks seems to remember a youth in which color was no bar to happiness, and at times even became the spur to adventure. Color furnishes the plot devices of the story without predetermining the moral judgments, and in this sense the book stands somewhat outside the current stream of "race" novels in which the Negro is shown primarily as victim.

Here, Uncle Tom is buried, but the age of protest has not yet arrived, I think we can assume that Mr. Parks gives us an accurate picture of a Negro community in a small Kansas town in the nineteen-twenties. By accepting an inferior status, the Negro was "accommodated" in a white society, although at a price he did not fully realize. Indeed, the "responsible" Negroes—those who would comprise the leadership of their race today—relied on their own strong sense of religious values to see them through; this is certainly the picture we get of Newt Winger's parents, Jack and Sarah. They do not especially resent white people as such, and they are quite ready to condemn the transgressor among themselves. Only incidentally do they play the color game.

This is a rambling sort of novel held together by a string of melodramatic events. It opens with a whirlwind of action in which young Newt Winger is caught in a cyclone and seduced by an older girl as they wait out the storm in a barn. Things are bound to seem a little tame after this, and during the next year or so Newt settles down to a fairly conventional boyhood. He steals peaches, gets himself a girl, has his problem with the schoolteacher, and earns money by working for Jake Kiner, a white farmer. Jake is killed one day by a drunken Negro. Unknown to the authorities. Newt is the only eyewitness to the slaying.

On circumstantial evidence, another man (white) is tried for the murder—but Newt's conscience gets the better of him and his testimony frees the innocent defendant. In so doing he condemns a Negro (who commits suicide before he can be brought to trial) in order to save a white man who himself is not much good. The story ends with the murderer's son seeking revenge on Newt who, in turn, is saved from death by the timely appearance of the town constable.

This is the sort of plot that you can take or leave alone, and my own inclination is to leave it alone. The real value of the novel is in its insight into group mores, the fact, for example, that Negroes are (or at least were) more concerned with their own internal problems than with social justice. Although Mr. Parks does not blink the injustices that were obviously present, he seems at pains to redress these in terms of the individually admirable white person. Conversely, because he knows the Negro background so well, his Negro villain comes across more convincingly than the evil white man, who is merely comic.

All in all, it is as if Mr. Parks wanted to make sure that no one would accuse him of loading the dice—of writing, in other words, as a Negro. And no one will, although I suspect that he might have written a more stirring novel if he had.

> *David Dempsey, "Witness to a Killing," in* The New York Times Book Review, *September 15, 1963, p. 4.*

Edwin M. Yoder, Jr. (essay date 1966)

[*In the following essay, Yoder summarizes* A Choice of Weapons, *noting: "This is an excellent introduction to what it must have been like to be black and ambitious—and poor—in the America of a generation ago. . . ."*]

It would console one's conscience to believe that the "choice of weapons" which enabled Gordon Parks to surmount the stigma of color and become a celebrated photographer is a live option for every gifted American Negro. But for every Parks whose pilgrim's progress ends at Time, Inc., or with the performance of one of his compositions in a Venice concert hall, perhaps dozens are stifled by poverty, dope, despondency, or the dead-end of some despairing ideology like that of the Black Muslims. "We shall overcome," chants the civil rights anthem; but let those who think the conquest easy begin with this book.

An artist's autobiography naturally deals with wounds and bows—with traumas and their part in shaping a craft. For Parks all other wounds are overshadowed by his involuntary error of having been born the wrong color. And the shattering experiences of his youth and young manhood were imposed not by the stupidities of authority or circumstance but by the ritual insensitivity of the clean, white, and well-fed.

You begin in Kansas, the youngest son of an immense brood born to a mother whose strength is stern, proud Methodism. One day she comes home, "spitting blood," to die. The matriarchy collapses. Only the "choice of weapons" suggested in the title remains as a legacy from the mother "who placed love, dignity, and hard work over hatred." Your brother-in-law in St. Paul throws you out and tosses your cardboard suitcase through a window into the snow. For shelter there is the all-night trolley; for food, in desperation, a pigeon the dogs killed, roasted over burning newspapers in a freezing street.

School, a luxury for the merely poor, becomes difficult and then impossible. Piano-playing, waiting tables, other odd jobs stave off starvation. But just as a break comes with a dance band, the Depression renders bands superfluous and throws you upon the alien world of Harlem, where you learn to fight rats with shoes and are very nearly arrested for pushing dope. The CCC offers another brief respite, and finally a Rosenwald Fellowship makes possible a photographer's job with the Farm Security Administration. Full of hope you come to Washington, only to find that the Capital, too, is a white man's domain. World War II comes, the FSA is absorbed into the Office of War Information, and just as you set off overseas to photograph the exploits of a Negro air corps unit you discover that publicity, too, is for white heroes only. Through it all, the reminders of race are present hourly. Whether you clean vile spittoons in a Chicago flophouse or try to buy a topcoat at a modish Washington department store, the epithet "black bastard" lurks, spoken or implied, in numberless encounters.

After 274 pages of this, relieved only by sporadic kindness or a stroke of good luck, the ending in wartime Harlem as black people "button up" against "the hawk over the ghetto" is abrupt and merciful. Appropriately, there is no resolution, although we know that this particular Christian made it out of his own Slough of Despond. But we know also that for too many—like the hapless killer whose gas-chamber execution is vividly described in the prologue—it ends in a catch for the hawk.

This is an excellent introduction to what it must have been like to be black and ambitious—and poor—in the America of a generation ago, when nearly every door was sealed to Negroes as never before or since in American history. Mr. Parks writes simply and incisively, although an unnecessary tremolo occasionally sounds when it is least expected, as if a tiny corner of the author's keen sensibility harbored a thwarted soap-opera writer. Perhaps it does; there could be worse subjects.

But then, much of the power of *A Choice of Weapons* derives from one's realization that for Mr. Parks "success" was not wildly unlike the vision of white middle-class America: good pay and comfort, dignity, a shot at recognition. It was not as a febrile prophet, after all, but as a humorous human being who liked to make music and photos and looked to society to respect and reward his ambition that he braved the insults and the rats and choked back moments of fury and despair. Let us not so condescend as to call this vision commonplace; none is, really. It was at least usual enough, however, as to make astounding and heart-sickening the obstacles Mr. Parks faced in its realization.

> *Edwin M. Yoder, Jr., "No Catch for the Hawk," in* Saturday Review, *Vol. XLIX, No. 7, February 12, 1966, p. 40.*

Susan Rice (essay date 1969)

[*In the following excerpt, Rice describes the movie version of* The Learning Tree *as "primitive."*]

Gordon Parks is a still photographer. He directed *The Learning Tree,* his first motion picture. It is still born. Dare I say primitive? Gordon Parks is black. If he wasn't nobody would pay much attention to his picture. But he is, and everybody is giving the film much more attention and praise than it deserves....

I am also sorry that the first massive, lavish, technicolor, mass distributed film by a black man should be so reassuring...like *Green Pastures.* Parks' remembrance of his boyhood is unaffected but middle-brow, like The Supremes doing Frank Sinatra tunes. The only charitable thing I can think of to say about it is that it is free of self-pity and bombast.... *The Learning Tree* has some of the stiltedness and some of the sensitivity of Truman Capote's childhood reminiscences. Does the idea of a black Truman Capote strike you as oddly as it does me? Does the world *need* another Capote of any color? Let's try another. I think Parks sees himself as a mini Orson Welles. In addition to directing, he wrote the screenplay, from his novel of the same name, and scored the film. I guess I am scoring it as well. Only God can make a tree.

> *Susan Rice, in a review of "The Learning Tree," in* Take One, *Vol. 2, No. 3, January-February, 1969, p. 25.*

Joseph Morgenstern (essay date 1969)

[*In the following excerpt, Morgenstern praises* The Learning Tree *as an "even-tempered piece of autobiography" but describes its film adaptation as an "uneven piece of film craftsmanship."*]

The pleasures of *The Learning Tree,* an awkward but greatly affecting movie, are all bound up with nostalgia for a vanished land in which barefooted farm boys could do cartwheels through unbounded fields of yellow flowers, in which a preacher could implore the Lord to "deliver our young from cigarettes, from dancing, from drinking, from flapper skirts," in which an amorous young man could give his girl a bottle of violet water and a card, especially made up to go with it, that said: "Roses are red, violets are blue, sugar is sweet and so are you."...

Parks has made, among several other things, a predictably pictorial period piece in soft-spoken Technicolor. He has made a lovely small movie about boyhood; not black boyhood or white boyhood so much as human boyhood, the maybehood that follows babyhood. He has also made a movie about the perilous plight of a black boy, confronted constantly by the sudden, sometimes violent, death of friends and family, who's still naive enough or brave enough to believe in the future.

The outward trappings of his life are as reassuringly bourgeois as the outside of a Watts bungalow—a cohesive family dominated by a strong, warm mother, church picnics, white shirts to school, some white friends, even a white piano teacher for a privileged black few in his community. In reality, though, the whites have the upper hand—on occasion the upper fist—and blacks are firmly steered away from dangerously white aspirations. The gifted young high-school student learns from his white teacher, just as Malcolm Little did in *The Autobiography of Malcolm X*, that Negro children are simply not college material.

With every reason in the world to lash out at the world, the younger Parks moves through it cleverly, carefully, while the older Parks recalls it as a world in which whites had no exclusive claim on vice and blacks had no exclusive claim on virtue.... *The Learning Tree* is an astoundingly even-tempered piece of autobiography, given the melodramatic violence of its author's youth. It is also an uneven piece of film craftsmanship....

In a few minor roles and scenes ... the performances are tentative and Parks's direction is sloppy or distracted. Surprisingly enough for a photographer of Parks's achievements, he relies heavily on dialogue where pictures alone would have turned the trick.

Apart from the sumptuous photography, *The Learning Tree* has little of the gloss and velocity we've come to expect from fashionably modern movies. At times it turns downright clumsy. I don't know what else to say about the clumsiness except that it's there and that it doesn't matter very much in the end. What matters most is the abiding presence of a good man telling a good story about a boy who was himself, a boy who remains alive, kicking and growing long after the movie ends.

> Joseph Morgenstern, "Boy's Life," in News-week, Vol. LXXIV, No. 6, August 11, 1969, p. 74.

Mel Watkins (essay date 1979)

[*In the following essay, Watkins presents an overview of* To Smile in Autumn, *concluding that the work is a "gracious self-portrait" of its author.*]

Gordon Parks's autobiographical novel *The Learning Tree* and his earlier memoir, *A Choice of Weapons,* focused on his adolescence as a poor youth in Kansas and on his struggle to overcome the barriers of discrimination and fashion a career as a photographer. In this book Mr. Parks has moved beyond "the bitterness of those times" to chronicle the years at the top of his profession as one of Life magazine's more celebrated photographers, as well as to detail the experiences of a variegated career that has brought him recognition as a composer, author and film director. *To Smile in Autumn* spans the years from 1943 to the present, and takes Mr. Parks through three marriages, several trips around the world and into the lives of some of the most renowned and influential figures of the past 35 years.

Mr. Parks's achievements would be exceptional no matter what his background, but when compared with the bleakness and hardship of his childhood they seem nothing less than outsized. Although a high-school dropout, he became a member of *Life* magazine's award-winning photography staff only five years after arriving in New York in 1943. His photographs and

writing for *Life*—covering subjects as diverse as Harlem street gangs, Paris fashions, Winston Churchill, the Ingrid Bergman-Roberto Rosellini love affair, and the civil-rights movement—were consistently acclaimed. But Mr. Parks's talents went far beyond journalism. While on assignment at *Life*'s Paris bureau in the early 1950's, his previously neglected interest in poetry and classical music became a near-obsession. Out of that drive came several books of poetry and a piano concerto, which was performed in the courtyard of Doges' Palace in Venice in 1955. The publication of *The Learning Tree* in 1963, written in little more than a year, instantly sparked interest in Hollywood, and in 1968 filming began; Mr. Parks served as producer, director and writer of both the script and the score. Subsequently he directed three other movies. And even after his departure for Hollywood he continued to do still photography for *Life* and other magazines.

Unlike Mr. Parks's two previous autobiographical works, which dwelled on the difficulty of attaining success, *To Smile in Autumn* is about the triumph of achievement, the abundance and glamour of a productive life. The memoir is dotted with memories of Mr. Parks's casual and intimate brushes with the rich and famous: his durable friendship with Gloria Vanderbilt; lunch with Richard Wright at Maxim's; a chat with Gen. Dwight D. Eisenhower at Allied headquarters; Frank Sinatra's appearance at a piano recital given by Mr. Parks's daughter; brandy with Winston Churchill and Anthony Eden aboard the Queen Mary; a bizarre tennis match with King Farouk in France; traveling with Malcolm X and visiting Eldridge Cleaver during his exile in Algiers.

One of the most interesting sections, on Mr. Parks's relationship with Duke Ellington, is also perhaps the most revealing. "Ellington had always been my hero," he writes. "Unlike other Black Hollywood stereotypes he never grinned, he smiled; he never shuffled, he strode.... At his performances we young blacks sat high in our seats, wanting the whites to see us; to know that this handsome, elegant, sharply dressed man playing that beautiful, sophisticated music was one of us." This admiration for Ellington is not surprising: Of all the personalities in the book it is the suave, sophisticated demeanor of the Duke that most closely approximates Mr. Parks's own. And it is that manner, decidedly urbane and charming, that makes this memoir so readable and entertaining.

There are, however, some problems. Mr. Parks's elegant narrative style, which includes a sampling of his poetry and extracts from a diary he kept in Paris, is sometimes at odds with the subjects he addresses. Mr. Parks acknowledges this in a description of returning to his hotel after leaving the Oakland headquarters of the Black Panthers: "I looked around at the sumptuous restaurants, salons, and boutiques that sharply defined the gap between the Panthers' world and the world they wanted to change. And for a few uncomfortable moments I felt out of place, disloyal, even traitorous. Then

Parks with actors on the set of The Learning Tree.

the elevator door opened and swallowed me, and up I went toward a hive of carpeted floors, soft beds, and snow-white sheets." Here, as with his comments on his journalistic involvement with Harlem street gangs, the Black Muslims and a destitute Harlem family, the impression is one of discontinuity, something like hearing Bobby Short play a Mississippi Delta blues.

But this contradiction appears perhaps inevitably in the memoirs of any successful American black man, and ultimately it causes only brief pause in an otherwise engaging memoir. Gordon Parks emerges here as a Renaissance man who has resolutely pursued success in several fields. His memoir is sustained and enlivened by his urbanity and generosity. (He is seldom critical of former associates or colleagues, with the notable exception of anecdotes about King Farouk and the *Ebony* magazine publisher Johnny Johnson.) Liberally supplemented with Mr. Parks's own photography, *To Smile in Autumn* is a gracious self-portrait. Its tone bespeaks an attitude perhaps best exemplified by Duke Ellington's ritual greeting to his audience: "We love you madly!" Mr. Parks handles the approach with nearly as much savoir-faire as his spiritual mentor.

Mel Watkins, "Renaissance Photographer," in The New York Times Book Review, *December 23, 1979, p. 7.*

James Monaco (essay date 1979)

[*In the following excerpt, Monaco surveys Parks's* Flavio, The Learning Tree, Shaft, Shaft's Big Score, The Super Cops, *and* Leadbelly, *focusing on the last-named film.*]

[Gordon Parks, Sr.] made a short, *Flavio,* about a boy in a Brazilian *favela,* in 1965. It was well received, but it took him more than three years to put together his first feature, *The Learning Tree* . . . . Finally Hollywood was ready for its first prominent Black director.

The Learning Tree (1968) based on Parks's own memoirs, is a visually stunning evocation of his childhood in Kansas in the twenties. Because the setting is Midwestern, the story is also rather novel, successfully avoiding the clichés and truisms of growing up Black in the South, or in a Northern ghetto. Yet, Parks's childhood wasn't particularly dramatic—no great traumas—and so *Learning Tree* is rather static, a fact which would have caused no problems if the film had been European, but which did not do much for his reputation as a bankable director in late-sixties Hollywood.

The emphasis in the moving-picture industry had always been on "moving" rather than "picture," and Parks's superb training as a still photographer wasn't of much use to him commercially in 1968, when Hollywood was just learning, through the use of new filmstock and techniques, that movies didn't have to be breathlessly paced to be attractive; that audiences would buy the "picture," too.

So Parks set out to show he could do "movies." The proof, **Shaft** (1971), was irrefutable. *Cotton Comes to Harlem* had introduced the form of Blaxploitation action films; **Shaft** added the all-important tone. The film was tough, lean, cool, hip, angry, and in the end even wise. Black audiences understood immediately that Richard Roundtree's heroic exploits as private eye John Shaft were a commentary on decades of white detective films as well as being entertaining in themselves. Most important: at last there was a real Black hero on the screen. Parks did one sequel, **Shaft's Big Score,** in 1972 . . . , and a more general urban cop film, **The Supercops** (1974), unusual in being one of extremely few non-Black films directed by a Black. Parks refused to be ghettoized as a filmmaker, just as he had refused to be ghettoized as a *Life* photographer.

Having paid his dues to the commercial film establishment, Parks was finally able to return to a more personal project. (pp. 196-97)

[**Leadbelly** is] a magnificent telling of an historical episode with strong mythic overtones. **Leadbelly** was just the sort of film Parks was meant to make. His experiences as photographer, musician, and novelist combine to create a film that works well on all three levels.

Like most mythic stories, this biography of Huddie Ledbetter—"Leadbelly"—the master of the twelve-string guitar, potentially verges on cliche. It takes someone of Parks's particular talents to avoid those pitfalls. He does so by confronting the mythic material head-on rather than apologizing for it. The film has a classic narrative structure: strong, simple, direct, and pointed. In short, it's very much like Leadbelly's own music.

It's grounded in humiliation. (Texas Governor Pat Neff comments after Leadbelly has performed for him: "Ain't nothin' can sing like a darkie when he puts his mind to it!") It opposes that oppression with the elemental politics of survival. (Dicklikker, Leadbelly's prison buddy, explains: "Ya suit yerself to the situation. When they wants to kill ya, just livin' is winning.") Ultimately, **Leadbelly** is a triumph of will . . . . **Leadbelly** provides a legitimate historical high of the sort we seldom get any longer from mainstream American movies, made by people who have lost (or never had) a sense of the vitality and meaning of the politics of existence.

Parks can bring it off because, first, he understands the strength of Leadbelly's music. He has also guided [the actors] . . . to an extraordinary level of performance. Along with his cinematographer, Bruce Surtees, he has in addition created a breathtakingly elemental imagery for the film—full of earth, air, sun, sweat, and color—that's almost insolent it is so powerful.

Most important, perhaps, is the groundbase of the film. What gave Leadbelly's songs their special power was the people whose stories they told. The same must be said for Parks's film. He made a movie about people, and the people give **Leadbelly** its mythic energy. (pp. 198-99)

> James Monaco, "The Black Film (and the Black Image)," in his American Film Now: The People, the Power, the Money, the Movies, *New American Library, 1979, pp. 185-214.*

Publishers Weekly (essay date 1990)

[*In the following* Publishers Weekly *review, a critic examines* Voices in the Mirror.]

Poor, jobless and hungry in Harlem in the early 1930s, Parks went on to achieve distinction as a photographer, film director, writer, poet, composer and painter. Born in a small Kansas town in 1912, he became the first black photographer at *Life* and *Vogue,* and later, Hollywood's first black director and screenwriter. His exhilarating, inspirational autobiography, **Voices in the Mirror: An Autobiography,** provides a searing view of what it's like to be black in America. Careening from the "hate-drenched city" of Washington, D.C., in the 1940s, to New York, "that jungle of uncertainty," to postwar Paris, Rio and Birmingham, Ala., Parks sets down his impressions of civil rights and black power struggles, his encounter with Third World poverty and meetings with Eisenhower, Churchill, Malcolm X, Sugar Ray Robinson, Ingrid Bergman, to name a few. He is guarded and defensive in discussing his three marriages, but succeeds in drawing the reader into the peaks and anguish of his "complex, transitory, bittersweet existence."

> A review of "Voices in the Mirror: An Autobiography," in Publishers Weekly, *Vol. 237, No. 41, October 12, 1990, p. 52.*

FURTHER READING

"Reporter with a Camera." *Ebony* 1, No. 8 (July 1946): 24-6.

> Brief biography of Parks, focusing on his career as a photographer.

Kramer, Hilton. "Art: Empathy of Gordon Parks." *The New York Times* (4 October 1975): 19.

Reviews *Moments without Proper Names,* concluding that the studies of "black suffering and of response to suffering" are Parks's best photographs.

Moore, Deedee. "Shooting Straight: The Many Worlds of Gordon Parks." *Smithsonian* 20, No. 1 (April 1989): 66-72, 74, 76-7.
Biography of Parks, chronicling the author's life as photographer, autobiographer, and filmmaker.

————. "'Martin'." *American Visions* 4, No. 6 (December 1989): 34-9.
Discusses the making of Parks's *Martin.*

Redding, Saunders. "In America." *The New York Times Book Review* (13 February 1966): 26.
Review of *A Choice of Weapons.* The critic writes: *"A Choice of Weapons* is not the overwrought, introspective and gut-wrenched jeremiad of a martyr to racial bigotry and hatred. It is, rather, a perspective narrative of one man's struggle to realize the values...he has been taught to respect."

Villagran, Nora. "Parks Extends a Helping Hand." *Detroit Free Press* (9 January 1991): 4C.
Highlights Parks's life and achievements and briefly reviews *Voices in the Mirror.*

Okot p'Bitek
1931-1982

Ugandan poet, essayist, novelist, translator, and editor.

One of East Africa's best-known poets, Okot p'Bitek helped redefine African literature by emphasizing the oral tradition of the native Acholi people of Uganda. His lengthy prose poems, often categorized as poetic novels, reflect the form of traditional Acholi songs while expressing contemporary political themes. In the preface to his essay collection *Africa's Cultural Revolution* (1973), p'Bitek explained: "Africa must re-examine herself critically. She must discover her true self, and rid herself of all 'apemanship.' For only then she can begin to develop a culture of her own.... As she has broken the political bondage of colonialism, she must continue the economic and cultural revolution until she refuses to be led by the nose by foreigners."

p'Bitek's respect for ancestral art forms was established during his childhood in Gulu, Uganda, where his father, a school teacher, was an expressive storyteller and his mother was considered a great singer of Acholi songs. An outstanding student, p'Bitek composed and produced a full-length opera while still in high school. At the age of twenty-two he published his first literary work, a novel in Acholi entitled *Lak tar miyo kinyero wi lobo* (1953; title means "Are Your Teeth White? Then Laugh!"). After studying at King's College in Budo, p'Bitek played on Uganda's national soccer team while maintaining a position as a high school teacher. In the summer of 1956 he participated in the Olympic Games in London; he remained in England to study at several institutions, including the Institute of Social Anthropology in Oxford and University College, Wales. He was first recognized as a major new voice in African literature in 1966 when he published *Song of Lawino: A Lament.* In the same year he was named director of the Uganda National Theater and Cultural Center, where he founded the highly successful Gulu Arts Festival, which celebrates the traditional oral history, dance, and other arts of the Acholi people. Political pressures, however, forced p'Bitek from his directorship after two years. He moved to Kenya, where, with the exception of frequent visits to universities in the United States, he remained throughout the reign of Ugandan dictator Idi Amin. After founding the Kisumu Arts Festival in Kenya and later serving as a professor in Nigeria, p'Bitek eventually returned to Makerere University in Kampala, Uganda, where he was a professor of creative writing until his death in 1982.

Widely regarded as p'Bitek's most famous work, *Song of Lawino* is a plea for the preservation of Acholi cultural tradition from the encroachment of Western influences. The prose poem is narrated by Lawino, an illiterate Ugandan housewife, who complains bitterly that her university-educated husband, Ocol, has rejected her and his own Acholi heritage in favor of a more modern lifestyle. Perceiving his wife as an undesirable impediment to his progress, Ocol devotes his attention to Clementina, his Westernized mistress. Throughout the work, Lawino condemns her husband's disdain for African ways, describing her native civilization as beautiful, meaningful, and deeply satisfying: "Listen Ocol, my old friend, / The ways of your ancestors / Are good, / Their customs are solid / And not hollow...." She laments her husband's disrespect for his own culture and questions the logic of many Western customs: "At the height of the hot season / The progressive and civilized ones / Put on blanket suits / And woollen socks from Europe...." In an interview, p'Bitek noted of the protagonist of *Song of Lawino*: "Lawino realizes that we are evolving too rapidly away from our historical and cultural roots. Her song is a challenge for African leaders and scientists: You learned from white books, but do you link this imported knowledge to Africa? Be aware of your own background." In contrast, *Song of Ocol* (1970) expresses Ocol's disgust for African ways and the destructive force of his self-hatred: "Smash all these mirrors / That I may not see / The blackness of the past / From which I came / Reflected in them." Rather than reflecting the superiority of Western civilization, Ocol's voice has been characterized as an enraged, violent outpouring against Africa and African culture. Bernth Lindfors observed: "His fanatical [Westernization] and rejection of himself have prevented him from developing into a creative human being. He has lost not just his ethnic identity but his humanity."

p'Bitek's next major work, *Two Songs: Song of Prisoner and Song of Malaya* (1971), won the Kenya Publishers Association's Jomo Kenyatta Prize in 1972. Widely praised for its political significance, *Song of Prisoner* describes the anguish of a convicted criminal as he suffers from depression, delusions, and claustrophobia. The specific nature of the prisoner's crime remains unclear: he first claims that he was arrested for loitering in the park but later asserts that he has assassinated a political leader who he describes as "a murderer / A racist / A tribalist / A clanist / A brotherist." Although he frequently presents himself as a hero, the ambiguous narrator also reveals intense feelings of impotence and anxiety: "I am an insect / Trapped between the toes / Of a bull elephant." Interpreting *Prisoner* as an allegory for the turbulent political climate in East Africa during the 1970s, Tanure Ojaide stated: "[p'Bitek's] viewpoint in *Prisoner* is pessimistic about Africa's political future, for there is no positive alternative to the bad leader. The poet sees the need to eradicate a repressive regime, but he fears that the successor could be equally bad or worse." In contrast, *Song of Malaya* (which loosely means "Song of Whore") is narrated by a prostitute whose strength and stable personality prevails as she exposes the hypocrisy of those who condemn her. Several critics have interpreted the narrator's voice as symbolizing tolerance for human diversity. Wrote Bernth Lindfors: "[The narrator] is the great social equalizer, humanity's most effective democratizer because she mixes with high and low indiscriminately. All who come to her are reduced to the same level."

In his later years p'Bitek focused on translating African literature, and in 1974 he published *The Horn of My Love,* a collection of Acholi folk songs about death, ancient Acholi chiefs, love, and courtship. The later *Hare and Hornbill* (1978) is a collection of folktales presenting both humans and animals as characters. Praising p'Bitek's translation of *The Horn of My Love,* Gerald Moore commented: "Those familiar with [p'Bitek's] own poetry, especially *The Song of Lawino,* will recognize here the indigenous poetic tradition in which that fine work is embedded."

Eulogized as "Uganda's best known poet" in his London *Times* obituary, Okot p'Bitek had a distinguished career in the fields of sport, education, and the arts. He sought, in his role as cultural director and author, to prevent native African culture, especially that of his native Acholi, from being swallowed up by the influences of Western ideas and arts. While serving as director for the Uganda National Theater and Cultural Center, he proclaimed in an interview: "The major challenge I think is to find what might be Uganda's contribution to world culture.... [W]e should, I think, look into the village and see what the Ugandans—the proper Ugandans—not the people who have been to school, have read—and see what they do in the village, and see if we cannot find some root there, and build on this." He further explained his feelings about the influence of Western culture on his own: "I am not against having plays from England, from other parts of the world, we should have this, but I'm very concerned that whatever we do should have a basic starting point, and this should be Uganda, and then, of course, Africa, and then we can expand afterwards."

(For further information about p'Bitek's life and works, see *Black Writers; Contemporary Authors,* Vols. 107, 124; and *Major 20th-Century Writers.*)

PRINCIPAL WORKS

Lak tar miyo kinyero wi lobo? (novel) 1953
Song of Lawino: A Lament (prose poem) 1966
African Religion in Western Scholarship (nonfiction) 1970
Song of Ocol (prose poem) 1970
Song of a Prisoner (prose poem) 1971
Religion of the Central Luo (nonfiction) 1971
The Revelations of a Prostitute (prose poem) 1971
Two Songs: Song of Prisoner and Song of Malaya (prose poems) 1971
Africa's Cultural Revolution (essay collection) 1973
The Horn of My Love [translator] (folk songs) 1974
Hare and Hornbill [translator] (folktales) 1978

* The title of this work may be translated "Are Your Teeth White? Then Laugh!"

Okot p'Bitek with Jan Kees van de Werk (interview date 1981)

[*The interview below originally appeared in an expanded form in the liberal magazine* NRC Handelsblad. *Here, p'Bitek discusses the importance of understanding and preserving traditional African culture.*]

[Jan Kees van de Werk]: *What does* **Song of Lawino** *say to the reader?*

[Okot p'Bitek]: Lawino realizes that we are evolving too rapidly away from our historical and cultural roots. Her song is a challenge for African leaders and scientists: You learned from white books, but do you link this imported knowledge to Africa? Be aware of your own background.

We must return to the village elders, take off our shoes, and respectfully listen to what they tell us. I take first-year students to the villages without pens, paper, or tape recorders. Afterward they must recall what they saw and learned—what elders told them about the original rite of a dance, for instance. When they have shown that they tried to understand the meaning without prejudice or preconceived Western ideas, we can discuss it further, in English, if necessary. The golden rule is, "Keep your mouth shut and don't ask questions." They reflect the preconceptions of the questioner.

Until recently social anthropology was the accomplice of colonialism, providing the colonizer with information that would insure efficient control and exploitation of the colonized peoples. Western science was used to justify the colonial system; it created the myth of the "primitive savage" who had to be civilized and converted. Now overreaction to the arrogance of Western science is becoming evident among African theologians, who are trying to prove that African gods have all the characteristics of the Christian god.

You once wrote of the two different groups in Africa: the dominant minority, which rules the Government; and the majority of undernourished villagers.

I may have drawn that distinction too sharply. In any event people are better off in the villages than in the shantytowns of the cities. The center of Nairobi is the image of a European city; it is the tomb of the rich surrounded by shantytowns.

The confrontation between rich and poor takes place in the villages, not in the cities. Both rich and poor return on weekends to the villages where their families live. The rich officials meet the poor beggars in their mothers' villages. In the evening when everyone gathers indirect questions are asked, such as, Has our village produced sons who do not help their brothers? In this manner the consciences of the rich are put under pressure.

Is oral literature as alive now as it was in your childhood?

Acoli tradition is very much alive. We commemorate my mother's death in June. By singing about her memory we come closer to the mystery of life.

I really wrote *Song of Lawino* as a response to the creativity of my mother, who almost drowned me with her songs. Finally I said, "Now you must listen to *my* song." But she was not satisfied; there was no music in it. I had already become the victim of written literature.

You have to make and perform oral literature with your entire body. In essence *Song of Lawino* and *Song of Ocol* should not be read but performed—not in theaters, but in the market places. My father told very lively and expressive horror stories of hissing snakes with feathers on their heads that turn into whips that can kill. When the storyteller confronts us with ourselves in the personification of the hot blooded elephant or the sly hare, we laugh and get to know ourselves better.

You once wrote, "For the millions of rural dwellers in Nigeria, Kenya, and Uganda, the novels of [African writers] are as insignificant as the unexpected rain in the dry season, because they do not reach the millions for whom they were written."

A conflict exists between language and communication. I wrote *Song of Lawino* in my own language so it could flourish independent of the paper it was written on. If you write in English a large group of people are excluded.

Is the Amin era being reflected in literature?

There are many plays about that era, and popular music as well. The ever-returning question is, "How did it get so far, and will we let it happen again?"

> *Okot p'Bitek and Jan Kees van de Werk, in an interview in* World Press Review, *Vol. 28, No. 8, August, 1981, p. 62.*

Bernth Lindfors (essay date 1984)

[*In the following excerpt, Lindfors studies p'Bitek's oral poetry, focusing on themes of social, cultural, and political life in Africa.*]

When Okot p'Bitek surprised the world with *Song of Lawino* in 1966, he was recognized immediately as a major African poet. No other African writer—except possibly Christopher Okigbo of Nigeria—had made such an indelible impact with his first volume of verse, creating at one stroke a new poetic idiom so entirely his own. Most African poets writing in English and French were cultural mulattoes seeking self-consciously to fuse the two disparate traditions of verbal creativity on which they had been nurtured.... But Okot p'Bitek was refreshingly different. When he sang, no European echoes could be heard in the background. His *Song of Lawino* was the first long poem in English to achieve a totally African identity.

This was no accident, considering Okot's education, cultural interests and literary inclinations. After attending high school in Uganda, earning a Certificate of Education at Bristol University and studying law at the University of Wales in Aberystwyth, he went on to Oxford where he worked for a B. Litt. at the Institute of Social Anthropology. It was here that he wrote a thesis on Acoli and Lango traditional songs, a formal academic study which must have forced him to take a closer look at the structure, content and style of songs he had heard and sung as a young man growing up in Uganda. This project, completed three years before the publication of *Song of Lawino,* may have suggested to him a new way of singing in English.

Okot appears to have developed an interest in music, song, literature and traditional culture while very young and to have sustained this interest throughout his life. As a schoolboy at King's College, Budo, he composed and produced an opera, and in 1953, when only 22 years old, he published his first literary work. *Lak tar miyo kinyero wi lobo (Are Your Teeth White? Then Laugh),* a novel in Acoli. After completing his undergraduate education in Britain, he returned to Uganda and joined the staff of the Extra-Mural Department at Makerere University College, a job which enabled him to carry out further research on the oral literature of the peoples of northern Uganda and to found and organize an annual Gulu Festival of the Arts. In 1966 he was appointed Director of the Uganda National Theatre and Cultural Centre in Kampala, where he did much to promote local cultural activities. At the end of 1967 he joined the Western Kenya section of Nairobi University College's Extra-Mural Department and immediately became the moving force behind the first Kisumu Arts Festival held in December 1968. Then, in the academic year 1969-70, he accepted a one-year appointment as Fellow in the International Writing Program at the University of Iowa, a position which enabled him to write full time. A year later he became attached to the University of Nairobi as Research Fellow at the Institute of African Studies and part-time Lecturer in Sociology and Literature. He remained at the University of Nairobi until 1978, a year during which he held visiting appointments at both the University of Texas at Austin and the University of Ife in Nigeria. In 1979, after Idi Amin Dada was overthrown, he returned once more to Makerere University where he was associated with the Institute of Social Research until his untimely death on 20 July 1982.

Throughout his busy academic and professional career, Okot p'Bitek never stopped writing. His enormously successful *Song of Lawino* was soon followed by three other long poems of the same genre: *Song of Ocol* (1970), *Song of Prisoner* and *Song of Malaya* (the latter two were published together in *Two Songs,* 1971). He also published two scholarly works, *African Religions in Western Scholarship* (1971) and *Religion of the Central Luo* (1971), one of which may have been written originally as his D. Phil. thesis in religion at Oxford. Another book, *Africa's Cultural Revolution* (1973), is a collection of some of the essays he wrote for East African periodicals, magazines and newspapers between 1964 and 1971. Since these essays contain several of Okot's most candid statements on African culture, they provide an excellent introduction to some of the ideas embedded in his poetry.

In the preface to *Africa's Cultural Revolution* Okot says that his essays are part of the revolutionary struggle in Africa 'dedicated to the total demolition of foreign cultural domination and the restoration and promotion of Africa's proud culture to its rightful place'. In order to achieve these worthwhile nationalistic goals,

> Africa must re-examine herself critically. She must discover her true self, and rid herself of all 'apemanship'. For only then she can begin to develop a culture of her own. Africa must redefine all cultural terms according to her own interests. As she has broken the political bondage of colonialism, she must continue the economic and cultural revolution until

she refuses to be led by the nose by foreigners. We must also reject the erroneous attempts of foreign students to interpret and present her. We must interpret and present Africa in our own way, in our own interests.

Okot's aim as a writer was to assist in this vital task of cultural redefinition. Okot's essays range widely over such varied topics as literature, philosophy, religion, politics, history, education, sex and pop music. But underlying them all is an insistence on the validity and dignity of indigenous African culture. Okot wanted Africans—especially educated Africans—to accept their Africanness and stop mimicking non-African customs, traditions, fashions and styles which are entirely inappropriate and even rather ridiculous in an African setting. Only by affirming the integrity of their own cultural identity will Africans find happiness and genuine fulfilment. As Ngugi wa Thiong'o puts it in an introduction to these essays, Okot 'is simply and rightly saying that we cannot ape and hope to create'. Okot desires to release the creative potential of Africa by making Africans conscious and proud of their own rich cultural heritage.

In his essays on literature, Okot begins the process of cultural redefinition by questioning the western conception of literature itself. He points out that "in western scholarship, literature means the writings of a particular time or country, especially those valued for excellence of form or expression. This definition, with its emphasis on "writing", implies that literature is the exclusive preserve of human societies which have invented the art of writing.' In place of this 'narrow and discriminatory definition' Okot advocates adopting a more 'dynamic and democratic' notion of literature as an art embracing 'all the creative works of man expressed in words.' This would take in oral as well as written performances because 'words can be spoken, sung or written. The voice of the singer or the speaker and the pen and paper are mere midwives of a pregnant mind. A song is a song whether it is sung, spoken or written down.' By redefining literature in this way, Okot was able to demonstrate that Africa possesses one of the richest literary cultures in the world.

He also emphasized that literature in Africa is a living social art. It is not a collection of old classics that one reads alone or studies diligently at school in order to pass examinations and win certificates. It is an intensely expressive activity which aims at publicly communicating deeply felt emotions. Sometimes it may be designed to amuse, sometimes to instruct, but the best literature never fails to make profound impact on the whole community. It is a totally democratic art which attempts to reach everyone within earshot. There must always be direct communication between the artist and his audience and full participation by all present. This means that the African literary artist cannot afford to indulge in deliberate obscurity. He produces his art not for art's sake but for society's sake.

Song of Lawino was created in this spirit. It is a thoroughly indigenous poem in form, content, style, message and aesthetic philosophy. Okot took the songs he knew best—Acoli and Lango traditional songs of praise and abuse, joy and sorrow, sympathy and satire—and made use of their rich poetic resources in composing an original anthem in honour of Africa. The result was something both old and new because while Okot exploited many of the conventions of oral art, he also invented a novel literary genre which had never been seen in African writing before. He did this first in his own mother tongue and then in English, claiming to have 'clipped a bit of the eagle's wings and rendered the sharp edges of the warrior's sword rusty and blunt, and also murdered rhythm and rhyme' in the process of translation. Like a traditional poet he was trying to reach the widest possible audience because he felt he had an important idea to impart. And like a literary artist he was still experimenting with his verbal medium in an effort to find a uniquely appropriate idiom to carry his message. *Song of Lawino* is thus a hybrid achievement, a successful sustained blending of oral and literary art in a long poem remarkably innovative in conception and design yet immanently African in orientation.

Much of the Africanness of the poem resides in its imagery, ideology and rhetorical structure. It is an oral song sung by an illiterate Ugandan housewife who complains bitterly about the insults and ill-treatment she receives from her university-trained husband. Being an unschooled village girl, Lawino speaks in the earthy idiom of the rural peasantry and sees everything from the perspective of a country cousin. She cannot understand why her husband Ocol follows western ways and why he rejects her for clinging to the traditions of her people. She knows nothing about ballroom dancing, cooking on a modern stove, and reading clocks, books or thermometers, and sees no reason why she should learn such strange skills when she can get along perfectly well without them. She has been exposed to a few Christian beliefs and teachings but these she found either incomprehensible or profoundly perplexing. Why can't she be allowed to follow her own ways? Why must Ocol abuse and punish her for being African? These are the questions Lawino asks repeatedly as she recounts her husband's brutality and cruel words. Recalling the time Ocol branded her and her kinsfolk as ignorant, superstitious fools, she laments:

> My husband's tongue
> Is bitter like the roots of the *lyonno* lily,
> It is hot like the penis of the bee,
> Like the sting of the *kalang!*
> Ocol's tongue is fierce like the arrow of the
>   scorpion,
> Deadly like the spear of the buffalo-hornet.
> It is ferocious
> Like the poison of a barren woman
> And corrosive like the juice of the gourd.

Everything Lawino says is rooted in the reality she has mastered, the world she knows. She speaks in a language which reveals an intimate knowledge of rural African life. Obviously such a perceptive observer is neither ignorant nor foolishly superstitious. Lawino's imagery alone refutes Ocol's accusation.

Okot's strategy throughout the poem is to contrast the natural grace and dignity of traditional African ways with the grotesque artificiality of modern habits and practices that educated Africans have copied from Europe. The primary target is Ocol's 'apemanship' but Okot gradually widens the focus of Lawino's complaints to embrace much larger social, political and religious issues arising from rabid, unthinking westernization. Okot once described *Song of Lawino* in an interview as

> a big laugh by this village girl called Lawino, laughing at modern man and modern woman in Uganda. She thinks that the educated folk are spoiled, in the sense that they don't belong, they don't enjoy fully the culture of the people of Uganda, and she thinks that if only these educated people could stop a little bit and look back into the village they would find a much richer life altogether.

Lawino is able to provide a window on both African worlds because she is the product of one and a prisoner in the other. Like Alice in Wonderland, like Gulliver, like Medza in Beti's *Mission to Kala*, she discovers herself in a strange new universe and reacts strongly to anything that deviates from her own cultural expectations and prejudices. But a major difference in her case is that most of her audience—western as well as African—does not share her cultural perspective but rather that of Ocol, the modern man she is laughing at. She forces such readers to see themselves from an entirely different point of view and to join in the laughter. By mirroring modern manners through her own distorted ethnocentric lens, Lawino serves as a catalyst of satire.

But she also becomes a victim of satire because occasionally there are significant discrepancies between her words and deeds. For instance, after beginning a devastating assault on the appearance of Ocol's modern girlfriend Clementine, she pauses briefly to assure her audience that her motives are pure:

> Do not think I am insulting
> The woman with whom I share my husband!
> Do not think my tongue
> Is being sharpened by jealousy.
> It is the sight of Tina
> That provokes sympathy from my heart.
>
> I do not deny
> I am a little jealous.
> It is no good lying,
> We all suffer from a little jealousy.
> It catches you unawares
> Like the ghosts that bring fevers;
> It surprises people
> Like earth tremors:
> But when you see the beautiful woman
> With whom I share my husband
> You feel a little pity for her!

She then resumes her attack with gusto, ridiculing Tina's dried-up breasts and padded brassière, insinuating she has aborted or killed many children in her long lifetime, and scoffing at her slim 'meatless' figure. Obviously Lawino is more than a little jealous of the woman she claims to pity.

Okot carefully counterpoints Lawino's lapses into pure invective with her gentle, nostalgic reflections on traditional African life. These frequent changes in mood and tempo reveal the softer side of her personality while reinforcing her emphasis on differences between the old and the new. Lawino's sympathies always lie with tradition, and through graphic images and telling details she is able to communicate her enthusiasm for the customs and practices of her people. She describes a civilization which is wholesome, coherent, deeply satisfying to those born into it, and therefore naturally resistant to fundamental change. Her angry tirade against Tina is followed by a rosy account of how rivals for a man's love behave in Acoli society and then by a level-headed appeal to Ocol politely asking him to come to his senses and stop rejecting his own heritage.

> Listen Ocol, my old friend,
> The ways of your ancestors
> Are good,
> Their customs are solid
> And not hollow
> They are thin, not easily breakable
> They cannot be blown away
> By the winds
> Because their roots reach deep into the soil

This is the theme of Lawino's entire song.

But because she tends to sing it too stridently, because she refuses to make the slightest effort to adjust to modern ways, because she remains so intractably old-fashioned, Lawino eventually exposes herself as a tribal chauvinist who is as limited in vision as her husband Ocol. Sometimes she is conscious of her inflexibility, as when she admits she cannot 'cook like a white woman' or 'dance the white man's dances' because she has never cared to learn such revolting skills. On other occasions she appears to be totally unaware of the strength of her cultural prejudices, and this naïvety sets her criticism of others in an ironic light. For example, she showers insults on Tina's lipstick, powder, perfume, wig and artificially dyed and straightened hair, yet in the very next breath goes on to extol Acoli customs of tattooing, body-painting, body-scenting and hairdressing. Her aim may be to condemn Tina's apewomanship and to ridicule Ocol's perverse preference for western odours and adornments, but she does not seem to realize that she is simultaneously betraying the absurdity of her own dogmatic Acolitude. Her unconscious undercutting of her own argument is a classic example of reflexive satire: the use of satire to satirize the satirist.

This is not to say that her attacks on the follies of westernized Africans are invalid or unjustified. Lawino has a keen eye for human stupidity, and her common sense does not allow her to be easily taken in by pretence

and affectation. She views Ocol and Tina not as her superiors but as ordinary human beings who are struggling desperately to prove themselves superior by adopting western ways. Since she does not understand such ways, she raises fundamental questions about their logic and propriety which westerners and westernized Africans never bother to ask. For instance, she wants to know why

> At the height of the hot season
> The progressive and civilized ones
> Put on blanket suits
> And woollen socks from Europe,
> Long under-pants
> And woollen vests,
> White shirts;
> They wear dark glasses
> And neck-ties from Europe.

She also can't imagine what pleasure these people take in smoking, drinking, kissing and other unclean, unnatural acts. Lawino regards such habits as foolish and unhealthy. Those who indulge in them ought to be avoided, not admired or emulated.

Even more difficult for Lawino to fathom are western habits of mind. Why should Ocol reckon time by consulting a clock when there are much more natural signs by which to measure the passing of a day? Why should he want to give his children Christian names when Acoli names are more meaningful? Why should he place so much faith in western medicine and prayer and scorn the remedies offered by herbalists and diviners? Why should politicians who are working towards the same goals oppose one another? By asking these questions Lawino focuses attention on some of the arbitrary and seemingly irrational aspects of western behaviour which would very likely baffle any non-westerner encountering them for the first time. She forces us to recognize the illogicality of our ways. Her incomprehension is both a warning and a protest against cultural arrogance.

What makes Lawino a more sensible person than Ocol is her acceptance of the validity of other cultures, despite her personal aversion to them. She does not insist, as Ocol does, that everyone conform to her own cultural pattern. She realizes that westerners will behave as westerners, and though she would clearly prefer Africans to behave as Africans, she is content to let Ocol eat western foods and adopt western eccentricities so long as he reciprocates with equal tolerance for her traditional preferences. She would like to see her husband return to the Acoli lifestyle he had once enjoyed, but if that is impossible (as it appears to be), then let him at least respect her right to remain loyal to the ways of her ancestors. At one point she sums it all up by saying

> I do not understand
> The ways of foreigners
> But I do not despise their customs.
> Why should you despise yours? . . .
> The pumpkin in the old homestead
> Must not be uprooted!

Lawino's 'lament' is a plea for tolerance, understanding and respect for African culture.

The success of **Song of Lawino** rests primarily on Okot's creation of a convincing persona to articulate his ideas. Lawino's vibrant personality animates the entire poem, giving it the energy and earthiness appropriate to an iconoclastic assault on post-colonial 'high' culture. Only a woman of her peasant origins could reject westernization so totally. Only a scorned wife of her particular matrimonial temper could denounce her husband so passionately yet yearn to win back his love. There may be inconsistencies in her conduct and huge self-contradictions in her argument, but these simply make her a more believable human being. She wins us over by the honest eloquence of her emotion, the primitive force of her tongue.

Yet we must never forget that she is a persona and that Okot may not have shared all her views. **Song of Lawino** is a long dramatic monologue deliberately placed in the mouth of an invented character, and to understand its true meaning we must carefully appraise the singer as well as the song. Lawino presents a persuasive case for African tradition because she is able to perceive salient absurdities of modern African life through eyes unclouded by formal education or acculturation to western ways. But though she sees clearly, her vision is limited by her own narrow cultural prejudices to a single, circumscribed point of view, and she has real difficulty seeing beyond her Acoli nose. This makes a good deal of her testimony suspect, for it is impossible to trust impassioned polemics brimming with so much overstatement and exaggeration. Lawino's argument, though tempered with unconscious irony, is just too one-sided.

This may have been why Okot decided to write **Song of Ocol** as a reply to Lawino. By giving Ocol a chance to state his own case, Okot could examine the same social, political and cultural issues from a totally different point of view. And in the process of ostensibly redressing the balance of a biased conjugal debate, he could make clever use of satire to reassert basically the same position he had advocated in **Song of Lawino.**

In singing his song, Ocol exposes himself as exactly the type of person Lawino had described—an angry, insensitive, impatient opportunist intent on destroying African traditions and institutions in the name of progress. He hated everything black because he associates blackness with backwardness and primitivism.

> What is Africa
> To me?
>
> Blackness,
> Deep, deep fathomless
> Darkness;
>
> Africa,
> Idle giant
> Basking in the sun,
> Sleeping, snoring,
> Twitching in dreams;

> Diseased with a chronic illness,
> Choking with black ignorance,
> Chained to the rock
> Of poverty . . .
>
> Mother, mother,
> Why,
> Why was I born
> Black?

In order to overcome his feelings of self-hatred and inferiority, Ocol is ready to uproot Lawino's pumpkins, burn mud huts, imprison witches and village poets, hang professors of African studies and obliterate indigenous cultural treasures. His aim is to

> Smash all these mirrors
> That I may not see
> The blackness of the past
> From which I came
> Reflected in them.

Much of Ocol's song is an inventory of what he intends to destroy. He speaks as a member of the ruling class that came to power after Independence with the ambition of transforming a former colony into a modern nation state. In order to bring 'civilization' to their part of the world, these westernized African leaders are planning to demolish the Old Homestead and build a New City complete with statutes of European explorers, missionaries and kings. Their notion of national progress is further imitation of Europe.

Nothing Ocol says wins our sympathy. He seems so intent on ravaging the countryside and throwing harmless people into prison in order to achieve a worthless goal that it is impossible to view him in a friendly light. He is obviously a blackguard obsessed with a desire to prove himself white. He displays no love or tenderness towards his fellow man and possesses no traits worthy of admiration. Indeed, one wonders why Lawino wants him back!

As Ocol speaks, his own words condemn him, making him the butt of ridicule. For example, after outlining a strategy for wiping out African culture and traditions and replacing them with western ways, he asks an African ambassador at the United Nations to

> Tell the world
> In English or in French,
> Talk about
> The African foundation
> On which we are
> Building the new nations
> Of Africa.

Ocol also claims to hate poverty but does nothing to help the poor, even though he has grown wealthy as a politician. His major concern as a public servant is not with the public welfare but with keeping thieves and trespassers off his vast country estate. He is a rich landed aristocrat in a poor underdeveloped country, a contrast which points up the disparity between his nationalistic ideals and parasitic practices. Virtually every line he speaks betrays him as an arch-hypocrite.

By the time we finish *Song of Ocol* we are aware that Lawino was right: Ocol's 'apemanship' has turned him into a monster. If he had managed to retain a healthy respect for African traditions, he might have been a better person and a far more constructive influence on his society. His fanatical westernization and rejection of himself have prevented him from developing into a creative human being. He has lost not just his ethnic identity but his humanity.

Thus *Song of Lawino* and *Song of Ocol,* though structured as a debate, actually present two sides of the same coin; they may face in opposite directions but they have precisely the same ring. Ocol's argument is undercut so completely by irony that it reinforces Lawino's position. And Okot, by removing himself from the quarrel between his personae, is able to establish an independent stance some distance from the ground Lawino defends. He advocated neither an atavistic return to Acoli customs and traditions nor a total abandonment of western ways. His aim appeared to be to help educated Africans—his readers, in fact—appreciate their rich cultural heritage so they can create a new culture equally meaningful and relevant to Africa.

Okot's next song was much more ambitious. Instead of carrying the cultural debate further, he turned to an explosive new political subject and treated it in a deliberately equivocal fashion. He used the same basic poetic form—an emotionally charged dramatic monologue—but invested it with such complex irony that its moral centre was difficult to discern. The poem has aroused considerable controversy in East Africa and is likely to go on provoking lively discussion for some time to come. Brief and puzzling, it has all the fascination of a conundrum.

Song of Prisoner begins as the anguished soliloquy of a man who appears to have been brutally beaten and thrown into prison for the most trivial of offences: vagrancy and loitering in the City Park. As he sits there counting his wounds and cursing his captors, he seems a victim of injustice and oppression. He broods on thoughts of his starving children, complains of his own hunger and thirst, and frequently lashes out at those he imagines to be responsible for his misfortunes. He even goes so far as to accuse his dead father of not having married a woman from the right clan, thereby foisting bad genes on all his descendants; then he turns around and accuses his mother of the same catastrophic matrimonial misjudgement. He also imagines his wife to be sleeping with a 'big chief' who drives a Mercedes Benz, and this vision gives him a macabre urge to 'drink human blood' and 'eat human liver'. Imprisonment is obviously driving him insane.

Not until the middle of the poem do we learn the real reason he has been locked up: he is a hired assassin who has killed the Head of State. Though he claims to have done this out of love for his country, his charge that the leader was 'a traitor, a dictator, a murderer, a racist, a tribalist, a clannist, a brotherist,...a reactionary, a revisionist, a fat black capitalist, an extortioner, an exploiter' sounds suspiciously like programmatic revolutionary rhetoric. Perhaps the prisoner is the heroic liberator he claims to be; perhaps he is the dupe of sinister forces in his society. In evaluating his conduct, we have only his own half-demented words to go by.

And next we hear him shouting that he had been a Minister in the Government, in fact he had been the one responsible for 'Law and Order...Peace and Goodwill in the land'. He asks for his gold pen so he can write to his children and parents and send them fat cheques. He now appears to have changed character completely, picking up a new set of parents along the way and leapfrogging from the depths of proletarian squalor to the heights of bourgeois luxury. Indeed, he has been transmuted into another Ocol. Could this be the same prisoner we had seen and heard earlier? If so, has he gone irretrievably mad? What accounts for his sudden, magical transformation?

Okot does not stop to answer these questions before moving into the final section of the poem, which contains a morbid appeal for oblivion as a distraction from despair. The prisoner says he wants to be free so he can sing, drink, dance and fornicate until he forgets the anguish of his insignificance. He knows that he has no future and that his children will never go to school or have a chance to escape wretched poverty. His only hope for release from these depressing thoughts lies in total debauchery:

> I want to drink
> And get drunk,
> I do not want to know
> That I am powerless
> and helpless,
> I do not want to remember anything.
>
> I want to forget
> That I am a lightless star,
> A proud Eagle
> Shot down
> By the arrow
> Of Uhuru!

The poem's internal contradictions generate a confused response. Should we feel sympathy for this prisoner, or disgust? Is he worthy of pity, approbation or condemnation? Was his crime noble or base? Okot leads us first towards one conclusion, then towards another until we are trapped in the labyrinth of the prisoner's complex personality. By encouraging us to make judgements which we later feel compelled to reverse, Okot makes us realize how difficult it is to distinguish between good and bad in contemporary Africa. We applaud the guerrilla 'freedom fighters' who boldly take the law into their own hands, yet we are appalled by the hard-fisted tactics of military regimes founded with the same disregard for individual liberties. The political assassin is seen as a national hero by some and as a self-seeking rogue by others. Many who feel oppressed may themselves be ruthless oppressors. Okot seems to be saying that in the confusion of post-Uhuru Africa, justice, honour, loyalty, morality—all the great social and political virtues—may be subject to reinterpretation according to the exigencies of the moment and the bias of the interpreter. There are no longer any fixed truths, only competing ideologies. This may be a cynical conclusion and perhaps even a gross misreading of Okot's intention, but when confronted with such rich ambiguity in a literary work, it is easy for a reader to go astray. The fact that the poem has already stirred so much controversy suggests that it invites many different interpretations.

Although most critics have assumed that *Song of Prisoner* is the song of a single prisoner, there is some evidence suggesting that it may have been conceived as a medley of various voices. Okot is reported to have said that the 'Soft Grass' episode involving the Minister and the gold pen is an interpolation by 'a man in the next cell, whom the Prisoner overhears'. If this is so, what is to prevent us from identifying other lyrics which seem out of character as songs sung by other prisoners? Perhaps *Song of Prisoner* actually represents the communal wailings of an entire cell block. This would make the poem less complex psychologically but certainly no less damning as an indictment of contemporary African experience. Despite flashes of gallows humour, it remains a very gloomy song.

Song of Malaya, which is pared with *Song of Prisoner* in *Two Songs,* provides boisterous comic relief. The prostitute who sings it is good-natured, proud of her profession and tolerant of all mankind. Like a public convenience she invites men of every description to enter and make use of her facilities. No one is barred or refused service. She is the great social equalizer, humanity's most effective democratizer because she mixes with high and low indiscriminately. All who come to her are reduced to the same level. She functions as the world's lowest common multiplier.

And for this very reason she is in a good position to expose cant and hypocrisy. Her song is a series of rebukes to her critics—to the chief who accuses her of giving him venereal disease, to the wife who is unhappy about sharing her husband with a whore, to the priest who preaches that monogamy is morality, to the schoolmaster who calls her children bastards, to the brother who despises her yet buys the services of other prostitutes, to the policeman who arrests her even though he was her customer the night before. Malaya answers their charges with common sense and good humour, pointing out their own failings and moral weaknesses in the process. Each of her replies ends with words of encouragement to her fellow professionals and lay workers:

> Sister *Malayas*
> Wherever you are,
> Wealth and health
> To us all.

As in *Song of Lawino* the strategy of the monologue is to juxtapose two different world views, one a commonly accepted perspective and the other a somewhat unortho-

dox outlook, and to slant the argument in such a fashion as to demonstrate the moral superiority of the latter. In *Song of Malaya* we find ourselves agreeing that prostitution seems a wholesome profession when compared with marriage, priesthood, teaching, law enforcement and other occupations which are no better ethically and spiritually than the imperfect human beings who take them up. The prostitute is at least self-reliant, open and unpretentious—a much healthier person psychologically than those who condemn her. She embraces all who come to her, never attempting to deny pleasure to those who are willing to pay the price. Her message, like Lawino's, is one of tolerance for human diversity. She accepts whatever seems natural and genuine, rejecting only the patently artificial and perverted. Malaya is clearly more moral than her society.

Some of the criticism directed at Okot as a commentator on East African society has asserted that his analysis of contemporary social problems is shallow, for he was more an entertainer than an incisive social scientist or political reformer. [In *The Last Word: Cultural Synthesism*], Taban lo Liyong has charged him with playfulness and insincerity:

> I see more of the frivolous and more of the jester in these [sociological and anthropological] works. Only rarely do I see an Okot with tight lips and protracted visage. . . . Okot with a political temper is better than Okot the skeptic posing as a champion for dying and dead customs he doesn't believe in. These are useful only as means for giving play to sarcasm, and making fun of other people's ways in mock-revenge for their destruction of the ways of his own people, again in which he does not seriously believe.

Ngugi wa Thiong'o has expressed the view that Okot was rather short-sighted for he failed to look at the root causes of East Africa's social problems: 'While I agree with p'Bitek's call for a cultural revolution, I sometimes feel that he is in danger of emphasizing culture as if it could be divorced from its political and economic basis. . . Can we be ourselves when our economic life is regulated by forces outside Africa? More recently Andrew Gurr, echoing Ngugi and quoting Frantz Fanon, has complained [in *Writers in Exile: The Creative Use of Home in Modern Literature*] that Okot's diagnosis of social ills 'does not go below the surface of the problem . . . [He] is fussing over the outworn garments of the past, not the teeming present'. These critics wanted Okot to probe more deeply into the body politic and expose the sources of its sickness instead of merely mocking the bizarre convulsions of a delirious, moribund society. They would have liked him to behave as a doctor rather than as a clown.

Yet Okot's strident style of satiric singing won him a wider audience than any political propaganda would have done, and he achieved this immense popularity without pulling any of his punches. Indeed, his four outspoken songs compel us to listen to voices we would not ordinarily heed. Original in form, technique and idea, these vivid lyrical soliloquys captivate the imagination and provoke the intellect while advancing half-ironic arguments that radically challenge some of our basic cultural assumptions. Our immediate reaction to such audacity may be to laugh in astonishment, but Okot has a talent for forcing us to think as we laugh. He never lets us rest comfortably in mindless complacency. This makes him an unsettling writer, indeed a very revolutionary artist, for his constant questioning teaches us entirely new ways of seeing ourselves and others. By singing comically and occasionally off-key, he draws attention to serious social disharmonies which require adjustment and correction. He wrote not merely to amuse but to instruct and guide his people. He once said that a truly African literature must have 'deep human roots' and deal 'honestly and truthfully with the problems of the human situation'. Okot p'Bitek, in striving to produce this kind of literature, has become one of Africa's major creative writers. He was a serious clown who provoked regenerative laughter. (pp. 144-56)

> *Bernth Lindfors, "The Songs of Okot p'Bitek," in* The Writing of East and Central Africa, *edited by G. D. Killam, Heinemann Educational Books Ltd., 1984, pp. 144-58.*

Tanure Ojaide (essay date 1986)

[*In the following excerpt, Ojaide examines opposing voices in p'Bitek's poetry.*]

Okot p'Bitek, who died in 1982, is one of the best known African poets. After the long domination of the African literary scene by West Africans, p'Bitek stormed the "literary desert of East Africa" with *Song of Lawino* in 1966. This was followed by *Song of Ocol* and *Song of a Prisoner.* His poems, "songs," are apparently very close to traditional African poetry. The Ugandan poet makes use of personae to express his views on the modern African socio-political scene. His *Song of Lawino, Song of Ocol,* and *Song of a Prisoner* are some of the best known personae in African poetry today.

p'Bitek's use of personae, masks, has made his viewpoint difficult to establish. Little or no critical attention has been paid to the poet's viewpoint in these poems. Critics like G. A. Heron and Edward Blishen have so far tended to focus on each of the personae without a synthesis of the three personae so as to propose the poet's own attitude to these characters. [In *The Poetry of Okot p'Bitek*] Heron says that "Lawino, Ocol, and the prisoner do represent the predicament and many of the attitudes of certain social groups in recent Ugandan history." However [as Norman Friedman noted in his "Point of View in Fiction"], it is necessary to know what the poet himself feels about these representative characters, since "the relationship between the author's values and attitudes, their embodiment in his work, and their effect upon the reader, have been and continue to be of crucial concern," and more so in Uganda and the rest of black Africa where the political culture is relatively young. In this article I intend to examine the personae of these three "songs," the way they function thematically

and stylistically, and from the discussion propose the poet's viewpoint.

Lawino seems to be the most likable character of the three. She represents the indigenous authentic African way of life. On the other hand, Ocol is a detestable character because he is presented as a cultural renegade. And the Prisoner is presented as mentally unstable and not reliable. Thus, the poet's viewpoint in *Lawino* is both romantic and realistic, in *Ocol* ironic, and in *Prisoner* ambivalent and pessimistic.

Lawino is the poet's voice in *Lawino.* The poem begins with "My Husband's Tongue is Bitter" in which Lawino recounts what her husband, Ocol, says about her, her people, and black people in general. Ocol is

> a modern man,
> A progressive and civilized man,

who "has read extensively and widely", and despises Lawino because she is antiquated, illiterate, pagan, physically ugly ("the owl type"), and unintelligent. Consequently, she is said to be "blocking his progress." (p. 371)

Two opposing values are thus presented in *Lawino.* Lawino picks different aspects of culture and uses each to show herself, Ocol, and Tina to bring out the differences between her and her cultural adversaries. Lawino does not condemn Western culture per se, but she strongly abhors Africans who copy alien ways indiscriminately. In "The Graceful Giraffe Cannot Become a Monkey," she states how nature has decreed differences to form various racial traits. To Lawino,

> Ostrich plumes differ
> From chicken feathers,
> A monkey's tail
> Is different from that of the giraffe,
> The crocodile's skin
> Is not like the guinea fowl's,
> And the hippo is naked, and hairless.
> The hair of the Acoli
> Is different from that of the Arabs;
> The Indians' hair
> Resembles the tail of the horse;
> It is like sisal strings...
> A white woman's hair
> Is soft like silk;
> It is light
> And brownish like
> That of the brown monkey,
> And is very different from mine.
> A black woman's hair
> Is thick and curly.

Beginning with nature, Lawino logically demonstrates the uniqueness of racial qualities. When one group forsakes its own nature and imposes on itself alien values, there is incongruity. That is why it is unnatural for an African woman with "thick and curly" hair to try to make it "soft like silk" like a white woman's. Tina, with whom Lawino shares her husband, "fries" her hair to make it look like a white woman's, and this results in her resembling

> A chicken
> That has fallen into a pond;
> Her hair looks
> Like the python's discarded skin.

Blacks who forsake their natural ways become artificial and weird. Tina and her "modern" types

> fry their hair
> In boiling oil
> As if it were locusts,
> And the hair sizzles
> It cries aloud in sharp pain
> As it is pulled and stretched.
> And the vigorous and healthy hair
> Curly, springy and thick
> That glistens in the sunshine
> Is left listless and dead
> Like the elephant grass
> Scorched brown by the fierce
> February sun.
> It lies lifeless
> Like the sad and dying banana leaves
> On a hot and windless afternoon.

There is something suicidal in the act of deliberately killing one's "vigorous and healthy" self. Besides, there is something demoniacal and strange in frying hair in boiling oil. By implication, Lawino emphasizes that white women are beautiful with their own kind of hair, and the strangeness creeps in with black women transposing to themselves what is not naturally theirs. Moving from one aspect of difference to another, Lawino uses hair, beauty, dance, food, love, religion, and politics to establish the dichotomy between herself and Ocol and Tina. She follows the simple, natural African way which she imbues with dignity, humility, innocence, respect, authenticity, and pride. She does not "fry" her hair; she does not bleach her skin to look lighter than she really is. She dances vigorously in the open and in light and will not commit abortion. Besides, she has a name which is meaningful to her unlike Clementine, called Tina for short, who has a meaningless alien name.

The borrowed ways are presented through Ocol and Tina's lifestyles as disrespectful, shameful, artificial, and degrading. She implies that those Africans who want to erase their natural traits such as hair and complexion are suffering from feelings of inferiority. In *Lawino,* Lawino is like a mother asking her children to behave respectfully. She tells Ocol that "To behave like a child does not befit you." She is like Mother-Earth lamenting her defilement by her erring children, Ocol and Tina.

The poet puts effective rhetorical devices at Lawino's disposal in stating her case against Ocol and Tina. She uses animal imagery to describe the two ways of life. She describes traditional African ways with the bull and the giraffe. The bull is associated with royalty and courage, while the giraffe has beauty and gracefulness. Unlike the bull and the giraffe which have positive qualities, repulsive animals such as the python, hyena, ostrich, and monkey describe Tina's ways. Lawino also uses negative sensuous imagery to show how despicable Tina looks. As she rubs cosmetics to become lighter, she smells like carbolic. Besides, lipstick has made her lips look like "raw yaws" and an "open ulcer," and because she starves to be slim, her bones rattle. Furthermore, Lawino uses logic in her arguments on the need for the inviolability of racial identity. She uses images of nature to prove that earth race has its own unique traits.

In spite of Ocol's criticism of Lawino as illiterate and unintelligent, one does not accept her in that bad light because, by carefully reasoning out the natural differences among peoples, she shows that she is knowledgeable and intelligent. Part of the subtlety in Lawino lies in what she does not condemn in Ocol and Tina. She does not, for instance, condemn Africans wearing Western dress. She is also silent on such amenities as electric light and pipe-borne water. What she is against is affectation and artificiality in manners and modes of life.

Lawino's position, therefore, in *Lawino* is clear. She defends the traditional African way of life and opposes the Africans who adopt white people's ways which are naturally not meant for them. Her refrain in the song if "Let no one uproot the Pumpkin from the old homestead." The pumpkin is the totemic symbol of the natural life led by the people. Somehow, Lawino's plea for the pumpkin to remain where it has been shows that she is not open to change. However, as I have stated earlier, her silence on certain aspects of Western life could be interpreted to mean her advocacy of selected aspects of foreign ways of life. On rare occasions, Lawino seems to condemn anything alien and that does not help her image as a defender of authentic ways in any region of the world. Her attitude toward Western dance and food illustrates this narrow-mindedness. According to her, in Western dances,

> Each man has a woman
> Although she is not his wife,
> They dance inside a house
> And there is no light.
> Shamelessly, they hold each other
> Tightly, tightly,
> They cannot breathe....
>
> Men hold the waists of the women
> Tightly, tightly....
> And as they dance
> Knees touch knees;
> And when the music has stopped
> Men put their hands in the trouser-pockets.

Narrow-minded and exaggerated as these lines may seem, they are meant to show the sharp contrast between the vigorous, healthy, and innocent dance in the arena and the unhealthy, immoral, and repressive dance of the "White People." Lawino seems bent on stopping the spread of what she considers a corrupting influence among her people. It is the same attitude she shows toward foreign food. When she hears that foreigners eat frogs, shells, tortoise, and snakes, she vomits. Such prejudice on her part is meant to show that her African food is as good as, if not better than, foreign dishes.

Lawino presents Ocol as misbehaving in spite of his so-called education. He does not respect his in-laws and his black people. Ocol is only quoted in *Lawino* as having said certain things. For a balanced view of the parties, Taban lo Liyong suggested [in "Lawino is Unedu"] that Okot p'Bitek should give Ocol and Tina a chance to defend themselves in the light of Lawino's complaints. Since Ocol and Tina stand for the same values, *Song of Ocol* becomes their joint response to Lawino.

Lawino's major complaint against Ocol is his hatred of African ways and things and his copying Western ways of life indiscriminately. In *Ocol,* the reader learns that Lawino is at least not wrong about Ocol's disrespect for African ways. In fact, the harsh tone of his condemnation of Africa suggests he hates Africa and all that is African far worse than Lawino relates. He considers Lawino a "defeated General" and her song mad bragging. Ocol's "song" lacks reason and logic. He says that his group

> will plough up
> All the valley,
> Make compost of the pumpkins
> And the other native vegetables.

Ocol does not say what he will plant in the valley. If he wants to destroy the pumpkins and other native vegetables, does he not betray a sense of unreality in believing that vegetables are bad because they are native? Ocol so hates blackness that he asks,

> Mother, mother,
> Why,
> Why was I born
> Black?

He rejects entirely the African past that once nurtured him. He wildly orders his people to

> Smash all these mirrors
> That I may not see
> The blackness of the past
> From which I came
> Reflected in them.

The mirror image is significant as it exposes Ocol's fear of reality. The mirror naturally reflects what is before it, and Ocol's refusal to see his past shows him as psychologically unbalanced. This is quite unlike Lawino who has self-recognition since she accepts certain deficiencies in the old ways she advocates. For instance, she admits that

> Ring-worm sometimes eats up
> A little girl's hair
> And this is terrible.

but she feels that since nature has identified human traits and ways, it is unnatural and wrong, for example, for an African woman to use the white people's ways of beautifying herself, since the two concepts of beauty are different.

What is revealing in Ocol's "defence" is that, unlike Lawino who goes into specific cultural aspects, he generalizes. In *Lawino,* Lawino quotes Ocol as saying:

> Black people are primitive
> And their ways are utterly harmful
> Their dances are mortal sins
> They are ignorant, poor and diseased.

These are stock descriptions of Africans in colonial books which Ocol reads. Ocol is like a participant in a debate who spends all his time generalizing about the bad aspects of his opponent. However, that one side is bad does not exonerate his own side from what he has been accused of. Besides, his side could be worse than the bad side of his opponent. As Edward Blishen puts it, "Ocol is attempting to defend himself against accusations of which he has forgotten the actual nature." One expects Ocol to defend Tina's hair style, her starving to be slim, her bleached skin, wigs, suggested abortion, and alien name, and his own Roman Catholicism, his readings, and especially his involvement in the party politics which brings disunity to his people. But he does not.

In the later sections of *Ocol,* Ocol talks like one of the few exploiters of Uhuru. He has acquired "sheep" and other things, and he is contemptuous of the "cowardly fools" who are afraid to take part in politics. Even if one agrees that certain persons refuse to participate actively in politics, should Ocol boast of being in the exploiting class in his country? Ocol goes on to celebrate as heroes Leopold of Belgium who plundered the Congo and Bismark who presided over the sharing of Africa to colonial powers. By this time Ocol's exploitative, fascist, and reactionary nature is revealed. He strays from his criticism of Africa and her past unexpectedly to celebrate the African environment he wants destroyed. There is nostalgic passion as he recollects

> That shady evergreen *byeyo* tree
> Under which I first met you
> And told you
> I wanted you,
> Do you remember
> The song of the *ogilo* bird
> And the chorus
> Of the grey monkeys
> In the trees nearby?

These are, perhaps, the most tender lines in *Ocol.* This seems to suggest that subconsciously, Ocol is fighting against himself and what he likes. And this may partly be responsible for his lack of specifics. Rather ironically, Lawino who is illiterate is more subtle than Ocol the educated man who generalizes unintellectually.

Who then is Okot p'Bitek's voice, Lawino or Ocol or neither of the two? From the two "songs," Lawino seems to be far more likable than Ocol. She is like a heroine championing the cause of her people's culture, unlike Ocol, who discards his roots and even hails Leopold of Belgium and Bismark of Germany, which places him on the side of colonialists and plunderers. One learns after listening to both Lawino and Ocol that Lawino is not as bad as Ocol says she is—she is natural and her vast knowledge enables her to compare the ways of her people with other people's. She sees the differences among Blacks, Whites, Arabs, and Indians. Taban lo Liyong is far from right in saying that "Lawino is the doomed villain of her lament, and that the whole thing is an ironic praise of Ocol by his anachronistic wife." Contrary to Liyong's view, the poet treats Lawino with realistic intensity. It seems that Lawino knows more than we expect her to, and if this means that p'Bitek intrudes into Lawino's personality, especially in the comments on politics and Roman Catholicism, it shows that Lawino is p'Bitek's double. That the poet imbues his likes and dislikes into Lawino's "song" demonstrates how fascinated he was with the personality of Lawino.

In addition, it seems that the rhythm of *Lawino* is more lively and charged compared to that of *Ocol.* This is not surprising since there is a lot of passion involved in celebration and this is more so when the subject of celebration is imbued with romantic qualities. *Lawino* combines both romanticism and realism. The cultural heritage is described romantically as in

> When the daughter of the Bull
> Enters the arena
> She does not stand there
> Like stale beer that does not sell,
> She jumps here
> She jumps there.
> When you touch her
> She says "Don't touch me!"

As Lawino romanticizes her heritage, she realistically presents the deterioration from the cultural ideal because of the aping of alien ways by such cultural renegades as Ocol and Tina. In "The Graceful Giraffe Cannot Become a Monkey," there is movement towards a climax as the rhythm intensifies, and mood, tone, and meaning become fused. In some of the sections I have already quoted and in

> My breasts were erect.
> And they shook
> As I walked briskly,
> And as I walked
> I threw my long neck
> This way and that way
> Like the flower of the lyonno lily
> Waving in a gentle breeze . . .
>
> I was the Leader of the girls
> And my name blew
> Like a horn.
> Among the Payira.
> And I played on my bow harp
> And praised my love

there is great poetic energy which is unmatched in *Ocol* or *Prisoner.* It seems the personality of the poet has passed into Lawino flowing round and round what she says. If it is true that p'Bitek started as early as 1954 to write what turned out to be *Lawino* twelve years later, the poet in the long period could have unconsciously passed into his heroine his own feelings. The pre-independence and independence years from 1954 to about 1965 were a period of intense nationalistic fervour in Uganda and other parts of Africa. Unlike the long period which went into the writing of *Lawino* (first written in Acholi and translated by the author into English), there does not seem to be such effort in *Ocol* (1970) and *Prisoner* (1971) which are shorter, hurried, and less intense.

Unlike *Lawino* which is a mixture of romance and realism, *Ocol* is mainly ironic. Ocol so aligns himself to such obnoxious parties like Leopold and Chancellor Bismark and the exploiting class in his country that he becomes despicable. Ocol's "song" is neither a lament not a celebration, unlike Lawino's. His is a wild outpouring against Africa. Ocol rages that

> We will uproot
> Each tree
> From the Ituri forest
> And blow up
> Mount Kilimanjaro,
> The rubble from Ruwenzori
> Will fill the Valleys
> Of the Rift,
> We will divert
> The mighty waters
> Of the Nile
> Into the Indian Ocean.

This is demagogic rage in which the speaker is unable to make a connected statement about the ways he is embracing. The question is not of forests and mountains, since they exist everywhere. There is the suggestion that Ocol does not understand the ways of the people he is copying, since many white people love forests, mountains, and rivers. Or he is somewhat accurately following those Whites who exploit nature for water, metal, oil, and other resources. What is significant in the rage is his fight against nature, which looks like a mad enterprise. Ocol does not build; he wants to destroy. There is something farcical in him; he sees Africa as a "large arc / Of semi-desert land", and yet he points at his sheep, "that golden carpet / Covering the hillside."

p'Bitek distances himself from Ocol, a sharp contrast to Lawino, whom the poet imbues with much of his likes, dislikes, and knowledge. p'Bitek makes Ocol an ineffective spokesman for his position, and the persona is to be seen critically. This does not mean that the poet accepts Lawino wholesale, for some aspects of her attack are more convincing than others. In any case, the poet seems to be so fascinated by Lawino that he uses the mask of Ocol to say what he does not believe in. Lawino seems to be the self of the poet and her "song" impresses us as conveying genuine feelings. Ocol, on the other hand, looks like the poet's anti-self. The poet uses the anti-self mask to express a contrary view of Lawino's stance. The tension between traditional African ways and indiscriminately borrowed alien ways lies beneath **Lawino** and **Ocol.**

Song of a Prisoner further extends the complexity of the poet's viewpoint. The poet does not make his mouthpiece a credible alternative to the ruler who was assassinated but whose government could not be toppled. There is ambivalence in the poetic viewpoint in that while political change is necessary in the corrupt and tyrannical situation presented in the poem, another order represented by the Prisoner is potentially selfish, materialistic, and tyrannical.

Prisoner is an angry complaint by the Prisoner against those who imprisoned him. The Prisoner sees himself as a victim of the Establishment. He has eliminated a leader who had been

> . . . a traitor
> A dictator
> A murderer
> A racist
> A tribalist
> A clanist
> A brotherist.

Furthermore, the leader was corrupt and was

> A reactionary
> A revisionist
> A fat black capitalist
> An extortioner
> An exploiter.

This cataloguing helps to establish the hideous image of the former leader. These are politically emotive names which the Prisoner calls the late ruler. The Prisoner thus indirectly sees himself as better than the negative names he gives the assassinated leader. Because the leader was very bad, the Prisoner is angry with his jailers who do not appreciate the good he has done for the people of his country. The point is that those who have thrown him in jail are of the same political persuasion as the former leader. It is naive for him to think that those he wants to remove from power violently will treat him kindly. In any case, the reader is tempted to praise the Prisoner who single-handedly removed the head of a repressive regime. The assassinated leader's tyranny touched the common people, since

> A stone wall
> Of guns
> Surround our village,
> Steel rhinoceroses
> Ruin the crops
> In the fields
> And sneeze molten lead
> Into the grass-thatched huts,
>
> Roaring kites
> Split the sky
> And excrete deadly dungs
> On the heads

> Of the people,
> Pots and skulls
> Crack . . . .

From the catalogue of atrocities perpetrated by the former leader, the Prisoner looks like a hero.

However, the Prisoner does not deserve the cloak of heroism he fantasizes as rightly belonging to him. He accepts money for the assassination and tries to play down his role as a hireling by presenting himself as a saviour. He admits that "I did not do it / For the money." Why did he accept money at all? He also talks of "those who hired me." He is a hireling and not a revolutionary, selflessly fighting against the prevailing atrocities in his land in order to bring about a more wholesome government to benefit the people. He is thus not the betrayed hero he says he is.

The Prisoner is not consistent on why he is in jail. Sometimes it seems as if he shot the former leader, but at another time he seems to have been jailed for his views. And once he gives the impression of being arrested for loitering unlawfully in a park. These inconsistencies in the Prisoner's role and defense jar his claims to heroism. The poet seems to emphasize the negative aspects of the Prisoner as the Prisoner emphasizes the negative aspects of the assassinated leader.

Rage as the Prisoner does against the Establishment and his people's inability to appreciate his act, he himself will not make a positive alternative to the leader he killed. He is highly egotistical, and he wants songs, celebrations, and fame. It is his kind that created personality cults, and in African politics such a personality is almost synonymous with dictatorship. He is guilty of some of the very things he accuses the slain leader of. This is ironical as he is not aware of his own qualities, which the reader knows. He is clannish and tribalistic like the slain leader. He chastises both his father and mother rudely for marrying outside their clans. He also accuses the dead leader of being a capitalist, but he is either one already or desires to be one himself. After all, he has a gold pen even in prison. Besides, he wants to send a "fat cheque" to his parents; and he says he drinks whiskey at home. He is morally lax, as he wants to sleep with "experienced prostitutes." He also wishes to sleep with his wife's sister, an act which in traditional African culture is morally repugnant.

Furthermore, the Prisoner is a traitor among his people. In the 1960s and 1970s the main concerns of Africa, especially through the O.A.U., were the decolonization of the continent and the eradication of apartheid. But here is a man who wants to dance the dance of colonialists and neocolonialists, and is eager to drink apartheid wine. By embracing the colonial and apartheid stigmas, the Prisoner exposes himself as a traitor among his Ugandan people. By saying that he is

> A proud Eagle
> Shot down

By the arrow
Of Uhuru

he seems to prefer colonialism to political freedom. He tries to gloss over his true self by evoking self-pity. He calls himself

. . . an insect
Trapped between the toes
Of a bull elephant.

Many metaphors and similes of this kind contrast his impotence with the might of the political Establishment.

The inconsistencies of the Prisoner show him as manic. His attitude to his parents shows a lot of contradictions. He is illogical and irrational. He is mentally deranged, as he wants to exume the bones of his parents to burn. Whether prison conditions have affected his mental condition or not, the poet does not tell. Perhaps, the poet wants the reader to see the Prisoner's illogicality as being exacerbated by his detention. But if the protester is a madman, what is the end of his confused protest? The poet shows a negative attitude to the Prisoner, whom he criticizes for not being better in many ways than the leader of the Establishment he wants to replace.

The poet's view point in *Prisoner* is pessimistic about Africa's political future, for there is no positive alternative to the bad leader. The pessimism is made bleak by the poet's ambivalence in the treatment of the Prisoner. The question is, which way Africa? None yet in *Prisoner.* The poet sees the need to eradicate a repressive regime, but he fears that the successor could be equally bad or worse.

From the preceding analysis, it is clear that Okot p'Bitek uses style and themes to define the poet's relationship with the speakers of the poems. The mixture of romance and realism in *Lawino* and Lawino's knowledge in spite of her illiteracy, together with her generally likable character, help to make her the most positive of the three personae. She condemns copying alien ways which are natural distortions and affirms the authenticity of her people's ways which she accepts may not be the best in the world. Ocol confirms Lawino's portrayal of him as a cultural sell-out. Having got Western education, Ocol's eyes "opened," and he started to turn against his roots. His position is most appalling since he is the son of the Bull. The poet suggests that when the Western way of life is accepted by the African in its entirety without consideration for relevant aspects, the receiver develops self-hatred. Lawino has some weaknesses and there could be some truth in Ocol's statements, but his generalizations do not help to make his case for Africans copying Western ways convincing. Ocol is the poet's mask but only a mask to avoid embarrassment and raise questions about what he unconvincingly sees as the drawbacks of African peoples.

The poet, therefore, advocates authenticity among his people without being obtusely zenophobic. He seems to be saying in *Prisoner* that as Africans rule themselves, he would like oppressive regimes to be removed, but not by false revolutionaries riding on the waves of popular discontent to satisfy their personal hunger for power. The three personae stand for ideas which are relevant in the discussion of the problems of contemporary Africa. They are, in a way, aspects of the poet's consciousness. The poet seems consistently concerned about his people as he endorses Lawino while he underscores the attitudes of Ocol and the Prisoner with irony and ambivalence respectively. (pp. 372-82)

Tanure Ojaide, "Poetic Viewpoint: Okot p'Bitek and his Personae," in Callaloo, Vol. 9, No. 2, Spring, 1986, pp. 371-83.

Ndubuisi C. Osuagwu (essay date 1988)

[*In the following essay, Osuagwu discusses the blending of traditional African poetic forms with modern experience in p'Bitek's songs.*]

A discussion of Okot p'Bitek as a traditional poet in modern garb calls for a definition of concepts. The concepts involved are the 'traditional' and the 'modern.' For the purpose of this paper, traditional poetry refers to the poetry of the people in the African countryside. It could be written; it could be performed. When written, the form, theme, appeal, style, including language must be able to send spontaneous ripples of passion down the nervous system of the average countrysider.

On the other hand, the 'modern' refers to those experiences which have come as a result of urbanisation, colonialism, Western technology and education. It also includes the decadence which follows these factors.

A consideration of p'Bitek in the light of the topic of this paper will be better rewarded by considering, as a point of departure, the background and training which have influenced his art. A great singer and dancer after the Acholi types, his loyalty to the Acholi culture, language and art had a harmonious development with his personality. Thus even while still in secondary school p'Bitek composed and directed a full length Opera.

In 1953, he published a novel in the Lwo language of the Acholi people, *Lak Tar Kinyero Wi Lobo (Are your Teeth White? Then Laugh)*. This was followed three years later by the first draft of the original Lwo traditional poetry, *Wer Pa Lawino (Song of Lawino)* which for obvious reasons colonial publishing houses rejected.

The bard's first degree thesis was devoted to the oral literature of the Acholi and Lango. Between his secondary school days and 1966 when the final draft of *Wer Pa Lawino* was written, p'Bitek was devoted to both studying and experimenting on Lwo traditional poetry.

His father was reputed as a good storyteller who was very witty in his use of proverbs. His mother was a great singer thirty four of whose songs the poet has presented in *Horn of My Love.* The early influence of his parents on his development was greatly re-inforced by his active involvement in the study and practice of his traditional poetry. Commenting on the nature of English education in Acholiland in p'Bitek's time, Gerald Moore observes [in *Twelve African Writers*]:

> A number of teachers... were themselves singers and players of the 'nana', the seven-stringed boat-zither which is the favourite instrument of the Acholi poet. These teachers were just in time to collect songs from some of the great pre-colonial singers, as well as composing many new ones of their own.... Thus the new educated class in Acholiland contained many who refused to let English education turn them aside from the language and literature of their own people.

From the poet's background, therefore, we discern a conscious objective in his training which culminated in his maturity as, not just a poet but, a traditional poet.

The world view of the bard's songs is the world view of the Acholi traditional society occasionally tinted by contemporary experience. A central issue in *Song of Lawino* is the disruption of the marriage institution. In the Acholi (as well as African) traditional society, marriage is regarded as a sacred union. There is room for polygamy in the sense that love is conceived as sharing, and what there is to share is the husband's love. But then, the first wife is not without her due recognition. In fact, there is an Acholi proverb which says, 'Your first wife is your mother.' It is the negligence of this recognition that Lawino is so bitter about. It is the cause of the marital disharmony in Ocol's family. This situation elicits a song from Lawino.

> Listen Ocol, you are the son of a Chief,
> Leave foolish behaviour to little children
> It is not right that you should be laughed at in a
>   song
> Songs about you should be songs of praise!

In *Song of Prisoner* we also note the lament of the disruption of family union which the prisoner suffers. The effect of prostitution on the matrimonial institution is also harped on in *Song of Malaya.*

The harmonious existence of the traditional society with the environment and the closeness of man to nature are usually celebrated in this world view. The recognition of this reality in his poetry is significant. For instance, Lawino shares such intimate and fond relationship with pots, grinding stones, Acholi dances, cooking stones, and describes them with such passion that we notice how much a part of her environment these things are.

The Acholi community like any other African community is one which conceives of time in terms of the natural rhythm of life. Man's leisure is dictated by the rhythm of work. We can therefore understand Lawino's concern about Ocol's relation to time. Time according to Lawino is not exhaustible and a natural rhythm of life dictates the time for various human activities. People do things in obedience to the rhythm of the day, the rhythm of the weeks, and even months. Precisely, in a traditional society, the concept of time is the concept of work.

Through her criticism of Ocol's addiction to artificial time, Lawino hints at the issues of dignity and collective consciousness which are integral parts of a traditional society. Ocol's new understanding of time makes him step from the position of the leadership expected of him to isolationism. The prisoner of the *Song of Prisoner* would want to break out of prison to join in traditional dances and rites. He recognises and emphasises the traditional value in collective consciousness.

Childbirth and children are significant issues in the community. They prop up marriage. A fruitful marriage leads to satisfaction and confidence on the part of the man, and the joy of motherhood on the part of the woman. The community also shares in the joy. We understand, therefore, Lawino's praise of manhood, fertility and the virtues of procreation in the Acholi culture. Even the Malaya emphasises this when she in *Song of Malaya* sings of the deception of men into believing that they are the fathers of their bastard children.

In the same vein, the Malaya condemns women who 'eat lizard eggs' to avoid bearing children. Within this world-view we appreciate Lawino's concern about Ocol's impersonal interaction with his children. The cries and coughs of children are fondly responded to and with pride by parents. It is therefore, extraordinary to fail to love and cherish children. Thus, Lawino asks:

> What is sweeter
> Than the cries of children?

Lullabies and reference to children's songs in *Song of Prisoner* underline the world view of the poems on children.

Song of Prisoner, written in what one might call movements, spans over fifteen of such movements. The title of each movement for p'Bitek sums up the central poetic image. The choice of the titles is equally significant. Almost all pick strings of the traditional Acholi community environment and experience: 'dung of chicken,' 'wounded crocodile', 'black mud', 'sacred rock', 'soft grass', 'cattle egret', 'undergrowth', etc., stir up images of common experience in the Acholi traditional society.

The celebration of bravery and strength is common experience, too. Traditional societies of the Eastern and Central Africa are known for their celebration of military exploits, war, and the like in their praise poetry. The philosophy behind such celebration underlines the competitive spirit of the people in such matters. Thus, a remembrance of one's prowess, bravery and previous exploits, acts as fuel to one's ambition and concept of his ability. It is within this philosophical and traditional Acholi reality that the prisoner's violent outbursts can be appreciated:

> See the muscles
> Of my arms,
> I can break your neck,
> Do you realise that?

Do you know
I was a footballer
And a boxer?
I have been a wrestler
And a runner,
I am a great hunter,
I have killed three buffaloes
And a hippopotamus
Single-handed . . .

The pattern of, and the spirit underlying the out-burst are purely traditional. Okot p'Bitek however understands that the times are modern and therefore extends this traditional poetic form to accommodate certain modern experiences which the traditional society has become accustomed to. Thus, the prisoner is not only an accomplished brave man within the traditional context but also a 'footballer' and a 'boxer' (modern forms of sports).

The Acholi world strongly believes in witchcraft which is considered as a crime not only against the individual but also against society. Witches are mischievous and therefore not to be allowed in the society. p'Bitek also accommodates this religious belief in his songs. Thus in an effort to assert his innocence the prisoner says:

Brother,
I am not a witch,
I was not caught
Dancing stark naked
Around your house . . .

The extended family system is revered usually within the society of p'Bitek's poetry. Blood relationship, as in the real traditional society, is traced and emphasised within the clan. p'Bitek's poetry celebrates this reality when Lawino condemns people and circumstances which tend to strain or sever such ties. Ocol and his brother, we are told, do not see 'eye to eye' because of party differences. Modern politics and the attendant obsession with material gains from political positions lead brothers into forgetting traditional values and the ethnic or lineage warmth that are supposed to bind them. Sharing and caring no longer exist. Sings Lawino,

Ocol does not share
Millet bread with his brother
Water from the public well
Is the only thing they share!
Ocol does not enter
His brother's house
You would think
There was homicide between them
That has not been settled . . .

This development is further expressed when the prisoner presents the prevalence of political thuggery, elimination of opponents and the travesty of justice which feature in modern politics. The mean confidence with which he peels off the prevailing ironies of the new system is significant.

. . . The best lawyers
Will defend me,
Our black nationalist judges

And those who hired me
Will set me
Free . . .

The new party politics does not make sense in the traditional community as the real issue is the material deprivation of the peasantry. Hence, Lawino contends:

If only the parties
Would fight poverty
With the fury
With which they fight each other
If disease and ignorance
Were assaulted
With the deadly vengeance
With which Ocol fights his mother's son
The enemies would have been
Greatly reduced by now.

The prisoner's concern is vehemently expressed when he contemplates the comfort of the Chief's dog against the background of his children's hunger and disease.

The fight for Uhuru was meaningful for the Acholi traditional society only in the context of the traditional concept of freedom. Freedom for the traditional society meant more than chasing the colonial masters out of power. It meant freedom in all its ramifications; freedom from oppression, exploitation. The irony which followed the achievement of Uhuru is the source of disillusionment for the society. Uhuru becomes synonymous with police brutality, exploitation, oppression of the peasantry and the lowly by the few inheritors of the white man's institution of power. Opportunists exploit the situation to oppress the true heroes of Uhuru. This Acholi experience is articulated in p'Bitek's poetry. He asks in desperation:

What is Uhuru
When all my thoughts
Are deep and silent rivers
Blocked up by concrete walls
Of fear and black suspicions?

He cannot understand this situation of freedom when he asks—

How can I think freely
When the very air
Has ears larger then
Those of the elephant
And keener than the bones
Of the 'ngege' fish?
Why are the words I speak
Captured and locked up
In a safe?

Freedom of speech of the individual is seen in the light of the poet's freedom in the traditional society. The poet is revered and even expected to speak out on behalf of the people. He could criticise those in authority without running any risks of incarceration. A poet who keeps 'silent in the face of tyranny' is considered irrelevant to the society.

Lawino also cannot understand the talk about Uhuru when materialism and power lead brothers into discordant existence, when murders and hatred reign all over the place. She asks:

> Is this the unity of Uhuru?
> Is this the Peace
> That Independence brings?

The prisoner, a spokesman for all prisoners of body and conscience, therefore longs for the real Uhuru, the real freedom. For him, real freedom is in the uninhibited communion with the traditional environment, with nature. He wants to 'breathe the air' of his own choice, 'Wake up early / Before the morning birds / Begin to sing'; Walk 'On the soft grass / Of the "olet" grazing ground / And share the sleepy air / With the cows and goats'; sleep 'With the sand / At the sea shore'.

Although p'Bitek leans much on the side of tradition, he does recognise the problem of book-illiteracy. He is aware that only a small percentage of the population of his society can read what he writes. As a result he devotes some time to certain experiences commonly shared by the literate group which he presents in the character of Ocol. This affords the 'modern' group the opportunity to introspect. Translating some of his works from the indigenous language into English and writing the others straight in English, the poet is able to reach this 'modern' audience.

To Okot p'Bitek the 'modern' (Western-educated) Acholi man tends to stir up

> ... a feeling of pity similar to the one
> the freed slaves of eighteenth-century America
> drew as a result of the near-zero nature of
> their cultural status.

S.E. Ogude commenting on the extent of the confusion of the freed slave contends that:

> The transition or more properly, the transformation from slave to free man did not indeed involve a change in cultural status ... The result was that the initial reaction of the freed slave (and this also holds true for the colonial people) was not to gather the shreds of his shattered cultural history, or to embark on a voyage of self-discovery, but to take the easy way out: to wear the garb of his erstwhile masters.

My contention is that Ogude could easily have had this in mind in that attempt to interpret what could be aptly described as the Ocol mentality in p'Bitek's poetry. And it is the poet's mentality that the poet's 'modern' audience commonly share.

The poet's allusions to the 'minister', in 'Big Chief' in *Song of Prisoner,* like the role of Ocol in *Song of Lawino* and *Song of Ocol* are made to draw attention to the failure of the Acholi (African) elite in spite of hard-won opportunities. Of course, their failure is measured using the yardstick of the traditional Acholi values.

Institutionalised prostitution, as we note in *Song of Malaya* (whore), Western system of democracy and politics are some of the other experiences which the poet identifies as modern and which make sense to a modern audience. The modern judicial system with all its pride in the nature of Western Law as an ass; christianity featuring its various contradictions; urbanisation and expensive western-type farms are some of the modern elements which Okot p'Bitek includes in his poetry.

The inclusion of these elements in p'Bitek's poetry makes it relevant to the modern reading audience. It helps to situate the poetry in contemporary times.

The characters of Ocol, Clementine (in *Song of Ocol* and *Song of Lawino*) 'Big Chief', the 'Minister', the Malaya (in *Song of Prisoner* and *Song of Malaya*) are recognisable in the modern society and among the modern black elites to whom the poet directs his songs.

The inclusion of these modern elements and characters, the mode of presentation of his poetry, etc., provide Okot p'Bitek with the garb of modernity which his poetry needs to be completely relevant to the contemporary society.

It is significant, however, that these modern features of his poetry are accommodated only within the thematic framework of his art. His aesthetic values, artistic techniques, style and form of his poetry are basically traditional. In other words, whereas elements of his modern garb could be found in WHAT he says, his traditional, artistic essence is found in HOW he says it—his techniques, his style, the form of his poetry—and this constitutes the sum total of the concept of the poet in the traditional society. What p'Bitek has consciously done is to extend the form and techniques, the frontiers of traditional poetry to accommodate the new experiences which constitute modernity.

Perhaps, one should assume this as a point of departure from which we could look at Okot p'Bitek's literary techniques against the background of the traditional society.

Okot p'Bitek's poetry is written in the song tradition of the Acholi traditional society. He insists that his poems are songs and emphasises this when he dedicates *Song of Ocol* to his father and mother who he acknowledges first, taught him to sing. The poems adopt the various forms of traditional songs which exist in his society. An illustration of this can be found in parts of his poetry which approximate to the satirical verse forms and songs of abuse of the Acholi people. Lawino, in her description of her rival, Clementine sings:

> Her lips are red-hot
> Like glowing charcoal,
> She resembles the wild cat
> That has dipped its mouth in blood,
> Her mouth is like raw yaws
> It looks like an open ulcer
> Like the mouth of a field ...

The origin of this form of satire can be better appreciated when compared with an Acholi satirical verse which the poet presents in *Horn of My Love*:

> His eyes died long ago,
> You can see clouds in them;
> The death of the eyes of the teacher.
> Clouds are visible in them, Oh;
> His eyes died long ago;
> The teacher does not leave his glasses behind;
> His eyes died long ago;
> You can see clouds in them.

Satirical songs are functional within the traditional set-up. In his poetry Okot p'Bitek adopts traditional satirical forms to moral ends. Lawino sings us a song for the unfortunate mother whose daughter is useless and mannerless.

> The mother of the beautiful girl
> Dies on the way to the well
> As if she has no daughter
> Her girl has no manners
> What is to be done?
> The mother of the girl
> Dies on the grinding stone
> In the bush to collect firewood!

Okot p'Bitek also adopts the dirge in his poetry. The form of the dirge he adopts to mourn the death of the dictator in *Song of Prisoner* is that which abuses the dead.

> Let the people
> Drink and dance,
> Let them rejoice,
> For
> The corrupt dictator
> Is dead.
> The noose on their necks
> Is cut...

Commenting on dirges that attack the dead, p'Bitek says,

> The body of the dead person is always treated with great respect and fear, and the burial rites are conducted with dignity and restraint. But in this group of songs the Acholi turn upon the dead with a viciousness which is not easy to explain.

The close similarity between the dirge quoted above from *Song of Prisoner* and another Acholi dirge which p'Bitek presents in *Horn of My Love* is significant and illustrates the fact of a common source for p'Bitek's poetry and traditional poetry in the Acholi society.

> The witch is dead;
> It is good that he is dead.
> You, Ulula,
> Touch his penis,
> See if it is cold and soft...
> Ee, the witch is dead, and it is good news.

In *Song of Lawino,* the dirge form is further exploited. Lawino mourns the 'loss' of her husband to the traditional society using the dirge,

> O, my clansmen
> . . . .
> Let us mourn the death of my husband
> The death of a Prince
> The ash that was produced
> By a great fire!
> O, this homestead is utterly dead...

Besides original creations of his own along the traditional forms, Okot p'Bitek also picks up existing Acholi traditional songs which he modifies in parts and fuses into his poetry. Examples abound as a comparison of his own recreations in his poetry with the original versions published in his anthology of Acholi songs (*Horn of My Love*) will illustrate. The first is the Love song which Lawino sings.

> She has taken the road to Nimule
> She will come back tomorrow
> His eyes are fixed on the road
> Saying, Bring Alyeka to me
> That I may see her...

The original version as presented in *Horn of My Love* goes thus:

> She has taken the path to Nimule;
> She will return tomorrow
> As she walked away her buttocks danced
> Bring Alyeka, let me see her...

The original version is much longer than that presented in *Song of Lawino.* The poet changes some of the phrases, omits whole lines and adds new ones perhaps to suit the immediate needs of his poetry and audience. In that case, he demonstrates the contention that creativity is given fullest realisation in performance as performance demands the poet's sense of judgment *vis-a-vis* his audience and other inevitable factors.

Commenting on the unique style and overwhelmed by the successful application of traditional poetic techniques which form the basis of Okot p'Bitek's poetry, Gerald Moore asks:

> What are the courses of this extraordinary style, with the unfailing freshness and sharpness of its images, its range of mood, its ability to gather up and convey to us whole distinctive way of life in work and play, in sorrow and in joy?

The effectiveness of p'Bitek's traditional poetic style is not in question. However, it will be interesting to note aspects of his style.

Okot p'Bitek is aware that the world of his poetry is the world of non-native speakers of the English language. He endeavours to communicate to his audience in the most intimate of languages. Hence he presents his earliest songs in the Lwo language. As he endeavours to capture a wider African audience, he translates these works into English while at the same time endeavouring to capture as much as possible the typical traditional Acholi idiomatic and rhetorical usages. To achieve this end, the poet flexes and bends the English language to accommodate those aspects of his society's linguistic heritage which contribute to the status of his art as traditional. It is, therefore, not accidental that the prisoner expresses his lot thus:

> Big Chief
> Is dancing my wife
> And cracking
> My sacred rock,

In the ordinary sense, the first two lines are an un-English expression. Those same lines contain a high degree of semantic violation. Human beings do not usually form the object of the verb to dance. Notwithstanding the un-Englishness of the construction coupled with the attendant violation of semantics, the expression makes a world of meaning to the African audience. The image it conjures is very sharp. The last two lines are very idiomatic and quite profound with meaning within the context of the world of this poem. Other examples of this flexibility of language abound throughout the poems.

I had mentioned semantic violations as if they were not within the realm of poetic eloquence. The fact is that within the traditional society, the poet exercises unlimited linguistic freedom which he exploits to create effect. Semantic violations are therefore used not only to create vivid images but also to excite the audience. The violations can come in the form of exaggerations, comparison of unrelated things, etc. The end result is what the poet strives at, and that is poetic eloquence.

We are excited and our imagination fired when p'Bitek's prisoner informs us:

> There is a carpenter
> Inside my head,
> He knocks nails
> Into my skull,

and when he complains,

> My penis
> Is an elephant's trunk
> Vomiting blood
> Like a woman
> In her moon ....

The violation of semantics in the lines quoted above consists in the presentation of the naturally impossible. What the poet achieves here is eloquence, poetic eloquence which has come through the firing of our imagination. We imagine the impossible situation where a carpenter can be accommodated in a human skull; where a penis can be extraordinary in its size. There is, therefore, a conscious play on fantasy. The audience is transported beyond the realm of reality. This is a level of intensification, a technique which the traditional poet finds invaluable.

Invocations are lavishly used in the poems to achieve immediacy. Their use also underlines the nature of rhetorical usages in the everyday life of the traditional African. Lawino does invoke her 'clansmen'; In *Song of*

Prisoner, invocations of the clan and clansmen are also made. This technique is an element of direct address which gives a dramatic effect to what is said. In addition to the clansmen, the ancestors are also invoked. There is in fact a lavish use of the elements of direct address and dramatic evocations. Lawino uses this very often. In any case that is the general style in the songs.

Okot p'Bitek's fictional characters pose as if addressing other characters directly. There are of course interruptions in this posture when the personae invoke a third party. The prisoner addresses various groups of persons and individuals. He also addresses even his dead father.

> You
> My old man
> Rotting in the earth,
> What an idiot
> You were.

There are many other such direct addresses: 'Wife / Wife / Are you asleep ...'; 'Wake up / You pressmen of the world'...; 'You Waiter', etc. We note the constant use of the second person pronoun in such direct addresses.

In *Song of Malaya,* it is the same style. The Malaya addresses the various groups that constitute her customers. When a third party is invoked, the second person pronoun is generally avoided and the party is addressed by name or title. This is illustrated when the whore interrupts her direct address to her customers to address her co-professionals:

> Sister Whores
> Wherever you are ...

The dramatic effect of these invocations is the best p'Bitek can achieve through the medium of writing. In using the device, there is an awareness of the fact that traditional poetry is better realised through performance. Hence he approximates to this essence of performance.

The characterisation techniques adopted by the poet are those used by traditional artists. Generally, in the traditional society, because of the closeness of man to nature and his environment, inanimate objects and abstract concepts are personified. Lawino tells us about grinding stones. There is the 'sister stone'; there is also the 'mother stone' which she describes thus:

> The mother stone
> Has a hollow stomach,
> A strange woman
> She never gets pregnant;
> And her daughter
> Never gets fatter ...

The Malaya could also personify the noise she hears made by another whore's bed thus:

> The soft drumming on the
> dancing mattress
> The bedstead gritting

her teeth . . .

The use of metaphors and metaphorical descriptions in Okot p'Bitek's poetry conjures up primal images. There is no room for artificial or cosmetic images. This adds to the traditional status of his poetry. In many cases, the metaphors are extended to achieve intensification of his poetic eloquence. The prisoner's description of his fate is full of extended metaphors. For instance he says of the wound in his head:

> Look at the laughing wound
> In my head
> Its cracked negro lips
> Painted with dirty brown Ochre

and tells us that his nose

> Is a broken dam,
> Youthful blood leaps
> Like a cheetah
> After a duiker

Occasionally the symbolism implied in the metaphors is humorous. For instance, when the Malaya advises her sister Malayas to remember to carry their 'boxing gloves' in their hand-bags the audience is tempted to smile. The neologism stirs up the image of sports and their associations. The allusion is germane and recognisable. The elements of wit and humour are rendered with great vigour.

Armed with powerful and compelling imagery, the poet's voice is elegaic in places with a sensibility grounded in the natural and perceived world of the Acholi. To achieve intensity in his poetic oratory, the poet incorporates praise chants and praise names. Ocol is the 'son of a bull', Lawino is the 'daughter of a bull', etc.

p'Bitek organises his lines to achieve intensity of thought or climax of experience. There is a certain level of listing which comes to a climax of experience towards the end of his lines. In addition, the poet makes a vast use of repetitions and parallel phrasing to achieve a cumulative effect. Talking about his children's education the prisoner says:

> My children are
> Not among them,
> My children do
> Not go to school
> My children will
> Never go to school.

The repetition of 'my children' coupled with the parallel involved in the alternating lines leads to the climax of the prisoner's thoughts of the impossibility of his children going to school.

In addition to the use of repetitions and parallel phrases, the bard adopts the use of short lines to aid memorisation which traditional poetry is capable of achieving during performance. At times he uses single-word lines also to ensure the reader's attention and to remove boredom.

There is also the element of the traditional sage reflecting on the present decadence, on communal memories pleading, questioning, telling, cautioning, and pointing things out to the younger and less wise members of the community. Sometimes he mocks, contemplates, challenges, using illustrations and admonitions from the traditional community repertory.

The success of the poet's traditional poetic forms, style and techniques is measured in his clear achievement of the poetic image which has been made possible through the various levels of intensification which he applies.

Precisely, Okot p'Bitek qualifies as a traditional poet albeit in modern garb as he bases the modern elements in his poetry on the technical repertory of traditional African literature. What we experience in his poetry is a modernism the emergence of which is from a clearly traditional African poetic tradition. Chinweizu and the others hold that,

> The artist in traditional African milieu spoke for and
> to his community. His imagery, themes, symbolisms
> and forms were drawn from a communally accessible
> pool. He was heard. He made sense.

My contention is that Okot p'Bitek as a poet could not be justly conceived in any language short of the above. In addition, he has in his poetry ensured continuity between traditional and modern poetry as we find him relevant in contemporary times in spite of his style. (pp. 13-28)

> *Ndubuisi C. Osuagwu, "A Traditional Poet*
> *in Modern Garb: Okot p'Bitek," in* The
> Literary Criterion, *Vol. XXIII, Nos. 1-2,*
> *1988, pp. 13-29.*

FURTHER READING

Moore, Gerald. "Songs from the Grasslands." *The Times Literary Supplement,* No. 3807 (21 February 1975): 204.
    Review of p'Bitek's *The Horn of My Love,* highlighting the author's Acholi heritage and praising his translation of traditional songs.

Ngugi wa Thiong'o. "Okot p'Bitek and Writing in East Africa." In his *Homecoming: Essays on African and Caribbean Literature, Culture and Politics,* pp. 67-77. London: Heinemann Educational Books, 1972.
    Focuses on p'Bitek's role in promoting awareness of East Africa's cultural tradition.

Ofuani, Ogo A. "Okot p'Bitek: A Checklist of Works and Criticism." *Research in African Literatures* 16, No. 3 (Fall 1985): 370-83.
    Bibliography of works by and about p'Bitek.

————. "The Traditional and Modern Influences in Okot p'Bitek's Poetry." *The African Studies Review* 28, No. 4 (December 1985): 87-99.
> Explores the influence of traditional and modern African culture on p'Bitek's verse.

————. "Digression as Discourse Strategy in Okot p'Bitek's Dramatic Monologue Texts." *Research in African Literatures* 19, No. 3 (Fall 1988): 312–40.
> Academic analysis of p'Bitek's use of digression in his dramatic monologues.

Ogunyemi, C. O. "In Praise of Things Black: Langston Hughes and Okot p'Bitek." *Contemporary Poetry* 4, No. 1 (1981): 19-39.
> Examines the works of Okot p'Bitek and Langston Hughes, focusing on their reversal of culturally biased myths about blacks in Africa and America.

————. "The Song of the Caged Bird: Contemporary African Prison Poetry." *Ariel* 13, No. 4 (October 1982): 65-84.
> Discusses the theme of imprisonment in the works of several authors, including p'Bitek.

Ward, Michael R. "Okot p'Bitek and the Rise of East African Writing." In *A Celebration of Black and African Writing,* edited by Bruce King and Kolawole Ogungbesan, pp. 217-31. Zaria: Ahmadu Bello University Press, 1975.
> Discusses the renaissance of East African writing, emphasizing the influence of p'Bitek's *Song of Lawino.*

Weinstein, Mark. "The Song of Solomon and *Song of Lawino*" *World Literature Written in English* 26, No. 2 (Autumn 1986): 243-44.
> Compares p'Bitek's use of metaphor in *Song of Lawino* to that in Song of Solomon.

Adam Clayton Powell, Jr.

1908-1972

American orator, autobiographer, and essayist.

Known primarily as a United States Congressman from Harlem, Powell was the first black member of the House of Representatives from the East. As a politician and a militant African-American leader, he made strong gains in the struggle for racial equality. Yet his career was marred by scandal. He was both pastor and playboy: a flamboyant, paradoxical, and charismatic figure who generated enormous controversy. Powell documented his views of American race relations in *Marching Blacks* (1945), which he termed "an interpretive history of the rise of the black common man." He also published a collection of sermons, *Keep the Faith, Baby!* (1967), and an autobiography, *Adam by Adam* (1971). Powell's works, though not particularly well-known, nevertheless illuminate an important figure and period in American history.

Powell was born in New Haven, Connecticut, in 1908. Shortly after his birth his family moved to New York City, where his father, Adam Clayton Powell, Sr., was made pastor of the Abyssinian Baptist Church. When the church moved to Harlem in 1923, Powell was exposed to the ideas of Jamaican-born black-rights champion Marcus Garvey and began attending meetings of black nationalist groups. "Marcus Garvey was one of the greatest mass leaders of all time," Powell later wrote. "He was misunderstood and maligned, but he brought to the Negro people for the first time a sense of pride in being black." During the Depression, Powell became a leader in his own right. He led a series of demonstrations against department stores, bus lines, hospitals, the telephone company, and other big businesses in Harlem, forcing them to hire blacks. He became chairman of the Coordinating Committee on Employment and organized picket lines outside the executive offices of the 1939-40 World's Fair, thereby gaining jobs at the fair for hundreds of black workers.

Powell also organized social and welfare programs at the Abyssinian Baptist Church, including a vocational guidance clinic as well as a soup kitchen and relief operation that supplied food, clothing, and fuel for thousands of Harlem residents. He served as the leader of the militant Harlem People's Committee and quickly earned a reputation, according to Simeon Booker in a 1967 *Ebony* magazine article, "for scrap, for agitation and for stinging rebuke." People began calling him "the Angry Young Man" and "Fighting Adam." Booker credited him with singlehandedly changing the course of national black affairs. In 1941 Powell was elected to the New York City Council. After serving four years on the council, Powell went to Congress as the representative of central Harlem. In Washington the new legislator continued his fight against racial discrimination. Al-

though unwritten prejudicial rules excluded him from such public places as dining rooms, steam baths, and barber shops, Powell defiantly made use of these facilities, often with his entire staff in tow. In one incident, a fellow representative, John E. Rankin from Mississippi, called Powell's election a "disgrace" and vowed never to "let Adam C. Powell sit by me" in the House chamber, which has open seating. Powell responded by calling Rankin's presence "distasteful" and commenting that only two people were fit to sit by Rankin: Hitler and Mussolini. Powell later recorded in *Adam by Adam* that "whenever Rankin entered the Chamber, I followed after him, sitting next to him or as close as I could. One day the press reported that he moved five times." In Congress Powell debated furiously with Southern segregationists, challenged discrimination in the armed forces, and wrote the Powell Amendment—an attempt to deny federal funds to projects that tolerated discrimination. Booker disclosed that Powell "upset tradition on Capitol Hill—against the wishes and combined efforts of many of his colleagues. Like no other Negro, except possibly the late Malcolm X, Adam knew how to anger, to irritate and to cajole his white counterparts."

Powell tackled a variety of causes. He fought for the admission of black journalists to the Senate and House press galleries; introduced legislation to ban racist transportation; and brought to the attention of Congress the discriminatory practices of such groups as the Daughters of the American Revolution (DAR). As chairman of the House Committee on Education and Labor, a position that made him perhaps the most powerful black in America, Powell's record was extraordinary. Under his direction the committee passed forty-eight major pieces of social legislation, including the 1961 Minimum Wage Bill, the Manpower Development and Training Act, the Anti-Poverty Bill, the Juvenile Delinquency Act, the Vocational Educational Act, and the National Defense Educational Act.

Booker asserted, however, that as Powell "became influential, powerful and dominating...he frequently clashed with Democrats, government officials, labor and educational leaders, and even the President on segregation and discrimination policies. While Southern chairmen blocked civil rights legislation at will, Adam tried to bottle major legislation whenever he felt it needed some anti-bias safeguards. This tactic brought him into open conflict with the 'white power structure.'" The resulting tense situation and Powell's record of high absenteeism brought upon him severe censure from his fellow legislators. This criticism was exacerbated by his reputation as a playboy and the accusation that he misused public funds by keeping on his payroll a receptionist with whom he was personally involved. His colleagues also charged him with tax evasion and junketeering. In response, Powell asserted: "The things other Congressmen try to hide, I do right out in the open. I'm not a hypocrite."

Powell's flamboyant public image and boastful nature severely damaged his career, however. When Powell called one of his constituents, Mrs. Ester James, a "bag woman" (a collector of graft for corrupt police), she sued him. Powell was found guilty of civil contempt but avoided arrest by appearing in New York City only on Sundays when summonses could not be served. Powell was convicted of criminal contempt in 1966 and took up residence on the Bahamian island of Bimini. In response to this conviction and other charges of misbehavior, a select committee of representatives investigated Powell, and on March 1, 1967, the House voted 307 to 116 to exclude him from the ninetieth Congress. Powell thus became the first committee chairman to be expulsed from the House in 160 years. Nevertheless, in a special election to fill his vacant seat two months later, Powell was overwhelmingly voted to his former position by his constituents. Ultimately, he paid the damages to Mrs. James and was then reseated in Congress in January 1969. Powell, however, was fined for misuse of funds and stripped of his seniority.

During this time, white liberals with whom Powell had worked abandoned him while black leaders rallied to his defense. The split marked a breach in the civil rights movement, which Francis E. Kearns analyzed in *Commonweal* magazine in 1967: "The chief significance of Adam Clayton Powell's recent difficulties with Congress lies not in the state of the Congressman's personal fortunes or even in the constitutional question of whether the House may deny a district representation by its duly elected Congressman.... Clearly Powell's censurable behavior hardly approaches in gravity the misconduct of some other Congressmen who have escaped punitive action.... The unseating of one of the most powerful Negro politicians in American history at the very time when a battery of editorialists are urging the Negro to temper his militancy is hardly likely to demonstrate that legislative action offers a viable alternative to mob action in the streets."

Six months after Powell's return to Congress, the Supreme Court ruled that the 1967 House decision to exclude the errant politician had been unconstitutional. He told reporters at the time: "From now on, America will know the Supreme Court is the place where you can get justice." But Powell's political career was coming to an end. In 1969 he was defeated by Charles B. Rangel in a Democratic primary after having been hospitalized for cancer. Powell died in 1972.

Powell's works were as controversial as his life. In *Marching Blacks*, Powell wrote about race relations in the United States, warning that blacks would "not stop until a people's democracy is born out of the rotten, decaying political life of America." Reviewing the work, Frank Adams wrote of Powell's "intemperance" and "intransigence" and called the book "the battle cry of an embittered man who avows the hope that his cause will triumph without bloodshed, but warns that only the conscience of white America can prevent another civil war...." Powell took the title of his sermon collection, *Keep the Faith, Baby!,* from a phrase he had earlier made his trademark. Although this work was widely praised, at least one critic, David Poling, documented enough similarities to other famous sermons to suggest that *Keep the Faith, Baby!* was not entirely Powell's original work. Powell's autobiography had a mixed reception. One critic described *Adam by Adam* as an "impenitent apologia," while Martin Kilson found the book "deficient in serious self-analysis." Kilson nevertheless praised Powell as "a discerning observer of American politics, both at the city and national levels, as well as of the pattern of cruel defeats and illustrations that surround the life of the ghetto Negro."

Although Powell's life often overshadows his works, his writing reveals the views of an important black political leader. As Representative Rangel said of his predecessor: "He was the only idol we had in those days in Harlem. He was audacious power and all of us thought, when we entered politics, that we wanted to be like Adam. God must have sent him, because we'll never see another like him."

(For further information about Powell's life and works, see *Black Writers* and *Contemporary Authors,* Vols. 33-36, 102.)

PRINCIPAL WORKS

Marching Blacks: An Interpretive History of the Rise of the Black Common Man (essay) 1945; revised edition, 1973
The New Image in Education: A Prospectus for the Future by the Chairman of the Committee on Education and Labor (essay) 1962
Keep the Faith, Baby! (sermons) 1967
Adam by Adam (autobiography) 1971

Frank S. Adams (essay date 1946)

[*In the following essay, Adams reviews* Marching Blacks, *labeling Powell a "spokesman for the 'New Negro.'"*]

As a boy of 10, Adam Clayton Powell Jr. stood on a chair and traced on his grandfather's back the P branded into his flesh in the days of slavery. It left him with a fierce resolve not to rest until he had wiped that brand from his memory, and from the conscience of white America. This angry volume, [*Marching Blacks,*] which he calls "An Interpretive History of the Black Common Man," is dedicated to that purpose.

"I am a radical and a fighter," he says of himself. His book and his record both bear witness to the truth of that characterization. This is no calm, dispassionate study of America's most difficult problem, but the battle cry of an embittered man, who avows his hope that his cause will triumph without bloodshed, but warns that only the conscience of white America can prevent another civil war from being fought with all the fury of the war that freed the slaves.

Despite—or perhaps because of—his highly emotional approach to the problem Dr. Powell has become in recent years one of the leading spokesmen for what he calls "the new Negro." His record of achievement and his demonstrated popularity among his people make worthwhile a careful examination of the goal to which he seeks to take them, and the methods and tactics by which he plans to reach it.

At the age of 37 he is already a national figure. He is the pastor of the largest Negro church in the world, with more than 10,000 adherents. So idolized is he in Harlem that he was elected to Congress without opposition—the first member of his race to be elected from New York State—after he had won the Democratic, Republican and American Labor party nominations. He is the publisher of a Harlem newspaper, "The People's Voice."

Master of a fiery eloquence that visibly stirs his Harlem audiences to peaks of emotion, he has been called by his enemies "a Communist-controlled rabble-rouser." Some of his own statements make it understandable how such charges could gain currency. To him one of the great contributions of the Scottsboro case was the emergence of communism as a power fighting for the rights of poor people. "Today there is no group in America, including the Christian Church, that practices racial brotherhood one-tenth as much as the Communist party," he writes.

A Doctor of Divinity himself, Dr. Powell says that at the time of Pearl Harbor "Christianity had been abolished" among 15,000,000 brown Americans, who "pitied the white folks' Christianity, their class system and decadent politics, their fears born of self-indulgence, injustice and oppression." "The great wedge that keeps America split asunder is the hypocrisy of the Christian church," he says, and the black people "will not stop until out of the rubble of present day religion there rises an edifice that includes all races, all creeds and all classes."

A member of Congress, bound by oath to support and defend the Constitution of the United States, Dr. Powell nevertheless warns that the Negroes will not stop "until a people's democracy is born out of the rotten, decaying political life of America," and "from the confusion created by enemies within the working class movement there comes a workers' society predicated upon a people's democracy." If America reverts to "normal, peace-time pseudo-democracy," then America is doomed.

The American Federation of Labor, he says, is the greatest drawback to a developing democracy, and is "a disgrace to the working class movement." He believes the hour is rapidly approaching when the Negro is going to ask the Congress of Industrial Organizations to have a showdown fight with the A. F. of L., for until the controlling clique of the A. F. of L. has been driven from power democracy will suffer.

"Both the black and the white Socialist would rather see the Negro continue as a second-class serf than cooperate with any movement with which Communists were associated, regardless of how insignificant was the role that the Communist played," Dr. Powell sneers, ignoring the historical background for the reluctance of Socialists to allow themselves to be used to pull Communist chestnuts out of the fire.

Dr. Powell does not limit his hatreds to white men and their organizations. One of his principal targets is the slave caste system that developed among the Negroes, under which the house Negroes spied upon and betrayed the field Negroes. Today the field Negro is in the ascendancy and means to stay there, he writes, while the house Negroes, except for a few "Uncle Toms," are trying to ingratiate themselves with the Negro masses.

Even more vicious than the divisions of the caste system, he declares, was the separation of light-skinned and dark-skinned Negroes. The taboo against intra-racial marriages between light and dark Negroes was more rigorous in some communities than that against interracial marriages, Dr. Powell tells us. The light-skinned Negroes and mulattoes established an upper class that retained its dominant position until the depression years of the last decade.

Harlem was a cesspool before the riots of March 19, 1937—the first race riot ever started by Negroes, Dr. Powell says. But, he avers, the Negro has never lost a race riot; some progress, some token improvement, has always followed, and this was no exception. Out of the Harlem riot a new Negro was born, who came to learn and practice the power of nonviolent social action.

The picket line, the boycott and the ballot are the weapons for such action, he says. In the four years before Pearl Harbor the picket line and the boycott were used to support the slogan, "Don't buy where you can't work," directed against Harlem merchants who refused to employ Negroes. The campaign brought 10,000 jobs and $10,000,000 in pay to Harlem Negroes, Dr. Powell says; he envisions its application on a nation-wide scale.

> Even a group as poor as the Negroes, if it controls its mass purchasing power, can force the mightiest of corporations to reconsider its policy. True, we are only 10 per cent of the population, but the margin of profit today is under 10 per cent. The Negroes can smash that margin of profit, or at least so cut it that the strongest corporation will be willing to talk to their representatives.

But the South, Dr. Powell says bitterly, is hopeless. Negroes aren't wanted in the South. Five to eight million Negroes must migrate from the South in the immediate post-war years, he believes; 1,000,000 to New York, 500,000 to Philadelphia, 250,000 to Boston, 750,000 to Detroit and Chicago, and 2,000,000 to Los Angeles and San Diego, until the backbone of the Southern economy has disappeared and a profound change in the South's philosophy has been brought about.

Six possible solutions to the Negro problem—eradica-tion, isolation, deportation, separation, integration and assimilation—have all been supported by Negroes at various times, Dr. Powell says. But today all but a handful of Negroes are convinced that the only solution is integration. Taking cognizance of Dr. Myrdal's find-ing that the chief cause of discrimination is the white fear of intermarriage, he says that to the black man social equality means equality in health, housing and recreational and cultural facilities. His answer will not still the fears of those who believe that the ultimate result of social equality, regardless of the present desires of black people, is bound to be intermarriage—a view that does not justify continued discrimination but does cast doubt on the possibility of any completely satisfac-tory solution of the problem.

Many good causes have had intemperate advocates. Whether such intemperance, in the long run, advances or retards the cause in which it is exerted is not susceptible to precise determination. Dr. Powell, like William Lloyd Garrison and John Brown, would brook no compromise. It is greatly to be hoped that his intransigence will have a happier outcome than did theirs.

> *Frank S. Adams, "A Spokesman for the 'New Negro'," in* The New York Times Book Review, *February 3, 1946, p. 3.*

H. A. Overstreet (essay date 1946)

[*In the following review of* Marching Blacks, *Over-street praises the work as a "fighting book."*]

[**Marching Blacks**] is a fighting book—a non-violent fighting book. It is also a victory book, for there are in its pages no doubts about the outcome. The marching blacks are marching—and the direction is not back to slavery.

> On December 7, 1941 [writes Congressman Po-well] America for the first time in its history enlisted upon two wars simultaneously. One was a world war and the other a civil war. One was to be a bloody fight for the preservation and extension of democracy on a world basis—the other a bloodless revolution within these shores against a bastard democracy.

These last two are not pleasant words for some white ears. For the black man to say it straight out that our democracy is illegitimate spawn will rouse fury among white-supremacy folk. Yet Mr. Powell has chapter and verse for his indictment. "The sneak attack of the Japanese upon our mid-Pacific base was no more vicious than the open attacks that had been waged consistently ... against the Declaration of Indepen-dence, the Constitution and the Bill of Rights." And, as he later shows, that are today being waged by Congress-men in their fight against the Negro's right to fair employment practices.

The author calls his book "an interpretive history of the rise of the black common man;" and he dedicates it "to the freedom fighters of the earth, at home and abroad, black and white, Jew and Gentile, Protestant and Catholic." The book is written in the context of a world fight for freedom. We are, as he rightly tells us, waging a civil war that extends all over the world—a war between those who insist upon their right to push others around, and those who, with a new passion of energy, insist that others shall no longer be pushed around.

The book tells the story of the Negro's growth "not in terms of statistics, population, and wealth, but in terms of his increasing mass power." This power, the writer says, is a new phenomenon. Negroes have hitherto failed chiefly because of divisions among themselves: differ-ences as to policy—between those who would appease the white man and those who would fight him; between those who would beg favors of him and those who would demand rights; between those who would resign themselves to be meek hewers of wood and drawers of water in a white man's society and those who would aspire to any level of profession or occupation of which their minds were capable. There were the divisions, too, of caste and class. Negroes imitated the snobbery of the whites, looking down upon their darker or their poorer fellows from heights of lighter color or greater wealth.

Dr. Powell tells a story of Negro unification that is amazing both as a fact and as a portent of the future. If he is correct in his account (and he brings fact after fact to support his contention), the Negro is no longer powerless. In achieving his own unification—in becoming the "mass Negro"—he has found his essential weapon of offense and defense.

But the Negro does not stand alone. A growing number of whites are marching beside him. This, obviously, is as it should be. Negro nationalism has no place where equality is the word. For where equality is the word there must be an equality of fighting valor. Whites and blacks must fight side by side. In this book they are shown, in instance after instance, fighting and moving ahead together.

For the white reader who is well minded toward the Negro but who is still unclear about the distance we must go before the racial issue approaches a solution this book should be illuminating reading. In few books is the ugliness of racial injustice so vividly and succinctly described; in few is the case so clearly stated for the fact that race prejudice is a poison that kills dignity and decency in the souls of race haters.

In the final part of the book, Dr. Powell proposes a strategy of mass migration from the South. Here opinions will seriously differ. To some persons, a mass migration of Southern Negroes into the already congested slums of Northern cities, particularly at a time when anti-Negro sentiment has been roused among Northern whites, would appear to be a grave mistake. Successes, such as those the author describes, along political lines would seem to such persons to be far more effective.

Representative Powell, Chairman of the House Committee on Education and Labor, at a news conference.

The author's bitterness against the betrayal of Christianity by the churches should be read by all churchmen. Defiantly he asserts:

> The first duty of the blacks ... is to Christianize religion ... Negro religionists refuse to be divided by the age-old antagonisms of the white church—Protestantism of Luther was of dubious doctrine. The Protestantism of the postwar world will be a Protestantism of protest. Based upon the spirit, it will cut across all existing lines of communion. It will be a religion of one faith, one people and one world, and not a provincial ecclesiasticism. It will recognize goodness in all the religions of the earth, and will not strive to place Christianity on a competitive basis but on a cooperative one. This is the religion of the new man the world over, black and white, brown and yellow.

(p. 34)

H. A. Overstreet, "Striding Down Freedom Road," in The Saturday Review of Literature, *Vol. XXIX, No. 6, February 9, 1946, pp. 34, 36.*

David Poling (essay date 1967)

[*In the following essay, Poling offers a mixed review of* Keep the Faith, Baby!, *praising Powell's ability to write terse, topical sermons but suggesting that Powell "borrowed" material from noted sermon writers.*]

Adam Clayton Powell has successfully mixed politics and religion for the last twenty-five years. Although the House of Representatives has derailed his political career momentarily, the role of preacher is as strong as ever. *Keep the Faith, Baby!* is a collection of sermons, meditations, and speeches delivered at the Abyssinian Baptist Church in Harlem. Here we have a glimpse of the style, interests, and themes of Powell in the pulpit in contrast to the playboy of Bimini, Cutty Sark and milk fame.

Will the Reverend Powell be asked to conduct seminary classes on preaching or sermon construction? I doubt it. But he has to be considered above average in ability to relate scripture to the needs and problems of everyday life. There is a directness, an economy of words that eludes too many preachers. The strongest sermons are fashioned around social issues that have swirled about the church in more than a decade: capital punishment, McCarthyism, civil rights, God is Dead, and, of late, Black Power.

He describes his own ground rules:

> I believe it is the business of the preacher to say an eternal word in a contemporary setting; to say a permanent word in a changing world; to help those who enter the doors to have not only a sense of history but a sense of the age.

In the sermon on capital punishment he notes that the rich usually go free while the poor go to the graveyard.

> In this decade we must move still further. The gallows, the gas chamber, the electric chair, should be relegated to our museums; to their appointed places along with the rack, the thumbscrew, the guillotine, and other discarded instruments of primitive injustice.

A thunder-and-lightning sermon on McCarthyism came right to the point when Powell said, "It is a reflection of the moral irresponsibility of the church which condones him, the press which praises him, and the large numbers of American people who follow him." As strong as this piece was, it seemed rather late in the fray: November 29, 1959.

We come to the best and the worst of this book for faith-keeping babies: respectively Powell's attitude toward Black Power and his slighting of Vietnam. If the ground rules have not changed on Powell's definitions, many people would be able to subscribe to his interpretation and promotion of Black Power: He writes:

> ...black power is not anti-white.
> Black power incorporates everybody who wishes to work together, vote together, and worship together.... Violence must play no part in its fulfillment....
> After years and years of rioting, black people should realize by now that when we burn up the neighborhood dry cleaners in a riot or a rebellion, we set our own clothes on fire.... Whites must join hands with blacks to achieve the full freedom of the Guaranteed Society because they are determined to get their full measure of freedom.

Powell's civil rights-Black Power statements have none of the yakety-yak that he has been feeding the public via press and TV interviews from the decks of *Adam's Fancy.* Vietnam, however, is a large shameful gap in Powell's sermons. Apparently his war is in Rhodesia and South Africa, not with troops in the jungles of Southeast Asia.

One of Pastor Powell's difficulties is giving credit to original sources. Quotation marks are about as rare as his appearances in Harlem. In his sermon, **"The Temptation of Modernity,"** the text is Matthew 4: 1-10, the account of Jesus's temptation in the wilderness. Fascinating parallels develop between Powell's discourse and George A. Buttrick's exposition in Vol. VII of the *Interpreter's Bible.*

> POWELL:
> Let us now examine these temptations of Jesus' day and of today. For as Browning said in his *Aristophanes' Apology,* "When the fight begins with himself, a man's worth something." ... Men and steel are alike uncertain until they are tested.

> BUTTRICK:
> ... It is a chance to rise as much as it is a chance to fall. "When the fight begins within himself, a man's worth something," for men and steel are alike uncertain until they are tested. (Browning, "Bishop Blougram's Apology")

> POWELL:
> I want you to note the Old Testament doctrine of

the devil. He is a personal devil. And let us admit that the temptations that beset us today are personal persuasions.

BUTTRICK:
Notice the O.T. doctrine of the devil. He is personal. Are not the seductions that beset us personal persuasions, and not merely of ourselves?

POWELL:
I love the story about Dwight Moody during a crisis; he wouldn't pray while others did, and when they upbraided him he said, "Brethren, I'm all prayed up."

BUTTRICK:
When Dwight L. Moody was upbraided because he failed to attend a prayer meeting in the midst of threatened shipwreck, he replied: "I'm prayed up."

POWELL:
Jesus did not center His mission on an economic crusade. He did not forsake the Cross for a bakeshop. Man does live by bread, but not by bread alone.

BUTTRICK:
Jesus would not center his mission in an economic crusade. He would not live merely for time, or forsake a Cross for a bakeshop. Man does live by bread ... but man does not live by bread alone.

POWELL:
I like the story I heard in Transjordan of a hungry Arab who suddenly finds a treasure in the midst of the desert and cries, "Alas, it is only diamonds!"

BUTTRICK:
The famished Bedouin, finding treasure in the desert, cried, "Alas, it is only diamonds."

POWELL:
Carlisle [*sic*] in his great *Sartor Resartus,* Book II in the ninth chapter, says, "Not all the finance ministers, upholsterers, and confectioners of Europe in joint stock company, could make one shoeblack happy for more than a couple of hours."

BUTTRICK:
Carlyle said that not all the "Finance Ministers and Upholsterers and Confectioners of modern Europe ... in joint stock company," could "make one shoeblack happy ... above an hour or two." (*Sartor Resartus,* Bk. II., ch. ix.)

POWELL:
Jesus might be able to shake a shallow generation out of its indifference, its unbelief.
     Noble spirits are always tempted to be sensational for the sake of God. God is not proved by sleight of hand.... How often we try!

BUTTRICK:
He might startle a shallow generation out of its indifference into sudden belief. Noble spirits are tempted to the sensational for the sake of God.... God is not improved by sleight of hand: the soul has its own testimony, and God is his own interpreter ... man has no right to force God's hand. How often we try....

POWELL:
At that very moment the Romans had a garrison in

every town, crushing with taxes and ruthlessly oppressing the people.

BUTTRICK:
At that moment the Romans had a garrison in every sizeable town, by which they levied crushing taxes and ruthlessly suppressed any attempt at revolt.

These are examples of the curious duplications that crop up in **Keep the Faith, Baby!**

In the sermon "**Are You the Right Size?**" Pastor Powell takes the wrong measurements. He tries to ease Halford Luccock's sermon into his own book but it just doesn't fit. At first it seemed just a coincidence of text and title but then Luccock's illustrations and skillful way of saying things kept breaking through. Small wonder. Luccock, who taught at Yale Divinity School for twenty-five years until his retirement in 1953, was the preacher's preacher for almost a half-century. In his book of sermons, *Marching Off the Map,* appears the sermon "On Being the Right Size." Compare the two:

POWELL:
I sat the other day talking to a very wealthy young woman. She talked literally for hours. I couldn't get a word in. In this earth-shaking hour the important people for her were Helena Rubinstein, Elizabeth Arden, Hattie Carnegie, Emily Post, Lilly Daché, Fanny Farmer, and Betty Crocker. They are all good gals but they are too small for our world.

LUCCOCK:
I have heard one woman talk voluminously on several occasions—when the exits were blocked and I couldn't get away. She made it clear that in her mind there is a little private Pantheon, in which are all the people who really count in her diminutive world. Here are some: Helena Rubinstein, Elizabeth Arden, Hattie Carnegie, Emily Post, Lilly Daché, Fannie Farmer, and Betty Crocker! They are all good girls! But it is a microscopic world.

Luccock never went to Bimini but it appears he has been heard frequently in Harlem. *Vide:*

POWELL:
I can take an electric micrometer and measure one ten thousandth of an inch. I can peek into one of the new giant telescopes and see a galaxy of stars a thousand light-years away.

LUCCOCK:
For there are incredible instruments today which can measure everything, from one ten-thousandth of an inch to a galaxy of stars a thousand light years away.

POWELL:
"A small animal has resistance to gravity relatively ten times greater than its driving force." That's why a fly can walk on a ceiling or a mouse can fall a thousand feet and only be slightly dazed.

LUCCOCK:
"A small animal has resistance to gravity relatively ten times greater than the driving force." Hence, flies can walk on the ceiling, and a thousand-foot

fall, which would kill a man, or even a rat, will give a mouse only a slight daze . . .

POWELL:
Our question for this morning is: 'What is the right size of mind and heart to fit our day and our world?"

LUCCOCK:
Our simple question is this: what would be the right size of mind and heart to fit our day and our world?

POWELL:
Through motion pictures and television we can hear a pin drop in Europe and a bomb drop in Asia. Do we have minds that match our eyes and our ears?

LUCCOCK:
Ears, that in New York can hear a pin drop in New Zealand, or a bomb drop in Korea! There is need of minds to match the eyes and ears.

POWELL:
Anyone who fits snugly and smugly into a small world of individual interests is the wrong size.
I call upon you this morning to take the most momentous journey in the world—from "I" to "We."

LUCCOCK:
Anyone who fits snugly into a small world of merely individual interests is the wrong size—too small . . . . We are all called upon to take the most momentous journey in the world, the journey from "I" to "We."

POWELL:
When the rich young fool purred to Jesus his self-satisfaction over his prosperity in three short sentences he used the word "I" or "my" thirteen times. Jesus said, "Thou fool."

LUCCOCK:
When the Rich Fool purrs his self-satisfaction over his prosperity, in three short sentences he uses the words "I" or "my" thirteen times! For him, at least, thirteen was an unlucky number! For God said, "Thou fool!"

POWELL:
We need people today who are the right size to fit the globe, the only size that has any survival value.

LUCCOCK:
Again, consider the need of people the right size to fit a globe. That is the only size that has any survival value.

POWELL:
One person with his mind made up can push a lot of folks around.

LUCCOCK:
Casey, the ex-preacher in Steinbeck's *Grapes of Wrath*, put it truly and forcibly: "One person with their minds made up can push a lot of folks around."

POWELL:
The empty promises of Communism make no appeal to well-fed Americans, but they are of tremendous appeal to the hungry, landless and hopeless millions of Asia, Africa and Latin America.

LUCCOCK:
The empty promises of Communism make no appeal to well-fed people in the United States. They have a tremendous appeal to the hungry, landless, hopeless millions of Asia, people with little or nothing to lose.

POWELL:
If we are to be the right size for our day, we must be tall enough to bump the sky.

LUCCOCK:
If we are to be the right size for our day and its demands, we must be tall enough to bump the sky.

Now we must consider Powell as politician, playboy, and preacher. Like some of his colleagues, he has discovered that it is one thing to preach and quite another to publish. Dean Liston Pope of Yale once said to his students before an examination: "I trust no one will glance at another's paper, for lo, if he does, some Saturday night he will take another man's sermon." (pp. 86, 89-90)

David Poling, "Powell in the Pulpit," in Saturday Review, *Vol. L, No. 16, April 22, 1967, pp. 86, 89-90.*

Martin Kilson (essay date 1971)

[*In the following review, Kilson evaluates Powell's autobiography,* Adam by Adam, *maintaining that Powell does not assess himself rigorously enough in the work.*]

The political style of America's black leaders varies as much as the style of its white leaders. It ranges from the soft-spoken businesslike pragmatist to the exhibitionistic, back-slapping demagogue, with infinite variation between these polar extremes. White leadership in this century has had numerous examples of the exhibitionistic demagogue, especially among the urban ethnic politicians (Irish, Jewish, Italian, Polish) and among white-racist, Protestant leaders in the South. This type has also existed among Negro leaders in this century, primarily among those who emanate from the racially segregated urban quarters that developed outside the South consequent to the mass migration of Southern blacks from World War I onward.

In fact, what I call the exhibitionistic or demagogic style, characterized by the uncompromising articulation of the bitter frustrations experienced by all sectors of the black ghetto, was indispensable to the emergence of independent Negro leadership in American cities in the years following World War I. This style, basically a black-racialist style, afforded the Negro politician the means for his own political base, outside the established political arrangements. Through the manipulation of black racialism, the Negro politician induced the emergence of latent political resources within black ghetto

Powell as pastor of the Abyssinian Baptist Church in Harlem.

institutions such as churches and fraternal bodies, within mutual-aid groups in the working class and professional associations like the National (Negro) Bar Association and the National (Negro) Medical Association. In this way, then, some of the first Negro-controlled political organizations in American cities were built, including those of Negro politicians like William Dawson (third Negro elected to Congress in this century, 1942-1970) who, having carved out a political base by manipulating black racialism, eventually discarded the demagogic style for the businesslike pragmatist style.

The political career of Adam Clayton Powell Jr., the main concern of *Adam by Adam,* was a model of the successful articulation of black racialism in American politics. Powell, unlike the late Representative William Dawson, clung to the demagogic style throughout his career—shrewdly amending and recasting it through different phases in the growth of racial consciousness among urban Negroes.

Unfortunately, *Adam by Adam,* like most political autobiographies, is deficient in serious self-analysis. Powell exhibits little capacity either to perceive the mainsprings (personal, emotional, parental, social) of his political style or to sustain any systematic analysis of the behavior emanating from this style. Yet Powell is a discerning observer of American politics, both at the city and national levels, as well as of the pattern of cruel

defeats and frustrations that surround the life of the ghetto Negro.

Born in 1908, within several years of the commencement of sizable Negro migration from the South to Northern cities, Powell, the son of an upper-middle-class Baptist clergyman who had speculated successfully in Harlem real estate, was reared in an era when thousands of blacks began facing the problems of urban adjustment. They were maliciously harassed and impeded at every turn by anti-Negro, white city machines—bureaucrats, politicians, police. Powell observed the perpetual failure of every strata within the Harlem ghetto to sustain leadership long enough to make a dent in the ghetto's massive pathologies and frustrations.

Upon completing college in 1930, Adam Clayton Powell Jr. was unexpectedly launched into New York City politics. This occurred when he responded favorably to requests from several leading Negro medical doctors (led by Dr. Ira McCown, later the physician of the New York State Boxing Commission) to help end blatant racial discrimination against Negro doctors at Harlem Hospital, a city institution. Run exclusively by white doctors and administrators (largely Irish), the Harlem Hospital served a largely Negro clientele. By the 1930's this clientele, especially the working and lower classes, had their usual frustrations compounded by massive unemployment caused by the Great Depression. It was to this sector of the clientele that Adam Clayton Powell Jr. turned for the leverage necessary to influence a change in the white supremacist practices of Irish doctors and administrators in Harlem Hospital.

Powell, gifted at oratory and popular arousal, pioneered the tactics of mass (and angry) direct action against white-supremacist institutions; by his reckoning he enticed 6,000 of "the people of the streets, the failures, the misfits, the despised, the maimed, the beaten, the sightless and the voiceless" to march on Harlem Hospital and City Hall. In this initial political act Powell discovered the political style and tactics that were to characterize his political career.

Powell entered national politics in 1944, when he was elected to Congress, the first Negro elected from the East in this century. In Congress he encountered situations that reinforced his attachment to militant racialism and the demogogic political style. Initially, Powell, "the first bad Nigger in Congress"—as he styles himself in the autobiography—encountered pervasive white supremacy in the facilities of Congress, something he shared with the three other Negro politicians who preceded him (Oscar DePriest, 1928-1934, Arthur Mitchell, 1934-1942, and William Dawson). But Powell suffered the white racist life style of the United States Congress poorly. He lashed out against it frequently, restraining his bitterness and aggression only when political prudence dictated, which was not very often.

Powell also began to understand that acquiescence to Congress's racist life style or adaptation of the businesslike pragmatist style that governed its political relationships would destroy his political independence. He would be required to make peace with the city and county machines which, through regular and predictable resources, controlled the lifeline of Congressmen. Pliant Congressmen, as most are, are ensured reelection in this manner, all things given; William Dawson, initially an exponent of black racialism who turned pragmatist, had guaranteed himself nearly 30 years of Congressional office. Yet Powell, aided by the independent resources of his church (the Abyssinian Baptist Church) and its 11,000 communicants was willing to forgo the benefits of compliance to Congressional political style. He alone in the years before sizable Negro representation in Congress (currently 13 blacks are there) used national politics as a platform for articulating the black racialist view of the Negro's status in American society.

Finally, Powell discovered in Congress that liberalism was a doubtful political method and style for solving the weaknesses of Negroes in American society. The willingness of liberal Congressmen in the Democratic party, under the New Deal, to sacrifice the needs and interests of Negroes whenever the decisive power formations in Congress considered these interests expendable annoyed Powell deeply. He displayed throughout his career much less ability to compromise this matter than did his Negro Congressional peers. To do so appeared to him a matter of life and death. When he gained the chairmanship of the powerful House Education and Labor Committee in 1961, to the chagrin of white liberals in Congress, he periodically attached pro-Negro amendments—popularly called 'Powell amendments'—to crucial legislation from his Committee. This caused serious delay in enactment of such legislation, modification of it, or, occasionally, defeat.

But Powell's political style was also compounded of personal ingredients. Though *Adam by Adam* fails to grapple with these in a coherent fashion, it offers morsels of insight. First, Powell is a man of more than usual vanity—evidence of which is plentiful in this autobiography—and the demagogic political style seems endemic to that characteristic. Powell appears, in fact, to consider himself a savior to the politically weak and poor Negro masses; though he often affected this posture merely as a political technique, exploiting the widespread tendency of the black lower classes to elevate political leaders to messianic status on many occasions. Powell seems to have internalized a messiah complex.

Furthermore, Powell relates in the autobiography how he suffered throughout boyhood and young manhood a gnawing urge to find an area of legitimate activity in which he could match the professional success of his father. The resort to politics by such men is not uncommon. In one of its aspects, politics, according to Talcott Parsons, is functionally diffuse, requiring few specialized resources; thus men with Powell's need to achieve and his charismatic talents pursue politics almost naturally.

But the personal sources of Powell's political style extend even further. Throughout the autobiography he describes a deep-seated, often manic, need to deviate from expected behavior. Politics affords more opportunity for fulfillment for such an impulse than other avocations. Politics also has pitfalls and booby-traps for those who would use it this way, but reject the discipline inherent in the unique reciprocity of the political process.

Powell, alas, never comprehended the kind of discipline that is basic to politics. The result was preordained: Powell, after 22 years in Congress, was stripped of his committee chairmanship by his white peers—motivated by a combination of white racism and perturbance at his political style. He would have been unseated had not the Supreme Court reinstated him.

In 1970, after nearly 30 years in Congress, Powell was defeated for re-election by a Negro member of the New York State Assembly, Charles Rangel. Predictably, nowhere in the autobiography does Powell seriously analyze his defeat. Like other political messiahs, Powell is above rigorous political analysis. If he clings to this perspective, we have certainly seen the last of Adam Clayton Powell Jr., the first United States Congressman from Harlem. (pp. 4, 16, 18)

> *Martin Kilson, in a review of "Adam by Adam," in* The New York Times Book Review, *November 7, 1971, pp. 4, 16, 18.*

FURTHER READING

Brooks, Albert N. D. "Profile of a Fighter." *The Negro History Bulletin* XX, No. 8 (May 1957): 170, 191.
   Brief biography of Powell. Brooks concludes: "In spite of his detractors [Powell's] record of public service suggests that personal gain has not been a major objective in his life."

Frazier, E. Franklin. "The Black Common Man." *The Nation* 162, No. 7 (16 February 1946): 201-02.
   Generally favorable review of *Marching Blacks,* calling it a work "characterized by shrewd insights, novel and unwarranted interpretations of historical facts, and much justifiable indignation."

Garland, Phyl. "I Remember Adam." *Ebony* XLV, No. 5 (March 1990): 56, 58, 60, 62.
   Examines Powell's political legacy.

Hamilton, Charles V. *Adam Clayton Powell, Jr.: The Political Biography of an American Dilemma.* New York: Atheneum, 1991, 448 p.
   Biography of Powell, focusing on his flamboyant political life. Hamilton traces the rise and fall of Powell from his early days in Harlem to his position as

chairman of the House Committee on Education and Labor in Washington, D. C.

Kilson, Martin. "Adam Clayton Powell, Jr.: The Militant as Politician." In *Black Leaders of the Twentieth Century,* edited by John Hope Franklin and August Meier, pp. 259-75. Urbana: University of Illinois Press, 1982.

Explores Powell's career as a militant member of Congress, attempting to reconcile his flamboyant life-style with his ability to "harness political power for useful ends."

Lewis, Claude. *Adam Clayton Powell.* Greenwich, Conn.: Fawcett Publications, Inc., 1963, 127 p.

Biography analyzing Powell's paradoxical image as statesman and playboy.

Review of *Adam by Adam,* by Adam Clayton Powell, Jr. *The New Yorker* 47, No. 39 (13 November 1971): 202-03.

Brief review of Powell's autobiography, labeling it "an impenitent apologia."

Dudley Randall

1914-

(Full name Dudley Felker Randall) American poet, short story writer, editor, critic, and publisher.

Called Detroit's First Poet Laureate, Randall is the founder of Broadside Press, a Michigan-based publishing company that helped launch the careers of many black poets, including Etheridge Knight and Haki R. Madhubuti (formerly Don L. Lee). "As publisher of Detroit's Broadside Press between 1965 and 1977," observed Suzanne Dolezal, "Randall provided a forum for just about every major black poet to come along during those years. And dozens of anthologies include his own rapid, emotional lyrics about Detroit's bag ladies, lonely old drunks, strapping foundry workers and young women with glistening, corn-rowed hair." R. Baxter Miller explained Randall's importance and influence in the black poetry movement thus: "Beyond Randall's contributions as a poet, his roles as editor and publisher have proven invaluable to the Afro-American community."

Randall's interest in poetry has been life-long. Born in Washington, D.C., the son of a minister and a teacher, he wrote his first poem when he was four years old, moved to Detroit when he was nine, and saw his poems first published in the *Detroit Free Press* when he was thirteen. A bright student, Randall graduated early. After working in Ford's River Rouge foundry for five years and serving in the army, he returned to school and earned a master's degree in library science from the University of Michigan. Randall, who became the reference librarian for Wayne County, also became fluent in Russian, visited Europe, Africa, and Soviet Russia, and later translated many Russian poems into English.

Critics regard Randall's poetry as a bridge between the works of earlier black writers and of the writers of the 1960s. "Exploring racial and historical themes, introspective and self-critical, [Randall's] work combines ideas and forms from Western traditional poetry as well as from the Harlem Renaissance movement," Miller noted. In an essay on Randall in *Black American Poets between Worlds, 1940-1960,* he elaborated: "Although attracted to the poetry of antiquity, including classical conventions, he also gives his energetic support to modern originality.... Black American literary art has benefited from his great talent and love for fifty years." Randall's first book of poetry, *Poem Counterpoem* (1966), contains ten poems by Margaret Danner and ten by Randall. *Cities Burning* (1968) focuses on the poet's urban environment and political turmoils of the 1960s. The third and more inclusive collection *More to Remember: Poems of Four Decades* (1971) displays Randall's artistic breadth in poems that address universal themes and explore "contradictions in human psycholo-

gy and the black arts movement," according to Miller. Later collections *After the Killing* (1973), *Broadside Memories: Poets I Have Known* (1975), *A Litany of Friends: New and Selected Poems* (1981), and *Homage to Hoyt Fuller* (1984) show Randall's polished craftsmanship. Reviewing *After the Killing*, Frank Marshall Davis declared: "Dudley Randall again offers visual proof of why he should be ranked in the front echelon of Black poets."

Broadside Press—Randall's other contribution to black poetry in America—began in 1963. Randall had composed the poem "The Ballad of Birmingham" after a bomb exploded in an Alabama church, killing four children. "Folk singer Jerry Moore of New York had it set to music, and I wanted to protect the rights to the poem by getting it copyrighted," the publisher recalled in *Broadside Memories: Poets I Have Known.* Leaflets, he learned, could be copyrighted, so he published the poem as a broadside, a single sheet of paper that could be printed and sold for a minimal price. Randall's

"Dressed All in Pink," composed after John F. Kennedy's assassination, also recorded by Moore, became number two of the Broadside series, which was to include close to one hundred titles by 1982.

Randall became a book publisher when poets at a Fisk University conference nominated him to collect and publish poems about Malcolm X. The result was *For Malcolm: Poems on the Life and Death of Malcolm X* (1967). By that time, aware that major publishers were seldom accepting works by young black poets, Randall became dedicated to publishing works by emerging black authors. Indeed, Randall's encouragement was essential to the writing careers of several black poets. Etheridge Knight, for example, was in prison when he contributed three poems to the Broadside anthology *For Malcolm,* and Randall's visits "convinced a hesitant Knight of his talent," Dolezal reported. Randall published first books for Knight and for Haki R. Madhubuti, two poets who now enjoy international acclaim.

Altogether, the press produced nearly sixty volumes of poetry and criticism under Randall's tenure, all showcasing black writers, who rewarded his dedication by remaining loyal to Broadside even when larger publishing houses with generous promotion budgets beckoned. Gwendolyn Brooks insisted that Randall, not Harper & Row, would publish her autobiography; Sonia Sanchez preferred Broadside to the Third World Press, the small press founded by Madhubuti. Poet Nikki Giovanni explained to Dolezal: "Broadside was neither mother nor father of the poetry movement, but it was certainly midwife. Dudley understood the thrust of the movement, which was essentially vernacular. He . . . allowed his poets to find their own voices. That was the charm of Broadside."

As a poet and publisher, Randall helped revitalize black poetry in America. Yet by 1977, his determination to supply low-priced books to stores already in debt to him brought the small press, also deeply in debt, to the crisis point. The Alexander Crummell Memorial Center, a church in Highland Park, Michigan, bought the press, retaining Randall as its consultant. Though the poets he once encouraged have found other publishers since the sale, Randall continues to be concerned for new poets and anticipates the publication of more new works when the press revives. But Dolezal concluded that whether that hope materializes, "Randall's achievement remains intact." Furthermore, as the poet told *New York Times* contributor Harold Blum, there is always plenty to do: "[A poet] can change the way people look and feel about things. And that's what I want to do in Detroit."

(For further information about Randall's life and works, see *Black Writers; Contemporary Authors,* Vols. 25-28; *Contemporary Authors New Revision Series,* Vol. 23; *Contemporary Literary Criticism,* Vol. 1; and *Dictionary of Literary Biography,* Vol. 41: *Afro-American Poets since 1955.*)

PRINCIPAL WORKS

"The Ballad of Birmingham" (poetry) 1965
"Dressed All in Pink" (poetry) 1965
Poem Counterpoem [with Margaret Danner] (poetry) 1966
For Malcolm: Poems on the Life and Death of Malcolm X [coeditor with Margaret G. Burroughs] (poetry) 1967
Cities Burning (poetry) 1968
Black Poetry: A Supplement to Anthologies Which Exclude Black Poets [editor] (poetry) 1969
Love You (poetry) 1970
"The Black Aesthetic in the Thirties, Forties and Fifties" (essay) 1971; published in periodical *The Black Aesthetic*
Black Poets [editor] (poetry) 1971
More to Remember: Poems of Four Decades (poetry) 1971
After the Killing (poetry) 1973
Broadside Memories: Poets I Have Known (nonfiction and poetry) 1975
A Capsule Course in Black Poetry Writing [with Gwendolyn Brooks, Keorapetse Kgositsile, and Haki R. Madhubuti] (nonfiction) 1975
A Litany of Friends: New and Selected Poems (poetry) 1981
Homage to Hoyt Fuller (poetry) 1984
Golden Song: The Fiftieth Anniversary Anthology of the Poetry Society of Michigan, 1935-1985 [coeditor with Louis J. Cantoni] (poetry) 1985

R. Baxter Miller (essay date 1986)

[*Miller edited the 1986 study* Black American Poets between Worlds, 1940-1960, *a collection of critical essays. In the following excerpt, he profiles Randall's poetry and comments on his remarkable contribution to the promotion of black writing.*]

Dudley Randall, poet, librarian, and publisher, is one of the most important Black men of letters in the twentieth century. A child during the Harlem Renaissance, he was himself a leading poet of the subsequent generation of Black writers, and he later became a pioneer of the Black literary movement of the 1960s. His own work, so accomplished technically and profoundly concerned with the history and racial identity of Blacks, benefits from the ideas and literary forms of the Harlem Renaissance as well as from the critical awareness of the earlier Western Renaissance. Although he borrows eruditely from the sources, he culturally transforms them. Through the founding of the Broadside Press and his brilliant editorial work there, he made available to a wide audience the work of fellow poets such as Hayden, Danner, Brooks, and Walker. The variety of such writers indicates that Randall's publishing was in no sense programmatic or intent upon a particular kind of poetry. Indeed, his own skill, so firmly rooted in literary history, is as different in its assumptions from the more formalistic verse of a Brooks or a Danner as it is from the folk and religious poems of Walker. But Randall combines his own poetic credo with that of other poets to create a broad tolerance in what he publishes. In other words, he makes an active commitment to Black literature in general. (p. 77)

[Randall] has helped to deepen the technical breadth and authenticity of Black poetry. Collaborator and mentor during the Black Arts Movement (1960-75), Randall infused his own ballads with racial history.... Boone House, a cultural center founded by Margaret Danner in Detroit, was "home" to Randall from 1962 through 1964. *There* Randall and Danner read their own work each Sunday, and over the years the two of them collected a group of their poems. When Randall edited the Broadside anthology *For Malcolm X,* the prospects for publication encouraged him to bring out the collaborative book as well. Entitled *Poem-Counterpoem* (1966), it became the first major publication of Broadside Press.

Perhaps the first of its kind, the volume contains ten poems, alternately each by Danner and Randall. Replete with social and intellectual history, the verses stress nurture and growth. In "**The Ballad of Birmingham**" Randall compares racial progress to blossoming. Through octosyllabic couplets and incremental repetition, including a dialogue between a mother and her daughter, he achieves "dramatic reversal," as Aristotle would call it, as well as epiphany. Based on historical incident, the bombing in 1963 of Martin Luther King Jr.'s church by white terrorists, eight quatrains portray one girl's life and death. (Four girls actually died in the bombing.) When the daughter in the poem asks to attend a Civil Rights rally, the loving and fearful mother forbids her to go to the rally. Allowed to go to church instead, the daughter dies anyway. Thus, the mother's concern was to no avail, for an evil world has no sanctuary, either in the street or in the church. After folk singer Jerry Moore read the poem in a newspaper, he set it to music, and Randall granted him permission to publish the lyrics with the tune.

"**Memorial Wreath,**" a Randall lyric of celebration, profits from well-structured analogues. Some imply the processes of resurrection, love, and blossoming. Others draw parallels between ancestry, suffering, and sacrifice; still others liken blues to racial continuity, to the inseparability of pain and beauty, and to the irony of racial experience, including art itself. Finally, when the speaker ultimately addresses his spiritual ancestors, the images come from the American nineteenth century. The more dramatically conceived and frequently anthologized ballad "**Booker T. and W. E. B.**" presents one voice's call and another's response. In alternating stanzas in the poem the two Black leaders (1856-1915; 1868-1963) express opposite views. While Booker T. Washington favors agriculture and domestic service, Du Bois emphasizes the human quest to learn liberally. Despite

Washington's focus upon property, Du Bois proposes dignity and justice. Randall, who tries to present each man realistically, favors Du Bois, to whom the narrator gives the last line intentionally. A free verse, "**For Margaret Danner / In Establishing Boone House**" (December 1962), fuses quest and rebirth into benediction: "May your crocuses rise up through winter snow." And the speaker in "**Belle Isle,**" the last lyric, addresses the poet's calling, "the inner principle . . . endowing / the world and time . . . joy and delight, for ever."

During the first Black Writer's Conference at Fisk University in the 1960s, Randall met Margaret Burroughs, founder and director of the Du Sable Museum of African American History in Chicago. When he called her regarding the anthology *For Malcolm X,* his previous study had prepared him well. He was aware, as most Americans were not, that the father of Russian literature, Aleksander Pushkin, had African origins through a maternal grandfather. Randall, who had learned the Russian language after the Second World War, was able to read the literature in the original, which not only impressed him as much as had the work of Latin and French poets, but had moved him to undertake some translations, notably "Wait for Me" and "My Native Land" by K. M. Siminov.

On his return from Russia and once again at home in Boone House, Randall plunged into cultural activities and met some emerging and important Black writers. He attended art exhibits, jazz sessions, and monthly readings of poetry. Authors read from a new anthology, *Beyond the Blues* (1962), and from a special issue of *Negro History Bulletin* (October 1962). Randall befriended fellow poets Betty Ford, Harold Lawrence, and Naomi Long Madgett as well as Edward Simpkins and James Thompson.

In 1966 Randall met the celebrated poet Gwendolyn Brooks. When a reading club in Detroit invited her to read at Oakland University, he requested that several English teachers meet her at the train station. When he himself finally greeted her after the reading, she was surprised. From book reviews in *Negro Digest,* she had thought him fierce, but he had proved pleasantly mild: "I thought you were terrible, but you're all right." While the two poets took snapshots together, she threw her arms happily around her new friend's shoulders, and, asked later to submit a poem for the new Broadside series, she granted him permission to republish "We Real Cool." He would bring out her pamphlets *Riot* (1969), *Family Pictures* (1971), and *Aloneness* (1971). At first he declined to issue her autobiography, *Report from Part One* (1972), because he believed that Harper and Row could better promote the volume. When Brooks disagreed, he finally conceded the argument, and, upon the publication, Toni Cade Bambara responded enthusiastically on the front page of the *New York Times Book Review.*

With a favorable evaluation of Audre Lorde's first book, *The First Cities* (1966), in *Negro Digest,* Randall followed her progress in *Cables or Rage* (London: Paul Breman, 1970), but, when asked to publish her third book, *From A Land Where Other People Live*, he found himself overbooked. Brooks intervened on Lorde's behalf, however, and he finally relented. The volume, which came out under his imprint in 1973, was nominated for a National Book Award. After the ceremonies in New York he and Lorde went backstage to meet the poet Adrienne Rich. As he paused at the breast-high platform and wondered how to mount it, Lorde gave him a hand, "How's that," she asked, "for a fat old lady?" A representative for Rich's publisher drove the two in a limousine to a cocktail party at the Biltmore Hotel, and Randall wondered secretly when Broadside might afford the luxury of a limousine. Although Lorde had promised to take him on the Staten Island ferry and show him her house in the area, they had celebrated too late; no time would be left during the next morning.

At the writer's conference at Fisk, Randall had strengthened the professional associations that would assure the publication of verses by established poets such as Hayden, Tolson, and Walker in the Broadside series. Securing from Brooks the permission to use the colloquial verse, "We Real Cool," he published the first group—"Poems of the Negro Revolt," a distinguished collection. Although he had the tendency at first to issue famous poems for popular dissemination, a reviewer in *Small Press* suggested that he might serve contemporary writing better by printing previously unpublished verse.

Randall, while at the conference at Fisk, had seen Margaret Burroughs' sketches and heard Margaret Walker rehearse her afternoon reading; as he listened to Walker read about Malcolm X, he observed that most Black poets were writing about Malcolm, and Burroughs proposed that Randall edit a collection on the subject. When Randall invited her to co-edit the volume, she accepted, and David Llorens promised to announce the anthology in *Negro Digest* (later *Black World*). Randall received the first submission a few days later.

For Malcolm X brought Hayden, Walker, and Brooks together with the younger writers LeRoi Jones (Imamu Baraka), Larry Neal, Sonia Sanchez, and Etheridge Knight. Randall, through collaboration with them, learned about the magazines, *Soulbook* and *Black Dialogue*, but problems with the printer delayed publication until June 1967. At Fisk, Randall had seen a slim girl with David Llorens, and, when he returned to Detroit, he received a letter from Nikki Giovanni, who requested a copy of *For Malcolm X* to review in the college publication edited by her. Although *For Malcolm X* did not appear until 1967, after her graduation from Fisk, she reviewed the book for a Cincinnati newspaper. During the book signing by contributors at Margaret Burroughs' museum, he met Haki Madhubuti (then Don L. Lee) and later received a copy of Madhubuti's *Think Black*. The younger poet had himself published 700 copies and sold them all in a week. When he and Randall read for a memorial program at a Chicago high school, Randall advised the new friend, "Now Don,

read slowly, and pronounce each word distinctly," Because Madhubuti read first and earned a standing ovation, Randall humorously promised himself to read thereafter "before, not after Don." When visiting Detroit, Madhubuti usually went by Randall's home. Although all business agreements between the two poets were oral, Madhubuti clearly regarded them as binding, for he refused to sign with Random House, and when his second book, *Black Pride* (1968), was completed he asked Randall to provide an introduction. In 1969 Randall brought out Madhubuti's *Don't Cry, Scream* in both paperback and cloth editions, the latter then a first for Broadside, though he himself would later publish a similar edition of *For Malcolm X.*

Over the years Randall won professional warmth from Sonia Sanchez, one of the contributors to *For Malcolm X.* In his poetry class at the University of Detroit she had wondered whether to publish with Third World Press, Madhubuti's firm, or with Broadside, which she finally chose. When Randall had a heart murmur, Sanchez sent him various teas, and, chiding him for smoking, she drove him to bookstores in New York. When he flew to Africa in 1970, she and Nikki Giovanni went to the motel to see him off. For consistent dedication to Black American poetry, Randall won personal and communal loyalty.

Yet Dudley Randall remains a poet in his own right. *Cities Burning* (1968) captures his zeitgeist. Here the visionary lyrics and apocalyptic revelations concern urban riot, generational opposition, and Black image-making. "**Roses and Revolutions,**" a prophetic lyric in free verse written in 1948, addresses both the Civil Rights Movement and personal conscience. Two other poems, "**The Rite**" and "**Black Poet, White Critic**," clarify in two brief quatrains Randall's theory of art. "**The Rite**" presents initially a dramatic dialogue and a narrative reflection which in turn give way to the conflict between the old and the young. Symbolically, the drama reenacts the Oedipal struggle between fathers and sons, for to some degree even rebels must cannibalize themselves off the very traditions they seek to overthrow. And insofar as revolutionaries or pseudo-revolutionaries themselves (Randall published many of their works) must emerge at least in part from precisely such tradition, destroying it completely would mean self-effacement. While the writer or any artist wants personal innovation, the younger author internalizes the older one, just as youth seeks to supersede and displace old age. Where such rebellious youth relives the inescapable lessons of the past, for the type of human existence itself never changes, so change itself, even revolution as espoused by militant Blacks in the sixties and early seventies, is necessarily incomplete. In "**Black Poet, White Critic**" the poet's drama becomes more racially focused as the detached narrator works through humorously to an interrogative punch line. Advising the poet to write "safely," the critic cautions against the subjects of freedom and murder. Moved by "universal themes and timeless symbols," the arbiter proposes a verbal portrait of the "white unicorn," and in quipping back ("a *white* unicorn?"), the narrator underscores the subjectivity of beauty.

Two other poems, "**The Idiot**" and "**The Melting Pot**," reveal Randall's technical range. The first, a humorous monologue, blends psychological depth with colloquial tone in order to portray police brutality. The police officer, who has called the speaker a Black "boy," punches him in the face and drags him to the wall. Here the officer searches and cuffs him. Sufficiently angry to chastise the police, the narrator relents because, "I didn't want to hurt his feelings, / and lose the good will / of the good white folks downtown, / who hired him." The irony is complex. The speaker feigns courage, but the rationalization signifies true cowardice. Why did the "good" people downtown hire the demonstrably bad policeman? The speaker's reasoning, ill-suited to an answer, breaks down. Rather than see others in true fashion, the idiot chooses doubly to blind himself. Almost hopelessly naive to white hypocrisy, he misreads direct racism as well. In eight rhymed quatrains "**The Melting Pot**" illustrates the ironic myth of the American mainstream to the protagonist, Sam. From the present-

Front cover of Randall's 1971 collection of poems.

ed fable, including the wordplay and rhyme, the comic ballad leads to an ultimate epiphany, for thrown out of the American crucible a thousand times, Sam reconfirms, "I don't give a da... / Shove your old pot. You can like it or not, / but I'll be just what I am."

Through poems such as "**A Different Image**," Randall acknowledges the influence of African and Caribbean poets. Schooled well in Négritude, a philosophy espoused by French-speaking Blacks since 1945, he deepens Black experience into universal meaning. In 1968 he brought out James Emanuel's first book of poetry, *The Treehouse and Other Poems* and issued Nikki Giovanni's second book, *Black Judgment*. In the reprinting of Margaret Danner's *Impressions of African Art Forms*, a facsimile of the 1960 original, he redistributed the only known volume devoted entirely to the subject of African aesthetics. During 1969 he published books by poets Jon Eckels, Beatrice Murphy, Nancy Arnez, and Sonia Sanchez, as well as those by Marvin X, Keorapetse Kgositsile, and Stephany. Randall served as instructor of English at the University of Michigan in 1969 and from then until 1974 served as poet in residence at the University of Detroit. For a while at the University of Ghana, he studied African arts. Then he visited Togo and Dohemy. From 1970 through 1976 he completed an appointment to the advisory panel of the Michigan Council for the Arts.

His literary career has prospered; the fourteen poems in **Love You** (1970) achieve more thematic and formal focus than in his previous poetry. With scholarly range, he writes the poem of celebration, the monologue, and the short visionary lyric. Attentive to transitory love-making, as well as to the discrepancy between appearance and reality, he observes well the tension between the tangible and the intangible. Sometimes he uses skillful similes to verbalize a speaker's personal joy; he employs Steinesque wordplay. Through structured dramatic situations, he projects personal advice and consolation for fellows. "**The Profile on the Pillow**," a well-crafted verse, compares the narrator's trace of the lover's silhouette to the mature poet's commitment to humanity. Set against the race riots of the late sixties, the narrator-lover echoes clearly Brooks's speaker ("The Second Sermon on the Warpland"): "We may be consumed in the holocaust, / but I keep, against the ice and the fire, / the memory of your profile on the pillow." Although love is intangible, the reader recognizes it through the writer's use of tangible light. Retreating from chaotic history, one person asks the other to "step into the circle of my arms," withdrawing from the metaphorical whirlwind and fire, from physical and emotional exhaustion.

For Dudley Randall the early 1970s meant a balanced and personal retreat. Written from the thirties through the sixties, the poems in **More to Remember** (1971) comprise his first comprehensive collection. Although the individual verses are not arranged chronologically, each group represents a particular decade of his work. While times changed, the biting irony and humor developed. *Poem, Counterpoem* (1966) contains only the verses appropriately paired with Danner's, and *Cities Burning* (1968) has only those which reveal a disintegrating era. Then the most indispensible of his volumes, the latter includes the subjects of kindness and cruelty, incredible harvests, diversely classical forms, and natural beauty. Here Randall explores some contradictions in human psychology and in the Black Arts Movement, and, still a thinking poet, in doing so he displays artistic breadth. Adding to the literary strategies from earlier volumes, he draws upon personification, and though despite some occasional and prosaic overstatement he keeps a sharp ear. In deftly manipulating his point of view, Randall writes the lyric or the parable equally well. In "**The Line Up,**" a poem in four quatrains, a police inquiry is written as an extended metaphor. Here one views the worth of various literary periods while the verse employs a double voice. There is, on the one hand, the common speech of accused criminals, including the murderer, the young pimp, and the dirty old man, yet on the other hand, the speaker maintains an ironic detachment; he believes that the investigators ask the wrong questions. Although the police indict many people and record their crimes, the officers themselves hardly understand, nor can they explain the motives.

"**Interview,**" possibly the most sustained and brilliant of the generational poems, portrays an entrepreneur turned philanthropist. As the old man explains his principles to an intruding young reporter, an ambivalence is clearly apparent. The newsman, who has crossed a protective moat and scaled a barbed wire fence, suggests boldly the mirror-image of the philanthropist himself at an earlier age. And in provoking the speaker's own credo, the youngster hears the man repudiate cynicism. The benefactor, self-trained in industry and discipline, avows to "Not snivel ... prove to those / Who could not take the world just as they found it / And therefore lack the power to change it at all / That one old, greedy and predacious villain / Can do more good ... than ... their years of whining and complaining."

"**On a Name for Black Americans,**" a politically angry sermon, stresses self-reliance as well. "The spirit informs the name, / not the name the spirit." While Randall suggests the name Du Bois temperamentally as well as ideally, he pragmatically implies Benjamin Franklin and Booker T. Washington. From childhood he remembers that Blacks worked hard once to have *Negro* capitalized, and he never considered the word derogatory. Although some Blacks have attempted to demean the term by using lower case or by applying it only to the submissive fellows, he still asserts that "what you are is more important than what you are called ... that if you yourself, by your life and actions, are great ... something of your greatness will rub off ... dignify ... actions affect words ... In a more limited sense ... words affect actions."

The distinction between appearance and reality pervades *More to Remember*. "**Put Your Muzzle Where Your Mouth Is (or shut up)**" addresses sarcastically a theoretical Black revolutionary. Loudly telling others to kill, he has murdered none himself, and the protagonist who shouts "Black Power" in the poem "**Informer**" similarly deludes the listeners who overlook his whispers to the FBI. "**Abu**" reveals the contradictions through low burlesque, for the activist who has apparently decided to blow up City Hall advertises in the *New York Times*. Right in front of the FBI infiltrators, he promises to assassinate a white liberal who gave "only" half a million dollars to the NAACP, but, asked to comment later, "Says nothing 'bout that Southern sheriff / killed three black prisoner / 'cept, he admired him / for his sin / cerity." So consumed with self-hatred, Abu is a self-acknowledged coward, for his posture and rhetoric are less dangerous than foolishly deceptive. He criticizes readily some white liberals who pose no obvious threat, but he rationalizes away the need to confront the racist who does so. He is as hypocritical as is the protagonist in "**militant Black, Poet,**" who hangs himself after a white suburbanite downplays the "militant's" bitterness. Finally, the poem "**Ancestors**" exposes the revolutionary's own elitist tendencies. While such people fantasize about royal heritage, they demean humble origins. In "**On Getting a Natural (For Gwendolyn Brooks),**" the volume's final poem written in December 1969, Randall's speaker celebrates the humanist. At first too humble to admit her own charisma ("beauty is as beauty does"), Brooks blossoms into racial awareness, and her epiphany rings true.

In *More to Remember* the description concludes with Randall's aesthetic theory. In "**The Ascent**" he has represented the poet as visionary, and in "**The Dilemma (My poems are not sufficiently obscure? To please the critics—Ray Durem),**" he has revealed once more the tension in the artist, the modifier of both literary tradition and classical form. Whether from traditionalists or revolutionaries, the artist asserts intellectual independence. The appropriately titled "**The Poet**" illuminates the type. Sloppily dressed and bearded, the writer reads when he should work. Imagining a poem, he would rather turn a profit and convert to "outlandish religions"; he consorts with Blacks and Jews. Often disturbing the peace, a "foe of the established order," he mingles with revolutionaries. In a satirical ploy the narrator plays temporarily the bigot's part: "When will you [the poet] slough off / This preposterous posture / And behave like a normal / Solid responsible / White Anglo Saxon Protestant." Randall's artist philosophizes more than he lives ("**The Trouble with Intellectuals**"), but he feels deeply ("**Mainly By the Music**").

Especially from 1972 through 1974, Randall contributed much to Black American culture. He participated in a poetry festival, "The Forerunners," codirected by Woodie King at Howard University in 1972. He bolstered indirectly the early success of the Howard University Press, which would issue the proceedings, and in Washington he heard Owen Dodson read from a wheelchair. He listened to Sterling Brown present "Strong Men." A recipient of the Kuumba Liberation Award in 1973, Randall participated in the seminar for socio-literature in the East West Culture Learning Institute at the University of Hawaii. He had established himself, says Addison Gayle, as one "who came to prominence, mainly, after the Renaissance years, who bridged the gap between poets of the twenties and those of the sixties and seventies ... began the intensive questioning of the impossible dream, the final assault upon illusion that produces the confrontation with reality, the search for paradigms, images, metaphors, and symbols from the varied experiences of a people whose history stretches back beyond the Nile."

Dudley Randall marks well the transition over six decades. His next pamphlet, *After the Killing* (1973), often assumes the style and voice of the younger poets. Although most of the verses included are recent, some are older ones. "**To the Mercy Killers**" appears with some poems completed during the sixties and seventies. Here Randall experiments with typographical lyrics and sharpens Juvenalian satire. Despite others' inclinations toward modern compression, he avoids the direction of Wallace Stevens and Gwendolyn Brooks as well as the visionary sweep of Walt Whitman and Langston Hughes. Pausing occasionally for sexual deliberations, he lays bare intraracial prejudice and semantic deceptions. "**Words Words Words**" criticizes Black activists who constantly favor white and light-skinned women. When the expressions belie the deeds, Randall's speakers toy with ambiguities. While one Black says "fag—" means something else, another adds that "mother" does as well. The narrator concludes that "maybe black / doesn't mean black, / [two line space] but white." The double space underscores the pause and insight.

The title poem, a parable, infuses murder with the solemnity of biblical myth. The literary world transmutes the poet's life into fable, for the historical Randall lived through World War II and Viet Nam. As in Robert Hayden's "In the Mourning Time," the speaker distills Black anger into ritual. Supposedly dedicated to ultimate peace, the bloodthirsty man kills other people, whose children in turn kill his own. Another bloodthirsty one, three generations later, repeats the original's words: "And after the killing/there will be [triple or quadruple space] peace." The blank space implies human extinction or an undesired solution. "**To The Mercy Killers**" translates the ritual more clearly into social portraits of totalitarianism and abortion, though neither subject may be fully intended. One man reclaims sarcastically the glowing life from others, the self-appointed gods who would destroy him. Elsewhere Randall's narrator states aphoristically: "There are degrees of courage. / One man is not afraid to die. / A second is not afraid to kill. / A third is not afraid to be merciful."

With energy and commitment, Randall demonstrates Black self-determination now. Influenced more by modernist techniques, he discusses the love of writing and the joy of publishing. Despite the fun of teaching, he expects his professional and literary career to take new turns. While not tearing up his work, he writes only in the days he has time. He composes the poems in his head and then writes them later–sometimes while lying down or driving along the freeway.

Randall believed that young Black poets should be free from publishers like Random House and Morrow and, despite the emergence of new talents, that older poets should continue to be active. While abandoning sonorousness in his own art, he attempted looser forms and more colloquial diction. Wanting a widely diverse audience, Randall worked for richness and philosophical depth. To achieve freedom and flexibility he declined partnerships as well as incorporations, for he feared that stockholders would demand profits, would lower quality, or would publish prose. While his income from the press went into publishing new poetry volumes, Randall paid royalties to other poets. He confessed, "I am not well qualified to operate in a capitalistic society. I came of age during the Great Depression, and my attitude toward business is one of dislike and suspicion. Writers who send me manuscripts and speak of 'making a buck' turn me off." Although dedicated to ideals, Randall remembered well the pragmatic lessons from the Black Renaissance. When the Depression came in the thirties, white publishers had dropped Blacks who earlier had been popular, so Randall recommended that Afro-Americans "build a stable base in their own communities."

In "**Coleman A. Young: Detroit Renaissance**" the speaker advocates communal rebirth. Aware of contemporary mechanization, he still acknowledges the value of wisdom. The historical sweep, suggesting both racial and human consciousness, spans 3,000 years. The final lines allude at once to Langston Hughes' *Montage* and Shakespeare's *Tempest*:

> Together we [human community] will build
> a city that will yield
> to all their hopes and dreams so long deferred.
> New faces will appear
> too long neglected here;
> new minds, new means will build a brave new
>   world.

The rhythmically intoned "long" and the repetitive "new" achieve sound inflections, ones rare indeed in more formal Black poetry. Even the words of Shakespeare's Miranda ("brave new world") assume a bluesesque depth and a suspended sharpness in half-stepped musical climbs.

Randall's recent book, *A Litany of Friends* (1981), demonstrates an intellectual depth of themes used and technical mastery of the poetic form. Of the eighty-two poems collected, twenty-four are reprints, and forty-eight are new. Six poems appeared first in *Poem, Counterpoem* (1966), four in *Cities Burning* (1968), one in *Love You* (1970), fourteen in *More To Remember* (1971), and nine in *After the Killing* (1973). Grouped topically, the verses demonstrate Randall's technical skill.

Randall enlarges the humanness of poetry written in English. Sensitive to Robert Hayden's historical allusions, he employs the sea-death imagery of Alfred Lord Tennyson, and he alludes equally well to Thomas Gray's graveyard school or to the blues tradition of Langston Hughes and Sterling Brown. Responsive to both romance and tragedy, Randall achieves the lyrical as well as the dramatically stoic poem. Creating both inner and outer voices, the private persona and the detached narrator, he reveals human consciousness.

In the sustained title poem of forty lines, Randall celebrates other people. Here are family members and fellow artists who helped him through a severe personal depression in the mid-seventies. While metaphors and similes emphasize kinship as well as journey, familial embrace signifies communal ritual. The ceremonial tone leads back through Black America to Africa. Without the mention of last names, the speaker thanks Gwendolyn Brooks for remembering him and sending gifts. He praises the late Hoyt Fuller for respecting him as a man rather than as a hero. In his mind he hears Etheridge Knight tell him to confront the pain and to transcend it. While the speaker thanks Audre Lorde for writing and sending donations, the narrator praises Sonia Sanchez, who phones him and sends herbs. So, friendship inspires personal restoration.

Two other poems, "**My Muse**" and "**Maiden, Open,**" suggest Randall's erudition. Well-versed in the poetic themes and forms of antiquity as well as in the English Renaissance, he shows the ambivalence of art and eternal love. In the seven stanzas of "**My Muse**" (October 1, 1980), he blends Greek sources with African sound. While the muse ("Zasha") inspires the poet, his verses come either in tenderness or wrath. The speaker observes classical analogues between the African muse, Catullus' Lesbia, and Shakespeare's dark lady as well as Dante's Beatrice and Poe's Annabel Lee. Restored to her rightful place in human mythology, the African muse appears as, "My Zasha / Who will live for ever in my poems / Who in my poems will be forever beautiful." The blackness is sublime. Through the analogue between the poem and the damsel, "**Maiden, Open**" places eternalness equally against the enchanted landscape: "who ever tastes the poet's lips / Will never grow old, will never die...."

More political poems such as "**A Leader of the People (for Roy Wilkins),**" written April 18, 1980, and "**A Poet Is Not a Jukebox**" distill racial history into literary type. Although Wilkins, an NAACP leader, was still alive then, today the verse marks an appropriate threnody. Dramatized in two voices, the optimistic one written in roman type and the pessimistic one expressed in italics, the poem contrasts Wilkins with the skeptical narrator. And, on a second level, it sets up Wilkins' two selves, one visionary and the other pragmatic. Wilkins acknowledges a commitment to self-respect and independence, but the negative voice assures him that sacrifice earns the enduring hatred of men and women. When Wilkins answers he will risk hatred for love, the

counterpart argues that others will rebuke him. Whereas Wilkins agrees to bear scorn and pride for the sake of Blacks, the other responds demonically so. Although Wilkins reaffirms the mission to withstand the enemies and save the people, the pessimist finished introspectively: "It is not your enemies who will do these things to you, / but your people."

When the emphasis falls less upon betrayal than endurance, "**A Poet Is Not a Jukebox**" reaffirms an artistic independence. After writing a love poem, the speaker must defend the choice to a militant inquirer. Why, she asks, doesn't he portray the Miami riot? Now self-removed from social upheaval, he has worked lately for the Census and listened to music. In ignoring television, he has avoided the news as well. As a statement about artistic freedom, the poem leads through totalitarianism to a complexly human statement. The writer must achieve personal and emotional range, for out of love and the commitment to happiness and joy, he "writes about what he feels, what agitates his heart...."

Apparently Randall edits in the same manner. While some scholars would view Randall today primarily as a publisher, others think of him as a man of letters. While he fails to shape his talent into polished rhythms and compressed images, he writes keenly in the ballad and sonnet forms, and in prophetic verse, he experiments in the parable and fable. Although attracted to the poetry of antiquity, including classical conventions, he also gives his energetic support to modern originality. While enabling him to perceive the love often overlooked in the poetry and life of Sonia Sanchez, his sensitive ear also helps him to appreciate the epic tone and Christian analogue in verses by Etheridge Knight, Sonia's former husband. Whether or not Dudley Randall is a great poet in his own right, Black American literary art has benefited from his great talent and love for fifty years. (pp. 78-91)

> *R. Baxter Miller, "'Endowing the World and Time': The Life and Work of Dudley Randall," in* Tennessee Studies in Literature, *Vol. 30, 1986, pp. 77-92.*

D. H. Melhem (essay date 1990)

[*In the following essay from her award-winning* Heroism in the New Black Poetry *(1990), Melhem discusses Randall's poetry and involvement with Broadside Press. A slightly different version of this essay appeared in* Black American Literature Forum *in 1983 under the title "Dudley Randall: A Humanist View."*]

"I never thought of myself as a leader," says Dudley Randall in his soft, vibrant voice. Yet the historical impact of Broadside Press, begun in Detroit in 1965 "without capital, from the twelve dollars I took out of my paycheck to pay for the first Broadside," attests to the modesty of his statement. Despite Randall's "silence" between 1976 and 1980, when the Press foundered as a result of overgenerous publishing commitments and subsequent debt; despite his depression during those years (he wrote no poetry until April of 1980), Broadside Press—which now continues in the hands of Hilda and Donald Vest—remains his edifice and achievement. It gave opportunity to dozens of unpublished as well as published Black writers (including all the poets in this study except Jayne Cortez). It produced *Black Poetry: A Supplement to Anthologies Which Exclude Black Poets* (1969), the first such anthology to appear under the imprint of a Black publisher. It revived and adapted the concept of the broadside, developed as a polemical device during the Puritan Revolution in seventeenth-century England. Randall's broadsides, many of them printed on oversized paper and decorated as works of art, suitable for framing, often served both aesthetics and rhetoric. But his deep concern was always for the best poetry, "the best words in the best order," as he has stated, invoking Samuel T. Coleridge. An extension of this interest has been the Broadside Poets Theater, a distinguished series of readings inaugurated by Randall in August 1980. Drawing Black poets from across the country, it has become his chief commitment to the arts.

Randall began his career as a writer in 1927, at age thirteen. That year he published a sonnet on the "Young Poets' Page" of the *Detroit Free Press,* winning first prize of a dollar. Music, religion, politics, and poetry were meshed early in his consciousness. Born on January 14, 1914, in Washington, D.C., he is the third (and the sole survivor) of the five children of Arthur George Clyde and Ada Viola (Bradley) Randall. The poet recalls going with his mother to a band concert in Towson, Maryland, when he was a child: "I was so impressed by the big bass drums and the big bass horns that I composed words about them to the melody of 'Maryland, My Maryland,' which the band had played. This is the earliest instance I can remember of my composing a poem." Randall's father, a politically oriented preacher who managed the campaigns of several Black office seekers after the family moved to Detroit, took him and his brothers to hear W. E. B. Du Bois, Walter White, James Weldon Johnson, and others.

In high school Randall developed skill in prosody, which he advises poets to study. Although he writes often in free verse, he does so by choice, not necessity.

> I believe there's an ideal, Platonic line for every thought. The job of the poet is to find it. In traditional verse, it's easier, as there's already a pattern given. Free verse is harder, as there's no given pattern for the line, and the poet has to find the one perfect line out of billions of possibilities. Therefore, the poet who hasn't mastered traditional verse and doesn't know a trochee from a hole in the ground, won't know what to look for or how to select when lines come into his mind. The line I like best in **"Ballad of Birmingham"** is the line in sprung rhythm, "but that smile / / was the last smile," where the 2 spondees balance each other. Most free verse is bad, as is most traditional verse, but there's more bad free

> verse than traditional verse. I always scan my free verse, and I know what rhythms I'm using, and why.

> The spareness of my ballads comes from Black folk poetry—spirituals & seculars—as well as from English folk poetry.

Randall also noted that Henry Wells's *Poetic Imagery Illustrated from Elizabethan Literature* (1924), which classifies images, was an important stylistic influence, as were classical meters and French forms. He has translated some of Catullus into the hendecasyllabics and Sapphic strophes of the original. In translating, whether from Aleksandr Pushkin or Konstantin M. Simonov or Paul Verlaine, Randall tries to render the form as well as the content. His most ambitious project, the "translation" of Chopin preludes and waltzes into "songs without words"—lyrics so totally expressive of the music that they would merge with it—lies ahead. In addition to earning a bachelor's degree at Wayne University (now Wayne State) in 1949 and a master's in library science at the University of Michigan in 1951, Randall has gone on to complete course requirements for a master's degree in the humanities at Wayne State. The Chopin translations may become the thesis for that second master's.

Listening to classical music helps Randall to write. Although he recommends that the poet read widely, "in any language you know," he agrees with Dorothea Brande's suggestion in *Becoming a Writer* (1937) that a wordless occupation, one that is rhythmical and monotonous, helps the creative process. He is not prescriptive about subject matter: "You write what you can," he says.

Randall's feeling for working-class people was deepened by his years at the Ford Motor Company in Dearborn, Michigan (1932-37). **"George"** commemorates the experience. In 1935 he married Ruby Hands, and soon a daughter, Phyllis Ada, was born. He was employed at the U.S. Post Office in 1938 and worked there—with time out during World War II—until 1951, when he took his first library position. A second marriage took place in 1942. Inducted into the army in July 1943 and trained in North Carolina and Missouri, Randall was sent overseas in February 1944. As a supply sergeant in the headquarters detachment of the Signal Corps, he served in the Philippines and in various islands of the South Pacific. Although he saw no active combat, he was close to those who did. His **"Pacific Epitaphs,"** from *More to Remember,* epitomizes that tragic time.

The poet shies away from the label "pacifist," yet he is strongly antiwar; see especially the title poem of his 1973 collection *After the Killing* and the "War" section of *A Litany of Friends.* Sadly, he likens war to an ongoing family feud and states, "I would say that conciliation is better than revenge." He does accept the designation "humanist." He tells of meeting Arna Bontemps in the 1960s at the Black Writers' Conference sponsored by the University of Wisconsin: Randall, upon asking permission to join a group seated in the cafeteria, was told by

Bontemps, "Yes, Dudley, since you're the only humanist here." Like [Gwendolyn] Brooks, Randall sees people in terms of "family" and remains a family-oriented man. Numerous letters to his daughter, correspondence he prizes, contain his own drawings of his Pacific surroundings during the war, including lizards, sand crabs, and flying fish. His devotion to his third wife, Vivian Spencer, a psychiatric social worker whom he married in 1957, is made manifest in later poetry.

When Randall was discharged in 1946, he returned home to go back to school and his post office job. After receiving his master's degree from Michigan, he worked continuously as a librarian: at Lincoln University in Jefferson City, Missouri, from 1951 to 1954; at Morgan State College in Baltimore to 1956; in Wayne County Federated Library System in Detroit to 1969, and at the University of Detroit, where he was also Poet-in-Residence, to 1976. During those years he received many honors, among them the Wayne State Tompkins Award, for poetry in 1962 and for poetry and fiction in 1966, and the Kuumba Liberation Award in 1973. Both the University of Michigan and Wayne State have named him a Distinguished Alumnus, and in 1977 he received awards from the International Black Writers' Conference and the Howard University Institute of Afro-American Studies. The following year the University of Detroit conferred upon him the honorary degree of Doctor of Literature. He is modestly but deeply proud of becoming, in 1981, the first Poet Laureate of Detroit.

The 1960s were critically formative years for Randall, as they were for all the poets in this study. Two stunning events in late 1963, the racist bombing of a church that resulted in the death of Black Sunday school children, and the assassination of John F. Kennedy, inspired the poems that were to become Randall's first broadsides. The **"Ballad of Birmingham"** and **"Dressed All in Pink"** began the Broadside Series and Broadside Press in 1965. Both poems were set to music by Jerry Moore; they were later included in **Cities Burning.**

Another step in the history of the Press was marked by Randall's meeting with Margaret Danner at a party for the late Hoyt Fuller, editor of the journal *Black World* and then of *First World.* Danner had founded Boone House, the important Black arts center which, from 1962 to 1964, existed as a forerunner of similar projects later launched with government assistance. The two poets conceived **Poem Counterpoem,** a unique series of their paired poems that was released in 1966. In May 1966 Randall attended the first Writers' Conference at Fisk University in Nashville. There he met Margaret Burroughs, with whom he developed the idea of the **For Malcolm** anthology (1967). As Randall observes, the press grew "by hunches, intuitions, trial, and error." At the Conference, he obtained permission from Robert Hayden, Melvin B. Tolson, and Margaret Walker to use their poems in the Broadside Series. He wrote to Gwendolyn Brooks and obtained her consent to publish "We Real Cool." Of this first group of six broadsides, Randall observes, " 'Poems of the Negro Revolt' is, I

think, one of the most distinguished groups in the Broadside Series, containing outstanding poems by some of our finest poets."

The most significant act of confidence accorded Randall and Broadside Press was made by Gwendolyn Brooks when, in 1969, she turned to it for the publication of *Riot.* Randall acted as Brooks's editor and was especially helpful in organizing her autobiography, *Report from Part One.* Brooks, in turn, assisted in the selection of poems for Randall's **More to Remember** (1971), rewriting the preface and eliminating a number of pieces he had planned to include (he now wishes he had excluded even more). The warm friendship inspired both poets. In 1970, Randall dedicated his book **Love You** "to Gwendolyn, an inspiration to us all."

Randall's democratic instincts are offended by what he calls "poet snobs." In a forthright, unpublished poem about the period of his depression, he caustically contrasts some poets' affectation of slovenliness with his own genuine reluctance to care for his body when he was despairing of life itself. With ribald wit he lists the authentic "credentials of dirtiness" and defends his present choice to dress well for public appearances. He feels strongly that poets should be interested in other people. "Shy and self-centered" in his early years, he gradually gained what he refers to as "negative capability" (adapting John Keats's phrase) by thinking of whatever person he meets instead of himself. Randall admires writers in whom he sees this capacity.

Though his humanism remains unaltered, Randall's thinking has undergone some modification over the years, partly as a result of his travels. He still does not "connect" with organized religion (although in *Contemporary Authors,* 1977, he listed his affiliation as Congregational), but his political tone seems more circumspect. "No," he told me in Detroit, as he drew at his pipe and leaned back in a living room chair, "I'm not a socialist. I went to Russia, and I think people are just human beings all the world over." Randall was referring to his 1966 trip with eight other artists to the Soviet Union, France, and Czechoslovakia. He was disturbed about the censorship and treatment of Aleksandr Solzhenitsyn and Osip Mandelstam. In 1970 he visited Togo and Dahomey in Africa and studied African arts at the University of Ghana. That trip enriched his consciousness. Its residue may be seen in his current taste in dress, like his favored orange cap and bright, sometimes African clothing. Yet the impressions revealed contradictions:

> Africa is a very big place. It is very hard to try to sum it up .... I think, moreover, that it is very unwise for a person to talk as if he knows a country after visiting it for only a short time and getting only superficial impressions. An instant expert! There were some contradictions. One of them, for example, was being part of an audience that was two-thirds Black, and the African speaker referred to us as "you white folks," which may give you some idea of how ... this person looked upon Black Americans. Yet I wouldn't generalize and say that every African had

this attitude. In the villages that we visited, for example, they said: "We know that you are our brothers who were taken away from us, and now you are coming back to see the land where your fathers lived, and we welcome you back."

Randall agrees with Haki Madhubuti that whites have been responsible for numerous depredations, but he does not put all whites into the same category. Though he notes wryly that poor whites, who face many of the same problems that Blacks encounter, can be just as prejudiced as those who are more affluent, he continues hopeful that people's attitudes can be altered and that "you can raise anybody's consciousness." Randall maintains his integrationist stance because "we're all human beings." He thinks it important, however, to promote Black solidarity, "to align yourself with those who are like you and in like condition."

Before founding Broadside, Randall was published in various magazines; wider recognition came with the appearance of his work in prestigious anthologies: Rosey E. Pool's *Beyond the Blues* (1962); *American Negro Poetry,* edited by Arna Bontemps (1963); and Langston Hughes's *New Negro Poets: U.S.A.* (1964). It was the Hughes anthology (which bears a foreword by Gwendolyn Brooks) that first presented **"The Southern Road"** (later reprinted in **Poem Counterpoem** and **A Litany of Friends**), a brilliant poem in the strict and now rarely employed form of the ballade. An important French innovation of the fourteenth and fifteenth centuries the ballade is identified with the poetry of Francois Villon, whose work was characterized by intelligence, precision, and realism. Randall's own advice to poets (which appears in *Contemporary Authors,* 1977), begins: "Precision and accuracy are necessary for both white and black writers." David Littlejohn cites **"The Southern Road"** as "a sophisticated rendering of the return-to-the-South theme."

The ballade, usually in three stanzas of eight lines each plus an envoi of four, utilizes three end-rhymes and takes as its refrain the last line of the first stanza. Randall uses a stately iambic pentameter line, and his skill controls the emotionally charged material:

> There the black river, boundary to hell,
> And here the iron bridge, the ancient car,
> And grim conductor, who with surly yell
> Forbids white soldiers where the black ones are.
> And I re-live the enforced avatar
> Of desperate journey to a dark abode
> Made by my sires before another war;
> And I set forth upon the southern road.

Randall connects "the black river" of Black life with ancient myth: the "grim conductor" is Charon who, ironically, enforces segregation. The poet becomes the incarnation and epiphany of his forefathers in a pilgrimage of identity toward life and death.

The second stanza describes the destination, the paradoxical "land where shadowed songs like flowers swell / And where the earth is scarlet as a scar." Because the

poet's blood has been shed here, he will claim the land: "None can bar / My birthright." The dual vision persists in the third stanza:

> This darkness and these mountains loom a spell
> Of peak-roofed town where yearning steeples soar
> And the holy holy chanting of a bell
> Shakes human incense on the throbbing air
> When bonfires blaze and quivering bodies char.
> Whose is the hair that crisped, and fiercely glowed?
> I know it; and my entrails melt like tar
> And I set forth upon the southern road.

Darkness and firelight, the sacred and the profane, spiritual immortality and physical death, redemption and murder vie dramatically as the poet, feeling himself ablaze ("I know it"), presses on. The tar simile merges poet with lynch victims, who were often tarred and then set afire. "Human incense" strikes a bitter irony in the religious context. Half-rhyme, used only in this stanza, sharpens the intellectual and visual contrasts among *soar, air, char, tar.*

In the closing quatrain, Randall invokes the land:

> O fertile hillsides where my fathers are,
> From which my woes like troubled streams have flowed,
> Love you I must, though they may sweep me far.
> And I set forth upon the southern road.

Significantly, the earth remains fertile, nourished by the poet's grief and blood, emblems of his people's suffering. The statement passionately affirms Randall's belief in the democratic potential of the United States, his conviction that "conciliation is better than revenge." The poem's refrain gains a semantic increment subtly from stanza to stanza and so transforms from the first, where it functions narratively, to the second, where it asserts a claim, to the third, where it makes a heroic gesture. In the envoi it becomes a measure of love as Randall moves to the simple declarative of the close. The last line suggests the poet as separate yet strengthened by his experience, like Whitman's "simple, separate person" who can "yet utter the word Democratic, the word En-Masse." This poem may be contrasted with the title poem of Sterling A. Brown's *Southern Road* (1932)—reprinted in Randall's useful anthology **The Black Poets** (1971)—which is a blues ballad in dialect expressing a chain gang member's hopeless view of his life.

Cities Burning (1968), the first collection of Randall's own poems, whose cover design and stark colors of red, black, and white resemble those of Brooks's *Riot,* reflects the revolutionary spirit of the sixties. Of its twelve poems, half—including the most polemical—are in free verse; the rest are rhymed. **"Roses and Revolutions,"** written in 1948, sets the tone:

> Musing on roses and revolutions,
> I saw night close down on the earth like a great dark wing,
> and the lighted cities were like tapers in the night,

and I heard the lamentations of a million hearts
regretting life and crying for the grave.

The Whitmanic line and inflection draw the free verse
to an affirmative close. There, the poet's prophetic
vision of a future in which "all men walk proudly
through the earth, / and the bombs and missles lie at the
bottom of the ocean / like the bones of dinosaurs buried
under the shale of eras," is confirmed by its radiance, in
which will "burst into terrible and splendid bloom / the
blood-red flower of revolution." The coupling of revolution and blossom invokes the Brooks of the "Second
Sermon on the Warpland" and her counsel to youth:
"Conduct your blooming in the noise and whip of the
whirlwind."

Randall's interest in other art forms appears in **"Primitives,"** which compares the attempt of abstract art
(Picasso is suggested) and modern poetry, especially the
typographically experimental, to deal with the threat
and hideous reality of modern warfare. His lyrical
"Augury for an Infant," addressed to his granddaughter,
Venita Sherron, closes the volume hopefully, seeing the
infant as "infinite possibility." But the strongest poems,
apart from the first, employ the lyrical understatement
of Black folk poetry, the terseness of blues, "ballards,"
spriuals, and seculars, and of old English ballads like
"Edward, Edward," "Lord Randal," and "The Twa
Corbies," where deep feeling compresses into rhythm,
rhyme, and the tragic frame. **"Dressed All in Pink"**
begins quietly, with a specific reference to John F.
Kennedy's ride though Dallas with his wife, Jacqueline,
and Governor John Connally on November 22, 1963,
and an allusive one to Camelot, land of the Kennedy
dream:

> It was a wet and cloudy day
> when the prince took his last ride.
> The prince rode with the governor,
> and his princess rode beside.

Randall's formal mastery gives a spondaic emphasis to
"last ride" in the only second line of any stanza thus
distinguished in the seven-stanza poem. Having progressed through the shooting, the piece closes: "and her
dress of pink so delicate / a deep, deep red is dyed." The
facts, ordered within the music and noble simplicity of
the genre, elevate into myth.

The **"Ballad of Birmingham,"** on the page opposite the
Kennedy poem, complements both subject and genre
with a similar spare dignity. Like the assassination of
the president, the bombing of the Sixteenth Street
Baptist Church on September 15, 1963, took place in
the year of heightened civil rights protests. This "Negro
Revolt" or "Black Rebellion" had culminated in the
March on Washington in August by over 200,000 Black
and white citizens, who had been stirred by Martin
Luther King's "I have a dream" speech at the steps of
the Lincoln Memorial. The following month, the Birmingham tragedy took the lives of four little girls at
Sunday School and injured other children. The attack

aroused nationwide grief and indignation, which the
events in Dallas would soon intensify.

Randall focuses upon one child, personalizing both the
horror and its context. The girl asks her mother's
permission to participate in a freedom march. The
mother, fearing the police dogs "and clubs and hoses,
guns and jails," protectively refuses and, in searing
irony, suggests that her child go to Sunday School
instead, where she will be safe. Dramatic tension builds
as the mother lovingly dresses the child for church and
smiles to think of her daughter "in the sacred place."
Then she hears the explosion: "her eyes grew wet and
wild. / She raced through the streets of Birmingham /
calling for her child." The murder, as if too terrible for
description and thus augmented by mystery, powerfully
registers in this vignette of maternal anguish. The poem
conveys the dreadful lesson: no place is sacred or safe in
such a time and place. The name of Birmingham, a city
then regarded as the "capital" of segregation, becomes a
symbol: "Birmingham becomes any city or town in
which the oppressed Black is killed out of racial
prejudice." [John T. Shawcross, "Names as 'Symbols' in
Black Poetry," in *Literary Onomestics Studies,* 1978].

Publication of the anthologies *For Malcolm* and *Black
Poetry,* the addition of Gwendolyn Brooks, Don L. Lee,
Sonia Sanchez, Etheridge Knight, Nikki Giovanni, and
other important writers to the regular list, along with
Broadside Series authors such as Robert Hayden, LeRoi
Jones, Margaret Walker, and Melvin B. Tolson, enhanced the prestige of the Press as the unquestioned
leader in Black publishing. In *Black Poetry,* Randall
reprinted from *Poem Counterpoem* his own popular
"George" and **"Booker T. and W. E. B."** The latter
imagines a dialogue between Booker T. Washington,
epitome of the industrious, conservative Negro who
accepts a subservient position—"Just keep your mouth
shut, do not grouse, / But work, and save, and buy a
house"—and W. E. B. Du Bois, the intellectual progenitor of the Civil Rights Movement, who disagrees: "For
what can property avail / If dignity and justice fail?"
Randall clearly and accurately represents both sides,
although, as he acknowledges wryly, Du Bois has the last
word: "Speak soft, and try your little plan, / But as for
me, I'll be a man."

"George," on the other hand, a workingman's tribute in
free verse, describes a foundry co-worker who once gave
Randall his "highest accolade: / You said: 'You not
afraid of sweat. You strong as a mule.'" Years later,
visiting the old man in a hospital ward, the poet
poignantly returns the compliment.

In 1970, an important year for Randall, he traveled to
Africa, and his volume of love poems, *Love You,* was
published in London. Of the book's fourteen pieces, a
few seem occasionally overwhelmed by ardent felings.
Others show the application of his fine lyricism to free
verse, as in **"The profile on the pillow,"** and to metrical
verse, in which **"Black magic"** seems to *sing* its refrain
of "Black girl, black girl." **"Faces"** lauds the beauty of

ordinary, aging features shaped by experience, "not only crocus faces / or fresh-snowfall faces / but driftwood faces, grooved by salt waters."

"Sanctuary," the last poem, mainly in iambic pentameter with deliberately varied stresses, offers particular interest for its whirlwind imagery, recalling Brooks's "Second Sermon on the Warpland," and its compounding ("nation-death-and-birth"), another heroic device of Brooks. **"This is the time of the whirlwind and the fire"** also reverts to the introductory poem, **"The profile on the pillow,"** where tender memory remains, despite possibilities that

> Perhaps
> you may cease to love me,
> or we may be consumed in the holocaust,
> but I keep, against the ice and the fire,
> the memory of your profile on the pillow.

This opening poem may be considered as companion to Brooks's "An Aspect of Love, / Alive in the Ice and Fire" (*Riot,* 1969), a title which alludes in mild irony to Robert Frost's "Fire and Ice." Brooks, like Randall, offers a tentative hope that personal love will endure.

It should be noted that Randall's use of the strong word "holocaust," which has acquired in this century the connotation of genocide, refers specifically to the widely held belief among Blacks, after the riots of the sixties, that the government was preparing concentration camps for their confinement, even extermination. The poet conveys an awareness of fatal peril that will hurl the lovers "with the other doomed spirits / around and around in the fury of the whirlwind"—an allusion to Dante's meeting, in his *Inferno,* with the lovers Paolo and Francesca, whose passion dooms them to be tossed forever by stormy winds. Brooks, on the other hand, uses the whirlwind as a symbol of social change.

Randall's energies converged in high gear upon a full edition, *More to Remember: Poems of Four Decades* (the 1930s through the 1960s), published by Third World Press the following year and dedicated to Don L. Lee. The collection shows a wide range of interests, prosodic skill, and experimentation, its poems almost evenly divided between rhyme and free verse—the latter featured in polemical pieces and the later poems. The main thrust is political and humane and includes lively commentary on poets and poetics. The book is organized by decades into four sections. The first, "The Kindness and the Cruelty," begins significantly with **"For Pharish Pinckney, Bindle Stiff During the Depression,"** dedicated to the brother of Randall's second wife, Mildred. At one time, the youth had lived as a boxcar-riding hobo who "learned the kindness and the cruelty / of the land that mothered and rejected you." Here the ambivalence of the Black experience in the United States may be generalized to include all those oppressed by poverty (see the expanded version in *A Litany of Friends*). Other poems celebrate youth in forms close to the traditions of seventeenth- and eighteenth-century English poetry. **"Shape of the Invisible,"** a cinquain after

Adelaide Crapsey yet showing Japanese influence, effectively measures poetic feet (1, 2, 3, 4, 1):

> At dawn
> Upon the snow
> The delicate imprint
> Left by the sleeping body of
> The wind.

"Incredible Harvests," the second section, marks an enhancement of poetic power and a life that encompasses fatherhood, love and other problems, wartime service, reflections on police arrest (see the blues ballad **"Jailhouse Blues,"** and **"The Line-Up"**), and frequently politics. Here the poet attends more closely to visual elements, most notably in **"Pacific Epitaphs."** The abbreviated and irregular length of these seventeen impressions epitomizes the brief lives of the dead and of their tombs, scattered among Pacific islands. Deep feeling compresses into epigram and understatement, as in **"Halmaherra,"** **"Laughing I left the earth. / Flaming returned,"** and **"Guadalcanal":**

> Your letter.
> These medals.
> This grave.

Avoiding sentimentality, the poems convey a dignity of grief while employing the restraint of, ironically, the Japanese haiku or tanka. Randall himself points out the additional influences of Edgar Lee Masters's *Spoon River Anthology* and of *The Greek Anthology,* which share a mode that is, in his words, "simple, spare, suggestive."

Yet the poet's lyricism does not fail him. Following **"Pacific Epitaphs,"** **"The Ascent"** memorably describes an airman's view of the earth as he moves

> Into the air like dandelion seed
> Or like the spiral of lark into the light
> Or fountain into sun . . . .
> ....
> We poise in air, hang motionless, and see
> The planet turn with slow grace of a dancer.

"Coral Atoll" extends the meditation on natural beauty in the wartime scene and ends with a line that suggests Randall's ideal of poetic form at the time: "Have died into a perfect form that sings." One recalls Keats's "die into life" in speaking of Apollo (*Hyperion,* 1.130).

In several ways, by contrasting form and relating content, Randall emphasizes the senseless recurrence of war and the timeless fraternity of its dead. **"Helmeted Boy"** addresses a youth killed in battle:

> Your forehead capped with steel
> Is smoother than a coin
> With profile of a boy who fell
> At Marathon.

As in **"Pacific Epitaphs,"** the brevity of the lines conveys the brevity of life.

The third section, "If Not Attic, Alexandrian," is the shortest yet displays an interesting variety of technique. It represents the 1950s, Randall notes, "when the nation was quiescent under President Eisenhower, and poetry was under the dominance of the Eliot/academic establishment." It takes its title from **"The Dilemma,"** subtitled with a quotation from the late Ray Durem, "My poems are not sufficiently obscure / to please the critics." In a Shakespearean sonnet, the speaker ironically claims that he cultivates his irony in order to be as confusing as the times. "So, though no Shelley, I'm a gentleman, / And, if not Attic, Alexandrian." Thus, tongue in cheek, Randall presents a poem not marked by simple refinement (Attic) but concerned with technical perfection (Alexandrian).

Other sonnets in this section include **"Anniversary Words,"** in the even stricter Petrarchan form, addressed to the poet's wife: "You who have shared my scanty bread with me / and borne my carelessness and forgetfulness / with only occasional lack of tenderness, / who have long patiently endured my faculty / for genial neglect of practicality." Apologia and appreciation, the poem may be instructively compared and contrasted with **"For Vivian,"** a more recent tribute (1983), published and then "calligraphized" in 1984, the poet notes, as Broadside No. 94:

> Me, this snoring, belching, babbling semblance of
>   man kind,
> What woman could refrain from laughing at?
> Or, caring more, quietly take her hat
> And leave? Yet, these four and twenty years
> You've stayed, though not without heart wring
>   and tears.
> For which my thanks. And bless your love which
>   binds.

The third section also contains the poet's aesthetic credo **"Aim,"** which calls for "words transparent as the air, / which hint the whole by showing the part clear." Randall comments that this poem shows his "liking for a classically natural style, without distracting eccentricities and obscurities."

"Interview" presents another technical surprise. In a dramatic monologue in blank verse after the fashion of Robert Browning—its sixty lines constituting Randall's longest published poem—a rich, elderly man (Henry Ford?) explains his tax-exempt research foundation and his life's philosophy to a brash reporter. He grants the interview in order to

>   prove to those
> Who could not take the world as they found it
> And therefore lack the power to change it at all
> That one old, greedy, and predacious villain
> Can do more good in the world than all of them
> In all their years of whining and complaining.

The portrait renders the shadowy grays as well as the clear blacks and whites of existence.

The relatively long closing section, "And Her Skin Deep Velvet Night," takes its title from **"On Getting a Natural (For Gwendolyn Brooks),"** the tribute that ends the volume. Mordantly amusing, **"Ancestors"** questions: "Why are our ancestors / always kings or princes / and never the common people? ... Or did the slavecatchers / steal only the aristocrats / and leave the fieldhands / laborers / streetcleaners / garbage collectors / dishwashers / cooks and maids / behind?" The democratic Randall tolerates neither snobbery nor intolerance. In **"Aphorisms,"** written with Blakean simplicity (Randall approves the comparison), he warns, "He who vilifies the Jew / next day will slander you. / / He who calls his neighbor 'nigger' / upon your turning back will snigger," and ends on a religious note: "While he who calls a faith absurd / thrusts the spear into his Lord."

The majority of the remaining poems in this group share a political nexus. **"Hymn"** expresses horror over "our worship" of the atomic bomb, which may end life on earth. **"The Trouble with Intellectuals"** and **"The Intellectuals"** were inspired by the difference between the Mensheviks who talked and the Bolsheviks who acted. A number of the poems scold the excesses of Black Nationalism and level criticisms of arrogance, extremism, and hypocrisy at some Black activists.

But there are tributes, too. The syncopated **"Langston Blues"** presents a moving elegy for one who brought "laughter from hell." And the closing poem praises Brooks's adoption of a natural hairstyle and becomes an encomium of her beauty combined in spirit, action, and appearance: "And now her regal wooly crown / declares / I know / I'm black / AND / beautiful."

In 1973 Randall published *After the Killing,* dedicated to the memory of a loyal Broadside worker, Ruth Elois Whitsitt Fondren. The fifteen poems, whose variety of subject matter accompanies the turn to even more free verse (only two are rhymed), show increased versatility in Randall's use of the form, to allow for more lyricism as well as argument. **"African Suite,"** the opening poem in five parts, gives Randall's impression of an Africa still racist and describes his feelings at visiting a Ghana castle that once held slaves. Some pieces apply Randall's critical humor to Blacks as well as to humanity in general, continuing the tact of *More to Remember.*

"After the Killing," the title poem, evokes the Brooks metonymic, heroic style: " 'We will kill', said the bloodthirster, / 'and after the killing / there will be peace.' " Although Randall will not call the poem pacifistic, it does dramatize the absurdity of war, preventive or retaliatory, and of the arms race. **"To the Mercy Killers,"** a Shakespearean sonnet, powerfully affirms life to the end: "if ever mercy move you murder me, / I pray you, kindly killers, let me live." **"For Gwendolyn Brooks, Teacher,"** utilizes spondaic energy and a spare meter: "You teach / without talk. / / Your life / is lesson. / / We give / because you do, / / are kind / because you are. / / Just live. / We will learn." Randall ends the book with a translation, an earlier poem, **"I Loved You Once"** (Ya vas lyubil), from Pushkin, described in an editor's footnote as "the Russian of African descent who is credited for making the Russian language live again."

After emerging from his silence in 1980, in 1981 Randall published *A Litany of Friends: New and Selected Poems,* his first book in eight years. Its moving title poem of dedication, autobiographical, identifies those many poets, friends, and family members who helped him morally, spiritually, and financially during his depression. The long-awaited book, which may be viewed in part as transitional, surprised some, pleased and dismayed others. It comprises excellent selections from previous years and volumes, interfaced with new or newly appearing poems in both free verse and conventional forms. **"Verse Forms,"** written in free verse, defends the sonnet: "A sonnet is an arrow. / Pointed and slim, it pierces / The slit in the armor." (Compare Gwendolyn Brooks's earlier admonition in "The Second Sermon on the Warpland": "not the pet bird of poets, that sweetest sonnet, / shall straddle the whirlwind.")

"A Litany of Friends," also in free verse, was begun April 1, 1980; along with **"The Mini Skirt,"** written on April 4, and **"To an Old Man,"** a sonnet written on Easter Sunday, two days later, it inaugurates the revived creative flow. The three poems, while they reflect the personal emphasis of much of the poetry, Black and white, of the seventies, reveal Randall's psychic energy shaping the two main categories of the new works: humanist concerns (in sections titled "Friends," "War," "Africa," and "Me") and love poetry (in "Eros," which, followed in number by "Friends," contains the bulk of the new poetry).

Part III, "War," offers a distinguished set from *More to Remember,* including **"Pacific Epitaphs."** Among the new or newly appearing antiwar poems are **"Games,"** a fine Petrarchan sonnet variant on boys' war games transposed into real battle, and **"Straight Talk from a Patriot,"** a satirical quatrain on the Vietnam War. Of two translations from the Russian of Konstantin M. Simonov, the exquisitely achieved **"My Native Land (Rodina),"** in six rhymed quatrains of iambic pentameter, personalizes patriotism. Randall's translations, for which his skill and temperament seem equally suited, confirm the breadth of his consciousness.

The introductory section, "Friends," reveals the warmth of the poet, who can write with stirring compassion of his dog (**"Poor Dumb Butch"**); with lyricism of his students (**"My Students"** is a series of fifteen haiku); and with imaginative appreciation of fellow Black poets (**"The Six,"** from 1975). At times the conventional form strains art into conventional registers, but when it succeeds, it does so notably. Randall comments: "Some of the love poems I wanted to sound simple and naive: 'For love converts away from sad,' using the adjective *sad* as a noun; 'And never mind receive,' using the verb *receive* as a noun, the object of the verb *mind.*"

What has disturbed some readers more than the uneven quality of certain pieces is their content. Part II, "Eros," has incurred the most criticism, partly for its unabashed indulgence in sensual appreciation and its occasional Elizabethan inflection (as in **"Maiden, Open"** and **"May and December: A Song"**). But Randall replies: "Poets strain against barriers. Wordsworth attacked Pope's 'poetic diction.' Now, no contemporary poet would be caught dead using 'poetic diction' like 'maiden,' 'bower,' 'sigh.' It's this new interdiction that I fight. Call it 'The New Romanticism,' if you will. I fight for the right to use 'romantic' diction as much as the Black poets of the 1960s fought to use street language."

"The Mini Skirt" typifies the relaxed, Rabelaisian mode. Health of both ego and libido return here in force as the poet delights in his own recovery. The mischievous iconoclast appears in **"The New Woman,"** a reply inscribed "to M. H. W. and D. H. M." (Mary Helen Washington and me), "who said that my poem **'Women'** was sexist." Hence, from the mildly amusing "I like women they're so warm & soft & sweet / Touch one & her skin yields like the flesh of a peach" of the older poem, **"The New Woman"** shifts to "I like women they're so hard & tough & strong / Feel their muscle it's hard & hairy as a coconut," and charges on to a hilarious reversal of the first poem's images and values. An intriguing found poem, **"The Erotic Poetry of Sir Isaac Newton,"** convincingly adapts *The Motion of Bodies* (1687) to free verse. **"Translation from Chopin"** —Prelude Number 7 in A Major, Opus 28—the first published sample from Randall's intended project, seems to dissolve into the poignancy of the piece when read accompanied by the music.

Some of Randall's friends and fellow poets had expected stirring political broadsides, calls for justice, and exhortations to Black unity. Several wondered, as he observes in the militant apologia **"A Poet Is Not a Jukebox,"** "But why don't you write about the riot in Miami?" In this rebuttal, forthright in free verse, Randall admits ignorance of Miami because of his immediate needs to revive his economic and creative life. But his defense turns into a spirited offense. He warns that

> Telling a Black poet what he ought to write
> Is like some Commissar of Culture in Russia
>   telling a poet
> He'd better write about the new steel furnaces in
>   the Novobigorsk region,
> Or the heroic feats of Soviet labor in digging the
>   trans-Caucasus Canal,
> Or the unprecedented achievement of workers in
>   the sugar beet industry who exceeded their
>   quota by 400 per cent (it was later discovered
>   to be a typist's error).

Randall's unfailing humanity empathizes with the Russian poet who may be devastated by his mother's dying of cancer, or by other personal matters. Further, states Randall, as the broadside becomes an aesthetic manifesto,

I'll bet that in a hundred years the poems the
  Russian people will read, sing, and love
Will be the poems about his mother's death, his
  unfaithful mistress, or his wine, roses, and
  nightingales,
Not the poems about steel furnaces, the trans-
  Caucasus Canal, or the sugar beet industry.
A poet writes about what he feels, what agitates
  his heart and sets his pen in motion.
Not what some apparatchnik dictates, to promote
  his own career or theories.

Randall maintains his freedom to choose, in his own
time, his own subjects, those which move him personally, including Miami. He goes on to defend writing about
love and, with extravagant seriousness, offers love as a
sociopolitical prescription. He sardonically notes that
"If Josephine had given Napoleon more loving, he
wouldn't have sown / the meadows of Europe with
skulls." In closing the poem and the book, Randall
insists:

A poet is not a *jukebox.*
A poet is *not* a jukebox.
A *poet* is not a jukebox.

So don't tell *me* what to write.

The revolutionary action of poets has ever been freely to
create from their deepest psychic sources. Defending
himself, ably and with humor, Randall affirms his own
center, his humanist core. One anticipates that as the
poet retrieves and reshapes the extensions of his daily
life, he will again articulate the range of interests that
have made him, in the words of R. Baxter Miller, "one
of the most important Black men of letters in the
twentieth century." The reader will welcome his courageous heart, its wit, lyricism, and humane expansiveness. (pp. 41-60)

> *D. H. Melhem, "Dudley Randall: The Poet
> as Humanist," in her* Heroism in the New
> Black Poetry: Introductions & Interviews,
> *The University Press of Kentucky, 1990, pp.
> 41-60.*

FURTHER READING

Nicholas, A. X. "A Conversation with Dudley Randall."
Black World XXI, No. 2 (December 1971): 26-34.
  Randall discusses his poetry and the evolution of
  Broadside Press.

Ishmael Reed

1938-

(Full name Ishmael Scott Reed; has also written under pseudonym Emmett Coleman) American novelist, poet, essayist, editor, and critic.

A highly original satirist and writer of experimental fiction, Reed is best known for novels that assail aspects of Western religion, politics, and technology. Reed's writing is distinguished by dynamic, playful language—for example, he prefers phonetic spellings to standard orthography, uses capitalization for emphasis, and substitutes numbers for words in the text. Although he writes about injustices engendered by Western civilization, he is primarily concerned with establishing an alternative black aesthetic, which he terms Neo-Hoo-Dooism. This concept is a syncretism of aspects of voodoo and other cultural traditions that Reed hopes will forge a multicultural aesthetic to purge African-Americans and Third World peoples of Western conditioning. Although his works and the Neo-HooDoo Aesthetic have offended some groups and provoked the ire of critics Houstin A. Baker, Jr., Addison Gayle, Jr., and Amiri Baraka, Reed is widely regarded as a revolutionary force in American writing.

Reed was born in Chattanooga, Tennessee, in 1938 and moved with his mother to Buffalo, New York, in 1942. He lived there for twenty years, beginning his college education in night school at the State University of New York at Buffalo. While in night school Reed wrote a short story entitled "Something Pure," in which Jesus returns as an advertising agent with a unique sales strategy that causes him to be ridiculed and scorned. The story attracted the attention of an English professor who subsequently helped Reed become a full-time student at the university. Yet Reed eventually left SUNY-Buffalo in 1960 because he lacked funds; he worked for a local newspaper briefly but soon left Buffalo. "Buffalo couldn't hold on to me," Reed explained in the introduction to *Shrovetide in Old New Orleans: Essays* (1978), "and so I ended up in New York, green, country, and ready to write. I started writing visionary poetry and began to hang out with a group of writers called the Umbra Workshop. Some of them formed the aesthetic and intellectual wing of the Black Power movement." In New York City Reed also founded the *East Village Other,* considered "The Mother" of underground newspapers. According to Henry Louis Gates, Jr., "Reed's New York period was crucial in his evolution as an artist, marked by ... an emerging national identity among black and white writers, organization of the 1965 American Festival of Negro Art, and the writing, in 1965 and 1966, of his first novel, *The Free-Lance Pallbearers,* published a year later to a remarkable critical reception."

The Free-Lance Pallbearers (1967) is a parody of the confessional style that has characterized much black fiction since the slave narratives of the eighteenth century. The novel's young hero, Bukka Doopeyduk, undergoes a chaotic search for self-awareness in a power-obsessed, white-ruled society called HARRY SAM. In his attempt to assimilate into HARRY SAM, he learns that one must be one's own master, yet he is powerless to apply this knowledge and is ultimately crucified. In his next work, *Yellow Back Radio Broke-Down* (1969), Reed introduced his Neo-HooDoo concept. Two precepts underlie Reed's concept: 1) the HooDoo idea of syncretism, or the combination of beliefs and practices with divergent cultural origins, and 2) the HooDoo concept of time. HooDoo (or voodoo as it is called in its country of origin, Haiti) is a syncretic religion, absorbing all that it considers useful from other West African religious practices. It was formed to combat degrading social conditions by dignifying and connecting people with helpful supernatural forces, and the religion thrives because of its syncretic flexibility, its ability to take even ostensibly negative influences and transfigure them. Reed turned this concept of syncretism into a literary method that combines aspects of "standard" English, including dialect, slang, argot, neologisms, and rhyme, with less "standard" language, whose principal rules of discourse are taken from the streets, popular music, and television. Concerning the HooDoo concept of time, Reed emphasized that time is not linear: dates are not often ascribed to "past" events in his works, and "past" and "present" overlap. The concepts of time and syncretism are central to *Yellow Back Radio Broke-Down*. The title—street-talk for the elucidation of a problem—means that the racial and oligarchical difficulties of an Old West town, Yellow Back Radio, are explained, or "broke down," for the reader. A spoof of Western pulp fiction, *Yellow Back Radio Broke-Down* is about the forces of intuition and irrationality, represented here by the Loop Garoo Kid, the Neo-HooDoo hero, in conflict with those of rationalism and science, as embodied by Drag Gibson.

Reed extended his Neo-HooDoo philosophy in *Mumbo Jumbo* (1972) and *The Last Days of Louisiana Red* (1974). Both novels are parodies of the mystery genre in which a detective, Papa LaBas (representing the voodoo deity Legba), attempts through voodoo to combat spells cast by the white establishment, which seeks to anesthetize the artistic and political black communities. LaBas also wishes to rebuild an aesthetic from the remains of black literary and cultural history. *Mumbo Jumbo,* set in Harlem and New Orleans during the 1920s, depicts the battle between two ideologies—Jes Grew, the instinctive black cultural impulse, and Atonism, the repressive, rationalist Judeo-Christian tradition. At the novel's conclusion, Jes Grew wanes after its sacred text is burned, but LaBas warns that the black ideology will reappear some day to make its own text: "A future generation of young artists will accomplish this," says LaBas, referring to the writers, painters, politicians, and musicians of the 1960s. Houston A. Baker, Jr., called *Mumbo Jumbo* "the first black American novel of the last ten years that gives one a sense of the broader vision and the careful, painful, and laborious 'fundamental brainwork' that are needed if we are to define the eternal dilemma of the Black Arts and work fruitfully toward its melioration.... [The novel's] overall effect is that of amazing talent and flourishing genius."

Reed's next novel, *The Last Days of Louisiana Red,* is set in Berkeley, California, during the 1970s and revolves around Louisiana Red, a destructive mental state that afflicts certain black militants. The novel concerns LaBas's investigation into the murder of Ed Yellings, the black discoverer of a cancer cure and the creator of the Solid Gumbo Works, a business that uses voodoo to fight Louisiana Red. A subplot involves a black radical feminist group called the Moochers, who conspire with white males to subdue black men. This theme is prevalent throughout Reed's work and has prompted feminists to criticize him harshly. *The Last Days of Louisiana Red* also drew criticism from advocates of the Black Aesthetic. Objecting to Reed's satire of black cultural nationalists in the novel, Baker wrote: "Ishmael Reed is at it again, wolfing, ranking, badmouthing, putting down those who stand in the way of love, harmony, common sense, and the neo-hoodoo way.... He considers himself one of the middle class achievers of Black American culture, and he has lamented that the culture wants to destroy its achievers. Concerned primarily with his own survival, he turns on the culture and destroys it with satire."

In his next novel, *Flight to Canada* (1976), Reed lampooned the slave narrative and, particularly, Harriet Beecher Stowe's novel *Uncle Tom's Cabin.* The major plot of *Flight to Canada* involves the escape of Raven Quickskill from his owner, Massa Arthur Swille, and Swille's efforts to capture Quickskill. The historical Canada is the eventual destination where Quickskill and other slaves wish to arrive when they flee Virginia, but this historical Canada is not the heaven slaves think, and pray, it will be. Yet in the face of the depressing stories about Canada from his friends Leechfield, Carpenter, Cato, and 40s, Quickskill will not relinquish his dream. For him, Canada is personified beyond the physical plane—it is a metaphor for happiness, be it "exile, death, art, liberation, or a woman," writes Quickskill in the novel. Henry Louis Bates commented that "*Flight to Canada* is a major work, perhaps Reed's most 'intelligent' novel. One senses here a sort of ending for this aspect of his earlier fiction: for the search for The Word, which Reed began in *Mumbo Jumbo,* has realized itself finally in the successful search for the Text—the text that at all points comments upon itself."

Reed has continued to satirize in subsequent novels, occasionally analyzing the American political and economic systems. In *The Terrible Twos* (1982), Reed distorted Charles Dickens's *A Christmas Carol* into a dark satire on racism and greed during the Ronald Reagan-lead 1980s, equating the selfishness and destructive tendencies of the United States with those traditionally displayed by two-year-old children. Reed's next novel, *Reckless Eyeballing* (1986), is a caustic satire of literary politics. Reed castigated what he perceived as a conspiracy between white male publishers and black female writers to subjugate black men by incorporating negative depictions of them into their work. Ian Ball, a black male writer in Reed's novel, responds to the poor reception of his earlier play, *Suzanna,* by writing *Reckless Eyeballing,* a play sure to please those in power with its vicious treatment of black men. ("Reckless eyeballing" was one of the accusations against Emmett Till, the young Chicago black who was murdered in Mississippi in 1953 for "looking and whistling at a white woman.") In 1989, Reed published a sequel to *The Terrible Twos.* In *The Terrible Threes,* he speculated on the future and presented a nation that descends into chaos after the neo-Nazi president of the United States discloses a White House plot to expel all minorities as well as poor and homeless people and to institute a fundamentalist Christian state.

In addition to his novels, Reed has written several volumes of poetry. In such collections as *Conjure: Selected Poems, 1963-1970* (1972), *Chattanooga: Poems* (1973), and *New And Collected Poetry* (1988), he combined black street argot with elements of mythology, voodoo, and pop culture. Yet his fiction has attracted the most critical attention, and that attention has often been negative. Critics are rarely satisfied with Reed's Neo-HooDooism. Darryl Pinckney contended: "Reed's 'Neo-HooDooism' is so esoteric that it is difficult to say what he intends by it, whether it is meant to be taken as a system of belief, a revival of HooDoo, the Afro-American form of Haitian VooDoo, or, as he has also suggested, as a device, a method of composition." Feminists have attacked his harsh portrayals of women and objected to his allegations that there is a conspiracy between white men and black women to oppress black men. Reed's satire of black characters has drawn criticism from architects of the Black Aesthetic: critics Baraka, Baker, and Gayle have accused the author of needlessly attacking a noble cause by lampooning figures in the Black Power and Black Arts movements. Furthermore, commentators have called Reed's works "crazy," "cute," and "living proof that the bacteria of the pop culture has entered the literary world." Reed responded to such reactions in the introduction to *Shrovetide in Old New Orleans*: "Many people have called my fiction muddled, crazy, incoherent, because I've attempted in fiction the techniques and forms painters, dancers, film makers, musicians in the West have taken for granted for at least fifty years, and the artists of many other cultures, for thousands of years. Maybe I should hang my fiction in a gallery, or play it on the piano."

Despite adverse reactions to his works, Reed is committed to satirizing American society—specifically its supposed cultural arrogance and subsequent neglect of those who are not "vital people," or members of the dominant culture or moneyed class. In addition to writing, Reed promotes young writers through his "Before Columbus" coalition, an "anti-Nazi" venture that publishes unknown writers of all ethnicities. Of Reed's role as an innovative force in American literature, Derek Walcott noted: "He alters our notion of what is possible. His importance to our use and understanding of language will not be obvious for many years."

(For further information about Reed's life and works, see *Black Writers; Contemporary Authors,* Vols. 23-24; *Contemporary Authors New Revision Series,* Vol. 25; *Contemporary Literary Criticism,* Vols. 2, 3, 5, 6, 13, 32, 60; *Dictionary of Literary Biography,* Vols. 2, 5, 33; *Dictionary of Literary Biography Documentary Series,* Vol. 8: *The Black Aesthetic Movement;* and *Major 20th-Century Writers.*)

PRINCIPAL WORKS

The Free-Lance Pallbearers (novel) 1967

The Rise, Fall, and...? of Adam Clayton Powell [as Emmet Coleman with Myrna Bain, Steve Cannon, and Clark Whelton] (essays) 1967
Yellow Back Radio Broke-Down (novel) 1969
catechism of d neoamerican hoodoo church: Poems (poetry) 1970
19 Necromancers from Now [editor] (anthology) 1970
Conjure: Selected Poems, 1963-1970 (poetry) 1972
Mumbo Jumbo (novel) 1972
Chattanooga: Poems (poetry) 1973
The Last Days of Louisiana Red (novel) 1974
Flight to Canada (novel) 1976
A Secretary to the Spirits: Poems (poetry) 1977
Shrovetide in Old New Orleans: Essays (essays) 1978
God Made Alaska for the Indians: Essays (essays) 1982
The Terrible Twos (novel) 1982
Reckless Eyeballing (novel) 1986
New and Collected Poetry (poetry) 1988
Writin' Is Fightin': Thirty-Seven Years of Boxing on Paper (essays) 1988
The Terrible Threes (novel) 1989

Neil Schmitz (essay date 1974)

[*In the following excerpt from one of the most important works of criticism yet published about Reed, Schmitz analyzes Neo-HooDooism and applies the concept to Reed's first three novels.*]

In his first novel, **The Free-Lance Pallbearers** (1967), Ishmael Reed emphatically declares what he will *not* do as a Black writer. Bukka Doopeyduk's narrative retells the tale told by countless Black heroes in Afro-American literature of their journey into the heart of whiteness only to deride its formulary disclosures and protests. Yet in parodying this confessional mode (the denouement of Doopeyduk's tale is his own crucifixion), Reed also attacks those Black writers who adopt fashionable approaches to experimental writing, who strive to be "Now-here" in "Nowhere." To turn from the stiffening form of the traditional novel James Baldwin shares with John Updike only to fall into the linguistic despair of William Burroughs or the elaborate glosses of metafiction is an artistic fate Reed has taken great pains to avoid. And therein lies the problem that has informed his subsequent fiction, **Yellow Back Radio Broke-Down** (1969) and **Mumbo Jumbo** (1972). How does one comprehend the significance of Burroughs' narrative form, write in the parodic manner of Thomas Pynchon and Donald Barthelme, and at the same time hold an opposed view of history, an optative, almost Emersonian sense of the dawning day? In his collection of poetry, **Conjure** (1972), Reed unequivocally asserts that Neo-HooDoo, this new direction in Afro-American literature, constitutes "Our Turn," a radical severance of his destiny as a writer from the fate of his White contemporaries. Appropriately the final poem, **"introducing a new loa,"** transforms Burroughs' emblematic nova, the dying light of Western civilization, into a "swinging HooDoo cloud," the birth of a new Africanized universe of discourse. "I call it the invisible train," he writes, "for which this Work has been but a modest schedule."

The course of Reed's experimentation with narrative has thus increasingly involved his conception of Neo-HooDoo as a literary mode. My purpose in this essay is simply to take him at his word—the considerable claim that he has found a way of writing fiction unlike those decreative and self-reflexive fictive modes in which his White contemporaries seem imprisoned. Reed is careful, of course, not to establish Neo-HooDoo as a school. It is rather a characteristic stance, a mythological provenance, a behavior, a complex of attitudes, the retrieval of an idiom, but however broadly defined, Neo-HooDoo does manifest one constant and unifying refrain: Reed's fiercely professed alienation from Anglo-American literature. Ultimately, then, Neo-HooDoo is political art, as responsible as Richard Wright's *Native Son,* but without Wright's grim realism or the polemical separatism that characterizes Imamu Baraka's work. For Reed the problem is to get outside the "Euro-Am meaning world" (Baraka's term) without getting caught as an artist in a contraposed system. . . . In Reed's fiction, particularly the novels after *Pallbearers,* this rigorous denial of the "dominant culture" and its critical values has led to paradoxes and ambiguities that are exceptionally "good" in the terms of "that traditional critique." One can invent myths, invoke legends, change his name and dress, but he cannot will himself into another language. And it is specifically literary language with its seductive devices, its forms and rhetoric, that pulls the self-styled exile back into the consciousness he professes to despise. More than any other contemporary Black writer, Reed seems aware of this dilemma, the difficulty of fashioning an art form that will liberate him from the double consciousness signified by the hyphen between Afro and American. Yet this liberation is the objective of *Pallbearers,* the meaning of its negations, and the challenge of his later fiction.

As the narrator of *Pallbearers,* Doopeyduk speaks literally from the grave. The scat-singing voice that introduces the novel does not belong to the Doopeyduk who speaks within the narrative duration of *Pallbearers.* In killing off that latter Doopeyduk, Reed murders a style, the Black writer's appropriation of what D. H. Lawrence (in a different context) called "art-speech." Doopeyduk's attempt to fashion his discourse in formal English only reveals his stupidity, an ignorance not of correct grammar or proper diction, but of his world. For the language in which he invests his feelings and perceptions is a dead language. He speaks to his wife, the combustible Fannie Mae, as though he were translating a text, and her response is appropriately ribald. It is not, however, just the White man's "art-speech" in the Black man's voice that Reed burlesques. He attacks as well the conventions of Afro-American literature, its traditional modes of rendering and interpreting Black experience. . . . The structure on which Reed relies in this narrative, which

he inflates and explodes, is the structure of Richard Wright's *Black Boy,* Ralph Ellison's *Invisible Man,* and the many subsequent books like them: *"read growing up in Soulsville first of three installments/or what it means to be a backstage darky."* Reed delivers the obligatory scenes of such confessional fiction with studied vulgarity. . . . The rites of passage established by Wright, Ellison, and Baldwin in their fiction are stripped of their dramatic force and reduced to the pratfalls of a burlesque routine. (pp. 126-28)

At his best . . . Reed achieves the surrealistic brilliance of Burroughs' skits in *Naked Lunch.* But between these extremes the prose often stalls in orthographical and grammatical posturing—misspelling for the hell of it. Finally, then, the problem with Doopeyduk's posthumous voice is that it is too obviously worked, too strained in its license. Burroughs' ability to transform street language, the idiom of the junk world, into powerfully stated and precise metaphors, a figurative language as dense and complex as any other in literature, remains the modern epitome of an accomplished colloquial style, an excellence Reed fails to attain in *Pallbearers.* What he does achieve, however, is the elliptical flow and quick displacements of Burroughs' narrative, the cutting edge of Burroughs' cold understanding of modern reality. The Hobbesian question—"Wouldn't you?"—posed in *Naked Lunch* as the resolution to the Algebra of Need is rephrased throughout *Pallbearers . . . .* Yet if Reed manages to erase the whiteness in his writing (the well-wrought form and rhetoric that won Baldwin so much critical praise) and breaks conclusively with the traditional novel, he does not emerge with a contrary Black style. The language of *Pallbearers* is an orchestration of idiolects, conflicting types of speech that caricature their speakers, but no single voice rules this contrived discordance. . . .

Yellow Back Radio constitutes Reed's attempt to reconstruct a coherent perspective and viable form from the necessary wreckage of *Pallbearers.* Armed with supernatural "connaissance," the magic of poetry, the Loop Garoo Kid replaces Doopeyduk, the hapless victim, at the center of Reed's fiction. "One has to return," Reed writes in the introduction to *19 Necromancers,* "to what some writers would call 'dark heathenism' to find original tall tales, and yarns with the kind of originality that some modern writers use as found poetry—the enigmatic street rhymes of some of Ellison's minor characters, or the dozens. I call this neohoodooism; a spur to originality . . . ." Neo-HooDoo as an experimental mode [is] the concept that informs *Yellow Back Radio . . . .* In its syncretistic composition, its diversity of gods and forms of worship, its avoidance of dogmatic structures, voodoo is Reed's reality-model, the known world forever hidden from the gaze of Westerners. Within it Loop is invulnerable; sheltered by ritual, aided by the endless resources of Nature, and empowered by the full possession of his body. (pp. 130-32)

The problem in *Yellow Back Radio* is to translate voodoo in a singular way of writing, to dislodge it from its status as a cultural myth and make it instead a state of consciousness. As we shall see, Reed does not write mythically—he writes about writing mythically.

If only in theory, then, Neo-HooDoo represents a new direction (so Reed argues) for the Black writer, an escape from the decadence of Anglo-American literature that reverses the path historically taken by Black writers and intellectuals in the United States. (p.132)

But where are the "original folk tales" and native idioms in Reed's fiction? How far indeed does Neo-HooDoo (both as myth and mode) take him from established literary canons? His discourse in *Yellow Back Radio* and *Mumbo Jumbo* curves in and around colloquial Black English, which serves him as a stylistic device, not as a language. It is withal a learned and allusive discourse as mixed in its diction as Mark Twain's. His forms are not narrative legends taken from an oral tradition, but rather the popular forms of the Western and the Gangster Novel.... *Yellow Back Radio* is a Black version of the Western Burroughs has been writing in fragments and promising in full since the fifties. Not only is the content of the fiction eclectic in its composition, but Loop's performance as a *houngan* in it has a good deal of Burroughs' "Honest Bill." For the core of his narrative, Reed borrows almost intact the sociological drama Norman Mailer describes in *The White Negro*—that migration of White middle-class youth in revolt against the values of their own culture toward the counter-culture of Black America—and then weaves into this phenomenon a barely disguised account of the student uprisings at Berkeley and other campuses. The shooting at Kent State comes after the publication of *Yellow Back Radio,* but it is accurately prefigured in the book. (pp. 132-33)

Into this revised Western,...Reed pours all the bitterness of present history. Certain Blacks betray Loop for the same dubious rewards that prompted Apache scouts to lead the cavalry to Geronimo. Official Washington is as blind and uncaring about the student massacre in the hinterland as it was during the Indian Wars of the 1880s. And like the Sioux after their crushing defeat at Wounded Knee, the victims of Gibson's peace (the students and Black militants of the sixties) dream apocalyptic dreams, create a drug culture (peyote/LSD), and retreat into themselves. So the narrative unfolds and draws to its necessary end. The only hold-out, the last authentic outlaw, is the artist, the worker of spells, Loop as necromancer. Yet in expanding the scope of the narrative in the final section to give Loop his mythopoeic due, Reed loses the bite of his allusive framework. The ending (Loop on the scaffold about to be hanged) presents a dazzling array of blackouts, bizarre Warholian bits, one-liners. But the laughter at the center of all this hilarity is so cold in its nihilism that it chills the book's critical perspectives.... [The] history that gives Reed his narrative line in *Yellow Back Radio* runs out on him.

When the Pope arrives near the end of the narrative..., the book dissolves into lectures.... In effect, the Pope's arrival restores the hyphenated consciousness Reed seeks to annul in his fiction. It is the Pope who fills us in, who makes the connections that enable us to see how and why Loop works as a character. *Yellow Back Radio* thus turns into a book *about* Neo-HooDooism. And every explanation, every concealed footnote, betrays the artifice of the myth. Reed's mythopoeic lore is as arcane as the cryptic references strewn about in Burroughs' fiction. And his art, it would seem, bears as much relation to James Brown doing the "Popcorn" or Jimi Hendrix stroking his guitar as does T. S. Eliot's, whom Reed consigns in his manifesto to the graveyard of Christian culture....

In [*Mumbo Jumbo*] Reed concentrates on the Harlem Renaissance of the twenties (Langston Hughes, Countee Cullen, et al).... *Mumbo Jumbo,* then, is primarily an historical narrative, a tragicomical review of what went wrong in the twenties.... As such, the book is also an ingenious dissertation on the nature of Afro-American art, a dissertation with a program for the revival of that art.

By fracturing his narrative into a series of sub-texts (there is even a romance, Earline's love for Berbelang), Reed solves some of the problems that arise in *Yellow Back Radio,* notably the problem of introducing a great amount of mythological information....Each story generates its own point of view... and gives Reed the ability to range widely over the dramatic possibilities within his myth. Similarly the diversity of these interpretations reflects the subtlety and complex nature of the Harlem Renaissance. (pp. 134-36)

Readers unfamiliar with the leading figures and notable disputes of the Harlem Renaissance will have a difficult time with *Mumbo Jumbo*.... Unlike *Yellow Back Radio,* where Reed's focus often seems simplistic and his energies diffused, *Mumbo Jumbo* swirls with the taut intricacy of a Jacobean revenge play. (p. 137)

[Though] Reed mercilessly attacks Eliot and Ezra Pound in *Conjure* as "Jeho-vah Revisionists," the archpriests of "atonist" literature, *Mumbo Jumbo* is as brocaded with mythic, literary, and historical allusions as either [*The Waste Land*] or the *Cantos*.... His fiction has become increasingly complex, learned, and witty (*Mumbo Jumbo* has a bibliography that extends for five pages).... In a sense, the problem with *Mumbo Jumbo* is that it is not mumbo jumbo at all. (p. 138)

Reed's Neo-HooDooist moves finally along the same metafictive angle that Pynchon and Barthelme take in their fiction, probing folklore and myth with the same seriocomic intent, to wrench from them their own truths. What distinguishes Reed's Neo-HooDooist is his adamant optimism, his belief that "print and words are not dead at all"..., the ringing note on which Reed ends his preface. (p. 139)

Neil Schmitz, "Neo-HooDoo: The Experimental Fiction of Ishmael Reed," in Twentieth Century Literature, *Vol. 20, No. 2, April, 1974, pp. 126-40.*

Ishmael Reed (essay date 1978)

[*On March 10, 1974, Reed interviewed himself in Berkeley, California. In the following excerpt from a 1978 revision of this self-interview, he discusses the writing of* Mumbo Jumbo *and* Yellow Back Radio Broke-Down, *comments on other black writers, and explains why he is "so mean and hard."*]

[Question]: *What went into the writing of* **Mumbo Jumbo?**

[Answer]: Intuition, intellect, research, maybe even communicators from the psychic field. I was amazed the number of times I would play my hunches about a particular historical event and then be able to go out and prove it. I wanted to write about a time like the present or to use the past to prophesy about the future—a process our ancestors called necromancy. I chose the twenties because they are very similar to what's happening now. This is a valid method and has been used by writers from time immemorial. Nobody ever accused James Joyce of making up things. Using a past event of one's country or culture to comment on the present. Of course when an American writer does it it's called "nostalgia" by people who see the American past as unworthy as a subject. I bet if you were writing about England of a hundred years ago—the kind of programs they broadcast on so-called Public Television, where they're using taxpayers' money to promote the "grandeur" of the Western past, they wouldn't call it "nostalgia." Or if you were writing about nineteenth-century Russia, the literature a whole wing of eastern criticism champions because that's where their parents came from and it's their "ethnic literature," their "homefolks" literature (the same people put down others for promoting their ethnic studies and ethnic arts and turning away from the "classics").

Anyway, getting back to the parallels—there was a postwar economic crisis, you had government scandal, (on page 69 of the paperback edition of **Mumbo Jumbo** there's a photo of the Watergate conspirators and the book was submitted on *January 31, 1971!* which is written after the last line in the book) there was an epidemic of "negromania" sweeping through America then, "The Jazz Age," there was a black writing renaissance, Egypt was on the ascendancy as it is now—important excavations were made in the twenties. And there are other parallels. The black cultural and political spectrum was similar.

I think I might have a touch of sync or synchronization ability (the ability to have insight into the similar form emanating from disparate entities or mediums is the way I see it). I get an average of three sync flashes per week. Last week I was trying to remember the name of a historian who was the best on the Monroe Doctrine. It occurred to me that he was heir to the Fannie Farmer candy fortune and I said Fannie Farmer and somebody on the radio said, "Fannie Farmer."

My mother is the clairvoyant of the family. She has the gift of precognition and she communicates with apparitions of deceased relatives who bring her important news, prophecies, and, of course, fortune.

Thousands upon thousands of blacks have these abilities. The slave masters always marveled at their communications system. I am beginning to believe that a large number of blacks are able to communicate with each other telepathically. I wouldn't be surprised if it turns out that Afros have a larger percentage of people with these *psi* abilities than other groups, among whom we find about 10 per cent of the people with these abilities. It may be that a large percentage of Western people with such abilities were slaughtered (nine million people in two centuries). When the Catholic Church wiped out those who rivaled its authority as the supreme residue of "supernatural" powers—you know, witches. Natural selection set in and most of the people who remain were benumbed.

Hotbeds of paganism, like Germany and Russia, resisted. Notice how Solzhenitsyn recently referred to Marxism as a Western idea. As Ionesco recently pointed out, Marxism is rooted in the Christian tradition. Solzhenitsyn's remarks can be interpreted as those of a Russian pagan getting back at the Church of Rome.

My reading leads me to believe that HooDoo or as they say in Haiti and other places "VooDoo" or "Vodoun" was always open to the possibility of the real world and the psychic world intersecting. They have a principle for it: Legba (in the U.S., "LaBas"). Physicists have discovered an element called neutrinos that can pass through walls (ghosts?). When I said this at Queens College some of the students and their Marxist teachers sniggled. You see, Marxists know all of the laws of Nature. They have the knowledge of the theoretical god of Western philosophy; this is why they can call people and events "irrelevant"—they're omniscient.

Anyway, there were sections of **Mumbo Jumbo** which were written in what some people call "automatic" writing or the nearest thing to it. Writing is more than just the act of typing. I think you get a lot of help from heritage, you know, "voices," the existence of which may be proven through the use of tape recorders. Work in this strange field began with a scientist named Friedrich Jurgeson.

One of the strangest events that happened about **Mumbo Jumbo** was the refusal of a museum in Rome to give me permission to use the picture of a Negroid Osiris they chipped off the wall of an Egyptian pyramid like the vandals they are; yet they got the gumption to call people "uncivilized." When they first received permission forms to use it they were delighted but when they saw the author's photo they refused. My agent went to

Rome and called the director about using it and the director wouldn't even reply. The photo appears in a book called *Black Eros* published by Lyle Stuart, I think. They let him use it but refused me permission.

Another mysterious episode occurred when Doubleday held up the book for a whole year. The book was submitted on January 31, 1971, and was supposed to be published in August of 1971 and it was held up until August of 1972. It would take an Archibald Cox to find out the reason why. I think I know. Of course, Bantam ruined the cover I did for **Mumbo Jumbo** just as they ruined Yvonne Williams' cover for **Yellow Back Radio Broke-Down.** The vice-president of Bantam called me and wanted to know what I doing for the Soledad Brothers. He was calling me from his air-conditioned office in Manhattan. I told him that I sympathized with the Soledad Brothers but my main job I felt was to humble Judeo-Christian culture. He said, "Oh."

Well, Bantam ruined the cover and messed up the book I guess because when you come down to it they are loud and don't have too much class. I just did a book with little bitty "chump change" that makes their whole list look like a thirteen-center hamburger you buy off the New Jersey freeway.

It always amazes me when some jeremiad hi-yellow "black" person would say, "Niggers can't do nothin right. The white man is the one." Did you know that Nixon wanted to retaliate against the Premier of North Korea when he shot down an American plane and killed over thirty men? Nixon couldn't because the Sixth or Seventh Fleet was being used for the filming of *Tora Tora Tora.*

Anyway **Mumbo Jumbo** got through despite an attempt to bury it.

Were you on "dope" or "drunk" when you wrote **Yellow Back Radio Broke-Down?**

The title **Yellow Back Radio Broke-Down** was based upon a poem by Lorenzo Thomas called *Modern Plumbing Illustrated,* which was published in a magazine called *East Side Review* (1966) which lasted one issue. I based the book on old radio scripts in which the listener constructed the sets from his imagination—that's why radio, also because it's an oral book, a talking book; people say they read it aloud, that is, it speaks

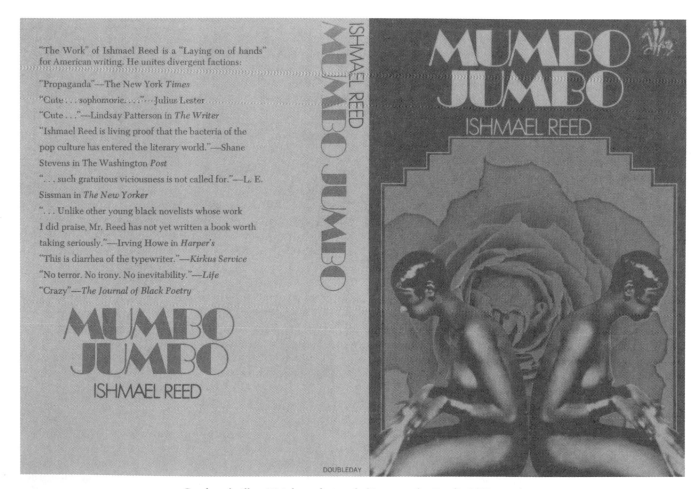

Reed and Allen Weinberg designed this cover for Reed's 1972 novel.

through them, which makes it a loa. Also radio because there's more dialogue than scenery and descriptions. "Yellow Back" because that's what they used to call old West books about cowboy heroes—they were "yellow covered books and were usually lurid and sensational," and so the lurid scenes are in the book because that is what the form calls for. They're not in there to shock. "Broke-Down" is a takeoff on Lorenzo Thomas' *Illustrated*. When people say "Break it down" they mean to strip something down to its basic components. So **Yellow Back Radio Broke-Down** is the dismantling of a genre done in an oral way like radio. The "time sense" is akin to the "time" one finds in the psychic world, where past, present, and future exist simultaneously. A generation from now, when people read my work, they will say—ho-hum, so what else is new?

That is because they will have become accustomed to a way of thinking that's considered "way-out" or even "crazy" now, just as Be-bop was considered "way-out" in the forties, but is now used as background music on very conventional television detective shows.

The funniest thing that happened about **Yellow Back** was its rave review in a magazine called *Western Roundup,* a rodeo magazine. I've never rode a horse in my life. That's really rich because "Yellow Back" writers were usually dudes from the East like me. The cowboys would read their books and begin to ape the exaggerations of themselves they read. A case of life imitating art. And so you see I wasn't "crazy" or "on dope" but extremely conscious of form when I wrote that book as Roland E. Bush and others have realized and pointed out. (pp. 130-34)

Why are you so hard on James Baldwin and Ralph Ellison?

I think that within the framework of Judeo-Christian culture James Baldwin is a great writer. What annoys me is the fact that he's a hustler who tries to come on like Job. He is undeniably a very ambitious man and the way he hops over here from the South of France and comments on "radical chic" issues—these junkets seem to occur always when he has a book coming out. Right now he's lending his prestige to an upper middle-class liberal hobby of going into jails and bringing out some of the worst elements of blacks and setting them up as cannon fodder, you know, not humans but "armed projectiles." We just lost Marcus Foster, whose only crime was that he was trying to do the best job he could do. But this anti-middle class, read anti-black achievers, which comes from places like Howard University and the South of Paris is negative and poisonous. I don't know any group in the world that would want to ice its most skilled people. The Arabs recently attributed their success to turning from "rijal al thiqa," people of confidence, to people of knowledge, "rijal al marifa": engineers, physicians, scientists, skilled navigators, and aviators. Did you know that the woman who runs the computer controlling five or so missile carriers is black? People should read *Ebony*'s feature "Speaking of Peo-

ple" as well as rhetorical losing prophecies of doom and gloom. I was in jail but it certainly wasn't for mugging, raping, or hitting some old person on the head with a brick or gunning down the operators of a Mom and Pop store. I was there for telling a cop he was taking a bribe. They beat me at the Ninth Precinct. I had my Selma all alone and *Life* wasn't there to cover it. I was just another nigger taking his lumps.

While some of my critics were reading Albert Camus and Hegel at Howard University I was living in the notorious Talbert Mall Projects on Spring Street in Buffalo, New York, 1960. My parents recently had their car stolen and they saw it parked in front of Talbert Projects but the police were scared to go in there to arrest anybody. Hard-working black people are the ones who are bearing the brunt of all of this intellectual romanticism concerning the "Political Prisoner," read "The Street Nigger" or "The Field Nigger." This abuse of the term by people like Baldwin and Professor Angela Davis harms the cause of those who are truly political prisoners not to mention the 27,000 aesthetic and "occult" prisoners they have locked up somewhere in the Midwest in institutions. People the society judges to be insane because they challenge it.

Dickens said that you can judge a society by the conditions of its prisons. That must mean that American society is pretty scummy. I know about the Skinner-inspired "behavior modification" programs and the experiments that are conducted on prisoner guinea pigs. I know about the brutality and the sadism; I know all about what the inside of American prisons resemble, but what are you going to do with somebody who comes into your house, rips off your stuff, and hits your mama on the head with a blackjack?

Baldwin does damage, I think, by not being informed that the majority of blacks in New York City, Detroit, and Chicago want Law and Order because they're the ones who have to pay with brain concussions for all of this radical chic stuff promoted from places that are so staked out with doormen and electronic gadgets that only God can enter the lobby. Everybody can't live on Central Park West or be chauffeur driven through Harlem. So it's easy for him to hop on the plane, come over here, and take up a cause. Before I call someone a "political prisoner" I would have to know what they're in for first.

Ralph Ellison has given interviews in which he puts down younger writers for lack of "craftsmanship"—no specifics, no suggestions, just lack of "craftsmanship." He'll write sly attacks against Afro-American writers but from what he has said his idea of craftsmanship is merely giving the synopsis of a Hemingway or Faulkner novel he's read. Telling what the story is about is not "craftsmanship," that's a plot, one aspect of "craftsmanship." In fact, if he were only interested in plot he might reward everyone with a technical discussion of whether plot is "story line" or whether plot is based upon causality, the way one event logically follows another. I hate to say this, but his comments on younger writers do not concern "craftsmanship" but are more like rhetoric, the kind of thing his friends accuse younger Afro-American writers of indulging in. They recognize rhetoric because they are champs at it. What I am saying is that someone ought to do an interview with him in which he is pressed to say exactly what he means about lack of craftsmanship, giving specifics, examples, and suggestions—I mean citing authors and the specific ways in which they lack craftsmanship. That way he would be performing a wise service—to these young authors who according to him lack craftsmanship.

Have you ever received an honorary degree or grant or an award for your writing?

I haven't received an honorary degree or grant but I was recently made an honorary pope by the Savarian Illuminati, for the writing of **Mumbo Jumbo,** which according to the sealed papers I received in the mail was founded in A.D. 1090 by Hassan i Sabbah. They read the book and didn't think it was "muddled" as one of the "Sister" critics thought. I get my strongest criticism from some of the "Sisters." I guess this is because they want me to improve and do better, God bless them. (pp. 135-37)

What is your opinion of recent black poetry?

Much of it is successful. One of the glaring problems, however, is that there isn't as much variety among the critical approaches as there is in the writing the critics are examining. Of course some of the critics only examine the writing of a particular school of black poetry and play like that's the whole thing, like other schools and individuals don't exist. I mean, how could somebody look at the black poetry of the last twenty years (I'm reluctant to call it black since most of the most inflated of the reputations—inflated by a magazine that has been pushing skin lighteners for twenty years—were people who are by my observation very "fair-skinned" and some of these people come on the "blackest"; I hate to bring this up but we're supposed to be "scientists" aren't we?) and say that black poetry is directed to the end of "Freedom and Liberation" and based upon "black speech and music" when an examination would show that the majority of language material is American or English and that the poets and novelists have been influenced by not only music but graphics, painting, film, sculpture—all disciplines and all art forms—and write about all subjects.

They say music because they are socialist realists and music is the most popular art form of the masses. You can be influenced by music while you're asleep but reading is hard work. Of course listening to Cecil Taylor, Bill Dixon, and others is hard work, too, but when these critics talk about "music" they don't mean those musicians; they wouldn't be calling on "the people" to do hard work, they want to make it easy for them and a lot of nonsense that goes down stems from their desire. They are basically social workers and not critics.

Now, if these social realist critics were so interested in "Freedom and Liberation" why would they jive around with the recent cultural history of a people they're supposed to be championing— depriving them of the knowledge of how rich and varied their culture is and was? Why, if they were so hot about "black poetry" would they omit any reference to major figures who were responsible for its development: Calvin Hernton, Lorenzo Thomas, Joe Johnson, Albert Haynes, Charles and William Patterson? Why do they hardly mention the *Umbra* poets, who were writing black poetry in the early sixties? Why would they leave out some of the excellent poets who've been writing since then in favor of promoting one particular school that originates from the screaming wing of the New York School of poets, "personalism," and borrows so much from the examples of the Black Mountain poets that you can't pick up an anthology without someone like Richard Ellman saying black poets would be nowhere if it were not for Olson, Williams, Ginsberg, et al., which is just about as mischievous as someone saying black female poets are superior to black male poets, as Kenneth Rexroth wrote in *American Poetry in the Twentieth Century,* published by Herder and Herder, p. 158. (pp. 140-42)

The writing establishment is now Afro-American and critics who can't see that are social realists and Christians who love to lose anyway. Notice how much they talk about losing: "Nigger, you incapable of doing anything, the white boys is the one that's smart." I cut out clippings of achievements of Afro-Americans for the last two years and I find them to be impressive, some staggering: Dr. Cooke, Afro-American scientist, part of a three-man team that isolated a human cancer virus at Cornell—I call him Dr. Cooke because UPI failed to give his first name. I'll bet if he was some unskilled liberator seduced into a wild scheme by upper-class carpetbaggers you would have gotten his first name and front-page picture.

Anyway, the field nigger got all the play in the sixties. This field nigger romanticism came out of places like Howard University, which is apparently a hotbed of lumpen, field nigger, proletariat, professional street nigger chic. Maybe it's about time people started paying attention to other types of slaves and free blacks from the past. Maybe this generation should listen to shoemakers, masons, bakers, brick and tile makers, inventors, butchers, scientists, cabinetmakers and upholsterers, carpenters and joiners, fishermen and oystermen, harness and saddlemakers, tailors, printers, dentists, barbers, physicians, teachers, musicians, architects, and others. They were there, too, and maybe they have a lesson to teach the present.

No matter what his critics say about him, Booker T. Washington's Tuskegee is still there.

Why you so mean and hard?

Because I am an Afro-American male, the most exploited and feared class in this country. All of the gentlemen, all of the ones who tried to be nice, are in the cemetery or sitting on a stoop humiliated and degraded waiting for someone to hand them a bowl of soup or waiting for the law some woman has called on them. (I'd be willing to bet that half the men at Attica who were wiped out were there on domestic charges.)

With few exceptions, men of most races, not just whites, fear or are curious about his powers. Opportunistic Africans and West Indians like the one *Esquire* put up to call Afro-American intellectuals "empty-headed" are imported by mischievous whites to preside over his political and cultural life, and to stifle his rage and show him up. Even Derek Walcott permits somebody like Selden Rodman to quote him as saying, "There's nothing whiter than an American black, once he has money . . . ."

When will Afro-Americans learn that they are alone and no one cares about them unless they can use them? Russia sold them out; China sold them out; Cuba is preparing to embrace Nixon; the African countries they point to as "socialistic" buy ads in Western newspapers begging for Western capital. It's amazing how uninformed some Afro-American "charismatic" leaders are—they get away with it because Afro journalists don't ask them tough questions and seem to bend over backwards to embrace their point of view.

Anyway, the tragedy of the Afro-American male is that he can't articulate the full extent of his oppression. If I say I am oppressed by "honkies" or "the system" the crowd roars and the popcorn is passed all around and gulped down. But if I say that "whites" are not the only ones who believe in the cultural and intellectual inferiority of the Afro-American male, if you get what I mean, and cite evidence, I'm censored by both white and black publications. Maybe in these hard times ahead we can get into some hard questions about this other oppression—this silent oppression. (pp. 143-44)

> *Ishmael Reed, in his* Shrovetide in Old New Orleans, *Doubleday & Company, Inc., 1978, 293 p.*

Lizabeth Paravisini (essay date 1986)

[*In the following excerpt, Paravisini examines* Mumbo Jumbo *as a parody of the detective novel.*]

The reader familiar with Ishmael Reed's fiction will recognize his novels as parodies of popular narrative forms: *The Last Days of Louisiana Red* follows the structure of the whodunit; *Yellow Back Radio Broke-Down* shatters the conventions of the western; *Flight to Canada* is a revision of the fugitive slave narrative. In these works, parody, which is usually restricted to the imitation and distortion of literary texts, becomes a medium for social and literary satire. One consistent element in Reed's fiction to date has been his use of parody—which is directed inward, toward the text—to examine the extra-literary systems that are the province of satire. Nowhere does Reed blend his parodic and

satiric intentions better than in *Mumbo Jumbo,* where he parodies a narrative form (the detective novel) whose identifying quality (the rational search for knowledge) is identical to the social, religious and philosophical principles he finds objectionable in Western culture. *Mumbo Jumbo* is both a satire of Western culture's concern with rationality and an example of the reorientation of older traditions possible under Reed's aesthetics of Neo-Hoodooism. (p. 113)

Because of the formulaic nature of the genre, a successful detective novel must adhere carefully to the expected pattern in order to fulfill the reader's expectations. Deviating from the pattern means transcending the genre [as Tzvetan Todorov observes]:

> As a rule, the literary masterpiece does not enter any genre except perhaps its own; but the masterpiece of popular literature is precisely the book that best fits its genre. Detective fiction has its norms; to develop them is to disappoint them: to "improve upon" detective fiction is to write "literature," not detective fiction.

Mumbo Jumbo "improves upon" detective fiction by following its structure while undermining its rationalistic suppositions. In this work, Reed's readers are challenged to the task of interpretation by the evocation of their expectations for a detective story before these expectations are disappointed. They are disappointed primarily by *Mumbo Jumbo* not being a tale of "methodical discoveries by rational means" of the circumstances of a mystery. There are "discoveries" and "means" in the text, but they are hardly "methodical" or "rational" in the way expected of detective fiction.

Structurally, however, the novel follows the pattern expected of the genre being parodied. The model of detective fiction chosen by Reed is that of the thriller, the type of narrative usually associated with the hard-boiled American tradition. Thrillers differ from whodunits—the most common type of detective fiction—in that they de-emphasize the discovery of the identity of the criminal as the chief aim of the plot, and focus instead on the unraveling of complex webs of conspiracy and murder. Thrillers are characterized by "rapid action, colloquial language, emotional impact, and the violence that pervades American fiction," leaving aside the "static calm, the intricate puzzle and ingenious deductions" of the whodunit [according to George Grella].

In *Mumbo Jumbo* Reed has written a story that, at least structurally, reads like a thriller. The plot is a fairly elaborate one that begins with an outbreak of the Jes Grew epidemic, a psychic condition which embodies the freedom and vitality of the Afro-American heritage. The epidemic is in search of its text, which it must find if it is not to evaporate. The text is in the hands of Hinckle Von Vampton, the librarian of the ancient order of the Knights Templar, who is himself being sought by the Wallflower Order. They, in turn, want to find and destroy the text and "sterilize Jes Grew forever." To avoid detection, Hinckle has selected fourteen people and paid them a monthly salary to send the text around to each other in a chain. (pp. 114-15)

Although structurally Reed follows the basic narrative pattern expected of a thriller, his use of the elements of the genre within this structure systematically undermines the reader's acceptance of **Mumbo Jumbo** as a typical detective story. This systematic undermining takes three forms: the first is the use of the dialectical pattern of detective fiction as the framework for the presentation of the author's views on Western culture; the second is the breaking of the internal rational logic of the process of detection; the third is the consistent use of humor to underscore those aspects of Western culture (and detective fiction) Reed finds amusingly objectionable.

The dialectical structure of the thriller is the ideal vehicle for Reed's argument that throughout history, Western culture (which he identifies with Christianity) has used its power to suppress non-Christian cultural manifestations because their sensuality and irrationality were incompatible with Western thought. The novel's main plot offers Reed's evaluation of the fate of Black culture in White America, taking as its basis what Reed calls "the major aesthetic tragedy of Afro-American life in the 20th century—the disappearance of New Orleans Old Music." In **Mumbo Jumbo,** the ultimate "crime" that PaPa LaBas and Black Herman must prevent is the destruction of Black aesthetic roots (roots which link Afro-American culture to ancient African religion) which are threatened by the representatives of Western culture: the Knights Templar, "the discredited order which once held the fate of Western civilization in its hands," and the aptly named Wallflower Order. Both stand for what Reed calls elsewhere the "worst facet of Christianity, its attempt to negate all other modes of thought and to insist upon a singularity of moral and ethical vision." The dialectics are those of logic, squareness, lethargy and lack of feeling on the one hand; and emotion, mystery, intuition, and movement on the other. To counter the Christian-Western view of the world, Reed offers Black American folklore and language, African religion and myth. In **Mumbo Jumbo,** they are embodied in the Jes Grew epidemic, a psychic condition which causes the host to do "stupid sensual things," to go into a state of "uncontrollable frenzy.". . . The efforts to destroy the Text needed for the epidemic to fulfill itself are thus charged with symbolic significance, as are Hinckle's efforts to create a Talking Android who

> . . . will tell the J. G. C.'s that Jes Grew is not ready and owes a large debt to Irish Theater. This Talking Android will Wipe That Grin Off Its Face. He will tell it that it is derivative . . . . He will describe it as a massive hemorrhage of malaprops; illiterate and given to rhetoric.

These efforts support PaPa LaBas' "conspiratorial hypothesis" about a secret society molding the consciousness of the West.

This hypothesis is sustained by the novel's best-developed sub-plot, which is built around the same concept of cultural dialectics. The Mu'tafikah are "artnappers" bent on plundering museums (here called centers of art detention) and returning "detained" art to the countries of origin. The "conspiracy" (headed by Berbelang and bringing together a multi-ethnic group of art students) is Reed's comment on the diverging Western and non-Western views of the role of art in society. For the Mu'tafikah, the holding of collections of African, Egyptian, and Amerindian art in American museums has broken the links of these objects with nature, ritual, and mystery. This break is seen as the result of a concerted effort to destroy the fabric of non-Western cultures.

PaPa LaBas and Black Herman's "rational sober" account of Hinckle's crime provides the historical framework in which the Western/non-Western confrontation has developed. The elaborate explanation is offered through a sweeping account of Western culture's on again/off again struggle against non-Western cultures, a struggle which begins with Aton's displacement of Osiris and does not end with the destruction of the Jes Grew text. The conspiracy is unveiled in **Mumbo Jumbo** through the use of historical and pseudo-historical documentation: the background information on the Knights Templar, the murder of Osiris and the defeat of Aton, the villainy of Moses, Warren Harding's involvement in the plot against Jes Grew, the news blackout on the attack on Port-au-Prince by the U.S. Marines, the theory of the orchestration of the 1930's depression as the means of curtailing the progress of Black aesthetics in this country.

Historical and pseudo-historical elements are interwoven in the text in the manner usually found in spy thrillers. Here, their role is that of unveiling a confrontation that is cultural rather than criminal but which (since it is presented within the dialectical structure of the detective story) emerges as an ethical confrontation of good (non-Western) versus evil (Western culture).

Throughout the novel, Reed points to the West's concern with rationality as the most salient characteristic separating Western and non-Western cultures. Detective fiction, depending as it does on the rational search for truth, epitomizes the culture Reed satirizes in the text. In **Mumbo Jumbo,** Reed sets out to undermine the role of rationality both thematically (by revealing the folly of those characters who act rationally) and structurally (by making his search for truth not dependent on logic or reason). Unlike the traditional detective, whose identifying feature is his ability to connect bits of information in logical patterns through his powers of deduction, Reed's detectives rely on intuition, "knockings" and ritual to arrive at the truth. PaPa LaBas is an "astro-detective" practicing his Neo-HooDoo therapy in his Mumbo Jumbo Kathedral; Black Herman is a noted occultist. Both are detectives of the metaphysical. (pp. 116-19)

Through these "detectives of the metaphysical" Reed systematically undermines the rational search for knowledge that characterizes detective fiction. The systematic undermining of the process of detection is accomplished primarily by making the process dependent on chance and intuition. (p. 119)

The dependence on chance and intuition constitutes an important structural break since the rationalistic exercise that is detective fiction does not allow for the intervention of either. Chance and intuition have no legitimacy within the rules of the genre since they break the internal logic of the narrative pattern to which the reader of this type of fiction is accustomed.

The critique of Western culture's concern with rationality implicit in the rejection of the rational process of detection also motivates Reed's attack on Freudian psychology as defender of the rational as opposed to the natural forces in the human psyche. Reed contends that Freud's lack of harmony with the natural world made him unable to see the validity of irrational manifestations. (p. 120)

The rejection of the prototypes of detective fiction, as well as the rejection of the rational process of detection, are underscored in the novel through the consistent use of humor. Humor is, in fact, one of the basic elements of Reed's Neo-HooDoo aesthetic, as well as one of the basic elements of Black culture threatened by Western culture. . . . (p. 122)

In *Mumbo Jumbo,* the chief source of humor is the parody of the conventions of detective fiction and film. The examples of such parodic exercises abound: there is the gang war in Harlem between Buddy Jackson and "the Sarge of Yorktown" over a numbers and speak operation which ends with Jackson marching the Sarge to the subway, exhorting him to leave Harlem and "never darken the portals of our abode again": or the Cagney-movie atmosphere of the scenes between the Sarge and Biff Musclewhite, former police commissioner on the take, in one of which the Sarge is gunned down, half of his head scattered in the neighboring dinner plates. The genre is satirized in the parodic portrayal of the Knights Templar as ineffectual gangsters, and of Hinckle and Safecracker as bumbling musclemen. The assembly of suspects which leads to the identification of the culprit, a "must" in the classic detective story, is elaborately parodied in a scene which finds PaPa LaBas and Herman gate-crashing a high society party to arrest Hinckle and Safecracker, only to have the guests refuse to hand them over until they "explain rationally and soberly what they are guilty of."

The humorous themes and techniques Reed uses in these parodic scenes are linked to those of Black comedians such as Dick Gregory, Moms Mabley, Flip Wilson, Godfrey Cambridge, and Richard Pryor, who use their ethnicity as a source of humorous material. (pp. 122-23)

Thematically, perhaps more important models for Reed are Negro militants like Rap Brown and Jennifer Lawson, whose brand of humor "lays bare the artificiality of the adherence to the Judeo-Christian ethics in America"—the central theme of Reed's fiction. The following example from one of Lawson's comic routines parallels Reed's theme and comic rhythm in *Mumbo Jumbo:*

> Yeah, Christianize me and colonize me.
> Make me your slave and bring me your Jesus . . .
> The constitution said I was three-fifths of a
> person.

In Reed's novel, as in the work of these comedians, humor is an integral part of the critique of society and fiction implicit in the "dialogue" nature of parody. . . . (p. 123)

In *Mumbo Jumbo,* this critique of fiction and reality through humor is systematically dialectical (as is to be expected in a parody of a genre whose basic structure is dialectical) and thematically consistent. Humor, both technically and thematically, stems from the basic contention behind the plot of detection—the critique of the disconnection of Western culture from nature (itself an irrational force) and its insistence on rationality as its foremost principle.

This critique extends to the concept of time in the novel:

> Time is a pendulum [LaBas explains]. Not a river.
> More akin to what goes around comes around;

a view which moves the work away from the linear concept of time detective fiction shares with the Christian concept of history. Both the plotting of the typical detective novel and the Judeo-Christian apocalyptic view of history "presuppose and require that an end will bestow upon the whole duration and meaning" [according to Frank Kermode]. The end of *Mumbo Jumbo* both negates the final restoring of order and justice of detective fiction and reaffirms the aesthetic break away from the Western aesthetic code. The pyrrhic victory of PaPa LaBas and Black Herman—pyrrhic because they unveil the conspiracy but fail to save the epidemic and its text—is met with hope for the rebirth of Jes Grew in a more receptive aesthetic environment; an environment which is being created by texts like *Mumbo Jumbo* which embody the creating and liberating aesthetics of Neo-HooDooism.

Mumbo Jumbo thus becomes one of Reed's most important contributions to the reinterpretation of Afro-American experience and culture evident in current historiography and sociology. Among Black American writers, this reinterpretation has often taken the form of parodies of detective fiction. (p. 124)

The parody of detective fiction has allowed these writers to move away from the logocentrism of Western models that has characterized interpretations of Afro-American culture and literature and towards an affirmation of that experience in texts that are not submissive to Western models. The "carnivalization" of these models (to use the term coined by Mikhail Bakhtin) has allowed these writers "to concentrate inventive freedom, to permit the combination of a variety of different elements and their rapprochement, to liberate from that prevailing point of view of the world, from all that is humdrum and universally accepted." As *Mumbo Jumbo* shows, the transformation of literary texts through parody leads to alternative structures which allow writers to supersede and reorient older traditions. (pp. 124-25)

> *Lizabeth Paravisini, "'Mumbo Jumbo' and the Uses of Parody," in* Obsidian: Black Literature in Review, *Vol. 1, Nos. 1 & 2, Spring-Summer, 1986, pp. 113-27.*

Darryl Pinckney (essay date 1989)

[*In the following excerpt, Pinckney surveys Reed's novels.*]

The slave narratives tell of spirits riding people at night, of elixirs dearly bought from conjure men, chicken bones rubbed on those from whom love was wanted, and of dreams taken as omens. Harriet Tubman heeded visions which she described in the wildest poetry. VooDoo, magic, spirit worship as the concealed religious heritage of the black masses, and literacy, control of the word as a powerful talisman, are among the folk sources of what Ishmael Reed calls the "Neo-HooDoo aesthetic" of his polemical essays, contentious poems, and pugnacious, elliptical fictions.

Reed's "Neo-HooDooism" is so esoteric that it is difficult to say what he intends by it, whether it is meant to be taken as a system of belief, a revival of HooDoo, the Afro-American form of Haitian VooDoo, or, as he has also suggested, as a device, a method of composition. Mostly Neo-HooDooism seems to be a literary version of black cultural nationalism determined to find its origins in history, just as black militants of the 1960s invoked Marcus Garvey or the slave rebellions. Neo-HooDooism, then, is a school of revisionism in which Reed passes control to the otherwise powerless, and black history becomes one big saga of revenge.

Black writers, Leslie Fiedler once pointed out, have been attempting to "remythologize" themselves and black people since the time of Jean Toomer, but in Neo-HooDooism writing itself becomes an act of retribution. Reed puts a hex or a curse on white society, or on any group in black life that he doesn't like simply by exposing them to ridicule: the whammy hits Rutherford B. Hayes, Millard Fillmore, Lincoln, Woodrow Wilson, black nationalists, black Maoists reading "Chinese Ping-Pong manuals," black feminists, white feminists, white radicals, television, what he conceives of as secret societies of Anglos, the master caste, and those who control the canon, the dreaded C word, and ignore Asian-American, Native American, and Hispanic literature, and get Afro-American literature all wrong. There

is also much beating up of Christianity and the Catholic Church.

Fantastic in plot, satirical in tone, colloquial in style, and always revolving around what Zora Neale Hurston identified as the "wish-fulfillment hero of the race" in folklore, Reed's novels, with one smooth black after another blowing the whistle on covert forces that rule the world, are latter-day trickster tales with enough historical foundation to tease. . . .

Many black intellectuals in the 1960s sought to rehabilitate their identity through Islam, Black Power, or the principles of Ron Karenga, who held that black art must show up the enemy, praise the people, and support the revolution. Words were seen as weapons and whites were accused of "the intellectual rape of a race of people," but Reed was too quirky to become merely a black separatist. At his most rhetorical he claims to have a multinational, multi-ethnic view of the United States. He concocted his personal brand of chauvinism, one designed to dispense with the black writer's burden of interpreting the black experience.

The ground under the naturalistic problem novel of the 1940s, which depended on oppression for its themes, was eroded by the possibilities of the integration movement, and it led black writers in the 1950s to turn inward. But the black revolt of the 1960s brought a resurgence of protest literature. Though Reed shared its anti-assimilationist urges, maybe he didn't want to sound like everyone else who was hurling invective against the injustices in American society. Reed's work aims to dissolve or transcend the dilemma of the double consciousness of the black writer as an American and as a black that has characterized black writing since the slave narratives. Chester Himes, half of whose ten novels are hardboiled detective stories from which Reed got a great deal, complained in his autobiography, *The Quality of Hurt* (1973), that white readers only wanted books in which black characters suffer. "Fuck pain," Reed said. "The crying towel doesn't show up in my writing."

To disarm racism and make room for his comic sense of the irrational, to free himself from the tradition of the black writer's double consciousness, Reed got rid of the confessional voice, the autobiographical atmosphere of Afro-American literature, "those suffering books" about the old neighborhood in which "every gum drop machine is in place." His first novel, *The Free-Lance Pallbearers* (1967), is a fitful, irreverent parody of the literature of self-discovery. The narrator, Bukka Doopeyduk, a luckless believer in "the Nazarene Creed," lives in a place called HARRY SAM, which is ruled by SAM, who is rumored to eat children, has been enthroned on a commode in a motel for thirty years, and rants about "all the rest what ain't like us."

The novel is madly scatological, waste overruns everything. Doopeyduk, "a brainwashed Negro" of the projects who listens to Mahler, becomes, by accident, a media star until he witnesses the "sheer evil" of SAM—

performing backroom anal sex. He then tries to grab power, fails, and is crucified on meat hooks.

Along the way to doom Doopeyduk meets opportunistic black leaders, voyeuristic white radicals, academics, slum lords, television talk show hosts, all of whom Reed lampoons. Given the climate of the late 1960s, with antipoverty programs like HARYOU and best sellers about the inner city in which self-exploration often had an element of self-exploitation, Reed's baiting of almost everyone has the calculated exhibitionism of funky stand-up comedy. For outrageousness, Reed's only peer is Richard Pryor.

There isn't much in this novel that Reed won't try to take the piss out of, including the legacy of *Black Boy* and *Invisible Man;* reports about the Vietnam War; the Book of Revelations; and militant rhetoric, which comes off as sell-out entertainment for masochistic white audiences. (p. 20)

Reed makes fun of VooDoo in *The Free-Lance Pallbearers.* Doopeyduk's wife's grandmother takes conjure lessons through the mail under the "Mojo Retraining Act," and while studying for her "sorcery exams" tries to shove her granddaughter in the oven to practice an exercise from the "witchcraft syllabus." VooDoo is part of the pervasive corruption in HARRY SAM, one more ridiculous thing about life.

But in his second novel, *Yellow Back Radio Broke-Down* (1969), Reed is serious about possession and spells, at least as a pose, though he is capable of saying anything to be sensational. Here in order to get away from white fiction as a model, and to return to a "dark heathenism," Reed puts Neo-HooDooism to the forefront in place of the crying towel of his experience as a black man in America. Anything that Reed approves of historically he says comes from HooDoo. "HooDoo is the strange and beautiful 'fits' the Black slave Tituba gave the children of Salem." Ragtime and jazz were manifestations of HooDoo, messages from the underground, and in his own day Neo-HooDoo signs are everywhere, like charges in an electric field.

Reed's Neo-HooDooism shares the syncretism of its model. Just as VooDoo absorbs Catholic saints to represent its spirits, Neo-HooDooism is comfortable enough with a California out-of-it-ness to become "a beautiful art form of tapestry, desire, song, good food, healthful herbs." Tall tales of how the weak overcome the strong through wit, toasts of the urban tradition, "positive" humor, and other "neo-African" literary forms—the entire folk tradition is, to Reed, a vast reservoir of HooDoo ideas to which he, its conservator, hopes in Neo-HooDooism to add "fresh interpretations" by "modernizing its styles."

Yellow Back Radio Broke-Down is a full-blown "horse opera" (spirits ride human hosts), a surrealistic spoof of the Western with Indian chiefs aboard helicopters, stagecoaches and closed-circuit TVs, cavalry charges of taxis. The wish-fulfillment hero in this novel is the Loop Garoo Kid, A HooDoo cowboy, not only "a desperado so ornery he made the Pope cry and the most powerful of cattlemen shed his head to the Executioner's swine," but also a trickster Satan. Loop Garoo conducts "micro HooDoo masses" to end "2000 years of bad news." He fights ranchers, the US government, and then Pope Innocent on behalf of the youth of Yellow Back Radio, an intersection of historical and psychic worlds, a beleaguered town where the rule of the elders has been temporarily overthrown by an anarchist revolt that resembles the counterculture of the late Sixties. The Pope wants Loop to "come home," to make peace with the Big Guy.

Like Reed's subsequent novels, *Yellow Back Radio Broke-Down* is about many things and all at once. Pages flash with allusions to great issues of the moment, the novel seems to unravel, to carelessly shed its best layers, in order to get to an impatient message: the hero must not suffer, must win out over the whites in power, or at least dazzle them to a draw. Black magic, and black culture, must be recognized as a force as powerful as any other. (pp. 20, 22)

But curiously, while Reed approaches historical black culture with the enthusiasm of one who has just come across an off-beat work that supports his anti-establishment convictions on current matters, like whether the police have a hard job or whether black militants are anti-achievement in their vilification of the black middle class, he does not hesitate to go against received black opinion, to deplore the lack of skepticism among his black critics, as if each side of his mouth were aimed at a different audience and his purpose were to discomfort both.

He can find the good fight anywhere, often with other black writers. "Even the malice and vengeance side of HooDoo finds a place in contemporary Afro-American fiction," Reed says, a fish in its own water. Already in his second novel Reed is defending himself against the Black Aesthetic critics, the followers of the Black Arts movement, the "field niggers" who got "all the play" in the 1960s, denounced individualism, and endorsed the line that there was a uniform black experience, that blacks have only one language, that of their liberation. Reed has the Loop Garoo Kid meet up with Bo Shmo, a "neo-socialist" who tells Loop that he's too abstract, "a crazy dada nigger" whose work is just "a blur and a doodle." Loop says:

> What's your beef with me, Bo Shmo, what if I write circuses? No one says a novel has to be one thing. It can be anything it wants to be, a vaudeville show, the six o'clock news, the mumblings of a wild man saddled by demons.

Bo Shmo says:

> All art must be for the end of liberating the masses. A landscape is only good when it shows the oppressor hanging from a tree.

Dear Black History Musuem ;

        If- Mr. ~~Houston~~ (Baker) wants to be ~~known~~ (known) as " real Black people "
in the"movement" - any " movement." He wants to achive this at the expense
of my Work and his review is unsubstanial, ~~and ignorant~~ ; it is a stern
lecture to me as if I were a student , and he , the chairman of my
department . This is not the case !

        Mr. Baker wants to be " right on" even if it means
defending any wretch , any lout , or tramp who who preys upon Afro-
Americans , the kind of uncritical , indiscriminate , thought which has
left a segement of a generation in shambles. (intellectual + moral)

        Every poll i've read , including those in <u>Black World</u>
and <u>Jet</u> , as well as discussions I've had with Afro-Americans of all
classes in many cities of the United States leads me to believe that
there is a discrepancy between the political thought of " real Black
people" and those opinions held by a handful of chirstian-socialist
intellectuals and Professors " crouching under the veil (ugh!)"of
the " Black Christ" and most recently," The Black Lenin."

        This desceepancy is furthur revealed on such questions (in political thought)
as crime against Afro-Americans. The "intelligentsia" which represents
maybe 2% of Afro-americans want to titty feed this element (criminal) and if this
element says we got an ideology then it gets a jar of osterized jams
besides. That's christian. ~~The masses of Afro-americans say i cut you,
you cut me . That's African.~~

        The " intelligentsia" ~~which now is~~ (now) saying/thre masses
are behind , and we tried to work with the middle class and that didn't
work , let;s form the Upper Ten society and by us some jeans and Mao
T-shirts like thry do up town ~~on the Plaza~~ (Park Ave.) these days. ~~It~~ (The intelligentsia) sees the
real enemy as stuff like " ~~the ruling class~~" (Imperialism) or " ... the vileness and
corruption at the root of the racialistic american society" ; abstarct
caterpillar-like monosyllabic ghoses and hobgoblins from the chirstian
hall of missionary , you know , what the front office calls
" The Humanities." ~~I mean, is Picasso the Lawrence Welk of African art
or not ?~~

        play (playwrights) The rank and file ~~view~~ " real Black people," view the
enemy as Walter Cotton's " Candyman" in The"Candy Man Dance"; a heroin
salesman whom " real Black People" do in at the end. They see the
" real enemy"as the one who took the old woman's social security check
or the crud who shot a woman in the head and left her to die because she
didn't recognize him and dismissed him as just another ~~punk~~." (seedy character)

*First page of Reed's draft of "HooDoo Munifesto #2: The Baker-Gayle Fallacy," in which Reed responds to Houston Baker's
negative review of* The Last Days of Louisiana Red.

Reed says he uses "the techniques and forms painters, dancers, film makers, musicians in the West have taken for granted for at least fifty years, and artists of many other cultures for thousands of years," but this seems a device to protect the structural weaknesses of his madcap novels. Reed does not create characters, he employs types to represent categories, points of view. Plot, however, he has in overabundance, ever since his most ambitious novel, *Mumbo Jumbo* (1972), in which he began to use the detective story as the vehicle for his history of the Western world according to Neo-Hoo-Dooism.

What Reed probably finds most congenial about the suspense genre, in addition to its law of cause and effect, is the recognition scene in the library where the hero makes arrests and explains how he solved the case, which in *Mumbo Jumbo* means a lengthy deposition on the mysteries of black culture. The exposition comes as a relief because of the complexity of the narrative, the noisy feeling of several voices going on at the same time. *Mumbo Jumbo* is dense with subplots, digressions, hidden meanings, lectures ("The Book of Mormon is a fraud. If we Blacks came up with something as corny as the Angel of Moroni . . ."). It is packed with epigrams, quotations, newsclips. The written text is interpolated with reproductions of drawings and photographs, illustrations that function as a kind of speech. Reed even appends a long bibliography about VooDoo, dance, Freud, art, music, ancient history, presidents, as if to say, "If you don't believe me look it up."

Mumbo Jumbo is set in the 1920s because of the parallels between the "negromania" that swept America during the Jazz Age and that of the late 1960s. A HooDoo detective, PaPa LaBas, tries to track down the source of the phenomenon Jes Grew, as the nationwide outbreak of dancing and bizarre behavior—"stupid sensual things," "lusting after relevance," and "uncontrollable frenzy"—is called. Jes Grew knows "no class no race no consciousness," and causes people to speak in tongues, hear shank bones, bagpipes, kazoos. It is "an anti-plague" that enlivens the host, fills the air with the aroma of roses. This creeping thing, like Topsy, "jes grew," as James Weldon Johnson said of ragtime, and in *Mumbo Jumbo* it could mean many things in black culture. "Slang is Jes Grew."

In trying to give black feeling an ancient history, Reed reaches back to unexpected allies like Julian the Apostate who foresaw the "Bad News" of a Christian Europe, and eventually into Egyptian myth, to Set's murderous jealousy of his brother, Osiris. Reed believes that the past can be used to prophesy about the future, "a process our ancestors called necromancy," and in *Mumbo Jumbo* the earthiness of black culture and the repressiveness of white societies are a legacy of Set's uptightness.

The message of *Mumbo Jumbo* is difficult to grasp because of an abstraction on which the action of the novel hinges. "Jes Grew is seeking its text. Its words.

For what good is a liturgy without a text?" An elite military group that defends the "cherished traditions of the West" successfully conspires to contain Jes Grew, to keep it from uniting with its text, its key of truth, which Reed calls the Book of Thoth, "the 1st anthology by the 1st choreographer." Jes Grew withers away without this text, but LaBas goes on with his obeah stick into the 1960s to tell college audiences about the good times that almost were and might be.

That the nature of the lost text is left for us to conjecture makes it hard to guess what Reed has in mind here as the written tradition for what he sees as the Neo-HooDoo aesthetic. The novel is anticlimactic, though Reed may mean that the mysteries of black culture can't be written down, that Jes Grew must remain in the air, always possible, but beyond the page. In fact, the suggestiveness of *Mumbo Jumbo* has made it a rich mine among poststructuralists who see it as a handbook of signs, a textbook of signifiers on prejudices about the quality of blackness since Plato, and an example of black literary autonomy. It has also been read as a critique of the Harlem Renaissance for its failure to come up with a distinct Afro-American voice.

Reed's novels after *Mumbo Jumbo* are variations on the theme of a total license that is not as liberating as it would seem. In them the hold of Neo-HooDooism begins to fade, or sinks into their soil. The later novels resort more to riddles, and reduce the detective novel to a hasty cycle of situation and exposition. The targets narrow. *The Last Days of Louisiana Red* (1974) puts PaPa LaBas in Berkeley. He rescues a HooDoo business, the Solid Gumbo Works, which performs good deeds, offers its clients a cure for cancer, and almost finds a cure for heroin addiction. This time HooDoo doesn't do battle with white theocrats, but with bad HooDoo, Louisiana Red, as practiced by the Moochers.

This is a satire on the hustlers of Black Power politics, with rallies and veiled references to posters of Huey Newton in his chair . . . . The plot involves opportunists in North African exile, a preacher who because he can't preach uses $100,000 of audiovisual equipment, and Minnie the Moocher, a heroine oppressed by the exaltation of her followers. (pp. 22-3)

Reed also draws on *Antigone* for this novel, offering a timid sister, brothers who slay each other, and a chorus, or Chorus, an "uncharacterized character," a vaudevillian in white tails, like Cab Calloway, who complains that his role declined because Antigone talked too much. Instead of being one who would not yield to earthly authority, a woman who did not believe that a man's death belonged to the state, Antigone, to Reed, is a selfish girl who wanted to have things her way. "You wrong girl," Reed says in a poem, **"Antigone, This Is It,"** "you would gut a nursery to make the papers," which makes her sound more like Medea. Nevertheless, she represents to Reed implacable hostility toward men and misuse of a woman's powers. Minnie the Moocher, Antigone's comic reincarnation, and her followers, dupes of the handed-down, hammered-in philosophy of the inferiority of slaves, are accused of not being able to "stand negro men attempting to build something: if we were on the corner sipping Ripple, then you would love us." (p. 23)

In *Flight to Canada* (1976), Reed's takeoff on the antebellum South, black women are also prominent among the boogey persons who get theirs. A black mammy in velvet, loyal to the incestuous, necrophiliac master, claims that Jesus got tired of Harriet Beecher Stowe, who ripped off *Uncle Tom's Cabin* from the narrative of Josiah Henson, and therefore caused one of her sons to be wounded in the war and the other to get "drownded." The light-skinned overseer tells the master, "I armed the women slaves. They'll keep order. They'll dismember them niggers with horrifying detail." The fugitive hero, Raven Quickskill, has a beautiful Indian lover and when they enter a tavern two of the female slaves help begin to "let out their slave cackle, giving them signifying looks." No black matriarchy for Reed.

In a **"Self-Interview"** in *Shrovetide in Old New Orleans* (1978) [see excerpt dated 1978] Reed asks himself, "Why you so mean and hard?"

> A. Because I am an Afro-American male, the most exploited and feared class in this country. All of the gentlemen, all of the ones who tried to be nice, are in the cemetery or sitting on a stoop humiliated and degraded and waiting for someone to hand them a bar of soap or waiting for the law some woman has called on them.

This is as much a flashback to the Sixties when the black male was an envied species as it is a reminder of current statistics about the low life-expectancy of black men.

Reed can't resist excess, overstating his case even when he has a valid one, as in *Reckless Eyeballing* (1986), another whodunit busy with plot, about the historical distortions of feminism. Whereas his quarrel in the books of the Seventies was with the Stalinesque rigidity of black aesthetic writers, he now takes on black women writers who have received attention, as if Alice Walker's finding the goddess within her were a distraction from his story of black men versus white men....

The Terrible Twos (1982) and its sequel, his most recent novel, *The Terrible Threes,* are set in the not-so-distant future mostly to undress the Reagan years. The detective in both books, Nance Saturday, who gets lost in the thick plots, remains aloof from the madness of trying to make it in the new white world, and becomes celibate out of a fear of infection. Neo-HooDooism itself has been pushed offstage entirely by a sort of Gnostic sect of questionable sincerity.

Reed is aware of the shift in the country's attention during the Eighties. *The Terrible Twos* opens with the "Scrooge Christmas of 1980," when it feels good to be a white man again and whites aren't afraid to tell blacks they aren't interesting anymore. There are more press-

ing problems. Reed's campaign to mention everything that has gone wrong in America results in a narrative that is all over the place, as if he were trying to work in everything from crime against the environment to offenses against the homeless. Instead of suspense or satire one is confronted with an extended editorial rebuttal.

The Terrible Twos is a souped-up version of *A Christmas Carol.* The northern hemisphere isn't "as much fun as it used to be." Hitler's birthday has become a national holiday, but the White House is alarmed by the number of "surplus people," worries that the world will turn "brown and muddy and resound with bongo drums" and the "vital people" will be squeezed out. A conspiracy unfolds to nuke New York and Miami and blame the destruction on Nigeria. Meanwhile, oil companies control Christmas, the Supreme Court grants one store exclusive rights to Santa Claus, and the economy depends on every day being Christmas for the "vitals." The conspiracy is threatened by the followers of Saint Nicholas and his servant or rival in legend, Black Peter. Saint Nicholas converts the President, a former model, by taking him to hell where Truman is the most tormented. The President is declared incapacitated when he reveals the conspiracy.

America has worsened in the new novel, *The Terrible Threes.* The temperature has dropped, larceny fills every heart, mobs roam the cities in search of food, evangelists who believe Jews and blacks are the children of the devil control the government and hope to establish a Christian fundamentalist state. "Who needs the yellows, the browns, the reds, the blacks?" These people are "the wastes of history." Saint Nicholas and Black Peter, a figure similar to Reed's earlier renegade heroes, compete to enlighten and to help people, and nearly bring back an age of liberalism until Lucifer himself interferes. To top it off, extraterrestrials, contemptuous of human beings, have their own plans for earth.

In this latest novel Reed writes of a country that has lost its soul, but he, too, seems uncertain of direction. His picture of "Scroogelike" America, "kissing cousin" of South Africa, of yuppies for whom the buck is the bottom line, of black people marooned in drug neighborhoods, is extremely bleak. Even Black Peter is chastised, ambivalent, exhausted. The extraterrestrials come like an afterthought, as if Reed were making a last-ditch effort to deny power over the future to Neo-HooDoo's opponents. His work has always had a certain bitterness, but that was part of its fuel. Compared to his reconstruction of recent American history as a sequence of Terribles (the first one, Reed says, began on November 22, 1963), of genocidal policies and cover-ups, his previous novels seem almost utopian.

But the problem with his parodies of the obvious and the obscure, his allegorical burlesques, pastiches of the fantastic—the problem with this gumbo (his analogy) is that he can't move beyond their negations. Neo-HooDooism needs what Reed would call Anglo unfreedom the way Christianity needs Judas's lips or, as the movie says, the way the ax needs the turkey. Similarly, Reed may have declined to take on the old-fashioned subject of the Afro-American's double consciousness, but his fictions are as dualistic in their representations of the egalitarian versus the hierarchical, HooDoo versus the Cop Religion. They buzz with conspiracy theories that pretend to explain the world, with the determination to set the world straight about the hypocrisy of "patriotic history." "Jefferson Davis died with a smile on his face." Paranoia, Burroughs said, is just having the facts, but a few facts are not as dangerous as Reed would have us think.

Reed's subjects involve large cultural questions, but often the transplant from the headlines is the quickest of operations. His novels are entirely of their day, nostalgic in their defiance of "the Judeo-Christian domination of our affairs," and vividly recall the era when the lightness of blackness was a revelation, when blacks were the catalysts of social change. Neo-HooDooism gave Reed a way to work with this, to reimagine it. Back then, in the **"Neo-HooDoo Manifesto,"** Reed could describe it as the "Now Locomotive swinging up the Tracks of the American Soul."

The shift in the cultural climate, the loss of that moment, may help to explain why in the Terribles Reed's remarkable fluency has dried up. The supporting atmosphere is missing, without which his books are suddenly vulnerable. This fluency, this back talk, is what animates Reed's work, for Neo-HooDooism is not the sort of mysticism or system that provides a language of symbols or infuses imagery, it has no widening gyres, no junkie codes. It is Reed's language that carries his mission of exasperation—the old black faith in the power of the word. . . .

Whether Reed's fictions are arguments for the reenchantment of Afro-American literature, are unmaskings of Western culture by written formulation, or are self-congratulatory texts about HooDoo as an untainted supply of material does not change the fact that his literary separatism is doomed to obsolescence because Afro-American writing only comes to life as a junction of traditions. Reed questions not only the social reality presented in Afro-American literature, but also the narrative tradition itself. To do so, he takes shelter in the black oral tradition without realizing that it makes him no more free than contemporary white novelists. Reed often speaks of his hero as "scatting," or uses Charlie Parker as an example of the Neo-HooDoo artist, free of the rules, blowing, improvising, and this wish-fulfillment hero becomes a stand-in for Reed himself, the black writer floating far above an alien tradition in which he doesn't feel at home. But perhaps there's no way back, for black writers, to an innocent folk state. The writers of the Harlem Renaissance inadvertently discovered that there is no literary equivalent to dance or music, and no reconciliation either.

Once it's written down, the oral tradition becomes literature, as Neil Schmitz pointed out, and the experience of the black man in the library intervenes with the experience of the black man in the street, in Reed as much as it does in any other black writers. Reed's Neo-HooDoo tales are not as tall as the ones blacks used to tell. Still there's much to say for his own tales: after all, not to make fun of racist absurdities is to be still afraid of them. (p. 24)

Darryl Pinckney, "Trickster Tales," in The New York Review of Books, *Vol. XXXVI, No. 15, October 12, 1989, pp. 20, 22-4.*

FURTHER READING

Fox, Robert Elliot. "Ishmael Reed: Gathering the Limbs of Osiris." In his *Conscientious Sorcerers: The Black Postmodernist Fiction of Leroi Jones/Amiri Baraka, Ishmael Reed, and Samuel R. Delany,* pp. 39-92. Westport, Conn.: Greenwood Press, 1987.
> Detailed analysis of Reed's novels.

Harris, Norman. "The Gods Must Be Angry: *Flight to Canada* as Political History." *Modern Fiction Studies* 34, No. 1 (Spring 1988): 111-23.
> Examines the impact of narrative viewpoint and time on character development in *Flight to Canada,* explaining how these factors underscore aspects of African-American political history.

Klinkowitz, Jerome. "Ishmael Reed's Multicultural Aesthetic." In his *Literary Subversions: New American Fiction and the Practice of Criticism,* pp. 18-33. Carbondale, Ill.: Southern Illinois University Press, 1985.
> Explicates Reed's literary aesthetic in the novel *The Terrible Twos* and in the essay collection *God Made Alaska for the Indians.*

Lee, Robert. "Black Christmas." *The Listener* 123, No. 3155 (8 March 1990): 31.
> Appraises *The Terrible Twos* as "a surreal American update of *A Christmas Carol*" and mentions the recent republication of *The Free-Lance Pallbearers,* "the first of Reed's self-styled HooDoo novels."

Martin, Reginald. "An Interview with Ishmael Reed." *The Review of Contemporary Fiction* 4, No. 2 (Summer 1985): 176-87.
> Interview with Reed, who discusses his works, his conflicts with critics and feminists, and the concept of Neo-HooDooism.

————. "The FreeLance PallBearer Confronts the Terrible Threes: Ishmael Reed and the New Black Aesthetic Critics." *MELUS* 14, No. 2 (Summer 1987): 35-49.
> Surveys critical opinion of Reed, especially the views of such proponents of the Black Aesthetic as Houston A. Baker, Jr., Addison Gayle, Jr., and Amiri Baraka.

————. *Ishmael Reed and the New Black Aesthetic Critics.* London: MacMillan Press, 1988, 120 p.

Discusses Reed's role as a catalyst of the new Black Aesthetic movement that revolutionized African-American literature in the 1960s.

Mason, Theodore O., Jr. "Performance, History, and Myth: The Problem of Ishmael Reed's *Mumbo Jumbo*." *Modern Fiction Studies* 34, No. 1 (Spring 1988): 97-109.

Analyzes *Mumbo Jumbo*, concluding: "In *Mumbo Jumbo*, Reed takes up more than he is able to handle and invites a degree of scrutiny that the novel simply cannot withstand. It breaks apart under the vastness of its own intentions."

McConnell, Frank. "Ishmael Reed's Fiction: Da Hoodoo Is Put on America." In *Black Fiction: New Studies in the Afro-American Novel since 1945,* edited by A. Robert Lee, pp. 136-48. New York: Barnes & Noble, 1980.

Traces the influence of Reed's Neo-HooDoo aesthetic on his novels.

Myers, George, Jr. "Tissue of Interpretations." *American Book Reviews* 10, No. 6 (January-February 1989): 13, 23.

Review of Charles Johnson's *Being & Race* and Reed's *Writin' Is Fightin': Thirty-Seven Years of Boxing on Paper,* of which Myers comments: "Collecting 18 essays, reviews, and newspaper articles, *Writin' Is Fightin'* documents the best jabs of a novelist who still can be a contender in satiric fiction."

Nazareth, Peter. Review of *New and Collected Poems,* by Ishmael Reed. *World Literature Today* 63, No. 4 (Autumn 1989): 684.

Brief review of Reed's 1988 collection of poems, calling the author "one of the most versatile and prolific of contemporary American writers."

Watkins, Mel. "An Interview with Ishmael Reed." *The Southern Review* 21, No. 3 (July 1985): 603-14.

Reed discusses writers and critics of African-American literature as well as *Reckless Eyeballing.*

Jacques Roumain

1907-1944

Haitian poet, novelist, journalist, essayist, and short story writer.

Roumain was a leader of a group of young Haitian intellectuals who, during the late 1920s and the 1930s, sought Haitian autonomy and an end to the American military occupation of Haiti. His writings support his belief in "art for people's sake" and in negritude. He is best known for the militant, racially conscious poetry of *Bois de'ébène* (1945; *Ebony Wood*) and the coalescence of Marxist theory and artistic expression in the novel *Gouveneurs de la rosée* (1944; *Masters of the Dew*).

Roumain was the oldest of eleven children of a land-owner and the grandson of former Haitian president Tancrède Auguste. A member of the upper middle class, he attended school in Port-au-Prince and in 1921 was sent to Grünau, Switzerland, to complete secondary school. There he read works by Friedrich Nietzsche, Arthur Schopenhauer, Charles Darwin, and Heinrich Heine and studied the art and philosophy of the Near East. An introspective and sometimes melancholy student, he wrote poetry but also participated in athletic activities, observing that sports satisfied something of the "excess of life which I have." From Grünau he went to Zurich and prepared for advanced studies in engineering, but somewhat abruptly he decided to study agronomy in Spain to prepare himself to develop his grandfather's land in Haiti. By 1927, mounting Haitian opposition to American occupation lured Roumain home to join activists fighting for Haitian nationalism.

In 1927 Roumain helped found the Haitian reviews *La trouée: Revue d'intérêt général* and *La revue indigène: Les arts et la vie* with the goal of educating Haitian youth about politics and culture. *La trouée* proposed to confront national issues, but Roumain found its literary standards weak and its expression of political ideas to run counter to its stated orientation, so he resigned by the journal's second issue. *La revue indigène* was more successful: it published poetry and fiction by Roumain and other Haitians as well as French and Latin American literature in translation. Roumain also contributed to the leftist newspaper *Le petit impartial,* published by George Petit, who, with Roumain, helped lead the *Ligue de la jeunesse patriote haitien,* established to unite divergent social levels of Haitian youth. After an article highly critical of the French clergy appeared in *Le petit impartial,* Roumain and Petit were arrested and held for seven months. Soon after their release they were again arrested, charged with scheduling an unauthorized meeting of more than twenty people.

A series of strikes and civil disorders in Haiti during 1929 and 1930 led the U.S. government to appoint a commission to arrange a peaceful transition to a new, more popular government. Recognized as a nationalist leader, Roumain was among a group of opposition representatives who met with the U.S. commission and chose Eugene Roy as the new provisional president of Haiti in 1930. Roy appointed Roumain head of the Department of the Interior, a position he resigned within a few months to campaign for Sténio Vincent, who won the first presidential election in late 1930 and reappointed Roumain to his former post. During this period Roumain published *La proie et l'ombre* (1930), *Les fantoches* (1931), and *La montagne ensorcelée* (1931). These works evidence Roumain's strong sense of the division between the mulatto Haitian middle class into which he was born and the black masses with whom he sympathized and identified. His disenchantment with the nationalist government, which had effected no appreciable change in the economic and social conditions of the peasants, reinforced his growing attraction to Marxism. He met with American Communist party officials in the United States; this, along with his refusal to accept another government post, brought Roumain under suspicion, leading to surveillance of his movements and inspection of his mail and packages. Late in 1932 a letter by Roumain detailing a proposed strike by Haitian laborers against the American Sugar Company was confiscated by government officials. Roumain's subsequent imprisonment was given wide press coverage, inspiring strongly negative sentiment toward him and others who promoted communist ideology. Upon release, Roumain declared his allegiance to communism and founded the Haitian Communist Party. In 1934 he was arrested on the grounds that he participated in an anti-government communist conspiracy; a military tribunal sentenced him to three years in prison. Communism was outlawed in 1936, and after his release from prison Roumain fled with his wife and son to Belgium.

In Belgium Roumain studied pre-Columbian art and history; after moving to Paris in 1937, he studied ethnology and related subjects. While in Paris he associated with such antifascist journalists and intellectuals as André Gide, Romain Rolland, and Louis Aragon and wrote articles and fiction for European journals. In 1939 Roumain left Paris for the United States. He began graduate courses in anthropology at Columbia University but soon left for Cuba at the invitation of the communist poet and journalist Nicolas Guillén. After working for a short time as a journalist in Cuba, he returned home to Haiti, which was now under a new government that had offered amnesty to political exiles. Roumain soon established the Bureau d'Ethnologie to oversee the study of items found at various archaeological sites in Haiti. He was later appointed chargé d'affaires to Mexico. Roumain died of a heart attack at the age of thirty-seven in 1944.

Roumain's poetry and fiction, though limited in quantity by the author's political activities, arrests, and emigrant existence, reflect the author's changing political ideas and growing knowledge of world literature. The early poetry shows the influence of French Romanticism. "Pluie," "Midi," and other animistic poems employ animals and nature to express human, typically melancholy, emotions. In other works, a lone poet or prophet seeks to understand the universe, aspiring to deep knowledge but ultimately despairing of its attainability. This despair is often evoked through mystical or celestial imagery that contrasts light with darkness. Critics noted that while many of these works use traditional forms, others introduce free verse and surrealist elements. In later revolutionary and militant poetry, Roumain became almost obsessed with theme, linking nationalism and negritude with Creole patois and rhythms and images based on African music and dance. Among this later verse, the title poem in *Ebony Wood* makes metaphorical reference to the human "logs" stacked in ships and transported to build the new world; "Nouveau sermon nègre," one of Roumain's anticlerical poems, attacks a white-dominated church that brainwashes converts into oppression and servility; and "Sales nègres" invokes a catalog of derogatory labels designed to denigrate Africans, Asians, Jews, and other ethnic and religious groups.

Unlike his poetry, Roumain's fiction was from the beginning concerned with Haitian problems. *La proie et l'ombre* and *Les fantoches* examine the psychology of a "lost generation" of young intellectuals unable to accept the old ways and unequipped to replace them. Their search for identity leads them to petty and sordid diversions in Port-au-Prince after dark. *La montagne ensorcelée* is set in a peasant village far removed from the urban environment of the early works. While the tension between passivity and action is again central, this novel is especially notable for Roumain's ambiguous attitude toward voodooism. Unlike works of the time that sensationalized specific aspects of voodoo, *La montagne ensorcelée* neither ridicules nor exploits the practice but instead seriously examines its importance to the Haitian peasant. Carolyn Fowler considered Roumain's shifts in narrative voice, which she regarded as masterfully imperceptible, to be responsible for the ambiguity in the novel: for example, French is used by an objective narrative voice, Creole by the "rational" voice of the peasants who have been exposed to other ways of thinking, and patois by the uneducated peasants, who represent a provincial viewpoint.

Roumain's masterpiece is *Masters of the Dew*. The hero of the work, Manuel, rallies feuding villagers to work together and irrigate their drought-stricken land. Although eventually killed by a jealous rival, the leader refuses to name the murderer as he dies, safeguarding the peasants' fledgling unity. Touching on a number of themes important to Roumain (nationalism, communism, romantic love, effective leadership, agricultural reform, and true friendship), *Masters of the Dew* is admired for its masterful synthesis of indigenous Haitian language, music, and folklore. "The novel is a beautiful, exact and tender rendering of Haitian life, of the African heritage, of the simple, impulsive, gravely formal folk, of the poetry and homely bite of their speech, of Congo dances, tropical luxuriance, the love of a land and its people," stated B. D. Wolfe.

Roumain introduced to literature the distinctive psychological viewpoint of the Afro-Haitian. Answering critics who consider Roumain's works nothing more than ideological tracts, J. Michael Dash stated: "[Roumain's] concern with the individual will and the quest for spiritual fulfillment show the extent to which he was very much a Romantic individualist rather than an ideologue whose main interest was conformity to Marxist ideals. It was really his strong moral conscience that drove him to the secular creed of Marxism.... Ultimately Roumain emerges as a modern artist concerned with the fate of the creative imagination in a world of broken continuities."

(For further information about Roumain's life and works, see *Black Writers; Contemporary Authors,* Vols. 117, 125; and *Twentieth-Century Literary Criticism,* Vol. 19.)

PRINCIPAL WORKS

La proie et l'ombre (short stories) 1930
Les fantoches (novel) 1931
La montagne ensorcelée (novel) 1931
Gouverneurs de la rosée (novel) 1944
  [*Masters of the Dew,* 1947]
Bois d'ébène (poetry) 1945
  [*Ebony Wood,* 1972]
Oeuvres choisies (essays, poetry, and fiction) 1964

Langston Hughes and Mercer Cook (essay date 1947)

[*Hughes was one of the leading figures of the Harlem Renaissance. Cook, an American critic, editor, and essayist, lived in Haiti and wrote and translated works about Haitian literature and culture. In the following excerpt from their introduction to* Masters of the Dew, *Hughes and Cook praise Roumain's literary achievements.*]

Roumain belonged to one of the first families of Haiti. His grandfather, Trancrède Auguste, had been president of the Republic. Money and position were part of Roumain's heritage. In addition, he had been blessed with the physique of an athlete and the features of a god. It would have seemed only natural for him to adopt the smug, ostrich-like attitude, still prevalent in a few Haitians of his class, who have chosen to ignore the realities of racism and exploitation. Instead, at the outset of his career, he served notice of his militancy by writing polemics inspired by the intense nationalism which the American occupation of his country provoked.

A logical outgrowth of this nationalism was the *Revue Indigène,* which Roumain founded in 1927, thereby inaugurating the new Haitian literature with its increasing awareness of things Haitian, of the African rather than the French background.

> 'Tis a long, long road to Guinée
> And death will guide you there.

So began one of his poems of this period . . . . Likewise, in one of his best known lyrics, **"When the Tom-Tom Beats,"** . . . he asked:

> Do you not feel the sweet magic of the past?
> It is a river which carries you far away from
> the banks and leads you towards the ancestral
> forests.

Other poems, mostly of social protest, appeared in various periodicals, anthologies, and in *Bois d'Ebène,* a booklet of verse posthumously published by the author's widow. In this collection, there is a forceful refrain characteristic of Roumain's revolt:

> que les nègres
> n'acceptent plus
> n'acceptent plus
>
> d'être vos niggers
> vos sales nègres.

Roumain's unusual scientific training, obtained at the Musée de l'Homme and elsewhere, found expression in several monographs, many articles, and in the Haitian Bureau of Ethnology, which he created. As early as 1930 he tried his hand at fiction. His first works—*La Proie et l'Ombre* and *Fantoches*—dealt with the Haitian scene, but in a manner that reflected the influence of the French Decadents. Dominated by a sense of futility and pessimism, these volumes treated primarily of the so-called elite Haitian. The following year, with the publication of *La Montagne Ensorcelée,* he discovered his most effective medium: the peasant novel. Exile, scientific research, imprisonment, the organization of the Haitian Communist Party, and incessant anti-Fascist activity, prevented further experiments in fiction until the Lescot government named him chargé d'affaires in Mexico City, a kind of honorary banishment that would at least keep him out of prison and provide leisure for writing.

Masters of the Dew (Gouverneurs de la Rosée) was written during Roumain's sojourn in the Mexican capital, and published in Haiti shortly after his death. When it became known in Haiti that we were about to translate the novel, offers of assistance came spontaneously from so many admirers of Jacques Roumain that we are unable to name them all. If *Gouverneurs de la Rosée* was to appear in a foreign language, they wanted to help make the translation as faithful as possible. (pp. vii-ix)

> Langston Hughes and Mercer Cook, in an introduction to Masters of the Dew by Jacques Roumain, translated by Langston Hughes and Mercer Cook, Reynal and Hitchcock, 1947, pp. vii-x.

Edmund Wilson (essay date 1949)

[*Wilson was an American critic who wrote widely on cultural, historical, and literary issues. In the following excerpt from an essay originally published in 1949, he discusses the relative merits of several of Roumain's works.*]

I have read only four books of Roumain, two of them, posthumously published, belonging to his late Communist period. *Bois-d'Ebène* . . . is a collection of poems, or rather of declamations, which somewhat parallels Aimé Césaire's *Cahier,* but fails of the latter's effect of passionate and cruel veracity. Roumain here invokes for the Negro a self-vindication and self-liberation which are simply his own special version of that now too familiar apocalypse, the victory of the proletariat. Except for a few happy images, *Bois-d'Ebène* seems to me unimportant as literature. So does his novel, *Gouverneurs de la Rosée* . . . , which—one assumes, through the efforts of the Communists—has been translated into English, under the title **Masters of the Dew.** This is simply the inevitable Communist novel that is turned out in every country in compliance with the Kremlin's prescription. You have the struggle against the bourgeoisie, the summons of the exploited to class solidarity, the martyr who dies for the cause—in this case, scientific irrigation. The Creole-speaking peasant hero is fired by a social idealism which he is supposed to have learned from a comrade on the sugar plantations of Cuba, but which he expounds with a *Daily Worker* eloquence that would scarcely have been possible in Creole. When one compares **Gouverneurs de la Rosée** with Lespès' *Les Semences de la Colère,* one sees that the experienced agronome (who has evidently been reading Malraux), though he, too, has allied himself with the Communists, has limited himself to observed fact and allowed himself only such sentiments as may be aroused in a sympathetic official by the spectacle of the trials of the peasants, whereas the radical man of letters, Roumain, has indulged himself in a Marxist fantasy. It is quite evident that Jacques Roumain did not know the black peasants well. But he did know the Mulatto bourgeoisie, to which he himself belonged, and his earlier novel, **Les Fantoches**..., which deals with the élite of Port-au-Prince, throws so much light on its subject that one regrets it should not have been projected on a more extensive scale. A blasé young man of society aroused to a rabid race-consciousness by the attentions of a visiting Frenchman to his beautiful financée—whom, however, he loves only half-heartedly—and her touching but useless attempt to restore his confidence in her by telling him in Creole that she loves him; the strange experience of one of the guests at a big evening party in a splendid house, when he walks by mistake into a sordid chamber, where the grandfather, an aged general, is found setting up lead soldiers and muttering about campaigns—these scenes have been lived and felt. The attempt to make contact with the people—one is often reminded in Haiti of pre-revolutionary Russia—is dramatized more convincingly by one of the episodes in writing **Gouverneurs de la Rosée.** Here a black girl who has put up a fight against the amorous son of her Mulatto employers is rescued from the misery to which they have consigned her by an upper-class intellectual, who demonstrates his exceptional nobility by taking her to live with him without making her sleep with him. Another earlier short novel of Roumain's, *La Montagne Ensorcelée*..., is somewhat more convincing than **Les Gouverneurs,** because it does take account of the beliefs of the peasants and not merely of their economic situation. (pp. 115-17)

Edmund Wilson, "Haiti," in his Red, Black, Blond and Olive; Studies in Four Civilizations: Zũni, Haiti, Soviet Russia, Israel, *Oxford University Press, Inc., 1956, pp. 71-146.*

Naomi M. Garret (essay date 1954)

[*In the following excerpt, Garret discusses Roumain's poetic ideals and comments on the themes and techniques the author employed in his works.*]

Roumain was haunted by a vision of a united Haitian people, a vision which dominated his actions and obsessed his mind; he knew that this could be achieved only by securing a better life for the oppressed masses. As a result, he turned his back upon a life of luxury to become a social menace to his class and a spokesman for the inarticulate masses. His courageous fight for the Haitianization of the total culture of his country won for him the enviable position of uncontested leader of the young intellectuals of Haiti. (p. 107)

In an interview with one of his group, Roumain sets forth his ideas on poetry. For him a poem is a drama which alone is the source of emotion. This dramatic emotion is not to be confused with the artistic emotion that results from satisfaction of a thought well turned; he exacts more than this of a poem. What he wants, he says, is "la force vibrante qui secoue. Le moteur." He cites his **"Cent mètres"** as an example.... In his conception, a poet is "un être qui vit... C'est le barde antique, adossé aux colonnades et déversant le trop plein de ses sensations. Et c'est pourquoi je me refuserai volontairement à suivre toute règle. Cet oiseau, qu'est la poésie, meurt, en cage."

Relative to the form of a poem, Roumain believes that this should be decided by the prevailing practices of an age. He has no mistaken idea that his group will hit upon the "final form" of Haitian poetry; he knows that they will be considered "vieux jeu" by younger generations.

As one of the leaders of the movement to reconcile Haitians with themselves and with their background, Roumain's ideas on the literature of his country are important. Like others of the young Pléiade, he condemns the past writers of Haiti for their lack of breadth in vision and absence of interest in the people. He credits them with having read French authors only, and only a few of those, whose renown had reached the island republic. He laments their failure to show any interest in the literature of the rest of the world or to keep abreast of the march of literary ideas. (pp. 107-08)

Roumain agrees with Normil Sylvain that it is natural and advisable for Haitian poets to follow the French masters in the forms chosen for their verse. Both of them refute the idea that the French can furnish models of "sensibilité" for Haitians and they advise the study of the works of people whose backgrounds contain elements similar to theirs. Therefore, Roumain advocates the inclusion of Latin-American poets in the reading of intelligent Haitians....

To assist in the education mentioned above, Roumain translated for the readers of *La Revue indigène* selections from several Latin-American poets....

Roumain proves to be the first of his group to become acquainted with the Negro poets of the United States and to realize that their ideas and ambitions are similar to those of Haitians. (p. 109)

Roumain reveals in his poetry the disillusionment, the unrest, and the despair which characterized [his] generation. In **"Insomnie,"** one sees the poet in a state of depression, overwhelmed by a fatigue that is more the result of a heavy heart than of physical exertion. He seems to find rest only in accepting the condition that he is powerless to throw off.... (p. 110)

Roumain's desire for the Haitianization of the literature of his country is exemplified in the source of most of the subjects of his poetry. These he found in the traditions and beliefs of the Haitian masses. One of his best known poems, **"Sur le chemin de Guinée,"** is based upon the belief, popular among the peasants, that the soul returns to Guinea after death. The poem abounds with the things the peasant hopes to find upon his return to his ancestral home.... The unusual figures of speech—the singular images of sound, sight, and even smell—added to the rhythm of the poem imbue it with a surprising and touching beauty. (pp. 110-11)

The novel, *Gouverneurs de la rosée* ..., which is considered by some critics as the best work of fiction to come from Haiti, bears out his saying that "Quelle que soit mon oeuvre, c'est à mon sol que je la dédierai." It is a superbly written work growing out of the peasant life of his country. *Bois-d'Ebène,* a small volume of poems, was published by his widow in 1945. Three of these are of special significance; for, they show the later and more militant Roumain who believed firmly in the principle of equality of man, a principle by which he lived and for which he would have willingly died.

The title poem begins by recalling to the Negro, that erstwhile article of commerce, his sufferings and depredation in all parts of the world, "depuis que tu fus vendu en Guinée," of the wanton slaughter of blacks on their long trek from their homeland.... They were strengthened by their songs of suffering and of deliverance, songs that were surpassed in power only by the silence of the blacks.... It was a silence caused by lynchings and other brutal and savage acts; but this silence, more cutting than the sharpest blade, louder than a cyclone of wild beasts, will not be stilled. It is a formidable power which rises and calls for

> vengeance et châtiment
> un raz de marée de pus et de lave
> sur la félonie du monde
> et le tympan du ciel crevé sous le poing
> de la justice.

Roumain, who could have easily elected to cast his lot among the more privileged, prefers instead to embrace the fate of these exploited pariahs:

> POURTANT
> je ne veux être que de votre race

ouvriers paysans de tous les pays.

And here, he changes his perspective and alters the aim of his art. A Comintern inspired view of the uniting of the working classes of all nations into a revolutionary international force supersedes his desire for the joining together of the forces of all Haitians into a power for the progress of his country and race.... (pp. 112-14)

"Bois-d'Ebène," written in Brussels June 1939, is brutal in its implications and thought provoking as a commentary upon contemporary civilization.

"Sales nègres" speaks in a similar vein of revolt for

> les nègres
> les niggers
> les sales nègres
> ... en Afrique,
> en Amérique.

and elsewhere, who have been relegated to conditions of degradation and humiliation. All institutions which have aided and abetted the exploitation of the underprivileged are attached. The Church, which has taught humility and resignation to the "sort maudit" of these outcasts, has not been spared. Since they have never been accepted on terms of equality with the other children in the so-called Christian faith, it is useless for them to continue.... (p. 114)

The poet sees the end of the unequitable position of these victims of ignorance and hatred brought about by the revolt of all blacks from the black belts of the United States, the cane fields of the Antilles, and the jungles of Africa. And they will not be alone.... (pp. 114-15)

"Nouveau sermon nègre" strengthens the protest against the Church, its practices and its teachings. Church policy has assigned a new role to Christ; He has been taken from the cross where He was crucified between thieves and placed in the den of the thieves whose traits He has assumed.... Just as the Church has reversed its character, Negroes will change the character of their songs; revolt will supplant acceptance and resignation.... (pp. 115-16)

Jacques Roumain whose command of English acquainted him with the black poets in the United States found in them kindred souls, fighting the same battles as he. He felt a close kinship with Langston Hughes who shared his interest in the common man and whose poems sound a protest against the lot of the latter.... It may not be safe to claim that Roumain was directly influenced by the American; it is a fact, nevertheless, that their themes and emotions are the same. Both are preoccupied with the masses instead of with the individual and recognize that the problems of all the underprivileged are similar. They shared a friendship based upon a common cause. One of Roumain's most touching poems is entitled **"Langston Hughes."**

Roumain, in whose veins the blood of his African ancestors had run very thin, cherished this part of his heritage and devoted much energy to ennobling it in the eyes of his compatriots, some of whom were much more skeptical. Turning his back upon material wealth, he dedicated his life to his ideals. He who refused all laws of expediency and of class sang to the country of his forefathers:

> Afrique j'ai gardé la mémoire Afrique
> tu es en moi
> Comme l'écharde dans la blessure
> Comme un fétiche au centre du village.

He begged her to use his gifts in her fight for redemption.... (pp. 116-17)

Loved and respected by his group and worshipped by his younger followers, Jacques Roumain has exerted more influence upon the poets among the latter class than any other member of the Pléiade of *La Revue indigène.* (p. 117)

> *Naomi M. Garret, "Representative Poets of the Renaissance: Poets of 'La Revue Indigène',"* in her The Rennaissance of Haitian Poetry, *1954. Reprint by Présence Africaine, 1963, pp. 86-147.*

Beverley Ormerod (essay date 1977)

[*In the following excerpt, Ormerod examines Roumain's combination of literary and sociopolitical concerns in* Masters of the Dew.]

A recurrent problem of French Caribbean writing is the difficulty of combining purely literary concerns with those of a strong socio-political commitment. Many a *roman à thèse,* here as in metropolitan France, has been more preoccupied with depicting social injustice or historically inspired neurosis than with creating a delicately-wrought work of the imagination. Jacques Roumain's *Gouverneurs de la rosée* may seem, on first acquaintance, to fall into the didactic category, to be a fictional companion piece to the militantly Marxist poems of the same author's *Bois-d'Ébène.* In bold, simple terms, the plot unfolds the story of a Haitian canecutter (familiar figure of Caribbean oppression, emblem of the centuries of slavery), who returns from fifteen years in Cuba to preach a doctrine of protest, self-help and cooperative action to the apathetic, divided and exploited peasants of his native village. The message is transposed from a proletarian to a rural setting, but its political source is readily identifiable. Yet the way in which the revolutionary goal is expressed lifts the reader away from politics to poetry and indicates the strong elements of myth and ritual which underpin the novel: "Nous ferons l'assemblée générale des gouverneurs de la rosée, le grand coumbite des travailleurs de la terre pour défricher la misère et planter la vie nouvelle."... Earth and *coumbite,* dew and water, dust and drought are the recurrent symbols through which the hero's adventure is invested with a legendary quality.

The central situation of the novel recalls one of the most ancient mythical motifs: that of the Waste Land. Pre-Christian vegetation cults, as Frazer and later anthropologists have contended, were based upon the concerns of peoples living in hot and often arid regions, dependent upon rain, or, later, irrigation, for the successful pursuit of their agricultural activities. Roumain, who studied at the Institut d'Ethnologie in Paris and undertook research under Paul Rivet of the Musée de l'Homme; who later founded the Haitian Bureau d'Ethnologie and published two anthropological monographs, would certainly have been familiar with the patterns of vegetation myth. Gods who free imprisoned waters, who fall sick and provoke a state of drought, or whose sexual activities are associated with irrigation, are familiar figures in the legends of India and Mesopotamia. (pp. 123-24)

It is immediately apparent that the plight of Fonds-Rouge echoes that of the Waste Land. "Nous mourrons tous ... —et elle plonge sa main dans la poussière"...: from the opening paragraph of the novel, dust and drought are associated with death. The village and the surrounding rural landscape are desolate, the rust-coloured earth laid bare. Parched humans and animals are assailed by the scorching breath of the wind, and by the harsh cries of the crows that circle obsessively above the diseased cactus hedges. The ravaged earth and all her attributes are presented in metaphors of human suffering and torture.... In an extension of the metaphor, the drought is associated with loss of sexual fulfilment through the image of the earth as a woman abandoned by her lover.... The sexual deprivation suggested here echoes the castration of Adonis and the legendary king's loss of virility; it also establishes by implication a paradigm of the ideal relationship between the peasant and his land, that of lover and mistress which prevailed in the days of the *coumbite,* when, "par un labeur viril"..., men forced the earth to yield up its fruits for their pleasure. Even the logical explanation for the drought—the persistent deforestation of the hillsides by the villagers—is expressed in terms of this sexual image.... (pp. 124-25)

It is the hero of the novel, Manuel, who perceives this betrayal of the earth and assumes the rôle of her lover: "je suis planté dans cette terre, je suis lié à cette terre."... And here the motif of the Waste Land is assimilated into that broader pattern which Joseph Campbell, in *The Hero with a Thousand Faces,* has termed the monomyth. In the standard monomyth the hero undergoes the processes of separation from the everyday world, mystical initiation or supernatural adventure, and triumphant return as a superior being, often bringing back a divine reward. This archetypal pattern is evident at more than one level of the novel. At the narrative level, the hero has already gone through separation from his village and taken part in a collective crisis of self-awareness during his years in Cuba, where the canecutters are for the first time conscious of being exploited and prepared to take militant strike action to improve their working conditions. It is because of this initiation into the world of politics and class struggle that Manuel is no longer able, on his return to Haiti, to accept passively the poverty and natural disasters which beset the villagers, their exploitation by the petty figures of rural authority, and their attitude of patient resignation with is fostered by voodoo and Catholicism alike. He brings with him the seeds of revolutionary change. Light shines on his forehead when he returns home..., and this is not only because he is a Christ-figure, an "Emmanuel", as Michel Serres has shown in his study of the novel's Christian imagery, but also because he is an instrument of socio-political illumination. Like Zola's Étienne in *Germinal,* haloed in moonlight as he preaches socialism to the rapt crowds of miners in the forest meeting, Manuel sheds light.... (pp. 125-26)

At a further level, however, where narrative merges into myth and symbol, Manuel's initiatory adventure is the discovery of the spring, and the reward which he brings back is the promise of water, of restored fertility, of a renewal of the "vie tarie"... of Fonds-Rouge. The image of light recurs in the context of this gift of water..., as it will do, with unmistakeable Christian symbolism, in the context of Manuel's sacrificial death.... But although Manuel's blood flows to expunge the fratricidal quarrels of the past; although, in renouncing vengeance, he brings peace and good will to the divided village, the novel is not the wholehearted "reprise sans lacune des *Testaments* de la tradition chrétienne" which Serres... maintains it to be. Christianity is used in a literary way by Roumain, as a source of traditional symbols; but as a religious system it is derided by his hero, who predicates a paradise where black angels launder the clouds and tidy up after storms, while white angels sing all day or blow into their conventional little trumpets.... After the death of Manuel even the devout Annaïse sees God as pitiless and unjust, deaf to black prayers, as destructive as the drought...—and old Antoine assents to this rejection of Christian faith with his ironic "Le Bondieu est bon, dit-on. Le Bondieu est blanc, qu'il faudrait dire."... Roumain has indeed incorporated important elements of the Christian myth: the idea of a lost Eden (symbolised in the novel by the African-inspired *coumbite*), the parallel between blood and water, the death of a redeemer figure. But Manuel's sacrifice is not made to save his fellow-men from original sin: in forsaking vengeance his obsessive thought is that he must save the water, must not imperil the irrigation scheme which is to restore the land. When, in describing his burial, the novel picks up the Biblical theme of Christ's love for the world, the traditional phrase is given an ironically literal twist: "ces nègres emportent le cercueil, ils emportent leur frère vers cette terre qu'il a tellement aimée, qu'en vérité, il est mort pour elle".... If we examine more closely the symbolic value of the earth, the *coumbite,* and the water and dew of the novel, we shall see that Manuel's death, and his relationship with Annaïse, suggest rituals which go back beyond Christianity to the ancient forms of vegetation cult out of which the Christian concept of a redemptive sacrifice was itself to emerge.

We have seen that the drought-ridden, barren earth is personified as a woman deprived of sexual satisfaction. From the moment of his return, Manuel enters into a relationship with the land based on his perception of it.... He visualizes the social reform of rural Haiti in terms of a faithful and intimate interaction between the labourer and his plot of earth: images of divorce and desertion... express with imperative urgency the plight of those who abandon the land. But the earth is not an easy conquest: like a long-pursued seduction, his patient search for a source of water reflects and moves parallel to his persistent courtship of the hesitant Annaïse. His discovery of the spring is described in terms of sensual excitement: he is like a boy going to his first lovers' rendez-vous, and when he is sure of success, his intense delight finds expression in amorous physical gesture:

> Manuel s'étendit sur le sol. Il l'étreignait à plein corps:
> "Elle est là, la douce, la bonne, la coulante, la chantante, la fraîche, la bénédiction, la vie."
> Il baisait la terre des lèvres et riait....

(pp. 126-27)

This symbolic union with earth and water reflects the mythical association of human fertility with that of the land. Ritual springtime couplings in the fields were common in ancient civilizations, which believed that the release of human sexual energy aided the germination of the seed and also provoked rain. Manuel's subsequent sexual union with Annaïse, who lies on the earth above the hidden spring to receive his embrace, repeats in human terms the mystical moment of his finding of the water, and thus assumes a symbolic, ritual nature. Serres... asserts that the human coupling represents a cosmic union between sun (Manuel) and water (Annaïse). It is difficult to perceive any association, other than the light symbolism mentioned above, between the hero and the sun; but Manuel is certainly the lover of the water. Annaïse hails him as "Maître de l'eau (qui) connais toutes les sources, même celle qui dormait dans le secret de ma honte"...; the fusion of natural and human worlds here picks up the earlier motif of Manuel's desire for the Haitian peasant to assume mastery over his recalcitrant female environment.... (p. 128)

The notion of fertility in the novel is also related to the lost ritual of the *coumbite,* where, in a survival of African tradition, a team of labourers, led by a drummer whose song set the tempo for their digging, used to work together in the fields for the benefit of all the village. Old Bienaimé's memories of the *coumbite* are of a time of plenty, when men went out early in the morning into the lush Guinea grass, barefoot in the cool dew and the gentle light of dawn, amid a landscape whose rich beauty was a reminder of sensual delight.... The *coumbite,* at once formal ritual and informal comradeship, and a last link with the lost paradise of African Guinea, symbolised the harmony of man with earth and of man with his human neighbour. The ritual is destroyed by a quarrel over land inheritance which ends in a murder

..., and this violent loss of fraternity is associated with the coming of the drought and its allied symbols.... In Manuel's vision of the future, *coumbite,* water, reconciliation and fertility are inseparably linked.... (pp. 128-29)

Water is the pivot of the story at the literal level; as Serres ... has demonstrated, it assumes a symbolic quality in the denouement through its associations with the Passion of Christ, whose blood is the water of life, and whose self-sacrifice upon the Cross finds many echoes in the circumstances of Manuel's death. A close reading of the novel shows that water and blood are also associated in earlier incidents. Attacked and brutally beaten by the Cuban rural police during his canecutting years, Manuel is sustained by an inner defiant notion of endurance "comme une source de sang, la rumeur inépuisable de la vie."... He visualizes the future irrigation canals as a network of veins bringing life to the very depths of the earth.... The murder which has divided the village into two hostile factions is like a stream of blood which cannot be crossed...; in persuading them to unite once more for the irrigation project, Manuel presents the water itself as a literal means of redeeming the past bloodshed: "l'eau lavera le sang et la récolte nouvelle poussera sur le passé et mûrira sur l'oubli."... In a further symbolic function, stagnant water represents the physical suffering caused by the drought...—and also the state of alienation in which the villagers live.... In contract to these stagnant pools, the living water will surge through the future canals, as the words of Manuel now flow with hope and promise, "clair comme l'eau courante au soleil."... Water also symbolises the control of one's destiny: the exploited Cuban canecutters own no water save their own sweat...; Hilarion fears the irrigation project because it will make the villagers independent of his exploitative money-lending... and, petty tyrant to the last, plans to impose a tax upon the new canals.... These notions of freedom and renewal through water are summed up in the title of the novel, where water is present in its most poetic form, as dew.

The ambition of being "gouverneur de la rosée" suggests, by its use of the old term for the former colonial ruler, an assumption of independence by the black peasantry at the socio-political level. Implicit in the phrase, however, is the gaining of a god-like authority over the forces of life and death. In the Old Testament, product of a warm and sometimes rainless region, dew has a vital symbolic value: the bestowing of dew is a blessing from God (as in Deut. 33:13), and the withholding of it is a curse. In a typical instance of divine retribution, the fellow-citizens of the prophet Haggai are punished with drought for failing to rebuild God's temple: "Therefore the heaven over you is stayed from dew, and the earth is stayed from her fruit" (Haggai 1:10). Likewise old Délira sees God, in syncretic conjunction with the voodoo *loa,* as having control over water and human life.... (pp. 129-30)

Manuel's dying vision of the dew projects into the future old Bienaimé's dream of past fruitfulness—"un champ de maïs à l'infini, les feuilles ruisselantes de rosée"...—and by willing the renewal of the *coumbite,* he enables the drought of Fonds-Rouge to become part of a positive cycle of suffering and renaissance. The delicate beauty of the dew encapsules the amorous relationship between Manuel and the earth. Dew is associated with the pride of the labourer gazing at his fields..., and with the joy of his wife going out at sunrise to gather the fruit of their land...; it is the reward of the peasant who keeps faith with the earth and thus gains control over his own destiny—"un travailleur de la terre sans reproche, un gouverneur de la rosée véritable."... Dew stands for fruitfulness, like the water which brings fertility to the land, like Manuel who brings fertility to Annaïse.... On the final page of the novel, the child stirs within Annaïse as the first water flows through the canal towards Fonds-Rouge, and the villagers, led once more by their drummer, run alongside shouting and singing with pride. Thus Manuel's death takes its place beside those of the ancient vegetation gods, Tammuz, Attis and Adonis, who, suffering their yearly ritual death and resurrection, symbolise the eternal cycle of sterile winter and fruitful spring, of collective mourning and rejoicing.... It is in the light of these traditions that we should view the apotheosis of Roumain's Manuel, whose resurrection is envisaged not in the asexual terms of Christian immortality, but in a sensual fusion with nature.... (pp. 131-32)

> Beverley Ormerod, "Myth, Rite and Symbol in 'Gouverneurs de la rosée'," in L'Esprit Créateur, *Vol. XVII, No. 2, Summer, 1977, pp. 123-32.*

Melvin Dixon (essay date 1979)

[In the following excerpt, Dixon discusses Roumain's use of folk material to "evoke the African presence" in his works.]

Edward Brathwaite has distinguished four kinds of New World literature that evoke the African presence: (1) a rhetorical literature, which uses Africa as a mask and only says the word "Africa" or invokes a dream of the Congo, Senegal, Niger, and other place names; (2) the literature of African survival, which "deals quite consciously with African survivals in Caribbean society" but does not reconnect them with the great tradition of Africa; (3) the literature of African expression, "which has its root in the folk, and which attempts to adapt or transform folk material into literary experiment"; and (4) the literature of reconnection by writers who have lived in Africa and the New World and who "are consciously reaching out to rebridge the gap with the spiritual heartland."

Most important of these developments, and the one most applicable to our study, is the "literature of African expression," for here the writer attempts to remake himself as he transforms folk material into literary experiment. Illustrating this process of self-discovery is Haitian Jacques Roumain, who took as models for his own literary expression the blues references of Langston Hughes, the sermons of James Weldon Johnson (**"Nouveau Sermon nègre"**), and his native Creole culture. Within this pattern of shared influence across linguistic lines one can speak of a cross-fertilization, an intertextuality among works of New World black literature. Not only was Roumain to learn from Hughes about the transformation of musical forms and folk material, but Hughes learned from Roumain, by translating his poetry, how to convey the peculiar Haitian assonance and sonority in English. In this respect, the poems "The Negro Speaks of Rivers" and **"Guinea"** present opportunities for interesting structural and thematic comparisons.

Both poems invest language with the power of transforming external folk material, atavistic reference, and the speaking voice itself. The speaker in Hughes's poem discovers a personal identity through his participation by means of language in an African past and a New World present. His racial knowledge is not abstract or romantic but grounded in personal and group behavior to create and re-create history. "I've known rivers," the poem begins, *because*

> I bathed in the Euphrates when dawns were young
> I built my hut near the Congo and it lulled me to
>   sleep
> I looked upon the Nile and raised the pyramids
>   above it.

Action within the past gives the poem an authentic voice for the present and rescues the work from an inappropriately romantic perspective. Man actively participates in human history. He earns his identity through the creation of civilization. The history outside him—rivers "older than the flow of human veins"—becomes his through the poem's near incremental repetition of the phrase "my soul has grown deep like the rivers."

Roumain, in a similar lyrical language, charts a journey into the future based on what the speaker in **"Guinea"** has inherited from the past. The word "Guinea" resonates for a Haitian audience not only because it signifies Africa but also because it identifies the popular belief in Haitian folklore that upon death one will journey to Guinea and join the ancestors. The lyrical tone of the poem differs from the more religious language of James Weldon Johnson's "Go Down Death," or Sterling Brown's more colloquial "Sister Lou," but, nevertheless, it initiates Roumain's search for a figurative language to express the form and feeling of his people. The poem is descriptive of one speaker's journey and prescriptive and instructive in the imperative mood for his audience:

> C'est le lent chemin de Guinée
> La mort t'y conduira
> Voici les branchages, les arbres, la forêt
> Ecoute le bruit du vent dans ses longs cheveux
>   d'éternelle nuit.

> C'est le lent chemin de Guinée
> Tes pères t'attendent sans impatience
> Sur la route, ils palabrent
> Ils attendent
> Voici l'heure où les ruisseaux grelottent comme
>   des chapelets d'os

> C'est le lent chemin de Guinée
> Il ne te sera pas fait de lumineux accueil
> Au noir pays des hommes noirs:
> Sous un ciel fumeux percé de cris d'oiseaux
> Autour de l'oeil du marigot
>   les cils des arbres s'écartent sur l clarté
>   pourrissante.
> Là, t'attend au bord de l'eau un paisible village,
> Et la case de tes pères, et la dure pierre familiale
>   où reposer enfin ton front.

> It's the long road to Guinea
> Death takes you down
> Here are the boughs, the trees, the forest
> Listen to the sound of the wind in its long hair
>   of eternal night

> It's the long road to Guinea
> Where your fathers await you without impatience
> Along the way, they talk
> They wait
> This is the hour when the streams rattle
>   like beads of bone

> It's the long road to Guinea
> No bright welcome will be made for you
> In the dark land of dark men:
> Under a smoky sky pierced by the cry of birds
> Around the eye of the river
>   the eyelashes of the trees open on decaying
>   light
> There, there awaits you beside the water a quiet
>   village,
> And the hut of your fathers, and the hard
>   ancestral stone
>   where your head will rest at last.

In the repetition of the droning phrase "C'est le lent chemin de Guinée," Roumain establishes a link to Haitian folk culture. And in his use of the "o" sound for near rhyme and rhythm, he approximates the open vowel sounds of the Creole language, as in "La mort t'y conduira."

When Langston Hughes translated the poem, he was particularly sensitive to this use of language and approximated the texture of the open, sonorous speech. Instead of the literal translation of the line to read "death will lead you there," he chose the sonorous, alliterative line "death takes you down" to maintain thematic clarity and to preserve the tonal quality of the language. The speaker in Roumain's original text, as in the translation, discovers a language through which he can experience death on the literal level and passage from the New World to Africa on the symbolic level. His experience is visual and aural: "Here are the boughs, the trees, the forest / Listen to the sound of the wind in its long hair / of eternal night." The speaker comes to know how the wind is animated, personified. And having established a primary contact with nature, he then discerns the voices of his fathers that accompany his passage through a decaying light that signifies no bright welcome. But rather than feeling an existential gloom, the speaker discovers "a quiet village" beside the water and the ancestral stone upon which he will rest. The repeated "long road to Guinea" suggests a passage that will test the speaker and, as in Hughes's "Negro Speaks of Rivers," make his presence one of active and earned behavior until he endures the darkness of his own fears and earns the rewarding, soft darkness of eternal rest.

Roumain's voice in the poem is that of a learned observer, instructing the uninitiated, who may still need to find—in the folk belief of spiritual and cultural redemption—comfort from the psychic dislocation and abandonment of his past in the New World. By its reference to Africa, Hughes's subjective voice affirms, indirectly, the historical, the folkloric, and, directly, the spiritual journey. Roumain is still groping for language that connects more fully to this rite of passage.

Roumain and Hughes were familiar with each other's work, but when Roumain began to write he composed melancholic, meditative verse that described his feelings of alienation upon his return to Haiti from his education abroad. Roumain's early poetry shows his search for a language to illuminate Haitian reality as the poet's own national identity. Other writers of the *Revue Indigène* were helpful to him, but so were writers of the Harlem Renaissance like Hughes and Countee Cullen. When interviewed by the review, Roumain suggested that Haitian writers become more aware of the flourishing North American black poetry. Years later, Roumain described indirectly how he learned from Hughes to depict the black figurative language of the blues. (pp. 33-7)

Roumain's sensitivity to colloquial speech, music, and folklore as a basis for indigenous figurative language is evident in his long, major poem, *Bois d'ébène* and surfaces again as a rhythmic device in his more political piece, **"Sales Nègres" ("Dirty Negroes")** .... But the creation of the peasant novel was Roumain's greatest achievement in Haitian letters. *Gouveneurs de la rosée* ..., translated by Langston Hughes and Mercer Cook as *Masters of the Dew* ..., shows Roumain's masterful transformation of Creole language, music, and folklore into literary experiment.

In *Masters of the Dew* we encounter the peasant greeting of "Honor," which is answered by "Respect" when one peasant visits another. Roumain transforms that dialogue in the text to indicate an exchange of greeting between Manuel, the protagonist, and his homeland of Fonds Rouge. The hero, after fifteen years of working in the cane fields of Cuba, returns to his drought-stricken village and finds water to irrigate the land. The community, however, is divided by a family feud that prevents the peasants from working cooperatively to build an aqueduct now that water is found. Roumain's use of the oral exchange "Honor-Respect" establishes an internal dialogue between Manuel and himself, and an external one with Nature, with whose life forces he renews his primal covenant and from whom he eventually gains

redemption in his martyrdom and sustenance for his community:

> (Manuel) was dull of happiness despite the stubborn thoughts that haunted him. He wanted to sing a greeting to the trees: "Growing things, my growing things! To you I say 'Honor!' You must answer 'Respect,' so that I may enter. You're my house, you're my country.

(pp. 38-9)

Roumain's achievement—transforming specific oral, musical, and folk forms into literature—links him to Hughes in the United States, Guillén in Cuba, and Léopold Sédar-Senghor in Senegal. Oral traditions, transformed, are the cultural elements shared by these black writers. They accomplish the very dictum articulated earlier by Jean Price-Mars that "nothing will be able to prevent tales, legends, songs come from afar or created, transformed by us, from being a part of us, revealed to us as an exteriorization of our collective self." (p. 40)

> *Melvin Dixon, "Rivers Remembering Their Sources," in* Afro-American Literature: The Reconstruction of Instruction, *edited by Dexter Fisher and Robert B. Stepto, The Modern Language Association of America, 1979, pp. 25-43.*

Carolyn Fowler (essay date 1980)

[*In the following excerpt from her 1980 biography of Roumain, Fowler examines themes and motifs in the author's poetry and fiction.*]

Jacques Roumain's portrayal of the aimlessness of bourgeois existence in *La Proie et l'ombre,* and the implications in his *Les Fantoches* that the "boue gouvernementale" of Haitian politics will remain a real problem after the departure of the marines, were appreciated by his contemporaries, but these works are not typical of the prose literature of the period. *La Proie et l'ombre,* a collection of short stories, appeared in late 1930. (p. 73)

All four stories [in *La Proie et l'ombre*] show essentially the same thematic preoccupations. The protagonists are all young urban intellectuals roaming aimlessly about Port-au-Prince, caught in the empty monotonous pettiness of their existence. Their despair stems from their sense that there is something missing in their lives. They should be capable of more. They are inadequate heroes, incapable of reaching beyond their lives. They realize this in a sudden moment of truth. (p. 77)

The theme of these ... stories is therefore none other than that already encountered in most of Roumain's poetry of 1927-29. His poetry reflected the hero in various settings: the romantic hero, sensitive, lonely and unhappy; the cosmic hero, just as lonely but reaching beyond himself into the vastness of space, the only bright spot in a universe shrouded in darkness; the valiant hero, fighting for rightful control of his destiny in the society of his compatriots. The hero now, in the early prose, becomes spokesman for a kind of Lost Generation, unable to find fulfillment in the old values and unable to find any new ones, and so existing in a vacuum. It is not the vacuum which ultimately destroys these heroes, but their lucidity about their condition.

But it is not only in the theme that this first prose seems closely related to the early poetry. Certain motifs recur, some of which have appeared in the poetry. Rhythmic buildups into lyric tirades at the moment of lucidity and a use of the self very reminiscent of the lyric or the epic *moi* of Roumain's poetry are also evidence that Roumain's mind is still functioning to a great extent in the poetic mode.

The most impressive of the motifs is the light-darkness antithesis already seen in so much of the poetry. Darkness is announced in the collection's title and enshrouds most of the stories. Occasionally, an image will recall a similar one depicted in the poetry. In **"La Veste"**:

> Saivre...regarda par le fenêtre. La pluie faisait fondre la lumière du réverbère. De fines aiguilles d'or tombaient. Derrière, la grande nuit vague, le grand silence noir....

> (Saivre...looked out of the window. The rain was melting the light from the street lamp. Fine needles of gold were falling. Behind, the great vague night, the great black silence.)

We are reminded of the image of the beloved in **"Attente"**:

> O les yeux douloureux d'épier le ruisseau d'or
> Que verse sur l'asphalte le réverbère borgne.

> (O the eyes sad to watch the golden stream which the one-eyed street lamp spills over the asphalt.)

In both passages night, darkness and rain represent vast unending gloom and eternal unfulfilled waiting but are accompanied by the one contrasting spot of light.

Other images found in the poetry seem to repeat themselves with great insistence in the early prose. In reading **"Fragment d'une confession,"** one finds oneself immersed in the same poetic universe as in **"Calme,"** where the lonely hero, after attempting to reach beyond, finally succumbs.... (pp. 77-8)

[**"Fragment d'une confession"**] also associates silence and space with suspension in time, an association found in much of the early poetry. Expressions such as "courbè sur le passé" suggest the body's futile efforts to escape its contingencies and recall other expressions such as "un homme courbé sur ses désirs morts" (**"Calme"**). The past participate "courbé" recalls other verbs: "je me penche hors de moi" (**"Insomnie"**). The image of the "acrobate tendant les bras vers le but" in this story strongly recalls the images in the early poetry of the outstretched arms, symbolizing the effort sustained, the source of strength called upon to reach the goal. When the arm motif recurs a few paragraphs later, it reveals the failure of the poet's individual effort. And it is at this juncture that the comforting presence of the beloved is invoked:

> ...Ah, que s'ouvre cette porte et entre une femme aux pas hésitants; qu'elle vienne avec ce mystérieux sourire que je ne connus jamais jusqu'à mon front pesant et mes bras inutiles....

> (...Ah, that that door might open and a woman enter on hesitant steps; that she might, with that mysterious smile that I never knew, come up to my heavy brow and useless arms....)

Again, we are reminded of certain of Roumain's early poems, which also invoke the comforting presence of the beloved. In the paragraph following, the motif of the hands also appears, symbolizing, as in the poetry, human contact in love:

> Mon Dieu, que s'ouvre cette porte et entre un tout petit enfant et vienne jusqu'à mes genoux et que j'entende sa douce voix malhabile et qu'il mette ses mains puériles sur mon vieux visage. Mon Dieu, peut-être m'aimera-t-il?...

> (Dear Lord, that that door might open and a very small child come to my knees and that I might hear his sweet, stumbling voice and that he might put his childish hands on my old face. Perhaps, dear Lord, he would love me?)

The story from beginning to end involves the reader in Benoît Carrère's nocturnal quest, up to the moment of final exhaustion at daybreak, when the reader is suddenly catapulted out of the character's private emotional universe by the sudden shift into third-person narrative. The effect is very much like the rhythmic buildup in poems like **"Cent mètres"** and **"Appel,"** which implicates the reader in the internal drama of the protagonist and releases him suddenly at the end from involvement in the hero's destiny. **"Fragment d'une confession"** is short, broken up into short stanzaic paragraphs. Given all these considerations, it is perhaps valid to raise the question whether **"Fragment d'une confession"** is not really, after all, a poem.

"Préface à la vie d'un bureaucrate," on the other hand, presents an entirely different case. It has a plot, which, however tenuous, functions toward the resolution of a central "problem" announced by the title. It contains as well the usual dialogue and narrative passages and the characterization associated with prose fiction. Yet a lyric interlude interrupts the action toward the end of the story, and at that point the same motif, conveying the same message as in **"Fragment d'une confession,"** reappears. (pp. 79-80)

The stories of *La Proie et l'ombre* often evoke gloom and monotony, not solely through surrounding darkness but also through tableaux of an overcast sky and of the sea. Light has an altogether different meaning when it is the diffuse light of day rather than a concentrated spot of light generated by or associated with the solitary, searching hero. In these stories, night typically fades into day, and the day is gloomy, a different form of monotony, as in the opening lines of **"Préface à la vie d'un bureaucrate."** . . . It is not the sunny tropics and the warm, blue-fringed beaches which we see in these stories, but the overcast sky, the murky grey water, the thin, drizzly rain . . . . (pp. 81-2)

If some of the motifs of *La Proie et l'ombre* repeat those of the poetry, others are new. We find over and over in these stories the lonely nocturnal walks through deserted streets contrasted with (sometimes immediately followed by) sudden immersion in a crowd of common folk. The noctambulation represents alienation, whereas the crowds of Creole-speaking blacks represent the Haitian identity which the alienated, intellectual, bourgeois heroes go out nightly in search of . . . . In **"Préface à la vie d'un bureaucrate,"** Michel, on waking, sees his raincoat still dripping from the night's rain, and it reminds him of the moment of his return home . . . We are not told why the dripping raincoat should remind Michel of his homecoming day, but the fact that the memory directly follows an allusion to nocturnal wanderings is perhaps significant, for it is the same juxtaposition of loneliness followed by sudden immersion in a crowd that we find in other passages in the prose of this period.

Less elaborate but more frequent is the recurrence of the forced smile or laugh. In almost every instance, laughter is hollow, the smile is a sneer or a pose, behind which bitter emptiness is discernible:

Daniel, in **"Propos sans suite"**:

> . . . il éclata de rire. La voix était blanche, tremblait et se brisa avec une sorte de rage . . . .
>
> Le rire fêlé recommençait . . .
>
> (. . . he burst out laughing. His voice was white; it trembled and broke with a kind of rage.)

Emilio, in **"Propos sans suite"**:

> Emilio fit une curieuse grimace: on eut dit que son rire s'était réfugié dans une ride subite qui tirait ses lèvres, amèrement . . . .
>
> (Emilio made a curious grimace: one would have said that his laughter had taken refuge in a sudden wrinkle which pulled at his lips bitterly . . .)

Michel, in **"Préface à la vie d'un bureaucrate"**:

> Il sourit de ce sourire qui lui était particulier: une sorte de rictus douleureux, qui tirait ses lèvres, d'un côté par deux rides divergents . . . .
>
> Un ricanement intérieur le déchire . . . .
>
> (He laughed that laughter which was peculiar to him: a kind of painful rictus that drew his lips to one side in two divergent wrinkles.
>
> An inner sneer tears at him)

Each succeeding image recalls the ones before it, establishing a kind of metaphoric resonance. The message of empty helplessness in the lives of these young men is transmitted as in Roumain's early poetry by the indirect means of motif symbolism.

Within the sordidness of the urban setting, here and there images and metaphors allude to the native fruits of Haiti. Such allusions are not usually gratuitous; they give the impression of lush growth and productiveness, of the overabundance resulting from natural, uninhibited growth. These metaphors seem to refocus on that which is indigenous, as contrasted with the gloomy artificiality of intellectualized urban life. Significantly, allusions to fruit occur in passages dealing with women, who themselves are symbols of hope and regenerative power. Sometimes that power is depleted, as in the case of the old peasant woman whom Michel, in **"Préface à la vie d'un bureaucrate,"** had glimpsed the day of his return. But more often, fruit and women still hold the promise of future growth. Crowds of common folk, women, and fruit all seem to represent the essence of Haiti and the source of Haitian life. This symbolism becomes more important as we go from *La Proie et l'ombre* to *Les Fantoches,* where it becomes more closely associated with certain characters and not with others . . . . (pp. 82-4)

Professor Mercer Cook has spoken of the influence of the French Decadents of the turn of the century in *La Proie et l'ombre.* Although Roumain does not speak of such an influence in any of his writings now available to us, certain parallels do exist between his early prose and the Decadents. In their nighttime wanderings, Roumain's young heroes often show a propensity for seeking out the dives and hovels of the city. Amid the stale smells of alcohol and cooking grease, the painted prostitutes and flotsam thrown in the sea and washed back up, they comment on man's dismal spiritual state. The heroes of *La Proie et l'ombre* share in common with the Parisians of the turn of the century a feeling that they are witnessing the empty culmination of a civilization. But it is doubtful that the *fin-de-siècle* ethic goes very deeply into the matrix of these stories. The young men of *La Proie et l'ombre* do not seek out depravity because of some genetic degeneracy; they do not seek it as a means of purification or of control over their destinies as do the heroes of the Marquis de Sade and their literary descendants. These young bourgeois of Port-au-Prince are far more humanitarian in their idealism. One is reminded by certain passages more of Baudelarian decadence and fallen angels. (p. 85)

In the heroes of *La Proie et l'ombre,* Jacques Roumain's contemporaries immediately recognized themselves and the author. Almost immediately, the obvious question was posed: Were these stories autobiographical? . . . Quite apart from any examination of its literary merits, young Haitians embraced *La Proie et l'ombre* as a kind of solace. The stories were an esthetization of an inner life which they could recognize as their own.

Carl Brouard avowed that even though only one of the stories was known to him, all of them *seemed* familiar. He agreed with Antonio Vieux that the collection was a "témoignage." But at the same time he implied that that testimonial, the result of Roumain's ability to analyse deep into human motivations, was also the result of Roumain's own analysis of himself.... (pp. 86-7)

[Contemporary] judgments seem to be making the same basic assumption. They all see Jacques Roumain the man as a repository for the feelings and aspirations of his generation. The inner life of Jacques Roumain, analyzed and revealed to his peers, reflects the inner life of all of them. The impulsion of the poet to use himself as model, to effect an esthetic reworking from the specific to the generic, is at the basis of these stories, as it was of the early poetry, and illustrates again their transitional nature. Unlike the poetry, however, these stories have specific characters who move about in more or less well-defined environments (and in the case of **"Préface à la vie d'un bureaucrate,"** must resolve certain problems). This explains why most readers have perceived and drawn meaning from *La Proie et l'ombre* on two levels.

While it seems safe to conclude that the individual soul's journey of the poet-prophet is also a testimony of the anguish of his contemporaries, the relationship between events in the life of the man, Jacques Roumain and those of certain of his characters is by no means as clear. There is strong evidence that certain of the actions and circumstances of some of the characters in *La Proie et l'ombre* parallel those of Jacques Roumain or certain of his associates. (pp. 88-9)

If, in *La Proie et l'ombre,* we find the indirect appeal to the sensitivities of the reader typical of poetry, we also find in it the direct appeal to the reader's powers of analysis typical of prose. While the indirect appeal constitutes an invitation to view the hero from within, to react as one with him, the direct appeal leaves us outside, scrutinizing, not only actions and the motivations for them, but also the milieu in which those actions unfold. In Roumain's first prose publication, the storyteller implicit in the novelist vies still with the impressionmaker implicit in the poet. In *Les Fantoches,* published in 1931, the storyteller comes more clearly into his own, creating more fully developed characters, who move in a better delineated environment and who exteriorize their feelings to a much greater extent through conversation. We find the same motifs of light and dark, of gloomy days and monotonous seas, of nocturnal walks and sudden crowds, of mirthless laughter and fruit and peasant women, as in *La Proie et l'ombre.* But it is more the characters and the opinions they enunciate which carry the theme in *Les Fantoches.*

Les Fantoches traces the lives of three young men: Marcel Basquet, *enfant gâté* of Port-au-Prince society; Santiague, the idealistic and dreamy poet; and Lefèvre, a sincere and dedicated politician. Around them circulate a host of secondary characters, the people who make up their milieu: Irène Estienne, Marcel's sweetheart; Michel Rey, whom we recognize from **"Préface à la vie d'un bureaucrate,"** but now older, resigned, and with a somewhat mellowed cynicism; Jeannette Lange, cool and calculating, who collects lovers almost in her husband's presence; Cosquer, the mathematician, who composes riddles on the theme of life; Albert Lecocq, a Frenchman and Marcel's persistent rival for the attentions of Irène; and Mlle Fattu, Irène's old-maid aunt, ever on the lookout for a suitable match for her ward. The story unfolds through a series of tableaux set in the last years of the American Occupation, just before the national legislative elections of October 1930. (p. 91)

We can recognize in *Les Fantoches* essentially the same theme as in *La Proie et l'ombre.* Lefèvre and Santiague state it in the last pages of the final chapter in a conversation where the word *fantoches* is used twice and which seems intended as the key to the whole book. There is, however, an important difference between this and the fiction published the previous year: the "A quoi bon?" of *La Proie et l'ombre* is no longer an answer but a question which a few courageous men muster enough courage to try to answer. (p. 98)

The book ... ends on a more optimistic note than any of the stories of *La Proie et l'ombre.* Marcel, Santiague, and Lefèvre, the principal characters, are the only ones whom we are privileged to glimpse from the inside. Each of the three has a "story" which is in some way resolved at the end: Lefèvre becomes a legislator, Marcel loses Irène, Santiague finds a kind of meaning to existence in befriending Charmantine. Both Marcel and Lefèvre are in conflict, Marcel with himself and Lefèvre with an irrational social system and the irrationality of man, which has spawned it. The poet Santiague has captured through disciplined mental work a kind of visionary equilibrium. He is at a psychological center between the two other men. He is neither happy nor fulfilled; but he is no longer in conflict. But it is Marcel's problem that draws the author's attention. Most of the action involves Marcel, and of the three it is he who must make the most meaningful journey. He is a typical Roumain hero.

Characterization in Roumain's work tends often to be symmetrical or antithetical. The tripartite division of the hero/protagonist in *Les Fantoches* is a case in point. Marcel shares with Santiague a talent for verbal expression. But whereas Santiague becomes absorbed in his writing, Marcel is undisciplined about it and does not believe in what he writes. (pp. 99-100)

Roumain's tendency to pair off opposing characters extends throughout the novel. Lefèvre is at antipodes in every way with his political opponent Marau. Lefèvre is an aristocrat; Marau is a parvenu. Lefèvre appeals to his audience's reason; Marau to its emotions. Lefèvre's motivations are selfless; Marau's are interested. Lefèvre is quiet and restrained; Marau is loud and boisterous.

Of the two writers, Santiague and Michel Rey, one is productive, the other is a failure. And Marcel wanders between these positive and negative poles. He is attracted very strongly to both. He goes from one to the other, and they both deliver exactly the same message to him: to beware of the empty life he is preparing for himself.

Marcel and Jeannette Lange complement each other in that both are cynical, destructive, and false. They seem to need to destroy in order to convince themselves that they exist. And indeed, they exist only as facades. If Mme Lange is hiding poverty and impotence behind the walls of her stately mansion, Marcel is a *poseur,* as he is called more than once in the novel, and more impressed by Pétion's genteel manners than with Christophe's accomplishments for the new nation of Haiti. Both are going on the pre-Occupation steam generated by their aristocratic backgrounds; the message seems to be that they are running on borrowed time.

Les Fantoches shows also certain affinities with the work of the French Decadents. Mme Lange in particular seems to represent the degenerate end of a noble line. Her seduction of Marcel (who is only one of many) betrays her sadistic character; seduction is her way of controlling and manipulating others. Unlike any of the heroes of *La Proie et l'ombre,* Marcel and Mme Lange purposely inflict pain and destruction. Marcel denies his love for Irène; the only way he can feel competent to cope with it is by turning on it. All of his acts are premeditated; blasé and cynical, he fits rather well a description of the decadent . . . . Of course, the parallel is again valid only on the surface: Marcel's decadent symptoms do not serve as a source of strength to him. Rather, they mask a profound inadequacy to cope with the world and with himself.

In the case of the young women, Roumain has set up an opposition in *Les Fantoches* which he does not pursue in the rest of his fiction. Jeannette Lange and Irène Estiènne, both upperclass, well educated, attractive, and intelligent, may have opposing souls, but this type of opposition does not recur in Roumain's female characterization. What does recur is the antithesis between the bourgeois and the peasant women.

These two classes are invariably cast as representatives of the two extremes of Haitian society: the artificial and the natural, the false and the true. Roumain's young intellectuals are thrown into a dilemma: their need for purity and national-racial identity on the one hand, for intellectual stimulation, fulfillment, and understanding on the other, causes them to fluctuate between one and the other pole. The women of the elite accept unquestioningly the life for which they are destined: a round of parties and evenings on the veranda sipping cool drinks, a world where grace, wit, charm and social standing are ultimate goals. Even Irène, for all her sympathy and intelligence, never gives any indication that she is at variance with these ideals. The women are bewildered and perplexed by the men, who are dissatisfied with that existence but can neither articulate nor actualize anything beyond it. These women are not unsympathetic characters; they are simply products of their upbringing,

unquestioning receptacles of the assumptions which rule the society in which they live.

The peasant women are receptacles also, but unlike their European-oriented, upper-class counterparts, they represent the indigenous Haitian. Roumain takes over a device which had existed in Haitian poetry since Oswald Durand, though lately given new life by the generation of 1927, and incorporates it into his fiction: He has his peasant women evoke the native fruits, the free and natural sensuousness and grace of living beings at peace with themselves and their identity. Thus, Charmantine's songs are a long litany of the fruits and streams of the Haitian countryside, and in the nurturing presence of the poet Santiague, they grow as freely and as naturally from her as fruit ripening and falling from a tree. Roumain has a tendency also to describe his peasant women—even the very old ones—in terms of fruits, as . . . with *La Proie et l'ombre.* Such descriptions are much rarer in the case of the young women of the bourgeoisie, who tend to be described more by their mannerisms, their background, their dress. But it is somehow these sophisticated women who emerge as the more credible, the more three-dimensional. The peasant women tend to remain passive, idealized symbols, whereas the bourgeois women act, speak, and *react* to those around them.

The highly developed characterizations in *Les Fantoches* have their beginning far back into the past. Certain characters form a continuity of types. Daniel, Michel Rey, Marcel Basquet are in the main really the same personality but with different names. The hopelessness and despair of each successive character is more elaborately and clearly depicted as those characters acquire more depth under the novelist's pen. We see Michel Rey in youth at his moment of truth, and again, years later, when he has made some sort of compromise with life. His existence clarifies the life ahead for Marcel. That Marcel is a younger edition of Michel is made quite clear in *Les Fantoches* in the beginning chapter where we see the two engaged in conversation at the bar.

Dialogue in Roumain's prose has two functions. Roumain's characters develop certain ideas in such a way that they seem to transmit a covert message to the reader. Roumain makes liberal "borrowings" from his own writing, from theories and experiences that have particularly impressed him or which he is in the process of thinking through. We find, for example, the Aztec god Huitzilopochtli associated in **"Corrida"** with other images of sacrifice. We find the same god called upon by Michel to illustrate the notion that Christianity shares certain essential traits with pagan rites. Years later, the notion of universal religious practices reappears in more thoroughly thought out form, and as revealed through anthropological investigation, in Roumain's pamphlet: *A Propos de la campagne "antisuperstitieuse".* And Jacques Roumain the dialectical materialist discussing history as spiral vs history as vertical motion in 1942 newspaper articles (**"Répliques au Révérend Père Foiset"**) recalls curiously Marcel Basquet in the copy room of the newspaper *Le Soir,* discussing the implacable determinism of nations and the *"parcours cyclique"* of history. In that same scene, Marcel is made to "borrow" the term *conscience raciale* in one of his essays. **"Conscience Raciale"** was the title Roumain had given to an essay on which he was working at the time *Les Fantoches* was published. Whether Roumain intended or not, he has invited the reader of *Les Fantoches* to alternate his attention between fictional circumstances and historical author, and thus have given further validity to discussion concerning the extent to which his works are autobiographical.

All of Roumain's literary efforts seem to be an extension of his own desire to do, his desire to push beyond. We see his own attempts to work out ideas and problems through the "borrowings" of his characters. Roumain's need to estheticize his own experiences in order to give ultimate meaning to his aspirations and his ability to sense the continuity between himself and his society rescue his work most of the time from being mere propaganda. (One might perhaps except most of the writings in *Le Petit Impartial.*) Partly because of this felt continuity between himself and others, partly because of the synthesis Roumain seems to have effected between his various activities and his literary expression, he does not distinguish greatly between what his characters do, feel, or say and what he himself does, feels, or says, or wants to convince others of. This synthetic nature of Roumain's own character is responsible for the inevitable (and by no means unjustified) perplexity on the part of the reader as to whether or not he is reading autobiography, whether certain passages at least may not contain autobiographical allusions, whether certain characters "are" Jacques Roumain.... Roumain's tendency to display his inner life through his characterizations is also responsible for the sermonizing quality of much of the dialogue; the long harangue on Christophe and the discussion near the end of *Les Fantoches* between Santiague and Lefèvre do not escape it.

Despite the more direct and overt presentation of theme through character and dialogue in *Les Fantoches,* motif symbolism still operates in this novel. Motifs are most noticeable in the final chapter. The hero Santiague appears at the beginning of the chapter, alone in a room bent over a table with a lamp providing the only bright arc of light, with the environing dark, and its negative associations, outside. Later in the scene, Lefèvre will look on Santiague's face and see it illuminated in that light. Santiague's lonely nocturnal walks, his sudden immersion in a crowd of common folk just before he stumbled onto Charmantine, and his alienation and recaptured identity through the peasant woman associated with fruits are all present in this last, important chapter.

The obvious symbolism behind the title is presented in several different ways in this last chapter. When Lefèvre comes in, he flops down into a chair, exhausted:

> Son attitude exprimait la plus grande lassitude. Ses bras pendaient des deux côtés du fauteuil comme ceux d'un pantin désarticulé....

> (His attitude expressed the greatest lassitude. His arms hung down both sides of the armchair like those of a disjointed puppet.)

Santiague, speaking of his loneliness, says he peoples it with the insignificant, wretched folk he meets in his noctambulations:

> Ainsi, je meuble ma vie de quelques personages, qu'à certaines heures je fais jouer devant mon imagination désoeuvrée ou pour me distraire de préoccupations importunes.
> Je distribue les rôles à cette petite troupe, j'invente son destin qui s'accomplit au gré de ma fantaisie. Ces fantoches m'amusent comme un Guignol....

> (Thus I people my life with a few characters, which, at certain hours, I parade out in front of my idle imagination or to distract me from harassing preoccupations.
> I distribute roles to this little troupe. I invent its destiny, which is accomplished according to the likings of my fantasy. These puppets amuse me like a Punch and Judy show.)

The reader will tend to identify Santiague, as a result of this speech, as a man whose mental discipline leads him to control rather than be controlled. The author has made us acutely conscious of puppets, and we are prepared for Lefèvre's statement, several pages later: "Vous êtes... le seul parmi nous... qui ne soit pas un fantoche."...(pp. 100-04)

Along with the greater preoccupation with characterization, satire increases. Roumain's gift for incisive commentary manifests itself in *La Proie et l'ombre* and in *Les Fantoches* in his portrayal of bourgeois existence... But there is also biting satire for the black Haitian aspiring to break into the middle class. Santiague remarks of the black politician, Aristide Marau, who speaks Creole to his mesmerized audience, that his father's name is Jean-Baptiste Philidor:

> Il (Marau) habite maintenant le Chemin des Dalles et grimpe lentement vers les hauts quartiers dont il prétend exécrer les riches habitants.... c'est un grimaud qui enrage de ne pouvoir faire sone petit mulâtre....

> (He [Marau] now lives on the Chemin des Dalles and climbs slowly toward the high sections of town, whose rich inhabitants he claims to loathe.... he's an ignoramus enraged at not being able to make his little mulatto baby.)

(pp. 104-05)

But the satire of Haitian modes of existence is most prevalent and most biting in Roumain's portrayal of middle-aged Haitian women of the upper classes. They are the repository of all that Roumain's young men resist—complacent mediocrity, ridiculous ignorance, unwarranted snobbery, fossilized modes of thought. Michel Rey's reaction before his mother-in-law is seen again in Marcel's identical response before the spectacle of his fiancée's aunt. In **"Préface à la vie d'un bureaucrate,"** Mme Ballin is proud of having, as she says, "vaincu l'atavisme." (That is, her features show no trace of her African ancestry.) . . . In *Les Fantoches,* Mlle Fattu has come onto the veranda expecting to find Lecocq, Irène's French suitor. Instead, she finds Marcel, but [is] unable to contain her admiration for Lecocq . . . . These women are faithful reflectors, incapable of independent thought or behavior. If the young women do not exactly show opposition to their set of values, they at least do not press with such determination; they, at least, attempt to understand their men. The dowagers make no such concessions, and Roumain renders them ridiculous.

Les Fantoches hangs together primarily because it maintains the same cast of characters and the same milieu from one chapter to another. But the book is not yet a fully developed novel, and this lack is primarily due to the sparseness of plot. *Les Fantoches* is really a series of scenes, the drama of which revolves around the life of Marcel, Santiague, and Lefèvre. As such, it is a story of love chanced and lost, of personal tranquility, and of public success and failure. But the weakness of the structure lies not so much in the lack of plot as in the fact that we are shifted from the private world of Marcel Basquet to that of the poet Santiague, then to that of Lefèvre. This occurs at the point where Santiague is deeply moved by his encounter with the old general hidden in the attic, and again at the end of the novel, when we enter the private world of Lefèvre for the first time as, moved by the story of Charmantine, he contemplates Santiague and we are allowed to see his thoughts.

There are no such structural defects in the case of *La Montagne ensorcelée,* which, on the contrary, handles admirably such shifts in point of view. Published the same year, and yet so different from *Les Fantoches, La Montagne ensorcelée* is a truly well-written and well-balanced story, with none of the stylistic excesses which, if they revealed a developing talent and an intelligent, well-read young author, had marred *La Proie et l'ombre* and *Les Fantoches.* (pp. 106-08)

> *Carolyn Fowler, in her* A Knot in the Thread: The Life and Work of Jacques Roumain, *Howard University Press, 1980, 383 p.*

Herman F. Bostick (essay date 1983)

[*In the following excerpt, Bostick surveys Roumain's development as a poet.*]

Any attempt to examine critically the poetry of Jacques Roumain will lead inevitably to a study of the life and careers of the man, so very closely are they intertwined. Poet, novelist, journalist, diplomat, politician, and ethnographer, Jacques Roumain succeeded, perhaps, better than any other writer of his generation according

to Roussan Camille, "in achieving by his engaging personality a very rare phenomenon: the complete harmony between life and ideas." The accuracy of Camille's observation becomes increasingly clear as one studies the creative works of Jacques Roumain. (p. 6)

Jacques Roumain's poetry was published in several different literary journals, prominent among which (in Haiti) were *La Trouée, La Revue Indigene, La Presse* and (in France) *Les Volontaires, Regards, Commune* and *Revue Littéraire Francaise pour la défense de la Culture.* Since Roumain did not give the dates of composition of his early poems, it is impossible to establish an accurate chronology for his poetry. Based on themes, tone, language and other stylistic features, Roumain's poetry may be classified as follows: (1) descriptive poems, (2) introspective poems, (3) poems of perseverance and self-sacrifice, (4) negritude poems, and (5) protest poems.

Roumain's descriptive poems are skillfully wrought miniature portraits of selected natural phenomena, such as a storm, a tropical afternoon, falling rain, the noon hour, etc. He uses as titles for most of his descriptive poems the particular phenomena that he will describe in the poems, i.e. **"Midi"** (noon), **"Pluie"** (rain), **"Apres-midi"** (an afternoon), and **"Orage"** (a storm).

Roumain's poem **"Pluie"** is a description of a rainstorm. This word portrait is achieved by use of a succession of audio and visual images. First he describes the rain monotonously strumming against the closed window. "La pluie, monotone dactylo, tapote aux fenêtres closes." Next, he says that the lights give off a shimmering rose glow in the thick darkness. "Des lumières tremblotent roses dans l'obscuritè dense." Giant snake-like streaks of lightning dance across a black sky. "Des éclairs, serpentine géants, dansent tordus à des pan de ciel noir." And finally, night spreads its wet veils over distant gardens where silently weeps the grief of roses that are losing their petals. "La nuit déploie ses voiles de moire sur les lointains jardins où pleure sans bruit le deuil des roses qui s'effeuillent." By the use of carefully selected images of sight and sound and in some cases feeling, Roumain presents in four sentences of varying length a spectacle of "sons et lumières." He compares the patter of rain to the continuous clatter of a typewriter in use. But Roumain subtly gives a degree of musicality to the patter of the rain in using the verb *tapoter* which means "to strum" as on a stringed instrument. To describe the glow of the lights in the thick darkness, he uses the verb *trembloter* which means "to quaver" or "to shiver," thus ascribing to an otherwise visual image audio and animate properties. The assigning of animate characteristics to a visual image is continued in the following line, "Giant snake-like streaks of lightning dance across a black sky." In the final lines of the poem night and roses take on human properties. Night spreads its wet veils over distant gardens and roses weep in sorrow over the loss of their petals.

In his descriptive poetry, Roumain utilizes repeatedly certain words, images, metaphors and other stylistic features which give to his poems a melancholy tone and an aura of gloom. These poems may be described as miniature portraits of varying shades of light and darkness. There is also the repeated use of the words *monotone, silence, silencieux, deuil,* as well as words with the sound *oi (noir, voile, moire, déploie)* considered in French as a dark sound.

While the influences of the French romantic poets are very evident in Roumain's descriptive poetry, unlike the French masters, he does not project himself into his descriptive poems. They are completely devoid of any personal references to the poet himself. And even though they are supposed to belong to the indigenist literary movement in Haiti, there is very little in any of these poems that identify them with that country or with its people.

In his poetry of introspection, Roumain becomes more personal. He is no longer content to paint impressionistic portraits of nature devoid of a personal and human dimension. While he continues to include descriptions of natural phenomena in his poems, they serve more as the setting or stimulus for the expression of his personal hopes, disappointments, anxieties or despair during a deeply troubled period of his life.

In an interview published in the *Revue Indigene,* Roumain described the function of poetry in the following words:

> For me, the poem contains a drama. And this dramatic aspect alone can disengage an emotion. That which one calls artistic emotion and which is only the satisfaction of a thing well said, is not enough for me. I demand more. I want the poem to be a vibrating force, a motor, which shakes.

It will be some time later before Roumain's poems begin to acquire that vibrating force. His poems of introspection are continuations of his descriptive poetry except for the poet's preoccupation with his own suffering. However, it is through these personal lamentations that Roumain as poet begins to emerge.

It is believed by some of Roumain's countrymen that the poet wrote many of his introspective poems while in prison. The titles of these poems (**"Anxiety," "Absence," "Darkness," "Mirage," "Insomnia"**) and their contents seem to support that belief. His introspective poems are short lamentations of one who is down but not out, who dares to cry if only in agony and despair.

> Hors
> Un homme courbé sur ses désirs morts
> je nu suis plus rien...
>
> (Save a man burdened down with his dead
>   dreams,
> I am no longer anything...)
>   **("Calme")**

In his poem, **"Insomnia,"** which is one of the poems believed to have been written in prison, Roumain presents a graphic picture of his physical isolation and his mental anguish. Using the poet's conception of a poem as a drama, one can identify in **"Insomnia"** the following scenes: (1) the decor or setting, (2) the protagonist's physical and mental suffering, (3) the protagonist's struggle for life and hope. In the opening scene, night descends upon the room like a black veil embroidered with stars. "La nuit entre dans la chambre, sombre voile brodé de'étoiles." The moon resembling a huge fruit teeters in his insomnia. "La lune est un gros fruit se balancant à mon insomnie." The nightingales of Hafiz are silent. "Les rossignols de Hafix sont morts." In scene two, the poet describes how the physical surroundings of isolation, silence, and darkness affect the protagonist. The silence appears to have a bluish hue. "Silence bleuâtre." The night seems endless and each hour drags on like a monotonous litany. "Nuit interminable. Chaque heure s'étire monotone comme une litanie." In the final scene, the protagonist describes his struggle to overcome his present state.

> I lean outside of myself to listen to a voice tenuous and sad like perfume. I am afraid of sleep. I want to think about my suffering and cradle myself in it as with a song. I stretch my hands toward you and I clutch the sky—and emptiness.

The act of stretching the hand or arms outward or leaning to grasp the stars or the sky may indicate the influence of existentialism upon Roumain's poetry. At the point in the poem when it appears that the protagonist will be crushed under the weight of his burden, he summons forth sufficient physical strength to act. It is this simple human act that sustains him and provides a ray of hope.

Between 1928 and 1930, Roumain wrote a small group of poems that differ significantly in theme, length and other stylistic features from his earlier poetry. In each of these poems, the poet introduces a sacrificial hero figure with whom he apparently identifies. In his poem, **"La Danse du poète-clown,"** the clown leaps into the ring and even though sad of heart and overcome with fever does a dazzling dance of whirls until his feet drag and his muscles snap. It is a dance to death. In his poem **"Cent Mètres,"** four runners enter a hundred yard dash race in which each one pushes himself beyond physical endurance in his effort to win. Roumain succeeds in **"Cent Metres"** in transforming a common athletic sport into a life and death drama. About this poem, he once explained:

> In **"Cent Mètres,"** I did not want to paint a picture, I am not a painter. I wanted to give life to what I had known. The fever. The delirious impressions. And the anxiety. To show the sorrowful depth of this drama of the track. The drama of nerves and muscles. From the time when the runners are crouched on their mark to the minute when they break the white ribbon which will make one of them a fine scarf.

The theme of the sacrificial hero is presented in three other of Roumain's poems, namely: **"Corrida"** (Bullfight), **"Le Chant de l'homme"** (Song of Man), and **"Appel"** (Appeal). In each poem, the central figure is required to go the proverbial "last mile." The hero suffers intensely and may even die in the end, but his suffering and death become redemptive acts. The quotation, "O Agni! toi qui flambes dans le sang du danseur éperdu!" used as a suprascript to **"La Danse du poète-clown"** announces the hero-martyr theme and further supports it.

During the years 1930-33, Jacques Roumain published his first negritude poems. Four in number, they bore the following titles: **"Sur le Chemin de Guinée"** (On the Road to Guinea), **"Quand bat le tam-tam"** (When the Tom-Tom Beats), **"Creole,"** and **"Langston Hughes."** In these poems, Roumain reverses the meaning of many of the images and symbols used in his early poetry. For example, night, darkness, rain, wind, river no longer symbolize the obscure, destructive, and/or unfathomable. But rather they now bespeak a sympathetic and positive cosmos of which the black poet, and by extension the black race, form an integral and necessary part of it. Similarly, symbols of whiteness will no longer represent purity, cleanness and beauty. In **"Quand bat le tam-tam"** the poet says,

> Your soul is the reflection in the murmuring
> waters
> where your fathers bent their dark faces.
> And the white man who made you a mulatto, it is
> this
> bit of scum, like spit, on the shore.

Here Roumain may be rejecting his French ancestry since he himself was a mulatto in the fullest sense of that term.

Roumain had been introduced to the poetry of Langston Hughes both in Europe and in Haiti before he met this Afro-American poet. He was deeply moved by this black poet from the United States who sang about black peoples. It is not surprising then that Roumain in his poem entitled **"Langston Hughes"** would highlight the common ancestral heritage of the black diaspora through the portrayal of a black male who savors the pleasures of women of easy virtues in Lagos, Dakar, Paris and Venice. The escapade of this traveler ends during the early morning hours in a cabaret in Paris as he calls out presumably to a black musician,

> Jouez se blues pou'moa
> O jouez ce blues pou'moa
>
> (Play those blues for me
> O play those blues for me)

("Langston Hughes")

Roumain ends the poem with the telling question, "Are you dreaming of the palm trees and songs of black paddlers in the dusk?"

The protagonist in **"Langston Hughes"** first rejects white American culture by refusing to mouth the familiar historical expression, "Lafayette, here we are!", usually said by white Americans upon arriving in Paris. But on the other hand, he affirms his African heritage by stating that the Seine River appears less beautiful to him than the Congo.

Roumain even tries to imitate the language, images, and rhythms of Langston Hughes' own poetry in his poem. There is the relaxed atmosphere of the cabaret, the casualness of the world traveler who knows his way with women of pleasure. He even attempts to reproduce the special way the Black American pronounces French by use of the clipped phrase "pou'moa." Roumain identifies with the protagonist in this poem (who is obviously meant to be Langston Hughes) by his use of the pronoun *tu* which in French expresses kinship or intimate friendship:

> *Tu* connus à Lagos ces filles
> Mélancoliques
> *Tu* vis la France...
> Tu as promené ton coeur nomad...
> de Harlem à Dakar

It should be borne in mind when reading Roumain's negritude poetry, that he never visited Africa. Therefore, the Africa he describes is the product of his creative imagination. His poem **"Sur le Chemin de Guinée"** is based on the belief reputed to have been held by some African slaves that said that when they died their souls would return to Guinea (Africa).

> It's the long road to Guinea
> Death will lead you there
> Here are the branches, the trees, the forest,
> Listen to the sound of the wind
> in its long strands of eternal night...
>
> It's the long road to Guinea
> Your fathers are patiently waiting for you
> on the way; they are talking.
> They are expecting you.
> Here are the boughs, the trees, the forest;
> Like a rosary of bones
> It's the long road to Guinea.
>
> No brilliant welcome will be made for you
> In the black country of black men
> Under a smoky sky pierced by the call of birds
> Around the eye of a tropical lake
> Eyelashes of trees open on decaying light
> There awaits you on the bank of the waters a
> peaceful village and the hut of your
> fathers and the hard ancestral stone
> where you will rest at last your head.

Of Roumain's negritude poetry, Jacob Drachler, author of *African Heritage* writes:

> In this poetry Africa appears as a lost paradise, an idyll of a vaguely remembered youth, where the self was undivided and unharnessed by the subsequent pervasive surveillance of a civilization alien to the poet's origins and his inspiration. It is important to realize that it is not an Africa geographically fixed and determined that is most significant

here ... Africa emerges from this poetry as a symbol of man in his pristine integrity, at one with himself and his world, a part of all he surveys.

In 1932, Jacques Roumain became disenchanted with the National Government of Haiti in which he held a position. He resigned his post and dedicated himself to organizing a Communist Party in Haiti. It was during this period that he came to the United States where he visited New York and Washington, D. C. While in New York, he met several of the celebrated figures of the Harlem Renaissance. But it seemed that the main purpose of his visit was to consult with officials of the Communist Party in the United States. His open espousal of Communism in Haiti led to his arrest, imprisonment and self-exposed exile in Europe.

It was during this period of exile in Europe that Roumain wrote his militant poetry. This corpus of revolutionary poetry consists of only three fairly long poems entitled: **"Bois d'ébenè"** (Ebony Wood), **"Nouveau Sermon Nègre"** (A New Black Sermon), and **"Sales Nègres"** (Dirty Blacks). These poems were first published in Europe. After Roumain's death, they were published in a single volume by his widow under the title, *Bois d'ébenè* (Ebony Wood) which is a metaphor for black men in the prime of life. The poem **"Bois d'ébenè"** is an epic which describes: (1) the secular history of the black race; and (2) the hope of the poet for black people and for the proletariat. Roumain begins **"Bois d'ébenè"** by addressing the black race.

> Black peddler of revolt
> You have known all the world's road
> Since you were sold in Africa ....
> ....
> ....
> But I know
> about the shrouds of silence on the branches
> of the cypress trees
> about petals of black clots of blood on
> blackberry bushes
> about those woods where they lynched
> my Georgia brother and the shepherd
> from Abyssinia

From this beginning in which he champions the black man's cause, Roumain moves to speak on behalf of the poet, the downtrodden everywhere without distinction of race:

> I want only to be your race
> workers, peasants in every country
> ....
> As the obstacles of physical features
> resolve themselves in the harmony of the face
> We proclaim unity in suffering and
> in revolt among all peoples on the
> entire face of the earth.

In **"Sales Negres"** Roumain declares that blacks will no longer accept a status of servitude vis-a-vis whites. In some of the most violent language to be found in French poetry, Jacques Roumain flings his revolt in the face of his white oppressors.

> Finished
> being in America
> Your negroes
> your blacks
> your dirty blacks
> For we have chosen our day
> We are on our feet
> All the damned of the earth
> All the justice seekers
> Moving on the attack ...
> To be done
> Once and for all
> With this world
> of negroes
> of blacks
> of dirty blacks

The poem **"A New Black Sermon"** is considered Roumain's most communistic poem in terms of its message. This poem may be divided into two parts. In part one, the poet exposes how the Church has degraded and disfigured the Christ who is presented here as black.

> They spat on your face
> Lord, our friend, our comrade
> ....
> They whitened His black face with spit
> of their cold contempt

Of the established church Roumain says:

> ... But today Christ is in the den of thieves and
> His arms stretched out in cathedrals
> shadow of the vulture.
> And in the basement of monasteries priests
> count the interests on thirty pieces of silver
> and the church's bell towers spit death on
> the hungry multitudes.

In part two of **"A New Black Sermon,"** Roumain presents his antidote to this scandalous state of affairs. First, he announces, "We will not forgive them, for they know what they do." He continues by enumerating other things that they will no longer do.

> No brothers, comrades
> We will pray no more
> We will sing the sad and hopeless
> spirituals no more.

This repetition of negatives intensifies the poet's announcement of what will be done to change the intolerable status quo.

> Another song rises from our throats
> We unfurl our red flag
> Stained with the blood of our people
> Under this banner we shall march
> Under this banner we are marching
> Arise wretched of the earth
> Arise prisoners of hunger ...

Roumain's protest poetry shows an angry Jacques Roumain. Gone are the dark and foreboding images of his descriptive poetry. Gone also are the sorrowful and vacillating cries of suffering expressed in his introspective poetry. They have been replaced by a strident denunciation of the status quo and an aggressive call to action to bring about a new social order based on freedom and international brotherhood. It is in his protest poetry that the life and goal of Roumain the poet and Roumain the political activist finally converge. Though militant, the poems of ***Bois d'ébenè*** are essentially optimistic. While he condemns the evil and corrupt, and calls for its destruction, he also challenges those who would join his cause in the words:

> We will rebuild . . .
> White worker of Detroit black sharecropper of
>   Alabama
> Countless multitudes in capitalistic enslavement
> Destiny places us shoulder to shoulder and by
> renouncing the antiquated evil of racial taboos
> We crush the debris of our isolation.

Shakespeare wrote, "The evil that men do lives after them,/The good is oft interred with their bones," The impact of Roumain's political activism in effecting a new day for the masses in Haiti virtually ended the day of his untimely death. It is his novels and poetry that have kept his memory alive. As Carolyn Fowler aptly states in her book, *A Knot in the Thread:*

> And if his socialist activism in Haiti may now, forty years later, be viewed with detached admiration, it is nonetheless true that such activism virtually disappeared with him . . . it is the field of literature which can most comfortably claim him as its own.

(pp. 7-14)

Herman F. Bostick, "From Romanticism to Militant Optimism: The Poetic Quest of Jacques Roumain," in The Langston Hughes Review, *Vol. II, No. 2, Fall, 1983, pp. 6-14.*

FURTHER READING

Bostick, Herman F. "Toward Literary Freedom: A Study of Contemporary Haitian Literature." *Phylon* XVII, No. 3 (Third Quarter 1956): 250-56.
   Cites Roumain as the single greatest influence on modern Haitian literature and culture.

Bradley, Francine. "Political Prisoners in Haiti." *The New Republic* LXXXII, No. 1060 (27 March 1937): 189.
   Letter written by the secretary of the Committee for the Release of Jacques Roumain urging readers to send letters of protest to help win Roumain's release from prison.

Clark, VèVè A. "Divine Metaphors of Order and Rage, A Manual for Joy: Jacques Roumain's *Gouverneurs de la rosée." Perspectives on Contemporary Literature* 10 (1984): 40-8.
   Close study of *Masters of the Dew,* focusing on two of its "central themes": order and rage.

Cobb, Martha K. "Concepts of Blackness in the Poetry of Nicolas Guillén, Jacques Roumain, and Langston Hughes." *CLA Journal* XVIII, No. 2 (December 1974): 262-72.
   Links Nicolas Guillén, Roumain, and Langston Hughes through common theme in their poetry.

Cook, Mercer. "The Haitian Novel." *The French Review* XIX, No. 6 (May 1946): 406-12.
   Examines the causes and results of the Haitian literary renaissance, describing *Masters of the Dew* as one of the most significant novels to appear in Haiti between 1939 and 1945.

Coulthard, G. R. *Race and Colour in Caribbean Literature,* pp. 39ff. London: Oxford University Press, 1962.
   Contains scattered discussions of Roumain's poetry and fiction.

Dash, J. M. "The Peasant Novel in Haiti." *African Literature Today,* No. 9 (1978): 77-90.
   Examines Roumain's fiction as a representative expression of the problems of the Haitian urban elite and the uniqueness of the indigenous peasantry.

————. "Jacques Roumain: The Marxist Counterpoint." In his *Literature and Ideology in Haiti, 1915-1961,* pp. 129-55. New York: Barnes & Noble, 1981.
   Examines shades of Marxism and Romanticism in Roumain's fiction, poetry, and ideological essays.

Dixon, Melvin. "Toward a World Black Literature and Community." *The Massachusetts Review* XVIII, No. 4 (Winter 1977): 750-69.
   Compares Roumain's *Masters of the Dew* with Claude McKay's *Banjo.*

Fowler, Carolyn. "Motif Symbolism in Jacques Roumain's *Gouverneurs de la rosée." CLA Journal* XVIII, No. 1 (September 1974): 44-51.
   Discusses *Masters of the Dew,* focusing on symbolism and recurring motifs.

————. "The Shared Vision of Langston Hughes and Jacques Roumain." *Black American Literature Forum* 15, No. 3 (Fall 1981): 84-8.
   Argues that Langston Hughes and Roumain shared "a vision of the function of art as the articulation of a people's condition, as a reflection of the culture which that people develops to cope creatively and to express their hope for the fulfillment of universal human aspirations."

Jahn, Janheinz. "'Indigenism' and 'Negrism'." In his *Neo-African Literature,* translated by Oliver Coburn and Ursula Lehrburger, pp. 214-38. New York: Grove Press, 1968.
   Compares the folklorist themes of Roumain's early poetry to his later poems.

Sonia Sanchez

1934-

(Born Wilsonia Benita Driver) American poet, playwright, author of children's books, short story writer, essayist and educator.

One of the major voices of black nationalism—the cultural revolution of the 1960s in which many black Americans sought an identity distinct from that of the white establishment—Sanchez is known for strong, idiomatic verse that mirrors her perception of black experience in America. In most of her works, including collections of poetry and stories for children, she presents positive role models and often harshly realistic situations in an effort to inspire her readers to improve their lives. Her use of idiomatic language, obscenities, and such verbal games as "the dozens" reflects urban, black English and lends a powerful edge to her works. She commented: "I write to tell the truth about the Black condition as I see it. Therefore I write to offer a Black woman's view of the world. How I tell the truth is a part of the truth itself.... What I learned in deciding 'how' to write was simply that most folks tend to think that you're lying or jiving them if you have to spice things up to get a point across. I decided along with a number of other Black poets to tell the truth in poetry by using the language, dialect, idioms, of the folks we believed our audience to be."

Born in Birmingham, Alabama, Sanchez was a shy child who rarely spoke because of a stutter. Her mother died when Sanchez was only a year old, and she was alternately raised by her grandmother and her father, who remarried several times. The defiant women in her family—one of whom Sanchez watched spit in the face of a driver who asked her to leave a bus because of her race—impressed upon the author at a young age the inner strength of blacks. In 1943 she moved with her father, Wilson L. Driver, to Harlem. Driver, a musician, took Sanchez to hear such prominent jazz artists as Billie Holiday, Billy Eckstine, and Art Tatum. After graduating from Hunter College, Sanchez studied creative writing under Louise Bogan, whose interest in the young poet encouraged her to pursue a literary career. Along with Haki R. Madhubuti (Don L. Lee) and others, Sanchez established a weekly writers' group that gave public readings. She soon began publishing poetry in small magazines and later in black periodicals. Committed to the black liberation movement of the 1960s, she supported the Congress of Racial Equality and was instrumental in establishing one of the first university-level black studies programs in the United States.

In her first two volumes of poetry, *Homecoming* (1969) and *We a BaddDDD People* (1970), Sanchez introduced themes to which she would return throughout her career: drug abuse in the black community, interracial relationships, and the importance of such role models as

Malcolm X, Nina Simone, and John Coltrane. Sanchez attributes her own personal and poetic development to these figures, too; her sharply punctuated and rhythmic early verse has been compared with the innovative improvisation of Coltrane, and she has credited Malcolm X with influencing her use of language. Sanchez commented: "A lot of our words and language came from Malcolm. He was always messing with the language and messing with people, and sometimes in a very sly kind of way demanding things of people and also cursing people out." Sanchez's poetry often deviates from Standard English, conforming instead to black speech patterns. By inserting extra letters in some words, dividing syllables by slashes, and breaking phrases into short lines, she provides dramatic accents and other clues that indicate how the poem should sound when read aloud.

Sanchez has long been interested in presenting her works before live audiences. She has given readings in Cuba, China, the West Indies, Europe, and on more than five hundred campuses in the United States. Of her popularity, Kalamu ya Salaam stated: "Sanchez developed techniques for reading her poetry that were unique in their use of traditional chants and near-screams drawn out to an almost earsplitting level. The sound elements, which give a musical quality to the intellectual statements in the poetry, are akin to Western African languages; Sanchez has tried to recapture a style of delivery that she felt had been muted by the experience of slavery. In her successful experimentation with such techniques, she joined . . . others in being innovative enough to bring black poetry to black people at a level that was accessible to the masses as well as enjoyable for them."

Sanchez was a member of Elijah Muhammad's Nation of Islam from 1972 to 1975. She stated that she joined the group because she wanted her children to see an "organization that was trying to deal with the concepts of nationhood, morality, small businesses, schools. . . . And these things were very important to me." While a member of the Nation, Sanchez continued to give public readings and voice her opinions about the direction of the organization. Some of her ideas, however, conflicted with those of the organization, which viewed women's roles as secondary to men's, and Sanchez left the Nation after three years. *A Blues Book for Blue Black Magical Women* (1973) and several poems in *Love Poems* (1973) were composed during this time and reveal a strong commitment to family and support for the black man.

A Blues Book for Blue Black Magical Women, which has been called "a spiritual autobiography," follows one woman's consciousness as she ages and explores her personal and social position within a black muslim community. The volume reveals what it is like to be female in a society that, according to Sanchez, "does not prepare young black women, or women period, to be women"; it also tells about the author's political involvements before and after her commitment to ethnic pride. While much of Sanchez's poetry is autobiographical in nature, critics have noted that she extends her personal experience to encompass that of all black people. Sanchez commented: "We must move past always focusing on the 'personal self' because there's a larger self. There's a 'self' of black people. And many of us will have to make a sacrifice in our lives to ensure that our bigger self continues." *Love Poems* contains many of the haiku Sanchez wrote during a particularly stressful period in her life. She embraced haiku as a powerful medium that allowed her to "compress a lot of emotion" into a few lines, as well as to express her increased interest in Eastern cultures. David Williams noted that the "haiku in [Sanchez's] hands is the ultimate in activist poetry, as abrupt and as final as a fist."

Although primarily recognized as a poet, Sanchez has also enjoyed success as a playwright and as a children's author. Many of her plays address the role of women in the black liberation movement, which often restricted women's activity to supporting black men, and such

dramas as *Sister Son/ji* (1969) and *Uh Huh; But How Do It Free Us?* (1974) have been identified as precursors of black feminist awareness.

Two of Sanchez's most recent volumes of poetry, the American Book Award winner *homegirls & handgrenades* (1984) and *Under a Soprano Sky* (1987), received overwhelming praise, with many commentators claiming that the poet had matured personally and stylistically without losing her political fervor. Her focus in many poems turned to drug addiction, homelessness, and loneliness, celebrating, according to Sanchez, "some homegirls and homeboys . . . who needed to be celebrated but never came through the Harlems of the world." Kamili Anderson wrote of her later style: "Sanchez has a penchant for enlisting words to imagery. She can mesmerize with scenarios that require readers to transfuse all of their senses, so much so that the ability to discern whether one is reading with the soul or with the eyes, or listening with the heart or the ears, is lost."

(For further information about Sanchez's life and works, see *Black Writers; Contemporary Authors,* Vols. 33-36; *Contemporary Authors New Revision Series,* Vol. 24; *Contemporary Literary Criticism,* Vol. 5; *Dictionary of Literary Biography,* Vol. 41; *Afro-American Poets since 1955; Dictionary of Literary Biography Documentary Series,* Vol. 8: *The Black Aesthetic Movement;* and *Major 20th-Century Writers.*)

PRINCIPAL WORKS

The Bronx is Next (drama) 1968; published in periodical *The Drama Review;* also published in *Cavalcade: Negro American Writing from 1760 to the Present,* 1971

Homecoming (poetry) 1969

Sister Son/ji (drama) 1969; published in *New Plays from the Black Theatre,* 1969

We a BaddDDD People (poetry) 1970

It's A New Day (poems for young brothas and sistuhs) (poetry) 1971

three hundred and sixty degrees of blackness comin at you: An Anthology of the Sonia Sanchez Writers' Workshop at Countee Cullen Library in Harlem [editor] (poetry) 1971

The Adventures of Fathead, Smallhead, and Squarehead (children's stories) 1973

A Blues Book for Blue Black Magical Women (poetry) 1973

Dirty Hearts (drama) 1973; published in *Breakout: In Search of New Theatrical Environments*

Love Poems (poetry) 1973

Uh Huh; But How Do It Free Us? (drama) 1974; published in *The New Lafayette Theatre Presents: Plays with Aesthetic Comments by Six Black Poets*

I've Been a Woman: New and Selected Poems (poetry) 1978

A Sound Investment and Other Stories (children's stories) 1980

Crisis in Culture: Two Speeches by Sonia Sanchez (speeches) 1983
homegirls & handgrenades (poetry) 1984
Under a Soprano Sky (poetry) 1987

Sebastian Clarke (essay date 1971)

[*In the following excerpt, Clarke discusses themes in* Homecoming *and* We a BaddDDD People.]

We are witnesses in an epoch where Black people all over the world are attempting to transform the legacy of the domination of "the economic mind over the imaginative", to destroy a history of submittance to a people of murderous rationalities and dispositions. The ramifications of these actions are that all segments of the Black population, whatever their profession might be, have to be utilized and given a function.

It is this *function* as it applies to art that should be examined in the works of the so-called Black artists. A great number of writers and poets have become victims to a deadened white philosophy: "art for art's sake", meaning that art has no function except that of "entertainment". The question is immediately raised as to the *meaning,* in terms of people's lives, of this "entertainment": is it merely to be *entertained* that we spend most of our lives running to and from the movie and theatre houses, the museums, etc., perpetually chained to the magic sounds of music?

I propose it is because man wants to be more than himself, he wants to transcend his individual, single "I", to relate it to the "we" of the community. It is for identification, meaning, illumination of the significance of his life that he seeks. It is not simply out of some insane and incomprehensible urge for "aesthetic" satisfaction/gratification, the appeasing of the senses, which is really the "low point" of all art, but for a fuller understanding of the nature of his life as man, as a human being, in relation to a larger world, outside and beyond himself.

It is for these profound reasons, as well as for a greater measure of political consciousness and control, that the present generation of Black writers and poets have begun to address their creations to the Black community. The white community does not reflect or represent their minds' idea of life; the very nature of their (whites') lives and their philosophical understanding of the world demonstrate their glorification of murder and death, and propose, further, the complete antithesis to the life-styles Black people *desire* to erect as monuments for their progeny. "We want life. We want to live", says a character in Imamu Baraka's play. The very foundation of Black writers' and poets' philosophy and motivation for a literature of commitment rests on their desire for a larger measure and quality of life, i.e., living.

Sonia Sanchez reflects this consciousness in her poetry. In fact, her very life-style is perpetually proposed as a link to the ideals and realisation of *blackness* which so profoundly pervades her work. She has said: "I think the prime thing with art, or being a writer, be it a playwright, a poet, or even a musician, etc., is to really show people what is happening in this country. And then show them they can change it". Her poem, **"the final solution"**, demonstrates the significance of her statements:

> . . . we the
> lead/ers of free
>   a/mer/ica
> say. give us your
>   hungry/
>   illiterates/
>   criminals/
>   dropouts/
>   (in other words)
>   your blacks
>   and we will
> let them fight
>   in vietnam
>   defending america's honor.
> we will make responsible
>   citi/
>   zens out of them or
>   kill them trying.

These are real, not imaginary, questions that the poet is preoccupied with. Her work, to a large extent, is centered on five principal levels of concern: (a) the white-woman-black man relationship; (b) Black man-woman relationship; (c) dope, as a reflection of one level of death; (d) politics and (e) loneliness and suicide, the introspection of self, the flight inwards, away from a world that is ever-menacing and cruel. These concerns, with the possible exception of loneliness and suicide, are more or less a reflection of the concerns of the other Black poets: Don L. Lee, Sterling Plumpe, Nikki Giovanni, Imamu Baraka and company. This significantly reflects Baraka's assertion that "the nation is our selves . . . whatever we are doing/is what the nation/is/doing/or/not doing". Immediately this unified preoccupation with specific themes has ramified meanings—that there is a related level of thought, of thinking, among the Black writers and poets of this generation which positively denies the historical "alienation" of writers, "artists", from their society, leaving that question of "alienation" to the rotting white Western mind, over-fed and comfortable.

As a contrast to her "politicalness", on a more intimate and personal level, Sonia sings:

> no sleep tonight
> not even after all
> the red and green pills
> I have pumped into
> my stuttering self or
> the sweet wine
> that drowns them.
>
>   this is
> a poem for the world

for the slow suicides
in seclusion.
somewhere on 130th st.
a woman, frail as a
child's ghost, sings.

It is the poetry of self's weakness, of the limitation of the
single self to transcend despair...

is everybody happy?
this is a poem for me.
i am alone.
one night of words
will not change
all that.

Commenting on that complex and controversial subject,
the Black man who emotionally relates to the white
woman because of the lack of pressure on his life, rather
than have any relationship with the Black woman, she
said:

It's a constant change. It's a constant struggle (. . .)
trying to be Black. And I think the brothers who have
really copped-out with white women have to answer
on the level of 'I can't find no sister'. Five years ago
I'd hear brothers say: 'I'm digging on a white chick,
cause there ain't no sister for me, sister'. I'd say:
'Well, man, I see a lot of sisters out here. And it
might require a little work'. I mean all relationships
be requiring work. You're not going to get somebody
who's completely perfect. But the white chick is a
sick chick, because she has no man. She turns to the
Black man, not because he is a very *heavy* man, but
more like a sexual object. She probably comes when
she sees him, or the idea of going to bed with him
upsets her so much, sexually. So it's an abnormal
relationship. They have pushed the Black man
around and say: 'We gon let you be a man'. But the
white woman keeps him in a very infantile kind of
situation. That's not a mature relationship between a
man and a woman. *You are responsible for each
other's actions.*

In both her books, *Homecoming,* and *We A BaddDDD
People* (both published by Broadside Press), there is a
continuous, but not monotonous, repetition of the
themes I have outlined. She has, consequently, been
accused of "creative unoriginality" and unable to attain
a "higher" level of "art". I maintain that the preoccupation with certain themes in the works of all "artists", be
they writers, painters, poets or musicians, is a reflection
of the constant preoccupation with Life, reality; it (the
art of repetition) is a rhythm in itself of "radial
synthesis" where each stress, emphasis, repetition is an
amplification of all that has become growth in us.
Rhythm, being the basis of Black Art, with meaning, the
most recognizable feature of the product, "at the root of
the struggle of Life between Death, being and nothing,
time and eternity", according to Father Mveng. Each
repetition reveals that human experience "is not a sum
of identical succeeding instants, but a totalization, in the
present, of all that has become growth in us."

To further illuminate this we can refer to Sonia's own
words:

Someone said to me recently, 'Well, you can't always
be talking about white-ness'. I said, 'Well, I might be
aware of white-ness. I might not have to be constantly talking about it. But I do get up every morning and
say we have an enemy, and that enemy is a cracker.
So I think we can't ever forget that we must
concentrate on blackness and liberation. We are
liberating ourselves from the oppressor, and the
oppressor is a cracker, is a devil, is a pig, which be
meaning that we always have to be aware of the
enemy. We can't just ignore him and let him go his
merry way, you know, because he's a very dangerous
mother. So we have to repeat them things all the
time'.

In the poem **"blk/chant"**, she says:

Yes, brothas and sistuhs.
          repeat every day
(as u reach
          for that scag
               reefers
                    wine
that send u spinnen into witeness
forgetten yo / blackness.)
          we programmed
fo death
          then may be we'll
begin to believe it.
          (that is
               if we still got time)
               u dig?

This same theme is repeated, but on a different level
and with a different sense of consciousness:

once i had a maaan
who loved me so he sed
we lived togetha, loved togetha
and i followed wherever he led

now this maaan of mine
got tired of this sloow pace
started gitten high a lot
to stay on top of the race

saw him begin to die
screeaamed. held him so tight
but he got so thin so very thin
slipped thru these fingers of might

last time i heard from him
he was bangen on a woman's door
callen for his daily high
didn't even care bout the score.

once i loooved a man
still do looove that man
want to looove that man again
wish he'd come on home again

need to be with that maaannn
need to love that maaaannnn
who went out one day & died
who went out one day & died.

There is also the nationalist/political strain that is a
constant theme of repetition in her poetry. Not only
does this consciousness reflect the "kill the honky"
preoccupation, but it questions the validity of Blacks
themselves who are supposed to be involved with
proposing the alternative to white insanity and death. In

fact, this theme reveals itself to be her present preoccupation. It moves away from the constant attacks on white society, to a dialogue with Black people, questioning the validity of their words in relation to their concrete lives, as lived, in motion.

```
          who's gonna make all
          that beautiful blk / rhetoric
          mean something.
                              like
          i mean
               who's gonna take
          the words
                    blk/is/beautiful
          and make more of it
          than blk/capitalism.
                         u dig?
          i mean
               like who's gonna
          take all the young/long/haired
          natural/brothers and sisters
          and let them
               grow till
                    all that is
          impt is them
                    selves
                         moving in straight/
          revolutionary/lines
                         toward the enemy
          (and we know who that is)
               like. man.
          who's gonna give our young
          blk/ people new heroes
               (instead of catch/ phrases)
               (instead of cad/ill/acs)
               (instead of pimps)
               (instead of white/whores) . . . etc.
```

(pp. 253-59)

Sonia is also very much concerned with the (white) woman liberation movement and its subversive relationship to Black women. Recently she said to me:

> One of the things a (black) woman can do without is trying to be a liberated white woman like they trying to do with this liberation thing. Black women have always had talents and Black people have always accepted the talents. Black men didn't think it emasculated them. Read *The Role Of The Muslim Woman In War*! I mean women had fought, just picked up guns and fought when their men had fallen. I think, finally, someone would have to come up and say: 'Look, there ain't woman's role as such, other than loving her man, respecting her King, raising them kids, and if she has a special talent, being able to use that special talent within the context of the nation'. It has nothing to do with anything else. But we get so messed up, cause at the core comes this woman liberation thing, and they tell you how oppressed you be. Black women ain't oppressed, it is Black people who be oppressed.

The ordering of the role the Black woman can play, as designated by Sonia, corresponds to the philosophy of the Bantu in relation to the three phases of evolution as Man as complete Man. First, she accepts that she is woman, the feminine dimension, which is an acceptation of the first principle—man, *Monad*, revealed in his masculinity; the second principle in man's evolution to becoming *humanised*, towards becoming a person, is revealed in woman, *Dyad*, fecundity; Man is now responsible to the other, but is not freedom, and is incomplete without *Triad*, child, i.e., without becoming mother. The complete cycle is Man-Woman-Child. These principles as designated by the Bantu, as unconsciously designated by Sonia, reveal the extent and degree to which the depth of an African sensibility still pervades her consciousness despite the severance from her native Africa for over four hundred years. This philosophy is essentially the key towards achieving harmony and unity within the Black family.

In terms of the stylistic quality of her writing, it is incontestable that she is one of the forerunners of the New Breed. The language and rhythm of her poetry reflect the language and speech-rhythm of Black people—revealing her most pristine desire as that of maximum communication to her audience in a language that they are not foreign to. One white critic said that the "young" Black writers are fakes because they use "word-acrobatics" in their writing. But the vibrations of Black people would have manifested themselves adversely if the "fakery" of these poets was a reality since the Black poets function within and for the Black community. Black people are a vibratory, emotional and all-feeling people, they are moved very much by their feeling-being. So that the rhetoric of this white critic has no foundation or relevance to the feelings of the Black poets' audience. In fact, the style, the writing style, of these Black poets is not unique or original—it is a very old form that has its tradition in white writers like William Carlos Williams and Lawrence Ferlinghetti. The *innovative difference* is that the style is transformed, is given creative life, by the uniqueness of the content of these poets' creations. It is much more relevant in terms of the specific reference to the lifestyles of Black people.

In terms of the negativism or positivism of Sonia's work there is one thing that is certain—that nowhere in her poetry is there a question of "identity" posed in any form. Sonia Sanchez has transcended that, and so have most of the other writers and poets of this generation; it has never been a question of a theme in her poetry. Hers is more significant and profound—like the releasing of the *id*, the demon of new Black Magic. It is a poetry of destiny, a declaration of self-determination, Black people are intrinsically being separated in their philosophy and essentially in their sensibility, as a nation, from the murderous, masochistic and decadent society that is called White America.

An alternative has been posed, a vision of a new society in its embryonic stages veering towards restoration to its traditional greatness, and a new generation will arrive and continue the work initiated by Imamu Baraka, Sonia Sanchez and the other Black writers and poets. (pp. 260-61)

Sebastian Clarke, "Black Magic Woman: Sonia Sanchez and Her Work," in Présence Africaine, *No. 78, Spring, 1971, pp. 253-61.*

George E. Kent (essay date 1975)

[*In the excerpt below, Kent, an American educator and nonfiction writer, reviews* A Blues Book for Blue Black Magical Women.]

Sonia Sanchez's latest book, *A Blues Book for Blue Black Magical Women*, possesses an extraordinary culmination of spiritual and poetic powers. It is in part an exhortation to move the rhythms of black life to a high peak through deep and deeper self-possession; in part an address to all, with specific emphasis upon women; in part, a spiritual autobiography. Actually, one gets trapped in rhetoric; the separate strands entwine themselves together and are pervasive, for the most part. The book consists of five parts: Part I, urging women to move out of false paths created by racism into the queenly existence of self-possession, purpose, direction; Part II, describing autobiographically Sonia's own psychological and spiritual evolution in the past; Part III, focusing on the present and giving her transition and rebirth to the Muslim vision; Part IV, a brief celebration of rebirth; and Part V, ringing with visions and celebrations. Although the spiritual journey finds its vitalizing point in a movement toward the Muslims, the spiritual and poetic power has nourishment even for the unready. In the book's conception of woman and her role, there seems to be both the influence of the Baraka group and that of the Muslims.

A Blues Book is a mountain-top type poem. That is, it is the poetic rhythms of one who has climbed from the valleys and is now calling others up from the low, the misted flats. A number of radical writers have attempted to create the mountain-top type, without sufficient awareness of the traps to be evaded. At the very least, it seems to require that one dislodge the ego from the center of one's concerns. If one has not dealt with the ego, if one is not really at the top or at one of the peaks, the ego whips out patronizing gestures and tones to the multitude.

It seems to me that the author has escaped such traps. I feel in the poems a genuine humbleness, love, and thankfulness, brightly leavening the exhortations. The voice is that of a struggler mindful of the journey and further humanized by it, an achievement emphasized by the confessional and testifying parts of the book.

One cannot presume to know the total struggle of the artist, but the resolutions of earlier strivings along certain lines seem to stand out. Earlier experiments with language and spelling seemed to be efforts to force the speaking voice to speak from the printed page. This volume achieves speaking tone by several devices: simplicity of diction, careful but undistracting uses of natural and mechanically induced pauses, extension of word sounds through spelling and capitalizations of certain letters, the breaking up of syntax, special arrangements of lines for sound and emphasis, and strategic varying of styles. Perhaps none of the devices is new to the author's poetry, but they here appear under further command and discipline.

The poetry, itself, benefits strongly from the poet's having felt out the music of words, so that a sure sense of how simple one can be and still retain the music is most always apparent. The opening lines will give some sense of this musical simplicity:

> We Black/woooomen have been called many
> things: foxes, matriarchs, whores,
> bougies, sweet mommas, gals,
> sapphires, sisters and recently Queens.
> i would say that Black/woooomen have been
> a combination of all these words because
> if we examine our past/history, at
> one time or another we've had to be like
> those words be saying.

This expository simplicity gives way to the more lyrical registrations of "young womanhood":

> as i entered into my
> young womanhood i became
> a budding of laughter. i
> moved in liquid dreams
> wrapped myself in a
> furious circuit of love
> gave out quick words
> and violent tremblings
> and kisses that bit
> and drew blood
> and the seasons fell
> like waterfalls on my thighs

The movement finally into the religious rebirth and the achievement of a new innocence abandons the simple nature imagery and creates songs involving images of light and devotion to Allah:

> WE ARE MUSLIM WOMEN
> dwellers in light
> new women created from the limbs of Allah.
> We are the shining ones
> coming from the dark ruins
> created from the eye of Allah:
> And we speak only what we know
> And do not curse God
> And we keep our minds open to light
> And do not curse God
> And we chant Alhamdullilah
> And do not curse God.

Perhaps one might quibble at the load of ideology direct statement is made to bear in Part I. An effort is made to deal with the direct statement-ideology situation by special emphasis upon sound pattern in lines and words and rhythmic variations. But, on the whole, the total book stands as a major achievement in both the use of technical resources and the presentation of a spiritual journey. (pp. 197-99)

George E. Kent, "Notes on the 1974 Black Literary Scene," in PHYLON: The Atlanta

University Review of Race and Culture, *Vol. XXXVI, No. 2, Second Quarter (June, 1975), pp. 194-99.*

Sonia Sanchez (essay date 1984)

[*In the following essay, Sanchez discusses her goals as a writer.*]

The poet is a creator of social values. The poet then, even though he/she speaks plainly, is a manipulator of symbols and language images which have been planted by experience in the collective subconscious of a people. Through this manipulation, he/she creates new or intensified meaning and experience, whether to the benefit or the detriment of his/her audience. Thus poetry is a *subconscious conversation,* it is as much the work of those who understand it and those who make it.

The power that the poet has to create, preserve, or destroy social values depends greatly on the quality of his/her social visibility and the functionary opportunity available to poetry to impact lives.

Like the priest and the prophet, with whom he/she was often *synonymous,* the poet in some societies has had infinite powers to interpret life; in others his/her voice has been drowned out by the winds of mundane pursuits.

Art no matter what its intention reacts to or reflects the culture it springs from. But from the very beginning two types of poetry developed. One can be called the *poetry of ethos* because it was meant to convey personal experience, feelings of love, despair, joy, frustration arising from very private encounter; the other *functionary poetry* dealt with themes in the social domain, religion, God, country, social institutions, war, marriage, and death in the distinct context of that society's perception.

To answer the question of how I write, we must look also to why I write. I write to tell the truth about the Black condition as I see it. Therefore I write to offer a Black woman's view of the world. How I tell the truth is a part of the truth itself. I've always believed that the truth concealed or clouded is a partial lie. So when I decide to tell the truth about an event/happening, it must be clear and understandable for those who need to understand the lie/lies being told. What I learned in deciding "how" to write was simply that most folks tend to think that you're lying or jiving them if you have to spice things up just to get a point across. I decided along with a number of other Black poets to tell the truth in poetry by using the language, dialect, idioms, of the folks we believed our audience to be.

The most fundamental truth to be told in any art form, as far as Blacks are concerned, is that America is killing us. But we continue to live and love and struggle and win. I draw on any experience or image to clarify and magnify this truth for those who must ultimately be about changing the world; not for critics or librarians.

Poetry's oldest formal ties were with religion. Humanity's first civilizations, it must be remembered, were theocratic and therefore religiously inspired. Thus were the ancient Black civilizations of the Nile, Mesopotamia, the Indus River, and Meso-America, societies in which religion as a *social vector,* not as *ritual,* exerted a prime force that motivated human action consciously and unconsciously.

Biblical scholars were poets. Marx was a poet. Mao was a poet. The Quran is poetically written. Black people lack such a centralized value network or system of thought. But this allows the poets of each age to contribute to the values of that age. I still believe that the age for which we write is the age evolving out of the dregs of the twentieth century into a more humane age. Therefore I recognize that my writing must serve a dual purpose. It must be a clarion call to the values of change while it also speaks to the beauty of nonexploitative age.

It is within this dual purpose that many of us see the Black aesthetic. For example, I chant in many of my poems. That chanting calls up the history of Black chanters and simultaneously has the historical effect of old chants: it inspires *action* and *harmony.* In one of my plays, **Sister Sonji,** Sonji is at a point of desperation or insanity or pretty close to it—which means that she is crying out in the night and no one listens or hears. She can sit in a rocking chair and sing a spiritual or she can chant the way *Sister Sonji* does when she knows she is almost gone or she is close to insanity. As she moves toward the deep end, she chants something that is ancient and religious. She chants her prayer. Her life. Her present. Her past. Her future. And a breath force comes back into her and with this chanting and on her knees she is reborn.

In **Sister Sonji** and **A Blues Book for Blue Black Magical Women,** I play with the concept of time. If I can give you a Black woman who is old, then is young, mature, and then old again, then I've dealt with time on some level. Then she becomes timeless. And we become timeless. Universal. When we understand the past and present in order to see our future. Therefore to see *Sonji* evolve into this old woman still full of hope, with no bitterness in terms of the children and the husband she has lost to war (time), with an understanding that if she can say to the audience *we dared to pick up the day* (time) *and make it night* (time); then to say can you or will you is a cry, a challenge to the audience to be timeless. And you will be timeless if you *be* about constant work and change. Black people will have no beginning or end if each generation does the job it must do to change the world.

Or in some poems I glorify the work or struggle of a sister struggler. Our poetic history needs to grow in this area, just as our consciousness needs to understand how to appreciate women as beautiful human beings.

In *A Blues Book for Blue Black Magical Women,* I attempt to show a Black woman moving/loving/living in America and the consequences of that movement. A "mountaintop" poem. George Kent [see excerpt dated 1975] says that *Blues Book* "possesses an extraordinary culmination of spiritual and poetic powers. It is in part an exhortation to move the rhythms of black life to a high peak through deep and deeper self-possession; in part, a spiritual autobiography." Kent said things that made me rethink/remember what I was doing at that time. I told D. H. Melham in an interview, "Yes. It's true. I was constantly climbing a mountain to get to that poem. And when I got there, two things could have happened. I could have said, 'Goody-goody-goody. I'm here. Look at the rest of you, you aren't.' However, after I was there, I looked up and saw another mountaintop, and then you realize what it's really all about on many levels."

But whatever the area or the issue, I see myself helping to bring forth the truth about the world. I cannot tell the truth about anything unless I confess to being a student, growing and learning something new every day. The more I learn, the clearer my view of the world becomes. To gain that clarity, my first lesson was that one's ego always compromised how something was viewed. I had to wash my ego in the needs/aspiration of my people. Selflessness is key for conveying the need to end greed and oppression. I try to achieve this state as I write.

Writing today in such a complex industrial age, with so many contradictions and confusions, is difficult. Many of us learned that to continue to write, we could not tell the truth and live a lie at the same time. So the values in my work reflect the values I live by and work for. I keep writing because I realize that until Black people's social reality is free of oppression and exploitation, I will not be free to write as one who's not oppressed or exploited. That is the goal. That is the struggle and the dream.

To bring my thoughts on how and why I write on down to elemental terms, the real nuts and bolts, I'll tell you how all of this gets done.

I must work a full-time job. Take care of a house and family. Referee or umpire at Little League games. Travel. Carry books when I travel. Work some more. Deal with illnesses and injuries. Help build the political organs within the Black community. Work on the car. Run for trains and planes. Find or create breaks. Then, late at night, just before the routine begins again, I write. I write and I smile as the words come drifting back like some reverent lover. I write columns for newspapers, poems, plays, and stories in those few choice hours before I sleep.

And they say leisure is the basis of culture.

(pp. 415-18)

Sonia Sanchez, "Ruminations/Reflections," in Black Women Writers (1950-1980), *edit-* ed by Mari Evans, Anchor Press/Doubleday, 1984, pp. 415-18.

Haki Madhubuti (essay date 1984)

[*Madhubuti (formerly Don L. Lee) is an American poet, short story writer, essayist, and critic. In the excerpt below, he surveys Sanchez's literary career.*]

There are few writers alive who have created a body of work that both teaches and celebrates life, even at its darkest moments. Sonia Sanchez does this and more throughout her many volumes of poetry, short stories, plays, and children's books. She is prolific and sharp-eyed. Her telescopic view of the world is seldom light, frivolous, or fraudulent. She is serious, serious to the point of pain and redemption. Her bottom line is this: she wants Black people to grow and develop so that we can move toward determining our own destiny. She wants us not only to be responsible for our actions but to take responsible actions. This is the task she has set for herself, and indeed she believes that what she can do others can do.

Her work is magic. Her scope and more often than not her analytical mind bring clarity and simplicity to the complicated. The brevity in her poetry has become her trademark.

> if i had known, if
> i had known you, i would have
> left my love at home.

She is a poet (and woman) of few but strong and decisive words. Her vision may sometimes be controversial; nevertheless, it is her vision. With a sharing heart and mind, she is constantly seeking the perfect, always striving with an enduring passion toward an unattainable completeness. (p. 419)

Sanchez writes poetry that is forever questioning Black people's commitment to struggle. Much of her work intimately surveys the struggles between Black people and Black people, between Blacks and whites, between men and women, between self and self, and between cultures. She is always demanding answers, questioning motives and manners, looking for the complete story and not the easy surface that most of us settle for. Her poetry cuts to the main arteries of her people, sometimes drawing blood, but always looking for a way to increase the heartbeat and lower the blood pressure. Her poetry, for the most part, is therapeutic and cleansing. Much of her work is autobiographical, but not in the limiting sense that it is only about Sonia Sanchez. She is beyond the problem of a consuming ego, and with her, unlike many autobiographical writers, we are not always aware of the protagonist's actual identity. Black experiences in America are so similar and the normal distinctions that set Black people apart are not always obvious to outsiders. This is to note that, for the most part, her experiences are ours and vice versa. She is an optimistic realist searching the alleys for beauty and substance.

As a Black woman writer who is political, she brings a critical quality to her work that can easily overpower the nonpolitical reader. She is a lover, but her love is conditional, reflective, and selective. She is not given to an emotional romanticism of her people. This is not to suggest that she is not fresh or spontaneous in her reflections, but to acknowledge that she has indeed experienced life at its roller-coaster fullest from Cuba to China, from New York City to San Francisco to the confusion and strength of the international Black world. Sanchez is not, in terms of mind-set or communication, a tea leaf reader or stargazer. She has the major poet's quality; she is a visionary, unafraid to implant the vision.

Sonia Sanchez respects the power of Black language. More than any other poet, she has been responsible for legitimatizing the use of urban Black English in written form. Her use of language is spontaneous and thoughtful. Unlike many poets of the sixties, her use of the so-called profane has been innovatively shocking and uncommonly apropos. Her language is culturally legitimate and genuinely reflects the hard bottom and complicated spectrum of the entire Black community. She has taken Black speech and put it in the context of world literature. This aspect of her work has often been overlooked. However, she, along with Baraka, Neal, Dumas, and a few others of the sixties poets, must be looked upon as a recorder and originator of an urban Black working language. Long before the discovery of Ntozake Shange, Sanchez set the tone and spaces of modern urban written Black poetry. In her early works, we can read and feel the rough city voices screaming full circle in all kinds of human settings, as in **"To Blk/Record/Buyers"**:

> don't play me no
> righteous bros.
>   white people
> ain't rt bout nothing
> no mo.
>   don't tell me bout
> foreign dudes
>   cuz no blk/
> people are grooving on a
> sunday afternoon
>   they either
> making out/
>   signifying/
>   drinking/
> making molotov cocktails/
>   stealing
> or rather more taking their goods
> from the honky thieves who
> ain't hung up
>   on no pacifist/jesus/
>   cross but
> play blk/songs
>   to drown out the
> shit/screams of honkies.   AAAH.
>   AAAH.   AAAH.   yeah.   brothers.
>   andmanymoretogo.

Language is one of the major tools used in the intellectual development of all people. The English language as the vehicle for communication in the United States varies from culture to culture. Part of the difficulty in communication between Blacks and whites is that whites do not listen to or respect serious communication from Blacks, and that whites do not understand, or prefer to ignore, voices of the majority of Blacks. Whatever the reason, Sanchez understands them, and speaks most forcefully and quite eloquently for herself, which is a creditable reflection of her community. Despite having located in academe (she is a tenured professor at Temple University), she has not separated herself from the roots of her people, and in most of her work we experience the urgency of Black life and a call for Black redemption and development.

She has effectively taken Black speech patterns, combined them with the internal music of her people, and injected progressive thoughts in her poetry. The best of the sixties poets always went past mere translation of the streets to transformation. Sanchez is a poet of enormous vision, and in each succeeding book one can view that vision deepening and broadening. She remains an intense and meticulous poet who has not compromised craft or skill for message. The content, the politics, are more effective because her language and style has enabled her to dissect the world in a fresh and meaningful manner.

All of Sanchez's books are significant: **Homecoming** (1969) for its pace-setting language, **We a BaddDDD People** (1970) for its scope and maturity. She displayed an uncommon ability for combining words and music, content and approach. The longer poems are work songs, and she continues to be devastating in the shorter works. **Love Poems** (1973), a book of laughter and hurt, smiles and missed moments, contains poems that expose the inner sides of Sanchez during the years 1964-73, in which she produces several masterworks. **A Blues Book for Blue Black Magical Women** (1974), her Black woman book, is a volume of sad songs and majestic histories. Her work becomes longer and balladlike. This book highlights Black women as mothers, sisters, lovers, wives, workers, and warriors, an uncompromising commitment to the Black family, and the Black woman's role in building a better world. **I've Been a Woman: New and Selected Poems** (1978) contains more than a decade of important work; it is truly an earth-cracking contribution. This book not only displays the staying power of Sonia Sanchez but also confirms her place among the giants of world literature. Throughout the entire body of her work, never apologizing, she affirms and builds a magnificent case for the reality of being Black and female, lashing out at all forms of racism, sexism, classism, just plain ignorance, and stupidity. It must be noted that she was taking these positions before it was popular and profitable.

A bringer of memories, Sanchez gives us just short of two decades of poetry which emphasizes struggle and history in poetic pictures; photographs, in which she as writer and participant was intimately involved. She does not let us forget. Her work is a reminder of what was, and is. She has experienced two lifetimes. Her poetic range is impressive and enlightening as she comments on subjects as diverse as Black studies and the Nation of Islam, from Malcolm X to Sterling Brown, unmistakably showing us that she is both player and observer in this world.

If you wish to measure the strength of a people, examine its culture. The cultural forces more than any other connector are the vehicles that transmit values from one generation to another. In studying Sanchez's poetry, we see a person immersed in her people's history, religion, politics, social structure, ethics, and psychology. She is forever pushing for Black continuation, as in **"For Unborn Malcolms,"** where she urges Black retaliation for white violence:

> its time
>   an eye for an eye
>   a tooth for a tooth
>   don't worry bout his balls
> they al
>   ready gone
>   git the word
> out that us blk/niggers
>   are out to lunch
> and the main course
> is gonna be his white meat.
>   yeah.

As a cultural poet, Sonia Sanchez is uniquely aware of the complexity and confusion of her people. She translates this world effectively, yet somehow even in her most down times, she projects richness and lively tomorrows. In the best of her work she is establishing tradition.

It would be condescending to state that she is original. She is so original she had difficulty getting published in the early days; her beauty and compactness of words are sometimes matched only by Carol Freeman and Norman Jordan. Nevertheless, although the major small journals that published Black poets exclusively and introduced the poets to each other and the community (*Journal of Black Poetry, Soul Book, Liberator* and *Negro Digest/Black World*) frequently provided a national outlet for Sanchez as well as other poets of her generation, Dudley Randall's Broadside Press was responsible for publishing Sonia Sanchez's early books as well as those of a good many of the sixties poets.

Sanchez delivers many aspects of Black life with a sharpness, a precision, that closely resembles rapping and signifying. In less skilled hands, this would not have worked, but Sanchez's strength has been to take the ordinary and make it art, make it memorable. The multiple sides of the poet were first demonstrated in her book *We a BaddDDD People* (1970), where she carefully and lovingly surveyed the Black world. The first section, "Survival Poems," is a mirror of our years. She comments on everything from suicide to her relationship to poet Etheridge Knight to whom she was married at the time. If there are any problems with *We a BaddDDD People* it may be with form. In a few of the poems, i.e.,

"A Chant for Young/Brothas and Sistuhs" she is too easy with the message; she does not force the reader to work or to reflect. The effectiveness of her use of slashes to separate words and lines is questionable.

> seen yo/high
>   on every blk/st in
> wite/amurica
>   i've seen yo/self/
> imposed/quarantined/hipness
>   on every
> slum/bar/
>   revolutionary/st

However, the form does work when the message doesn't overpower the style. Her poem **"There Are Blk/Puritans"** is an excellent example of irony and substance. She argues for a new and developed political awareness, demanding that her readers locate the actual profanity in their lives:

> there are blk/puritans
> among us
>   straight off the
> mayflower
>   who wud have u
> believe
>   that the word
> fuck/u/mutha/fucka
>   is evil.
>   un/black.
>   who wud
> ignore the real/curse/words
> of our time
>   like.   CA/PITA/LISM
> blk/pimps
>   nixonandco
> COMMUNISM.
> missanne
>   rocke/FELLER.
>   there
> are blk/puritans among us
> who must be told that
> WITE/AMURICA
>   is the
> only original sin.

Immediately noticeable in this poem are (1) a sense of history—getting off the *Mayflower* means Black people came from somewhere else—and suggests a polarity, an intragroup dichotomy; (2) questioning values—the system of exploiting capitalism vs. curse words, i.e., which is the real evil; (3) the use of Black language, blk, wud, mutha, fucka, wite, Amurica; (4) the negative effects of acculturation, blk/puritans/among us; and (5) an identification of the undeniable evils of this world: CA/PITA/LISM, blk/pimps, nixonandco, COMMUNISM, missanne, rocke/FELLER and WITE/ AMURICA. The spelling of America as AMURICA is to denote the murdering quality of this land, which, as she sees it, is the "original sin."

Throughout this section of *We a BaddDDD People*, Sanchez is concerned with Black-on-Black damage, especially in the area of social relationships, i.e., family:

> and i mean.

like if brothas
programmed sistuhs to love
instead of
        fucken/hood
                and i mean
if mothas programmed
                sistuhs to
good feelings bout they blk/men
and i
        mean if blk/fathas proved
they man/hood by
                fighten the enemy
instead of fucken every available sistuh.
and i mean
        if we programmed/loved/each
other in com/mun/al ways
                so that no
blk/person starved
        or killed
                each other on
a sat/ur/day nite corner.
then may
        be it wud all
come down to some
        thing else
like RE VO LU TION.
        i mean if
        like yeh.

It is interesting that in later books, especially *Love Poems* and *I've Been a Woman,* she forsakes syllable separation and overuse of page and concentrates more on the fresh juxtaposing of words within context. The overuse of the page and the seemingly confusing punctuation prevalent in *Homecoming* and *We a BaddDDD People* all but disappear in later poetry and are not highlighted in her selected poems.

Sanchez has always been the sharpest in locating the tragedies in our lives and she is not one to bite her tongue or forge false messages. She goes directly to the bone. Like a skilled chiropractor, she locates the spine and carefully and professionally makes the correct adjustments. In "**Present,**" from *A Blues Book for Blue Black Magical Women,*

            there is no place
        for a soft/black/woman.
        there is no smile green enough or
        summertime words warm enough to allow my
            growth.
        and in my head
        i see my history
        standing like a shy child
        and i chant lullabies
        as i ride my past on horseback
        tasting the thirst of yesterday tribes
        hearing the ancient/black woman
        me, singing hay-hay-hay-hay-ya-ya-ya.
                hay-hay-hay-hay-ya-ya-ya.
        like a slow scent
        beneath the sun . . .

She is always seeking fulfillment—bridging generations looking for answers, forever disturbing the dust in our acculturated lives. Her work represents cultural stabilizers at their best. As Geneva Smitherman noted in her book *Talkin and Testifyin: The Language of Black America:*

> What the new black poets have done, then, is to take for their conceptual and expressive tools a language firmly rooted in the black experience. Such terms and expressions enable the poets to use cultural images and messages familiar to their black audiences, and with great strokes of brevity, Black English lines and phrases reveal a complete story. (Such, of course, is the way any good poet operates; what is unique here is the effective execution of the operation in a black way.)

Much of Sanchez's poetry is painful and challenging; *that she continues to love is the miracle.* How can a Black man not be touched and moved by poems such as "**For Unborn Malcolms**" and "**Past**"? In the earlier work, there seemed to be little peace within her, and the forces that were tearing her apart ripped at our souls also. However, Sanchez cannot be boxed into any single category even though most of her work deals with some aspect of Black redemption. The book that represents this multifacetedness in addition to displaying other sides of the poet's nature is *Love Poems* (1973).

Love Poems is a startling and profound departure from Sanchez's other books. It's introspective and meditative. The poems are highly personal and complex. For the untried reader, some of the poems will require three and four readings. The book is less experimental, and she has basically made use of traditional poetic forms such as haiku and ballad. The poetry is delicate, rich, and very honest. There are illustrations to complement the poetry, and between the line drawings and the poems there is an air of quiet patience created.

Love Poems represents close to a decade of sunsets, hangovers, and travel. The woman, as poet, ignites in this book and brings forth fire and wood and most appropriately food. She continues this voice in *A Blues Book for Blue Black Magical Women,* yet in *Love Poems* there is a great tenderness, a willingness to touch the reader. She is seeking distilled communication, clearing paths so that nothing separates the poet from the reader. She succeeds beautifully; there are few obstacles; her form is relaxed, the lines easy, flowing. Her language has appropriate colorations, and the content is tridimensional: (1) an unusual yet effective openness, (2) razor-sharp brevity that painlessly cuts into the heart, and (3) a womanly seriousness—strong and unmoving—like trying to remove black from coal, an impossible task unless you destroy or burn the coal.

The titles of the poems are not descriptive; they are convenient identifiers as in "**July**":

        the old men and women
        quilt their legs
        in the shade
        while tapestry pigeons
        strut their necks.
        as i walk, thinking
        about you my love,
        i wonder what it is

to be old
and swallow death each day
like warm beer.

One can see a marriage beginning to break as she talks to us in **"Poem No. 2"**:

my puertorican
husband who feeds me
cares for me and loves me
    is trying to under
stand my Blackness.
so he is taking up
watercolors.

Much of the poetry is about the men in her life, and one immediately notices the change of attitude toward her father. From the poem **"A Poem for My Father"** of *We a BaddDDD People* to the two-part poem **"Father and Daughter"** of *Love Poems* there is an escalation of understanding that belies her young years. The earlier poem speaks of "perfumed bodies weeping/underneath you," and "when i remember your/deformity i want to/do something about your/makeshift manhood. i guess that is why/on meeting your sixth/wife i cross myself with her confessions." This poem is cold and unforgiving and seems to lack understanding. **"Father and Daughter"** of *Love Poems* (there is also another **"Father and Daughter"** in *I've Been a Woman*) is a compelling and unforgettable reading of emotions from the daughter, who states in Part One, "It is difficult to believe that we/even talked. how did we spend the night while seasons passed in place of words." However, the complexity of the love the poet feels for her father as well as the distance between them, and a newfound understanding, is inescapable in Part Two:

you cannot live hear and bend my heart
amid the rhythm of your screams. Apart
still venom sleeps and drains down thru the years
touch not these hands once live with shears
i live a dream about you; each man
alone. You need the sterile wood old age can
bring, no opening of the veins whose smell
will bruise light breast and burst our shell
of seeds, the landslide of your season
burns the air: this mating has no reason.
don't cry, late grief is not enough. the motion
of your tides still flows within; the ocean
of deep blood that downs the land. we die:
while young moons rage and wander in the sky.

The men in Sanchez's life have brought both joy and hurt and the experience is without a doubt a common thread that connects Black women to each other as well as to their men. All Black women have been influenced by Black men be they their fathers, brothers, lovers, husbands, sons, or friends; they affect the women in a multitude of ways both negative and positive, such as:

Now. i at
thirty. You at
thirty-two are
sculptured stains
and my death
comes with

enormous eyes
and my dreams
turn in deformity.

and the positive is thought-provoking:

and what of the old bearded man collecting
bottles who pulls a burlap bag behind?
if we speak of love,
what of his black body arched over the city
opening the scales of strangers
carrying the dirt of corners to his hunched corner?
if we know of love
we rest;
while the world moves wrenched by collection.

Love Poems was published during the period that Sanchez was a member of the Nation of Islam, and during those years the unofficial position of the NOI was to read little other than the recommended text. It is remarkable that there are only a few references in *Love Poems* that remind us of her religious conversion. One of the powerful things about the collection is that it defies ideological positioning, and the other quality is that the poems indicate that she seems to be at peace with herself. This peacefulness comes across in several memorable poems:

there are things sadder
than you and I. some people
do not even touch.

(pp. 420-29)

This book is almost too beautiful—a somewhat sad beauty containing lines and stanzas that other poets wish that they had written. In *Love Poems,* Sanchez is more lyrical in a subtle way. Her descriptive powers are full-blown; she is quietly dramatic, yet her slices of life are never soap-operaish or exploitative as in this haiku:

we grow up my love
because as yet there is no
other place to go

The book *I've Been a Woman: Selected and New Poems* flows, is river-like and thirst-quenching. It is a poet's book containing landscapes and mountains with few valleys. This collection is the history of Sanchez as poet—the poet consistently at her best, spanning the entire range of her talent. A carefully selected volume, it is a clear indication of the growth and genius of the poet. Selected poems, unlike a poet's collected poems, is not a life's work. It is more midlife, a middle years' comment of the poet as well as statements that suggest or indicate what is to come. (p. 430)

In this collection she includes another **"Father and Daughter"** that rocks with colors and intimate observations. It seems that her father will continue to be a subject of much discussion in future works. However, the poem that will undoubtedly live for ages is **"Kwa Mamu Zetu Waliotuzaa"** (For Our Mother Who Gave Us Birth). This work, the last piece in the collection, is a stunning three-part epic calling mothers (a special final tribute to Shirley Graham Dubois) to recapture sunlight and peace while acknowledging death . . .

> death is a five o'clock door forever changing time.
>   and it was morning without sun or shadow;
> a morning already afternoon. sky. cloudy with
>   incense.
>   and it was morning male in speech;
> feminine in memory.
> but i am speaking of everyday occurrences:
> of days unrolling bandages for civilized wounds;
> of gaudy women chanting rituals under a waterfall
>   of stars;
> of men freezing their sperms in diamond-studded
>   wombs;
> of children abandoned to a curfew of marble.

Yet, for the poet, "at the Center of death is birth" represents the real focus of her poetry. She is hungry for life. Trapped in America, she like us has had to make small compromises in position—not values—such as having race and economics determining where we live and work. As a seeker of truth, as a pathfinder in the area of communicative writing, Sanchez has few peers. She falls beautifully in the tradition of Gwendolyn Brooks, Margaret Walker, Langston Hughes, Zora Neale Hurston, Sterling Brown, and Shirley Graham Dubois.

She has few peers that can match the urgency, anger, and love found in her work. There are few who can look over two decades of work and feel good and pleased for taking the long, difficult road and coming out scared, but not cut, not devoid of future:

> i am circling new boundaries
> i have been trailing the ornamental
> songs of death (life
> a strong pine tree
> dancing in the wind
> i inhale the ancient black breath
> cry for every dying (living
> creature
>
> come. let us ascend from the
> middle of our breath
> sacred rhythms
> inhaling peace.

Sanchez has been an inspiration to a generation of young poets. In my travels, she, Mari Evans, and Gwendolyn Brooks are the women writers most often admired. Her concreteness and consistency over these many years is noteworthy. She has not bought refuge from day-to-day struggles by becoming a writer in the Western tradition. Her involvement in struggle has fueled her writing so that she is seldom boring or overly repetitious. Somehow, one feels deep inside that in a real fight this is the type of Black woman you would want at your side. In her work she brings clarity to the world and in so doing she, unlike many writers, transcends our conception of what a poet does.

There is no last word for a poet. Poets sign their own signatures on the world. Those who comment on their greatness do so only because greatness is often confused with the commonplace in this country. The singers of the new songs understand the world that is coming because they are the makers. Include Sonia Sanchez. (pp. 431-32)

> *Haki Madhubuti, "Sonia Sanchez: The Bringer of Memories," in* Black Women Writers (1950-1980), *edited by Mari Evans, Anchor Press/Doubleday, 1984, pp. 419-32.*

David Williams (essay date 1984)

[*In the following excerpt, Williams traces the development of Sanchez's poetic voice.*]

The title of Sonia Sanchez's first collection, *Homecoming,* marks with delicate irony the departure point of a journey whose direction and destination can now be considered. *I've Been a Woman,* her most recent book, invites such an appraisal, including as it does a retrospective of her earlier work as well as an articulation of a newly won sense of peace:

> shedding my years and
> earthbound now. midnite trees are
> more to my liking.

These lines contain an explicit reworking of images that dominate **"Poem at Thirty,"** one of the most personal statements in *Homecoming.* That early poem pulses with a terror rooted in a consciousness of age as debilitating. Midnight and traveling, images of perpetual transition, bracket the poem's fear:

> it is midnight
> no magical bewitching
> hour for me
> i know only that
> i am here waiting
> remembering that
> once as a child
> i walked two
> miles in my sleep . . .
> travelling. i'm
> always travelling.
> i want to tell
> you about me
> about nights on a
> brown couch when
> i wrapped my
> bones in lint and
> refused to move.
> no one touches
> me anymore . . .

In the new poems of *I've Been a Woman* Sanchez reevokes these images in order to establish her new sense of assurance. Midnight no longer terrifies; rootedness has succeeded sleepwalking as an emblematic image.

Correlating these poems in this way allows a useful perspective on the work of a poet whose development has been as much a matter of craft as it has been a widening and deepening of concerns. *Homecoming* largely satisfies Baraka's demand in "Black Art" for "assassin poems, Poems that shoot/guns"; but there is from the beginning an ironic vision in Sanchez's work that ensures that she differentiate between activist poetry and what she herself has labeled, in *We a BaddDDD People,* "black rhetoric." The difference is that between substance and shadow, between "straight/ revolutionary/lines" and "catch/phrases." And it is clear from Sanchez's work in *Homecoming* that she believes that the ideal poetry demands the practice of a stringent discipline. The poems in that collection are characterized by an economy of utterance that is essentially dramatic, like language subordinated to the rhythms of action. The verse of *Homecoming* is speech heightened by a consciousness of the ironies implicit in every aspect of Black existence. The poems read like terse statements intended to interrupt the silence that lies between perception and action.

In the title poem of the volume, Sanchez presents the act of returning home as a rejection of fantasy and an acceptance of involvement:

> i have returned
> leaving behind me
> all those hide and
> seek faces peeling
> with freudian dreams.
> this is for real.

The opposition set up is enriched by her perception of other dichotomies: between youth and maturity, between Blackness and "niggerness." And Sanchez also knows that for a while earlier she had chosen Blackness over "niggerness":

> once after college
> i returned tourist
> style to catch all
> the niggers killing
> themselves with
> three-for-oners
> with
> needles
> that cd
> not support
> their stutters.

She had been one of those "hide and seek faces" on the outside, looking in at the niggers; in the real world she is now a nigger:

> black
> niggers
>   my beauty.

This, the climax of the poem, is the real homecoming; and the opening lines, reread, acquire a new resonance:

> i have been a
> way so long...

The division of "away" by the line break turns the second line into an extraordinarily weighted phrase; it rings like the refrain of a spiritual. This is a homecoming from very far away. The poem's closing lines,

following the natural climax, provide an amplification of the earlier "now woman":

> i have learned it
> ain't like they say
> in the newspapers.

This truth, not learned in college, is at the core of a whole complex of meanings contained in the almost offhand casualness of the verse, which reads like transcribed speech.

"Homecoming" is a meditation meant to be overheard; the sense of an audience is a necessary part of the poem's meaning. Much of Sanchez's poetry in her first two collections is even more overtly dramatic, designed to be spoken as part of a larger performance in which silences and an implied choreography say as much as the actual words. "Summary," another focal point of the first collection, quickly abandons the initial pretense of being inner-directed:

> this is
> a poem for the world
> for the slow suicides
> in seclusion.
> somewhere on 130th st.
> a woman, frail as a
> child's ghost, sings.

The sibilances here are deliberately accusatory, and the simile is as generalized as it can be without becoming a cliché. The snatch of song that follows transforms the poem fully into what it is, a plaint for all the women (Cassandra, Penelope, Billie Holiday, Bessie Smith) who have been victims. Spoken in the accents of this specific Black woman, "Summary" is rooted in a sisterhood of angry pain. As the poem's rhythm begins to stutter, its linear form disintegrates into a scattershot catalogue in which numerous lives and experiences are summarized:

> life
> is no more than
>   gents
>   and
>   gigolos
>   (99% american)
> liars
>   and
> killers (199% american) dreamers
>   and drunks (299%
>   american)
>   i say
> is everybody happy/...

The emotion crests and breaks at this point, driven against a wall of futility. The voice falls back into the monotone with which the poem started—except that now it has been reduced to the barest of statements:

> this is a poem for me.
> i am alone.
> one night of words
> will not change
> all that.

The point, of course, is that these lines are more than just "a poem for me," and we are intended to perceive this. **"Summary"** is a performance in which an unobtrusive intelligence has acknowledged the presence of an audience.

The imagined response of this audience is occasionally crucial to the poems in **Homecoming,** some of which are, in essence, communal chant performances in which Sanchez, as poet, provides the necessary language for the performance. The perceptions in such poems are deliberately generalized, filtered through the shared consciousness of the urban Black. **"Nigger"** is the heard half of a dialogue with someone who can almost be visualized; his response seems to fill the gaps between the surges of speech, which gather confidence until the word "nigger" has been exorcised and the poem's initial claim has been made good:

> that word
> ain't shit to me
> man . . .

The coupled poems **"Black Magic"** and **"To a Jealous Cat"** pick up the "my man" refrain from **"Nigger"** and transform it. In that poem it has the weight of a public epithet, a designation for someone whose relationship with the voice in the poem could only be that of an adversary. In **"Black Magic,"** on the other hand, it has the warmth of a private endearment, a whisper in which both words are equally stressed (*"my man"*) and therefore become an assertion of possession as well as of pride. In the process the phrase "black magic" is itself transformed.

> magic
>   my man
> is you
>   turning
> my body into
> a thousand
> smiles . . .

In **"To a Jealous Cat"** the appellation remains private, but it is now the privacy of anger and disappointment. The poem is the second act in the drama of a human relationship, and it makes bitter and ironic play with the same elements that make **"Black Magic"** so celebratory:

> no one never told
> you that jealousy's
> a form of homo
> sexuality?

The lineation transforms "homosexuality" into an ironic shadow of the ideal sexuality earlier gloried in. At the same time the word is used as a bitter taunt:

> in other
> words my man
> you faggot bound
> when you imagine
> me going in and out
> with some other cat.
>   yeah.

In retrospect, the earlier question ("don't you/know where you/at?") acquires a new and savage significance, and when "my man" recurs it is cruelly ironic. As a consequence, the deceptively ordinary lines with which the poem closes are really an indictment:

> perhaps you ain't
> the man we thought.

It is significant that the pronoun here is "we" and not "I." The lines are meant to underscore the ambiguity with which "my man" has been invested; sexual identity becomes, by extension, a metaphor for self-awareness.

Poems such as **"Nigger"** and **"To a Jealous Cat"** demonstrate that, in one sense, Sanchez has been "earthbound" from the beginning. Her use of Black speech as the bedrock of her poetic language ensures that her imagery remains sparse and wholly functional, even when it is most striking, as in the final lines of **"For Unborn Malcolms"**:

> git the word
> out that us blk/niggers
>   are out to lunch
> and the main course
> is gonna be his white meat.

Even here, the spirit of this extended image remains true to its origins; it accords with the poem's characteristic tone of dramatized anger. Sanchez can break open the routine hipness of street talk with a single word that allows a glimpse into the complexities of some area of the Black experience:

> some will say out
> right
>   baby i want
>   to ball you
> while smoother
> ones will in
> tegrate your
> blackness . . .

"Integrate" is such a word; as used here, it sums up a whole history of betrayal and anger with a sharp wit that is itself characteristic of much of Sanchez's work. In **"Short Poem"** she recounts her man's praise of her sexiness; then, with impeccable timing, she delivers her assessment:

> maybe
>   i
>   shd
>   bottle
>   it
>   and
> sell it
> when he goes.

The ironic twist in the final line is reminiscent of such poems as "Widow Woman" and "Hard Daddy," where Langston Hughes uses the same device. Sanchez's wit is generally more cutting than Hughes', however. **"Small Comment"** is a deadly parody of the academic style of discourse; after successive restatements of the initial thesis have mired the poem in verbiage, the final "you dig" is devastatingly mocking. **"To Chuck"** is a different sort of parody; Sanchez offers a caricature of e.e. cummings, but the tone of the mockery is gentle. The poem, like **"Black Magic,"** is ultimately celebratory:

```
     i'm gonna write me
        a poem like
           e.e.
        cum
           mings to
        day. a
     bout you
           mov
     ing iNsIDE
           me touc
     hing my vis
           cera un
        til i turn
     in
        side out. i'
                 m
     go
        n n
           a sc
              rew
     u on   pap   er...
```

There is also something of self-parody here: Sanchez is obviously aware of the parallels between cummings' approach to poetic form and that favored by the militant young poets of the sixties. The feeling celebrated by the poem is genuine, however. Beneath their deliberate anarchy, the lines suggest that sexual commitment is a species of revolutionary act.

The poems in *Homecoming* and *We a BaddDDD People* lie along a spectrum bounded by two extremes. At one pole there are those poems that almost seem to have exploded from the force of the raw anger at their center; for **"The Final Solution"** and **"Indianapolis/Summer/1969/Poem,"** for instance, the visual shape on the page is the equivalent of a stutter:

```
     like.
        i mean.
           don't it all come down
     to e/co/no/mics.
           like it is fo
     money that those young brothas on
     illinois and
        ohio sts
           allow they selves to
     be picked up
        cruised around...
```

Poems like these appear to be still in the process of being composed; words seem to have not yet settled into place. The poem in flux is given to the reader, and the act of reading becomes an act of composition. At the other pole are those poems where Sanchez creates the sense of monotone by presenting a stream of meditation in which the individual semantic units flow into each other without any single word or image breaking the aural surface of the rhythm. In **"Poem at Thirty,"**

"Personal Letter No. 2," and **"Personal Letter No. 3"** the audience is relegated to insignificance. These poems are entries in a personal diary which is the extension, not the converse, of the communal scrapbook of being Black in America. The weariness of spirit they reveal finds its verbal counterpart in a vocabulary cadenced to a slower rhythm, one very different from the streetwise staccato of a poem like **"Indianapolis...."** **"Personal Letter No. 3"** is typical in this regard:

```
     no more wild geo
     graphies of the
     flesh. echoes. that
     we move in tune
     to slower smells.
     it is a hard thing
     to admit that
     sometimes after midnight
     i am tired
     of it all.
```

Midnight and travel: the emblems recur. They are mythic images that summon up vistas of Black history, even as they fix the particular anguish of an individual soul.

The most striking difference between *Love Poems* and Sanchez's earlier work lies in the widening of the range of her imagery. The world evoked in *Homecoming* and *We a BaddDDD People* is that of the urban nighttime, bereft of any glimpse of the natural landscape. From *Love Poems* on, images of trees, flowers, earth, birds, sea, and sky dot the verse. Sanchez, however, is very far from using them to suggest an idyllic universe; in fact, the natural world enters the verse of *Love Poems,* in particular, as part of a vision of an external reality in which things are out of kilter:

```
        this earth
     turns old
     and rivers grow lunatic
     with rain. how i wish
     i could lean in your cave
     and creak with the winds.
```

There are occasional instances of such images being used in a more upbeat fashion ("he/moved in me like rain"), but by and large they function as elements in an astringent lyricism that is a development of the mood of early poems such as **"Personal Letter No. 3"** and **"Poem at Thirty."** **"Father and Daughter"** is typical in this regard. The poem, which consists of paired sonnets whose formal structure acts as a brake on the emotional immediacy of the experience, closes with these lines:

```
     don't cry. late grief is not enough. the motion of your
     tides still flows within: the ocean of deep blood that
     drowns the land. we die: while young moons rage and
     wander in the sky.
```

This is a glimpse of apocalypse. The lines are reminiscent of Derek Walcott's "The Gulf," which ends with a frightening vision of America's future, and like Walcott's poem, Sanchez's turns upon the sense of a personal experience being magnified into a perception of an entire society. Ocean, earth, and moon, with their mythic associations, become the moving forces in this process. The imagery is the spark that ignites the poem.

The intensified lyricism of Sanchez's work partakes of the same economy of utterance that had marked her earlier poetry. If her use of the sonnet form in **"Father and Daughter"** represents an effort to compress emotion within a restraining mold, she carries that attempt even further in works such as **"Poem No. 4."** The supple urge of the verse strains against the compact, even form of the triplet used here; the poem succeeds precisely because of this tension:

> i am not a
>
> face of my
> own choosing.
> still. i am.
>
> i am . . .

Sanchez takes this principle of compression to its ultimate form in the haiku that punctuate *Love Poems.* In these, emotion has been concentrated and distilled into moments which capture the now and the then, the immediacy of an action as well as its intimations of change. Sometimes the act of compression is almost too drastic; the poem is pared down until there is little of real significance left:

> did ya ever cry
> Black man, did ya ever cry
> til you knocked all over?

There is no moment of intersection here, no sense of an abrupt discovery. At other times, however, Sanchez pulls off the haiku with tremendous authority, impaling a single perception with an image as definite and as inevitable as the climactic movement in a choreographed dance:

> O i am so sad, i
> go from day to day like an
> ordained stutterer.

Unlike imagist poetry, this does not depend for its meaning on the ripples set off by a static image. The simile generates its own energy, compelling us to partake in the emotion. The haiku represents for Sanchez the point at which the irreducible statement of personal assertion ("still. i am./i am.") converges with the ideal of "straight/revolutionary/lines." The haiku in her hands is the ultimate in activist poetry, as abrupt and as final as a fist.

But Sanchez is also concerned with experience as process, with the accumulation of small adjustments that constitute the data of individual and communal life. This concern involves more than just the juxtaposing of past and present; in **"Sequences"** and **"Old Words,"** Sanchez struggles to divine the almost insensible shifts that result in our present dilemmas. The latter poem, in particular, attempts no less than an explora-

tion of the growth of the malaise that Sanchez believes to be endemic in modern life:

> we are the dis
> enfranchised ones
> the buyers of bread
> one day removed
> from mold
> we are maimed
> in our posture . . .

Following this initial evocation of despair, Sanchez chronicles the race's (and humanity's) emotional history through a series of images that all connote a failure to communicate. Against these she places the iconic figures of Billie Holiday and Prez, both of whom tried to reach out through their music. They become, for Sanchez, part of a process of human history that has moved us from "herding songs" to "mass produced faces." In the penultimate section of the poem she summarizes the gradations in that process in a way that suggests a movement from life to death:

> Are we ever what we should be?
> seated in our circle of agonies
> we do not try to tune our breaths
> since we cannot sing together
> since we cannot waltz our eyes
> since we cannot love.
> since we have wooed this world
> too long with separate arias of revolution
> mysticism hatred and submission
> since we have rehearsed our
> deaths apart . . .

Each of these failures has contributed to our "maimed posture." The poem's facsimile of narrative catalogues the history of the human experience, then adds a somber coda:

> we have come to
> believe that we are
> not. to be we
> must be loved or
> touched and proved
> to be . . .

How we come to "believe that we are not" is the object of Sanchez's concern in her next collection, *A Blues Book for Blue Black Magic Women.* The principles and techniques of narrative dominate this volume. The poems, developing on the style of **"Sequences"** and **"Old Words,"** represent the fulfilment of a truth and a form that Sanchez had touched much earlier in such works as **"Summary," "Poem at Thirty,"** and **"Summer Words of a Sistuh Addict."** These early poems all turn upon the image of a woman as ghost, as mummy:

> i want to tell
> you about me
> about nights on a
> brown couch when
> i wrapped my
> bones in lint and
> refused to move . . .

The music that twines around her is a dirge whose nursery-rhyme lyrics mockingly underline her impotence; it is as if her anguish, ultimately inexpressible, has to be contained in formulas. In **Blues Book** Sanchez, submerging her personal self in a persona that is deliberately generalized, undertakes a ritual of acceptance, confession, cleansing, and rebirth.

In **"Past"** that ritual begins with a prayer for cleansing:

> Come ride my birth, earth mother
> tell me how i have become, became
> this woman with razor blades between
> her teeth.
>   sing me my history O earth mother...
> for i want to rediscover me. the secret of me
> the river of me. the morning ease of me...

The narrative is at the starting point of a movement back into the womb of memory, where the traumas of youth and adolescence can be relived. The verse leans heavily on repetition and incantation as the journey backward from woman to young girl is made. The movement is measured in terms of a descent into darkness—the darkness of the South, of remembered cruelty, of the savage games of adolescence:

> remember parties
> where we'd grindddddDDDD
> and grindddddDDDDD
> but not too close
> cuz if you gave it up
> everybody would know. and tell...
> then walking across the room
> where young girls watched each other
> like black vultures...

The backward movement of the narrative is finally arrested when this ritual of cleansing accomplishes its purpose of discovering how it all started:

> i walked into young
> womanhood. Could not hear
> my footsteps in the streets
> could not hear the rhythm of
> young Black womanhood.

This image is that of a ghost, the same ghost that haunts the lines of the early poems. The narrative has demonstrated *how* this state of nonbeing was reached. From this point the movement is in the other direction. **"Present"** moves us through a redefining of the now, up to the moment when this process conceives the possibility of the woman reborn:

> and my singing
> becomes the only sound of a
> blue/black/magical/woman. walking.
> womb ripe, walking. loud with mornings. walking.
> making pilgrimage to herself. walking.

The deadened senses are alive again; singing has replaced silence. The spirit of affirmation inherent in the blues creates the possibilities that are finally to become real in **"Rebirth,"** with its images of gestation:

> whatever is truth becomes known. nine
> months passed touching a bottomless sea.
> nine months i wandered amid waves
> that washed away thirty years of denial...
> nine months passed and my body
> heavy with the knowledge of gods
> turned landward. came to rest...
> i became the mother of sun. moon. star children.

What Sanchez does in **Blues Book** is to use a sense of history as a liberating device. The wasteland of the present and the immediate past is transformed and renewed as the narrative takes us back to an awareness of beginnings, a green world whose innocence can redeem our sense of sin. It is no accident that the poetry of **Blues Book** is both ritualistic and religious. To sing the blues is to affirm a racial truth. Lyricism here has the special purpose of achieving a communal sense of worship, and Sanchez is the shaman, the "blue black magic woman" whose words initiate that process. The weight of meaning in **Blues Book** thus rests on the narrative, on the actual sequence of the ritual, for it is only in this way that the experience of change can be concretized.

The new poems in *I've Been a Woman* benefit from the sense of continuity and evolution conferred by the earlier work. The impact of the section entitled "Haikus/Tankas and Other Love Syllables" is immeasurably enhanced by *Love Poems,* for instance; the new poems, drawing on a relatively limited stock of images (water in various forms, trees, morning, sun, different smells), are an accumulation of moments that define love, age, sorrow, and pride in terms of action. Particular configurations recur: the rhythms of sex, the bent silhouettes of old age, the stillness of intense emotion. But taken

Sonia Sanchez.

together, these poems are like the spontaneous eruptions that punctuate, geyserlike, the flow of experience.

The other new poems in *I've Been a Woman* consist of a series of eulogies, collectively titled "Generations," in which Sanchez explicitly claims her place among those who speak of and for Black people. There is a schematic balance operating here: the individual poems respectively eulogize Sterling Brown (age), Gerald Penny (youth), Sanchez's father, and the idea and reality of mothers. The synthesis implied in this design is enacted in the poetry itself; the imagery and rhythms of the verse in this section convey an overwhelming sense of resolution and serenity. The poems dedicated to Sterling Brown, however, seem overloaded with busy imagery. This is especially true of the first of the two. Cast in the form of a praise song, it presents Brown as a priest-poet and simultaneously implies Sanchez's awareness of her own membership in the tradition which Brown has so honorably helped to maintain. But the effect of the poem is to dilute our sense of Brown's significance, the succession of carefully wrought images, along with the overly schematic structure, gives the poem the feeling of an exercise.

The same cannot be said of the other poems in this section. The Gerald Penny eulogy, built around its song-prayer refrain, is a convincing celebration of a life. Its images—rainbow, yellow corn, summer berries—are felt metaphors of fulfillment, and its diction manages to avoid naïveté while maintaining an appropriate simplicity:

> I am going to walk far to the East
> i hope to find a good morning
> somewhere
>
> I am going to race my own voice
> i hope to have peace
> somewhere...

By the time the poem arrives at its final refrain, its language has enacted a measured movement to a point of calm.

> I do not cry
> for i am man
> no longer
> a child of your
> womb.
>
> There is nothing which does not
>   come to an end
> And to live seventeen years is good
>   in the sight of God.

This calm carries over into **"Father and Daughter,"** the final entry in a diary which began, in *We a BaddDDD People,* with **"A Poem for My Father."** In this early work the anger is open and raw:

> when i remember your
> deformity i want to
> do something about your
> makeshift manhood.

The vengeful rhythms of these lines allow no dialogue; but **"Father and Daughter,"** deliberately repeating the title of an earlier poem which ends in a vision of destruction, moves quietly into a portrayal of family. The grandchild who frolics between father and daughter is an emblem of generation and reconciliation, as is the image of snow melting into a river. The final lines, slowing the graceful rhythm of the poem, pointedly return to the image of the cross with which **"A Poem for My Father"** closes. **"Father and Daughter,"** which begins with the act of talking, concludes with a rejection of the gesture made in the earlier poem and an acceptance of a shared human frailty:

> your land is in the ashes of the South.
> perhaps the color of our losses:
> perhaps the memory that dreams nurse:
> old man, we do not speak of crosses.

The sense of reconciliation here evoked has its corollary in **"Kwa Mamu Zetu Waliotuzaa."** Alternating discursive, image-filled passages of verse with rhythmic, incantatory refrains, this poem enacts a ritual quest for peace that is finally attained through the hypnotic mantras of the closing lines.

> the day is singing
> the day is singing
> he is singing in the mountains
> the nite is singing
> the nite is singing
> she is singing in the earth...

This poem, as much as anything else in *I've Been a Woman,* actualizes the condition of being earthbound. The journey begun with *Homecoming* ends here, in a vision of earth and roots and parenting. (pp. 433-48)

> *David Williams, "The Poetry of Sonia Sanchez," in* Black Women Writers (1950-1980), *edited by Mari Evans, Anchor Press/Doubleday, 1984, pp. 433-48.*

Rosemary K. Curb (essay date 1985)

[*In the following excerpt, Curb discusses female roles in Sanchez's plays.*]

In 1960 when the first sparks of Black racial discontent were igniting the roaring conflagration of the Black Revolution, Sonia Sanchez was twenty-five. At twenty she graduated from Hunter College with a Bachelor of Arts and continued graduate study at New York University. She had been writing poetry since her childhood in Birmingham, Alabama. By the mid-sixties, Sanchez was raising two sons as a single mother and declaiming her poetry at Black Power Conferences in northern cities across the country. She was generally regarded as the leading female literary voice of Black Revolution.

In the now classic collection of the period titled *Black Fire,* edited by LeRoi Jones and Larry Neal, published in 1968, only four of the fifty-six poets included are women. Barbara Simmons has one poem, Lethonia Gee two, Carol Freeman three, and Sonia Sanchez four. **"To All Sisters"** by Sanchez succinctly presents the movement's orthodox position regarding the obligation of Black women to bolster Black male ego by reassuring Black men about their superior sexual power: "there ain't/no MAN like a Black man."

In most of her poetry and drama in the sixties, Sanchez promotes racial separatism, but she also hints at sexist oppression within the Black movement. Her recurring sub-motif, less popular with male revolutionaries than separatism, is the loneliness and sense of betrayal of Black women, loyal to the hope of a future Black nation, deserted by the men to whom they have given an almost religious allegiance. The lonely bitter female speaker in the more emotionally and rhetorically complex poem **"summary,"** [sic] published in *Black Fire,* apparently represents many Black women in America, even though she has not recognized the collective nature of her oppression nor the collective male benefit of keeping women separated from each other in their private anguish.

Most of the Black revolutionary plays by women and men in the sixties present a majority of male characters. When unrelated women are presented together, they are usually portrayed competing for male attention. (pp. 19-20)

In Black revolutionary drama in the sixties female characters are rarely portrayed cooperating on a project which primarily aids women. Rarely do we see women educating each other about male oppression and offering strategies for independence and autonomy. [In *Ain't I a Woman: Black Women and Feminism*] Bell Hooks analyzes the motives of the sexist male revolutionaries:

> Black leaders, male and female, have been unwilling to acknowledge Black male sexist oppression of Black women because they do not want to acknowledge that racism is not the only oppressive force in our lives. Nor do they wish to complicate efforts to resist racism by acknowledging that Black men can be victimized by racism but at the same time act as sexist oppressors of Black women.

About the same time that *Black Fire* appeared, Sonia Sanchez started writing plays because the longer dramatic form was useful when a poem could not contain her political message. The first published play by Sanchez appeared in *The Drama Review* special issue on Black Theatre, edited by Ed Bullins. The short play **The Bronx is Next** is set in Harlem in the midst of a racial revolution. Revolutionaries are burning all the buildings in a poor section to force the construction of livable housing units. A character called Old Sister, who is judged by the male leaders to be too attached to her oppressive past in Birmingham, is sent back to her apartment to go up in smoke with her possessions.

The play's other female character, called Black Bitch, projects the strident Sapphire stereotype so despised by male leaders of the movement as a threat to male superiority. The woman is devalued as both promiscuous, if not actually a professional prostitute, and non-separatist. Not only is she caught in a compromising intimacy with a white policeman, but she spews forth condemnation of Black men's abuse of Black women, to which the male leader responds, "Oh shit. Another Black matriarch on our hands." The leader immediately punishes and humiliates her with a brutal sexual assault and then sends her back to her apartment to burn in the holocaust. Although the Black Bitch character criticizes abusive men, she is portrayed as an enemy of the revolution who must be sacrificed for the future purity of the Black nation. In the context of the dramatic piece her complaints sound trivial and irrelevant if not downright Black-hating.

Sanchez created her second play **Sister Son/ji** for *New Plays From the Black Theatre,* edited by Ed Bullins. This dramatic monologue presents in flashbacks five periods in the life of a Black revolutionary woman. Although the single speaking character does not present herself as a feminist, she acknowledges woman's frequent devaluation by abusive men intoxicated with self-importance. As Son/ji grows from her first act of resisting racism to a sense of betrayal by male revolutionaries who seduce and abandon women to maturity borne of loss and survival, the reader/audience watches the character grow into solitary strength.

At the opening, the title character appears to be an old woman collecting her memories. With grey hair, bowed head, dragging feet, she turns and addresses the audience from her dressing table: "i ain't young no mo. My young days have gone, they passed me by so fast that i didn't even have a chance to see them. What did i do with them? What did i say to them? Do i still remember them? Shd i remember them?" She recalls sadly that all four of her sons are buried there in Mississippi, and she decides to "bring back yesterday as it can never be today." With costume and makeup transformations, she changes into a successively older character, while lighting changes punctuate each flashback.

As a young Negro woman of eighteen or nineteen in the first flashback, Son/ji breathlessly tells her boyfriend Nesbitt, who has come up for the weekend from Howard University, how she raged out of her political theory class at Hunter College because the "ole/bitch" professor could not distinguish her from the other two Black women in a class of twelve students. Son/ji's first assertion of Black pride and rebellion against passive white racism is tinged with woman-hating:

> she became that flustered red/ whiteness that ofays become, and said but u see it's just that—and i finished it for her—i sd it's just that we all look alike. yeah. well damn this class.

When the more conventional Nesbitt, fearful of offending white authority, apparently chides Son/ji for her impulsiveness, she replies: "it might have been foolish but it was right. After all at some point a person's got to stand up for herself just a little." Ironically Son/ji submits to Nesbitt's will to seduce her in the well-baited trap of his father's car and reluctantly loses her virginity. Aware of his insensitivity to Son/ji's loss and her desperate desire for his approval, she asks: "nesbitt do u think after a first love each succeeding love is a repetition?"

In the next flashback Son/ji remembers learning at a Black Power Conference "about blk/women supporting their blk/men, listening to their men, sacrificing, working while blk/men take care of bizness, having warriors and young sisters." Although Sister Son/ji calls the assymetry of the sexes within the movement "blk/love/respect between blk/men and women," the subtext of the orthodoxy demands female subservience to the male will to power.

While the ostensible purpose of asserting increased male dominance within the Black movement was to strengthen the race by glorifying Black masculinity and destroying the supposed Black matriarchy, Bell Hooks regards the promotion of patriarchy as a racist devaluation of Black women.

> By shifting the responsibility for the unemployment of Black men onto Black women and away from themselves, white racist oppressors were able to establish a bond of solidarity with Black men based on mutual sexism. White men preyed upon sexist feelings impressed upon the Black male psyche from birth to socialize Black men so that they would regard not all women, but specifically Black women as the enemies of their masculinity.

Sanchez illustrates Son/ji's growing consciousness of the selfish hypocrisy of male leaders by juxtaposing the public rhetoric of the meeting with Son/ji's private lament to the particular man whose power she is supporting:

> Is there time for all this drinking—going from bar to bar. Shouldn't we be getting ourselves together—strengthening our minds, bodies and souls away from drugs, weed, whiskey and going out on Saturday nites. alone. What is it all about or is the rhetoric apart from the actual being/doing? What is it all about if the doings do not match the words?

Just as she effectively counterpoints Son/ji's first act of rebellion against white racism with her submission to seduction, "the mutual love and respect" that Sanchez believes essential for the growth of Black families seems out of Son/ji's reach. She finds herself trapped: assertive behavior wins her the label "bitch," but continued passive behavior reaps only further abuse and desertion.

In the next brief scene, which begins softly and builds to a crescendo, Sister Son/ji seems to be breaking down. In her mania, she weaves Black Power slogans with fragments from radio shows and childhood games, personal pleas to the man in her life with public shouts against white racism.

> THE CRACKERS ARE COMING TO TOWN TODAY. TODAY TODAY. HOORAY. where are u man? hee. hee. hee. the shadow knows. we must have

an undying love for each other. it's 5 AM in the morning. i am scared of voices moving in my head. ring-around-the-honkies-a pocketful-of-gunsker-boomkerboomwehavenopains. the child is moving inside me. where are you? Man yr/son moves against this silence. he kicks against my silence. Aaaaaah. Aaaaaah. Aaaaaah. oh. i must keep walking. man, come fast. come faster than the speed of bullets—faster than the speed of lightning and when u come we'll see it's SUPER-BLOOD. HEE. HEE. HAA. FOOLED U DIDN'T IT? Ahhh- go way. go way voices that send me spinning into nothingness.

The absent but imagined deserting husband has become transformed in Sister Son/ji's fantasy into a Black macho superman. Her hollow laughter, which acknowledges the empty facade of masculinity, becomes increasingly chilling.

In the next scene Son/ji is an emotionally cool revolutionary warrior wearing a gunbelt and a baby carrier. She is preparing for an attack by the white forces by sending her younger children away from the battlefield with lunches, while her thirteen year old son Mungu fights and dies in the war. Son/ji resists accepting white people who have come to aid the Black revolutionary cause. In accord with Black Muslim tradition, she calls them "devils." Son/ji says that she does not "mind the male/devils here but the female/devils who have followed them." After grieving for her son, she calls for the expulsion of a "devil/woman" who has apparently attached herself to one of the Black warriors:

> have we forgotten so soon that we hate devils. that we are in a death struggle with the beasts. if she's so good. so liberal. send her back to her own kind. Let her liberalize them. Let her become a camp follower to the hatred that chokes white/america.

Sister Son/ji suggests executing the man if he tries to keep his white female lover in the camp. Michele Wallace, analyzing [in *Black Macho and the Myth of Superwoman*] the sudden increase of northern middle class white women going down South to battle for civil rights and becoming involved with Black men, conjectures that the women were eager to avoid being called racist. Inevitably Black women despised the influx of white women who were attracting Black male attention.

The third revolutionary play published by Sanchez in the sixties, ***Uh Huh; But How Do It Free Us?*** presents three scenes which have no narrative connection but which illustrate the oppression created by power imbalance implicit in sexual polarity. The oppressed women in each scene suffer as a direct result of male selfishness and vanity. The male antagonists in the first and third scenes are portrayed as less pernicious than the female competitors for male attention.

The absurdist middle scene throws light on the power struggles in relationships dramatized more realistically in the framing first and third scenes. In the absurdist scene four (Black) brothers and one white man ride rocking horses as a theatrical metaphor for their narcotic addictions. A Black woman and a white woman, both called whores and costumed appropriately, cater to the sado-masochistic fantasies of the men by whipping them and bringing them cocaine upon demand. The scene concludes with a bizarre "queen contest" between the Black whore and the character now called "white dude" prancing around the stage in drag and shouting, "See, I'm the real queen. I am the universe." Finally the white dude punches his opponent to the floor declaring, "Don't look at her. She's Black. I'm white. The rightful queen." The scene suggests that all women are servants and caretakers for all men, regardless of race, but that only Black men possess the true macho qualities inherent in the American masculine stereotype. White men easily degenerate into women.

The first and third scenes both centrally portray Black revolutionary leaders whose vanity requires the sexual and nurturing attention of several women. Malik's two wives, both pregnant, are not sufficient to feed his insecurity. The reassurance of conquest is luring him on to pursue other women. The conservative homebody Waleesha contrasts with younger revolutionary activist wife Nefertia. Despite his past attentions, Malik has apparently tired of both of them by the time the play opens. Michele Wallace notes that the inordinate value placed on Black masculinity tended to devalue Black women's humanity to such an extent that young Black women were dropping out of school because their boyfriends had convinced them that doing anything other than having babies and performing domestic chores was "counterrevolutionary."

The longer, more fully developed third scene dramatizes the dilemma of an unnamed Black man. Both costume and stage set illustrate the split allegiance of the revolutionary leader. His costume is half African dashiki and half white American business suit. One side of the stage is the apartment of a white woman, the Black man's weakness/addiction but also his source of material wealth. The other half is the apartment he shares with a Black woman who has come to California from New York to live and work for the revolution with him. As the Black woman becomes more well known in the movement, the Black man's interest in her and devotion to her decline:

> It's just hard for me, you know, to see you up there on stage gittin' all that applause. Makes me wonder why you chose me. After all, I'm not really famous yet. I'm working on it. But you, everybody knows you.

The frantic oscillation of the man called Brother between Black and white women finally reaches a climax on the evening he tries to be with both of them simultaneously. Although Brother refuses to accompany Sister to her reading, he promises to wait at their apartment for her return. Meanwhile he rushes over to his white woman lover, who is drowning her grief at her anticipation of losing Brother to Sister with Scotch and sleeping pills. Brother frantically tries to wake her.

> I am committed to you, lady. Don't nobody mean to me what you mean to me. C'mon, baby, you gonna

be all right. I'm you mannnn. Nothing can change that, you know. So what if she's having a baby. It's something she wanted. I guess it fulfills her as a Black woman, but it didn't bother you and me, baby. Not us. We were together before she came and we'll stay together.

Brother thanks the unconscious white woman for the money that put him through school, money that enables him to travel and dress well. He even says, "I'm a man because you've allowed me to be a man."

Although Brother seems to need the white woman's affection and approval as much as he needs her money, other Black men justified their involvement with white women not only as a means of gaining money to support themselves and the movement (a curious blend of masculine and political prostitution) but also used the sexual availability and willingness of white women, who "didn't put them down and made them feel like men" as a means of controlling or devaluing Black women. According to Michele Wallace, some Black men regarded a white woman as "a piece of the white man's property that he might actually obtain."

In the final confrontation with Brother, Sister unleashes her fury: "To you being a Black woman means I should take all the crap you can think of and any extra crap just hanging loose. That ain't right, man, and you know it too." Like Son/ji, Sister urges Brother to follow the puritan code of abstinence from alcohol, drugs, and tobacco that the revolution preaches. After the man makes his final exit, Sister decides not to leave him because she believes that he will change.

> He'll understand why a Black man must be faithful to his woman, so she'll stop the madness of our mothers repeating itself out loud.... I am the new Black woman. I will help the change to come. Just gots to rock myself in Blackness in the knowledge of womanly Blackness and I shall be.

All three Black revolutionary plays by Sonia Sanchez produced or published in the sixties portray Black women being abused by Black men. The two female characters in the first play are verbally condemned by the male revolutionaries and rewarded for their self-assertion of counterrevolutionary views with the "poetic justice" of extermination. The play does not present them as strong or even sympathetic characters.

Sister Son/ji, however, is portrayed as heroic in her solitary strength. Nevertheless, the man or men who abuse her are not presented as representatives of the oppressive system of patriarchy but as isolated flawed men. Thus Son/ji's struggle against masculine vanity is seen as an isolated dilemma. At no point does she acknowledge that any portion of her suffering results from a system of male domination which separates women from mutual struggle. Despite her name, Sister Son/ji seems bereft of loving and supportive sisters. She exhibits no hint of feminist consciousness or sense of solidarity with other women battling against patriarchy. Both Sister Son/ji and Sister in the third section of *Uh Huh; But How Do It Free Us?* survive alone. Even though the women are admirable, such dramatic portraits do not promote the liberation of Black women.

Bell Hooks explains how sexism within the male Black revolution camouflaged the need to struggle against women's oppression and silenced Black women from speaking out in their own behalf:

> Without a doubt, the false sense of power Black women are encouraged to feel allows us to think that we are not in need of social movements like a women's movement that would liberate us from sexist oppression. The sad irony is of course that Black women are often most victimized by the very sexism we refuse to collectively identify as an oppressive force.

Although none of the three revolutionary plays by Sonia Sanchez asserts a conscious feminist position, their portrayals of the victimization of strong women constitute a preliminary raising of consciousness. They dramatize the need for active cooperation among Black women in political struggle for sexual as well as racial justice. Chronologically the plays progress toward feminism. (pp. 20-8)

> Rosemary K. Curb, "Pre-Feminism in the Black Revolutionary Drama of Sonia Sanchez," in The Many Forms of Drama, Vol. V, edited by Karelisa V. Hartigan, University Press of America, 1985, pp. 19-29.

Kamili Anderson (essay date 1989)

[*In the following excerpt, Anderson reviews* Under A Soprano Sky.]

The name Sonia Sanchez may be the most undeservedly underspoken of contemporary women poets in America. Relative to her merits as both prolific poet (she has authored thirteen books) and social activist, widespread critical acknowledgment of Sanchez's talents has been remiss. No doubt this is a result of the boldly rhetorical nature of her work and her involvement with so-called "radical" Black literary and cultural factions. But her poetry, for its precision and insightfulness, warrants far broader recognition, no matter how belated.

Sanchez was a leading spokessister for the women's side of things in the defiant Black Arts literary upsweep of the 1960s and 1970s. It was often she who, even as a female follower of the Honorable Elijah Muhammad and the Nation of Islam, was the strongest feminist poetic voice in a cultural movement with strong sexist leanings. Noted for her dramatic and moving articulations of her own work, Sanchez now (she is in her fifties) presents an intriguing study in juxtapositioned extremes. Her poetry has burned consistently with a fierce but expertly controlled intensity. With each collection, that fire has burned hotter and cleaner.

Her latest and finest work, **Under a Soprano Sky,** is hot enough to melt rock, and it comes hard on the trail blazed by her previous book, **Homegirls & Hand Gre-**

nades. Although the poems in this collection are tempered and configured to scorching extremes, they are, simultaneously, her most introspective and intricate. They deal with age, AIDS, alienation awareness, Africa, and all of us, men and women.

Sanchez has a penchant for enlisting words to imagery. She can mesmerize with scenarios that require readers to transfuse all of their senses, so much so that the ability to discern whether one is reading with the soul or with the eyes, or listening with the heart or the ears, is lost.

This is deep, deep stuff that conjures and comingles the senses in a potpourri of images. "i shall spread out my veins," she writes, "and beat the dust into noise." "i hear the wind of graves moving the sky"; "hands breathing"; "my eyes put on more flesh" and "i hear the bricks pacing my window" are more of the same. "Under a soprano sky / a woman sings / lovely as chandeliers," sings the refrain from her title poem. Lovely and fiercely, she should add.

Under a Soprano Sky offers a full dose of a mature woman-poet rising to the height of her powers, a woman very much like the older Black women Sanchez writes respectfully of in **"Dear Mama"**: "women rooted in themselves, raising themselves in dark America, discharging their pain without ever stopping." This collection poses the "full moon of sonia/shining down on ya" to anyone who might take her or her sisters' visions lightly. With it comes the warning: "you gon known you been touched by me / this time."

Few poets write with more succinctness or intensity: Sanchez's expansive poems can incorporate guttural sounds insistent upon vocal rendition or be terse, taut haikus. Haikus such as those "for domestic workers in the african diaspora," "i works hard but treated / bad man. i'se telling you de / truth i full of it." and "for a black prostitute," "redlips open wide / like wound winding down on / the city / clotting." provide searing examples.

From **"fragment 3"** echoes the call:

> come all you late twenty
> year olds you young thirties
> and forties and fifties.
> O lacquered revolutionists!
> all you followers of vowelled
> ghosts painted on neon signs.
> O noise of red bones cascading dreams.
>
> come to conscripted black
> mounted on a cell of revelation
> come and salute death
> while the rust of tombs
> murmur old sonnets
> and my grave sinks with
> the pleasure of insects
> who wear no diadem.

Sonia Sanchez is a poet not to be disavowed further. Her work is high reality transformed into high rhetoric, transformed into high art. *Under a Soprano Sky* and the corpus of her work deserves a thorough reading that is worthy of her substantial and finely honed literary talents.

Kamili Anderson, "Giving Our Souls," in Belles Lettres: A Review of Books by Women, *Vol. 4, No. 2, Winter, 1989, p. 14.*

FURTHER READING

Gabbin, Joanne Veal. "The Southern Imagination of Sonia Sanchez." In *Southern Women Writers: The New Generation,* edited by Tonette Bond Inge, pp. 180-203. Tuscaloosa: University of Alabama Press, 1990.
    Discusses Sanchez's life and work, especially in relation to her upbringing in the South.

Joyce, Joyce Ann. "The Development of Sonia Sanchez: A Continuing Journey." *Indian Journal of American Studies* 13, No. 2 (July 1983): 37-71.
    Thorough examination of Sanchez's poetic development.

Leibowitz, Herbert. "Exploding Myths: An Interview with Sonia Sanchez." *Parnassus* 12 and 13, Nos. 2 and 1 (Spring/Summer and Fall/Winter 1985): 357-68.
    Interview with Sanchez on her use of language and her literary influences.

Melhem, D. H. "Sonia Sanchez: Will and Spirit." *Melus* 12, No. 3 (Fall 1985): 73-98.
    Interview exploring Sanchez's development as a writer.

Palmer, R. Roderick. "The Poetry of Three Revolutionists: Don L. Lee, Sonia Sanchez, and Nikki Giovanni." *CLA Journal* XV, No. 1 (September 1971): 25-36.
    Addresses Sanchez's attitude toward black identity and experience.

Saunders, James Robert. "Sonia Sanchez's *Homegirls and Handgrenades:* Recalling Toomer's *Cane.*" *Melus* 15, No. 1 (Spring 1988): 73-82.
    Analyzes *homegirls & handgrenades* as a response to Jean Toomer's *Cane.*

Tate, Claudia. "Sonia Sanchez." In her *Black Women Writers at Work,* pp. 132-48. New York: Continuum, 1983.
    Interview in which Sanchez recalls her association with the Nation of Islam.

Walker, Barbara. "Sonia Sanchez Creates Poetry for the Stage." *Black Creation* 5, No. 1 (Fall 1973): 12-14.
    Interview with Sanchez on *Sister Son/ji.*

Léopold Sédar Senghor

1906-

(Has also written under pseudonyms Silmang Diamano and Patrice Maguilene Kaymor) Senegalese poet, essayist, nonfiction writer, critic, editor, and author of children's books.

An influential statesman who served as President of the Republic of Senegal for twenty years following its independence from France in 1960, Senghor is an accomplished poet and essayist whose work affirms the rich traditions of his African heritage. Along with Aimé Césaire, he is best known as an outspoken proponent of negritude, a literary ideology that urges black people worldwide to resist cultural assimilation and to reclaim their African past. Many commentators have noted elements of both European and African culture in Senghor's poetry, attributing this synthesis to his French education and his long service in the French government. Robert W. July, however, contended that Senghor's works are not exclusive to one group. He argued that "the value of Senghor's poetry rests squarely on its own merits which are not parochial but universal.... Thus the special pleading of negritude fades before the eloquence of the poet whose humanity represents and refreshes us all."

Senghor was born in the predominantly Islamic province of Joal, French West Africa. Raised as a Roman Catholic, he attended French missionary schools in preparation for the priesthood but abandoned his religious studies in favor of the classics and modern literature. Upon graduation from the Lycée of Dakar in 1928, he earned a scholarship to study at the Sorbonne. While in Paris, he met the West Indian writers Aimé Césaire and Léon Gontran Damas, who introduced him to the works of Harlem Renaissance authors Claude McKay, Countee Cullen, and Langston Hughes. These writers' pride in African-American culture profoundly influenced Senghor's writings, as did the verse of French poets André Breton, Paul Claudel, and St.-John Perse. In 1933 Senghor became the first black African to graduate from the Sorbonne with the agrégé de grammaire, the highest degree granted in French education. The following year, with Césaire and Damas, he founded the literary and cultural journal *L'étudiant noir,* which helped delineate the principles of negritude and published the works of other francophone writers. During this period, Senghor also taught Latin, classical literature, and African history at several secondary schools in suburban Paris.

The poems in Senghor's first major collection, *Chants d'ombre* (1945), were written during the 1930s. Although largely traditional in structure and meter, these pieces evoke the intricate rhythmic patterns of songs from Senghor's native village. In such poems as "Neige sur Paris" and "Nuit de Sine," Senghor described the

loneliness and alienation he experienced during his first years in Paris. He also reflected upon his boyhood in Joal and devoted several poems to his parents and a maternal uncle. *Hosties noires* (1948) evidences Senghor's growing interest in Pan-Africanism and contains some of his strongest attacks on French colonialism. The majority of the poems in this collection relate his experiences as a soldier and prisoner of war while serving in the French Colonial Army during World War II. In the poem "Camp 1940," for example, Senghor recalled the fraternal bonds that he formed with black American and West Indian GIs during his incarceration. The poems "Aux tirailleurs Sénégalais" and "Désespoir d'un volontaire libre" celebrate the humility and endurance of Senegalese soldiers, whose battlefield experiences Senghor equates with the sufferings of their ancestors under colonialism. The angry, militant tone of the verse in this collection provoked some critics to label negritude a racist movement. With the advent of Fascism and Nazism in Europe, however, Senghor tempered his views. Jonathan Peters declared: "Senghor wishes that the threat to the free existence and expression of a national will and consciousness will be a lesson to France and the rest of Europe in dealing with colonies under their management and that the inhumanity of the encounter will give birth to a new and multi-cultural humanism."

Following World War II, Senghor became active in politics. In 1946 he became a Senegalese député in the French National Assembly in Paris, and in 1948 he formed the socialist party Bloc Démocratique Sénégalais in his own country. Senghor also remained involved in literary pursuits, playing a significant role in the establishment of the literary journal *Présence africaine* in 1947 and, a year later, editing *Anthologie de la nouvelle poésie nègre et malgache de langue française* (1948), which features the works of writers from the Caribbean, French West Africa, and Madagascar. He also published his own verse during this period, most notably the volume *Chants pour Naëtt* (1949), which contains love lyrics addressed to a woman whose physical attributes and spiritual temperament serve as metaphors of the African landscape.

Ethiopiques (1956) is regarded by many commentators as Senghor's most conciliatory collection of verse. The poems in this book were composed during the early 1950s, when Senghor served as French delegate to the United Nations General Assembly and was reelected to the French National Assembly. The sequences "Epîtres à la Princesse" and "La mort de la Princesse," which depict the courtship of a European princess by an African diplomat, were interpreted by several critics as allegories of Senghor's political orientation and his marriage to a French woman. Also included in *Ethiopiques* is the long dramatic poem "Chaka," which recounts the final days of the nineteenth-century Zulu warrior king who conquered South Africa through mass murder and tyranny. Based in part on Lesothan writer Thomas Mofolo's 1926 historical novel *Chaka,* Senghor's poem was regarded as a highly idealized and apologetic rendition of Chaka's ruthless exploits. John Reed and Clive Wake stated: "Chaka's excuse that it was necessary to destroy, like a farmer burning the bush before a new season, is a simile which it is impossible to apply in detail."

Senghor continued to publish poetry following his election as President of Senegal. *Nocturnes* (1961) contains a series of elegies discussing the nature of poetry and the role of the poet in contemporary society. This collection also reprints in its entirety Senghor's volume *Chants pour Naëtt* as a sequence of poems entitled "Chants pour Signare." *Selected Poems* (1964) made Senghor's most significant verse available in English translation. In a review of this volume, a critic for *Newsweek* observed: "Like Walt Whitman, Senghor taps private sources deep within himself to discover in his experience the consciousness of his people and the drama of his continent.... Conquest over despair, acceptance, and pride drive through the poems like a strong river, unifying them by its powerful currents."

After 1960 Senghor wrote chiefly political and critical prose that tied closely to the goals, activities, and demands of his political life. During this time he survived an attempted coup d'état staged in 1962 by Senegal's prime minister, Mamadou Dia. The following year Senghor authorized the Senegalese National Assembly to draw up a new constitution that gave more power to the president. Known for his ability to hold factions together, he remained in power—he was reelected in 1968 and 1973—despite more coup attempts, an assassination plot in 1967, and civil unrest in the late 1960s. Much of Senghor's writing from this era outlines the course he feels Africa must follow, despite upheavals. Commenting on the instability suffered by African nations after achieving independence, Senghor told *Time* magazine: "The frequency of coups in Africa is the result of the backwardness in civilization that colonization represented....What we should all be fighting for is democratic socialism. And the first task of socialism is not to create social justice. It is to establish working democracies." Senghor's views on socialism and politics are collected in several nonfiction works, including: *Rapport sur la doctrine et le programme du parti* (1959; *Report on the Principles and Programme of the Party*), *Liberté I: Négritude et humanisme* (1964; *Freedom I: Negritude and Humanism*), and *Ce que je crois: Négritude, Francité, et la civilisation de l'universel* (1988).

Senghor is revered throughout the world for political and literary accomplishments that span nearly six decades. It is widely believed that he was considered in 1962 for the Nobel Prize in Literature. When *Selected Poems* appeared in 1964, *Saturday Review* likened Senghor to American poet Walt Whitman and determined that the poems represented were "written by a gifted, civilized man of good will celebrating the ordinary hopes and feelings of mankind." The *Times Literary Supplement* called Senghor "one of the best poets now writing in [French]" and marveled at his "astonishing achievement to have combined so creative a life with his vigorous and successful political activities." Senghor's life, according to Jacques Louis Hymans, "might be summarized as an effort to restore to Africa an equilibrium destroyed by the clash with Europe." For those who see contradictions in Senghor's effort, Hymans observed that "one constant in his thought appears to surmount the contradictions it contains: universal reconciliation is his only goal and Africa's only salvation."

(For further information about Senghor's life and works, see *Black Writers; Contemporary Authors,* Vol. 116; and *Contemporary Literary Criticism,* Vol. 54.)

PRINCIPAL WORKS

"Le problème culturel en AOF" (essay) 1937; published
    in periodical *Paris-Dakar*
"Ce que l'homme noir apporte" (essay) 1939; published
    in periodical *L'homme de couleur*
Chants d'ombre (poetry) 1945

"Defense de l'Afrique noire" (essay) 1945; published in periodical *Esprit*

Anthologie de la nouvelle poésie nègre et malgache de langue française [editor] (poetry) 1948

Hosties noires (poetry) 1948

Chants pour Naëtt (poetry) 1949

La belle histoire de Leuk-le-Lievre (juvenile literature) 1953; also published as *La belle histoire de Leuk-le-Lievre: Cours élémentaire des écoles d'Afrique noire* 1961

Chants d'ombre-Hosties noires (poetry) 1956

*Ethiopiques (poetry) 1956; also published as *Ethiopiques: Poèmes,* 1974

Rapport sur la doctrine et le programme du parti (prose) 1959

[*Report on the Principles and Programme of the Party,* 1959; also published as *African Socialism: A Report to the Constitutive Congress of the Party of African Federation,* 1959]

Rapport sur la politique générale (prose) 1960

Léopold Sédar Senghor (poems and prose) 1961

Nation et voie africaine du socialisme (prose) 1961; also published as *Liberté II: Nation et voie africaine du socialisme,* 1971

[*Nationhood and the African Road to Socialism,* 1962; also published as *On African Socialism,* 1964]

Nocturnes (poetry) 1961

[*Nocturnes,* 1969]

Rapport sur la doctrine et la politique générale; ou, Socialisme, unité africaine, construction nationale (prose) 1962

Liberté I: Négritude et humanisme (prose) 1964

[*Freedom I: Negritude and Humanism,* 1974]

Poèmes (poetry) 1964

Selected Poems (poetry) 1964

Théorie et pratique du socialisme sénégalais (prose) 1964

Prose and Poetry (poetry and prose) 1965

Latinité et Négritude (prose) 1966

Négritude, arabisme, et Francité: Réflexions sur le problème de la culture (prose) 1967; also published as *Les Fondements de l'Africanité; ou, Négritude et Arabité,* 1967

[*The Foundations of "Africanité"; or, "Negritude" and "Arabité,"* 1971]

Politique, nation, et développement moderne: Rapport de politique générale (prose) 1968

Elégie des Alizes (poetry) 1969

Le plan du décollage économique; ou, La participation responsable comme moteur de développement (prose) 1970

Pourquoi une idéologie négro-africaine? (lecture) 1971

Lettres d'hivernage (poetry) 1973

La parole chez Paul Claudel et chez les négro-africains (prose) 1973

Paroles (poetry) 1975

Pour une relecture africaine de Marx et d'Engels (prose) 1976

Pour une société sénégalaise socialiste et démocratique: Rapport sur la politique générale (prose) 1976

Selected Poems = Poésies choisies (poetry) 1976

Liberté III: Négritude et civilisation de l'universel (essay) 1977

Selected Poems of Léopold Sédar Senghor (poetry) 1977

Poems of a Black Orpheus (poetry) 1981

Ce que je crois: Négritude, Francité, et la civilisation de l'universel (prose) 1988

*This work contains "Chaka," a poem adapted from Thomas Mofolo's 1926 novel about the Zulu warrior.

John Reed and Clive Wake (essay date 1964)

[*In the following excerpt from a 1964 introduction to Senghor's* Selected Poems, *Reed and Wake evaluate the poet's work, focusing on theme and technique.*]

Senghor's poetry is critically best examined not as the poetry of a new African poetic tradition because, though Senghor's poetry may be important for the foundation of such a tradition, speculation about it now can hardly throw light on Senghor's poetry itself. It is best examined as the work of a man in a particular situation making use of a French poetic tradition which is at hand. In fact the outstanding qualities of Senghor's work do come from the situation of the man himself. If we look at his situation at the moment, he is President of the Republic of Senegal. His life has been devoted and devoted with success to politics as well as to poetry.... The circumstances which enabled—almost one might say, drove—Senghor to become both poet and politician can be set out. They in turn have given a quality to his poetry—or enabled his poetry to retain qualities which are hard to find in European poetry. Perhaps the most important is the holding together without strain personal and public issues, a poetry which furnishes a myth and at the same time allows the poet to remain an acceptable hero of his own poetry.... We could say that the value of Senghor's poetry comes more from the combination of poet and politician than the combination of African and Frenchman but the two combinations in the end are inseparable, because the circumstance which has allowed Senghor to be both poet and politician without the one spoiling the other is precisely the circumstance that he is one of the small group of Africans with whom the French colonial policy of assimilation—half-heartedly believed in and only spasmodically applied—really took its course. It is because Senghor is an African so deep in the culture of the French language that he was for a time a teacher of French in a Parisian Lycée, that the personal nostalgia which gives rise to his earliest poetry must lead by way of a sentimental journey back to Africa, to political involvement. It is his possession of French culture which among his own people makes him one of a small group of leaders. The process of acquiring this culture takes him to Europe where he experiences not only exile but the peculiar predicament of having a black skin in a white society. It is through the culture whose acquisition has brought this predicament, that the predicament can be expressed. But this culture also gives the status of a leader, so that for Senghor the predicament is not personal, and not resolvable merely through poetic utterance but through political action.... The French gave to Senghor and those like him everything French culture could offer, not to enable them to carry their countries to independence but to make them Frenchmen, local dignitaries in the overseas provinces of France. The independence of Senegal was not foreseen by Senghor's teachers, nor indeed by Senghor himself until well into the 1950's. Even so, Senghor's life has been largely a working out of the inevitable if unforeseen logic of the French colonial policy of assimilation, and if it has provided the context for his whole achievement, it is also something which overtook him like his fate. He writes somewhere how his father used the white school to which he was eventually sent as a threat of punishment while his mother wept and pleaded that he was too young to go away. But if French culture was a fate that overtook Senghor, it was a fate of human devising. The negro in the New World finds his fate in his black skin. His destiny is being who he is. And although the society which despises him is of human devising and in the last resort his predicament comes from the human actions and decisions which made up the centuries of the slave trade, the literature of the New World negro expresses an existential rather than a social predicament. The only genuine poetry which emerges is defiant, and destructive. (pp. viii-x)

Senghor's white education was a preparation for leadership which led to personal problems which could only be resolved by the assumption of that leadership. But they could be solved in that way. Within this particular situation, private and public problems fall almost exactly together; a private personality and a public personality become compatible. Hence Senghor's cultivation of poetry did not render him incapable of taking the political action the situation demanded, his political offices have not meant the death of the poet; further, the poetry itself has a quality of being at the same time profoundly personal poetry and public poetry, a poetry in which the aspiration of his people, in which the generalized manifesto of new African consciousness are expressed. Poetry of this kind does not exist in Europe, and perhaps it cannot exist even in Africa outside the particular conditions which have surrounded Senghor's life. It is these conditions which give real validity to the literary concept of *négritude*. For Senghor, a scrupulous and honest, that is, poetical expression of himself, is also a political expression. Hence the criticisms which are made of this concept by some English-speaking Africans have a general validity, but fail to understand how the concept in circumstances different from their own can still be valid. Ezekiel Mphahlele, the South African critic, writes that the artist at work and the nationalist are not one and the same person. Usually they are not, but in Senghor they are.

Even in the earliest published verse, the personal is never separated from the larger situation from which the personal situation arises: a racial, political and colonial situation. The main themes in *Chants d'Ombre* (1945) are exile, the loneliness and homesickness of an African student in Paris in the 1930's.... [The] nostalgia for the paradise of childhood with its 'innocence of Europe' brings an awareness of a conflict between his African heritage and European culture. This conflict is felt personally, but not only as a personal problem—it is also the problem of the conflict between Africa and Europe. His own role as the spokesman for his people is already present. Poems which take their rise in the evocation of mood or in erotic experience, like **"Nuit de Sine"**, reach their conclusion in a mood of impatience, as if all this only reminded the poet of a task of speaking on behalf of others which has still to be achieved.... The conflict is traced most fully in **"For Koras and Balafong"**, where Soukeina and Isabella, sister and foster-sister, stand for Africa and Europe. If he had to choose one and reject the other, he says he would choose Soukeina, but the very imagery of sister and foster-sister shows that Senghor does not expect to be driven to make this choice. It is his good fortune to live in a situation where colonialism resolves into affirmatives and not negatives. He can take with both hands, and his poetry finds a fullness of expression to correspond to the fullness of his cultural position, just as his theoretic writing on *négritude* postulates an ultimate all-inclusiveness in the concept of the Culture of the Universal. At the same time, the poetry although it is autobiographical never has that sharpness which is the tone of the individual at war with the world found in some European poetry. Even at its most bitter, Senghor's poetry is poetry of fulfilment rather than of decision. Though he rejects much of Western civilization, Senghor is a poet at ease in two cultures, unlike many modern European poets and indeed some African poets, who are at ease in none. Even his task of expressing the vision of his native culture through the means and methods of an acquired culture sets him problems which are much more immediately rewarding in their solution than the problem which faces an original artist in Europe who often has to express a new vision through the means and methods of a culture that upholds an older and incompatible vision. This is why so much modern poetry contains destructive elements—ugliness, cacophony, nonsense—which are necessary before anything new can be said. These destructive elements are absent from Senghor's poetry. Now and then we catch an echo of the idiom of surrealism, but Senghor's poetry in its use of language and in its attitude towards the civilization of its time is at the opposite pole from surrealism. (pp. x-xii)

To the period of the War belongs much of Senghor's bitterest but also most moving poetry. He joined the French Army as a private soldier, was captured by the Germans and remained in the prison camp *Front-Stalag 230* until 1942. The War confirms Senghor's loyalty to France, and through that loyalty he finds a new solidarity with his own people and also with the common people of France. Yet military life reveals the continuing prejudice against the blackman, and one of the themes of the second collection of poems, *Hosties Noires* (1948) is the humiliation of the African soldier. In the camps Senghor celebrates the humility and endurance and creativity of his own people. Europe in its distress has needed to use them and will not be able to turn them away from their part in building the new world. A mythic battle in the future is foreseen, but it is not a war of African against European, but a great revolutionary struggle of all the oppressed peoples and the white workers who belong with them. Much of the poetry is still personal, but Senghor has taken on the impersonality of the African soldier. The heroes of this volume are the *tirailleurs* of Senegal, and Senghor in his own person finds justification in being their poet.... ***Chants pour Naett,*** first published in 1949, and afterwards republished as part of the volume ***Nocturnes*** (1961), under the title ***Chants pour Signare,*** is a series of short love poems. The woman addressed is in a way identified with Africa, as the women in his earlier poetry are almost always seen and expressed in terms of landscape. The image usually has strongly maternal characteristics. Love is a going back to the emotional world of Africa and of childhood, a retreat from the harsh bright demands of the West. These poems seem written from inside Africa, and the nostalgia of exile and the bitterness of the despised soldier are mostly absent, and with them much of the emotional turbulence of the earlier verse. These poems are less rhetorical, less violent, less public. Although the literal meaning is often obscure, the tone is without ambiguity and the quality of imagery and melody is rich. (p. xiii)

In ***Ethiopiques,*** a collection published in 1956, the lyrical quality in his previously highly personal poetry has become the self-confident rhetoric of the man who represents his people, who has become their trumpet. Even in the poems of the group called **"Épîtres à la Princesse"**, which are the only ones in the volume which seem to be personal in subject matter, he takes up, perhaps half playfully, the position of a leader in an old-fashioned traditional Africa of the imagination. It is not that there is no distinction between public and private life, but the poems occur at that point when a private friendship seems to have public implications. They are about two people who, like medieval sovereigns, in their personal relations establish symbolically the relations between their realms. Senghor is once more the hero of his own poetry, but not now as a person in a predicament or a man discovering solidarity with his fellows, but as their symbol, speaking for them with an air of confidence, as personal and impersonal as an hereditary monarch.

In the **"Épîtres à la Princesse"**, Senghor presents himself, the poet-ruler, in a poetic world built up out of his own personal relationships and African history, owing something perhaps to the princes who found cities in Saint-John Perse's *Anabase*. There is, however, another image used by Senghor in which this notion of the compatibility of the poet and the ruler is deeply challenged—the image of Chaka the Zulu. Senghor's dramatic poem about Chaka is inspired by the remarkable historical novel written in Sesuto by Thomas

Mofolo and published in 1926.... Mofolo, a Christian and writing before it was fashionable to glorify every aspect of the African past, sees Chaka as a bloodthirsty tyrant and at the end a crazy megalomaniac. Yet he is also born under a curse, led astray by supernatural soliciting, a figure not unlike Macbeth. Senghor chooses the moment at the very end of Chaka's life, and makes him a martyred figure, a man who has sacrificed himself body and soul for his people. Critics have objected to this cavalier use of history, and yet the attempt to reinterpret historical figures in a startling way is not unusual, even outside poetry, and Senghor does not in fact do violence to any of Mofolo's events.... [Senghor's **"Chaka"**] fails as a justification of Chaka's actions and read in this way is quite intolerable. Chaka's excuse that it was necessary to destroy, like a farmer burning the bush before a new season, is a simile which it is impossible to apply in detail. However, Senghor is not really concerned with Chaka's actions; his drama is without action and concerns Chaka's state of mind alone, and so we must see the death of Noliwe, for example, not as the death of another human being, but as the sacrifice Chaka himself makes, giving up what he loves and even his power to love.

In this poem, Senghor is less concerned with the crimes which those who have power may have to commit, than with the sacrifices of love and of their real creativity which they may have to make.... [He] makes Chaka a poet who has to sacrifice his poethood to undertake the liberation of his people. In reading the poem, it is difficult to avoid seeing Senghor himself as Chaka and at the same time noticing how different Senghor's own situation seems to be. We notice it is the White Voice that identifies poet and politician.

> My word, Chaka, you are a poet... a fine speaker, a politician...!

Chaka himself distinguishes them. A politician is a man of action alone, he killed the poet in himself. He was dead himself before the first of his victims. Yet in the second part of the poem, set now not against the accusing White Voice but against the Chorus and its leader, Chaka is once more established in his poethood. The politics of violence becomes the politics of a new kind of creation through rhythm. Chaka is no longer the Lion, the Elephant, the Buffalo, but the athlete, the dancer, the lover. Power is against the vocation of the poet, but it is also the testing and the purgatory of the poet. Chaka, who has been called by the White Voice the poet of the Valley of Death, is declared Poet of the Kingdom of Childhood, creator of the words of life. The poet who died to make the politician, lives again and the politician dies. Chaka's own definition of the poet in his last utterance is 'the one-who-accompanies, the knee at the side of the drum, the carved drumstick.' The poet is in this sense not incompatible with the political leader, because the poet is not a creator, but the spokesman; he speaks for his people. As earlier in Senghor's verse, we find the repeated image of the trumpet, the ambassador.

Alternatively, though not the creator, he provides the rhythm for the creative activities of the whole people.

In his most recent poems, the **"Odes"**, Senghor seems to treat more directly the problems of the nature of poetry and the sources of poetic inspiration. The direct but antithetic imagery of the **"Elegy of Midnight"** deals with the aridity and the creativity of the poet. Poetry springs from childhood, into which the poet must be born again. But it also springs from the sleep of death. In the **"Elegy of the Circumcised",** he tells how poetry affirms life and overcomes the fear of death, but only by surrendering to the process of life. The poem must give up structure, become only rhythm. Poetry lives only if the words are allowed to go. (pp. xiv-xvi)

A comparison between Senghor's **"Elegy of the Waters"** and Claudel's Ode **"L'Esprit et l'Eau"** immediately suggests itself. As we have seen, there is no point in trying to isolate Senghor's poetry from the tradition of French poetry; it is difficult to see how recognizable poetry can be written in any language without reference to the poetic traditions already existing in that language. As a poet of the French literary tradition, Senghor is not an innovator. The reasons for this have been discussed earlier in this introduction. We could say Senghor is a poetic innovator in an African poetic context, but not in the European. On the other hand, he enters the French poetic tradition at a point where it was most open, the point at which an awareness of the world outside Europe and the excitement of non European culture was powerfully felt, in the poetic tradition of Paul Claudel and Saint-John Perse. Senghor is of course not an imitator, and he has said that the material for **Chants d'Ombre** and **Hosties Noires** was already in his drawer before he discovered Saint-John Perse. Still, he recognizes them as cognate poets: Claudel, the professional diplomat, living most of his adult life outside France, an expert on oriental civilizations; Saint-John Perse, also a career diplomat, also living almost continuously outside France, preoccupied with the theme of exile. Yet both these poets are profoundly European, in the sense that traditional European values are stressed in their work. They are poets whose sentiments are patriotic and reactionary, poets of civilization, men who were able to combine eminent careers in the public service with poetic creativity. Senghor's poetry shares with theirs the freedom from regular metrical form, a use of language which is rhetorical, drawing on rich but not eccentric sources of vocabulary and dependent on highly charged words, like 'blood', 'gold', and 'night', elaborating a few central images and symbols.

The differences are, however, important. Senghor, like them, is a poet of civilization, but his attitude is less arrogant, less insistent, more humane. His work is also more intensely personal than the French poets'. Claudel and Saint-John Perse have not written the kind of occasional verse which makes up most of Senghor's collections. At the same time Senghor's poetry is less egotistical. It is also in its sympathies both aristocratic and popular, profoundly traditional, not only in the African context, but also in the European, and at the same time revolutionary. Senghor has been called the poet of unity. It would perhaps be more correct to call him the poet of reconciliation, which is not the same thing. This conciliation is not only found in the thought and feeling of the poetry, but also in its techniques. It is not a poetry of paradox, of sharp metaphysical distinctions, or far-fetched imagery which suddenly reveals similarities in unexpected places, and at the same time, unexpected contradictions. It is poetry without wit. It is poetry in which the great commonplace symbols are used, sometimes conventionally, sometimes idiosyncratically, but never rigidly to create absolute distinctions. Night and day, black and white, become ambiguous. This is helped by the way in which European languages impose a symbolism of white and black which an African tends to repudiate, as Sartre points out in his essay *Orphée Noir*. Senghor's poetry, like his cultural philosophy, is inclusive, rather than exclusive. His world is ultimately without negation, which means that the relation between the word and the reality is always a direct one. Nothing can be defined by negatives. Nothing can be mentioned in a poem to be excluded. Hence poetry is a listing of things, a bringing of them together, in a relationship which is not structural or architectural, but rhythmic and living. A speaking of names is intended to establish a relation.

> And I repeated your name: Dyallo!
> And you repeated my name: Senghor!
> **("Mediterranean")**

The word, as in African thought, and indeed in all the prephilosophic thought of Europe, is active and creative; the master of language is the master of things.

Poetry of this kind is hard to find in English, where the use of wit and of definition by exclusion has had a triumph much more complete than in France, and where so much of our poetry is devoted to suggesting the disquietingly unsure relationship between language and reality. The nearest equivalent in the English language to the idiom which Senghor uses is the idiom of Whitman and his followers. Indeed Whitman is an indirect source of Senghor's style, for his work was an important influence around the turn of the century on the whole school of free-verse writing in France from which Senghor derives. (pp. xvii-xix)

Some passages in Senghor sound very like Whitman. Others sound like Robinson Jeffers. But there is a certain French literary quality about his work which makes it wrong to model the style of a translation closely on existing poetry in English. Senghor's language is not archaic, although he does permit himself now and then surprising archaisms in vocabulary, but it is impossible to render him into an altogether colloquial modern English idiom. His heightened rhetorical language in English often sounds turgid. On the other hand the direct use of language means that much of his poetry can survive direct translation. Like Saint-John Perse he is attractive to the translator, though his verse in translation, like Saint-John Perse's, is not immediately attractive to the English reader. Even T. S. Eliot's version of the *Anabase* would be perplexing to read on its own as an English poem. (p. xix)

John Reed and Clive Wake, in an introduction to Selected Poems *by Léopold Sédar Senghor, translated by John Reed and Clive Wake, Atheneum, 1964, pp. vii-xix.*

Sylvia Washington Bâ (essay date 1973)

[*In the following excerpt, Washington Bâ examines the concept of negritude in Senghor's poetry.*]

In his prefatory remarks to the appendix of *Nocturnes,* Senghor states his intention of writing first of all for his people. Yet what of these same illiterate "peasants" to whom his poetry remains inaccessible? He explains further the full import of his declaration: it is by reaching French-speaking Africans that he will best be able to reach the French and, ultimately, all men. His mission is to bear witness to what he believes to be his truth, a duty he has admirably fulfilled in many capacities. In fact, his mission is twofold. He must galvanize the forces of his own people so that they too may respond to the call of their spokesman. (p. 152)

The messianism of Senghor's poetry is the pivotal element that makes it "at the same time profoundly personal poetry and public poetry, a poetry in which the aspiration of his people, in which the generalized manifesto of new African consciousness are expressed." Not only does he foretell deliverance from political and cultural bondage, he also leaves no doubt as to the evangelistic role of his poetry, frequently using the literal translation of the word "gospel": good news. His sense of the moral excellence of his mission and his faith in the efficacy of the poetic word in the realization of the future cause him to assume a vindicatory tone in affirming his role.

> Such my answer and my two-headed scepter:
> Lion's jaws and Sage's smile.

Force and wisdom: such are the black poet's talents and duties in regard to his own people. But Senghor's ultimate aim is the elaboration of the values of negritude and their participation in the "Civilization of the Universal," the panhuman convergence toward which mankind is tending. Before such a civilization can be realized, there remains a crucial issue to be reckoned with: the so-called crisis of western civilization. Not only must the black poet lead his own people to salvation; all poets are called upon to re-establish true humanistic values, to lead man back to himself. The poet's mission is redemption, the revival of hope by the prophecy of man's victory over brute force. The poet's tool is language. He alone can manipulate the magic of the creative power of the word, he alone can reveal the moral value of words that has been obscured by the function of utility. Chaka laments the fact that the white

man arrived bringing civilization but also "the naked word." Senghor quotes Teilhard de Chardin on the subject: "The more the world becomes rationalized and mechanized, the more it needs 'poets' as the saviors and leaven of its personality."

That true human values have been stifled by the technological civilization of the west is the subject of much concern and discussion. Moralists decry the imbalance between technical perfection and moral disarray; men of religion note the despiritualization rampant in modern existence, both in the strict sense of organized religion and in the broad sense of human spiritual values. Surrounded by his Frankensteins, the contemporary western man is the victim of alienation from his humanity in much the same way that the black man has known alienation from society. By an ironic twist of history, the colonizer has brought upon himself the very fate to which he subjected the colonized and is victimized by the results of the very force in whose name he launched his undertaking: progress.

> It was the year of Discovery. From their eyes they spit yellow fire. And the waters of the rivers flowed with gold and sweat. The capitals were bursting with them. The naked men were reduced to slaves, and the parents sold their children for one guinea coin.
>
> Then it was the year of Reason. From their eyes they spit red fire. And hatred knotted men's necks in twisted ganglions, and the soldiers bathed in the mud of the blood. The executioners and the learned were decorated; they had found the way to kill a man twice.
>
> Then it will be the year of Technology. From their eyes they will spit white fire. The elements will separate and aggregate governed by mysterious attractions and repulsions. The animals' blood and the plants' sap will be but whey. The white men will be yellow, the yellow men white, all will be sterile.

Senghor's résumé-prophecy accurately depicts the devolution of the double process of alienation and the interaction of practical aims and means and their concomitant moral results. The politico-economic rationale of slavery and colonization nurtured avarice and hate, with its intellectual counterpart of racism, and the entire process culminated in the moral sterility of dehumanized technology.... It must be this atrophied, devitalized condition that accounts not only for the modern *taedium vitae* but also for the deplorable and shocking connection between progress, technology, and science and death and destruction, between material wealth and injustice and oppression. As Senghor has remarked, "Civilization" is not the exploits of outer space per se. If such exploits are devoid of human values and purposes, they will only contribute further to the "barbarism of civilized men." It is at this point that negritude transcends its narcissistic and combative aspects and becomes constructive. Senghor believes that the black man's culture should be recognized as real and valid as a matter of human justice, but primarily because the values of negritude can be instrumental in the reintegration of positive values into western civilization and the reorientation of contemporary man toward life and love. (pp. 153-56)

Before the west can be expected to welcome the values of negritude, it has a right to know exactly what the term embraces and the extent of its objective validity.... Senghor's definition of the concept as the sum of these cultural values is deceptively simple and is based on a certain assumption that is obviously valid in his own experience but that demands substantiation when applied universally and seemingly on the basis of color alone. Superficial or biased reading of Senghor's essays and poems can leave us with erroneous or contradictory impressions. Random reading of critical commentary on Senghor's writings tends to leave us in a quandary also. We may be faced with analyses based on any of several of Senghor's pronouncements on the subject, most of them quite profound and in a variety of contexts. Or, we may encounter critics who insist upon assessing literary merits by political criteria; appreciations too strongly governed by personal preferences and temperaments; or reviewers unequipped to understand the many facets of Senghor's formation, situation in history, and vocation as poet and statesman. A convenient method for evaluating negritude is the consideration of the two main elements that constitute it and under which all the themes, concepts, and connotations may be grouped. These two divisions are what may be described as (1) situational or historical negritude and (2) the more basic theory of essential negritude.

Historical negritude concerns generally the fact of being black in a white world, and specifically the twentieth century's awakening to that fact. The origins of racial prejudice are disputed, but the fact constitutes a historical reality responsible for the common heritage of all black men. If this heritage was not brought about initially because of color, it has been perpetuated on that basis and is at the heart of the contemporary black existence. Whatever sociological, cultural, or ideological expressions of black men are rooted in that heritage may be grouped under the descriptive tag of negritude. The twentieth-century black *évolué*'s awareness of his situation, which produced the contemporary search for identity and self-assertion, is the pivotal moment of negritude. The negritude movement, itself a product of history, is at the crossroads and must reckon with its heritage in terms of its future. (pp. 158-59)

Essential negritude as advanced by Senghor is a far more controversial concept, since the idea of a black African personality, a black specificity, is based on the explosive notion of race. This word is so highly charged in contemporary human relations that the slightest reference to it risks interpretation out of all proportion to reality. The Nigerian poet and playwright, Wole Soyinka, has countered with his now famous sally ridiculing the idea of a tiger's having to proclaim his tigritude. Jean Ghéhenno protests that he could no more believe in the values of negritude than in those of "whiteness": "The human spirit has no color." Their point is clear enough but is based on the sophism that

avoids the affirmation of the supremacy of European values implicit in the refusal to recognize African culture. Ideally, the necessity of values' having to be specified as white or black should never exist, but in view of the division produced by history, it is rather naïve to expect the black man to vindicate his humanity without first vindicating that aspect of it that has been so discredited.... In a wry though not entirely unfounded remark, LeRoi Jones (Imamu A. Baraka) points out the folly of a hasty judgment on negritude: "... It is usually made to seem by European commentators like the crafts program of the Black Muslims." Before countering with the cry of "antiracist racism," we would do well to understand what Senghor means by race and how he links race-color with an avowed humanistic ideology. (p. 160)

The principal issue is one of definition, since connotation and usage often extend terms beyond their true meaning. In the very strictest sense, race is a matter of homogeneity: the continuity of a physical type. Race defines a physical community presenting an ensemble of common hereditary physical traits. The term that properly applies to a cultural community, which may be but most often is not biologically homogeneous, is "ethnic group." A purely historical phenomenon, this reality addresses itself to the socio-psychological aspect of a group, its psycho-cultural properties. (p. 161)

No discussion of race can overlook the fact that racial purity is a rare thing. Though history has somewhat obscured the fine details of racial components, it has left one aspect to assume the role of prime differentiating factor: pigmentation. For this reason, and especially in the case of the black man, the realities of *race, ethnic group,* and *culture* have come to designate one reality. Negritude defined as "the same reaction to the same events" among blacks throughout the world transcends the geographical factor in favor of the historical factor.

What happens to the claim of universal essential negritude in the instance of North and South American blacks centuries removed from their origins? Senghor takes this into account, recognizing that a different cultural milieu eventually exerts decisive influence, but notes that he is less struck by the permanence of physical traits among blacks of the Americas than by the permanence of characteristic psychic traits *in spite of* the new milieu. Though segregation may account for this permanence of traits to some extent, it is not the sole factor in view of the case of Latin American blacks who have known less absolute forms of segregation. The black diaspora poses the problem of the chicken and the egg: which came first? To what extent has perpetuating cultural values and attitudes served to maintain characteristic psychic traits and to what extent has the permanence of the black man's psycho-physiological make-up contributed to the perpetuation of his cultural expression?

Black American writers and intellectuals are divided in their views on the reality of race in regard to culture.

Senghor had an ally in Langston Hughes whom he quotes as saying just after World War I: "We, the creators of the new generation, want to give expression to our *black personality* without shame or fear...."
... Some who object to Senghor's views on the permanence of racial traits do so on the basis of what they believe to be the implications of such views. They feel that the affirmation of such permanence is synonymous with a denial of their cultural "American-ness." There is a difference of emphasis that explains the divergence of views. Because of the separatist connotations of the idea of a black specificity and the American blacks' experience with separatist views, some are wary of such an attitude. They interpret Senghor's ideas as meaning that they should cultivate their "blackness" to the exclusion of their "American-ness." Others, among them many voices of the "new black youth" of America, champion the separatist notion, though their complete line of thinking would not be seconded by Senghor. (pp. 161-63)

[For] those who are unconvinced of the validity of essential negritude, Senghor has yet another angle, which is aesthetic or stylistic negritude. In his famous *Anthologie de la nouvelle poésie nègre et malgache de langue française,* he says: "... what makes the negritude of a poem is less the theme than the style, the emotional warmth that gives life to the words, that transmutes the *parole* into *verbe.*" In his preface to this *Anthologie,* "Orphée noir," Sartre makes an observation which, despite his noble intentions and often brilliant insights, attests to some confusion on his part in regard to negritude. After quoting this same remark of Senghor's, Sartre says: "We could not be better advised that negritude is neither a state nor a definite ensemble of vices and virtues, of intellectual and moral qualities, but a certain affective attitude toward the world." Many, including Senghor himself, have seized upon the final phrase of this observation as the most succinct and accurate definition of essential negritude, yet no one has taken issue with Sartre on the rest of his statement in the light of Senghor's elaboration of the philosophy of negritude. (pp. 165-66)

Any consideration of essential negritude and its validity ultimately rests upon the validity of Senghor's analysis of black African culture as based on the philosophy of life forces. The unity of this culture must be established before its principles and values can be presumed to be transmitted and maintained throughout the black world. Dissenting voices among black Africans themselves, especially inhabitants of former British colonies, refute the very foundation of negritude, on the basis of the diversity of African personalities. These objections are not based solely on whatever formative influences the various colonial powers may have exerted on African ways of life; they refer to profound cultural differences that predate sustained contact with the west. They object to the notion of a "single archetypal African culture," which the Haitian writer Jacques Stéphen Alexis suggests is "an idealised portrait of Senghor's own local Serer culture." One of the most outstanding of

African writers, the South African Ezekiel Mphahlele, is one of the most vociferous and derisive critics of Senghor's views, objecting to his "pretension to a mystical unified whole." Though Senghor's fervor in regard to negritude may smack of the mystical, this term would hardly be applicable to his views on the basic cultural unity of black Africa. "Despite these differences and contrasts, of which any serious student of African culture soon becomes aware, there are underlying similarities between cultures of neighboring African peoples and in the processes of culture change for sub-Saharan Africa as a whole...." This situation poses no problem when we consider an obvious analogy: European civilization and its German, Spanish, French, Italian, etc., components. The individuality of each people sacrifices nothing to their general "European-ness"; "... serious inquiry does not hesitate to trace the mainstreams of the European heritage to their sources, nor to seek the common cultural ground on which Western men stand." (pp. 167-68)

One very noticeable problem which characterizes much of the adverse criticism of negritude is the unwillingness or inability of many commentators to go beyond a certain superficial approach to language and ideas. Only such a failing could account for the censure of a sort of popular folklorism when Senghor means culture as he has defined it. There is the same tendency to read traditionalism for moral tradition, retrogression for "moral rearmament," and racism for the cultivation of negritude, of which love is set forth as one of the primary virtues. This backfires when the commentators are faced with such Senghorian ideas as the opposition of European discursive reason and black African intuitive reason or the primacy of rhythm. Out of the context of his detailed analysis of black African culture according to his definition of culture, these ideas inevitably seem to be nothing more than infuriating corroborations of traditional, distorted views on black Africa. There can be no fruitful dialogue with Senghor until some commentators abandon their superficial approach to his ideas.

The most marked difference between Senghorian negritude and the ideology of younger militant poets is precisely the element and tone of militancy. Senghor is definitely of another generation, that of discovery and elaboration. This present generation finds Senghor's philosophy outmoded from various points of view. (pp. 169-70)

Senghor's love of France adds an ironic note to his campaign on behalf of black African culture. To condemn this affection is to lose sight of the fact of Senghor's and his generation's unique position in history. It was they who had to adjust to the realization that the education afforded them by assimilationist policy was at once a singular opportunity, an indispensable means of achievement, and a falsification of themselves. That Senghor was able to avail himself of the good in this situation and use it against the evil of the same situation, yielding to only a temporary bout with "antiracist racism" is no negligible achievement. The way in which negritude has been misunderstood and misinterpreted is rather forcefully demonstrated by the fact that the same ideology can be accused of racism and nonmilitancy, of reactionary views because Senghor hopes to build a future on moral force derived from the past. (p. 170).

The younger generation finds little "relevance" in Senghor's poetry. His dream of the kingdom of child-hood is too divorced from the aspirations and realities of their Africa today to touch those actively involved in contemporary progress and turmoil.... [These] youn-ger blacks are more for dynamic change than for continuity. They reproach Senghor for not living up to the tradition he professes to uphold: "In the African traditions which Senghor quotes incessantly, it is the bards who galvanize the warriors' energies. Toward what destinies is this writer trying to lead the African people by the grace of poetry?" Though Sartre pro-claimed black poetry a revolutionary force by its very existence and Senghor deemed the First World Festival of Negro Arts "an undertaking much more revolution-ary than the exploration of the cosmos," cultural revolution does not conform to the idea of revolution entertained by those who would have poetry engagé. There is another irony in the fact that Senghor's political commitment has interrupted his poetic vocation. It is generally true that there was more black African poetry published before independence than after and that the impetus supplied by that cultural means was instrumen-tal in bringing about that independence. And it is true that all writing is a commitment.

In the current atmosphere of tension and showdown in places where the black struggle is at a white heat, the attitude of "action now" is understandable.... But such action, brought about by violence if need be, is still not the final solution. Progress cannot exist in a void and Senghor's cultural militancy seeks to provide the neces-sary framework for meaningful change, identity, and self-realization. (pp. 171-72)

There is some truth in the observation that Senghor's poetry has lost much of its actuality in relation to the Africa of today and the approach to her problems. What was revelation in 1945 is now history. The quarrel is not with the quality of Senghor's poetry as poetry but rather that today's world demands more than pure poetry. Senghor thinks differently: "Poetry is not prose. Poetry does not aim at efficacy; it is, by virtue of which it is efficacious, ripping out the soul and turning it inside out like tripes in the sun." But the idyllic world of his poetry seems to the younger poets a deformed image of the present instead of an inspirational view of the past. This aspect of Senghor's poetry and its counterpart in his political ideology pose a problem not only for younger Africans but also for some of his contemporaries who, for various reasons, cannot understand the value of a vision of the past in the elaboration of the future.

One of the most poignant examples of the inability to appreciate an idyllic past is the case of the South African Ezekiel Mphahlele, who finds that Senghor's poetry "reflects a defective poetic vision." ... It is incontesta-ble that Senghor's belief in the regenerative power of a "return to the sources" is possible because he had the grace of knowing a kingdom of childhood such as he describes and of fulfilling himself in the way he so ardently advocates to his fellow Africans. Negritude as a romantic myth can remain so for those who have no such past to which to relate or who can not sympathize with Senghor's brand of cultural militancy. Negritude is a myth for Senghor also, but in the etymological sense of the word: it is explanatory and fundamental, inspira-tional and operative. Since a golden age is part of every literary tradition, he feels that Africa is entitled to hers. (pp. 173-74)

The militant realists take issue with the idealized picture of purity and innocence that Senghor paints in his analyses and poetic images of black African society. Certainly he is far too intelligent to do so with intent to deceive the world and Africans themselves. It would seem rather that he assumes that the realities of poverty, ignorance, squalor, internecine rivalries, witchcraft, superstition, cannibalism, graft, greed, ambition, etc., are too well known to require emphasis, having already received their fair share of it. He prefers to outline the ideal in the hope—itself ideal—of judging what is best, although potential, in man and thereby realizing that potential. To the pragmatist, Senghor's way is a terribly roundabout, intellectualist way of helping Africans, Africa, and the black man in general. The conception of freedom differs greatly among men and strikingly so between Africans of former British and French colonies. The English-speaking African cannot understand the Gallic penchant for systematizing thought and actions into movements and "isms." His pragmatic view dis-penses with cultural and intellectual luxuries and attacks the problem at hand by the most direct, most efficient means. (pp. 174-75)

Prospective negritude is the final step in the long progression from narcissistic through combative and constructive negritude. Borrowing Gaston Berger's "philosophy of the distant future," which studies the future of the world in an effort to predict its evolution, Senghor situates negritude in the universal context that would be its fulfillment. The development and increas-ing complexity of the sciences and of communications, and the universal effects of wars and balance of power, inevitably bring continents, races, and nations into contact with one another. The exchange of ideas, goods, and techniques necessarily results from this contact, and tends to lead toward a planetary civilization whose only hope for survival will be in the symbiosis of all civilizations. According to Senghor, each civilization has cultivated only fragments of the total human reality; the ideal civilization of the twenty-first century, the "Civilization of the Universal," would welcome the positive values and virtues of each civilization in a symbiosis of "giving and receiving." "True culture is being firmly rooted and being uprooted. Firmly rooted in the native land, in one's spiritual heritage. But, being uprooted: open to the rain and the sun, to the enriching contributions of foreign civilizations."

A Wolof proverb says, "Man is the remedy of man." The black problem is a universal problem and black culture has ramifications throughout the world. Too often we choose to ignore very real parallels in underdevelopment. The Third World is certainly economically underdeveloped, but the Great Powers suffer from spiritual and moral underdevelopment no less debilitating. For these deficiencies, negritude proposes remedies in the form of humanizing virtues. "The 'Civilization of the twenty-first century'... will surely be *superindustrial,* that is, technological. It will be *humanism* or *barbarism,* depending on whether or not the peoples of the Third World, and among them the black peoples, will have brought to it their contributions."

During his most recent visit to the United States, Senghor challenged America to become the prototype of the civilization of the future:

> ... you have all the necessary ingredients, it is you who can give it a truly universal dimension. Your population is composed of every major European and Asian ethnic group, but even more important, those from Africa as well .... Thus it is the Americas, more particularly the United States, which already anticipates the world of the twenty-first century and holds in its strong but faltering hands not only its own destiny, but the destiny of the entire world. For it is the destiny of America to summon negritude to its rightful place in the civilization of the twenty-first century.

(pp. 179-80)

Sylvia Washington Bâ, in her The Concept of Negritude in the Poetry of Léopold Sédar Senghor, *Princeton University Press, 1973, 305 p.*

Gerald Moore (essay date 1980)

[*In the excerpt below, Moore discusses how Senghor's political and personal life have influenced his literary work.*]

[Léopold Sédar Senghor] is many things to many men. The points at which his mind or his life touch those of others are exceptionally various; as must be the case with any man who claims equal eminence as poet, scholar, and statesman. Among African presidents, Senghor shares this distinction with Agostinho Neto of Angola, a man for whom he had little political sympathy, and it must be said of both men that the policies they pursued in power are very much those we would expect from their poetry. Senghor's preoccupation with acknowledging an equal heritage from Africa and from Europe, the constant search in his poetry for the keynote of reconciliation, are the marks also of his astute but accommodating foreign policy, of his almost limitless

collaboration with France. And his poetic claim to representative status, as the champion of his people, is matched by the skill with which he has dominated Senegalese political life for over twenty years. The revolutionary fire and passionate aspiration of Neto's poetry, by contrast, should also prepare us for the very different kind of struggle the Angolan people have had to undergo, and the very different political leadership they have enjoyed .... Both wrote like men who confidently expected to play a leading part in the affairs of their countries. It is even possible that Africa would have little time for a prominent poet who did not have such expectations.

This representative note is struck very early in Senghor's work, in these lines from **"The Return of the Prodigal Son"**:

> Tomorrow I take the way of Europe, way of the ambassador
> In longing for my black country.

Exile, then, is seen neither as escapism nor as the search for a purely personal advantage, but as a duty and a sacrifice. It is no accident that Senghor is a Senegalese, for his career embodies the Senegalese dilemma. (pp. 17-18)

As both a beneficiary and a victim of the assimilationist educational system, Senghor felt its effects from the age of seven, or perhaps earlier, through the influence of an already *assimilé* father, a Catholic in a predominantly Moslem society, and a prosperous trader in a land of widespread poverty. The intention and the effect of the system was to distance the child step-by-step from his own culture and values, exposing him at the same time to the very real seductive power of French civilization, ranging from the tangible delights of red wine (a specially favoured import), good bread and *charcuterie* to the more rarefied ones of Voltaire's prose or Rousseau's libertarian sentiments. This alienation from oneself, coupled with the prolonged exile in France then necessary to any higher education, called forth the counter-assertion of negritude, but it was a counter-assertion made very much in the intellectual terms, as well as in the language of the conqueror. The ambivalence of Francophone African policies is one which lies also at the heart of negritude itself. Senghor is not only the leading theoretician of negritude, of the black personality and its unique qualities, but also one of the leading practitioners of those black policies which often tie Dakar, Abijan and Libreville so intimately to France that they sometimes seem only a Métro ride from Paris, rather than so many thousands of miles on the map.

To recognize this ambivalence is not to belittle Senghor as a poet, but to prepare ourselves for an understanding of the conflicting materials out of which his poetry and his life have been built. It's more than fifty years since the young Senghor arrived in France; more than forty since his first poems and critical essays began to appear. His work contains within itself much of the tension, anguish, hope and striving which characterized Senegalese and African experience during those same years.

Senghor was one of the first Africans to pursue a French academic education to a high level, and the first to complete his *agrégé,* the state qualification for teaching in senior schools.... In his boyhood he moved among the Serere farmers and fishermen of the district, listening to the tales of the poets and the old women about the ancient Africa which preceded the French conquest.... This was a period of his life which was to achieve great significance in retrospect, a period which he is constantly opposing to the velleities of 'assimilation', using it as a kind of touchstone of original virtue and sincerity; it is his 'kingdom of childhood'. Dominant in the memory of those years is the figure of his maternal uncle Tokô'Waly, who was his principal instructor in the traditional culture of the savannahs.... (pp. 21-2)

But from the age of seven Senghor began an intensive study of the French language.... In 1928 he sailed for France to continue his studies at the Lycée Louis-le-Grand and the Sorbonne in Paris. Here he was soon joined by Aimé Césaire, seven years his junior, and the two men began the long series of conversations and experiments which, as they saw it, prepared them for the task of 'giving a tongue to the black races'. Another acquaintance of this period was Léon Damas of French Guiana. None of these three men began to publish until the late 1930s; they had first to master the strange status of the 'assimilated' man living in a society to which he does not belong. We discover from Senghor, as later from Camara Laye, that the overwhelming impression of the star pupil from French Africa who won his way to Paris was one of isolation. Only in this new context did he discover the fallacy that had underlain his whole education: he was not and could never be a Frenchman. He had therefore to settle down and rediscover what it was to be an African. To this task he was able to bring all the intellectual curiosity, the mastery of language and the knowledge of literature which were the abiding and noble parts of the education he had been given. The supreme irony of 'assimilation' is that it has inadvertently contributed more than anything else to this process—the rediscovery of Africa. (pp. 22-3)

The style which Senghor made for himself actually owes little to the scornful whiplash of Césaire's poetry, or to the staccato lines and typographical tricks of Damas, inspired partly by the latter's reading of American poetry. But Césaire undoubtedly exercised a powerful and liberating influence on Senghor through his intellect and personality, an influence which Senghor has generously acknowledged in his memorable **"Letter to a Poet"**.... Curiously, despite the passionate warmth of this poem, Senghor casts Césaire very much in his own image; for it is the African poet who more habitually sings of 'Ancestors, Princes and Gods' and whose verse 'breathes like the night'. Césaire is far more the poet of blazing tropical noon, of volcanic menace and the dry crack of the tornado. (pp. 23-4)

With Césaire he began to develop the new literary programme of negritude, which demanded of its poets a strong verbal rhythm, a wealth of African allusions and a general exaltation of 'the African personality'. The true past of the black man must be rediscovered beneath the layers of colonial history, his culture vindicated, and his future prepared. Senghor alone, however, insisted upon the musical aspect of rhythm, even demanding that his poetry should be recited to the accompaniment of African instruments. Almost at once we find him creating, through the use of the long line, that rolling, deep-breathed sound which distinguishes all his verse. (pp. 24-5)

In *Chants d'Ombre* Senghor had already asserted not only his personal music but the major preoccupations which haunt his verse to this day. Chief among these is his insistence on communion with the dead, with the ancestors and defeated princes of his people, from whom his own education sought to isolate him. How far this is a poetic attitude, how far a deep conviction, it is impossible to say. Senghor, in any case, has expressed unforgettably the classical African view of the dead as the principal force controlling the living, benevolent but watchful. In a poem like **"In Memoriam"**, he invokes the dead from his lonely exile in Paris, seeking to draw strength from their company and example.... Here the dead serve as a bridge between Senghor and everything which his education has turned him away from. By mingling the names of the Seine, the river of Paris, with those of his homeland (Sine, Gambia, Saloum) he stresses the universality of their presence. Looking out from his attic window, he suddenly sees the blood of the French conquest filling the narrow streets; but he sees also the presence which can reconcile him with his strange white brothers. It is to the dead, or in other poems, to his mother, that he seeks to justify his present life, his present interests, his apparent immersion in the affairs of a Parisian savant.... (pp. 28-9)

This, then, is 'negritude upright'. With this key Senghor has unlocked his lips and sent forth a river of rich sombre melody. Yet as we read on into his second volume, *Hosties Noires* (*Black Wafers,* 1945), we do begin to wonder how far Senghor's negritude can be seen as embodying what Wole Soyinka has called a genuine 'self-apprehension', an untrammelled apprehension of himself as an African. Sometimes it seems to contain a suspiciously large element of apprehension in terms of the Other. It must be remembered that Senghor's early years in Paris coincided with those in which many white scholars, such as Maurice Delafosse, Georges Balandier and Marcel Griaule, were saying the same sort of things about black personality and civilization that Senghor was saying. Even Catholic racist writers like Charles Maurras were at least in agreement about the profound differences between white and black cultures, even if they went on to rationalize from this a hierarchy of values with France at the top. But the whole tendency of Senghor's mind is towards synthesis rather than separation. Having established the unique qualities of African cultures, his desire is not to hold them in isolation, but to pool them in what he calls 'The Civilization of the Universal'. This notion, derived in part from the biologist Teilhard de Chardin, regards human cultures as organic and evolutionary, with a tendency to combine themselves into new wholes.

It seems that Senghor's construct of 'La Civilization Négro-Africaine' (Black African Civilization), a construct made up essentially in exile, is built not only out of materials remembered from his childhood, but out of his reactions to such writers as those just mentioned. It is partly an argument with Europe, rather than a free, spontaneous expression; and perhaps this is inevitable, because Senghor's public life in these years was frequently one of argument. As a professor of French language and literature in the *lycées* of Tours and Paris, a position which he occupied from 1935 to 1940, the poet must have felt the continual need to assert his difference if he were not to sink entirely into the imposed role of a Black Frenchman. Such an assertion, though humorously made, can be found in the poem, **"Que M'accompagnent Koras et Balafong"** (**"Let Koras and Balafong Accompany Me"**), written during those years.... (pp. 29-30)

But in *Hosties Noires* the poet's position has become still more ambivalent than that of the black shepherd of blond heads, for if Senghor was not obliged to remain in France after his graduation (he had not yet entered parliamentary politics), he carried his allegiance to the French part of his heritage still further by taking French citizenship and by volunteering to fight a war which many black intellectuals regarded as an irrelevance, except in so far as it might indirectly further African liberation. (pp. 30-1)

Senghor, who swiftly found himself a prisoner-of-war in German hands, could only mourn the thousands of Senegalese riflemen who fell on the battlefields of Europe, as others were later to fall in Indo-China and Algeria, fighting in what was now quite clearly the imperial interest of France. But, despite the warmth and compassion of these poems, perhaps he might have done better to tell the soldiers, as Léon Damas had already done, to 'go and invade Senegal!'

It is these anomalies which make much of the more public, less personal poetry of *Hosties Noires* difficult to read, and which culminate in the last stanzas of the closing poem, **"Prayer for Peace"**. After enumerating some of the worst colonial excesses of France and Europe, Senghor cries:

> Bless this people who have brought me Your Good News, Lord, and opened my heavy eyelids to the light of faith.
> They have opened my heart to knowledge of the world, showing me the rainbow in the new faces of my brothers.

(p. 31)

Here, as elsewhere in *Hosties Noires,* Senghor's perpetual search for reconciliation has betrayed him; he appears before us with a paper dagger and an ingratiating smile. It is assimilation rather than negritude which triumphs in such writing.

His poetry is often at its best when he abandons the search for reconciliation and is content to register a single emotion without too much care for the consequences. The love poems of *Chants pour Naëtt* (*Songs for Naëtt*) (1949) have this quality of abandon and seem to derive a lot of their rhythmic energy from it. Senghor's verse here moves faster than usual and his imagery glows with an extraordinary warmth.... A different but equal satisfaction can be found in a poem like **"New York"** from *Ethiopiques* (1956). This achieves a completely acceptable stance of negritude by its sincere and illuminating opposition of downtown Manhattan and Harlem. The structure of this poem is extremely successful, with its explosive opening, its gradual mounting sense of dry sterility, its sudden transition to the refreshing warmth and smell of Harlem, and the splendid broad gesture which ends it.... A similar strength and wholeness are achieved when Senghor turns aside from his long love affair with France, from his obsession with being 'Ambassador of the Black Peoples', and plunges himself into communion with his childhood, with his native landscape, with the broad night of the savannah, with all that he associates with his ancestors. Here the poet has no need to justify or excuse anything. He is serene, and this serenity fills his verses with its quiet music. In such a mood Senghor's sincerity marks the page and he writes unforgettably. The following lines are taken from *Ethiopiques,* a volume in which too much space is devoted to lamentations of exile—and now it is exile *from* Europe that the poet is lamenting, exile from all that is symbolized by 'the Princess de Belfort' (a synonym for his second wife, a Norman aristocrat). But in this extract of his poem, **"Pour Khalam"**, Senghor breaks free from all that, and rediscovers his purest vein of introspection:

> I don't know when it was, I always confuse childhood with Eden
> As I mix up Death and Life—a bridge of kindness joins them.

(pp. 32-4)

Notable also in *Ethiopiques* is the stronger drive of Senghor's rhythm, which now develops a shorter breath and a more regular fall. His poem **"L'Absente"** yearns for the coming of spring to the dry savannah and equates it with the long-predicted arrival of the Queen of Saba ('The Absent') from the East. Perhaps this Ethiopian figure symbolizes for him the integration of his Christian faith and his African identity, just as the rape of Ethiopia in 1935-6 symbolizes the continued spoliation of the continent.... (p. 34)

Here the more regular fall of the metre is countered by the forward rush of the poem. But turning from *Ethiopiques* to *Nocturnes* (1961), one is conscious of a certain slackening of energy. Nowhere is this more evident than in the poet's decision to republish the *Chants pour Naëtt,* originally issued in 1949 in honour of his black wife Ginette Eboué, and to suppress all mention of their original subject, Naëtt. The effect is to render the poems less compelling as the expression of a passionate lyrical urge.

Also, the five Elégies which follow the love-songs, and complete the volume, despite a sombre richness of sound, do occasionally collapse into unabashed nostalgia and escapism.... The tendency of these poems is more and more in divergence from the tendency of his actual life-style, for the Presidential Palace in Dakar represents a more drastic exile from the Kingdom of Childhood than even his Parisian exile did. The poetry has become compensation for the time and energy his public life now consumes.

The composition of the Elégies coincides with the years 1957 to 1959, when Senghor was becoming almost entirely absorbed in affairs of state, and when he was fighting vainly to arrest the deliberate balkanization of West Africa by the French government by means of the *loi cadre,* which encouraged the growth of petty 'independent' territories, relying heavily on French military and financial support. His success in dominating Senegalese political life for twenty years has been marred by his failure to achieve a wider association with his neighbours, even if one doubts whether the achievement of a greater federation would significantly have altered the conservative and pro-French bent of his foreign policy.

These twenty years of power, though rich in policy statements and refinements of his theoretical position, have been thin in poetry. But what poet has not found public life to be the enemy of the muse? The harvest of those years, at any rate, is represented by the thirty short poems published with his collected volume in 1973, as **"Lettres de l'Hivernage"**. The title can only be translated as "Letters of the Rainy Season", since Senghor specifically tells us that, in his region, 'l'Hivernage' is not winter, but summer and the advent of autumn. He now addresses Africa, not as a poet, but as a statesman. Hence, the quieter, more domestic tone of these poems, which no longer carry the burden of the writer's hopes, ambitions and concerns. They do not merely express escapism, as happened occasionally with the Elégies, but they are an escape by their very nature from the incessant anxiety and activity of statesmanship.... (pp. 34-6)

Senghor once defended himself from the charge of exoticism in a somewhat mannered essay, **"As the Manatees go to Drink at the Source"**. There he argued that he was writing primarily for an African audience, to whom such words as *kora, balafong, dyali* and *khalam* were familiar. If they were exotic to the French reader, that was not his concern. They were not in intention picturesque, but descriptive;

> For all is sign and sense at the same time for the African Negro; each being, each thing; but also the matter, the form, the colour, the smell and gesture

and rhythm and tone and timbre: the colour of the lappa, the shape of the kora, the design of the bride's sandals, the steps and gestures of the dancer, the mask and so on.

Reading such passages, the suspicion grows that what Senghor is describing is the unifying faculty of the artist in man, not specifically in African man. The enemies of spontaneity and passion move amongst us all, and they do not always carry white masks. But Senghor's claim that he writes primarily for his people, although dismissed by Reed and Wake [see excerpt dated 1964], has perhaps been validated by events. When he began writing in Paris over forty years ago, it is probable that his readership, beyond the immediate circle of his friends, was largely French. But with the spread of literacy in French over those same years, with the public readings which are a feature of his life in Dakar, with the ascent of Senghor himself to a position of international fame, it seems likely that his poetry is now and will for many years remain among the best known in Africa. (pp. 36-7)

Gerald Moore, "Assimilation or Negritude," in his Twelve African Writers, *Indiana University Press, 1980, pp. 17-38.*

Alfred J. Guillaume, Jr. (essay date 1989)

[*In the following excerpt, Guillaume explores motive, motif, and content in Senghor's poetry.*]

If the Harlem Renaissance of the 1920s served as the catalyst for the "New Negro" in the United States, the Negritude movement of the 1930s in Paris sparked a similar renewal for black students from Africa and the Caribbean, who rejected the assimilation of European values and redefined themselves as children of Africa. The journey to the ancestral sources ("pèlerinage aux sources ancestrales") began in 1932 with the publication of *Légitime Défense,* a Communist and surrealist journal that opposed the bourgeoisie. Founded by Etienne Léro, Jules Minnerot, and René Ménil, all from the Antilles, the journal extolled black values and culture. But it was the 1934 literary journal *Etudiant Noir,* of Aimé Césaire, Léon Damas, and Léopold Sédar Senghor, that gave birth to Negritude, the second Negro Renaissance.

Although Césaire coined the word, Senghor, the poet/politician, became Negritude's principal apostle, promoting it in his poetry and essays as well as integrating it into his political posture. Senghor defined Negritude as the "sum total of black cultural values." This ideology was as much a reaction against the imposition of European culture as a celebration of African civilization. Through Negritude, the black rediscovers the self and reaffirms the riches of his own heritage.

This reawakening of blackness by the students in Paris did not develop in isolation. The Harlem writers were a major source of inspiration. For Senghor, to proclaim one's blackness, one's Negritude, was to reclaim one's humanity. The Harlem Renaissance writers had done so, and Senghor read them voraciously, even translating some of their work. He admired particularly Langston Hughes, whom he met for the first time in 1959 as a delegate to the U.N. General Assembly. In a letter to Mercer Cook on 8 September 1967, Senghor states that Hughes "... is the greatest Negro-American poet.... He was, without doubt, the most spontaneously Negro poet. In other words, he best fulfilled the notions I have of black cultural values, of Negritude. I believe, moreover, that Langston felt everything that linked us—Césaire, Damas, and me—to him."

This spontaneity that Senghor speaks about is emotion; this, he says, is the special quality that makes one black. His statement "emotion is black, reason is Greek" ("l'émotion est nègre, comme la raison hellène") is now legendary and has caused much consternation among African literati who feel that Senghor's theories reinforce ideas that the Negro is inferior. Nevertheless, Senghor insists that emotion enables blacks to grasp an object intuitively in its totality, its interior as well as its exterior composition. This unique reaction, according to Senghor, supersedes rational consciousness and is a surreal participation of subject and object. He calls this phenomenon an "attitude of abandon, assimilation, not domination: attitude of love."

In a 1976 interview with Senghor, I asked him to clarify what he meant by object. His response was that "the European seeks to dominate nature, as Descartes once said. He transforms it to serve his own needs, whereas the Negro-African considers nature as reality of the object, of that which is in front of and which is beyond him; he blends into this reality." To further illustrate his point, Senghor recalled a dance of the bull that he witnessed at the home of President Houphouet-Boigny of the Ivory Coast: "The bull's movements bring forth fertility. Through his movements and gesticulations, [the dancer] allows himself to be seized by the bull's force. The dancer is totally identified with the object, bull. In contrast, the Albo-European sets himself apart from the object; he analyzes it; he uses it as an instrument. The black man abandons himself into the object to live its essence. This is called emotion." Hence, for Senghor, the black man lives the object. There is a symbiosis of the real world and the imagination. In his response to nature as assimilator, he expands himself as subject and object.

That the Harlem Renaissance writers expressed a sensual celebration of life, is, according to Senghor, due to their African heritage. That they demonstrated a continuity of a past musical heritage (the link between the tom-tom and the swing of the trumpet), an outpouring of religious sentiment (the correlation between the African's respect for the cosmic forces and his ancestral dead and the Negro-Americans' image of God) is due to their shared Negritude.

Senghor's Negritude is a revalidation of the humanistic elements of African society. From Africa's innocence a new order of fraternal love and respect will emerge. Nowhere is this more apparent than in Senghor's poetic evocation of childhood. Through the exploration of this distant reality, Senghor rediscovers the lost world of unrestrained happiness. His intention is twofold: to become an individual mind united with nature and to retain the continuity that he associates with an African feeling for life. This emphasis on intensity and communion is the source of a profound feeling that progresses beyond personal fulfillment and in his poetry is often linked to a sociopolitical vision. Beginning with the emptiness of his Parisian environment experienced as a student, Senghor visualizes a fuller life for himself and all oppressed people through childhood innocence.

This retreat into memories of childhood is a rejection of Europe and a return to family, the ancestors, and the land, all of which represent a restoration of beauty and simplicity. This quest is not simply romantic idealization but a tangible reality that the poet can recall at will: "I only need to name things, the elements of my childhood universe, in order to prophesy the City of Tomorrow, that will rise from the ashes of the past. That's the poet's mission." In order to purify himself from the "contagions of being civilized" ("contagions de civilisé") (**"Que m'accompagnent kôras et balafong"**), Senghor uses the imagination to dissolve all conflicts between himself and the external world; he recreates the oneness with nature that he experienced as a child, thus maintaining an indissoluble link with the splendor of African life. He says of himself and of the other students exiled in Paris: "We walked, equipped with the miraculous arms of double vision, piercing the blind walls, discovering, recreating the marvels of the Childhood Kingdom. We were re-born through Negritude." His poetry inevitably leads to the complex questions of his attitudes toward Europe and of the poetic and social function which he as a writer assigns himself.

In Senghor's mind the innocence of Africa is somehow the guardian of the innocence that Europe has lost:

> At the turn in the road, the river, blue in the cool
>   September fields
> A Paradise that protects from fevers a child with
>   eyes as bright as two swords
> Paradise my African childhood, which kept watch
>   over the innocence of Europe
>   (**"Que m'accompagnent kôras et balafong"**)

According to Senghor, the freshness of childhood assures the triumph of what poetic reverie reveals, the possibility of a future society of universal brotherhood. Although he does not explain in detail how this will happen, childhood innocence is thus broadened to include the promise of Africa's sociopolitical future. What is certain is that his prophetic vision involves a transcendence whereby the Europeanized psyche of the poet dies in order to be purified in the child:

> Oh! to die to childhood, may the poem die[,] the
> syntax disintegrate, may all the inessential
> words be swallowed up.
> The weight of the rhythm suffices, no need of
> words-cement to build on the rock the City of
> Tomorrow.
> ("Elégie des circoncis," *Nocturnes*)

These lines from an elegy recall a youth's initiation rites but also the poet's re-initiation into the childlike universe that he associates with a new society.

Senghor's messianic quest, as poet and politician, is to seek the New Day, the Clear Dawn of the New Day ("Aube transparente d'un jour nouveau") that will include the emancipation of all colonized peoples and oppressed workers. This metaphor of the "Clear Dawn" is of utmost importance in his ideology and is the conclusion of **"A l'appel de la race de Saba"** (*Hosties Noires*), a poem that shows the complexities of Senghor's vision of Africa, nature, and politics. It demonstrates how in the poet's mind the return to the African experience of his childhood is identical to the struggle for liberation. Part I of the poem introduces themes of exile and nostalgia; Part II shows how the poet's memory of family and community preserved him from the evils of European society. Parts III and IV express Senghor's desire to unite Africa and Europe, but also reveal the danger of becoming an *assimilé*. But against that risk is the need to engage in the communal combat for freedom. The poem thus demonstrates how, in Senghor's mind, the return to the African experience of his childhood is identical to the struggle for liberation.

The child motif is a symbol of Senghor's political vision. This is especially evident in **"The Return of the Prodigal Son"** (**"Le Retour de l'Enfant prodigue"**), a poem that contrasts the childlike world with the destructiveness of war, the "mud of civilization" ("la boue de la Civilisation"), that Senghor had known during his sixteen years of separation from Africa. Like a number of other poems, it is a stormy attack on the oppressive aspects of European society, but the poet asserts that he is preserved from hatred and favors fraternity. He is willing to die for his people, but realizes that he can best serve as "Master of Language—Nay, name me its ambassador" ("Maître de Langue—Mais non, nomme-moi son ambassadeur"). He must stop European destruction of nature and resurrect his own past: "I resurrect my earthly virtues!" ("Je ressuscite mes vertus terriennes!"). Again, it is clear that Senghor's poetic-political undertaking springs from his adherence to the values of his African childhood:

> Oh! to sleep once more in the clean bed of my
> childhood
> Oh! once more the dear black hands of my mother
> tucking me to sleep
> Once more the bright smile of my mother.
> Tomorrow, I will again take the road to Europe,
> the road of my embassy
> Homesick for my black native land.

Often in Senghor's poetry, his political mission presents certain ambiguities that appear to contradict this idealistic conception of justice inspired by childhood nostalgia, but a complete treatment of these issues is beyond the scope of this essay. It is instructive to note that in **"Que m'accompagnent kôras et balafong,"** an early poem, Senghor's cleansing of the physical and psychic assimilation of European culture and his ultimate victory to restore Africa's dignity and nobility are not without violence and retribution. The poet as Archangel and trumpeter of justice purges his people of centuries of slave trade with a sword that spills the blood of colonizers into Europe's rivers. Similar ambiguities between Senghor the African and Senghor the European parallel the conflicts between Senghor the politician and Senghor the poet. These are especially apparent in the dramatic poem **"Chaka."**

Written about a Zulu chief who fought the whites early in the nineteenth century, the poem attempts at first to justify the use of violence to defend primitivistic values. Divided into two sections (*chants*), the poem is an apology for Chaka, who caused many Africans to suffer. Accused by the *Voix blanche* of killing Nolivé, an embodiment of woman-Afrika, Chaka responds, in the first *chant,* that her death is an act of love and ultimately the liberation of his people from European aggression. Her death is a new life that assures the continuity of African civilization. She is a sacrificial victim of the politician in his fight against the oppressor. A man of action and fortitude, Chaka destroys the poet within him. Both deaths are necessary for the liberation of the African people. Politics is Chaka's calvary, but it is an unselfish response to racism, exploitation, and colonialism. In spite of the suffering brought upon his people by the "Pink Ears" ("Roses-d'oreilles"), Chaka insists that his mission is not one of hate, but one of reconciliation and love.

In the second *chant,* however, Chaka loses his political persona and becomes Senghor, the poet. The violence-love of the first section is replaced by childhood-love that glorifies Africa's renaissance. As poet, Chaka envisions the serenity of childhood as a sociopolitical symbol of universal peace. Chaka is praised as a hero. His love for his people culminates in the sexual bond between him and Nolivé, a union that celebrates the living forces of African society. He is the prophet of a new order and the creator of life, a mission for which he was prepared by the serenity of childhood and the loneliness of exile.

From the union of lover and beloved, poet and Africa, arises the "new world" in an act of universal creativity. How this will come about remains unexplained. Perhaps it is mere mystification. Within the poem, however, it involves an ultimate triumph. Chaka's death is somehow an augury to the resurrection of the Africa to which Senghor aspires and to the creation of a future society void of oppression.

Senghor's vision of childhood, his idealization of an Africa of innocence and primeval goodness might appear diluted by his affection for France: "I have a strong weakness for France" ("...j'ai une grande faibless pour la France") (**"Prière de paix,"** *Hosties Noires*). And he wrote further: "Ah! don't say that I don't love France...." ("Ah! ne dites pas que je n'aime pas la France....") (**"Poème liminaire,"** *Hosties Noires*). In fact, the series of poems, **"Epitres à la Princesse"** (*Ethiopiques*), written to a European princess and involving themes of love, separation, and death, seems to compromise his fidelity to Africa and to his mission. And yet he makes it clear in **"Que m'accompagnent kôras et balafong"** that if at any time he were forced to choose, he would choose Africa:

> But if I must choose at the moment of ordeal
> I would choose the verse of the rivers, of the
>   winds and of the forests
> The assonance of plains, and of streams.
> I would choose the rhythm of the blood of my
>   unclothed body
> I would choose the trill of the balafongs and the
>   euphony of the strings.
> I would choose my weary black people, my
>   peasant people.

He reminds those who may consider him a servant of white European culture that before he was a teacher of French boys and an obedient civil servant, he was a child of Africa, nourished by the rich traditions of his people. The message of Senghor's Negritude, then, is that the humanity of Africa is preferable to the mechanization of Europe.

Some critics believe that Senghor's vision of Negritude fails because it appears to perpetuate the myth of the inferior Negro. Kofi Anyidiho, for example, referring to Senghor's romantic quest, states, "The only problem...is that he chooses the wrong myths for the cause of Negritude he claims to be championing. Not only are his myths compromised by his reliance on anthropological views of Africa; they conform too well to all the old stereotypes of colonialism, with their emphasis on the irrational, the sensuous, the luxuriant, the dark, the ingenuous, the compulsively self-giving." Negritude, according to Stanislas Adotevi, is pure propaganda and "a panacea the president-poet uses for problems of government... an opium." Frederick Ivor Case calls it a "philosophic aberration," and asserts that "the concept of Negritude cannot be the answer to any situation pertaining to the reality of the black masses."

Yet fifty years after the founding of the Negritude movement, Senghor still tenaciously views it as the path to universal culture, conceiving his own childhood and youth as an ageless symbol of Africa's past, present, and future, a vibrant Africa, where rests the promise of mankind.

(pp. 271-78)

Alfred J. Guillaume, Jr., "Negritude and Humanism: Senghor's Vision of a Universal Civilization," in The Harlem Renaissance: Revaluations, *Amritjit Singh, William S. Shiver, Stanley Brodwin, eds., Garland Publishing, Inc., 1989, pp. 271-80.*

FURTHER READING

Markovitz, Irving L. "A Bibliographical Essay on the Study of Ideology, Political Thought, Development and Politics in Senegal." *A Bibliography on African Affairs* 3, No. 4 (April 1970): 5-15.
    Comprehensive bibliography of Senghor's work.

Michaud, Paul. "Senghor: 80 Plus and Busier than Ever." *New African* 234 (March 1987): 14-15.
    Discusses Senghor's many activities since stepping down as president of Senegal.

Scheub, Harold. "Soukeîna and Isabelle—Senghor and the West." In *Africa & the West: Intellectual Responses to European Culture,* edited by Philip D. Curtain, pp. 189-230. Madison: The University of Wisconsin Press, 1972.
    Explores theme and motif in Senghor's poetry, claiming that it is Senghor's humanistic vision rather than "racial justification" that characterizes the poet's work.

Wake, Clive. "L. S. Senghor and Lyrical Poetry." In *European-Language Writing in Sub-Saharan Africa,* edited by Albert S. Gérard, pp. 462-75. Budapest: Akadémiai Kiadó, 1986.
    Evaluates Senghor's poctry, calling Senghor "the undisputed initiator of modern African writing."

Ntozake Shange

1948-

(Born Paulette Williams) American dramatist, novelist, poet, and essayist.

American writer Shange, best known for the "choreopoem" *for colored girls who have considered suicide/ when the rainbow is enuf* (1975), won praise for combining poetry, prose, music, and dance in the stage production of this work. In her dramas, novels, and poetry—which are often amalgamations of literary genres and media—Shange draws upon her experiences as an African-American woman to write innovatively and passionately on racial, political, and feminist issues. She is particularly noted for her portrayal of black women and her criticism of discrimination against them in American society. Shange explained in a 1983 interview: "I feel that as an artist my job is to appreciate the differences among my women characters.... Our personalities and distinctions are lost. What I appreciate about the women whom I write about, the women whom I know, is how idiosyncratic they are. I take delight in the very peculiar or particular things that fascinate or terrify them."

Born to Paul T. Williams, a surgeon, and Eloise Williams, a psychiatric social worker and an educator, Shange—originally named Paulette Williams—was raised with the advantages available to the black middle class. Her childhood was filled with music, literature, and art. Dizzy Gillespie, Miles Davis, Chuck Berry, and W. E. B. Du Bois were among the frequent guests at her parents' house. On Sunday afternoons Shange's family held variety shows. She recalled them in a self-interview published in *Ms.*: "my mama wd read from dunbar, shakespeare, countee cullen, t.s. eliot. my dad wd play congas & do magic tricks. my two sisters & my brother & i wd do a soft-shoe & then pick up the instruments for a quartet of some sort: a violin, a cello, flute & saxophone. we all read constantly. anything. anywhere. we also tore the prints outta art books to carry around with us. sounds/images, any explorations of personal visions waz the focus of my world." Yet the careers she chose for herself—war correspondent and jazz musician, to name two—were dismissed by her family as "'no good for a woman'," she told interviewer Stella Dong. She chose to become a writer because "there was nothing left." Frustrated and hurt after separating from her first husband, Shange attempted suicide several times before focusing her rage against society and its treatment of black women. While earning a master's degree in American Studies from the University of Southern California, she took her African name: Ntozake (pronounced En-to-ZAH-ki), which means "she who comes with her own things," and Shange (pronounced SHONG-gay), which means "she who walks like a lion." Since then she has sustained a triple career

as an educator, a performer/director in New York and Houston, and a writer whose works draw heavily on the frustrations of being a black female in America. "I am a war correspondent after all," she told Dong, "because I'm involved in a war of cultural and esthetic aggression. The front lines aren't always what you think they are."

Shange's first drama, *for colored girls who have considered suicide / when the rainbow is enuf,* was originally produced off-Broadway. This "choreopoem," as Shange described it, is a cycle of poems combined with music and dance. Shange explored the sufferings and joys of seven African-American women and rejoiced in their ability to share and overcome their sorrows. Jacqueline Trescott noted that *for colored girls* "became an electrifying Broadway hit and provoked heated exchanges about the relationships between black men and women. ... When [it] debuted, [it] became the talk of literary circles. Its form—seven women on the stage dramatizing poetry—was a refreshing slap at the traditional, one-two-three-act structures." Even though plays combining

1688

poetry and dance had already been staged by Adrienne Kennedy, Mel Gussow argued that "Miss Shange was a pioneer in terms of her subject matter: the fury of black women at their double subjugation in white male America." Yet Shange was faulted for her unsympathetic treatment of black men, who are depicted as obstacles to the social and spiritual freedom of black women. Most critics, however, viewed the play as an affirmation of the human will to survive. Toni Cade Bambara maintained that Shange "celebrates the capacity to master pain and betrayals with wit, sister-sharing, reckless daring, and flight and forgetfulness if necessary. She celebrates most of all women's loyalties to women."

Shange has written numerous other plays, including *Spell #7* (1979) and her adaptation of a Bertolt Brecht drama, *Mother Courage & Her Children* (1980). *Spell #7* is about a group of black theatrical performers who discuss the racism they face in the entertainment world. Through poetic vignettes blended with song and dance, Shange explored her characters' feelings. *Spell #7* is structurally and thematically similar to *for colored girls,* but it relies more on such conventional elements as dialogue and plot development. Like much of her work, Shange's *Mother Courage & Her Children* met with mixed reviews. Shange changed the play's setting from seventeenth-century Europe to the post-Civil War United States, and she portrayed Mother Courage as a black woman selling her wares during the battles between United States Cavalry units and American Indians. In a common reaction to the drama, Frank Rich commented: "To fulfill her mission of resetting *Mother Courage* in black America, [Shange] seems to have seized on some events that superficially correspond to those of Brecht's play without carefully considering how those events would square with the true meaning of the original text."

After the production of *Mother Courage,* Shange began to concentrate on writing novels and poetry. Her collections of poetry, like her theater pieces, are highly original. Her first collection, *Nappy Edges* (1978), contains fifty poems and is too long, according to Harriet Gilbert. Nevertheless, the critic maintained, "nothing that Shange writes is ever entirely unreadable, springing, as it does, from such an intense honesty, from so fresh an awareness of the beauty of sound and of vision, from such mastery of words, from such compassion, humor and intelligence." Shange takes extreme liberties with the conventions of written English in her poetry, using nonstandard spellings and punctuation. Some reviewers have argued that these innovations present unnecessary obstacles to readers of *Nappy Edges, A Daughter's Geography* (1983), and *From Okra to Greens: Poems* (1984). Explaining her "lower-case letters, slashes, and spelling," Shange has said that "poems where all the first letters are capitalized" bore her. "I like the idea that letters dance . . . ," she added. "I need some visual stimulation, so that reading becomes not just a passive act and more than an intellectual activity, but demands rigorous participation." Her idiosyncratic punctuation assures her "that the reader is

not in control of the process"; she wants her words in print to engage the reader in a kind of struggle and not be "whatever you can just ignore." The spellings, she said, "reflect language as I hear it . . . . The structure is connected to the music I hear beneath the words."

Shange has taken liberties with the conventions of fiction writing, too. In her first full-length novel, *Sassafrass, Cypress & Indigo* (1982)—an expansion of her novella *Sassafrass* (1976)—Shange wove narrative, poetry, recipes, magic spells, and letters to tell of three sisters and their relationships. Sassafrass attaches herself to Mitch, a musician who uses hard drugs and beats her; she leaves him twice but goes back to him for another try. Cypress, a dancer in feminist productions, at first refuses to become romantically involved with any of her male friends. Indigo, the youngest sister, retreats into her imagination, befriending her childhood dolls, seeing only the poetry and magic of the world. The music she plays on her violin becomes a rejuvenating source for her mother and sisters. "Probably there is a little bit of all three sisters in Shange," Connie Lauerman suggested, "though she says that her novel is not autobiographical but historical, culled from the experiences of blacks and from the 'information of my feelings'." Shange's second novel, *Betsey Brown* (1985), is a semiautobiographical work set in St. Louis during the late 1950s, when that city began to integrate its schools. Betsey is a thirteen-year-old black girl who enjoys a comfortable home life. When she is bused to an integrated school across town, she becomes aware of differences between blacks and whites. Shange is especially concerned with Betsey's reconciliation of her cultural heritage and her new environment. Although critics had mixed views about *Betsey Brown,* many praised the novel for its depiction of the black middle class. Claudia Tate also noted a change in Shange's writing with *Betsey Brown.* "Most of Shange's characteristic elliptical spelling, innovative syntax and punctuation is absent from *Betsey Brown,*" wrote Tate. "Missing also is the caustic social criticism about racial and sexual victimization. . . . *Betsey Brown* seems also to mark Shange's movement from explicit to subtle expressions of rage, from repudiating her girlhood past to embracing it, and from flip candor to more serious commentary."

Critics have detected a change in Shange's attitudes over the years, but the author herself has asserted that she is as angry and subversive as ever but not as powerless, "because I know where to put my anger, and I don't feel alone in it anymore." Shange continues to produce dramas, poetry, and novels in her own innovative style. Deborah R. Geis described Shange's unique works: "Shange has created a poetic voice that is uniquely her own—a voice which is deeply rooted in her experience of being female and black, but also one which, again, refuses and transcends categorization. Her works articulate the connection between the doubly 'marginalized' social position of the black woman and the need to invent and appropriate a language with which to articulate a self."

(For further information about Shange's life and works, see *Black Writers; Contemporary Authors,* Vols. 85-88; *Contemporary Authors Bibliographical Series,* Vol. 3; *Contemporary Authors New Revision Series,* Vol. 27; *Contemporary Literary Criticism,* Vols. 8, 25, 38; *Dictionary of Literary Biography,* Vol. 38: *Afro-American Writers after 1955: Dramatists and Prose Writers;* and *Major 20th-Century Writers.*)

PRINCIPAL WORKS

for colored girls who have considered suicide/ when the rainbow is enuf: A Choreopoem (drama) 1975
Sassafrass: A Novella (novella) 1976
Natural Disasters, and Other Festive Occasions (poetry and prose) 1977
A Photograph: A Still Life with Shadows/ A Photograph: A Study of Cruelty (drama) 1977; revised as *A Photograph: Lovers-In-Motion,* 1979
Where the Mississippi Meets the Amazon [with Thulani Nkabinda and Jessica Hagedorn] (drama) 1977
From Okra to Greens: A Different Kinda Love Story (drama) 1978
Nappy Edges (poetry) 1978
Black & White Two-Dimensional Planes (drama) 1979
Boogie Woogie Landscapes (drama) 1979
Spell #7 (drama) 1979
*Mother Courage & Her Children (drama) 1980
Some Men (poetry) 1981
Three Pieces (dramas) 1981
Sassafrass, Cypress & Indigo (novel) 1982
A Daughter's Geography (poetry) 1983
From Okra to Greens: Poems (poetry) 1984
See No Evil: Prefaces, Essays & Accounts (essays) 1984
Betsey Brown: A Novel (novel) 1985
Ridin' the Moon in Texas: Word Paintings (poetry) 1987
Three Views of Mt. Fuji (drama) 1987

*This drama is an adaptation of Bertolt Brecht's *Mother Courage and Her Children.*

Ntozake Shange (essay date 1977)

[*Shange "interviewed" herself for* Ms. *in 1977. In a prefatory comment she explained: "i can't quite remember how many questions or journalists or people have happened to me in the last year. i can't even remember everything i've said. i know i tried to convey my perceptions of the world, of men & women, music & language, as clearly as I cd, but poets who talk too much can trip over their own syllables. can become absurd.... so here i have a chance to talk to myself (which i really do). all the time / i'm asking myself. what the hell is going on with you. i'll share this now with you. a conversation with all my selves." In the following excerpt from this "conversation," she discusses influences on her work.*]

[Question]: *why did you always want to be an ikette?*

[Answer]: there waz a time in my life when rhythm & blues waz my only reality. from the time i was eight until i was about thirteen years old i wd sit by the radio in st. louis & listen to george logan's show, till my mother insisted i had enuf of that niggah music. saturdays were spent at vashon high school or at sumner high school (all colored) watching jackie wilson tear his clothes off, dancing in the aisles to ben e. king, the olympics, the shirelles. the only black folks with a public aura were on the stage. now i cd never really sing, but i've always been able to "shake that thing." ike & tina turner were big big big in st. louis. the ikettes got ta wear lil slinky skirts & be on the stage where smokey robinson wd bend over & whisper abt "bad girls." "she's not a bad girl because she wants to be free / uhmmm, she wants to be free." that waz what i wanted / to be free to dance & smile at the people having such a good time listening to tina turner talk abt "i'm justa fool / you know i'm in love." i imagine her songs were for me what edna st. vincent millay's sonnets were for a terribly romantic lil white girl thirty years ago.

but how did you get from tina turner & the chantelles to bebop & poetry?

my mother & father went to europe, cuba, haiti, and mexico. they kept their friends around me from nigeria, togo, haiti, cuba, india, the phillippines, france & mexico. i heard so many languages, so many different kinds of music. visits from dizzy gillespie, chico hamilton, sonny til & chuck berry. i played a solo violin concert in the fifth grade. i cdnt tell the difference tween notes & letters. an "a" waz an "a" like a "b" waz another way of saying something. "i live in language / sound falls round me like rain on other folks." we usedta have sunday afternoon family variety shows. my mama wd read from dunbar, shakespeare, countee cullen, t.s. eliot. my dad wd play congas & do magic tricks. my two sisters & my brother & i wd do a soft-shoe & then pick up the instruments for a quartet of some sort: a violin, a cello, flute & saxophone. we all read constantly. anything. anywhere. we also tore the prints outta art books to carry around with us. sounds / images, any explorations of personal visions waz the focus of my world. st. louis waz just desegregating herself, while i grew. sometimes a langston hughes poem or a bobby timmons tune waz the only safe place i cd find.

that might explain yr lifestyle. why you move so much & rarely keep a house more than a year.

yes, it might. my parents were so mobile during my early childhood. i waz accustomed to traveling, since we moved so many times: from trenton, to upstate new york, to alabama, back to trenton, to st. louis & again back to trenton, before i waz thirteen. i never expected to have anywhere in particular to call home. the spaces i occupied in los angeles, boston, san francisco, & new york from 1969 till now have congealed, to the extent that i relate to those seventeen flats as one. they all look the same. the hangings i wove. the photos of the same friends. the same records. the same pots & pans. i surround myself with essentially the same people wherever i go.

we usedta call ourselves the COMIC-DU-WOP COMMUNE. poets mostly & some musicians. thulani, jessica hagedorn, nashira & pepo ntosha, pedro pietri, papoleto melendez, etnairis rivera, gylan kain, & carol lé sanchez, & paul vane, roberto vargas, alejandro murghia, victor hernandez cruz & tom cusan. we are all so transient. nothing changes too much for any of us. we write poems. we read the poems. we find out who pays money to read the poems. we go there. we read to each other, drink wine, walk the streets with each other making poems. we like to fall in love & be poets. i'm not sure anybody enjoys our stuff as much as we do. or even if people realize how essential poems are to our existence.

you mentioned a number of male writers. how do you account for yr reputation as a feminist, if you listen to & get nourishment from all these men?

(i laugh.) some men are poets. they find wonderment & joy in themselves & give it to me. i snatch it up quick & gloat. some men are poets. they fall prey to despair & ruin. when i feel sad, i go off with them / carrying my sorrow on a leash. some men are poets & then, some men are just men who simply are not worth the time it takes to forget a bad idea. i stay far from them: i hear there is an epidemic of vacuity whenever they open their mouths.

wd you be willing to mention names?

no.

well. how do you explain loving some men who write & some men who play music & some men who are simply lovable, when yr work for almost three years has been entirely woman-centered?

i can do a lot of things. we all can. women haveta. i waz not able to establish the kind of environment i thot my work needed when i read with men all the time. you haveta remember there's an enormous ignorance abt women's realities in our society. we ourselves suffer from a frightening lack of clarity abt who we are. my work attempts to ferret out what i know & touch in a woman's body. if i really am committed to pulling the so-called personal outta the realm of non-art. that's why i have dreams & recipes, great descriptions of kitchens & handiwork in *sassafrass, cypress & indigo.* that's why in *for colored girls* . . . i discuss the simple reality of going home at nite, of washing one's body, looking out the window with a woman's eyes. we must learn our common symbols, preen them and share them with the world. the readings i usedta do with david henderson, conyus, bob chrisman, paul vane, tom cusan, roberto vargas & all the others at the coffee gallery, the intersection, & s.f. state were quite high. but the readings at the women's studies center, with the third world women's collective, international women's day affairs, with the shameless hussy poets, these were overwhelmingly intense & growing experiences for me as a woman & as a poet.

the collective recognition of certain realities that are female can still be hampered, diverted, diluted by a masculine presence. yes. i segregated my work & took it to women. much like i wd take fresh water to people stranded in the mojave desert. i wdnt take a camera crew to observe me. i wdnt ask the people who had never known thirst to come watch the thirsty people drink.

i believe my work waz nourished & shaped to a large degree by the time i spent with women. in san francisco i waz isolated in this very close community of creative women. rosalie alphonso, elvia marta, paula moss, halifu, ifa iyaun, laurie carlos, mari, wopo holup, j.j. wilson: all these women had something to do with *for colored girls* at one stage or another / have given me courage & insight. no one thinks men relating as artistic collaborators is weird. we assume artists need the energy of other artists. look at the music of the art ensemble of chicago, air, or the world saxophone quartet, the chi-lites. that's all cool / they are all men. but women artists exploring what we are in the world is still considered "breaking away" from normal. groups like isis, gang-bang, sagaris, the women's film festival, daughters inc. aren't included in normal. but we need ourselves to take care of ourselves. it's as simple as that.

some white people think lorraine hansberry influenced you; since she didn't, who did help you understand yr craft?

around 1966 / abt the time i went to barnard i thot leroi jones (imamu baraka) waz my primary jumping-off point. that i cd learn from him how to make language sing & penetrate one's soul, like in *the dead lecturer, the system of dante's hell,* & *black magic poetry.* then i found myself relating technically to ishmael reed, particularly in terms of diction & myth, as in *yellow back radio broke-down* & *mumbo jumbo.* then i discovered the nostalgia david henderson can make so tangible; our immediate past as myth. & here comes pedro pietri, allowing language to create a world that can't exist outside his poems. i find victor hernandez cruz shows me how to say anything i thot i saw.

jessica hagedorn on the other hand puts the worlds we both share in a terribly personal & cosmopolitan realm. her book, *dangerous music,* says to me that complicated notions can be explicated by rhythm. we can approach difficult concepts with ourselves; there is no need to go the route of iowa to get a sophisticated poem. all the years i've been writing i've spoken constantly with thulani, whose poetry sustains me as much as my own. thulani teaches me to take risks. her familiarity with the new black music & her understanding of a woman's relationship to the universe continually push me to refuse to be afraid of what i am feeling.

then there is clarence major who has let fantasy loose for me. let me see language with no more responsibility than to give me an image / however contorted, private & bizarre. clarence's stuff, like his novel *reflex & bone structure*, is breaking the linear tradition in black literature, moving us from narrative to the crux of the moment.

i've learned so much from latin americans too: julio cortazar, manuel puig, octavio paz, mario vargas llosa, miguel angel asturias, réné dépestre, gabriel garcía márquez, jacques roumain, léon damas. i get a western hemispheric reference that saves me from what is insidious in north american & european literature / the suggestion that black people exist only as vehicles for white people's fantasies. the technical skill & brilliance of the characterizations of garcía márquez have raised my expectations of how well a reader shd know a person / place.

& then there is neruda ...

i thot you said all art forms contributed to yr development?

i didn't say it yet. i thot abt saying that what dianne mcintyre's sounds-in-motion dance company does with cecil taylor's music gives me the right to put the axis of a poem off balance & hold. i wanted to say i learn abt lyricism from david murray's saxophone & romare bearden's collages. i wanted to insist i've learned abt beauty from carmen delavallade's dancing & albert ayler's music.

yes, but what do you believe a poem shd do?

quite simply a poem shd fill you up with something / cd make you swoon, stop in yr tracks, change yr mind, or make it up. a poem shd happen to you like cold water or a kiss.

one more thing. what is it like to be you?

good. good. sometimes more trouble than i like to handle cuz i didn't take care of myself the way i cd have had i known i waz worth loving. but then i have a bunch of raucous memories i have survived to giggle abt / that has to be awright. i am becoming less afraid of who this "zaki" is. (pp. 35, 70, 72)

Ntozake Shange, "Ntozake Shange Interviews Herself," in Ms., Vol. VI, No. 6, December, 1977, pp. 34-5, 70, 72.

Carol P. Christ (essay date 1980)

[*In the following excerpt from her 1980 study* Diving Deep and Surfacing: Women Writers on Spiritual Quest, *Christ examines the poetry of* for colored girls who have considered suicide / when the rainbow is enuf.]

A gutsy, down-to-earth poet, Ntozake Shange gives voice to the ordinary experiences of Black women in frank, simple, vivid language, telling the colored girl's story in her own speech patterns. Shange's gift is an uncanny ability to bring the experience of being Black and a woman to life. Those who hear or read her choreopoem *for colored girls who have considered suicide / when the rainbow is enuf* may feel overwhelmed by so much reality, so much pain, so much resiliency, so much life force. They may even feel they have actually lived through the stories they have heard.

Like Adrienne Rich, Shange is acutely aware of the nothingness experienced by women in a society defined by men. But Shange is also aware of a double burden of pain and negation suffered by women who are Black in a society defined by *white* men—where Black women are not even granted the ambivalent recognition some white women receive for youth and beauty or for being wives and mothers of white men. Shange's poem also reflects the double strength Black women have had to muster to survive in a world where neither being Black nor being a woman is valued.

Though Shange's forte is the vivid re-creation of experience, *for colored girls* is more than the simple telling of the Black girl's story. It is also a search for the meaning of the nothingness experienced and a quest for new being. In Shange's poems the experience of nothingness is born of the double burden of being Black and a woman, but the stories she tells bring a shock of recognition to every woman who has given too much of herself to a man. The heart of the experience of nothingness in *for colored girls* is a woman's loss and debasement of self for love of a man. But what makes Shange's poems more than just another version of *Lady Sings the Blues*—a theme of sorrow and survival too familiar to Black women (and white women)—is Shange's refusal to accept the Black woman's sorrow as a simple and ultimate fact of life. She probes for a new image of the Black woman that will make the old images of the colored girl obsolete. Shange envisions Black women "born again" on the far side of nothingness with a new image of Black womanhood that will enable them to acknowledge their history while moving beyond it to "the ends of their own rainbows."

For colored girls began as a series of separate poems, but as it developed Shange came to view "these twenty-odd poems as a single statement, a choreopoem." ... In a sense the dialogical form of Shange's play re-creates the consciousness-raising group of the women's movement, where in sharing experiences and stories, women learn to value themselves, to recognize stagnant and destructive patterns in their lives, to name their strengths, and to begin to take responsibility for their lives. The sense of dialogue in Shange's choreopoem is an invitation to the women in the audience to tell their stories. What emerges is a tapestry of experiences, interwoven with a sense of plurality and commonality.

The title of the choreopoem provokes questions. Why did Shange use the outdated term "colored," which Black people abandoned as oppressive in the sixties? How is the rainbow enough? And what does a rainbow have to do with suicide? In a television interview,

Shange explained why she used "colored girls" in the title of her poem. She spoke of the importance of Black self-definition, of taking pride in dark skin and African heritage. She said that her own name, "Ntozake," is an African name she chose as a way of affirming her African roots. But, she said, it was also important to affirm her American ancestors. She recalled that her grandmother's last words to her were that she was a precious "little colored girl." Thinking about this made Shange realize that "colored" was not only a term used by whites to define Blacks, but also a term of endearment in the Black community. To reclaim the name "colored girl" was to reclaim her relationship to her grandmother, a part of her story. The juxtaposition of "colored girl" with "rainbow" enables Black women to see the varied tones of their skin as a reflection of the glorious hues of the rainbow, not as a color to be borne in shame. And, though colored girls have considered suicide because they have been abused by white society and Black men, this need no longer be the case. "The rainbow" is now understood as an image of their own beauty, and it "is enuf."

Shange further explained the meaning of the enigmatic last line of her title, when she said, "One day I was driving home after a class, and I saw a huge rainbow over Oakland. I realized that women could survive if we

Program for the Broadway production of Shange's award-winning drama.

decide that we have as much right and as much purpose for being here as the air and mountains do." Here Shange describes a kind of mystical insight—being does not require justification, it just is. Within the poem, Shange restates the last line of the title, "but are movin to the ends of their own rainbows." ... This restatement extends the mystical insight further: after recognizing their grounding in being, Black women must begin to create their own reality, for example, by creating symbols like the rainbow to express their infinite beauty.

For colored girls begins with a poem spoken by the lady in brown about the importance of naming and celebrating experience in song and story.... Only when her song is sung, her story told will the Black woman know her potential. She will be "born" as a human being for the first time, because she will be aware of herself as a person with value and a range of choices. (pp. 97-100)

In order to sing a colored girl's song, Shange must re-create the language of her experience, a language which, in its concrete particularity, has almost never been spoken. Black women's voices have been negated by the standard (white) English grammar that has forced Black people to fit their experiences into alien language patterns. Black women's experiences have also been negated by a literary tradition that celebrates the experiences of white men. Shange ignores standard grammar in her effort to capture the nuances of Black women's speech patterns and experience.... The idiom of this Black girl's life is reflected in speech patterns, choice of words, details of description, spelling, and punctuation (or rather lack of it).... Shange's poems also reflect her notion that Black speech is close to music, an understanding expressed in the mixed genre choreopoem in which music, dance, and spoken word are woven together. (pp. 100-02)

The poems in *for colored girls,* when taken as a whole, describe a spiritual journey through the particularities of a Black woman's experience. In this journey an alternation of joy, despair, and reconstitution of self proceeds circularly, musically, rather than linearly. Shange's women move through hope, defeat, and rebirth in several of the poem sequences, until in the last the lady in red experiences a crescendo of despair that leads to a dramatic rebirth of self and a more certain awareness of the self's grounding in larger powers of life and being. The poems in *for colored girls* celebrate the Black woman's life force and capacity for love. They confront her defeat and celebrate her resilience. They provide her with alternatives to the image of the Black woman as either helpless and defeated, a "sorry" colored girl, or as strong and resilient, "impervious to pain." ... In her search for new images, the Black woman cannot simply adapt images from the white man, the Black man, or the white woman, because none of these images of being human reflect the fullness of her humanity, the affirmation of both her color and her sex. To search for new images of self is to ask anew the old questions: What is it to be human? Do we need relationships? Sex? What is the relation between body and soul? Shange seeks answers to these questions as she explores the Black woman's experience in her poems.

The first several poems in *for colored girls* create a mood of youthful optimism, playfulness, and joy in being alive. The serious note of the opening poem is interrupted by the singing of the childhood song, "mama's little baby," the reciting of a playful rhyme, and a game of tag. This lighter note, which carries over into the next two poems, expresses Shange's perception that the Black girl's childhood does not always prepare her for the struggles and hard times of her adult experience. (pp. 103-04)

["Graduation nite"] tells the story of a girl's first sexual initiation. While the girl's lower class and sometimes violent environment ... is evident in her tale, the story is a positive one. Graduation was an exuberant rite of passage for her, and she sang inside.... (p. 104)

The following poem, **"now I love somebody more than,"** tells the story of the lady in blue's teen-age fascination with the Caribbean rhythms of Puerto Rican musician Willie Colon. Though this poem too has its serious moments, including a reference to Black self-hatred and color caste systems..., the poem as a whole is joyous. Beginning with the first "ola"... and moving through vivid descriptions of her dancing..., the poem is an invocation to the spirit of music and dance that has brought so much joy to a colored girl's life. (pp. 104-05)

While the first two poems celebrate Black women's life force, the next poem, **"no assistance,"** tells of their abuse. The lady in red tells how she loved a man who didn't appreciate her.... What makes the story of the lady in red more than the age-old female complaint about abuse by men is humor, anger, and insight.... Seeing her actions with humor creates a distance from pain and allows her to express her anger and to take responsibility for ending the affair.... Because she sees herself as responsible for letting herself be abused, she sees her power to refuse to be a victim.... The anger expressed in her last words to this man is the anger of a woman who has realized she doesn't need to waste her time on a man who doesn't value her. Her story calls up feelings of pain and outrage that such an obviously creative and funny woman has not been able to find a man to appreciate and love her. (pp. 105-06)

The next two poems speak of painful violations of women's bodies in rape and hack abortion. All the women speak the rape poem together, affirming that unfortunately this is not an individual story.... The picture created by Shange's poem is brutal but true. The stark simple lines of the poem and their harsh rhythm contrast effectively with the mood of joy expressed in the first two poems and deepen the feelings of pain and outrage that were introduced in **"no assistance."** Shange creates a mood, preparing the audience to experience ever deeper nothingness in a Black woman's story.

In **"abortion cycle #1"** Shange re-creates a woman's terror during an illegal abortion. The poem begins cryptically as four of the women shriek "eyes," "mice," "womb," "nobody," evoking a feeling of terror. The rest of the poem, spoken by the lady in blue, is a collage of images of pain, disgust, fear, shame.... These images capture the feeling of violation, the pain of an abortion without anesthesia: it felt like something huge and powerful was inside her womb, like death was coming out of all her orifices.... This woman's secret shame recalls the opening poem, where it was stated that as long as the Black woman's story is not told, she will hear nothing but "maddening screams // & the soft strains of death."... In sharing her story, the lady in blue can begin to break out of her isolation.

In the next several poems, **"sechita," "toussaint,"** and **"one,"** Shange turns the audience to three individual stories which, while not without their own painful dimensions, are not as devastating as the stories of rape and back-room abortion. (pp. 106-08)

The alternation of naming Black women's strengths and naming their abuse and suffering continues in the next poem, **"i useta live in the world."** In this poem Shange contrasts the universe of free Africa with its "waters ancient from accra / tunis // cleansin me / feedin me"... with Harlem where "my ankles are covered in grey filth // from the puddle neath the hydrant." ... Black women in Harlem not only live in poverty and filth but also suffer verbal and physical abuse from men who assuage their shattered egos by abusing women.... The ultimate degradation she suffers is the knowledge that she must become violent like her surroundings if she is to survive.... (pp. 109-10)

The next poem, **"pyramid,"** considers women's complicity in their oppression.... It is an old story of women considering men more important than their friendships with each other. In this case, the women betray a close bond between each other for a man who doesn't even care about any of them.... Shange concludes the poem with the two women comforting each other.... The strongest love between them is their love for each other.... Shange celebrates the bond of sisterhood between women as a more reliable source of support than romantic fantasies about men.

In the next series of poems, **"no more love poems"**..., which form the reflective introspective center of the choreopoem, Shange explores the experience of nothingness created by women's dependence on men. In what to me is the most profound poem in *for colored girls,* the lady in orange (originally played by Shange) sings a "requiem for myself / cuz i // have died in a real way."... The death she suffered was caused by self-denial and self-deception.... In these lines Shange expresses an understanding of why women take abuse from men without complaining: it is just too painful to admit that men have the upper hand in many relationships and that they abuse the women who love them. The young Black girl who knows that she will suffer on account of her race often tries to deny that she will also suffer on account of her sex. However, to begin to admit the depth of her pain and experience of nothingness is the beginning of the road to self-acceptance for every woman. (pp. 110-11)

In the final poem of **"no more love poems,"** the poet confesses her inability to make her experience congruent with her philosophy. Indeed the disparity between her vision and her reality begins to drive her mad: "i've lost it / / touch with reality" . . . , she confesses. She ponders again the alternatives and admits she does not have the answer. . . . Though she has not found a solution, she has achieved clarity about the problem and confidence in her own values and worth. She will not be likely again to deny her pain or to take abuse in relationships. She may not be able to find a man to love her, but she can at least refuse to be a victim, and this is an important step. The other women join her in her refusal to take abuse, asserting that their love is too "delicate," "beautiful," "sanctified," "magic," "saturday nite," "complicated," and "music" to have thrown back in their faces. Their joint affirmation has more power than an individual assertion because in celebrating their sisterhood with each other, each woman hears her value affirmed by the others.

Their resolution not to take abuse is put into practice in the next poem, the story of a woman who "made too much room" for a man and apparently considered herself worthless when he left her. The title line of the poem, **"somebody almost walked off wid alla my stuff"** . . . , is a metaphor that works on several levels. On the literal level it may refer to a man who stole some of a woman's things and attempted to sell them for money. On a sexual level, "stuff" is a euphemism for a woman's sexuality and refers to the man's failure to appreciate her giving of her body. And on the psychological level, the line refers to a man taking advantage of a woman's vulnerability and need for love. More than a lament, this poem is a celebration of a woman's self-respect and resolve not to abase herself for a man. The poem's humor stems from the literal elaboration of the central metaphor. . . . The lady in green enjoys her metaphor so much that she even begins to imagine this man has taken all her unique individuality, including her gestures and the identifying marks on her body. . . . In creating a catalogue of her "stuff" she comes to value herself in all her particularity. Instead of being turned in on herself, her anger is directed at the man who didn't appreciate what she had to offer. . . . Though rightly angry at the man, her anger is not a plea for him to love her as she thinks she deserves to be loved. Rather it is the anger of a woman who is learning finally to nurture and value herself. "My stuff," she says, "is the anonymous ripped off treasure // of the year." . . . Her list of what she treasures in herself is healing because she affirms her whole self, not just the self that has been primped and pampered to meet male approval. Shange deliberately celebrates aspects of her self that flout cultural ideals of female attractiveness: her immodesty, when she gives her crotch sunlight; her flawed body, including "calloused feet" and a "leg wit the // flea bite"; her unfeminine personality expressed in "quik

language" . . . ; and her unfeminine female smells, when she "didnt get a chance to take a douche." . . . (pp. 112-14)

The lady in blue wonders what the lady will do if this man comes back saying he's sorry. This provokes the women to join together in creating a litany of excuses men give when they say they're sorry. . . . the lady in blue replies, "one thing i dont need // is any more apologies." . . . Instead of continuing to live out the forgiving female role, she expresses in yet another particular way the women's joint decision to take no more abuse.

At last able to affirm themselves as they are, colored, and sometimes sorry, open and in need of love, the women face a final challenge as the lady in red tells the story of Crystal and Beau Willie Brown. The story begins in the room of Beau Willie, a Vietnam veteran sent to "kill vietnamese children" . . . , who returned "crazy as hell" . . . and addicted to drugs. Not unaware of the oppressive forces that turned Beau Willie crazy, the lady in red focuses on his tragic interaction with Crystal . . . , who with their children takes the brunt of Beau Willie's rage. (pp. 114-15)

The lady in red breaks the silence with her cry, "i was missin somethin." . . . Her cry reminds everyone of the loss of her children. The other women deepen her cry, adding, "somethin so important," "somethin promised." . . . The lady in blue finally names what is missing—"a layin on of hands," to which the other ladies respond, "strong," "cool," "movin," "makin me whole," "sense," "pure," "all the gods comin into me / layin me open to myself." . . . Their words describe the sensations felt in a laying on of hands, an ancient healing ritual that is often practiced in evangelical sects in poor white and poor Black communities. The ladies explain that a laying on of hands is not sex with a man, or a mother's comforting touch, but a touching in which powers larger than the self are channeled into the one being healed. The laying on of hands ritual affirms the self's position in a community and in the universe, and suggests to her that she is not alone, that other humans—in this case women—and the very powers of being support her life and health. The laying on of hands in a community of women celebrates the power of sisterhood and sharing as one of the keys to a woman's moving through the experience of nothingness.

In the last poem, the lady in red describes how a woman, possibly Crystal, moves through nothingness to new being. Having contemplated suicide, this woman "fell into a numbness" . . . , but a mystical experience in nature brought her back to life. . . . Like Shange felt after her experience with the rainbow, the lady in red could conclude, "we are the same as the sky. We are here, breathing, living creatures, and we have a right to everything."

The final words of the lady in red, which are picked up and sung gospel style by the other women, are an incredible affirmation of her own power of being: "i found god in myself // and i loved her / i loved her fiercely." . . . These words express the affirmation of self, of being woman, of being Black, which is at the heart of *for colored girls* . . . . These final lines express Shange's conviction that the Black woman's quest for being is grounded in the powers of being. Though she has moments of despair that make her consideration of suicide logical, the powers of being in nature and sisterhood aid the Black woman in moving through nothingness. More than just a statement of self-affirmation, this woman's finding God in herself is an acknowledgement of her self's grounding in larger powers. (pp. 115-17)

To say "i found god in myself // and i loved her / i loved her fiercely" is to say in the clearest possible terms that it is all right to be a woman, that the Black woman does not have to imitate whiteness or depend on men for her power of being. This affirmation is a clear vision of new being on the far side of nothingness. (p. 117)

> Carol P. Christ, "'I Found God in Myself . . . & I Loved Her Fiercely': Ntozake Shange," in her Diving Deep and Surfacing: Women Writers on Spiritual Quest, *Beacon Press*, 1980, pp. 97-118.

Deborah R. Geis (essay date 1989)

[*In the following excerpt, Geis surveys Shange's dramatic work, exploring her use of monologue.*]

Ntozake Shange's works defy generic classifications: just as her poems (published in *Nappy Edges* and *A Daughter's Geography*) are also performance pieces, her works for the theater defy the boundaries of drama and merge into the region of poetry. Her most famous work, *for colored girls who have considered suicide/ when the rainbow is enuf,* is subtitled "a choreopoem." Similarly, she has written *Betsey Brown* as a novel and then again (with Emily Mann) in play form, and her first work of fiction, *Sassafrass, Cypress & Indigo,* is as free with its narrative modes—including recipes, spells, letters—as Joyce was in *Ulysses.* Perhaps more so than any other practicing playwright, Shange has created a poetic voice that is uniquely her own—a voice which is deeply rooted in her experience of being female and black, but also one which, again, refuses and transcends categorization. Her works articulate the connection between the doubly "marginalized" social position of the black woman and the need to invent and appropriate a language with which to articulate a self.

In their revelation of such a language, Shange's theatrical narratives move subtly and forcefully between the comic and the tragic. A brief passage from *for colored girls* underscores the precarious path between laughter and pain which Shange's characters discover they are forced to tread:

> distraught laughter fallin
> over a black girl's shoulder

> it's funny/it's hysterical
> the melody-less-ness of her dance
> don't tell nobody, don't tell a soul
> she's dancin on beer cans & shingles

The images associated with the word *hysterical* in this passage show the multilayered and interdependent qualities of the "black girl's" experience: *hysterical* connotes a laughter which has gone out of control, a madness historically—if not accurately—connected with femaleness. Moreover, the admonition "don't tell nobody, don't tell a soul" suggests the call to silence, the fear that to speak of her pain will be to violate a law of submission. The onlooker will aestheticize the dance or call attention to its comic qualities rather than realize the extent to which the dance and the laughter are a reaction against—and are even motivated by—the uncovering of pain.

The key here is the complexity, for Shange, of the performative experience. In her plays, especially *for colored girls* and *spell #7,* Shange develops her narration primarily through monologues because monologic speech inevitably places the narrative weight of a play upon its spoken language and upon the performances of the individual actors. But she does not use this device to develop "character" in the same fashion as Maria Irene Fornes and other Method-inspired playwrights who turn toward monologic language in order more expressively to define and "embody" their characters both as women and as individuals. Rather, Shange draws upon the uniquely "performative" qualities of monologue to allow her actors to take on *multiple* roles and therefore to emphasize the centrality of *storytelling* to her work. This emphasis is crucial to Shange's articulation of a black feminist aesthetic (and to the call to humanity to accept that "black women are inherently valuable") on two counts. First, the incorporation of role-playing reflects the ways that blacks (as "minstrels," "servants," "athletes," etc.) and women (as "maids," "whores," "mothers," etc.) are expected to fulfill such roles on a constant basis in Western society. Second, the space between our enjoyment of the "spectacle" of Shange's theater pieces (through the recitation of the monologues and through the dancing and singing which often accompany them), and our awareness of the urgency of her call for blacks/women to be allowed "selves" free of stereotypes, serves as a "rupturing" of the performance moment; it is the uncomfortableness of that space, that rupture, which moves and disturbs us.

In **"takin a solo/ a poetic possibility/ a poetic imperative,"** the opening poem of *Nappy Edges,* Shange argues that just as the great jazz musicians each have a recognizable sound and musical style, so too should the public develop a sensitivity to the rhythms and nuances of black writers and that the writers themselves should cultivate "sounds" which distinguish them as individuals. She writes:

> as we demand to be heard/ we want you to hear us.
> we come to you the way leroi jenkins comes or cecil
> taylor/ or b.b. king. we come to you alone/ in the
> theater/ in the story/ & the poem. like with billie

holiday or betty carter/ we shd give you a moment
that cannot be recreated/ a specificity that cannot be
confused. our language shd let you know who's
talkin, what we're talkin abt & how we cant stop
sayin this to you. some urgency accompanies the test.
something important is going on. we are speakin.
reachin for yr person/ we cannot hold it/ we dont
wanna sell it/ we give you ourselves/ if you listen.

Although Shange's remarks were intended to address the
larger issue of Afro-American writing, her words hold
true for the speakers of monologue in her plays as well,
for the monologue is another way of "takin a solo." For
Shange's actors/characters (it is sometimes difficult to
draw the distinction between the two, as the actors
frequently portray actors who in turn portray multiple
characters), monologues issue forth with the same sense
that "some urgency accompanies the test" and that, in
delivering the speeches, they are "reachin for yr person." In this respect the characters seem to aspire
toward a specificity which would make them stand as if
independent of their author. But the hallmark of the
very "imperative" which Shange has announced in the
first place is the unmistakable sense that all of the
speakers' voices are ultimately parts of one voice: that of
Shange, their creator and the play's primary monologist
or storyteller.

All of Shange's theatrical pieces, even *a photograph:
lovers in motion* and *boogie woogie landscapes,* unfold
before the audience as collections of stories rather than
as traditionally linear narratives; the events are generated less from actual interactions as they unfold in the
"present" of the play (except perhaps in *a photograph*)
than from the internal storytellers' *recreations* of individual dramas. The implied privilege of the storyteller
to create alternate worlds, as well as the fluidity of the
stories themselves and the characters in them, relies
heavily upon the immense power that African and Afro-
American tradition have assigned to the spoken word.
According to James Hatch, Africans traditionally believe that "words and the art of using them are a special
power that can summon and control spirit." Furthermore, as Geneviève Fabre explains in *Drumbeats Masks
and Metaphor*:

> The oral tradition holds a prominent place in Afro-
> American culture. For slaves (who were often forbid-
> den to learn to write) it was the safest means of
> communication. It provided basic contact with Afri-
> ca as a homeland and a source of folklore, a contract
> also between ethnic groups unified under a common
> symbolic heritage, between generations, and finally,
> between the speaker and his audience.... Because
> the oral tradition has long remained a living practice
> in Afro-American culture, the dramatic artist has
> been tempted to emulate not only the art and
> techniques of the storyteller, but also his prestigious
> social function—that of recording and reformulating
> experience, of shaping and transmitting values, opin-
> ions, and attitudes, and of expressing a certain
> collective wisdom.

Shange takes the notion of exchange and collectivity
among storytellers even further in her use of the space in
which her pieces are performed. Monologue creates

"narrative space"; Shange depends upon the power and
magic of the stories within her plays to create the scenes
without the use of backdrops and other "theatrical"
effects. *for colored girls* is the most "open" of the plays
in this sense, as it calls for no stage set, only lights of
different colors and specific places for the characters to
enter and exit. *boogie woogie landscapes* conjures up the
mental images of the title within the confines of Layla's
bedroom: "there is what furniture a bedroom might
accommodate, though not too much of it, the most
important thing is that a bedroom is suggested." Although the sets of both *spell #7* and *a photograph* are
fairly specific (a huge minstrel mask as a backdrop and,
later, a bar in lower Manhattan for the former; a
photographer's apartment for the latter), they still call
for this space to be reborn in different imaginary ways
as the characters come forth and tell their stories.

for colored girls, Shange's first major theater piece,
evolved from a series of poems modeled on Judy
Grahn's *Common Woman*. The play received its first
performances in coffeehouses in San Francisco and on
the Lower East Side of Manhattan; eventually, it attracted critical and public attention and moved to the New
Federal Theater, the Public Theater, and then to Broadway in 1976. *for colored girls* draws its power from the
performances—in voice, dance, and song—of its actors,
as well as from the ways it articulates a realm of
experience which heretofore had been suppressed in the
theater; the "lady in brown" speaks to the release of this
suppression when she says near the beginning of the
piece:

> sing a black girl's song
> bring her out
> to know her self
> ...she's been dead so long
> closed in silence so long
> she doesn't know the sound
> of her own voice
> her infinite beauty

The instruments for releasing and expressing the "infinite beauty" of the "black girl's song" become the
characters, who do not have names and specific identities of their own (except through their physical presences), but rather take on multiple identities and
characters as the "lady in brown," "lady in red," "lady
in yellow," etc. These "ladies" put on the metaphorical
masks of various characters in order to enact the
"ceremony" of the play, which gathers them together in
a stylized, ritualistic fashion. The ritual is a religious one
to the extent that the participants turn to the "spirit"
which might be best described as the black female
collective unconscious; it is a celebratory one in that
their immersion in it is ultimately a source of joy and
strength. In this sense the ritual is a festival that depends
as much upon the bonds of the group as it does upon
individual expression; Fabre makes this connection
explicit when she says that "the group...takes possession of space and enlarges it to express communion."

As the characters assume their different "masks," we see them enact a complex series of microdramas, some joyful and others painful. So it is that the "lady in purple" narrates the tale of Sechita, who "kicked viciously thru the nite/ catchin' stars tween her toes," while the lady in green "plays" Sechita and dances out the role. Both of these characters "are" Sechita, for the identity of this character within a character merges in the spoken narration and the accompanying movement. Yet it also becomes clear in the course of the play that these actors/ characters are *not* simply assuming masks or roles for the sake of a dramatic production; they must enact the "dramas" and wear the "masks" of black women every day of their lives. Shange has taken on the difficult task, then, of universalizing her characters in the play without allowing them to fall into roles that are essentially stereotypes. She discusses the need for this balance between the "idiosyncratic" and the "representative" in an interview with Claudia Tate:

> I feel that as an artist my job is to appreciate the differences among my women characters. We're usually just thrown together, like "tits and ass," or a good cook, or how we can really "f—" [*sic*]. Our personalities and distinctions are lost. What I appreciate about the women whom I write about, the women whom I know, is how idiosyncratic they are. I take delight in the very peculiar or particular things that fascinate or terrify them. Also, I discovered that by putting them all together, there are some things they all are repelled by, and there are some things they are all attracted to. I only discovered this by having them have their special relationships to their dreams and their unconscious.

At times the storytellers within *for colored girls* seem to be putting on "masks" of humor which they wear, as part of the assumption of a role or character, in order to create a way of channeling the fear and anger they experience into the mode of performance. For instance, in one monologue the lady in red expresses the pain of a rejected love with a sardonic "itemization" of what she had been through:

> without any assistance or guidance from you
> i have loved you assiduously for 8 months 2 wks
>   & a day
> i have been stood up four times
> i've left 7 packages on yr doorstep
> forty poems 2 plants & 3 handmade notecards i
>   left
> town so i cd send to you have been no help to me
> on my job
> you call at 3:00 in the mornin on weekdays
> so i cd drive 17 1/2 miles cross the bay before i go
>   to work
> charmin charmin
> but you are of no assistance

The disruptive power of this and other "comic" narratives in the play comes from the realization that what we are laughing at, though merely amusing and exaggerated on the surface, has an underside of bitterness and even torment. Often the shift from humor to pathos is so sudden that the effect is as if we have been slapped, which is precisely the way Shange describes the transi-

tion to the story on "latent rapist bravado" ("we cd even have em over for dinner/ & get raped in our own houses/ by invitation/ a friend"). Helene Keyssar points out in *The Curtain and the Veil* that the spectator is likely to overlook the pain in favor of the humor in the play's earliest vignettes, but as the work moves into such searing narratives as the lady in blue's story of an abortion, we begin to feel increasingly uncomfortable with our own laughter. The candor of the speakers combined with the persistent irony, says Keyssar, "prevents the display of emotion from becoming melodramatic and allows the spectators a vulnerability to their own feelings that can renew their ability to act with others in the world outside the theater." But there is also another way to view this generation of "vulnerability": as a result of the disjunction between the guise of humor and the realization that such moments in the play are actually imbued with pain and anger, the spectator experiences the feeling of having entered an uncomfortable "space" between the two strategies of performance. Like Brecht, Shange seems to believe that inhabiting such a "space" causes the audience to question its own values and beliefs; unlike Brecht, though, she engages the emotions directly in this process. She says in her interview with Tate, "I write to get at the part of people's emotional lives that they don't have control over, the part that can and will respond."

The most emotionally difficult (and most controversial) monologue in the play in terms of this vulnerability is the "Beau Willie Brown" sequence, the only story with a male protagonist. It concerns Beau Willie, a Vietnam veteran who beats up Crystal, the mother of their two children, so many times that she gets a court order restraining him from coming near them. When Beau Willie forces his way into Crystal's apartment and insists that she marry him, she refuses, and he takes the children away from her and holds them out on the window ledge. In the devastating final moments of the story, the lady in red, who has been telling the story, suddenly shifts from referring to Crystal in the third person to using "I":

> i stood by beau in the window/ with naomi reachin
> for me/ & kwame screaming mommy mommy from
> the fifth story/ but i cd only whisper/ & he dropped
> em

It is as if, in this wrenching moment, the lady in red has abandoned the sense that she is "acting out" a story; she "becomes" the character she has been narrating. As she closes the space between her role as narrator and the character of Crystal, this moment of the story itself brings to an end the distancing effect created by Shange's use of spectacle up to this point: the piece is no longer an "entertainment" but a ritualized release of pure feeling which is experienced rather than "performed."

Because of the resonance of the "Beau Willie Brown" story, *for colored girls* seems on the brink of despair; instead, though, the intensity and raw emotion of the lady in red's/Crystal's narrative serves to bring the

Ntozake Shange.

women together and to acknowledge the strength they derive from each other. They characterize this final affirmation in religious terms, but it is a piety derived from within rather than from an outward deity:

> a layin' on of hands
> the holiness of myself released
> . . . i found god in myself
> & i loved her/ i loved her fiercely

Janet Brown justly indicates the need for a movement toward such a resolution when she says that the "successful resolution to the search for autonomy is attributable first to the communal nature of the struggle." However, these last two sequences of the play have come under fire by some critics because they feel that Shange had ultimately failed to translate the personal into the political. Andrea Benton Rushing criticizes Shange's isolation in *for colored girls* "from salient aspects of black literary and political history," the "shockingly ahistorical" way it seems to ignore "white responsibility for our pain," and its final "rejection of political solutions." Similarly, Erskine Peters is appalled

by the apparent manipulativeness of the "Beau Willie Brown" monologue:

> This climax is the author's blatantly melodramatic attempt to turn the work into tragedy without fulfilling her obligations to explore or implicate the historical and deeper tragic circumstances. There is a very heated attempt to rush the play toward an evocation of pity, horror, and suffering. The application of such a cheap device at this critical thematic and structural point is an inhumane gesture to the Black community.

Rushing and Peters raise a valid issue when they say that *for colored girls* is not a direct and forceful indictment of white supremacist politics, at least not in as immediate a sense as *spell #7.* But Peters' accusation that Crystal's story constitutes a "cheap device" which turns the play into a pseudotragedy seems unfounded, for such an argument ignores the declaration of community which comes at the end of the play in response to the individual pain which reached its peak in the "Beau Willie Brown" narrative. Indeed, one might argue that the placement of this story before the play's closing ritual is Shange's attempt to avoid having the spectator convert the final moments into cathartic ones—for as Augusto Boal argues so convincingly in *Theater of the Oppressed,* catharsis can have the "repressive" or "coercive" effect of lulling the spectator into complacency. Or, as Michael W. Kaufman says of the black revolutionary theater of Baraka, Reed, and others, "The very notion of catharsis, an emotional purgation of the audience's collective energies, means that theatre becomes society's buffer sponging up all the moral indignities that if translated into action could effect substantial change." If the ending of the play is dissatisfying because it seems to be administering a palliative to the audience, that is precisely the point: Shange is suggesting the sources of possible strength and redemption by having the characters *perform* the play's closing "ritual." But since the "Beau Willie Brown" story has closed the gulf between narrator and narrative, this final "performance" *cannot* be only a "show." Just as the "ladies" are no longer playing "roles," the spectacle of their concluding ritual automatically conveys a sense of urgency which—coupled with the sheer emotional impact of the "Beau Willie Brown" sequence—prevents the audience from experiencing the ending as cathartic.

Kimberly Benston discusses black American theater's movement away from European-American structures and toward African-rooted ones in terms of the shift from *mimesis*/drama to *methexis*/ritual. Not only, she claims, does the ritual create a sense of community, as we have discussed in *for colored girls,* but it also breaks down the barriers that have traditionally existed between the performers and the spectators. This is perhaps why, in the opening of Shange's *spell #7* (1979), there is a "huge blackface mask" visible on the stage even while the audience is still coming into the theater. Shange says that "in a way the show has already begun, for the members of the audience must integrate this grotesque, larger than life misrepresentation of life into their pre-show chatter." We might say that she thus attempts to erase distinctions between "play" and "audience": not only does the performance address the spectators, but in this case the spectators are also forced to "address" the performance. At the beginning of the play, the performers parade in minstrel masks identical to the huge one which looms overhead; they eventually shed their masks and pose instead as "actors" (or actors playing actors who, in turn, play at being actors), but the image of the minstrel mask is a sign that even modern black actors are still often conceived of as little more than minstrels. As the actor/character Bettina complains, "if that director asks me to play it any blacker/ i'm gonna have to do it in a mammy dress."

Shange, then, makes the minstrel-masking into a ceremony of sorts in the opening scene of *spell #7,* and the resemblance of the giant minstrel face above the stage to an African voodoo mask is wholly intentional. At the same time, though, the blackface masks that the actors wear at the beginning of the play also invoke the *travesty* of a ceremony, for the masks represent the "parts" each must play (in the Western tradition) in order to get a job. Shange connects this to her feelings about her own "masking" in an interview with Tate:

> It was risky for us to do the minstrel dance in *spell #7,* but I insisted upon it because I thought the actors in my play were coming from pieces they didn't want to be in but pieces that helped them pay their bills. Black characters are always being closed up in a "point." They decided, for instance, that *spell #7* by Zaki Shange is a feminist piece and therefore not poetry. Well, that's a lie. That's giving me a minstrel mask.... We're not free of our paint yet! The biggest moneymakers—*The Wiz, Bubblin' Brown Sugar, Ain't Misbehavin'*—are all minstrel shows.

In the course of the play, though, the actors/characters also use "masking" in a different way; they try on various "masks" or roles, as in *for colored girls,* to perform the monologues and group pieces that provide both mirrors and alternatives for the various "selves" they create under pressure from a society governed by white values and images. So, for instance, one of the nameless and faceless performers behind a minstrel mask at the beginning of the play becomes the actor Natalie in the next scene, who in turn "becomes" Sue-Jean, a young woman who desperately wants a baby, as she and Alec (another of the "minstrels" revealed as actor/character) alternate in narrating her story while she mimes it out.

Unlike *for colored girls, spell #7* makes use of a central storyteller figure, Lou, who "directs" the monologues which are performed in the course of the play. It is appropriate that Lou is a magician, for even the title of *spell #7* (the subtitle of which is "geechee jibara quik magic trance manual for technologically stressed third world people") refers to magic making. In his opening speech, though, Lou warns of the power (and danger) of "colored" magic:

> my daddy retired from magic & took

> up another trade cuz this friend a mine
> from the 3rd grade/ asked to be made white
> on the spot

> what cd any self-respectin colored american magi-
>   cian
> do with such an outlandish request/ cept
> put all them razzamatazz hocus pocus zippity-
>   doo-dah
> thingamajigs away   cuz
> colored chirren believin in magic
> waz becoming politically dangerous for the
>   race . . .

> all things are possible
> but ain't no colored magician in his right mind
> gonna make you   white
> i mean
>   this is blk magic
> you lookin at
> & i'm fixin you up good/ fixin you up good &
>   colored

The image of the narrator as "magician" implies that the storytellers themselves will be under the control of a certain "author"; yet as the actors perform their pieces, the stories seem at times to slip away from a guiding narratorial force and to become deeply personal. In a sense, the performers threaten to overpower the narrator in the same way that the third grader's request to be made white is beyond the power of Lou's magician father: the stories take on a kind of magic which is independent of their "director," and yet to enter this realm may be painful and perilous. Lou, then, is like a surrogate author who is responsible for the content of the play, but who also cannot fully control what happens to it once the performers begin to take part.

Lou's position in relation to the performers is most fully evident when, after Lily becomes wholly absorbed in her monologue about the network of dreams she has built around her image of her hair, he stands up and points to her. Shange indicates in the stage directions that Lou "reminds us that it is only thru him that we are able to know these people without the 'masks'/the lies/ & he cautions that all their thoughts are not benign, they are not safe from what they remember or imagine." He says, partly to Lily and partly to the audience:

> you have t come with me/ to this place where
>   magic is/
> to hear my song/ some times i forget & leave my
>   tune
> in the corner of the closet under all the dirty
>   clothes/
> in this place/ magic asks me where i've been/ how
>   i've
> been singin/ lately i leave my self in all the wrong
>   hands/
> in this place where magic is involved in undoin
>   our masks/ i
> am able to smile & answer that.
> in this place where magic always asks for me
> i discovered a lot of other people who talk without
>   mouths
> who listen to what you say/ by watchin yr jewelry
>   dance
> & in this place where magic stays

you can let yrself in or out
but when you leave yrself at home/ burglars &
     daylight
thieves
     pounce on you & sell your skin/ at cut-rate on
     tenth avenue

The "place where magic is" means, within the most literal context of the play, the bar where the actors meet and feel free to try on various roles. But it is also the theater, and the implication is that, as such, it is both a safe place and an unsafe place: certain inhibitions are lifted and certain feelings can be portrayed, but one risks vulnerability in exposing one's memories and emotions. Finally, "this place where magic is" marks the space in which the actor/writer/artist allows creativity to happen. The impulse to safeguard it—"lately i leave my self in all the wrong hands"—echoes the fear of loss which Shange turns into a similar set of metaphors in the "somebody almost walked off wid alla my stuff" poem in *for colored girls.* But something interesting occurs as the result of Lou's delivery of this speech: although he designs it to reinforce his power as the play's magician/narrator, its effect is to establish *him* as being in a position not altogether different from that of the other characters, for the speech reveals his vulnerability, his disguises and defenses, and his need to inhabit a "safe" place in which to create.

If Lou is indeed addressing the audience as well as Lily, the implication is that he is inviting the spectator to become similarly vulnerable. Not surprisingly, then, the play's two "centerpiece" monologues attempt—as in *for colored girls*—to take hold of the spectator in the gap that the performers create between the "safe" region of spectacle/entertainment and the "unsafe" region of pain and emotional assailability. In the first of the two monologues, Alec tells of his wish for all of the white people all over the world to kneel down for three minutes of silence in formal apology for the pain that they have given to black people:

> i just want to find out why no one has even been able
> to sound a gong & all the reporters recite that the
> gong is ringin/ while we watch all the white people/
> immigrants & invaders/ conquistadors & relatives of
> london debtors from georgia/ kneel & apologize to
> us/ just for three or four minutes. now/ this is not
> impossible.

Of course, the image is an absurd one, and Lou calls attention to this when he responds to Alec, "what are you gonna do with white folks kneeling all over the country anyway/ man." The humor in Alec's rather extreme proposal is undercut, however, by the suffering which stands behind such a request. Perhaps the most savage example of anger transferred to the realm of the comic, though, and one which cannot fail to disturb the audience, is Natalie's "today i'm gonna be a white girl" monologue. She takes on the voice of the vacuous and hypocritical "white girl" who flings her hair, waters her plants, and takes twenty Valiums a day:

> . . . i'm still waiting for my cleaning lady & the lady
> who takes care of my children & the lady who caters

my parties & the lady who accepts quarters at the bathroom in sardi's. those poor creatures shd be sterilized/ no one shd have to live such a life. cd you hand me a towel/ thank-you caroline. i've left all of maxime's last winter clothes in a pile for you by the back door. they have to be cleaned but i hope yr girls can made gd use of them.

Freud says in *Jokes and Their Relation to the Unconscious* that the ability to laugh at something is interfered with when the "joke" material also produces a strong affect and so another emotion "blocks" one's capacity to generate laughter; for this reason, it is not surprising that the "white girls" in the audience at whom this monologue is aimed may feel too angry at Natalie's speech to consider it funny. Or they may laugh because they distance themselves from the reality of her words. Similarly, the very intensity of Natalie's emotions as she speaks this piece shows both the amount of pain which gradually interferes with her ability to sustain the joking tone of her own speech at the end and the intensified need for release through humor which her bitterness engenders. As Freud indicates,

> precisely in cases where there is a release of affect one
> can observe a particularly strong difference in expen-
> diture bring about the automatism of release. When
> Colonel Butler answers Octavio's warnings by ex-
> claiming 'with a bitter laugh': '*Thanks* from the
> House of Austria!' his embitterment does not prevent
> his laughing. The laugh applies to his memory of the
> disappointment he believes he has suffered; and on
> the other hand the magnitude of the disappointment
> cannot be portrayed more impressively by the dra-
> matist than by his showing it capable of forcing a
> laugh in the midst of the storm of feelings that have
> been released.

It is also striking that the play's final monologue, spoken by Maxine, comes forth because she is "compelled to speak by natalie's pain" (i.e., after Natalie delivers the "white girl" monologue). As in *for colored girls,* the play's penultimate sequence seems to be different in tone from the earlier monologues—and again, the effect is a closure of the "gaps" we have discussed. Here Maxine speaks of the way her world was shattered when she realized as a child that blacks were not exempt from the diseases, crimes, and so on, that white people experienced. She closes with a description of her decision to appropriate gold chains, bracelets, and necklaces as a symbol of "anything hard to get & beautiful./ anything lasting/ wrought from pain," followed by the shattering remark that "no one understands that surviving the impossible is sposed to accentuate the positive aspects of a people." Lou, as "director" of the action, freezes the players before they can fully respond to Maxine's words, and he repeats the closing portion of his opening speech: "And you gonna be colored all yr life/ & you gonna love it/ bein colored/ all yr life." As the minstrel mask reappears above them, he leads the actors in the chant "colored & love it/ love it being colored." Shange notes in the stage directions that the chant is a "serious celebration, like church/ like home." Her words are entirely appropriate to the dual nature of the ending: it is true that the characters are celebrating themselves, but the resonance of the preceding monologue, which was fraught with pain—as well as the overwhelming presence of the minstrel mask—recalls the anger and frustration which also underlie their chant. The characters, then, are imprisoned in the stereotypes and social position which the world has assigned to them, but like the women in *for colored girls* they call for unity as a source of strength. Their chant of "colored & love it/ love it bein colored" suggests that they intend to escape from their prison by redefining it so that it is no longer a prison. But the possibility remains that for the time being the escape may be only a partial one. As Shange writes in "unrecovered losses/ black theater traditions," the minstrel face which descends is "laughing at all of us for having been so game/ we believed we cd escape his powers."

Spell #7's ultimate vision may be more cynical than that of *for colored girls,* but its call for redefinitions is one which echoes throughout Shange's theater pieces. She invites a reconsideration of role-playing which suggests that in the process of acting out the various "masks" that blacks/women are *expected* to assume, one undergoes an experience of interior drama. Liberated through monologic language and by dance, song, etc., which release different, richer, more complex characters and experiences, the very nature of role-playing has been appropriated as a tool for "performing a self." She sees role-playing as a way simultaneously to give her characters an archetypal fluidity and to confront role-oriented stereotypes. On some level Shange's characters are always aware that they are speaking to an audience; perhaps this emphasis is an acknowledgement of the sense that women—as John Berger discusses in *Ways of Seeing*—are always the objects of vision and so are constantly watching themselves being watched. Rather than decentering the position of authorship in her plays by providing a sense that the characters are as if "self-created," though, Shange appears to share Michelene Wandor's view that deliberate attention to the author's role as "storyteller" provides a backbone, a controlling structure, for the play. Interwoven with this is a revision of spectacle as a vehicle for amusement; Shange's interpretation of "spectacle" insists upon questioning both the *mode* of performance which lures the audience's attention (as in the minstrel show at the beginning of *spell #7*) and the *subtext* of the spectacle itself. The monologue, then, is both an object for transformation and a means by which transformations can occur. Above all, Shange feels passionately that "we must move our theater into the drama of our lives." Her works attempt to speak, in the way that she says Layla's

unconscious does in *boogie woogie landscapes,* of "unspeakable realities/ for no self-respecting afro-american girl wd reveal so much of herself of her own will/ there is too much anger to handle assuredly/ too much pain to keep on trucking/ less ya bury it." (pp. 210-24)

Deborah R. Geis, "Distraught Laughter: Monologue in Ntozake Shange's Theater Pieces," in Feminine Focus: The New Women Playwrights, *edited by Enoch Brater, Oxford University Press, Inc., 1989, pp. 210-24.*

FURTHER READING

Hinds, Diana. "Like Cold Water or a Kiss." *Books,* No. 2 (May 1987): 11.
Brief prose portrait of Shange.

Phillips, Alice H. G. "Calling for the Right Kind of Power." *The Times Literary Supplement,* No. 4437 (15-20 April 1988): 420.
Review of *Nappy Edges* with Alice Walker's *Once* and Audre Lorde's *Our Dead Behind Us.* Phillips notes of Shange's collection of poetry: "Those out of sympathy with Shange's technique, or her spelling, may not appreciate her more searching poems on racism, old age, the exploitation of women by men and vice versa. But at its best her method can achieve both serious humour and deep seriousness."

Strandness, Jean. "Reclaiming Women's Language, Imagery, and Experience: Ntozake Shange's *Sassafrass, Cypress & Indigo." Journal of American Culture* 10, No. 3 (Fall 1987): 11-17.
Examines *Sassafrass, Cypress & Indigo,* noting: "Shange, by reclaiming the old and developing new metaphors for women's experience, creates female characters who differ significantly from previous female protagonists in nineteenth and twentieth century literature."

Wheatley, Patchy. "Waiting for Change." *The Times Literary Supplement,* No. 4314 (6 December 1985): 1406.
Review of *Betsey Brown* that concludes: "[By] interweaving Betsey's story with those of the various generations of her family and community Shange has...produced something of wider significance: a skilful exploration of the Southern black community at a decisive moment in its history."

Wole Soyinka

1934-

(Full name Akinwande Oluwole Soyinka) Nigerian dramatist, poet, novelist, critic, translator, editor, autobiographer, and short story writer.

Recipient of the 1986 Nobel Prize for Literature, Soyinka has been called Africa's finest writer. The Nigerian playwright's unique style blends traditional Yoruban folk-drama with European dramatic form to provide both spectacle and penetrating satire. Soyinka stated that in the African cultural tradition, the artist "has always functioned as the record of the mores and experience of his society." His plays, novels, and poetry all reflect that philosophy: they serve as a record of twentieth-century Africa's political turmoil and struggle to reconcile tradition with modernization. Eldred Jones stated in his book *Wole Soyinka* that the author's work touches on universal themes as well as addressing specifically African concerns: "The essential ideas which emerge from a reading of Soyinka's work are not specially African ideas, although his characters and their mannerisms are African. His concern is with man on earth. Man is dressed for the nonce in African dress and lives in the sun and tropical forest, but he represents the whole race."

As a young child, Soyinka was comfortable with the conflicting cultures in his world, but as he grew older he became increasingly aware of the pull between African tradition and Western modernization. Aké, his village, was mainly populated with people from the Yoruba tribe and was presided over by the *ogboni,* or tribal elders. Soyinka's grandfather introduced him to the pantheon of Yoruba gods and to other tribal folklore. His parents were key representatives of colonial influences, however: his mother was a devout Christian convert and his father a headmaster for the village school established by the British. When Soyinka's father began urging Wole to leave Aké to attend the government school in Ibadan, the boy was spirited away by his grandfather, who administered a scarification rite of manhood. Soyinka was also consecrated to the god Ogun, an explorer, artisan, and hunter in Yoruban folklore. Ogun is a recurring figure in Soyinka's work and has been named by the author as his muse.

Soyinka published some poems and short stories in *Black Orpheus,* a Nigerian literary magazine, before leaving Africa to attend the University of Leeds in England. There his first play was produced. *The Invention* (1955) is a comic satire about an incident that causes South Africa's black population to lose their black skin color. Unable to distinguish blacks from whites and thus enforce its apartheid policies, the government is thrown into chaos. "The play is Soyinka's sole direct treatment of the political situation in Africa," noted Thomas Hayes. Soyinka returned to Nigeria in

1960, shortly after independence from colonial rule had been declared. He began to research Yoruban folklore and drama in depth and incorporated elements of both into his next play, *A Dance of the Forests* (1960).

A Dance of the Forests was commissioned as part of Nigeria's independence celebrations. In the play, Soyinka warned the newly independent Nigerians that the end of colonial rule did not mean an end to their country's problems. It shows a bickering group of mortals who summon up the *egungun* (spirits of the dead, revered by the Yoruba people) for a festival. They have presumed the *egungun* to be noble and wise, but they discover that their ancestors are as petty and spiteful as any living people. "The whole concept ridicules the African viewpoint that glorifies the past at the expense of the present," suggested John F. Povey in *Tri-Quarterly.* "The sentimentalized glamor of the past is exposed so that the same absurdities may not be reenacted in the future. This constitutes a bold assertion to an audience awaiting an easy appeal to racial heroics." Povey also praised Soyinka's skill in using dancing, drumming, and singing to reinforce his theme: "The dramatic power of the surging forest dance [in the play] carries its own visual conviction. It is this that shows Soyinka to be a man of the theatre, not simply a writer."

After warning against living in nostalgia for Africa's past in *A Dance of the Forests,* Soyinka lampooned the indiscriminate embrace of Western modernization in *The Lion and the Jewel* (1966). A *Times Literary Supplement* reviewer called this play a "richly ribald comedy" that combines poetry and prose "with a marvellous lightness in the treatment of both." The plot revolves around Sidi, the village beauty, and the rivalry between her two suitors. Baroka is the village chief, an old man with many wives; Lakunle is the enthusiastically Westernized schoolteacher who dreams of molding Sidi into a "civilized" woman. In *Introduction to Nigerian Literature,* Jones commented that *The Lion and the Jewel* is "a play which is so easily (and erroneously) interpreted as a clash between progress and reaction, with the play coming down surprisingly in favour of reaction. The real clash is not between old and new, or between real progress and reaction. It is a clash between the genuine and the false; between the well-done and the half-baked. Lakunle the school teacher would have been a poor symbol of any desirable kind of progress.... He is a man of totally confused values. [Baroka's worth lies in] the traditional values of which he is so confident and in which he so completely outmaneouvres Lakunle who really has no values at all."

Soyinka was well established as Nigeria's premier playwright when in 1965 he published his first novel, *The Interpreters.* The novel allowed him to expand on themes already expressed in his stage dramas and to present a sweeping view of Nigerian life in the years immediately following independence. Essentially plotless, *The Interpreters* is loosely structured around the informal discussions between five young Nigerian intellectuals. Each has been educated in a foreign country and has returned hoping to shape Nigeria's destiny. They are hampered by their own confused values, however, as well as by the corruption they encounter everywhere. Some reviewers likened Soyinka's writing style in *The Interpreters* to that of James Joyce and William Faulkner. Others took exception to the formless quality of the novel. Nevertheless, Neil McEwan pointed out that for all its flaws, *The Interpreters* is "among the liveliest of recent novels in English. It is bright satire full of good sense and good humour which are African and contemporary...." He further observed that although *The Interpreters* does not have a rigidly structured plot, "there is unity in the warmth and sharpness of its comic vision. There are moments which sadden or anger; but they do not diminish the fun."

The year 1965 also marked Soyinka's first arrest by the Nigerian police. He was accused of using a gun to force a radio announcer to broadcast incorrect election results. No evidence was ever produced, however, and the PEN writers' organization launched a protest campaign, headed by William Styron and Norman Mailer. Soyinka was released after three months. He was next arrested two years later, during Nigeria's civil war. Soyinka was completely opposed to the conflict, especially to the Nigerian government's brutal policies toward the Ibo people who were attempting to form their own country, Biafra. He traveled to Biafra to establish a peace commission composed of leading intellectuals from both sides; when he returned, the Nigerian police accused him of helping the Biafrans buy jet fighters. Once again he was imprisoned. This time Soyinka was held for more than two years, although he was never formally charged with any crime. Most of that time he was kept in solitary confinement. When all of his fellow prisoners were vaccinated against meningitis, Soyinka was passed by; when he developed serious vision problems, he was again ignored by his jailers. He was denied reading and writing materials, but he manufactured his own ink and began to keep a prison diary, written on toilet paper, cigarette packages, and in between the lines of the few books he secretly obtained. Each poem or fragment of journal he managed to smuggle to the outside world became a literary event and a reassurance to his supporters that Soyinka still lived, despite rumors to the contrary. Published as *The Man Died: Prison Notes of Wole Soyinka* (1972), the author's diary constitutes "the most important work that has been written about the Biafran war," according to Charles R. Larson. He wrote: "*The Man Died* is not so much the story of Wole Soyinka's own temporary death during the Nigerian Civil War but a personified account of Nigeria's fall from sanity, documented by one of the country's leading intellectuals." Soyinka was released in 1969 and left Nigeria soon after, not returning until a change of power took place in 1975.

Many literary commentators sense that Soyinka's work changed profoundly after his prison term. His work now focused on the war and its aftermath and was darker in tone. For example, Soyinka's second novel, *Season of Anomy* (1973), expresses almost no hope for Africa's future. According to John Mellors in *London Magazine*: "Wole Soyinka appears to have written much of *Season of Anomy* in a blazing fury, angry beyond complete control of words at the abuses of power and the outbreaks of both considered and spontaneous violence.... The plot charges along, dragging the reader (not because he doesn't want to go, but because he finds it hard to keep up) through forest, mortuary and prison camp in nightmare visions of tyranny, torture, slaughter and putrefaction. The book reeks of pain.... Soyinka hammers at the point that the liberal has to deal with violence in the world however much he would wish he could ignore it; the scenes of murder and mutilation, while sickeningly explicit, are justified by...the author's anger and compassion and insistence that bad will not become better by our refusal to examine it."

Like *Season of Anomy,* Soyinka's postwar plays are considered more brooding than his earlier work. *Madmen and Specialists* (1970) is called "grim" by Martin Banham and Clive Wake in *African Theatre Today.* In the play, a doctor—who is trained as a specialist in torture—returns home from the war and uses his new skills on his father. The play's major themes are "the loss of faith and rituals" and "the break-up of the family unit which traditionally in Africa has been the foundation of society," according to Larson. Names and events in the play are fictionalized to avoid censorship, but Soyinka has clearly "leveled a wholesale criticism of life in Nigeria since the Civil War: a police state in which only madmen and spies can survive, in which the losers are mad and the winners are paranoid about the possibility of another rebellion. The prewar corruption and crime have returned, supported by the more sophisticated acts of terrorism and espionage introduced during the war." Larson concluded: "In large part *Madmen and Specialists* is a product of those months Soyinka spent in prison, in solitary confinement, as a political prisoner. It is, not surprisingly, the most brutal piece of social criticism he has published." In a similar tone, *A Play of Giants* (1984) presents four African leaders—thinly disguised versions of Jean Bedel Bokassa, Sese Seko Mobutu, Macias Ngeuma, and Idi Amin—meeting at the United Nations building, where "their conversation reflects the corruption and cruelty of their regimes and the casual, brutal flavor of their rule," disclosed Hayes. In Hayes's opinion, *A Play of Giants* demonstrates that "as Soyinka has matured he has hardened his criticism of all that restricts the individual's ability to choose, think, and act free from external oppression.... [It is] his harshest attack against modern Africa, a blunt, venomous assault on...African leaders and the powers who support them."

Soyinka's work is frequently described as demanding but rewarding reading. Although his plays are widely praised, they are seldom performed, especially outside of Africa. The dancing and choric speech often found in them are unfamiliar and difficult for non-African actors to master. Most recently, Soyinka has published two books: *Mandela's Earth, and Other Poems* (1988) and *Isarà: A Voyage around Essay* (1989). He is currently the chairman of the editorial board of *Transition,* a literary magazine revived in 1991 for the purpose of "exchanging opinions and ideas, with Africa at its center." Along with Henry Louis Gates, Jr., and Kuame Anthony Appiah, Soyinka published the first new issue in May 1991. Critics are already calling *Transition* an important forum for black writers. Yet, as Hayes summarized, Soyinka's importance and influence lie elsewhere: "[Soyinka's] drama and fiction have challenged the West to broaden its aesthetic and accept African standards of art and literature. His personal and political life have challenged Africa to embrace the truly democratic values of the African tribe and reject the tyranny of power practiced on the continent by its colonizers and by many of its modern rulers."

(For further information about Soyinka's life and works, see *Black Writers; Contemporary Authors,* Vols. 13-16; *Contemporary Literary Criticism,* Vols. 3, 5, 14, 36, 44; and *Dictionary of Literary Biography Yearbook: 1986*).

PRINCIPAL WORKS

The Invention (drama) 1955
The Lion and the Jewel (drama) 1959
A Dance of the Forests (drama) 1960
The Trials of Brother Jero (drama) 1960
Three Plays (dramas) 1962
Five Plays (dramas) 1964
The Strong Breed (drama) 1964
Camwood on the Leaves (radio play) 1965
The Interpreters (novel) 1965
Kongi's Harvest (drama) 1965
The Road (drama) 1965
Idanre, and Other Poems (poetry) 1967
Poems from Prison (poetry) 1969; also published as *A Shuttle in the Crypt* [enlarged edition], 1972
Three Short Plays (dramas) 1969
Madmen and Specialists (drama) 1970
Plays from the Third World: An Anthology [editor] (dramas) 1971
The Man Died: Prison Notes of Wole Soyinka (prose) 1972
The Bacchae of Euripides: A Communion Rite (drama) 1973
The Jero Plays (dramas) 1973
Season of Anomy (novel) 1973
Collected Plays. 2 vols. (dramas) 1973-74
Poems of Black Africa [editor] (poetry) 1975
Death and the King's Horseman (drama) 1976
Myth, Literature, and the African World (essays) 1976
Ogun Abibiman (poetry) 1976
Opera Wonyosi (drama) 1977
Aké: The Years of Childhood (autobiography) 1981
Requiem for a Futurologist (drama) 1983
A Play of Giants (drama) 1984
Six Plays (drama) 1984
Mandela's Earth, and Other Poems (poetry) 1988
Isarà: A Voyage around Essay (prose) 1989

Adrian A. Roscoe (essay date 1971)

[*Roscoe, an English critic and professor of African literature, is the author of* Mother Is Gold: A Study in West African Literature *(1971). In the following excerpt from this work, he examines the contrasts between traditional African culture and Western influences in Soyinka's poetry and drama.*]

Soyinka is a poet of twilight zones, be they between night and day or day and night, life and death, or death and life. They are areas of transition for which he has an abiding fascination; for they are those areas in which he can most fully explore certain basic facts about life and death. *The Road* alone is enough to suggest that no other poet or dramatist in the English language has explored so extensively, and with such rapt fascination, that shrouded middle passage between death, fleshly dissolution, and arrival in the other world.

Grey, then, is a dominant colour. Soyinka calls a whole section of *Idanre and Other Poems grey seasons;* but the colour, in fact, pervades his work as a whole. In **'I think it Rains'**, a poem whose tension springs from its subtle opposition of wet and dry, fruit and sterility, we find the stanza:

> I saw it raise
> The sudden cloud, from ashes. Settling
> They joined in a ring of grey; within
> The circling spirit . . . .

One can see, too, that the ideas implied by [the] choice of colour are borne also by words like 'wisps', 'smoke', 'febrile', and 'ashes'. In **'Season'**, we find 'wood-smoke', 'shadows from the dusk' and 'the wilted corn plume'. **'In Memory of Segun Awolowo'** ends with the lines

> Grey presences of head and hands
> Who wander still
> Adrift from understanding.

(pp. 49-50)

Soyinka, who would agree with Pound's dictum about loading the language of verse with as much meaning as it can bear, is often a difficult poet. He dictates the terms on which a reader must approach him; and, apart from an occasional explanatory note, no concessions are offered. To complicate matters further, Soyinka is a poet for whom the traditional Yoruba cosmology is a potent fact in his imaginative life, and, thus, in the art he creates. Without a working knowledge of the Yoruba background, his work cannot fully be understood; and this presents a handicap even to non-Yoruba Nigerians. The Yoruba cosmology, embodied in Ifa, the traditional religious system of his people, constantly underlies his work and has provided growth points for his artistic development. An essential point about Soyinka, then, and one which firmly marks him off from his fellow West African poets, is that *he is still working within a traditional system*; a system which allows him to explore the problems of creation and existence from a philosophical home base. He has not felt obliged to cast off traditional thinking and dress himself in the tattered remnants of alien philosophies. Not for Soyinka the myth-building problems of Yeats or Blake's desperate cry, 'I must create a system or be enslaved by another man's.' And this, perhaps, is why his scorn of negritude has always sounded so confident. Its disciples' prideful strutting was, in any case, a natural target for his satiric mind; a mind that seems always to have been convinced of man's absurdity, his innate imperfection, and the futility of his grandiose assertions. There was something further. More acutely than anyone else, Soyinka seemed to detect an element of the spurious in negritude's professed objective of reaching back for cultural roots. Christian and westernised, its disciples were, in effect, reaching back for what was no longer there. There was a celebration of convenient symbols and trophies from the past—the external *bric à brac* that could easily be appealed to—but not the *essence* of the past, its systems of thought, which had been discarded for ever. Where

they hoped to assert their African-ness by praise poems for the mask or in verse sung to African instrumental accompaniment, Soyinka has worked with the essence itself. He has never renounced it; his appeal to it is spontaneous and natural. Nor is this mere lip service, for he is imaginatively engaged with a tradition that still happens to be alive. He is the only West African poet who, in this philosophical sense, can be said to do so. Hence his complete lack of nostalgia, his lack of that melancholy recollection of a dying world that marks so much West African verse. One cannot wax nostalgic about current affairs. With Soyinka there is no problem of authenticity.

This is not to say that he rejects the modern world with its new insights and its expanding scientific knowledge. His education in Nigeria and England has enabled him to absorb much that is modern; he is learned in the modern disciplines, and his style itself—recognisably modern—is evidence of absorption and adaptation. A modern grafting has been performed on a vigorous traditional plant. Or, to state it in his own way, he has achieved 'the ideal fusion—to preserve the original uniqueness and yet absorb another essence'. It means that Soyinka's work can be both strongly local and excitingly universal. (pp. 50-1)

There is an attractive human-ness about Ifa, for its gods lived among men, and usually shared man's foibles. It also offers a convincing reading of the universe, especially in its insistence on a divine balance of forces, which, as a rule, ensures harmony, but which results in chaos when the balance is disturbed. Ifa has not only survived; it has become modernised. Such is its flexibility that Sango, the god of thunder and lightning, has, with perfect ease, become also the god of electricity. Ogun, a god of prodigious power and responsibility, the deity associated with iron and metals generally, with war, exploration, artisans, and creativity, is now also the god of the roads and the god of workers. He would preside as naturally over Ibadan's Department of Metallurgy as Jeremy Bentham over the London School of Economics. There is, then, in Ifa, besides its human-ness, an open-ness and flexibility which have allowed it to survive into the modern world. It also enjoys what Sowande calls 'a Diversified Unity, and not a Unified Diversity likely to come apart at the seams'. (pp. 51-2)

'Idanre', Soyinka's account of Ogun's creation pilgrimage to the earth, is, to date, by far his most extensive and ambitious poem. Firmly based in the traditional Ifa system and containing within itself those main lines of thought that have marked Soyinka's verse throughout his career, this is a darkly powerful piece of work that in parts has a strong flavour of the mythopoeic about it. (p. 56)

Ogun is the rather satanic hero of the poem. Since he is 'the septuple one', the god who carries seven gourds with him into battle, it is not unfitting that the poem should be divided into seven sections. The first is *deluge . . .* , a scene of violent primeval activity, where, in a raging storm and Cimmerian darkness torn only by lightning flashes, earth is in the process of creation.... In the fury of this storm, the first of the actual season (Ogun's season) in Nigeria, and, for the poet's purpose, seen as the first storm of creation, Ogun is beginning his pilgrimage to earth. He is the god of the creative essence—the rain he brings promises new life. He is also of course the god of war who tempers his promise of life abundant with the threat of death. It is a sort of bloody conferring of life and death together. (pp. 56-7)

There is violence in the first section; but it is violence fraught with the promise of life. In the second section, ... *and after,* the promise, in keeping with the strangely dual nature of Ogun, is not completely fulfilled; or at least, it is fulfilled and then instantly blighted. The threat of doom hangs over a scene that appeared to be growing increasing 'blissful'. We thus find stanzas celebrating the joy of Ogun's coming balanced, inevitably, by stanzas insisting on the bloody side of his mission. The wine girl, for example, who, Soyinka tells us, is a representational fusion of Sango and Ogun, first appears in a scene of relaxed, sunny happiness.... But this rich serenity is shattered in an instant when, in the very next stanza, the girl appears as the dead victim of a hideous car smash. The lovely wine girl becomes 'a greying skull / On blooded highways', her lone face filled with sadness. Only moments before, Ogun, as the god of creation and of the harvest, had smiled his peace upon her; now, as the god of the road, as the god of war, he greedily slaughters her.... After some fine surrealistic writing, in which the poet describes some childhood fantasies, the section ends with Ogun bringing order to the world. He makes harmony out of dissonance, imposes a pattern on chaos, teaches the whole of creation to dance and sing.... (pp. 57-9)

Ogun's path, ... his pilgrimage to earth, is an annual event, 'one loop of time'. The same point is made more firmly in the third section, *pilgrimage.* The journey Ogun is making is both his first pilgrimage and the annual pilgrimage he has been making ever since. This is how the Yoruba account for the seasons, and for the strange flow of human existence which is marked by waves of joy and waves of sadness, waves of plenty and waves of drought, waves of life and waves of death—all following, one after another, in an endless cyclical motion. (p. 59)

After section four, which describes Ogun and the gods settling down to an earthly existence, we reach section five, *the battle.* As its name suggests, it is given over to the bloodier side of Ogun's life on earth. As the poet explains, Ogun, having reluctantly been made king of Ira, gets drunk while leading his men into battle. Instead of destroying the enemy, he turns on his own warriors and wreaks appalling carnage among them. His men shout to try and bring him to his senses; but all to no avail.... He is called a murderer, a cannibal; but the cries fall on deaf ears. 'His being incarnate', says the poet, 'Bathes in carnage, anoints godhead/In Carnage.' To the cries of help, Esu, the troublesome god of fate,

who also happens to be present, will not listen either.... Eventually, the drunken god grows sober; he realises his mistake: 'Passion slowly yielded to remorse'.... Aside from its mythic basis, its attempt to explain a universal pattern, this section clearly has a contemporary relevance. (pp. 59-60)

Section six, *recessional,* is an important stage in the poem's development, and one in which the more personal statement, the conclusions drawn from the night's experience, are emphasised. It recounts the return journey, the poet coming home from his night spent in the woods and rain. The night is ending; so, too, its furious cataclysmic upheavals. Dawn approaches. One central reflection seems to emerge from the night's events. While the previous sections of the poem have been insisting on the cyclic pattern of Ogun's pilgrimage, its eternal inevitability, Soyinka now seems to ask: Are we, in fact, slaves to this pattern? Is it really so inevitable? Can it, indeed, be broken? In a sense, the Yoruba system within which Soyinka is working, itself provides one answer. For, as Soyinka reminds us, the Yoruba believe that Atunda, slave to the first deity, 'Either from pique or revolutionary ideas ... rolled a rock down on his unsuspecting master, smashing him to bits, and creating the multiple godhead.' The significance of this is that Atunda's action created diversity. Hence, Ogun, though a monstrously powerful god is, after all, only one god among many; his annual visitation, and the mixed blessings associated with it, represents but one pattern, though, of course, an important one. But Atunda brings a promise of diversity, variety of patterns; and he is praised heartily for it. The section becomes not only a celebration of diversity, but a vigorous plea for it. It is only a short step now to an *apologia* for the artist's independence, for the importance of uniqueness, of individuality. There is a plea for boldness, new directions, unfettered private growth and exploration—a plea, above all, for freedom in myriad forms.

Incredibly, we find that Ogun, who seems to be all things to all men, can help here: is he not a bold innovating character himself? Is he not, after all, the god of adventurers and explorers? (p. 61)

The emphasis in section seven, *harvest,* returns to the promise of peace and plenty. Parts here read like a magnificent fulfillment of J. P. Clark's poem 'The Year's First Rain', which ended with an image of the earth 'Swollen already with the life to break at day'. Ogun withdraws into the forests, there is 'A dawn of bright processions', and then ...:

> The first fruits rose from subterranean hoards
> First in our vision, corn sheaves rose over hill
> Long before the bearers, domes of eggs and flesh
> Of palm fruit, red, oil black, froth flew in sun
>   bubbles
> Burst over throngs of golden gourds.

This is writing of a rare sensuous quality, unequalled by any other West African poet. Soyinka is describing the promise fulfilled, the promise heralded by the storm and the bloodshed. Reflecting on his country's sad contemporary history, which has paralleled Ogun's bloody pilgrimage, he laments that it is this and 'the brief sun-led promise of earth's forgiveness' that are awaited to round out, to complete, the cycle. Yet even in this final section, Ogun's dual nature as creator and killer, and the doom of repetition that he symbolises, are insisted on; for the closing stanza of this dark poem states that the golden harvest is already, in its egregious ripeness, moving towards decay, towards 'resorption in His alloy essence'. The cycle must go on.

The poem, then, with its dark backcloth and its epic resonances, provides convincing testimony not only to Soyinka's stature as a poet, but also to his ability to work within the traditional Ifa system. That there was something both timely and timeless about its inspiration is suggested in Soyinka's Preface . . . :

> *Idanre* lost its mystification early enough. As events gathered pace and unreason around me I recognised it as part of a pattern of awareness which began when I wrote *A Dance of the Forests*. In detail, in the human context of my society, *Idanre* has made abundant sense. (The town of Idanre itself was the first to cut its bridge, its only link with the rest of the region during the uprising of October '65.) And since then, the bloody origin of Ogun's pilgrimage has been, in true cyclic manner most bloodily reenacted.

(p. 63)

Wole Soyinka is West Africa's finest dramatist. Here is a man richly endowed with literary skill, whose work, which has poured forth abundantly in a career still in its early stages, bears the marks of a refined sensibility, stringent critical standards, and, above all, great creative energy. . . . As we have seen, by temperament a satirist, he moves about the West African scene like some marvellously gifted Malcontent, fiercely thrusting at the corruption, intrigue, and vaulting ambition which he witnesses on every side. And his blows strike home, for on two occasions he has been sent to prison.

His education and training, in Africa and the United Kingdom, partly account for his position as the West African dramatist in whom the theatrical traditions of Europe and the homeland are most successfully synthesised (though perhaps symbiosis is a more appropriate word, since both traditions are strongly alive in him). London critics have said that his roots go deep into western traditions and that he is following at a distance in the footsteps of men like Jonson and Webster. While they are right in believing that Soyinka has been receptive to such influences, it must be emphasised at the same time that his work is essentially African in material and inspiration. As our discussion of his verse revealed, Soyinka is a Yoruba who acknowledges his roots and clings to them; he is not, in any sense of the word, *déraciné*. (p. 219)

The following examination of Soyinka's works is divided into three sections. The first will discuss Soyinka as a satirist and take *Dance of the Forests* and *The Road* for special treatment; the second treats of Soyinka's interest in language as an instrument of satire; and the third offers a detailed examination of the plays' synthesis of features African and western.

'Satire in the theatre', Soyinka observed in 1965, 'is a weapon not yet fully exploited among the contemporary dramatists of Nigeria, fertile though the social and political scene is for well-aimed barbs by the sharp, observant eye.' . . . But Soyinka's interest in satire does not stem from that *annus horribilis,* 1965. One of his early poems, **'Telephone Conversation'**, published in 1962, was a memorable sally into this field, drawing applause from many sides, and especially from the South African critic Ezekiel Mphahlele. Even earlier, however, came *A Dance of the Forests,* written for Nigeria's Independence Celebrations, and performed by The 1960 Masks, Soyinka's own company; it is the most complex satirical play which the author has so far written. Here indeed was a stroke of bold imagination that pointed up the breadth, depth and sincerity of Soyinka's vision; for in a play offered to a nation on the euphoric occasion of its Independence, the immediate victim of the satire is that nation itself; in a play ostensibly celebrating a country's birth, the talk is all of death, delusion, and betrayal. Indeed, flying in the face of all the cherished teachings of negritude, Soyinka has chosen to de-romanticise his people and their history with a boldness scarcely paralleled since the days of Synge and O'Casey. (p. 220)

We learn at once that Soyinka's vision ranges far beyond the present, even if this is his immediate concern; his theme is a large one, his frame of reference nothing less than the past, present, and ongoing stream of human existence. There is to be, then, a great gathering of the tribes at a momentous time in their history. It is a fitting occasion for the nation to show its medals and resurrect its trophies—a time to recall historic heroism of the sort that will provide inspiration for future endeavour. 'The accumulated heritage—that is what we are celebrating', declares Council Orator Adenebi . . . . Such is the spirit of the occasion; such the pride and hope of a nation at a great turning point in its history. But Soyinka possesses the satirist's passionate, almost pathological, obsession for the truth. Those heady with the excitement of the present must be bullied into setting their experience within the framework of historical fact; they must be allowed to glimpse some of the abiding truths of the human condition. Those who stand in the present and drug themselves with memories of former glories, like Orator Adenebi, whose absurd musings spiral ever further away from reality, must be faced with the grim reality behind their dreams.

The living, then, are anxious to call up from the dead a host of mighty heroes, celebrate the Gathering of the Tribes with a vision of past splendour; and in an empty clearing in the forest (with a starling piece of stagecraft), the soil breaks and there arise from the dead two pathetic human figures—a sorry link indeed 'for the season of rejoicing'. The Dead Man has behind him a wretched history of misery, thwarted hopes, and betrayal; The Dead Woman, his wife, sorrowful, and pregnant 'for a hundred generations', has an equally miserable past, and is soon to be delivered of a half-child, her baby who symbolises the future.

Soyinka allows us to see the details of their past in a Faustian recreation of the Court of Mata Kharibu, a mythical king who represents the 'glorious' history to which the living look back with nostalgia. Soyinka's purpose here is clear, for, as he observes elsewhere, the past 'clarifies the present and explains the future'. As Soyinka sees it, Africa's past is a sadly inglorious one. Thus, here in this shrine of historic magnificence, in this reign to which living Africans look back with pride, we find a whore as queen, and a king unrivalled in barbaric ferocity; a king who will brook no opposition to his every whim, who fears, like all tyrants, the independent mind, and will sell into slavery even his most devoted subjects. Dead Man is one of them, sold for a cask of rum because he dared to think for himself and suggest that he and the king's warriors should only go to war in a just cause. A figure of mutating significance, Dead Man is here representative of ordinary, thinking, reasonable mankind. (pp. 221-22)

Dead Man's history also includes involvement with the slave-trade, Africa's most traumatic historical experience. Soyinka gives his audience the brutal truth that the Kharibus of Africa's past had as much blood on their hands as the white slavers. At this point in a play notable for its Janus-like viewpoint, we begin to find Africa's inglorious past pointing a finger towards the present and the future.... There is a strong hint that Africa too easily accepts its chains, be they inflicted by strangers or brothers. More startling, however, is the clear implication that the chains are, and always have been, a permanent feature of the landscape. The 'new' ship in which Kharibu and all his ancestors would be proud to ride suggests modern forms of slavery that the author's fellow Africans are blindly accepting. It is as though Soyinka sees the whole of African history in the crushingly powerful image of a great slave galley sailing down the straits of time, from the dim past down to the present and on towards the horizon of the future. (pp. 223-24)

And what of the present? 'The pattern is unchanged,' says Dead Man, who was 'one of those who journeyed in the marketships of blood', and who is now visiting the modern world of the living. It is a lesson in disillusionment, for, as he is at one point reminded, 'Your wise men, casting bones of oracle/Promised peace and profit/New knowledge, new beginnings after toil...' Treated abominably in the past, he and his wife are abominably treated in the present. The bearers of bitter truth about an inglorious history, they are given at the Gathering of the Tribes the cold welcome of beggars at a feast.... It is a measure of the subtlety of Soyinka's art that the satire here works on two levels; for this shocking treatment of guests, and, furthermore, guests from the dead (we have stressed their importance often enough), is immediately recognised as a flagrant violation of rules of conduct upon which African societies pride themselves. At a more profound level, we are meant to witness in this behavior not only a wilful blindness to the truth about the past, but also an arrogant rejection of that past as it is enshrined in these two representative figures....

The experience of Dead Man and his wife is clear enough. It is a case of *plus ça change*. Men treated each other appallingly in the past; they treat each other appallingly in the present; they will treat each other appallingly in the future. (p. 224)

Such, then, is Soyinka's message for the happy occasion of Nigeria's Independence Celebrations—a sobering reminder of some basic, and abiding, truths about mankind in general and about Africans and their history in particular. Events since 1960 have proved with a vengeance the accuracy of at least that part of his vision which dealt with the future. But in addition, *A Dance of the Forests* supplies proof, if proof is needed, that Soyinka saw the need for national self-criticism six years before Achebe raised the subject as a matter of urgency in the pages of *Présence Africaine*. Soyinka's satiric vision is a curious affair—partly Swift's savage indignation, partly the Conradian 'horror', and partly the Wordsworthian lament over 'what man has made of man'. It informs every part of this difficult but remarkable play.

An equally difficult and powerful piece of satire is Soyinka's *The Road* published in 1965. From the very title of the play (a work that stands in relation to pieces such as *The Lion and the Jewel* like *Hamlet* to *Twelfth Night*), one realises that here is a further exploration of a subject which has fascinated Soyinka throughout his literary career. [The] road here is a fertile central motif. At one level it is any Nigerian road beside which the main scenes of the play are acted or danced. At another level, it is the proverbial road of life, along which all men must travel, individually or collectively as nations. Closely associated with this is the idea of the road of progress, a notion lightly ridiculed in Soyinka's poem **'Death in the Dawn'**. Above all, however, it is the road between life and death which runs precisely through that hazy landscape between this world and the next that so fascinates Soyinka. Along this highway the dead must travel.

Watching over the road, lurking behind all the events of the play, is Ogun, the greedy god who feeds on the butchery that the roads daily provide. Ogun lives on death and needs feeding regularly. The lorry drivers in the play are his devotees, their festival is his festival. Significantly, during their masquerade in his honour, they carry a dog tied to a stake as a sacrificial offering. Ogun's driver followers are notorious killers of dogs that stray onto the road.... But Ogun shows little care for his own (one recalls the manner in which he slew his warriors when king of Ira). Hence so many of the road's 'heroes' in the play—Zorro, Akanni the lizard, Sigidi Ope, Sapele Joe, Saidu-Say, Indian Charlie, Humphrey Bogart, Cimmarron Kid, Muftau, and Sergeant Burma—are dead. Hence so many of the play's central figures are probing towards death, or are actually dead and undergoing decomposition, their voices ghosting forth from this twilight zone in a most unnerving manner....

[Soyinka chooses] a middle ground, a sort of no-man's land belonging neither to the world of the flesh nor the spirit.... (p. 228)

This dark middle area, reminiscent of many of Soyinka's poems, effortlessly grows suggestive of ideas other than those of death and dissolution. It suggests, for example, the overall position of Africa, caught, in Mabel Segun's memorable words, 'hanging in the middle way'. Soyinka portrays a hideous mingling of cultures that he finds in this middle state, though he does so with a complexity, a subtlety, and a revulsion, unparalleled in those innumerable publications that exhibit the cultural clash through stale commonplaces.

Professor himself is the best illustration of this. With his Victorian outfit of top hat and tails, all threadbare, with his academic title, earned through prowess in forgery, with his past connection with the Christian church, and his clear leanings towards Ifa, he is a sort of amphibious creature, neither right African nor right European; neither wholly spiritually oriented nor wholly materialistic. We have mentioned already the psychological problems of modern Africa: there are definite suggestions of schizophrenia or mere lunacy in Professor, and Soyinka wants us to notice them. A veritable aura of symbolism surrounds this weird scoundrel. It is no mere chance that he is dressed in Victorian garb. In part, presumably, Soyinka is making the common joke that Africa follows absurdly, at a distance, the fashions of Europe, and never actually catches up. Similar jibes are found in Achebe and Nicol. But he is also hinting that Professor represents the first real nineteenth-century encounter with the West, and furthermore, the subsequent history of that encounter. Hence, almost everything about this creature is betwixt and between. He is partly a genuine seeker after the Word, which means here knowledge of the essence of death, and partly a genuine criminal, bold, selfish, and rapacious. It is the sort of contradiction that suggests the familiar Afro-European dichotomy.... (p. 229)

If Professor is an unpleasant mingling of Africa and Europe, so, too, are the play's drivers and thugs. They are men with names inspired by American crime and western films, men like Say Tokyo Kid who can affect a tough Chicago gangster's drawl ('I don give a damn for that crazy guy and he know it') yet sing traditional Yoruba praise songs and worship Ogun. With his tough talk, his alleged scorn for Professor's spiritualism (belied by his belief that there are 'a hundred spirits in every guy of timber' he carries), Say Tokyo represents an ugly

fusion of the traditionally African and the hard-headed materialism of an alien culture. (p. 230)

The play is also a bitter attack on Nigerian society as a whole: here is a scathing criticism of *A Dance of the Forests* in a wormier form. It is as though Soyinka, in his deliberate choice of the Agemo idea, is trying to say that he sees the whole of his contemporary society dissolving into the rottenness and stench of death. Apart from Murano, who is deaf, dumb, dead (and therefore, impotent), there is not a single undiseased figure in the play. The whole dark scene is pervaded by vice and greed in all its forms. The sun never seems to rise in this play. It is a picture of unrelieved gloom and decadence, where a dog-eat-dog morality rules supreme.... To complete this revolting picture, Soyinka ensures that a representative of all ranks of society is included: his country must be seen to be corrupt from top to bottom. The law, as represented by Particulars Joe, is corrupt in the most blatant manner; the Church stands as an empty shell behind the entire play, irrelevant and powerless. Chief-in-Town, a modern version of the traditional Oba, is a political representative who keeps a gang of thugs in hire and distributes opium. The common people, like Samson and Kotonu, prey on one another like hyenas.

The Road is Soyinka's writing on the nation's wall. He draws a society that is on the road to death and dissolution, a society for which there seems no hope. Perhaps, like Professor, who speaks of death as 'the moment of our rehabilitation', this society will have to die before it learns the truth. Rebirth is only possible after the descent from life is complete. This movement itself is foreshadowed by the mask at the end of the play which sinks slowly until 'it appears to be nothing beyond a heap of cloth and raffia.'

In *A Dance of the Forests* and *The Road,* a whole nation was under attack. In other plays, too, the satirical element has figured strongly; but there it is not a whole society but particular members of it who come in for abuse. Soyinka particularly loathes those who possess power and use it dishonestly, those whose selfishness drives them to keep the people in a state of ignorance and subservience.

In *The Swamp Dwellers,* Kadiye is the target, a fat village priest who remains 'smooth and well-preserved' even in time of drought by exploiting the simple piety of those whom he represents before the local god. He lies upon the land and 'choke(s) it in the folds of a serpent'. In *The Trials of Brother Jero,* Jeroboam himself is under attack, an eloquent fraud working as a Beach Prophet and striding the boards like some strange character from mediaeval times. He cuts a striking figure with his heavily-bearded face, his rod of office, long flowing hair, white gown and fine velvet cape—all of them aids to deceit. The West African scene is alive with weird scoundrels of this sort. In a lighter vein, *The Lion and the Jewel* focuses its attack on Lakunle, a westernised schoolteacher who appears ridiculous with his modicum of book learning, his complete vacuity of wisdom and his preposterous arrogance; he is a man who feels elevated enough to call his people 'a race of savages' and sees himself as the prophet of a new order. Despising ancestral ways, he is determined to drag his community into the vulgar daylight of the modern world. Soyinka would probably call *The Lion and the Jewel* a recreational piece. But *Kongi's Harvest* appeared during the years of Nigeria's gathering storm and strikes a more urgent and 'engaged' note. At the heart of his country's afflictions he sees politicians with their lust for power and their illiberal vision. He has stated elsewhere that it is not the continent's writers but its politicians who have shaped 'the present philosophy, the present direction of modern Africa', and he asked, 'is this not a contradiction to a society whose great declaration of uniqueness to the outside world is that of a superabundant humanism? Hence *Kongi's Harvest,* theatrically a rather dull play, is a fierce onslaught on West Africa's modern breed of politicians, and especially on Kongi himself, the President of Isma and a modern version of Mata Kharibu complete with all the image-making paraphernalia of the twentieth century .... After the more general satire of *A Dance of the Forests* these, then, are some of the individual victims chosen as targets in the plays that have followed. (pp. 231-33)

Reaping the harvest of a past dominated by the spoken word, Soyinka is deeply interested in the rhetorical arts. Hence no doubt his special penchant for the dramatic form and the appearance in each of his plays of at least one outstanding orator. We usually find, too, a carefully ordered range of linguistic styles, which not only affords Soyinka a necessary variety of voices, but constitutes a basic item in his satirical armour as well ....

As a satirist vitally concerned about language and style, Soyinka stands in line with distinguished predecessors. It is enough to recall the names of Skelton, Swift, Pope, and Sterne to establish how consistently the great satiric tradition of English letters has opposed itself to the abuse of language. (p. 234)

Where historically the abuse of language has been decried mainly in its literary manifestations, satire in the modern world has attacked its debasement by propagandists and political machinery. George Orwell, the twentieth century's Swift, provides a useful example. In Orwell's view, the decline of a language 'must ultimately have political and economic causes'; bad politics encourage the abuse of language, and the slovenliness of our language leads to woolly thinking. (p. 235)

Now, Orwell and Soyinka can be taken as kindred spirits .... We have already cited Soyinka's complaint that 'the present philosophy, the present direction of modern Africa was created by politicians' (including men who felt it necessary on two occasions to strip him of his freedom). It is not surprising, therefore, that politicians and their abuse of language should become a theme of his plays.

Kongi's Harvest offers perhaps the best example. Here traditional African politics, which placed the power of ruling in the hands of local chieftains, is being ousted by the politics of Kongi with his passion for dictatorship in the modern style. It is a familiar case of the traditional ways in conflict with the forces of change. The old order is represented by Oba Danlola and his followers, whose choice of language sharply marks them off from Kongi's party of modernists. Their style has a concreteness of metaphor and imagery which recalls the traditional Yoruba verse .... (p. 236)

The difference between the era which Danlola represents and Kongi's new dispensation is seen in the play as largely one of language. Having dismissed Danlola and his followers as 'a backward superstitious lot', Kongi is firmly committed to building a political machine that is recognisably modern and recognisably western. Hence, the linguistic style which Soyinka gives to the tyrant and his minions is fraught, not with the metaphor and proverbial wisdom of Old Africa, but with the 'washer words' and politico-scientific jargon of the modern world. (p. 237)

Thus, Kongi's harvest is to be 'a harvest of words', and Soyinka will shape his satire accordingly. Kongi has decided that there must be a deliberate break with the past—essentially a political break of course, but involving a cultural and linguistic break as well .... The effort is hard to sustain, and of course Soyinka's point is that their new style is a gross affectation; but on the whole, they succeed and we hear the familiar jargon that a man like Orwell loathed so passionately. 'Progressive forces', 'a step has already been taken in that direction', 'contemporary situation', 'reactionary', 'positive stamp', 'scientific image', 'positive scientificism', 'so-called wise ones', 'clean break'—the cliches pour forth, and one half expects to hear 'consensus', 'escalation', 'dialogue', 'credibility gap', and 'all-time highs' thrown in for good measure. (pp. 238-39)

The whole movement of the play is towards the great Festival of the New Yam, traditionally the responsibility of Danlola; Kongi plans to 'secularise' this event, ceremonially ring out the old order, and assert his supremacy as the fountainhead of all meaningful power in the country .... In the event, the show is a fiasco, and the play ends in the style of Danlola, though he is on his way into exile when the curtain falls. (p. 240)

Lakunle's style in *The Lion and the Jewel* is a clear window through which we see his worthless values. This is a much less serious play than *Kongi's Harvest,* but nevertheless the style given to Lakunle represents a deliberate attempt to reflect the encroachment of western values upon African mores.

Lakunle, the torch-bearer of modernity in his community, is in love with Sidi, an unlettered village nymph; but the foxy old Bale of the village, Baroka, wants her too, and the play becomes an amusing struggle between these rivals, who represent, once again, the old order and the new. Lakunle is a fervent disciple of romantic love (that recent western import into West African society) and a champion of all those freedoms for which the feminists have struggled. He sketches for his beloved the splendid life that will be hers if only she will consent to marry him without his paying the traditional bride price.... Sidi of course is disgusted with this 'strange unhealthy mouthing' and retreats, leaving Lakunle to complain wearily and comically.... This is all light satire, but it has its point. The conflict is between the champions of two worlds, and Baroka, the spokesman of tradition, wins the fight; the modern, westernised representative not only loses but is the laughing stock of the play. It is as if Soyinka, even in this gay comedy, cannot resist taking sides; as if he, in company with satirists in general, is on the side of conservatism, seeing in tradition a bedrock of sanity that will defy the swirling torrents of change and revolution. But it is not as simple as this, for Soyinka's very achievement consists in his own coming to terms, artistically, with the modern world. A clue to his real position probably lies in the fact that it is largely the trivia, that superficies of western life that Lakunle espouses—western life observed at one remove in the streets of Lagos. Thus, Soyinka is no doubt saying to his people, 'Don't throw away your heritage (which still has much to offer you) for the glossy manifestations of western life. Look at Lakunle and see how absurd it would be.' (pp. 240-42)

The Trials of Brother Jero is dominated by the personality and style of the holy fraud himself, whose oratory is cultivated to deceive, whose rhetoric serves duplicity rather than divinity.... As usual, the play uses two contrasting styles. Jero's is one, and the second belongs to the plain folk who are his victims. Their language is as humble as their status, and in moments of deepest sincerity it becomes mainly West African pidgin. In the ... scene on the beach, an emotional prayer session is in progress under the direction of Chume, the assistant prophet whose wife Jero has seduced. The petitions are frankly materialistic but, coming from the poor, touchingly human for all that. They are punctuated regularly with Amens, and the whole effort builds to a tremendous climax as these humble people whip up their emotional fervour.... (pp. 243-44)

Thus we can understand Soyinka's fundamental interest in language. Language as a key to man's inner being; language as a mirror of social standing; language as an instrument of deceit and oppression; language as a device for sheer entertainment; language as a vehicle for man's deepest utterances; language as a source of comedy; language as an instrument of satire—Soyinka is keenly aware of all these facets and explores them energetically in his plays.

Although Soyinka's work reveals a definite blending of African and western elements, the basic material out of which the plays are fashioned is overwhelmingly indigenous. The elements of African pre-drama, for instance, are here in force, as a brief survey of the plays will reveal.

Soyinka's first play was called, significantly, **A Dance of the Forests,** and its opening words indicate that it is meant to partake of the nature of a dance. The resurrected ancestors were rejected by the living 'So I took them under my wing', says Aroni. 'They became my guests and the Forests consented to dance for them.' And the dance, thus, is a common feature throughout the play. The villagers dance around the totem carved for the festivities, there is the dance of the Half-Child, offspring of the Dead Woman, and a dance by the god Eshuoro and his jester, called the Dance of the Unwilling Sacrifice. Ritual is added to dance at one point when a dancer is followed by a young girl acting as an acolyte who sprinkles the dancing area as she goes. This itself is followed shortly by a solemn recitation by a dirgeman, urging everyone to stand back and 'Leave the dead/Some room to dance', and then by Agboreko's oracular consultation. At the climax of the play we find the ceremonial masking of the three 'earthly protagonists', who, ridden and possessed by the various spirits which the Interpreter calls up, 'chorus' the future in the manner of the religious masks of Egungun and Voodoo.

The Lion and the Jewel is a lively combination of dancing, singing, and drumming. A particularly memorable feature is the Dance of the Lost Traveller, a re-enactment in mime form of an important event occurring prior to the time period of the play, and about which the audience must be informed. It was the unexpected visit of a Lagos photographer whose car broke down as it passed near the village. Sidi chooses villagers to dance the different parts of 'devil horse' (car) and python; and persuades Lakunle (warmly African beneath his western veneer) to dance the part of the stranger.... The stranger's arrival and short stay in the village are then mimed, and, to simulate the car wheels, four dancers roll the upper halves of their bodies to the accompaniment of throbbing drums.

In the same play, Baroka wins Sidi by spreading abroad a rumour that he is impotent—a rumour that leads to the performance and a frankly sexual 'dance of virility', carried out exclusively by the ladies. It is a wild triumphant affair in which the Bale's sexual life from his days of great potency to his final 'defeat', is acted out with enormous gusto. Sadiku, his eldest wife, leads a dancing group of younger women in pursuit of a male, who rushes about, dancing in tortured movements as defeat draws near, and is finally 'scotched', to the unbounded delight of the ladies. It is a bold piece of theatre (made nicely ironic by having the dancers burst on stage at precisely the moment of Sidi's seduction) which not even Aristophanes could have bettered.

In the other plays, too, traditional elements feature strongly. **Kongi's Harvest,** for example, reaches a grand climax at the Yam Festival, which is a veritable orgy of feasting, dancing, chanting, and parading, all to the frenzied accompaniment of dozens of pounding pestles. As we have seen in **The Road,** Soyinka's note *For the Producer* with its reference to the mask idiom, is evidence enough of the tradition in which he is working.

A play replete with dirge and praise singing, and which contains a festival in honour of Ogun, god of iron, it serves to indicate how deeply the roots of Soyinka's art are sunk in African traditional practice.

But the most interesting example of how Soyinka uses pre-dramatic material can be found in **The Strong Breed,** a dark, powerfully moving play built around the scapegoat idea, one of the most ancient conventions devised by social man for the easing of his collective conscience. In the village of the play, there is a New Year's Eve ritual in which the evil of the old year is cleansed away for the beginning of the new. The theme is introduced by a sick girl, who appears dragging an effigy or 'carrier' that is to be beaten, hanged, and burnt so that it will carry away her illness.... It is a clear example of pre-drama at the heart of a most moving play.

Traditional material, then, features strongly. What of those elements borrowed from the West? Some of these are extremely simple, yet fundamental. For instance, the plays have a text, and, therefore, a fixed form, which in itself is a basic departure from traditional practice. The improvisation of the early Yoruba troupes would be unthinkable in any of the Soyinka plays which we have discussed. Again, the texts are in English and the plays are designed for western stages rather than for the traditional open square.

There are, too, several techniques learnt from European practice that give Soyinka's art a flexibility and freedom it would otherwise lack. A day in the life of Brother Jero, introduced to the audience by the Prophet himself, and then acted out by him, represents a device more likely to have been learnt from Brecht or Pirandello than from Africa. The flashback technique, for which Soyinka has been criticised by Martin Esslin, is likewise a western borrowing.... A divided stage is used in the first section of **Kongi's Harvest,** for the play alternates between two scenes; it is a device used memorably in the Isherwood-Auden play *On the Frontier,* and, of course, it is common in films and in television plays. Soyinka might have borrowed it from any one of these sources; there is no evidence of it in the dramatic tradition inherited from his forefathers. His plots, too, reveal an ingenuity inspired more perhaps by Ben Jonson than by indigenous models. Certainly there is no plot in Yoruba Folk Opera to match the complexity of **The Lion and the Jewel** or **A Dance of the Forests.**

Western influence emerges, too, in the matter of characterisation. Soyinka's figures have a degree of psychological depth and complexity which vernacular drama has never achieved. Professor, in **The Road,** to take but one illustration, is a distinctly African personality in a distinctly African play, but the bewildering complexity of his character, the shadows of the past that enshroud it, its aura of insanity, its weird admixture of the criminal and spiritual—all this is felt to have been made possible only by Soyinka's knowledge and imitation of western dramatists.

Soyinka has rapidly emerged as West Africa's most distinguished dramatist, and indeed he is beginning to claim attention as one of the foremost English-speaking playwrights of our time. As a satirist he is certainly in the front rank. As a poetic dramatist, he has few equals. (pp. 244-48)

> *Adrian A. Roscoe, "Drama" and "Progress in Verse," in his* Mother Is Gold: A Study in West African Literature, *Cambridge at the University Press, 1971, pp. 13-70, 176-248.*

Bernth Lindfors (essay date 1981)

[*In the following excerpt, Lindfors reviews* The Bacchae of Euripides *and* Opera Wonyosi, *stating: "At times Soyinka looks more like a hitchhiker than a trailblazer.'*]

[Today Soyinka] is widely regarded as one of Africa's most original creative artists. He has defined his own distinctive idiom in drama, poetry, fiction and criticism, never allowing himself to fall too deeply under the sway of alien or autochthonous traditions of expression. In the marketplace of modern literature, where many convertible currencies are freely available, Soyinka owes surprisingly few traceable debts.

Yet in recent years he has published two plays that are undisguised adaptations of well-known European masterworks: **The Bacchae of Euripides,** which Soyinka "conceived as a communal feast, a tumultuous celebration of life," and **Opera Wonyosi,** an Africanization of John Gay's *The Beggar's Opera* and Bertolt Brecht's *The Threepenny Opera....* What is interesting to observe in both of these adapted works is the degree to which Soyinka modified the original texts in order to achieve his own ends. We might well ask, how much did he blatantly retain and how much did he transform in obedience to independent creative stresses?

The Bacchae of Euripides has already been commented on by a number of drama critics and scholars, the consensus view being that Soyinka succeeded in reinvesting the play with greater dimensions and complexity by introducing African elements that harmonize with the original theme but do not radically alter the nature of the drama. In other words, though he extended its basic structure and rearranged its furnishings, he did not tamper with its original design.... One might venture to say that in form as well as content Soyinka's **Bacchae** remains [a European drama].... (p. 22)

The same kind of statement could be made about **Opera Wonyosi,** which follows Brecht rather slavishly in places and transforms far less of *The Threepenny Opera* than Brecht's play transformed of John Gay's eighteenth century musical drama, *The Beggar's Opera.* Soyinka seems content to pour local palm-wine into European receptacles rather than devise wholly new containers for his home-brewed spirits. **Opera Wonyosi** is a very topical Nigerian satire, but it gains much of its thrust and momentum by delivering its message in a dependable, racy vehicle of foreign manufacture. Indeed, at times Soyinka looks more like a hitchhiker than a trailblazer.

Take the "character structure" of the opera, for instance. Soyinka does not bother to change the names of a number of his dramatis personae, retaining the traditional Captain Macheath (i.e., Mack the Knife), Hookfinger Jake, Police Commissioner "Tiger" Brown, Jimmy, Polly, Jenny, Sukie and Lucy. Even when he does introduce a new name, the name itself does not necessarily signal a change in the role or personality of the character to whom it is given.... The only new characters of any significance are representatives of various professions: a military man, colonel Moses; a university academic, Professor Bamgbapo.... One comically inflated character readily identifiable as a notorious contemporary personage is Emperor Boky, a hilarious caricature of Emperor Jean-Bedel Bokassa of the Central African Republic, whose imperial coronation, like that of the Queen in Brecht's rendition, serves as the occasion for Macheath's royal reprieve at the end of the melodrama, thereby providing the happy ending that Gay, Brecht and Soyinka sardonically agree light opera demands. (p. 23)

The songs Soyinka used in *Opera Wonyosi* came from a variety of sources, hardly any of which were African. He grafted new words onto well-known Euro-American tunes, much as Gay had done with old English airs in *The Beggar's Opera.* For instance, he borrowed Kurt Weill's famous score for the theme song, the "Moritat of Mackie the Knife," but changed Brecht's lyrics to suit his Nigerian audience.... Other melodies recognizable from Soyinka's lyrics include such popular favourites as "The Saint Louis Blues,"... and at least one Nigerian "highlife" tune, but there is no evidence that any traditional African songs or indigenous musical instruments were utilized. Musically *Opera Wonyosi* was an eclectic Western medley.

This is not to say that Soyinka's effort to adapt an alien art form was unsuccessful. *Opera Wonyosi* may have retained a Brechtian structure and a Gayish agility of wit, but Soyinka managed to turn the flavour of the farce into something characteristically African. Indeed, though all the action is presented as taking place in the Central African Republic, it is not difficult to identify specific Nigerian targets of his satire.... Military rule itself is mercilessly lampooned, and the charges brought against Colonel Moses at his trial—charges of arson, rape, assault, and murder...—have an uncomfortably close correlation with real happenings in postwar Nigeria.... Soyinka was tweaking some very prominent public noses, just as John Gay had done 250 years before. (pp. 24-5)

Soyinka's purpose in writing this opera was to satirize Nigeria in the mid-1970's, a period marked by military rule and an economic boom fueled by oil.... *Opera Wonyosi* apparently was meant to restore human communication.... Soyinka attempted to do this by hold-

ing up to ridicule and scorn many of the social atrocities committed in the morally confused postwar era. The story of Mack the Knife was a convenient peg on which to hang his charges against his countrymen, for the underworld ambience of such a traditional villain-hero was sufficiently distanced in time and place to provide a large-scale perspective on the subject of human depravity, thereby imbuing the dramatic action with a semblance of "universality," yet at the same time that ambience resembled so closely the cut-throat, dog-eat-dog atmosphere of the "high period of Nigeria's social decadence" that Mackie could be easily assimilated as a local folk-hero/villain. Nigerian audiences would not be likely to question the stylized squalor of the beggar's world portrayed in this opera, for that would be tantamount to denying the surreal dimensions of their own corrupted world. Soyinka had chosen an excellent warped mirror to reflect the absurdities of an unbalanced age. (p. 30)

It may be no mere coincidence that both Brecht and Soyinka reworked the story of Mack the Knife in a postwar era, for both must have felt that their countrymen had learned nothing from the horrors of the holocaust. Man's unreluctant return to depravity after such catastrophe must have struck them as dangerously idiotic. To show up this dark, benighted side of human nature, both turned to light opera, sugarcoating the bitter message they wished to convey to a complacent populace. By making people laugh at something absurdly close to home, they sought to make them think.

Brecht, however, fashioned his opera as a comment on the evil inherent in all mankind and reinforced by manmade institutions.... Soyinka, on the other hand, spoke primarily of the evils visible in Nigeria. Like Gay, he was striking out at specific targets in his own society, so his was a more topical satire than Brecht's. But whereas Gay was content to expose social evils without denouncing them or inquiring into their origins, Soyinka was interested in provoking his audience to raise questions about what their world was coming to and why.... Soyinka thus stands in a middle ground between Gay and Brecht. He has more social commitment than Gay but less pessimism than Brecht. He appears to believe that reform is possible so long as one can recognize and speak out against the evils that man brings upon man. *Opera Wonyosi* is his attempt to contribute to the reform of contemporary Nigeria through song, dance, and satirical laughter. (pp. 31-2)

Bernth Lindfors, "Begging Questions in Wole Soyinka's 'Opera Wonyosi'," in Ariel: *A Review of International English Literature, Vol. 12, No. 3, July, 1981, pp. 21-33.*

James Olney (essay date 1982)

[*In the following excerpt, Olney praises* Aké, *declaring that the book "is destined to become a classic of African autobiography."*]

[*Aké*] is destined to become a classic of African autobiography, indeed a classic of childhood memoirs wherever and whenever produced.

What Mr. Soyinka makes most vividly present is the living landscape of Aké, the Nigerian village where he grew up on a parsonage compound.... It is from the wonderfully colorful, agitated, aroma-laden markets, the likes of which one finds all across West Africa, that Mr. Soyinka distills the essence of the Aké of his memories....

In one of the finest chapters of *Aké,* Mr. Soyinka eulogizes the markets of his childhood. His mcmory is remarkable; he still seems able to hear the sounds, taste the flavors and smell the aromas of 35 and 40 years ago. Every sound and smell blended together in the evenings of Mr. Soyinka's childhood to form "part of the invisible network of Aké's extended persona." They are gone now, but once he could be sure of "Ibarapa's sumptuous resurrection of flavours every evening."...

Throughout his previous work, Wole Soyinka has insisted on the dual nature of the role performed by the African artist. The artist "has always functioned in African society...as the record of the mores and experience of his society *and* as the voice of vision in his own time." In *Aké* Mr. Soyinka rehearses his own vision even as he traces its roots in the experiences and people of his African childhood. The world that Mr. Soyinka recalls in *Aké,* that he creates or re-creates from memories of the past (for it is sadly different now), is a world of pervasive, indwelling spiritual presences.

A sense of these presences is felt as Mr. Soyinka recalls the people among whom he grew up: his mother and father...; his paternal grandfather, who was crucially important to Mr. Soyinka's education in Yoruba traditions.... But the importance of the spiritual world is seen more obviously in the descriptions of the *egúngún,* ancestral spirits who return in all their power and vitality when their masks are danced in festive procession and who represent the extended being of parents, grandparents and elders. Indeed, the *egúngún* even assert their presence through the organ in the Christian church.... (p. 7)

There is more than a little method in this mingling of African ancestors and the Christian deity. Mr. Soyinka sees this and other ritual performances as more or less successful attempts (Yoruba more successful, Christian less) at restoring to a condition of unity and cosmic balance the three interpenetrating, interdependent worlds of his traditional Yoruba (and more generally African) belief: the ancestors, the yet unborn and the living.

In addition to these three realms Mr. Soyinka distinguishes a "Fourth Stage," and throughout his work we find symbolic figures, spirits and objects that have an especially intimate tie to the stage that he calls "the numinous area of transition." The *egúngún,* who make the transition and bind the worlds of the living and the dead together with the dancing of their masks, belong to this Fourth Stage. But in *Aké* there are other examples: There is the girl named Bukola, who is an *àbikú* ("a child which is born, dies, is born again and dies in a repetitive cycle"); there are the wood spirits around the parsonage compound; there is Mr. Soyinka's little sister, whose death, on her first birthday, makes him expect some sort of universal cataclysm; there is the guava tree that Mr. Soyinka imagines to be *his* tree, inhabited by spirits that he can command.... Such symbolic figures and incidents in *Aké* perform the function of ordering and vitalizing the cosmos that they do in Mr. Soyinka's other work, whatever the mode. (pp. 7, 18)

For all its seriousness, *Aké* is not at all a solemn book. On the contrary, it is full of high good humor and a lyric grace. The book's structure is largely one of strung-together sketches and anecdotes....But even these sketches and anecdotes are used to describe and realize a world to which Mr. Soyinka's mature understanding and his dozen or so volumes of fiction, drama and poetry are deeply committed....

Through recollection, restoration and re-creation, he conveys a personal vision that was formed by the childhood world that he now returns to evoke and exalt in his autobiography. This is the ideal circle of autobiography at its best. It is what makes *Aké,* in addition to its other great virtues, the best available introduction to the work of one of the liveliest, most exciting writers in the world today. (p. 18)

> *James Olney, "The Spirits and the African Boy," in* The New York Times Book Review, *October 10, 1982, pp. 7, 18.*

Wole Soyinka with Anthony Appiah (interview date 1986-87)

[*The following interview was conducted in late 1986 or early 1987, soon after Soyinka had won the Nobel Prize for Literature. Here, Soyinka talks with Anthony Appiah about receiving the Nobel Prize and discusses his play* Death and the King's Horseman. *A variant form of this interview first appeared in 1987 in* The New Theater Review *under the title "Easing the Transition."*]

[Appiah]: *Now that you've had three months or so to think about it, can you tell us what you think the significance is of the award of the Nobel Prize, first of all to you and then to you as an African?*

[Soyinka]: To me, it's been hell. (Laughter). On one level, yes. I understand what Bernard Shaw meant when he was given the Prize and he said he could forgive the man who invented dynamite, but it took the mind of a devil to invent the Nobel Prize for literature. I share some of this feeling, but only to a certain extent. The other side of the coin, of course, is that it increases one's literary family, increases one's awareness of the need of many activities, many paths, many concerns of the common Earth we inhabit. It increases an awareness of the need of people to fasten onto a voice, a representative, and that refers to your question about Africa in particular. So, it's of great importance, I think, not so much to me as to the literary craftsmen of my continent, to those who share the longing for a brotherhood/sisterhood which transcends the African continent and reaches out into the diaspora. The way in which the Prize has been received by people all over the world, particularly the African diaspora—in the West Indies, in the United States, and across the various language boundaries—has reinforced my insistent conviction that the African world is not limited by the African continent.

I noticed that when you gave your Nobel lecture, you chose to discuss apartheid and southern Africa. Did you feel that that was a particularly important thing to do at that moment?

A lot of my writing has been concerned with injustice, with inhumanity, with racism, inside and outside of my immediate environment, which is Nigeria. This is a world platform, and I could not think of any more appropriate moment for voicing this particular level of my literary concerns. I thought it was most appropriate, yes.

How does it enhance or change your position when you're speaking within Nigeria?

I've always insisted that I do not accept any kind of double standards. I do not accept a distinction, excuses on behalf of either our own black oppressors or the white oppressors of our race. In other words, the more one emphasizes the oppression which we receive from outside, the more we obtain the moral strength and the moral authority to criticize our own black oppressors. So this is equally important. Many African heads of state sent messages, personal telegrams, telexes, etc., and for me this means they have already accepted the imperative of the moralities which guide my work. So now it becomes a little bit more difficult for many of them to say, "Oh, you are criticizing us to the outside world!" when they understand that a kind of moral authority attaches to events of this kind and they have identified themselves with it. Otherwise, I'll tell them, "Take back your congratulatory telegrams." (Laughter.)

I wonder if this wouldn't be a good moment to go back a bit in time and ask you to comment on **Aké,** *your book about your early childhood. Could you say something about the process of writing about your early life?*

You know, one recaptures certain aspects of some elements of smells and sounds, either by actually smelling and hearing them or by suddenly missing them, because something triggers off the memory. You suddenly realize that a certain slice of your life is disappearing, and you get a feeling that you want to set it down in one form or another. This period of my childhood belongs to that sudden realization of a lost period, a lost ambience, a lost environment. I don't like autobiographies, because they're mostly lies, but there's a period of

Front cover of Soyinka's 1976 collection of poems.

innocence in which one can write down things quite frankly. Even *Aké* is not totally truthful. (Laughs.) You have to expunge some things. You are embarrassed by some things, so you leave them out. But this is obviously more truthful because of the lack of inhibition than many other things I write about my life. It's not lying—you don't tell untruths, you just do not tell all the truth. It's part and parcel of the protection of human dignity. I've always been repelled by the general Euro-American habit of telling all, revealing all the dirty secrets of human relationships, even without asking permission of those who share this personal relationship with you. (Laughter, applause.)

So the childhood is one period in which there is really nothing much to hide, and I'd always wanted to set it down. I spoke to my publisher, he gave me a small advance, and I spent it. It took three years after that before I could enter the frame of mind to recapture this particular life in the way I wanted to set it down.

Aké was very successful in this country—it's a widely read book—, and that success makes plain how intelligible you have made the world of your childhood to those of us who in different ways didn't share it, because we lived either in other parts of Africa or in other parts of the world. There presumably are, however, problems in presenting your work, especially as a dramatist, because of the different traditions of interpretation of theater and performance in Nigeria, in West Africa, in Africa, and in the rest of the world. Could you reflect a little while on some of the ways in which these problems affect the production that you're now engaged in, **Death and the King's Horseman***?*

It's interesting that you ask that question apropos of *Aké*, because in one of the sessions with the company, some of the cast expressed their difficulty in finding a sort of corresponding experience in their own lives with the content, theme, and characters in ***Death and the King's Horseman.*** I have to confess that I was very impatient about this kind of difficulty. But, remarkably, one of the actresses—and a white one at that—said to the others, "Well, why don't you read *Aké?*" At least one portion is, in fact, very significant in terms of the position of the women in ***Death and the King's Horseman.***

But, as I said and admit freely, I have a very impatient attitude towards this. I grew up, as many of us did, on the fare of European literature. Even in school we didn't have too much problem understanding the worlds of William Shakespeare, Bernard Shaw, Galsworthy, Moliere, and Ibsen, and, frankly, I'm irritated when people from outside my world say they find it difficult to enter my world. It's laziness, it's intellectual laziness . . . especially today when communication is a matter of course. There are economic relations between all the nations of the world. I see in Nigeria millionaires, multi-corporations, a constant exchange of films, video tapes, radio, music; Fela comes here with his music. I find no difficulty at all in entering into Chinese literature, Japanese literature, Russian literature, and this has always been so. I think the barrier is self-induced. "This is a world of the exotic, we can not enter it." The barrier is self-created. By now it has to be a two-way traffic. There can be no concessions at all; the effort simply has to be made.

But at the same time the work of a director principally involves responsibility towards the audience. He must always find idioms, whether in the field of music, poetry, or scenography, to interpret what might be abstruse elements. The director must bring out images in concrete terms which are merely in verbal terms within the book. When he moves a play from one area to another, the director seeks certain symbols, certain representational images in order to facilitate—because you're encapsulating a history of a people within a couple of hours. If you take *Coriolanus* to Africa, it's the responsibility of the director to try to transmit the metaphors within that particular language, the visual images, in terms which cannot be too remote. But then again I believe that the audience must not be overindulged, and once as a director I feel I have satisfied

myself, that I've eased the transition, the rest is up to the audience. They can take it or leave it. (Applause.)

I take it that part of the passion of your remarks is in response to some of the ways in which your work has been received in the United States and in Europe, perhaps more in the United States.

I have to say Europeans are a little bit—if one can make comparisons—more receptive. Americans are very insular. I suppose that's because you have so many cultures in America, and Americans don't feel they have to go outside what is already here. But there's a great deal of insularity in America, and that applies not merely to culture, but to politics. Americans don't even make an attempt to understand the politics of outside nations. They think they do, but they do not. And I mean this on all levels. I speak not merely of the taxi driver who asked me, "Yea, what's happening, man. You're from Neegeria. Is that in Eer*an*?" (Laughter.) I find the same attitude even among university lecturers. Not so long ago there was a professional, very intelligent, highly trained, and I happened to remark that one of my ways of relaxing is just to go into the bush and do some hunting. And he said, "Oh, what do you use for hunting?" What he was asking was, "Is it clubs? Or bows and arrows?" I mean we've been fighting wars with cannons and guns in Africa for I don't know how long. I said, "No, it's catapult." (Laughter.) So, it's the same thing with culture. Americans are far more insular.

I'd like to talk a little more about **Death and the King's Horseman.** *Is this a political play, or would you rather read it as relatively apolitical, by contrast, for example, to* **A Play of Giants***?*

Of course there's politics in ***Death and the King's Horseman.*** There's the politics of colonization, but for me it's very peripheral. The action, the tragedy of ***Death and the King's Horseman*** could have been triggered off by circumstances which have nothing to do with the colonial factor—that's very important to emphasize. So it's political in a very peripheral sense. The colonial factor, as I insist, is merely a catalytic event. But the tragedy of a man who fails to fulfill an undertaking is a universal tragedy. I regard it as being far, far, far less political than *A Play of Giants,* yes.

You've said that **Horseman** *is fundamentally a metaphysical play. That might invite the speculation that it is a difficult play, since* metaphysical *is a word—I know this as a philosopher—which invites difficulties. Is there something you want to say, in advance of people's seeing it, about the metaphysical issues, the issues of death and transition, which the play addresses?*

All his life, the principal character, the Elesin Oba—the Horseman of the King—, has enjoyed certain unique privileges for a certain function. At the critical moment he fails to fulfill that function, so he's doomed. That's straightforward. But then, one asks, how is it that, in the first place, such a function was the norm for a community of people? We can ask that from this distance. And that's not so long ago. In fact, societies like this still exist.

I've given my company current examples from India, for instance, of human sacrifice and so on to the goddess Kali, which were in the newspapers quite recently. So one must begin by understanding what is the spiritual context of a people for whom this is not an aberration, not an abnormality, and one finds it in the world view, the metaphysical beliefs of the Yoruba people.

We believe that there are various areas of existence, all of which interact, interlock in a pattern of continuity: the world of the ancestor, the world of the living, and the world of the unborn. The process of transition among these various worlds is a continuing one and one which is totally ameliorated. For instance, the function of ritual, of sacrifice—whether it's a ram or a chicken—, the function of seasonal ceremonies, is in fact allied to the ease of transition among these various worlds.

So, in effect, death does not mean for such a society what it means for other societies. And it's only if one establishes this kind of context, through whatever symbolic means, that one can begin—distanced as you and I are from this particular kind of society, even if we are part of the world. It's only by exposing this world as a hermetic, self-regulating universe of its own that a tragedy of a character like Elesin can have absolute validity. So within that context, this is what enables him. For him it's not death.

At the same time, even journeying from New York to Boston is an activity of loss. You leave something behind. It involves a pain. How much you want to live in this world which you know very well, which is concrete, which one can only relate to in symbolic terms. And so for Elesin the difficulty does exist as a human being within this world. But he's been brought up to believe, and his whole community believes, in the existence of these various worlds which are secure and even concrete in their own terms. And his failure to make that transfer from one to the other, *that* really is the tragedy of Elesin.

You spoke just now of **Horseman** *as a tragedy, which of course it is. I think the concept of tragedy tends to get used in our culture very much and in a debased form and with very little sense of classical tragedy. You chose, very deliberately I think, to frame* **Horseman** *as a classical tragedy. Is that not a difficulty, turning once again to the problems of production? Is it not difficult to produce a tragedy for a contemporary American audience? Not because it's alien or exotic or African, but because the concept of tragedy required to enter this world is a distant one to many people?*

Yes. But that's only if one begins by accepting the European definition of tragedy. I remember my shock as a student of literature and drama when I read that drama originated in Greece. What is this? I couldn't quite deal with it. What are they talking about? I never heard my grandfather talk about Greeks invading Yoru-

baland. I couldn't understand. I've lived from childhood with drama. I read at the time that tragedy evolved as a result of the rites of Dionysus. Now we all went through this damn thing, so I think the presence of eradication had better begin. It doesn't matter what form it takes. (Applause.)

Nevertheless, whatever their origins, tragedy does have a specific, formal . . .

But I've never made a claim that I'm presenting tragedy in European terms. *Tragedy*—quite apart from the misuse of the word which we know about—whether we translate it in Yoruba or Tre or Ewe, I think we'll find a correlative somewhere in which we're all talking about the same thing. Just as the equivalent of the word *tragedy* in Yoruba can be debased in Africa, so it can be debased in Europe. But ultimately there is a certain passage of the human being, a certain development or undevelopment of the human character, a certain result in the processes of certain events which affects the human being which has that common definition of tragedy in no matter what culture. And it is to that kind of linguistic bag, that symbolic bag, which audiences in theater must attune themselves, whether it is Japanese tragedy or Chinese tragedy.

There may be difficulties, but I think they're very superficial. As I explained to some of my company, "You say you have difficulty looking for some parallel experience in America. But what do you call what happened to Richard Nixon? If ever there was a tragic character, that is it. Begin from there." (Laughter.) Just begin from there. We all have these experiences; it's universal. It's only in the details we differ. What happens to a man psychologically in terms of his valuation within the community in which he resides, the fall from—to use a cliché—grace to grass, that's the element of tragedy.

> *Wole Soyinka and Anthony Appiah in an interview in* Black American Literature Forum, *Vol. 22, No. 4, Winter, 1988, pp. 777-85.*

Tanure Ojaide (essay date 1988)

[*In the following excerpt, Ojaide examines African and Western influences in Soyinka's poetry.*]

A survey of Wole Soyinka's influences reveals the admixture of indigenous and foreign qualities in the poems. These influences affect the poet's materials, concepts, language, and technique. The poet combines traditional African and Western influences so dexterously that he creates a personal authenticity. (p. 767)

Soyinka makes use of Yoruba myths, superstitions, and beliefs in his poetry. There are references to Yoruba gods and what they represent, beliefs about the presence of ancestors who receive offerings from the living to protect them, and "the same child who dies and returns again and again to plague the mother."

Soyinka copiously exploits the Ogun myth. The dual-natured god, who manifests himself in seven ways, is "God of Iron and metallurgy, Explorer, Artisan, Hunter, God of war, Guardian of the Road, the Creative Essence. His season is harvest and the rains." The qualities of Ogun, a war monger and yet a shield to orphans, destructive and creative, form the background to **"Idanre"** and *Ogun Abibimañ.* Sometimes, as in **"Dawn,"** the myth is subtly used. In addition to Ogun, many gods, including Orunmila, Sango, Orisa-nla, and Esu, are alluded to in **"Idanre."** Soyinka chooses not Orunmila, principle of order, wisdom, and authority, as his divine mentor, but Ogun, the creative but destructive god; for to the poet, creation is paramount. Not only is Ogun a selfless explorer, but he possesses qualities relevant to a Third World country in this technological age. Yoruba myths enrich **"Dawn," "Death in the Dawn," "In Memory of Segun Awolowo," "Abiku," "Dedication," "Idanre," "Hunt of the Stone,"** and *Ogun Abibimañ.*

Interwoven with the myths and culture are the value system, the love of ceremonies, and the agrarian preoccupations of the people. Soyinka expresses the Yoruba value system of a successful life as combining wealth, children, and long life in **"Dedication."** The poem is based on *isomoloruko,* the naming ceremony, which is a Yoruba household celebration. **"Koko Oloro"** is a rendition of a "children's propitiation chant." The agrarian and religious society provides the poet materials for his poems in the form of food and sacrifices to the gods. There is emphasis on fertility and increase, and images of farming are abundant in **"Idanre."** Harvest in **"Idanre"** becomes a synthesis of social and religious activities.

Yoruba myths could prove obscure to the reader not conversant with the poet's native world picture—a possible problem Soyinka seems aware of in **"Idanre,"** where he appends notes to help the uninitiated reader. In some other poems for which the author provides no notes, the reader may lose the profundity of the expressions. M. J. Salt's explication of **"Dawn"** explains allusions and offers suggestions which are obvious to the reader knowledgeable in Yoruba myths but indiscernible to the non-Yoruba novice. It is only the initiate who will link "Death the scrap-iron dealer / Breeds a glut on trade. The fault / Is His of seven paths whose whim / Gave Death his agency" from **"In Memory of Segun Awolowo"** to the demanding Ogun, who destroys human beings on the very roads he is meant to guard. In fact, not every Yoruba-speaking person will detect these allusions, only persons versed in Yoruba myths, who might also be outsiders. These allusions give a traditional African character to the voice and viewpoint of the poet.

Soyinka is also much influenced by Yoruba poetic forms, which enrich his poetry. There are qualities of *Ifa, etiyeri, ijala,* and *oriki* poetic forms in *Idanre, A Shuttle in the Crypt,* and *Ogun Abibimañ. Ifa,* divination, is conducted by a medicine man called *babalawo,* who usually recommends that the patient perform sacrifices to counter the evil forces affecting him. *Ifa* has its own poetry, which is usually chanted. The *etiyeri* is a masquerader who performs in the evening and satirically attacks anti-social attitudes in the society. *Ijala* is poetry of hunters and blacksmiths, and it is usually in the form of chants. *Oriki* is a praise chant. These latter two forms involve a kind of praise, and the chant could also be termed an *oriki.*

According to Wande Abimbola, "Two of the most important and characteristic features of Ifa style are repetition and word-play." Puzzles, obscurity, and personification are also common in Ifa divination poetry. These features abound in Soyinka's poems. Repetitions of words, phrases, or lines occur in, among other works, **"Idanre," "O, Roots!"** and *Ogun Abibimañ.* There is a certain exuberance in Soyinka's use of words comparable to Ifa's. And the density of his poetry is in the tradition of Ifa, in which prophetic words are not to be taken literally.

Soyinka seems also to be influenced by the *etiyeri* tradition of Yoruba satire, in which the poet is a masquerader who wants to maintain the social and moral ideals of his environment. In that pursuit, he ridicules and accuses violators. Soyinka's early poems—some of the October 1966 poems of *Idanre* and many poems in *A Shuttle in the Crypt*—are perhaps indebted to this Yoruba tradition of satire. The poet's use of sarcasm, metaphors, repetitions, and refrains is also part of this poetic form. His use of abuse and curse, especially in **"Malediction,"** might be related to the *etiyeri.*

The poet is also indebted to the *ijala* poetry of hunters and to the *oriki* praise tradition. *Oriki* involves descriptions, eulogy, oblique references to events, appellation, epithets, hyperbole and apostrophe. These qualities are common in Soyinka's poetry, especially **"Idanre"** and *Ogun Abibimañ.* Ogun, "of seven paths," is variously "the silent blacksmith," "the lone one," and "the Creative Essence," who has a "large creative hand." These *oriki* features give dignity to the protagonists of Soyinka's poems, who are heroes in the Yoruba epic tradition. Homage and prayers, as in **"Dawn"** and **"O, Roots!"** respectively, are in the *oriki* tradition. In *ijala* poetry, there are invocations and salutations to powerful gods such as Ogun and Sango. Following this convention in *Ogun Abibimañ,* the poet calls on Ogun to assume generalship of the black freedom fighters and lead them to victory against a racist minority establishment. The poem's incantatory rhythm, repetitions, and Yoruba "figures" are influenced by *ijala* and *oriki* poetic forms.

Some of these possible influences on Soyinka from Yoruba poetic forms involve properties common to oral poetry in particular. Examples of hyperbole, metaphors, repetitions, and refrains abound not only in Yoruba poetry but in Ewe, Urhobo, and Zulu literatures, which are also oral. In the case of praise poetry, Soyinka absorbs both the Yoruba and Zulu praise conventions in

Ogun Abibimañ, where he appropriately seeks the combined efforts of Ogun and Shaka to assert black independence. Some of these Yoruba techniques are therefore universal, and might have been acquired from any oral literature. Even in a poem like **"Dedication,"** which is an undisguised model of the Yoruba naming ceremony, Soyinka does not always stick to the traditional meaning of symbols. He writes:

> . . . and leave this taste
> Long on your lips, of salt, that you may seek
> None from tears.

Salt here is meant to forestall tears, which have salt as part of their chemical content. This is a different, more scientific, meaning of *salt* than that which the Yoruba people traditionally take it to be. Abimbola, expressing the traditional belief on salt, says it

> could be regarded as the commodity which one must have in order to have the secret and important knowledge which can affect the choice of one's destiny in life. In other words, salt is synonymous with good, orderly and civilised life while lack of it represents primitive useless life. This is probably why salt is used during the christening ceremony of Yoruba children. Salt is synonymous with good, happy and sweet life.

Soyinka gives a personal touch to the traditional symbol.

The Yoruba tradition gives Soyinka an African identity, since the poetry shows a sense of cultural roots. The use of Yoruba materials is a nostalgic act which makes the African reader identify more readily with the poems. To the Western reader, Soyinka's poetry is an exotic medley. The Yoruba mythical allusions give profundity to the poetry; furthermore, the particular is made universal and the universal made particular in the Yoruba gods, who are local manifestations of classical gods. The local influences affect his technique in the use of repetitions, metaphors, and epithets, and partly fashion his viewpoint. I have already mentioned the Yoruba concept of a successful life expressed in **"Dedication."** Soyinka's attitude toward women seems to me traditionally African. His women are basically sources of sex and increase, and, consequently, he uses images of farming for sex. He is agrarian and ambivalent towards technology, looking back to an idyllic state. He perceives life in terms of farming, and there are many references to seeds, growth, and harvest. The poet is critical of technology, which to him is a shallow conception of life when compared to the profounder truths and power of nature.

Soyinka is, however, not influenced by Yoruba culture alone. His "book" education inevitably brought him into contact with Judeo-Christian and Western literary traditions. He was bound to come into contact with the Bible and Christianity in his elementary and secondary schools, since Religious Knowledge was a common subject. In *Aké* he recalls being taught the Bible. Soyinka may no longer be a practicing Christian, but the Biblical influence on him is strong. **"The Dreamer"** and **"Idanre"** refer to Christ, and Joseph and Potiphar's wife of Genesis are the subject of **"Joseph"** in *A Shuttle in the Crypt.* **"Easter"** in *Idanre* is based on a Christian concept. In "the lone figure" poems of *Idanre,* Christ is the archetype of the lonely and prophetic individual unacknowledged until after his death. The poet himself is a Christ figure in **"Journey."** The many references to bread, as in **"Ikeja, Friday, Four O'Clock"** *(Idanre)* and **"Relief"** *(A Shuttle in the Crypt),* are related to Christ's feeding multitudes with a few loaves of bread. He uses wine in **"Journey"** with a Biblical undertone. Besides, "Usurpers hand my cup at every / Feast a last supper" *(Shuttle)* has Christ's last supper with his apostles as its source. **"Space"** subtly alludes to Noah's ark, and Lazarus is mentione in **"Seed."** The poet also alludes to Herod and Elijah in *A Shuttle in the Crypt.* Lamenting the destruction in his country, the poet says "tares / Withhold possession of our mangled lawns," an apparent reference to one of Christ's parables.

Soyinka has doses of both traditional African and Judeo-Christian religions which come out in his work now and then. Judeo-Christianity affords him materials for allusions and metaphors, and does not appear as a force against which he struggles, unlike Okigbo, Awoonor, and Okot p'Bitek; he does not satirize Christianity. His absorptive personality blends the Christian tradition into his being. Religious words such as *canonization, martyr, saint,* and *baptism* appear in the poems to broaden and universalize the experiences the poet attempts to convey.

The curriculum of the English departments at the Universities of Ibadan and Leeds in Soyinka's undergraduate days would have included Shakespeare and the Elizabethans, the metaphysical poets, Jacobean dramatists, and twentieth-century writers such as W. B. Yeats, Ezra Pound, T. S. Eliot, Dylan Thomas, and James Joyce. If my own studies in the English department at Ibadan some dozen years later are a reflection, a bachelor's program in English would have made Soyinka intimate with major British and a few American writers. Soyinka has also taught literature at Lagos, Ibadan, and Ile-Ifé, and this would have exposed him to many literary figures and schools.

The poet's knowledge of Western literatures filters into his poetry, affecting his technique, allusions, and literary concepts. His preface to *Idanre* is a variation of a speech in Shakespeare's *Tempest.* One of his archetypes is Hamlet, and in his poem **"Hamlet,"** he makes reference to one of Macbeth's speeches. Soyinka's obsession with death and violence seems Jacobean. Apart from the Yoruba tradition of satire, he may have borrowed a leaf from the neo-classical tradition of Swift, Pope, and Dryden. He has a poem, **"Gulliver,"** in which he likens his mistreatment by the Nigerian establishment in the crisis years to Gulliver's in Lilliput. And there is a Miltonian echo in **"Idanre."** Soyinka's practice is that of the epic poet inspired by the muse—with him, Ogun. He is spokesman for the black race in *Ogun*

Abibimañ. The elegies on Fajuyi, Banjo, and Okigbo are reminiscent of Milton's *Lycidas.*

"Every young man's heart," Malraux says, "is a graveyard in which are inscribed the names of a thousand dead artists but whose only actual denizens are a few mighty, often antagonistic, ghosts." Soyinka shares characteristics of the modernist tradition, such as fragmentation and allusiveness, with Yeats, Pound, Eliot, and Joyce. The early poems of Yeats were chants, and he makes use of Celtic myths and legends of the Irish people. Soyinka himself has absorbed Yoruba incantatory rhythms. Two of Yeats's poems, "On a Political Prisoner" and "Prayer for My Daughter," have a bearing on Soyinka's **"Prisoner"** and **"Dedication."** Soyinka quotes Yeats in the third part of *Ogun Abibimañ* to convey his contradictory attitude toward violence. To Yeats violence is negative; not so to Soyinka if it is the only means to defeat repression and racial indignity. Soyinka's difficulty, use of the objective correlative and persona, and advocation of non-narcissism on the part of the poet are comparable to the modern conventions of Ezra Pound and T. S. Eliot. He is familiar enough with Pound apparently to accuse Okigbo of regrouping Pound's images around the oil-bean and the nude spear. In **"Flowers for my land,"** where there is a waste land motif, his "I do not / Dare to think these bones will bloom tomorrow" echoes Eliot. There is a subtle allusion to the Holy Grail legend in **"Vault centre."** His density and use of compound words appear Joycean. He wrote a poem, **"Ulysses,"** for his Joyce class, an indication that he taught *Ulysses* and is familiar with Homer. He explores the quest theme, alludes to Circe's transformation of Ulysses' companions to swine, and alludes to Scylla and Charybdis. Soyinka's "wine-centred waves" and "swine-scented" in that poem are light variations of Homer's description of the sea as "wine-dark waves." His **"By Little Loving"** is modeled on Thomas Blackburn and reveals an awareness of contemporary British poetic trends.

Soyinka's essays and creative work reveal a voracious reader of Western literatures. Soyinka is an exception to the typical African intellectual whom Chinua Achebe describes as reading a few uninspiring British novels. His passion for drama brought him into contact with Greek and European dramatists. References to Antigone, the Stygian mysteries, and Lethe are part of the classical culture underlying his work. The Greek dramatists (Sophocles, Euripides, and Aeschylus) would particularly have appealed to the Yoruba-raised poet because of their similar attitude toward gods and tragedy. Hence his equating Yoruba gods to Greek gods and his references to Dionysus and Prometheus are not surprising. Here is a ready synthesis of African and European cultures in which the local is universalized and the universal simultaneously localized.

The poet's study, work, and travels have broadened his awareness. He uses foreign seasons to express himself. He talks of "Sudden winter" in **"Death in the Dawn"** and refers to autumn in **"Massacre October '66."** These references give variation and universal dimension to the poetry. His social observations in Britain inspired some of his early poems: **"Telephone Conversation," "My Next-Door Neighbor," "The Immigrant,"** and **"And the Other Immigrant."** He has been to Holland, the United States, West Germany, and Ghana, among other countries. During his sojourn in Ghana in the mid-1970s he wrote *Ogun Abibimañ, abibimañ* being an Akan word for the land of Black peoples. **"Around Us Dawning"** and **"Luo Plains"** are travel poems. The travels have given him fresh experiences and enriched his sensibility.

Two other possible influences on Soyinka's poetry are his work in the theatre and his relationship with his Nigerian literary colleagues J. P. Clark and Christopher Okigbo. He spent eighteen months with the Royal Court Theatre as a play reader. He founded the 1960 Masks in Nigeria. In addition to writing plays, he has directed and taken part in many productions of his plays and in those of other writers. His practical interest in the theatre may thus be responsible for the dramatic dialogue in **"Telephone Conversation,"** the boasting of **"Abiku,"** and the stage comments in the early poems. He describes the behavior of government and prison officers in theatrical terms in **"Purgatory."**

Okigbo, Clark, and Soyinka were close colleagues at Ibadan and read poems to each other. Soyinka's **"Abiku"** seems to be in deliberate opposition to Clark's "Abiku." Soyinka has a love-hate attitude toward Okigbo: He is not impressed by Okigbo's *Heavensgate* and *Limits,* as his sarcastic comments in *The American Scholar* (1963) reveal. However, he praised him after his death. Some of the poems of *A Shuttle in the Crypt,* especially **"O, Roots!",** have the incantatory rhythm which characterizes Okigbo's poetry. Okigbo's egocentricism may have driven Soyinka into distancing himself from his subject. If these speculations on Soyinka's relations to Clark and Okigbo are valid, it means the poet's contemporary colleagues inclined him to go in a different direction in ideas and poetic concepts. In his opposite positions in relation to Clark's "Abiku" and Okigbo's narcissism, Soyinka projects virile and valid alternatives.

The degrees of explicit Yoruba and Western influence vary in Soyinka's poetry. Apart from **"Koko Oloro"** and **"Dedication,"** which are based on Yoruba tradition, and "the lone figure" poems and **"Journey,"** based on Western concepts, most other poems combine African and Western features more subtly and unevenly. The Yoruba influences help create the poet's celebratory and critical voices. The Western influences seem to be stronger in the contemplative poems. The Western poetic tradition is behind the poet's use of formal stanzas and rhymes. The special appeal of compound words, epithets, possessives, metaphors, personifications, alliterations, and repetitions can be attributed to a combination of Yoruba and European modernist influences. The Western influences give his voice and viewpoint an intellectual accent.

But there is another aspect to Soyinka's poetry. History, especially Nigerian, has dictated the direction of Soyinka's writing. Independence brought with it a sense of nationalism which influenced the poet's use of materials from his culture as he had not done before in Britain. The Nigerian crisis and the poet's imprisonment have also affected his voice and viewpoint. The killings he describes in **"Massacre October '66"** convinced him of the bestiality of man. He describes the then military leader as selfish, tyrannical, bloodthirsty, and hypocritical. The anti-Gowon poems are mainly satirical. The voice of the poet in *A Shuttle in the Crypt* is somber due to the reality of experience. In *A Shuttle in the Crypt* the poet is no longer an observer and witness who is sometimes distant, as in the early poems and in *Idanre,* but is a victim. As he says in **"Ulysses,"** practical experience is shocking, unlike toying with concepts:

> It was a crystal cover on the world
> A rake of thunders showered its fragments
> To a slow dissolve in hailstones, and I was
> Held awhile to its truthfulness of transcience.

It is out of this devastating experience that the poet gains insight. The increasingly dark vision of the poet which develops up through *A Shuttle in the Crypt* does not preclude positive lessons. The poet's sense of history also gave birth to *Ogun Abibimañ,* which was inspired by Samora Machel's declaration of war against the then minority-ruled Rhodesia.

For Wole Soyinka, the Yoruba, Nigerian, and African as well as the Judeo-Christian, Western literary and social influences are integrated into one confident personality. There is no conflict in his use of indigenous and foreign materials and techniques. Though the Western reader may be uneasy about the Yoruba myths and the African may be tasked by the range of Soyinka's allusions and modernist techniques, the poems are an expression of an individual's complex sensibility. The two main sources of influences give variety and vitality to the poetry. The variety is not indiscriminate but a unity-in-variety. There is tension between the unity and the variety, a quality which gives vigor to the poetry. Like the Ogun he reveres, Soyinka in his poetry is a fusion of polar qualities. He is at once modern and conservative. His influences are blended into a new authenticity consonant with a native-culture-conscious Nigerian intellectual who is Western-educated and widely traveled. Soyinka acknowledges the "limited amount of originality in the creative ideas. Innovations have a slightly larger scope but ultimately what we all do mostly is the renovation and development of existing ideas." Soyinka's influences do not make him a less original poet; he is as original as any poet can be in the totality of his work. (pp. 768-76)

Tanure Ojaide, "Two Worlds: Influences on the Poetry of Wole Soyinka," in Black American Literature Forum, *Vol. 22, No. 4, Winter, 1988, pp. 767-76.*

Jonathan Coe (essay date 1990)

[*In the following essay, Coe favorably reviews Soyinka's most recent works:* Isarà: A Voyage around Essay *and* Mandela's Earth, and Other Poems.]

Nothing speaks louder about British insularity than the fact that we tend to be impressed by Booker rather than Nobel prizewinners. *Isarà* is Soyinka's first major prose work since he won the Nobel prize in 1986, and while it would be idle to expect it to make the bestseller lists, it certainly ought to win a few more admirers for this most accessible of African writers—particularly as it is being issued in tandem with a paperback of his newly-topical poems inspired by Nelson Mandela.

In truth the most exhilarating aspect of reading Soyinka is the contact it affords, not with a different culture, but with a different attitude towards language. One of his poems in *Mandela's Earth* describes the experience of arriving in New York and being confronted by a poster:

> This film star / space star /
>   mayor or porn queen
> Toothsomely pledges: "New
>   York loves you!"
> Forgive my innocence, does
>   New York know me?
> The word has turned mere
>   gesture in N.Y.

This disdain for a use of language which can turn words into "mere gestures" informs Soyinka's prose as much as his verse. In *Aké,* his childhood memoir (published in 1981), he recalled a visit made when he was a young boy to the market outside Ibara, and his awe and excitement at the profusion of items on display: "it did not seem possible that there was so much thing in the world!"

The whole book was infused with this sense of raw physicality, made feasible by an unflinching respect for words which required that economy be prized over sentimental "gestures." *Isarà* is in some ways a sequel to *Aké,* which introduced us to his mother, Wild Christian, and his father, the schoolmaster nicknamed Essay. Soyinka himself does not appear; however the book describes events which took place before he was born— and the perspective is not that of a child but of an impersonal narrator. Intended as "a tribute to 'Essay' and his friends and times," Isara observes the shifting preoccupations of a group of contemporaries, all of them (in Soyinka's punning phrase) "Ex-Ilés" from their native town, over a period of 15 years.

Its starting point, apparently, was a tin box in which Soyinka found some of his father's documents: "a handful of letters, old journals with marked pages and annotations, notebook jottings, tax and other levy receipts, minutes of meetings and school reports, programme notes of special events, and so on." Around these he has constructed a series of semi-fictional (and often very funny) episodes foregrounding some of the political, intellectual and financial concerns which would have been current in Western Nigeria before and after the Second World War.

Its central characters are the schoolmaster, Soditan Akinyode, and a college drop-out called Sipe who has since gone on to become an energetic and erratically successful entrepreneur. Sipe sets up a benevolent fund for his friends but finds his ambitious schemes constantly thwarted by their unworldliness: a plan to invest in Belgian bonds comes to nothing when Soditan starts agonising over the moral objections ("trust the teacher to run into a reference to an ancient instrument by a British knight who had uncovered unspeakable cruelties by the Belgians in the Congo!"). Although specific in period and location, this account of the compromises of liberal capitalism coming up against the wobbly dictates of idealism is handled with a boisterous subtlety which preserves its relevance intact.

Throughout the book, Soyinka feelingly evokes a society whose very cultural identity has been called into question by colonialists. Sometimes this is brought home by large-scale comic incidents—such as the much hyped recital of Western classical music which reduces its entire audience to a torpor—and sometimes by telling turns of phrase, as when one of Soditan's former pupils admits "I can bomb the English language worse than Hitler and no one will complain." At such moments you realise that, for these people, violence done to property and violence done to language are two sides of the same coin.

There are critics on the left in Nigeria who accuse Soyinka of failing to take an explicit political position, but from a British perspective this claim seems hard to understand. Soditan expresses irritation at one point with the coyness of the British—"they had this tendency towards apologetic, even tentative, language in straightforward matters."

The issues treated in *Isarà* are rarely straightforward, and its language is never tentative or apologetic. Instead of offering a merely wistful or elegiac portrait of a lost father-figure, it pays him an even more handsome tribute: it celebrates the life of the mind, and nails down a moment in history, with a wit, accuracy and intelligence which our own writers would do well to emulate.

Jonathan Coe, "Riches in a Box," in Manchester Guardian Weekly, *April 8, 1990, p. 26.*

FURTHER READING

Amuta, Chidi. "From Myth to Ideology: The Socio-Political Content of Soyinka's War Writings." *The Journal of Commonwealth Literature* XXIII, No. 1 (1988): 116-29.

Examines Soyinka's work written before the Nigerian Civil War (1967-70).

Badejo, Diedre L. "Unmasking the Gods: Of Egungun and Demagogues in Three Works by Wole Soyinka." *Theatre Journal* 39, No. 2 (May 1987): 204-14.
Explores the motif of masking/unmasking in three of Soyinka's plays: *A Dance of the Forests, Opera Wonyosi,* and *A Play of Giants.*

Bernstein, Richard. "African Oriented: Reviving a Magazine of Change and Ideas." *The New York Times* (14 May 1991): B1.
Discusses Soyinka's role in reviving *Transition* magazine.

Booth, James. "Myth, Metaphor, and Syntax in Soyinka's Poetry." *Research in African Literatures* 17, No. 1 (Spring 1986): 53-72.
Studies meaning and technique in Soyinka's poetry, concluding: "Brilliant and assured in tone as Soyinka's poetry undoubtedly is, it is also... metaphorically irresponsible and syntactically messy. And these are poetic sins of no small order."

David, Mary T. "The Theme of Regeneration in Selected Works by Wole Soyinka." *Black American Literature Forum* 22, No. 4 (Winter 1988): 645-61.
Examines the theme of regeneration in *The Interpreters, Season of Anomy,* and *The Man Died.*

Euba, Femi. "Soyinka's Satiric Development and Maturity." *Black American Literature Forum* 22, No. 3 (Fall 1988): 615-28.
Considers *Opera Wonyosi* and *A Play of Giants,* calling the latter work Soyinka's best satirical play.

Gibbs, James. "'A Storyteller on the *Gbohun-Gbohun*': An Analysis of Wole Soyinka's Three Johnny Stories." *Research in African Literatures* 20, No. 1 (Spring 1989): 50-9.
Examines Soyinka's "Johnny Stories," three short stories that "represent a step in the emergence of Soyinka as a writer, or at least as a storyteller on the gbohun-gbohun (radio)."

Haynes, John. "Giving a Twist to the Circle." *The Times Literary Supplement,* No. 4538 (23-29 March 1990): 307.
Favorable review of *Mandela's Earth, and Other Poems,* focusing on theme.

Maduakor, Obiajuru. "Soyinka as a Literary Critic." *Research in African Literatures* 17, No. 1 (Spring 1986): 1-38.
Evaluates Soyinka as a critic. Maduakor distinguishes and discusses four types of essays in Soyinka's *Myth, Literature, and the African World*: Incidental Essays, Ritual Essays, Essays on Ideology and Social Vision, and Controversies.

Naidoo, Beverley. "The Hedge of Bitter Almonds." *The Times Educational Supplement,* No. 3866 (3 August 1990): 16.
Review of *Mandela's Earth, and Other Poems.* The critic concludes: "This is a wide-spanned, rich collection from a great poet who combines urbanity with

vigour and searing wit with a passionate commitment to unpeeling human truths."

Tucker, M. Review of *Isarà: A Voyage around Essay,* by Wole Soyinka. *Choice* 27, No. 10 (June 1990): 1686.

Favorably reviews *Isarà,* stating: "The book is both thrilling lyricism and a reverberating consciousness of the conflicts of temporal behavior spread against unchanging spiritual need."

Wallace Thurman

1902-1934

(Full name Wallace Henry Thurman; also wrote under pseudonyms Patrick Casey and Ethel Belle Mandrake) American novelist, dramatist, editor, scriptwriter, short story writer, critic, and poet.

Thurman was a central figure in the Harlem Renaissance and one of its severest critics. Famous for his self-described "erotic, bohemian" lifestyle and regarded as a maverick by his contemporaries, Thurman often used satire to accuse blacks of prejudice against darker-skinned members of their race. He also rejected the belief that the Harlem Renaissance was a substantial literary movement, claiming that it produced no out-standing writers and that those who were critically acclaimed often exploited—and allowed themselves to be patronized by—whites. Thurman's fiction is noted for its controversial subject matter and for its vivid depiction of Harlem's "low life," a motif first popularized by Carl Van Vechten in his novel *Nigger Heaven.* Although Thurman's works are frequently heavy-handed and superficial in their approach, they offer a rare, behind-the-scenes portrait of Harlem during the 1920s.

Born and raised in Salt Lake City, Utah, Thurman attended the University of Utah for a year before transferring in 1922 to the University of Southern California at Los Angeles. He first learned of the Harlem Renaissance while working as a columnist at a black-oriented newspaper. Inspired by the critical interest accorded New York's black artists and writers, Thurman founded *Outlet,* a little magazine intended to generate a similar literary movement on the West Coast. Thurman's publication survived only six months, how-ever, and in 1925 he moved to Harlem at the height of the Renaissance. In New York City Thurman took a job as a reporter and editor at *The Looking Glass,* then became managing editor of the *Messenger,* where he published short fiction by Langston Hughes and Zora Neale Hurston. Thurman left the *Messenger* in the autumn of 1926 for a circulation manager's position at a white-owned periodical, *World Tomorrow.* He later joined the editorial staff at Macaulay Publishing Company as a reader, where he advanced to editor in chief.

In the summer of 1926 Hughes asked Thurman to edit *Fire!!,* a magazine that Hughes and writer Bruce Nugent were planning. Zora Neale Hurston, the poet and essayist Gwendolyn Bennett, and the visual artist Aaron Douglas were members of the editorial board. Accord-ing to their statement in the foreword to the premiere issue, *Fire!!* was intended to "satisfy pagan thirst for beauty unadorned" and would provide a literary forum for younger black writers who wanted to stand apart from the older, venerated black literati. Thurman agreed to edit the magazine, and he contributed the short story "Cordelia the Crude" to its first issue. Despite such a promising beginning, however, *Fire!!* ceased publication after its first issue due to financial difficulties and a fire that destroyed its editorial office. In addition, the publication received derisive reviews from such estab-lished black critics as W. E. B. Du Bois and Benjamin Brawley and was virtually ignored by the white literary establishment. Two years later, Thurman published *Harlem: A Forum of Negro Life,* a more moderate, general-interest magazine also devoted to displaying works by younger writers. Like its predecessor *Fire!!,* however, *Harlem* failed after its premiere issue.

In 1929 Thurman wrote his first play, *Harlem: A Melodrama of Negro Life in Harlem,* in collaboration with William Jourdan Rapp, a white free-lance writer. The play, which opened on Broadway and ran for ninety-three performances, is about a southern black family that relocates to New York City in search of better economic opportunities but encounters instead unemployment, racial bias, and urban squalor. *Harlem* received mixed reviews, ranging from "exciting" to "vulgar." Many blacks condemned the play for its focus on the seedier elements of life, including illicit sex, wild parties, and gambling. R. Dana Skinner noted "the particular way in which this melodrama exploits the worst features of the Negro and depends for its effects solely on the explosions of lust and sensuality," yet Theophilus Lewis considered *Harlem* "a wholesome swing toward dramatic normalcy."

The title of Thurman's first novel, *The Blacker the Berry* (1929), is taken from the African-American folk-saying "the blacker the berry, the sweeter the juice," but its usage has been interpreted as ironic because of the work's attack on intraracial prejudice. Emma Lou Morgan, the protagonist, is a dark-skinned girl from the Midwest who is looked down upon by her fairer family and friends. When she attends school in California, she is likewise discriminated against because of her skin color, propelling her to move to Harlem where she believes she will be accepted. Emma Lou's expectations are soon shattered; consumed by self-hatred, she begins using hair straighteners and skin bleaching creams and takes on the attitudes of the fairer-skinned blacks who have degraded her. She in turn snubs darker men, believing them to be intellectually inferior and takes up with Alva, a man who is light-skinned but cruel and irresponsible. After discovering Alva in a lover's em-brace with another man, Emma Lou realizes how hypocritical she has become. Initial reviews of *The Blacker the Berry* were less than positive; most critics viewed the work as choppy and occasionally incoherent. Some commentators, however, have detected subtle autobiographical connotations in the novel. Robert Bone contended that "no one who has read *The Blacker the Berry* will doubt that source of this self-hatred was [Thurman's] dark complexion."

Thurman realized that his own writings, while offering distinct and often compelling sketches of African-American life, fell short of the literary excellence he demanded. He addressed this concern in his second novel, *Infants of the Spring* (1932). The work's central character, Raymond Taylor, is a young black author who is trying to write a serious novel in a decadent, race-conscious atmosphere. Taylor resides in a boardinghouse, nicknamed "Niggeratti Manor," with a number of young blacks who pretend to be aspiring authors. The whole of Harlem's artistic coterie—the bohemian fringe, patronizing whites, and Thurman's friends and associates Alain Locke, Zora Neale Hurston, Langston Hughes, and Bruce Nugent—is bitterly satirized, and Thurman suggested that these and other writers have destroyed their creativity (and the Harlem Renaissance movement in general) by leading such self-destructive lives. He also insisted that black writers are further impeded by patronizing white critics who praise everything they produce, regardless of quality, as innovative and brilliant. *Infants of the Spring* garnered criticism similar to that of *The Blacker the Berry;* unlike Thurman's first novel, however, which was considered too objective, *Infants of the Spring* was judged overly subjective and its author overly argumentative. Yet reviewers praised Thurman for his candid discussion of the movement and the contradictory standards that propelled and sustained it. Martha Gruening observed: "[*Infants of the Spring*] is a bitter and extreme statement and, like all such statements, inevitably only a partial one, but its quota of truth is just that which Negro writers, under the stress of propaganda and counterpropaganda, have generally and quite understandably omitted from their picture."

The Interne (1932), Thurman's third and final novel, was written in collaboration with Abraham L. Furman, a white author Thurman met while working at Macaulay's Publishing Company. The book focuses on the daily activities at an urban hospital—some commentators contended that Thurman's model was City Hospital on Manhattan's Welfare Island—as seen through the eyes of a young white doctor, Carl Armstrong. In his first three months at the hospital, Armstrong's ideals are shattered by his encounters with corrupt medical and administrative staffs. For a time the protagonist yields to this environment, but he soon realizes his own loss of ethics and saves himself by opening a medical practice in a rural area. Critics could not agree whether Thurman's accounts of medical misconduct were based on fact; many claimed that the novel had no semblance of reality while others stressed that the incidents were actual, if unusual and sensational.

After the publication of *The Interne* Thurman left Harlem for a scriptwriting position at Bryan Foy Productions in Hollywood. He lived wantonly and drank excessively. He completed two scripts, *Tomorrow's Children* and *High School Girl,* both low-budget,

"social realism" pieces whose theatrical releases were overshadowed by such films as *It Happened One Night* and *Imitation of Life.* Thurman failed to secure a writing position at a major motion picture studio, and, in poor health, he returned to New York City in May 1934 in a state of disillusionment and pessimism. While at a reunion party with his Harlem friends, he collapsed and was taken to City Hospital, where he died seven months later of complications relating to tuberculosis. In 1940, Thurman's old friend Langston Hughes paid tribute to him in his autobiography, *The Big Sea:* "Wallace Thurman wanted to be a great writer, but none of his own ever made him happy.... [He] contented himself by writing a great deal for money, laughing bitterly at his fabulously concocted 'true stories.' ... He thought the Negro vogue had made us all too conscious of ourselves, had flattered and spoiled us, and had provided too many easy opportunities for some of us to drink gin and more gin, on which he thought we would always be drunk."

(For further information about Thurman's life and works, see *Black Writers; Contemporary Authors,* Vols. 104, 124; *Dictionary of Literary Biography,* Vol. 51: *Afro-American Writers from the Harlem Renaissance to 1940;* and *Twentieth-Century Literary Criticism,* Vol. 6. For related criticism, see the entry on the Harlem Renaissance in *Twentieth-Century Literary Criticism,* Vol. 26.)

PRINCIPAL WORKS

Negro Life in New York's Harlem (nonfiction) 1928
The Blacker the Berry: A Novel of Negro Life (novel) 1929
Harlem: A Melodrama of Negro Life in Harlem [with William Jourdan Rapp] (drama) 1929
Infants of the Spring (novel) 1932
The Interne [with Abraham L. Furman] (novel) 1932
Tomorrow's Children (screenplay) 1934
High School Girl (screenplay) 1935

*Both films were released by Brian Foy productions.

Theophilus Lewis (essay date 1929)

[*An American critic, essayist, and short story writer, Lewis wrote for numerous African-American and Roman Catholic publications over the course of fifty years. In the excerpt below, he reviews Thurman's play* Harlem, *deeming it "a wholesome swing toward dramatic normalcy."*]

Harlem, a spirited melodrama by William Jourdan Rapp and Wallace Thurman, introduces an innovation in the treatment of Negro character on the American stage, and if it turns out to be a box office success its influence on the trend of Negro drama will be of far greater significance than its intrinsic merit as a play. Before the production of **Harlem,** all the so-called Negro plays, except *The Emperor Jones* and *Lulu Belle,* show that their authors went to exceptional pains to discover unusual and quaint types for dramatic representation. Their quest has not been for authentic Negro character but for "colorful" types. It is true that only selected types are suitable for dramatic treatment; but they should be selected for their virility, not for their oddity....

Harlem, because it emphasizes "I will" character instead of the gypsy type of Negro, is a wholesome swing toward dramatic normalcy. Its characters are not abnormal people presented in an appealing light but everyday people exaggerated and pointed up for the purposes of melodrama. This is a sound orthodox theatrical practice, and if **Harlem** proves to be as profitable as it is entertaining other playwrights will be encouraged to adopt its methods with the result that Negro drama will be changed from an aberrant to a normal form....

[The] character portrayed in **Harlem** is superior to the types pictured in the preceding Negro play.... What is of more importance to the Negro sociologist as well as the dramatist is the higher type of women presented in **Harlem.** For example compare Cordelia with Bess, the most vividly portrayed female character in *Porgy.* In Bess we have the woman who wants to be good but who is unable to follow her better impulses.... In Cordelia we have a purposeful woman who is determined to have her way regardless of the havoc that follows in her wake. She is not a victim of men; men are her victims. She is an immoral woman while Bess, strictly speaking, is unmoral. Bess, to state the matter in concrete terms, is first cousin to a boar's bride while Cordelia, Lady Macbeth and Hedda Gabler are sisters under the skin.

As a specimen of theatrical craftsmanship, aside from its portrayal of character, **Harlem** is a well made play which shows very few flaws of construction. The authors had to strain a bit to make the second act long enough but they met the problem in a way that does not result in any conspicuous sagging of suspense. The background and atmosphere are genuine and are so logically interwoven with the plot that only one character is a superfluous loose end.

> *Theophilus Lewis, "If This Be Puritanism,"*
> *in* Opportunity, *Vol. VII, No. 4, April, 1929,*
> *p. 132.*

W. E. Burghardt Du Bois (essay date 1929)

[*An American civil rights leader, educator, and man of letters, Du Bois is a major figure in twentieth-century American history. He was founder of the National Association for the Advancement of Colored People (NAACP) and edited the organization's periodical* The Crisis *from 1910 to 1934. Considered the "dean" of the Rear Guard intellectuals whose works initiated the Harlem Renaissance in the 1920s, he deplored the movement in black literature toward exploiting sordid aspects of African-American culture. Du Bois and Thurman were literary opponents; according to Phyllis R. Klotman, "Du Bois seemed offended at the mere mention of [Thurman's magazine* Fire!!*J." In the following review of* The Blacker the Berry, *Du Bois, while admitting personal bias towards the author, contends that the novel "may be promise and pledge of something better."*]

It is a little difficult to judge fairly Wallace Thurman's **The Blacker the Berry.** Its theme [of intraracial prejudice] is one of the most moving and tragic of our day....

[It] is the plight of a soul who suffers not alone from the color line, as we usually conceive it, but from the additional evil prejudice, which the dominant ideals of a white world create within the Negro world itself. (p. 249)

This is the theme, but excellent as is the thought and statement, the author does not rise to its full development. The experience of this black girl at the University is well done, but when she gets to Harlem she fades into the background and becomes a string upon which to hang an almost trite description of black Harlem.

The story of Emma Lou calls for genius to develop it. It needs deep psychological knowledge and pulsing sympathy. And above all, the author must believe in black folk, and in the beauty of black as a color of human skin. I may be wrong, but it does not seem to me that this is true of Wallace Thurman. He seems to me himself to deride blackness; he speaks of Emma's color as a "splotch" on the "pale purity" of her white fellow students and as mocking that purity "with her dark outlandish difference". He says, "It would be painted red—Negroes always bedeck themselves and their belongings in ridiculously unbecoming clothes and ornaments."

It seems to me that this inner self-despising of the very thing that he is defending, makes the author's defense less complete and less sincere, and keeps the story from developing as it should. Indeed, there seems to be no real development in Emma's character; her sex life never becomes nasty and commercial, and yet nothing in her seems to develop beyond sex.

Despite all this, the ending is not bad, and there is a gleam of something finer and deeper than the main part of the novel has furnished. One judges such a book, as I have said, with difficulty and perhaps with some prejudice because of the unpleasant work in the past to which the author has set his hand. Yet this book may be promise and pledge of something better, for it certainly frankly faces a problem which most colored people especially have shrunk from, and almost hated to face. (pp. 249-50)

> *W. E. Burghardt Du Bois, "The Browsing*
> *Reader: 'The Blacker the Berry',"* in The
> Crisis, *Vol. 36, No. 7, July, 1929, pp. 249-50.*

Martha Gruening (essay date 1932)

[*In the following excerpt, Gruening describes* Infants of the Spring *as "an ironic, mordant, and deeply honest book."*]

There is no mistaking the grimness of [Thurman's] attitude toward artistic and literary Harlem, the Negro Renaissance, and those on both sides of the color line who have made it possible. [In *Infants of the Spring*] Mr. Thurman has written an ironic, mordant, and deeply honest book. I know of no other story of Negro life, unless it is Claude McKay's *Banjo,* which reflects with such authenticity the clash of views among Colored People themselves as to the function and achievements of Negro artists in a white world. If one excepts George Schuyler, Thurman is the only Negro writer who has made any attempt to debunk the Negro Renaissance. There is need of such debunking. The Negro Renaissance has produced some first-rate work. It has also produced a great deal which is mediocre and pretentious and which has been almost ludicrously overpraised and ballyhooed....

The narrative framework of the story is slight, a series of episodes in the life of a group of artists and dilettantes who, for a while, occupy the same house in Harlem and who all, in one way or another, find frustration. Their experiences are revealed to a large extent in the give and take of conversation and it is in these conversations that the virtue of the book largely resides....

Infants of the Spring is not a great book but it is an important one. Like Mr. Thurman's earlier *The Blacker the Berry,* and unlike much of the output of contemporary Harlem, it is written with no weather eye on a possible white audience. There have been few other books equally honest in their description of certain phases of Negro life—Langston Hughes's *Not Without Laughter* and Claude McCay's *Home to Harlem* come to mind in this connection—but no other Negro writer has so unflinchingly told the truth about color snobbery within the color line, the ins and outs of "passing" and other vagaries of prejudice.... [He] tells the world what all intelligent Negroes know but generally admit only among themselves. It is a bitter and extreme statement and, like all such statements, inevitably only a partial one, but its quota of truth is just that which Negro writers, under the stress of propaganda and counterpropaganda, have generally and quite understandably omitted from their picture. By its inclusion Thurman has taken an important step away from mere racial self-consciousness toward self-realization.

> Martha Gruening, "Two Ways to Harlem," *in* The Saturday Review of Literature, *Vol. VIII, No. 34, March 12, 1932, p. 585.*

Langston Hughes (essay date 1940)

[*Hughes, a seminal figure in African-American literature, was a catalyst of the Harlem Renaissance movement. Called "the Poet Laureate of Harlem" by Carl Van Vechten, he integrated the rhythm and mood of jazz and blues music into his work and employed colloquial language in an effort to capture the essence of black American culture. Hughes worked with Thurman on the ill-fated magazine* Fire!!, *and Thurman helped Hughes with the publication of his first short stories. In the following excerpt from his 1940 autobiography* The Big Sea, *Hughes offers a brief tribute to Thurman's life and career.*]

The summer of 1926, I lived in a rooming house on 137th Street, where Wallace Thurman and Harcourt Tynes also lived. Thurman was then managing editor of the *Messenger,* a Negro magazine that had a curious career. It began by being very radical, racial, and socialistic, just after the war.... Then it later became a kind of Negro society magazine and a plugger for Negro business, with photographs of prominent colored ladies and their nice homes in it.... I asked Thurman what kind of magazine the *Messenger* was, and he said it reflected the policy of whoever paid off best at the time.

Anyway, the *Messenger* bought my first short stories. They paid me ten dollars a story. Wallace Thurman wrote me that they were very bad stories, but better than any others they could find, so he published them.

Thurman had recently come from California to New York. He was a strangely brilliant black boy, who had read everything, and whose critical mind could find something wrong with everything he read. (pp. 233-34)

Thurman had read so many books because he could read eleven lines at a time. He would get from the library a great pile of volumes that would have taken me a year to read. But he would go through them in less than a week, and be able to discuss each one at great length with anybody. That was why, I suppose, he was later given a job as a reader at Macaulay's—the only Negro reader, so far as I know, to be employed by any of the larger publishing firms.

Later Thurman became a ghost writer for *True Story,* and other publications, writing under all sorts of fantastic names, like Ethel Belle Mandrake or Patrick Casey. He did Irish and Jewish and Catholic "true confessions." He collaborated with William Jordan Rapp on plays and novels. Later he ghosted books. In fact, this quite dark young Negro is said to have written *Men, Women, and Checks.*

Wallace Thurman wanted to be a great writer, but none of his own work ever made him happy. *The Blacker the Berry,* his first book, was an important novel on a subject little dwelt upon in Negro fiction—the plight of the very dark Negro woman, who encounters in some communities a double wall of color prejudice within and without the race. His play, *Harlem,* considerably distorted for box office purposes, was, nevertheless, a compelling study—and the only one in the theater—of the impact of Harlem on a Negro family fresh from the South. And his *Infants of the Spring,* a superb and bitter study of the bohemian fringe of Harlem's literary and artistic life, is a compelling book.

But none of these things pleased Wallace Thurman. He wanted to be a *very* great writer, like Gorki or Thomas Mann, and he felt that he was merely a journalistic writer. His critical mind, comparing his pages to the thousands of other pages he had read, by Proust, Melville, Tolstoy, Galsworthy, Dostoyevski, Henry James, Sainte-Beuve, Taine, Anatole France, found his own pages vastly wanting. So he contented himself by writing a great deal for money, laughing bitterly at his fabulously concocted "true stories," creating two bad motion pictures of the "Adults Only" type for Hollywood, drinking more and more gin, and then threatening to jump out of windows at people's parties and kill himself. (pp. 234-35)

About the future of Negro literature Thurman was very pessimistic. He thought the Negro vogue had made us all too conscious of ourselves, had flattered and spoiled us, and had provided too many opportunities for some of us to drink gin and more gin, on which he thought we would always be drunk. With his bitter sense of humor, he called the Harlem literati, the "niggerati." (p. 238)

> *Langston Hughes, "Harlem Literati," in his* The Big Sea: An Autobiography, *1940. Reprint by Hill & Wang, 1963, pp. 233-41.*

Robert Bone (essay date 1965)

[*A noted American critic, Bone is the author of* The Negro Novel in America *(1958; revised edition, 1965) and* Down Home: Origins of the Afro-American Short Story *(1975). In the following excerpt from the first-named work, he briefly surveys Thurman's* The Blacker the Berry *and* Infants of the Spring.]

"The blacker the berry, the sweeter the juice"—so runs the Negro folk saying. In a mood of bitter irony, Thurman borrows this phrase for the title of his novel about a dark girl who is the victim of intraracial prejudice. From the moment that Emma Lou enters the world—a black child rejected by her own parents—her pigmentation is a constant source of pain. (p. 92)

Emma Lou's real tragedy is that she accepts the values of the system which torments her. Her use of bleaching agents, for example, betrays her unconscious belief in the magical power of a fair complexion. As the novel unfolds, she outgrows this crippling frame of reference and comes to recognize that her main enemy is within: "What she needed now was to accept her black skin as being real and unchangeable." This theme of self-acceptance is typically Renaissance: to be one's dark-skinned self and not a bleached-out imitation is the essence of emancipation. But Thurman's hard-won victory (the conflict he is acting out, through Emma Lou, is clear enough) does not prove to be decisive. His second novel [*Infants of the Spring*] shows him to be incapable of

holding his feelings toward the race in stable equilibrium.

Infants of the Spring is a neurotic novel, in which Thurman broods introspectively on the "failure" of the Negro Renaissance. (pp. 92-3)

[The] canker of Bohemianism, in Thurman's eyes, . . . threatened to nip the New Negro Movement in the bud. The symbolic setting of his novel is Niggerati Manor, where colored artists, writers, and musicians live in various stages of decadence and sterility. The central characters are Paul, a symbol of dissipated genius, and Ray, a young writer who struggles to free himself from an obsessive race-consciousness. Much of the "action" consists merely of dialogue, which serves to convey the author's impressions of the Negro Renaissance.

After a series of satirical sketches of leading Renaissance personalities, the novel draws to a depressing close. Paul commits suicide in such a manner that his masterpiece is destroyed. A drawing on the title page of the ruined manuscript pictures Niggerati Manor with a foundation of crumbling stone . . . . The dream of the Negro Renaissance was, for Thurman, to end thus in disillusion and despair. The tone of the novel is too bitter, however, and Thurman's sense of personal failure too acute, to accept his critique of the Renaissance at face value.

It was appropriate enough that Thurman should seek to become the undertaker of the Negro Renaissance; at the time, he was busy digging his own grave with bad gin. His self-hatred, and the suicidal impulses which it engendered, were the central facts of his later years. No one who has read *The Blacker the Berry* will doubt that the source of this self-hatred was his dark complexion. The old struggle for self-acceptance, which Thurman had apparently won through Emma Lou, is reopened and finally abandoned through the character of Ray. "Eventually," Ray remarks, "I'm going to renounce Harlem and all it stands for." This mood of renunciation pervades *Infants of the Spring.* In his wholesale indictment of the Renaissance generation, Thurman was simply working out his self-destructive impulses on the level of a literary movement. (pp. 93-4)

> *Robert Bone, "The Harlem School," in his* The Negro Novel in America, *revised edition, Yale University Press, 1965, pp. 65-94.*

Daniel Walden (essay date 1987)

[*In the excerpt below, Walden surveys Thurman's career, focusing on the social and racial climate that influenced it.*]

Although New York City in the 1920s was for most whites a joyous, expanding metropolis, for many blacks, Wallace Thurman among them, it was a city of refuse, not a city of refuge. Growing up at a time when many Americans—after World War I—were eager to get back what Warren Harding would call "normalcy," Thurman reached Harlem at the moment when white Americans looked to black America, north of 110th Street and along Lexington and Convent Avenues, as the bastion of primitivism and earthiness. Some whites came to gape, some to laugh, but many came to seek exuberant escape in the so-called exotic primitivism of Negro cabaret life. As Langston Hughes exclaimed in *The Big Sea,* "thousands of whites came to Harlem night after night, thinking the Negroes loved to have them there, and firmly believing that all Harlemites left their houses at sundown to sing and dance in cabarets, because most of the whites saw nothing but the cabarets, not the houses."

During these years, nearly all the black writers and artists drifted to New York. As might be expected most were drawn by the promise of New York City as a center where art and literature would flourish. In Hughes' contemporary opinion, what was important was that black writers spoke their own words, their own truths, no matter whether blacks, or whites, were pleased or offended. For in this decade, publishers opened their doors to black authors and poets and artists. What was significant was that in New York City the NAACP, *The Crisis, Opportunity,* and several black newspapers flourished. As early as 1920, W. E .B. Du Bois pointed out, Claude McKay, Langston Hughes, Jean Toomer, Countee Cullen, Anne Spencer, Abram Harris and Jessie Fauset had already been published in *The Crisis.*

Of the whites drawn to Harlem and to black life, only a minority were interested in the discovery and development of black talent. For black writers and artists the 1920s represented an era or opportunities and hopes. It was the decade in which the writers replaced apologetics and militancy and racial propaganda with their own voices as the *raison d'être.* True, Walter White's *Fire in the Flint* (1924), W. E. B. Du Bois' *Dark Princess* (1928), and George Schuyler's *Slaves Today* (1931) maintained an offensive, anti-racist posture. But most writers tried to be writers; following the advice of Henry James (whether they had read him or not), they let their stories unfold and their characters evolve out of their stories. In some cases, the psychology of caste and the racial experience, echoing Charles Chesnutt's early models, became dominant aspects; for Rudolph Fisher, the everyday life of blacks in Harlem, linked to the trauma of Southern exposure to Northern urbanism, was played out much as everyday life was depicted by other authors. And, in Carl Van Vechten's *Nigger Heaven* (1926), a white novelist so successfully portrayed blacks in urban New York that he called up the most violent pros and cons of the period, and to a certain extent set out the parameters within which all black novelists would be judged. A "blow in the face" to Du Bois, *Nigger Heaven* was "an absorbing story" to James Welden Johnson: Gwendolyn Bennett coined "Van Vechtenizing around," to describe the ways in which tourists saw Harlem. As Hugh Gloster put it, no matter the negative criticism, the pull of the exotic exerted an influence hard to deny. It is in the grip of all these forces that Wallace Thurman, with William Jordan Rapp,

produced *Harlem* (1929), a play dealing with life in the ghetto, *The Blacker the Berry* (1929), and *Infants of the Spring* (1932).

Wallace Thurman, "the most symbolic figure of the Literary Renaissance in Harlem," brilliant, consumptive, desperate, was the focal point for black Bohemia in the late 1920s. The inner circle included Rudolph Fisher, M.D., writer, Langston Hughes, poet, and Zora Neale Hurston, novelist. They knew the great ones, W. E. B. Du Bois, James Welden Johnson, Carl Van Vechten; and they knew the other Renaissance writers and critics, George Schuyler, Countee Cullen, Jean Toomer, Arna Bontemps, Alain Locke, Benjamin Brawley, and Charles S. Johnson. It was Du Bois, Locke and Brawley who contended that a true renaissance in black literature was in the making. The inner circle wished it were true but had their doubts. Of them all, Thurman's desire to become "a *very* great writer like Gorki or Thomas Mann," said Langston Hughes, stuck out like a sore thumb. Unfortunately, the strong feeling that he was "merely a journalistic writer" made him melancholy, suicide-prone, and disillusioned; his self-hatred engendered by his dark complexion, and his reliance on bad gin, were by-products of the despair which marked his decline and early death after a brilliant and promising career. (pp. 201-03)

Although Van Vechten's emphasis on jazz, sex, atavism and primitivism was rejected in many quarters, his influence was profound. It is in this context that Wallace Thurman in 1929 published *The Blacker the Berry,* a study of interracial color prejudice operating upon Emma Lou Morgan, daughter of a light-skinned mother whose family motto was "whiter and whiter every generation" until their grandchildren would be able to pass and race would no longer be a problem. Feeling the burden of blackness, as Wallace Thurman did, his character Emma Lou is further depressed when she learns that it was her color that forced the estrangement of her mother from her second husband. Leaving Boise, Idaho, as close as Thurman apparently could get in urban tone to Salt Lake City, Emma Lou attends the University of Southern California (also paralleling Thurman's career), and tries to get a job in Harlem. Denied employment because she is so dark, she falls in love with a mulatto-Filipino, Alva, but her obsession with color drives him off. After finishing college at the City College of New York, she tries again to help Alva, who is now an alcoholic and burdened by an idiot child, and is again rejected. Emma Lou, seemingly an ordinary, normal person in every way, is apparently the victim of color prejudice, in both white *and* black America.

Thurman, probably influenced by *Nigger Heaven* or by the prevailing disposition to portray Harlem in its most vivid colors, describes Harlem's cabaret life, the rent parties, speakeasies (this was during Prohibition), vaudeville shows and ballroom dances as they were. But his emphasis on sex, alcohol, dancing, and gambling makes the balance disappear. Even serious fictionalized discussions with Langston Hughes (Tony Crews) and Zora Neale Hurston (Cora Thurston) turn into reinforcements of the author's already apparently set opinions. During a discussion with Campbell Kitchen (clearly modeled on Carl Van Vechten), we read that it was Van Vechten who "first began the agitation in the higher places of journalism which gave impetus to the spiritual craze . . . It was he who sponsored most of the younger Negro writers, personally carrying their work to publishers and editors." In spite of Thurman's disinclination to give Du Bois, Locke, and Johnson credit for *their* pioneering work, it is true that Van Vechten can be credited with earnest spadework. Significantly, in his novel Thurman was most angry at those blacks who perpetuated discrimination against blacks, especially black women. The doggerel verse he quotes is eloquent testimony to that: "Yaller gal rides in a limousine; / Brownskin gal rides the train. / Black gal rides in an ol' oxcart, / But she gits there jes' the same."

Thurman, contrary to the emerging literary style, made a dark-skinned girl his protagonist. Black, except for the followers of Marcus Garvey, did not become fashionable or popular until the 1960s. On the other hand in all fairness it has to be said that Thurman's point was that prejudice and racism existed within the black community, not that there was an inherent advantage in blackness. Given the growing belief that "white was right," as Mrs. Morgan put it, it was not surprising that Emma Lou's color led to her mother's rejection; in turn, following the practice of many dark-skinned women (and some men), Emma Lou used skin whiteners and hair straighteners and preferred light-skinned men. At the end, if one accepts the proviso that experience is the best teacher, Emma Lou has come to terms with her identity and her color.

Unfortunately, the title, taken from an old Negro folk saying, "The blacker the berry, the sweeter the juice," has to be taken ironically, bitterly. For the point has to be made, Emma Lou was too black, too conscious of her blackness; it had to dawn on her, as it did on Thurman eventually, that the fault lay only partially in her color. As Thurman put it, "what she needed to do now was to accept her black skin as being real and unchangeable, to realize that certain things were, and would be, and with this in mind, begin life anew, always fighting, not so much for acceptance by other people but for acceptance of herself." But this also seems to mean that *The Blacker the Berry,* while inspired by a man's talent and commitment, failed because it lacked subtlety and complexity.

In his second novel, *Infants of the Spring,* the focus is on Niggeratti ("Nigger" plus "literati") Manor, a huge residence cut up into studios for black artists and writers. Actually both blacks and whites live there, most of them unproductive, along with their retinues. Raymond Taylor, a talented writer hampered by his excessive race consciousness, Samuel Carter, a white militant desiring martyrdom, Eustace Savoy, a black singer hesitant about singing Negro spirituals, Pelham Gaylord, a painter and poet of little talent, Paul Arbian, a black, dissipated, homosexual painter, and Stephen Jorgenson, a white obsessed with, then repelled by, black women and primitivistic Harlem, make up the cast. Unfortunately, as Thurman's Taylor puts it, except for Jean Toomer, "the average Negro intellectual and artist has no goal, no standards, no elasticity, no pregnant germ plasm." On the other hand, when the avowed brains and talent of the Negro Renaissance are brought together, their substantive essence is lost in the heat of a socio-political debate over Pan-Africanism, activism or personal self-expression. In common with Langston Hughes's words in "The Negro Artist and the Racial Mountain," whose views he would surely have known, Thurman opted for individuality. "Let each seek his own salvation." Similarly, in accord with Shakespeare's *Hamlet,* that "The canker galls the infants of the spring / Too oft before their buttons be disclosed," Thurman castigated Renaissance artists' and writers' exploitation of the whites from downtown who supported the Renaissance so long as it could remain Niggeratti Manor. In the most sarcastic tones, one of his black characters says, "Being a Negro writer in these days is a racket and I'm going to make the most of it while it lasts."

Thurman was one of the fledgeling writers of the Renaissance. As a character like Raymond Taylor he could imaginatively interact with, and comment on, the personalities integral to the times. Knowing that "The American Negro . . . was entering a new phase in his development," that he "was about to become an important factor in the artistic life of the United States," Raymond still clung to the belief that unless he, or Paul, or others "began to do something worth while, there would be little chance of their being permanently established." The point is that among the emotional arguments, in the midst of the calls for a turn or return to "pagan inheritance," or "Marxism," it is Thurman's balanced view that we admire today. Answering Dr. Parkes (who reflects Alain Locke), the noted college professor who calls for a return to Africa to resurrect "our pagan heritage," as well as Fenderson, who complains about everything, and Madison, who uses Lenin as his role-model, Cedric (Eric Walrond), backed up by Raymond (Thurman), heatedly comments: "Well . . . why not let each young hopeful choose his own path? Only in that way will anything at all be achieved?"

Thurman, brooding and magnetic, to a significant degree ridiculed the Renaissance of which he was part. While he was at the center of this movement, he denounced the quality of the literature because it laid at best a shaky foundation for the future. He looked for reasons within himself and the race. "That ninety-nine and ninety-nine hundredths per cent of the Negro race is patently possessed and motivated by an inferiority complex," he wrote, is a central cause. That he had the talent but not the greatness of theme and expression so needed was another. Given such rationales, not trying was an escape. Yet, as he expressed it in *The Blacker the Berry,* he also wrote it in *Infants of the Spring,* and this must be accepted as vintage Thurman: "Individuality is what we strive for. Let each seek his own salvation."

In Thurman's vision the Renaissance was doomed to fail. "At first glance," it is affirmed at the end of *Infants,* "it could be ascertained that the skyscraper [Niggeratti Manor] would soon crumble and fall, leaving the dominating white lights in full possession of the sky." Given this assumption, Thurman felt that black writers should not be propagandists but writers, that they should not be race writers. It is not surprising that his persona, Raymond, is told that "race to you means nothing. You stand on a peak.... Propaganda you despise. Illusions about Negroes you have none." Nor is it surprising that shortly after *Infants* was published, Thurman, emancipated from everything but himself, liquor, T.B., and despair, died. (pp. 204-07)

Thurman, Robert Bone has written, was the aspiring undertaker of the Negro Renaissance [see except dated 1965]. Consistent with Countee Cullen's advice that the job of the Negro writer was "to create types that are truly representative of us as a people," he tried to remain true to himself; but he misused satire, he paraded his pet hates and he was, finally, too heavy-handed in his writing. On the other side, driven by his anger, his sense of rejection, his consciousness of color, and the realization that there was no resolution in sight, he ended *Infants* on a positive note. Although Paul slashed his wrists with a Chinese dirk, Thurman's forced ending concluded that art would be produced by individuals of talent who were willing to work hard with the self-consciousness that defied crippling doubt.

Thurman undeniably was a writer of power and talent. An insider in the Harlem literary circles, he was even referred to as one of the central pivots of the Harlem Renaissance. Yet when Thurman is weighed as a writer, it is certain that he will be found wanting. Unable to control the rich literary material with which he worked, he consistently imposed a morbid look on his characters and developed stories and novels so atomized that he ultimately wound up at cross purposes with himself. His irony was well placed, whether in **"Cordelia the Crude"** in *Fire,* 1 (November 1926), or in **Harlem** (1929). In the latter work, a simple Southern mother seeing her family torn apart by the vagaries of Harlem, by the "sweet-back" of the "hot-stuff man," by lotteries and vice, by the necessity of having rent parties, is helpless to intervene; religion and family are her refuge of last resort. Cordelia, caught up in the wild life of the city, is almost destroyed by poverty and the city. It was a startlingly realistic drama. It was also a very successful, overly melodramatic play about the harshness of life and black disillusionment. In Edith Isaacs's opinion, "Violent and undisciplined as the play was, it left a sense of photographic reality."

In the same way, Thurman's talent burst out in *The Blacker the Berry* and *Infants of the Spring.* In debunking the "Negro Renaissance," in parading his pessimism, Thurman exemplified how strongly he felt about the enduring quality of the literature of the Harlem writers. He believed, as one of his characters phrased it in *Infants of the Spring,* "Being a Negro writer in these days is a racket, and I'm going to make the most of it while it lasts." No wonder Langston Hughes described him as having a prodigious capacity for gin, though he detested it; no wonder Hughes wrote that Thurman liked being a Negro but thought it a great handicap. Most significantly, as a very dark-skinned black man who met discrimination everywhere, he set out to record honestly and realistically black life in Harlem, but wound up compromising his principles. As Margaret Perry says, "he usually settled for capitalizing on its exotic-erotic elements in order to succeed." Unhappy when forced to be with blacks, rejected so often when with whites, he wrote, "I was fighting hard to refrain from regarding myself as martyr and an outcast." Yet it was both the martyr and outcast that dominated the content and the style of his writing. In the end he exhausted himself trying to please the public while at the same time trying to write with a New Negro honesty. (pp. 208-09)

Thurman's pessimism dominates his satire. The cancer that gnawed at his vitals, the cancer of Bohemianism, was a combination of color, caste and dilettantism. If he had the talent, his heavy-handedness, mixed with equal parts of disillusion and despair, of himself and the alleged achievements of the 1920s, overcame his native ability. "The most self-conscious of the New Negroes," writes Robert Bone, "he ultimately turned his critical insight against himself and the wider movement with which he identified." Wanting to be a very great writer, he seems to have known he was merely a journalist. Melancholy, suicide-prone, he tried to say but ended up shouting that phoniness in the Harlem Renaissance was rampant even as he insisted, with Emersonian firmness, that capitulation to badges and names, to large societies, and dead institutions must give way to the free and individual spirit. Where he meant to write fiction, he wrote criticism; he wrote didactically. He failed, but he failed magnificently.

In December 1934, both Rudolph Fisher and Wallace Thurman died. In Dorothy West's eyes, years after the event, Thurman's death "was the first break in the ranks of the New Negro." Ironically, Thurman, who liked to drink gin, but *didn't* like to drink gin, died of T.B. in the charity ward of City Hospital, Welfare Island, New York. He would like to have believed, as he put it in *The Blacker the Berry,* that everyone must find salvation within one's self, that no one in life need be a total misfit, but he could not totally break with his sense of gloom and despair and rejection and self-abnegation. In terms of his literary contributions, he was one of the significant but less than major figures of the Renaissance. However, to quote Mae Gwendolyn Henderson, "His significance,... far exceeds the work he left behind. Not only was he tremendously influential upon the younger and perhaps more successful writers of the period, but his life itself became a symbol of the New Negro Movement." (pp. 209-10)

Daniel Walden, "'The Canker Galls . . . ,' or, The Short Promising Life of Wallace Thurman," in The Harlem Renaissance Re-examined, *edited by Victor A. Kramer, AMS Press, 1987, pp. 201-11.*

FURTHER READING

Brown, Sterling. "The Urban Scene." In his *The Negro in American Fiction,* pp. 131-50. 1937. Reprint. Port Washington, N.Y.: Kennikat Press, Inc., 1968.
> Analysis of Thurman's "devil's advocate" role in exposing intraracism in *The Blacker the Berry* and the failure of the Harlem Renaissance in *Infants of the Spring.*

Gloster, Hugh. "The Van Vechten Vogue." In his *Negro Voices in American Fiction,* pp. 157-73. Chapel Hill: University of North Carolina Press, 1948.
> Discusses the satirical aspects of *The Blacker the Berry* and *Infants of the Spring.*

Henderson, Mae Gwendolyn. "Portrait of Wallace Thurman." In *The Harlem Renaissance Remembered,* edited by Arna Bontemps, pp. 147-70. New York: Dodd, Mead & Co., 1972.
> Biographical and critical overview.

Huggins, Nathan Irvin. "Art: The Ethnic Province." In his *Harlem Renaissance,* pp. 190-243. New York: Oxford University Press, 1971.
> Brief discussion of Thurman's intent in *Infants of the Spring,* which Huggins calls "one of the best written and most readable novels" of the Harlem Renaissance.

Perkins, Huel D. "Renaissance 'Renegade'?: Wallace Thurman." *Black World* XXV, No. 4 (February 1976): 29-35.
> Examines Thurman's criticism of the Harlem Renaissance. Perkins maintains that the author was a significant and constructive critic of the movement and not, as some commentators have charged, a disloyal and rebellious member.

West, Dorothy. "A Memoir of Wallace Thurman: Elephants Dance." *Black World* XX, No. 1 (November 1970): 77-85.
> Biographical sketch that details Thurman's years in Harlem, bringing into focus his early enthusiasm for the Renaissance and the reasons behind his later skepticism and disillusionment.

Melvin B. Tolson

1898?–1966

(Full name Melvin Beaunorus Tolson) American poet, journalist, and dramatist.

Tolson, an American poet, challenged divisions of race and class in American society and expressed optimism about the possibility of achieving economic and racial equality among all disadvantaged groups. Mariann B. Russell observed: "Concerned with the underdog in general and with the Black underdog in particular, he saw words as weapons in the war against social ills.... [His] lyric encompassed a social, metaphysical, and communal burden."

Tolson was born in Moberly, Missouri. His father, a Methodist minister, moved his family from place to place throughout Missouri and Iowa during Tolson's childhood. Tolson early developed a love for literature, publishing his first poem in an Iowa newspaper at the age of fourteen, and was elected senior-class poet at his high school. He attended Fisk University for a year and then Lincoln University in Pennsylvania, where he became active in public speaking and debate. His speaking skills brought him national recognition when he was debate coach at Wiley College in Marshall, Texas; his successful debate teams often subverted "the color line" of segregation by defeating teams from such prestigious institutions as the University of Southern California and Oxford University. During this period Tolson also examined social issues in "Caviar and Cabbage," his weekly column in the *Washington Tribune,* outlining the concerns and interests of blacks during the Great Depression and World War II. At the age of fifty-four, Tolson was elected mayor of Langston, Oklahoma, an office he held for four terms. He died in 1966.

As a graduate student at Columbia University in 1931, Tolson was strongly influenced by black artists of the Harlem Renaissance as well as by the potential for interracial unity he perceived in Harlem. His poetry collection *A Gallery of Harlem Portraits* (posthumously published in 1979) is an epic depiction of the racial and cultural diversity of Harlem: "Radicals, prizefighters, actors and deacons, / Beggars, politicians, professors and redcaps, / Bulldikers, Babbitts, racketeers and jig-chasers, / Harlots, crapshooters, workers and pink chasers...." Reflecting Tolson's Marxist political views, the poems in *A Gallery of Harlem Portraits* repudiate class divisions created by economic disparity, revealing the author's concern for the rights of the working class: "Then a kike said: *Workers of the world, unite!* / And a dago said: *Let us live!*... / WE ARE THE UNDERDOGS ON A HOT TRAIL!" Tolson's attempts to publish the collection were unsuccessful, and it remained in manuscript for forty years. He first received critical recognition in 1939 when his poem "Dark

Symphony" won a national poetry contest judged by acclaimed writers Frank Marshall Davis, Arna Bontemps, and Langston Hughes. Unlike *A Gallery of Harlem Portraits,* "Dark Symphony" focuses exclusively on the historical experiences and accomplishments of African-Americans. The poem's tone is optimistic, affirming black achievements: "Out of abysses of Illiteracy, / Through labyrinths of Lies, / Across waste lands of Disease... / We advance!..."

Tolson expanded the motif of historical experience in his collection *Rendezvous with America* (1944), which focuses on prejudices that have corrupted American history and the strength the United States derives from its multiple races and heritages. In a characteristically positive outlook, Tolson predicted the emergence of class unity from the chaos and destruction of the 1930s and 1940s. An optimistic tone also pervades *Libretto for the Republic of Liberia* (1953), a long poem written when the author was Poet Laureate of Liberia. Here, Tolson portrayed Liberia as a symbol of universal brotherhood and freedom. He also warned of the instability created by colonialism and the constant struggle for economic dominance, comparing fluctuations of international power to a ferris-wheel. In his column "Caviar and Cabbage," he explained: "On the merry-go-round all seats are on the same level. Nobody goes up; therefore, nobody has to come down.... Racial superiority and class superiority produce the hellish contraption called the Ferris-Wheel of history."

Tolson long wished to write an epic poem about the history of black America from its African origins to the present. Although the planned work was to encompass five books, the author completed only the first volume, *Harlem Gallery: Book I, The Curator* (1965), before his death. Set in a Harlem art gallery, the poem explores the difficulties and conflicts experienced by black artists in white-dominated America. The museum curator, a man of African, Irish and Jewish heritage, and his friend Dr. Nkomo, a native African, debate the nature of the relationship between the artist and his environment. Praising the work's eclectic combination of classical and oral traditions, Rita Dove asserted: "Tolson's extravagant verbiage pays homage to the essence of 'style'—he mixes colloquial and literary references as well as diction; irony and pathos, slapstick and pontifications sit / side by side." Although *Harlem Gallery: Book I* was more widely reviewed than Tolson's earlier works, it suffered criticism for its incorporation of a complex, culturally diverse structure at a time when many black writers were supporting a literary aesthetic of more distinctly African origins. Some commentators asserted that Tolson's poetry was subjected to the same critical biases and labeling he depicted as impediments to black artists in *Harlem Gallery:* "Poor Boy Blue, / the Great White World / and the Black Bourgeoisie / have shoved the Negro Artists into the white and not-white dichotomy, / the Afroamerican dilemma in the arts— / the dialect of / to be or not to be / a Negro."

Tolson's skillful delineation of character, his ability to turn discussions of aesthetics into social commentary, his breadth of vision, and his deftness with language garnered critical acclaim as well as controversy. Admitting that *Harlem Gallery* presents the same complexity and involved syntax that rendered Tolson's earlier works somewhat inaccessible, Blyden Jackson asserted that "nevertheless [it] is a fine product of the imagination.... [Tolson] achieved a memorable presentation of the human comedy and of human values." Responding to other critics' neglect of Tolson's work, Robert Donald Spector declared: "Here is a poet whose language, comprehensiveness, and values demand a critical sensitivity rarely found in any establishment.... Whatever his reputation in the present critical climate, Tolson stands firmly as a great American poet."

(For further information about Tolson's life and works, see *Black Writers; Contemporary Authors*, Vols. 89-92, 124; *Contemporary Literary Criticism*, Vol. 36; and *Dictionary of Literary Biography*, Vols. 48, 76.)

PRINCIPAL WORKS

Rendezvous with America (poetry) 1944
Fire in the Flint (drama) [adapted from Walter S. White's novel of the same title] 1952
Libretto for the Republic of Liberia (poetry) 1953
Harlem Gallery: Book I, The Curator (poetry) 1965
A Gallery of Harlem Portraits (poetry) 1979
Caviar and Cabbage: Selected Columns by Melvin B. Tolson from the Washington Tribune, 1937-1944 (newspaper columns) 1982

Rita Dove (essay date 1985)

[*In the following excerpt, Dove discusses Tolson's epic poem* Harlem Gallery, *challenging the negative critical response it received upon publication.*]

When Melvin B. Tolson published part I of his projected epic poem, **Harlem Gallery,** in 1965, critical response was immediate and controversial. Whereas the mainstream literati (read: white) were enthusiastic, proclaiming Tolson's piece as the lyrical successor of *The Waste Land, The Bridge,* and *Paterson,* proponents of the rapidly solidifying Black Aesthetic were less impressed. Part of the controversy was sparked by Karl Shapiro's well-meaning Foreword. "Tolson writes and thinks in Negro," Shapiro pronounced, prompting poet and essayist Sarah Webster Fabio to remark:

> Melvin Tolson's language is most certainly not "Negro" to any significant degree. The weight of that vast, bizarre, pseudo-literary diction is to be placed back into the American mainstream where it rightfully and wrongmindedly belongs.

Shapiro describes **Gallery** as "a narrative work so fantastically stylized that the mind balks at comparisons." Divided into 24 sections corresponding to the letters in the Greek alphabet, **Harlem Gallery** contains allusions to Vedic Gods, Tintoretto, and Pre-Cambrian pottery, as well as snippets in Latin and French. No wonder some of his black contemporaries thought he was "showing off."

To be sure, the timing was bad for such a complex piece. The Civil Rights movement was at its peak, and Black Consciousness had permeated every aspect of Afro-American life, including its literature. Black writers rejected white literary standards, proclaiming their own Black Aesthetic which extolled literature written for the common people, a literature that was distinctly oral, using the language patterns and vocabulary of the street to arouse feelings of solidarity and pride among Afro-Americans.

Although Shapiro prefaced his precocious linguistic analysis with a righteous outburst against the "liberal" politics of American tokenism, the suspicion had already been raised that M. B. Tolson was the white critics' flunky. "A great poet has been living in our midst for decades and is almost totally unknown..." Shapiro exclaimed; Paul Breman, however, in his contribution to *Poetry and Drama, The Black American Writer* (vol. II), declared "[Tolson] postured for a white audience, and with a wicked sense of humour gave it just what it wanted: an entertaining darkey using almost comically big words as the best wasp tradition demands of its educated house-niggers."

Who *was* this Tolson? Could he be the same man appointed Poet Laureate of Liberia and commissioned to write the *Libretto for the Republic of Liberia* in celebration of Liberia's Centennial? Allen Tate had written a patronizing introduction to this piece; conversely, William Carlos Williams salutes the *Libretto* in *Paterson.* Could the "white man's darkie" be the same man who taught at black colleges all his life, the teacher who gleefully watched his debate students defeat the debate team at Oxford? Could he be the same poet who said, "I will visit a place T.S. Eliot never visited"? And is this that most "unNegro-like" voice that Fabio protested:

> but often I hear a dry husk-of-locust blues
> descend the tone ladder of a laughing goose,
> syncopating between
> the faggot and the noose:
> "Black Boy, O Black Boy,
> is the port worth the cruise?"
> *Harlem Gallery*

Tolson's virtuoso use of folk talk and street jive was forgotten whenever the readers stumbled across more "literary" allusions like "a mute swan not at Coole." In the controversy over racial loyalties and author's intent, nobody bothered to read *Harlem Gallery* on its own terms. The poem—and the story it tries to tell—got lost in the crossfire.

Harlem Gallery, Book I: The Curator is the first part of a proposed five-part poem delineating the odyssey of the black man in America.... In *Book I: The Curator* (the only book Tolson completed before his death in 1966), the role of the black artist is examined on several levels. The narrator, a Mulatto of "afroirishjewish origins" and ex-Professor of Art, is curator of the Harlem Gallery. His gallery allows him ample opportunity to observe the shenanigans of the black bourgeoisie; his dealings with starving artists such as John Laugart, as well as his friendship with other black cultural figures, give him glimpses into all strata of black life. The Curator's alter ego, Dr. Nkomo, is his stronger, more prideful counterpart; taken together, their observations form a dialectic of the position of blacks—and most specifically, the black artist—in white America.

The Curator muses on the predicament of being black and an artist in America. "O Tempora, / *what* is man?" he asks in **"Beta"**; "O Mores, / what *manner* of man is this?" Spliced into this highly stylized ode are little stories—dramatic monologues, vignettes—which serve to illustrate the philosophical stance of the more discursive parts. These stories exhibit classical narrative techniques, as well as several storytelling "riffs" which are rooted in the Afro-American oral tradition.

The lives of three black artists are limned. The first, the half-blind, destitute painter John Laugart, we first meet in **"Zeta."** In his search for new work to show, the Curator visits Laugart in his "catacomb Harlem flat." The character sketch of Laugart is as gritty and muscular as anything in Dickens:

> His sheaf of merino hair
> an agitated ambush,
> he bottomed upon the hazard of a bed—
> sighing:
> "The eagle's wings,
> as well as the wren's,
> grow weary of flying."
> His vanity was a fast-day soup—thin, cold.

Laugart has just finished his masterpiece, *Black Bourgeoisie,* a painting the Curator feels is certain to arouse the ire of the patrons of his gallery. Yet Laugart refuses to compromise his art in order to pay the rent. The consequences—related in a dry postscript—"He was robbed and murdered in his flat, / and the only witness was a Hamletian rat."

John Laugart's tragic fate is sandwiched between the shimmering overture of the first five sections and the underworld glimmer of the Harlem of the Thirties. The Curator leaves Laugart to his chill vigil and stops in at Aunt Grindle's Elite Chitterling Shop to shoot the philosophic bull with his ace boon coon, Doctor Obi Nkomo. They are next seen at a *Vernissage* at the Harlem Gallery, where sublimated versions of black history and its heroes hanging on the wall provide ironic contrast to the ignominious private lives of the prospective buyers, exemplified by Mr. Guy Delaporte III, "the symbol / of Churchianity" to the "Sugar Hill elite."

"Hey man, when you gonna close this dump?" cries Hideho Heights as he bursts into the hushed gallery. Our second black Artist, the "poet laureate of Harlem," is boisterous and irreverent. He stops his good-natured ribbing only long enough to declaim his latest poem, a tribute to "Satchmo" Armstrong. Those sections of *Harlem Gallery* devoted to Hideho Heights display a virtuoso rendering of narrative layers—a tribute, perhaps, to Heights's own extravagant linguistic paeans. In the section **"Mu,"** the scene at the Zulu Club provides a backdrop to Hideho's recitation of his rather militant version of the John Henry ballad. This story-within-a-story, however, is interrupted by the anecdotes of the "Zulu Club Wits," whose tableside conversation ranges from an anecdote about service in a Jim Crow restaurant to an animal fable reminiscent of Brer Rabbit (which draws its spirit from Africa) about the mistreated minorities in America: Hideho relates the "strange but true" story of the sea-turtle and the shark. Driven by hunger to swallow the sea-turtle whole, the shark is utterly helpless as the "sly reptilian marine" "gnaws / ...and gnaws...and gnaws... / *his* way to freedom."

The dialogues in the Zulu Club scenes show how close Tolson's baroque surface mirrors typical black street speech. When Heights pinches a "fox," she whirls around and "signifies" on him:

> "*What* you smell isn't cooking," she said.
> Hideho sniffed.
> "Chanel No. 5," he scoffed,
> "from Sugar Hill."

Hideho Heights's John Henry poem ("The night John Henry is born an ax / of lightning splits the sky, / and a hammer of thunder pounds the earth, / and the eagles and panthers cry!") is right in the tradition of great black ballads, as well as incorporating the bawdiness ("Poor Boy Blue! Poor Boy Blue! / I came to Lenox Avenue, / but I find up here a Bitchville, too!") of a "toast." In her excellent study on black speech patterns, *Talkin and Testifyin: The Language of Black America,* Geneva Smitherman describes the toast:

> Toasts represent a form of black verbal art requiring memory and linguistic fluency from the narrators. Akin to grand epics in the Graeco-Roman style, the movement of the Toast is episodic, lengthy and detailed.... Since the overall narrative structure is loose and episodic, there is both room and necessity for individual rhetorical embellishments and fresh imaginative imagery.... the material is simply an extension of black folk narrative in the oral tradition.

In fact, the whole of **Harlem Gallery** is very much like the Toasts to Shine and Stag-o-lee, those mythic "bad-men" heroes in black oral tradition. In Tolson's case, however, his hero is the archetypal Black Artist.

Many of Tolson's narrative techniques are based on devices exclusively rooted in the Afro-American tradition. "Metaphors and symbols in Spirituals and Blues / have been the Negro's manna in the Great White World," sighs one Zulu Club wit; perhaps the most vivid declaration of this appears in **"Iota"**:

> In the Harlem Gallery, pepper birds
> clarion in the dusk of dawn
> the flats and sharps of pigment-words—
> quake the walls of Mr Rockefeller's Jericho
> with the new New Order of things,
> as the ambivalence of dark dark laughter
> rings
> in Harlem's immemorial winter.

The third Harlem artist is Mister Starks, conductor of the Harlem Symphony orchestra. Mister (his mother gave him the first name "Mister" so that whites would have to address him with respect) appears in sections **"Rho," "Sigma," "Tau"** and **"Upsilon."** To relate the circumstances of Stark's mysterious death, Tolson uses all the devices of the criminal drama, right down to the Smoking Gun and the Deep Dark Secret Revealed in the Secret Papers.

"Rho" begins with a phone call from the police station. "O sweet Jesus, / make the bastard leave me alone!" a hysterical Heddy Starks screams. The Curator recalls how Mister Starks met Heddy, then a striptease dancer called "Black Orchid," and how she used "The intelligentsia of Mister's bent" as "steps on the aerial ladder / of the black and tan bourgeosie."

Next comes a flashback to the day of Starks's death. He has sent a copy of his Last Will and Testament to his friend Ma'am Shears, owner of the Angelus Funeral Home. Fearing the worst, she phones to discourage him: "It's not like Black folks to commit suicide," she pleads. Stark's only response is a dry repartee: "Aren't we civilized yet? The Will contains explicit instructions for Starks's funeral, as well as an admonishment to his wife to turn over to the Curator the manuscript she has "possessed / with malice aforethought." Seven pages after Heddy's hysterical phone call, we learn why she is phoning: "arrested at a marijuana party / and haunted in her cell," she has decided to give the manuscript to the Curator and make "her peace with God."

Starks is found with a bullet in his heart; the gun is found in the toilet bowl of a character named Crazy Cain. Now we know "who-dun-it," but we don't know anything about the murderer. For that information we need to read the manuscript, a collection of poetical portraits written by Starks and titled *Harlem Vignettes.*

The section **"Upsilon"** is comprised entirely of these vignettes, which begin with a painfully honest self-portrait. Starks is aware that he has compromised his talents, writing boogie-woogie records when he should have been pursuing the excellence of his one triumph, the *Black Orchid Suite.* The *Harlem Vignettes* are incisive thumbnail sketches of many of the characters already encountered in **Harlem Gallery,** including John Laugart, Hideho Heights, and the inscrutable Curator. In Crazy Cain's sketch we learn that Mister Starks had fired him from the Harlem Symphony; he was also the illegitimate son of Black Orchid and Mr. Guy Delaporte III.

Can I get a Witness? Because what Tolson has been doing all along is testifying, which is nothing more than to "tell the truth through story." The *Vignettes* are important not only as an advancement of the plot, but for their function as narrative history—in designing them, Tolson is a sort of literary counterpart to the African griot, the elder assigned the task of memorizing tribal history.

There are a host of other characteristics typical of black speech which appear in **Harlem Gallery**—mimicry, exaggerated language, spontaneity, bragadoccio. There is one narrative technique, however, which informs the overall structure of Tolson's piece. Smitherman calls this mode of presentation "narrative sequencing" and observes that many Afro-American stories are actually abstract observations about the larger questions of life rendered into concrete narratives:

> The relating of events (real or hypothetical) becomes a black rhetorical strategy to explain a point, to persuade holders of opposing views to one's own point of view.... This meandering away from the "point" takes the listener on episodic journeys and

over tributary rhetorical routes, but like the flow of nature's rivers and streams, it all eventually leads back to the source. Though highly applauded by blacks, this narrative linguistic style is exasperating to whites who wish you'd be direct and hurry up and get to the point.

Tolson doesn't stop there, but employs another important technique of black / African storytelling—what Smitherman calls "tonal semantics": using rhythm and inflection to carry the *implication* of a statement. "Oh yes, it *bees* that way sometimes," an old blues lyric goes; Tolson syncopates his passages by erratic line lengths strung on a central axis, thus propelling our eye down the page while stopping us up on short lines:

> The school of the artist
> is
> the circle of wild horses,
> heads centered,
> as they present to the wolves
> a battery of heels...

Harlem Gallery is composed according to Tolson's **"S-Trinity of Parnassus"**—the melding of sound, sight and sense. Sound refers to the oral nature of the poem— "Just as sound, / not spelling, / is the white magic of rhyming in the poet's feat..." Tolson meant for his lines to be read aloud; the visual impact of the centered lines contributes to the forward thrust that a lively oral recitation would possess. "Sense" refers to both meaning and the sensory aspect of language.

Tolson's extravagant verbiage pays homage to the essence of "style"—he mixes colloquial and literary references as well as diction; irony and pathos, slapstick and pontification sit side-by-side. And if we look closely at **_Harlem Gallery_'s** dazzling array of allusions—one component of what Sarah Webster Fabio calls Tolson's "vast, bizarre, pseudo-literary diction,"—we find no favoritism for any social or cultural group.... If anything, Tolson is deliberately complicating our pre-conceived notions of cultural—and, by further implication, existential—order.

Even the title of Tolson's poem can be taken a thousand different ways. Its primary meaning—the art gallery in Harlem which the Curator runs—is embellished by a host of secondary connotations: 1) the peanut gallery (cheaper balcony seats in a movie theater, where blacks were relegated in segregated establishments); 2) the art gallery as symbol, suggesting a reading of the poem as a series of *portraits* (an earlier Tolson work, *A Gallery of Harlem Portraits,* is similar to Mister Starks's *Harlem Vignettes* in that it is more a collection of portraits than a tale); 3) the sense of gallery as a promenade; Tolson's characters certainly "exhibit" themselves, and Tolson makes a case for the hero as stylist; for Hideho Heights, Mister Starks, the Curator and Doctor Nkomo, style *is* being. This importance of "style" finds its more popular counterparts in the lyrics of James Brown and the hot "cool" image of Prince; you make do with what you got, you take an inch and run with it. As Ronald Walcott says in his essay "Ellison, Gordone and Tolson: Some Notes on the Blues, Style and Space":

> For Melvin Tolson, the victories attainable through style are not only real, considerable and worthy of record, but they are indicative as well of his people's invincible sense of the possible...; style, if one takes it seriously as an expression of vision, *is* substance, insofar as it reflects and determines one's experience, assessment and response being what experience, after all, is about.

Harlem Gallery is not merely a showcase for Tolson's linguistic and lyrical virtuosity; neither is it a hodge-podge of anecdotes and small lives set like cameos in the heavy silver of philosophical discourse. It is to be viewed *not* as the superficial "Sugar Hill elite" inspect the art works hanging at the exhibition in the Curator's gallery. Rather, the lives of John Laugart, Hideho Heights and Mister Starks should be seen as illustrations of the three possibilities / alternatives for the black artist. One can embrace the Bitch-Goddess Success (personified by Hedda Stark / "Black Orchid"), as did Mister Starks: "My talent was an Uptown whore," he says of himself, "my wit a Downtown pimp." One can, like Laugart, remain uncompromising and be spurned by one's own. Or one can lead a double life, producing crowd-pleasers (which don't necessarily have to lack aesthetic principles) while creating in secrecy the works one hopes will last. The Curator discovers Hideho's double life one night when he takes the poet home, dead-drunk in a taxi; on the table the Curator discovers a poem "in the modern idiom" called *E. and O. E.*— which happens to be the title of a psychological poem for which Tolson received *Poetry* magazine's Bess Hokin award in 1952.

Where does Tolson place himself in this "trinity that stinks the ermine robes"? Certainly not with Mister Starks, although he is sympathetic to Starks's weakness. And, similarities notwithstanding, he does not identify himself with the Poet Laureate of Harlem. Although he admires Hideho's flair and to a great extent believes in Heights's aesthetic manifesto ("A work of art is a two-way street, / not a dead end, / where an artist and a hipster meet. / The form and content in a picture or a song / should blend like the vowels in a diphthong...") Tolson certainly didn't hide his "difficult" poems from the public.

Tolson's meditation on the plight of the black American artist emerges most vividly in **"Psi."** The Curator sees his place in America quite clearly. "Black Boy," he begins, "let me get up from the white man's Table of Fifty Sounds / in the kitchen; let me gather the crumbs and cracklings / of this autobio-fragment / before the curtain with the skull and bones descends." The kitchen is the place for servants, but it is also the place where scraps of song and gossip blend to become a marvellous "kitchen talk."

Paradoxically it is John Laugart, the artist given least space in *Harlem Gallery,* who most exemplifies Tolson's own sense of artistic responsibility. And though Tolson didn't die destitute and anonymous—in fact, he received the annual poetry award of the American Academy of Arts and Letters a few months before his death in 1966—he was misunderstood by many of those he loved most, by those to whom he dedicated his energies in the creation of his last work—the black intellectuals. No one understood this predicament better than Tolson himself. As he has the Curator say near the end of *Harlem Gallery:*

> Poor Boy Blue,
> the Great White World
> and the Black Bourgeoisie
> have shoved the Negro Artist into
> the white and non-white dichotomy,
> the Afroamerican dilemma in the Arts—
> the dialectic of
> to be or not to be
> a Negro.

(pp. 109-17)

Rita Dove, "Telling It Like It I-S 'IS': Narrative Techniques in Melvin Tolson's 'Harlem Gallery'," in New England Review and Bread Loaf Quarterly, *Vol. VIII, No. 1, Autumn, 1985, pp. 109-17.*

Mariann B. Russell (essay date 1986)

[*In the following excerpt, Russell explores the evolution of style in Tolson's poetry.*]

[Tolson] does not belong to that stream of Anglo-American poetry which is purely lyric, expressing directly and mellifluously the poet's own emotions. He concerns himself, on the contrary, with social issues as the barebones of life. His style comes closer to oratorical rhetoric than to song, and his poem is generally public rather than confessional.

The son of a "fighting preacher"—"I used to watch my Dad in the pulpit and feel proud ... "—Tolson was himself a great speaker and debate coach as well as a director of theater. Concerned with the underdog in general and with the Black underdog in particular, he saw words as weapons in the war against social ills. Closely linked to the Afro-American oral tradition and the personal commitment to fighting injustice, he shaped a Christo-Marxist worldview. As in the poetry of others the thirties, his lyric encompassed a social, metaphysical, and communal burden.

Over the years he had four books of poetry published. The first, written about 1934, was brought out posthumously. *A Gallery of Harlem Portraits,* as it was called, contained verses about Harlemites. His next book, was *Rendezvous with America* (1944), a collection somewhat influenced by World War II; his third volume, *Libretto for the Republic of Liberia* (1953), was written after he had been chosen the poet-laureate of the country so named. In "academic" style the booklength ode celebrates the African nation. His final volume, *Harlem*

Gallery (1965), was another booklength ode, intended as the beginning of an epic about the American Black. (pp. 1-2)

The first book, *Portraits,* responds to the remark by a fellow student, himself German-American: "Say, we've never had a Negro epic." Tolson finds precedent for the genre in the Anglo-American literary heritage. His models are, among others, Longfellow, Whittier, Milton, Tennyson, and Poe. (pp. 2-3)

When Tolson presents in *Portraits* approximately two hundred characters significant of the Black community, his worldview becomes clear. The tragicomic tone emanates from the assumption that "the basis of racial prejudice in the United States is economic" (*Caviar and Cabbage*). He sees the Harlem community, with its great variety of types, classes, and colors, not as the exotic area of "jungle-bunny" fame but as the subject of an "earthy, unromantic and sociological literature." Throughout the book, indirectly and sometimes directly, Tolson advocates the union of the masses, poor white and poor Black, as the solution to racial and class discrimination. The final goal of proletarian unity is an apocalyptic democracy—classless, multiracial, multicultural—an attainable utopia.

The hero of *Portraits* is the "underdog," who might some day understand and assume his own destiny. Those Harlemites who already have such knowledge are more directly heroic. The group includes Big Jim Casey and Zip Lightner, proletarian heroes who live for the union of Black and white workers. But the particularly flawed hero is Vergil Ragsdale who, as his name suggests, is the poet of the people. He shares their exploited condition. Though there are more effective artists, he appears at greatest length. His perspective may most approximate Tolson's view then:

> Harlem, O Harlem,
> City of the Big Niggers,
> Graveyard of the Dark Masses,
> Soapbox of the Red Apocalypse ....
>
> *(Portraits)*

Sustained by gin and cocaine, Vergil, the dishwasher at Manto's cafe, dreams of completing his epic poem to Harlem. Although he truly foresees his own pathetic death from tuberculosis, he does not predict the real tragedy: an ignorant landlady will burn the poem, his raison d'être, as trash. Still, this character articulates and represents his people's condition as well as imagines their retribution. His life is ambiguous, as is his heroism.

The style of these poems suits Tolson's epic intention. Characters, presented in short vignettes of about a page, represent the great variety of Harlem humanity, from Peg Leg Snelson to Mrs. Alpha Devine to the Black Moses. As with the poems in *Spoon River,* each of these short ones ends with a climax, a dramatic event, a revelation, a statement, or, in many instances, a blues verse. Tolson, influenced by the imagists, relies on presentation more than on commentary. The larger poetic structure of the entire book, however, lacks variety as poem after poem is introduced mechanically. The diction characterizes occasionally the people in dialect and blues, but the larger voice is the narrator's. The latter speaks of the "little man" as victim but assumes an appreciative tone. The poem presents nobly the techniques of survival in a blues style.

Tolson's next book, *Rendezvous with America,* continues the epic intention in a different vein. As the author broadens his thematic concerns from Harlem to various places in America and to the world at large, the social concerns deepen. The subject here is man—Black and white—as revealed through economics, sociology, and psychology. But the heroes are still political and artistic. Such poets as Sandburg and Whitman set precedents for Tolson's celebration of human potential, despite the actual corruption, inequality, and injustice in still flawed America. Democracy, true justice, and multiculture continue to engage him: "These States breed freedom in and in my bone: / I hymn their virtues and their sins atone" (*Rendezvous*).

The epic strain here is less obvious than in *Portraits.* Under the impetus of World Ward II, Tolson sees good and evil written large in human affairs. Celebration of American promise and human potential go hand in hand with the praise of such historical figures as Nat Turner, Frederick Douglas, and Harriet Tubman. The book is replete with heroic figures (and some villains) who become symbolic in the literary context—Daniel Boone, Joe Dimaggio, Thomas Paine, Abraham Lincoln, and many more.

How then do these hymns to America and humanity differ from the art in Rockefeller Center during the 1930s or from Fourth of July oratory? Although the poetry emphasizes American ideals, it escapes from being merely patriotic encomia. The poetry is skillfully grounded in realistic observation. In many poems from **"Ex-Judge at the Bar"** to **"Vesuvius,"** Tolson illustrates the "idols of the tribe"—those deliberately fostered myths of race, caste, and class that separate mankind. His optimism takes root in the faith that the masses will eventually see through the snares, shams, and hypocrisies to a republican ideal. His ironic—sometimes satiric—tone works against any blind faith in the American dream; he reveals frequently through incident, character, or animal imagery the gulf between the dream and reality.

By now he has worked out for himself a poetic ideal. He refers to the "'3 S's of Parnassus'—Sight, Sound, and Sense." Sight concerns the look of a poem on a page. He experiments frequently with centered placement, especially of short lines, to emphasize his point. At other times he works a short line against a longer one for visual effect. His second "S" refers to sound. Sensitive to the ear, he writes poetry to be read aloud—he seldom uses an eye-rhyme. His frequent use of parallelism encompasses both sound and sight. The last "S" means

"sense," meaning and imagination—chiefly the use of figurative language. Tolson's tropes depend on often startling associations or similarities, frequently using personifications and synechdoche to link seemingly opposed realities in a kind of imaginative dialectic.

Some examples of Tolson's figurative language appear in the long title poem, **"Rendezvous with America"**: "his bat cuts a vacuum," "surfed in white acclaim," "scaling the Alpine ranges of drama with the staff of song," "blue-printing the cabala of the airways," "imprisoning the magic of symphonies with a baton," "enwombing the multiple soul of the New World." Although some of these metaphors are not entirely satisfactory, they do illustrate the quality and kind of Tolson's imagery. (pp. 3-5)

Throughout *Rendezvous,* with few exceptions (there are very few private poems), Tolson practices oratorical rhetoric and evinces social concern. Here the reader encounters a variety of styles in the four long poems, **"Rendezvous with America," "Dark Symphony," "Of Men and Cities,"** and **"Tapestries of Time."** There is still greater experimentation in the short poems grouped in sections including free verse, Shakespearean sonnet, ballad, and ballade. One poem in iambic monometer, **"Song for Myself,"** is a poetic tour de force, as the diversity in poetic forms increases.

Even where there may be a dramatic incident, or a striking character in the short poems, it has a parabolic effect in building to a climax. The effective **"Ballad of the Rattlesnake"** is framed by another poem which portrays Black and white sharecroppers. Although they extend now beyond the specific Harlem community, Tolson's concerns remain now in the deeper structure, the same as those in *Portraits* earlier, but they take shape in both conventional and unconventional metrics. In the long and more complex poems, he uses devices that are both poetic and oratorical, including repetition with variation, striking metaphors, and wide-ranging allusions. He subsumes the Black sermon into the artistic voice, and it readdresses the cultural concern. The rhetorical triangle which binds the folk source, the independent imagination, and the appreciative audience continues unbroken.

Besides the American promise and the proletarian expectation, there is another heroic element. Here appears the figure of the bard. **"The Poet"** portrays a generalized figure who, though largely disregarded in his time, looks uncaringly into the nature of things:

> An Ishmaelite
> He breaks the icons of the Old and New
> . . . .
> The poet's lien exempts the Many nor the Few

and

> A champion of the People versus Kings—
> His only martyrdom is poetry:
> A hater of the hierarchy of things—

Freedom's need is his necessity.

(Rendezvous)

The proud "Ishmaelite" and "anchoret" intuits a "bright new world." Heroic in insight, he dedicates himself to the communication of his vision, which penetrates custom. He reincarnates the Vergil Ragsdale figure, but without the same locale and pathetic circumstances. In *Rendezvous* the Ethiopian Bard of Addis Ababa is equally a kind of prophet. From insight into contemporaneity, he foresees the "bright new world." Lyric vision and social celebration merge.

> His name is an emblem of justice
>   Greater than *lumot* of priest . . . .
> The seven league boots of his images
> Stir the palace and marketplace.
>
> *(Rendezvous)*

These two, poet and prophet, fuse in Tolson's great man or genius. Tolson saw heroes and villains as representative of human potential for greatness and evil. To serve this social vision, his style evolved with many of the characteristics of oratorical rhetoric.

During his time spent at Columbia University (1931-32) and Greenwich Village (1930s), Tolson became acquainted with the first wave of the moderns represented by Sandburg, Hughes, and Masters. On his own he discovered Eliot's *The Waste Land* and later Crane's *The Bridge* which, according to Mrs. Tolson, "showed her husband that he was 'on the wrong road.'" He therefore set out, still on his own, to come to terms with this academic style:

> Imitation must be in technique only. We have a rich heritage of folklore and history. We are a part of America. We are a part of the world. Our native symbols must be lifted into the universal. Yes, we must study the techniques of Robert Lowell, Dylan Thomas, Carlos Williams, Ezra Pound, Karl Shapiro, W. H. Auden. The greatest revolution has not been in science but in poetry. We must study such magazines as *Partisan Review,* the *Sewanee Review, Accent,* the *Virginia Quarterly.* We must read such critics as Crowe Ransom, Allen Tate, Stephen Spender, George Dillon and Kenneth Burke.

In the period between the publication of *Rendezvous* and the writing of *Libretto,* Tolson included in his eclectic reading the moderns who set the tone of the two decades between the world wars. The reading and the public occasion of Liberia's centenary resulted in the style and content of *Libretto.* In the poem packed with Eliotic notes, we have Tolson's venture in a style aimed at the literary caviar.

Here his view extends from Liberia and Africa to the world. The hero is, symbolically, Liberia, one of only two uncolonized nations in Africa then. Tolson reflects on this historical fact, on Liberia's contribution to Allied efforts in World War II, and on the history of this republic founded by American Blacks freed from slavery; he therefore celebrates its national identity. The epic qualities from *Portraits* and *Rendezvous* reappear here in a different context. Liberia, historically exploited by France and England, aids these two countries by supplying rubber and providing airports during the war. The campaign against "fascists" becomes almost a holy war. Liberia, the name and motto signifying freedom, emerges as both real and symbolic. Transcending racial and economic biases, it foreshadows Africa's triumph in the world. Tolson thus fuses epic material and "academic" style.

The poem is either an ode or a series of eight odes. The titles of metrically varying sections range the diatonic scale from "Do" to "Do." The sections are thematically and symbolically interconnected in the ode form:

> Metrically, the term ode usually implies considerable freedom in the introduction of varied rhythmic movements and irregularities of verse-length and rhyme-distribution. There is something "oratorical" about a true ode; and its irregularities may be conceived of as produced by its adaptation to choric rendition or to public declamation, either actual or imagined . . . . Primarily, it [ode] refers to the context and spirit of a poem, implying a certain largeness of thought, continuity of theme, and exalted feeling.

Tolson, faced with the problem of writing an occasional poem about a little-known nation, turns deliberately to the ancient form. (pp. 7-9)

Tolson's last book of poetry, *Harlem Gallery,* fuses the early subject matter of *Portraits* with his later techniques. Although he presents mechanically more than two hundred Harlemites in *Portraits,* he abandons the strategy here in favor of a much more dynamic one. A number of poems are thematically integrated into the one irregular ode. A different letter of the Greek alphabet labels each of the twenty-four poems in order, just as the names of notes mark *Libretto.* Both poems work toward a signed and structured climax.

The ode incorporates Tolson's epic principle. He has viewed *Harlem Gallery: Book I, the Curator* as the first of five works that would delineate Afro-American history from the African origins to the contemporary world. (p. 12)

The style of [*Harlem Gallery*] is more dynamic than that in *Libretto.* The new mode, with allusiveness and complexity of metaphor, image and symbol, excludes verbiage. Here emerge greater mastery and flexibility. The poems project their themes through a flux of character, interaction, and talk. The peripatetic Curator goes to Laugart's apartment, Aunt Grindle's Chitterling Shop, the Harlem Gallery, and the Zulu Club. He hears or knows about the happenings at the police station, the Haha Club, and the Angelus Funeral Home. His wanderings focus the geography of Harlem. His thoughts about the characters, life, and art are projected in both discursive and narrative cantos. At once a dramatic persona and an undramatized prophet like Eliot's Tiresias, he represents the consciousness through which the ode is played. In a sense he "makes" the "autobio-fragment"—the ode itself—literally humanize intellect and oratory. The poem ends then with the achievement of the metonym:

> The allegro of the Harlem Gallery is not a chippy
>   fire,
> for here, in focus, are paintings that chronicle a
>   people's New World odyssey
>   from chattel to Esquire!

> (*Harlem Gallery*)

Some indication of how Tolson's poem works can be seen in the first canto. In **"Alpha,"** one hears the voice of the Curator for the first time. The basic symbols appear in the first two lines:

> The Harlem Gallery, an Afric pepper bird, awakes
>   me at a people's dusk of dawn.

The Harlem Gallery, like the pepper bird native to Africa, stirs the Curator to action. He must envision the ode, the "autobio-fragment," at a people's dusk of dawn, the transition between night and morning symbolically figuring a new socio-economic age. Here the Afro-American will attain his full stature. The ode itself will both prophetically and aesthetically help to usher this in.

Then the poem evokes some Third World challenges to the "Great White World," the former being the social equivalent to the Curator's craft. Introspectively, the Curator turns to himself, faces the task, and sees himself as flawed, being comic where seriousness is called for, being serious when comedy is required. He shares humankind's meandering approach to the necessary search for true freedom. He envisions the task again, now hearing "a dry husk-of-locust" blues asking "Black Boy, O Black Boy, / is the port worth the cruise?" Inhibitions based on self-doubt harden the task; to maintain the integrity of self, humanity, and race proves nearly too much. The "clockbird's jackass laughter" haunts his effort. Challenged by the pepper bird, but mocked by the clockbird, he reveals the spirit of transitional man in a transitional world.

As in **"Alpha"** the entire ode centers in irregular rhyme, internal rhyme, alliteration, assonance, and consonance. Major symbols in the ode, such as Harlem Gallery, African pepper bird, Dusk of Dawn, and clockbird, recur now. The Buridan's ass and "the gaffing *To ti"* have appeared earlier in different genres, but images of the Hambletonian gathering for a leap, the apples of Cain, and barrel cactus are fresh. Here closes the decade long evolution in his worldview as an Afro-American, for his craft subsumes and perfects his oratory.

But with an epic intention, why does he abandon the folk model for the academic one? Why, if so committed to the Black and white masses, does he write in the style of the literary elite?

Perhaps *Harlem Gallery* is not exclusively for the elite. Here one reads and enjoys with persistence more than with erudition. Or, maybe Tolson regards the style as a criterion of excellence. Perhaps he wants to master the technique but to maintain his Afro-American experience. A final answer comes from Tolson, himself one of the "crafty masters of social conscience":

> Today
> The Few
> Yield Poets
> Their due;
> Tomorrow
> The Mass
> Judgment
> Shall Pass.

> (*Rendezvous*)

> (pp. 13-15)

Mariann B. Russell, "Evolution of Style in the Poetry of Melvin B. Tolson," in Black American Poets between Worlds, 1940-1960, *edited by R. Baxter Miller, The University of Tennessee Press, Knoxville, 1986, pp. 1-18.*

Melvin B. Tolson, Jr. (essay date 1990)

[*In the following excerpt, Tolson's son discusses his father's life and poetic career.*]

"Black Crispus Attucks taught / Us how to die / Before white Patrick Henry's bugle breath / Uttered the vertical / Transmitting cry: / 'Yea give me liberty or give me death . . . .'" These words still reverberate in this sixty-sixth year of the celebration by African Americans of "Black History Month." They [these words from **Dark Symphony**] express the importance that the struggle against socioeconomic and cultural racism held for Melvin B. Tolson in his lifetime and in the works he left to what he called "the vertical audience," that of the ages. This poet, orator, teacher of English and American literatures, grammarian, small-town mayor, theater founder and director, debate coach was born on 6 February 1898 in Moberly, Missouri, the son and nephew of Methodist preachers. The family moved frequently in Missouri and Iowa to the different churches his studiously intellectual but autodidact father pastored.

Tolson often said that in his earliest youth he was dedicated to the palette. However, he was permanently deterred from this path by his mother's encounter with a bohemianly attired painter who, attracted by the boy's ability, spoke of taking him to Paris! . . . Subsequently turning to literature, Tolson said that his first poem, **"The Wreck of the Titanic,"** was published about 1912, when the family lived in Oskaloosa, Iowa. A favorite teacher encouraged him as early as 1915 or 1916, when the family resided in Mason City, Iowa. The earliest copies of the poet's work were discovered by Robert Farnsworth, who has done the most extensive research on Tolson's life, having published a definitive biography in 1984. He discovered two short stories and two poems written by the then class poet for the *Lincolnian,* the yearbook of Lincoln High School in Kansas City, Missouri. Tolson was attending high school there while the family lived near his father's church in Independence. These short stories and poems appear in the 1917 and 1918 editions of the yearbook, in which his future career is predicted to be that of "Poet and Playwriter" (*sic*). The feature poem dedicated to his graduating class of 1918 is grandiloquently entitled **"The Past, Present and Future"** and is already distinctively "Tolsonian" in imaginative thrust and language.

> Fair muses, from Olympia's wind-kissed height,
> Inspire our souls with (thy) eternal flame
> That we may sing of this sad hour aright,
> A song full worthy of our Mater's name.
> In sooth, it pains our hearts to break the ties
> That grip us to our friends in warm embrace.
> However Time, who like a meteor flies,
> Has hurled us hence, this tearful time to face.

Later lines, such as "Our hearts beat fast, our eyes flame with desire! / Our souls long for the battle-smoke of strife!" are also typical of the action-filled language and oratorical tone of the later poetry. (p. 395)

The five stanzas of eight iambic-pentameter lines in the *Lincolnian* show a relative ease in the manipulation of *a b a b* rhymes and may be said to substantiate Tolson's own oft-repeated opinion that "poets are made though technique must be taught." It is obvious, despite the clichés and infelicities of form, that the poet of *Harlem Gallery: Book I, The Curator* of 1965 is already present almost fifty years earlier. The poetic direction is already set toward the rich imagery and allusive language of the later period.

In his junior year at Lincoln University, outside Philadelphia, Tolson married Ruth Southall of Charlottesville, Virginia. After graduation in 1923, a son was born and the family moved to Marshall, Texas, on the edge of the oilfield district, where Tolson had a job as English teacher at Wiley College, a small Methodist Episcopal school. Two more sons and a daughter were born during these years. Coincidentally, about a mile away in the same town was a second small black college, Bishop, supported by the Baptist Church. The total student population of the two colleges might occasionally have reached one thousand, though rarely.

In the pantheon of black colleges of this pre-civil-rights era Wiley College was regarded with something like envy and awe by the Negro population of the South. Its prestige was unrivaled west of the Mississippi, and Tolson quickly grew to be one of the intellectual stars of this environment. For the next few years he expended the enormous store of energy in his five-foot-six-inch, 130-pound frame in several directions. He coached the junior-varsity football team, expounding for many years afterward on the strategies he devised to defeat the larger, better-fed varsity players. He played hard, competitive tennis with faculty and students, again proclaiming the advantages of strategy. He trained competitive orators and coached championship debate teams,

among whose opponents were the University of Oklahoma (an interracial "first"), Oxford University, and the University of Southern California. He directed the college theater group and helped found the black intercollegiate Southern Association of Dramatic and Speech Arts, for whose festival contests he and his students wrote and presented plays. His students called him "the Little Master" and told and retold (sometimes apocryphal) stories, admiring his debater thrusts of intelligence in discussions—often on the open campus—with students and other professors and his disregard for the clothing amenities associated with being a college professor in those more formal days. (pp. 395-96)

Debate remained a vital part of Tolson's teaching life until falling into swift discontinuance just before World War II, about the time the subjects that had furnished the substance of its adversarial roles became too immediately relevant to be "debated." In the midst of this and other activities, Tolson had worked on his Master of Arts degree at Columbia University but finished his thesis only on the eve of Hitler's invasion of France. The subject of his thesis was **"The Harlem Group of Negro Writers,"** and the degree was awarded in 1940. He knew personally some of the Harlem Renaissance figures and, while at Columbia, was inspired to write a sonnet about Harlem. A roommate, according to Tolson, ridiculed the idea of fitting Harlem into a sonnet, and this comment made him think of composing a longer work in the years that followed.

He was back teaching at Wiley College in the early thirties and busy at work on his poetry about Harlem. To encompass the vastness of the community, he finally decided on a framework inspired by *Spoon River Anthology* (1915). Edgar Lee Masters had used the device of a stroll through a graveyard and the epitaphs on headstones to introduce his poetic population. Tolson combined his own early interest in painting and the prominence of this art during the Harlem Renaissance to create another device that would allow a similar scope of poetic presentation. The resulting collection of some 340 poems, *A Gallery of Harlem Portraits,* unsuccessfully made the rounds of publishing houses for several years, after which time Tolson abandoned further attempts, putting the manuscript in a trunk. Some forty years later, in 1979, the publication of approximately half of the "portraits" was finally brought about by Robert Farnsworth. Because of a similarity in titles when Tolson took up the theme again (in *Harlem Gallery: Book I, The Curator* of 1965), there is often confusion of the two on the part of readers and oral commentators of Tolson's work.

The poet himself speaks of the influence of Masters, Browning, and Whitman on *A Gallery of Harlem Portraits.* Another, more obvious influence, which is perhaps taken for granted in African American poetry of the period, is the blues.

> Troubled waters, troubled waters,

Done begin to roll.
Troubled waters, troubled waters,
Gittin' deep an' col'.
Lawd, don't let dem troubled waters
Drown ma weary soul.

The New Year comes, the Old Year goes.
What's down the road nobody knows.
I play my suit with a poker face,
But Father Time he holds the ace.

Most of the "portraits" contain blues inserts, both original and traditional. Tolson recalled several times sitting up late at night with Sterling Brown, the poet, the two drinking and delightedly competing at the invention of blues lyrics—never, unfortunately for us, written down or otherwise recorded.

In the same vein, Tolson was renowned as a raconteur, the veracity of whose minutest details sometimes took second place to dramatic effect. Although a few instances of his speaking or being interviewed exist, he would not allow his sons to record the oral history which he recounted so enthusiastically and entertainingly (the body tape recorder was still a thing of the future). These accounts were a gold mine of experiences on debate tours and travels to dramatic festivals in the segregated South and North, as well as encounters with famous, infamous, and ordinary people. We meet many of these events and people, however, in *A Gallery of Harlem Portraits* and in subsequent works published during his lifetime: *Rendezvous with America* (1944), *Libretto for the Republic of Liberia* (1953), and *Harlem Gallery* (1965).

The "portraits" range through all the classes, colors, and past and present careers imaginable in the Harlem of the twenties and thirties.

Dusky Bards,
Heirs of eons of Comedy and Tragedy.
Pass along the streets and alleys of Harlem
Singing ballads of the Dark World: . . .
. . . .
Radicals, prizefighters, actors and deacons,
Beggars, politicians, professors and redcaps,
Bulldikers, Babbitts, racketeers and jig-chasers,
Harlots, crapshooters, workers and pink-chasers
Artists, dicties, Pullman porters and messiahs . . .
The Curator has hung the likenesses of all
In *"A Gallery of Harlem Portraits."*

Between these two stanzas from the introductory poem **"Harlem"** are eight assorted stanzas of blues lyrics which comment on the relations between men and women, blacks and whites, the powerful and the powerless. Although he espoused the antibourgeois attitude of the artist that has pervaded Western civilization since the late nineteenth century in France, Tolson had not yet done the extensive study or held the hours-long discussions he was to have with his friend and colleague Oliver W. Cox, who came to Wiley in 1938, or the author-editor V. F. Calverton. Nevertheless, in a book-length study of the 1965 **Harlem Gallery** Mariann Russell shows that the earlier "portraits" attribute poverty to the same socio-economic conditions as does

the later work, and they too call on the "underdogs of the world to unite."

While he was composing **Portraits,** Tolson was also writing prose. By the summer of 1937 he had written two plays. One, a musical comedy-drama title *The Moses of Beale Street,* was done in collaboration with Edward Boatner, the famous arranger of spirituals, who also taught at Wiley. The two were partly inspired by the continued success of the miracle play *The Green Pastures,* though they placed many of their scenes in Hell rather than Heaven. An agent agreed to represent them, and Tolson left the manuscript, later lost, with his collaborator while he returned to begin the school year in Marshall.

In May 1938 he began contributing a weekly column to the *Washington Tribune,* an African American newspaper in the District of Columbia. Farnsworth selected one hundred from the seven years' worth of columns and secured their publication in a 1982 volume whose title, **Caviar and Cabbage,** echoed that of the column. There are also records of one-act and three-act plays, one of which was a dramatization of *Black No More,* a novel by Walter White of the NAACP, which was finally performed at a 1952 convention of the Association.

After beginning the newspaper column, Tolson started work on a novel called *Dark Symphony,* of which some ninety-six pages remain. However, at the suggestion of poet Frank Marshall Davis, he entered a 126-line poem in the poetry contest sponsored by the 1940 American Negro Exposition in Chicago. He gave the title **"Dark Symphony"** to the poem, which was awarded first prize by the jury composed of Davis, Arna Bontemps, and Langston Hughes. The opening lines of my essay quote the opening lines of the poem, which is Tolson's most popular work. The first seventeen lines were even used as the frontispiece for the 1976 Schlitz Brewing Company's "Famous Black Americans Historical Calendar." I am sure the poet would have been delighted!

"Dark Symphony" is divided into sections bearing the names of musical notations.

Allegro Moderato
Black Crispus Attucks taught
Us how to die. . . .

Lento Grave
The centuries-old pathos in our voices
Saddens the great white world. . . .

Andante Sostenuto
They tell us to forget
The Golgotha we tread. . . .

Tempo Primo
The New Negro strides upon the continent
In seven-league boots. . . .

Larghetto
None in the Land can say
To us black men Today. . . .

Tempo di Marcia
Out of abysses of Illiteracy,

Through labyrinths of Lies,
Across waste lands of Disease. . .
We advance!. . . .

The musical notations characterize in varying degrees the tone of each of the sections of the poem. In **"Dark Symphony"** Tolson also returns to the cultivation of patterns of rhyme, a practice he had abandoned in *Gallery* except in the blues lyrics. He alternates rhyme with blank-verse sections. This poem is the longest that he had written to this time and is an example of the increasing lengthiness of the major poems he will write hereafter.

"Dark Symphony" appeared in the September 1941 issue of *Atlantic Monthly* and was read by Mary Lou Chamberlain, who later left *Atlantic* and became a member of the editorial board of Dodd, Mead. She suggested Tolson submit a manuscript for publication, the composition of which resulted in *Rendezvous with America* (1943). Other shorter and longer poems were written for the book. One of the shortest is **"My Soul and I,"** dedicated to Tolson's wife and containing only twelve lines. It is a quietly lyrical love poem, one of the very few he ever wrote, in a vein that is counter to his natural intellectual exuberance. The longest poem in the volume, **"Tapestries of Time,"** in eight sections, contains 369 lines in strophes of varying lengths and rhyme schemes. Furthermore, the collection contains several experiments in form: rhyming lines of only two syllables (**"A Song for Myself"**); a pantoum, a Malay fixed-form poem adapted by Baudelaire (**"The Furlough"**); a section of twelve sonnets. There are vignettes based on his work with black and white sharecroppers who wanted to form a union in Harrison County, scenes of life in the pre-civil-rights South, materials from African history and folklore, references to contemporary events, and reflections on the role of the artist in society. All these are themes that recur throughout his prose and poetry.

In 1947 Tolson left Wiley College for Langston University in Langston, Oklahoma, at the invitation of another of his fine debaters, Hobart Jarrett, then chairman of the English Department, and at the urging of his family. He was forty-nine years old and had just been named Poet Laureate of the Republic of Liberia, West Africa. The original sponsors of Liberia, the American Colonization Society, had also founded Lincoln University, of which his friend and schoolmate Horace Mann Bond had recently become president. The Poet Laureate was to compose a celebratory poem for the centennial of the founding of Liberia. As the poem he originally planned grew in length and complexity, Tolson was obliged to compose another, shorter poem that arrived in time for the celebration.

"DO"

Liberia?
No micro-footnote in a bunioned book
Homed by a pendant
With a gelded look:
You are
The ladder of survival dawn men saw

In the quicksilver sparrow that slips
The eagle's claw!

Seven strophes at the beginning of this book-length ode of 770 lines ask the meaning of Liberia. In seven lines each of roughly similar appearance we are told what Liberia is not, then what it is. The irregularly metered lines rhyme *a b a b* and are centered on the page, a practice which comes to dominate completely the final work of Tolson's career, *Harlem Gallery* (1965). In the *Libretto* this visual structure alternates with other, different patterns as well as with non-rhymed sections. The divisions of the ode bear the names of the diatonic musical scale.

Sometimes before beginning the composition of the ode, Tolson had encountered modern poetry and the New Criticism of Eliot, Pound, Ransom, Tate, Brooks, et alia. His own natural bent toward the intellectual, toward the attempt—like Paul Valéry—to render poetic creation as willed an activity as possible, was instantly attracted by the new techniques, though not by the ethos of their practitioners. For him, as for other artists, inspiration was a "given" with whose materials the poet consciously and conscientiously labored to produce a work of art. Techniques could be adapted to the expression of any ideology. Tolson felt the artist as artist made the greatest contribution to his people by creating the finest art object to express their liberation. As he was to say years later during a 1966 writers' conference at Fisk University: "A man has his biology, his sociology, and his psychology—and then he becomes a poet!. . . I'm a black poet, an African-American poet, a Negro poet. I'm no accident."

By the time of his work on the *Libretto* Tolson had begun to limit his extracurricular activities. There were occasional dramatic productions, no athletic activities, fewer though still frequent public addresses (such as those travelling with Roscoe Dunjee, founder-publisher of the Oklahoma City *Black Dispatch,* championing the cause of Ada Lois Sipuel Fisher), and no regular news columns: the emphasis was now principally on the writing of poetry. His reading and study of modern verse and criticism had become even more voracious as he taught himself the newer techniques and adapted them to his own talents. Thus the *Libretto,* though obviously influenced by the modernism of the period, is unlike the poetry of any of his contemporaries. It has lost none of its exultant belief in the final triumph of the "little people" and the achievement of political and socio-economic justice. Like Aimé Césaire, whose *Cahier d'un retour au pays natal* (1947) masterfully utilizes the techniques of surrealism, Tolson remains a poet in blackness. He was fully aware of the difficulties this text presented and supplied pages of notes at the end of the book. In conversations with me he stated that he knew he was "dicing with Fate" in trying to force entrance into the "canon," but he was certain that, like Stendhal, he would be vindicated in time. He felt that he could do it and relished the challenge; so it had to be done!

Libretto underwent constant revision, and Allen Tate finally provided a very complimentary preface. At the same time, Tolson was busy writing other poetry, which appeared in print before the publication of *Libretto* in 1953. (Duke Ellington was the Composer Laureate of Liberia for the same centennial, for which he produced the provocative "Liberian Suite.") The last section of the final **"DO"** presents "The Futurafrique, the chef-d'oeuvre of Liberian Motors," "The United Nations Limited" (a train), "The Bula Matadi" (a luxurious ocean liner), "Le Premier des Noirs, of Pan-African Airways." The ode closes on this vision of Liberia:

> The Parliament of African Peoples signets forever
> the Recessional of Europe and
> trumpets the abolition of itself:
> and no nation uses *Felis leo* or
> *Aquila heliaca* as the emblem of
> *blut und boden;* and the hyenas
> whine no more among the bar-
> ren bones of the seventeen sun-
> set sultans of Songhai; and the
> deserts that gave up the ghost
> to green pastures chant in the
> ears and teeth of the Dog, in
> Rosh Hoshana of the Afric
> calends: *"Honi soit qui mal y pense!"*

Nine years passed between the publication of *Rendezvous with America* and *Libretto for the Republic of Liberia.* Twelve years would elapse before the publication of Tolson's third and final collection of verse, *Harlem Gallery: Book I, The Curator.* Despite the time and labor required for the composition of the 340 poems of *A Gallery of Harlem Portraits,* he had not, when he decided to come back to the idea, reexamined the original manuscript merely to rework it. In the earlier work there is only a one-line mention of the Curator, but he becomes the principal character of the 1965 *Harlem Gallery.* Furthermore, by the time of the composition of the latter work Tolson's original idea had expanded to include the whole history of the diaspora of African Americans. He now planned to write five volumes, with books 2-5 to be titled respectively *Egypt Land, The Red Sea, The Wilderness,* and *The Promised Land.* However, operations for cancer and deteriorating health during and after the writing of *The Curator* prevented any further work. Progress on this volume was indeed facilitated by the refusal of his wife to consent to his running for a fifth term as mayor of Langston City!

"Alpha"

> The Harlem Gallery, an Afric pepper bird,
> awakes me at a people's dusk of dawn,
> The age alters its image, a dog's hind leg,
> and hazards the moment of truth in pawn.
> The Lord of the House of Flies,
> jaundice-eyed, synapses purled,
> wries before the tumultuous canvas,
> 'The Second of May'—
> by Goya:
> the dagger of Madrid
> vs.
> the scimitar of Murat.

> In Africa, in Asia, on the Day
> of Barricades, alarm birds bedevil the Great
> White
> World,
> A Buridan's ass—not Balaam's—between no oats
> and
> hay.

(pp. 396-99)

The five projected volumes [of *Harlem Gallery*] were to trace the odyssey of black Americans from Africa to the twentieth-century New World, "from chattel to Esquire," words which close the first volume. The point of view is not that of the artist, as in the original *Portraits,* but that of the Curator, who talks and meditates encyclopedically on race, art, artists, and the Gallery. We learn of the difficulties he has in dealing with "the bulls of Bashan," the moneyed Gallery supporters led by Mr. Guy Delaporte III, president of Bola Boa Enterprises, Inc. There are conversations with artists and friends, many of them similar to characters and names in *Gallery of Harlem Portraits* or combinations of characters from that work and real life.

After five sections dedicated to the ideas of observations of the Curator, we meet John Laugart (in **"Zeta"**), a "half-blind painter, / spoon-shaped like an aged parrot-fish." He lives in "a catacomb Harlem flat / (grotesquely vivisected like microscoped maggots) / where the caricature of a rat / weathercocked in squeals / to be or not to be / and a snaggle-toothed toilet / grumbled its obscenity." Laugart has painted a masterpiece, *Black Bourgeoisie,* "a synthesis / (savage-sanative) / of Daumier and Gropper and Picasso," which the Curator is certain "will wring from [the Regents'] babbitted souls a Jeremian cry!" The Curator hangs the work anyway, and "Before the *bête noire* of [the painting], Mr. Guy Delaporte III takes his stand / a wounded Cape buffalo defying everything and Everyman!" Later [Laugart] was robbed and murdered in his flat, / and the only witness was a Hamletian rat."

In Aunt Grindle's Elite Chitterling Shop (**"Eta"**) we meet the Curator's alter ego, Dr. Obi Nkomo, native African Africanist versed in the knowledge and culture of the West, who uses irony to comment on and often challenge the Curator's opinions. It is obvious that the poet sympathizes with them both and uses Nkomo to gain a perspective different from that of the Curator. Often, as a skillful debater, Tolson places the reader in a dilemmatic position before contrasting ideas of the Curator and the "signifying" Nkomo. The latter is also the vehicle for Tolson to incorporate African materials like those he has previously used in prose and poetry. (pp. 399)

The following are a few of the more important characters of *Harlem Gallery:* Snakehips Briskie, (**"MU"**), dancer, who Convulsively, unexampledly / ... began to coil, to writhe / like a prismatic-hued python / in the throes of copulation"; Black Diamond, "heir presumptive to the Lenox Policy Racket"; Shadrach Martial Kilroy, "president of Afroamerican Freedom"; Hedda

Starks, alias Black Orchid (**"RHO"**), "a striptease has-been / of the brassy-pit-band era," but who had possessed a "barbarian bump and sophisticated grind / (every bump butted by the growl of a horn)"; Mister Starks, "from Onward, Mississippi— / via Paris, Texas, via Broken Bow, Oklahoma," whose mother named him "Mister" "Since every Negro male in Dixie was / either a *boy* or an *uncle*." (Starks was pianist-composer of the "Black Orchid Suite" and poet of the manuscript *Harlem Vignettes*.) There are also dozens of "walk-on" characters who people the Harlem of this volume, and space-time allusions are not limited to the Renaissance era.

After a brief, rare "writer's block," Tolson was able to "end" the volume. In **"PSI"** he has the Curator address first "Black Boy" and then "White Boy" on the subject of racial lies, myths, and stereotypes. **"OMEGA"** addresses them both at once, proclaiming the existence of flowers of hope that bloom in the ghetto despite the flowers of death in the white metropolis: "In the black ghetto / the white heather / and the white almond grow, / but the hyacinth / and the asphodel blow / in the white metropolis!" Then he calls on the Seven Sages of ancient Greece ("O Cleobulus, / O Thales, Solon, Periander, Bias, Chilo, / O Pittacus") to "unriddle the phoenix riddle of this." The poem closes on this tribute to the Gallery and to African Americans:

> Our public may posses in Art
> a Mantegna figure's arctic rigidity;
> yet—I hazard—yet,
> this allegro of the Harlem Gallery
> is not a chippy fire,
> for here, in focus, are paintings that chronicle
> a people's New World odyssey
> from chattel to Esquire!

(p. 400)

Melvin B. Tolson, Jr., "The Poetry of Melvin B. Tolson (1898-1966)," in World Literature Today, *Vol. 64, No. 3, Summer, 1990, pp. 395-400.*

FURTHER READING

Bérubé, Michael. "Avant-Gardes and De-Author-izations: *Harlem Gallery* and the Cultural Contradictions of Modernism." *Callaloo* 12, No. 1 (Winter 1989): 192-215.
    Discusses *Harlem Gallery*, exploring Tolson's use of modernist techniques.

Hansell, William H. "Three Artists in Melvin B. Tolson's *Harlem Gallery*." *Black American Literature Forum* 18, No. 3 (Fall 1984): 122-27.
    Examines the main characters of *Harlem Gallery*.

Mootry, Maria K. "'The Step of Iron Feet': Creative Practice in the War Sonnets of Melvin B. Tolson and Gwendolyn Brooks." *Obsidian II: Black Literature in Review* 2, No. 3 (Winter 1987): 69-87.
    Explores expressions of social concern in Tolson's *Rendezvous with America*.

Schroeder, Patricia R. "Point and Counterpoint in *Harlem Gallery*." *CLA Journal* XXVII, No. 2 (December 1983): 152-68.
    Discusses narrative structure and imagery in *Harlem Gallery*.

Smith, Gary. "A Hamlet Rives Us: The Sonnets of Melvin B. Tolson." *CLA Journal* XXIX, No. 3 (March 1986): 261-75.
    Critical analysis of Tolson's sonnets.

Thompson, Gordon E. "Ambiguity in Tolson's *Harlem Gallery*." *Callaloo* 9, No. 1 (Winter 1986): 159-70.
    Studies complex imagery and structure in *Harlem Gallery*.

Jean Toomer

1894-1967

American poet, short story writer, dramatist, and essayist.

Toomer's greatest contribution to literature is *Cane* (1923), an innovative volume of avant-garde poetry, short stories, drama, and prose vignettes that explores African-American culture and spirituality in the rural South and the urban North. Toomer conceived *Cane* as an elegiac work commemorating a folk culture rooted in nature and myth that he believed would soon be superseded in a waxing industrial age. The child of mixed-race parents, Toomer rejected racial chauvinism and the label "black author"; rather, he considered himself the representative of a new "American" race made up of elements of all humanity, and many of his writings reflect this universalist philosophy. *Cane* has been hailed since its release as one of the greatest works of the Harlem Renaissance period, and critics have praised Toomer for his rich use of language and symbol. Although his later work, which reflected his increasing interest in mysticism and metaphysics, never attained the critical stature of *Cane,* Toomer is now regarded as a seminal figure in the canons of both African-American and Modernist literature.

Born in Washington, D.C., Toomer described his ancestry as "Scotch, Welsh, German, English, French, Dutch, Spanish, with some dark blood"; his grandfather was black, his mother of mixed race, and his father a white Georgia farmer. Toomer spent much of his childhood in an affluent white section of Washington, relatively free from racial prejudice, in the home of his maternal grandfather, P. B. S. Pinchback, a prominent Louisiana politician of the Reconstruction era. After the death of Toomer's mother in 1909, the Pinchbacks experienced extreme financial losses, requiring the family to move to a modest black neighborhood. Toomer's experience in both black and white society offered him an unusual perspective on racial identity. Early in his life he concluded that he was neither black nor white—a conviction that deeply affected both his literary career and the course of his life.

As a young man, Toomer lived a transient existence, studying various subjects at several universities and working a number of jobs. He enjoyed a literary apprenticeship for several months in 1919 and 1920 in Greenwich Village, where he met such prominent New York intellectuals as Edwin Arlington Robinson and Waldo Frank. In the fall of 1921, Toomer accepted a temporary teaching position in Sparta, Georgia, a rural Southern town that gave him the opportunity to discover his black roots. He further explored his heritage on a tour of the South with Frank in 1922. This exposure to the South inspired much of *Cane.*

Shortly after the publication of *Cane* in 1923, Toomer became a follower of George Gurdjieff, an Armenian mystic whose philosophy aspired toward the achievement of "objective consciousness": awareness of one's status as part of a larger, universal being. Toomer embraced this philosophy, believing that modern man had become alienated from the world around him. Toomer spent the summer of 1924 at the Gurdjieff Institute in Fontainebleau, France, and devoted the next several years to proselytizing Gurdjieff's philosophy in the United States. When he began writing regularly again in the late 1920s, Toomer's work was dominated by Gurdjieffian metaphysics, not by African-American issues. This alienated publishers who had wished to associate the author with the Harlem Renaissance, an affiliation Toomer had always resisted. Toomer spent the rest of his career in obscurity, unable to get much of his work published, although he continued to write prolifically. After his conversion to Quakerism in 1940, he renounced Gurdjieff and wrote on Christian themes.

He died in 1967, two years before the republication of *Cane* and the subsequent revival of interest in his work.

In *Cane*, which is divided into three sections, Toomer contrasted the passionate, nature-bound life of rural African-American Southerners with the numbness and ineffectuality of urban black Northerners in order to demonstrate his belief that materialism and restrictive social values leave individuals spiritually crippled. Employing a structure often compared to musical composition, Toomer unified *Cane*'s various pieces with recurring themes and motifs and with poetic elements borrowed from gospel and blues music. In the first section of *Cane*, Toomer interwove six stories with twelve poems, using imagery drawn from nature to create lyrical, impressionistic, and often mystical portraits of six Southern women. Images of sunset, dusk, ripening fruit, and canefields in the stories "Karintha," "Becky," "Carma," and "Fern" suggest the richness of a passing way of life, while ghosts, full moons, and fire in "Esther" and "Blood-Burning Moon" announce its dissolution. By turns strong and vulnerable, exotic and ordinary, innocent and misunderstood, Toomer's women convey the essence of an era that was soon to be altered by encroaching cultural change. In "Song of the Son," a poem that has been deemed central to *Cane*'s thematic development, Toomer declared, "for though the sun is setting on / A song-lit race of slaves, it has not set; / Though late, O soil, it is not too late yet."

Cane's second section, which comprises seven prose sketches and five poems, shifts in setting to the urban North of Chicago and Washington, D.C. In "Seventh Street," the opening piece, Toomer established the frantic tone and urban landscape that characterize this section. His rhythms, ragged and jazz-influenced, contrast with the flowing, lush texture of the first section. Houses, alleys, asphalt streets, machines, theaters, and nightclubs function as symbols of confinement that limit growth and thwart self-understanding. In his examinations of sexual and emotional relationships between men and women in such stories as "Avey," "Theater," "Box Seat," and "Bona and Paul," Toomer challenged the conventions of modern industrialized society, illustrating how a pseudo-culture robs one of lifegiving, creative instincts and uproots one from the nurturing provided by the soil.

Cane's third section consists of "Kabnis," Toomer's longest and most sustained piece, which incorporates the themes of both sections one and two. Variously described by critics as a play, novella, and short story, "Kabnis" is a thinly veiled autobiographical portrait of an educated but spiritually confused Northern black who travels to the South to teach school in a small rural town. "Kabnis" focuses on various men who each embody some part of the black experience: Kabnis, an idealist inflated by bourgeois white values and disillusioned with his race; Lewis, a man of intelligence and stature who accepts his history; Hanby, a school principal who plays the aristocrat among his people; and Father John, an old black made wise by the experience of slavery and by intimacy with his heritage. Critics have seen in these and other figures the dilemma of the black American caught between conflicting and alienating lifestyles and values. There is little agreement, however, whether Toomer effectively resolved in "Kabnis" the conflicts he so skillfully evoked. Some critics have argued that Toomer achieved his goal by suggesting that blacks can help themselves by returning to their spiritual roots. Other reviewers claimed that Toomer ends *Cane* inconclusively at best, with each of the characters in "Kabnis" either despairing of the future or resigned to it.

Cane drew early critical interest because of its engaging approach to subject and its experimental form. Critics recognized that *Cane* is neither a diatribe on racial relations nor a strident reformist doctrine, as were many works by other Harlem Renaissance writers, but is instead a lyrical, passionate, and artistic creation. The influence of Sherwood Anderson and Waldo Frank, acknowledged by Toomer, is evidenced in the centrality of folk life; Toomer also attributed his work to the influence of the Imagist poets whose economy of line and image he praised and emulated.

Critic Robert Jones separated Toomer's post-*Cane* career into two periods: the "Objective Consciousness" period, in which his work reflects the philosophy of Gurdjieff, and the "Religious" period following his conversion to Quakerism. The Gurdjieffian works espouse the elevation of human consciousness through asceticism, communion with nature, and reflection on the interconnectedness of the universe. During Toomer's "Religious" period, he adopted the Quaker belief in "quietism," a passive submission of the self to God. Throughout both phases, his belief in the need for the breakdown of racial and ethnic divisions remained a constant concern in both his writing and in his personal life. Very few of the post-*Cane* works were published, although some were collected in the posthumous *The Wayward and the Seeking: A Collection of Writings by Jean Toomer* (1980); the remainder of Toomer's manuscripts, which include several novels, volumes of autobiography, and plays, are housed at Fisk University in Nashville, Tennessee.

Only a few of Toomer's post-*Cane* works have garnered critical attention, notably "The Blue Meridian," a long poem that heralds the coming of a united human race, spiritually enlightened and free of artificial barriers; critics have compared this work to the poetry of Walt Whitman in its vision of a transcendental identity common to all humans. However, many critics dismiss Toomer's work after *Cane* as sermonizing and lacking in the lyrical quality of his younger work; they suggest that Toomer, who always displayed a philosophical bent in his writing, allowed his intellectual agenda to overwhelm his aesthetics. Many were also disappointed with his refusal to expand upon the African-American themes of *Cane*, and Toomer himself blamed these expectations for his later commercial and critical frustrations. He wrote: "*Cane* was a song of an end. And why no one has seen and felt that, why people have expected me to write a second and a third and a fourth book like *Cane* is one of the queer misunderstandings of my life."

Darwin T. Turner concluded his introduction to the 1975 edition of *Cane* with this observation: "*Cane* was not Jean Toomer's total life; it was perhaps merely an interlude in his search for understanding. No matter what it may have been for him, *Cane* still sings to readers, not the swan song of an era that was dying, but the morning hymn of a Renaissance that was beginning."

(For further information about Toomer's life and works, see *Black Writers; Concise Dictionary of American Literary Biography, 1917-1929; Contemporary Authors,* Vols. 85-88; *Contemporary Literary Criticism,* Vols. 1, 4, 13, 22; *Dictionary of Literary Biography,* Vols. 45, 51; *Major 20th-Century Writers;* and *Short Story Criticism,* Vol. 1. For related criticism, see the entry on the Harlem Renaissance in *Twentieth-Century Literary Criticism,* Vol. 26.)

PRINCIPAL WORKS

Cane (poetry, short stories, and drama) 1923
Essentials (aphorisms) 1931
The Flavor of Man (lecture) 1949
*The Wayward and the Seeking: A Collection of Writings
      by Jean Toomer* (poetry and short stories) 1980
The Collected Poems of Jean Toomer (poetry) 1988

Waldo Frank (essay date 1923)

[*An American novelist, critic, and editor, Frank was a founder of* Seven Arts, *a distinguished magazine of leftist politics and avant-garde literature. After meeting Toomer in 1920, he became the young author's mentor and was instrumental in launching his career. In the following excerpt, taken from his foreword to the first edition of* Cane, *Frank acclaims Toomer's evocation of the South and praises him for choosing an aesthetic, rather than racially provincial, approach to the work.*]

Reading [*Cane*], I had the vision of a land, heretofore sunk in the mists of muteness, suddenly rising up into the eminence of song. Innumerable books have been written about the South; some good books have been written in the South. This book *is* the South. I do not mean that *Cane* covers the South or is the South's full voice. Merely this: a poet has arisen among our American youth who has known how to turn the essences and materials of his Southland into the essences and materials of literature. A poet has arisen in that land who writes, not as a Southerner, not as a rebel against Southerners, not as a Negro, not as apologist or priest or critic: who writes as a *poet.* The fashioning of beauty is

ever foremost in his inspiration: not forcedly but simply, and because these ultimate aspects of his world are to him more real than all its specific problems. He has made songs and lovely stories of his land . . . not of its yesterday, but of its immediate life. And that has been enough.

How rare this is will be clear to those who have followed with concern the struggle of the South toward literary expression, and the particular trial of that portion of its folk whose skin is dark. The gifted Negro has been too often thwarted from becoming a poet because his world was forever forcing him to recollect that he was a Negro. The artist must lose such lesser identities in the great well of life . . . . The French novelist is not forever noting: "This is French." It is so atmospheric for him to be French, that he can devote himself to saying: "This is human." This is an imperative condition for the creating of deep art. The whole will and mind of the creator must go below the surfaces of race. And this has been an almost impossible condition for the American Negro to achieve, forced every moment of his life into a specific and superficial plane of consciousness.

The first negative significance of *Cane* is that this so natural and restrictive state of mind is completely lacking. For Toomer, the Southland is not a problem to be solved; it is a field of loveliness to be sung: the Georgia Negro is not a downtrodden soul to be uplifted; he is material for gorgeous painting: the segregated self-conscious brown belt of Washington is not a topic to be discussed and exposed; it is a subject of beauty and of drama, worthy of creation in literary form.

It seems to me, therefore, that this is a first book in more ways than one. It is a harbinger of the South's literary maturity: of its emergence from the obsession put upon its minds by the unending racial crisis—an obsession from which writers have made their indirect escape through sentimentalism, exoticism, polemic, "problem" fiction, and moral melodrama. It marks the dawn of direct and unafraid creation. And, as the initial work of a man of twenty-seven, it is the harbinger of a literary force of whose incalculable future I believe no reader of this book will be in doubt.

How typical is *Cane* of the South's still virgin soil and of its pressing seeds! and the book's chaos of verse, tale, drama, its rhythmic rolling shift from lyrism to narrative, from mystery to intimate pathos! But read the book through and you will see a complex and significant form take substance from its chaos. Part One is the primitive and evanescent black world of Georgia. Part Two is the threshing and suffering brown world of Washington, lifted by opportunity and contact into the anguish of self-conscious struggle. Part Three is Georgia again . . . the invasion into this black womb of the ferment seed: the neurotic, educated, spiritually stirring Negro. As a broad form this is superb, and the very looseness and unexpected waves of the book's parts make *Cane* still more *South,* still more of an aesthetic equivalent of the land.

What a land it is! What an Aeschylean beauty to its fateful problem! Those of you who love our South will find here some of your love. Those of you who know it not will perhaps begin to understand what a warm splendor is at last at dawn.

> A feast of moon and men and barking hounds,
> An orgy for some genius of the South
> With bloodshot eyes and cane-lipped scented mouth
> Surprised in making folk-songs....

So, in his still sometimes clumsy stride (for Toomer is finally a poet in prose) the author gives you an inkling of his revelation. An individual force, wise enough to drink humbly at this great spring of his land...such is the first impression of Jean Toomer. But beyond this wisdom and this power (which shows itself perhaps most splendidly in his complete freedom from the sense of persecution), there rises a figure more significant: the artist, hard, self-immolating, the artist who is not interested in races, whose domain is Life. The book's final Part is no longer "promise"; it is achievement. It is no mere dawn: it is a bit of the full morning. These materials...the ancient black man, mute, inaccessible, and yet so mystically close to the new tumultuous members of his race, the simple slave Past, the shredding Negro Present, the iridescent passionate dream of the To-morrow...are made and measured by a craftsman into an unforgettable music. The notes of his counterpoint are particular, themes are of intimate connection with us Americans. But the result is that abstract and absolute thing called Art. (pp. vii-xi)

> *Waldo Frank, in a foreword to* Cane *by Jean Toomer, 1923. Reprint by University Place Press, 1967, pp. vii-xi.*

Robert Bone (essay date 1965)

[*Bone, an American critic and educator, wrote the critical histories* The Negro Novel in America *(1958; revised edition, 1965) and* Down Home: The Pastoral Impulse in Afro-American Short Fiction *(1975). In the following excerpt, he provides an overview of* Cane, *examining thematic unities in the work.*]

The writers of the Lost Generation, as John Aldridge has observed, "were engaged in a revolution designed to purge language of the old restraints of the previous century and to fit it to the demands of a younger, more realistic time." Stein and Hemingway in prose, Pound and Eliot in poetry, were threshing and winnowing, testing and experimenting with words, stretching them and refocusing them, until they became the pliant instruments of a new idiom. The only Negro writer of the 1920's who participated on equal terms in the creation of the modern idiom was a young poet-novelist named Jean Toomer.

Jean Toomer's *Cane* is an important American novel. By far the most impressive product of the Negro Renaissance, it ranks with Richard Wright's *Native Son*

and Ralph Ellison's *Invisible Man* as a measure of the Negro novelist's highest achievement. Jean Toomer belongs to that first rank of writers who use words almost as a plastic medium, shaping new meanings from an original and highly personal style. Since stylistic innovation requires great technical dexterity, Toomer displays a concern for technique which is fully two decades in advance of the period. While his contemporaries of the Harlem School were still experimenting with a crude literary realism, Toomer had progressed beyond the naturalistic novel to "the higher realism of the emotions," to symbol, and to myth. (pp. 80-1)

In spite of his wide and perhaps primary association with white intellectuals, as an artist Toomer never underestimated the importance of his Negro identity. He attained a universal vision not by ignoring race as a local truth, but by coming face to face with his particular tradition. His pilgrimage to Georgia was a conscious attempt to make contact with his hereditary roots in the Southland. Of Georgia, Toomer wrote: "There one finds soil in the sense that the Russians know it—the soil every art and literature that is to live must be embedded in." This sense of soil is central to *Cane* and to Toomer's artistic vision. "When one is on the soil of one's ancestors," his narrator remarks, "most anything can come to one."

What comes to Toomer, in the first section of *Cane,* is a vision of the parting soul of slavery:

> ...for though the sun is setting on
> A song-lit race of slaves, it has not set;
> Though late, O soil, it is not too late yet
> To catch thy plaintive soul, leaving, soon gone.

The soul of slavery persists in the "supper-getting-ready songs" of the black women who live on the Dixie Pike—a road which "has grown from a goat path in Africa." It persists in "the soft, listless cadence of Georgia's South," in the hovering spirit of a comforting Jesus, and in the sudden violence of the Georgia moon. It persists above all in the people, white and black, who have become Andersonian "grotesques" by virtue of their slave inheritance. Part I of *Cane* is in fact a kind of Southern *Winesburg, Ohio*. It consists of the portraits of six women—all primitives—in which an Andersonian narrator mediates between the reader and the author's vision of life on the Dixie Pike.

There is Karintha, "she who carries beauty" like a pregnancy, until her perfect beauty and the impatience of young men beget a fatherless child. Burying her child in a sawdust pile, she takes her revenge by becoming a prostitute; "the soul of her was a growing thing ripened too soon."

In **"Becky"** Toomer dramatizes the South's conspiracy to ignore miscegenation. Becky is a white woman with two Negro sons. After the birth of the first, she symbolically disappears from sight into a cabin constructed by community guilt. After the birth of the second, she is simply regarded as dead, and no one is surprised when the chimney of her cabin falls in and buries her. Toward Becky there is no charity from white or black, but only furtive attempts to conceal her existence.

Carma's tale, "which is the crudest melodrama," hinges not so much on marital infidelity as on a childish deception. Accused by her husband of having other men ("No one blames her for that") she becomes hysterical, and running into a canebrake, pretends to shoot herself. "Twice deceived, and the one deception proved the other." Her husband goes berserk, slashes a neighbor, and is sent to the chain gang. The tone of the episode is set by the ironic contrast between Carma's apparent strength ("strong as any man") and her childish behavior.

Fern, whose full name is Fernie May Rosen, combines the suffering of her Jewish father and her Negro mother: "at first sight of her I felt as if I heard a Jewish cantor sing....As if his singing rose above the unheard chorus of a folksong." Unable to find fulfillment, left vacant by the bestowal of men's bodies, Fern sits listlessly on her porch near the Dixie Pike. Her eyes desire nothing that man can give her; the Georgia countryside flows into them, along with something that Toomer's narrator calls God.

"Esther" is a study in sexual repression. The protagonist is a near-white girl whose father is the richest colored man in town. Deprived of normal outlets by her social position, she develops a neurotic life of fantasy which centers upon a virile, black-skinned, itinerant preacher named King Barlo. At sixteen she imagines herself the mother of his immaculately conceived child. At twenty-seven she tries to translate fantasy into reality by offering herself to Barlo. Rebuffed and humiliated, she retreats into lassitude and frigidity.

Louisa, of "Blood-Burning Moon," has two lovers, one white and the other colored. Inflamed by a sexual rivalry deeper than race, they quarrel. One is slashed and the other is lynched. Unlike most Negro writers who have grappled with the subject of lynching, Toomer achieves both form and perspective. He is not primarily concerned with antilynching propaganda, but in capturing a certain atavistic quality in Southern life which defies the restraints of civilized society.

Part II of *Cane* is counterpoint. The scene shifts to Washington, where Seventh Street thrusts a wedge of vitality, brilliance, and movement into the stale, soggy, whitewashed wood of the city. This contrast is an aspect of Toomer's primitivism. The blacks, in his color scheme, represent a full life; the whites, a denial of it. Washington's Negroes have preserved their vitality because of their roots in the rural South, yet whiteness presses in on them from all sides. The "dickty" Negro, and especially the near-white, who are most nearly assimilated to white civilization, bear the brunt of repression and denial, vacillating constantly between two identities. Out of this general frame of reference grow the central symbols of the novel.

Toomer's symbols reflect the profound humanism which forms the base of his philosophical position. Man's essential goodness, he would contend, his sense of brotherhood, and his creative instincts have been crushed and buried by modern industrial society. Toomer's positive values, therefore, are associated with the soil, the cane, and the harvest; with Christian charity, and with giving oneself in love. On the other side of the equation is a series of burial or confinement symbols (houses, alleys, machines, theaters, nightclubs, newspapers) which limit man's growth and act as barriers to his soul. Words are useless in piercing this barrier; Toomer's intellectualizing males are tragic figures because they value talking above feeling. Songs, dreams, dancing, and love itself (being instinctive in nature) may afford access to "the simple beauty of another's soul." The eyes, in particular, are avenues through which we can discover "the truth that people bury in their hearts."

In the second section of *Cane*, Toomer weaves these symbols into a magnificent design, so that his meaning, elusive in any particular episode, emerges with great impact from the whole. "Rhobert" is an attack on the crucial bourgeois value of home ownership: "Rhobert wears a house, like a monstrous diver's helmet, on his head." Like Thoreau's farmer, who traveled through life pushing a barn and a hundred acres before him, Rhobert is a victim of his own property instinct. As he struggles with the weight of the house, he sinks deeper and deeper into the mud....(pp. 81-5)

The basic metaphor in "Avey" compares a young girl to the trees planted in boxes along V street, "the young trees that whinnied like colts impatient to be free." Avey's family wants her to become a school teacher, but her bovine nature causes her to prefer a somewhat older profession. Yet, ironically, it is not she but the narrator who is a failure, who is utterly inadequate in the face of Avey's womanhood.

In "Theater" Toomer develops his "dickty" theme, through an incident involving a chorus girl and a theater-manager's brother. As John watches a rehearsal, he is impressed by Dorris' spontaneity, in contrast to the contrived movements of the other girls. He momentarily contemplates an affair, but reservations born of social distance prevent him from consummating his desire, except in a dream. Dorris, who hopes fleetingly for home and children from such a man, is left at the end of the episode with only the sordid reality of the theater.

"Calling Jesus" plays a more important role than its length would indicate in unifying the symbolism of the novel. It concerns a woman, urbanized and spiritually intimidated, whose "soul is like a little thrust-tailed dog that follows her, whimpering." At night, when she goes to sleep in her big house, the little dog is left to shiver in the vestibule. "Some one...eoho Jesus...soft as the bare feet of Christ moving across bales of Southern cotton, will steal in and cover it that it need not shiver, and carry it to where she sleeps, cradled in dream-fluted cane."

In **"Box Seat"** Toomer comes closest to realizing his central theme. The episode opens with an invocation: "Houses are shy girls whose eyes shine reticently upon the dusk body of the street. Upon the gleaming limbs and asphalt torso of a dreaming nigger. Shake your curled wool-blossoms, nigger. Open your liver-lips to the lean white spring. Stir the root-life of a withered people. Call them from their houses and teach them to dream." (p. 85)

The thought is that of a young man, whose symbolic role is developed at once: "I am Dan Moore. I was born in a canefield. The hands of Jesus touched me. I am come to a sick world to heal it." Dan, moreover, comes as a representative of "powerful underground races": "The next world-savior is coming up that way. Coming up. A continent sinks down. The new-world Christ will need consummate skill to walk upon the waters where huge bubbles burst." (p. 86)

The feminine lead is played by Muriel, a school teacher inclined toward conventionality. Her landlady, Mrs. Pribby, is constantly with her, being in essence a projection of Muriel's social fears. The box seat which she occupies at the theater, where her every movement is under observation, renders her relationship to society perfectly. Her values are revealed in her query to Dan, "Why don't you get a good job and settle down?" On these terms only can she love him; meanwhile she avoids his company by going to a vaudeville performance with a girl friend.

Dan, a slave to "her still unconquered animalism," follows and watches her from the audience. The main attraction consists of a prize fight between two dwarfs for the "heavy-weight championship"; it symbolizes the ultimate degradation of which a false and shoddy culture is capable. Sparring grotesquely, pounding and bruising each other, the dwarfs suggest the traditional clown symbol of modern art. At the climax of the episode the winner presents a blood-spattered rose to Muriel, who recoils, hesitates, and finally submits. The dwarf's eyes are pleading: "Do not shrink. Do not be afraid of me." Overcome with disgust for Muriel's hypocrisy, Dan completes the dwarf's thought from the audience, rising to shout: "JESUS WAS ONCE A LEPER!" Rushing from the theater, he is free at last of his love for Muriel—free, but at the same time sterile: "He is as cool as a green stem that has just shed its flower."

Coming as an anticlimax after **"Box Seat," "Bona and Paul"** describes an abortive love affair between two Southern students at the University of Chicago—a white girl and a mulatto boy who is "passing." The main tension, reminiscent of Gertrude Stein's *Melanctha*, is between knowing and loving, set in the framework of Paul's double identity. It is not his race consciousness which terminates the relationship, as one critic has suggested, but precisely his "whiteness," his desire for knowledge, his philosophical bent. If he had been able to assert his Negro self—that which attracted Bona to him in the first place—he might have held her love.

In **"Kabnis"** rural Georgia once more provides a setting. This is the long episode which comprises the concluding section of *Cane*. By now the symbolic values of Toomer's main characters can be readily assessed. Ralph Kabnis, the protagonist, is a school teacher from the North who cringes in the face of his tradition. A spiritual coward, he cannot contain "the pain and beauty of the South"; cannot embrace the suffering of the past, symbolized by slavery; cannot come to terms with his own bastardy; cannot master his pathological fear of being lynched. Consumed with self-hatred and cut off from any organic connection with the past, he resembles nothing so much as a scarecrow: "Kabnis, a promise of soil-soaked beauty; uprooted, thinning out. Suspended a few feet above the soil whose touch would resurrect him."

Lewis, by way of contrast, is a Christ figure, an extension of Dan Moore. Almost a T. S. Eliot creation ("I'm on a sort of contract with myself"), his function is to shock others into moral awareness. It is Lewis who confronts Kabnis with his moral cowardice. (pp. 86-7)

Halsey, unlike Kabnis, has not been crushed by Southern life, but absorbed into it. Nevertheless, his spiritual degradation is equally thorough. An artisan and small shopkeeper like his father before him, he "belongs" in a sense that Kabnis does not. Yet in order to maintain his place in the community, he must submit to the indignities of Negro life in the South. Like Booker T. Washington, whose point of view he represents, Halsey has settled for something less than manhood. Restless, groping tentatively toward Lewis, he escapes from himself through his craft, and through an occasional debauch with the town prostitute, whom he loved as a youth.

Father John, the old man who lives beneath Halsey's shop, represents a link with the Negro's ancestral past. Concealed by the present generation as an unpleasant memory, the old man is thrust into a cellar which resembles the hold of a slave ship. There he sits, "A mute John the Baptist of a new religion or a tongue-tied shadow of an old." When he finally speaks, it is to rebuke the white folks for the sin of slavery. The contrast between Lewis and Kabnis is sharpened by their respective reactions to Father John. Through the old slave, Lewis is able to "merge with his source," but Kabnis can only deny: "An' besides, he aint my past. My ancestors were Southern bluebloods."

In terms of its dramatic movement **"Kabnis"** is a steep slope downward, approximating the progressive deterioration of the protagonist. Early in the episode Kabnis is reduced to a scarecrow replica of himself by his irrational fears. His failure to stand up to Hanby, an authoritarian school principal, marks a decisive loss in his power of self-direction. Gradually he slips into a childlike dependence, first on Halsey, than on the two prostitutes, and finally on Halsey's little sister, Carrie Kate. In the course of the drunken debauch with which the novel ends, Kabnis becomes a clown, without dignity or manhood, wallowing in the mire of his own self-hatred. The stark tragedy of **"Kabnis"** is relieved only by the figure of Carrie Kate, the unspoiled child of a new generation, who may yet be redeemed through her ties with Father John.

A critical analysis of *Cane* is a frustrating task, for Toomer's art, in which "outlines are reduced to essences," is largely destroyed in the process of restoration. No paraphrase can properly convey the aesthetic pleasure derived from a sensitive reading of *Cane.* Yet in spite of Toomer's successful experiment with the modern idiom—or perhaps because of it—*Cane* met with a cold reception from the public, hardly selling 500 copies during its first year. This poor showing must have been a great disappointment to Toomer, and undoubtedly it was a chief cause of his virtual retirement from literature. Perhaps in his heart of hearts Jean Toomer found it singularly appropriate that the modern world should bury *Cane.* Let us in any event delay the exhumation no longer. (pp. 87-9)

> Robert Bone, "The Harlem School," in his The Negro Novel in America, *revised edition, Yale University Press, 1965, pp. 65-94.*

Patricia Chase (essay date 1971)

[*Chase is an American poet and critic. In the following excerpt from an essay first published in* CLA Journal *in 1971, she discusses* Cane's *female characters.*]

If the fabric of *Cane* is the life essence and its meaning behind absurdity, then Toomer's women characters are the threads which weave *Cane* together. Like the form in which Toomer chose to express himself, his women characters are no less rare and sensual. Perhaps they are all the same woman, archetypal woman, all wearing different faces, but each possessing an identifiable aspect of womanhood. Each is strange, yet real; each wears a protective mask of indifference; each is as capable of love as well as lust; and each is guilty of or victimized by betrayal—of herself or of a man. There is no aspect of woman that Toomer does not weave inextricably into his archetypal woman, and in the end, through Carrie K., he has fashioned out of flesh and also failure his vision of womankind.

Toomer moves his women characters, as he changes the locus of *Cane,* from South to North and back to the South again. All of the women reflect their environment, are mirrored in it and react to it. Some belong to themselves (Carma, Karintha, Avey); others belong to the rich earth of Georgia (Fern, Becky, Esther, Louisa); and the rest belong to the whitewashed conformity and death-in-life of the North (Dorris, Muriel, Bona). If Toomer poses a question through one woman, he often answers that same question, or makes his statement through another. If Carma, in her ferocity and natural drive, does not understand her responsibility for her actions and their consequences, then Louisa most clearly does. If Karintha and Fern are the existential questions, of being or nonbeing, of identity vs. nonentity, then Avey is the statement of survival through acceptance and indifference. If Becky is reality in the face of absurdity, then Esther is absurdity in the face of reality. If Dorris mirrors the question of finding life sustenance in the North, then Muriel is the answer.

Toomer's thread of meaning begins weaving itself in Karintha, who is "perfect as dusk when the sun goes down." If Toomer is fashioning an archetypal woman, he begins with the first feminine quality, beauty:

> Her skin is like the dusk on the eastern horizon,
> O cant you see it, O cant you see it,
> Her skin is like dusk on the eastern horizon
> ...When the sun goes down.

Karintha is passionate and fierce, bursting with vitality and life, but she grows ripe too soon. She is suffused, even as a child, with an almost tangible sexuality and sensuality, but she suspends herself just out of reach of those who want her. Like many of Toomer's women, she is not to be possessed. Toomer paints Karintha in gentle brushstroke words: "Her sudden darting past you was a bit of vivid color, like a black bird that flashes in light." Karintha seems to be holding the promise of life's secret, but just out of reach. Like the baby that "fell out of her womb," she exists in a haze of sweet smoke. In the rural South, poor, with nothing to *do,* she is very much free to *be.* She belongs simply to herself and to "the Georgia dusk when the sun goes down." Karintha is a question, a provocative overture to a rehearsal of human experience.

If Karintha is Toomer's existential question, then Fern and finally Avey are the statement to that question. In Fern Toomer expands on the quality of beauty in a woman. Her face "flowed into her eyes. Flowed in soft cream foam and plaintive ripples, in such a way that wherever your glance may momentarily have rested, it immediately thereafter wavered in the direction of her eyes." Fern is alluring yet elusive. Through Fern, Toomer deals with the concept of beauty for its own sake in a woman. Men see in her eyes what they want to see, mystery and a yet unfulfilled desire. In his desire and fascination the young man says of her: "They were strange eyes. In this, that they sought nothing—that is, nothing that was obvious and tangible and that one could see, and they gave the impression that nothing was to be denied.... Fern's eyes desired nothing that you could give her; there was no reason why they should withhold.... When she was young, a few men took her, but got no joy from it." Perhaps behind her beauty there was nothing else. Her promise, it appeared, was just out of reach, and: "As you know, men are apt to idolize or fear that which they cannot understand, especially if it be a woman." In Fern, Toomer is building a myth of woman, endowing her with mysticism and an ineluctability that make men want to do some "fine, unnamed thing" for her. But Fern lacks external identity. She *is* her beauty. It is her only gift from life. Yet Fern is the only one who accepts this. Others weave myths about her to sustain themselves, and then with vague guilt, having used her to escape oppressive passion or ennui, or perhaps to escape—for a moment—themselves, they weave myths and dreams protectively about her in payment for their use of her. "A sort of superstition crept into their consciousness of her being somehow above them." In her dissertation, "Jean Toomer: Herald of the Negro Renaissance," Mabel Mayle Dillard makes the point that men are "struck by an attachment to Fern that transcends all reality." But no one really touches Fern, if there is anything to touch. She is waiting, it seems, for something that will never come, and she knows it. She belongs to the soil of Georgia and the scent of the cane. There is no choice involved. So in waiting, Fern has *become* all that life has given her—her beauty—and her being is dreamy and drugged by the day-to-day life that is her reality and her prison. Said Toomer in a letter to his friend, Waldo Frank. "In Karintha and Fern the dominant emotion is a sadness derived from a sense of fading, of a knowledge of one's futility to check solution . . ." In the same letter he says, "The supreme fact of mechanical civilization is that you become part of it or get sloughed off or under." (pp. 389-91)

What he hints at in Karintha and Fern, Toomer states outright through Avey, the existential woman. Unconcerned, indifferent, living in the here and now, "lazy and easy as anything," she is an earthy but enigmatic woman. Like Karintha and Fern, Toomer describes Avey in terms of her allure and her elusiveness. She is a mystique to the adolescent boys who see her as floating among, but somehow above, them. Avey is a woman already, but they are not yet men and cannot have her. The young man in love with Avey says, "I'd meet her on the street, and there'd be no difference in the way she said hello. She never took the trouble to call me by my name . . . . She'd smile appreciation, but it was an impersonal smile, never for me." Later, when they are older, he says wistfully, "But though I held her tightly in my arms, she was way away." Like Karintha and Fern she came and went as she pleased, leaving always a scent of unfulfilled promise behind her. She is silent and knowing, surprised by none of life's traps and betrayals. Like Fern and Karintha men are tempted to weave myths about her and to "idolize and fear that which they cannot understand, especially if it be a woman." Avey, like Fern and Karintha, seems to hold the key to some secret, that if men only knew what, would make them free. However, if Avey is heavy with sensual promise, it is not through her own design. It is simply what men *choose* to see in her, not being able to understand her for what she is. Not being able to really know Avey or possess her, the persona (perhaps speaking for the author) wishes to protect her from the sordid side of life to explain her to herself. But she has already experienced life and has come to grips with it on her own terms. Life has been real enough and brutal enough for Avey that she has seen it for its absurdity and hypocrisy, come to workable terms with it, and thus can no longer be wounded by it. She has been so blown about willy-nilly by life that she knows her powerlessness against

circumstance. But to her would-be lover she is "lazy and indolent . . . " (pp. 392-93)

In moving from the black world (the South) to the white world (the North) in **Cane,** Toomer passes consciously through the grey world of Esther and Becky, a purgatory of miscegenation. Through both Becky and Esther, Toomer limns women who bear the burden of society's vision of race mixing. In Becky he is dealing with the creator; with Esther, the creation. If Becky is reality in the face of absurdity, then Esther is absurdity in the face of reality. Becky, who is white, is rejected because she bears two illegitimate black sons; Esther is rejected because she is neither black nor white, and her mind becomes equally gray. Becky is relegated to her world through her actions; Esther fashions a world of fantasy for lack of a real one. Becky is reality. Esther is illusion.

Becky has borne two black sons. As a result she is ostracized by both the black and white communities. In their guilt for rejecting her, they scurry desperately but furtively to provide her with food, shelter, and a cloak of anonymity. Those who weave a myth of mysticism about Fern and Avey also endow Becky with a supernatural myth, laying their burden of guilt upon her. She is feared by them since she is the mirror within which they must see their own narrowness and cruelty. Becky is said to exude "vitality," but it is nothing so qualitative as that; hers is simply bone-hard determination to survive. Her survival for so long in the face of rejection and score proves her strength and the validity of her existence. The author's description of Becky is merely a sketchy framework for his purpose, for **"Becky"** reveals the bleak reality of the human experience, more than the woman. In Toomer's style, she *is* the experience. Of course, the crumbling of Becky's house is most symbolic; perhaps it caves in from the oppressive weight of a whole town's guilt. And it is interesting that in the face of rejection and ostracism, Becky chooses to stay in this rural southern town while it is the people of the community who really flee from Becky, who holds the mirror of their weaknesses.

Toomer's other "grey world" woman, Esther, is a woman without racial or sexual identity. She lacks the color, both literally and figuratively, of Fern, Karintha, Louisa, Carma, and Avey. Having been bleached of the color to which she has birthright, black, she has also been robbed of its quality. She is of neither world in color and neither world in mind. Belonging nowhere, Esther builds her own world through fantasy. All of her plans are sketchy and unsure. Even her dreams are bits and pieces of fantasy, never whole or complete. In her loneliness and emptiness, both as a person and as a woman, she reaches out for depth and the reality of living, personified for her by King Barlo, but she has little save fantasy to offer him. She sees Barlo as her deliverer—from loneliness to love, from barrenness to fulfillment, from greyness to blackness, from nonentity to identity. In her solitude, and out of her need, she creates an impossible myth about Barlo, and in the end, it is the myth she desires, not the man. Face-to-face with

King Barlo (fantasy faced with reality) she sees that he is a man, not a myth, and since her life is built on myths and fantasy, she cannot relate to him. Esther leaves with numb acceptance of her life stretching out before her empty and meaningless. She "steps out" then of whatever shreds of realness she may have had into a world where "there is no air, no street, and the town has completely disappeared." With no alternative left, Esther steps finally into the world of madness, where no identity is required. Her mind is indeed a "pink meshbag filled with babytoes." Perhaps Esther symbolizes the part of woman that needs myth to survive in an alien and frightening world, sexual myth as well as male myth. For many women these myths are reality. Society makes them reality, and many cannot choose but believe. And like Esther, for them, the myth becomes the man. And the life. Everlasting. (pp. 393-94)

From the depth and natural life force of the South, Toomer moves his women characters and their lives to the fast-moving world of the urban North—industrial, cold, anonymous. If Toomer characterizes through primitive woman a reaction to life in the South, then Dorris, Muriel, and, to an extent, Bona typify the life of the whitewashed North.

Dorris, with her beauty and vitality, exemplifies all that the North represents, but in **"Theater,"** she takes up arms in her dancing and passionately presents herself to the world, asking for love in return. She gives herself over to the rhythms of life, through her dancing, hoping to draw John into the dance of life and into her:

> I've heard em say that men who look like him (what does he look like?) will marry if they love. O will you love me? And give me kids, and a home, and everything? . . . Dorris dances. She forgets her tricks. She dances. Glorious songs are muscles of her limbs. And her singing is of canebrake loves and mangrove feastings.

Dorris tries with all her being to clutch the feelings of the man, John, whose black body is separated from his consciousness, which is white-washed and melancholy like the North. As Lieber points out, John does not accept or rejoice in his black heritage, is estranged from it, and cannot love Dorris on her terms. His mind is a prison of the shaft of white light; he has been whitewashed by the white people, standards, and racism of the North, where, because of his blackness, his manhood is denied. Thus he cannot love, and without love, Dorris is in turn robbed of her womanhood. The dank whiteness of the North, its cold, its people, and its "dry smell of dry paste and paint and soiled clothing" will make Dorris dry and brittle herself. She will become, without love, a dancing doll, groping for feeling and empathy, laboring to survive as a woman where there is no survival possible.

Muriel is John's counterpart in a woman. Starched, retreating, disguising her selfness behind the walls of a prim, white house, Muriel worries constantly about "what people think" and becomes the prisoner of that cliché. At the first hint of something real and of value,

Dan and his desire, she backs away in fear. Dan, trying desperately to retain his identity in the disgusting conformity of urban life, tries to free Muriel from her prison of fear. "For once in your life youre going to face whats real, by God—." But Muriel pushes him away.

> Muriel fastens on her image. She smoothes her dress. She adjusts her skirt. She becomes prim and cool. Rising, she skirts Dan as if to keep the glass between them . . .

Muriel has sold herself to play a minor part in a sham, white-washed world. She wants Dan, but not in a real or honest way. She wants him sexually, but is not free enough to enjoy her own sexuality. Since she is not free enough to give herself to him, she fantasizes rape and violence, anything but real loving. Like an adolescent, she wants to call what she wants by another name. Dan recognizes her for what she is, a slave to convention.

> Muriel—bored. Must be. But she'll smile and she'll clap. Do what youre bid, you she-slave. Look at her. Sweet, tame woman in a brass box seat. Clap, smile, fawn, clap. Do what youre bid . . .

For the real sexual love that she wants, Muriel accepts the symbolic grappling of midgets on a stage. "They charge . . . . They pound each other furiously. Muriel pounds." And for her orgasm she sees "cut lips and bloody noses." For love, she accepts hate; for sex, blood. In a grotesque parody of afterlove, a battered midget comes out holding flowers and a mirror, within which Muriel is refused her reflection, since she has none. Instead, the midget presents her with bloody roses as a mocking memento.

Like Muriel and Dorris, Bona, a white girl from the South transplanted to the North, is colorless and washed by conformity. In her search for meaning in life and in the "white experience," she is in love with Paul's blackness, but not Paul himself. Like John, a victim of white-washing, Paul has not embraced his racial identity and all that it involves. As Robert Bone asserts in *The Negro Novel in America,* it is Paul's inability to assert his Negro self that makes the potential love affair "an abortive one." As the white woman face-to-face with, and attracted to, the black man, Bona is confused and unsure. She symbolically dances about Paul on the basketball court, testing her feelings and measuring his.

> She whirls. He catches her. Her body stiffens. Then becomes strangely vibrant, and bursts to swift life within her anger . . . . He look at Bona. Whir. Whir. They seem to be human distortions spinning tensely in a fog. Spinning..dizzy..spinning . . . Bona jerks herself free, flushes a startling crimson, breaks through the bewildered teams, and rushes from the hall.

An extrovert herself, Bona is irresistibly drawn to Paul, who is quiet, pensive, and deep. She wants to know him, but with her preconditioned vision of him, she does not see him at all. Their experiences and their lives have been kept so rigidly apart for so long by society that they are strangers and do not know how to reach out to each other as man and woman. The gulf between them is far too wide, from black to white, from man to woman, and from real to real. In **"Bona and Paul"** Toomer is no longer dealing with absurdity in the face of reality, or reality in the face of absurdity, but one reality in the face of another. (pp. 397-400)

With his statement in **"Bona and Paul"** and with Paul's realization (perhaps a reflection of Toomer's own agonizing battle with identity), Toomer is ready to move back again to the source—the deep South. Here, through Kabnis, he extends his question of identity to a statement through woman. Quietly and surely, through Carrie K., Toomer makes his final statement of woman and her role. Carrie K., unlike some of the other women characters in **Cane,** is able to accept herself and her cultural experience totally, with action as well as reaction. She is young and shy, yet knowing. She is able to understand equally the young man, Kabnis, denying yet searching for his identity, as well as she understands the old man, Father John, who is the container and the reflector of the black experience for which Kabnis searches: "She is lovely in her fresh energy of the morning, in the calm, untested confidence and nascent maternity...." Carrie K. believes not only in herself, but in the validity of all human experience. She is the bridge between the old and the new, and between fantasy and reality. Toomer seems to present, through Carrie K., his total vision of woman—not withdrawing, but advancing toward the future carrying the relevant past, i.e., Father John, with her. Through her Toomer makes his final statement of woman as a bridge, not only between man and man, but as a bridge between man and himself. This is most evident when Father John, the "mute John the Baptist of a new religion—or tongue-tied shadow of an old," vouchsafes "... th sin th white folks 'mitted when they made th Bible lie." Infuriated, Kabnis retorts,

> "So thats your sin. All these years t tell us that th white folks made th Bible lie. Well, I'll be damned.. Lewis ought t have been here. You old black fakir—"

Carrie K. then responds to Kabnis:

> "Brother Ralph, is that your best Amen?" She turns him to her and takes his hot cheeks in her firm cool hands. Her palms draw the fever out. With its passing, Kabnis crumples. He sinks to his knees before her, ashamed, exhausted. His eyes squeeze tight. Carrie presses his face tenderly against her...

Without fear and with intuitive perception, Carrie K. accepts the validity of *all* human experience without judgment or contempt. She is, in her compassion and acceptance, the link between the man and his soul.

Toomer begins with Karintha and her beauty, and ends with Carrie K. and her profundity, as **Cane** culminates in the vision and meaning of human experience. Through his reflections of a woman's reaction to living, through many women and the faces they wear, Toomer has woven a vision of woman that is real and valid, because they are.

This vision culminates in Carrie K. She is all of his women in one self-actualizing woman. She is **Cane.**

> Her skin is like the dusk on the eastern horizon,
> O cant you see it, O cant you see it,
> Her skin is like dusk on the eastern horizon
> ... When the sun goes down.

(pp. 400-02)

Patricia Chase, "The Women in 'Cane'," in Jean Toomer: A Critical Evaluation, *edited by Therman B. O'Daniel, Howard University Press, 1988, pp. 389-402.*

Alan Golding (essay date 1983)

[*Golding is an American educator and critic. In the following excerpt, he relates the poetry and short stories of* Cane *to Toomer's personal search for racial and spiritual identity.*]

> Some critics have viewed [*Cane*] as an experimental novel; others as a miscellany, composed of poetic, dramatic, and narrative elements; still others as a work *sui generis,* which deliberately violates the standard categories. The problem is complicated by the fact that parts of *Cane* were published independently as poems, sketches, and stories. This would suggest that Toomer thought of them as separate entities, whatever their subsequent function in the overall design.

Thus Robert Bone summarizes the field of critical responses to **Cane** [in his *Down Home: A History of Afro-American Short Fiction from Its Beginnings to the End of the Harlem Renaissance,* 1975]. Yet, in whatever way they have finally categorized Jean Toomer's collage of character vignettes, poetry, song, short story, and drama, critics have generally argued that the book exhibits various kinds of unified design. The action throughout occupies either the same setting (Parts 1 and 3 occur in Sempter, Georgia, a fictionalized Sparta) or the same *kind* of setting (Part 2 moves among various Northern cities, including Washington, D.C., and Chicago). This tripartite structure based on place provides some overall shape and readers have also noted various strains of thematic and stylistic unity in the work.

If we accept that Toomer did try to shape his "separate entities" into an "overall design," then this question arises: Why? What was he after in his efforts to forge **Cane's** fragments into a whole? I suggest that he was striving for more than a solely esthetic unity. Toomer organizes **Cane** around a pattern of balanced but unresolved poles—between rural South and urban North, black emotionalism and white intellect, female sensuality and male mind. Like most such polarities these appear, from one angle, facile and rather simplistic, and it reflects negatively on Toomer that they are not post hoc critical contrivances, that they can easily be found in **Cane.** Yet at the same time these poles embody powerful social and personal conflicts: that of Southern, rural, black culture facing assimilation into a predominantly white, urban, Northern culture, and that of

Toomer's own mixed racial identity. I shall argue that Toomer's drive to make the pieces of *Cane* balance or cohere enacts on the formal level his struggle to reconcile both the contradictory spirits of North and South and the black and white within himself.

Toomer's search for personal and racial identity so strongly forms the basis of his art that the work after *Cane* disintegrates once he feels he has reached his goal of spiritual and racial harmony in discovering Gurdjieff's Unitism in 1924. He dissociated himself from racial fiction to the extent of refusing James Weldon Johnson permission to use some of the *Cane* poems in a revised edition of *The Book of American Negro Poetry* in 1930, on the grounds that they were neither black nor white but simply "American" poems. In fact, Toomer refused to be included in several Negro anthologies around this time, and was angry with Alain Locke for publishing parts of *Cane* in the Harlem Renaissance manifesto, *The New Negro*. Yet asserting his black identity may have cost him the chance to publish a novel, *Transatlantic*, in 1929. In 1941 he gave permission for two selections from *Cane* to appear in an anthology of black literature, *The Negro Caravan*.

Thus the evidence on whether Toomer considered himself black remains inconclusive. In an unpublished essay, **"The South in Literature,"** written partly to promote *Cane*, he describes himself as "of Negro descent." In a 1922 letter to Sherwood Anderson he alludes to his art as having the didactic impulse to guide "the youth of the [black] race": "But I feel that in time, in its social phase, my art will aid in giving the Negro to himself. In this connection I have thought of a magazine. . . . The need is great." Yet Toomer did not identify with blacks after writing *Cane*. The book seems to have functioned as an elegy not only for the black folk spirit but for Toomer's own blackness. As George Kent says, "Toomer may have represented the kind of racial consciousness that for a brief interval is *most* intense *precisely* because it is about to *disappear*." Toomer's temporary identification with blacks apparently released his art, as he himself admits in 1922: "Within the last two or three years, however, my growing need for artistic expression has pulled me deeper and deeper into the Negro group." *Cane* represents what Bone calls "a momentary deviation" from a consistent, lifelong pattern of challenging racial categories. Even around the time of writing *Cane* Toomer did little to encourage the Harlem Renaissance, and in a 1930 diary he writes "I am to decrystallize these [racial] divisions and make possible the widespread consciousness of the American race."

Cane shows Toomer in 1923 intellectually an American and emotionally a black. His later writings displace this conflict from the racial to the spiritual plane and increasingly emphasize personal, spiritual integration independent of race: "Themosense (thought *and* emotion *and* sensing) is the inner synthesis of functions, which represents the entire individual and gives rise to complete action." In *Cane* Toomer writes as a black man—but as the first black writer to attempt collapsing racial categories in literature by consistently applying white artists' formal experiments to black themes of racial disenfranchisement, oppression, and identity. Until *Cane*, black fiction had been represented by the straightforwardly realistic novels of Charles Chesnutt, Paul Laurence Dunbar, James Weldon Johnson, and W. E. B. DuBois. Certainly Johnson's *The Autobiography of an Ex-Coloured Man* (1912) deals with similar modes of communal black experience (oral tales, music and dance, religious oratory, lynchings) to *Cane*. Certainly DuBois's *The Souls of Black Folk* (1903) offers, in short sketches occasionally linked by songs, a Northerner's narrative travelogue of the rural South. But *Cane* advanced on these works by pursuing such modernist prose techniques as the breakdown of continuous narrative into juxtaposed fragments, an emphasis on psychological over narrative realism, snatches of plot more symbolic than literal, and the elevation of governing metaphors to almost mythic status (compare Jake Barnes's groin wound or, later, Faulkner's bear to Toomer's use of cane and dusk). Clearly these techniques are not the prerogative of white writers, but they had never before appeared so sustainedly in black writing as they did in *Cane*. (pp. 197-201)

We often talk of "organic" form as "musical" form, and indeed *Cane* has been described as having a musical unity, especially in the systematic repetition and contrast of its images and themes. Munson notes that Toomer once thought of becoming a composer and discusses **"Karintha"** as a structural model for many of the stories. This piece opens with a song, presents its theme, breaks into song once more, develops the theme further, and continues to alternate prose and "song" or poetry, with each shift qualifying the previous development. Readers have variously related *Cane*'s repetition of images to late nineteenth-century symphonies and jazz improvisations, as broad a range as one could wish for under the general rubric of "musical form." The common feature in these diverse descriptions is that which Munson proposed, an alternation between theme and refrain or variation on the theme. But one need not look as far as symphonies or jazz to find this pattern—only as far as the work song, spirituals, and call-and-response preaching which comprise much of *Cane*'s content.

In constantly redefining its own verbal components, this cross-referential or repetitive structure also redefines the relationship between individual experience and that of the race. Thus it reflects Toomer's own vacillating sense of racial identity. The cross-referentiality occurs both within and between particular pieces. Within a piece, choric descriptive phrases such as those in **"Karintha"** or **"Blood-Burning Moon"** resonate with increasing richness against the main action and place the individual protagonist's experience within a broader context of racial experience. Karintha's "skin is like dusk on the eastern horizon," and the repetition of this simile accumulates to connect her awakening sexuality with that time of day when, in the world of *Cane*, the black soul paradoxically awakens. The ominous "blood-burning moon" in the story of that title comes to govern not only Tom Burwell's fate but that of his people, "showering the homes of folk" in the Georgia town; its influence builds as the image is repeated.

Between pieces, Toomer mixes forms so that each piece may comment on the other. The structure of Part 1 of *Cane* consists of a prose piece followed by two poems which refer both backward to the preceding and forward to the following prose pieces. This poetry qualifies or provides an alternative perspective on the prose sketches. It often reminds us of hardship or pain in the midst of beauty, of suffering in acceptance, reflecting Toomer's ambivalence about his roots. In **"Reapers,"** for example, "a field rat, startled, squealing bleeds,/His belly close to ground," cut by a scythe. This image shows the more threatening side of the beauty-pain duality present in **"Karintha,"** where Karintha "carries beauty, perfect as dusk when the sun goes down" but also "stoned the cows, and beat her dog, and fought the other children." Then the two elements come together in **"November Cotton Flower,"** a description already attributed to Karintha: winter cold sets in, the soil fights drought, birds die, yet suddenly "the flower bloomed." The poems continue to reflect on the prose narratives throughout Part 1. The anonymous suffering of **"Face,"** her "Brows— / recurved canoes / quivered by the ripples blown by pain," generalizes the immediate, personalized pain of **"Becky,"** and the poem's imagery is echoed later in **"Fern":** "Face flowed into her eyes. Flowed in soft cream foam and plaintive ripples." This movement from particular (**"Becky"**) to general (**"Face"**) also occurs between **"Carma"** and **"Song of the Son,"** and further typifies the oscillating movement of Part 1. **"Carma"** raises questions of individual freedom—"Should she not take others?"—which stimulate the more generalized **"Song of the Son,"** where the freedom at stake is that of a whole race.

Toomer's Georgia is saturated in song and his synesthetic metaphors aim at a Symbolist identification of image and object, of self and environment: "Pungent and composite, the smell of farmyards is the fragrance of the woman. She does not sing; her body is a song. She is in the forest, dancing." But most importantly for our argument, he uses musical form, actual black songs and musical imagery, to identify with the black part of himself and with the culture that *Cane* portrays. Thus music serves a social as well as an esthetic function for Toomer and for his black characters. In the Northern stories of Part 2, a number of characters—the jazz singers of **"Seventh Street,"** the narrator of **"Avey,"** Dan Moore, Dorris, Paul—use dance or song to release themselves from social restraints, express themselves, and assert their blackness. His Southern blacks make "folk-songs from soul sounds" and thus activate "race memories" of their African origins. And as a phase of black culture fades ("just before an epoch's sun"), these songs also record the meaning of that culture: "Caroling softly souls of slavery,/What they were, and what they are to me."

As that sun declines, then, Toomer uses musical imagery not only to celebrate an ideal but also to mourn its loss: the ideal of the black soul preserving its traditions through folk songs and spirituals. Toomer had learned in his 1922 Georgia visit that spirituals were dying, mocked even by certain of the Southern blacks themselves, and he had learned that many rural blacks cheerfully embraced urbanization:

> But I learned that the Negroes of the town objected to them [folk songs and spirituals]. They called them "shouting." They had victrolas and player-pianos.... With Negroes also the trend was towards the small town and then towards the city—and industry and commerce and machines. The folk-spirit was walking in to die on the modern desert. That spirit was so beautiful. Its death was so tragic.

And in the withering of this folk-spirit Toomer may have sensed the withering of his own art. Only a few months after *Cane's* publication he summarized the spirit of his book as a spirit of fading: "a sadness derived from a sense of fading, from a knowledge of my futility to check solution.... The folk-songs themselves are of the same order: the deepest of them, 'I ain't got long to stay here.'" *Cane* marked the end of a culture and of the only significant phase of Toomer's art:

> *Cane* was a swan-song. It was a song of an end. And why no one has seen and felt that, why people have expected me to write a second and a third and a fourth book like *Cane,* is one of the queer misunderstandings of my life.

The music of *Cane* does not bring harmony; the differences between black and white culture and Toomer's ambivalent relationship to those differences remain key notes. Toomer wrote in his autobiography that the "tensions" which "arise from natural oppositions"—and which arise in human society, itself "a situation of tensions of forces," in the form of cultural conflict—"should eventuate in constructive crises." **"Box Seat"** offers an integrated statement of life's source in oppositions:

> Life bends joy and pain, beauty and ugliness, in such a way that no one may isolate them. No one should want to. Perfect joy, or perfect pain, with no contrasting element to define them would mean a monotony of consciousness, would mean death.

(pp. 202-05)

So far I have discussed how certain kinds of formal oscillation within individual pieces and within the large divisions of *Cane* reflect Toomer's wrestling with the future of Southern black culture and with his own racial identity. On a larger scale, contrasts between Parts 1 and 2 of *Cane* reflect that same wrestling. For example, Southern blacks' move from a rural past to an urban future appears through opposed geographical locations: the Georgia of Part 1, where Toomer's blacks have their roots, and the Northern cities of Part 2, where those roots are severed. To illustrate this severing of roots Toomer reverses the image patterns of Part 1 in the urban settings of Part 2. Fresh, clean pine becomes the "stale soggy wood of Washington." Fragrant Southern air contrasts with "smells of garbage and wet trash" or "the scent of rancid flowers," the "smell of dry paste, and paint, and soiled clothing." When the Washington air is sweet, it is sweet not with cane but with "exploded gasoline." Vegetative imagery becomes mechanical, soft lines become hard and metallic, and the color of steel blue recurs. Images of burial or confinement dominate Part 2: characters find themselves trapped in vestibules, theaters, basements, cars. Houses, narrow alleys, machines, and nightclubs all cramp movement and block communication.

A further contrast between Parts 1 and 2, between South and North, exists in Toomer's different handling of female sexuality. Part 1 shows sexuality withered (Esther), suffering (Becky), or abused because of its very fecundity (Karintha, Carma, Fern). Yet with the exception of Esther these women have an inner strength and aloof self-sufficiency which carries them beyond the pain and stress of their immediate circumstances. They rarely talk, in contrast to the constant self-justification of the Northern women. The women of Part 2, both black and white, have channeled their sexuality into social formulas. In **"Box Seat"** Muriel says to herself that "the town wont let me love you, Dan" and "I'm not strong enough to buck it"; Bona refuses to kiss Paul because he hasn't said he loves her.

Similarly, the free spontaneity of Southern music has been twisted in the Northern cities into music-hall parodies like "Li'l Liza Jane." The spiritual is now a brassy march, the music "moans," "throws a fit," and crashes. All natural rhythms have been manipulated into social, noninstinctual forms. The city holds no roots for the black and substitutes only factory smoke for the sinuous, fetal, or animal motion of the pine smoke which "curls up and spreads" throughout Part 1. Encountering "a portly Negress" in a city theater, Dan Moore would like to believe that "Her strong roots sink down and spread under the river and disappear in blood-lines that waver south." But the woman does not conform to Dan's notions of her: "He is startled. The eyes of the woman don't belong to her. They look at him unpleasantly."

Toomer's Northern characters are mostly hamstrung by an overdeveloped sense of self which does not afflict the characters of Part 1: "Muriel fastens on her image." Accordingly the soft color tones of the South are transformed into violent colors and bright, mechanical light. In **"Theater"** a shaft of bright light serves as a metaphor for the intellectual system which creates the rift between John's mind and his body:

> John's mind coincides with the shaft of light. Thoughts rush to, and compact about it. Life of the house and of the slowly awakening stage swirls to the body of John, and thrills it. John's body is separate from the thoughts that pack his mind.

John, the theater manager's brother, appears, like Paul in **"Bona and Paul,"** to be a surrogate Toomer, the rift

between white intellectuality and black sensuality mirroring Toomer's own experience: **"Theater"** was written out of a two-week stint Toomer served as manager of Washington's Howard Theatre. (pp. 206-08)

The split that many of Toomer's characters feel between mind and body, white and black experience, rural origins and an urban present only makes explicit a separateness already visible in the stance of his narrators. The narrator of Part 1 is an uprooted Northerner, mediating between the action and the reader. In **"Fern,"** for instance, he visits "the soil of ... [his] ancestors" and returns north with the story of Fern, which he tells to a Northern audience "against the chance that ... [they] might happen down that way." Such an outsider feels particularly transient in the South in his attempts to involve himself in a way of life of which he knows he is not ultimately part. In fact the most fully developed attitude in *Cane* is that of what Munson calls "the spectatorial artist." This stance demands that Toomer face one central conflict of his identity and his art: how to both observe and participate in black culture? (p. 209)

Ralph Kabnis is *Cane*'s central example of the spectatorial artist. Part 3, named after him, translates the imagistic, psychological, and social tensions of Parts 1 and 2 into an intellectual debate in an attempt to resolve them. It originated as one of the dramas with which Toomer experimented throughout the 1920s and in which, influenced by reading Shaw, he sought to achieve social satire in a lyric style. (One such drama is a companion piece to **"Kabnis"**: in *Natalie Mann,* from 1922, a racially mixed writer, Nathan Merilh, uses black folk songs in creating an art which he hopes will bring blacks to greater self-awareness.) Toomer's purpose in his plays required a technique new to American theater, flexible and nonrepresentational. **"Kabnis"** employs the expressionist technique of positing characters as human or social types. Toomer wishes to examine possible ways of being black, so the social milieu in which Kabnis moves covers a wide range: the ancient black slave John, the working craftsman Halsey, the bourgeois school supervisor Hanby with his Booker T. Washington rhetoric, the Northern black radical Lewis, the traveling minister Layman, the innocent girl Carrie, the whores Cora and Stella, the shouting church congregation. The social strata and range of attitudes scattered throughout Parts 1 and 2 are thus concentrated in one story.

Kabnis's outsider position, his failure to gain access to this society, dramatizes Toomer's final inability to reconcile the cultures of South and North. Kabnis dreams of giving words to "the face of the South," but short-circuits his own vision by resisting the contact with the Georgia earth that could release that vision: he listens to night winds "against his will" and feels himself "suspended a few feet above the soil whose touch would resurrect him." I have shown how Toomer denied his own racial ancestry after writing *Cane.* Kabnis—of whom Toomer wrote to Frank, "Kabnis is *Me*"—does the same. A racially ambiguous Northern visitor in the

South, he rejects the black heritage that throws him into such conflict:

Kabnis: . . . An besides, he [Father John] aint my past. My ancestors were Southern blue-bloods—

Lewis: And black.

Kabnis: Aint much difference between blue an black.

Lewis: Enough to draw a denial from you. Cant hold them, can you?

Master; slave. Soil; and the overarching heavens. Dusk; dawn. They fight and bastardize you.

Early in **"Kabnis"** the lullaby-cum-spiritual "rock a-by baby" attempts to unite Kabnis's conflicting racial roots by integrating black and white. But the song lives in a fragile condition somewhere between falling and stability and is framed by poles of peace and violence:

> The half-moon is a white child that sleeps upon the tree-tops of the forest. White winds croon its sleep-song:
>
> > rock a-by baby..
> > Black mother sways, holding a white child on her bosom.
> > when the bough bends..
> > Her breath hums through pine-cones.
> > cradle will fall..
> > Teat moon-children at your breasts,
> > down will come baby..
> > Black mother.
>
> Kabnis whirls the chicken by its neck, and throws the head away. Picks up the hopping body, warm, sticky, and hides it in a clump of bushes.

Such violent language occurs only in **"Kabnis,"** expressing the confusion of a character who can face neither the pangs of real human and social involvement (which would mean accepting his black roots) nor the loneliness of detachment (accepting his difference from the Southern black community). Toomer wrote that "*Cane* was born in the agony of internal tightness, conflict and chaos." Nowhere does that chaos show more than in **"Kabnis,"** where Toomer most urgently tries to order it. (pp. 210-12)

His final visionary tableau does suggest that Toomer saw **"Kabnis"** resolving *Cane's* oppositions, but it contradicts his characters' recurrent failure to bind together the fragments of their experience. The tableau almost canonizes the generational extremes of Southern black culture, its past (Father John) and its future (Carrie), and leaves us with the sun, a "gold-glowing child," rising "from its cradle in the tree-tops of the forest" and offering the town "a birth-song." This scene emphasizes the regenerative side of the nature that *Cane* celebrates. The passage is packed with the impressionistic images of Part 1: shadows of pines, dreams, music. But Kabnis's antilyrical hardness is still too much with us for this ending convincingly to effect any racial or spiritual integration. *Cane's* return to the geographical world of

Part 1 is all the more poignant because Kabnis and Toomer himself are not part of that social world.

Cane abounds in images of a new age for blacks failing to be born. In Part 1 Becky loses her sons, the narrator loses Fern, Carma loses her husband, Esther loses Barlo, Louisa loses Tom Burwell and Bob Stone. In Part 2, John loses Dorris, Dan loses Muriel, Paul loses Bona, and Avey is an "orphan-woman." Finally in **"Kabnis,"** white lynchers impale a living black fetus on a tree; and Carrie, whose "nascent maternity" might have represented the race's future, is left alone once Lewis gives up hope of effecting change and returns North. Prose and poetry, white and black, North and South, the three parts of the book—these remain unreconciled both within Toomer and within his culture. The formal tour-de-force of *Cane* finally can only reflect, but not resolve, its author's conflicts. (pp. 213-14)

> *Alan Golding, "Jean Toomer's 'Cane': The Search for Identity through Form," in* Arizona Quarterly, *Vol. 39, No. 3, Autumn, 1983, pp. 197-214.*

Robert Jones (essay date 1987)

[*Jones, an American educator and critic, coedited* The Collected Poems of Jean Toomer *(1988). In the following excerpt, he offers an overview of Toomer's poetic career. This essay has been specially edited for inclusion in* Black Literature Criticism.]

Jean Toomer's popularity as a writer derives almost exclusively from his lyrical narrative *Cane.* He shows himself there to be a poet, but few are aware of the extensive and impressive corpus of his other poems. His poetic canon may be classified into three categories: the individually published poems, the poems first published in *Cane,* and the mass of over 100 unpublished poems. To date, however, there has been no attempt to assemble a standard edition of Toomer's poetical works, nor has there been any comprehensive study of his poems. Yet it is, perhaps, through the lens of his poetry that we are provided the most revealing commentaries on Toomer as artist and philosopher.

Toomer's poetry spans more than three decades and evolves in four distinct periods: the Aesthetic Period (1919-August 1921), marked by Imagism, improvisation, and experimentation; the Ancestral Consciousness Period (September 1921-1923), characterized by forms of racial consciousness and Afro-American mysticism; the Objective Consciousness Period (1924-1939), defined by Gurdjieffian idealism and "being consciousness"; and the Religious Period (1940-1955), distinguished by Christian Existentialism, owing to an espousal of Quaker religious philosophy. His poetic canon, then, constitutes a direct dramatization of consciousness, a veritable phenomenology of the spirit.

Toomer's career as a poet began long before the publication of *Cane.* Between 1919 and 1921 he experimented with several forms of poetry, including haiku, lyrical impressionism, and "sound poetry." The major influences on his artistic and philosophical development during this period were Orientalism, French and American Symbolism, and Imagism. (pp. 253-54)

The best examples of the Imagist poetry from this period are **"And Pass," "Storm Ending," "Her Lips Are Copper Wire,"** and **"Five Vignettes."** A sustained impressionistic portrait of twilight fading into darkness, **"And Pass"** images a picturesque sea setting in two brief movements, each introduced by "When." The poem concludes in a moment of visionary awareness, as the poet's imagination is suddenly arrested by the passing clouds, the fleeting and majestic "proud shadows." Concomitant with the poet's sense of exaltation comes a sense of his own loneliness and mortality, as "night envelops/empty seas/and fading dreamships."

Also richly impressionistic in design, **"Storm Ending"** unfolds as an implied comparison between two natural phenomena, thunder and flowers, although imagery remains the crucial vehicle of meaning:

> Thunder blossoms gorgeously above our heads,
> Great, hollow, bell-like flowers,
> Ambling in the wind,
> Stretching clappers to strike our ears . . .
> Full-lipped flowers
> Bitten by the sun
> Bleeding rain
> Dripping rain like golden honey—
> And the sweet earth flying from the thunder.

This scene captures the momentous return of sunshine and tranquility to nature following a tempest, as the sound of thunder fades into the distance.

In **"Her Lips Are Copper Wire"** desire generated by a kiss is compared to electrical energy conducted between copper wires, here imagined as lips. The evocative and sensuous opening lines, addressed to an imaginary lover, well illustrate Pound's Doctrine of the Image:

> Whisper of yellow globes
> gleaming on lamp-posts that sway
> like bootleg licker drinkers in the fog
>
> and let your breath be moist against me
> like bright heads on yellow globes . . .

Toomer's **"Five Vignettes"** is a series of imagistic sketches modeled after Japanese haiku poetry. The first is a seascape portrait of "red-tiled ships" shimmering iridescently upon the water. The ships are "nervous," under the threat of clouds eclipsing their watery reflections:

> The red-tiled ships you see reflected,
> Are nervous,
> And afraid of clouds.

The second vignette images a dynamic tension between stasis and motion:

> There, on the clothes-line
> Still as she pinned them,
> Pieces now the wind may wear.

The third vignette images an old man of ninety, still living courageously, "eating peaches," and unafraid of the "worms" which threaten his very existence. The fourth is reminiscent of an Oriental proverb, especially in its idea that suffering teaches wisdom; and the fifth images a Chinese infant, as well as our common humanity:

> In Y. Den's laundry
> A Chinese baby fell
> And cried as any other.

Vignettes four and five are as "moral" as they are imagistic, each in its own way commenting on the universal human condition. As we shall see, these "message-oriented" lyrics signal a subtle shift in Toomer's pre-*Cane* aesthetic which is more conspicuously apparent in the poems **"Banking Coal"** and **"Gum."** The basis for this shift from an imitative toward an affective theory of art is most clearly articulated in Toomer's 1921 review of Richard Aldington's essay on Imagism, "The Art of Poetry."

Toomer with his Uncle Bismarck, who encouraged his early interest in literature.

Several of the poetic sketches recall the linguistic impressionism of Gertrude Stein's *Tender Buttons,* especially **"Face"** and the quartet **"Air," "Earth," "Fire,"** and **"Water."** In *Tender Buttons,* Stein attempted to defamiliarize our automatized linguistic perceptions by creating a noun headnote without naming it, as she illustrates in "A Carafe, That Is a Blind Glass":

> A kind in glass and a cousin, a spectacle and
>   nothing strange
> A single hurt color and an arrangement in a
>   system to pointing
> All this and not ordinary, not unordered in not
>   resembling.
> The difference is spreading.

This lyrical sketch is reminiscent of a riddle: "What is made of glass (and its 'cousin') but is different from a drinking glass in the way it spreads (bulbously) at the bottom?" The answer would be a carafe. Like Stein, Toomer attempted to register precise nuances of perception and name them with a unique word or phrase. Here he renders an image of the noun headnote "Face":

> Hair—
> silver-gray,
> like streams of stars
> Brows—
> recurved canoes
> quivered by the ripples blown by pain,
> Her eyes—
> mists of tears
> condensing on the flesh below

(pp. 254-56)

In the months between September of 1921 and December of 1922, Toomer wrote the poems in *Cane,* evocative of an empathetic union between the spirit of the artist and the spirit of Afro-American mysticism. Indeed, in describing the formal design in *Cane,* what he termed "the spiritual entity behind the work," Toomer indicated that he viewed the book, at least retrospectively, as a mandala: "From the point of view of the spiritual entity behind the work, the curve really starts with '**Bona and Paul**' (awakening), plunges into '**Kabnis,**' emerges in '**Karintha,**' etc. swings upward into '**Theater**' and '**Box Seat,**' and ends (pauses) in '**Harvest Song.**'" The mandala, a symbol of integration and transmutation of the self in Buddhist philosophy, is an arrangement of images from the unconscious to form a constellation. Usually a formalized, circular design containing or contained by a figure of five points of emphasis, each representing the chief objects of psychic interest for the maker, a mandala functions to unite the conscious intellectual perceptions of its creator with his or her unconscious psychic drives and intuitions. A mandala, then, is both an instrument of the self's awakening and a chart of its spiritual evolution. In accordance with Toomer's spiritual design, the poems which begin this mandalic cycle—**"Reapers," "November Cotton Flower," "Cotton Song," "Song of the Son," "Georgia Dusk," "Nullo," "Conversion,"** and **"Portrait in Georgia"**—represent celebrations of ancestral consciousness, whereas the ones which end the cycle—**"Beehive," "Prayer,"** and **"Harvest Song"**—chronicle the poet's loss of empathetic union with Afro-American consciousness.

The poems which begin the cycle celebrate Afro-American culture and lament its disappearance. Written in iambic pentameter couplets, **"Reapers"** depicts black workers in a rural field setting. The first half of the poem describes "the sound of steel on stone" as the reapers "start their silent swinging, one by one." The second half contrasts this human activity with the sharp efficiency of a mechanical mower, which kills a field rat with machine-like precision and continues on its way. The contrast between the human and the mechanical emphasizes not only the displacement of black workers by machines, but also the passing of an era. The poem ends with a lament for the destruction of nature by the machine: "I see the blade,/Blood-stained, continue cutting weeds and shade."

Also written in iambic pentameter couplets, **"November Cotton Flower"** is a variation of the Italian sonnet. The octave images a late autumn setting, the end of the cotton season. Drought ravages the land as birds seek water in wells a hundred feet below the ground. The sestet describes the blooming of a November cotton flower amid this arid and barren scene, an event perceived to be supernatural by the local inhabitants: "Superstition saw/Something it had never seen before." The concluding couplet reveals the poem to be an extended metaphor, completing the analogy of the flower's mystery and sudden beauty in terms of a beautiful and spontaneous brown-eyed woman: "Brown eyes that loved without a trace of fear/Beauty so sudden for that time of year." Like the November cotton flower, the woman is an anomaly within her depressed and rustic environment.

"Cotton Song" belongs to a subgenre of Afro-American folk songs which captures the agony and essence of slavery. The poet uses music—the work song itself—to symbolize the medium by which slaves transcended the vicissitudes of slavery. Moreover, it is precisely spiritual freedom which engenders thoughts of political freedom:

> Cotton bales are the fleecy way
> Weary sinners bare feet trod,
> Softly, softly to the throne of God,
> We ain't agwine t wait until th Judgement Day!

"Song of the Son" and **"Georgia Dusk"** are swan songs for the passing Afro-American folk spirit. **"Song of the Son"** develops in two movements, with images of sight, sound, and smell. The first movement invokes images of smoke and music. Once stately Georgia pines have been reduced to smouldering sawdust piles; smoke spiraling toward heaven is the by-product of their former grandeur. Similarly, the "parting soul" of the Black American folk experience has been reduced to an evening song which, like the smoke, carries throughout the valley of cane. The poet is imaged as the prodigal son, returning "just before an epoch's sun declines" to capture in art the fleeting legacy of a "song-lit race of slaves." The second movement develops as an extended metaphor of slaves as "deep purple ripened plums,/Squeezed, and bursting in the pine-wood air." The imagery recalls the cloying state of fruit as it passes into the oblivion of the post-harvest. Yet the spectatorial poet is able to preserve "one plum" and "one seed" to immortalize both the past and the passing order in art.

In **"Georgia Dusk"** the sky relents to the setting sun and night, in a "lengthened tournament for flashing gold." In this nocturnal setting, "moon and men and barking hounds" are engaged in "making folk-songs from soul sounds." As in **"Song of the Son,"** wraiths of smoke from a "pyramidal sawdust pile" symbolize the passing of an era supplanted by industry, ". . . only chips and stumps are left to show/The solid proof of former domicile." With the advent of dusk, however, comes a heightened sense of the black man's union with the spiritual world, "with vestiges of pomp,/Race memories of king, and caravan,/High-priests, and ostrich, and a ju-ju man." These mystical moments inspire the people to sing, their voices resonating and passing throughout the piny woods and the valley of cane. The poet concludes with an invocation to the singers: "Give virgin lips to cornfield concubines,/Bring dreams of Christ to dusky cane-lipped throngs." The juxtaposition of secular and religious imagery symbolizes the mystical power of Afro-American folk music to harmonize the earthly (the "cornfield concubines" and "dusky cane-lipped throngs") and the heavenly ("sacred whispers," "virgin lips," and "dreams of Christ").

"Nullo," "Conversion," and **"Portrait in Georgia"** are Imagist in form and design. **"Nullo"** captures the fiery, iridescent beauty of golden, sun-drenched pine needles' falling upon a cowpath in a forest at sunset. The poet effectively arrests the stillness and solitude of the moment: "Rabbits knew not of their falling,/Nor did the forest catch aflame." **"Conversion"** images the spirit of Afro-American culture—the "African Guardian of souls"—as compromised and debased by Western influences, "drunk with rum,/Feasting on a strange cassava,/yielding to new words and a weak palabra/of a white-faced sardonic god." **"Portrait in Georgia"** is reminiscent of **"Face,"** in which Toomer attempts to render a vision of the poem's title. This Georgian portrait, however, is one of a lynched and burned black woman:

> Breath—the last sweet scent of cane,
> And her slim body, white as the ash of black flesh
>   after flame.

The sonnet **"Beehive"** discloses a shift in the poet's consciousness from spiritual identification to spiritual alienation. This lyric develops in two movements as an extended metaphor of the poet as exile in Eden. The first movement depicts the world as a black beehive, buzzing with activity on a moonlit, silvery night. The second movement, however, describes the spectatorial poet's estrangement, when he characterizes himself as an unproductive and exploitative "drone,/Lipping ho-ney,/Getting drunk with silver honey." Although he has tasted the "silver honey" of Afro-American culture, he is nevertheless unable to bridge the gap between himself and his fellow workers, unable to "fly out past the moon/and curl forever in some far-off farmyard flower."

"Prayer" describes a waning of the spirit, and of the creative powers, which results from a dissociation of inner and outer, soul and body: "My body is opaque to the soul./Driven of the spirit, long have I sought to temper it unto the spirit's longing,/But my mind, too, is opaque to the soul." This failure of the spirit, and of its creative powers, is reflected metapoetically in the lines "I am weak with much giving./I am weak with the desire to give more."

Completing the mandalic or spiritual design, **"Harvest Song"** dramatizes the poet's loss of empathetic union with the essence of Afro-American culture and consciousness. Ironically titled, **"Harvest Song"** describes an artist's inability to become one with the subjects of his art, as well as his inability to transform the raw materials of his labor into art. Reminiscent of Robert Frost's "After Apple-Picking," **"Harvest Song"** develops as an extended portrait of the poet as reaper. Although the poet/reaper has successfully cradled the fruits of his labor, when he cracks a grain from the store of his oats, he cannot taste its inner essence. In vain, he attempts to stare through time and space to understand the sources of his inspiration; he also tries to make up the physical distance by straining to hear the calls of other reapers and their songs. But his dust-caked senses preclude any meaningful or helpful intervention. The "knowledge of hunger" he fears is the failure of consciousness and of the creative impulse. Thus, he is reluctant to call other reapers for fear they will share their truly inspiring grains, grains he is unable to assimilate. "It would be good to hear their songs . . . reapers of the sweet-stalk'd/cane, cutters of the corn . . . even though their throats/cracked and the strangeness of their voices deafened me." Still, he beats his soft, sensitive palms against the stubble of the fields of labor, and his pain is sweeter and more rewarding than the harvest itself. He is then comforted by the pains of his struggles, although they will not bring him knowledge of his hunger.

A major unpublished poem that is also a product of this period is the mystical and evocative **"Tell Me,"** which contains nature imagery evocative of the local-color poems in *Cane*, although it was inspired by the majestic mountains and the scenic Shenandoah River near Harpers Ferry. Written in three four-line stanzas of rhymed iambic pentameter, this poem unfolds with a series of apostrophes to the "dear beauty of the dusk," as the poet implores the spirit of nature to share with him its dark and mysterious essence.

Shortly after the publication of *Cane* in October of 1923, Toomer began studying the austere idealism of the Greek-Armenian mystic Georges Gurdjieff, and in 1924 he attended the Gurdjieff Institute for the Harmonious

Development of Man at the Château de Prieuré in Fontainebleau, France. Toomer sailed back to America after two months, but returned to the Gurdjieff Institute in 1926, 1927, and 1929. Yet despite the rigorous demands engendered by his devotion to Gurdjieff, Toomer continued writing and assembling his poetry. Indeed, as we shall see, poetry provided an artful medium for imaging his ideas on the phenomenology of "Objective Consciousness." While Gurdjieffian philosophy is arcane and obscure, we need not concern ourselves with its esoterica in order to formulate its major tenets as they relate to Toomer. (pp. 257-62)

In terms of the nature of consciousness, the "ordinary man," Gurdjieff tells us, "is a three-brained being," his ontological status shared among three autonomous centers: physical, emotional, and intellectual. In some people the center of gravity is located in the moving center; in others, in the intellectual or emotional center. Beyond these centers, however, there exist higher levels of "objective consciousness," which Gurdjieff calls the "higher emotional center" and the "higher thinking center." On these levels of mystical awareness, the self is the recipient of a miraculous "energy" from a non-material source, in direct communion with the supernatural. In religious philosophy, this state of consciousness is called "illumination," "enlightenment," or "epiphany." In the words of Richard Gregg, "There is a blending of subject and object, a mutual absorption, a forgetting of everything else; there is often delight, and exaltation, an enthusiasm, a rapture, a deep and abiding joy .... It is not knowing from without; it is a knowing from within. It is not knowing about; it is unitive knowledge. Unitive knowledge is much more complete and deeper than knowing about." ...

[It] is important to understand Gurdjieff's conception of art, particularly in the light of an affective aesthetic which generally characterizes the poetry Toomer wrote during this period. Gurdjieff's art aesthetic is perhaps most clearly revealed in his theory of "Objective Art":

> I measure the merit of art by its consciousness, you by its unconsciousness. A work of objective art is a book which transmits the artist's ideas not directly through words or signs or hieroglyphics but through feelings which he evokes in the beholder consciously and with full knowledge of what he is doing and why he is doing it.

In view of this aesthetic and its influence on Toomer, it would be appropriate to surmise that the poetry of this period was written to inspire higher consciousness. Yet we must also keep in mind that Toomer had already declared his preference for affective over emotive art as early as 1921, in his review of "The Art of Poetry."

Toomer's "Objective Consciousness" poetry may be grouped into three categories: poems on being consciousness and self-integration, such as **"The Lost Dancer," "Unsuspecting,"** and **"White Arrow"**; poems revealing mysticism (**"At Sea"** and **"The Gods Are Here"**) and "New American" consciousness (**"The Blue Meridian"**); poems on consciousness of the self that is the cosmos, as represented by **"Peers"** and **"Living Earth"**; and poems on consciousness of the self that is humanity, as represented by **"Men"** and **"People."**

"The Lost Dancer" expresses the poet's quest for unity of being and self-integration in terms of the failure of idealism. The dancer/artist figure is "lost" because he is unable to discover a "source of magic" whereby he can transcend the rigorous imperatives of subject/object dualism—inner and outer, essence and personality, self and world, art and life—, here symbolized by the metaphysical "vibrations of the dance" and the physical "feet dancing on earth of sand":

> Spatial depths of being survive
> The birth to death recurrences
> Of feet dancing on earth of sand;
> Vibrations of the dance survive
> The sand; the sand, elect, survives
> The dancer. He can find no source
> Of magic adequate to bind
> The sand upon his feet, his feet
> Upon his dance, his dance upon
> The diamond body of his being.

Unity of being, then, follows when the dancer is able to synthesize "the birth to death recurrences/Of feet dancing on earth of sand" (object) with "the diamond body of his being," the prismatic brilliance of inner essence (subject), to form a unified complex, the transcendental self. (pp. 252-64)

Both **"At Sea"** and **"The Gods Are Here"** offer expressions of mystical experiences. **"At Sea"** dramatizes an ephemeral and fleeting moment during which the poet is transfixed by the awesome power and beauty of the sea. During this mystical state of consciousness, he experiences a "pang of transcience," when the spirit of the universe briefly reveals itself in the life and order of the cosmos:

> Once I saw large waves
> Crested with white-caps;
> A driving wind
> Transformed the caps
> Into scalding spray—
> "Swift souls," I addressed them–
> They turned towards me
> Startled
> Sea-descending faces;
> But I, not they,
> Felt the pang of transcience.

"The Gods Are Here" develops as an extended contrast between two forms of asceticism, both of which release the soul from bondage and permit its union with the divine: There is the hermit on a mountain among the wilds of nature and the poet within the domestic environment of society:

> This is no mountain
> But a house
> No rock of solitude
> But a family chair,
> No wilds
> But life appearing

As life anywhere domesticated,
Yet I know the gods are here,
And that if I touch them
I will arise
And take majesty into the kitchen.

A minor classic in American literature, **"The Blue Meridian"** is a Whitmanian affirmation of democratic idealism, a poetics for democracy. In describing the original text of this poem, Toomer reveals his "New American" or millennial consciousness: "I wrote a poem called 'The First American,' the idea of which was that here in America we are in the process of forming a new race, that I was one of the first conscious members of this race." Toomer believed that his own blend of ethnic strains, like America's melting pot itself, conferred upon him a mystical selfhood and a transcendental vision of America. Like Walt Whitman, he believed that there is a central identity of self which is the foundation of freedom, that each individual is unique and yet identical with all, and that democracy is the surest guarantee of individual values. And, like Whitman, he attempted to resolve the conflict between individual and society at the transpersonal level by positing his own self, "the first American," as the self of all beings. Toomer's Adamic conception of himself as one of the first conscious members of a united human race is, then, the very cornerstone of his "First American" or "New American" consciousness. Such an exalted mind, carrying with it the conviction of absolute novelty, recalls the "Cosmic Consciousness" of Canadian psychologist R. M. Bucke. "Along with the consciousness of the cosmos," writes Bucke, "there occurs an intellectual enlightenment which alone would place the individual on a new plane of existence—would make him almost a member of a new species." Having formulated an identity, Toomer, as the new American Adam, proceeds to become the maker of his own conditions by projecting a model society. According to R. W. B. Lewis, the American Adam *projects* a world of order and meaning and identity into either a chaos or a vacuum; he does not *discover* it." This is precisely what Toomer does in *The Blue Meridian and Other Poems*:

When the spirit of mankind conceived
A new world in America, and dreamed
The human structure rising from this base,
The land was a vacant house to new inhabitants,
A vacuum compelled by nature to be filled
Spirit could not wait to time select,
Weighing in wisdom each piece,
Fitting each right thing into each right place
But had to act, trusting the vision of the possible.

(pp. 264-66)

In the summer of 1938 Toomer moved to Bucks County, Pennsylvania, where he was almost immediately attracted to Quakerism. During his apprenticeship with the Society of Friends, he immersed himself in Quaker religious philosophy and wrote numerous essays on George Fox and Quakerism. In 1940, he joined the Society of Friends. His interest in Quaker religious philosophy sprang from his own idea that the Society of Friends provided a radical venture beyond Objective Consciousness to a vital and transforming religious faith:

Quakers assembled, I had been told, for silent worship and waited for the spirit to move them. This appealed to me because I had practiced meditation. Years before I had read a brief account of George Fox that impressed me. I had heard of the Quaker reputation for practicing what they preached.... Prior to coming into contact with Friends I had been convinced that God is both immanent and transcendent, and that the purpose of life is to grow up to God; that within man there is a wonderful power that can transform him, lift him into new birth; that we have it in us to rise to a life wherein brotherhood is manifest and war impossible.

In order to define the poetry of this period as Christian Existential, two factors must be considered. In the first place, Toomer envisioned Quaker religious philosophy as a bridge between two (Kierkegaardian) levels of consciousness, the ethical or social concerns of Objective Consciousness and the religious or theistic concerns of Christianity. Indeed, in 1938 he sought to reconcile Gurdjieffian idealism with Quakerism by organizing a cooperative of both Quakers and lay individuals called Friends of Being. As we shall see, the ostensible conflict remains as the basis for a pervasive Christian Existentialism. In the second place, in contrast with Gurdjieffian idealism, Quakerism and Christian Existentialism comprise fundamentally the same religious philosophy. In temperament and philosophy, Toomer's consciousness is perhaps best described as Christian Existential. And it is precisely this consciousness which is the genesis of his spiritual odyssey as a Quaker poet.

The meditative verses and confessional lyrics from this period render a vision of man as alone, estranged from society, the universe, and God. Reflecting an evolution in the poet's spiritual consciousness, these poems fall into several categories: confessional lyrics manifesting subtle tensions between Being Consciousness and Quaker Consciousness, as in **"Desire"**; meditations regarding mediation between the self and God, such as **"The Chase"** and **"Cloud"**; confessional lyrics on asceticism, such as **"Motion and Rest"**; and lyrical verses of orthodox Quakerism, such as **"To Gurdjieff Dying,"** **"The Promise,"** and **"They Are Not Missed."**

In **"Desire,"** conflicting claims of consciousness are imaged as two types and levels of love. The poem opens with religious allusions to "suffering" and "the opened heart," symbolic of the Sacred Heart. The imagery then shifts to reflect the poet's Being Consciousness: "I seek the universal love of beings;/May I be made one with that love/And extend to everything I turn towards that love." The conflict between the "ethical" exigencies of agapé and the "moral" concerns of Logos are conditionally reconciled in favor of the latter in the closing lines of this poem:

In this new season of a forgotten life
I move towards the heart of love
    Of all that breathes;

I would enter that radiant center
and from that center live.

The image of white birds in flight dramatizes the poet's quest for spiritual mediation in **"The Chase,"**

As the white bird leaves the dirty nest,
Flashes in the dangling sky,
And merges in the blue up there,
May my spirit quit me,
And fly the beam straight
Into thy power and thy glory.

"Cloud" employs a variation of the five-line tanka to speculate on the "livid cloud" which separates man from the "salient light" of Quaker religious faith.

"Motion and Rest" images white birds coming to rest in rendering a tranquil portrait of asceticism:

I have watched white birds alight
On a barn roof
And come to rest, instantly still,
Effortlessly relaxed and poised,
In them no trace of former motion.
So would I come to rest
So should we come to rest
At quiet time.

Within the Society of Friends, "Quietism" refers to a mystical state of consciousness wherein one experiences annihilation of the will and passive absorption of the Inner Light. The metaphor of motion and rest thus effectively dramatizes two contrasting states of consciousness: the realm of the world, with its emphasis on social engagement, and the realm of the spirit, which emphasizes quietistic contemplation.

"To Gurdjieff Dying" is a carefully crafted Italian sonnet, with variations in rhyme scheme. The poem employs end rhymes in the opening and closing lines of both the octave and the sestet, with intermediate iterating end rhymes, while retaining the conventions of iambic pentameter. A profound repudiation of Gurdjieff, this sonnet demonstrates the poet's devout acceptance of Quaker religious faith. The octave disparages Gurdjieff for "Knowing the Buddhic law but to pervert/Its power of peace into dissevering fire." He is also described as a seducer "coiled as serpent round the Phallic Tau/And sacramental loaf" and as a false prophet, "Son of the Elder Liar." The sestet further reproves Gurdjieff for having "deformed the birthbringings of light/Into lust-brats of black imaginings,/Spilling Pan-passions in the incarnate round/Of hell and earth." The concluding lines invoke the "Lords of the Shining Rings/Skilled in White Magic," the authority of religion itself, to "Save even Gurdjieff from his hell forthright." Light and dark imagery here effectively contrasts the "black imaginings" of Gurdjieffian idealism and the "white magic" of religious faith. (pp. 267-69)

Toomer's poetic canon constitutes a study in the phenomena of the spirit, not only in its revelations of spiritualist philosophies—Orientalism, Afro-American

Mysticism, Gurdjieffian Idealism, and Quakerism—but in its formal expression of the poet's highest goals—to essentialize and spiritualize experience. "I am not a romanticist," wrote Toomer, "I am not a classicist nor a realist, in the usual sense of these terms. I am an essentialist. Or, to put it in other words, I am a spiritualizer, a poetic realist. This means two things. I try to lift facts, things, happenings to the planes of rhythm, feeling, and significance. I try to clothe and give body to potentialities" (**"Reflections of an Earth-Being"**). He describes the mystical ecstasy of poetic creation in terms of an epiphanical experience: "A flash bridges the gap between inner and outer, causing a momentary fusion and wholeness. Thus poetry starts, at least to me." Yet, in the end, he viewed poetry not as sheer aesthetic pleasure, but as a means of enlarging one's heart and consciousness. In his own words, "Poems are Offerings. Gifts to me I give to you." (pp. 270-71)

Robert Jones, "Jean Toomer as Poet: A Phenomenology of the Spirit," in Black American Literature Forum, *Vol. 21, No. 3, Fall, 1987, pp. 253-73.*

FURTHER READING

Bontemps, Arna. "The Negro Renaissance: Jean Toomer and the Harlem Writers of the 1920s." In *Anger and Beyond: The Negro Writer in the United States,* edited by Herbert Hill, pp. 20-36. New York: Harper & Row, 1966.
Explores the influence of *Cane* on African-American literature.

Bradley, David. "Looking behind *Cane.*" *The Southern Review* 21, No. 3 (July 1985): 682-94.
Bradley reminisces about his first encounter with *Cane* and examines conflicts concerning race and art that affected Toomer during the composition of the work.

Braithwaite, William Stanley. "The Negro in Literature." *The Crisis* 28, No. 5 (September 1924): 204-10.
Surveys African-American literature, declaring: "of all the writers I have mentioned . . . , the one who is most surely touched with genius is Jean Toomer, the author of *Cane.*"

Brinkmeyer, Robert H., Jr. "Wasted Talent, Wasted Art: The Literary Career of Jean Toomer." *The Southern Quarterly: A Journal of the Arts in the South* 20, No. 1 (Fall 1981): 75-84.
States that with the exception of *Cane,* all of Toomer's literary work is tainted by a preoccupation with mysticism and philosophy. Brinkmeyer questions whether, in many of Toomer's later pieces, "he really has a story to tell, or whether his work is merely a coathanger on which to hang his philosophical wardrobe."

Bush, Ann Marie, and Mitchell, Louis D. "Jean Toomer: A Cubist Poet." *Black American Literature Forum* 17, No. 3 (Fall 1983): 106-08.

Examines similarities among the aesthetic goals of Toomer and those of cubist visual artists, arguing that Toomer, like the cubists, renders his subjects in the form of multiple, fragmented images.

Christensen, Peter. "Sexuality and Liberation in Jean Toomer's 'Withered Skin of Berries'." *Callaloo* 11, No. 2 (Summer 1988): 616-26.

Discusses homoerotic imagery in Toomer's short story "Withered Skin of Berries," terming the story "a celebration of the redeeming power of love and sex."

Davis, Charles T. "Jean Toomer and the South: Region and Race as Elements within a Literary Imagination." In *The Harlem Renaissance Re-examined,* edited by Victor A. Kramer, pp. 185-200. New York: AMS Press, 1987.

Attributes the artistic success of *Cane* to Toomer's having "discovered his blackness" by spending time in rural Georgia.

Du Bois, W. E. B. "The Younger Literary Movement." *The Crisis* 27, No. 4 (February 1924): 161-63.

Discusses sexual themes in *Cane* and, while professing puzzlement over some of its more oblique narratives, praises it as the first work of a gifted artist.

Hughes, Langston. "Gurdjieff in Harlem." In his *The Big Sea,* pp. 241-43. New York: Alfred A. Knopf, 1945.

Recounts Toomer's attempt to teach the philosophy of Gurdjieff in New York City.

Kerman, Cynthia Earl, and Eldridge, Richard. *The Lives of Jean Toomer: A Hunger for Wholeness.* Baton Rouge: Louisiana State University Press, 1987, 411 p.

Detailed biography emphasizing Toomer's quest for spiritual enlightenment.

McKay, Nellie Y. *Jean Toomer, Artist: A Study of His Literary Life and Work, 1894-1936.* Chapel Hill: University of North Carolina Press, 1984, 262 p.

Analyzes the "growth, development, and decline of Jean Toomer as a literary artist."

Reckley, Ralph, Sr. "The Vinculum Factor: 'Seventh Street' and 'Rhobert' in Jean Toomer's *Cane.*" *CLA Journal* 31, No. 4 (June 1988): 484-89.

Identifies the stories "Seventh Street" and "Rhobert" as "linchpins" in *Cane,* contending that they function as thematic links.

Rice, Herbert W. "Repeated Images in Part One of *Cane.*" *Black American Literature Forum* 17, No. 3 (Fall 1983): 100-05.

Suggests that the lines on the title page of *Cane* ("Oracular, / Redolent of fermenting syrup, / Purple of the dusk, / Deep-rooted cane") are repeatedly echoed in the imagery of the first section of the work.

———. "An Incomplete Circle: Repeated Images in Part Two of *Cane.*" *CLA Journal* 29 (June 1986): 442-61.

Examines imagery in the second section of *Cane.*

Rusch, Frederik L. "Jean Toomer's Early Identification: The Two Black Plays." *MELUS* 13, Nos. 1-2 (Summer 1986): 115-24.

Analyzes Toomer's plays *Balo* and *Natalie Mann,* which Rusch states embody many of the same concerns as the stories and poems of *Cane.*

Thompson, Larry E. "Jean Toomer: As Modern Man." In *The Harlem Renaissance Remembered,* edited by Arna Bontemps, pp. 51-62. New York: Dodd, Mead, 1972.

Examines Toomer's search for identity in his life and work.

Watkins, Patricia. "Is There a Unifying Theme in *Cane?*" *CLA Journal* XV, No. 3 (March 1972): 303-05.

Interprets *Cane* as a study of alienation.

Desmond Tutu

1931-

(Full name Desmond Mpilo Tutu) South African orator, sermonist, and essayist.

Recipient of the 1984 Nobel Peace Prize, Anglican archbishop of Capetown, and one of the world's foremost critics of South Africa's apartheid government, Tutu has collected two volumes of speeches and sermons: *Crying in the Wilderness: The Struggle for Justice in South Africa* (1982) and *Hope and Suffering: Sermons and Speeches* (1983). "Like all great preachers," wrote Joshua Hammer, "his every speech and press conference is a blaze of emotion, his every gesture a drop of oil fueling the oratorical fire. Waving his arms, punching the air like a boxer, the elfin... figure draws in his followers with a stream of whispers, shouts and sobs, punctuated with roars of laughter."

Since the 1970s, Tutu has campaigned vigorously for the abolition of apartheid, South Africa's system of government that defines and allocates political power and privileges to people on the basis of skin color and ethnic background. Tutu himself first encountered apartheid while growing up in the western Transvaal mining town of Klerksdorp. He stated that at first the constant racial taunts of the white boys were not "thought to be out of the ordinary," but that as he got older he "began finding things eating away at [him]." Recalling one incident in which he heard his father referred to as "boy," Tutu remarked: "I knew there wasn't a great deal I could do, but it just left me churned.... What he must have been feeling... being humiliated in the presence of his son. Apartheid has always been the same systematic racial discrimination: it takes away your human dignity and rubs it in the dust and tramples it underfoot."

In 1943 the Tutu family moved to Johannesburg, where Tutu's father became a teacher and his mother a cook at a missionary school for the blind. The new surroundings greatly affected young Tutu, especially the school. Not only was he deeply moved by the dedication and service shown by staff members, but it was here that he met Father Trevor Huddleston, who would become his most influential mentor and friend. A leading British critic of South Africa's apartheid system, Huddleston served as the parish priest of Sophiatown, a black slum district of Johannesburg. Tutu recalled his first meeting with the priest: "I was standing with my mother one day, when this white man in a cassock walked past and doffed his big black hat to her. I couldn't believe it—a white man raising his hat to a simple black labouring woman." Following a bout with tuberculosis, Tutu resumed his education and entered the School of Medicine at Witwatersrand University with the intention of becoming a doctor. He was forced to drop out of medical school, however, when he could no longer afford the tuition fees. He began training as a teacher instead. Tutu

received his B.A. from the University of Johannesburg in 1954 and taught high school in Johannesburg and Krugersdorp until 1957, when he resigned in protest of government plans to introduce a state-run system of education especially intended for students in black districts. Limiting both the quality and extent of education, the system was considered by many to be deliberately second-rate. The same year, inspired by the ideals of his mentor Huddleston, he began theological studies with the priests of the Community of Resurrection, the Anglican order to which Huddleston belonged.

Following ordainment as priest in 1961, Tutu worked in small Anglican parishes in England and South Africa. He continued his education and, in 1966, received a master's degree in theology from King's College, London. In 1972 he accepted a position in England as associate director of the Theological Education Fund. Thoroughly enjoying his role, he traveled extensively throughout Asia and Africa and presided over the allocation of World Council of Churches scholarships.

Thoughts of South Africa and the discrimination faced by his black countrymen seemed to surface continually, however. Finally, in 1975, Tutu decided to return to his homeland and "contribute what I could to the liberation struggle," he explained. Upon returning, his presence and commitment to the cause of black Africans was felt almost immediately.

Choosing to live in his parish in Lesotho, Tutu monitored closely the feelings of his congregation and the local community. In an atmosphere of mounting racial tension, he attempted to pacify angry black youths, encouraging them to seek change through peaceful means. In 1976 he met with black activist Nhato Motlana in an effort to curb violent riots in the black township of Soweto on the outskirts of Johannesburg. He also wrote to the incumbent South African Prime Minister Balthazar J. Vorster, warning him of the dangerous situation in Soweto. Tutu later claimed that Vorster dismissed his letter as a ploy engineered by political opponents. On June 16, 1976, however, racial tension exploded into racial violence as black demonstrators met untempered reprisal from white security forces. Six hundred blacks were shot to death in the confrontation. The tragic events of the Soweto riots focused the world's attention on the antiapartheid struggle in South Africa. For Tutu the increasing number of violent confrontations between blacks and security forces marked a change in his perception of his own involvement. Following the riots he began to use his growing influence to initiate peaceful negotiation. This was not done in deference to the government, however. Tutu had become a highly visible and vocal critic.

In 1979 Tutu voiced a major condemnation of the South African government before an international audience. In an interview for a Danish television program, he called on the government of Denmark to cease buying South African coal as a sign of support for the antiapartheid cause. The appeal moved people in other countries as well to consider implementing economic sanctions against South Africa. Tutu's actions brought him serious government reprisals. When he returned from Denmark in 1979, authorities seized his passport: a move generally seen as a warning of possible imprisonment—the fate of two previous government critics, Nelson R. Mandela and Victor Tambo—or expulsion from the country. Tutu ignored the signal, however, and continued his antiapartheid campaign. The South African government eventually returned his passport in January 1981 but confiscated it again in April. Thereafter Tutu was allowed to travel outside South Africa only with the government's permission and special travel documents that listed his nationality as "undetermined."

It was during a permitted stay in the United States, on October 16, 1984 that Tutu received word that he was the 1984 Nobel peace laureate. Part of the Nobel citation read: "It is the committee's wish that the Peace Prize now awarded to Desmond Tutu should be regarded not only as a gesture of support to him and to the South African Council of Churches of which he is leader, but also to all individuals and groups in South Africa who, with their concern for human dignity, fraternity and democracy, incite the admiration of the world." According to *Time* magazine, "much of white South Africa reacted grumpily or indifferently to the news." Said Tutu, in response: "You feel humble, you feel proud, elated and you feel sad. One of my greatest sadnesses is that there are many in this country who are not joining in celebrating something that is an honor for this country." He would later reassure his followers: "Despite all that the powers of the world may do, we are going to be free."

Many of Tutu's orations have been collected in *Crying in the Wilderness: The Struggle for Justice in South Africa* and *Hope and Suffering: Sermons and Speeches.* *Hope and Suffering* contains Tutu's writings from 1976 to 1982. Divided into four sections—"Introducing South Africa," "Liberation as a Biblical Theme," "Current Concerns," and "The Divine Intention"—the collection chronicles "the evil of apartheid and the yearnings for freedom of blacks in South Africa," according to critic John F. Whealon. Whealon added that "*Hope and Suffering* illustrates well the unique dynamic that is Desmond Tutu, who is blunt, fearless, filled with faith and courage, charismatic." In *Crying in the Wilderness,* Tutu pleaded for non-violent change in South Africa but warned that unless conditions improve, there will be more "blood riots" in the streets. "[Tutu] stoutly denies that he is preaching Marxism or Communism," Eugene A. Dooley summarized of the work. "Instead he pleads for justice against inhuman life conditions."

(For further information about Tutu's life and works, see *Black Writers* and *Contemporary Authors,* Vol. 125.)

PRINCIPAL WORKS

Crying in the Wilderness: The Struggle for Justice in South Africa (speeches, sermons, and interviews) 1982

Hope and Suffering: Sermons and Speeches (sermons and speeches) 1983

The Words of Desmond Tutu (quotations) 1989

Eugene A. Dooley (essay date 1982)

[*In the following excerpt, Dooley reviews* Crying in the Wilderness.]

Bishop Desmond Tutu, a brilliant Anglican cleric, is easily the most influential black leader in South Africa. He is no mere demagogue, either, but rather a scholarly Church orator who has chosen the task of convincing the white people of his land that apartheid is cruel, counter-productive, anti-social and anti-Scripture. He is devastatingly logical in showing not only that the white religious sects hypocritically misrepresent their Christian faith but also in scoring the bigoted policies of political leaders who refuse to budge from their consistent cruelty toward the black natives.

Since blacks there outnumber the white five-to-one, it stands to reason that the whites had better read the handwriting on the wall. Their powerful sun is setting, and they had better institute some cooperative efforts to establish a better social order for their land. The Roman Catholic Archbishop, Denis Hurley, O.M.I., of Durban, has been saying that for many years past, and his voice was also one "crying in the wilderness for justice" until very recently when he summoned all his auxiliaries to push for a crusade for Justice and Rights.

[*Crying in the Wilderness*], subtitled "The Struggle for Justice in South Africa," contains many of Tutu's speeches, press releases and sermons. He stoutly denies that he is preaching Marxism or Communism, though some whites are using that as a scare tactic against him. Instead he pleads for a system that will allow emerging tribes to be given a system where men will not be tossed into horrible prisons for merely asking simple rights, pleading for justice against inhuman life conditions. Some white leaders, he says, are totally unChristian in their arbitrary use of police powers. All the black wish, he says, are the abolition of the hated apartheid, along with the human right to work for better home life and family security. Whether the whites like it or not, he says that the day is surely coming when black people there will have political power, and that day can come without bloody riots if the whites are willing to sit down and negotiate. Black Africa is awakening daily, and the whites cannot deny it. The Bishop is optimistic that a peaceful solution can be reached.

> *Eugene A. Dooley, in a review of "Crying in the Wilderness," in* Best Sellers, *Vol. 42, No. 8, November, 1982, p. 313.*

Huston Horn (essay date 1985)

[*In the following review, Horn examines the strengths and shortcomings of* Hope and Suffering.]

With the resolute confidence of an Old Testament psalmist, South Africa's Bishop Desmond Tutu [in *Hope and Suffering*] raises impassioned cries against his nation's white-skinned oppressors. They may hold the blacks in thrall for now, but surely God in his time will bring apartheid crashing down. But, while his Anglican anger roils like dense smoke from the printed page, a beckoning, reconciling light shines through it. Notwithstanding the intransigent foes he faces, Tutu's gaze rarely wanders from a benign, visionary South Africa ruled together by blacks and whites. Nothing less, the bishop holds, would fit God's prescription for humanity.

To those familiar with the thought and writing of the winner of 1984's Nobel Peace Prize, this will sound like vintage Tutu, and so it is. Since most of the bishop's

energy goes into spoken words denouncing the plight of South Africa's tyrannized black majority, the book before us is in fact a collection of sermons and speeches delivered by him in the early '80s and late '70s. Published first in Johannesburg in 1983, it now comes in an edition opportunely produced (and casually edited) by William B. Eerdmans within weeks of the peace prize announcement. Celebrity apparently is more marketable than an enthusiasm for justice.

While a warmed-over work it may be, the bishop's preachments have contemporary relevance and ring. For one thing, so little seems to have been accomplished since Tutu took up his assault on apartheid years ago. "What have we got to show for all our talk of peaceful change? Nothing!" he told a black South African reporter just the other day. For another (and better) thing, Tutu's style is literate and readable, his ironic wit no less than his irenic wrath.

"One rule about South Africa that has the validity of a Euclidian axiom," Tutu writes, "is the one stating that on any major matter, you can be sure that most White South Africans will be ranged on one side and the majority of Black South Africans will be found on the opposite one.... Following the application of this rule, Blacks knew they were in trouble when their White compatriots went into transports of ecstatic delight and joy when Mr. Ronald Reagan won the 1980 U.S. Presidential elections."

Even back then, Tutu was pessimistic about Ronald Reagan's vaunted "constructive-engagement" approach to the government of South Africa, "a policy of appeasement with ... the most vicious system since Nazism." And, after a recent White House meeting with the President, Tutu had not changed his mind. Those soothing claims that the lot of blacks in South Africa is on the rise—in sports, in the creation of international hotels and restaurants, in the removal of discriminatory signs—are without substance, Tutu writes.

"It is a charade because ... they are mere concessions that depend on the whim of those who have political power," he says. Put simply, it is that political power that blacks must share if they are ever to have true liberty.

And, as he looks at the world about him and sees how the United States *sometimes* contends with tyranny, as it did in imposing sanctions against martial law in Poland, the bishop comes to a doleful conclusion: "The U.S. Government does not really care about Blacks. Poles are different. Poles are White."

Hope and Suffering reflects its author's strengths, but in spite of them, somehow, it is unsatisfying. Perhaps it is too recent to be history; too dated to be news. One must still scan the daily papers regularly to see, for example, if the White House ever will adopt a stern policy against apartheid; if those 119 U.S. corporations doing business in South Africa ever will exert economic pressure to effect political change for the voteless blacks; if, indeed, humane and moral stirrings ever will arise in South Africa's minority white government.

A more irritating flaw in **Hope and Suffering** is the editorial abandon (some items dated, some not; some items introduced by explanatory notes, some not); the book seems to have been rushed into print ere the Nobel bloom was off the bishop.

> *Huston Horn, in a review of "Hope and Suffering: Sermons and Speeches," in* Los Angeles Times Book Review, *January 27, 1985, p. 2.*

John F. Whealon (essay date 1985)

[*In the following essay, Whealon offers a section-by-section study of* Hope and Suffering.]

Publicity about the writer of this book has exceeded any publisher's fondest dreams. **Hope and Suffering** was published in South Africa in 1983, and in Britain and the United States in 1984. Then the author, Bishop Desmond Tutu, General Secretary of the South African Council of Churches, gained international attention as winner of the 1984 Nobel Peace Prize and then again as Johannesburg's first black Anglican bishop.

This book, a compilation and editing of some of Tutu's sermons and writings from 1976 to 1982, begins with considerable biographical material. There is an authoritative foreword by Anglican Bishop Trevor Huddleston, himself a veteran of the South African racial struggle. And there is an eloquent introduction by the Rev. Buti Tlhagale, a Roman Catholic priest from Soweto. All writings in this book refer to the evil of apartheid and the yearnings for freedom of blacks in South Africa. Therefore the book's title, **Hope and Suffering.** The various writings are presented in four separate chapters or sections.

The first section, entitled "Introducing South Africa," describes in detail the moral evil that apartheid is: "Blacks forming 80 percent of the population were relegated to 13 percent of the land. They enjoyed none of the rights that citizens take for granted in a democracy—they had to carry passes; they were subjected to influx control measures; they lived in segregated areas little better than ghettoes; they received a segregated education with glaring disparity in annual government expenditure per capita between black and white (at present it is in the order of 1:10)."

The second section, from my viewpoint, shows Tutu at his best and strongest. The chapter "Liberation as a Biblical Theme" focuses on the biblical teachings and the theology underlying his public stance against apartheid. He was a seminary teacher, and that dimension of his life is shown here. From the Old Testament he treats at length the Exodus theme, with deliverance from oppression and journeying to the Promised Land of Freedom as applicable to the South African blacks. He talks of the Jews in exile, developing at that time the

Deutero-Isaian future exodus theme and the P account of creation in Genesis. From the New Testament he shows how Matthew presents Jesus as the new Moses, the new Joshua, the liberator of peoples. And in a challenging fashion, he holds up this theological teaching on the immorality of apartheid to the Christian Government of South Africa and to the Dutch Reformed Church that gives biblical support to apartheid. Tutu is solid and updated in his biblical bases. He shows the hopeful, courageous spirit of Romans 8.

The third section, "Current Concerns," presents the bishop's personal and pointed comments on the political scene in South Africa and in the United States. Impatient for change now, he is strongly critical of any temporizing measures in the Reagan Administration and in the current South African Government. Perhaps it was the abundant acronyms, local names and references, so mystifying to this foreigner. Anyway I thought the bishop better as a theologian than as a political commentator. The final section, "The Divine Intention," contains personal religious testimony about the Will of God in the present South Africa trials. This chapter is deeply spiritual.

Hope and Suffering illustrates well the unique dynamic that is Desmond Tutu, who is blunt, fearless, filled with faith and courage, charismatic. At this critical time in his nation's history, he is the right man in the right place. Once in a comparable struggle for racial equality, the Rev. Martin Luther King Jr. served as the inspiring moral leader. May Bishop Desmond Tutu be protected and given more authority by his Nobel Prize and status as bishop. And may his dream of racial equality and freedom for his people soon come true. (pp. 349-51)

> *John F. Whealon, in a review of "Hope and Suffering: Sermons and Speeches," in* America, *Vol. 152, No. 16, April 27, 1985, pp. 349-51.*

Patrick Jordan (essay date 1985)

[*In the following review, Jordan comments on Tutu's theme in* Hope and Suffering: *"the abhorrent evil of the South African system."*]

Bishop Tutu has said elsewhere the church has five marks: it is one, holy, catholic, apostolic, and suffering. In this brief collection of addresses and sermons [**Hope and Suffering**], he describes the sufferings of South Africa's majority black population under apartheid. He proposes, but does not detail, a prophetic vision for societal change there, and simultaneously offers his personal example of enduring hope, one capable of sustaining the long-suffering in movements of human rights everywhere.

Desmond Tutu's theme is singular and unabashed: the abhorrent evil of the South African system. His theological method is here likewise singleminded: liberation-exodus is the lens by which to examine and weigh the apartheid situation. The bishop speaks with flowing ease and ready passion. What he has to say is not always couched in irenic terms. On occasion, he caricatures opponents, a fact not likely to engender their trust. He is firmly set as to his goals: the solution must be political. "Either there is going to be power-sharing or . . . we must give up hope of peaceful settlement in South Africa." The international community must bring economic pressure to bear on Pretoria. Finally, Tutu and his people are watching. "When we are free," he writes, "we will remember those who helped us to get free." It is that deliverance which animates Tutu. It is a hope assured, and richer than mere words. (pp. 477-78)

> Patrick Jordan, in a review of "Hope and Suffering: Sermons and Speeches," in Commonweal, Vol. CXII, No. 15, September 6, 1985, pp. 477-78.

Bonganjalo Goba (essay date 1986)

[*In the excerpt below, Goba delineates Tutu's conception of liberation theology.*]

Those of us who have listened and have been taught by Archbishop Tutu, know that he is a serious biblical theologian. His theological vision is grounded in a profound faith that believes that the God of the Bible is on the side of the down-trodden, the oppressed or if you like, the wretched of the earth. This vision is reflected in his sermons, speeches and even conversations which reflect a deep spirituality whose characteristics are utter devotion and trust in God who has been revealed in Jesus Christ; and a deep concern for those who suffer and are victims of oppression. The Biblical ethos informs and shapes Archbishop Tutu's theological vision. This is a point which is misunderstood by those who think his statements and actions are motivated by political ambition.

But his theological vision is grounded in his understanding of the church. He makes the following observation about the church [in *Hope and Suffering: Sermons and Speeches*]:

> The Church of God must produce a relevant theology which speaks to hopelessness and despondency. The Church of God must declare the Lordship of God and of Christ—that God is the Lord of History and of this world despite all appearances to the contrary, that He is God of justice and cares about oppression and exploitation, about deaths in detention, about front-end loaders, squatters' shacks, about unemployment and about power.

Archbishop Tutu's biblical vision of a God who is concerned about the plight and suffering of people moves him to be part of God's liberating mission in the South African context. We can say it is this obedience to the divine call of a God who cares so much for the wretched, that moves Archbishop Tutu to engage so forcefully in the struggle for authentic liberation. This involvement and passionate call for justice in this land is a response of obedience to God who in Jesus Christ

has come to liberate the world. It is a response of faith; but one that challenges the structure of bondage in the South African apartheid society. Archbishop Tutu's moral outrage against apartheid is the product of his deep faith in a God who cares for people irrespective of who they are. Apartheid, according to Archbishop Tutu, is not simply contrary to the gospel, but it is demonic in that it breeds suffering and chaos.

It is this theological vision that influenced and inspired some of us to engage in black theological reflection within the South African context. As a special tribute to Archbishop Tutu I want to share with you some of his major theological concerns, as expressed in his sermons, speeches and lectures. In no way will I suggest that these can be arranged systematically; but I propose to give a broad outline of these theological concerns as well as reflect on them. In doing so, I am also inviting young budding black theologians to address themselves to some of these issues. I want to reflect on two of his major theological concerns, a response to the challenge he has posed to the black Christian community:

(a) A concern to develop a biblical theology of liberation.

(b) A call for the church to be a community of liberation.

Archbishop Tutu is basically a biblical theologian. By this I want to suggest that the foundations of his theological hermeneutic are grounded in the liberating message of the Bible. To illustrate this point let me quote from one of his statements [in *Hope and Suffering*]:

> Where there is injustice, exploitation and oppression then the Bible and the God of the Bible are subversive of such a situation. Our God, unlike the pagan nature gods, is no God sanctifying the *status quo*. He is a God of surprises, uprooting the powerful and unjust to establish His Kingdom. We see it in the entire history of Israel.

Archbishop Tutu makes numerous references to the Bible as part of the development of his theological hermeneutics. Unfortunately this biblical hermeneutics thrust in his theology is not developed in the form of a theological treatise—but merely as a crucial ingredient in his theology. I want to show why this theological concern is crucial to the way we do theology in the South African context. (pp. 61-3)

There is renewed interest in the study of the Bible particularly using methods from the Social Sciences. More biblical scholars are turning to Sociology and Sociology of Knowledge in their attempt to unravel the early social world of both the Old and the New Testaments. I believe this is a very important development which hopefully will shed new insights on the significance of the Bible for theology and preaching. This will also enable us to appreciate why certain Biblical themes have attracted the attention of particularly those who engage in the theology of liberation, especially the theme of the Exodus. As the scope of this essay does not permit me to examine these new developments, I will focus my attention on one aspect, that is, viewing scripture as a liberating word and then use it as a basis for understanding the place of the Bible in black theological reflection.

One of the prevailing misconceptions about the theology of liberation is that this kind of theology is inspired purely by radical ideologies such as nationalism and Marxism, and not the Bible. We need to examine this misconception in order to put the record straight. What we must recognize is that one of the central themes of the Bible is liberation/salvation. What theology of liberation has succeeded to impress on our minds is that the God of the Bible is the God of liberation. Daniel Migliore in his book *Called to Freedom* makes the following observation:

> Liberation theology finds the centre of Scripture in its story of God's liberating activity. In the Old Testament God's saving action is focussed in the Exodus, the liberation of a people from political, cultural and religious bondage. By this event God has become known as the liberating God. 'I am the Lord your God, who brought you out of the land of Egypt, out of the house of bondage' (Ex. 20:2).

Because of this basic theological thrust Migliore has suggested that the Bible should be interpreted (a) historically, (b) theocentrically, and (c) contextually.

Let us examine what he means by these three categories. (a) To interpret the Bible historically plays an important role in theology, or preaching for that matter, in that it compels the exegete to take seriously the particularity of God's actions. This approach enables us to appreciate the liberating acts of God in history. But more than this consideration, it enables us to appreciate the problems and the limitations of the early Christian community.

We come to understand the possibilities that remained as a challenge to that community. As Migliore states, "To interpret the Bible historically is to see in its narratives not only memories of past events but promises of new possibilities." The point which Migliore emphasizes is that in studying the past of God's liberating activity, we are challenged to understand its implications for the present. But further, this approach enables us to link our present struggle with that of the early Christian community.

I believe Archbishop Tutu, as a biblical theologian, has been very conscious of this principle in his work. He displays a very strong consciousness that the God of the Bible acts within human history. That God sides concretely with the wretched of the earth within the historical context of their struggle. For Archbishop Tutu the incarnation is a historical event that signals God's determination to liberate humanity from oppression and dehumanization. The God of the Bible acts in history to liberate humanity, this is the message of the ministry of Jesus Christ. In one of his important sermons delivered at Steve Biko's funeral he made the following statement:

Yes, the God Jesus came to proclaim He was no neutral sitter on the fence. He took the side of the oppressed, the poor, the exploited, not because they were holier or morally better than their oppressors.

No, He was on their side simply and solely because they were oppressed. Yes, this was the good news Jesus came to proclaim—that God was the liberator, the one who set free the oppressed and the poor and exploited. He set them free from all that would make them less than he wanted them to be, fully human persons as free as Jesus Christ showed Himself to be. And so all the mighty works which Jesus performed, healing the sick, opening the eyes of the blind, forgiving the sins of all sinners, were to set them free so that they could enjoy the glorious liberty of the children of God. And His followers believed He would restore the Kingdom again to Israel. He would set them free from being ruled by the Romans and give them back their political independence.

For Archbishop Tutu God is involved in the struggle of the oppressed. God takes sides within a specific historical context. This principle is important for it compels whoever reads the Bible to contextualize.

The other important point which Migliore makes is that the Bible should be interpreted theocentrically. This principle, I believe, is so central to our theological hermeneutic that without it, it becomes impossible to engage in any meaningful biblical exegesis. Migliore makes the following observation about this:

> Scripture must be interpreted theocentrically; however, the meaning of "God" is radically redefined in the biblical story of liberation.

> The central actor in the biblical drama is God, Scripture witnesses to the reality of God, to the purpose of God, to the kingdom of God. The content of the biblical story is God's faithfulness in acts of judgment and mercy, in the covenant with the people of Israel and in the history of Jesus. The biblical narrative has many aspects, but in the midst of the many aspects is the central theme: the mystery of the faithful God who takes up the cause of justice, freedom, and peace on behalf of the creation oppressed by sin and misery. Scripture witnesses on the promise of God even in the midst of judgment. It declares God's benevolence toward us even in the depth of our sin: "While we were yet sinners Christ died for us" (Rom. 5:8). Scripture proclaims the decisive ratification of all God's promises in the resurrection of the crucified Jesus. "For all the promises of God find their Yes in him" (II Cor. 1:20).

Reading his articles or listening to Archbishop Tutu one gets an interesting insight about how his theology is centred on the notion of God. For Archbishop Tutu God is alive and involved in the struggle of the oppressed. It is thus the God of liberation of the exodus who is the source of his prophetic piety. God is not just an idea but becomes the vision the embodiment of a real liberating presence in the world. In one of his sermons Archbishop Tutu made the following observation:

> So let us remind ourselves again and again just what kind of God our God is. He is always there. He has

always been there. So don't despair. No matter how long it may take or seem to be. He is there. He hears, He cares and will act. We must not doubt that He will take our side and that He will rescue us and lead us out of bondage, out of our slavery, out of our poverty, out of our suffering. He will make us His own people to worship Him and He is almighty. Nothing will eventually stop Him.

This vision of a God who takes sides is so real for Archbishop Tutu, God is not neutral for in Jesus Christ He identifies with the poor and the oppressed. This theocentric approach, I believe, is reflected in most theologies of liberation. Liberation theologians are so conscious of this God who liberates the wretched of the earth. I believe this principle is a pivot on which our hermeneutic is based for without this profound consciousness of a God who is involved in the struggles of humanity, there would be no theology or theologies of liberation.

The other important principle that Migliore mentions in his book is that the Bible must be interpreted contextually. He makes the following observation about this:

> Scripture must be interpreted contextually; however, the context of our interpretation must be increasingly open to and inclusive of the yearnings of the whole creation to be free.

> The context of our interpretation of Scripture will always include and will frequently begin with our now personal awareness of captivity and yearning for freedom and new life: with our own anxiety, guilt, frustration, alienation, loneliness and despair.

I believe that Archbishop Tutu has been very faithful to this principle. For in his sermons and speeches he interprets the Bible contextually. For him the Bible is so relevant to every situation of life. The word of God addresses the South African situation. It is the word that unravels the contradictions and the evils of the political system of apartheid. Speaking about the church he makes the following statement:

> The church in South Africa must be a prophetic church which cries out 'thus saith the Lord' speaking up against injustice and violence, against oppression and exploitation, against all that dehumanizes God's children and makes them less than what God intended them to be. The Church of God in this context must show forth the features of the Lord and Master who tied a towel around His waist to wash the feet of His disciples.

This concern with the present contest of oppression and suffering is reflected in his theological vision. As he attempts to interpret the word of God contextually, he at the same time proclaims its promise for liberation in the here and now. Through Archbishop Tutu, God speaks so powerfully to the South African situation. It is this commitment that has earned Archbishop Tutu both enemies and friends.

So what we see in this brief analysis is the development of a biblical vision that addresses itself to the current political struggle of the oppressed. The Word of God addresses itself to the plight of the poor and the oppressed. It is not only the word but the word made flesh in the liberating ministry of Jesus Christ. What we see in Archbishop Tutu's theological vision is the development of an incarnational approach in which God's concern becomes alive through the commitment of those who serve God in the world today. In this, Archbishop Tutu succeeds to make the Bible relevant to the struggle of authentic human liberation. I believe Archbishop Tutu must be given credit for this, for the Bible has been silent for a very long time in our struggle for liberation within the South African context. (pp. 63-7)

Bonganjalo Goba, "A Theological Tribute to Archbishop Tutu," in Hammering Swords into Ploughshares: Essays in Honor of Archbishop Mpilo Desmond Tutu, *edited by Buti Tlhagale and Itumeleng Mosala, 1986. Reprint by Africa World Press, Inc. and William B. Eerdmans Publishing Company, 1987, pp. 61-71.*

FURTHER READING

Bierman, John. "A Skeptical View: Tutu Decries the Pace of Reforms." *Macleans* 102, No. 11 (13 March 1989): 22.
  Interview with Tutu on political reforms in South Africa.

Tutu, Desmond. "No One Will Stop Us . . . ." *The Unesco Courier* 43, No. 6 (June 1990): 37-8.
  Tutu responds to questions on the possibility of a democratic South Africa.

Amos Tutuola

1920-

Nigerian novelist, short story writer, and playwright.

With his first published novel, *The Palm-Wine Drinkard and His Dead Palm-Wine Tapster in the Deads' Town* (1952), Tutuola became the first Nigerian writer to achieve international recognition. His works draw freely from traditional Yoruban folktales and are written in nonstandard English, often influenced by the grammar and vocabulary of Tutuola's native language, Yoruba. The early appearance of a laudatory review by acclaimed poet Dylan Thomas influenced critical reception of *The Palm-Wine Drinkard*, and the ensuing attention gave Tutuola's books a cultlike status in the West. This novel remains his best-known work and has been translated into fifteen languages. Early Nigerian critics expressed doubt about Tutuola's writing ability, complaining that his work was ungrammatical and unoriginal and imitated the work of D. O. Fagunwa, a Yoruban chronicler of tales in the vernacular. While Tutuola's subsequent works received comparatively less attention from Western critics, Nigerians now appreciate his unique style and have reclaimed Tutuola as an innovative storyteller who has perpetuated and recreated their folktales.

The son of a cocoa farmer, Tutuola completed only six years of school. He worked as a blacksmith in the Royal Air Force in Lagos from 1942 to 1945, after which he unsuccessfully attempted to open his own blacksmith shop. Following a year of unemployment, he found a job as a messenger at the Department of Labor in Lagos. He was prompted to write his first novel after reading an advertisement placed by a Christian publisher that had printed collections of African stories. He commented in an interview: "[The] time I wrote [*The Palm-Wine Drinkard*], what was in my mind was that I noticed that our young men, our young sons and daughters did not pay much attention to our traditional things or culture or customs. They adopted, they concentrated their minds only on European things. They left our customs, so if I do this they may change their mind...to remember our custom, not to leave it to die.... That was my intention." He wrote the first draft in two days, and the manuscript eventually reached a British publisher who printed it eight years later. Upon receiving *The Palm-Wine Drinkard*, Tutuola remembered, the publishers contacted him: "[They] were wondering whether I found the story fallen down from somebody because it is very strange to them. They wondered because they were surprised to see such a story...they wanted to know whether I had made it up or got it from somebody else." Tutuola continued to work as a messenger for ten years, writing in his spare time.

Tutuola's works typically concern a naive or morally weak character who is either inspired or forced to embark on a spiritual journey. During the journey, he or she encounters danger, confronts spirits from the underworld, and has sudden insights that enable him or her to live a more pious life. The title character in *Simbi and the Satyr of the Dark Jungle*, (1956), for example, is a wealthy, young girl who decides that she must experience "poverty" and "punishment." She is kidnapped and, in her various attempts to return home, follows "The Path of Death" to such fantastical places as "The Town Where Nobody Sings," "The Sinners' Town," and "The Town of the Multi-Coloured People"; when she returns home, she realizes that she should no longer disobey her mother. Because of their spiritual themes, allegorical characters, and symbolic plots, Tutuola's works have been called mythologies or epics rather than novels, and many critics have compared his use of mythology and epic quests to patterns in John Bunyan's *Pilgrim's Progress* or Jonathan Swift's *Gulliver's Travels*. While some critics have dismissed Tutuola's works as simple retellings of local tales, other have noted that the stories present universal themes and complex cosmologies. The protagonists' quests are seen as mythical encounters with gods, fanciful flights of imagination, or Tutuola's personal exploration of the psyche. Charles R. Larson commented: "Tutuola's imagination is frequently a bridge between the internal and the external world (the ontological gap), between the real and the surreal, between the realistic and the supernatural...."

Tutuola employs many techniques associated with oral traditions in his novels and stories. Specific episodes, for example, are often repeated for emphasis, and Tutuola embellishes well-known tales with personal interpretations and modern situations. According to Michael Thelwell: "[Tutuola's] is a traditional imagination wandering—much like his narrator in the Land of the Spirits—through the cultural chaos of modern urban Nigeria." Characteristic of his modern, fantastical creatures is "the television-handed goddess," whom the palm-wine drinkard encounters on his travels. The mixing of contemporary concepts with traditional stories has been seen as evidence of Tutuola's sensitivity to social and environmental changes in Nigeria. While he adapts his tales to modern experience, his works are also tinged with the loss of former Nigerian spiritual beliefs. He commented: "I wrote to tell of my ancestors and how they lived in their days. They lived with the immortal creatures of the forest.... But now the forests are gone. I believe the immortal creatures must have moved away."

Perhaps the most unique aspect of Tutuola's novels is his unconventional use of the English language: skewed syntax, sometimes broken English, and idiosyncratic diction. For example, Tutuola wrote in *The Palm-Wine Drinkard*: "[If] I were a lady, no doubt I would follow him to wherever he would go, and still as I was a man I would jealous him more than that...."; his usage of "jealous" as a verb reflects Yoruban grammatical constructs, in which adjectives and verbs are often interchangeable. Edward Blishen noted the effect of Tutuola's style: "The language is wonderfully stirring and odd: a mixture of straight translation from Yoruba, and everyday modern Nigerian idiom, and grand epical English. The imagination at work is always astonishing.... And this, not the bargain, is folklore not resurrected, but being created fresh and true in the white heat of a tradition still undestroyed." Although some admirers hail Tutuola as the founder of Nigerian literature, most critics agree that his literary style and method are highly personal and have had little influence on subsequent writers in Nigeria. He now enjoys a wide international readership and his works are commonly read in Nigerian schools.

(For further information about Tutuola's life and works, see *Black Writers*; *Contemporary Authors*, Vols. 9-12; *Contemporary Authors New Revision Series*, Vol. 27; *Contemporary Literary Criticism*, Vols. 5, 14, 29; and *Major 20th-Century Writers*.)

PRINCIPAL WORKS

The Palm-Wine Drinkard and His Dead Palm-Wine Tapster in the Deads' Town (novel) 1952
My Life in the Bush of Ghosts (novel) 1954
Simbi and the Satyr of the Dark Jungle (novel) 1956
The Brave African Huntress (novel) 1958
The Palm-Wine Drinkard (drama) 1958
Feather Woman of the Jungle (novel) 1962
Ajaiyi and His Inherited Poverty (novel) 1967
The Witch-Herbalist of the Remote Town (novel) 1981
The Wild Hunter in the Bush of the Ghosts (short stories) 1982; revised edition, 1989
The Village Witch Doctor and Other Stories (short stories) 1990

Dylan Thomas (essay date 1952)

[*Thomas was a Welsh poet, short story writer, scriptwriter, and essayist. In the following excerpt from a 1952* Observer *review of* The Palm-Wine Drinkard and His Dead Palm-Wine Tapster in the Deads' Town, *he introduces Tutuola to Western readers.*]

[*The Palm-Wine Drinkard*] is the brief, thronged, grisly and bewitching story, or series of stories, written in young English by a West African, about the journey of an expert and devoted palm-wine drinkard through a nightmare of indescribable adventures, all simply and carefully described, in the spirit-bristling bush. From the age of ten he drank 225 kegs a day, and wished to do nothing else; he knew what was good for him, it was just what the witch-doctor ordered. But when his tapster fell from a tree and died, and as, naturally, he himself "did not satisfy with water as with palm-wine," he set out to search for the tapster in Deads' Town.

This was the devil—or, rather, the many devils—of a way off, and among those creatures, dubiously alive, whom he encountered,... [was] a "beautiful complete gentleman" who, as he went through the forest, returned the hired parts of his body to their owners, at the same time paying rentage, and soon became a full-bodied gentleman reduced to skull.

Luckily, the drinkard found a fine wife on his travels, and she bore him a child from her thumb; but the child turned out to be abnormal, a pyromaniac, a smasher to death of domestic animals, and a bigger drinkard than its father, who was forced to burn it to ashes. And out of the ashes appeared a half-bodied child, talking with a "lower voice like a telephone." (There are many other convenient features of modern civilised life that crop up in the black and ancient midst of these fierce folk legends, including bombs and aeroplanes, high-heel shoes, cameras, cigarettes, guns, broken bottles, policemen.) There is, later, one harmonious interlude in the Faithful-Mother's house, or magical, technicolour nightclub, in a tree that takes photographs; and one beautiful moment of rejoicing, when Drum, Song, and Dance, three tree fellows, perform upon themselves, and the dead arise, and the animals, snakes, and spirits of the bush dance together. But mostly it's hard and haunted going.... (pp. 7-8)

The writing is nearly always terse and direct, strong, wry, flat and savoury; the big, and often comic, terrors are as near and understandable as the numerous small details of price, size, and number; and nothing is too prodigious or too trivial to put down in this tall, devilish story. (p. 8)

> *Dylan Thomas, "Blithe Spirits," in* Critical Perspectives on Amos Tutuola, *edited by Bernth Lindfors, Three Continents Press, 1975, pp. 7-8.*

Margaret Laurence (essay date 1968)

[*Laurence was a Canadian novelist, short story writer, poet, essayist, and reporter. In the following excerpt, she argues that the quest theme in Tutuola's novels mirrors the author's own psychological explorations.*]

Amos Tutuola's strangely poetic writing was quick to gain recognition in England and America, but in his own country it was at first widely criticised because of its bizarre use of English and because Tutuola was dealing with a past which many people were trying to forget, a past associated with the old gods and the spirits of forest and village, an ancestral past whose traditions for many of the present generation had lost their powers of reasurrance while still retaining some powers of fear and threat. Nowadays Tutuola's work is recognised and admired by a whole generation of more sophisticated Nigerian writers, who no longer feel the need to deny their roots, but Tutuola has little in common with these young intellectuals either. His writing does not belong to any mainstream. It is neither contemporary nor traditional. It is, really timeless and quite individual, although Tutuola has been greatly influenced by his Yoruba background. (p. 126)

He is in a sense an epic poet who as a man belongs nowhere, and this isolation is both his tragedy and his artistic strength....

The Yoruba culture is rich in folk tales, stories of gods and spirits, talking animals, magic charms, and powers, people who are transformed into gazelles or fish or birds. Tutuola draws deeply upon the folk tales and myths of his own people, using this material in a way that is strictly his own, sometimes taking snatches of Yoruba tales or characters from Yoruba mythology and recreating them in his own fantastic manner, sometimes combining past and present in such creatures as the Television-Handed Ghostess. He is able to use the Yoruba tales in a variety of ways because they are genuinely his, and often he does not seem to be using them consciously at all. They are simply his frame of reference, the terms in which he naturally tends to think.

The tone of Tutuola's writing also resembles that of many Yoruba tales, for it is both humorous and poetic, and it fluctuates between a portrayal of beauty and lightness and a portrayal of grotesque ugliness....

[Whatever] his sources, in his best work Tutuola makes something new from his material. He writes very much out of himself, and his writing stands alone, unrelated to any other Nigerian writing in English. There is a tremendous courage about the man, for he has been able to go on alone, remaining true to an inner sight which perceives both the dazzling multicoloured areas of dream and the appalling forests of nightmare.

Tutuola's first book [*The Palm-Wine Drinkard*] is his masterpiece. It takes the form of an odyssey, a journey into the underworld which the hero undertakes in order to prove himself. It is really a journey of the spirit, in which the hero meets the monster-creations of his own mind, suffers torments, wins victories and finally returns to his own country, able now to rule it because of the wisdom his experiences have given him and because of the power he has gained through the terrors he has overcome. It is, of course, a classic journey, found in the mythologies of all cultures. It has been compared to Orpheus in the underworld, to Bunyan's *Pilgrim's Progress*, to Dante, to the journey of Odysseus. (pp. 127-28)

[*My Life in the Bush of Ghosts*] approaches and in some ways even surpasses *The Palm-Wine Drinkard* in the grotesque quality of its visions, although the work as a whole is not as powerful as the first. 'Bush', to a West African, means the rain-forest or what Europeans and Americans might call the jungle. 'Ghosts' in this book are not the spirits of dead persons, but rather spirits who have never lived as people but have always inhabited their own spirit world which coexists with ours.

The hero is lost from his home and enters the Bush of Ghosts as a boy of seven. He emerges as a man many years later. [The critic] Gerald Moore sees the story as a kind of *rite de passage*, an initiation, and undoubtedly this is so. As well, however, the story is a journey into the depths of the subconscious. Tutuola may not have intended it to be this; indeed, if he had intended it, it probably would not have worked out that way, for this type of exploration has to be done out of necessity, not calculation. The book appears to be a painful setting down of the publicly suppressed areas of the mind. In this fictional guise, the forbidden can be looked at, and the horrifying or appalling side of the self can be brought into the open. The 'self' in this sense means all our selves, for although the forest looks (and is) different to every pair of eyes, it is there in varying shapes and forms for us all. Few are brave enough to look at it, and fewer still to record it.

It is a grim world we are shown here. There is an obsession with pain, flogging, humiliation, torture, excreta. The torments of the hero are feared but also masochistically sought. The image of the mother is an interesting and ambiguous one, for the boy keeps thinking of his own mother with warmth and affection, yet he encounters such repulsive mother-types as the Flash-Eyed Mother, whose entire attention, significantly enough, is taken up with the snarling and evil-looking infant heads which are sprouting all over her body, and who therefore neglects all her other ghost children, including the hero, who has been taken into the community as one of her family. (pp. 132-33)

The deep split in the mind between the old gods and the new is expressed poetically and with great power. Tutuola never in this book actually names the old Yoruba gods—in fact, he hardly ever refers to them as gods at all. The old gods inhabit his writing in the form of spirits and ghosts, and most of these are frightening. . . . The hero of the story fears all these ghosts very much indeed, yet he repeatedly seeks their company. He cannot get away from them. The attitudes to Christianity, as they appear in this book, are mixed, to say the least. The conflicts which are laid bare here are the same conflicts as those described by Achebe in *Things Fall Apart* and *Arrow of God*, but in the work of Tutuola the clash between religions is not being described as such and is perhaps not even recognised as such. It is brought out in quite a different way, in terms of the main character's suffering, a suffering which only if it is viewed very superficially can be believed in as being merely external adventure. The hero puts a yearning faith in the Christian God. He is always saying 'as God is so good—'. At one point he discovers his long-dead cousin in the tenth Town of Ghosts, and finds that the cousin has set up a mission. The mission sign—humorously and yet in a way almost heartbreakingly—reads, THE METHODIST CHURCH OF THE BUSH OF GHOSTS. Rarely has dichotomy been expressed in so few words.

The unacknowledged resentment against Christianity comes out almost with a sense of relief and release, like someone speaking a long-forbidden obscenity in order to break its haunting power. This resentment is perhaps not so very difficult to grasp, for it is directed against the religion which severed several generations of Africans from their own past. It appears in odd forms—sometimes by taking Christian rituals and turning them inside out or upside down. (pp. 133-34)

The old religions of Africa have combined with Christianity in some peculiar ways. The two have also clashed—and clashed tragically—within the individual minds of men. The whole story of this conflict is only now beginning to emerge clearly. A writer such as Achebe deals with it by trying to understand it and perceive it, by re-creating it within the personalities of his characters, characters who are not himself but who exist as themselves. This is the method of the novelist. Tutuola's method is poetic and intuitive. Here we get the conflict raw. Whether or not he means it to be there, it *is* there. (p. 135)

The ending [of *My Life in the Bush of Ghosts*] is enigmatic. 'This is what hatred did.' This conclusion does not seem to make sense in the external context, but it has specific meaning if it is viewed as another direct and indeed tragic statement from the inner world. *My Life in the Bush of Ghosts* is the work of someone who has walked in the pit of hell, and who has been courageous enough to open his eyes while he was there. . . .

[*Simbi and the Satyr of the Dark Jungle*] concerns the learning of wisdom through ordeal. It is not as strong a story as either *The Palm-Wine Drinkard* or *My Life in the Bush of Ghosts*, but much of it is written in a sprightly manner which is partly produced by the appearance of more conversation than the previous books contained.

Simbi is Tutuola's only book not written in the first person. He succeeds best with a first-person narration, as though he were able in this way to get inside the personality of the central character and to write with the unfailingly true sound of a human voice.

Simbi is the daughter of a wealthy woman. She is an only child and has been brought up in luxury. She is also naturally gifted, being a lovely girl and having a fine singing voice. But Simbi grows weary of her pleasant life, and longs to experience '. . . the "Poverty" and the "Punishment"'. She prays to know the meaning of poverty and punishment, and her dangerous prayer is quickly answered. (p. 136)

As with so much of Tutuola's work, under the lightness and humour, under the descriptions of enchanted places [in *Simbi*], there lies the continuing theme of pain, dreaded and yet sought. (p. 138)

[*The Brave African Huntress*] is something of a disappointment. It is altogether thinner in texture, not so richly imaginative as his first three books, although there are flashes of the old style—for example, in chapter headings such as The Animal That Died But His Eyes Still Alive (the heroine prudently salvages the animal's skull with its glowing eyes and uses it as a night light), or in beautifully expressive phrases such as 'Whisperly the king spoke—'. (pp. 138-39)

[Despite] the frequently humorous tone of the surface, the main underlying theme [of *Feather Woman of the Jungle*] is a masochistic one. For the story's hero the goal is to be achieved only through pain and humiliation, suffering which he is compelled to seek, not really for its own sake but in order that the enduring of it may permit the gates to be opened to the desired end. (pp. 145-46)

Amos Tutuola has a way of combining the macabre and the beautiful, the horrifying and the humorous, the familiar and the mysterious. One of the most impressive things about him when he is at his best is the vitality of his writing and the completely unstudied and casual way in which he makes his dramatic effects. (p. 146)

Essentially, however, the themes are dark ones, themes which can in no sense be said to exclude any one of us . . . . [The] magic is never mock-up, never a sham—it is always the real thing. But if Tutuola's books are for children [as some critics suggest], it is only in the same way that *Gulliver's Travels* was once thought to be.

Tutuola's books are not really novels. They are episodic and they follow the classical lines of the sagas found in all cultures. He writes best when most intuitively and most intensely inward. His forests are certainly and in detail the outer ones but they are, as well, the forests of the mind, where the individual meets and grapples with the creatures of his own imagination. These creatures are aspects of himself, aspects of his response to the world into which he was born, the world to which he must continue to return if he is to live as a man. (pp. 146-47)

> Margaret Laurence, "A Twofold Forest: Amos Tutuola," in her Long Drums and Cannons: Nigerian Dramatists and Novelists, *Macmillan, London, 1968, pp. 126-47*

David Arnason (essay date 1975)

[*Arnason is a Canadian poet, short story writer, educator, critic, and an historian. In the excerpt below, he addresses Tutuola's position in Nigerian literature.*]

The Palm Wine Drinkard burst onto the world literary scene in 1952, and was an immediate and smashing success. This was balanced by Tutuola's cool reception by Nigerian critics, who felt that the quaintness of Tutuola's style was the chief appeal to outsiders, and that he was read with condescension. Most western critics deny that they treat Tutuola condescendingly, and attempt to prove their point by treating Nigerian critics with condescension, mocking their aspirations towards progress and culture.

There is right on both sides. **The Palm Wine Drinkard** is an excellent book and the style is refreshing and interesting. At the same time, it is also a very limited style, and the Nigerians are quite right in pointing out that it is not a model to be held up for young Nigerians to emulate. Nigerians are very sensitive about language. They live in a country in which dozens of languages are spoken and wisely or not, they have chosen English as their official language. This in itself creates other problems. Each speaker brings to bear upon English the stress, rhythm, intonation, sounds and structure of his native tongue . . . . Thus certain features of Tutuola's language, his conversion of adjectives into verbs ("I would jealous him"), the strange time sense created by his adverbial uses of "there", and his special use of conjunctives are not so much inventive as they are natural forms to him. This is not to deny inventiveness to Tutuola, but to point out that some of the criticism raised by his countrymen is not merely unreasonable . . . .

The objection of Tutuola's style is not so much a criticism of **The Palm Wine Drinkard** as a thing in itself, but a criticism of it as a model, and this is an important distinction. It would be a mistake to suggest that the verve and dynamism of Tutuola's style are purely the felicitous result of a marriage of Yoruba and English. If this were so, any partly educated Yoruba writing in English could be expected to produce an equally captivating style, and this is clearly not the case. There is a great deal of inventiveness and intuitive awareness of the possibilities of English in Tutuola's work . . . .

Tutuola is an impressive stylist . . . .

In fact, the elements which lend dynamism and power to Tutuola's style are the same elements which make for power in any more conventional style: a terse economy of means, vivid and concrete language, sure and descriptive detail, and original and imaginative imagery. (p. 56)

[However,] Tutuola succeeds not because of his idiosyncratic English, but in spite of it.

It cannot be denied, of course, that at various points Tutuola's blending of Yoruba sentence structure and English vocabulary produces strikingly powerful and original effects. These are, however, felicitous accidents and should not be used as a gauge of Tutuola's capacity to handle language. His use of the word "drinkard" may indeed be an inspired blending of the English "drinker" and "drunkard" to create a new concept of the man who drinks too much, but to whom may not be applied the pejorative connotations of the world "drunkard". More likely though, it is simply an error resulting from the fact that in spoken Yoruba the vowel sound "u" as in "drunkard" does not exist. Nor are all his singular usages so fortunate. His use of the word "patentee" to refer to those who treat patients in a hospital is unclear and confusing.

The second point on which Western and Nigerian critics tend to disagree is on the nature of Tutuola's talent. At the extremes, some Western critics find a totally inventive talent, creatively discovering universal themes. They draw parallels between Tutuola and such writers as Dante, Spencer, and Bunyan and marvel at such untutored genius. The extreme position of his detractors is that Tutuola has no talent; that his work is for the most part a slavish imitation of [D. O.] Fagunwa, or else a bad retelling of Yoruba folk tales, full of error and unwelcome innovation . . . .

Tutuola did read *Pilgrim's Progress* in 1948, just two years before he wrote **The Palm Wine Drinkard**, and the similarities between the two may thus be presumed less than coincidental . . . . [As] the evidence gathers, it appears that all of the incidents in **The Palm Wine Drinkard** are based on folk tales and myths . . . .

The truth of the matter, I think, lies somewhere in the middle. Tutuola is neither a great and inspired original creator nor a dull and slavish imitator. His is what Joseph Campbell calls a syncretic imagination. It reconciles opposites and creates syntheses. His method is eclectic, drawing from all sources and merging wildly disparate elements into a wholly believable unity. The syncretic imagination functions at every level of Tutuola's art. It is, first of all, apparent in the style. With no apparent difficulty Tutuola combines imagery drawn from a pre-industrial, animistic and magic-based cultural sensibility with imagery drawn from an industrial, monotheistic, and scientific cultural sensibility.... [The] pattern of imagery reaches its ultimate point in Tutuola's second book *My Life in The Bush of Ghosts* in which appears a wonderful monster, The Television Handed Ghostess.

The syncretic imagination functions at the level of narrative as well. Dozens of dualities are reconciled in the sweep of the story. The spiritual world and the human world are merged. The hero of the book is a mortal, but he is also "Father of Gods". (p. 57)

At the deepest level operates what Joseph Campbell in *The Masks of God* calls "syncretic monotheism". The monsters, spirits and gods of the bush operate without apparent conflict in a universe in which the Christian God is also apparently present and operative; though by no means to be presumed to have more power than any of the other gods. For example, when the spirits of Unreturnable Heavens Town leave the hero and his wife buried to their necks and prey to the evil whims of children, the Christian God intervenes to save them....

It is Tutuola's ability to synthesize all elements of the African experience into a cohesive form that is his chief claim to genius. *The Palm Wine Drinkard* is not a kind of gothic novel which requires suspension of belief so that we can vicariously experience nameless terrors. It creates a believable world in which terror is functional, and in which the monsters are infused with the human elements that make them terrible.

It remains, finally, to discuss the form of the book. It is called a novel, though that seems inappropriate. The story exists outside of the societal web, and most of the judgments we customarily make about novels are simply irrelevant. Judgements about characterization, setting, thematic unity and social relevance are of little importance in discussion of *The Palm Wine Drinkard*....

In fact, *The Palm Wine Drinkard* is a saga. When any preliterate, oral society becomes literate and begins to write out of its own experience, its attempts to transmit the material from the old oral tradition into the new literary mode produce an heroic form that may be broadly called the saga. Roughly equivalent forms have occurred in most cultures that have managed to emerge to the literate level on their own or have managed to escape being completely overwhelmed by another dominating culture.

A comparison of *The Palm Wine Drinkard* with the early Icelandic sagas provides a great number of interesting similarities. The early Icelandic sagas are based on the folk tales and myths of an earlier oral culture, as is *The Palm Wine Drinkard*. The Icelandic saga-writer did not create essentially new material, but transformed the stories of the bardic tradition, giving them his individual shape. It would appear that Tutuola has done just this; like the saga-writer he has relied on a story telling tradition, but has given his own particular treatment to the traditional material. The sagas are picaresque, episodic works, in which the supernatural is operative, and in which the heroes often have magical powers themselves. All of this can be said equally of *The Palm Wine Drinkard*. The heroes of the sagas often encounter dreadful monsters with whom they do battle.... The basic pattern of most of the sagas is the form of the quest, and that is the form that Tutuola employs....

The chief difference between *The Palm Wine Drinkard* and other sagas is that they are written in the vernacular languages, while *The Palm Wine Drinkard* is written in the language of the dominant culture. This is a significant fact....

As it is, Tutuola's work remains a fascinating example of the natural evolution of a literature. In other circumstances it might have been the key to a developing literature. Under present circumstances it appears to be a dead end. Tutuola's English has not the resources to serve as a stylistic model for younger writers. His saga form and his folk tale material are unlikely to be used again in anything like the form he uses them. Nigeria is rapidly becoming a modern, industrialized state, and new gods are in the ascendant. (p. 58)

> David Arnason, "Amos Tutuola's 'The Palm Wine Drinkard': The Nature of Tutuola's Achievement," in Journal of Canadian Fiction, *Vol. III, No. 4, 1975, pp. 56-9.*

Chinua Achebe (essay date 1978)

[*Achebe is a celebrated Nigerian novelist, short story writer, poet, essayist, and editor. In the following excerpt, he examines Tutuola's juxtaposition of work and play in* The Palm-Wine Drinkard and His Palm-Wine Tapster in the Deads' Town.]

[Tutuola] is the most moralistic of all Nigerian writers.... [He] has his two feet firmly planted in the hard soil of an ancient oral and moral tradition.

Of course Tutuola's art conceals—or rather clothes—his purpose, as good art often does. But anybody who asks what the story is about can hardly have read him. And I suspect that many people who talk about Tutuola one way or another have not read him.

The first two sentences in *The Palm-Wine Drinkard* tell us what the story is about:

> I was a palm-wine drinkard since I was a boy of ten years of age. I had no other work more than to drink palm-wine in my life.

The reader may, of course, be so taken with Tutuola's vigorous and unusual prose style or by the felicitous coinage, *drinkard,* that he misses the social and ethical question being proposed: What happens when a man immerses himself in pleasure to the exclusion of all work; indeed raises pleasure to the status of work and occupation; when he says in effect: Pleasure be thou my work! *The Palm-Wine Drinkard* is a rich and spectacular exploration of this gross perversion, its expiation through appropriate punishment and the offender's final restoration. (pp. 25-6)

Nothing in all this is particularly original. What is so very impressive is Tutuola's inventiveness in creating new and unexpected circumstances for the unfolding of the theme. For example Tutuola makes the interesting point that those whose personal circumstance removes for them the necessity for work are really unfortunate and deprived and must do something to remedy their lack. This is demonstrated rather dramatically by that mysterious, and in the end quite terrible, personage, the Invisible Pawn, otherwise known as Give and Take, who comes to the Drinkard out of the night and tells how he has always heard the word "poor" without really knowing it and asks for help in order to make its acquaintance. Tutuola is saying something quite unusual here for in the estimation of the world, poverty is a great misfortune and those born into affluence are accounted lucky. But here is Tutuola saying that a man whose circumstance has insulated him from want has a need to go out and actively seek and undergo its punishment for a season in order to make his life meaningful and complete. Simbi, a character in Tutuola's later book [*Simbi and the Satyr of the Dark Jungle*] has, like the Drinkard, a much too easy childhood and deals with it by going in search of hardship. The Drinkard has too much appetite and too little wisdom to recognize his predicament unaided and is forced by fate into dealing with it. (p. 27)

Even a moderately careful reading of *The Palm-Wine Drinkard* reveals a number of instances where Tutuola by consistently placing work and play in close sequence appears quite clearly to be making a point.

In the episode of the Three Good Creatures we see how music relieves the Drinkard and his wife of the curse of their half-bodied baby. They have just danced non-stop for five days and find themselves unexpectedly rid of their intolerable burden. But right away they also realize that after the dance the life of struggle must be resumed and its details attended to . . . . [The] poet/drinkard who has just sung a lofty panegyric to the three personifications of music, and danced for five days without pausing even to eat, now suddenly becomes a practical man again concerned with money and "food etc." He carves a paddle, turns himself into a canoe and his wife into a boatman. At the end of the first day they have garnered seven pounds, five shillings and three pence from ferrying passengers across the river. (One small point here; the Drinkard is a magician and from time to time does exploit his supernatural powers, but he always has

to combine this ability with honest-to-God work. So although he can turn himself into a canoe, he still needs to carve a real paddle!)

If this episode were the only instance in the book where Tutuola makes the point of restoring the ascendancy of work after a binge one would probably not be justified in attaching particular significance to it, striking though it certainly is. But we do find Tutuola returning again and again to the same motif. In fact later in the book there is another "special occasion" involving Drum, Dance and Song again. This time the merriment is to celebrate the deliverance of the Red People from an ancient curse and the founding of their new city. Even Drum, Dance and Song surpass themselves on this occasion. Such was the power of their music that "people who had been dead for hundreds of years rose up and came to witness." . . . The cosmic upheaval unleashed by the three primogenitors of music is only quelled and natural order restored after they have been banished permanently from the world so that only the memory of their visit remains with mankind. Quite clearly the primal force of their presence has proved too strong for the maintenance of the world's work. Immediately after their gigantic display and banishment Tutuola switches abruptly and dramatically to the theme of work to clinch the point. . . . [It] becomes possible, I believe, to see the proper balance between work and play as a fundamental law of Tutuola's world, and the consequences of its infringement as the central meaning of the book.

In addition to the primary balance between work and play in the grand design of *The Palm-Wine Drinkard* we notice also a subordinate or secondary system of interior balances between particularly harsh sectors of the Drinkard's ordeal and recuperative periods of rest. Compared to the sectors of hardship the periods of respite are few and brief—a justifiable disparity in view of the Drinkard's early life of indolent frivolity. But though brief the intervening episodes of rest/play are very striking and are best portrayed in the White Tree, Wraith Island and Wrong Town. Of these three the White Tree yields the richest harvest of interpretation and I should like to take a minute and look at it a little closely.

Not surprisingly this episode takes place after the Drinkard and his wife have endured the most savage torture of the entire journey at the hands of the sadistic inhabitants of Unreturnable-heaven's Town. It thus seems quite appropriate that after such a surfeit of suffering the travellers should enjoy their most elaborate rest at this point. But the ease and luxury they do encounter in the White Tree surpass all expectations. Free food and drink in a cabaret atmosphere and a gambling casino are among the amenities of this European-style haven of conspicuous consumption. Predictably the Drinkard very quickly relapses into his old addictions . . . . And naturally he loses the will for the quest so that when Faithful Mother tells him that it is time to resume the struggle, he begs to be permitted to stay in the Tree forever. She tells him that this is impossible. Then he makes a second plea—for her to accompany them to the end of the journey. Again she says no. Totally disconsolate the Drinkard contemplates a third possibility: death. But even that escape is also impossible for them because they have already sold their death.

I think that what Tutuola is saying here is very important for an understanding of the meaning of the story. The three ways in which the pilgrim might seek to evade the rigours of a dangerous quest are taken up in turn and rejected: he may not prolong the interlude of rest and enjoyment at the inn; he may not be assisted to arrive at his destination without the trouble of travelling; he may not opt out of the struggle through premature death.

As the Drinkard and his wife resume their journey there is even an oblique suggestion that their recent experience in the White Tree has been of the insubstantial nature of a dream.

> ... it was just as if a person slept in his or her room, but when he woke up, he found himself or herself inside a big bush.

If we accept this suggestion the implication may well be that play though a necessary restorative is only a temporary and illusory escape from the reality of waking life which is work with its attendant pain and suffering.

The Drinkard's fault, as we said earlier, is that he attempted to subvert the order of things and put play in the place of work. He does this because he has an appetite which knows no limit or boundary. His punishment is exact and appropriate. He is launched on a quest in which he wages adequate struggle to compensate for his previous idleness. While he is undergoing this learning process he is shown many positive examples from other people of what his own life should have been. (pp. 27-30)

[Perhaps] the most striking object lesson for the Drinkard is the terrible son born from his wife's swollen thumb. Although the Drinkard may not know or acknowledge it this child is like a distorting mirror reflecting his father's image in unflattering proportions. He is really Palm-Wine Drinkard, Junior. He has the same insatiable appetite, the same lack of self-control and moderation, the same readiness to victimise and enslave others. He is of course an altogether nastier person than his father but the essential elements of character are the same.

There is a secondary theme which runs beside that of work and play and finally meets and merges with it. This is what I have called the theme of boundaries. As the Drinkard and his wife leave Wraith Island the friendly inhabitants accompany them to the frontier and then stop. And we are told by the Drinkard that "if it was in their power they would have led us to our destination, but they were forbidden to touch another creature's land or bush." (p. 30)

There are numerous other instances in the book where boundaries play a decisive role in the plot. For instance a monster may be pursuing the travellers furiously and then suddenly and unexpectedly stops at some frontier such as a road. And we have a variant of the same basic idea in the case of Give and Take who "could not do anything in the day time"—an observation of a boundary erected in time rather than space. And finally the Drinkard is to learn on setting foot at last on Dead's Town that "it was forbidden for alives to come to the Dead's Town"—an example of what we might half-seriously call an existential boundary.

What all this means is that here in this most unlikely of places, this jungle where everything seems possible and lawlessness might have seemed quite natural, there is yet a law of jurisdiction which sets a limit to the activity of even the most unpredictable of its rampaging demons. Because no monster however powerful is allowed a free run of the place, anarchy is held at bay and a traveller who perseveres can progress from one completed task to the domain of another and in the end achieve the creative, moral purpose in the extra-ordinary but by no means arbitrary universe of Tutuola's story.

This law of boundaries operates more subtly but no less powerfully at other levels in *The Palm-Wine Drinkard.* A boundary implies a duality of jurisdictions both of which must be honoured if there is to be order in the world. Tutuola suggests that promise and fulfilment constitute one such duality, for a promise is no less than a pledge for future work, a solemn undertaking to work later if one can play now. Consequently we find that Tutuola never allows a broken promise to go unpunished. There are quite a few examples of such breach and punishment in the book.... (pp. 30-1)

[We] can also apply the concept of boundaries to the dual jurisdictions of work and play. Because the Drinkard's appetite knows no limit or boundary he takes and takes without giving and allows play not just to transgress but wholly and totally to overrun the territory of work. His ordeal in the jungle of correction changes him from a social parasite to a leader and a teacher whose abiding gift to his people is to create the condition in which they can overcome want and reliance on magic, and practise again the arts of agriculture, and produce by their own work the food they need. (pp. 31-2)

Relevance is a word bandied around very much in contemporary expression, but it still has validity nonetheless.... Tutuola speaks ... strongly to our times. For what could be more relevant than a celebration of work today for the benefit of a generation and a people whose heroes are no longer makers of things and ideas but spectacular and insatiable consumers? (p. 32)

Chinua Achebe, "Work and Play in Tutuola's 'The Palm-Wine Drinkard'," in Okike, No. 14, September, 1978, pp. 25-33.

Eustace Palmer (essay date 1979)

[*In the following excerpt, Palmer comments on the genre of Tutuola's major works.*]

In order to establish [Tutuola's] position in African literature and to estimate him properly, it is essential to be clear about the genre in which he wrote. It has been too facilely assumed, particularly in the western world, that he wrote novels. Yet, however flexible we may be in our definition of the novel or in the choice of criteria for its evaluation, it will be difficult, if not impossible, to find a definition or set of criteria which will enable us to describe the works of Tutuola as novels. To attempt to make a serious evaluation of Tutuola as a novelist is to apply to his works a body of assumptions to which they are incapable of rising and to do a grave disservice to his reputation. For Tutuola is not a novelist, but a brilliant teller of folk tales. In order to answer the objections of most African readers we have to concede that his language is not quite up to standard, and not just deliberately so; but we can then go on to suggest that within the genre of the folk tale this deficiency does not matter—in fact, it is, in a sense, a positive asset. Similarly, we have to agree with most African readers that Tutuola is not strikingly original, but we can then go on to assert that whereas realism and originality are expected of the formal novel, the teller of folk tales is expected to take his subject matter and the framework of his tales from the corpus of his people's traditional lore.

The most useful approach to Tutuola, then, is to regard him as working within the African oral tradition. The folk tale is common property belonging to the people as a whole; it is an expression of their culture and their social circumstances. The teller of folk tales knows that the framework of the story he is about to tell is already known to a majority of his hearers; but he knows equally that his reputation as a teller will depend on the inventiveness with which he modifies and adds to the basic framework of the tale. For within the basic framework the teller is allowed considerable room for manoeuvre. His audience, knowing the details of the tale already, will look forward, not to his accuracy, but to the extent and effectiveness of his improvisations and modifications, to the skill with which he makes use of facial expressions, gestures, pauses and rhetorical devices and creates suspense and excitement. While using the inherited framework, the brilliant teller of folk tales transforms them into something uniquely his own.

Tutuola is precisely such an author. Taking his stories direct from his people's traditional lore, he uses his inexhaustible imagination and inventive power to embellish them, to add to them or alter them, and generally transform them into his own stories conveying his own message. It is obvious that most of the stories in his works come direct from the oral tradition. (pp. 12-13)

In most of the stories the accents of the story teller are clearly discernible. For instance, at the end of the entire story of the Palm-Wine Drinkard, Tutuola, reverting to the third-person omniscient, says: 'That was how the story of the Palm-Wine Drinkard and his dead palm-wine tapster went.' It has been generally recognized that this is the way in which most folk tales are concluded. It is also to the oral tradition that we owe the apparently unnecessary repetitiveness at certain points in Tutuola's stories. Is this not typical of the practice of the story teller who wants to make sure that his audience do not forget certain important points in the story and therefore feels obliged to recapitulate? (pp. 13-14)

A look at some of the Tutuolan stories derived from the oral tradition will demonstrate how he transforms them into something uniquely his own. (p. 14)

[In *The Palm-Wine Drinkard*] Tutuola's adaptations [of] and additions [to traditional folk tales] are considerable and they are generally of three kinds: there are the additions he makes to draw attention to the Drinkard's power and skill in rescuing the lady; there are those which deepen the moral dimension of the tale; and finally there are those which increase the suspense and fascination that the audience of an oral tale would naturally expect. At the start Tutuola makes the skull hire his clothes and the other parts of his body, thus conferring on him a certain dignity and independence; he is clearly a force for the Drinkard to reckon with. Then the girl does not merely escape because the head is rendered powerless or because some wind blows her home, for it is essential that the Drinkard should be the agent of rescue in order to call attention to his tremendous powers of resilience and courage from the start of the tale. In line with this purpose, Tutuola does not merely strip the 'complete gentlemen' down to a mere skull or head, thus emphasizing the deceptiveness of appearances; he makes the skull a most formidable character and adds the paraphernalia of the other skulls and the entire episode of the Drinkard's ingenious and successful rescue bid. If the skull is a formidable character, he meets an equally formidable opponent in the Drinkard. Tutuola also adds the detail of the girl's disobedience of her father, her wilful rejection of other suitors and her insistence on following the skull in spite of his warnings, in order to make the girl herself ultimately responsible for the disaster that almost overtakes her, and thus to sharpen the moral point. Then he heightens the girl's fascination with the gentleman for the benefit of his audience and colours the gentleman's description in such terms that the audience's interest is aroused . . . . But although Tutuola has a moral intention he is a good enough artist to realize that the moral point should not be made overtly; consequently he tones down the overt moralizing found in the other versions where the girl is virtually asked what lessons she has learned from her experiences. (pp. 16-17)

It is in ways such as these that Tutuola cleverly adapts and transforms the inherited stories, welding them into the framework of the themes of his own books. Skilful story teller that he is, the additions not only add depth of meaning, but also heighten suspense, create humour and fascination, and generally attempt to capture the spirit of folk tales as they are actually told.

It is an integral part of Tutuola's handling of the traditional that he quite unashamedly incorporates into it elements from the modern technological world, thus imparting new vitality and interest. Moving with perfect ease within the imaginary fantastic world of the traditional, he is yet able to endow his creatures with modernistic trappings, thus attuning them to modern sensibilities. (p. 18)

Tutuola also transforms the traditional by means of exaggeration. Fantasy and exaggeration are hallmarks of his art. They are also, of course, hallmarks of the folk tale, though Tutuola's details are perhaps the most fantastic and exaggerated that will be found anywhere in the world of the folk tale. His monstrous creatures, particularly the wicked ones, always perform the most extraordinary feats. (p. 19)

Although a large number of Tutuola's stories come from the oral tradition, there is no doubt that many others have been concocted by his own fertile imagination. Having been steeped in the wonders of traditional lore, he shows himself quite adept at inventing his own mythology and so colouring it that it looks even more fantastic than folklore. We think of the sheer fantasy of the 'spirit of prey' who kills an animal each time he closes his eyes, of the strange inhabitants of the 'Unreturnable Heavens Town' who climb a ladder before leaning it against a tree, and wash their domestic animals but leave themselves dirty. In *My Life in the Bush of Ghosts* there is the monstrous figure of the Flash-eyed Mother—so obviously the product of Tutuola's fantastic imagination—who alone fills the town like a vast hill. (pp. 19-20)

Although tribute must be paid to Tutuola's inventiveness, the point must still be made that his imagination is essentially almost childlike. These fantastic creatures appear at times like the bugbears conjured up by the child's imagination which is haunted or delighted by stories of the monstrous, the fantastic and the incredible. The description of the repulsive-smelling ghost in *My Life in the Bush of Ghosts* is surely the product of a childlike imagination. When the hero marries a ghostess in a ceremony which looks very much like an imitation of a church wedding, the total effect seems rather like childlike daydreaming. Only a childlike imagination could make the Faithful Mother inspect a guard of honour specially arranged for her by the Flash-eyed Mother. Take the references to killing away, and the Big Bird's ranting in *The Brave African Huntress* looks rather like two boys bragging about their physical prowess. The impression of simple-mindedness it creates is reinforced by the style in which it is couched. (p. 20)

It is now time to discuss Tutuola's language in some detail. While his style has proved objectionable to many West African readers, Tutuola has had many stout defenders from the western world. Ulli Beier talks about the vigour and freshness he brings to the language by his refusal to be merely correct; Harold Collins, endorsing Beier's further claim that Tutuola's innocent approach allows him to distort the language to suit his own purposes, goes on to suggest himself that 'Tutuola's innocent manhandling of our language gives results that are extremely interesting for language study; they suggest the malleability of the language, the possibilities in the language for creative expansion, for freshness and the assimilation of alien ideas' [see excerpt dated 1969]; and Ronald Dathorne asserts that 'Tutuola's English is a sensible compromise between raw pidgin (which would be unintelligible to European readers) and standard English... He is a conscious craftsman, who knows where his own talents lie.' All these views suggest that Tutuola has perfect control of the language and chooses to manipulate it in his own way for very laudable reasons. Nevertheless, we still have to make certain discriminations if our criticism is to be valuable, however great our admiration for Tutuola. It is now generally recognized that the West African writer, forced to write in a language which is not his own, and which is often inadequate to accommodate his insights, will bend it to suit his own purposes. But no less a person than Chinua Achebe has warned that this kind of manipulation of the language can only be done from a position of strength by writers who are competent in its use, not from a position of weakness. It is idle to pretend that Tutuola deliberately distorts the language to suit his own purposes or that he consciously fashions a sensible compromise between raw pidgin and standard English to meet the predilections of his European readers. Tutuola does not 'refuse to be merely correct'; he would have found it difficult to be correct, given his standard of education which did not proceed beyond the elementary stage. (pp. 20-1)

Tutuola's English is demonstrably poor; this is due partly to his ignorance of the more complicated rules of English syntax and partly to interference from Yoruba. But it would be a serious mistake to deprecate this as a weakness in his art or to use it as an excuse for invalidating it completely. For by one of those strange accidents of fate, the language ideally suits the genre of the oral tale. It is the language of the speaking voice telling a tale in a particular situation, exaggerating, elaborating, repeating, explaining and inevitably making numerous errors; but all these add to the vigour and colour of the tales. In reading Tutuola's works we are aware of a voice talking and we unconsciously make the same allowances that we would make for a normal speaker. (p. 25)

[Tutuola's] place in African letters is assured because he represents the transition from an oral to a written literature. He has put down his tales on paper, but he has captured as brilliantly as anyone could the nuances, the techniques and effects of the oral tale. Few other writers of fiction have followed his example and it will be a very brave critic indeed who will say categorically that his work leads in a straight line to the novel. (pp. 34-5)

Eustace Palmer, "Amos Tutuola," in his The Growth of the African Novel, *Heinemann Educational Books Ltd., 1979, pp. 11-35.*

Abiola Irele (essay date 1981)

[*In the following excerpt, Irele explores the influence of Yoruban culture on Tutuola's works.*]

There is a great amount of misunderstanding involved in the reputation that Tutuola has enjoyed outside Nigeria, and especially in Western countries. It was thought that he had created a new form of expression, a new kind of novel, whereas in fact ... he merely took over a form developed out of the folk tradition to a new level of expressiveness by Fagunwa. It was even imagined that the universe of his narratives bore some kind of relationships to that which the surrealists, each in his own way, sought to evoke from the subliminal reaches of the individual consciousness. His limitations with regard to the English language in which he expressed his works were also valorized.... In short, Tutuola has been admired for his 'quaintness', for the apparent ingenuousness of his style and of the content of his novels.

Now, quaintness, as such, is not and cannot be a value. To make matters even clearer, we must go further and say that on the specific point of language, the limitations of Tutuola are limitations and constitute a real barrier, sometimes even a formidable one, both for him as an artist, and for his readers. Tutuola obviously does not dominate his linguistic medium and there is no use pretending that this is an advantage. The truth is that we arrive at an appreciation of Tutuola's genuine merit, *in spite of* his imperfect handling of English, not because of it. (pp. 182-83)

There is nothing to wonder at therefore in the poor and often hostile reception which his work has received in Nigeria, especially among literate Yoruba. This is something that has surprised and worried Tutuola's foreign admirers. A good part of this reception has admittedly been obtuse, but a little reflection and some understanding of the cultural context in which Tutuola's work has been received at this end is enough to show that the sudden acclaim showered on Tutuola could not but make little impression upon a public long familiar with the works of Fagunwa—in other words, with the original thing, presented in the singular felicities of Fagunwa's handling of Yoruba. It needs to be said and recognized that the shift from Fagunwa in Yoruba to Tutuola in English cannot but represent, at least at the first flush, a disappointing experience for the Yoruba-speaking reader familiar with the work of Fagunwa, so that it needs closer attention to arrive at a response to the writings of Tutuola adequate to his peculiar genius. (p. 183)

It is clear that much of the praise and acclaim that have been lavished upon Tutuola belong more properly to Fagunwa who provided not only the original inspiration but indeed a good measure of the material for Tutuola's novels. The echoes of Fagunwa in Tutuola's works are numerous enough to indicate that the latter was consciously creating from a model provided by the former.... [Despite] its derivation from the work of Fagunwa, Tutuola's work achieves an independent status that it owes essentially to the force of his individual genius. The development that he has given to the form he took over from the earlier writer has the character of a brilliant confirmation.... [The] fact that needs to be made more evident is that Tutuola possesses a power of the imagination which breaks through the limitations of his language and which, properly considered, compels our adhesion to his vision and our recognition of him as an original artist. (p. 184)

The distinction of Tutuola, as Gerald Moore has observed, resides in his visionary powers. The Orphic significance which Moore has drawn out of his writing is indeed important, and it is useful to observe that it lies at the end of the high road of myth which his imagination, at one in this respect with that of his culture, traverses with such zest and assurance. But its importance also arises from the fact that it is the dominant element in the individual apprehension of Tutuola the artist and not, as is the case with Fagunwa, in the individual expression of a collective consciousness. The difference I am making between the two writers may perhaps appear a specious one, particularly to readers who have a direct acquaintance with Fagunwa in the original. But I believe it to be real, and that it is fair to say that where Fagunwa achieves a personal reorganization of the traditional material, and is thus able to put his stamp on this material in his own writings—aided especially by his gift of language—one feels that with Tutuola, there is a total *reliving* of the collective myth within the individual consciousness. The artist is here at the very centre of his material and of the experience that it communicates. (pp. 184-85)

It is perhaps possible to articulate this impression that one receives from Tutuola's novels in a more precise way by pointing to the imagery that he employs. The most cursory study of his works shows the constant recurrence of images built upon the play of light through the entire range of the colour spectrum. His imagination can indeed be qualified as being characteristically luminous, for his visual imagery constantly communicates a sense of brilliant intensity.... (p. 185)

The 'Television-handed ghostess' of *My Life in the Bush of Ghosts* affords ... [a] memorable example, among many others, of this constant engagement of Tutuola's perceptions and sensibility with the phenomenon of light.

Tutuola's imagery suggests the nature of his experience and gives an indication of the temper of his imagination. His vision is that of a dreamer, in the sense in which Eliot described Dante as a dreamer; that is, of a seer of visions. The imagery reflects an unusual capacity for perceiving and realizing in concretely sensuous terms a certain order of experience that lies beyond the range of the ordinarily 'visible'. And in this ability to give body to the fruits of his unusually productive imagination, Tutuola also displays the multiple facets of a sensitivity keenly attuned to the marvellous and the mysterious.

Tutuola cannot be considered a mystic in the ordinary Western understanding of the word because although his visions are personal, they do not involve a withdrawal from the world, but on the contrary, in terms of the culture in which his mind functions, a more active involvement with that scheme of reality that binds the everyday to the extraordinary in a lively reciprocity. (pp. 185-86)

The heightened capacity for vision in this primary sense also accounts for that other aspect of Tutuola's imagination that impresses itself upon our attention, what one might term its expansiveness. Tutuola's imagination is not only 'outsize', it tends towards a constant comprehensiveness.... There is at work in the densely packed atmosphere of his narrative an unrestricted play of the imagination and at the same time a strong sense of artistic involvement, a deep identification on the part of the writer with the products of his imagining spirit. (p. 186)

It is this keen participation by Tutuola in his own evocations that seems to me to set him off from Fagunwa. In all Fagunwa's stories, a distance seems to separate the characters and events that he presents from the deepest feelings of the author himself. This impression of a dissociation between the narrative content and the writer's response is reinforced by Fagunwa's habit of didactic reflections and constant asides to his audience.... With Tutuola, on the other hand, we get the impression that he is himself the hero of his own stories, and we feel that they relate primarily to his own immediate sense of humanity and proceed from his own immeasurable appetite for experience rather than from a more general social and moral awareness. (pp. 186-87)

Tutuola's experience, then, is very personal, and his vision particularized; nonetheless, the elements that furnish the substance of his writings derive in a recognizable way from his culture. His work relates in a much freer and more dynamic way to the Yoruba narrative tradition than that of Fagunwa, but there is the channelling of the elements through the form created by his great predecessor.... Fagunwa has had imitators and followers writing in the Yoruba language, but none of them manifests the genius of Amos Tutuola. (p. 187)

> *Abiola Irele, "Tradition and the Yoruba Writer: D. O. Fagunwa, Amos Tutuola and Wole Soyinka," in his* The African Experience in Literature and Ideology, *Heinemann Educational Books Ltd., 1981, pp. 174-97.*

Nancy J. Schmidt (essay date 1982)

[*Schmidt is an American editor, educator, essayist, and short story writer. In the following excerpt, she reviews* The Witch-Herbalist of the Remote Town.]

Although Tutuola includes numerous proverbs and proverbial references in *The Witch-Herbalist of the Remote Town*, as in his other narratives, they are not used to reinforce a consistent moral message. Rather, they are used in a variety of narrative contexts to support different moral values, instead of as chapter headings and reinforcements of Tutuola's major moral messages, as in *Ajaiyi and His Inherited Poverty.* Good and evil, right and wrong, are not consistently defined in *Witch-Herbalist.*

Witch-Herbalist, like all of Tutuola's narratives, combines elements of Yoruba oral literature with the realities of the modern world. The contemporary political world is evident from the opening sentences of the narrative.... However, contemporary politics are not as explicitly a part of the action in *Witch-Herbalist* as in *Ajaiyi and His Inherited Poverty,* although they are implicitly a part of the background of the action. There are numerous references to townspeople and "wild" people of the jungle, each with their assumed superiority over the other. In addition, customs of numerous different "races" are mentioned, and specific references are made to the Tiv, Igbo, and Yoruba. The problems of political ethnicity are clearly implicit in Tutuola's narrative to anyone familiar with contemporary Nigerian politics.

The fusion of Yoruba and Christian religious elements is also evident in *Witch-Herbalist,* as in Tutuola's other narratives. Although there is no explicit institution such as the Methodist Church in the Bush of Ghosts found in *My Life in the Bush of Ghosts,* the fusion is evident in the person of the Witch–Herbalist and her Hall of Assembly. The *Witch-Herbalist* is called Omnipotent, Omnipresent, and Omniscient Mother; she speaks the language of birds, beasts, and all human groups, so she has no need of an interpreter. Yet she has "fearful" characteristics so typical of Tutuola's monsters, being so old as to be "a deathless old woman" and very young and beautiful at the same time, many different kinds of voices, a "strange and fearful," "beautiful" frock that includes no woven cloth, and she rests her feet on two tigers.

In the Hall of Assembly of the Witch-Herbalist or the Omniscient Mother there is an altar and a "mighty organ." The organist looks like a big red bird. A "mighty bell" that sounds "like that of the church," calls the "burdensome people" to the Hall. In the Hall the people "did not pray to the witches but to the God Almighty" and sing from the Gospel Hymn Book. The people also make sacrifices, dance, and are served "delicious food and drinks" from the "kitchens" which are not too far away. The rituals that the Witch-Mother performs are those of an herbalist, often accompanied by speeches that combine Christian rhetoric and Yoruba proverbs.

The style in which *Witch-Herbalist* is written will be familiar to readers of Tutuola's other narratives, yet there are some subtle, and perhaps significant stylistic differences. The creatures that the hero meets on his journey to Remote Town are described in familiar Tutuolan terms with thick veins protruding from their necks, smelling sores, long, bushy beards, terrible cries, etc. The "etc." has become an increasingly frequent part of Tutuola's descriptions; the descriptions are shorter and more is left to the reader's imagination. Although Tutuola describes colors associated with a creature's appearance or dress in his other narratives, in *Witch-Herbalist* he often uses the term "multicolor" instead of designating colors, or simply says "different kinds of colors," instead of naming any colors. Furthermore, the hero meets some of the creatures more than once, including the Abnormal Squatting Man of the Jungle and the Crazy Removable-Headed Wild Man, thus reducing the variety of creatures that Tutuola describes. Few of the creatures are described in as vivid detail as those in the *Palm-Wine Drinkard* or as the Satyr in *Simbi and the Satyr of the Dark Jungle.*

Tutuola often uses two synonymous words as a repetitive stylistic device of oral narrative and, perhaps, to clarify the meaning of his story. However, in *Witch-Herbalist,* Tutuola actually defines words in parenthetical sentences.... Why he chooses to define some Yoruba terms and not others is not clear, but the definitions suggest either that Tutuola is becoming increasingly removed from an audience with whom he shares a common cultural background or that his editor introduced the definitions. Although the definition of Yoruba terms is present in *Ajaiyi and His Inherited Poverty,* it is even more conspicuous and is sometimes intrusive in the narrative in *Witch-Herbalist.*

The characters in Tutuola's narratives are interested in counting and often refer to things as "uncountable." In *Witch-Herbalist* "uncountable" is one of a number of words including "terrible" "multi-color," "horrible," "race," "lovely," "etc." that is used excessively. Whereas the hero of *Witch-Herbalist* is positively obsessed with counting twinklings [a Yoruban unit of time], whether they be in the hundreds or "sixtieths of a twinkling," he rarely makes references to calendar time. As a result the reader is occasionally told that some event happened two years ago, when the preceding narrative seems to have covered a few days or weeks at most. Such inconsistencies are not common in Tutuola's other narratives where counting is developed into a "fine art."

Witch-Herbalist continues some stylistic trends found in *Ajaiyi and His Inherited Poverty*.... Tutuola's grammatical constructions continue to become more in line with standard Oxford English. There are only a few grammatical "errors" in *Witch-Herbalist.* More significantly, there are fewer unusually constructed words of the type that are so common in Nigerian chapbooks and which so intrigued European reviewers of *The Palm-Wine Drinkard.* Many descriptive terms used in his other narratives are simply reused in new contexts in *Witch-Herbalist.* It appears that either Tutuola's creative imagination is flagging or his editor felt compelled to standardize and homogenize his English.

Tutuola's presence is very evident in *Witch-Herbalist,* but the strength of his presence and his imagination are not as strong as they once were. His narrative skill is still evident in the smooth, rapid flow of much of the narrative. However, the return journey from Remote Town is lacking both in descriptive and narrative interest, as well as in events that explain why the hero drinks the soup the Witch-Herbalist has prepared for his wife and forbidden him to drink. The concluding incident when the hero returns from the dead following his pregnancy and sacrifice to the god of the river is anticlimactic. Although the concluding incident restores the hero to his status as hero of Rocky Town, it contributes to the diffuseness of the latter part of the narrative, as well as to the moral ambivalence of the narrative. Neither Tutuola nor his hero seem to be able to take a consistent moral stand, a characteristic that is distinctly different from Tutuola's other narratives.

The differences between *Witch-Herbalist* and Tutuola's other narratives probably are related to many factors. They may reflect contemporary Yoruba culture, Tutuola's changing attitude toward Yoruba and Nigerian cultures as well as his changing position in Yoruba and Nigerian cultures, the difficulties of writing an oral narrative for an audience to whom oral narratives are becoming less familiar and less related to daily behavior, and the editorial policies for publishing African fictional narratives in the 1980s. (pp. 67-9)

> Nancy J. Schmidt, "The Return of Amos Tutuola," in Africa Today, *Vol. 29, No. 3, 1982, pp. 65-9.*

John Haynes (essay date 1990)

[*In the excerpt below,* Haynes *reviews* The Wild Hunter in the Bush of the Ghosts *and* The Village Witch Doctor and Other Stories.]

Although *The Palm Wine Drinkard* was Amos Tutuola's first published novel, he had written *The Wild Hunter in the Bush of the Ghosts* earlier, in 1948, and sent the exercise-book manuscript to Faber and Faber where it stayed until 1982, when Three Continents Press issued a limited scholar's edition with a facsimile of Tutuola's handwriting. In 1983, while attending the International Writers' Workshop at Iowa, Tutuola was asked to prepare the present edition. In his foreword, Bernth Lindfors writes:

> He went through the typescript of the original version carefully, correcting obvious errors and restructuring several episodes. I was asked to lend a hand in the revision and to supervise computerized typesetting of the final text.

Lindfors' phrasing is a little unfortunate in that it may give the impression to some readers, not in possession of the earlier text, that some scholarly tinkering has been going on. We are reassured that "what is being presented here is basically the same old *Wild Hunter* in more modern dress", but all this does sound a little jaunty at a time when African writers and critics are increasingly wary of the role of western scholars and publishers in handling their work. "This transformation" [*sic*], Lindfors concludes, "achieved by means of the latest technological miracles, is very much in keeping with the spirit of the story."

Is it? It is only in a very superficial sense that Tutuola deals in "miracles". His cosmology is one that undermines the western notion of the "miracle" as a bizarre deviance from the stable, solid world of western rationalism and literary naturalism.

The Wild Hunter, like *The Palm Wine Drinkard,* challenges this whole cultural scenario and draws on vernacular Yoruba writing. In *The Palm Wine Drinkard* Tutuola carried the challenge into the very structure of his prose by using a non-standard kind of English which, though sometimes taken as a quaint index of semi-literacy, was in fact, as Chinua Achebe has pointed out, a conscious choice. *The Wild Hunter* is in standard English but with tellingly non-standard deployment of the "bureaucratese" of his civil service years. Thus if you want to get into heaven you need the official letter from, of all places, the office of the Devil, who would

> forward the letter to the record office in heaven without delay.... The Devil suggested that the person should use two envelopes. He or she should write his or her name and address on the back of one of the two envelopes, and the correct postage stamps should be affixed to it.

Like a good mission-school précis writer he cites exact dates and numbers, but not in quite the clerical spirit. He uses them for ironically precise approximations. A stream is "about seventeen feet wide", in heaven "the yard was about four thousand miles square". The colonial clerk's precision is mocked by being seen, from the clerk's point of view, in its true pointlessness. This is Nigeria. This is the Bush. In a naturalistic story, setting limits the options of the characters. In the Bush anything at all can happen. Tutuola can always produce any situation he wants whatever, at any point. What compels his reader's interest is neither the "naivety" of the writing, nor the bizarre ghosts he concocts, but his sheer intensity and worry about his hero's spiritual quest.

The Village Witch Doctor and Other Stories is a collection of fables, also in standard English, all much slighter than *The Wild Hunter* and more readily assimilable to a comfortable western view of African quaintness; as also, more worryingly, to the sentiment that the Zulu poet, Mazisi Kunene, put into the mouth of Shaka: that conquered nations end up with a literature of children's fables about animals. Not all Tutuola's fables are about animals. They deal with tricksters, devious juju-men, often with an explicit moral about the wages of disobedience. The story of Tortoise's degeneration from a promising, handsome young man to an armed robber who sells his own town to an enemy and then foments civil war there will remind Nigerians of the betrayal in high places of the promise that independence seemed once to hold, and the subsequent descent into civil war and poverty.

John Haynes, "Precise Approximations and Trickster Tales," in The Times Literary Supplement, *No. 4546, May 18-24, 1990, p. 534.*

FURTHER READING

Collins, Harold R. *Amos Tutuola.* New York: Twayne Publishers, 1969, 143 p.
    Overview of Tutuola's life and career.

Larson, Charles R. *The Emergence of African Fiction*, revised edition, pp. 102-12. Bloomington: Indiana University Press, 1972.
    Discusses difficulties the non-African encounters in Tutuola's fiction, focusing on the author's use of oral tradition and his unconventional representation of time.

Lindfors, Bernth. "Amos Tutuola: Literary Syncretism and the Yoruba Folk Tradition." In *European-Language Writing in Sub-Saharan Africa*, edited by Albert S. Gérard, Vol. 2, pp. 632-49. Budapest: Akadémiai Kiadó, 1986.
    Examines the influence of oral and written literary traditions on Tutuola's novels.

Moore, Gerald. "Amos Tutuola: A Nigerian Visionary." *Black Orpheus*, No. 1 (1957): 27-35.
    Thorough study of Tutuola's early work.

Thelwell, Michael. "'The Gods Had Perished:' Tutuola's *Palm-Wine Drinkard*." In his *Duties, Pleasures, and Conflicts: Essays in Struggle*, pp. 208-17. Amherst: The University of Massachusetts Press, 1987.
    Explores Tutuola's personal background and its influence on *The Palm-Wine Drinkard*.

Derek Walcott

1930-

(Full name Derek Alton Walcott) West Indian poet, playwright, critic and journalist.

Walcott is highly regarded for poetry and plays that focus on the opposing African and European influences of his colonial West Indian heritage. His poetic language reflects this cultural division, employing both the formal, structured language of Elizabethan verse and the colorful dialect of his native island, St. Lucia. While embracing the literary tradition of England, Walcott frequently denounces the exploitation and suppression of Caribbean culture that has resulted from colonial rule. His acclaimed poem "A Far Cry from Africa" delineates the theme of uncertain identity that has dominated his poetic career: "I who am poisoned with the blood of both, / Where shall I turn, divided to the vein? / I who have cursed / The drunken officer of British rule, how choose / Between this Africa and the English tongue I love?"

Walcott was born on St. Lucia, a small island in the West Indies. He has characterized his childhood as "schizophrenic," referring to the divided loyalties associated with his African and English ancestry and the fact that he grew up in a middle-class, Protestant family in a society that was predominantly Roman Catholic and poor. His mother, a teacher actively involved in the local theater, strongly influenced his artistic development, and although his father died when he was still an infant, Walcott drew inspiration from the poems and numerous watercolor paintings he left behind. Walcott explained: "[My father's paintings] gave me a kind of impetus and a strong sense of continuity. I felt that what had been cut off in him somehow was an extension that I was continuing." Walcott's childhood ambition was to be a painter; in his autobiographical poem *Another Life* (1973), he and his friend, the painter Dustin St. Omer, vowed to record the unique atmosphere of the Caribbean through their art: "we would never leave the island / until we had put down, in paint, in words... / all its sunken, leaf-choked ravines, / every neglected, self-pitying inlet...." Walcott, having developed an affinity for the English literature he read in school, began writing poetry at an early age, often imitating such writers as W. H. Auden, T. S. Eliot, and Dylan Thomas. When he was eighteen, he financed the publication of *Twenty-Five Poems* (1948), his first poetry collection. While studying literature at St. Mary's College in St. Lucia and at the University of West Indies in Jamaica, he completed two more volumes of poetry and produced *Henri Christophe* (1950), a historical play written in verse. A later historical play entitled *Drums and Colours* (1958) brought Walcott both critical recognition and a Rockefeller Fellowship to study theater in the United States. Upon his return to the Caribbean, he became intensely

involved in Trinidad's artistic community, writing reviews and organizing the Trinidad Theatre Workshop, where several of his plays were produced during the 1950s and 1960s. Since the 1970s, Walcott has divided his time between the West Indies and the United States, where he has taught at Yale, Columbia, and other universities.

The importance of understanding and preserving West Indian culture is a prominent theme in Walcott's works. Many of his plays, often called "folk-dramas," are firmly rooted in the common life and language of the West Indies and evoke Caribbean dialect and legends. *Ti-Jean and His Brothers* (1958), for example—a work strongly influenced by the African art of storytelling—is about a humble, sensible boy named Ti-Jean who succeeds in outwitting the devil. Walcott explained his use of folklore and dialect: "The great challenge for me was to write as powerfully as I could without writing down to the audience, so that the large emotions could be taken in by a fisherman or a guy on the street, even if he didn't understand every line." *Dream on Monkey Mountain* (1967), often considered Walcott's most successful play, won an Obie Award in 1971. Many critics interpreted the drama as a metaphorical work in which the downtrodden consciousness of a colonized society is symbolized through the hallucinations of Makak, an aging charcoal maker and vendor. In an interview, Walcott described the main character of the play: "Makak comes from my own childhood. I can see him for what he is now, a brawling, ruddy drunk who would come down the street on a Saturday when he got paid and let out an immense roar that would terrify all the children .... This was a degraded man, but he had some elemental force in him that is still terrifying; in another society he would have been a warrior."

Commentators have emphasized Walcott's portrayal of the Caribbean as a society of uncertain heritage, as a "new world" in which the artist may help shape a cohesive cultural identity. *Another Life* celebrates such an artistic opportunity: "we were the light of the world! / We were blest with a virginal, unpainted world / with Adam's task of giving things their names." Yet while Walcott's poetry expresses the potential for developing a unique identity out of the diversity of the West Indies, it also reveals the author's fear that island culture will be overwhelmed by British dominance and expanding tourism. In *The Star-Apple Kingdom* (1979) Walcott declared: "One morning the Caribbean was cut up / by seven prime ministers who bought the sea in bolts— / one thousand miles of aquamarine with lace trimmings, / one million yards of lime-coloured silk...." The poem "St. Lucie" laments the loss of French patois to the national language of English: "Come back to me / my language / Come back, / cacao, / grigri, / solitaire, / ciseau." Many of Walcott's later poems depict the artist as an outcast from the West Indian community, estranged from both African and European heritage. In the 1987 poem "The Light of the World," Walcott expressed his sense of alienation and futility as a poet: "There was nothing they wanted, nothing I could give them / but this thing I have called 'The Light of the World'."

Anger associated with the injustices of colonial rule is another common motif in Walcott's poetry. Reviewers praised the poem "The Schooner *Flight*," in which Shabine, a smuggler, sailor and poet of racially mixed heritage, feels exiled by his own past: "I met history once, but he ain't recognize me, / a parchment Creole, with warts / like an old seabottle, crawling like a crab / through the holes of shadow cast by the net...." Discussing the impact of colonial history on the Caribbean identity, Walcott stated: "At great cost and a lot of criticism, what I used to try to point out was that there is a great danger in historical sentimentality.... The whole situation in the Caribbean is an illegitimate situation. If we admit that from the beginning that there is no shame in that historical bastardy, then we can be men. But if we continue to sulk and say, 'Look what the slave-owner did,' and so forth, we will never mature." *Omeros* (1990), Walcott's acclaimed epic poem, is a

historical and literary pilgrimage into West Indian history. Reinventing Homer's *Odyssey*—he cast West Indian fishermen, prostitutes, and landlords in such classical roles as Achilles, Helen, and Hector—Walcott explored various world cultures, tracing their influence on the present identity of the Caribbean people. Oliver Taplin observed: "Throughout the poem, as in the mind, there are persistent reflections on the historical events that have directly and indirectly shaped the characters' lives: the brutal attacks of the slaves on Achille's African forebears, of Europeans on native Americans, of French warships against British when the Windward Islands were first colonized.... But Mr. Walcott recalls these scenes of death and suffering with the objective sympathy of a Homer, who tells what happened to Trojans as well as Greeks."

(For further information about Walcott's life and works, see *Black Writers; Contemporary Authors*, Vols. 89-92; *Contemporary Authors New Revision Series*, Vol. 26; *Contemporary Literary Criticism*, Vols. 2, 4, 9, 14, 25, 42; and *Dictionary of Literary Biography Yearbook, 1981*.)

PRINCIPAL WORKS

Twenty-Five Poems (poetry) 1948
Epitaph for the Young: A Poem in XII Cantos (poetry) 1949
Henri Christophe: A Chronicle in Seven Scenes (drama) 1950
Harry Dernier: A Play for Radio Production (drama) 1951
The Sea at Dauphin: A Play in One Act (drama) 1953
Wine of the Country (drama) 1953
Ione: A Play with Music (drama) 1957
Drums and Colours: An Epic Drama (drama) 1958
Ti-Jean and His Brothers (drama) 1958
Malcochon; or, Six in the Rain (drama) 1959
In a Green Night: Poems, 1948-1960 (poetry) 1962
Dream on Monkey Mountain (drama) 1967
The Gulf and Other Poems (poetry) 1969
In a Fine Castle (drama) 1970
Another Life (poetry) 1973
The Charlatan (drama) 1974
The Joker of Seville (drama) 1974
O Babylon! (drama) 1976
Sea Grapes (poetry) 1976
Selected Verse (poetry) 1976
Remembrance (poetry) 1977
Pantomime (drama) 1978
The Star-Apple Kingdom (poetry) 1979
The Fortunate Traveller (poetry) 1981
Selected Poetry (poetry) 1981
Midsummer (poetry) 1984
Collected Poems, 1948-1984 (poetry) 1986
Three Plays (drama) 1986
The Arkansas Testament (poetry) 1987
Omeros (poetry) 1990

Joseph Brodsky (essay date 1983)

[*Below, poet Joseph Brodsky argues that Walcott should be considered a great poet of the English language, not just a regional artist.*]

[For the thirty years that Walcott has been writing, critics have] kept calling him "a West Indian poet" or "a black poet from the Caribbean." These definitions are as myopic and misleading as it would be to call the Saviour a Galilean. The comparison may seem extreme but is appropriate if only because each reductive impulse stems from the terror of the infinite; and when it comes to an appetite for the infinite, poetry often dwarfs creeds. The mental as well as spiritual cowardice, obvious in the attempts to render this man a regional writer, can be further explained by the unwillingness of the critical profession to admit that the great poet of the English language is a black man. It can also be attributed to degenerate helixes, or, as the Italians say, to retinas lined with ham. Still, its most benevolent explanation, surely, is a poor knowledge of geography.

For the West Indies are an archipelago about five times as large as the Greek one. If poetry is to be defined by physical reality, Walcott would end up with five times more material than that of the bard who also wrote in a dialect, the Ionian one at that, and who also loved the sea. When language encounters the absence of a heroic past a situation may emerge whereby the crest of a wave arrests the mind as fully as the siege of Troy. Indeed, the poet who seems to have a lot in common with Walcott is not English but rather the author of the *Iliad* and the *Odyssey,* or the author of "On the Nature of Things." The need to itemize the universe in which he found himself gives Walcott's descriptive powers a truly epic character; what saves his lines from the genre's frequent tedium, though, is the sparseness of his realm's actual history and the quality of his ear for the English language, whose sensibility in itself is a history.

Quite apart from the matter of his own unique gifts, Walcott's lines are so resonant and stereoscopic precisely because this "history" is eventful enough, because language itself is an epic device. Everything this poet touches reverberates like magnetic waves whose acoustics are psychological and whose implications echo. Of course, in that realm of his, in the West Indies, there is plenty to touch—the natural kingdom alone provides an abundance of fresh material; but here is an example of how this poet deals with that most *de rigueur* of all poetic subjects—the moon—which he makes speak for itself:

> Slowly my body grows a single sound,
> slowly I become
> a bell,
> an oval, disembodied vowel,
> I grow, an owl,
> an aureole, white fire.

(from **"Metamorphoses, I/Moon"**)

And here is how he himself speaks *about* this most poetic subject—or rather, here is what makes him speak about it:

> . . . a moon ballooned from the Wireless Station.
>   O
> mirror, where a generation yearned
> for whiteness, for candour, unreturned.

(from **"Another Life"**)

(p. 39)

To put it simply, instead of indulging in racial self-assertion, which no doubt would have endeared him to both his potential foes and his champions, Walcott identifies himself with that "disembodied vowel" of the language which both parts of his equation share. The wisdom of this choice is, again, not so much his own as the wisdom of his language—better still, the wisdom of its letter: of black on white. He is like a pen that is aware of its movement, and it is this self-awareness that forces his lines into their graphic eloquence:

> Virgin and ape, maid and malevolent Moor,
> their immortal coupling still halves the world,
> He is your sacrificed beast, bellowing, goaded,
> a black bull snarled in ribbons of its blood.
> And yet, whatever fury girded
> on that saffron-sunset turban, moon-shaped
>   sword
> was not his racial, panther-black revenge
> pulsing her chamber with raw musk, its sweat,
> but horror of the moon's change,
> of the corruption of an absolute,
> like white fruit,
> pulped ripe by fondling but doubly sweet.

(from **"Goats and Monkeys"**)

This is what a "sound colonial education" amounts to; this is what having "English in me" is all about. With equal right, Walcott could have said that he has in him Greek, Latin, Italian, German, Spanish, Russian, French: because of Homer, Lucretius, Ovid, Dante, Rilke, Machado, Lorca, Neruda, Akhmatova, Mandelstam, Pasternak, Baudelaire, Valéry, Apollinaire. These are not influences—they are the cells of his bloodstream. And if culture feels more palpable among urine-stunted trees through which "a mud path wriggles like a snake in flight," hail the mud path.

And so the lyrical hero of Walcott's poetry does. Sole guardian of the civilization grown hollow at the center, he stands on this mud path watching how "a fish plops, making rings / that marry the wide harbour" with "clouds curled like burnt-out papers at their edges" above it, with "telephone wires singing from pole to pole / parodying perspective." In his keen-sightedness this poet resembles Joseph Banks, except that by setting his eyes on a plant "chained in its own dew" or on an object, he accomplishes something no naturalist is capable of—he animates them. To be sure, the realm needs it, not any less than he does himself in order to survive there. In any case, the realm pays him back, and hence lines like:

> Slowly the water rat takes up its reed pen
> and scribbles leisurely, the egret
> on the mud tablet stamps its hieroglyph...

This is more than naming things in the garden—it is a bit later. Walcott's poetry is Adamic in the sense that both he and his world have departed from Paradise—he, by tasting the fruit of knowledge; his world, by its political history.

"Ah brave third world!" he exclaims elsewhere, and a lot more has gone into this exclamation than simple anguish or exasperation. This is a comment of language upon a more than purely local failure of nerve and imagination; a reply of semantics to the meaningless and abundant reality, epic in its shabbiness. Abandoned, overgrown airstrips, dilapidated mansions of retired civil servants, shacks covered with corrugated iron, single-stack coastal vessels coughing like "relics out of Conrad," four-wheeled corpses escaped from their junkyard cemeteries and rattling their bones past condominium pyramids, helpless or corrupt politicos and young ignoramuses ready to replace them while talking revolutionary garbage, "sharks with well-pressed fins / ripping we small fry off with razor grins"; a realm where "you bust your brain before you find a book," where, if you turn on the radio, you may hear the captain of a white cruise boat insisting that a hurricane-stricken island reopen its duty-free shop no matter what, where "the poor still poor, whatever arse they catch," where one sums up the deal the realm got by saying, "we was in chains, but chains made us unite, / now who have, good for them, and who blight, blight," and where "beyond them the firelit mangrove swamps / ibises practicing for postage stamps."

Whether accepted or rejected, the colonial heritage remains a mesmerizing presence in the West Indies. Walcott seeks to break its spell neither by plunging "into incoherence of nostalgia" for a nonexistent past nor by finding for himself a niche in the culture of departed masters (into which he wouldn't fit in the first place, because of the scope of his talent). He acts out of the belief that language is greater than it masters or its servants, that poetry, being its supreme version, is therefore an instrument of self-betterment for both; i.e., that it is a way to gain an identity superior to the confines of class, race, and ego. This is just plain common sense; this is also the most sound program of social change there is. But then, poetry is the most democratic art—it always starts from scratch. In a sense, a poet is indeed like a bird that chirps no matter what twig it alights on, hoping there is an audience, even if it's only the leaves.

About these "leaves"—lives—mute or sibilant, faded or immobile, about their impotence and surrender, Walcott knows enough to make you look sideways from the page containing:

> Sad is the felon's love for the scratched wall,
> beautiful the exhaustion of old towels,
> and the patience of dented saucepans

seems mortally comic....

And you resume the reading only to find:

> ...I know how profound is the folding of a napkin
> by a woman whose hair will go white....

For all its disheartening precision, this knowledge is free of modernist despair (which often disguises one's shaky sense of superiority) and is conveyed in tones as level as its source. What saves Walcott's lines from sounding hysterical is his belief that:

> ...time that makes us objects, multiplies
> our natural loneliness...

which results in the following "heresy"

> ...God's loneliness moves in His smallest creatures.

No leaf, either up here or in the tropics, would like to hear this sort of thing, and that's why they seldom clap to this bird's song. Even a greater stillness is bound to follow after:

> All of the epics are blown away with leaves,
> blown with careful calculations on brown paper,
> these were the only epics: the leaves....

The absence of response has done in many a poet, and in so many ways, the net result of which is that infamous equilibrium—or tautology—between cause and effect: silence. What prevents Walcott from striking a more than appropriate, in his case, tragic pose is not his ambition but his humility, which binds him and these "leaves" into one tight book: "...yet who am I...under the heels of the thousand / racing towards the exclamation of their single name, / Sauteurs!..."

Walcott is neither a traditionalist nor a modernist. None of the available -isms and the subsequent -ists will do for him. He belongs to no "school"; there are not many of them in the Caribbean, save those of fish. (One would be tempted to call him a metaphysical realist, but then realism is metaphysical by definition, as well as the other way around. Besides, that would smack of prose.) He can be naturalistic, expressionistic, surrealistic, imagistic, hermetic, confessional—you name it. He simply has absorbed, the way whales do the plankton or a paintbrush the palette, all the stylistic idioms the north could offer; now he is on his own, and in a big way.

His versatility in different meters and genres is enviable. In general, however, he gravitates to a lyrical monologue and to a narrative. That and his verse plays, as well as his tendency to write in cycles, again suggest an epic streak in this poet, and perhaps it's time to take him up on that. For thirty years his throbbing and relentless lines have kept arriving on the English language like tidal waves, coagulating into an archipelago of poems without which the map of contemporary literature would be like wallpaper. He gives us more than himself or "a world"; he gives us a sense of infinity embodied in the language as well as in the ocean, which is always present in his poems: as their background or foreground, as their subject, or as their meter.

To put it differently, these poems represent a fusion of two versions of infinity: language and ocean. The common parent of the two elements is, it must be remembered, time. If the theory of evolution, especially the part of it that suggests we all came from the sea, holds any water, then both thematically and stylistically Derek Walcott's poetry is the case of the highest and most logical evolution of the species. He was surely lucky to be born at this outskirt, at this crossroads of English and the Atlantic where both arrive in waves only to recoil. The same pattern of motion—ashore, and back to the horizon—is sustained in Walcott's lines, thoughts, life.

Open a book by Walcott, and see "...the grey, iron harbour / open on a sea-gull's rusty hinge," hear how "...the sky's window rattles / at gears raked in reverse," be warned that "At the end of the sentence, rain will begin. / At the rain's edge, a sail...." This is the West Indies, this is that realm which once, in its innocence of history, mistook for "a light at the end of a tunnel / the lantern of a caravel" and paid for that dearly: it was a light at the tunnel's entrance. This sort of thing happens often, to archipelagos as well as to individuals: in this sense, every man is an island. If, nevertheless, we must register this experience as West Indian and call this realm the West Indies, let's do so, but let's also clarify that we have in mind the place discovered by Columbus, colonized by the British, and immortalized by Walcott. We may add, too, that giving a place a status of lyrical reality is more imaginative as well as a more generous act than discovering or exploiting something that was created already. (pp. 40-1)

Joseph Brodsky, "On Derek Walcott," in The New York Review of Books, *Vol. 30, No. 17, November 10, 1983, pp. 39-41.*

Paul Breslin (essay date 1987)

[*In the following excerpt, Breslin examines form and theme in several of Walcott's best-known works.*]

The publication of Derek Walcott's **Collected Poems 1948-1984** offers an occasion to reflect on the career of a poet widely (and justly) recognized as among the best writing in English. Although reviewers have praised Walcott lavishly, his work has attracted surprisingly little sustained criticism, and general studies of contemporary poetry seldom mention him. The North American critic, lacking detailed knowledge of Caribbean literature and history, is tempted to romanticize Walcott as an exotic, a bird of tropical splendor who shames, by his brilliant plumage, the drab language of his colleagues to the north. Although I have been unable, for the occasion of this review, to acquire such detailed knowledge either, I have found that taking a first step

toward such knowledge helps enormously in understanding Walcott's poetry and in assessing his achievement. (p.168)

Walcott's **Collected Poems** opens with **"Prelude,"**written in 1948, when he was eighteen years old. In retrospect, its title seems more appropriate than he could possibly have known when he chose it, for this poem not only hints at themes that reverberate through much of his work, it shows him already aware of an intersection between characteristic modernist attitudes and his own experience. The first three lines seem consciously aimed at the genre of Caribbean pastoral:

> I, with legs crossed along the daylight, watch
> The variegated fists of clouds that gather over
> The uncouth features of this, my prone island.

By a Cranean logic of metaphor, the island lies "prone" on its face, its "uncouth features" turned down; if it tries to get up, it will be knocked down again by those "fists of clouds." This imagery insists on the powerlessness, rather than the beauty or vitality, of the place, despite the tourists with binoculars who "think us here happy."

The diffidence of the last three stanzas reflects not only the poet's youth, but also his sense of belonging to a "lost" culture, "Found only / In tourist booklets," or "in the blue reflection of eyes / That have known cities." The poet who must become imagining subject belongs to a culture that has been defined only as the object of European perceptions, European intentions. And yet the language by which he registers this diffidence comes straight from the dominant literary tradition: "I go, of course, through all the isolated acts, / Make a holiday of situations. / Straighten my tie and fix important jaws." This is Prufrock speaking, or the Crane of "Chaplinesque."

At eighteen, Walcott was still borrowing more than he was re-imagining, but he progressed rapidly. In **"A Far Cry From Africa,"** one hears a momentary echo of Auden ("Statistics justify and scholars seize / The salients of colonial policy"), but the poem has an unmistakable unity of style. It confronts a language of moral statement, reminiscent of neo-Augustan satire, with the metaphorical daring and elided logic of modern symbolism. Thus it can accommodate lines such as "The violence of beast on beast is read / As natural law, but upright man / Seeks his divinity by inflicting pain" alongside its animistic opening: "A wind is ruffling the tawny pelt / Of Africa. Kikuyu, quick as flies, / Batten upon the bloodstream of the veldt." Thematically, too, the poem concerns the confrontation of opposites: Walcott, "divided to the vein," cannot bring himself to condone the terrorism of the Kikuyu during the Mau Mau rebellion, even though he condemns the British colonialism against which the Kikuyu fight. The precedent of modernist primitivism, which rummaged *The Golden Bough* for vanished gods in order to restore contact with the elemental forces of the earth, gives Walcott his language for the African and tribal side of the dilemma; the neo-Augustan language of moral statement gives him a language for his distance from this part of his heritage.

In such poems as **"Tales of the Islands,"** Walcott experimented with juxtapositions of dialect and standard English. We have been listening to "college boys" talking pretentiously about art and politics, and witnessing a "fête" at which "savage rites" are re-enacted "For the approval of some anthropologist," when Walcott slips into the vernacular:

> Poopa, da' was a fête! I mean it had
> Free rum whisky and some fellars beating
> Pan from one of them band in Trinidad.

Even one of the literary types gets drunk enough to descend from the acrolect while "quoting Shelley with 'Each / Generation has its angst, but we has none.'" The vernacular ironically corrects the stuffiness of the "college boys" and the self-consciousness of the anthropologist: to reconstruct the rites of the past is to serve "history," but to turn from the anthropologists to the steel band from Trinidad is to enter the living present of "tradition," for which the vernacular provides a language. But for Walcott, the choice between acrolect and basilect is not narrowly allegorical: there is a living present to be found in the great English poets as well as in the regional life. In **"Orient and Immortal Wheat,"** one finds a subtler juxtaposition:

> So heaven is revealed to fevered eyes,
> So sin is born, and innocence made wise,
> By intimations of hot galvanize.

The first two lines, with their lofty language of generalization, aim at moral universality. They recall the tradition of meditative verse in English, extending back to Marvell and beyond, and it is hard to hear "intimations" in the third line without thinking of Wordsworth's Ode. But with "hot galvanize," we are back in the landscape as well as the idiom of the islands: Walcott has before him, as material for his spiritual analogies, the cheap metal roofs of the village houses. Here, the juxtaposition does not undercut the loftiness of the previous lines, but rather confers dignity on the local landscape.

These early poems, and others such as **"Goats and Monkeys,"** **"Laventille"** (dedicated to V. S. Naipaul) and **"The Glory Trumpeter"** force us to complicate the distinction between the Adamic and the historical that Walcott would later make in **"The Muse of History."** In these, the path to Adamic disencumberment must be cleared by recognition and exorcism of history. In order to become Adamic, the poet must first become historical. So in **"Goats and Monkeys,"** Walcott must first see Othello as a fantasy spun out of racial fear: kissing Desdemona, Othello "is Africa, a vast sidling shadow / that halves your world with doubt"; their union mates "Virgin and ape, maid and malevolent Moor." In order to claim, at the end of the poem, that Othello is "no more / monstrous for being black," Walcott must first disentangle our perception of him from the historical burden of racial stereotype: Othello's "fury ... was not his racial, panther-black revenge / ... but horror of the moon's change, / of the corruption of an absolute." Othello is monstrous in his unforgiving horror of mutability—which is essentially Platonic idealism, a Greek rather than Moorish idea.

In **"The Muse of History,"** Walcott claims that "it is not the pressure of the past that torments great poets but the weight of the present"; in **"Laventille,"** however, one cannot look at the present without recognizing that the pressure of the past has shaped it:

> The middle passage never guessed its end.
> This is the height of poverty
> for the desperate and black;
>
> climbing, we could look back
> with widening memory
> on the hot, corrugated-iron sea
> whose horrors we all
>
> shared. [...]

The poem ends with an ambiguous image of simultaneous death and birth, as if to suggest that only through escape from this crippling past, that "withheld / us from that world below us and beyond" can the poet recover a lost Adamic freedom: "We left / somewhere a life we never found." Until then, the poet must struggle toward a difficult emergence, still wrapped in the "swaddling cerements" of a colonial history.

In most of his early poems (by which I mean those included in the **Selected Poems** of 1964), Walcott writes exclusively from a Caribbean perspective. The plane that takes him toward "the final north" at the end of **"Tales of the Islands"** heads into the unknown; there is a poem called **"Return to D'Ennery: Rain,"** but it says nothing of the place *from which* the poet has returned. **"Bleecker Street, Summer"** treats Greenwich village as pastoral, as if to require the great world for its pastoral idealization of the Caribbean. And **"A Letter from Brooklyn"** turns out to be about a letter written *to* the poet by a woman in Brooklyn who once knew his father. **"The Glory Trumpeter,"** one of the finest early lyrics, reveals Walcott no longer entirely "withheld," as in **"Laventille,"** from the world "beyond" the Caribbean. In the closing stanza, Eddie, the trumpeter of the title, has

> turned his back
> On our young crowd out fêting, swilling liquor,
> And blew, eyes closed, one foot up, out to sea,
> His horn aimed at those cities of the Gulf,
> Mobile and Galveston, and sweetly meted
> Their horn of plenty through his bitter cup
> In lonely exaltation blaming me
> For all whom race and exile have defeated,
> For my own uncle in America,
> That living there I never could look up.

Like the poet, Eddie inhabits two cultures, but is at ease within neither. He has turned his back on his West Indian compatriots to aim his horn across a literal and figurative Gulf, toward North American cities too far away to hear him; and yet the jazz he plays comes from the part of North America where Mobile and Galveston are; it is *their* horn of plenty. It is as foreign to the "young crowd" as Walcott's complex and allusive style must be to many West Indian readers. Back from America, the poet feels guilty for having become relatively assimilated, but in America he remains an outsider, the unwelcome relative of the uncle he "never could look up."

By the time he wrote **"The Gulf,"** Walcott's sense of dual citizenship had been much extended. As in the conclusion of **"Tales of the Islands,"** the poet is in an airplane, but this time he is leaving the United States, not the Caribbean. As it begins its flight, "friends diminish"; the poet is attached to the United States, as he is to the Caribbean, though still he has "no home." If the poem shows Walcott still further assimilated into the English-speaking world outside the islands, it also shows him working, in a more particularized way than previously, from the historically concrete toward the universally symbolic. **"The Gulf,"** which is literally the Gulf of Mexico beneath the airplane, becomes the vehicle for a set of parallel metaphors. It is also the detachment, further depicted in the plane's departure from the earth, of the soul in meditation: "So, to be aware / of the divine union the soul detaches / itself from created things." It is the poet's sense of a lingering "gulf" between himself and both the island culture from which he came and the larger world into which he has ventured. And finally, it turns out that in the United States, too, there is a gulf: the poem was published in 1969, when the nation appeared to be coming apart at the seams:

> The Gulf, your gulf, is daily widening.
>
> each blood-red rose warns of that coming night
> when there's no rock cleft to go hidin' in
> and all the rocks catch fire, when that black
>   might,
>
> their stalking, moonless panthers turn from Him
> whose voice they can no more believe, when the
>   black X's
> mark their passover with slain seraphim.

The apocalyptic language of this passage may seem dated, but in other respects, this poem wears well. I find most fascinating its implication that the dream of transcendence—of "divine union," a universality encompassing the divisions of black and white, Caribbean and cosmopolitan identities—arises precisely when the pressure of history becomes most acute, and seems to drive toward an impasse. Only after confronting his historical predicament and finding no way out of it can he turn from history altogether and recover, unexpectedly, the lost Adamic identity:

> Yes, somehow, at this height,
>
> above this cauldron boiling with its wars,
> our old earth, breaking to familiar light,
> that cloud-bound mummy with self-healing scars

peeled of her cerements again looks new.

One is reminded of the "swaddling cerements" in the last line of **"Laventille."**

Perhaps this is the time for me to say that, much as I admire Walcott's poetry, I am uncomfortable with claims to Adamic transcendence of history, to claims of elemental kinship to the earth that circumvent cultural mediation. To be sure, no poet could go on writing without the faith that poetry finally transcends the historical pressures that impinge on its making; but that "finally" is an important qualification. To skip the intervening steps is to invite the faults of bombast and bardic pretentiousness into one's poetry, and it must be admitted that they often visit Walcott's. There is a thin line between magniloquence and grandiloquence, and if **"A Far Cry from Africa," "The Glory Trumpeter,"** and most of **"The Gulf"** manage to stay on the right side of it, a great many poems, early and late, do not, or do so only intermittently. Walcott's chief gift (like Robert Lowell's) is for the brilliant phrase, the mighty line, the heart-stopping passage; the architectural virtues have come less easily to him.

All this is by way of preface to my reservations concerning *Another Life,* an autobiographical sequence in twenty-three verse "chapters" that occupied Walcott from 1965 to 1972 and takes up some thirty percent of the space in his *Collected Poems.* It tells the story of Walcott's life from childhood to his first successes as a poet and departures into the wider world. It begins promisingly, with evocative descriptions of the setting. The third chapter seems to launch the narrative proper when it describes a cast of village characters, with names from A to Z, as "the stars of my mythology," and likens them to figures in Homer. But only a few of these ever reappear in the poem, and only to take marginal roles. Instead of narrating, Walcott becomes fixated on landscape, on the sacredness of the artist's vocation, and on the intensity of his own feelings. The poem does indeed have a structure, as Edward Baugh demonstrates in his fine monograph study of it. But it is not a narrative structure: the poem is knit together by continuities of imagery, and it progresses not by narration but by a sequence of tableaux.

Another Life is a long, ambitious poem, and I can only sketch, on this occasion, my reasons for considering it on the whole a failure, albeit a noble and interesting one. To begin with, it lacks any hierarchy of intensity; reading *Another Life* is rather like listening to an organist who leaves the diapason stop on for the whole recital.... [Walcott] drives unrelentingly at the sublime. As a result, foreground is hard to distinguish from background, key points of arrival from incidental detail. When the young Walcott encounters the *First Poems* of the Jamaican poet George Campbell, he *tells* us that it is an important moment, from which "another life it seemed would start again"; it is the first time that he, who had wished to shed his own blackness, finds a literary depiction of black people as "sacred" rather than brutish beings. But Walcott-as-autobiographer has already been hammering away for a hundred lines or so with language like this:

> The groves were sawn
> symmetry and contour crumbled,
> down the arched barrack balconies
> where colonels in the whisky-coloured light
> had watched the green flash, like a lizard's tongue
> catch the last sail, tonight
> row after row of orange stamps repeated
> the villas of promoted civil servants.

However dazzling such passages may be in isolation, they leave Walcott with nowhere to go when he wants to intensify his language to meet a special intensity in his experience. The fire that destroyed Castries in 1948, the mystical epiphany of his fourteenth year described in Chapter 7, even the suicide of Harold Simmons, art-teacher and father-figure of Walcott's youth, ought to stand out as moments of crisis, but they are all but lost in the general furor of Walcott's language.

My second difficulty with *Another Life,* related to the first, concerns its thinness of incident. One can understand that Walcott, unwilling to surrender to the "muse of history," wants to distill the essential and universally-resonant from the particulars of experience. But I am not asking for confessional detail. Even though one can barely discover, by reading *The Prelude,* that Wordsworth lost both his parents by the age of thirteen, the milieu is solidly present: one can see his Cambridge and his London, and one can at least glimpse the village life of the Lake Country. In *Another Life,* everything seems ready to turn into myth or metaphor before it is first solidly *there;* whereas Joyce plays the mythical against the quotidian in *Portrait of the Artist as a Young Man* or *Ulysses,* Walcott seems impatient with the literal. Autobiography can be highly selective in what it includes; it can fictionalize and distort; it can be disingenuous as the day is long. But it cannot afford an essential blankness of incident, and that is what troubles me in *Another Life.* The style has been asked to do all the work; the intense excitement that the style claims to feel has been severed from its occasion, for the characterization of the authorial "I" and of his first love Anna is so abstract as to prevent the tracing of emotion to motive. The passages concerning the friendship with Gregorias (Walcott's name for the painter Dunstan St. Omer) are the ones that wear best; although Gregorias has been quite consciously treated as a figure worthy of legend, we see the man at work, in despair and in triumph, and the characterization seems rooted in experience as no other in the book really is.

But I do not wish to dwell on the flaws of *Another Life;* Walcott has given us four volumes of poetry since, and I would like to close by considering two of the finest poems from these: **"The Schooner *Flight*"** and the well-nigh perfect lyric, **"The Season of Phantasmal Peace."** The first (along with the equally fine **"The Star-Apple Kingdom"**) shows Walcott able to write a long poem that sustains the level of his finest shorter works. The second was assumed bodily into the *Norton Anthology of Poetry*

soon after its appearance in *The Fortunate Traveller,* and the editors, not always judicious in their canonization of new work, are to be congratulated for recognizing this poem at once.

"The Schooner *Flight*" is Walcott's most inspired experiment in dialect mixed with the Marlovian "mighty line." This time Walcott attempts autobiography at a remove, through the obviously fictional character of Shabine, smuggler, sailor and poet. Like Walcott, Shabine feels himself to be an exile: "I had no nation now," he says, "but the imagination." And yet he remains attached to the islands he leaves: "if loving these islands must be my load, / out of corruption my soul takes wings." Shabine, no less than Walcott, seeks to be purged of history; his voyage becomes a baptismal "sea-bath," a return to the primal relation of Adamic man and the history-less elements. But like Walcott also, Shabine cannot be purged of history other than by re-experiencing it. He encounters a phantom slave ship; passing Dominica, he cannot help recalling the fate of the Carib Indians: "Progress is something to ask Caribs about," he tells his friend Vince. "They kill them by millions, some in war, / some by forced labour dying in the mines." And finally, like Walcott, Shabine feels caught between white and black, between the cynicism of the colonial governments and the cynicism of the new governments that have replaced them. Racially mixed, he carries the contradictions of the region within himself: "I have Dutch, nigger, and English in me, / and either I'm nobody, or I'm a nation."

Whereas *Another Life,* undecided whether to tell what happened or to condense narration into iconic symbols, thrashes and sprawls, **"The Schooner *Flight*"** deciding in favor of the iconic, has admirable compression. The purgational voyage of the *Flight* tests Shabine, first by the painful recollection of history and then by the climactic storm in which the captain becomes a black Christ: "crucify to his post, that nigger hold fast / to that wheel, man, like the cross held Jesus / and the wounds of his eyes like they crying for us." The voyage sustains narrative movement, building toward the ending when Shabine, having accomplished his sea-change, is finally at peace: "I wanted nothing after that day."

The economy of means afforded by the convention of spiritual voyage is one strength of **"The Schooner *Flight*"**; another is the marvelously inventive satirical wit that Walcott unleashes here. One had seen only brief flashes of this comic talent in earlier poems; here it is fully evident:

> I met History once, but he ain't recognize me,
> a parchment Creole, with warts
> like an' old sea-bottle, crawling like a crab
> through the holes of shadow cast by the net
> of a grille balcony; cream linen, white hat.
> I confront him and shout, "Sir, is Shabine!
> They say I'se your grandson. You remember
>   Grandma,
> your black cook, at all?" The bitch hawk and spat.
> A spit like that worth any number of words.

If Walcott can stick it to the colonialists, he can also be hard on cant about revolution: "In the 12:30 movies the projectors best / not break down, or you go see revolution," So much for revolutionary fervor, if it can be quieted by an afternoon movie.

"The Season of Phantasmal Peace" contains not a word of dialect; if **"The Schooner *Flight*"** stands as Walcott's most successful incorporation of the vernacular, the shorter poem is the finest expression of his aspiration to universality, to being a poet of the world rather than of a particular region of it. The poem's ravishingly lofty language risks Walcott's familiar faults of bombast and overreaching, but his time, with perfect tact, the poem recognizes the limits of its own yearnings for the sublime and pulls back from the brink of excess. As the title itself tells us, the poet knows that the gorgeous vision he is about to show us is at best a transitory glimpse of an unattainable transcendence, and perhaps even a glimpse of an illusory transcendence that exists nowhere at all. The poem subtly sustains this awareness:

> Then all the nations of birds lifted together
> The huge net of the shadows of this earth
> in multitudinous dialects, twittering tongues,
> stitching and crossing it. They lifted up
> the shadows of long pines down trackless slopes,
> the shadows of glass-faced towers down evening
>   streets,
> the shadow of a frail plant on a city sill—

The grandeur of scale immediately conveyed by "all" and "huge" may tempt us to envision the net dragging the massive skyscrapers and pines free of the earth and raising them into the air, but it is only their shadows that the net can hold, not their substance.

If the revelation is ethereal, leaving the things and ourselves, "the wingless ones," still earthbound, it is also obscure:

> And men could not see, looking up, what the wild
>   geese drew,
> what the ospreys trailed behind them in silvery
>   ropes
> that flashed in the icy sunlight . . .

"Drew" has the primary meaning of "pulled"; it is parallel with "trailed." But it also has a secondary meaning: whatever figure the geese "drew" in their movement through the sky, we were unable to see it; if they were trying to give us a sign from the transcendent realm they inhabit, we from our earthly vantage point, could not read it. The net is protective, "covering this world / like the vines of an orchard, or a mother drawing / the trembling gauze over the trembling eyes / of a child fluttering to sleep." This simile prompts the recollection that, first of all, the net's protection cannot be imagined except in analogies of earthly, fallible protection; and, second, that if the protection turns out to be illusory, the "net" takes on a different meaning, more akin to its literal use: no fish wants to be caught in a net, just as no one wants to be taken in by an illusion. To be sure, the poem affirms the epiphanic moment as valuable, how-

ever brief: "for such as our earth is now, it lasted long." But it does not encourage sentimental illusions, especially if read in the context of other poems from *The Fortunate Traveller* such as **"North and South"** and **"The Spoiler's Revenge,"** which depict earthly conflicts still very far from reconciliation.

By concentrating on these two poems, I mean only to show the range of Walcott's recent accomplishment; there is much else in the last four volumes that is nearly as good. Despite the fact that he has sometimes been overpraised and idealized, and despite his chronic temptation to the grandiose and overwrought, sometimes more *is* more. His best poems use the full resources of English in a way that most contemporary work—clipped, prosy, and understated—does not even attempt to do. He deserves his reputation as one of the best poets writing in English, but our praise would be more sincere if it extended to imitation. Despite the gulf between Walcott's Caribbean and our workshop-ridden literary culture, he can teach us that we do not have to starve our language in the name of authenticity; he can remind us, with Blake, that you do not know what is enough until you know what is more than enough. (pp. 173-82)

> *Paul Breslin, "'I Met History Once, But He Ain't Recognize Me': The Poetry of Derek Walcott," in* TriQuarterly 68, *No. 68, Winter, 1987, pp. 168-83.*

Mark A. McWatt (essay date 1988)

[*In the following excerpt, McWatt examines Walcott's development of a distinctly Caribbean form of literature, emphasizing the author's theme of artistic isolation.*]

The work of Derek Walcott must be seen in terms of his relationship to the islands and sea of the Caribbean; to the sense of people and place that awakened and forged his talent, and to the social and educational environment is which it matured. Some of the most famous voices that sing the poet's praises abroad seem (deliberately?) oblivious to his Caribbean context, and can therefore sound somewhat hollow and distorted. Joseph Brodsky, the Nobel prize-winning poet and friend of Walcott, quarrels with those who speak of him as a 'West Indian poet' or as a 'black poet from the Caribbean', and he himself prefers to think of Walcott simply as 'the great poet of the English language' [see excerpt dated 1983].

Yet, for West Indian readers and critics there is much more to be considered than what Seamus Heaney refers to as Walcott's 'deep and sonorous possession' of the English language, or how he ranks with other English-language poets world-wide. In the first place, for the West Indian audience and critic, Walcott is not only—or even primarily—a poet, but also a man of the theatre, a playwright and the founder of important theatre movements in the region. It is probable that many more

West Indians have seen his plays than have read the poems. This perception of a double Walcott—poet and playwright—is itself important, as it suggests the several aspects of 'doubleness' associated with the West Indian identity. Part of our response to Walcott involves a complex dynamic of self-recognition whereby we reciprocate his own sense of writing for his people by seeing ourselves in his personae and characters as well as in the 'schizophrenic' author behind them.

In the opening sections of the poem **"The Schooner Flight"** we find the red-nigger persona, Shabine, stealing away at dawn from his home, his sleeping mistress and his island; as he gets into the taxi that is taking him to his departing ship, the driver recognises him:

> 'This time, Shabine, like you really gone!'
> I ain't answer the ass, I simply pile in
> the back seat and watch the sky burn
> above Laventille pine as the gown
> in which the woman I left was sleeping,
> and I look in the rearview and see a man
> exactly like me, and the man was weeping
> for the houses, the streets, that whole fucking
>   island.

These lines of Shabine can be seen as expressing Walcott's own feelings about the islands of the Caribbean: there is the fierce, almost corrosive love for the physical beauty, for the familiar streets and houses; the domestic attachment to home and woman and yet the movement away, and the tears of frustration and betrayal caused by this wrenching. The paradox of the moment's emotions is also conveyed in the split between observing self and image in the mirror, and the sense of doubleness proliferates in the simultaneity of tears and bravado, the fineness of sensibility and the coarseness of language—the expletive and the breaking heart. All of these dualities powerfully embody the familiar (but eternally real) problems of West Indian identity as well as the particular relationship between the writer and his island home.

On 23 January 1930 Derek Alton Walcott was born in Castries, St. Lucia. As a mulatto he was aware from very early of his double heritage, of black and white ancestors; this split was reinforced by other factors such as his methodist, middle-class upbringing on an island that was largely Catholic and poor, and in particular by the colonial education which emphasised the formal language at the expense of dialect, and which taught the tradition of English literature from the classics to the moderns. This is not to say that Walcott was particularly troubled by this heritage; his was a fairly common West Indian position, in which it was easy to accept the paradoxes. Walcott himself says: 'In that simple, schizophrenic boyhood one could lead two lives: the interior life of poetry, the outward life of action and dialect.'

Walcott's great sensitivity to the literature he read at school—which included a sense of its power and the significance it bestowed on people and place—filled him with the urge to recreate his island home; as a painter he tried to capture it on canvas, as a poet he longed to

summon it to the kind of life and power he discerned in the poetry he read. In **Another Life,** his long autobiographical poem, he tells how he and his friend Gregorias (the artist, Dunstan St Omer) swore

> that we would never leave the island
> until we had put down, in paint, in words,
> as palmists learn the network of a hand.
> all of its sunken, leaf-choked ravines,
> every neglected, self-pitying inlet
> muttering in brackish dialect ...

This exuberant love for the island and the need to sanctify it in song—along with the significant experiences of his youth—comes across clearly in his earliest poetry. Walcott published privately, and within the region, his first three collections of poems; these were **25 Poems** (1948); **Epitaph for the Young: XII cantos** (1949); and **Poems** (1951).

It was, however, over a decade later that Walcott began to be known internationally, with the publication in 1962 of **In a Green Night: Poems 1948-1960.** Among the earlier poems in this collection is **'A City's Death by Fire'**, about the fire that destroyed Castries in 1948:

> After that hot gospeller had levelled all but the
>   churched sky
> I wrote the tale by tallow of a city's death by fire
>   . . .

Here one can see the deliberate assumption of the role of poet and, as Walcott carries out his self-set task, the diction and imagery echo the English poets he had been reading—particularly Dylan Thomas: the 'churched sky' becomes 'the bird-rocked sky' in a later line and the poet walks 'among the rubbled tales'. Later poems in the collection suggest the poetry of seventeenth-century England, with references to John Donne and Thomas Traherne. The title-poem echoes a line from Andrew Marvell's 'Bermudas', and that echo is reinforced throughout, with the diction and the measured formality of seventeenth-century verse, by the image of the orange tree which dominates the poem and becomes, by the end, a metaphysical conceit.

In this volume the young poet is obviously experimenting with styles, learning his craft; and yet the voice remains true to the Caribbean setting, and authentic in terms of the West Indian experience. In **'A Sea-Chantey'**, Odysseus and 'Cyclopic volcanoes'—summoned easily from the poet's familiarity with the classics—are balanced with the names of Caribbean islands and island schooners. The poem goes on to unite all in a litany that movingly evokes the calm of the island sabbath, ending with the thrice-repeated line: 'the amen of calm waters'. In other poems he is concerned as much with Caribbean man and society as with the landscape; **'Tales of the Islands'** is a virtuoso performance by the young poet, a sequence of ten sonnets which depict not only various examples of the physical landscape of the Caribbean, but also aspects of the psychological landscape as well, while the human characters such as Cosimo de Chrétien and Miss Rossignol struggle with the bewildering or sinister legacies of West Indian history. But perhaps the most important poems in the collection, in terms of the divided nature of the West Indian personality, are **'Ruins of a Great House'** and **'A Far Cry From Africa'**. In the former, Walcott juxtaposes the artistic spirit and achievements of seventeenth-century England with its appetite for bloody conquest and slaves in the Caribbean. Through a careful meditation on the transience of life and power, he arrives, almost in spite of himself ('so differently from what the heart arranged'), at a curious hollowness and vulnerability at the heart of imperial conquest, and therefore at a sense of compassion for all. In **'A Far Cry From Africa'** he uses the Mau Mau struggle in Kenya as an occasion for reflecting on his dual ancestry; he declares himself 'divided to the vein', unable to choose between 'this Africa and the English tongue I love'. This is an important theme to which Walcott returns in later poems such as **'Verandah'** and in some of the plays.

Walcott's sense of the theatre grew out of his perception of the theatrical all around him as a boy: in the street-corner revivalist meetings at night, lit by gas-lamp and complete with song and music and dramatic conversions; in the lives of the poor whose freedom he envied; and in the derelict characters of the city whose flamboyant physical and mental defects suggested the magic of the theatre. So, apart from beginning 'marathon poems on Greek heroes', Walcott would play at theatre with his brother Roderick (also a noted dramatist): 'little men made from twigs, enacting melodramas of hunting and escape.' Walcott's first play was **Henri Christophe,** produced in 1950 by the St Lucia Arts Guild, which Walcott himself had helped to found. The play is important because of its perception of West Indian history and of the West Indian hero; Christophe afforded the young playwright the opportunity of writing about a West Indian king in the manner of Shakespearean and Jacobean drama. As with the early poetry, the style and language of this first play are derivative and experimental; the characters (including illiterates) speak in the still and remote language of Jacobean drama: all this serves, nevertheless, to portray again that split between white mind and black body which Walcott reads as part of the West Indian condition. His handling of the events of the play as 'one race's quarrel with another's God' reinforces this theme and remains true to the vision of a divided West Indian psyche.

In 1950 Walcott left St Lucia on a scholarship to the University College of the West Indies, in Jamaica, where he received a BA in English, French and Latin. In Jamaica Walcott directed a student production of **Henri Christophe** and published **Poems,** the aforementioned early volume of poetry. After leaving university he worked for a few years in teaching and journalism in Grenada, Trinidad and Jamaica, before settling in Trinidad in 1959. The move to Trinidad was an important one for several reasons: The Trinidadian population was large enough and the society sufficiently varied and sophisticated to allow a creative writer the freedom to function; Trinidad's traditions of carnival and calypso were important in the development of Walcott's later drama, and it was in Trinidad that he founded the most important theatrical group, the Little Carib Theatre Workshop, which he honed into a fine company of actors and the perfect vehicle for his own plays. The name of the group was later changed to the Trinidad Theater Workshop.

After a few shorter plays which suggested various influences, including classical Greek drama and J M Synge, Walcott completed his apprenticeship as a playwright and found his own authentic dramatic idiom in two superb plays, **Ti-Jean and his Brothers** and **Dream on Monkey Mountain.** Unlike Christophe, the protagonists in these plays have no royal pretensions, but are heroes in the folk tradition. Ti-Jean is the third son of the folk tale who succeeds where his elder brothers fail, but he is also the true revolutionary who overthrows white colonial rule, for Walcott's devil is also the old man of the forest and the white planter, both of whom are tricked by Ti-Jean's cunning and resourcefulness. Yet it is a folk cunning, and the resourcefulness of the peasant, making use of the powers of the forest creatures and the wisdom of his mother. Similarly, Makak, the ugly charcoal burner of **Dream on Monkey Mountain,** using his own resources of imagination and the richness of experience, undertakes the purifying dream of his people, wherein he undergoes suffering but emerges with a clear sense of self and identity, and rid of his fear and hatred of whiteness. It is a revolutionary dream, like Ti-Jean's actions, and these folk heroes suggest strategies for survival and success in the Caribbean context. The plays also represent Walcott's concern for, and involvement with, the community. Through an involvement with the folk and the community the hero arrives at a true sense of self, whereas in the poems the movement seems to be in the opposite direction—through a contemplation of self towards a vision of community.

In **The Castaway and Other Poems** (1965) and **The Gulf** (1970), we see concern with the self as isolated, separated from the outside world and having to forge links with that world. This balances the folk themes of the drama and it seems that, at this stage of Walcott's career, the duality or schizophrenia is reflected in the split between poetry and drama. The figure of the castaway alone on his beach suggests the loneliness of the artist, trying to make sense, not only of his world, but of himself in relation to it, whether it be the fertile horrors of a swamp, in the poem of that name, or the squalor of a teeming slum, as in **'Laventille'**, where the poet is isolated by his sense of history and the peculiar depth of his feeling. In **'Crusoe's Island'** there are images of the castaway, the hermit and the artist, all suggesting the same condition, all emphasising separation and the failure of community. At the end of the poem the community is present in the children of Tobago, on the beach or returning for vespers, but the poet cannot reach or change them:

> . . . nothing I can learn
> From art or loneliness

Can bless them as the bell's
transfiguring tongue can bless.

The poet has killed God, his competitor, and cannot
join their simple community of faith, he can only write
about them—art becomes the substitute for community,
or the consolation for its loss. In *The Gulf* the poet
remains isolated; he cannot dance to the carnival music
in **'Mass Man'**, the 'coruscating, mincing fantasies' of
the themes and costumes of the bands are no match for
the historical ghosts that dance in the poet's memory
and he plays instead the whipped slave hanging from a
gibbet, his mind already on Ash-Wednesday. The poet's
art becomes one of atonement, not so much for history
as for the forgetfulness and waste of the carnival culture.
The separation between poet and society is further
emphasised in **'Blues'**, where he is beaten when he
approaches a gang of black youths in the American
south, and in the title-poem, where he meditates on the
USA and its history from behind the window of a plane
flying over the Gulf of Mexico. In the collection, the gulf
becomes a metaphor for all kinds of separation and for
the gap between the poet and the people and places he
loves.

Another Life (1973), Walcott's autobiographical poem, is
an important landmark in his work because it supplies
details of his artistic development and early career in St
Lucia, while developing some of the themes and concerns of his poetry in *The Gulf,* speculating on the nature
of art and memory. All is expressed in a tough, flexible
medium that proves as suitable for the sparkling flights
of lyricism as it is for the narrative or meditative
sections and the passages of pure invective. Apart from
tracing important relationships which the young writer
enjoyed (notably with the painters, Harry Simmons and
Dunstan St Omer), the poem shows his love for the
island and its people. He tells of an incident, an
epiphany, that occurred 'in the August of my fourteenth
year': wandering in the hills above the town he succumbs to a sudden wave of pity for the island and its
people:

> ...I felt compelled to kneel,
> I wept for nothing and for everything,
> I wept for the earth of the hill under my knees,
> for the grass, the pebbles, for the cooking smoke
> above the labourer's houses like a cry...
> ...For their lights that shine through the hovels
>   like litmus...

These are the love and the tears that Shabine experiences as he leaves Trinidad in **'The Schooner *Flight*'**.
Such intimate revelations of feeling are balanced in the
poem by Walcott's more public voice, the voice he uses
to castigate the philistinism of Caribbean society which
allows its artists to die in poverty and neglect. The whole
of the poem's chapter 19, entitled **'Frescoes of the New
World II'**, is a scathing indictment of governments and
other institutions in the regions which betray their
people in order to feather their own nests or to play
games of power. The chapter is probably the finest piece
of poetic invective in West Indian literature. The poet
consigns to the sulphurous hell of Soufrière:

> all o' dem big boys, so, dem ministers,
> ministers of culture, ministers of development,
> the green blacks, and their old toms,
> and all the syntactical apologists of the Third
>   World
> explaining why their artists die
> by their own hands, magicians of the New Vision
> Screaming the same shit.

Living in Trinidad in the late 1960s, with the growing
Black Power movement which culminated in the uprising of 1970, Walcott's concern with questions of politics
and ideology—and the prominence of these themes
within his work—inevitably grew. These topics are
treated in poems such as **'Junta'**, in *The Gulf,* and
'Parades Parades', in *Sea Grapes* (1976); but it is
perhaps in the collection *The Star-Apple Kingdom* (1980)
that this theme really comes to the fore. Shabine in **'The
Schooner *Flight*'** is seen to be the victim of a corrupt
minister for whom he smuggled scotch—and was made
the scapegoat after the minister's investigation of himself. In the title-poem of the collection, which Walcott
wrote after reading *The Autumn of the Patriarch* (1975)
by Gabriel García Márquez, there is a wonderful
portrait of the regional prime ministers cutting up the
Caribbean sea like bolts of blue and green cloth and
selling it 'at a mark-up to the conglomerates', much as
Garcia Márquez's dictator had sold the sea and was
forced as a result to live on the edge of a vast bowl of
dust. The mood of Walcott's poem echoes the troubled
mood of Jamaica under the Manley government. The
sinister female figure in the poem, who calls herself the
revolution and whose lineage is Latin and Catholic,
suggests nevertheless the curious strength of Jamaican
women and embodies both the hope and the menace of
that time.

The political themes also figure in Walcott's plays of this
later period. One of Walcott's ambitions of this time
seems to have been to write a successful Broadway
musical: in collaboration with Galt MacDermot (who
was responsible for the music of the Broadway hit,
Hair), he wrote *The Joker of Seville* (1974) and *O
Babylon* (1976). Neither play found its way to Broadway, but *O Babylon* is important for its portrayal of the
Rastafarians of Jamaica and their struggle against the
Babylon of exploitative big business, the police and the
narrow attitudes of middle-class society towards them.
These two plays are also significant in that they were the
last two plays performed by the Trinidad Theater
Workshop under Walcott's direction; he broke with the
Workshop in 1976. Two later plays, *Remembrance*
(1977) and *Pantomime* (1978) also engage with political
themes. The main protagonist of the former, Albert
Perez Jordan, has lost his elder son in the 1970 Black
Power uprising and remains bewildered and scornful of
a political conviction he cannot understand. In this play
Walcott explores, with satirical insight but also with
compassion, the gap between the mental attitudes and
the political awareness of Perez Jordan and his children;

between his 'real' foreign war and their playing at revolution; between the dedication and sense of purpose he felt as a teacher, and the aimlessness of the younger generation (his younger son is an artist who paints an American flag on the roof). The other play, *Pantomime,* is a kind of black/white fable where Walcott explores the humour and irony in the two characters' reversal of the roles of Robinson Crusoe and Friday. It is a reprise of several themes—that of the castaway, of racial division (black body/white mind) and West Indian identity, and the larger theme of illusion and reality. Like Ti-Jean or Makak, the characters struggle through to an understanding not only of themselves and their relationship to each other, but also of the forces and attitudes historically responsible for the social divisions of the Caribbean; the humour in the play balances a serious message concerning the encounter of slave and colonial master and all the consequent problems of that relationship.

After his break with the Theatre Workshop in Trinidad Walcott turned his attention increasingly to the USA, where he took up sessional teaching assignments at US universities. Since 1981 he has been teaching creative writing at Boston University and returning to the Caribbean as often as he can. His most recent poetry reflects this new 'doubleness' as he is now a poet of 'North' and 'South' (the titles of the structural divisions in *The Fortunate Traveller,* 1981) and of 'Here and Elsewhere' (*The Arkansas Testament,* 1987). In *The Fortunate Traveller* the poem, 'The Spoiler's Return', is important not only for its masterful depiction of Trinidadian Calypso culture or for its political and social satire, but also because it represents perhaps the high point of Walcott's handling of dialect in his poetry. He began experimenting with this tentatively in a few lines of poems such as the sonnet in 'Tales of the Islands', which begins: 'Poopa da' was a fete!' It developed slowly in the poetry (although the dialogue in many of the plays was largely dialect), to the point where it has become a natural, flexible and sophisticated poetic medium in 'The Schooner *Flight*', which Seamus Heaney describes as 'epoch-making' precisely for this reason; he says that Walcott has discovered 'a language woven out of dialect and literature, neither folksy nor condescending . . . evolved out of one man's inherited divisions and obsessions'. 'The Spoiler's Return' duplicates this achievement. Here is Spoiler explaining how the devil (a fan of his kaiso) has let him return to Port of Spain:

> I beg him two weeks leave and he send me
> back up, not as no bedbug or nor flea,
> but in this limeskin hat and floccy suit,
> to sing what I did always sing: the truth.
> Tell Desperadoes when you reach the hill,
> I decompose, but I composing still . . .

A feature of the latest poetry is Walcott's increasing concern with the figure of the poet, and the business of writing poetry itself. From his earliest poems his work was sprinkled with metaphors about writing poetry, or about the kind of poetry he sought to write, but the tendency towards a portrait of the poet writing, towards a bleak self-contemplation or self-questioning, has become marked in the latest collections. This can be seen in a poem such as 'Hotel Normandie Pool' from *The Fortunate Traveller,* but by the time we come to the collection entitled *Midsummer,* this is the mode that predominates:

> At the Queen's Park Hotel, with its white, high-
>   ceilinged rooms
> I reenter my first local mirror. A skidding roach
> In the porcelain basin slides from its path to
>   Parnassus.
> Every word I have written took the wrong ap-
>   proach.
> I cannot connect these lines with the lines in my
>   face.

The same seems to hold true for the latest drama, as in the play *A Branch of the Blue Nile* (1986), which involves characters who are playwrights and actors, and a play within a play. Perhaps this is another aspect of the autobiographical urge evident in *Another Life,* or part of the proliferating complexity of character or of the ambiguities at the heart of the creative urge, that Walcott himself sees so clearly in chapter 9 of the autobiographical poem.

One poem in Walcott's very latest volume, *The Arkansas Testament,* takes us back to the poet's undying love for islands and people that has been a constant throughout his career. It takes us back to the August epiphany in his fourteenth year, to Shabine weeping for his island, to Spoiler, coming back from Hell to try to save his beloved Trinidad. The poem is 'The Light of the World', in which the poet takes a trip with the peasants of his native St Lucia in a mini-bus. He looks around and loves them all—one women he considers the light of the world; he is in tune with the features and rhythms of their lives, but still remains unable to participate fully, distanced by vocation, by a habit of perception. When the poet gets off at his stop the following final scene occurs:

> Then, a few yards ahead, the van stopped. A man
> shouted my name from the transport window.
> I walked up towards him. He held out something.
> A pack of cigarettes had dropped from my pocket.
> He gave it to me. I turned, hiding my tears.
> There was nothing they wanted, nothing I could
>   give them
> but this thing I have called 'The Light of the
>   World.'

But the gift is indeed valuable, and the giver worthy. With his accumulated fame and honours, living as ever between two worlds, Walcott remains the poet of the Caribbean people, of islands and of sea. (pp. 1607-15).

Mark A. McWatt, "Derek Walcott: An Island Poet and His Sea," in Third World Quarterly, *Vol. 10, No. 4, October, 1988, pp. 1607-15.*

Anthony Kellman (essay date 1989)

[*In the following excerpt, Kellman discusses* The Arkansas Testament, *focusing on Walcott's ambiguous feelings about his Caribbean homeland.*]

Divided into two parts—"Here" and "Elsewhere"—the poems [in Walcott's *The Arkansas Testament*] contain subjective/objective declarations concerning the poet's place in his homeland (the Caribbean) and in other, more northern places where he often sojourns. Walcott's two testaments are both Old and New, underlining the book's structural parallel with the Bible. "Here" can be seen as an Old Testament—the poet's origins and past life in the Caribbean, while "Elsewhere"—a New Testament—articulates his current experiences in the United States, where he works.

What links the two geographically disparate parts of the book is the poet's sense of personal invisibility, and his disappointment, at times even despair, at the human condition. Walcott's is a continuing quest to integrate two selves fashioned by his African and European ancestries. Because he is neither and always "Here" and "Elsewhere," Walcott, time and time again, finds himself an outsider, an Everyman figure, "schizophrenic, wrenched by two styles" (**"Codicil," *The Castaway,*** 1965).

From his sense of historical alienation in *The Castaway* and *The Star Apple Kingdom* (1979); through *The Fortunate Traveller* (1981), who is fortunate only in the sense that he is in a position to escape places when they become unbearable, but who is hounded by guilt complexes; through his penultimate collection, *Midsummer* (1984), where, in **"Gaugin,"** he concedes his regret that "I left (The Caribbean) too late," Walcott seems to be wrestling with his Janus double-sided vision. He uses this schizophrenic reality of Caribbean Man in order to testify to the failures of regional Independences to sustain artists there. In a bid to find his place / the poet's place in a world of arrogance, pride, upside-down values and racism, Walcott presents a personal Testament which is universal in its implications, and which challenges the reader to be more open in terms of relationships, racial and otherwise.

As he has done recently in the openings of his books, Walcott returns, in the poem **"The Lighthouse,"** to the Caribbean, his island home, St. Lucia, where "Stars pierce their identical spots / over Castries...." Apparently, nothing has changed. The domino-slamming men in the rum shops share the same ribald jokes, while "Unaging moonlight falls / on the graves." The tightly-structured meter of this long poem suggests the tenseness and apprehension the poet feels on returning home. The imagery of the poem also reflects his psychological precariousness. The full moon is described as "A coin tossed once overhead, / that stuck there, not heads or tails."

The personas in this poem, very reminiscent of V.S. Naipaul's hopeless characters, are the dispossessed: men who have become victims of historical legacies of attrition and post-Independence victimization. There are drunks; an actor "lost in the post office! Stripped / A superfluous character written out of script"; and children running down crooked streets, some falling, most taking "the straight / road from their galvanised hell."

In **"The Three Musicians,"** a parody of the tale of the Biblical wise men, three down-and-out musicians go house-to-house on Christmas Day, serenading neighbors for food and drink. These men, who "eat in silence... belt out two straights, / then start singing like shite," are pitied by the master of the house who "feels / that his heart will burst" at the sight of these three "kings."

Another character, the persona in **"A Letter From the Old Guard,"** who has served with Lord Alexander in the Sudan, is reduced to an arthritic night watchman. It is Remembrance Day, and the elderly man reflects proudly on his days in the colonial army. Today, he has very little to show for his heroic exploits and attributes his fate to the failures of the new Independences. He states with some bitterness: "Then we get Independence all of a sudden / and something went. We can't run anything / ...we black people."

The dots of stars that mottle the sky in **"The Lighthouse,"** suggesting ellipsis or incompleteness, are the points where the poet resumes his exploration of his island/history/self with each return. The fact that Walcott consistently makes this effort at coming to terms with his heritage is a hope in itself.

Not only does Walcott have a stubborn love for his homeland, but he is also extremely courageous in his quest for stability and wholeness, considering that his responses to the region are often tinged—sometimes laced—with terror and dread. In **"Cul De Sac Valley,"** he notes that "the forest runs / sleeping, its eyes shut," and that "Pigeon Island / pins the sea in its claws." This disturbing imagery underlines the poet's fear of Caribbean leaders bounding into the twenty-first century through the dark—(the blind leading the blind?)—and is articulated, I think, out of a sense of responsibility and concern for his homeland.

In **"Gros Islet,"** the poet's bitterness (or perhaps it is more his disappointment) reaches new intensity and outspokeness. Here, "There is no wine..., no cheese, the almonds are green, / the grapes bitter, the language is that of slaves." And in **"White Magic,"** white myths are praised for their authenticity, whereas the local ones are denounced as being unoriginal, based on ignorance. Walcott writes:

> ...the deer-footed, hobbling hunter, Papa Bois,
> he's just Pan's clone, one more translated satyr
> ....
> Our myths are ignorance, theirs is literature.

The last poem in Part 1 of the book, **"The Light of the World,"** highlights Walcott's feelings of guilt for having "left" the Caribbean. He says: "I had abandoned them, ...left them to sing Marley's songs of sadness...." Yet, he loves his people's warm neighborliness, and feels as though he "might suddenly start sobbing on the public transport" in which he is travelling. He thinks that he has abandoned them and also that they have abandoned him. Specifically, he feels that he should have given them something more tangible, but all that he can give them is "This thing I have called 'The Light of the World.'" In short, Walcott implies that what he will give his people (and perhaps this is the best possible gift that he can truly give) are his poems, his art.

There are some beautiful poems in Part 2 of this collection as well. This section's title poem, **"Else-where,"** examines the effects of war. It becomes a parody of a pastoral. Children waddle in streams, there are old men nearby, women squatting by a river, and "a stick stirring up a twinkling of butterflies." Above this scene, in contrast, "flies circle their fathers." **"Salsa,"** is a satirical comment on the Americanization of San Juan; **"The Young Wife,"** an elegy written to a man whose wife has died of cancer; **"For Adrian,"** about an old subject—departures. All these poems are tightly structured, using Walcott's innovative ballad meter.

While there are these fine poems in this part of the book, the section, overall, is not as assured as Part 1. Too often, it seems as though Walcott has not fully assimilated the nuances of the northern cultures that he writes about. Although always skillfully crafted, several of the poems here are half-glimpsed clichéd sketches. In this section, one gets a sense of travelogue writing, mere reportage, particularly in the disappointing title poem.

This thirteen-page poem describes the poet's sojourn in Arkansas, a racially segregated state. He feels himself "homesick / for islands with fringed shores," and although very acute in his observations of the physical surroundings of the place, he lacks an authoritative tone. The main point of this long poem, however, and one which makes the link between the two sections, is that "I was still nothing." The poet is exiled both "Here" and "Elsewhere." In the Caribbean, he is alienated as an artist; in Arkansas, because he is a black man. Once, in a cafeteria, "I looked for my own area," he writes. "The muttering black decanter / had all I needed; it could sigh for / Sherman's smoking march to Atlanta / or the march to Montgomery." The sunshine in Arkansas is cold. Fearing rejection, the poet asks: "Will I be a citizen / or an afterthought of the state?"

The fear of regional rejection drove Caribbean writers to the Metropolis in the 1950s and 60s and is still driving New Generation writers to the U.S.A. and Canada—that is, those who can leave. It is this sense of rejection at home which is at the heart of Derek Walcott's disappointment in the Caribbean. (pp. 605-07)

The hope in *The Arkansas Testament* is that while the wandering poet may be nothing, by that very nothingness he has the potential to contain and be everything. The book is also a testament to the need for

people—whether Caribbean or North American—to be less parochial and provincial in their outlooks on life. As Walcott states in **"Tomorrow, Tomorrow"**:

> To have loved one horizon is insularity;
> it blindfolds vision, it narrows experience.

(p. 608)

Anthony Kellman, "Testimony from Here and Elsewhere," in Callaloo, *Vol. 12, No. 3, Summer, 1989, pp. 605-08.*

Sean O'Brien (essay date 1990)

[*In the following essay, O'Brien analyzes Walcott's epic poem* Omeros.]

Much of the splendour of Derek Walcott's poetry is to be found in his writing about the sea. The epic *Omeros* may prove to be the consummation of his love affair with water. It begins with the hero, Achille, explaining how canoes are cut down from the forest of St Lucia and ends with his return to shore and the words "the sea was still going on." *Omeros* is, in one sense, a work in praise of its capacity to do just that. The sea has "no memory of the wanderings of Gilgamesh / or whose sword severed whose head in *The Iliad*. / It was an epic whose every line was erased / yet freshly written." It "never altered its metre to suit the age, a wide page without metaphors. / Our last resort". In *Omeros,* land itself tends to become ocean, especially the island's windy forests, while desks and floors are covered with charts or the maps made by sunlight and leaf-shadow. Human identities are themselves shifted and transformed by real or imagined voyages. The act of speech itself is described in oceanic terms. When the poet is told the word "Omeros" by the Greek girl who seems the poem's shadowy inspiration, he provides its Creole etymology:

> *O* was the conch-shell's invocation, *mer* was
> both mother and sea in our Antillean patois,
> *os,* a grey bone, and the white surf as it crashes
>
> and spreads its sibilant collar on a lace shore.
> Omeros was the crunch of dry leaves, and the
>   wash
> that echoes from a cave-mouth when the tide has
>   ebbed.

The "Homeric coincidence" of this marine voice with an island "once named Helen", and now named for a blind saint, provokes the poem, not "for kings floundering in the lances of rain but the prose / of abrupt fishermen cursing over canoes."

From this account, and from the names of the central figures (Achille, Hector, Philoctete and Helen), it might be supposed that *Omeros* recasts Homeric materials directly into a Caribbean setting. If this were simply the case, Walcott's detractors could enjoy a field-day at the expense of those tendencies summarized in Stewart Brown's (largely favourable) essay "Spoiler: Walcott's People's Patriot": namely, Walcott's alleged Eurocentricity, his arrogant individualism, and his inability "because of his class, culture and philosophy to 'ground' with West Indian people." But *Omeros* is a complex work, both structurally and in its repeated examination of perennial themes in Walcott's work—identity, exile, how history is suffered and survived, and the obligations of the artist—in which he is hardly sparing to himself. It might be further objected that the rehearsal of error is luxury of a kind, and as E. A. Markham, in his anthology *Hinterland,* has pointed out, "many of Walcott's early statements have been taken not as the privileged glimpse inside a writer's mind trying to relate achievements to objectives, but as literary manifestoes". Part of the subject of *Omeros,* however, is the problem of getting past "literature" to achieve, in the words of an early poem, **"Islands"**, "Verse crisp as sand, clear as sunlight, / Clear as the cold wave, ordinary / As a tumbler of island water." *Omeros* is also informed by love and humility, the subjects of the superb **"The Light of the World"**, from Walcott's previous collection, *The Arkansas Testament,* where the beautiful unknown woman on the crowded island bus at night is surely a forerunner of Helen as she appears in *Omeros.*

The first three of the seven books of *Omeros* tell of the quarrel between the fishermen Achille and Hector, of Helen's desertion of Achille for Hector, and of their friend Philoctete, incurably injured by a cut from an anchor. Their town also contains the blind seer Seven Seas and the wise woman Ma Kilman. Helen's doings in particular are observed by Plunkett, her former employer, retired RSM and pig farmer, who, like the poem in general, identifies her with the island. In search of a history for the place he studies the naval engagement in which the French treasure ship Ville de Paris was sunk by the British and in doing so discovers the death, in the same battle, of a Midshipman Plunkett, thereby finding for himself and his wife, Maud (who spends much of her time at embroidery), the son whom life has not allowed them. The despairing Achille is also drawn to the past, diving for the treasure (guarded, it is said, by a one-eyed octopus) in hopes of winning Helen back. These events, veering between the literal and the visionary, are complemented by two comic episodes, the one broad and the other sour—the cyclone, depicted as a syncretizing knees-up for the gods, and the short-lived activities of Maljo's United Love Party, which opposes itself to the island's "identical" capitalist and Marxist factions. After the shindig which marks the flowering and imminent extinction of the ULP, Achille, in despair at Helen's absence, suffers sunstroke and undergoes a return to Africa, drawn on by the flight of the ocean-going swift to encounter his ancestor Afolabe to witness the enslavement of the tribe, the torments of the slave passage:

> the fading sound of their tribal name for the rain,
> the bright sound of the sun, a hissing noun for the
> river,
> and always the word "never", and never the word
> "again".

That Walcott is trying to win back ground from the novel is apparent not only in the variety and ingenuity of the narrative, but in his or his persona's constant presence in the poem, whether invoking Omeros or encountering his dead father in the streets of the island capital. The latter episode is one of many fine set-pieces. It dramatizes the intersection of the then-and-thereness of the barber's shop and political conversation with the sense of historical scale which accompanies the arrival of a liner for coaling. Teams of local women walk "like ants up a white flower-pot"; as the poet's father states, "the / infernal anthracite hills showed you hell early." The feet of the women are identified with those of verse, and the son's duty is "to give those feet a voice".

Although the personal exile begun at the close of the third book has many reverberations in the remainder of the poem, it seems uncertain whether the more extensive autobiographical material which occupies much of the fourth and fifth books is successful or wholly necessary. There is a slackening of impetus and—despite the appearance of Omeros in the guise of a tramp outside St Martin in the Fields—there are occasions when Walcott lapses into the "writing" noted by Seamus Heaney in the weaker moments of *The Fortunate Traveller* (1982). The meditative passage on Ireland, for instance, drawn from a visit to Glen-da-Lough, is reminiscent of MacNeice having a thin time. Nor am I convinced that the material concerned with the destruction of the Sioux (seen as analogous to the vanished Aruacs of the Caribbean) is fully meshed with the poem as a whole. Yet the sorrows, frustrations and insights addressed in the book's centre are a preparation for return. As the poet's father states in a further meeting in a colder climate, "in its travelling all that the sea-swift does, / it does in a circular pattern". To "have seen everything and been everywhere" is a way of renewing attachment to the sight of a "sail leaving harbour and a sail coming in", and the implied possibility of refreshed inspiration is confirmed in the opening chapter of the sixth book:

> Ah, twin-headed January, seeing either tense:
> a past, they assured us, born in degradation,
> and a present that lifted us up with the wind's
>
> noise in the breadfruit leaves with such an elation
> that it contradicts what is past! . . . .

What remains of the central narrative is largely concerned with reconciliation and healing. Ma Kilman finds the appropriate root (grown from a seed carried by a bird from Africa) to heal Philoctete: bathed in a cauldron, he also discovers his name. Hector, tempted away from the sea, becomes a daredevil taxi-driver and dies on the road. The pregnant Helen returns to Achille, who is himself to die beyond the book's pages. Plunkett recovers from the death of Maud, whose coffin is draped with her embroidery of the island's birds. The botched modernization of the island—another familiar Walcott theme—is seen taking place. Yet as these events are resolved, their author undergoes an inquisition by Omeros, whom he encounters on the shore. This familiar compound ghost, part wooden beam, part Homeric bust, part mulatto Charon, part plain speaker, states: "Forget the gods... and read the rest.... / A girl smells better than the world's libraries'". Their subsequent tour of the island involves a visit to a volcanic Purgatory rich in politicians and poets, and Walcott himself barely escapes their fate, restored to the world with a damning enquiry:

> You tried to render
> their lives as you could, but that is never enough:
> now in the sulphurs' stench ask yourself this
> question,
>
> whether a love of poverty helped you
> to use other eyes, like those of that sightless stone?

Walcott has referred to his sense of himself as a member of a "guild", a contributor to a greater literary whole, and has also spoken on his pleasure at being told that he sometimes sounds like someone else. There are Auden-esque moments in *Omeros,* and some of the duller passages sound like Lowell. More strikingly, the etymology of "Omeros", the encounters with the poet's father and the Dantesque passages in Purgatory seem, like some of the work in *The Arkansas Testament,* to build on suggestions from Heaney, though these are so far expanded as to render the idea of simple indebtedness a marginal one. As throughout his work, Walcott is preoccupied here both with European-derived tradition and the claims of home. In a recently published interview with David Montenegro in *Partisan Review* he argued that "when you enter a language, you enter a kind of choice which contains in it the political history of the language, the imperial width of the language, the fact that you are either subjugated by the language or you have to dominate it. So language is not a place of retreat, it's not a place of escape, it's not even a place of resolution. It's a place of struggle." The struggle Walcott undertakes in *Omeros* in one sense resembles Achille's or Plunkett's: that is, to know history and overcome it, as Achille does on his return to the island, reconciled to the dead Hector, or as Plunkett, beached at the end of an empire, attempts to do. Significantly, Walcott supplies the funeral oration for Hector which Achille himself cannot make, and in so doing brings back to mind the passengers at the close of **"The Light of the World"**: "There was nothing they wanted, nothing I could give them / but this thing I have called 'The Light of the World'". *Omeros,* then tries to speak for a people unaware of the story it tells.

Omeros is a problematic poem. For some, the very limited use of patois may condemn it. For others, although Helen may be so fundamental a literary presence as to resist appropriation, there may be something uneasy in Walcott's preoccupation with *seeing* her, and with her physical beauty, however intimately she comes to represent the island. From time to time there is also a suspicion that discursive material is being forced into verse, while the prominence given to matters of artistic conscience might seem misplaced. But having said this, *Omeros* is an extraordinarily ambitious under-

taking, clearly founded in the conviction that poetry is an urgent task and an art which should be capable of whatever the imagination requires. Walcott's powers of evocation seem inexhaustible: the virtual omnipresence of the sea never threatens to become formulaic, while the motifs of lace, the forest, the conch-shell and the flight of birds gain in suggestiveness as the poem travels through its several thousand lines. The narrative episodes—in particular Achille's voyages—are compelling in themselves, and in its movements through time and memory and between the external and interior worlds the poem is satisfyingly mysterious. St. Lucia, by this account, is, as Kavanagh put it, one of the world's "important places", one that "held all ... of paradise, / with no other sign but the lizard's signature, / and no other laurel but the *Laurier-canelle's*". With *Omeros* Derek Walcott has thrown down an intimidating challenge to the Old World's dispirited centre. (pp. 977-78)

Sean O'Brien, "In Terms of the Ocean," in The Times Literary Supplement, *No. 4563, September 14-20, 1990, pp. 977-78.*

FURTHER READING

Atlas, James. "Derek Walcott: Poet of Two Worlds." *The New York Times Magazine* (23 May 1982): 32, 34, 38-9, 42, 50-1.
  Biographical discussion of Walcott's career.

Bedient, Calvin. "Derek Walcott, Contemporary." *Parnassus: Poetry in Review* 9, No. 2 (Fall-Winter 1981): 31-44.
  Analysis of *The Fortunate Traveller,* arguing that its sense of dislocation and lack of authority reflects a pervasive trend in contemporary literature.

Birkerts, Sven. "Derek Walcott." In his *The Electric Life: Essays on Modern Poetry,* pp. 265-72. New York: William Morrow and Company, 1989.
  Reprint of an essay that originally appeared in *The New Republic* on January 23, 1984, in which Birkerts analyzes the structure of Walcott's *Midsummer.*

Brown, Lloyd W. "Caribbean Castaway New World Odyssey: Derek Walcott's Poetry" *The Journal of Commonwealth Literature* 11, No. 2 (December 1976): 149-59.
  Focuses on Walcott's theme of artistic odyssey.

Dove, Rita. "Either I'm Nobody, or I'm a Nation." *Parnassus: Poetry in Review* 14, No. 1 (1987): 48-76.
  Thorough discussion of works included in Walcott's *Collected Poems.*

Fido, Elaine Savory. "Value Judgements on Art and the Question of Macho Attitudes: The Case of Derek Walcott." *Journal of Commonwealth Literature* XXI, No. 1 (1986): 109-19.
  Feminist critical analysis of Walcott's poetry, arguing that his imagery often implicitly simplifies women.

Fox, Robert Elliot. "Big Night Music: Derek Walcott's *Dream on Monkey Mountain* and the 'Splendours of Imagination'." *The Journal of Commonwealth Literature* XVII, No. (1982): 16-27.
    Examines the metaphorical structure of *Dream on Monkey Mountain*.

Heaney, Seamus. "The Language of Exile." *Parnassus: Poetry in Review* 8, No. 1 (Fall-Winter 1979): 5-11.
    Review of Walcott's *The Star-Apple Kingdom*.

Hirsh, Edward. Interview with Derek Walcott. *The Paris Review* 28, No. 101 (Winter 1986): 197-230.
    Walcott discusses his artistic development and his career as a poet and dramatist.

Ramsaran, J. A. "Derek Walcott: New World Mediterranean Poet." *World Literature Written in English* 21, No. 1 (Spring 1982): 133-47.
    Focuses on the influences contributing to Walcott's development of a distinctly West Indian literature.

Taylor, Patrick. "Myth and Reality in Caribbean Narrative: Derek Walcott's 'Pantomime'." *World Literature Written in English* 26, No. 1 (Spring 1986): 169-77.
    Critical analysis of Walcott's *Pantomime*.

Thompson, John. "Old Campaigners." *The New York Review of Books* 23, No. 16 (14 October 1976): 33-4.
    Review of Walcott's *Sea Grapes*.

Alice Walker

1944-

American novelist, short story writer, essayist, poet, critic, editor, and author of children's books.

The author of the Pulitzer Prize-winning novel *The Color Purple* (1982), Walker writes about the black woman's struggle for spiritual wholeness and sexual, political, and racial equality. Although most critics categorize her writings as feminist, Walker rebuffs the label, describing her work and herself as "womanist." She defines this term as "a woman who loves other woman....Appreciates and prefers woman's culture, woman's emotional flexibility...and woman's strength....*Loves* the spirit....Loves herself. *Regardless."* For this reason, some critics have faulted Walker's fiction for its unflattering portraits of black men. However, most applaud her lyrical prose, her sensitive characterizations, and her gift for rendering beauty, grace, and dignity in ordinary people and places.

Much of Walker's fiction is informed by her Southern background. She was born in Eatonton, Georgia, a rural town where most blacks worked as tenant farmers. At age eight she was blinded in her right eye when an older brother accidentally shot her with a BB gun. Because her parents did not have access to a car, Walker did not receive medical attention until several days after the accident, thereby creating irrevocable damage to the eye. Walker spent most of her childhood withdrawn from others because of her disfigurement and began writing poetry to ease her loneliness. She commented later that because of this incident, she "began to really see people and things, to really notice relationships and to learn to be patient enough to care about how they turned out." In 1961 Walker won a scholarship to Spelman College in Atlanta, where she became involved in the civil rights movement and participated in sit-ins at local business establishments. In 1963, she transferred to Sarah Lawrence College in Bronxville, New York, graduating from there in 1965. She spent the following summer in Mississippi as an activist and teacher and met her future husband Melvyn Leventhal, a Jewish civil rights attorney. Walker and Leventhal married in 1967 in New York City and resumed their activist work in Mississippi, becoming the first legally married interracial couple to reside in Jackson, the state capital. They divorced in 1976. Since then Walker has focused more on her writing and has taught at various colleges and universities.

Walker's first novel, *The Third Life of Grange Copeland* (1970), introduces many of her prevalent themes, particularly the domination of powerless women by equally powerless men. In this work, which spans the years between the Depression and the beginnings of the civil rights movement in the early 1960s, Walker chronicled three generations of a black sharecropping family and

explored the effects of poverty and racism on their lives. Because of his sense of failure, Grange Copeland, the family patriarch, drives his wife to suicide and abandons his children to seek a better life in the North. His legacy of hate and violence is passed on to his son, Brownfield, who eventually murders his wife. At the novel's conclusion, Grange returns to his family a broken yet compassionate man and attempts to atone for his past transgressions with the help of his granddaughter, Ruth. While some reviewers accused Walker of reviving stereotypes about the dysfunctional black family, others praised her use of intensive, descriptive language in creating believable characters.

Walker's next novel, *Meridian* (1976), a tale of perseverance and personal sacrifice set during the 1960s, is generally regarded as one of the best novels about the civil rights movement. Here Walker explored conflicts between traditional African-American values handed down through slavery and the revolutionary polemic espoused by the Black Power movement. The title

character is a college-educated woman who commits her life to helping Southern blacks gain political and social equality. She joins an organization of black militants but is forced to leave the group when she refuses to condone its violent actions. Meridian remains devoted to her activist work, however, and later becomes a legendary leader throughout the South, continuing the work of such historical figures as Harriet Tubman and Sojourner Truth. While several critics admonished Walker for depicting Meridian as a mythic figure, Marge Piercy responded: "Is it possible to write a novel about the progress of a saint? Apparently, yes. With great skill and care to make Meridian believable at every stage of her development, Walker also shows us the cost."

Walker's next novel, *The Color Purple,* placed Walker among the most important contemporary American writers and made her an overnight literary celebrity. Presented in an epistolary style, the novel traces thirty years in the life of Celie, a poor Southern black woman who is vicitimized physically and emotionally by both her stepfather and her husband. While in her teens, Celie is repeatedly raped by her stepfather, who sells the two children she bears him. Celie is eventually placed in a loveless marriage with Albert, a widower she addresses as "Mister," who for the next three decades beats her and torments her psychologically. Celie writes letters describing her ordeal to God and to her sister Nettie, who escapes a similar fate by serving as a missionary in Africa. Celie eventually finds solace through her friendship and love for Albert's mistress, Shug Avery, a charismatic blues singer who gives her the courage to leave her marriage. At the novel's end, Celie is reunited with her children and with Nettie.

Walker earned nearly unanimous praise for *The Color Purple,* especially for her accurate rendering of black folk idioms and her characterization of Celie. Peter S. Prescott echoed the opinion of most reviewers when he called Walker's work "an American novel of permanent importance, that rare sort of book which (in Norman Mailer's felicitous phrase) amounts to 'a diversion in the fields of dread'." *The Color Purple* and its subsequent film adaptation in 1985 led to controversy among the black intelligentsia, however, particularly for its negative portraits of black men. Darryl Pinckney unflatteringly equated Walker's novel with Harriet Beecher Stowe's *Uncle Tom's Cabin,* stating: "[Like] Stowe's, Walker's work shows a world divided between the chosen (black women) and the unsaved, the 'poor miserable critter' (black men), between the 'furnace of affliction' and a 'far-off, mystic land of . . . miraculous fertility'." Richard Wesley, however, disputed charges of bias against black males in Walker's novel. He contended that Walker "is reminding many of us men of our own failures. She is reminding women of *their* failures as well. She is saying that Black is Beautiful, but not necessarily always *right.*"

Walker's recent work, *The Temple of My Familiar* (1989), is an ambitious novel recording 500,000 years of human history. The novel's central character, Miss Lissie, is a goddess from primeval Africa who has been incarnated hundreds of times throughout history. She befriends Suwelo, a narcissistic university professor whose marriage is threatened by his need to dominate and sexually exploit his wife. Through a series of conversations with Miss Lissie and her friend Hal, Suwelo learns of Miss Lissie's innumerable lives and experiences—from the prehistoric world in which humans and animals lived in harmony under a matriarchal society to slavery in the United States—and regains his capability to love, nurture, and respect himself and others. Critics generally dismissed *The Temple of My Familiar* as at best a minor work. Most reviewers took issue with Walker's speculative interpretation of the origins of patriarchal societies and found her discourses on racial and sexual relations pretentious and offensive. Yet J. M. Coetzee commented: "We should read [the novel] as a fable of recovered origins, as an exploration of the inner lives of contemporary black Americans as these are penetrated by fabulous stories . . . . Nevertheless, history is not just storytelling . . . . Africa has a past that neither the white male nor Ms. Walker can simply invent."

Walker is also considered an accomplished poet. Darwin Turner described her verse as "moderately open forms which permit her to reveal homespun truths of human behavior and emotion." Walker's first collection, *Once: Poems* (1968), includes works written during the early 1960s while she attended Sarah Lawrence College. Some of these pieces relate the confusion, isolation, and suicidal thoughts Walker experienced when she learned in her senior year that she was pregnant. In her second volume, *Revolutionary Petunias and Other Poems* (1971), Walker addressed such topics as love, individualism, and revolution while recounting her years in Mississippi as a civil rights activist and teacher. *Goodnight, Willie Lee, I'll See You in the Morning* (1979) contains verse that celebrates familial bonds and friendships. Walker's most recent collection of poetry, *Her Blue Body Everything We Know* (1991), focuses on the "political and personal issues of race, gender, environment, love, hate and suffering," according to reviewer Lisa Failer.

In addition to her novels and poetry, Walker has also published two volumes of short stories, *In Love and Trouble: Stories of Black Women* (1973) and *You Can't Keep a Good Woman Down: Stories* (1981), both of which evidence her womanist philosophy. *In Search of Our Mothers' Gardens: Womanist Prose* (1984) and *Living by the Word: Selected Writings, 1973-1987* (1988) are collections of essays written throughout Walker's career; they focus on such topics as the environment, animal rights, and nuclear war. Walker is also the author of two books for children, *Langston Hughes: American Poet* (1974) and *To Hell with Dying* (1988).

Walker is one of the most prolific black women writers in America. Her work consistently reflects her concern with racial, sexual, and political issues—particularly with the black woman's struggle for spiritual survival. Addressing detractors who fault her "unabashedly feminist viewpoint," Walker explained: "The black woman is one of America's greatest heroes.... Not enough credit has been given to the black woman who has been oppressed beyond recognition." Walker's insistence on giving black women their due resulted in *The Color Purple,* one of the most widely read novels in America today. "Perhaps even more than Walker's other works," educator Barbara T. Christian announced, "[*The Color Purple*] especially affirms that the most abused of the abused can transform herself. It completes the cycle Walker announced a decade ago: the survival and liberation of black women through the strength and wisdom of others."

(For further information about Walker's life and works, see *Black Writers; Concise Dictionary of American Literary Biography, 1968-1988; Contemporary Authors,* Vols. 37-40; *Contemporary Authors New Revision Series,* Vols. 9, 27; *Contemporary Literary Criticism,* Vols. 5, 6, 9, 19, 27, 46, 58; *Dictionary of Literary Biography,* Vols. 6, 33; *Short Story Criticism,* Vol. 5; and *Something about the Author,* Vol. 31.)

PRINCIPAL WORKS

Once: Poems (poetry) 1968
The Third Life of Grange Copeland (novel) 1970
Revolutionary Petunias and Other Poems (poetry) 1971
Five Poems (poetry) 1972
In Love and Trouble: Stories of Black Women (short stories) 1973
Langston Hughes: American Poet (juvenile nonfiction) 1974
Meridian (novel) 1976
Goodnight, Willie Lee, I'll See You in the Morning (poetry) 1979
"Porn at Home" (essay) 1980; published in periodical *Ms.*
You Can't Keep a Good Woman Down: Stories (short stories) 1981
*The Color Purple (novel) 1982
Horses Make a Landscape Look More Beautiful: Poems (poetry) 1984
In Search of Our Mothers' Gardens: Womanist Prose (essays) 1984
Alice Walker Boxed Set—Fiction: The Third Life of Grange Copeland, You Can't Keep a Good Woman Down, and In Love and Trouble (novel and short stories) 1985
Alice Walker Boxed Set—Poetry: Good Night, Willie Lee, I'll See You in the Morning; Revolutionary Petunias and Other Poems; Once, Poems (poetry) 1985
"Cuddling" (short story) 1985; published in periodical *Essence*
"Kindred Spirits" (short story) 1985; published in periodical *Esquire*
"Olive Oil" (short story) 1985; published in periodical *Ms.*

"Not Only Will Your Teachers Appear, They Will Cook New Foods For You" (essay) 1986; published in periodical *Mendocino Country*
Living by the Word: Selected Writings, 1973-1987 (essays) 1988
To Hell with Dying (juvenile fiction) 1988
The Temple of My Familiar (novel) 1989
Her Blue Body Everything We Know (poetry) 1991

*This work was made into a movie in 1985, starring Whoopi Goldberg, Oprah Winfrey, and Danny Glover.

Mary Helen Washington (essay date 1979)

[*In the following excerpt, Washington examines the depiction of women in Walker's work.*]

From whatever vantage point one investigates the work of Alice Walker—poet, novelist, short story writer, critic, essayist, and apologist for black women—it is clear that the special identifying mark of her writing is her concern for the lives of black women. (p. 133)

[There] are more than twenty-five characters from the slave woman to a revolutionary woman of the sixties [about whom she has written]. Within each of these roles Walker has examined the external realities facing these women as well as the internal world of each woman.

We might begin to understand Alice Walker, the apologist and spokeswoman for black women, by understanding the motivation for Walker's preoccupation with her subject. Obviously there is simply a personal identification.... Moreover her sense of personal identification with black women includes a sense of sharing in their peculiar oppression. (p. 134)

Walker understands that what W.E.B. Du Bois called double consciousness... creates its own particular kind of disfigurement in the lives of black women, and that, far more than the external facts and figures of oppression, the true terror is within; the mutilation of the spirit *and* the body. Though Walker does not neglect to deal with the external *realities* of poverty, exploitation, and discrimination, her stories, novels, and poems most often focus on the intimate reaches of the inner lives of her characters; the landscape of her stories is the spiritual realm where the soul yearns for what it does not have. (p. 135)

The true empathy Alice Walker has for the oppressed woman comes through in all her writings.... Raising an ax, crying out in childbirth or abortion, surrendering to a man who is oblivious to her real name—these are the kinds of images which most often appear in Ms. Walker's own writing.... (pp. 136-37)

What particularly distinguishes Alice Walker in her role as apologist and chronicler for black women is her evolutionary treatment of black women; that is, she sees the experiences of black women as a series of movements from women totally victimized by society and by the men in their lives to the growing developing women whose consciousness allows them to have control over their lives. (p. 137)

Walker's personal construct of the black woman's history [is] the woman suspended, artist thwarted and hindered in her desires to create, living through two centuries when her main role was to be a cheap source of cheap labor in the American society....

Most of Walker's women characters belong to the first part of the cycle—the suspended woman.... [These] are women who are cruelly exploited, spirits and bodies mutilated, relegated to the most narrow and confining lives, sometimes driven to madness. (p. 139)

In **"The Child Who Favored Daughter,"** the father presides over the destruction of three women in his family: his own wife, whom he drives to suicide after beating and crippling her; his sister, named Daughter, whose suicide is the result of the punishment her family exacts after she has an affair with a white man; and his own daughter, whom he mutilates because she will not renounce her white lover. To understand the violence of this man toward these three women in his family, author Walker makes us know that it is the result of an immense chaos within—the components of which are his impotent rage against the white world which abuses him, his vulnerable love for his child and his sister, both of whom chose white lovers. He is so threatened by that inner chaos that the very act of violence is a form of control, a way of imposing order on his own world. By killing his daughter, he has at once shut out the image of Daughter which haunts him, he has murdered his own incest, and he has eliminated the last woman who has the power to hurt him. (pp. 141-42)

Walker [has] explored the tragedies in the lives of Black women—the tragedy of poverty, abuse from men who are themselves abused, the physical deterioration—but there is greater depth in Walker's exploration because not only does she comprehend the past lives of these women but she has also questioned their fates and dared to see through to a time when black women would no longer live in suspension, when there would be a place for them to move into.

In the second cycle of Walker's personal construct of the history of black women are the women who belong to the decades of the forties and fifties, those decades when black people (then "Negroes") wanted most to be part of the mainstream of American life even though assimilation required total denial of one's ethnicity. (pp. 142-43)

The women in this cycle are also victims, not of physical violence, but of a kind of psychic violence that alienates them from their roots, cutting them off from real contact.

The woman named Molly from Walker's poem **"For My Sister Molly Who in the Fifties"** is the eldest sister in a poor rural family in Eatonton; she is, in fact, Alice Walker's sister and Walker is the child narrator of the poem mourning the loss of her talented and devoted "Molly." When Molly first comes home on vacation from college, she is very close to her brothers and sisters, teaching them what she has learned, reading to them about faraway places like Africa. The young narrator is enraptured by Molly, spellbound by the bright colorful sister who changes her drab life into beauty....But being a child, the narrator does not realize or suspect the growing signs of Molly's remoteness. Molly goes off to the university, travels abroad, becoming distant and cold and frowning upon the lives of the simple folks she comes from .... From her superior position [Molly] can only see the negatives—the silent, fearful, barefoot, tongue-tied, ignorant brothers and sisters. She finds the past, her backward family, unbearable, and though she may have sensed their groping after life, she finally leaves the family for good. (pp. 143-45)

The women of the second cycle are destroyed spiritually rather than physically, and yet there is still some movement forward, some hope that did not exist for the earlier generation of American black women. The women in this cycle are more aware of their condition and they have greater potential for shaping their lives, although they are still thwarted because they feel themselves coming to life before the necessary changes have been made in the political environment—before there is space for them to move into. The sense of "twoness" that Du Bois spoke of in *The Souls of Black Folk* is perhaps most evident in the lives of these women; they are the most aware of and burdened by the "double consciousness" that makes one measure one's soul by the tape of the other world. (p. 145)

The women of the third cycle are, for the most part, women of the late sixties, although there are some older women in Walker's fiction who exhibit the qualities of the developing, emergent model. Greatly influenced by the political events of the sixties and the changes resulting from the freedom movement, they are women coming just to the edge of a new awareness and making the first tentative steps into an uncharted region. And although they are more fully conscious of their political and psychological oppression and more capable of creating new options for themselves, they must undergo a harsh initiation before they are ready to occupy and claim any new territory. (p. 146)

Besides political activism, a fundamental activity the women in the third cycle engage in is the search for meaning in their roots and traditions. As they struggle to reclaim their past and to re-examine their relationship to the black community, there is a consequent reconciliation between themselves and black men.

In Sarah Davis, the main character of Walker's short story, **"A Sudden Trip Home in the Spring,"** we have another witness to the end of the old cycles of confusion and despair. Her search begins when she returns home to the South from a northern white college to bury her father. She is an artist, but because of her alienation from her father, whom she blames for her mother's death, she is unable to paint the faces of black men, seeing in them only defeat.... Through a series of events surrounding her father's funeral, Sarah rediscovers the courage and grace of her grandfather and reestablishes the vital link between her and her brother. Her resolve at the end of the story to do a sculpture of her grandfather... signifies the return to her roots and her own personal sense of liberation. This story, more than any other, indicates the contrast between the women of the second cycle who were determined to escape their roots in order to make it in a white world and the emergent women of the third cycle who demonstrate a sense of freedom by the drive to reestablish those vital links to their past. (pp. 147-48)

> Mary Helen Washington, "An Essay on Alice Walker," in Sturdy Black Bridges: Visions of Black Women in Literature, edited by Roseann P. Bell, Bettye J. Parker, and Beverly Guy-Sheftall, Anchor Press, 1979, pp. 133-49.

Gloria Steinem (essay date 1982)

[*In the following excerpt, Steinem—a well-known American feminist—praises Walker's skills as a writer, noting* The Color Purple *as the author's greatest literary achievement.*]

There must be thousands of people scattered around this country, each one of whom thinks only she or he knows how necessary and major a writer Alice Walker is.

Even "writer" may be too distant a word. Traveling and listening over the years, I've noticed that the readers of Alice Walker's work tend to speak about her as a friend: someone who has rescued them from passivity or anger; someone who has taught them sensuality of self-respect, humor or redemption.

"I've been a much better person," said an angry young novelist to a roomful of his peers, "since I've been under the care and feeding of Alice Walker's writing." (p. 35)

"While I'm reading her novels, I'm completely unaware of her style," said a literary critic who is a writer herself. "It's unpretentious and natural, like a glass that contains whatever she wants you to see. Yet I can read a few paragraphs of hers and know immediately: That's Alice." (pp. 35, 37)

I've heard many such comments over the past decade or so.... I don't hear the usual celebrity question: what is Alice really like? Readers feel that know her personally from her writing. But lives touched by her work form a small secret network on almost every campus and in many cities and towns.

Of course, the existence of such readers, even unknown to each other, means that Alice Walker is not a secret writer. Her two novels, three books of poetry, and two short story collections have sold and been reviewed respectably....

But her visibility as a major American talent has been obscured by a familiar bias that assumes white male writers, and the literature they create, to be the norm. That puts black women (and all women of color) at a double remove. Only lately have writers like Toni Morrison or Maya Angelou begun to escape those adjectives that are meant to restrict, not just describe. Toni Cade Bambara, June Jordan, Paule Marshall, Ntozake Shange, and other valuable current writers are still missing from the mainstream (and the mainstream is missing them) because of this bias against the universality of what they have to say. So are all the Zora Neale Hurstons and Nella Larsens of the past whose works have been allowed to pass out of print and out of mind.

Even with Black Studies, Women's Studies, and other new courses now trying hard, it's going to take many years to change academic habits that still expect American readers to cross boundaries of country, time, and language to identify with Dostoevsky or Tolstoy, but not to walk next door and meet Baldwin or Ellison; that still assume women can identify with male protagonists, but that there's something perverse about the other way around.

As usual, however, the people are way ahead of their leaders—and readers are ahead of their book reviewers. It's true and important that a disproportionate number of people who seek out Alice Walker's sparsely distributed books are black women.... But white women, and women of diverse ethnic backgrounds, also feel tied to Alice Walker. The struggle to have work and minds of our own, vulnerability, our debt to our mothers, the price of childbirth, friendships among women, the problem of loving men who regard us as less than themselves, sensuality, violence: all these are major themes of her fiction and poetry. (In *The Third Life of Grange Copeland,* her first novel, she exposed violence against women by their husbands and lovers. It was 1970, years before most women had begun to tell the truth in public about such violence, and her novel paid a critical price for being ahead of its time.) In fact, she speaks the female experience more powerfully for being able to pursue it across boundaries of race and class.

And she never gives in. No female character is ever allowed to disappear behind a sex role, any more than she would allow a black character to sink into a stereotype of race.

As the young novelist said, "I've become a much better person..." and that seems to be a frequent reaction of her readers who are black men. They comment on her clear-eyed rendering of the rural black South in which many of them grew up, her loving use of black folk

English, and her understanding of what goes right and wrong between men and women.

It's true that a disproportionate number of her hurtful, negative reviews have been by black men. But those few seem to be reviewing their own conviction that black men should have everything white men have had, including dominance over women; or their fear that black women's truth-telling will be misused in a racist society; or their alarm at her "lifestyle," a euphemism for the fact that Alice was married for 10 years to a white civil rights worker. (p. 37)

As for white male readers, the main problem seems to be a conviction that her books "aren't written for us." Given the fears expressed by those black male critics, it's ironic that white men's reactions often center on the increased understanding of black rage, and a new conviction that they themselves have been deprived of seeing the world whole. In fact, Susan Kirschner, an English professor who made a study of all the reviews of **Meridian,** concluded that the only critic to examine seriously the moral themes of the novel, not just respectfully describe its plot, was Greil Marcus, a white reviewer writing in *The New Yorker.* (pp. 37, 89)

I've suspected for a long time that a convention of all the atomized Alice Walker readers in the country might look surprisingly big and diverse. It might look something like the world.

In fact, her readers may be about to find each other, and discover their numbers greatly increased, in the light of new public attention. *The Color Purple,* Alice Walker's third and latest novel, could be the kind of popular and literary event that transforms an intense reputation into a national one.

For one thing, the storytelling style of *The Color Purple* makes it irresistible to read. The words belong to Celie, the downest and outest of women. Because she must survive against impossible odds, because she has no one to talk to, she writes about her life in the guise of letters to God. When she discovers her much-loved lost sister is not dead after all but is living in Africa, she writes letters to Nettie instead. The point is, she must tell someone the truth and confirm her existence....

The result is an inviting, dead-honest, surprising novel that is the successful culmination of Alice Walker's longer and longer trips outside the safety of Standard English narration, and into the words of her characters. Here, she takes the leap completely. There is no third person to distance the reader from events. We are inside Celie's head.

And Celie turns out to be a no-nonsense, heartrending storyteller with a gift for cramming complicated turns of events and whole life histories into very few words. Like E. L. Doctorow in *Ragtime,* the rhythm of the telling adds to the momentum of suspense—but what he did with an episodic style and pace of chapters, Celie can do with the placement of a line, a phrase, a verb....

Reviewers should also understand why Alice Walker has always preferred to describe her characters' speech as "black folk English," not "dialect"; a word she feels has been used in a condescending, racist way. When these people talk, there are no self-conscious apostrophes and contractions to assure us that the writer, of course, really knows what the proper spelling and grammar should be. There are no quotation marks to keep us at our distance. Celie just writes her heart out, putting words down the way they feel and sound. Pretty soon you can't imagine why anyone would bother to write any other way.

The second pleasure of *The Color Purple* is watching people redeem themselves and grow, or wither and turn inward, according to the ways they do or don't work out the moral themes in their lives. In the hands of this author, morality is not an external dictate. It doesn't matter if you love the wrong people, or have children with more than one of them, or whether you have money, go to church, or obey the laws. What matters is cruelty, violence, keeping the truth from others who need it, suppressing someone's will or talent, taking more than you need from people or nature, and failing to choose for yourself. It's the internal morality of dignity, autonomy, and balance.

What also matters is the knowledge that everybody, no matter how poor or passive on the outside, has these possibilities inside. (p. 89)

By the end of the novel, we believe that this poor, nameless patch of land in the American South is really the world—and vice versa. Conversations between Celie and Shug have brought us theories of philosophy, ethics, and metaphysics; all with a world vision that seems more complete for proceeding from the bottom up. The color purple, an odd miracle of nature, symbolizes the miracle of human possibilities.

In the tradition of Gorky, Steinbeck, Dickens, Ernest Gaines, Hurston, Baldwin, Ousmane Sembene, Bessie Head, and many others, Alice Walker has written an empathetic novel about the poorest of the poor.... But, unlike most novels that expose race or class, it doesn't treat male/female injustice as natural or secondary. (And unlike some supposedly feminist novels, it doesn't ignore any women because of race or class.) Just as unusual among books about the poor and powerless, it is not written *about* one group, *for* another. The people in this book could and would enjoy it, too.

It's hard to imagine anyone in the country this novel couldn't reach.

But will it? (p. 90)

Gloria Steinem, "Do You Know This Woman? She Knows You: A Profile of Alice Walker," in Ms., *Vol. X, No. 12, June, 1982, pp. 35, 37, 89-94.*

Robert Towers (essay date 1982)

[*In the following excerpt, Towers praises Walker's use of black dialect in* The Color Purple *but points out certain "inadequacies" in the work.*]

There is nothing cool or throwaway in Alice Walker's attitude toward the materials of her fiction. The first book by this exceptionally productive novelist, poet, and short-story writer to come to my notice was *Meridian* (1976), an impassioned account of the spiritual progress of a young black woman, Meridian Hill, during the civil-rights struggle of the 1960s and its aftermath. . . . Though beset by serious structural problems and other lapses of craft, *Meridian* remains the most impressive fictional treatment of the "Movement" that I have yet read.

In *The Color Purple* Alice Walker moves backward in time, setting her story roughly (the chronology is kept vague) between 1916 and 1942—a period during which the post-Reconstruction settlement of black status remained almost unaltered in the Deep South. Drawing upon what must be maternal and grandmaternal accounts as well as upon her own memory and observation, Miss Walker, who is herself under forty, exposes us to a way of life that for the most part existed beyond or below the reach of fiction and that has hitherto been made available to us chiefly through tape-recorded reminiscences: the life of poor, rural Southern blacks as it was experienced by their womenfolk. (p. 35)

I cannot gauge the general accuracy of Miss Walker's account [of Celie's life] or the degree to which it may be colored by current male-female antagonisms within the black community. . . . I did note certain improbabilities: it seems unlikely that a woman of Celie's education would have applied the word "amazons" to a group of feisty sisters or that Celie, in the 1930s, would have found fulfillment in designing and making pants for women. In any case, *The Color Purple* has more serious faults than its possible feminist bias. Alice Walker still has a lot to learn about plotting and structuring what is clearly intended to be a realistic novel. The revelations involving the fate of Celie's lost babies and the identity or her real father seem crudely contrived—the stuff of melodrama or fairy tales.

The extended account of Nettie's experience in Africa, to which she has gone with a black missionary couple and their two adopted children, is meant to be a counterweight to Celie's story but it lacks authenticity—not because Miss Walker is ignorant of Africa . . . but because she has failed to endow Nettie with her own distinctive voice; the fact that Nettie is better educated than Celie—and a great reader—should not have drained her epistolary style of all personal flavor, leaving her essentially uncharacterized, a merc reporter of events. The failure to find an interesting idiom for a major figure like Nettie is especially damaging in an epistolary novel, which is at best a difficult genre for a twentieth-century writer, posing its own special problems of momentum and credibility.

Fortunately, inadequacies which might tell heavily against another novel seem relatively insignificant in view of the one great challenge which Alice Walker has triumphantly met: the conversion, in Celie's letters, of a subliterate dialect into a medium of remarkable expressiveness, color, and poignancy. I find it impossible to imagine Celie apart from her language; through it, not only a memorable and infinitely touching character but a whole submerged world is vividly called into being. Miss Walker knows how to avoid the excesses of literal transcription while remaining faithful to the spirit and rhythms of Black English. I can think of no other novelist who has so successfully tapped the poetic resources of the idiom. (p. 36)

> Robert Towers, "Good Men Are Hard to Find," in *The New York Review of Books, Vol. XXIX, No. 13,* August 12, 1982, pp. 35-6.

Thadious M. Davis (essay date 1983)

[*In the following excerpt from an essay originally published in* The Southern Quarterly *in 1983, Davis examines the theme of search for self-identity in Walker's work.*]

Walker's heritage and history provide a vehicle for understanding the modern world in which her characters live. "Because I'm black and I'm a woman and because I was brought up poor and because I'm a Southerner, . . . the way I see the world is quite different from the way many people see it," she has observed to Krista Brewer: "I could not help but have a radical vision of society . . . the way I see things can help people see what needs to be changed." Her vision, however, is a disturbing one to share. Walker relies upon sexual violence and physical abuse to portray breaches in black generations. Typically, she brings to her work a terrible observance of black self-hatred and destruction. While Walker does not negate the impact of a deleterious past, she rarely incorporates white characters as perpetrators of crimes against blacks. Her works simply presume, as she states, that "all history is current; all injustice continues on some level." Her images of people destroyed or destroying others originate in a vision of cultural reality expressed matter-of-factly, such as in the poem from *Revolutionary Petunias,* **"You Had to Go to Funerals":** "At six and seven / The face in the gray box / Is nearly always your daddy's / Old schoolmate / Mowed down before his / Time." Walker's racial memory of a tangible, harsh reality succeeds in focusing experience, holding it fixed, and illuminating some aspects of brutality that might well be overlooked or obscured. (p. 40)

One scene in *Meridian* delineates the everyday quality of familial rage in Walker's fiction. A woman who believes that her family and community, as well as the racial barriers and social order of the South, have all combined to rob her of a full life irons into her children's and husband's clothes her frustrations and her creativity. Instead of loving her family openly or accusing anyone explicitly, she uses her ordinary domestic chore to enclose her children in "the starch of her anger," as Walker labels it. This character, Mrs. Hill, includes her children in her victimization, and in the process she excludes them from any meaningful, close relationship with her. The result is a tension- and guilt-ridden existence, both for Mrs. Hill and for her family. The scene suggests how personal outrage and anger stemming from social and historical forces (particularly ignorance, discrimination, racism, exploitation, and sexism) become warped and distorted in Walker's world.

In fact, Walker has discussed her writing, and need to write, in terms that articulate her deflection of rage and her reconciliation with it. After the birth of her daughter, she put her frustrations and her energy into her work: "Write I did, night and day, *something,* and it was not even a choice, . . . but a necessity. When I didn't write I thought of making bombs and throwing them . . . . Writing saved me from the sin and *inconvenience* of violence—as it saves most writers who live in 'interesting' oppressive times and are not afflicted by personal immunity." She does not have to add that her writing absorbed the violence, especially emotional violence, in the lives of her characters. Walker's recollection and the scene from *Meridian* add a situational

context to the prevalent violence and excessive pain found in all of her fiction, but they do not fully address the motivational context for the choice of family as the expressive vehicle.

Walker creates a multiplicity of permanently maimed and damaged souls within the family structure who feel no pressure for responsible living or assume exemption from the demands of responsibility. There may be occasions of optimism or hope, for example, when Sarah, a Southern black art student in **"A Sudden Trip Home in the Spring,"** returns from New York for her father's funeral, she comes, with the help of her brother, to understand her father's life after years of resenting his flaws, and she resolves to learn how to make her grandfather's face in stone. But more pervasive in Walker's fiction is despair: women who commit suicide, such as the wife in **"Her Sweet Jerome,"** who sets fire to herself and her marriage bed; men who main or kill, such as the father in **"The Child Who Favored Daughter,"** who cuts off his daughter's breasts; people who allow themselves to become animals, such as Brownfield in *The Third Life of Grange Copeland,* who, accepting a "nothingness" in himself, shoots his wife in the face while his children watch; and people who simply give up on life, such as Myrna in **"Really, Doesn't Crime Pay?"** who spends her days softening her hands and thwarting her husband's desire for a child.

Walker assumes that by revealing negative actions and violent encounters, she may be able to repair the damage done by unreflective people who are unable to recognize that their actions have more than personal consequences, that they may rend bonds between generations and thus affect all members of a family, community, race, or society. In her depictions of abuse and violence, Walker takes the risk of misrepresenting the very people whom she seeks to change. Yet her unrelenting portraits of human weaknesses convey her message that art should "make us better." . . . Her message, postulated in her novels, is that the breaches and violations must be mended for health and continuity, for "survival *whole,*" as her character Grange Copeland declares.

Reparation or redemption may be undertaken by a single individual in whom Walker vests the responsibility for survival, because it is the action of a single individual that has caused the breakdown of experience or identity in private lives, and ultimately in the public or social life of the group. Individual characters acting alone become repositories of decent behavior, as well as harbingers that the messages embedded in the lives of generations of blacks will not be lost. One example is Elethia, a young woman who masterminds the retrieval of "Uncle Albert," a mummified black man who is all teeth, smiles, and servitude as a decoration in the window of a "whites only" restaurant, despite the reality of his having been a rebellious slave whose teeth were knocked out for his efforts to remain human. Elethia knows that Uncle Albert's denigration to a subservient happy waiter cannot be allowed. She and her cohorts

Walker at age six.

break the plate glass, reclaim the mummy, burn it, and save the ashes. She aims to rid the world of all false, stereotypical images of blacks, especially men, and to recover the past, rectify its misrepresentations, and preserve the truth for future generations. Elethia realizes that the work will not end with rescuing Uncle Albert, but that it will extend over her lifetime. Walker's individual Elethias understand that breaches may have occurred between succeeding generations, but that progress in the present and towards the future depends upon reconstruction of the bridges that, as Carolyn Rodgers says in her poem "It Is Deep," one generation has "crossed over on." Although **"Elethia"** is not one of Walker's most successful stories, it adheres to her belief that the world, her reality, is filled with connections, oftentimes unsuspected connections, which she as an artist can illuminate.

Walker believes that as a writer she must work towards a larger perspective, which she describes as "connections made, or at least attempted, where none existed before, the straining to encompass in one's glance at the varied world the common thread, the unifying theme through immense diversity, a fearlessness of growth, of search, of look, that enlarges the private and the public world." For her, one way of structuring "the common thread" is by means of generations; she values the strength and purpose black generations have given to her writing, but she refuses to reduce their meanings to platitudes or to ignore the complexities of their lives. (pp. 41-3).

Walker treasures and preserves in her works not merely her parents' faces and her own, but those of her grandparents and great-grandparents and all her blood and social relatives as well. For instance, in the poem from *Goodnight Willie Lee* entitled **"talking to my grandmother who died poor (while hearing Richard Nixon declare 'I am not a crook'),"** she concludes: "i must train myself to want / not one bit more / than i need to keep me alive / working / and recognizing beauty / in your so nearly undefeated face." It is in her grandmother's "so nearly undefeated face" that Walker reads at what cost her people have survived. (p. 44)

Because of her conception of art and the artist, as well as her recognition of the value of her mother's stories and her family's faces, Walker displays an enormous sympathy for the older generation of Southern women ("Head-ragged Generals") and men ("billy club scar[ed]"), whose lives were sacrifice.... The poem ["The Women"] celebrates the generation that preceded Walker's own, those men and women who opened doors through which they themselves would never pass and who were unafraid to attempt personal and social change in order to restructure subsequent generations. Walker acknowledges their achievement, but also their adversities.

Her older men, in particular, have experienced troubled, difficult lives, such as those of Grange Copeland and Albert in *The Color Purple.* These men have been abusive in their youths, but they come to an essential understanding of their own lives and their families' as they learn to be reflective, responsible, and expressive individuals. Although they may seem to reflect her anti-male bias, they are more significant as portrayals of Walker's truth-telling from a particular perspective that is conscious of their weaknesses—weaknesses that they distort into violence against other blacks, especially women and children—and conscious, too, of their potential for regeneration. Walker's men to whom sexuality is no longer an issue are redeemed by learning to love and assume responsibility for their actions. In presenting these men, Walker first depicts what has come to be the stereotypes of blacks, essentially those set destructive patterns of emotional and psychological responses of black men to black life, their women, children, friends, whites, and themselves. Then she loosens the confines of the stereotype and attempts to penetrate the nexus of feelings that make these lives valuable in themselves and for others.

Much of the redemption, nevertheless, is only potential as Walker portrays it. The nameless husband in *The Color Purple* becomes "Albert" in his later years, because, like Grange Copeland in Walker's first novel, he discovers reflection which makes him a defined person who can accept the responsibility for his mistakes and the suffering he has caused, especially his abusive treatment of his wife whom he had denigrated.... Despite his contemplative demeanor at the end of the novel, Albert remains in the realm of potential. His apparent psychological return to roots, though inadequately motivated, is primarily a portent of a healing process.

Walker names this healing a "wholeness" in her essay, **"Beyond the Peacock: The Reconstruction of Flannery O'Connor,"** in which she, like her characters, returns to her roots in order to regenerate herself and to comprehend the pervasive impact of social environment. Her attitude is clear in the poem from *Once,* **"South: The Name of Home,"** which opens: "when I am here again / the years of ease between / fall away / The smell of one / magnolia / sends my heart running / through the swamps. / the earth is red / here— / the trees bent, weeping / what secrets will not / the ravished land / reveal / of its abuse." It is an environment that is not without a history of pain, but it nonetheless connects generations of blacks to one another, to a "wholeness" of self, and to "the old unalterable roots," as in **"Burial":** "Today I bring my own child here; / to this place where my father's / grandmother rests undisturbed beneath the Georgia sun / ... Forgetful of geographical resolutions as birds / the farflung young fly South to bury / the old dead." One key to "wholeness," even if it is rarely achieved, is the development of self-perception by means of generational ties to the land.

The achievements and dreams that emerge from the connected experience of generations are expressions of freedom and beauty, of power and community. The primary dream, usually voiced in terms of the creation of art, is that of freedom to be one's own self, specifically to be one's own black self and to claim, as do Walker's blues singers Shug Avery in *The Color Purple* and Gracie Mae Still in **"Nineteen Fifty-Five,"** one's own life for one's self and for future generations.

Walker transforms the individual, so much a part of the special characteristics used to define the white South, into a person who is black and most often female. In the one-page story **"Petunias"** from *You Can't Keep a Good Woman Down,* she individualizes an unnamed woman with a history and a sense of herself. The woman writes in her diary just before her death in an explosion of a bomb her son intends for the revolution: "my daddy's grandmama was a slave on thc Tcarslee Plantation. They dug up her grave when I started agitating in the Movement. One morning I found her dust dumped over my verbena bed, a splinery leg bone had fell among my petunias." This woman and others in Walker's canon are the stereotyped, the maimed, the distorted blacks who still rise, as Maya Angelou entitles one of her works, "Still I Rise." These characters become redeemed as individuals with an indelible sense of self. But that act of rising out of the depths of degradation or depression is accomplished by means of the person's coming to terms with the truth of his or her community, with his or her social and historical place among others who have suffered, grieved, laughed, and lusted, but who miraculously have held on to dignity and selfhood. Characters, such as Sammy Lou, a woman on her way to the electric chair for killing her husband's murderer, pass on a powerful legacy of individual identity; Sammy Lou leaves her children the instructions: "Always respect the word of God," and "Don't yall forget to *water* my purple petunias."

Walker operates within this legacy. She keeps before her the vision of her own mother, who cultivated magnificent flower gardens, despite her work from sun up to dark either in the fields or as a domestic for less than twenty dollars a week. Walker refers to her mother's gardens as her "art," "her ability to hold on, even in simple ways." That garden is her recurrent metaphor for both art and beauty, endurance and survival; it is essentially, too, Walker's articulation of the process by which individuals find selfhood through examining the experiences of others who have proceeded them. (pp. 45-7)

In her first novel, *The Third Life of Grange Copeland,* three generations of Copelands converge to create Ruth's identity, and three generations form the stages or lives of the patriarch and title character, Grange Copeland. When any one member of the Copeland family or of a particular social generation of blacks (from 1920 to 1960) ignores the dynamics of family structures or forgets the historical perspective that the structures are maintained through necessity and love, he or she loses the capacity for primary identifications with race, family, and community, and loses as well the major basis for defining one's self and one's humanity. The most detailed illustration presented in the novel is Brownfield, the son of Grange and a member of the middle generation in the work.

Brownfield Copeland becomes one of "the living dead, one of the many who had lost their souls in the American wilderness." He reduces his murder of his wife to a simple theorem: "*He liked plump women. . . . Ergo,* he had murdered his wife because she had become skinny." Because of his twisted logic, Brownfield "could forget (his wife's) basic reality, convert it into comparisons. She had been like good pie, or good whiskey, but there had never been a self to her." Not only by means of the murder itself, but also by the process of his reasoning about it, he strips himself of his humanity when he negates his culpability with the negation of his wife's existence as a human being.

Brownfield's physical death sadly, though appropriately in Walker's construction, comes at the hands of his father Grange and over the future of his daughter Ruth. But his spiritual death occurs much earlier "as he lay thrashing about, knowing the rigidity of his belief in misery, knowing he could never renew or change himself, for this changelessness was now all he had, he could not clarify what was the duty of love." He compounds one of the greatest sins in Walker's works, the refusal or inability of change, with his dismissal or meaning in family bonds. Ironically, his death makes possible the completion of change in his daughter's life that had been fostered by his father, who late in his life understood the necessity of moving beyond the perverted emotions constricting the lives of the Copelands.

In *Meridian,* Walker's second novel, the heroine divests herself of immediate blood relations—her child and her parents—in order to align herself completely with the larger racial and social generations of blacks. Meridian Hill insists that although seemingly alone in the world, she has created a fusion with her generation of activist blacks and older generations of oppressed blacks. The form of the work, developed in flashbacks, follows a pattern of Meridian's casting off the demands made by authority and responsibility within the conventional family and traditional institutions. Unlike Brownfield's rejection of responsibility, the rupture in this novel is ultimately positive, despite its being the most radical and mysterious instance of change and acceptance in Walker's fiction. It is positive because the novel creates a new basis for defining Meridian's self and for accepting responsibility for one's actions. In fact, the controlling metaphor is resurrection and rebirth, an acting out of the renewal impossible for Brownfield. By the end of the novel, Meridian's personal identity has become a collective identity. . . . In spite of her painful private experiences, Meridian is born anew into a pluralistic cultural self, a "we" that is and must be self-less and without ordinary prerequisites for personal identity. And significantly, because she exemplifies Walker's recurrent statement of women as leaders and models, Meridian leaves her male disciple Truman Held to follow her and to await the arrival of others from their social group.

Truman's search, structurally a duplication of Meridian's, is part of personal change that is more necessary for men than for women in Walker's fiction and that becomes social change through the consequences of actions taken by individuals who must face constraints, as well as opportunities, in their lives, but must also know why they act and what the consequences will be. Truman resolves to live the life of an ascetic so that he might one day be worthy to join Meridian and others "at the river." (pp. 48-50)

Perhaps Walker's third novel most effectively conveys her messages and evidences her heritage as a black Southern writer. In *The Color Purple,* which won the Pulitzer Prize for fiction in 1983, she takes a perspectivistic or "emic" approach to character delineation and cultural reality. She sees and portrays a world from the inside outward; she uses the eyes of Celie, a surnameless, male-dominated and abused woman, who records her experiences in letters. Celie is not a "new" character in Walker's fiction; she is similar to one of the sisters in **"Everyday Use,"** the bride in **"Roselily,"** and the daughter in **"The Child Who Favored Daughter,"** but unlike these other silent, suffering women characters, Celie writes her story in her own voice. She tells her life as only she has known it: a girl, merely a child, raped by her stepfather whom she believes is her natural father; that same girl bearing his two children only to have them stolen by him and to be told that they are dead; the denial and suppression of that girl's actual background and history, as well as her letters from her sister.

In Celie's epistles, Walker makes her strongest effort so far to confront the patterns in a specified world and to order and articulate the codes creating those patterns. In effect, she uses the uncovered patterns to connect, assimilate, and structure the content of one human being's world and relationship to that world. Celie writes letters—her story, history—to God and to her sister Nettie. She writes out of desperation and in order to preserve some core of her existence. In love and hope, she writes to save herself....Celie writes from the heart, and grows stronger, more defined, more fluent, while simultaneously her intensely private, almost cryptic style develops into a still personal, subjective style, but one which encompasses much more of the lives surrounding her.

While social interactions and institutions typically define human reality, these do not ultimately define Celie's. She is isolated and alone, despite the numbers of family members and others impinging upon her world. Slowly and cautiously, she builds a reality that is different, one based upon her singular position and the abstractions she herself conceives in the course of her everyday life. Her inner life is unperverted by the abuse and violence she suffers. Only when she has formulated the outlines of her private identity in writing does her interaction with others become a significant factor in making sense of social codes in the public world. When she reaches her conclusions, she has rejected most of the available social models for personal identity; she is neither Shug Avery, the hardliving blues singer who gives and takes what she wants in being herself, nor is

she Nettie, her sister who can experience the wider world outside the social environment of her childhood. Yet, Celie passionately loves both of these women, and has tried at different stages to emulate them. Celie's own subjective probings lead her to confirm her individual interpretation of herself and of her situational contexts. Nonetheless, she does arrive, as invariably a Walker bearer of responsibility must, at her place in the spectrum of life, her relationship to others, and her own continuity.

Celie affirms herself: "I'm pore, I'm black, I may be ugly and can't cook, a voice say to everything listening. But I'm here." Her words echo those of Langston Hughes's folk philosopher, Jesse B. Semple (Simple): "I'm still here... I've been underfed, underpaid,.... I've been abused, confused, misused.... I done had everything from flat feet to a flat head.... but I am still here.... I'm still here." Celie's verbal connection to Hughes's black everyman and the black oral tradition extends her affirmation of self, so that it becomes racial, as well as personal, and is an actualization, rather than the potentiality that most often appears in Walker's work. Celie *is,* or in her own black folk English, she *be's* her own black, nappy-haired, ordinary self in all the power and pain that combine in her writing to reveal the girl, the female becoming totally a woman-person who survives and belies the weak, passive exterior her family and community presume to be her whole self. Her act of writing and affirming is magnificent. It is an achievement deserving of celebration, and perhaps not coincidentally, it is Walker's first "happy ending," not only for her character Celie, but for most of her fictional family as well. (pp. 50-2)

Despite her concentration on the brutal treatment of black women and the unmitigated abuse of children, Walker believes in the beauty and the power of the individual, and ultimately of the group. And because she does, she is willing to gamble on ways of articulating her unique vision. She is not always successful; the experimental stories of *You Can't Keep a Good Woman Down* are an example, as are the unconvincing letters from Celie's sister Nettie in Africa. However, even in the less effective works, Walker validates the necessity of struggling out of external constrictions to find meaning in one's own life. It seems quite appropriate that both her dedication and statement at the end of *The Color Purple* reaffirm and invoke the spirits of people who fill her head and her work with their voices and their presence, with the selves that come to *be* within the pages of her writing.

Certainly, in the composition of much of her work so far, Alice Walker must have felt as she did while writing **"The Revenge of Hannah Kemhuff,"** a work inspired by one of her mother's own stories: "I gathered up the historical and psychological threads of the life my ancestors lived, and in the writing...I felt joy and strength and my own continuity. I had that wonderful feeling that writers get sometimes...of being with a great many people, ancient spirits, all very happy to see me consulting and acknowledging them, and eager to let me know through the joy of their presence, that indeed, I am not alone." Perhaps this consoling vision of interconnections is one reason why Alice Walker can capture the deep layers of affirmative and destructive feelings in human beings who must live and make their lives known, and why she can compel readers to heed their messages. (pp. 52-3)

> *Thadious M. Davis, "Alice Walker's Celebration of Self in Southern Generations," in* Women Writers of the Contemporary South, *edited by Peggy Whitman Penshaw, University Press of Mississippi, 1984, pp. 39-53.*

Trudier Harris (essay date 1984)

[*In the following excerpt, Harris evaluates* The Color Purple, *stating of the work: "To complain about the novel is to commit treason against black women writers, yet there is much in it that deserves complaint . . . ."*]

The Color Purple has been canonized. I don't think it should have been. The tale of the novel's popularity is the tale of the media's ability, once again, to dictate the tastes of the reading public, and to attempt to shape what is acceptable creation by black American writers. Sadly, a book that might have been ignored if it had been published ten years earlier or later has now become *the* classic novel by a black woman. That happened in great part because the pendulum determining focus on black writers had swung in their favor again, and Alice Walker had been waiting in the wings of the feminist movement and the power it had generated long enough for her curtain call to come. . . . While it is not certain how long Alice Walker will be in the limelight for *The Color Purple,* it is certain that the damaging effects reaped by the excessive media attention given to the novel will plague us as scholars and teachers for many years to come.

The novel has become so popular that Alice Walker is almost universally recognized as a spokeswoman for black people, especially for black women, and the novel is more and more touted as a work representative of black communities in this country. The effect of the novel's popularity has been detrimental in two significant and related ways. Response to its unequaled popularity, first of all, has created a cadre of spectator readers. These readers, who do not identify with the characters and who do not feel the intensity of their pain, stand back and view the events of the novel as a circus of black human interactions that rivals anything Daniel Patrick Moynihan concocted. The spectator readers show what damage the novel can have: for them, the book reinforces racist stereotypes they may have been heir to and others of which they may have only dreamed.

The other, equally significant, detrimental effect is that the novel has been so much praised that critics, especially black women critics, have seemingly been reluctant to offer detailed, carefully considered criticisms of it. While that may be explained in part by the recent publication of the novel and by the limited access black women critics traditionally have had to publishing outlets, these possible explanations are partly outweighed by the fact that the novel has been so consistently in the public eye that it takes great effort not to write about it. *The Color Purple* silences by its dominance, a dominance perpetuated by the popular media. Those who initially found or still find themselves unable to speak out perhaps reflect in some way my own path to writing about the novel. From the time the novel appeared in 1982, I have been waging a battle with myself to record my reaction to it. For me, the process of reading, re-reading, and re-reading the novel, discussing it, then writing about it has reflected some of the major dilemmas of the black woman critic. To complain about the novel is to commit treason against black women writers, yet there is much in it that deserves complaint . . . . After all, a large number of readers, usually vocal and white, have decided that *The Color Purple* is the quintessential statement on Afro-American women and a certain kind of black lifestyle in these United States. (p. 155)

When I started asking black women how they felt about the book, there was a quiet strain of discomfort with it, a quiet tendency to criticize, but none of them would do so very aggressively. We were all faced with the idea that to criticize a novel that had been so universally complimented was somehow a desertion of the race and the black woman writer. Yet, there was a feeling of uneasiness with the novel. Instead of focusing upon the specifics of that uneasiness, however, most of the black women with whom I talked preferred instead to praise that which they thought was safe: the beautiful voice in the book and Walker's ability to capture an authentic black folk speech without all the caricature that usually typifies such efforts. They could be lukewarm toward the relationship between Celie and Shug and generally criticize Albert. However, they almost never said anything about the book's African sections until I brought them up. Do they work for you? Do you see how they're integrated into the rest of the novel? Does the voice of Nettie ring authentic and true to you? Only when assured that their ideas would not be looked upon as a desertion of black femininity would the women then proceed to offer valuable insights.

For others, though, silence about the novel was something not to be broken. One Afro-American woman critic who has written on contemporary black women writers told me that she would never write anything on the novel or make a public statement about it. Quite clearly, that was a statement in itself. Her avowed silence became a political confirmation of everything that I found problematic about the novel.

But shouldn't black women allow for diversity of interpretation of our experiences, you may ask? And shouldn't we be reluctant to prescribe a direction for our black women writers? Of course, but what we have with this novel is a situation in which many black women object to the portrayals of the characters, yet we may never hear the reasons for their objections precisely *because they are black women.* (pp. 155-56)

In Gloria Steinem's article on Alice Walker and her works, especially **The Color Purple,** which appeared in *Ms. Magazine* in June of 1982 [see excerpt dated 1982], Steinem reflects her own surprise at Walker's achievement; her response is condescending at times to a degree even beyond that latitude that might be expected in such works. She praises Walker for generally being alive, black, and able to write well. (p. 156)

Steinem focuses on the language and the morality in Walker's novel. The language I have no problem with, but then I am not one of the individuals who assumes that black women have difficulty with folk idiom. Celie's voice in the novel is powerful, engaging, subtly humorous, and incisively analytic at the basic level of human interactions. The voice is perfectly suited to the character, and Walker has breathed into it a vitality that frequently overshadows the problematic areas of concern in the novel.... The form of the book, as it relates to the folk speech, the pattern and nuances of Celie's voice, is absolutely wonderful. The clash between Celie's conception and her writing ability, however, is another issue. I can imagine a black woman of Celie's background and education talking with God, as Mariah Uphur does in Sarah E. Wright's *This Child's Gonna Live,* but writing letters to God is altogether another matter. Even if we can suspend our disbelief long enough to get beyond that hurdle, we are still confronted with the substance of the book. *What* Celie records—the degradation, abuse, dehumanization—is not only morally repulsive, but it invites spectator readers to generalize about black people in the same negative ways that have gone on for centuries. Further, how Celie grows and how she presents other characters as growing is frequently incredible and inconsistent to anyone accustomed to novels at least adhering to the worlds, logical or otherwise, that they have created.

When I read lines such as "...I'm so beside myself," "She look like she ain't long for this world but dressed well for the next," "Look like a little mouse been nibbling the biscuit, a rat run off with the ham," and "Scare me so bad I near bout drop my grip," I felt a sense of déjà vu for all the black women who made art out of conversation in the part of Alabama where I grew up.... That part of Celie I could imagine. And one might even understand, at least initially, her fear of her stepfather and the underdeveloped moral sense that leads to inactivity in response to abuse. Her lack of understanding about her pregnancy is also probable within the environment in which she grew up; as many black girls/women during those years were taught that babies were found in cabbage heads or in hollow logs.

But those years and years and years of Celie's acquiescence, extreme in their individuality, have been used too readily to affirm what the uninformed or the ill-informed believe is a general pattern of violence and abuse for black women. That is one of the dangerous consequences of the conceptualization of that powerful voice Celie has.

One of the saddest effects and the greatest irony of that voice is that, while it makes Celie articulate, it has simultaneously encouraged silence from black women, who need to be vocal in voicing their objections to, as well as their praises for, the novel. As Celie's voice has resounded publicly, it has, through its very forcefulness, cowed the voices of black women into private commentary or into silence about issues raised in the novel.

The voice led to Steinem's celebration of the wonderful morality in the novel, yet what she finds so attractive provides another source of my contention with the book. Steinem asserts that morality for Walker "is not an external dictate. It doesn't matter if you love the wrong people, or have children with more than one of them, or whether you have money, go to church, or obey the laws. What matters is cruelty, violence, keeping the truth from others who need it, suppressing someone's will or talent, taking more than you need from people or nature, and failing to choose for yourself. It's the internal morality of dignity, autonomy, and balance." What kind of morality is it that espouses that all human degradation is justified if the individual somehow survives all the tortures and uglinesses heaped upon her? Where is the dignity, autonomy, or balance in that? I am not opposed to triumph, but I do have objections to the unrealistic presentation of the path, the *process* that leads to such a triumph, especially when it is used to create a new archetype or to resurrect old myths about black women.

By no means am I suggesting that Celie should be blamed for what happens to her. My problem is with her reaction to the situation. Even slave women who found themselves abused frequently found ways of responding to that—by running away, fighting back, poisoning their masters, or through more subtly defiant acts such as spitting into the food they cooked for their masters. They did something, and Celie shares a kinship in conception if not in chronology with them. (pp. 156-57)

I found so many white women who joined Steinem in praising the novel that I read it again just to recheck my own evaluations. Then, since I was on leave at The Bunting Institute at Radcliffe and had access to a community of women, the majority of whom were white, I thought it would be fitting to test some of my ideas on them. Accordingly, I wrote a thirty-three-page article on the novel and invited women in residence at the Institute to come to a working paper session and respond to what I had written. My basic contentions were that the portrayal of Celie was unrealistic for the time in which the novel was set, that Nettie and the letters from Africa were really extraneous to the central concerns of the novel, that the lesbian relationship in the book represents the height of silly romanticism, and that the epistolary form of the novel ultimately makes Celie a much more sophisticated character than we are initially led to believe....

During that session, I discovered that some white women did not like the novel, but they were not the ones controlling publications like *Ms.* One white woman commented that, if she had not been told the novel had been written by a black woman, she would have thought it had been written by a Southern white male who wanted to reinforce the traditional sexual and violent stereotypes about black people. That comment affirmed one of my major objections to the thematic development of the novel: The book simply added a freshness to many of the ideas circulating in the popular culture and captured in racist literature that suggested that black people have no morality when it comes to sexuality, that black family structure is weak if existent at all, that black men abuse black women, and that black women who may appear to be churchgoers are really lewd and lascivious.

The novel gives validity to all the white racist's notions of pathology in black communities. For these spectator readers, black fathers and father-figures are viewed as being immoral, sexually unrestrained. Black males and females form units without the benefit of marriage, or they easily dissolve marriages in order to form less structured, more promiscuous relationships. Black men beat their wives—or attempt to—and neglect, ignore, or abuse their children. When they cannot control their wives through beatings, they violently dispatch them. The only stereotype that is undercut in the book is that of the matriarch. Sofia, who comes closest in size and personality to the likes of Lorraine Hansberry's Mama Lena Younger and comparable characters, is beaten, imprisoned, and nearly driven insane precisely because of her strength.

The women had fewer comments on the section on Africa, but generally agreed that it was less engaging than other parts of the novel. I maintained that the letters from Africa were like the whaling chapters in *Moby Dick*—there more for the exhibition of a certain kind of knowledge than for the good of the work. (p. 157)

Other women from that session also commented on Walker's excessively negative portrayal of black men—not a new criticism leveled against her—and some thought the lesbian relationship was problematic. There were others, though, who couldn't see what all the fuss was about, who said that they had simply enjoyed reading the novel. I had no trouble with their enjoyment of the novel as a response to reading it; my problems centered on the reasons for their finding it so enjoyable. Those who did generally mentioned the book's affirmation: that Celie is able to find happiness after so many horrible things have happened to her. That is a response that would probably please Walker, who has indicated that the character Celie is based on her great-grand-mother, who was raped at twelve by her slaveholding master. In reparation to a woman who had suffered such pain, Walker has explained: "I liberated her from her own history.... I wanted her to be happy." It is this clash between history and fiction, in part, that causes the problems with the novel.

On the way to making Celie happy, Walker portrays her as a victim of many imaginable abuses and a few unimaginable ones. Celie is a woman who *believes* she is ugly, and she centers that belief on her blackness. While this is not a new problem with some black women, a black woman character conceived in 1982 who is still heir to the same kinds of problems that characters had who were conceived decades earlier is problematic for me—especially since Celie makes a big deal of how ugly she believes she is. But, you may say, how can a woman affirm any standard of beauty in an environment in which men are so abusive? Allowance for the fact that Celie is "living" in the 1940s really does not gainsay the criticism about this aspect of her conception. I would say in response that Nettie was there during Celie's early years, and Nettie apparently has a rather positive conception of herself. If Celie believes her about some things, why not about others? Instead, Celie gives in to her environment with a kind of passivity that comes near to provoking screams in readers not of the specta-tor variety who may be guilty of caring too much about the characters. Before she can be made to be happy, Celie is forced to relive the history of many Afro-American women who found themselves in unpleasant circumstances, but few of them seem to have undergone such an intuitive devaluation of themselves....I can imagine Celie existing forever in her situation if some-one else did not come along to "stir her root life," as Jean Toomer would say, "and teach her to dream." It is that burying away of the instinctive desire to save one's self that makes me in part so angry about Celie—in addition to all those ugly things that happen to her. Plowing a man's fields for twenty years and letting him use her body as a sperm depository leaves Celie so buried away from herself that it is hard to imagine anything stirring her to life—just as it is equally hard to imagine her being so deadened. Ah—the dilemma.

Celie does have an awareness of right and wrong that comes from outside herself—as well as the one she will develop from her own experiences. She knows that Albert's abuse of her is wrong just as she knew her stepfather's sexual exploitation of her was wrong. And she does go to church; whether or not she believes what she hears, certainly something of the Christian philoso-phy seeps into her consciousness over the years. There are guidelines for action, therefore, to which she can compare her own situation and respond. Also, consider-ing the fact that she cannot have children with Albert, the traditional reason for enduring abuse—one's chil-dren—is absent in her case. So why does she stay? (pp. 157-58)

From the beginning of the novel, even as Walker presents Celie's sexual abuse by her stepfather, there is an element of fantasy in the book. Celie becomes the ugly duckling who will eventually be redeemed through suffering. This trait links her to all the heroines of fairy tales from Cinderella to Snow White. Instead of the abusive stepmother as the villain, the stepfather plays that role. He devalues Celie in direct proportion to Nettie's valuing of her; unfortunately, as an inexperienced rather than an adult godmother, Nettie lacks the ability to protect Celie. The clash between youth and age, between power and powerlessness begins the mixed-media approach of the novel. Celie's predicament may be real, but she is forced to deal with it in terms that are antithetical to the reality of her condition. (p. 159)

The fabulist/fairy-tale mold of the novel is ultimately incongruous with and does not serve well to frame its message. When things turn out happily in those traditional tales, we are asked to affirm the basic pattern and message: Good triumphs over evil. But what does *The Color Purple* affirm? What were all those women who applauded approving of? It affirms, first of all, patience and long-suffering—perhaps to a greater degree than that exhibited by Cinderella or by the likes of Elizabeth Grimes in James Baldwin's *Go Tell It on the Mountain.* In true fairy-tale fashion, it affirms passivity; heroines in those tales do little to help themselves. It affirms silence in the face of, if not actual allegiance to, cruelty. It affirms secrecy concerning violence and violation. It affirms, saddest of all, the myth of the American Dream becoming a reality for black Americans, even those who are "dirt poor," as one of my colleagues phrascd it, and those who are the "downest" and "outest." The fable structure thereby perpetuates a lie in holding out to blacks a non-existent or minimally existent hope for a piece of that great American pie. The clash of characters who presumably contend with and in the real world with the idealistic, suprarealistic quality and expectations of fairy-tale worlds places a burden on the novel that diffuses its message and guarantees possibilities for unintended interpretations.

With its mixture of message, form, and character, *The Color Purple* reads like a political shopping list of all the IOUs Walker felt that it was time to repay. She pays homage to the feminists by portraying a woman who struggles through adversity to assert herself against almost impossible odds. She pays homage to the lesbians by portraying a relationship between two women that reads like a schoolgirl fairy tale in its ultimate adherence to the convention of the happy resolution. She pays homage to black nationalists by opposing colonialism, and to Pan Africanism by suggesting that yes, indeed, a black American does understand and sympathize with the plight of her black brothers and sisters thousands of miles across the ocean. And she adds in a few other obeisances—to career-minded women in the characters of Mary Agnes and Shug, to born-again male feminists in the character of Albert,

and to black culture generally in the use of the blues and the folk idiom. (p. 160)

I *will* teach *The Color Purple* again—precisely because of the teachability engendered by its controversiality. I will be angry again because I am not a spectator to what happens to Celie; for me, the novel *demands* participation. I will continue to react to all praise of the novel by asserting that mere praise ignores the responsibility that goes along with it—we must clarify as much as we can the reasons that things are being praised and enumerate as best we can the consequences of that praise. I will continue to read and re-read the novel, almost in self-defense against the continuing demands for discussions and oral evaluations of it. Perhaps—and other black women may share this response—I am caught in a love/hate relationship with *The Color Purple;* though my crying out against it might be comparable to spitting into a whirlwind in an effort to change its course, I shall nevertheless purse my lips. (pp. 160-61)

Trudier Harris, "On 'The Color Purple', Stereotypes, and Silence," in Black American Literature Forum, *Vol. 18, No. 4, Winter, 1984, pp 155-61.*

Richard Wesley (essay date 1986)

[*In the excerpt below, Wesley addresses the "men-bashing" controversy surrounding* The Color Purple. *He concludes: "As an African-American male, I found little that was offensive . . . in either the novel or the movie."*]

Although shut out as a winner at the 1986 Academy Awards, [*The Color Purple*] is easily the best-known and most controversial film of the 1985-86 movie season. Alice Walker, creator of the story, has been praised on one side as a major heroine and giant in American literature, and vilified on the other as a traitor to her race, a marginal talent upon whom praise is heaped because she is a woman, and as a pawn/weapon employed by white men to subjugate black men, whom they view as their natural enemy in the continuing struggle over male power.

In a strange and wonderful way, these wildly divergent reactions are a testament to the power and talent of Alice Walker. Like the best writers of any era, she has probed deeply into the soul of the nation in which she was bred and, in doing so, has brought to light our country's dark secrets.

As an African-American male, I found little that was offensive as far as the images of black men portrayed in either the novel or in the movie goes, though there were times I did think, "Alice Walker doth protest too much."

What angers black men as they read [*The Color Purple*], or watch the film version, is that *all* the black men are portrayed as fools; the women are portrayed as noble and long-suffering. If they have any weaknesses, they are weaknesses seemingly brought about by their long association with these foolish men. Walker had a point to make, and she had no need to include those black men who, with the help of the women in their lives, raised large families, sent their children off to school and into productive lives.

Black people from poor, impoverished southern rural backgrounds can tell endless stories about such men. They were not from middle-class backgrounds, nor did they have much in the way of education. They lived just down the road from where Celie and Mister lived. Many black men were upset that Alice Walker chose to paint a picture in which these men did not exist. I was not "upset," but I was disappointed. (p. 62)

We may understand the sociological conditions that might explain Mister, but there are some black men who are going to be brutes no matter what the circumstances of their lives. Mister behaves the way he does because he can get away with it. He has the power. He reflects the prevailing attitudes of male privilege. As long as black men seek to imitate the power structure that crushes them, as long as black women support this sad act of imitation and intimidation, and as long as black women submit to the idea that they have done something to deserve a lowly status in life and in the eyes of their husbands, then the morbid relationship of Celie, the oppressed, and Mister, the oppressed oppressor, will continue to be played out in homes all across America.

My feelings about **The Color Purple** put me directly at odds with many black artists, social leaders, civic leaders, and ordinary citizens all over the United States who *do* have enormous problems with the novel and with the film. That is their prerogative and I respect it.

What I do not respect, however, is the behavior of others in my community who have taken it upon themselves to be guardians of the black image. (pp. 62, 90)

These image tribunes are most often black males, usually in their thirties and older. They almost always seem to base their attacks on political concepts developed in the community during the turbulent days of the 1960s. For these men, the Black Power ideology of that time has remained sacrosanct and is in no need of revision. Part of the ideology requires black men and women to pull together. However, the unity of black men and women can only exist if the man *leads*. Therefore the woman must "submit": remain silent on sensitive issues. You do not "disrespect" your man in public, that is, criticize him in public, or speak too loudly about things that matter to you, or interrupt him when he is conversing with friends or colleagues on "serious" issues. A woman must always defer to her man and subjugate her will to his.

Few black men in their right minds will come out and couch their objections to Walker's novel in those terms, but you can hear echoes of those sentiments in much of their criticism of her: Walker is airing dirty linen in

public. She is reminding many of us men of our own failures. She is reminding women of *their* failures as well. She is saying that Black is Beautiful, but not necessarily always *right*. A lot of people do not want to hear that.

I find all this especially surprising given that in past years when black male authors such as Chester Himes in *The Primitive* or John A. Williams in *The Man Cried I Am* decried both directly and indirectly the black woman's lack of faith and support of them, no one said a word. We should never forget that the 1950s and 1960s were a time when many black male authors rose to prominence by writing plays and novels in which black women were portrayed as castrating shrews who stunted their sons' growth by criticizing and denigrating them at every opportunity. The silence at the time was deafening.

If black women writers such as Gayl Jones, Audre Lorde, Ntozake Shange, or Alice Walker are to be hounded from one end of the country to the other for decrying the insensitivity of black men to black women, then should not those black male writers such as Ishmael Reed be brought before some of these "image tribunals" to account for *their* literary transgressions? But more important, there should be *no* "tribunals" *at all*. No one in America—and black America, especially—should be telling writers what they may or may not say. Writers are the antennae of any society. They have to speak when others dare not. The years-long stagnation of the once-vital Black Arts Movement of the 1960s and 1970s is only the latest example of what can happen when ideology is allowed to dominate thought. (pp. 90-1)

Richard Wesley, "'The Color Purple' Debate: Reading between the Lines," in Ms., Vol. XV, No. 3, September, 1986, pp. 62, 90-2.

Alice Walker with Jean W. Ross (interview date 1988)

[*The following interview, conducted by telephone in 1988, first appeared in* Contemporary Authors New Revision Series, Vol. 27. *Here, Walker recounts the writing of* The Color Purple *and discusses her other novels, short stories, and poetry.*]

[Ross]: *Before* **The Color Purple,** *which won you both the Pulitzer and the American Book Award and was made into a very popular movie, you had to your credit two earlier novels, two short story collections, four volumes of poetry, and a respectable body of essays and critical writing. Has* **The Color Purple** *brought a large general readership to your other writings?*

[Walker]: Yes. I would say that I now reach many more people.

You've described the way the characters of **The Color Purple** *came to you, demanding first that you move from Brooklyn to a quieter place and finally that you give up* *just about everything else to listen to their voices. Were any of them difficult to capture once you had settled into the conditions they seemed to require?*

I wasn't trying to capture them; it was really just the opposite, more a matter of being in a place where they could be free, where they wouldn't *feel* captured, they wouldn't feel pressed, they wouldn't feel anything but just at home. Partly that is because they are all parts of myself, composites and memories and reconstructions, with lots of help from the intangibles.

Did the characters go away completely after you finished the book?

I have to explain that describing them as voices and spirits coming to me is a way of making it easier for people who don't write to understand what it feels like actually to create something. I do feel visited; all of my characters are absolutely right there in the house with me, and I often think about what one or the other one would say about something, or how something would look to them, or what would make them laugh and what would make them cry. I think of how they would say things. In a sense, then, they're always with me. They have lives, so they're still talking and commenting; they're still company for me. But they're not necessarily saying things that I will write. They're just free.

How early did you know the story would take the epistolary form?

I think almost from the beginning, just because that is so organic. It was the only thing I could use to keep Nettie and Celie connected, since Nettie was in Africa and Celie was in Georgia. There was no telephone; Celie would not have been able to use a telegraph machine. They had letters, and that was it. So the decision about the form was fairly simple.

*There has been some very vocal resentment of the way you've portrayed your men. In the essay **"In the Closet of the Soul,"** collected in your new book, **Living by the Word,** you responded to that. Do you see the resentment as positive in some ways?*

Yes, I think it has been wonderful. It has given a lot of people an insight into the art, if you can call it an art, of criticism itself, because many people who never thought about it before, many people who have actually read my work and who had a very different response to all of it than the critics had, now have an understanding of some of the things that critics do in criticizing work—things that have nothing to do with the work or the writer, but have to do with whatever subject matter the critics are themselves interested in projecting. Sometimes they're just capitalizing on the publicity of somebody else's work; they inject themselves and use it as a platform.

How much of a hand did you have in the movie?

I was a consultant; I was available to them for questions, and I advised them on as many things as they could think of and as I could think of. They used a lot of my

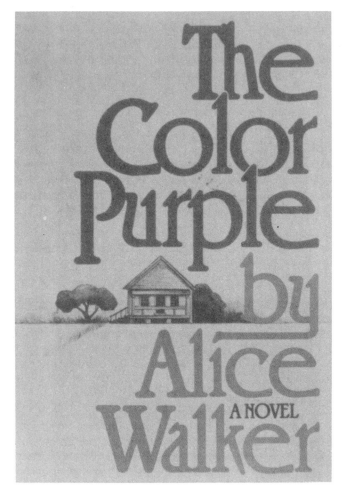

Dust jacket of Walker's most acclaimed work.

suggestions from the script I had written. I spent as much time on the set as I could, which turned out to be about half the time.

In your interview with John O'Brien that was originally published in Interviews with Black Writers, *you said that not a single line of the first draft for* The Third Life of Grange Copeland, *your first novel, ended up in the book. Has your other writing been revised anywhere near so heavily?*

It's been a totally different experience each time. In fact, **The Color Purple** was written originally almost entirely the way it appears in the book. There was an article in the *New York Times Magazine* for which they photographed some of the manuscript pages, and they're really identical in most cases with the final book. I think it had to do with the kind of solitude I wrote it in.

I wrote **The Third Life of Grange Copeland** while living in Mississippi in the middle of incredible racial turmoil, and sometimes terror and silence and craziness. That was also the time of giving birth—I finished the book three days before my daughter was born. And I moved several times while I was writing that book. It was a very different kind of writing. I was trying to capture something—then I *was* trying to capture something: partly the slipping away of a way of life. That was what I was trying to capture for myself, to remember a way of life that was changing and at the same time write this book which looks at, among other things, a lot of violence now in families and a lot of love in families and intergenerational relationships. It was very different. They're all very different.

Reviewing your second novel, **Meridian,** *for* Newsweek, *Margot Jefferson noted that you have "a Southern writer's love for storytelling." You have written about your mother's stories and what they've meant to you. Do you feel that your roots as a writer go back to that tradition?*

Yes, I do. And beyond my own mother, I think the South has always been a place where the oral tradition has been given credit. It's been respected. Before television, the storyteller was it. The storyteller and the musician were deeply loved. When you saw them coming down the road, you knew that you had a good evening ahead of you. This is true in so many parts of the world today. We go to Bali a good bit (we've been twice and hope to go again), and it's like coming back to the same culture that I grew up in. They tell stories, and the storyteller is respected. They present shadow puppets and little plays and dramas. Their culture is still very folk-oriented.

Your poetry was the first thing published. Had you been writing poetry since the injury to your eye when you were eight, which you've said paradoxically enabled you "really to see people and things"?

I think the poetry that I actually *call* poetry didn't start coming until I was a teenager. Then at Spelman College I started writing poetry in a more conscious way and actually published some poems in the college magazine. I started writing fiction when I transferred to Sarah Lawrence.

In **"How Poems Are Made/A Discredited View"** (Horses **Make a Landscape Look More Beautiful**) *there's the verse "Letting go / in order to hold on / I gradually understand / how poems are made." Has the process of making poetry, or your feelings about it, changed over the years you've been doing it?*

I think so. I haven't actually considered how the process has changed, but I think that my poems today are more about the world outside myself. It is more definitely a poetry of reclaiming ancient, global connections that I wasn't aware of when I was younger. I love writing poetry—it must be the next best thing to singing beautifully.

How well do you think black women are doing in terms of self-image and of actually having a strong voice in society?

I think they're doing well. Obviously there are so many black women and white women and Native American women who aren't doing well, who are having more children than they can take care of and bad relationships and no money and no jobs. But, given where we are in the United States, the racism and the sexism and the economy and the predominant culture, which is not affirming of us, I think black women do remarkably well and manage to have very strong voices and very positive hearts. In my life, I tend to see a lot of these women.

You're a champion and master of black folk speech. Would you comment on the problems involved in preserving that heritage while needing to deal on most levels in standard English? What sort of mix seems ideal to you?

I use them both naturally. In speaking to you, I speak in the language we both understand, and it's perfectly easy to do. But when I'm speaking to my mother it's in black folk English; and if my grandmother and grandfather were alive and I were speaking to them, I'd do the same. It's the language they spoke, and we'd understand that. Sometimes in speaking to people who are my peers but would have parents and grandparents like mine and would therefore understand the old language, I use the language of my grandparents. It's very cozy; it immediately creates a world. We know immediately where we're from, who our people are. It's like having your own country.

For me, speaking the old language is a matter of loving it. There's almost no other way that I can see my grandmother's face. I have no clear photograph of her; and even if I did, it wouldn't work as well as using her language. When I use her language, I can see her face, I can smell her kitchen, and I can feel her hands. All of that is in the language.

In teaching black literature, there's a similar problem, which is to retain the feeling for its special qualities while presenting it as a real part of the larger body of literature. What thoughts do you have on teaching it?

The ideal is to have a teacher who loves it and really understands its value. I think it's always fairly useless for people to try to teach something that they don't care about or that they think is not what they should be teaching. In a way, I wonder if it could ever be taught really well in schools by just anyone; I tend to think not. I think that our literature, like Native American literature, should be taught by people who love it. That is the way it will have a life. I say that partly because I sometimes run into teachers who teach my work and who obviously resent it. They resent the work, they resent my point of view, they resent having to teach women, they resent having to teach black people. In that case, it would be just as well not to have them try to do it, but to have people who really love it, and really understand it, do it.

Do you find the growing body of critical writing on black literature cogent and useful, by and large?

I don't read much of the awful criticism, where the intention of the critic is to wound or maim. I think a lot of criticism has become very debased, that it's not helpful. It's not helpful to the writer, it's not helpful to the reader, and it's not even helpful to the critic, because there's so much meanness, often, and a real inability to get into the heart of the writer and try to see the world through the heart of the writer. But of course there's some really astonishingly wonderful criticism being written and published. I recently received an amazing book called *Conjuring: Black Women, Fiction, and Literary Tradition*, edited by Marjorie Pryse and Hortense Spillers. I also see on my desk Mary Helen Washington's latest book, *Invented Lives: Narratives of Black Women 1860-1960*. And there are many other excellent critics doing exemplary work: critics who are as interested in nurturing and healing the reader as the writer is. I think of Sherley Anne Williams, Deborah McDowell, Barbara Christian, Lorraine Bethel (a superb critic from whom not enough is heard). I thank the Goddess for these scholars!

You wrote in the 1970 essay **"Duties of a Black Revolutionary Artist,"** *now collected in* **In Search of Our Mother's Gardens,** *"My major advice to young black artists would be that they should shut themselves up somewhere away from all debates about who they are and what color they are and just turn out paintings and poems and stories and novels." Would you revise that at all eighteen years later?*

No, because in that it is assumed that the rest of the time they are right in the middle of life, of struggle, of everything else that's happening in the world. I know from my own experience that it's very hard to create something whole in the midst of a society in which everything is fragmented. You do have to get away and take those long walks and sit by the the water and let your self come to you. One of the great dangers in a society that is so fragmented, so chaotic, is the loss of the self and the filling in of what would have been the self with TV. What you often have is a society full of people who are empty of themselves but full of television. This will never create art; this will only create more Big Macs to munch.

Tell me about your publishing venture Wild Trees Press, and how it's going.

It's going well, but I think we're going to be shifting to something else. We've published six books now, and it's very difficult because we're only three people. My partner and I are both writers, and we're both working on books—actually we've just finished two books of our own. We have just published a book by a Balinese painter. He came here from Bali last night and is downstairs now. We're going to launch his book over the next couple of weeks. But it takes an awful lot of energy, and a lot of money; it takes a lot of our time. So I think we're going to rest from it for a bit and maybe do something else or just concentrate on our own work. We haven't decided. It's been great, though. It's been a wonderful experience to publish beautiful books and be on the other side of the publishing process; we're now learning what publishers are up against in dealing with writers.

Gloria Steinem, in her Ms. *article on you in June, 1982 [see excerpt dated 1982], testified to the closeness your readers feel to you. Do you hear a great deal from them?*

I do. I get lots and lots of letters, and generally I just *feel* them. They write, and when I see them in this part of the world, Northern California, I'm always aware of my community, the people who support me and the people who tell me that they've been moved or touched by reading something that I've written, or that some aspect of their lives has been changed by it. This is very good. In fact, during the critical attacks that people made on me and **The Color Purple**—especially the movie, when that came out—I was aware of the presence of those people who support me. The negative criticism was more than balanced by the hundreds of letters that came from people who testified out of their own lives to say, This happened to me when I was five, I was so happy to have something I could look at that was outside of myself, and yet I could see myself in it; that made it easier for me to deal with stuff that I hadn't wanted to look at for thirty years. And so on.

It's obvious from what you've written about them that your mother's gardens have served you well as both inspiration and metaphor. Do you tend a garden of your own now, a literal garden?

I do, yes—a literal garden. In fact, just last week I planted a hundred more onions, my first batch of corn, my tomatoes, my beans, my eggplant, my artichokes, everything. I do garden, and it's lovely.

Is the quiet place still the environment you need to do your thinking and writing in?

Yes. The first thing I did, even before I could afford it, was find some acreage up in the northern part of the state with a little shack on it. It was literally a shack, actually sliding down the hill, it was so shacky. But I knew that I had to have a place that I could retire to, in the sense of getting away: *repair* to, as people used to say. It's been good; it's been the best thing I've ever done, next to having my daughter.

Besides **Living by the Word,** *there's the new children's book made from your earlier short story* **"To Hell with Dying"** *and, I believe, another children's book in the works.*

Yes. The next children's book is *Finding the Green Stone*, and it will be illustrated by the same wonderful illustrator who collaborated with me on the last one, Catherine Deeter.

What's beyond that that you can talk about—or is it still and always a matter of waiting for the voices?

My new novel. I can't talk about it, but I've finished it, and it's called *The Temple of My Familiar.* It's about the last five hundred thousand years. Beyond that there are several other things planned. But I can't ever talk about work that's ahead; that seems to curtail my sense of freedom. And it doesn't really involve voices; it just involves more time. (pp. 471-74)

> *Alice Walker with Jean W. Ross, in an interview in* Contemporary Authors, New Revision Series, Vol. 27, *edited by Hal May and James G. Lesniak, Gale Research Inc., 1988, pp. 471-74.*

David Nicholson (essay date 1989)

[*In the excerpt below, Nicholson expresses his disappointment with* The Temple of My Familiar, *describing it as "a fragmented hodge-podge."*]

With *The Temple of My Familiar,* Alice Walker seems to have been striving to write a *big* book, the kind writers used to feel they had to write at a certain point in their careers—a significant book jampacked with compelling characters and dealing with the great social and political issues of an age. It would be nice to report that Walker has succeeded, but reading this new novel is much like watching a little girl parade, all dressed up in her mother's clothes and high heels. One may applaud her cuteness, but it is awfully hard to take her seriously.

The central problem is that this is not a novel so much as it is an ill-fitting collection of speeches, a *faux*-hip tract for the New Puritanism, a manifesto for the Fascism of the New Age. *The Temple of My Familiar* has no plot in the conventional sense of the word, only a series of strung-together stories in which things happen without rhyme or reason. There are no characters, only types representative of the world Walker lives in or wishes could be. And there is no dialogue between these characters. Instead, they are politically correct speeches grounded in knee-jerk feminism (which Walker calls "womanism") and the same catalogue of goofy California enthusiasms—vegetarianism, crystals, massage, psychology, talking to plants, trees and animals, past life regression—that characterized to wretched excess her recent collection of essays, *Living by the Word.*

As it has no conventional structure, it is difficult to summarize *The Temple of My Familiar.* There are several couples: Carlotta (daughter of a widowed Latin American refugee) and Arveyda (a musician reminiscent of the rock star Prince); Hal and Lissie, two older people originally (though this is never quite made clear) from the South Carolina Sea Islands and now living in Baltimore; and Suwelo (a professor of American history who has adopted an African name) and Fanny, his former wife, a woman in search of herself.

Walker's theme appears to be the difficulty of love, the pain men and women must pass through to find themselves and each other, for each of these couples must confront and overcome some internal crisis. It's worth noting here that, as this is womanist fiction, women suffer, but do no wrong. Men though, are dangerous children infatuated with power and violence, except for those few willing to allow their mates the "space" to search for some mysterious personal fulfillment, and those (even fewer) who have given up their anger and aggression for the satisfaction of bread-baking, vegetarianism, shawl-wearing and soft, plant-fiber sandals.

All of this—the individual passages from fragmentation to wholeness, even the New Age inanities—might be more meaningful had Walker made the characters' dilemmas more powerful. But nothing is dramatized sufficiently, only told flatly with a marked absence of passion. We are told, for example, that there is something missing in Arveyda's life because he does not know who his father is, but not shown how this loss affects him. We are told, not shown, that Carlotta is bereft when she learns that her mother and Arveyda have slept together. And we are told of, and not shown, the disintegration of Suwelo and Fanny's marriage because of Fanny's quest for freedom.

Then, too, Carlotta and Arveyda and Hal and Lissie and Suwelo and Fanny spend page after tiresome page talking to each other. . . . Yet somehow, despite all the talk, despite the ranging among the centuries and from country to country, none of the conflict, none of the dilemmas these people find themselves caught between ever becomes very real. One reads, but does not believe.

It is hard, of course, to be moved by the despair of characters blessed with such material goods as saunas, whirlpool baths, sailboats, country homes in Marin County and recording studios in town homes with views of the Golden Gate Bridge. In the end, however, it is of more consequence that the characters fail to move us because Walker has denied them their integrity—their contrariness, their freedom to be wrong. Instead, she has imposed her consciousness upon them. Many of the stories are told in the first person but, oddly enough, none of the characters sounds like himself; all—from Guatuzocan-born Carlotta to Hal to Fanny—sound alike. After a while the reader realizes that this is the voice of a West Coast intellectual, perhaps even the voice of Walker herself.

The Color Purple, Walker's best-selling novel, was also told in the first person and contained, in germ, some of the same themes. The difference there was that Celie's and Nettie's voices were so real, so right, the reader was willing to overlook the shift in point of view midway through the novel and its dishonest, anachronistic happy ending. Here there are only glimmers of the tough forthrightness that characterized *The Color Purple,* glimmers of what might have been, had Walker not fallen victim to her own publicity or had her editor been courageous enough to save her from her own excess. What Walker has given us [in *The Temple of My Familiar*] is a fragmented hodge-podge, and that is all the more sad because so much of her earlier work was so good, breaking ground that allowed black women (and men) to look at themselves and their lives in new ways. (pp. 3, 5)

> David Nicholson, "Alice Walker Trips," in Book World—The Washington Post, *May 7, 1989, pp. 3, 5.*

Lisa Failer (essay date 1991)

[*In the following excerpt, Failer offers a mixed review of Walker's most recent book of poetry,* Her Blue Body Everything We Know.]

In the preface to this book of collected and new poems [**Her Blue Body Everything We Know**] Alice Walker writes: "In keeping faith with Poetry's honest help to me, I have not deleted or changed—beyond a word or two—anything I have written, though greatly tempted at times to do so.

"The young self, the naive self, the ill or wounded self, the angry and hurt self, appear doubly vulnerable now, in light of my unexpected bonus of years, and the experience they have brought me. I embrace them all, as Poetry has embraced me."

Within this very personal definition of poetry lie both the strengths and the weaknesses of Walker's verse. When the poems succeed, they evoke a kind of raw beauty; when they fail, it's for lack of polish.

But with each successive collection, Walker is able to comfortably mix experience and art. As the poet moves in her own life from marriage to motherhood, and as these and other relationships break apart or strengthen, the emotions and the poetry grow more sophisticated and ambiguous, less naively uniform.

While in this new collection the poems take on the political and personal issues of race, gender, environment, love, hate and suffering, the middle and later work speaks with more authority. The poems, though often angry, penetrate appearances to reveal the underlying complexities. Love becomes not just love but a little bit of hate, and hate carries with it the promise of forgiveness, as in the poem **"Good Night, Willie Lee, I'll See You in the Morning"**:

> Looking down into my father's
> dead face
> for the last time
> my mother said without
> tears, without smiles
> without regrets
> but with civility
> "Good night, Willie Lee, I'll see you
> in the morning."
> And it was then I knew that the healing
> of all our wounds
> is forgiveness
> that permits a promise
> of our return
> in the end.

The new poems in the last section of the book, as a whole, are not Walker's strongest. Yet themes of reconciliation that resound through the collection appear here as poignant hopes for the future: for a planet on which all beings can be comfortable, for societies that can accept new leaders who will heal the political world and connect us to our beginnings, from which, it is implied, we can start again.

Her Blue Body Everything We Know is a huge and varied collection. But from the naive to the mature, the work possesses a wholeness. If it doesn't exhibit unflinching poetic genius, it does point to a life in which poetry has always been spoken.

> Lisa Failer, "Lifetime Collection Reveals the Metrical Alice Walker," in Detroit Free Press, *May 19, 1991, p. 7H.*

FURTHER READING

Bobo, Jacqueline. "Sifting Through the Controversy: Reading *The Color Purple.*" *Callaloo* 12, No. 2 (Spring 1989): 332-42.
> Discusses the controversy surrounding *The Color Purple* and public reaction to the film.

Bradley, David. "Novelist Alice Walker Telling the Black Women's Story." *The New York Times Magazine* (8 January 1984): 25-37.
> Extensive biographical profile of Walker, interspersed with critical analysis of her work.

Callaloo 12, No. 2 (Spring 1989).
> Special issue devoted to Walker, with essays and reviews by Theodore O. Mason, Jr., Joseph A. Brown, and Keith Byerman.

Coetzee, J. M. "The Beginnings of (Wo)man in Africa."
The New York Times Book Review (30 April 1989): 7.
> Mixed review of *The Temple of My Familiar.* The critic concludes: "*The Temple of My Familiar* is a novel only in a loose sense. Rather, it is a mixture of mythic fantasy, revisionary history, exemplary biography and sermon. It is short on narrative tension, long on inspirational message."

Fowler, Carolyn. "Solid at the Core." *Freedomways* 14, No. 1 (First Quarter 1974): 59-62.
> Discusses the strengths and weaknesses of *In Love and Trouble.*

Hollister, Michael. "Tradition in Alice Walker's 'To Hell with Dying'." *Studies in Short Fiction* 26, No. 1 (Winter 1989): 90-94.
> Summary and critical overview of Walker's short story for children "To Hell with Dying."

Iannone, Carol. "A Turning of the Critical Tide?" *Commentary* 88, No. 5 (November 1989): 57-9.

Examines critical response to *The Color Purple* and *The Temple of My Familiar.* Of the former work, the critic writes: "One cannot help thinking that the reason critics managed to applaud *The Color Purple* in the teeth of so many flaws was itself political—the necessity to welcome the voice of a poor black woman, and a lesbian at that, into the mainstream of contemporary literature."

Ingoldby, Grace. "Fall Out." *New Statesman* 108, No. 2791, (14 September 1984): 32.
Explores characterization in *You Can't Keep a Good Woman Down.*

Petry, Alice Hall. "Alice Walker: The Achievement of the Short Fiction." *Modern Language Studies* 19, No. 1 (Winter 1989): 12-27.
Evaluates Walker's short stories, concluding that Walker is an uneven writer.

Pollitt, Katha. "Stretching the Short Story." *The New York Times Book Review* (24 May 1981): 9, 15.
Praises Walker's willingness to explore controversial topics in *You Can't Keep a Good Woman Down* but faults her perceived tendency to depict all black women as victims of racism and sexism.

Margaret Walker

1915-

(Full name Margaret Abigail Walker Alexander) American poet, novelist, and critic.

A writer whose career spans five decades, Walker experienced first-hand two of the most exciting periods in the history of black American literature: the Harlem Renaissance of the 1920s and the Black Aesthetic Movement of the 1960s. She began her career under the guidance of Langston Hughes in the 1930s and has since emerged as a "literary mother" to a crop of new writers like Nikki Giovanni, Alice Walker, and Sonia Sanchez. Walker's reputation as a writer rests chiefly on *For My People* (1942), *Jubilee* (1966), and *Prophets for a New Day* (1970)—three works that reflect Walker's long-standing devotion to the heritage of black American culture.

"I was born on the seventh day of the seventh month of the year," Walker told an interviewer in 1988. "My mother was her mother's seventh child, and my father was his mother's seventh child. I am the child of the parents of seven, and my grandmother said, 'You are born lucky'." Margaret Abigail was born in 1915 in Birmingham, Alabama, to Reverend Sigismund C. Walker and Marion Dozier Walker. As a child she developed a deep and abiding interest in books and literature. In the 1920s she began reading the works of the Harlem Renaissance poets—particularly Langston Hughes—and started writing poems herself when she was twelve years old. "I think Langston's poetry and his life have influenced me remarkably from the time I was a child," she recalled. "I saw him first when I was about sixteen years old and halfway through college. He read my poetry and encouraged me to write." Walker maintained a friendship with Hughes for the next thirty-five years. W. E. B. Du Bois further encouraged Walker by publishing her poem "I Want to Write"—formerly "Daydreaming"—in the *Crisis,* the magazine he founded, when Walker was nineteen years old. In this early work Walker stated: "I want to write / I want to write the songs of my people. / I want to hear them singing melodies in the dark. / I want to catch the last floating strains from their sob-torn throats. / I want to frame their dreams into words; their souls into notes."

Walker attended Northwestern University and, in her senior year, became involved with the WPA Writers' Project, where she developed a friendship with Richard Wright. Both writers benefited greatly from the relationship; Walker helped Wright do research for *Native Son,* and Wright, in turn, helped Walker revise and refine her poetry. In 1939, however, Wright abruptly ended his relationship with the poet. In *A Poetic Equation: Conversations between Nikki Giovanni and Margaret Walker* (1974), Walker recalled: "Some mutual 'friends' told him some kind of lie. They said that I had said

something. I don't know what they told him, but he became inarticulate with rage." Wright later wrote to Walker, but she refused his letters. After leaving the WPA, Walker returned to school and obtained a master's degree from the University of Iowa. Two years later, in 1942, she published her first collection of poetry, *For My People.* Winner of the Yale Younger Poets Series Award, the poems in *For My People* honor ordinary blacks who, "faced with terrible obstacles which haunt Black people's very existence, not only survive but prevail—with style," according to Eugenia Collier.

Walker followed *For My People* with *Jubilee,* a historical novel about a slave family during and after the Civil War. The novel took Walker thirty years to complete. During these years, she married a disabled veteran, raised four children, taught full time at Jackson State College in Mississippi, and earned a Ph.D. from the University of Iowa. The lengthy gestation, she asserted, partly accounts for the book's quality. As she told

Claudia Tate in *Black Women Writers at Work*, "Living with the book over a long period of time was agonizing. Despite all of that, *Jubilee* is the product of a mature person." She continued: "There's a difference between writing about something and living through it. . . . I did both." The story of *Jubilee*'s main characters Vyry and Randall Ware was an important part of Walker's life even before she began to write it down. As she explained in *How I Wrote "Jubilee"* (1972), she first heard about the "slavery time" in bedtime stories told by her maternal grandmother. When old enough to recognize the value of her family history, Walker took initiative, "prodding" her grandmother for more details and promising to set down on paper the story that had taken shape in her mind. Later on, she conducted extensive research on every aspect of the black experience during the Civil War. "Most of my life I have been involved with writing this story about my great-grandmother, and even if *Jubilee* were never considered an artistic or commercial success I would still be happy just to have finished it," she revealed.

Critical reactions to *Jubilee* were mixed. Granting that the novel is "ambitious," *New York Times Book Review* contributor Wilma Dykeman deemed it "uneven." Arthur P. Davis, writing in *From the Dark Tower: Afro-American Writers, 1900-1960*, suggested that the author "has crowded too much into her novel." Even so, countered some reviewers, the novel merits praise. Abraham Chapman of the *Saturday Review* appreciated the author's "fidelity to fact and detail." In the *Christian Science Monitor*, Henrietta Buckmaster commented, "In Vyry, Miss Walker has found a remarkable woman who suffered one outrage after the other and yet emerged with a humility and a moral fortitude that reflected a spiritual wholeness." Dykeman concurred: "In its best episodes, and in Vyry, *Jubilee* chronicles the triumph of a free spirit over many kinds of bondages." In 1977, eleven years after the publication of *Jubilee*, Walker accused Alex Haley of plagiarizing from the work to create his best-selling novel *Roots*. The charges were later dropped, but Walker still refers to that incident as the "*Roots* fiasco" and has written a poem entitled "Ripoff *Roots* Style."

Prophets for a New Day, Walker's next work, is another book of poetry. Unlike the poems in *For My People*, which, in a Marxist fashion, names religion an enemy of revolution, *Prophets for a New Day* "reflects a profound religious faith," according to Collier. "The heroes of the sixties are named for the prophets of the Bible: Martin Luther King is Amos, Medgar Evars is Micah, and so on. The people and events of the sixties are paralleled with Biblical characters and occurrences. . . .The religious references are important. Whether one espouses the Christianity in which they are couched is not the issue. For the fact is that Black people from ancient Africa to now have always been a spiritual people, believing in an existence beyond the flesh." Perhaps more importantly, in all the poems, continued Collier, Walker depicted "a people striking back at oppression and emerging triumphant."

Since completing *Prophets for a New Day*, Walker has published *October Journey* (1973) and *This is My Century: New and Collected Poems* (1988)—two collections of poetry—and *Richard Wright, Daemonic Genius: A Portrait of the Man, A Critical Look at His Work* (1988). She is currently working on a sequel to *Jubilee* and an autobiography. When not writing, she often gives lectures on black literature and about the writers she has known: James Weldon Johnson, Langston Hughes, Countee Cullen, Zora Neale Hurston, W. E. B. Du Bois, Richard Wright, and Arna Bontemps. Over the years, some black writers have accused Walker of not being "political enough" in her writings. Joyce Pettis disagrees; she calls Walker an invaluable "chronicler of the black experience." Walker herself stated: "I have no desire to separate myself from what I am. . .from my race, from my gender, from my nationality, and from my consciousness. I'm black, woman, writer; I'm very Black Nationalist."

(For further information about Walker's life and works, see *Black Writers; Contemporary Authors*, Vols. 73-76; *Contemporary Authors New Revision Series*, Vol. 26; *Contemporary Literary Criticism*, Vols. 1, 6; and *Dictionary of Literary Biography*, Vol. 76: *Afro-American Writers, 1940-1955*.)

PRINCIPAL WORKS

*"Daydreaming" (poetry) 1934; published in periodical *Crisis*
For My People (poetry) 1942
Ballad of the Free (poetry) 1966
Jubilee (novel) 1966
Prophets for a New Day (poetry) 1970
How I Wrote "Jubilee" (prose) 1972
October Journey (poetry) 1973
A Poetic Equation: Conversations between Nikki Giovanni and Margaret Walker (conversations) 1974
Richard Wright, Daemonic Genius: A Portrait of the Man, A Critical Look at His Work (nonfiction) 1988
This is My Century: New and Collected Poems (poetry) 1988

*This work was later retitled "I Want to Write."

Lester Davis (essay date 1967)

[*In the following essay, Davis favorably reviews* Jubilee, *stating that the book is an indictment of "bigotry, intolerance and slavery."*]

If you read *Gone With The Wind*, or saw the Hollywood version of it, you would not have required a Ph.D. or a superior intellect to have arrived at the conclusion that there was something "rotten in the State of Denmark." The concept of a people enslaved without brutality and cruelty is somehow alien to common human experience. Nevertheless, there has always been a tendency in significant areas of American thought to accept the concept of the benevolent and beautiful white mistress and the indolent and docile Negro slave whose loyalty and devotion to his master were second only to his devotion to a God whose emissaries counselled him to turn the other cheek and look to the day of his deliverance to the land of milk and honey.

Margaret Walker, in her epic, historical, and thoroughly researched novel, *Jubilee,* presents a somewhat different picture. One overlooks her sometimes trite and often stilted prose style and is entranced and ensnared by vivid vignettes of sordid yet thought-provoking reality. The heroine, Vyry, is a mulatto slave born of her master's weakness in the exercise of his ownership prerogatives. She assumes heroic proportions in her relentless struggle for freedom, dignity, and fulfillment. The reader who is white is forced to experience shame, guilt and revulsion. The reader who is black is angered but given a sense of pride in his heritage of struggle and suffering.

Jubilee will probably never stake any claim for inclusion on a list of the world's great books. It is a good forthright treatment of a segment of American history about which there has been much hypocrisy and deliberate distortion. It has a flavor of authenticity which is convincing and refreshing.

For its heroine, Miss Walker reaches into the annals of her own family background and presents Vyry, her great-grandmother, a woman of exceptional moral and physical strength with an innate capacity for logical reasoning. Through the thoughts and actions of Vyry from her early childhood to mature adulthood, the reader learns much about the social, economic and political structure of the plantation system prior to and following the Civil War. The picture is sordid, brutal and sometimes depressing. But it does not compromise with reality. It makes few concessions to the conscience of white America.

There are revealing insights into the economic stratification of the plantation system. The master of the big house is lord of all he surveys and exercises total control over his vast domain and all who must function within his orbit. At the bottom of the economic strata is the poor "white trash" who is the instrument of his oppressive rule. Hence, Grimes, the sadistic overseer of the Dutton plantation, in his generous application of the lash, not only protects the master's interests but gives cruel vent to his own frustrations which are born of the hopelessness and futility of his social and economic position.

His vast land and slave holdings give Dutton sufficient political power to guarantee him a seat in the Georgia legislature. Hence, he has neither the time, inclination or moral strength to protect Vyry from the wrath of his wife who resents the slave-girl's striking resemblance to her own daughter Lillian.

The mistress of the Dutton plantation bears no resemblance to Scarlett O'Hara. She does much to mar the picture of gracious, benevolent and humane southern white womanhood. She rules her domain with precision and abject cruelty. Vyry survives in spite of Big Missy's efforts to destroy her physically, emotionally, and spiritually.

Slaves who attempted escape, if caught, were either killed by being ripped to pieces by the dogs or strapped to the whipping-post and brutally whipped almost to the point of death. Vyry was no exception. She received seventy lashes—more than enough to kill the average person—but she survived to see the South's destruction and the coming of freedom for the slaves. As she stands naked but tall on the auction block, one is reminded of the enigmatic Kipling's racist apology for British colonialism; the concept of the white man's burden. "Though I've belted you and flayed you, By the livin' Gawd that made you, You're a better man than I am, Gunga Din."

Vyry was an unusual and remarkable woman but her ordeal of suffering and torture was neither unique nor exclusive to her sex or race. The havoc and devastation of the Civil War brought freedom for the slave but suffering and misery for the whole South. The system of feudal agrarianism based on rich profits in cotton and human indignity was inhuman and cruel. It died a slow and agonizing death and left a heritage of wounds and scars that still have not healed.

The story of Vyry's long and eventful life won a Houghton Mifflin Literary Fellowship award for Miss Walker. *Jubilee* is not escape reading. It is gripping and absorbing, but thought-provoking. Its message is clear and concise. The will for freedom can never be denied. There is majesty and dignity in the lowliest of men. Vyry eventually finds peace and happiness in freedom, with the love of her husband and children in her own home. In the inane ramblings of her demented, white half-sister we see the irony of her final triumph over her oppressors.

The story is told without bitterness or rancor. In the end, Vyry negates hatred or feelings of revenge. She does not present the false picture of one who stoically turns the other cheek but she recognizes that future salvation lies in the unity of black and white. It is bigotry, intolerance and slavery which are indicted in *Jubilee.* (pp. 258-60)

Lester Davis, "The Passing of an Era," in Freedomways, *Vol. 7, No. 3, Summer, 1967, pp. 258-60.*

R. Baxter Miller (essay date 1981)

[*In the following excerpt, Miller examines biblical references in Walker's* For My People *and* Prophets for a New Day. *Of Miller's essay, Walker once stated: "I [am] so proud of [this] piece. . . ."*]

Margaret Walker learned about Moses and Aaron from the Black American culture into which she was born. As the daughter of a religious scholar, she came of age in the depression of the thirties, and like those of Margaret Danner, Dudley Randall, and Gwendolyn Brooks, her career has spanned three or four decades. Much of her important work, like theirs, has been unduly neglected, coming as it does between the Harlem Renaissance of the 1920's and the Black Arts Movement of the 1960's. Most indices to literature, Black American and American, list only one article on Margaret Walker during the last seven years.

Walker knew the important figures of an older generation, including James Weldon Johnson, Langston Hughes, and Countee Cullen. She heard Marian Anderson and Roland Hayes sing, and she numbered among her acquaintances Zora Neale Hurston, George Washington Carver, and W.E.B. Du Bois. What does the richness of the culture give her? She finds the solemn nobility of religious utterance, the appreciation for the heroic spirit of Black folk, and the deep respect for craft. Once she heard from the late Richard Wright that talent does not suffice for literary fame. She took his words to heart and survived them to write about his life, his self-hatred, and his paradoxical love for white women. She knew, too, Willard Motley, Fenton Johnson, and Arna Bontemps. Her lifetime represents continuity. From a youthful researcher for Wright, she matured into an inspirational teacher at Jackson State University, where she preserved the spirit of her forerunners, the intellect and the flowing phrase, but she still belongs most with the Black poets whose careers span the last forty years. Her strengths are not the same as theirs. Margaret Danner's poetry has a quiet lyricism of peace, a deeply controlled introspection. No one else shows her delicacy of alliteration and her carefully framed patterns. Dudley Randall's success comes from the ballad, whose alternating lines of short and longer rhythms communicate the racial turmoil of the sixties. He profits from a touching and light innocence as well as a plea and longing of the child's inquiring voice; purity for him too marks an eternal type.

In *For My People* Walker develops this and other types in three sections, the first two divisions with ten poems each and the last segment with six. The reader experiences initially the tension and potential of the Black South; then the folk tale of both tragic possibility and comic relief involving the curiosity, trickery, and deceit of men and women alike; finally, the significance of physical and spiritual love in reclaiming the Southern land. Walker writes careful antinomies into the visionary poem, the folk secular and the Shakespearian and Petrarchan sonnets. She opposes quest to denial, historical circumstances to imaginative will, and earthly suffering to heavenly bliss. Her poetry purges the southern ground of animosity and injustice which separate Black misery from Southern song. Her themes are time, infinite human potential, racial equality, vision, blindness, love and escape, as well as worldly death, drunkenness, gambling, rottenness, and freedom. She pictures the motifs within the frames of toughness and abuse, fright and gothic terror. Wild arrogance, for her speakers, often underlies heroism, but the latter is more imagined than real.

The myth of human immortality expressed in oral tale and in literary artifact transcends death. The imagination evokes atemporal memory, asserts the humanistic self against the fatalistic past, and illustrates, through physical love, the promise of both personal and racial reunification. The achievement is syntactic. Parallelism, elevated rhetoric, simile, and figure of speech abound, but more deeply the serenity of nature creates solemnity. Walker depicts the sun, splashing brook, pond, duck, frog and stream, as well as flock, seed, wood, bark, cotton field, and cane. Still, the knife and gun threaten the pastoral world as, by African conjure, the moral "we" attempts to reconcile the two. As both the participant and observer, Walker creates an ironic distance between history and eternity. The Southern experience in the first section and the reclamation in the second part frame the humanity of folk personae Stagolee, John Henry, Kissie Lee, Yallah Hammer, and Gus. The book becomes a literary artifact, a "clean house" which imaginatively restructures the southland.

But if Dudley Randall has written "The Ballad of Birmingham" and Gwendolyn Brooks "The Children of the Poor," Walker succeeds with the visionary poem. She does not portray the gray-haired old women who nod and sing out of despair and hope on Sunday morning, but she captures the depths of their suffering. She recreates their belief that someday Black Americans will triumph over fire hoses and biting dogs, once the brutal signs of White oppression in the South. The prophecy contributes to Walker's rhythmical balance and vision, but she controls the emotions. How does one change brutality into social equality? Through sitting down at a lunch counter in the sixties, Black students illustrated some divinity and confronted death, just as Christ faced His cross. Walker deepens the portraits by using biblical typology, by discovering historical antitypes, and by creating an apocalyptic fusion. Through the suffering in the Old and New Testaments, the title poem of *For My People* expresses Black American victory over deprivation and hatred. The ten stanzas celebrate the endurance of tribulations such as dark murders in Virginia and Mississippi as well as Jim Crowism, ignorance, and poverty. The free form includes the parallelism of verbs and the juxtaposition of the present with the past. Black Americans are "never gaining, never reaping, never knowing and never understanding." When religion faces reality, the contrast creates powerful reversal:

> For the boys and girls who grew in spite of these things to be man and woman, to laugh and dance and sing and play and drink their wine and religion and success, to marry their playmates and bear children and then die of consumption and anemia and lynching.

Through biblical balance, **"For My People"** sets the White oppressor against the Black narrator. Social circumstance opposes racial and imaginative will, and disillusion opposes happiness. Blacks fashion a new world that encompasses many faces and people, "all the adams and eves and their countless generations." From the opening dedication (Stanza 1) to the final evocation (Stanza 10) the prophet-narrator speaks both as Christ and God. Ages ago, the Lord put His rainbow in the clouds. To the descendants of Noah it signified His promise that the world would never again end in flood. Human violence undermines biblical calm, as the first word repeats itself: "Let a new earth rise. Let another world be born. Let a bloody-peace be written in the sky. Let a second generation full of courage issue forth. . . ."

"We Have Been Believers," a visionary poem, juxtaposes Christianity with African conjure, and the Old Testament with the New, exemplified by St. John, St. Mark, and Revelation. The narrator ("we") represents the Black builders and singers in the past, for Walker seeks to interpret cultural signs. The theme is Black faith, first in Africa and then in America. As the verse shows movement from the past to the present, the ending combines Christianity and humanism. With extensive enjambment, the controlled rhapsody has a long first sentence, followed by indented ones that complete the meaning. The form literally typifies Black American struggle. The long line is jolted because an ending is illusory, and the reader renews his perusal just as the Black American continues the search for freedom. The narrator suggests the biblical scene in which death breaks the fifth seal (Revelation 6:11). There the prophet sees all the people who, slain in the service of God, wear garments as the narrator describes them.

The authenticating "we" is more focused than either Ellison's in *Invisible Man* or Baldwin's in *Notes of a Native Son.* Their speakers are often educated and upwardly mobile people who move between White and Black American worlds. Walker's, on the contrary, are frequently the secular and religious "folk" who share a communal quest. She blends historical sense with biblical implication: "Neither the slaver's whip nor the lyncher's rope nor the / bayonet could kill our black belief. In our hunger we / beheld the welcome table and in our nakedness the / glory of a long white robe." The narrator identifies Moloch, a god of cruel sacrifice, and all people who have died for no just cause. She prepares for the myth that dominates the last three parts of the poem, the miracle that Jesus performed on the eyes of a blind man. After He instructs him to wash them in the pool of Siloam, the man sees clearly (John 9:25). Another allusion suggests the miracle that Christ worked for the afflicted people near the Sea of Galilee. Walker's narrator knows the legend, but awaits the transformation (Mark 7:37). The waiting prepares for an irony phrased in alliteration: "Surely the priests and the preachers and the powers will hear. . ./. . .now that our hands are empty and our hearts too full to pray." This narrator says that such people will send a sign—the biblical image of relief and redemption—but she im-

plies something different. Although her humanism embraces Christianity, she adds militancy and impatience. Her rhetoric illustrates liquid sound, alliteration, and assonance: "We have been believers believing in our burdens and our / demigods too long. Now the needy no longer weep / and pray; the long-suffering arise, and our fists bleed / against the bars with a strange insistency."

The impatience pervades **"Delta,"** which has the unifying type of the Twenty-Third Psalm. Although the first part (ll. 1-35) presents the blood, corruption, and depression of the narrator's naturalistic world, the second (ll. 36-78) illustrates the restorative potential of nature. High mountain, river, orange, cotton, fern, grass, and onion share the promise. Dynamic fertility, the recleansed river (it flowed through swamps in the first part), can clear the Southern ground of sickness, rape, starvation, and ignorance. Water gives form to anger, yet thawing sets in. Coupled with liquidity, the loudness of thunder and cannon implies storm; the narrator compares the young girl to Spring. Lovingly the speaker envisions vineyards, pastures, orchards, cattle, cotton, tobacco, and cane, "making us men in the fields we have tended / standing defending the land we have rendered rich and abiding and heavy with plenty." Interpreting the meaning of earth can help to bridge the distance between past decay and present maturity when the narrator celebrates the promise:

> the long golden grain for bread
> and the ripe purple fruit for wine
> the hills beyond for peace
> and the grass beneath for rest
> the music in the wind for us
> and the circling lines in the sky
> for dreams.

Elsewhere a gothic undercurrent and an allusion to Abel and Cain add complexity; so does an allusion to Christ and transubstantiation. Rhetorical power emerges because the harsh tone of the Old Testament threatens the merciful tone of the New one. Loosely plotted, the verse recounts the personal histories of the people in the valley. Still, the symbolical level dominates the literal one, and the poem portrays more deeply the human condition. The narrator profits from the gothicism which has influenced Ann Radcliffe, Charles Brockden Brown, and Edgar Allan Poe. Just as Walker's pictures create beauty for the African-American, they communicate a grace to all who appreciate symmetrical landscapes. The tension in her literary world comes from the romantic legacy of possibility set against denial: "High above us and round about us stand high mountains / rise the towering snow-capped mountains / while we are beaten and broken and bowed / here in this dark valley." Almost no rhyme scheme exists in the poem, but a predominance of three or four feet gives the impression of a very loose ballad. The fifth stanza of the second part has incremental repetition, as the undertone of Countee Cullen's poem "From the Dark Tower" heightens the deep despair, the paradox of desire and restraint: "We tend the crop and gather the harvest / but not for ourselves do we sweat and starve and spend. . ./

here on this earth we dare not claim. . ." In the stanza before the final one the reader associates myth and history. While the narrator remembers the Blacks unrewarded in the Southern past, the imagery suggests Christ and transubstantiation. The speaker, however, alludes mainly to Abel slain by Cain (Genesis 4:10): "We with our blood have watered these fields / and they belong to us." Implicitly the promise of the Psalmist ("Yea though I walk through the valley of the shadow of death") has preceded.

In four quatrains, **"Since 1619"** strengthens Old Testament prefiguration. Aware of World War II, the narrator illuminates human blindness. She emphasizes the inevitability of death and the deterioration of world peace. With anaphora she repeats the Psalmist: "How many years. . .have I been singing Spirituals? / How long have I been praising God and shouting hallelujahs? / How long have I been hated and hating? / How long have I been living in hell for heaven?" She remembers the Valley of Dry Bones in which the Lord placed the prophet Ezekiel, whom He questioned if the bones could live. Whereas in the Bible salvation is external and divine, here the transformation comes from within. The poem contrasts moral renewal to the spiritual death during World War II and the pseudo-cleanliness of middle-class America. Written in seven stanzas, the verse has four lines in the first section and three in the second. Initially the poem portrays the ancient muse, the inspiration of all poetry, and later it illustrates poverty, fear, and sickness. Even the portrait of lynching cannot end the narrator's quest for cleanliness. Although Americans face death, they will continue to seek solace through intoxication and sex. The beginning of the poem foreshadows the end, but the directness in the second section supplants the general description in the first. The middle-class Americans in the first part have no bombing planes or air-raids to fear, yet they have masked violence and ethnocentric myth: "viewing weekly 'Wild West Indian and Shooting Sam,' 'Mama Loves Papa,' and 'Gone By the Breeze!'" Calories, eyemaline, henna rinse, and dental cream image a materialistic nation. With a deeper cleanliness, the speaker advises the reader within an ironic context: "Pray for second sight and the inner ear. Pray for bulwark against poaching patterns of dislocated days; pray for buttressing iron against insidious termite and beetle and locust and flies and lice and moth and rust and mold."

The religious types in the second and third sections of *For My People* rival neither those in the first section nor those in *Prophets for a New Day*. When Walker ignores biblical sources, often she vainly attempts to achieve cultural saturation. Without biblical cadences her ballads frequently become average, if not monotonous. In **"Yalluh Hammer,"** a folk poem about the "Bad Man," she manages sentimentality, impractical concern, and trickery, as a Black woman outsmarts the protagonist and steals his money.

But sometimes the less figurative sonnets are still boring. **"Childhood"** lacks the condensation and focus to develop well the Petrarchan design. In the octave a young girl remembers workers who used to return home in the afternoons. Even during her maturity, the rags of poverty and the habitual grumbling color the Southern landscape still. Despite weaknesses, the poem suggests well a biblical analogue. As the apostle Paul writes "When I was a child, I spake as a child: but when I became a man, I put away childish things" (I Corinthians 13:11), Walker's sonnet coincidentally begins, "When I was a child I knew red miners. . ./ I also lived in a low cotton country. . .where sentiment and hatred still held sway / and only bitter land was washed away." The mature writer seeks now to restore and renew the earth.

In *Prophets* Walker illustrates some historical antitypes to the Old Testament. Her forms are the visionary poem, free verse sonnet, monody, pastoral, and gothic ballad in which she portrays freedom, speech, death, and rebirth. Her major images are fire, water, and wind. When she opposes marching to standing, the implied quest becomes metaphorical, for she recreates the human community in th spiritual wilderness. She looks beneath any typological concern of man's covenant with God, and even the pantheistic parallel of the Southerner's covenant with the land, to illuminate man's broken covenant with himself. The human gamut runs from death ("mourning bird") to the potential of poetry ("humming bird"). Poetry recreates anthropocentric space. The speaker depicts the breadth through dramatic dialogue, sarcasm, and satire. Even the cold stone implies the potential for creative inspiration or Promethean fire. The narrator verbally paints urban corruption in the bitter cold and frozen water. Her portrait images not only the myth of fragmentation and dissolution, but the courage necessary to confront and transcend them. Her world is doubly Southern. Here the Old South still withstands Northern invasion, but the Black South endures both. One attains the mythical building beyond (sounds like Thomas Wolfe), the human house, through fire. Form is imagined silence. Poetry, both catharsis and purgation, parallels speaking, crying, and weaving. The center includes geometric space and aesthetic beauty. To portray anthropocentric depth is to clarify the significance of human cleansing.

Although the sonnets and ballads in *For My People* are weak, the typological poems in *Prophets for a New Day* envision universal freedom. But neither Walker nor her reader can remain at visionary heights, for the real world includes the white hood and fiery cross. Even the latter image fails to save the poem **"Now,"** in which the subject is civil rights. Here both images of place and taste imply filth as doors, dark alleys, balconies, and washrooms reinforce moral indignation. The Klan marks "kleagle with a klux / and a fiery burning cross." Yet awkward rhythms have preceded. In shifting from three feet to four, the speaker stumbles: "In the cleaning room and closets / with the washrooms marked 'For Colored Only.'" The ear of **"Sit-Ins"** catches more sharply the translation of the Bible into history. Written in twelve lines of free verses, the lyric depicts the students at North Carolina A & T University, who in 1960 sat down at the counter of a dime store and began the Civil Rights movement. The speaker recreates Southern history. In the shining picture, the reader sees the Angel Michael who drove Adam and Eve from Paradise, but the portrait becomes more secular: "With courage and faith, convictions and intelligence / The first to blaze a flaming patch for justice / And awaken consciences / Of these stony ones." The implement that in the Bible and Milton symbolized Paradise Lost becomes a metaphor for Paradise Regained. In viewpoint the narrator gives way to the demonstrators themselves: *"Come, Lord Jesus, Bold Young Galilean / Sit Beside This Counter / Lord With Me."*

As with most of Walker's antitypical poems, **"Sit-Ins"** hardly rivals **"Ballad of the Free,"** one of her finest. The latter work portrays the heroic missions and tragic deaths of slave insurrectionists and excels through consistent rhythm as well as compression of image. At first the verse seems true to the title. Although the design of the typical ballad usually emphasizes a rhythmic contrast between two lines in succession, **"Ballad of the Free,"** stresses a contrast between whole stanzas. Of the twelve sections which comprise the poem, each of the four quatrains follows a tercet which serves as the refrain. The narrator adds a striking twist to St. Matthew (19:30; 20:16), in which Peter asks Jesus what will happen to people who have forsaken everything to follow Him. Christ replies that the social status will be reversed. Although He speaks about the beginning of the apocalypse in which all persons arc judged, Walker's narrator forsees the end of the apocalypse in which all are equal: "The serpent is loosed and the hour is come. . . ."

The refrain balances social history and biblical legend. The first stanza presents Nat Turner, the leader of the slave insurrection in South Hampton, Virginia, during 1831. After the first refrain, the reader recognizes Gabriel Prosser, whom a storm once forced to suspend a slave revolt in Richmond, Virginia. With a thousand other slaves, Prosser planned an uprising that collapsed in 1800. Betrayed by fellow bondsmen, he and fifteen others were hanged on October 7 in that year. After the first echo of the refrain, Denmark Vesey, who enlisted thousands of Blacks for an elaborate slave plot in Charleston, S.C., and the vicinity, appears in the fifth stanza. Authorities arrested 131 Blacks and four Whites, and when the matter was settled, thirty-seven people were hanged. Toussaint L'Ouverture, who at the turn of the eighteenth and nineteenth centuries liberated Haitian slaves, follows the second echo of the refrain. Shortly afterwards an evocation of John Brown intensifies the balance between history and sound. With thirteen Whites and five Blacks, Brown attacked Harper's Ferry on October 16, 1859, and by December 2 of that year, he was also hanged. In the poem, as in the Southern past, the death of the rebel is foreshadowed. Gifted with humane vision, he wants to change an inegalitarian South. But the maintainers of the status quo will kill, so the hero becomes the martyr.

In order to emphasize Turner as historical paradigm, the narrator ignores the proper chronology of L'Ouverture, Prosser, Vesey, Turner, and Brown. She gives little of the historical background but calls upon the names of legend. What does she achieve, by naming her last hero, if not a symmetry of color? The ballad that began with Black Nat Turner ends with White John Brown, for if action alone determines a basis for fraternity, racial distinction is insignificant.

For a central portrait of Turner, the verse moves backward and forward in both typological and apocalyptic time. As with the narrator of Hughes's "Negro Speaks of Rivers," the speaker can comprehend different decades. Because she is outside of Time, L'Ouverture and Brown, who come from different periods, appear to her with equal clarity. Until the eleventh stanza, the biblical sureness of the refrain has balanced history. The note of prophecy sounds in the slowness and firmness of racial progress: *"Wars and Rumors of Wars have gone, / But Freedom's army marches on. / The heroes' list of dead is long, / And Freedom still is for the strong."* The narrator recalls Christ (Mark 13:7) who prophesies wars and rumors of war, but foretells salvation for endurers. The final refrain interfuses with the fable and history: "The serpent is loosed and the hour is come."

"At the Lincoln Monument in Washington, August 28, 1963," presents analogues to Isaiah, Exodus, Genesis, and Deuteronomy. Written in two stanzas, the poem has forty-four lines. The speaker dramatizes chronicle through biblical myth, racial phenomenology, and Judaeo-Christian consciousness. She advances superbly with the participant to the interpreter, but even the latter speaks from within an aesthetic mask. The poetic vision authenticates the morality of her fable and the biblical analogue. The first stanza has twenty-eight lines, and the second has sixteen. As the speaker recalls the march on Washington, in which more than 250,000 people demonstrated for civil rights, she attributes to Martin Luther King, Jr., the leader of the movement, the same rhetorical art she now remembers him by. The analogue is Isaiah: "The grass withereth, the flower fadeth: but the word of our God shall stand for ever" (40:8). Two brothers, according to the fable, led the Israelites out of Egypt. Sentences of varied length complement the juxtaposition of cadences which rise and fall. The narrator names neither King as "Moses" nor King's youthful follower as "Aaron," yet she clarifies a richness of oration and implies the heroic spirit. King, before his death, said that he had been to the mountain top, and that he had seen the Promised Land. But the speaker literarily retraces the paradigm of the life; she distills the love of the listeners who saw him and were inspired: "There they stand. . ./ The old man with a dream he has lived to see come true."

Although the first eleven lines of the poem are descriptive, the twelfth combines chronicle and prefiguration. The speaker projects the social present into the mythical past. Her words come from a civil rights song, "We

Woke Up One Morning With Our Minds Set On Freedom." The social activist wants the immediate and complete liberation which the rhetorician (speaker and writer) translates into literary symbol: "We woke up one morning in Egypt / And the river ran red with blood. . ./ And the houses of death were afraid."

She remembers, too, the story of Jacob, who returns home with his two wives, Leah and Rachel (Genesis 30:25-43). Laban, the father-in-law, gave him speckled cattle, but now the narrator understands that Jacob's "*house* (Africa-America) has grown into a nation / The slaves break forth from bondage" (emphasis mine). In Old Testament fashion, she cautions against fatigue in the pursuit of liberty. Through heightened style, she becomes a prophet whose medium is eternal language. She has mastered alliteration, assonance, and resonance.

> Write this word upon your hearts
> And mark this message on the doors of your
>   houses
> See that you do not forget
> How this day the Lord has set our faces toward
>   freedom
> Teach these words to your children
> And see that they do not forget them.

Walker's poetry alludes subtly to King but refers to Malcolm X directly. The verse dedicated to Malcolm portrays him as Christ. Nearly a Petrarchan sonnet, the poem is not written in the five-foot line, but has several lines of four or six feet. Neither of the last two lengths usually characterizes the form, and even a concession of off-rhyme does not make a Petrarchan scheme unfold. The comments sound repetitious because they are. As with the earlier sonnet **"Childhood," "Malcolm"** appears at first to deserve oblivion because here, too, Walker fails to condense and control metrics. Still, the quiet appeal is clear. The Christ story compels rereading, and one finds it a meaningful experience. When Malcolm is associated with a dying swan in the octave, the narrator alludes to the Ovidian legend of the beautiful bird which sings just before death. Malcolm takes on Christ's stigmata: "Our blood and water pour from your flowing wounds."

Vivid and noble portraits of crucifixion, another type of martyrdom, give even more vitality to **"For Andy Goodman, Michael Schwerner, and James Chaney"** (hereafter **"For Andy"**), a poem about three civil rights workers murdered in Mississippi on June 21, 1964. The elegy complements seasonal and diurnal cycle through the reaffirmation of human growth and spiritual redemption. Despite the questionable value of martyrdom, sunrise balances sunset, and beautiful leaves partly compensate for human mutilation. In dramatic reversal, Walker's narrator uses the literary technique which distinguishes *Lycidas, Adonais,* and *When Lilacs Last in the Dooryard Bloom'd.*

The flower and the paradigmatic bird (lark, robin, mourning bird, bird of sorrow, bird of death) restore both an epic and elegiac mood. The reader half-hears the echo of the goddess Venus who mourns for Adonis; *mourning* and *morning,* excellent puns, signify the cycle and paradox of life. The short rhythm, two feet, and the longer rhythm, three or four, provide the solemn folksiness of a very loose ballad or free verse. With interior rhyme, the musical balance communicates quiet pathos: "They have killed these three / They have killed them for me." The gentle suggestion of the trinity, the tragic flight of the bird, and the slow but cyclical turning from spring to spring intensify the narrator's sadness and grief.

Just as **"For Andy"** shows Walker's grace of style, the title poem of *Prophets* illustrates that the Bible prefigures the eloquence. As with the earlier poem **"Delta," "Prophets"** resists paraphrase because it abstractly portrays Black American history. The poem has three parts. The first shows that the Word which came to the biblical prophets endures, and the next presents the actual appearance of the ancient vision to new believers. In the third part, the reader moves to a final understanding about tragic death. While the poet marks the recurrence of sacred light, fire, gentleness, and artistic speech, she contrasts White and Black, dark and light, age and youth, life and death. Some allusions to Ezekiel and Amos now fuse with others from Ecclesiastes and Isaiah. Amos tells of a prophet-priest of sixth century B.C., a watchman over the Israelites during the exile in Babylon, by the river of Cheber (Ezek. 1:15-20). As a herdsman from the southern village of Tekoa, Judah, he went to Bethel in Samaria to preach a religion of social justice and righteousness. He attacked economic exploitation and privilege and criticized the priests who stressed ritual above justice. Because Amos is Walker's personal symbol of Martin Luther King, Jr., she provides more background about him than about others. The reader knows his name, character, and homeland.

But Walker socially and historically reinvigorates the scriptures. She is no eighteenth-century Jupiter Hammon who rewrites the Bible without any infusion of personal suffering. She feels strongly and personally that the demonstrators in the sixties antitypify the Scriptures: "So today in the pulpits and the jails, / A fearless shepherd speaks at last / To his suffering weary sheep." She implies perseverance even in the face of death, and her speaker blends the images of the New Testament with those from *Beowulf.* Her lines depict the beast:

> His mark is on the land
> His horns and his hands and his lips are gory with
>   our blood
> He is death and destruction and Trouble
> And he walks in our houses at noonday
> And devours our defenders at midnight.

The literary word images fear and sacrifice more than immediate redemption. What shadows the fate of the good? The beast

>   has crushed them with a stone.
> He drinks our tears for water
> And he drinks our blood for wine;

He eats our flesh like a ravenous lion
And he drives us out of the city
To be stabbed on a lonely hill.

The same scene relives the crucifixion.

Walker draws heavily upon the Bible for typological unity. Of the twenty-two poems in *Prophets,* seven of the last nine have biblical names for titles, including **"Jeremiah," "Isaiah," "Amos-1963," "Amos (Postscript-1968)," "Joel," "Hosea,"** and **"Micah."** A similar problem besets all, although to a different extent. The aesthetic response relies on historical sense more than on dramatized language, and passing time will weaken the emotional hold. In **"Jeremiah,"** the narrator is conscious of both the fallen world and the apocalyptic one. She suggests Benjamin Mays, who has been a preacher and educator in Atlanta for over fifty years. Seeking to lift the "curse" from the land, Mays wants to redeem the corrupted city. The mythical denotation of the place—"Atlanta"—inspires the cultural imagination. Once a girl by that name lost a race to Hippomenes, her suitor, because she digressed from her course to pursue golden apples. Yet Walker's poem does more than oppose Mays to urban materialism. Through his articulation (the spoken word), he signifies the artist and the writer. The narrator who recounts the tale is an artist, too, since Walker's speakers and heroes mirror each other. Although Jeremiah appears as a contemporary man, he exists in a half-way house between legend and reality. Despite limitations, the final six lines of the verse combine myth and anaphora, where the speaker compares the imaginative and historical worlds more closely than elsewhere. Once destroyed by fire, Atlanta suggests Babylon, capital first of Babylonia and then of Chaldea on the Euphrates river. As the scene of the biblical Exile, the city represents grandeur and wickedness. The book of Psalms portrays the despair of the Israelites who sat down and wept when they remembered Zion. With an undertone of an old folk ballad, Walker builds a literary vision. While anaphora strengthens solemnity, the voice subsumes both narrator and prophet:

> My God we are still here. We are still down here
>   Lord,
> Working for a kingdom of Thy Love,
> We weep for this city and for this land
> We weep for Judah and beloved Jerusalem
> O Georgia! "Where shall you stand in the Judgment?"

Through the fire, the mark, and the word, **"Isaiah"** clarifies the typology which leads from **"Lincoln Monument,"** midway through the volume, to **"Elegy"** at the end. Jeremiah expresses himself in the public forum as well as on television. He resembles Adam Clayton Powell, Jr., a major Civil Rights activist in Harlem during the depression. Powell persuaded many Harlem businesses, including Harlem Hospital, to hire Blacks. As Chairman of the Coordinating Committee on Employment, he led a demonstration which forced the World's Fair to adopt a similar policy in 1939. He desegregated many Congressional facilities, Washington restaurants, and theatres. He proposed first the withholding of federal funds from projects which showed racial discrimination; he introduced the first legislation to desegregate the armed forces; he established the right of Black journalists to sit in the press galleries of the United States House of Representatives and in the Senate. As Chairman of the House Committee on Education and Labor in 1960, he supported forty-eight pieces of legislation on social welfare and later earned a letter of gratitude from President Johnson.

> In 1967, however, Powell's House colleagues raised charges of corruption and financial mismanagement against him. In January he was stripped of his chairmanship and barred from the House, pending an investigation. On March 1, 1967 Powell was denied a seat in the House by a vote of 307 to 116, despite the committee's recommendation that he only be censured, fined, and placed at the bottom of the seniority list. On April 11 a special election was held to fill Powell's seat. Powell, who was not campaigning and was on the island of Bimini and who could not even come to New York City because of a court judgment against him in a defamation case, received 74% of the Harlem vote cast [Peter M. Bergman and Mort N. Bergman, in *The Chronological History of the Negro in America*].

Even more clearly, the **"Amos"** poems reconfirm Walker's greater metaphor for Martin Luther King, Jr. The first of these two verses, twenty lines in length, portrays Amos as a contemporary shepherd who preaches in the depths of Alabama and elsewhere: "standing in the Shadow of our God / Tending his flocks over the hills of Albany / And the seething streets of Selma and of bitter Birmingham." As with the first **"Amos"** poem, the second **"Postscript (1968)"** is written in free verse. With only ten lines, however, the latter is shorter. King, the prophet of justice, appears through the fluidity and the wholesomeness of the "O" sound: "From Montgomery to Memphis he marches / He stands on the threshold of tomorrow / He breaks the bars of iron and they remove the signs / He opens the gates of our prisons."

Many of the short poems that follow lack the high quality found in some of Walker's other typological lyrics. **"Joel"** uses the standard free verse, but the historical allusion is obscure. **"Hosea"** suffers from the same problem. The Bible presents the figure as having an unfaithful wife, but Walker's poem presents a Hosea who, marked for death, writes love letters to the world. Is the man Eldridge Cleaver? The letters and the theme of redemption clearly suggest him, but one can never be sure. The legend could better suit the man. The last poem in *Prophets* appropriately benefits from some of Walker's favorite books such as Ecclesiastes, Isaiah, and St. John. **"Elegy,"** a verse in two parts, honors the memory of Manford Kuhn, professor and friend. Summer and sunshine give way to winter snow and "frothy wood," since the green harvest must pass. But art forms ironically preserve themselves through fire, and engraving comes from corrosion. Eternity paradoxically depends upon decay. The first section concerns the cycle of nature which continually turns; the second, an elaborate conceit, depicts people as ephemeral artists. Reminiscent of Virgil's *Aeneid,* Shelley's "The Witch of Atlas," and Danner's short lyric, "The Slave and the Iron Lace," Walker's second section begins:

> Within our house of flesh we weave a web of time
> Both warp and woof within the shuttle's clutch
> In leisure and in haste no less a tapestry
> Rich pattern of our lives.
> The gold and scarlet intertwine
> Upon our frame of dust an intricate design. . . .

Here are her ablest statement and restatement of the iamb. The "I" sound supports assonance and rhyme, even though the poem is basically free. At first the idea of human transitoriness reinforces *Ecclesiastes* which powerfully presents the theme. In a second look, however, one traces the thought to Isaiah (40:7): "The grass withereth, the flower fadeth: because the spirit of the Lord bloweth upon it. . . ." But the speaker knows the ensuing verse equally well: "The grass withereth, the flower fadeth; but the *word* [emphasis mine] of our God shall stand for ever" (40:8). Poetry, an inspired creation in words, is divine as well. To the extent that Kuhn showed Christ-like love and instruction for his students, his spirit transcends mortality. For any who demonstrate similar qualities is the vision any less true and universal? To Nicodemus, the Pharisee whom Jesus told to be reborn (John 3:8), the final allusion belongs.

> We live again
> In children's faces, and the sturdy vine
> Of daily influences: the prime
> Of teacher, neighbor, student, and friend
> All merging on the elusive wind.

Patient nobility becomes the poet who has recreated Martin Luther King, Jr. as Amos. She has kept the neatly turned phrase of Countee Cullen but replaced Tantalus and Sisyphus with Black students and sit-ins. For her literary fathers, she reaches back to the nineteenth-century prophets Blake, Byron, Shelley, and Tennyson. Her debt extends no less to Walt Whitman and to Langston Hughes, for her predecessor is any poet who forsees a new paradise and who portrays the coming. As with Hughes, Walker is a romantic. But Hughes had either to subordinate his perspective to history or to ignore history almost completely and to speak less about events than about personal and racial symbols. Walker, on the contrary, equally combines events and legends but reaffirms the faith of the spirituals. Although her plots sometimes concern murder, her narrators reveal an image of racial freedom and human peace. The best of her imagined South prefigures the future. (pp. 157-72)

> *R. Baxter Miller, "The 'Etched Flame' of Margaret Walker: Biblical and Literary Recreation in Southern History," in* Tennessee Studies in Literature, *Vol. 26, 1981, pp. 157-72.*

Eugenia Collier (essay date 1984)

[*In the following essay, Collier explores myth and ritual in Walker's poetry, defining the former as "the wellspring of racial memories" and the latter as "the actions, gestures, and activities which recur in a culture and which overlap with and result from myth."*]

"For my people everywhere. . . ," the reader began, and the audience of Black folk listened, a profound and waiting silence. We knew the poem. It was ours. The reader continued, his deep voice speaking not only *to* us but *for* us, ". . . singing their slave songs repeatedly: their dirges and their ditties and their blues and jubilees. . . ." And as the poem moved on, rhythmically piling on image after image of our lives, making us know again the music wrenched from our slave agony, the religious faith, the toil and confusion and hopelessness, the strength to endure in spite of it all, as the poem went on mirroring our collective selves, we cried out in deep response. We cried out as our fathers had responded to sweating Black preachers in numberless cramped little churches, and further back, as our African ancestors had responded to rituals which still, unremembered and unknown, inform our being. And when the resonant voice proclaimed the dawn of a new world, when it called for a race of *men* to "rise and take control," we went wild with ancient joy and new resolve.

Margaret Walker's **"For My People"** does that. It melts away time and place and it unifies Black listeners. Its power is as compelling now as it was forty-odd years ago when it was written, perhaps more so as we have experienced repeatedly the flood tide and the ebb tide of hope. The source of its power is the reservoir of beliefs, values, and archetypal characters yielded by our collective historical experience. It is this area of our being which defines us, which makes us a people, which finds expression *in Black art and in no other.*

Make no mistake: What we call the "universal" is grounded in particular group experience. All humans (except, perhaps, an occasional aberrant individual) share such fundamentals as the need for love, an instinct for survival, the inevitability of change, the reality of death. But these fundamentals are meaningless unless they are couched in specific human experience. And there is no person who is not a member of a race, a group, a family of humankind. Nobody exists alone. We are each a part of a specific collective past, to which we respond in a way in which no person outside the group can respond. This is right. This is good.

Margaret Walker has tapped the rich vein of Black experience and fashioned that material into art. By "Black experience" we refer to the African past, the dispersal of African people into a diaspora, and the centuries-long incubus of oppression. Included is the entire range of human emotion from despair to joy to triumph. The discussion here will be of Margaret Walker's use of this shared experience in her poetry.

Margaret Walker's signature poem is **"For My People."** Widely anthologized in Black collections and often read at dramatic presentations, it is the work most closely associated with her name. Some years ago, when I was involved in compiling an anthology of ethnic literature for high schools, the editor (white) refused to permit us to include this poem. It was too militant, he said. The man was unutterably wise: the poem thrusts to the heart of Black experience and suggests a solution that would topple him and the culture he represents from its position of power. White response to African American literature is often, and for obvious reasons, diametric to Black response; this poem is indeed a case in point.

"For My People" exemplifies Walker's use of Black myth and ritual. The poem first evokes the two mechanisms which have never been a source of strength to Black folk: music and religion. But even in the first stanza is implied a need to move beyond historical roles, for the "slave songs" are sung "repeatedly," the god (lower case) to whom the people pray is "unknown," and the people humble themselves to "an unseen power." Then the poem catalogues the rituals of the toil which consumes the life of the people, hopeless toil which never enables one to get ahead and never yields any answers. The stanza jams the heavy tasks together without commas to separate them, making them all into one conglomerate burden: "washing, ironing, cooking scrubbing sewing mending hoeing plowing digging planting. . . ." The poem rushes by, as indeed life rushes by when one must labor "never gaining never reaping never knowing and never understanding. . . ."

Walker now changes focus from the general to the specific—to her playmates, who are, by extension, all Black children playing the games which teach them their reality—"baptizing and preaching and doctor and jail and soldier and school and mama and cooking and playhouse and concert and store and hair and Miss Choomby and company. . . ." She shows us the children growing up to a woeful miseducation in school, which bewilders rather than teaches them, until they discover the overwhelming and bitter truth that they are "black and poor and small and different and nobody cared and nobody wondered and nobody understood. . . ." The children grow, however, to manhood and womanhood; they live out their lives until they "die of consumption and anemia and lynching. . . ."

The poem then returns to the wide angle of "my people" and continues its sweep of Black experience, cataloguing the troubled times wrought by racism.

The form of the first nine stanzas supports their message. Rather than neat little poetic lines, they consist of long, heavily weighted paragraphs inversely indented. The words and phrases cataloguing the rituals of trouble are separated by "and . . . and . . . and." There is little punctuation. Each stanza begins with a "for" phrase followed by a series of modifiers. Finally the long sentence, with its burden of actions and conditions, ends with one short, simple clause which leaves the

listener gasping: "Let a new earth rise." Five words. Strong words, each one accented. Five words, bearing the burden of nine heavy stanzas, just as Black people have long borne the burden of oppression.

The final stanza is a reverberating cry for redress. It demands a new beginning. Our music then will be martial music; our peace will be hard-won, but it will be "written in the sky." And after the agony, the people whose misery spawned strength will control our world.

This poem is the hallmark of Margaret Walker's works. It echoes in her subsequent poetry and even in her monumental novel *Jubilee.* It speaks to us, in our words and rhythms, of our history, and it radiates the promise of our future. It is the quintessential example of myth and ritual shaped by artistic genius.

The volume *For My People* is the fruit of the Chicago years in the 1930s when the young poet found her voice. A lifetime's experience went into the writing of the book: the violent racism of the deep South, her gentle and intelligent parents, her bitter struggle to retain a sense of worth despite the dehumanizing forces of Alabama of the 1920s and 1930s; her disillusionment at discovering that racial prejudice was just as strong in the Midwest, where she went to college, as in the South. After her graduation from Northwestern University in the mid-thirties, she went to Chicago to work at various jobs, including the Federal Writers Project. There her developing sensitivity was nurtured by her association with young artists and intellectuals, including Richard Wright. She became interested in Marxism and, like many of her contemporaries, saw it as the key to the accomplishment of the dream. After four years she left Chicago to study in the School of Letters of the University of Iowa. The poems in *For My People,* reflecting the thoughts, emotions, and impressions of all the years, were her master's thesis. After receiving her degree, she returned to Southern soil, this time to stay.

The South is an ancestral home of Black Americans. It is true, of course, that slavery also existed in the North and that Black people have lived from the beginning in all sections of this country. But collectively it is the South that is the nucleus of Black American culture. It is here that the agony of chattel slavery created the history that is yet to be written. It is the South that has dispersed its culture into the cities of the North. The South is, in a sense, the mythic landscape of Black America.

This landscape as portrayed vividly in this first important volume for the South is the psychic as well as the geographic home of Margaret Walker. The children in **"For My People"** play "in the clay and dust and sand of Alabama." The strong grandmothers in **"Lineage,"** who "touched earth and grain grew," toiled in the wet clay of the South. And the farm in Iowa reminds the poet of her Southern home. "My roots are deep in southern life," writes Walker in **"Sorrow Home,"** flooding the poem with sensual images of warm skies and blue water, of the smell of fresh pine and wild onion. "I want my body bathed in southern suns," she writes in **"Southern**

Song," "my soul reclaimed from southern land." This poem is rich in images of silver corn and ponds with ducks and frogs, of the scent of grass and hay and clover and fresh-turned soil.

Both poems portray what Eleanor Traylor calls the ruined world, the fragmented world of the American South, the ambivalence which ever haunts Black people. For the Southland is the "sorrow home, melody beating in my bone and blood!" And the speaker (for us all) demands, "How long will the Klan of hate, the hounds and the chain gangs keep me away from my own?" And the speaker, the collective "I," after portraying the peace and beauty of the Southland, pleads in graphic detail for undisturbed integration of the Self.

The poem that most completely exploits the motif of the South is the long poem **"Delta."** "I am a child of the valley," Walker asserts, and again the "I" is collective. The valley is both literal and symbolic. The images are realistic descriptions of an actual place. But the poem's essence is its symbolic meaning. The valley is, in the beginning, a place of despair, of "mud and muck and misery," hovered over by "damp draughts of mist and fog." Destruction threatens, for "muddy water flows at our shanty door/and leaves stand like a swollen bump on our backyard." Here the sounds are the dissonance of the honky-tonks, the despairing sounds of "the wailing/of a million voices strong." The speaker, in deep despair, demands that her "sorrowing sisters," "lost forgotten men," and a desperate people rise from the valley with a singing that "is ours."

This vision of hope recalls the fact that the generations-long labor of the people has made the valley theirs/ours. The snowcapped mountains tower high above the "beaten and broken and bowed" ones in "this dark valley." On the river, boats take away "cargoes of our need." Meanwhile, our brother is ill, our sister is ravished, our mother is starving. And a deep-seated rebelliousness surfaces from inside our collective self. Oppression increases with the destruction of a sudden storm, and the rape and murder of all we love leaves us "dazed in wonder." From this lowest of all points, when we are threatened with total loss, we realize our love for this place, and our right to it, precisely because it is "our blood" that has "watered these fields."

"Delta" encompasses the essence of Black myth in America. The valley depicts our traditional position as the most completely oppressed people in America; the mountains, snowcapped, are our aspiration for the fulfillment of America's promise—ever before us but totally beyond our reach. Again, the rituals of toil and despair and regeneration affirm the myth. The message of the poem is that we have bought our stake in this nation with our labor, our torment, and our blood. And nothing, nothing, can separate us from what is ours.

The poems of the South portray one level of the Black American ancestral home. Walker is not unaware of the scattered places worldwide which created the Black American. "There were bizarre beginnings in old lands for the making of me," she asserts in **"Dark Blood."** The "me" is both personal and collective as she refers not only to her own immediate ancestry in Jamaica but to the eclectic background of Black people—Africa, Asia, Europe, the Caribbean. "There were sugar sands and islands of fern and pearl, palm jungles and stretches of a never-ending sea." She will return "to the tropical lands of my birth, to the coasts of continents and the tiny wharves of island shores" to "stand on mountain tops and gaze on fertile homes below." This return is a psychic journey into the mythic past, a journey necessary for the Black American, for only by reuniting with the fragmented self can one become whole. On her return to the place of her physical birth, Walker writes, the "blazing suns of other lands may struggle then to reconcile the pride and pain in me." The poem thus encompasses space and time—continents and islands, antiquity and now. It thrusts deep into the Black American self.

In another section of the volume, Walker shows another aspect of our psyche: our folklore. Here the voice is that of the tale teller indigenous to Black America, especially the South, who reaches back ultimately to the people who swapped tales around the fire in ancient Africa. Using ballad forms and the language of the grass-roots people, Walker spins yarns of folk heroes and heroines: those who, faced with terrible obstacles which haunt Black people's very existence, not only survive but prevail—with style. There are the tough ones: Kissie Lee, who learned by bitter experience that one must fight back and who "died with her boots on switching blades"; Trigger Slim, who vanquished the terror of the railroad workers' mess hall, Two-Gun Buster; and the baddest of them all, Stagolee, who killed a white policeman and eluded the lynch mob. There are the workers: Gus the lineman, who handled his live wire and survived many certain-death accidents only to drown drunk, facedown in a shallow creek; and the most famous worker, John Henry, who "could raise two bales of cotton/with one hand anchored down the steamboat," but who was killed by a ten-pound hammer. There are the lovers: Sweetie Pie, done wrong by her lover Long John Nelson; the Teacher, whose "lust included all/Women ever made;" Yalluh Hammuh, who was defeated by jealous Pick Ankle and his girl friend May; Poppa Chicken, whose very presence on the street made the girls cry, "Lawdy! Lawd!" There are the supernatural elements throughout: old Molly Means, "Chile of the devil, the dark and sitch," whose ghost still "rides along on a winter breeze"; Stagolee's ghost, which still haunts New Orleans; Big John Henry, whom the witches taught how to conjure. These are all archetypes who recur repeatedly in Black American lore and are vital to the culture—mythic characters performing endlessly their rituals of defeat, survival, and triumph.

Contrasting with the ballads are the poems which end the volume: six sonnets. But even here the setting is the mythic landscape, the South of Walker's memory. It is peopled by "red miners" who labor incessantly and hopelessly, "painted whores," pathetic and doomed, and people who are hurt and bewildered, muttering protests against their oppression. The landscape is filled with tree stumps, rotting shacks of sharecroppers, and cold cities with tenements. The form of these poems supports their theme. For the dignified sonnet form, which emerges from a European vision of an orderly universe, substitutes here approximate rhyme rather than true rhyme, indicating that, for these people, the promise has been distorted.

The symbols in the *For My People* poems are elemental: sun, earth, and water. The sun is the primary symbol, appearing repeatedly. The sun is a beneficent force, radiating comfort; it is the source of healing. "I want my body bathed again in southern suns," she writes in **"Southern Song,"** "to lay my hand again upon the clay baked by a southern sun. . . ." In **"Dark Blood"** it is the "blazing suns of other lands" which bring together the scattered ancestry and "reconcile the pride and pain in me." Often the sun force is implied in the many agrarian images of growing grain or seeds planted with the expectation of fulfillment. In **"Sorrow Home"** the absence of the sun is symbolically significant. Declaring that "I was sired and weaned in a tropic world. . . .Warm skies and gulf blue streams are in my blood," the poet asserts her longing for the sun and the natural things it produces in contrast to the unnatural environment of the city: "I am no hot-house bulb to be reared in steam-heated flats with the music of 'L' and subway in my ears, walled in by steel and wood and brick far from the sky."

The most sustained reference to the sun is in the brief poem **"People of Unrest,"** where the speaker gazes "from the pillow" at the sun, the pillow seeming to symbolize lethargy or other conditions which prevent one from knowing one's potential and taking appropriate action. The sun is the "light in shadows"—hope when all seems hopeless. The day grows tall; it is time for action—for self-knowledge, for healing, for positiveness. We should seek joyfully the force which will make us whole and move us to positive action. For our curse of "unrest and sorrow," the sun will provide regeneration.

Earth and water are closely associated with sun. Soil, sun-warmed, is also healing. It is the womb from which springs nourishment for spirit as well as body. The sturdy, singing grandmothers "touched the earth and grain grew." The persona caught in the unnatural environment of the Northern city longs for unbroken rest in the fields of Southern earth, where corn waves "silver in the sun" **("Southern Song")**. We need "earth beneath our feet against the storm" **("Our Need")**. Water also is a life force, working with earth to produce nourishment and peace. The city-dwelling persona longs to "mark the splashing of a brook, a pond with ducks and frogs. . ." **("Southern Song")**.

But an imbalance between sun, earth, and water produces chaos. The valley, where there is little sun, yields "mud and muck and misery" **("Delta")**. The soil there is "red clay from feet of beasts." The red of the clay

suggests violence as "my heart bleeds for our fate." There is muddy water at our shanty door, and we are threatened by swollen levees. Rivers are the mode of transportation by which the fruits of our labor are taken from us. In the city, where there are "pavement stones" instead of warm earth and "cold and blustery nights" and rainy days instead of sun, the people shield themselves from that nature, brooding and restless, whispering oaths **("Memory.")**

The symbols of sun, earth, and water arise from racial memory of generations when nature, not Western technology, sustains life. The slave culture was an agrarian culture, and before that the African sun and earth and water in balance kept us living, in imbalance made us struggle against death. Walker uses these symbols in accordance with our history, tapping Black myth and ritual.

Something else particularly significant to Black people infuses the *For My People* poems: music. In poem after poem music is heard as a life-sustaining force. There are not only the rhythms of the long-paragraph poems and the ballads, but also the repeated references to music. It is music that reflects the emotional tone of many of the poems and often provides an essential metaphor. In **"Sorrow Home"** the music of the city is dissonant; the persona is plagued by the restless music propelling her toward home. Beneath it all is the melody of the South, the sorrow home, beating in her bone and blood. **"Today"** is itself a song, singing of the terrible images of a wartime world: "I sing these fragments of living that you may know by these presents that which we feared most has come upon us." In two poems Walker defies Black tradition. In **"For My People,"** the religious songs are called "dirges" and she demands that they disappear in favor of "martial songs." In **"Since 1619"** she demands impatiently, "How many years since 1619 have I been singing Spirituals?/How long have I been praising God and shouting hallelujahs?" Music, for Walker, is a medium for communicating her message, as it has been for Black people since the beginning of time.

The poems in *For My People* thus emerge from centuries of Black American myth and ritual. Tinged with the Marxism which influenced the young poet's thinking at the time, they nevertheless reflect not only the writer's own grounding in Black Southern tradition but the generations of racial experience which were the ingredients of that tradition. The major dynamic in the book is the tension between the natural beauty of the land and the unnatural horror of racism, the poet's longing for the South but dread of its oppression and violence. The book is a demand for revolution.

The major part of this essay is concerned with these poems because this critic feels that *For My People* is Margaret Walker's most vital contribution to our culture. It is the nucleus which produced her subsequent volumes. Nearly thirty years passed before Walker published another collection of poems. Meanwhile the nation had engaged in wars, declared and undeclared, and Black people's fortunes had risen and fallen several times over.

Prophets for a New Day (1970) was the fruit of the upsurge of rebellion of the 1960s; it was published by a major Black influence of the times, Dudley Randall's Broadside Press. The poems in this small paperback volume are Walker's tribute to the people, celebrated and unsung, who contributed their agony and sometimes their lives to freedom.

Here the Southern landscape has become the battleground for the struggle for civil and human rights. As in *For My People,* the poet contrasts nature's beauty with the horror of violence and oppression. The elemental symbols of sun, earth, and water have disappeared as the scene shifts to the cities, which are the backdrop for struggle and death. Jackson, Mississippi, where lie "three centuries of my eyes and my brains and my hands," is called "City of tense and stricken faces. . .City of barbed wire stockades." The sun is destructive here, for it "beats down raw fire." The jagged rhythms and uneven rhyme underscore the tension (**"Jackson, Mississippi"**). Birmingham, Alabama, is a place where beautiful memories, tinged with fantasy, contrast with the present reality of hatred and death (**"Birmingham"**).

The people on the mythic landscape are the heroes of that time. They are the "prophets." Some, like the children who were jailed, will not be remembered individually, but their collective effort is unforgettable history. Others are names whose very mention elicits floods of memories of that bitter time: Malcolm X, Martin Luther King, Medgar Evers, the three slain young civil rights workers. Walker has captured their heroism in poem after poem. She alludes often to specific events—the 1963 march on Washington, Dr. King's ringing speech there, the march on Selma, the dogs and fire hoses and cattle prods used against young and old nonviolent demonstrators, the murder of heroes. The poems are infused with rage, controlled and effective.

One difference from the *For My People* poems is immediately apparent: the biblical references in *Prophets for a New Day.* The early poems, consistent with their Marxist cast, saw religion as an opiate. **"Since 1619"** demands that "these scales fall away from my eyes" and that "I burst from my kennel an angry mongrel. . . ." In another poem from that volume, **"We Have Been Believers,"** she damns all Black religion, the "black gods from an old land" and the "white gods of a new land," ridiculing the faith of the people and insisting, "We have been believers believing in our burdens and our demigods too long." She demands revolution, which she apparently sees as the antithesis of religion. *Prophets for a New Day,* however, reflects a profound religious faith. The heroes of the sixties are named for the prophets of the Bible: Martin Luther King is Amos, Medgar Evers is Micah, and so on. The people and events of the sixties are paralleled with Biblical characters and occurrences. The title poem makes the parallel clearly. It begins,

seeing fire as paradigm in the burning bush of the Moses legend, the goals informing the lips of Isaiah, and as Nommo, or the Word, which inspires the prophets of today's "evil age." The religious references are important. Whether one espouses the Christianity in which they are couched is not the issue. For the fact is that Black people from ancient Africa to now have always been a spiritual people, believing in an existence beyond the flesh. African art, the music of the slave culture, and the fervor of urban storefront churches affirm the depth of this faith.

Prophets for a New Day, like its predecessor, is grounded in Black myth and ritual. It records the generation of the sixties' contribution to the history of bloody struggle against oppression and the soul-deep conviction that we—that all people—are meant by nature to be free.

Another volume, *October Journey,* a collection of poems from 1934 to 1972, was published by Broadside Press three years later. For the most part, I found these poems less impressive than the others. Some were occasional poems and some written in sonnet form, using formal diction, which this critic found artificial and lacking in spontaneity. Here I admit a personal bias: I have never found European structures such as the sonnet, nor poems written for specific occasions, to be sturdy enough vehicles to contain the weight of our centuries-long tragedy and triumph, nor of our vision which stretches from an African past to the future.

"October Journey," the title poem, is an exception. It is a fine work, rivaling the best poetry of our times in its imagery, its emotional appeal, and the way it burrows deep inside the reader. The poem is a journey into the mythic homeland. It begins with a warning fashioned out of folk beliefs, suggesting that for the traveler the "bright blaze" of autumn's rising is to be preferred to heady spring hours, or to what might be tempting summer nights; cautioning that broad expanses of water should be avoided during the full moon, and that some kind of protection should be carried. The message is that the finest journeys occur in October. Then follows a series of passionate images of the Southland in October, "when colors gush down mountainsides/and little streams are freighted with a caravan of leaves," and in all the seasons. The description is a collage of form and color and sun-earth-water. The speaker eagerly anticipates the return to the place of so many loving memories; such a return is necessary if one is to be whole. "The train wheels hum, 'I am going home, I am going home,/I am moving toward the South.'" But, as in Walker's other poems, the old ambivalence is there: ". . .my heart fills up with hungry fear. . . ." And when she arrives in homeland, the natural beauty of the place and the warmth of childhood memories are swallowed up in the dreadful reality of the ruined world, portraying brilliantly the withering of promise, the grief too deep and pervasive to be expressed, the dried blooming, the wasted potential, sullen facets of the profound. Again Walker has portrayed brilliantly the profound historical experience of Black people, the mythic past which lies just behind our eyes.

Margaret Walker is a profoundly important poet whose works plumb the depth of our racial experience. And our racial experience is a deeply human experience no less universal than that of our oppressors and, in fact, more important. For it takes inhumanity, greed, and technology to be an oppressor; but it takes all the attributes of godly humanity to survive oppression and to emerge as victorious human beings. Margaret Walker shows us the way. The power of her emotion and poetic craftsmanship transcends ideology and bares the struggle and strength which are integral to our individual and collective selves. Despite the many images of brutality inflicted upon us, Walker's vision from the beginning has been of a people striking back at oppression and emerging triumphant. Despite her avowed abhorrence of violence Walker has ever envisioned revolution. Rapping with Nikki Giovanni, Walker admitted that her feelings about Black people and the struggle for freedom were best encompassed in an early poem published in *Prophets for a New Day,* **"The Ballad of the Free."** This poem unites the old urge toward revolution and the militance of Christian teachings learned from her minister father. She evokes the champions whose blood colors our history: Nat Turner, Gabriel Prosser, Denmark Vesey, Toussaint L'Ouverture, John Brown. She repeats, in a stirring refrain, words that sing our most intimate racial self. The metaphor is that of a serpent loosed, and echoing Fanon, Walker prophesied that there is more to come than merely the last being first.

Margaret Walker's poetry has mined the depths of African-American racial memory, portraying a history and envisioning a future. Like all artists, she is grounded in a particular time and thus labors under particular limits of conscious perception. Her vision of the African past is fairly dim and romantic, in spite of various individual poems on ancestry. Consciously she sees African-Americans as a minority group in the United States of America, the stepchildren, rejected, oppressed, denied, brutalized, and dehumanized by the dominant group. But her poetry emanates from a deeper area of the psyche, one which touches the mythic area of a collective being and reenacts the rituals which define a Black collective self. When she was nineteen, Margaret Walker wrote:

> I want to write
> I want to write the songs of my people.
> I want to hear them singing melodies in the dark.
> I want to catch the last floating strains from their
>   sob-torn throats.
> I want to frame their dreams into words; their
>   souls into notes.
> I want to catch their sunshine laughter in a bowl;
> fling dark hands to a darker sky
> and fill them full of stars
> then crush and mix such lights till they become
> a mirrored pool of brilliance in the dawn.

And she has done just that. (pp. 499-510)

Eugenia Collier, "Fields Watered with Blood: Myth and Ritual in the Poetry of Margaret Walker," in Black Women Writers (1950-1980): A Critical Evaluation, *edited by Mari Evans, Anchor Press/Doubleday, 1984, pp. 499-510.*

Margaret Walker with Lucy M. Freibert (interview date 1986)

[*In the following 1986 interview, Freibert and Walker discuss the major influences on Walker's life and literary work. The interview took place at Walker's home in Jackson, Mississippi.*]

[Freibert]: *You have been a writer, teacher, activist, homemaker, and cultural analyst. What is the unifying role in your life?*

[Walker]: Well, I think that the feminine principle of being a daughter, a sister, a mother, and now a grandmother has been the motivating and inspiring agency. I think I said that first in a piece I wrote called **"On Being Female, Black, and Free"**—that being a woman is first, that when the doctor says "It's a she," that's the first thing.

Would you talk about some of the people who have influenced you the most?

Well, my parents had the first influence on me. They were teachers. My mother taught music, and my father taught religion and philosophy. My father had taught in high schools before he taught in college; he had taught many different subjects. He was a fine English scholar, but he was first and foremost a theologian. Hearing my father give his sermons, watching him prepare them, and seeing him exemplify in his daily life what he preached had an effect on me. My mother was a musician—just hearing her play and hearing that music every day had a real influence on me. But equally important was my grandmother. When I think of how I grew up, I think of the three of them.

My teachers until I was almost college age were mostly women. I had only one male teacher in grade school, and then in high school I had three or four male teachers. When I was in college, my freshman English teacher was a woman, a very fine teacher who had graduated from Northwestern. She told my parents they should send me to Northwestern, where they had gone to school. And then when I was sixteen, I saw Langston Hughes for the first time. He was one of the first black male writers influential on me. . . .Then I went to Northwestern when I was seventeen, and I had no more women teachers. The only woman who taught me at Northwestern taught hygiene. I was surprised to discover that black women teaching in black colleges in the South had far more position, prestige, and status than white women teaching in northern coed universities. The black woman on the black college campus can be anything she wants to be, but the faculties of Northwestern and Iowa showed me the lower status of white women teachers.

Three black men influenced you?

My three black writer friends didn't teach me formally in school but influenced my work very much. I read Langston Hughes first when I was eleven years old, and I saw him when I was sixteen. I knew him for thirty-five years. He was a close friend and a real influence. W. E. B. Dubois, whom I also saw for the first time when I was about seventeen at Northwestern, published my first poem in a national magazine, *Crisis*. It was called **"Daydream,"** but it's now called **"I Want to Write."** That was my dream—to write. And the third black man was Richard Wright, whom I met after I was out of college.

Did your parents directly encourage you to write?

Yes, they did. When I was twelve years old, my father gave me a daybook in which I could keep my poems, and told me to keep everything I wrote together, not to scatter my work. That motivated me to fill the book.

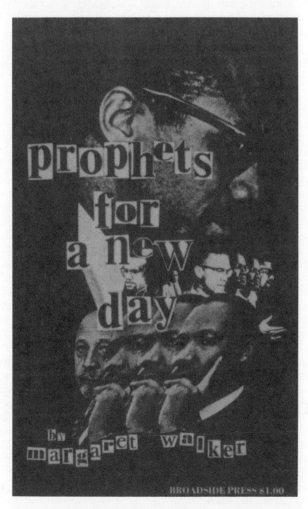

Cover of Walker's 1970 collection of poetry.

That became your journal, then?

Well, it wasn't really a journal. I started a journal when I was thirteen. My journals were kept in composition books. I think that I may be able to go back to them and use them for the autobiography. I have been blocking it out in my head and looking for a theme. I am sure that there will be passages from those journals that I will want to go back and remember and include in the autobiography.

Do you normally use materials from your journals in your literary works?

I think so, but it has been an unconscious thing. I was consciously writing journals. I wasn't consciously taking material from them to use in the books, except when I was working with the Richard Wright book. For that I went back to entries in my journals deliberately. I read his journals but wasn't allowed to quote directly from them. But I could quote from my own. The episode in which our friendship ended is recorded in the book in its entirety. I was a very young woman, in my very early twenties. As I look back on it now, the experience is as clear and concise and direct as I recorded it then. I have not changed a word in that journal entry. . . .

I am sure you are pleased to have the Wright book finished and to know that it will be coming out soon. Would you comment on the title you gave the book: **Richard Wright: A Daemonic Genius.**

I am using the Greek term "daemonic," and using it in an aesthetic sense. The creative genius of Wright was not orphic, and it was not, shall I say, visionary like that of Blake. It was daemonic in the way that we speak of the shield of Achilles made by Haiphaestus as being daemonic. Daemonic genius is genius driven by devils or demons but not purely Satanic. Wright was also like the god maker, the person of character and personality like Pygmalion. It's that kind of daemonic. I am not calling him a devil, although I think his widow must believe that's what I'm up to.

Your relationship with Wright ended rather abruptly. According to one report, you said that Wright picked your brains and then dismissed you.

[laughing] Well, I think feminists will grab that, but wait a minute, let's stop there. People have made a great deal over the friendship and the breaking up, and I don't look back now with any regret. I have written the book with a great deal of hard work and some pleasure, and I hope that it is going to be available soon. I suppose that I may have gotten a great deal from the Wright friendship. I know he got a lot from me. Whether he picked my brain—he may have tried to—I doubt that he could have thoroughly picked my brain.

Would you discuss the other works that you have in progress? I saw a rather lengthy list in your file over at the Jackson State library. It starts with Minna *and* Jim.

That's the sequel to *Jubilee.* I have only blocked that out. I haven't done any work on it.

And Mother Broyer?

I'm working on that now. I've done a hundred pages, and I'm in the second section of that. It is laid in four cities: it starts in Algiers, across the river from New Orleans, moves to Los Angeles, California, and then to Harlem, New York, and ends on the West Side of Chicago. Mother Broyer spends the first twenty-two or three or maybe twenty-five years in New Orleans, then about ten or twelve years in Los Angeles, about a year, six to eight or ten, maybe twelve to eighteen months in New York, and then spends the rest of her life in Chicago.

Then there's **This Is My Century.**

This is My Century is a book of my poetry. It is going to be the collected poetry. It will include five books: *For My People, Prophets for a New Day, October Journey, This Is My Century,* and *A Poem for Farish Street.*

And then you are working on the autobiography.

Yes, I have done a hundred pages on the autobiography, but I am going to have to rearrange and reorganize it in terms of the themes that I have in mind. . . .

Do you write on schedule, or do you just wait until the spirit moves you?

Well, I can write any time that I sit down to the typewriter or with my notebook. It depends on what I am writing. I really had a schedule that last year with *Jubilee,* in the last few months especially, but never before or since have I been able to get back to a schedule.

When you write poetry, do you carry the poem around in your head first, or do you start right out putting things on paper?

Regardless of the medium, whether you are a musician, a painter, a graphic artist, a plastic artist, or a sculptor, whether you are a writer or an architect, you begin the same way. Creative writing grows out of creative thinking, and nothing begins a work before the idea as a conceptualization; that is the beginning. All writers, all artists, all musicians, all people with creative talent begin with that creative thinking. They begin with conceptualization. You get an idea, and sometimes the whole process moves on mentally and unconsciously before it is given conscious artistic form, but the process begins with the idea.

Everything begins in the mind. You have an idea, and you may not know for a long time what form this idea is going to take or what you are going to say or how you are going to say it, but you have that first. For me it is intuitive. Some people are not intuitive. I'm intuitive. I in-tu-it. For me it begins with a concept, maybe before it is even an idea—a concept before it becomes thought or

idea. It may begin with a picture. For the musician, I am sure it begins with a musical motif or a sound that the musician hears or senses. It is a process using the sensory perceptions, I guess you would say. You perceive or conceive. You perceive what is outside. You conceive what is inside. And you move from the perception of a concept or thought or idea to a figuration and a configuration.

The poet has nothing but words and language to be used as tools. And the poet—I think my father taught me this—the poet in my instance uses rhetorical devices. I have been told by some poets and even by some teachers that I am too rhetorical. I cannot conceive of writing poetry without metaphor and simile, synecdoche, metonymy, hyperbole. I grew up with that, and my work is rhetorical, but I think it is rhetorical in the best sense of the word. I had teachers who tried to break me of the habit. My father taught me my first lessons in rhetoric from an old English book that he had brought to this country. It gave all the rhetorical forms. I don't think a poet writes simply in grammatically correct language. I think all the greatest poets in the world were rhetoricians, and I believe in the rhetoric. Paul Engle has criticized me for it. He said, "Margaret was just too rhetorical." I laughed, because I am still rhetorical, and I always will be.

That's what makes your voice so distinctive. What or who helped you to find your voice?

My father, really. I think Stephen Benét tells it in the introduction to *For My People.* It was not just that I heard the sermons my grandfather and my father preached, but it was that training my father gave me in the use of rhetoric. And I really didn't believe when I was a teenaged youngster growing up that you could write poetry without the use of simile and metaphor. I thought you had to use them. After I was older and had gained my own voice, I realized that I had read the Bible all my life and that the use of parallelism was what I had learned from the Bible: cataloguing and repetition and internal rhyme—not so much end rhyme, because that was what I had learned from ordinary poetry. I didn't think of the poetry in the Bible as ordinary. I thought it was extraordinary. And when Benét says you can feel these Biblical rhythms in my poetry, that is the greatest compliment he could give me. I think most of us in the South grew up on that Bible, the King James version of the Bible, as much as on reading Dickens and Sir Walter Scott. Because if you were a student in the South, you have read Scott, Dickens, the Bible, and Shakespeare, and you may have read Milton, because we are very Miltonic in the South. And these are the great influences in English and American literature. And just because we have learned to speak in cryptic language and monosyllabic sentences, making sentences out of monosyllabic words, that is no reason to drop rhetoric from poetry. I'm very certain that I am one of the few black writers who believes that strongly in rhetoric. But I can't help it. It's a part of my background.

I think the voices I have heard in the classics, whether it was the great English, American, or Continental poetry, carry with them not only the surge, the melody, and the rhythm of Biblical poetry, they also have power. And I have had people tell me that my words have power, the power that comes out of that Biblical background, that religious background that makes you aware that words are not just some idle spoken things but they should carry great meaning with them. My father taught me that poetry must have three qualities. It must have rhythm or music, but first it must have pictures or images, and third it must have meaning. And everything I write I test by those three standards. Are there any pictures here in the poetry? Do you see images? Do you feel the rhythms? Do you sense the power behind the meaning? Those are my three major standards. I was a long time coming to this in prose. I thought that prose was completely disconnected from poetry. I didn't grow up realizing that stories and novels and biography and autobiography had sometimes the same rhythms, the same images that poetry has. I was taught versification and scansion by masters. When I was at Northwestern, my teacher, Professor Hungerford, rigidly schooled me in versification and scansion. He has written a little book, *On Remembering the Rhythms.* He believed in that sweep, and he liked my poems. He said that in "JEAN LAFITTE, the Baratarian" I was writing like Keats, that I had that sensuousness that Keats had, that it came from my descriptive power in the pictures, the images, but it was also in the rhythm, because I wrote in couplets. But they were not heroic couplets; they were run-on Keatsian couplets. I was always determined to have meaning or power in these things.

The connection you made between poetry and prose shows up so well in **Jubilee.** *Almost every chapter is like a poem in itself.*

I appreciate your saying that because one critic said that my style was atrocious and that I had no poetry in *Jubilee.* I was amused at that. He said that the book wasn't interesting, was dull, and didn't have any sex in it. When I read that, I laughed because I said, "Millions of people do not agree with you."

Jubilee *was probably the earliest book to focus on the complexity of the relationship between black and white women.*

Well, I think that's what Minrose Gwin is talking about in *Black and White Women of the Old South.* She says that I do express that connection, that relationship. And I am sure they must be there because my audience consists of both black and white. And I have had many, many white people in the South tell me they relate to the book. They feel with the characters in there. They recognize people. And, of course, black folks tell me, "Oh, Vyry is everybody's grandmother." They love Vyry because they say, "She's just like my grandmother. She was like my grandmother was. Where does she come from?" They know her. They recognize her. It wasn't a simple, easy, quick task to bring her to life.

Was that perception of the black and white women's dilemma in your grandmother's story, or is that where your artistry comes in?

I think it was both. Of course, you know, I never say Vyry. Vyry was really Margaret, my great-grandmother, and Minna, who told me the story, was really Vyry. Her name was Elvira. My grandmother was a part of my raising, my rearing. She told me the story. The story, as she told it, reflected the relationship of my great-grandmother to all people around her, black and white. I think you recognize the humanistic value of Vyry because whether it's Aunt Sally or Mammy Sukey, whether it is Miss Lillian or Miss Lucy, you see the kinship of women. When the poor white woman in the house with the children has not been fed, Vyry feeds her, and she tells Randall Ware and Innes—the night that they talk and she shows her back—she says, "If any of those people came to my door in the mornin', no matter how bad they treated me, I would feed 'em. I would feed 'em."

One of the reviewers said that *Jubilee* is a powerful testament to Christianity, to Christian love, because the thing that we get from Vyry—and people don't want to believe it—is that out of outrage and violence and bitterness, she comes up with this Christian love and forgiveness. And you know, I was raised that way. My grandmother was that way. And she was Vyry's child. And I realized when I finished the book that I had never known Vyry, but I knew her daughter, and she was like Vyry. My mother said, "Oh, you've got my grandmother down. She was just like that." I said, "But you know I was really using grandma." Then she said, "Well Mamma was like grandma." And I said, "And my mother was like her mother." I'm like my mother. The older I get, the more I look like my mother and I think like my mother. My grandmother was just like her mother. Women are like their mothers.

And childbearing women—I have a daughter expecting—and I told her, "Women have their children the way their mothers had them." That's part of being a woman—in the difficulty of going into puberty, the problems of early marriage, or even when marriages don't last (because all marriages are not made in heaven), and divorce, which is perhaps the worst thing a woman can go through short of death itself, and the whole business of estrangement—in all these instances women follow the pattern of women who have gone before them.

But then we have an interesting thing happening, which has happened with the sexual revolution. We have women who look at the pain they have suffered and who have been through some excruciating sexual pain, that is, in their relationships with men and other women so that they determine to break the shackles, to do away with the ikons, and to avoid the stereotypes. And these women are speaking out more and more, but this is what the women's movement has meant. At first it was simply to break the terrible slavery of domestic bondage, where they were under the rule of the father and the husband, and they didn't dare cross them and be independent and think for themselves. And then they decided we want to be a part of the world around us. We want to be educated. We want to have our chance at careers. We want options. We don't all want to be married. We don't all want to have children. We want to be able to make a living without this father or husband.

And then we have seen this male domination go so far that we find women who have been brutalized in their marriage relationships or in their paternal relationships, and they moved out to what may *seem* a perversion of love—they found a bonding with other women. This is very obvious in our society today. It existed before, but we kept it hidden. We closed it off. We didn't want this to be a part of what the world knew about us, because then we became pariahs and were thrown aside.

It is a long way up for women from the status of women in ancient times, say in the time of Jesus, when a woman could be brought before Jesus and accused: "This woman was caught in the act of adultery, and Moses said stone such a one to death. What do you say?" I think that is the first move toward woman's liberation, when Jesus says, "Well, any man who has never sinned and who is not guilty of any woman, let him pick up the stone and throw first." He didn't say, "Where is the man who was with this woman?" He didn't say, "Well, I don't believe there should be one kind of standard or two." He just said, "Let the man without sin cast the first stone." And he looked around and all these men had moved away. He said to the woman, "Woman, where are your accusers?" She said, "Sir, I have none." He said, "Well, neither do I accuse you." In other words, "I know nothing about you. I haven't been guilty of it. So you may go on your way, but don't sin any more." (pp. 50-4)

How does your experience as a black woman writer compare with that, say, of Zora Neale Hurston, Nella Larson, or Gwendolyn Brooks?

I guess I have had some of the same problems they have had. You should compare me with a white woman writer, because there is where the great difference has been. I'm not an unfulfilled person in the same sense that Zora was. Zora was certainly a very great storyteller and very bright, a brilliant woman, but she didn't graduate from Columbia with a doctorate under Papa Boaz. Not that she wasn't as smart as Margaret Mead or Ruth Benedict. They were white, and she was black. There's where the contrast is. She didn't get the doctorate in anthropology. Well, I can say that I went to school, and I got the doctorate. Very few black people had done it at Iowa before I did, and very few have since, but I went back where I had gotten a master's and, though it was difficult, I managed to fulfill the requirements. And I got it. Therefore, that's one thing that Zora was frustrated in. I've not been frustrated.

Zora was married twice very briefly. Her marriages did not work out. I was married thirty-seven years to one man, and I have four children, eight grandchildren from that union. In that sense I am not frustrated at all. I know only one other person who has been married as long as I have to the same man, and that is Gwendolyn Brooks. Gwen was married to Henry Blakely in her very early twenties when first I knew her. They had a very brief separation, but while they were separated I think Gwen must have realized that Henry was always very good for her. They had two children together, a son and a daughter, and in that respect we are alike. Gwen is still married to Blakely. My husband is dead.

I never knew Nella Larson. I saw Zora as a child, but I never saw Nella Larson and knew little about her until I was an adult. I read Zora's books as they came out. I have since read Nella Larson's *Quicksand* and *Passing*. I don't care for her as much as I do for Zora, but I think she's a fine writer. I know almost nothing of her personal life. Zora was accused of sodomy, taken into court, and although she came out of it and was vindicated and proved innocent, it literally ruined her life and career. And I have not had that kind of awful situation.

There are three women from Georgia—two white and one black—whom I put in the same bag: Flannery O'Connor, Carson McCullers, whom I knew at Yaddo, and Alice Walker. I never knew Flannery O'Connor, but she went to the same school I went to in Iowa, and they told me about her. Those three women are from the same neck of the woods in Georgia. They are all three women of gothic imagination, all three writing of the violent South. It was Flannery O'Connor who wrote *The Violent Bear It Away.* Carson was writing things about grotesque people in *Ballad of the Sad Café,* and in *The Heart Is a Lonely Hunter* and *Reflections in a Golden Eye.* I would say even in *Clock Without Hands.* Flannery O'Connor's "Artificial Nigger," *The Violent Bear It Away, Everything That Rises Must Converge*—they can all be compared with Alice Walker's *Third Life of Grange Copeland, Meridian,* and *The Color Purple.* I'm not like any of those women. Those women have a different imagination. Those women have a different perspective. They have a different philosophy. I think they are all remarkable writers. I think that it will take many more years before we say these women were great artists. They were great craftswomen, virtuosos, but I don't think any one of those women can stand up now to the test of what I consider the great test of an artist— that you are willing to go back and read their books over and over again. I don't know. I do not personally enjoy reading them over and over again. I'm repelled by Flannery O'Connor's "Artificial Nigger." I don't think much even of *The Violent Bear It Away.* I think one of her best things is *Everything That Rises Must Converge.* Carson McCullers, who is around my age, died very much younger. I read *The Heart Is a Lonely Hunter* and liked that, but there were things in it I didn't like. And then she came out with *Reflections in a Golden Eye.* I would never read that book again. When she came up with *Clock Without Hands,* it was so painful I could hardly bear to read the whole book.

I had great difficulty with Alice Walker's *The Color Purple.* I do not like the book for many reasons. I think Alice's best work is *In Search of Our Mothers' Gardens.* It's a very beautiful book and a book that I can relate to and understand. *The Third Life of Grange Copeland* for me has many problems. The book *Meridian* includes my name, and I'm there as a character, and I don't exactly appreciate that. I can hardly make myself go back and look at *Meridian.* I think I feel about those books the way I feel about Faulkner's *Sanctuary.* At first I was just repelled. I like the kind of macabre humor that Faulkner uses, but then again, it is that same gothic imagination.

Now I find myself able to read and reread Eudora Welty, and she has a gothic imagination and she does sometimes deal with the grotesque and with things almost gruesome, but her *Delta Wedding* reflects that Delta language and you can hear that speech. Her folk things are truly authentic. I think she is a great artist. You see the difference? I can read her anytime. I would say that Eudora Welty's immortality is assured. I'm not sure about those three women from Georgia. I think that way up the road, they are going to be like Kate Chopin.

She's back now. My students love her. They loved Meridian, *also.*

A lot of people love and like Alice. I have known Alice, but I think that *The Color Purple* is a reflection on the black family as a whole, particularly on black men, that it is not even complimentary to black women, and certainly to black children. And I agree with those women out in California who said that it is not good reading for pre-adolescent children, that it should not be required reading in the grade schools and junior high schools.

I don't think it was intended for that.

But when the fight came up, the question came up as to censorship, and all of us are opposed to that. So you see there is a fine line there.

That is the most difficult thing to decide.

And that's what I'm saying. It is like saying Henry Miller is a great writer in *Tropic of Cancer* and *Tropic of Capricorn.* There is some filthy stuff there. There is some filthy vile stuff there. Now it depends on how you are judging. And I don't think literature should be judged on moral grounds. I think it should be judged on aesthetic grounds, and then you might say Henry Miller is a great writer.

Young writers like Nikki Giovanni and Sonia Sanchez rate you among the greats. Sonia calls you "a strong gust of woman."

Sonia is like a child of mine. Nikki and Sonia and Alice are my daughters' generation. Sonia is older than they by a few years, but they are still young enough to have been my daughters. I like all three of them personally.

Alice and Nikki and Sonia can write what I cannot write. I want to write very much about the Vietnam War, the sixties, and the seventies, but I ask myself over and over again, "What am I going to do with that vocabulary?" because it is a shocking, brutal kind. And the four-letter words, the drug scene, the violence and crime, the black nationalism, all that stuff. It's really not my cup of tea. I want to write about it because it's my son's generation. He went to Vietnam, and I think there needs to be a record of that. I don't know whether I am ever going to be able to put it down, because I cannot use the four-letter words and the language, and I cannot deal with the shock bit.

To skip backward a minute, what is it about Gwendolyn Brooks's Annie Allen *that so appeals to you? You have spoken so highly of that work.*

Well, I'll tell you what I liked about *Annie Allen* when I read it. I had read *A Street in Bronzeville,* which shows Gwen's talent very clearly, and it's a very good first book, but *Annie Allen* reflects very careful discipline, hard work, knowledge of the craft, and such an understanding of that adolescent girl as she does in *Maud Martha,* that I think the book is nothing short of superb. "The Anniad," which is in there, is to me a great piece. I have argued with Dudley Randell when I say it's written in rhyme royale. He says it's not the Chaucerian stanza, but I say it is. I think I know as well as Dudley. It is the Chaucerian line and stanza. And that's a very difficult stanza to write. I think Gwendolyn Brooks proved in *Annie Allen* that she was capable of most difficult forms, that she could write in the strictest meters and still keep the very wonderful flavor of black life and folklore. I think that's what's in *Annie Allen.* I think, too, that that book is a very well-crafted book. I think that Gwen is at her very best in *Annie Allen.* I think in this book she fulfills the promise of *A Street in Bronzeville.* You see in *Annie Allen* that she is an artist who understands the craft of poetry and the art of writing. And I think that aside from a number of the very flavorsome pieces in there, you don't see anything like it again until she comes to "Mecca." "Mecca" is another very fine piece.

I haven't seen any recent things of Gwen's to say that I like this or that, but Gwen wrote nine volumes of poetry. She says some of the stuff was for children and then did *Maud Martha,* which I think is a sensitive portrait. I wish she had done more of that sort of thing, but *Annie Allen* is superb. I think I have said it somewhere.

I'd like to get back to your poetry for just a moment. The French feminist critics talk about "writing from the body" these days. Early in the forties you wrote,

I want my careless song to strike no minor key; no fiend to stand between my body's southern song—the fusion of the South, my body's song and me.

Is there a connection here?

Well, I don't know whether I was thinking in the feminist vein when I said that, because I have said it over and over again, in both **"Southern Song"** and **"Sorrow Home."** What I'm saying, in a very sensuous, not sensual but sensuous, way is that I'm a creature of the South. When I wrote this I was in cold Chicago, and I didn't see grass and hay and clover in bloom. I didn't see red clay. I didn't smell the earth after the rain. All of this comes back to me, so I write about the South, and then I contrast, as I do frequently in poetry and prose. (I do it a lot in the Richard Wright book.) I contrast the ideal beauty of the land, the ambience of the South, and the horror of its violence and racial conflict. When I leave the physical beauty of the South, and when I talk about "my body's southern song—the fusion of the South, my body's song and me," I mean that I am a part of this whole process of nature, that when we come together I am complete and it is complete because it is a part of me and I am part of it. Now I want to see the dichotomy closed, the split ended. The social horror and the physical beauty are constantly there, and I talk about that in everything I write—the beauty of the South and the horror of this other society. (pp. 55-6)

Margaret Walker and Lucy M. Freibert, in an interview in Frontiers: A Journal of Women Studies, *Vol. IX, No. 3, 1987, pp. 50-6.*

FURTHER READING

Barksdale, Richard D. "Margaret Walker: Folk Orature and Historical Prophecy." In *Black American Poets between Worlds, 1940-1960,* edited by R. Baxter Miller, pp. 104-117. Knoxville: University of Tennessee Press, 1986.
    Evaluates the poems in *For My People,* stating that "the title poem is itself a singular and unique literary achievement."

Fabre, Michel. "Margaret Walker's Richard Wright: A Wrong Righted or Wright Wronged?" *Mississippi Quarterly: The Journal of Southern Culture* XLII, No. 4 (Fall 1989): 429-50.
    Attacks Walker's book on Richard Wright. The critic notes: "To put it bluntly, there is nothing new, in terms of literary criticism, in *Daemonic Genius.* This apparently neatly structured book, with catchy chapter titles and sub-titles, and the expected scholarly apparatus, appears on closer scrutiny to become a parody of scholarly criticism . . . . [This work] raises serious questions about Margaret Walker as writer and critic."

Giddings, Paula. "A Shoulder Hunched against a Sharp Concern: Some Themes in the Poetry of Margaret Walker." *Black World* XXI, No. 2 (December 1971): 20-25.

Studies common themes in *For My People* and *Prophets for a New Day.*

Gwin, Minrose C. "*Jubilee*: The Black Woman's Celebration of Human Community." In *Conjuring: Black Women, Fiction, and Literary Tradition,* edited by Marjorie Pryse and Hortense J. Spillers, pp. 132-50. Bloomington: Indiana University Press, 1985.
    Examines Walker's humanistic vision in *Jubilee,* concluding: "In *Jubilee* the black woman's forgiving gesture suggests not so much an abatement of black pain or lifting of white guilt. . .[but] that we can redeem ourselves by extending our sense of human community—whether white, black, male, female, South, North—in ever-widening circles."

Powell, Bertie J. "The Black Experience in Margaret Walker's *Jubilee* and Lorraine Hansberry's *The Drinking Gourd.*" *CLA Journal* XXI, No. 2 (December 1977): 304-11.
    Considers Hansberry's *The Drinking Gourd* and Walker's *Jubilee* as two works about American plantation slavery.

Rowell, Charles H. "Poetry, History and Humanism: An Interview with Margaret Walker." *Black World* XXV, No. 2 (December 1975): 4-17.
    Walker discusses early influences on her work and reveals her motive for writing *Jubilee.*

Review of *Jubilee,* by Margaret Walker. *The Times Literary Supplement,* No. 3409 (29 June 1967): 583.
    Mixed review of *Jubilee.* The critic notes: "Miss Walker does not really fulfil her own ambition. There are too many chunks of undigested history, too many conversations which casually mention the latest legislation as well as what is for supper. Much of the characterization is stereotyped and cliché-ridden. And some of the conclusions smack of Uncle Tom. But there are compensations. . . ."

Traylor, Eleanor. "Music as Theme: The Blues Mode in the Works of Margaret Walker." In *Black Women Writers (1950-1980): A Critical Evaluation,* edited by Mari Evans, pp. 499-525. Garden City, N.Y.: Anchor Press/Doubleday, 1984.
    Explores the blues motif in *Jubilee.*

————."'Bolder Measures Crashing Through': Margaret Walker's Poem of the Century." *Callaloo* 10, No. 4 (Fall 1987): 570-95.
    Overview of poems in Walker's *This is My Century.*

Ward, Jerry W., Jr. "A Writer of Her People: An Interview with Dr. Margaret Walker Alexander." *Mississippi Quarterly: The Journal of Southern Culture* XLI, No. 4 (Fall 1988): 515-27.
    Interview. Walker evaluates the work of Alice Walker, Amiri Baraka, and Sonia Sanchez.

Booker T. Washington

1856-1915

(Born Booker Taliaferro; later added surname Washington) American autobiographer, essayist, lecturer, and biographer.

Washington's *Up from Slavery* (1901) is a classic American autobiography that has long inspired black and white readers alike. A respected educator and founder of the Tuskegee Institute, Washington was one of the most important social thinkers of the early twentieth century. His 1895 speech before a racially mixed audience at the Atlanta Cotton States and International Exposition won him national recognition when he stated his basic philosophy: "In all things that are purely social we can be as separate as the fingers, yet one as the hand in all things essential to mutual progress." This accommodating racial policy appeased northern and southern whites during the discordant post-Reconstruction era and helped motivate many black Americans to become economically independent. However, Washington was often criticized by other prominent black intellectuals, most notably W. E. B. Du Bois—who had earlier supported him—for social policies that emphasized industrial education for black students while repudiating black political agitation. Today Washington is viewed by critics as a complex man whose "accommodation" policies were used in conjunction with covert political activities to improve the social and economic conditions of his race.

Washington was born in 1856 near Roanoke, Virginia, at Hale's Farm, where his mother was the slave cook of James Burroughs, a minor planter. His father was white and possibly a member of the Burroughs family. As a child Booker swept yards and brought water to slaves working in the fields. Freed after the Civil War, he and his mother went to Malden, West Virginia, to join Washington Ferguson, whom his mother had married during the war. Booker later added "Washington" to his name. In Malden young Washington helped support the family by working in salt furnaces and coal mines. He taught himself the alphabet, then studied nights with the teacher of a local school for blacks. In 1870 he started doing housework for the owner of the coal mine where he worked. The owner's wife, an austere New Englander, encouraged his studies and instilled in Washington a great regard for education. In 1872 he set out for the Hampton Institute, a school set up by the Virginia legislature for blacks. He walked much of the way and worked menial jobs to earn the fare to complete the five-hundred-mile journey.

Washington spent three years at Hampton, paying for his room and board by working as a janitor. After graduating with honors in 1875, he taught for two years in Malden, then returned to Hampton to teach American Indians as part of a special program. In 1881,

General Samuel Chapman Armstrong, the principal at Hampton, recommended Washington to the Alabama legislature for the job of principal of a new school for black students at Tuskegee. Washington was accepted for the position, but when he arrived in Tuskegee he discovered that neither land nor buildings had been acquired for the projected school, nor were there any funds for these purposes. Consequently, Washington began classes with thirty students in a shanty donated by a black church. Soon, however, he was able to borrow money to buy an abandoned plantation nearby and moved the school there.

Convinced that economic strength was the best route to political and social equality for blacks, Washington encouraged Tuskegee students to learn industrial skills. Carpentry, cabinetmaking, printing, shoemaking, and tinsmithing were among the first courses the school offered. Boys also studied farming and dairying, while girls learned cooking and sewing and other skills related to homemaking. Strong emphasis was placed on personal hygiene, manners, and character building. Students followed a rigid schedule of study and work and were required to attend chapel daily and a series of religious services on Sunday. Washington usually conducted the Sunday evening program himself. During his thirty-four-year principalship of Tuskegee, the school's curriculum expanded to include instruction in professions as well as trades. At the time of Washington's death from arteriosclerosis and extreme exhaustion in 1915, Tuskegee had an endowment of $2 million and a staff of 200. Nearly 2,000 students were enrolled in the regular courses and about the same number in special courses and the extension division. Among its all-black faculty was the renowned agricultural scientist George Washington Carver. So revered was Washington at Tuskegee that he was buried in a brick tomb, made by students, on a hill overlooking the Institute.

Although his administration of Tuskegee is Washington's best-known achievement, his work as an educator was only one aspect of his multifaceted career. Washington spent much time raising money for Tuskegee and publicizing the school and its philosophy. His success in securing the praise and financial support of northern philanthropists was remarkable. One of his admirers was industrialist Andrew Carnegie, who thought Washington "one of the most wonderful men . . . who ever has lived." Many other political, intellectual, and religious leaders were almost as laudatory. Washington was also in demand as a speaker, winning national fame on the lecture circuit. His most famous speech was his address at the opening of the Cotton States and International Exposition in Atlanta in September, 1895. Later known as the Atlanta Compromise, the speech contained the essence of Washington's educational and racial views and was, according to C. Vann Woodward, "his stock speech for the rest of his life." Emphasizing to black members of the audience the importance of economic power, Washington contended that "the opportunity to earn a dollar in a factory just now is worth infinitely more than the opportunity to spend a dollar in an opera house." Consequently he urged blacks not to strain relations in the South by demanding social equality with whites.

The Atlanta speech, Woodward noted, "contained nothing [Washington] had not said many times before . . . . But in the midst of racial crisis, black disenfranchisement and Populist rebellion in the '90s, the brown orator electrified conservative hopes." Washington was hailed in the white press as leader and spokesman for all American blacks and successor to the prominent abolitionist Frederick Douglass, who had died a few months earlier. His position, however, was denounced by many black leaders, including civil rights activist W. E. B. Du Bois, who objected to Washington's emphasis on vocational training and economic advancement and argued that higher education and political agitation would win equality for blacks. According to August Meier, those blacks who accepted Washington's "accommodation" doctrines "understood that through tact and indirection [Washington] hoped to secure the good will of the white man and the eventual recognition of the constitutional rights of American Negroes." The contents of Washington's recently released private papers reinforce the later interpretation of the educator's motives. These documents offer evidence that in spite of the cautious stance that he maintained publicly, Washington was covertly engaged in challenging racial injustices and in improving social and economic conditions for blacks. The prominence he gained by his placating demeanor enabled him to work surreptitiously against segregation and disenfranchisement and to win political appointments that helped advance the cause of racial equality. "In other words," Woodward posited, "he secretly attacked the racial settlement that he publicly sanctioned."

Among Washington's many published works is his autobiography *Up from Slavery,* a stirring account of his life from slave to eminent educator. Often referred to by critics as a classic, its style is simple, direct, and anecdotal. Like his numerous essays and speeches, *Up from Slavery* promotes his racial philosophy and, in Woodward's opinion, "presents [Washington's] experience mythically, teaches 'lessons' and reflects a sunny optimism about black life in America." Woodward added, "It was the classic American success story 'the Horatio Alger myth in black'." Praised lavishly and compared to Benjamin Franklin's *Autobiography, Up from Slavery* became a best-seller in the United States and was eventually translated into more than a dozen languages.

(For further information about Washington's life and works, see *Black Writers; Contemporary Authors,* Vols. 116, 125; *Something about the Author,* Vol. 28; and *Twentieth-Century Literary Criticism,* Vol. 10.)

PRINCIPAL WORKS

Black-Belt Diamonds: Gems from the Speeches, Addresses, and Talks to Students of Booker T. Washington (speeches) 1898

The Future of the American Negro (essays and speeches) 1899

A New Negro for a New Century [with N. B. Wood and Fannie Barrier Williams] (essays) 1900

The Story of My Life and Work [with Edgar Webber] (autobiography) 1900; also published as *An Autobiography by Booker T. Washington: The Story of My Life and Work* [revised edition], 1901; also published as *Booker T. Washington's Own Story of His Life and Work* [revised edition, with supplement by Albon L. Holsey], 1915

Up from Slavery [with Max Bennett Thrasher] (autobiography) 1901

Character Building: Being Addresses Delivered on Sunday Evenings to the Students of Tuskegee Institute by Booker T. Washington (essays and addresses) 1902

Working with the Hands: Being a Sequel to "Up from Slavery" Covering the Author's Experiences in

Industrial Training at Tuskegee (autobiography) 1904

Tuskegee and Its People: Their Ideals and Achievements [coeditor with Emmett J. Scott] (nonfiction) 1905

Putting the Most into Life (essays and addresses) 1906

Frederick Douglass [with S. Laing Williams] (biography) 1907

The Negro in the South: His Economic Progress in Relation to His Moral and Religious Development [with W. E. B. Du Bois] (essays and addresses) 1907

The Story of the Negro: The Rise of the Race from Slavery. 2 vols. (nonfiction) 1909

My Larger Education: Being Chapters from My Experience [with Robert E. Park and Emmett J. Scott] (autobiography) 1911

The Man Farthest Down: A Record of Observation and Study in Europe [with Robert E. Park] (nonfiction) 1912

The Story of Slavery (essay) 1913

Selected Speeches of Booker T. Washington [edited by E. Davidson Washington] (speeches) 1932

The Booker T. Washington Papers. 14 vols. [edited by Louis R. Harlan and Raymond W. Smock] (autobiography, essays, interviews, letters, and speeches) 1972-89

Booker T. Washington (lecture date 1895)

[*The following excerpt is from an address Washington delivered to a predominantly white audience at the Atlanta Exposition of 1895. Here, he summarizes his views on the role of blacks in American society. This speech is often referred to as the Atlanta Compromise.*]

Mr. President, Gentlemen of the Board of Directors and Citizens: One-third of the population of the South is of the negro race. No enterprise seeking the material, civil, or moral welfare of this section can disregard this element of our population and reach the highest success. I but convey to you, Mr. President and Directors, the sentiment of the masses of my race, when I say that in no way have the value and manhood of the American negro been more fittingly and generously recognized than by the managers of this magnificent exposition at every stage of its progress. It is a recognition that will do more to cement the friendship of the two races than any occurrence since the dawn of our freedom.

Not only this, but the opportunity here afforded will awaken among us a new era of industrial progress. Ignorant and inexperienced, it is not strange that in the first years of our new life we began at the top instead of at the bottom; that a seat in Congress or the state legislature was more sought than real estate or industrial skill; that the political convention or stump speaking had more attractions than starting a dairy farm or truck garden . . .

To those of my race who depend on bettering their condition in a foreign land or who underestimate the importance of cultivating friendly relations with the southern white man, who is their next-door neighbour, I would say cast down your bucket where you are, cast it down in making friends in every manly way of the people of all races by whom we are surrounded. Cast it down in agriculture, mechanics, in commerce, in domestic service, and in the professions. And in this connection it is well to bear in mind that whatever other sins the south may be called to bear, when it comes to business, pure and simple, it is in the south that the negro is given a man's chance in the commercial world, and in nothing is this exposition more eloquent than in emphasizing this chance. Our greatest danger is, that in the great leap from slavery to freedom we may overlook the fact that the masses of us are to live by the productions of our hands, and fail to keep in mind that we shall prosper in proportion as we learn to dignify and glorify common labour and put brains and skill into the common occupations of life; shall prosper in proportion as we learn to draw the line between the superficial and the substantial, the ornamental gewgaws of life and the useful. No race can prosper till it learns that there is as much dignity in tilling a field as in writing a poem. It is at the bottom of life we must begin, and not at the top. Nor should we permit our grievances to overshadow our opportunities.

To those of the white race who look to the incoming of those of foreign birth and strange tongue and habits for the prosperity of the south, were I permitted I would repeat what I say to my own race: 'Cast down your bucket where you are.' Cast it down among the 8,000,000 Negroes whose habits you know, whose loyalty and love you have tested in days when to have proved treacherous meant the ruin of your firesides. Cast down your bucket among these people who have, without strikes and labour wars, tilled your fields, cleared your forests, builded your railroads and cities, and brought forth treasures from the bowels of the earth, and helped make possible this magnificent representation of the progress of the South. Casting down your bucket among my people, helping and encouraging them as you are doing on these grounds, and to education of head, hand, and heart, you will find that they will buy your surplus land, make blossom the waste places in your fields and run your factories. While doing this, you can be sure in the future, as in the past, that you and your families will be surrounded by the most patient, faithful, law-abiding, and unresentful people that the world has seen. As we have proved our loyalty to you in the past, in nursing your children, watching by the sickbed of your mothers and fathers, and often following them with tear-dimmed eyes to their graves, so in the future, in our humble way we shall stand by you with a devotion that no foreigner can approach, ready to lay down our lives, if need be, in defense of yours, interlacing our industrial, commercial, civil, and religious life with yours in a way that shall make the interests of both races one. In all things that are purely social we can be as separate as the fingers, yet one as the hand in all things essential to mutual progress....

Nearly sixteen millions of hands will aid you in pulling the load upward or they will pull against you the load downward. We shall constitute one-third and much more of the ignorance and crime of the south, or one-third its intelligence and progress; we shall contribute one-third to the business and industrial prosperity of the south, or we shall prove a veritable body of death, stagnating, depressing, retarding every effort to advance the body politic.

Gentlemen of the Exposition: As we present to you our humble effort at an exhibition of our progress, you must not expect overmuch; starting thirty years ago with ownership here and there in a few quilts and pumpkins and chickens (gathered from miscellaneous sources), remember the path that has led us from these to the inventions and production of agricultural implements, buggies, steam-engines, newspapers, books, statuary, carving, paintings, the management of drug stores and banks, has not been trodden without contact with thorns and thistles. While we take just pride in what we exhibit as a result of our independent efforts, we do not for a moment forget that our part in this exhibition would fall far short of your expectations but for the constant help that has come to our educational life not only from the southern states, but especially from northern philanthropists, who have made their gifts a constant stream of blessing and encouragement.

The wisest among my race understand that the agitation of questions of social equality is the extremest folly, and that progress in the enjoyment of all the privileges that will come to us must be the result of severe and constant struggle, rather than of artificial forcing. No race that has anything to contribute to the markets of the world is long in any degree ostracized. It is important and right that all privileges of the law be ours, but it is vastly more important that we be prepared for the exercise of these privileges. The opportunity to earn a dollar in a factory just now is worth infinitely more than the opportunity to spend a dollar in an opera-house.

In conclusion, may I repeat that nothing in thirty years has given us more hope and encouragement, and nothing has drawn us so near to you of the white race, as this opportunity offered by this exposition; and here bending, as it were, over the altar that represents the results of the struggles of your race and mine, both starting practically empty handed three decades ago, I pledge that in your effort to work out the great and intricate problem which God has laid at the doors of the south, you shall have at all times the patient, sympathetic help of my race; only let this be constantly in mind—that while from representations in these buildings of the product of field, of forest, of mine, of factory, letters, and art, much good will come, yet far above and beyond material benefits will be that higher good, that, let us

pray God, will come, in a blotting out of sectional differences and racial animosities and suspicions, and in a determination, even in the remotest corner, to administer absolute justice, in a willing obedience among all classes to the mandates of law and a spirit that will tolerate nothing but the highest equity in the enforcement of law. This, coupled with our material prosperity, will bring into our beloved south a new heaven and a new earth.

> *Booker T. Washington, "A Plea for His Race" The* Constitution, *Atlanta, September 19, 1895, p. 4.*

James Creelman (essay date 1895)

[*The following excerpt is from a brief essay Creelman wrote for the* New York World *the day of the Atlanta Compromise. Here, he describes the emotional impact the speech had on both black and white members of the audience.*]

When Prof. Booker T. Washington, principal of an industrial school for colored people in Tuskegee, Ala., stood on the platform of the Auditorium, with the sun shining over the heads of his hearers into his eyes and his whole face lit up with the fire of prophecy, Clark Howell, the successor of Henry W. Grady, said to me: "That man's speech is the beginning of a moral revolution in America."

It is the first time that a negro has made a speech in the South on any important occasion before an audience composed of white men and women. It electrified the audience, and the response was as if it had come from the throat of a whirlwind. (p. 3)

There was a remarkable figure, tall, bony, straight as a Sioux chief, high forehead, straight nose, heavy jaws and strong, determined mouth, with big white teeth, piercing eyes and a commanding manner. The sinews stood out on his bronzed neck, and his muscular right arm swung high in the air with a lead pencil grasped in the clenched brown fist. His big feet were planted squarely, with the heels together and the toes turned out. His voice rang out clear and true, and he paused impressively as he made each point. Within ten minutes the multitude was in an uproar of enthusiasm, handkerchiefs were waved, canes were flourished, hats were tossed in the air. The fairest women of Georgia stood up and cheered. It was as if the orator had bewitched them. (p. 9)

I have heard the great orators of many countries, but not even Gladstone himself could have pleaded a cause with more consummate power than did this angular negro standing in a nimbus of sunshine surrounded by the men who once fought to keep his race in bondage. The roar might swell ever so high, but the expression of his earnest face never changed.

A ragged ebony giant, squatted on the floor in one of the aisles, watched the orator with burning eyes and tremulous face until the supreme burst of applause came and then the tears ran down his face. Most of the negroes in the audience were crying, perhaps without knowing just why. (pp. 9-10)

James Creelman, in an excerpt in The Booker T. Washington Papers: 1895-98, *Vol. 4, edited by Louis R. Harlan & others, University of Illinois Press, 1975, pp. 3-15.*

George N. Smith (letter date 1895)

[*The following excerpt is from one of the first expressions of opposition to Washington's Atlanta Compromise. by a black American. Here, Smith compares Washington unfavorably with Frederick Douglass, charging: "It is supreme folly to speak of Mr. Washington as the Moses of the race."*]

The Negro is made, indeed, of queer stuff. To compare Mr. Booker T. Washington with Frederick Douglass is as unseemly as comparing a pigmy to a giant—a mountain brook leaping over a boulder, to great, only Niagara. It seems that Mr. Washington, himself, and his friends would blush at the use of the name of the great Douglass in this connection. Mr. Washington has done a good work. So have hundreds of other young colored men in the south. He has attained some prominence as a collector of funds—simply this, nothing more. He has been more a creature of combinations and circumstances than a man who has wrung success, usefulness and fame from the clouds of adversity. (p. 345)

Leaving out "chickens from miscellaneous sources," the speech which Mr. Washington made at Atlanta has been repeated a hundred times by him . . . . His charge of theft against the Negro must make every race-lover hang his head with shame. It was unworthy of the occasion and a stab at his race. Was this like great Douglass? No, but the "old man eloquent" must have turned over in his grave, ashamed of the speaker.

The spirit of Douglass wept, 'but some people applauded'! No, no, Mr. Washington did not make a great speech. But the combinations and circumstances of the hour made it prominent. It was simply 'pushed' by cold business men, seeking the money success of the [Atlanta] exposition, to serve their ends. Mr. Washington was simply an instrument. Was this like the great Douglass? Was he ever an instrument in the hands of an organization seeking money gain? Money, money, money, is the sole purpose of the exposition. We will not deny that it has given the Negro a chance to 'show off' while the white man 'goes off' with the money bags, as usual.

Then did you ever stop to think that the press, loudest in praise of Mr. Washington, was most bitter in denouncing the great Douglass? Have you not seen in the same article in the last few weeks the praise of Washington and the curse of Douglass? 'And the Negroes applauded it.' Where is the blush of shame? Are we, indeed, a race of sycophants and time-serving scullions? (pp. 345-46)

Where is the memory of the immortal Daniel Alexander Payne, J. C. Price, Robert Brown Elliott and others? Did they say nothing? Did they do nothing? Where are Bishop Turner, B. K. Bruce, N. W. Cuney, Peter H. Clark, James Hill, of Mississippi, Fortune and others, whose manly, noble utterances and well-fought battles paved the way for Mr. Washington? These men have made the very heavens ring with their eloquence, while the old earth trembled beneath the tread of the hosts which they led up out of the Egypt of ignorance and oppression. Did you ever stop to think that the men who are exalting Mr. Washington see no good in these noble men? Did you ever stop to think that the newspapers which laud Mr. Washington curse these men?

It is supreme folly to speak of Mr. Washington as the Moses of the race. If we are where Mr. Washington's Atlanta speech place us, what need have we of a Moses? Who brought us from Egypt, through the wilderness to these happy conditions? The men mentioned above. Let us pray that the race will never have a leader, but leaders. Who is the leader of the white race in the United States? It has no leaders, but leaders. So with us.

Yes, Mr. Washington's Atlanta popularity is simply cat's paw. His speech was simply ordinary, cannot stand the test of fair criticism in cool moments, and will pass away with the excitement of the hour.

It is a sad mistake on the part of Mr. Washington's friends to undertake to boost him as the "Moses," "the Frederick Douglass," "the leader of the race," or to place his Atlanta speech among the "classics." (pp. 346-47)

George N. Smith in his letter of November 16, 1895, in The Journal of Negro History, *Vol. LV, No. 4, October, 1970, pp. 344-47.*

John Hope (lecture date 1896)

[*Hope was an American academic and university president. In the following excerpt from a speech delivered before the Nashville Negro Debating Society in February 1896, he attacks the propositions Washington set forth in his Atlanta Compromise. Earlier, Hope had turned down Washington's offer of a teaching position at Tuskegee Institute; with this address, he publicly challenged Washington at a time when other prominent blacks, notably W. E. B. Du Bois, strongly supported him.*]

If we are not striving for equality, in heaven's name for what are we living? I regard it as cowardly and dishonest for any of our colored men to tell white people or colored people that we are not struggling for equality. If money, education, and honesty will not bring to me as much privilege, as much equality as they bring to any American citizen, then they are to me a curse, and not a blessing. God forbid that we should get the implements with which to fashion our freedom, and then be too lazy or pusillanimous to fashion it. Let us not fool ourselves nor be fooled by others. If we cannot do what other freemen do, then we are not free. Yes, my friends, I want equality. Nothing less. I want all that my God-given powers will enable me to get, then why not equality? Now, catch your breath, for I am going to use an adjective: I am going to say we demand social equality. In this Republic we shall be less than freemen, if we have a whit less than that which thrift, education, and honor afford other freemen. If equality, political, economic, and social, is the boon of other men in this great country of ours, then equality, political, economic, and social, is what we demand. Why build a wall to keep me out? I am no wild beast, nor am I an unclean thing.

Rise, Brothers! Come let us possess this land. Never say: "Let well enough alone." Cease to console yourselves with adages that numb the moral sense. Be discontented. Be dissatisfied. "Sweat and grunt" under present conditions. Be as restless as the tempestuous billows on the boundless sea. Let your discontent break mountain-high against the wall of prejudice, and swamp it to the very foundation. Then we shall not have to plead for justice nor on bended knee crave mercy; for we shall be men. Then and not until then will liberty in its highest sense be the boast of our Republic.

> *John Hope, in a speech delivered before the Nashville Negro Debating Society on February 22, 1896, in* A Documentary History of the Negro People in the United States: From the Reconstruction Era to 1910, Vol. II, *edited by Herbert Aptheker, fourth edition, The Citadel Press, 1968, p. 758.*

Charles W. Chesnutt (essay date 1900)

[*Chesnutt was an American novelist and short story writer. In 1928 he was awarded the Springarn Medal, given annually by the NAACP, in honor of his "pioneer work as a literary artist depicting the life and struggles of Americans of Negro descent, and for his long and useful career as scholar, worker and free-man." In the following excerpt from an essay that first appeared in 1900 in* The Critic, *he reviews* The Future of the American Negro *and assesses Washington's role as a racial leader.*]

Mr. Booker T. Washington has secured so strong a hold upon the public attention and confidence that anything he has to say in his chosen field is sure to command the attention of all who are interested in the future of the American negro. This volume [*The Future of the American Negro*], which is Mr. Washington's first extended utterance in book form, cannot fail to enhance his reputation for ability, wisdom, and patriotism. It is devoted to a somewhat wide consideration of the race problem, avoiding some of its delicate features, perhaps, but emphasizing certain of its more obvious phases. The author has practically nothing to say about caste prejudice, the admixture of the races, or the remote future of the negro, but simply takes up the palpable problem of ignorance and poverty as he finds it in the South, and looking neither to the right nor the left, and

only far enough behind to fix the responsibility for present conditions, seeks to bring about such immediate improvement in the condition of the negro, and such a harmonious adjustment of race relations, as will lay the foundation for a hopeful and progressive future for the colored people. The practical philosophy of the book is eminently characteristic; it fairly bristles with the author's individuality.

As might be expected, much of the volume is devoted to discussing the importance of industrial education for the negro, of which the author is the most conspicuous advocate.... The argument for industrial education is not based upon any theory of the inferiority of the negro, which is beside the question, but upon the manifest conditions under which he must seek his livelihood.... It is to the building up of a substantial middle-class, so to speak, that industrial education and the lessons of industry and thrift inculcated by Mr. Washington are directed. He insists, somewhat rigidly, on the rational order of development, and is pained by such spectacles as a rosewood piano in a log school-house, and a negro lad studying a French grammar in a one-room cabin. It is hardly likely that Mr. Washington has suffered very often from such incongruities, and some allowance should be made for the personal equation of even a negro lad in the Black Belt. (pp. 114-15)

Mr. Washington is a pioneer in another field. He has set out to gain for his race in the South, in the effort to improve their condition, the active sympathy and assistance of the white people in that section. This is perhaps a necessary corollary to his system of education, for it is in the South that he advises the negroes to stay, and it is among their white neighbors that they must live and practise the arts they acquire. If Mr. Washington succeeds in this effort, he will have solved the whole problem. But he has undertaken no small task.... The student of history and current events can scarcely escape the impression that it is the firm and unwavering determination of the Southern whites to keep the negro in a permanent state of vassalage and subordination....

It is to be hoped that Mr. Washington may convince the South that the policy of Federal non-interference, which seems to be the attitude of the present and several past administrations, places a sacred trust upon the South to be just to the negro....

There will undoubtedly be a race problem in the United States, with all its attendant evils, until we cease to regard our colored population as negroes and consider them simply as citizens.... In the meantime, if the work led by Mr. Washington shall succeed in promoting better conditions, either by smoothing over asperities; by appealing to the dormant love of justice which has been the crowning glory of the English race—a trait which selfishness and greed have never entirely obscured; or by convincing the whites that injustice is vastly more dangerous to them than any possible loss of race prestige, Mr. Washington will deserve, and will doubtless receive, the thanks of the people of this whole nation. (pp. 115-16)

> Charles W. Chesnutt, in an extract from "The Negro World Looks at Washington," in Booker T. Washington, edited by Emma Lou Thornbrough, Prentice-Hall, 1969, pp. 114-16.

W. D. Howells (essay date 1901)

[*Howells, a turn-of-the-century American literary critic, was among the few mainstream white commentators of his day with an in-depth knowledge of works by black authors; he is credited with bringing poet Paul Laurence Dunbar to the attention of the American public. In the following excerpt, he praises Washington upon the publication of* Up from Slavery.]

Except for the race ignominy and social outlawry to which he was born, the story of Booker T. Washington does not differ so very widely from that of many another eminent American. His origin was not much more obscure, his circumstances not much more squalid, than Abraham Lincoln's, and his impulses and incentives to the making of himself were of much the same source and quality.... There is nothing more touching in his book [*Up from Slavery*] than the passages which record [his mother's] devotion and her constant endeavor to help him find the way so dark to her. There is nothing more beautiful and uplifting in literature than the tender reverence, the devout honor with which he repays her affection. His birth was a part of slavery, and she was, in his eyes, as blameless for its conditions as if it had all the sanctions. The patience, the fearless frankness, with which he accepts and owns the facts, are not less than noble; and it is not to their white fathers, but to their black mothers, that such men as Frederick Douglass and Booker Washington justly ascribe what is best in their natures.

The story of his struggle for an education is the story of Booker Washington's life, which I am not going to spoil for the reader by trying to tell it. He has himself told it so simply and charmingly that one could not add to or take from it without marring it. The part of the autobiography which follows the account of his learning to read and write, in the scanty leisure of his hard work in the West Virginia coal mines, and of his desperate adventure in finding his way into Hampton Institute, is, perhaps, more important and more significant, but it has not the fascination of his singularly pleasing personality. It concerns the great problem, which no man has done more than he to solve, of the future of his race, and its reconciliation with the white race, upon conditions which it can master only through at least provisional submission; but it has not the appeal to the less philosophized sympathies which go out to struggle and achievement. It is not such interesting reading, and yet it is all very interesting; and if the prosperity of the author is not so picturesque as his adversity, still it is

prosperity well merited, and it is never selfish prosperity. (pp. 281-82)

The dominant of Mr. Washington's register is *business;* first, last and all the time, the burden of his song is the Tuskegee Industrial Institute. There is other music in him, and no one who reads his story can fail to know its sweetness; but to Tuskegee his heart and soul are unselfishly devoted, and he does not suffer his readers long to forget it. He feels with his whole strength that the hope of his race is in its industrial advancement, and that its education must, above all, tend to that. His people must know how to read and write in order to be better workmen; but good workmen they must be, and they must lead decent, sober, honest lives to the same end. It was the inspiration of this philosophy and experience which enabled him, in his famous speech at the opening of the Atlanta Exposition [see excerpt above], to bring the white race into kindlier and wiser relations with the black than they had known before. Social equality he does not ask for or apparently care for; but industrial and economic equality his energies are bent upon achieving, in the common interest of both races. Of all slights and wrongs he is patient, so they do not hinder the negro from working or learning how to work in the best way. (p. 283)

White men rise from squalor almost as great as that which has left no taint upon the mind and soul of the born thrall, Booker T. Washington. But it must be remembered to his honor, and to his greater glory as a fighter against fate, that they rise in the face of no such odds as he has had to encounter. No prejudice baser than the despite for poverty bars their way. But the negro who makes himself in our conditions, works with limbs manacled and fettered by manifold cruel prepossessions. These prepossessions yield at certain points to amiability, to mildness, to persistent submissiveness, but at other points they yield to nothing.

In spite of them, though never in defiance of them, Booker T. Washington has made himself a public man, second to no other American in importance. He seems to hold in his strong grasp the key to the situation; for if his notion of reconciling the Anglo-American to the Afro-American, by a civilization which shall not seem to threaten the Anglo-American supremacy, is not the key, what is? He imagines for his race a civilization industrial and economical, hoping for the virtues which spring from endeavor and responsibility; and apparently his imagination goes no farther. But a less deeply interested observer might justify himself in hoping for it, from the things it has already accomplished in art and literature, a civilization of high aesthetic qualities.

As for the man himself, whose winning yet manly personality and whose ideal of self-devotion must endear him to every reader of his book, something remains to be said, which may set him in a true perspective and a true relation to another great Afro-American, whose name could not well be kept out of the consideration. Neither by temperament nor by condition had Frederick Douglass the charm which we feel when Booker T. Washington writes or speaks. The time was against him. In that time of storm and stress, the negro leader was, perforce, a fighter. The sea of slavery, from which he had escaped with his bare life, weltered over half the land, and threatened all the new bounds of the Republic. By means of the Fugitive Slave Law, it had, in fact, made itself national, and the bondman was nowhere on American soil safe from recapture and return to his master. Frederick Douglass had to be bought, and his price had to be paid in dollars by those who felt his priceless value to humanity, before he could be to it all that he was destined to become.

It would have been impossible that the iron which had entered into the man's soul should not show itself in his speech. Yet, his words were strangely free from violence; the violence was in the hatred which the mere thought of a negro defying slavery aroused in its friends. If you read now what he said, you will be surprised at his reasonableness, his moderation. He was not gentle; his life had been ungentle; the logic of his convictions was written in the ineffaceable scars of the whip on his back. Of such a man, you do not expect the smiling good humor with which Booker T. Washington puts the question of his early deprivations and struggles by. The life of Douglass was a far more wonderful life, and when it finds its rightful place in our national history, its greater dynamic importance will be felt.

Each of these two remarkable men wrought and is working fitly and wisely in his time and place. It is not well to forget slavery, and the memory of Frederick Douglass will always serve to remind us of it and of the fight against it. But it is not well to forget that slavery is gone, and that the subjection of the negro race which has followed it does not imply its horrors. The situation which Booker T. Washington deals with so wisely is wholly different from the situation which Douglass confronted, and it is slowly but surely modifying itself. The mild might of his adroit, his subtle statesmanship (in the highest sense it is not less than statesmanship, and involves a more than Philippine problem in our midst), is the only agency to which it can yield. Without affirming his intellectual equality with Douglass, we may doubt whether Douglass would have been able to cope so successfully with the actual conditions, and we may safely recognize in Booker T. Washington an Afro-American of unsurpassed usefulness, and an exemplary citizen. (pp. 287-88)

W. D. Howells, "An Exemplary Citizen," in The North American Review, *Vol. CLXXI-II, No. 537, August, 1901, pp. 280-88.*

W. E. Burghardt Du Bois (essay date 1903)

[*Du Bois was at the vanguard of the civil rights movement in America. One of his best-known works,* The Souls of Black Folk: Essays and Sketches *(1903), shocked many blacks when it first came out, for in it Du Bois announced his opposition to the conciliatory educational and social policies of Washington and his followers. Here, in an excerpt from* The Souls of Black Folk, *Du Bois assails Washington's doctrines, stating that their submissive attitudes relegate blacks to an inferior social position.*]

Booker T. Washington arose as essentially the leader not of one race but of two,—a compromiser between the South, the North, and the Negro. Naturally the Negroes resented, at first bitterly, signs of compromise which surrendered their civil and political rights, even though this was to be exchanged for larger chances of economic development. The rich and dominating North, however, was not only weary of the race problem, but was investing largely in Southern enterprises, and welcomed any method of peaceful cooperation. Thus, by national opinion, the Negroes began to recognize Mr. Washington's leadership; and the voice of criticism was hushed.

Mr. Washington represents in Negro thought the old attitude of adjustment and submission; but adjustment at such a peculiar time as to make his programme unique. This is an age of unusual economic development, and Mr. Washington's programme naturally takes an economic cast, becoming a gospel of Work and Money to such an extent as apparently almost completely to overshadow the higher aims of life. Moreover, this is an age when the more advanced races are coming in closer contact with the less developed races, and the race-feeling is therefore intensified; and Mr. Washington's programme practically accepts the alleged inferiority of the Negro races. Again, in our own land, the reaction from the sentiment of war time has given impetus to race-prejudice against Negroes, and Mr. Washington withdraws many of the high demands of Negroes as men and American citizens. In other periods of intensified prejudice all the Negro's tendency to self-assertion has been called forth; at this period a policy of submission is advocated. In the history of nearly all other races and peoples the doctrine preached at such crises has been that manly self-respect is worth more than lands and houses, and that a people who voluntarily surrender such respect, or cease striving for it, are not worth civilizing.

In answer to this, it has been claimed that the Negro can survive only through submission. Mr. Washington distinctly asks that black people give up, at least for the present, three things,—

First, political power,

Second, insistence on civil rights,

Third, higher education of Negro youth,—

and concentrate all their energies on industrial education, the accumulation of wealth, and the conciliation of the South. This policy has been courageously and insistently advocated for over fifteen years, and has been triumphant for perhaps ten years. As a result of this tender of the palm-branch, what has been the return? In these years there have occurred:

1. The disfranchisement of the Negro.

2. The legal creation of a distinct status of civil inferiority for the Negro.

3. The steady withdrawal of aid from institutions for the higher training of the Negro.

These movements are not, to be sure, direct results of Mr. Washington's teachings; but his propaganda has, without a shadow of doubt, helped their speedier accomplishment. The question then comes: Is it possible, and probable, that nine millions of men can make effective progress in economic lines if they are deprived of political rights, made a servile caste, and allowed only the most meagre chance for developing their exceptional men? If history and reason give any distinct answer to these questions, it is an emphatic *No.* And Mr. Washington thus faces the triple paradox of his career:

> 1. He is striving nobly to make Negro artisans business men and property-owners; but it is utterly impossible, under modern competitive methods, for workingmen and property-owners to defend their rights and exist without the right of suffrage.
>
> 2. He insists on thrift and self-respect, but at the same time counsels a silent submission to civic inferiority such as is bound to sap the manhood of any race in the long run.
>
> 3. He advocates common-school and industrial training, and depreciates institutions of higher learning; but neither the Negro common-schools, nor Tuskegee itself, could remain open a day were it not for teachers trained in Negro colleges, or trained by their graduates.

This triple paradox in Mr. Washington's position is the object of criticism by two classes of colored Americans. One class is spiritually descended from Toussaint the Savior, through Gabriel, Vesey, and Turner, and they represent the attitude of revolt and revenge; they hate the white South blindly and distrust the white race generally, and so far as they agree on definite action, think that the Negro's only hope lies in emigration beyond the borders of the United States. And yet, by the irony of fate, nothing has more effectually made this programme seem hopeless than the recent course of the United States toward weaker and darker peoples in the West Indies, Hawaii, and the Philippines,—for where in the world may we go and be safe from lying and brute force?

The other class of Negroes who cannot agree with Mr. Washington has hitherto said little aloud. They deprecate the sight of scattered counsels, of internal disagreement; and especially they dislike making their just criticism of a useful and earnest man an excuse for a general discharge of venom from small-minded opponents. Nevertheless, the questions involved are so fundamental and serious that it is difficult to see how . . . representatives of this group, can much longer be silent. Such men feel in conscience bound to ask of this nation three things:

> 1. The right to vote.

2. Civil equality.

3. The education of youth according to ability.

They acknowledge Mr. Washington's invaluable service in counselling patience and courtesy in such demands; they do not ask that ignorant black men vote when ignorant whites are debarred, or that any reasonable restrictions in the suffrage should not be applied; they know that the low social level of the mass of the race is responsible for much discrimination against it, but they also know, and the nation knows, that relentless color-prejudice is more often a cause than a result of the Negro's degradation; they seek the abatement of this relic of barbarism, and not its systemic encouragement and pampering by all agencies of social power from the Associated Press to the Church of Christ. They advocate, with Mr. Washington, a broad system of Negro common schools supplemented by thorough industrial training; but they are surprised that a man of Mr. Washington's insight cannot see that no such educational system ever has rested or can rest on any other basis than that of the well-equipped college and university, and they insist that there is a demand for a few such institutions throughout the South to train the best of the Negro youth as teachers, professional men, and leaders.

This group of men honor Mr. Washington for his attitude of conciliation toward the white South; they accept the "Atlanta Compromise" in its broadest interpretation; they recognize, with him, many signs of promise, many men of high purpose and fair judgment, in this section; they know that no easy task has been laid upon a region already tottering under heavy burdens. But, nevertheless, they insist that the way to truth and right lies in straightforward honesty, not in indiscriminate flattery; in praising those of the South who do well and criticising uncompromisingly those who do ill; in taking advantage of the opportunities at hand and urging their fellows to do the same, but at the same time in remembering that only a firm adherence to their higher ideals and aspirations will ever keep those ideals within the realm of possibility. (pp. 49-54)

In failing thus to state plainly and unequivocally the legitimate demands of their people, even at the cost of opposing an honored leader, the thinking classes of American Negroes would shirk a heavy responsibility . . . . The growing spirit of kindliness and reconciliation between the North and South after the frightful differences of a generation ago ought to be a source of deep congratulation to all, and especially to those whose mistreatment caused the war; but if that reconciliation is to be marked by the industrial slavery and civic death of those same black men, with permanent legislation into a position of inferiority, then those black men, if they are really men, are called upon by every consideration of patriotism and loyalty to oppose such a course by all civilized methods, even though such opposition involves disagreement with Mr. Booker T. Washington. We have no right to sit silently by while the inevitable seeds are sown for a harvest of disaster to our children, black and white. (pp. 55-6)

It would be unjust to Mr. Washington not to acknowledge that in several instances he has opposed movements in the South which were unjust to the Negro; he sent memorials to the Louisiana and Alabama constitutional conventions, he has spoken against lynching, and in other ways has openly or silently set his influence against sinister schemes and unfortunate happenings. Notwithstanding this, it is equally true to assert that on the whole the distinct impression left by Mr. Washington's propaganda is, first, that the South is justified in its present attitude toward the Negro because of the Negro's degradation; secondly, that the prime cause of the Negro's failure to rise more quickly is his wrong education in the past; and, thirdly, that his future rise depends primarily on his own efforts. Each of these propositions is a dangerous half-truth. The supplementary truths must never be lost sight of: first, slavery and race-prejudice are potent if not sufficient causes of the Negro's position; second, industrial and common-school training were necessarily slow in planting because they had to await the black teachers trained by higher institutions,—it being extremely doubtful if any essentially different development was possible, and certainly a Tuskegee was unthinkable before 1880; and, third, while it is a great truth to say that the Negro must strive and strive mightily to help himself, it is equally true that unless his striving be not simply seconded, but rather aroused and encouraged, by the initiative of the richer and wiser environing group, he cannot hope for great success.

In his failure to realize and impress this last point, Mr. Washington is especially to be criticised. His doctrine has tended to make the whites, North and South, shift the burden of the Negro problem to the Negro's shoulders and stand aside as critical and rather pessimistic spectators; when in fact the burden belongs to the nation, and the hands of none of us are clean if we bend not our energies to righting these great wrongs.

The South ought to be led, by candid and honest criticism, to assert her better self and do her full duty to the race she has cruelly wronged and is still wronging. The North—her copartner in guilt—cannot salve her conscience by plastering it with gold. We cannot settle this problem by diplomacy and suaveness, by "policy" alone. If worse come to worst, can the moral fibre of this country survive the slow throttling and murder of nine millions of men?

The black men of America have a duty to perform, a duty stern and delicate,—a forward movement to oppose a part of the work of their greatest leader. So far as Mr. Washington preaches Thrift, Patience, and Industrial Training for the masses, we must hold up his hands and strive with him, rejoicing in his honors and glorying in the strength of this Joshua called of God and of man to lead the headless host. But so far as Mr. Washington apologizes for injustice, North or South, does not rightly value the privilege and duty of voting, belittles the emasculating effects of caste distinctions, and opposes the higher training and ambition of our brighter minds,—so far as he, the South, or the Nation, does this,—we must unceasingly and firmly oppose them. (pp. 57-9)

W. E. Burghardt Du Bois, "Of Mr. Booker T. Washington and Others," in his The Souls Black Folk: Essays and Sketches, *tenth edition, McClurg, 1903, pp. 41-59.*

H. G. Wells (essay date 1906)

[*Wells was an English novelist, essayist, literary critic, and writer of short stories. In the following excerpt from an essay originally published in* Harper's Weekly *in 1906, he recounts a visit with Washington.*]

I have attempted time after time to get some answer from the Americans I have met, the answer to what is to me the most obvious of questions. "Your grandchildren and the grandchildren of these people [Negroes] will have to live in this country side by side; do you propose, do you believe it possible, that they shall be living then in just the same relations that you and these people are living now; if you do not, then what relations do you propose shall exist between them?"

It is not too much to say that I have never once had the beginnings of an answer to this question.... (p. 102)

I certainly did not begin to realize one most important aspect of this question until I reached America. I thought of those eight millions as of men, black as ink. But when I met Mr. Booker T. Washington, for example, I met a man certainly as white in appearance as our Admiral Fisher, who is, as a matter of fact, very white. A very large proportion of these colored people is more than half white. One hears a good deal about the high social origins of the Southern planters, very many derive undisputably from the first families of England. It is the same blood that flows in these mixed colored peoples' veins. Just think of the sublime absurdity, therefore, of the ban. There are gentlemen of education and refinement, qualified doctors and lawyers, whose ancestors assisted in the Norman Conquest, and they dare not enter a car marked white and intrude upon the dignity of the rising loan-monger from Esthonia....

But whatever aspect I recall of this great taboo that shows no signs of lifting, of this great problem of the future...there presently comes to my mind the browned face of Mr. Booker T. Washington, as he talked to me over our lunch in Boston. (p. 103)

He answered my questions meditatively. I wanted to know with an active pertinacity. What struck me most was the way in which his sense of the overpowering forces of race prejudice weighs upon him. It is a thing he accepts; in our time and condition it is not to be fought about. He makes one feel with an exaggerated intensity (though I could not even draw him to admit) its monstrous injustice. He makes no accusations. He is for taking it as a part of the present fate of his "people," and for doing all that can be done for them within the limit that it sets.

Therein he differs from Du Bois, the other great spokesman color has found in our time. Du Bois is more of the artist, less of the statesman; he conceals his passionate resentment all too thinly. He batters himself into rhetoric against these walls. He will not repudiate the clear right of the black man to every educational facility, to equal citizenship, and to equal respect. But Mr. Washington has statecraft. He looks before and after, and plans and keeps his counsel with the scope and range of a statesman. I use "statesman" in its highest sense; his is a mind that can grasp the situation and destinies of a people....

I argued strongly against the view he seems to hold that black and white might live without mingling and without injustice, side by side. That I do not believe. Racial differences seem to me always to exasperate intercourse unless people have been trained to ignore them.... "You must repudiate separation," I said. "No peoples have ever yet endured the tension of intermingled distinctness."

"May we not become a peculiar people—like the Jews?" he suggested. "Isn't that possible?"

But there I could not agree with him.... The colored people...are not a community at all in the Jewish sense, but outcasts from a community. They are the victims of a prejudice that has to be destroyed. These things I urged, but it was, I think, empty speech to my hearer. (pp. 103-04)

"I wish you would tell me," I said abruptly, "just what you think of the attitude of white America towards you. Do you think it is generous?"

He regarded me for a moment. "No end of people help us," he said.

"Yes," I said; "but the ordinary man. Is he fair?"

"Some things are not fair," he said, leaving the general question alone. "It isn't fair to refuse a colored man a berth on a sleeping-car. I? I happen to be a privileged person, they make an exception for me; but the ordinary educated colored man isn't admitted to a sleeping-car at all. If he has to go a long journey, he has to sit up all night. His white competitor sleeps. Then in some places, in the hotels and restaurants—it's all right here in Boston—but southwardly he can't get proper refreshments. All that's a handicap...

"The remedy lies in education," he said; "ours—*and theirs.*

"The real thing," he told me, "isn't to be done by talking and agitation. It's a matter of lives. The only answer to it all is for colored men to be patient, to make themselves competent, to do good work, to live well, to give no occasion against us. We feel that. In a way it's an inspiration." (pp. 104-05)

Whatever America has to show in heroic living today, I doubt if she can show anything finer than the quality of the resolve, the steadfast efforts hundreds of black and colored men are making today to live blamelessly, honorably and patiently, getting for themselves what scraps of refinement, learning and beauty they may, keeping their hold on a civilization they are grudged and denied....

But the patience the negro needs!

No, I can't help idealizing the dark submissive figure of the negro in the spectacle of America. He, too, seems to me to sit waiting—and waiting with a marvelous and simple-minded patience—for finer understandings and a nobler time. (p. 105)

> *H. G. Wells, in his extract from "The White World Looks at Washington: Two British Opinions," in* Booker T. Washington, *edited by Emma Lou Thornbrough, Prentice-Hall, 1969, pp. 102-05.*

Booker T. Washington (essay date 1915)

[*In the following excerpt from an essay published in* The New Republic *only days after his death, Washington offers his assurance that segregation laws are unnecessary because black Americans have no intention of mixing socially with white Americans. This essay, written after several years of discouraging setbacks in race relations, is considered one of Washington's harshest assessments of the white South.*]

In all of my experience I have never yet found a case where the masses of the people of any given city were interested in the matter of the segregation of white and colored people; that is, there has been no spontaneous demand for segregation ordinances. In certain cities politicians have taken the leadership in introducing such segregation ordinances into city councils, and after making an appeal to racial prejudices have succeeded in securing a backing for ordinances which would segregate the negro people from their white fellow citizens. After such ordinances have been introduced it is always difficult, in the present state of public opinion in the South, to have any considerable body of white people oppose them, because their attitude is likely to be misrepresented as favoring negros against white people. They are, in the main, afraid of the stigma, "negro-lover."...

Personally I have little faith in the doctrine that it is necessary to segregate the whites from the blacks to prevent race mixture. The whites are the dominant race in the South, they control the courts, the industries and the government in all of the cities, counties and states except in those few communities where the negros, seeking some form of self-government, have established a number of experimental towns or communities.

I have never viewed except with amusement the sentiment that white people who live next to negro populations suffer physically, mentally and morally because of their proximity to colored people. Southern white people who have been brought up in this proximity are not inferior to other white people. The President of the United States was born and reared in the South in close contact with black people. Five members of the present Cabinet were born in the South; and many of them, I am sure, had black "mammies."...

It is true that the negro opposes these attempts to restrain him from residing in certain sections of a city or community. He does this not because he wants to mix with the white man socially, but because he feels that such laws are unnecessary. The negro objects to being segregated because it usually means that he will receive inferior accommodations in return for the taxes he pays. If the negro is segregated, it will probably mean that the sewerage in his part of the city will be inferior; that the streets and sidewalks will be neglected, that the street lighting will be poor; that his section of the city will not be kept in order by the police and other authorities, and that the "undesirables" of other races will be placed near him, thereby making it difficult for him to rear his family in decency. It should always be kept in mind that while the negro may not be directly a large taxpayer, he does pay large taxes indirectly. (p. 113)

White people who argue for the segregation of the masses of black people forget the tremendous power of objective teaching. To hedge any set of people off in a corner and sally among them now and then with a lecture or a sermon is merely to add misery to degradation. But put the black man where day by day he sees how the white man keeps his lawns, his windows; how he treats his wife and children, and you will do more real helpful teaching than a whole library of lectures and sermons. Moreover, this will help the white man. If he knows that his life is to be taken as a model, that his hours, dress, manners, are all to be patterns for someone less fortunate, he will deport himself better than he would otherwise. Practically all the real moral uplift the black people have got from the whites—and this has been great indeed—has come from this observation of the white man's conduct. The South to-day is still full of the type of negro with gentle manners. Where did he get them? From some master or mistress of the same type....

Finally, as I have said in another place, as white and black learn daily to adjust, in a spirit of justice and fair play, those interests which are individual and racial, and to see and feel the importance of those fundamental interests which are common, so will both races grow and prosper. In the long run no individual and no race can succeed which sets itself at war against the common good; for "in the gain or loss of one race, all the rest have equal claim." (p. 114)

> *Booker T. Washington, "My View of Segregation Laws," in* The New Republic, *Vol. 5, No. 57, December 4, 1915, pp. 113-14.*

Marcus Garvey (essay date 1923)

[*Jamaican-born Garvey was one of the most prominent black-rights champions of his era. As founder of the Universal Negro Improvement Association (UNIA) he led a movement promoting greater unity for blacks throughout the world. This movement, which counted more than eight million followers at its zenith, was the key force in the back-to-Africa cause that influenced black politics and social activism in the second and third decades of the twentieth century. In addition, Garvey promoted black-oriented businesses, notably the Black Star Line of ships for transporting blacks who wanted to return to Africa. Garvey's first major project as an activist was the founding of a trades school in Jamaica. But the project, modeled after Washington's Tuskegee Institute, failed to develop successfully, and in time Garvey's views shifted away from promoting black unity solely through education and commerce. The following statement was first issued in 1923. In it, Garvey speaks of a new black spirit that transcends Washington's policies.*]

The world held up the great Sage of Tuskegee—Booker T. Washington—as the only leader for the race. They looked forward to him and his teachings as the leadership for all times, not calculating that the industrially educated Negro would himself evolve a new ideal, after having been trained by the Sage of Tuskegee.

The world satisfied itself to believe that succeeding Negro leaders would follow absolutely the teachings of Washington. Unfortunately the world is having a rude awakening, in that we are evolving a new ideal. The new ideal includes the program of Booker T. Washington and has gone much further.

Things have changed wonderfully since Washington came on the scene. His vision was industrial opportunity for the Negro, but the Sage of Tuskegee has passed off the stage of life and left behind a new problem—a problem that must be solved, not by the industrial leader only, but by the political and military leaders as well.

If Washington had lived he would have had to change his program. No leader can successfully lead this race of ours without giving an interpretation of the awakened spirit of the New Negro, who does not seek industrial opportunity alone, but a political voice. The world is amazed at the desire of the New Negro, for with his strong voice he is demanding a place in the affairs of men.

> *Marcus Garvey, "Booker T. Washington's Program," in his* Philosophy and Opinions of Marcus Garvey; or, Africa for the Africans, *edited by Amy Jacques Garvey, second edition, Frank Cass & Co. Ltd., 1967, p. 41.*

W. Edward Farrison (essay date 1942)

[*In the following excerpt, Farrison contends that Washington's theory of industrial education was a failure because he did not recognize the need for political power as a means to gain economic stability for black Americans. However, since Farrison wrote this essay, it has been discovered that Washington had strong political influence in the Roosevelt and Taft administrations, which he used to aid the careers of many black political appointees and leaders.*]

Although Mr. Washington is often accredited with developing a new theory of education, the lessons which he endeavored to teach were not new. His doctrine concerning work was essentially the same as the "gospel of labor" which Thomas Carlyle—whom he probably had not read extensively—had preached in spluttering and cryptic exclamations earlier in the nineteenth century. The lessons of economy and thrift, as everyone knows, had been promulgated in colonial America more than a hundred years before by that apostle of material comfort and progress, Benjamin Franklin—whom Mr. Washington, doubtless, had read. Moreover, Mr. Washington's teachings were of the very form and pressure of his time. Mr. Washington came forth at the time when a great many other Americans whose beginnings were unpromising, but whose opportunities were greater than his, were working diligently and shrewdly—if not always honestly—to make themselves gods of the very comfort and well-being and respectability for which Mr. Washington taught Negroes to strive. Incidentally, it may be noted that in a large measure Tuskegee was built and has thrived on the blessings of the gods of ease who during the Gilded Age enshrined themselves in temples of wealth and power.

It should also be noted that the idea of inculcating in Negroes lessons of industry, thrift, and economy by means of a school devoted to industrial education was not original with either Mr. Washington or General Armstrong. As Mr. Washington himself knew, the idea was much older than the Emancipation Proclamation; and as he also knew, his basic arguments in favor of industrial training for free Negroes had been set forth by Frederick Douglass in his proposal for the establishment of an industrial college for Negroes long before the Civil War. But in advising Negroes in the South to work to regain by an industrial efficiency suggestive of that advocated by Milton's Mammon what they lost by disfranchisement, Mr. Washington veered altogether away from Douglass's point of view.

In a half-dozen books, several articles, and numerous speeches Mr. Washington reiterated his views, frequently using the same phraseology and the same examples. Here and there he pointed to individual Negroes who had succeeded by means of industrial training, thrift, and tact. What these had done, he said, Negroes as a group could do. But he seemed to overlook the fact that these isolated instances were more often the exception than the rule and, therefore, proved little or nothing about the group, hampered as it was, and still is, by crushing circumstances which individuals now and then succeed in surmounting.

Almost fifty years have passed since Mr. Washington came into prominence as an educator and leader. In spite of notable industrial progress and economic advancement, and the make-believe of the over-optimistic, the masses of Negroes, especially in the South, are still living in poverty and ignorance. During the last fifty years but few of the blessings envisioned by Mr. Washington have come; and the economic and social, as well as the political, problems of the masses of Negroes still remain to be solved. If time has thus belied Mr. Washington's views, it is probably due less to chance than to their inherent weaknesses.

Granted that there is moral value as well as dignity in manual labor, and that economic independence may be achieved by industrial skill—though the depression of the 1930's leads one to wonder whether any amount or kind of education or training can guarantee economic security—how can the Negro secure to himself the benefits of his labor unless he has some influence in the determination of his value to his community as a worker? And how can he have this while, because of a lack of influence and power in the body politic, he can still work only at such jobs as are *given* to him? Obviously, one who is powerless to choose his job is equally as powerless to demand full reward for his labor. The very respectability and influence which Mr. Washington said Negroes could expect to have conferred upon them as rewards for industry and thrift are indeed the only desiderata by which Negroes can every achieve economic independence. Thus it appears that in Mr. Washington's argument ends and means were confused, and Negroes were urged to lift themselves by their own bootstraps.

As a result of the promulgation of Mr. Washington's views industrial training of a kind became a feature of Negro education in the South and has remained thus ever since. Numerous private and public institutions devoted wholly or partly to industrial training were established, and some schools already existing were tempted to add industrial departments. In **Working with the Hands** . . . , the principal work in which he tried to explain his program of education, Mr. Washington mentioned sixteen schools of this kind that grew out of Tuskegee.

Despite the increase in the number of industrial schools, however, industrial training has remained principally a verbal feature of Negro education—for reasons which one needs no philosopher's lantern to see. First, with but one or two exceptions the private schools have never been adequately equipped to offer thorough industrial training to anybody, and the one or two exceptions could accommodate only a negligible minority of those who might have profited by such training. Second, until recently, after industrial training was transformed into "mechanical arts" and "technical education," probably nowhere in the South was it given anything approaching adequate support out of public funds. The fact is, the sham industrial education provided for Negroes at public expense would have been altogether farcical if it had not had so many tragic aspects. There have been, of course, considerable improvements in recent years; but when one considers the changes which have been constantly taking place in organized industry, he becomes woefully conscious that public industrial education for Negroes in the South is still far from adequate. And as to equitableness, except in a few places there has hardly been any pretension to that. Witness the rapidity and aplomb with which vocational education on the secondary school level—the school level of the masses— was recently being provided for everybody except Negroes, until national defense became urgent.

Why have matters developed thus? Not because everybody has been naïve enough to believe that everything has been lovely, but because Negroes as a group have not been sufficiently influential and powerful politically to demand better consideration from those in control of public funds and public policies. The fact that the very kind of education advocated by Mr. Washington for the masses of Negroes and verbally supported by others has never really been made available demonstrates graphically one of the most palpable weaknesses in his argument. The very means—namely, industrial education—by which he taught the masses of the Negroes to achieve civil and political independence is itself a part of a larger end—namely, equal educational opportunities—towards which civil and political independence is the only sure means.

A belief held by many, especially by those who have never taken the trouble to read Mr. Washington carefully, is that he advocated industrial training for Negroes to the exclusion of liberal education. There are in his writings, to be sure, querulous criticisms of liberal education and its advocates, as in the latter half of the fifth chapter in **Up from Slavery** . . . and in the chapter "The Intellectuals and the Boston Mob" in **My Larger Education** . . . . But in spite of such criticisms this belief is erroneous. He believed profoundly in industrial education for the masses, but he also believed in liberal and professional education for some. In both his speeches and his published writings Mr. Washington repeatedly disclaimed the advocacy of any one kind of education to the exclusion of *all* other kinds, and there seems to be no reason to doubt his sincerity. In **Working with the Hands** he asserted:

> While insisting upon thorough and high-grade industrial education for a large proportion of my race, I have always had the greatest sympathy with first-class college training and have recognized the fact that the Negro race, like other races, must have thoroughly trained college men and women. There is a place and a work for such, just as there is a place and a work for those thoroughly trained with their hands.

This statement was ably supported by Mr. Washington's practice. As is well known, in developing his program at Tuskegee he found places and work for many who had been educated in the best liberal-arts traditions in Negro colleges as well as in famous Northern universities. However theoretical arguments might go, this was an actual step toward conjoining the two kinds of education for the betterment of the masses of Negroes.

Mr. Washington's frequent ridicule of the study of French, instrumental music, and foreign geography in dirty cabins was not an argument against liberal education. Plainly, it was not intended to be such. Rather, it was an argument against any kind of learning that did not meet the immediate needs of the learner. Unfortunately, it reminds one of the spurious "Mandy, is you done your Greek yet?" argument; but in substance and force it was one with the now familiar and generally accepted argument against teaching fudgemaking and embroidering as home economics where more practical matters of homemaking need to be emphasized. As an argument it was concrete, simple, familiar, and slightly humorous; and because of this very fact it was subject to easy overemphasis on the part of both Mr. Washington and his critics.

As it has been with many other pleaders for particular causes, so it was with Mr. Washington. His belief in industrial education became a faith which he defended short of discrediting all other faiths. In the light of his molding experiences his emphasis on industrial training, even though possibly out of proportion to its value, is understandable, if it was not altogether justifiable— which is also true of his early critics' attitudes towards him in the light of their backgrounds and experiences. He himself probably was not confused, but there was the danger that those who would follow him might be misled into putting too much emphasis on merely making a living and too little on living. Had Mr. Washington lived twenty years longer, he could hardly have missed seeing that no one kind of education is sufficient even for the masses of Negroes—unless the Negro is to remain some special kind of American and something less than an American citizen. Seeing this, great American that he was, Mr. Washington, doubtless, would have changed his philosophy of education and also his views as a "leader of the Negro people." Otherwise the ascription of greatness to him would have been a mistake. (pp. 314-19)

> *W. Edward Farrison, "Booker T. Washington: A Study in Educational Leadership," in* South Atlantic Quarterly, *Vol. XLI, No. 3, July, 1942, pp. 313-19.*

August Meier (essay date 1957)

[*In the following excerpt, Meier argues that Washington worked more actively for political and social rights for blacks than many of his critics have maintained.*]

Washington was associated with a policy of compromise and conciliation toward the white South that is not in keeping with the trend of our times. Yet Washington's own correspondence reveals such extensive efforts against segregation and disfranchisement that a re-evaluation of his philosophy and activities is in order.

Undoubtedly in reading Washington's books, articles, and speeches, one is most strongly impressed with the accommodating tone he adopted toward the white South. He minimized the extent of race prejudice and discrimination, criticized the airing of Negro grievances, opposed "social equality," accepted segregation and the "separate by equal" doctrine, depreciated political activity, favored property and educational qualifications for the franchise (fairly applied to both races), largely blamed Negroes themselves for their unfortunate condition, and counselled economic accumulation and the cultivation of Christian character as the best ways to advance the status of Negroes in American society. His ultimate ends were stated so vaguely and ambiguously that Southern whites mistook his short-range objectives for his long-range goals, although his Negro supporters understood that through tact and indirection he hoped to secure the good will of the white man and the eventual recognition of the constitutional rights of American Negroes.

Now, although overtly Washington minimized the importance of political and civil rights, covertly he was deeply involved in political affairs and in efforts to prevent disfranchisement and other forms of discrimination. For example, Washington lobbied against the Hardwick disfranchising bill in Georgia in 1899. While he permitted whites to think that he accepted disfranchisement, he tried to keep Negroes believing otherwise. In 1903 when Atlanta editor Clark Howell implied that Washington opposed Negro officeholding, the Tuskegeean did not openly contradict him, but asked T. Thomas Fortune of the leading Negro weekly, the New York *Age,* to editorialize, "We are quite sure that the Hon. Howell has no ground . . . for his attempt to place Mr. Washington in such a position, as it is well understood that he, while from the first deprecating the Negro's making political agitation and office-holding the most prominent and fundamental part of his career, has not gone any farther."

Again, while Washington seemed to approve of the disfranchisement amendments when he said that "every revised constitution throughout the southern States has put a premium upon intelligence, ownership of property, thrift and character," he was nevertheless secretly engaged in attacking them by legal action. As early as 1900 he was asking certain philanthropists for money to fight the electoral provisions of the Louisiana constitution. Subsequently he worked secretly through the financial secretary of the Afro-American Council's legal bureau, personally spending a great deal of money and energy fighting the Louisiana test case. (pp. 220-21)

Although he always discreetly denied any interest in active politics, he was engaged in patronage distribution under Roosevelt and Taft, in fighting the lily-white Republicans, and in getting out the Negro vote for the Republicans at national elections. He might say, "I never liked the atmosphere of Washington. I early saw that it was impossible to build up a race of which their leaders were spending most of their time, thought, and

energy in trying to get into office, or in trying to stay there after they were in," but under Roosevelt he became the arbiter of Negro appointments to federal office.

Roosevelt started consulting Washington almost as soon as he took office. The Tuskegeean's role in the appointment of Gold Democrat Thomas G. Jones to a federal judgeship in Alabama was widely publicized. Numerous letters reveal that politicians old and new were soon writing to Tuskegee for favors. Ex-congressman George H. White unsuccessfully appealed to Washington after the White House indicated that "a letter from you would greatly strengthen my chances." [His secretary, Emmet J.] Scott reported that the President's assertion to one office-seeker that he would consider him only with Washington's "endorsement" had "scared these old fellows as they never have been scared before." Some of the established politicians played along and were helped along. Thus P.B.S. Pinchback, at one time acting governor of Louisiana, was favored throughout the Roosevelt and Taft administrations. In the case of J. C. Napier, Nashville lawyer and banker, Washington first turned him down as recorder of deeds for the District of Columbia and minister to Liberia, then named him as one of two possibilities for consul at Bahia, later offered him the Liberian post which Napier now refused, and finally secured for him the office of register of the Treasury. Examples of Washington's influence could be multiplied indefinitely, for a number of port collectorships and of internal revenue, receiverships of public monies in the land office, and several diplomatic posts, as well as the positions of auditor for the Navy, register of the Treasury, and recorder of deeds were at his disposal. Among his outstanding appointments were Robert H. Terrell, judge of municipal court in Washington; William H. Lewis, assistant attorney-general under Taft; and Charles W. Anderson, collector of internal revenue in New York.

Furthermore, Roosevelt sought Washington's advice on presidential messages to Congress and consulted him on most matters concerning the Negro. Every four years, also, Washington took charge of the Negro end of the Republican presidential campaign, he and his circle, especially Charles Anderson, recommending (and black-balling) campaign workers and newspaper subsidies, handling the Negro press, advising on how to deal with racial issues, and influencing prominent Negroes.

If Washington reaped the rewards of politics, he also experienced its vicissitudes. From the start he was fighting a desperate and losing battle against the lily-white Republicans in the South. His correspondence teems with material on the struggle, especially in Louisiana and Alabama, and in other states as well. As he wrote to Walter L. Cohen, chairman of the Republican state central committee of Louisiana and register of the land office in New Orleans, on October 5, 1905: "What I have attempted in Louisiana I have attempted to do in nearly every one of the Southern States, as you and others are in a position to know, and but for my action, as feeble as it was, the colored people would have been completely overthrown and the Lily Whites would have been in complete control in nearly every Southern State."

Troubles came thick and fast after Taft's inauguration. The new President did not consult Washington as much as Roosevelt had done, and Washington exercised somewhat less control over appointments.... Not until 1911, after persistent efforts to convince the administration of the need for some decent plums in order to retain the Negro vote, were a few significant appointments finally arranged. The most notable was that of W. H. Lewis as assistant attorney-general—the highest position held by a Negro in the federal government up to that time.

In areas other than politics Washington also played an active behind-the-scenes role. On the Seth Carter (Texas) and Dan Rogers (Alabama) cases involving discrimination against Negroes in the matter of representation on jury panels, Washington helped with money and worked closely with lawyer Wilford Smith until their successful conclusion before the United States Supreme Court. He was interested in protecting Negro tenants, who had accidentally or in ignorance violated their contracts, from being sentenced to the chain gang. He was concerned in the Alonzo Bailey peonage case, and when the Supreme Court declared peonage illegal, confided to friends that "some of us here have been working at this case for over two years," securing the free services of "some of the best lawyers in Montgomery" and the assistance of other eminent Alabama whites.

In view of Washington's public acceptance of separate but equal transportation accommodations, his efforts against railroad segregation are of special interest. When Tennessee in effect prohibited Pullman space for Negroes by requiring that such facilities be segregated, he stepped into the breach. He worked closely with Napier in Nashville, and enlisted the aid of Atlanta leaders like W.E.B. DuBois. This group did not succeed in discussing the matter with Robert Todd Lincoln, president of the Pullman company, in spite of the intercession of another railroad leader, William H. Baldwin, Jr. And, though Washington was anxious to start a suit, the Nashville people failed to act. In 1906, employing Howard University professor Kelly Miller and Boston lawyer Archibald Grimké as intermediaries, Washington discreetly supplied funds to pay ex-senator Henry W. Blair of New Hampshire to lobby against the Warner-Foraker amendment to the Hepburn Railway Rate Bill. This amendment, by requiring equality of accommodations in interstate travel, would have impliedly condoned segregation throughout the country, under the separate but equal doctrine. The amendment was defeated, but whether owing to Blair's lobbying or to the protests of Negro organizations is hard to say.

It is clear, then, that in spite of his placatory tone and his outward emphasis upon economic development as the solution to the race problem, Washington was surreptitiously engaged in undermining the American race system by a direct attack upon disfranchisement and segregation; that in spite of his strictures against political activity, he was a powerful politician in his own right. The picture that emerges from Washington's own correspondence is distinctly at variance with the ingratiating mask he presented to the world. (pp. 222-27)

> *August Meier, "Toward a Reinterpretation of Booker T. Washington," in* The Journal of Southern History, *Vol. XXIII, No. 2, May, 1957, pp. 220-27.*

Martin Luther King, Jr. (essay date 1967)

[*A renowned American civil rights leader of the 1960s, King, like Washington, sought to bring about racial equality through nonviolent methods. However, in the following excerpt, King points out what he considers to be a basic flaw in Washington's approach to racism.*]

We must get rid of the false notion that there is some miraculous quality in the flow of time that inevitably heals all evils. There is only one thing certain about time, and that is that it waits for no one. If it is not used constructively, it passes you by.... (p. 128)

Equally fallacious is the notion that ethical appeals and persuasion alone will bring about justice. This does not mean that ethical appeals must not be made. It simply means that those appeals must be undergirded by some form of constructive coercive power. If the Negro does not add persistent pressure to his patient plea, he will end up empty-handed. In a not too distant yesterday, Booker T. Washington tried this path of patient persuasion. I do not share the notion that he was an Uncle Tom who compromised for the sake of keeping the peace. Washington sincerely believed that if the South was not pushed too hard, that if the South was not forced to do something that it did not for the moment want to do, it would voluntarily rally in the end to the Negro's cause. Washington's error was that he underestimated the structures of evil; as a consequence his philosophy of pressureless persuasion only served as a springboard for racist Southerners to dive into deeper and more ruthless oppression of the Negro. (pp. 128-29)

> *Martin Luther King, Jr., "The Dilemma of Negro Americans," in his* Where Do We Go from Here: Chaos or Community?, *Harper & Row, 1967, pp. 102-34.*

Theodore L. Gross (essay date 1971)

[*In the following excerpt, Gross argues that* Up from Slavery *is an admirable description of one man's success but fails as a work of literature.*]

Washington's work is the most famous slave narrative in our literature. Earlier autobiographies—notably Frederick Douglass' powerful indictment of slavery, *My Bond-*

age and My Freedom . . . —illuminate the Negro's attitude toward white supremacy in the nineteenth century, but *Up from Slavery* comes at a moment in American history which affords Washington a special opportunity to write a public document as well as a personal memoir—*Up from Slavery* is, at all times, directed to its white audience.

"I was born a slave on a plantation in Franklin County, Virginia," Washington records; "my life had its beginnings in the midst of the most miserable, desolate, and discouraging surroundings." With this straightforward, unpretentious opening, one is prepared for a faithful depiction of Negro life on the plantation—from the inside, as it were, and not through the benevolent, paternalistic eyes of Thomas Nelson Page or Joel Chandler Harris; one is prepared for an iconoclastic autobiography of real historic, if not aesthetic, value. But except for several descriptions of the impoverished condition of Washington's family, the early pages of *Up from Slavery* presents a picture of slavery no different essentially—no more human, or inhuman, as the case may warrant—from that of Page or Harris, and, moreover, one that is continually conditioned by Washington's optimism and religious faith . . . . (pp. 127-28)

The title of Washington's narrative suggests his inexorable optimism: he is interested in the Negro's movement away from slavery, up rather than through, a movement that in Washington's own case was effected by his "struggle for an education," He based his personal confrontation with white American, although at times it scarcely seems to be a confrontation, on the belief that "every persecuted individual and race should get much consolation out of the great human law, which is universal and eternal, that merit, no matter under what skin found, is in the long run, recognized and rewarded"; and the tension that exists in *Up from Slavery* is between Washington's unwavering self-belief, his tenacious self-reliance and idealism, and the society that excluded him. By accepting without question *laissez-faire* capitalism and by adopting those puritanic virtues—hard work, cleanliness, earnestness, and thrift— of the American culture which had suppressed the development of his race, he knew that he must succeed.

And from all practical points of view he did succeed. His life story is a lesson for persecuted people, a kind of primer on how to succeed in spite of your background. "As I now look back over my life," he reminds us, "I do not recall that I ever became discouraged over anything that I set out to accomplish." This unwillingness to be dismayed is reflected in his comments upon racial conditions in America: conditions are improving, movement is upward and away from slavery, the Negro simply has to improve himself to improve his situation . . . . Improvement is the keynote that is struck in *Up from Slavery,* an improvement that results from honest labor—"nothing ever comes to one, that is worth having, except as a result of hard work"—and Washington presents his simple lesson simply, earnestly, entirely unconscious of what seem to us platitudes, employing a

Washington, on a visit to New York.

bare, unpretentious, utilitarian prose that suits his practical ideas. His autobiography is characterized by the sentimental idealism of a good man—particularly of a good American—whose every line is poised deliberately between teaching and preaching.

One reads *Up from Slavery* as one reads a moral tract and not a work of literature, for it is infused with how life could be if only one were as virtuous, as selfless, as determined, as self-confident as Booker T. Washington himself. The book lies heavily in one's hands, for it lacks the essential ingredient of literature—the ingredient that Richard Wright's *Black Boy,* with all its obvious blemishes, possess—that is necessary for enduring autobiography: the complexity of the inner life. Toward the end of his autobiography, Washington confesses that "fiction I care little for. Frequently I have to almost force myself to read a novel that is on every one's lips. The kind of reading that I have the greatest fondness for is biography. I like to be sure that I am reading about a real man or a real thing." Although this is the natural bias of that kind of American who traditionally has considered fiction frivolous, it nevertheless suggests the imaginative dimension that is lacking in *Up from*

Slavery; and one concludes that Washington succeeded in life, if not in literature, precisely because he did not permit himself to explore the complex results of slavery on the Negro's sensibility in the late nineteenth century. (pp. 128-30)

> Theodore L. Gross, "The Black Hero," in his The Heroic Ideal in American Literature, *The Free Press, 1971, pp. 125-92.*

Louis R. Harlan (essay date 1972)

[*In the following excerpt, Harlan, editor of the* Booker T. Washington Papers *and author of a definitive biography of Washington, describes the early impact of* Up from Slavery.]

[*Up from Slavery,*] conceived and guided by some of the country's leading editors and publishers, was deliberately designed to enhance Washington's image among the general reading public as the spokesman of his race. It promoted his school, his social philosophy, and his career. Employing a better ghost-writer [than the one he had used for *The Story of My Life and Work*], writing more of the book himself, and having a clearer sense of purpose than in the earlier book, he produced a minor classic, read all over the world, widely translated, and continuously in print for successive generations. Its principal fault was also a cause of its popularity, that it presented Washington's experience mythically rather than with candor, and thus gave an overly sunny view of black life in America. (p. 245)

Up from Slavery was a *succès d'estime.* Reviewers uniformly commended the simplicity, directness, and eloquence of Washington's style. He presented himself to the world in a most pleasing image, and many reviewers compared Washington's autobiography with that of Benjamin Franklin. (p. 249)

A more significant measure of the success of a book was its impact on the lives of its readers. Black people particularly identified themselves with the protagonist and lived vicariously through his hardships, struggles, and success. A black attorney of Nashville wrote to Washington: "My early experience was very similar to your early ones. I only wish the similarity were kept up to this day." The book provided for many blacks a success model. If Washington could successfully transcend not only poverty but prejudice, any other black man could believe that he too could rise above his lowly beginnings. And despite his occasional humorous jibes at the "old-time" Negroes, Washington's account of his life exuded black pride and individual self-confidence.

Whites also found inspiration in the book. This was partly because the story appealed to certain universal qualities of human nature and the taste for a good narrative, but also because it was so full of goodwill toward whites. Many whites who felt twinges of guilt about their long history of oppression of Negroes

derived warm comfort from this evidence that a representative Negro did not hate them. (pp. 252-53)

As an elaborate exposition of Washington's racial philosophy, *Up from Slavery* completed the work of the Atlanta Compromise speech. It clothed Washington's message of accommodation and self-help in the classic success story, the Horatio Alger myth in black. From slavery there was no other direction than up, and Washington saw the hardships of his early life as a challenge to be up and doing, not as a deterrent. He presented himself simply but without false modesty as possessing all the virtues extolled by Cotton Mather, Poor Richard, and Ralph Waldo Emerson, and his life as a sting of anecdotes illustrating these virtues. To him as to his readers, his life seemed evidence of the capacity and future of his race and of mankind. Washington was the hero of his own life. His life promised black men as well as white men that they could find "acres of diamonds" in their own back yards—if they had any. Together, but for different reasons, white and black Americans welcomed Washington's faith that not through social conflict but through upward striving, white benevolence, and a benign Providence, his race could overcome, as he had overcome, the obstacles of the color line. (p. 253)

> Louis R. Harlan, "The Self-Made Image," in his Booker T. Washington: The Making of a Black Leader, *1856-1901, Oxford University Press, Inc., 1972, pp. 229-53.*

Houston A. Baker, Jr. (essay date 1972)

[*Baker is an authority on black American literature. In the following excerpt from his 1972 study* Long Black Song: Essays in Black American Literature and Culture, *he examines the "institutional frame of mind" manifested in* Up from Slavery.]

Washington felt that he had formed a social and educational philosophy that was compatible with the times; through his educational labors and his public pronouncements, he attempted to show that the educated black American could be a "useful" citizen, an improver of the community, a clean and well-mannered manual laborer of high moral character. Moreover, such a black man, he insisted, would not trouble himself with social equality.... The president, southern governors, and a host of politicians were grateful, enthusiastic, overwhelmed; while America went its imperialistic way in the Philippines, and white William Sumner and other race theorizers poured forth their doctrines, there was a black leader at home to keep the masses at peace. It must truly have seemed that God was in an American heaven and all was right with the Yankee world.

Even today, both revolutionaries and scholars who should know better take Washington's hand-and-finger metaphor ("In all things that are purely social we can be as separate as the fingers, yet one as the hand in all things essential to mutual progress.") as the whole of his teaching, and write off one of the most famous black Americans as a traitor on the basis of his 1895 address to the Atlanta Cotton States and International Exposition, which catapulted him to a position of national leadership. When we turn to *Up from Slavery,* however, we are forced to take another view, for Washington's autobiography is far more than an ameliorative treatise on race relations. The book is first of all a representative work in a major genre in the black literary tradition. Originally published in 1900 as *The Story of My Life and Work, Up from Slavery* ... was one of the last slave narratives published in America.

The first chapter rings a familiar note—it seems almost an imitation of Douglass's *Narrative.* The straightforwardness of the opening is the same ("I was born a slave on a plantation in Franklin County, Virginia"), the setting is again agrarian, and we see the familiar ironic equation of the status of slaves with that of the farm animals: "My mother, I suppose, attracted the attention of a purchaser who was afterward my owner and hers. Her addition to the slave family attracted about as much attention as the purchase of a new horse or cow." ... Finally, Washington assumes the "tragic mulatto" posture at the outset: "Of my father I know even less than of my mother. I do not even know his name. I have heard reports to the effect that he was a white man who lived on one of the near-by plantations." ... (pp. 86-7)

The similarities between Douglass and Washington are not surprising when we consider that Washington wrote one of the earliest biographies of Douglass and was familiar with his writing; nevertheless, we have similarity with a difference. Washington's view of slavery is quite unlike that of Douglass. The perspective in the first chapter of *Up from Slavery* is almost antebellum, considering the narrator's forgiving nature, his view of the positive good derived from slavery, and his discussion of the sadness felt by both master and slave when freedom arrived and parted their ways.... Heightening his antebellum tone, Washington speaks of the slave's fidelity, his willingness to lay down his life for his master, his sadness (his tears mingled with those of the master) when freedom came, and his desire, in some cases, to stay on the plantation after emancipation.

This is not to say, however, that Washington totally ignores the oppression and violence of slavery; he too talks of men reduced to brutes and treated as such, but in a tone which is, at best, compromising. More important though, is the institutional frame of mind that manifests itself throughout *Up from Slavery.* Slavery itself, as we have seen above, is designated as an "institution" and a "school," and at other points a "system" or a "net." Washington's book, therefore, like all slave narratives, begins with the "peculiar institution" of slavery, to which Washington juxtaposes another institution, the schoolhouse.... (pp. 87-8)

According to Washington, the institution was a failure; unhinged gates, broken window panes, unkempt gar-

dens, lack of refinement in diet, and general waste were the evidence of its inefficiency. The basis of Washington's condemnation is the inability of slavery to produce useful men, efficient operations, or social refinement. Ignorance, the absence of self-help, and the low value placed on self-reliance nurtured an unproductive institution. Surely the writer had imbibed his Benjamin Franklin, Ralph Waldo Emerson and Samuel Smiles, either by reading, or simply by breathing in the spirit of his age.

The dichotomy between the "peculiar" institution and the educational institution continues into the second chapter of *Up from Slavery*—"Boyhood Days." While we see that the work situation could encompass educational opportunities (Washington, like Douglass, learned his letters while doing manual labor), we also see the narrator assuming the role of trickster in order to escape work and get to school on time. Moreover, Washington philosophizes on education in this chapter and tells us of his own struggle for literacy. The motivation behind his struggle is obvious; education produces merit, and "Every persecuted individual and race should get much consolation out of the great human law, which is universal and eternal, that merit, no matter under what skin found, is in the long run recognized and rewarded." ... Washington's subscription to the maxim (which seems to contain but little truth) is understandable in the light of his age: when proscription is so severe that a group's chances of upward mobility seem almost nil and when its merit is studiously ignored, one alternative to despair or revolt is to predict that "in the long run" things will be better. Washington's movement, therefore, is toward "merit" and its corresponding recognition and reward. At one pole of his thoughts stands slavery, the opprobrious institution, and at the other stands Harvard, one of America's oldest and most renowned universities, from which he received an honorary degree in 1896. Institutions thus mark the depth and height of his perspective.

In the intermediate sections of *Up from Slavery* it is still the institution that delineates stages of development. In chapters two and three, for example, the salt and coal mining industries are accorded terse descriptions and negative comments. Mrs. Ruffner's home, however, where Washington worked as a "servant," receives a positive evaluation, because here he learned habits of cleanliness and was allowed to continue his education while working. The major feature of the Ruffner home, in fact, was its role as an educational institution: "the lessons that I learned in the home of Mrs. Ruffner were as valuable to me as any education I have ever gotten anywhere since." ... The truth of this statement is driven home when the narrator tells us of his cleaning the recitation room at Hampton: "It occurred to me at once that here was my chance. Never did I receive an order with more delight. I knew that I could sweep, for Mrs. Ruffner had thoroughly taught me how to do that when I lived with her." ... The significance of his accomplishment is expressed in institutional terms: "The sweeping of that room was my college examination, and never did any youth pass an examination for entrance into Harvard or Yale that gave him more genuine satisfaction." . . . (pp. 89-90)

From the time of his entry into college until he goes off to found a school of his own, one institution dominates the narrative. Hampton Institute and its educational concerns are always in the forefront in chapters three through six, and we are told what Washington learned about helping others, recognizing the dignity of labor, and aiding in the preparation of students (both black and red) for study at Hampton. It is in chapter seven, "Early Days at Tuskegee," however, that we witness the start of an interesting coalescence—the merger of a man and an institution. Washington and Tuskegee become almost inseparable for the remainder of *Up from Slavery.*

The growth of Tuskegee parallels the progress of its founder. Still a young and inexperienced man when he went to Alabama, Washington slowly achieved recognition as his institution grew in size and merit. We have almost a new beginning of the narrative at chapter seven, "Teaching School in a Stable and a Hen-house," since Tuskegee starts as a relatively loose-knit organization in agrarian quarters and a rural setting. As the work proceeds, however, it moves (with the school) toward greater urbanity and sophistication: the initial plantation setting becomes a "Southern Campus"; the original enrollment of thirty rural pupils becomes a body of students from twenty-seven states and territories of America and several foreign countries; the initial limited curriculum broadens to include thirty industrial departments; and the stable and henhouse become sixty-six buildings, "counting large and small." In a sense, Tuskegee almost seems to assume a life of its own; it is fed money, which is collected by Washington and his wives, and it grows into something beautiful and healthy . . . . While the school is growing, its founder is given recognition and reward, and he likewise grows in stature. The man and the institution complemented each other, but it was only through a multitude of men that Washington and Tuskegee were able to survive.

In one respect, *Up from Slavery* resembles the *Autobiography* of John Stuart Mill. Mill said at the outset of his work that he not only wished to record the important events of his life, but also to acknowledge the debts he owed to the great men of his age. Washington's autobiography is filled with acknowledgements to such men: General Samuel Armstrong, A. H. Porter, President McKinley, Andrew Carnegie, President Cleveland, and Charles Eliot are only a few. If at times these names read like a patron's list for a cultural event, they do indicate the degree of recognition the author received during his life, and they represent the sources of the nourishment of Tuskegee Institute as well as the great men of Washington's acquaintance.

As the institute grew, the behavioral patterns that it encompassed were perpetuated, expounded, and affirmed by the founder before large audiences. The result, of course, is that Tuskegee came, as all institu-

tions must, to stand for a particular behavioral pattern that was of value to the community as a whole. Those connected with, enrolled in, or responsible for the institution were considered affirmers of this pattern, and when we see some of the greatest names of Washington's time associated with Tuskegee, we can logically deduce that the school expressed, to a great extent, the values of its age. (pp. 90-2)

In light of his traditional American point of view, it is not difficult to see why, writing in the early twentieth century, Washington chose the progression from institution to institution as a means of developing his autobiography. America itself was making exemplary institutional leaps throughout the nineteenth century, and the educational institution was particularly important. The school constitues not only a "behavioral pattern" itself, but also an organization inculcating behavioral patterns. And Washington was able to found an institution that instilled an "American way of life" into black Americans.

Washington received perhaps his most fitting reward when his labors were recognized by one of the oldest institutions in America. The narrator seems aware of the appropriateness and momentousness of his honorary degree from Harvard, for he even arranges his autobiography so that the 1896 Harvard commencement is described, climactically, in the last chapter, while the 1899 trip to Europe is presented in the chapter before. The founder of an educational institution that perpetuated the "American way" standing before the representatives of the oldest and one of the most renowned universities in the country to receive meet homage—this is indeed a celestial position when it is juxtaposed against that peculiar institution with which *Up from Slavery* begins. And the upward path is paved by educational institutions and the men who breathed life (money and labor) into them.

Washington thus shared the American frame of mind in regard to institution-building, and as a champion of American virtues he received fitting reward for his labors. Yet it is not difficult to discover the sources of the vociferous condemnations of the Tuskegeean. The most significant charge concerns Washington's narrowness of scope; life is reduced, particularly in the later chapters of *Up from Slavery,* to a chronicling of grants, a recording of newspaper comments on the founder's speeches and awards, and a listing of famous men met and impressed. Moreover, there is a narrowness in the very behavioral pattern that Washington endorsed, a contraction of perspective indigenous to Tuskegee Institute and its founder, a narrowness revealed in the four characteristics that mark the ideal Tuskegee graduate, the ideal Washingtonian man—skill, high moral character, a sense of expediency, and a belief in the dignity of labor . . . . In *Up from Slavery* there is no orientation toward the future; no cherishing of the aesthetic, the abstract, or the spiritual; there is little belief in the value of institutions beyond educational (and philanthropic) ones. More significantly, there is no social idealism looking toward a day of complete liberation, when all men shall possess their freedom as equals. In *Up from Slavery* "spirit" is translated into dollar signs, idealism into manual labor, and the desire for "freedom now" into useful work.

One hates to think what D. H. Lawrence would have made of Booker T. Washington had he turned an eye upon him in *Studies in Classic American Literature.* Washington appears even more culpable than the Benjamin Franklin who emerges from Lawrence's essays, for he had not only a Puritan ethical monomania, but also a condemnatory zeal. He championed all the American values, but also condemned those institutions that attempted to deal with aspects of the human condition that Tuskegee did not encompass or encourage. The church, labor unions, political structures, idealistic educational enterprises, and creative writing are all belittled directly or by implication in Washington's autobiography. (pp. 92-4)

In a final analysis, however, we cannot write off as a myopic organization man the former slave who served as America's "black leader" for twenty years, built a thriving educational institution in the heart of a racist South, and aided thousands in the struggle for dignity. Washington's achievements would be considered great in any age or in any country, and in late nineteenth-century America they were just short of miraculous. Moreover, social scientists and historians such as Gunnar Myrdal, August Meier, and Louis Harlan have demonstrated that Washington was more complex than would appear from "the ingratiating mask" he presented to the world. (p. 94)

Further research is likely to modify our overall evaluation of the man, but new information cannot alter *Up from Slavery.* The social philosophy set forth in this autobiography and the manner in which it is presented indicate that the author was not as fine a champion of black American rights as he might have been. At a time when the broadest possible perspective and the greatest aid were needed in the black man's struggle for freedom and equality, Washington failed in one of the primary roles of the leader. He opened too few of the doors toward his followers' most sought-after goal; in fact, he closed the doors and barred the shutters on all that lay beyond the ultimate welfare and informing philosophy of his own autonomous, somewhat mechanized institution. By championing the value of education, however, and by producing a sort of Horatio Alger handbook of how to acquire an education and how to set up an educational institution, Washington was following in the path of men such as [David] Walker and Douglass, and anticipating Du Bois. In any meaningful examination of black literature and culture it is impossible to ignore *Up from Slavery,* the book that presents the man Washington and the institution Tuskegee. (p. 95)

> Houston A. Baker, Jr., "Men and Institutions: Booker T. Washington's 'Up from Slavery'," in his Long Black Song: Essays in

Black American Literature and Culture, *The University Press of Virginia, 1972, pp. 84-95.*

James M. Cox (essay date 1977)

[*In the following excerpt, Cox discusses* Up from Slavery *as both a personal document and a work of literary art, arguing that it ranks with Benjamin Franklin's* Autobiography *and Henry Adams's* The Education of Henry Adams.]

Up from Slavery is a resistant text. The autobiography of a prominent public figure, it almost affronts the literary critic with the bleak inertia of its prose. Its content is equally resistant—its didacticism, its self-gratulation, its facts, and its policies are all but in front of its form. Thus cultural historians will see it as representative of a time which they hope history has transcended; black militants will see it as the record of an Uncle Tom who made his way at the expense of his people; white liberals will see it in a light much the same but weaker. Representatives of all these constituencies would inevitably choose W.E.B. Dubois's *Souls of Black Folk* (1903) as a stronger piece of writing . . . . Yet the cultural fact to remember is that Dubois knew how powerful Booker T. Washington was, and in powerfully risking a counter-view to Washington's life and vision he initiated a dialectic upon the racial question which has no more been settled than the racial question itself has been settled. More important for my immediate purposes than the actual controversy between two black views of the racial question is the resistance which Washington's text raises against my own reflections on autobiography. It is not, first of all, Washington's only autobiography. A year before he published it, he had published *The Story of My Life and Work* . . . . It is not uncommon for an autobiographer to write two versions of his life. Dubois was to write at least three in his long life; so did Sherwood Anderson; so did Frederick Douglass . . . . Though such strategies allow the writer a chance for revision, each succeeding effort throws more and more into doubt his capacity for any secure point of view. The insecurity may keep him alive, but it diminishes the finality of each life that he writes.

Even here Washington is different. He wrote neither of his lives alone. Instead he supervised them, something in the manner of an overseer. *The Story of My Life and Work* was, as Louis Harlan points out in his biography of Washington, actually written by Edgar Webber, a black journalist whom Washington brought to Tuskegee in 1897 largely for the purpose of assisting him in his life story. But Washington was so busy and so exhausted that he took his first vacation, a trip to Europe, and did not oversee the final chapters of the manuscript. Webber on his part proved inadequate to the task, making many errors and resorting to the short-cut methods of padding the book with schedules, letters, and copies of speeches, which are in reality substitutions for the text rather than fulfillments or extensions of it. (pp. 246-47)

Even before Webber had finished the book, Washington was, according to Harlan, already planning another book, this time for the regular rather than the subscription trade; and this time he got a white journalist, Max Thrasher from St. Johnsbury, Vermont, to help him with the project. This time, too, Washington supervised the work every inch of the way, leaving Thrasher practically no freedom. He dictated to Thrasher on trains, took Thrasher's notes and in turn wrote his own draft of the autobiography, letting Thrasher check the manuscript. I have on occasion heard scholars of black studies point gloatingly to Thrasher's presence in the project as evidence of Washington's having been a captive to the white mind. It would actually be difficult to imagine a more reduced role than Thrasher was forced to play; even to call him a ghost, as Harlan does, is to use the term loosely. He seems much more like a slave to Washington's narrative. That fact, concealed from the text, provides both a starting point and index for scrutinizing the life story which Washington ordered for himself.

That story is, as everyone knows, one of the great success-stories of American history. Washington tells in the simplest, most straightforward terms of his rise from slavery to a position as leader of his people .... By dint of hard work, ceaseless diplomacy with the white population of Macon County, and unremitting perseverance in the face of ignorance, poverty, inertia, and doubt, he builds Tuskegee from nothing but dilapidated outbuildings of a ruined plantation into Tuskegee Normal and Industrial Institute. Money for the school comes primarily from white northern philanthropists; students come from the black population of the United States, though largely from the South; survival comes from Washington's carefully orchestrated interdependence between Tuskegee and the dominant southern whites. The climax of Washington's career, as he narrates it, is his speech at the Atlanta Exposition in 1895. That speech not only represents the achievement of an ex-slave addressing a largely white southern audience; it also marks Booker T. Washington's emergence as a national leader of his people.

That is the barest outline of Washington's story—or the story he chooses to tell. The way he tells it is simple and unadorned. His prose is reduced to an almost impoverished simplicity; metaphor is sparse; eloquence is all but absent; there is neither richness of texture nor complication of consciousness; even the simplicity never condenses into the energy of compression but retains an air of immobility being put into slow and steady motion. Although Washington was a successful public speaker and although the Atlanta speech (which he quotes in full in his text) shows oratorical flourish and declamatory urgency, the narrative throughout is characterized by what can best be called almost pure inertia.

In calling Washington's style purely inertial, I mean that he writes as if language were matter rather than energy. The words are things which, added one to another, do not record so much as they build the narrative life upon the line that the structure of his life has taken. Thus the events which Washington recounts are not so much dramatized as deadened into matter with which to make the narrative. They are being set steadily in place by the narrator, as if he were constructing the model of his life. The pain, fear, anguish, self-doubt, and anxiety which attended Washington's life are there, of course; but they are muted into the very matter of the narrative. This tendency to treat language as material causes Washington's narrative consciousness to seem literally housed in his narrative. If Washington is moving the blocks of his life into position, they seem to rest in place by their own weight.

That solid stability is one aspect of Washington's inertial style; but there is also motion—for Washington is moving his material into place. Yet here again he seems to be following the course of his life rather than directing it. The relatively strict chronology of autobiographical convention to which he adheres provides the form that draws him along. If he drove himself to make his actual life—and he explicitly indicates that he did— his belief in the existence of that life gives him the powerful illusion that it has created him as the narrator of it. This combination of conventional form and self-belief conveys the strong sense that Washington is pursuing the slow and steady motion of his life.

His use of chronological convention to order his life is but a reflection of his capacity to use time to make his life into a book just as he had used it to make his life as a man. His belief in the weight of his life puts all his language into a rhetorical rather than a dramatic or imaginary relation to that life. The solid reality to which his language refers now exists for language to use. If it was the result of desire, ambition, and fierce determination, it now becomes the matter from which Washington will read higher laws. Here again Washington's book is conventional, embracing as it does the moral and exemplary fatalities of autobiography. The exemplary autobiography is the secularized version of the Christian confessional form. The confessional form (with the exception of the revolutionary Rousseau!) denigrates the man by relating his conversion into God; the exemplary form converts godlike achievement into a model for man to follow. The one portrays the fallen child attaining to the spirit of the Father; the other becomes the model father to provide principles for the children. The one seeks goodness as truth, the other goodness as conduct. [Benjamin] Franklin's *Autobiography* is a classic example of the exemplary convention, and Washington is clearly Franklin's descendant. Having achieved success, he publishes his life as an example of the virtues he believes that he practised in gaining the high ground from which he writes.

If Franklin is almost disarmingly simple in his exemplary narrative, Washington is dismayingly simple in his. Franklin enunciates principles with sufficient ease to disclose the possibility that he lacks principle altogether; he can thus reveal an implicit amusement in his life of himself. Washington clings almost desperately to his virtues. What for Franklin is policy becomes gospel for Washington. Keeping his life under much stricter control than that of Franklin, Washington is constrained to reiterate his smaller number of principles—the principle of constant work, the principle of helping others to help themselves, and the principle of building a life from the ground up. Thus where Franklin takes pleasure in the disclosure of his principles—he even writes the autobiography in moments of leisure—Washington's principles are themselves his only pleasure. He hardly knows how to play. If Franklin's very model of himself is a gift that he easily bequeaths to posterity, Washington's life is all but asking for the reader's charity—as if he were waiting in the parlor for one more contribution.

Then one must confront Washington's idea of education. It is as single-minded as his adherence to the Protestant work ethic—and as unpopular to critics of his life and work. Believing that education for people on the bottom of society has to begin at the bottom, Washington wants the body and hands cleaned and disciplined before he cultivates the head. Foreign languages and even books themselves have little benefit in his eyes unless students are able to command a trade. He championed industrial education, and particularly he champions it in his autobiography, as a means of teaching his people how to work. This philosophy of education, reiterated throughout the book, galled blacks in Washington's own time, and it galls them all the more in our time when they can see, just as white readers can see, that this was a means of placating whites. Washington was assuring them, in effect, that Tuskegee graduates would know how to work more than they would know how to think.

These aspects of Washington's narrative make it singularly unprepossessing for both the literary and the cultural critic. They are there, and I could not wish them away even if I would. Yet a reader willing to encounter the book and give it a degree of consciousness—Washington's book, like his life philosophy, is going to ask for something—has a chance for revelations in Washington's inertial narrative.

First of all, there is the fact that Washington was born in *Franklin* County, Virginia. That inertial fact reveals its energy once we think of the book in relation to Franklin's autobiography. He was born a slave, but does not know his father, who is said to be a white man. Thus he has white blood from an unknown father. When he goes to Malden he has no name—but names himself Booker Washington, in a schoolroom. For all his matter-of-factness Washington does note that one of the advantages of having been a slave was his freedom to name himself. He even mentions other slaves taking names such as John S. Lincoln. But he chose Washington; at the time he did it he was no doubt attempting to follow a pattern he saw others pursuing. Yet in light of all that he was to do, the early act is charged with significance—a significance which Washington never stresses because he does not need to. George Washington was, after all, a Virginian who owned slaves yet was

the father of his country. Booker Washington is also a Virginian who has been a slave and has an unknown white father. In naming himself he lays claim to the white blood in him and relates himself to the father of his country. He himself clearly sees his original naming of himself as a promise of being a father to his people.

As for Washington's actual call to his vocation, here is what he says about it:

> One day, while working in the coal mine, I happened to overhear two miners talking about a great school for coloured people somewhere in Virginia. That was the first time I had ever heard anything about any kind of school or college that was more pretentious than the little coloured school in our town....
>
> As they were describing the school, it seemed to me that it must be the greatest place on earth, and not even Heaven presented more attractions for me at that time than did the Hampton Normal and Agricultural Institute in Virginia, about which these two men were talking. I resolved at once to go to that school, although I had no idea where it was, or how I was going to reach it. I remembered only that I was on fire constantly with one ambition, and that was to go to Hampton.

That quotation stands out in my context much more than it does in Washington's text. I have seen students read right through it, numbed by the patient plod of Washington's inertial style. Yet it is Washington's *calling,* as he makes unmistakably clear. The whole episode may be a fiction; certainly there would be no way to prove its actual existence, since the two men conversing were unaware of Washington's secret presence. In any event here is a *black boy in a coal mine* hearing his life's direction named, and any wish to call it a fiction seems to me merely a weak theoretical formulation in the face of Washington's capacity, from the established ground he has come to hold, to *make the facts of his life.* If his identity as ex-slave gave him the freedom to name himself and make that name a fact, his achievement as founder of Tuskegee gives him the freedom to make the fact of his call. He even shows that he is creating the fact when he intrudes the full name of Hampton, which the two men could hardly have named. When we consider that it is a coal mine, that he is black, that both he and the coal possess the implicit or inertial energy, we begin to see both the act and style of ***Up from Slavery.*** The inertia of the style produces the effect of an indeterminate consciousness on the part of Washington, the autobiographer. If I say that he intended the significance that I see, both the style and the skeptical readers reading it almost smile in my face, implicitly accusing me of trying to make a "symbol" of that passage. And of course the accusation is to a large extent right. That is why I am willing to leave it as a made or earned fact—inertial in its existence until it is put into relation to a consciousness prepared to invest it with dynamic energy.

Such a consciousness, once attracted to that inertia, feels the whole possibility of Washington's life about to come to life; relationships start up like rabbits from a blackberry patch. It was Henry Adams, after all, who in his dynamic *Education* determined to measure the line of force of American history in terms of coal production. And it is coal which to this very moment holds the inertial energy of all the weight of geological ages pressing down upon it to create the potential fire of civilization. Set against Henry Adam's autobiography of a failed education, Washington's calling to a successful education strikes sparks. Yet the very critic who would write a book on Henry Adams's art would likely smile indulgently at the comparison.

But let that go. The point is that coal is in the earth. It is the earth into which Booker T. Washington's life is driven and out of which it stands. In his slave cabin, which had no wooden floors, he tells us, there had been a hole where sweet potatoes were kept. When he comes up out of the coal mine to go to Hampton Institute, he makes his way to Richmond where, without enough money to get a meal or a room, he sleeps under a board sidewalk on the ground. Though beneath the pedestrians, he is yet on the earth. And when he ultimately goes to Tuskegee, the first thing he does is to acquire land on which to build his school from the ground up. He helps clear the fields of this farm—it is actually a ruined plantation—which his school is to occupy. The first building takes the place of the burned-down ruin of the original plantation house; he and his students "dig out the earth" where the foundations are to be laid. Washington is proud that the cornerstone is grounded in the great "black belt" of the South; he knows, and says, that the black belt refers both to the dark soil of the deep South and to the dark people who live there. All this is the ground of Washington's world—the ground where slavery had existed and the ground in which he is determined to found his school. Both his act of life and his vision of education are rooted in this land. (pp. 248-55)

All this is not to praise Washington's vision of education but to see that vision. His discipline is the measure of the rudimentary struggle to gain the ground on which education can be founded. That ground is in the South, under the political sway of whites who, having been dispossessed of their slave world, have nonetheless ridden out reconstruction to regain their damaged dominion. Washington is placating them. He has to; to do otherwise would be to abandon his school or go north to relocate it. His whole theory of education can justifiably be viewed as a promise to southern whites that Tuskegee graduates will not have big ideas; but it cannot justifiably be seen as simply that. The desperate order of the skilled hand, the toothbrush, the clean body, and the clean school is a great hope rooted in a great fear.

We might want to say that the hope represses the fear, but that simply isn't true. Fear is everywhere present in Washington's narrative. When he was a slave boy bringing food home late from the mill he feared that he would be caught in the dark and have his ears cut off by deserting soldiers. On the way to West Virginia with his mother and brothers, the family spent the night in an abandoned house, only to be frightened away by a blacksnake. Even when he names himself, he is in anxiety at not having a name as the teacher begins to call the roll. There is fear present in being "called" in the coal mine; thus he noiselessly creeps to hear the two men talking. He is glad to be called to be a teacher—partly out of fear of being called to be a preacher. He is afraid of the whites around Tuskegee and afraid of the whites in the North from whom he has to beg money, but most of all he is afraid of the psychological space he occupies between the two hostile camps. The space and the fear are almost one and the same thing. (pp. 256-57)

This fear never diminishes with Washington's success; if anything, it increases—not in intensity, since the inertial style precludes emotional crescendo, but in presence. For as Washington gains recognition, he is more and more exposed. Beyond fearing lack of money for Tuskegee from the North or resistance to the school from the South, he has to fear how his action as a public figure will be interpreted by his conflicting constituencies. In preparing to speak at Atlanta, he faces fear on every hand—fear of what southern whites may say, fear of whether he will hurt his school, fear of the visiting northern whites, and fear of the speaking act itself. That fear is, to be sure, a rhetorical background for the success of the speech, but it is also one of the great facts in Washington's book. He discusses his profound fear of public speaking—the fear that some single member of the audience may walk out, the performer's fear of going on stage, the gnawing anxiety of eating a multicourse dinner with the knowledge of having to give an after-dinner speech. When he at last takes his first vacation—the trip to Europe—he fears the luxuries, the dinners, the society, and the possible misunderstandings the Tuskegee community may have about his absence. As he ends the book he is very much on the defensive. He knows that Dubois and hundreds of northern blacks are raising their voices in criticism; he knows that the Tuskegee teachers and students are restive; and it seems to me that he profoundly knows that his own success is being accompanied by mounting victories of anti-negro legislation; for all his success and all his placation he knows about lynching and raises one last plea against it. He ends his book with an account of his triumphant welcome in Richmond, the capital of his native state, yet anyone sensitive to the narrative will feel Washington's anxious wonder whether he may have been as secure under the sidewalk as he is on top of it.

In citing this fear in the book, I am once again forced to distort the nature of its presence. The inertial style cannot and does not express it dramatically but contains it constantly. That, it seems to me, is the mastery of the inertial style. To speak of Washington's mastery may again provoke a smile. But my point in using the word is that Washington is a master. His whole book is devoted to coming up *from* slavery, not up against it. Slavery is the deep ground of his experience; to reject it totally would remove all possibility of becoming a master of the self—and self-mastery is what much of Washington's book is about. It is the iron discipline that he pursues, and it is the basis on which he builds a school and is its master. He becomes the master speaker who aspires to total control of his audience; the description of that control he leaves to white reporters, whose description of his galvanizing presence he almost self-servingly enters in the text.

It would be easy to misconstrue the figure of Washington as master. By converting it into a metaphor, I could jump on the bandwagon with Washington's innumerable critics and say that Washington is playing the role of white master on the old plantation, getting along with the white society of former masters, and making his students the same old black laborers on the new Tuskegee plantation. I have heard it said and I cannot quite unsay it. For Washington is deeply related to the old white world. He is a slave son of an unknown white father from that world; and even George Washington, the white father of freedom whom Washington "adopts" once he is free, did own slaves—a paradox which Henry Adams contemplated with almost paralyzed dismay.

The fact remains, however, that Booker Taliaferro Washington, if not all black, defines himself as black, not white. He determines to remain in a society which will aggressively see him as black. If the name he takes is white and the civilization which he is set on acquiring for himself and for his people is white, these are to be acquisitions, not being; they are property, not identity. They constitute a self to be moved and built, both in Washington's life and in his book. If it is possible to say that this model self is white, I think it equally possible to say that the white model self is Washington's very slave. It is simple, fiercely reduced in its outlines, kept rigidly in line, and controlled with an iron discipline. It has enormous dynamic energy which can only be implicitly seen.

The inertial style makes Washington seem like an old man, rather than a relatively young man. He was at most forty-five when it was published; he was only twenty-five when he went to Tuskegee. It is hard to believe, this youth so given over to age, this drive which moves so slowly. Yet it is just this slow and steady movement which is the black being of Washington—the being that he retained for himself, yet represents for his people. He does not create the motion; it has been created by the force which ended slavery. It is slow, but it is relentless: it is both a force and a fact—the emotion of identity and the motion of history—which cannot be stopped. Since it is everywhere present it cannot be revealed.

To have said so much may not prove that *Up from Slavery* is literature. I certainly cannot prove it so to anyone disposed to exclude it from the shelf of our "major" works of art. I do believe that it is a wonderful parallel text to Henry Adams's *Education,* just as I believe that it is a remarkable counterpart to Dubois's *The Souls of Black Folk.* (pp. 257-60)

James M. Cox, "Autobiography and Washington," in The Sewanee Review, *Vol. LXXXV, No. 2, Spring, 1977, pp. 235-61.*

William L. Andrews (essay date 1987)

[*The following excerpt is from a paper delivered at the session on "Slavery and the Literary Imagination" at the 1987 English Institute. Here, Andrews examines what has been termed the "accommodationist strategy" of* Up from Slavery.]

The pragmatism of the postbellum slave narrator stems primarily from his willingness to interpret and evaluate slavery according to its practical consequences in the real world of human action. While the antebellum narrative did not ignore the practical effects of slavery on blacks and whites in the South, it rested its antislavery case on religious and ethical absolutes like Bibb's "inevitable laws of Nature's God," or what William Craft called "the sacred rights of the weak." The postbellum narrator rarely appeals to such ideals or to the righteous indignation that let his antebellum predecessor condemn slavery so categorically. Instead he asks his reader to judge slavery simply and dispassionately on the basis of what Booker T. Washington liked to call "facts," by which the Tuskegean meant something other than empirical data. In *Up from Slavery,* as in many other postbellum slave narratives, a factual evaluation of slavery exploits what William James would later call the "practical cash-value" of the word, its significance in the present day. What slavery was in the past is not so important as what slavery means, or (more importantly) can be construed to mean, in the present. A factual view of slavery, for Washington, is concerned less with a static concept of historical truth, frozen in the past, than with the need for rhetorical power in the ever-evolving present. To the postbellum slave narrator, particularly Washington, slavery needed to be reviewed and reempowered as a concept capable of effecting change, of making a difference ultimately in what white people thought of black people as freedmen, not slaves. The facts of slavery in the postbellum narrative, therefore, are not so much what happened *then*—bad though it was—as what *makes* things, good things, happen now.

Looking the facts of the present (more than the past) in the face, Washington could justifiably call slavery a school in which black Americans had learned much about the necessity of hard work, perseverance, and self-help as survival skills in their difficult passage in the antebellum South. The fact of turn-of-the-century American "scientific" racism, which stereotyped "the Negro" as degraded, ignorant, incompetent, and servile, demanded that slavery be re-presented anew, not as a condition of deprivation or degradation, but as a period of training and testing, from which the slave graduated with high honors and even higher ambitions. Given the changed socio-political circumstances, it is not surprising to find the postbellum slave narrator treating slavery more as an economic proving ground than an existential battleground for southern black people. The slave past, if effectively represented, could provide the freedman and freedwoman with credentials that the new industrial-capitalist order might respect. By the turn of the century, blacks were realizing their need for a usable American past on which they could build. They could also see that southern whites needed to be reminded of who had built the Old South and who could help to build a New South as well. The agenda of the postbellum slave narrative thus emphasizes unabashedly the tangible contribution that blacks made to the South, in and after slavery, in order to rehabilitate the image of the freedman, not the idea of slavery, in the eyes of business America.

Although in some ways a typical postbellum slave narrative, *Up from Slavery* stands out today, as always, because of its articulation of an accommodationist strategy that, though by no means original, Washington managed to identify as his own. What we would call accommodationism, however, is what the Tuskegean would have termed realism. What are the sources of real power in the real world? asks the writer of *Up from Slavery.* In the antebellum slave narrative . . . , the answer is almost unanimous. Knowledge is power, and the fundamental source of knowledge is literacy, the ability to open one's mind to the words of others and to liberate other minds with a text of one's own. As an ex-slave and an educator, Washington pays lip service to the importance of reading in his own life and in the training of his people. But in his preferred persona as pragmatic student of power, he demotes men of the word and elevates men of action to the putative leadership of his people. The irony of the pre-eminent black speaker and writer of his day identifying himself as a man of real acts, not mere words, should not prevent us from recognizing the literary significance of Washington's antiliterary thesis. *Up from Slavery* is, in its own quiet and indirect—should I say sly?—way, a manifesto of a quasi-literary realism that attempts to restrict the traditional sovereignty of the black wordsmith by chaining the signifier to a preexistent signified and thus making the word merely reflective, rather than constitutive, of reality.

Washington's realism entails a radical distinction between deeds and words. "The actual sight of a first-class house that a Negro has built is ten times more potent than pages of discussion about a house that he ought to build, or perhaps could build." Action, Washington insists, produces things; discussion, by contrast, produces only more discussion. "Instead of studying books so constantly, how I wish that our schools and colleges might learn to study men and things!" The men Washington studies are, of course, white men of action and substance, like Andrew Carnegie, Collis P. Huntington, and William McKinley. In stark contrast with them are black men of words—in particular, southern politicians, preachers, and educators. These men, Washington argues, have too often made speaking and writing a refuge from doing, from working productively for the good of the race. As he surveys the recent history of his people, he finds that politicians stirred up in the people

only an "artificial" desire to hold public office; preachers inspired in literate black men only a self-serving "call to preach"; teachers merely pandered to "the craze for Greek and Latin learning" among pathetically ignorant blacks. Instead of doing tangible good, all this preaching and teaching and speech-making created in the minds of rural southern blacks a pernicious notion, namely, that an alternative resource of power existed to what Washington called the "real, solid foundation" of black advancement, the agrarian life. Even Washington had to acknowledge that the black community had traditionally revered the man of the word as "a very superior human being, something bordering almost on the supernatural" in the case of those who understood the mystery of foreign languages. Such men seemed not to require "the solid and never deceptive foundation of Mother Nature," that is, a grounding in the life of "the soil," to exercise power and excite envy among southern blacks. Washington's fear was that the example of Afro-American men of the word would encourage young blacks to believe that the route to black power was not hand-to-mouth, from act to word, but rather just the reverse, from performing word to reforming act. Washington pays inadvertent tribute to these black masters of the speech-act by noting that they "live by their wits" instead of by their hands and that the white South regards them with a perplexed and uneasy suspicion.

Few can read *Up from Slavery* today without recognizing that Washington also lived by his wits in a consummate manner. A former political stump speaker and student of the ministry, Washington clearly understood the power of the word in the mouth of an artful and ambitious black man. "I never planned to give any large part of my life to speaking in public," he blandly remarks, adding, "I have always had more of an ambition to *do* things than merely to talk *about* doing them." Yet no black man could have built Tuskegee Institute without knowing that action proceeds from speech and that speech is itself a most potent form of action. Washington acknowledges that he authorized the erection of Porter Hall, the first building on the Tuskegee campus, before he had the money to pay for it. He relied on his charm and good name in the community to secure loans to complete the edifice. He had no capital at all when he conceived of putting up the second building, but, as he offhandedly comments, "We decided to give the needed building a name" anyway. Naming the building Alabama Hall proved, of course, a shrewd political maneuver that helped to ensure the continuation of the state funding on which Washington depended so much in the early years. This speech-act alone, so reminiscent of the talismanic power of naming in the slave narrative tradition, belies Washington's insistence that words merely publicize deeds. Thus, even though he claims that he always "had a desire to do something to make the world better, and *then* be able to speak to the world about that thing" (emphasis mine), Washington had the wit to see that speaking makes doing possible and that reality is contingent on language, not the other way around.

Nevertheless, in an effort to subvert the "almost supernatural" status of the man of words in the black community, the author of **Up from Slavery** presents himself as a naturalist, arguing that only from a rootedness in "nature" does he derive the "strength for the many duties and hard places that await me" in the real world. Washington is not talking about communing with Nature in some romantic fashion. His need is more immediate and tangible: "I like, as often as possible, to touch nature, not something that is artificial or an imitation, but the real thing." Hence it is no surprise to find Washington depreciating belles-lettres and enthusing over newspapers as "a constant source of delight and recreation." Obviously, fiction, poetry, and drama are artificial and merely imitative of "the real thing." Only one kind of storytelling can satisfy Washington's appetite for realism, namely, "biography," for which he claims "the greatest fondness." Why he should prefer biography to all other kinds of reading is plain enough: "I like to be sure that I am reading about a real man or a real thing." But the way Washington prefaces his predictable desire for the "real thing"—"I like to be *sure*"—suggests that he knows that readers of biography do not always get what they expect or want, nor does biography always assure its readers of their ability to distinguish between the real and the artificial. Maybe this is one reason why Washington is at such pains in writing his own biography to portray himself as a plain and simple man of facts, "the real thing" among autobiographers, a man who represents himself as no more than what he is. Washington *knows* the prejudice in his white audience against the black men of words as truth-tellers; this is a major reason why he claims he is a man of acts and facts. By repeatedly declaring his "great faith in the power and influence of facts" and his conviction that one can touch the real thing in biography, Washington acts to shore up the foundation of **Up from Slavery,** which we can see is not so much grounded in real things as in linguistic demonstrations of realism.

Capitalizing on the postbellum slave narrator's pragmatic revision of the facts of slavery, **Up from Slavery** promulgates a concept of realism which challenges the traditional status of the sign in the Afro-American narrative tradition. By claiming a radical distinction between action and speech and by disclaiming language as anything more than a referential medium, Washington denies the performative dimension of representation. The consummate rhetorician, he tries to pass for a realist, we might say, since this lets him keep his agenda masked behind a semblance of nonrhetorical *vraisemblance.* If Washington could define the terms by which realism would be judged in Afro-American writing, then he could consign literary representation to a *reactive* status in Afro-American culture, thereby robbing it of the expressive power that the word had held in the black community since the antebellum era. The rise of Tuskegee realism then, foregrounded by the postbellum slave narrative and reinforced by numerous autobiographies of Washington's protégés, imitators, and admirers, discounts the hard-won victory of antebellum narratives like *My Bondage and My Freedom* and *Incidents in the*

Life of a Slave Girl, texts that liberated black narrative from an alienating and objectifying focus on the sign as a referent to an object—slavery—rather than a subject—the questing consciousness of the former slave. Tuskegee realism, ever respectful of Washington's much-heralded "gospel of the toothbrush," sanitizes the mouth of the speaking subject until it attains that acme of "unselfishness" which is, in Washington's eyes, the hallmark of every successful man of action. (pp. 68-73)

> *William L. Andrews, "The Representation of Slavery and the Rise of Afro-American Literary Realism, 1865-1920," in* Slavery and the Literary Imagination, *new series, no. 13, edited by Deborah E. McDowell and Arnold Rampersad, The Johns Hopkins University Press, 1989, pp. 62-80.*

FURTHER READING

Amann, Clarence A. "Three Negro Classics: An Estimate." *Negro American Literature Forum* 4, No. 4 (Winter 1970): 113-19.
> Comparative study of three autobiographies by black writers: *Up from Slavery, The Souls of Black Folk* by W. E. B. Du Bois, and *The Autobiography of an Ex-Colored Man* by James Weldon Johnson. Amann states that *Up from Slavery* is limited in scope and not as accomplished as Du Bois's *The Souls of Black Folk.*

Brawley, Benjamin. "The Maturing of Negro Literature." In his *The Negro Genius: A New Appraisal of the Achievement of the American Negro in Literature and the Fine Arts,* pp. 143-70. New York: Dodd, Mead, & Co., 1937.
> Discusses Washington's eloquence as a speaker.

Bresnahan, Roger J. "The Implied Readers of Booker T. Washington's Autobiographies." *Black American Literature Forum* 14, No. 1 (Spring 1980): 15-20.
> Studies intended reader response to *The Story of My Life and Work* and *Up from Slavery,* arguing that Washington's method in the autobiographies is "to tap the reader's own identity and then to modify it."

Calista, Donald J. "Booker T. Washington: Another Look." *The Journal of Negro History* XLIX, No. 4 (October 1964): 240-55.
> Maintains that Washington often wore a "mask of compromise" in order to achieve his long-range goal of advancement for black Americans.

Cox, Oliver C. "The Leadership of Booker T. Washington." *Social Forces* 30, No. 1 (October 1951): 91-7.
> Marxist study of Washington's career as a black leader. Cox argues that Washington collaborated with whites and promoted restraints on black social power. The critic adds: "Probably a collaborator of Washington's magnitude could never again be imposed upon the race because even the rural Negroes of the South are conditioned to respond negatively to him."

Dillard, James Hardy. "A Christian Philosopher: Booker T. Washington." *Southern Workman* LIX, No. 5 (May 1925): 209-14.
    Views Washington's Christian faith as the motivating force behind his ideas and methods for bringing about change in the social and economic circumstances of blacks.

Eddy, Sherwood, and Page, Kirby. "Freedom from Ignorance: Booker T. Washington." In their *Makers of Freedom: Biographical Sketches in Social Progress,* pp. 32-62. New York: George H. Doran Co., 1926.
    Discusses the political and economic climate during Washington's era and examines his accomplishments in relation to the beliefs of the time.

Friedman, Lawrence J. "Life 'In the Lion's Mouth': Another Look at Booker T. Washington." *The Journal of Negro History* LIX, No. 1 (October 1974): 337-51.
    Documents a "pattern" of "conflicting and equivocating rhetoric that characterized Booker T. Washington's active years." Friedman maintains that the material gains Washington is said to have achieved through covert tactics "[may] have been exaggerated."

Genovese, Eugene D. "The Legacy of Slavery and the Roots of Black Nationalism." *Studies on the Left* 6, No. 6 (November-December 1966): 3-26.
    Contends that Washington had an "enormous" influence on the social and political thinking of later black nationalists.

Gottschalk, Jane. "The Rhetorical Strategy of Booker T. Washington." *Phylon* XXVII, No. 4 (Winter 1966): 388-95.
    Examines Washington's weekly talks at Tuskegee Institute.

Harlan, Louis R. "Booker T. Washington and the *Voice of the Negro.*" The Journal of Southern History XLV, No. 1 (February 1979): 45-62.
    Discusses Washington's attempts to gain editorial control of the black journal *Voice of the Negro.*

———. *Booker T. Washington: The Wizard of Tuskegee, 1901-1915.* New York: Oxford University Press, 1983, 548 p.
    Book-length study of Washington's final years at Tuskegee Institute.

———. *Booker T. Washington in Perspective: Essays of Louis R. Harlan.* Edited by Raymond W. Smock. Jackson: University Press of Mississippi, 1988, 210 p.
    Collects Harlan's major essays about Washington.

Meier, August. "Booker T. Washington and the Negro Press: With Special Reference to the *Colored American Magazine.*" The Journal of Negro History XXXVIII, No. 1 (January 1953): 67-91.
    Discusses Washington's involvement with the black journals of his day, especially the *Colored American Magazine.*

Morris, Charles. "Booker T. Washington, the Pioneer of Negro Progress." In his *Heroes of Progress in America.* 2d rev. ed., pp. 335-44. Philadelphia: J. B. Lippincott Co., 1919.
    Biographical sketch of Washington.

Naipaul, V. S. "Reflections: How the Land Lay." *The New Yorker* 64 (6 June 1988): 94-100, 103-05.
    Studies how Washington put the precepts of *Up from Slavery* into practice at Tuskegee Institute and comments on the Institute's role in present-day American life. Naipaul also recounts a visit he made to the Tuskegee campus during the 1980s.

Pole, J. R. "Of Mr. Booker T. Washington and Others." In his *Paths to the American Past,* pp. 170-88. New York: Oxford University Press, 1979.
    Overview of Washington's life and literary career.

Roosevelt, Theodore. Preface to *Booker T. Washington: Builder of a Civilization,* by Emmett J. Scott and Lyman Beecher Stowe, pp. ix-xv. New York: Doubleday, Page & Co., 1916.
    Laudatory evaluation of Washington's social and political achievements for black Americans.

Spencer, Samuel R., Jr. *Booker T. Washington and the Negro's Place in American Life.* Boston: Little, Brown and Co., 1955, 212 p.
    Profiles Washington's career as an advocate of social and economic advancement for blacks.

Stepto, Robert. "Lost in a Cause: Booker T. Washington's *Up from Slavery.*" In his *From behind the Veil: A Study of Afro-American Narrative,* pp. 32-51. Urbana: University of Illinois Press, 1979.
    Detailed analysis of *Up from Slavery* as a classic work of African-American literature.

Thornbrough, Emma L. "Booker T. Washington As Seen by His White Contemporaries." *Journal of Negro History* LIII, No. 2 (April 1968): 161-82.
    Examines the reactions of Washington's white contemporaries to his racial programs.

Whitfield, Stephen J. "Three Masters of Impression Management: Benjamin Franklin, Booker T. Washington, and Malcolm X As Autobiographers." *The South Atlantic Quarterly* 77, No. 4 (Autumn 1978): 399-417.
    Comparative study of Franklin, Washington, and Malcolm X as men whose autobiographies were artfully crafted to create specific impressions of their authors.

Woodward, C. Vann. "Booker T. Washington in History." In *Booker T. Washington,* edited by Emma Lou Thornbrough, pp. 130-73. Englewood Cliffs, N.J.: Prentice-Hall, 1969.
    Explores the long-range influence and effects of Washington's social and economic policies.

Young, Alfred. "The Educational Philosophy of Booker T. Washington." *Phylon* XXXVII, No. 3 (September 1976): 224-35.
    Argues that Washington's philosophy of education reflected a "'black perspective of education' and that it functioned as a liberating force for the ubiquitous Afro-American."

Phillis Wheatley

1753?–1784

(Full name Phillis Wheatley Peters) West African-born American poet.

Wheatley was the first black person known to have published a volume of writings in North America. (Earlier, in 1761, Jupiter Hammon—a slave on Long Island—published a single broadside poem, "An Evening Thought: Salvation by Christ, with Penetential Cries.") Historically significant in American letters, Wheatley's *Poems on Various Subjects, Religious and Moral* (1773) was used as an exemplar of the power of education by proponents of equalitarian and abolitionist aims who hailed the collection as a product of a genius. The collection, composed largely of neoclassical elegiac poetry that displays the controlled rhythms and rhyme patterns popularized by Alexander Pope, has been variously regarded as brilliant and artistically inconsequential. Most modern assessments, however, recognize Wheatley's accomplishments as typical of the best second-tier poetry of her age.

Believed to have been born in West Africa (most likely in present-day Senegal or Gambia), Wheatley was purchased at a slave auction in 1761 by the wife of a wealthy Boston merchant who wanted a youthful personal maid to serve her in old age. Wheatley was about seven or eight years old when she arrived in America; she appeared frail and sickly, though her gentle, demure manner was considered charming. Once in the Wheatley household, the child displayed a curiosity and aptitude for learning that led her owners to abandon plans to train her as a servant in favor of educating her through Bible study. She made astonishing progress in her studies: within sixteen months Wheatley had mastered English and taken up classical and contemporary poetry as well as French, Latin, and Greek literature. By her early teens, she was already better educated than most upper-class Bostonians. As a result, she was offered exceptional privileges for a slave, most notably a private room furnished with a lamp and writing materials to be used should poetic inspiration come to her during the night. But such favoritism had its price: as numerous commentators have observed, Wheatley was forbidden from associating with other slaves.

Wheatley's first poem, "An Elegiac Poem, on the Death of that Celebrated Divine, and Eminent Servant of Jesus Christ, the Reverend and Learned George Whitefield," was published locally in 1770 as a broadside and a pamphlet. It was reprinted in newspapers throughout the American colonies and in England, bringing both national and international attention to the poet. On the advice of physicians, she sailed to England in 1773 with the Wheatleys' son Nathaniel to ease her asthma. Her reception in Britain pleased her enormously. Treated as a celebrity, Wheatley later recalled this visit as the high

point of her life. Among the admirers she met was the ardent English abolitionist Selina Hastings, Countess of Huntingdon, who became her patron and secured publication of *Poems on Various Subjects*. After being appointed an audience with King George III, Wheatley was forced to cancel the appearance when she was abruptly summoned to Boston to attend to her dying mistress. During the next few years the Wheatley family scattered throughout New England. Wheatley, having been freed three months before her mistress's death in March 1774, attempted to publish another volume of verse, but her efforts were unsuccessful despite personal and public praise by such men as Voltaire, George Washington, and John Paul Jones. In 1778 Wheatley married John Peters, a free black man who worked as a lawyer and grocer; he was called "a remarkable specimen of his race, being a fluent writer, a ready speaker." Yet financial difficulties led to Peters's incarceration in a Massachusetts debtor's prison, and his absence contributed to the death of their two infant children. Wheatley worked as a domestic in boardinghouses to support herself and a surviving infant. Untrained for menial labor and physically frail, she died in 1784, and her child, who died shortly afterward, was buried with her in an unmarked grave.

Wheatley was essentially an occasional poet who wrote elegies and honorific verse to commemorate the lives of friends and famous contemporaries as well as to celebrate important events, such as George Washington's appointment as commander in chief of the Revolutionary forces ("To His Excellency General Washington"). Although these poems feature Popian diction, meter, and rhyme patterns, Wheatley's strong technical skill sets her work apart from that of many of her contemporaries. One critic, Vernon Loggins, deemed her verse as perhaps the best in her time but agreed with J. Saunders Redding that her work unfortunately displays the genteel, artificial emotions characteristic of Pope's poetry as well. In addition to neoclassical influences, Christianity figures prominently in Wheatley's works; in "To Maecenas," "On Recollection," and other poems, Wheatley blends the two elements with what some critics consider Miltonic effect. Julian D. Mason and others have discussed this curious combination of neoclassicism and religion in terms of Wheatley's cultural environment.

When first published, *Poems on Various Subjects* was considered so extraordinary that the first edition was prefaced with signed testimony of such prominent Boston citizens as John Hancock, the Reverend Samuel Mather, and Thomas Hutchinson affirming its authenticity as the work of an African slave girl. Two eighteenth-century reviews presaged the conflicting assessments that were to characterize the body of Wheatley's poetry in coming years: a favorable review determined that although the poems themselves "display no astonishing power of genius," they have special merit because of their singular creator, while a negative appraisal asserted that "most of those [black] people have a turn for imitation, though they have little or none for invention." In the mid-nineteenth century Rufus Wilmot Griswold, noting the persistent partisanship of the two extremes, observed that *Poems on Various Subjects* is "quite equal to much of the contemporary verse that is admitted to be poetry by Phillis's severest judges," adding that "it would be difficult to find in the productions of American women. . . anything superior in sentiment, fancy, and distinction"—a view with which other critics have concurred.

Modern African-American critics have scrutinized Wheatley's verse for evidence of racial pride or defiance of bondage. During the 1920s, when protest literature spawned by the Harlem Renaissance was at its height, James Weldon Johnson noted that while "To the University of Cambridge, in New England" and "An Address to the Earl of Dartmouth" make reference to Wheatley's capture and separation from her family, the poet betrays an "almost smug contentment at her own escape therefrom" which "cannot but strike the reader as rather unimpassioned." J. Saunders Redding wrote of the "negative, bloodless, unracial quality in Phillis Wheatley," and Terence Collins has stated: "Wheatley's true legacy is the testimony her poetry gives to the insidious, self-destroying nature of even the most subtle, most gentle of racially oppressive conditions." Some critics have argued that Wheatley's subjects must be judged by examining the poetic models and social influences within her restricted sphere, noting the irony of her position as a pampered favorite of Boston's privileged class and of her enforced isolation from other slaves. At least one critic, Sondra O'Neale, has attributed conflicting views of Wheatley's race consciousness to an apparently intentional ambiguity and double meaning in the poetry in general and particularly in the religious verse, where for example, Wheatley refers to her fellow slaves as "Ethiopians," a racial and biblical term used as a symbol of ancestral awareness and self-esteem. O'Neale suggested that "through juxtaposition of. . . ancient concepts on the origin of race, Wheatley clearly implies that because Americans were ignoring Africa's status in biblical interpretations of 'chosen' nations, the slaves—denied knowledge of their inclusion in God's promises—were held in a psychological bondage even more demeaning than their physical enslavement."

Wheatley was a minor poet who followed the literary fashion of her age. Despite mixed views about her poetic gifts and likely potential under different circumstances, her poetry remains a point of departure for the study of black literature in America. James Weldon Johnson offered this caution: "[Wheatley's] work must not be judged by the work and standards of a later day, but by the work and standards of her own day and her own contemporaries. By this method of criticism [Wheatley] stands out as one of the important characters in the making of American literature, without any allowances for her sex or her antecedents."

(For further information about Wheatley's life and works, see *Concise Dictionary of American Literary Biography, 1640-1865; Dictionary of Literary Biography*, Vols. 31, 50; *Literature Criticism from 1400 to 1800*, Vol. 3; and *Poetry Criticism*, Vol. 3.)

PRINCIPAL WORKS

An Elegiac Poem, on the Death of That Celebrated Divine, and Eminent Servant of Jesus Christ, the Reverend and Learned George Whitefield (poetry) 1770

Poems on Various Subjects, Religious and Moral. By Phillis Wheatley, Negro Servant to Mr. John Wheatley of Boston (poetry) 1773

An Elegy, Sacred to the Memory of That Great Divine, the Reverend and Learned Dr. Samuel Cooper (poetry) 1784

Liberty and Peace: A Poem (poetry) 1784

Letters of Phillis Wheatley, the Negro-Slave Poet of Boston (letters) 1864

Life and Works of Phillis Wheatley. Containing Her Complete Poetical Works, Numerous Letters and a Complete Biography of This Famous Poet of a Century and a Half Ago (poetry and letters) 1916

The Poems of Phillis Wheatley (poetry) 1966; revised edition, 1989

London Monthly Review; or, Literary Journal (essay date 1774)

[*In the excerpt below from a 1774 review of* Poems on Various Subjects, *the anonymous critic deems Wheatley's poetry "merely imitative."*]

If we believed, with the ancient mythologists, that genius is the offspring of the sun, we should rather wonder that the sable race have not yet been more distinguished by it, than express our surprize at a single instance. The experience of the world, however, has left to this part of mythology but little probability for its support; and indeed, it appears to be wrong in its first principles. A proximity to the sun, far from heightening the powers of the mind, appears to enfeeble them, in proportion as it enervates the faculties of the body. Thus we find the tropical regions remarkable for nothing but the sloth and languor of their inhabitants, their lascivious dispositions and deadness to invention. The country that gave birth to Alexander and Aristotle, the conqueror of the world, and the greater conqueror of nature, was Macedonia, naturally a cold and ungenial region. Homer and Hesiod breathed the cool and temperate air of the Meles, and the poets and heroes of Greece and Rome had no very intimate commerce with the sun.

The poems written by this young negro bear no endemial marks of solar fire or spirit. They are merely imitative; and, indeed, most of these people have a turn for imitation, though they have little or none for invention.

The following short account of the Author is prefixed to the poems.

> Phillis was brought from Africa to America, in the Year 1761, between Seven and Eight Years of Age. Without any Assistance from School Education, and by only what she was taught in the Family, she, in Sixteen Months Time from her Arrival, attained the English Language, to which she was an utter Stranger before, to such a Degree, as to read any, the most difficult parts of the Sacred Parts of the Sacred Writings, to the great Astonishment of all who heard her.
>
> As to her Writing, her own Curiosity led her to it; and this she learnt in so short a Time, that in the Year 1765, she wrote a Letter to the Rev. Mr. Occom, the Indian Minister, while in England.
>
> She had a great inclination to learn the Latin Tongue, and has made some Progress in it. This Relation is given by her Master who bought her, and with whom she now lives.
>
> John Wheatley.
> Boston, Nov. 14, 1772.

She has written many good lines, and now and then one of superior character has dropped from her pen; as in the Epistle to Maecenas,

> The lengthening line moves languishing along.

And in the **"Thoughts on the Works of Providence"**;

> Or the sun slumbers in the ocean's arms.

In her verses to the Earl of Dartmouth, on his being appointed Secretary of State for the American department, she speaks of her own situation and country, which she seldom does in any other part of her poems. After bespeaking his Lordship's favourable sentiments in behalf of American liberty, she asks,

> Should you, my Lord, while you peruse my song,
> Wonder from whence my love of Freedom
>   sprung,
> Whence flow these wishes for the common good,
> By feeling hearts alone best understood,
> I, young in life, by seeming cruel fate
> Was snatch'd from Afric's fancy'd happy seat:
> What pangs excruciating must molest,
> What sorrows labour in my parent's breast?
> Steel'd was that soul and by no misery mov'd
> That from such a father seiz'd his babe belov'd:
> Such, such my case. And can I then but pray
> Others may never feel tyrannic sway?

We are much concerned to find that this ingenious young woman is yet a slave. The people of Boston boast themselves chiefly on their principles of liberty. One such act as the purchase of her freedom, would, in our opinion, have done more honour than hanging a thousand trees with ribbons and emblems. (pp. 30-1)

> *A review of "Poems on Various Subjects," in* Critical Essays on Phillis Wheatley, *edited by William H. Robinson, 1982, pp. 30-1.*

Thomas Jefferson (essay date 1782)

[*A member of the Continental Congress, author of the Declaration of Independence, and later the third president of the United States and founder of the University of Virginia, Jefferson was among America's foremost thinkers and statesmen during the early years of the American republic. During the Revolutionary War, he served as governor of Virginia, writing his famous* Notes on the State of Virginia *(completed in 1782) in response to a wartime questionnaire sent to American statesmen by a concerned French official. In the following excerpt from his* Notes, *Jefferson offers dismissive remarks about Wheatley's poetry.*]

Comparing [blacks] by their faculties of memory, reason and imagination, it appears to me that in memory they are equal to the whites; in reason much inferior, as I think one could scarcely be found capable of tracing and comprehending the investigations of Euclid; and that in imagination they are dull, tasteless, and anomalous. . . . never yet could I find that a black had uttered a thought above the level of plain narration; never saw even an elementary trait of painting or sculpture. . . . In music they are more generally gifted than the whites with accurate ears for tune and time, and they have been found capable of imagining a small catch. . . .

Misery is often the parent of the most affecting touches in poetry. Among the blacks is misery enough, God knows, but no poetry. . . . Religion, indeed, has produced a Phyllis Whately; but it could not produce a poet. The compositions published under her name are below the dignity of criticism. The heroes of the Dunciad are to her, as Hercules to the author of that poem. . . . (pp. 42-3)

> *Thomas Jefferson, "On the Unacceptability of Blacks in White America," in* Critical Essays on Phillis Wheatley, *edited by William H. Robinson, 1982, pp. 42-3.*

The Christian Examiner (essay date 1834)

[*In the excerpt below, the anonymous critic compares Wheatley's poetry to that of her white contemporaries and attempts to "record our tribute of praise in behalf of one who was an honor and ornament to her race and her kind."*]

[Phillis Wheatley's poetry] seems to us respectable, though not of a high order. Yet how many of the white writers of this country have enjoyed a transient reputation on much less intrinsic merit! What proportion of the rhymesters, who enrich our newspapers and magazines with their effusions, can write half so well as Phillis Wheatley? She had no assistance. Like one of her favorite authors, "she lisped in numbers, for the numbers came." She seemed to have begun to write verses as soon as she had sufficient command of the English language to express her ideas,—certainly before she could have known any thing of the rules of composition. Accordingly, we find some ill-constructed and harsh and prosaic lines, but not so many by half as in the verses of most of her contemporary American poets. That her lines are full of feeling, no one will deny who has read the extract we have already given. That she had considerable originality will be apparent from her epitaph on Dr. Sewall.

> Lo, here, a man, redeemed by Jesus' blood,
> A sinner once, but now a saint with God.
> Behold, ye rich, ye poor, ye fools, ye wise,
> Nor let his monument your heart surprise;
> 'T will tell you what this holy man has done,
> Which gives him brighter lustre than the sun.
> Listen, ye happy, from your seats above.
> I speak sincerely, while I speak and love.
> He sought the paths of piety and truth,
> By these made happy from his early youth.
> In blooming years that grace divine he felt,
> Which rescues sinners from the chains of guilt.
> Mourn him, ye indigent, whom he has fed,
> And henceforth seek, like him, for living bread;
> Ev'n Christ, the bread descending from above,
> And ask an int'rest in his saving love.
> Mourn him, ye youth, to whom he oft has told
> God's gracious wonders, from the times of old.
> I, too, have cause, this mighty loss to mourn,
> For he, my monitor, will not return.
> Oh, when shall we to his blest state arrive?
> When the same graces in our bosoms thrive?

Phillis had a peculiarity of intellect which is not often met with. Her memory was very ill regulated. That it must have been uncommonly strong, in some things, is self-evident, else how could she have acquired the English language in so short a time?—how could she have mastered the Latin? Yet in other matters it was very defective. It has been seen that she could remember but one solitary fact, connected with her life, previous to her seventh year. The memory of other children reaches much further back. When she composed, she could not retain her own composition in her mind, and was obliged either to lose it or commit it instantly to paper. We offer no solution of this anomaly, —it is enough that it must have been a great disadvantage to a person of literary pursuits.

Phillis Wheatley, we think, was a precocious genius, destined very rapidly to acquire a certain degree of excellence, and there to stop for ever. As mediocrity, or even moderate merit in song, is never tolerated, we dare not hope that her works will ever be very popular or generally read; for readers never take into account the disadvantages the writer may have labored under. It is not just that they should; for otherwise the land would be flooded with bad writings, to the exclusion and discouragement of good. It is little consolation to him, who has wasted his time and money in buying and reading a wretched production, to be told that it was written by an apprentice or a woman. We do not mean by this to express any disapprobation of the publication before us, but merely to say that, singular as its merits are, they are not of the kind that will command admiration. Still the work will live,—there will always be friends enough of liberty and of the cause of negro improvement not to let it sink into oblivion, and many will desire to possess it as a curiosity. We wish the publisher success, and, if any thing we can say shall contribute to it, we shall heartily rejoice. As a friend of the Africans and of mankind at large, we are happy to record our tribute of praise in behalf of one who was an honor and ornament to her race and her kind.

Born in a land of darkness, the grasp of the spoiler first woke her from the dream of her infancy. Ruthlessly torn from home and parents, no kind arm supported her head or ministered to her wants during the horrors of the middle passage. The crack of the whip, the screams of suffocating and famishing human beings, and the clank of chains were the lullaby of her childish slumbers. Ignorant, naked, and forlorn, she stood up in a foreign land to be sold, like a beast in the market, to strangers whose pity she had not even a voice to demand. A brighter dawn flashed on her mind. Her own intelligence and energy supplied the want of instruction. In the midst of the obloquy attached to her hue, she reached an intellectual eminence known to few of the females of that day, and not common even now. The treasures of literature became hers,—the gospel shone upon her. Grateful, humble, pious, and affectionate, prosperity made no change in her heart. Flattery could not make her vain,—pleasure diminished not her gratitude,— starvation and ill usage never turned her from her duty.

Her worthless husband never heard a syllable of reproach from the dying mother by the side of her dying child. She died in suffering and starvation, and is gone to take the rank which she earned, in a place where many who may despise her for a skin not colored like their own, will never come. (pp. 172-74)

"Phillis Wheatley's 'Poems'," in The Christian Examiner and General Review, *Vol. 16, No. LXII, May, 1834, pp. 169-74.*

James Weldon Johnson (essay date 1921)

[*Johnson was a newspaper editor, lawyer, U.S. consul to Nicaragua and Venezuela, and a Broadway songwriter; his song "Lift Every Voice and Sing" has been adopted as the African-American national anthem. Johnson is also known for the novel* The Autobiography of an Ex-Colored Man *(1912), which was originally published anonymously and later reissued under his name in 1927. In the following excerpt from his 1921 preface to* The Book of American Negro Poetry, *he provides a literary and historical overview of Wheatley's career.*]

Phillis Wheatley has never been given her rightful place in American literature. By some sort of conspiracy she is kept out of most of the books, especially the text-books on literature used in the schools. Of course, she is not a *great* American poet—and in her day there were no great American poets—but she is an important American poet. Her importance, if for no other reason, rests on the fact that, save one, she is the first in order of time of all the women poets of America. And she is among the first of all American poets to issue a volume. (p. 23)

Anne Bradstreet preceded Phillis Wheatley by a little over one hundred and twenty years. She published her volume of poems, *The Tenth Muse,* in 1650. Let us strike a comparison between the two. Anne Bradstreet was a wealthy, cultivated Puritan girl, the daughter of Thomas Dudley, Governor of [Massachusetts] Bay Colony. Phillis, as we know, was a Negro slave girl born in Africa. Let us take them both at their best and in the same vein. The following stanza is from Anne's poem entitled "Contemplation":

> While musing thus with contemplation fed,
> And thousand fancies buzzing in my brain,
> The sweet tongued Philomel percht o'er my head,
> And chanted forth a most melodious strain,
> Which rapt me so with wonder and delight,
> I judged my hearing better than my sight.
> And wisht me wings with her awhile to take my
>   flight.

And the following is from Phillis' poem entitled **"Imagination":**

> Imagination! who can sing thy force?
> Or who describe the swiftness of thy course?
> Soaring through air to find the bright abode,
> Th' empyreal palace of the thundering God,
> We on thy pinions can surpass the wind,

> And leave the rolling universe behind.
> From star to star the mental optics rove,
> Measure the skies, and range the realms above;
> There in one view we grasp the mighty whole,
> Or with new worlds amaze th' unbounded soul.

We do not think the black woman suffers much by comparison with the white. Thomas Jefferson said of Phillis: "Religion has produced a Phillis Wheatley, but it could not produce a poet; her poems are beneath contempt" [see excerpt dated 1782]. It is quite likely that Jefferson's criticism was directed more against religion than against Phillis' poetry. (pp. 24-5)

It appears certain that Phillis was the first person to apply to George Washington the phrase, "First in peace." The phrase occurs in her poem [**"To His Excellency General Washington"**] written in 1775. The encomium, "First in war, first in peace, first in the hearts of his countrymen," was originally used in the resolutions presented to Congress on the death of Washington, December, 1799.

Phillis Wheatley's poetry is the poetry of the Eighteenth Century. She wrote when Pope and Gray were supreme; it is easy to see that Pope was her model. Had she come under the influence of Wordsworth, Byron or Keats or Shelley, she would have done greater work. As it is, her work must not be judged by the work and standards of a later day, but by the work and standards of her own day and her own contemporaries. By this method of criticism she stands out as one of the important characters in the making of American literature, without any allowances for her sex or her antecedents.

According to *A Bibliographical Checklist of American Negro Poetry,* compiled by Mr. Arthur A. Schomburg, more than one hundred Negroes in the United States have published volumes of poetry ranging in size from pamphlets to books of from one hundred to three hundred pages. About thirty of these writers fill in the gap between Phillis Wheatley and Paul Laurence Dunbar. (pp. 25-6)

It is curious and interesting to trace the growth of individuality and race consciousness in this group of poets. . . . Only very seldom does Phillis Wheatley sound a native note. Four times in single lines she refers to herself as "Afric's muse." In a poem of admonition [**"To the University of Cambridge, in New England"**] she refers to herself as follows:

> Ye blooming plants of human race divine,
> An Ethiop tells you 'tis your greatest foe.

But one looks in vain for some outburst or even complaint against the bondage of her people, for some agonizing cry about her native land. In two poems she refers definitely to Africa as her home, but in each instance there seems to be under the sentiment of the lines a feeling of almost smug contentment at her own escape therefrom. . . . In the poem [**"To the Right Honorable William, Earl of Dartmouth"**], she speaks of freedom and makes a reference to the parents from whom she was taken as a child, a reference which cannot but strike the reader as rather unimpassioned. . . . (pp. 28-9)

The bulk of Phillis Wheatley's work consists of poems addressed to people of prominence. Her book was dedicated to the Countess of Huntington, at whose house she spent the greater part of her time while in England. On his repeal of the Stamp Act, she wrote a poem to King George III, whom she saw later; another poem she wrote to the Earl of Dartmouth, whom she knew. A number of her verses were addressed to other persons of distinction. Indeed, it is apparent that Phillis was far from being a democrat. She was far from being a democrat not only in her social ideas but also in her political ideas; unless a religious meaning is given to the closing lines of her ode to General Washington, she was a decided royalist:

> A crown, a mansion, and a throne that shine
> With gold unfading, Washington! be thine.

Nevertheless, she was an ardent patriot. Her ode to General Washington . . . , her spirited poem, **"On Major General Lee"** . . . , and her poem, **"Liberty and Peace,"** written in celebration of the close of the war, reveal not only strong patriotic feeling but an understanding of the issues at stake. (pp. 29-30)

What Phillis Wheatley failed to achieve is due in no small degree to her education and environment. Her mind was steeped in the classics; her verses are filled with classical and mythological allusions. She knew Ovid thoroughly and was familiar with other Latin authors. She must have known Alexander Pope by heart. And, too, she was reared and sheltered in a wealthy and cultured family,—a wealthy and cultured Boston family; she never had the opportunity to learn life; she never found out her own true relation to life and to her surroundings. And it should not be forgotten that she was only about thirty years old when she died. The impulsion or the compulsion that might have driven her genius off the worn paths, out on a journey of exploration, Phillis Wheatley never received. But, whatever her limitations, she merits more than America has accorded her. (p. 31)

> *James Weldon Johnson, "Preface to Original Edition," in* The Book of American Negro Poetry, *edited by James Weldon Johnson, revised edition, Harcourt Brace Jovanovich, Inc., 1931, pp. 9-48.*

Vernon Loggins (essay date 1931)

[*In the following excerpt, Loggins provides an overview of the styles and themes of Wheatley's works and appraises the poet's stature in American letters.*]

The main body of Phillis Wheatley's verse belongs to that class of poetry which we call occasional. Eighteen out of her forty-six poems which are known to have come down to us are elegies. It has been said that she wrote them as consolatory poems at the request of friends. Five are on ministers, two on the wives of a lieutenant-governor and a celebrated physician, and the rest on unknown persons, including a number of children who died in infancy. The material is in each instance conventional, true to the traditions of the elegy in an elegy-making age, especially in Boston, where the writing of poems of condolence and epitaphs had been in great vogue since the days of Anne Bradstreet and Urian Oakes. The treatment is in accord with neoclassical standards. Whatever feeling there is, is impersonal and artificial; the method for achieving effect is mainly that of hyperbole; the ornamentation is elaborate and sumptious, with frequent invocations of the Muses, allusions to pagan gods and Biblical heroes, overuse of personification, and pompousness of diction. **"To the Rev. Mr. Pitkin on The Death of His Lady,"** which suggests the general mood of the elegies, opens in this strain—

> Where Contemplation finds her sacred Spring;
> Where heav'nly Music makes the Centre ring;
> Where Virtue reigns unsullied, and divine,
> Where Wisdom thron'd, and all the Graces shine;
> There sits thy Spouse, amid the glitt'ring Throng;
> There central Beauty feasts the ravish'd Tongue;
> With recent Powers, with recent Glories crown'd,
> The choirs angelic shout her welcome round.

Six of the poems were inspired by public events of importance, such as the repeal of the Stamp Act, the appointment of Washington as commander-in-chief of the Revolutionary forces, the betrayal of General Lee into the hands of the British, and the return of peace after the close of the Revolution; and a number are on minor happenings, such as the voyage of a friend to England, and the providential escape of an acquaintance from a hurricane at sea. These, like the elegies, are affected, written with an exaggerated dignity, with a straining attempt to force high eloquence.

But not all of Phillis Wheatley's poems are occasional. Following the New England custom of versifying selections from the Bible, begun back in the early days when the *Bay Psalm Book* was compiled, she worked out paraphrases of eight verses from the fifty-third chapter of Isaiah, and of the passage in the first book of Samuel which describes David's fight with Goliath. It is unnecessary to say that her neoclassical couplets deaden entirely the fire of Isaiah's rhapsody; she was so far away from the true Biblical ardor that she opened the paraphrase by invoking the "heav'nly muse." Her **"Goliath of Gath"** is more successful. In hearing the following lines one might feel that he is listening to the steady music of the opening of Pope's version of the *Iliad:*

> Ye martial pow'rs, and all ye tuneful nine,
> Inspire my song, and aid my high design.
> The dreadful scenes and toils of war I write,
> The ardent warriors, and the fields of fight:
> You best remember, and you best can sing
> The acts of heroes to the vocal string:
> Resume the lays with which your sacred lyre,

Did then the poet and the sage inspire.

Also among her better achievements is the adaptation of that portion of the sixth book of Ovid's *Metamorphoses* which tells of Niobe's distress for her children. This classical paraphrase belongs to the small group of poems for which Phillis Wheatley did not look to her New England predecessors for models. Her pieces on abstractions, including **"Imagination," "Recollection,"** and **"Virtue,"** probably owe their subject matter to English rather than to American influences. And her companion hymns, **"Morning"** and **"Evening,"** place her among those eighteenth-century poets, numerous in England, who felt so greatly the splendors of Milton's "L'Allegro" and "Il Penseroso" that they attempted imitations.

What one most wishes Phillis Wheatley had done, she left undone: she wrote too rarely about herself. Her intimate personal interests were ignored. She composed verses on the deaths of those who meant little to her, but, so far as we know, she remained silent after the deaths of Mrs. Wheatley and Mrs. Lathrop and her own children. She dwelt at length on the common notions of her day regarding liberty, but she neglected almost entirely her own state of slavery and the miserable oppression of thousands of her race. In all of her writings she only once referred in strong terms to the wrongs of the Negro in America. The reference is in the poem addressed to the Earl of Dartmouth upon his appointment as George III's secretary for North America:

> Should you, my lord, while you peruse my song,
> Wonder from whence my love of Freedom
>   sprung,
> Whence flow these wishes for the common good,
> By feeling hearts alone best understood,
> I, young in life, by seeming cruel fate
> Was snatch'd from Afric's fancy'd happy seat:
> What pangs excruciating must molest,
> What sorrows labour in my parent's breast?
> Steel'd was that soul and by no misery mov'd
> That from such a father seiz'd his babe belov'd:
> Such, such my case. And can I then but pray
> Others may never feel tyrannic sway?

But with all of her outward neglect of self, Phillis Wheatley was too honest to veil her true personality in what she wrote. The sincerity of childhood and the delicacy of young womanhood, uniform in both the black race and the white, are constantly reflected, even when she is most artificial. Her gentle character, so often commented upon, lies revealed in every poem and letter.

But the dominant trait in the personality which her writings reveal is a capacity for intense religious faith. Without that faith she probably would never have written a line. She was not devout with the primitive adoration of a Jupiter Hammon, but with a belief balanced and controlled by Puritan training, such a belief as that of any other member of the Old South Church who might have seen worth in the emotionalism of George Whitefield. Every poem which was born in

her mind, even the adaptation from Ovid, came forth filled with religious feeling. Her letters to Obour Tanner are to a great extent dissertations on the mercies and goodness of God. The one wholly subjective poem which came from her pen, **"On Being Brought from Africa,"** proves what religion was in her life.

> 'Twas mercy brought me from my *Pagan* land,
> Taught my benighted soul to understand
> That there's a God, that there's a *Saviour* too:
> Once I redemption neither sought nor knew.
> Some view our sable race with scornful eye,
> "Their colour is a diabolic die."
> Remember, *Christians, Negros* black as *Cain,*
> May be refin'd, and join th' angelic train.

It is interesting to speculate what her thinking might have been if it had not been nurtured by the Puritanism of eighteenth-century Boston and by the simple doctrines of the Countess of Huntingdon's circle. But speculate as we will, we cannot conceive a philosophical system, whether based on the assumption that the savage is noble and superior or on any other assumption, which might have replaced her deep trust in the God of the Puritans.

That which is most important in a consideration of her work is her talent—a talent all the more difficult to explain because it is contradictory, in one response spontaneous and intuitive, and in another respect rational and exceedingly self-conscious. Her success in absorbing the music of Alexander Pope, master of England's neoclassical verse-makers, gives her poems their highest claim to distinction; and it seems that she was not aware of what she was doing when she achieved that success. We are told that there were three books in the Wheatley library for which she had a particularly strong affection—the Bible, a collection of tales from classical mythology, and Pope's Homer. Her first publication, the elegy on Whitefield, shows that she was familiar with Gray. We know that after her visit to England she possessed a Milton, and that after 1774 she owned a collection of Shenstone's poems. There is reason to believe that she read every poem which she could find, whether in book, magazine, newspaper, or broadsheet. But it was Pope's translation of Homer which taught her most. We have already noticed, in the quotation from **"Goliath of Gath,"** how near she could come to her great master's idiom whenever her subject matter gave her the opportunity. In writing the following lines from **"Thoughts on His Excellency Major General Lee,"** she was probably thinking of the first book of *Paradise Lost,* but it is Pope's music which she reproduced:

> While thus he spake, the hero of renown
> Survey'd the boaster with a gloomy frown,
> And stern reply'd: "O arrogance of tongue!
> And wild ambition, ever prone to wrong!
> Believ'st thou chief, that armies such as thine
> Can stretch in dust that heaven-defended line?"

Even in her one poem in blank verse, **"To the University of Cambridge, in New-England,"** a quotation from which has been given, the line, with its strong rise, marked caesura, and hastened fall, is that of Pope. Indeed, reproduction of Pope's versification characterizes all of her poems with the exception of the few which she wrote in lyrical measures. She lived during the age when the poetical fashion in America was to imitate Pope; and while John Trumbull, Timothy Dwight, Joel Barlow, the Philip Freneau of the political satires, and numerous others among her contemporaries caught more of his general spirit, she perhaps excelled them all in reproducing his rhythms. Her power to attain this place of eminence must be pronounced as due to her instinct for hearing the music of words, an instinct which was possibly racial. As in Jupiter Hammon and many other Negro poets, in her the strange sense for imitating sound exercised itself of its own will. She never mentioned Pope, and only rarely touched upon themes such as he treated; but before she began writing, she had read his Homer with her deep-searching ear open for impressions which were to endure. (pp. 22-7)

Like all neoclassical poets, she borrowed images freely. One finds in her poems the favorite eighteenth-century *clichés,* such as *vaulted skies, roving fancy, crystal shower, feathered warbler, smiling fields, graceful tresses,* and *pensive bosoms.* One also finds an imagination imitating with a remarkable accuracy. The images indicated by italics in the following lines are the invention of a mind working with precision and with a clean recognition of nice artistic adjustment:

> All-conquering Death! by thy resistless pow'r,
> *Hope's tow'ring plumage falls to rise no more!*
>
> *We trace the pow'r of Death from tomb to tomb,*
> And his are all the ages yet to come.
>
> *The frozen deeps may break their iron bands,*
> *And bid their waters murmur o'er the sands.*
>
> Aeolus in his rapid chariot drove
> *In gloomy grandeur from the vault above:*
> Furious he comes. His winged sons obey
> Their frantic sire, *and madden all the sea.*
>
> He drops the bridle on his courser's mane,
> *Before his eyes in shadows swims the plain.*
>
> *Swift thro' his throat the feather'd mischief flies,*
> Bereft of sense, he drops his head, and dies.

Images of like character abound in Phillis Wheatley's poems. They are not direct copies, and they cannot be created by a mind that is not a master of itself. They prove as well as the smooth music in Phillis Wheatley's verse her genius at imitation. And it is not too much to presume that if she had been taught by a Wordsworth, who would have convinced her of the value of turning to her sincere religious self for her subjects and of using an idiom drawn out of her own personality, her work would stand on its own merits rather than on the fact that she, a Negro and a slave, produced it. If she had not fallen under the sway of the New England elegists and of Pope and his school, she might today be considered one of the ornaments in American literature as well as one of the most interesting curiosities. (pp. 28-9)

Vernon Loggins, "The Beginnings of Negro Authorship, 1760-1790," in his The Negro Author: His Development in America to 1900, *1931. Reprint by Kennikat Press, Inc., 1964, pp. 1-47.*

J. Saunders Redding (essay date 1939)

[*Redding is a distinguished critic, historian, novelist, and autobiographer. His first book,* To Make a Poet Black *(1939), is a scholarly appraisal of African-American poetry that includes a historical overview as well as biographical information about individual poets. As one of the first anthologies of its type to be written by a black critic, this book is considered a landmark in criticism of African-American writers. In the following excerpt, Redding discusses the taming effect of Wheatley's upbringing upon her poetry.*]

There is no question but that Miss Wheatley considered herself a Negro poet: the question is to what degree she felt the full significance of such a designation. Certainly she was not a *slave* poet in any sense in which the term can be applied to many who followed her. She stood far outside the institution that was responsible for her. As for the question of degree, though she refers to herself time and time again as an "Ethiop," she seems to make such reference with a distinct sense of abnegation and self-pity. (pp. 8-9)

This attitude on the part of Miss Wheatley was the result of the training and conduct of her life. Treated as one of the Wheatley family on terms of almost perfect equality, petted and made much of, she was sagacious enough to see that this was due in part at least to her exotic character and sensitive enough to feel that her color was really a bar to a more desirable, if less flattering, attention. At best this life was not too dear to Phillis. She recounts the joys of the life to come in the strains of one who looks upon this life as though it were a strange and bitter preparation for an eternity of bliss. The Wheatleys adopted her, but she had adopted their terrific New England conscience. Her conception of the after-life was different from that of most of the slaves as we find it expressed in songs and spirituals. No contemplation of physical luxuries of feastings, jeweled crowns, and snowy robes enticed her. Her heaven must be a place of the purest sublimation of spirit. Less than this would serve but to remind her of this dark bourne of flesh and blood.

But if the degree to which she felt herself a Negro poet was slight, the extent to which she was attached spiritually and emotionally to the slaves is even slighter. By 1761 slavery was an important almost daily topic. The Boston home of the Wheatleys, intelligent and alive as it was, could not have been deaf to the discussions of restricting the slave trade.... Not once, however, did she express in either word or action a thought on the enslavement of her race; not once did she utter a straightforward word for the freedom of the Negro.

When she did speak of freedom in ["**To the Right Honorable William, Earl of Dartmouth**"], it was:

> Should you, my Lord, while you peruse my song,
> Wonder from whence my love of freedom sprung,
> Whence flow these wishes for the common good,
> By feeling hearts alone best understood,
> I, young in life, by seeming cruel fate
> Was snatch'd from Afric's fancied happy seat.

"Seeming cruel" and "fancied happy" give her away as not believing either in the cruelty of the fate that had dragged thousands of her race into bondage in America nor in the happiness of their former freedom in Africa. How different the spirit of her work, and how unracial (not to say unnatural) are the stimuli that release her wan creative energies. How different are these from the work of George Horton who twenty-five years later could cry out with bitterness, without cavil or fear.... (pp. 9-11)

It is this negative, bloodless, unracial quality in Phillis Wheatley that makes her seem superficial, especially to members of her own race. Hers is a spirit-denying-the-flesh attitude that somehow cannot seem altogether real as the essential quality and core of one whose life should have made her sensitive to the very things she denies. In this sense none of her poetry is real. Compared to the Negro writers who followed her, Miss Wheatley's passions are tame, her skill the sedulous copy of established techniques, and her thoughts the hand-me-downs of her age. She is chilly. Part of her chill is due to the unmistakable influence of Pope's neoclassicism upon her. She followed the fashion in poetry. Overemphasis of religion was a common fault of the time. She indulged it in poetic epistles, eulogistic verse, verses written in praise of accomplishments. Her ready submission to established forms was a weakness of the period. First and last, she was the fragile product of three related forces—the age, the Wheatley household, and New England America. Her work lacks spontaneity because of the first, enthusiasm because of the second, and because of the third it lacks an unselfish purpose that drives to some ultimate goal of expression.

And yet she had poetic talent, was in fact a poet. No one who reads ... **"Thoughts on the Works of Providence"** can deny it.... Judged in the light of the day in which she wrote, judged by that day's standards and accomplishments, she was an important poet. As a Negro poet she stands out remarkably, for her work lacks the characteristics of thought one would expect to find. (pp. 11-12)

> *J. Saunders Redding, "The Forerunners," in his* To Make a Poet Black, *1939. Reprint by Cornell University Press, 1988, pp. 3-18.*

Angelene Jamison (essay date 1974)

[*In the following excerpt, Jamison demonstrates how Wheatley's verse "is a product of a white mind, a mind that had been so engulfed in the education,* religion, values, and the freedom of Whites that she expressed no strong sentiments for those who had been cast into the wretchedness of slavery by those she so often praised with her pen.'*]

Phillis Wheatley was a poet of the latter half of the eighteenth century who happened to be Black. Despite her position as a slave and despite the growing interest in the slave issue in Bostonian circles, of which she was a marginal part, she did not address herself in any significant degree to the plight of her people. She wrote to Whites, for Whites and generally in the Euro-American tradition at that time. That is, Phillis Wheatley was influenced by neo-classicism. And much of her poetry reflects various stylistic characteristics of Alexander Pope and his followers. **"On Being Brought from Africa to America," "Hymn to Evening,"** and many of her other poems reflect her ability to use effectively Pope's heroic couplet. (pp. 408-09)

Among the themes which permeate the poetry of Phillis Wheatley are Christian piety, morality, virtue, death, praises of classical heroes, and a celebration of abstractions such as the poems **"On Recollection"** and **"Imagination."** There are very few poems in which Phillis Wheatley points to her experiences as a Black and a slave. Her poetry embraces white attitudes and values, and it characterizes Phillis as a typical Euro-American poetess. She was detached from her people and her poetry could never be used as an expression of black thought. (p. 409)

Since Phillis Wheatley wrote primarily for the Whites and since we are concerned with re-examining her life and works in terms of their significance to us, it is important to analyze the image that those for whom she wrote had of her. Many were astonished at the poetry of Phillis Wheatley and showered her with praises because they had not expected such capabilities from an African. This kind of response was typical of those Whites who were willing to recognize the talents of Blacks. To them, Blacks who made contributions were always the exception and never the general rule regardless of the circumstances under which Blacks made their contribution.

[In his introduction to *The Poems of Phillis Wheatley*] Julian D. Mason, Jr., cites several examples of Whites who spoke favorably of Phillis Wheatley. Among them were William Joseph Snelling, a Boston writer, whose comments appeared in the May, 1834 edition of *The Christian Examiner,* and John Edward Bruce who discussed Phillis in his essay, "Negro Poets," in the March 6, 1897 edition of *The Literary Digest of New York.* Snelling marveled at the level of intelligence reached by Phillis, but he felt that her poetry would receive lasting admiration from only those who were sympathetic towards Blacks. John Edward Bruce felt that she was an extraordinary young woman who did much to dispel the myth that Blacks were intellectually inferior.

Even though Snelling and Bruce made some positive comments about Phillis Wheatley, both were operating under the assumption that Blacks were inferior and incapable of intellectual pursuits. Neither saw her poetry as highly exceptional when compared to eighteenth century standards, but they were awed by the fact that here was a Black who could at least make attempts at expressing herself in poetry. And since Phillis' poetry was white-oriented, Snelling and Bruce seemed to have been convinced that she had intellectual potential.

Although Phillis Wheatley generally received some favorable comments from Whites during her lifetime and afterwards, there were also those Whites who harshly criticized her poetry purely on a racial basis. People like Thomas Jefferson were blinded by her color and their prejudices against Blacks. In his "Notes on Virginia" [see excerpt dated 1782], Thomas Jefferson said:

> Misery is often the parent of the most affecting touches in poetry. Among the Blacks is misery enough, God knows, but no poetry... Religion, indeed has produced a Phillis Wheatley; but it could not produce a poet. The compositions published under her name are below the dignity of criticism.

Many of the other so-called critics who ridiculed the works of Phillis Wheatley fall into the category of white racists who refused to recognize any merits in the contributions of Blacks.

More important to us than the attitudes of Whites toward Phillis Wheatley are those of Blacks, and here the attitudes are just as diverse as those of Whites. Perhaps the first Black to pay tribute to Phillis Wheatley was Jupiter Hammon who wrote a poem to her in 1778 entitled "An Address to Miss Phillis Wheatly (sic), Ethiopian Poetess, in Boston who came from Africa at eight years of age, and soon became acquainted with the gospel of Jesus Christ." By referring to her in his title as an "Ethiopian Poetess," Hammon acknowledged her ancestry and her creative abilities. However, the main thrust of the poem to Phillis Wheatley is that she should be thankful to God for "bringing thee from the distance shore, / To learn his holy word." It is implicit in the poem that Jupiter Hammon was much more concerned with Phillis' salvation than he was with her poetry, and he wanted Phillis to give all praises to God for any gifts she might have had.

More recent black critics of Phillis Wheatley have been more concerned with examining her image as a Black rather than saving her soul. Several critics have pointed to her ability to write poetry but they have critically questioned her race consciousness. J. Saunders Redding, in his book, *To Make A Poet Black,* says "... the extent to which she was attached spiritually and emotionally to the slave is even slighter" than the extent she felt herself a Negro poet. He goes on to say that "she is chilly," and he holds Pope's neo-classicism responsible [see excerpt dated 1939]. Benjamin Brawley also points to Phillis Wheatley's lack of reference to race, but he seems to feel that she had no alternative but to model herself after writers with which she was familiar.

Statements like those of J. Saunders Redding and Benjamin Brawley have been compounded by more militant critics and readers of Phillis Wheatley. After reading various poems of Phillis Wheatley, the first comment of most students is that she was not Black enough and of course they are correct. But, we must move beyond that kind of statement into re-examining the poetry in light of the implications of her lack of race consciousness to the development of black thought.

Phillis Wheatley was a woman of African descent. However, when examining certain poems where she makes direct and indirect references to herself as an African, it is obvious that she lacked pride in her heritage. Her reference to herself as an Ethiopian gives no evidence that she had embraced the culture from which was was taken; rather it was a means of humbling herself. In her poem **"To The University of Cambridge in New England"** she requested that the students take advantage of all the opportunities presented to them and guard themselves against sin. In the concluding lines of the poem she pleaded:

> Ye blooming plants of human race divine,
> An Ethiop tells you 'tis your greatest foe;
> Its transient sweetness turns to endless pain
> And in immense perdition sinks the soul.

Here she refers to the students, who were obviously white, as practically God-like, and she warns them against the pitfalls of evil. Her statement that "an Ethiop tells you . . ." reflects a lack of self-worth particularly within the context of the poem. If an Ethiop is aware of the danger of sin then certainly these "blooming plants of human race divine," those who belong to the best race, should also be aware. It would seem that Phillis, one who thought it necessary to warn these white students of the deadly potential of sin, would have included in her poem the greatest sin of slavery which had been committed upon her.

Her concept of herself as a poet was no better than her concept of herself as a Black. When writing poems to those for whom she had an extreme admiration, she felt it necessary to apologize for even attempting to address these Whites in poetic form. As a matter of fact, Phillis once implied in a response to the answer to a poem she had written to a gentleman in the Navy, that her poetry could never equal the poem she had received from him. In the same poem, after having placed herself in an inferior position, she states: "Then fix the humble Afric muse's seat / At British Homer's and Sir Isaac's feet." At this point, she is just humble and submissive enough to believe that the African muse belonged at the foot of the European.

Phillis Wheatley's self-image as it is reflected in her poetry is strongly related to her religious attitudes. The poem, **"On Being Brought from Africa to America,"** shows her gratitude for having been taken from what she perceived as a pagan land, brought to America and taught Christianity. Her lines, "Some view our sable race with scornful eye, / Their colour is a diabolic die," are indicative of some awareness of the existing atti- tudes of Whites toward Blacks. And in the last two lines of the poem, "Remember, *Christians, Negroes,* black as *Cain,* / May be refined and join th' Angelic train," she articulates that Blacks too have the opportunity to be saved. However, "Remember, *Christians, Negroes,* black as *Cain"* does not clarify whether she perceives Christians and / or Blacks can be black as Cain. The ambiguity indicates that possibly before Blacks can be equal to Christians, if ever, they must be refined. The lines also indicate Phillis Wheatley's acceptance of the curse of Cain and its racist implication.

To Phillis, God was an impartial and merciful Savior whose works deserved all praises from mankind. In the final lines of **"Thoughts on the Works of Providence,"** she muses, "To him, whose works array'd with mercy shine, / What songs should rise; how constant, how divine!" This God had been taught to Phillis Wheatley by Whites and her feelings toward Him enhanced her humbleness and submissiveness. Much of her poetry reflects the qualities she perceived as necessary in order to meet God's approval and, consequently, be received in heaven. Graciously and without question, Phillis Wheatley accepted the religion of the oppressor who had enslaved her. She never looked at her position as a slave as a contradiction to the goodness and graciousness of God.

Just as Phillis did not see a contradiction in the white man's concept of religion, neither did she see the contradiction in his concept of freedom. In no area does Phillis Wheatley's white orientation present itself more than in her poems dealing with freedom. In **"To His Excellency General Washington,"** after humbling herself and apologizing for what she perceived as possible inaccuracies in an introductory letter, Phillis Wheatley moves on to express her patriotism and her undying faith in the "honorable" General Washington. She praises his gallantry and sees him as "first in peace and honors," and "fam'd for thy valour, for their virtues more." (pp. 409-13)

In another poem, **"On Liberty and Peace,"** Phillis Wheatley sees Columbia as being firmly protected by Heaven in the quest for freedom and peace. She sees Britain, in its efforts to maintain control over the colonies, as a cruel and vicious menace, and she strongly supports other countries which come to the aid of the colonies in their fight for freedom. The blood that was shed in the war, the lives that were lost on both sides, the land that was destroyed were all necessary to Phillis because she felt heaven had ordained that Columbia be free, and as she points out "Freedom comes array'd with charms divine, / and in her Train Commerce and Plenty Shine." Throughout the poem, **"Liberty and Peace,"** she makes reference to the fact that some divine aid will always guide the path of Columbia, and that Columbia will be a model for peace.

> Where e'er Columbia spreads her swelling sails;
> To every Realm Shall peace her charms display,

> And Heavenly Freedom spread her golden ray.

Phillis saw the very country which enslaved her and other Blacks as one deserving some heavenly protection. How could she be so removed from the plight of her people and the attitudes towards her people as to glorify those who were responsible for that wretched condition of slavery? Did she feel that bringing peace to the colonies would bring peace and freedom to Blacks? It is clearly substantiated that she was brainwashed to the point of expressing totally the sentiments of Whites without giving any consideration to the fact that the white "heroes" of the American Revolution were con- cerned only about themselves. Blacks, to most of them, were a means of supplying labor and the questions of the freedom of Blacks had nothing to do with the freedom of Whites from the mother country.

Some readers of Phillis Wheatley might argue that her poem, **"To the Right Honourable William, Earl of Dartmouth, His Majesty's Principal Secretary of State of North America and C.,"** is a strong indication of her awareness of the position of Blacks in this country and her own plight particularly. From that poem, most refer to the following lines:

> Should you, my Lord, while you peruse my song,
> Wonder from whence my love of freedom sprung,
> Whence flow these wishes for the common good,
> By feeling hearts alone best understood,
> I, young in life, by seeming cruel fate
> Was snatch'd from Afric's fancy'd happy seat:
> What pangs excruciating must molest,
> What sorrows labour in my parent's breast?
> Steel'd was that soul and by no misery mov'd
> That from such a father seiz'd his babe belov'd:
> Such, such my case. And can I then but pray
> Others may never feel tyrannic sway?

In this stanza Phillis Wheatley seems to be trying to explain why she has concerned herself in her poetry with the freedom of the American colonies. Her reason which is weakly supported is that she was taken from her homeland, which she describes as "Afric's fancy'd happy seat." The implication here is that Africa may not have been as happy as imagined. Moreover, she talks about the pain and suffering endured by her parents but she never makes reference to having suffered herself. Slavery is not mentioned nor is it clearly implied. Also, as J. Saunders Reddings points out "'seeming cruel' and 'fancy'd happy' give her away as not believing even in the cruelty of the fate that had dragged thousands of her race into bondage in America nor in the happiness of their former freedom in Africa" [see excerpt dated 1939].

In the last two lines of this stanza she is obviously talking about Whites when she says, ". . . and can I then but pray / others may never feel tyrannic sway," because Blacks already felt this tyranny.

Thus, Phillis Wheatley's poem to the Earl of Dartmouth provides no evidence of her Blackness nor does it show that her orientation was anything other than white. She was a poet who happened to be Black and it is a mistake to refer to her as a Black poet. However, it is much to the credit of black people that a slave girl was able to get a book of poems published at such an early age and during the seventeen hundreds. But in any literary analysis of the poetry of Phillis Wheatley from a Black perspective, we must accept the fact that her poetry is a product of a white mind, a mind that had been so engulfed in the education, religion, values, and the freedom of Whites that she expressed no strong sentiments for those who had been cast into the wretchedness of slavery by those she so often praised with her pen. Any student who is exposed to Phillis Wheatley must be able to recognize that her poetry expressed the sentiments of eighteenth century Whites because her mind was controlled by them, her actions were controlled by them, and consequently her pen. (pp. 413-15)

Angelene Jamison, "Analysis of Selected Poetry of Phillis Wheatley," in The Journal of Negro Education, *Vol. XLIII, No. 3, Summer, 1974, pp. 408-16.*

Charles Scruggs (essay date 1981)

[*In the excerpt below, Scruggs examines the styles, themes, and concerns of Wheatley's poetry, setting aside the question of the author's race and social status.*]

[Whenever Phillis Wheatley's] poetry has been discussed as poetry, a "Romantic" bias has determined her critical reputation. Even in the twentieth century, criticism of her poetry has been shaped by prejudices inherited from the Romantic period. To listen to her modern critics, "neo-classicism" was the *bête noire* of her brief poetic career. Saunders Redding talks of the "chill . . . of Pope's neo-classicism upon her" [see excerpt dated 1939], and M. A. Richmond complains that "neo-classicism" was responsible for her artificiality. "Neo-classicism," says Richmond, encased Phillis Wheatley within the "tyranny of the couplet" and crushed her talent under "the heavy burden of ornamental rhetoric." The kindest thing that has been said of "neo-classicism" is that it taught her regularity.

Thanks to Donald Green *(The Age of Exuberance)* and others, we have become somewhat suspicious of the word "neo-classicism." Not only was this word invented by the nineteenth century but the concept itself cannot possibly encompass the richness and complexity of eighteenth-century art. Even when the term "neo-classicism" makes sense within a limited context, no student of the eighteenth century today would treat it as though it were synonymous with the contemporary meaning of "artificiality." In fact, as all students of the eighteenth century know, the word "artificial" presents an interesting historical irony. The eighteenth century ordinarily did not use the word "artificial" in a pejorative sense—although it could be used that way. Usually "artificial" meant "artful, contrived with skill."

That many of Phillis Wheatley's poems are "contrived with skill" is the basis of my argument in this paper. We are told that Phillis Wheatley was a bad poet because she lived in an age uncongenial, even hostile, to the true poetic sensibility. If she had been planted in better soil, such as the fertile ground of the Romantic period, then we would have had a real poet instead of a hothouse flower. Eighteenth-century poetry, these critics insist, was impersonal, stylized, and ornate; and the poetical fashions of this period were dictatorial and absolute. Thus in imitating the literary conventions of her day, Phillis Wheatley wrote poetry which is artificial and insincere. This view is wrongheaded because it fails to understand those literary conventions which it deplores. More precisely, it fails to take into account that eighteenth-century aesthetic thought made a distinction between artifice and artificiality, and not between sincerity and artificiality. Because Phillis Wheatley's critics have refused to recognize the artifice of eighteenth-century poetry, they have not seen the competent craftsmanship of Phillis Wheatley's poems. Not seeing the forest, they certainly cannot be expected to see the trees.

When Phillis Wheatley visited England in 1773, she was received there with more fanfare than she would ever receive in her lifetime in America. This reception is significant, because it tells us something about mid-eighteenth-century aesthetic taste. Arriving in London with her owner Susannah Wheatley, this humble young girl found herself courted and lionized by the city's literati. The Countess of Huntingdon became her patron; the former Lord Mayor of London presented her with a copy of *Paradise Lost;* and **Poems on Various Subjects** was actually published in England—primarily owing to Lady Huntingdon's efforts. These events have been described in detail, but no one has told us the reason for such lavish attention given to a lowly slave poet. The answer lies in England's fascination for poets who illustrated the principle of "natural genius." This principle can best be explained by the Latin aphorism, *poeta nascitur, non fit* ("a poet is born, and not made"). Although the idea of "natural genius" is at least as old as Pindar, it was given a new interpretation by the middle of the eighteenth century. This interpretation not only helps us to understand the English response to Phillis Wheatley, but it also enables us to see how she could use the idea of "natural genius" to her own poetical advantage.

As was the case with many ideas not his own, Joseph Addison popularized the concept of "natural genius" in the eighteenth century. In 1711, in *Spectator* 160, Addison had distinguished between two kinds of poetic genius. The first kind are those artists "who by the mere strength of natural parts, and without any assistance of art or learning, have produced works that were the delight of their own times and the wonder of posterity." The second kind are artists who "have formed themselves by rules and submitted the greatness of their natural talents to the corrections and restraints of art." Addison claims to make no invidious comparison between the two types of genius, but he does admit that there is something "nobly wild, and extravagant in ... natural geniuses that is infinitely more beautiful than all the turn and polishing of what the French call a *bel esprit,* by which they would express a genius refined by conversation, reflection, and the reading of the most polite authors." As Addison defined the term, "natural genius" implied an elitist view of the poet; some are born with this divine talent and others are not.

Addison never imagined that the idea of "natural genius" could be applied to a working-class poet. Nevertheless, at mid-century this concept was given a distinctly democratic twist. Some members of the English aristocracy became convinced that among the poor were to be found "mute, inglorious Miltons," who if only given the chance would burst forth in glorious song. Thus poets were seized upon because they were "unlettered," and in the thirty-five years or so before Phillis Wheatley began to write in the late 1760s, we find numerous examples of bards from the lower classes who were patronized by people of position. For example, Joseph Spence sponsored Stephen Duck, the "Thresher-Poet"; William Shenstone, Lady Mary Montague, and Lord Lyttelton encouraged James Woodhouse, the "Shoemaker-Poet"; Lord Chesterfield helped Henry Jones, the "Bricklayer-Poet"; and in a little more than a decade after Phillis Wheatley's death, Hannah Moore took Ann Yearsley under her wing, the poet known as Lactilla, the "Milkmaid-Poet."

Given this atmosphere, it is understandable that Lady Huntingdon became excited over the poetry of a young slave girl. To Lady Huntingdon, this was another example of "natural genius" among the impoverished classes. Furthermore, she knew that others would respond to this new manifestation of the "Unlettered Muse," and she therefore placed a picture of Phillis Wheatley on the frontispiece of *Poems on Various Subjects* in order to call attention to the author's humble station. (pp. 279-82)

This tradition of "natural genius" continues well into the nineteenth century and is the basis of Margaretta Odell's short biography of the African poet. A strange mixture of fact and fancy, Odell's *Memoir* (1834) is our major source of information about Phillis Wheatley's life [see Further Reading]. The myth which Odell expounds has its roots in eighteenth-century England. We learn, for instance, that as a young girl Phillis took to poetry as naturally as ducks take to water. Although people encouraged her to read and write, "nothing was forced upon her, nothing was suggested, or placed before her as a lure; her literary efforts were altogether the natural workings of her own mind." Also, she never had "any grammatical instructor, or knowledge of the structure or idiom of the English language, except which she imbibed from a perusal of the best English writers, and from mingling in polite circles. . . ." Furthermore, she was visited by visions in the night which awakened her and which she wrote down as poems. The next morning,

she could not remember these dreams which had inspired her to write poetry.

The extent to which Phillis Wheatley believed she was a "natural genius" is difficult to determine, but she did skillfully employ this public image of herself in her poetry. The appearance of the idea of "natural genius" in her poems presented a familiar paradox, as her age would have instantly recognized. In a poetical correspondence with Lieutenant Rochfort of His Majesty's Navy, Phillis Wheatley modestly disclaims the use of artifice, at the same time that she artfully defines the kind of poet she is and hopes to be.

Phillis Wheatley had written a poem, addressed to Rochfort, in which she had praised the sailor's martial valor, and Rochfort responded by sending her a poem of his own. In "The Answer," Rochfort eulogizes Phillis Wheatley by glorifying the country of her birth. Africa is depicted as a "happy land" where "shady forests . . . scarce know a bound." Here there are

> The artless grottos, and the soft retreats;
> "At once the lover and the muse's seats."
> Where nature taught, (tho strange it is to tell,)
> Her flowing pencil Europe to excell.

In these lines, Rochfort has romanticized Africa. Primitivistic and picturesque, this Africa is as unreal as the "dark continent" of the advertisement to *Poems on Various Subjects.* Rochfort sees Africa as the cause of Phillis Wheatley's power as a poet; the simple "artless" land has given birth to an "artless" poet. In later lines, he celebrates "Wheatley's song" as having "seraphic fire" and an "art, which art could ne'er acquire."

When Phillis Wheatley wrote a poetic reply to this poem, she employed the same motifs which Rochfort had used. She refers to Africa as a luxuriant "Eden." Then she humbly says of Rochfort's flattery:

> The generous plaudit 'tis not mine to claim,
> A muse untutor'd, and unknown to fame.

She laments further that her "pen . . . Can never rival, never equal thine," but she will nevertheless continue to study the best authors to improve her talent. She illustrates this thought by soaring into poetic flight:

> Then fix the humble Afric muse's seat
> At British Homer's and Sir Isaac's feet
> Those bards whose fame in deathless strains arise
> Creation's boast, and fav'rites of the skies.

It is easy to see that Rochfort and Phillis Wheatley are playing an elaborate game in these poems, with the assumptions on both sides well understood. Rochfort tells her that she is an "artless" poet, and she modestly agrees, only to prove his thesis that her "untutored" muse has the capacity for true "seraphic fire." She is the "artless" poet as wise *ingénue.*

It is worth noting that in the above passage, Phillis Wheatley says that she will worship at the shrines of

Pope and Newton, two of the greatest "bards" of the age. In section two of this paper, her indebtedness to Pope will become clear as she tries to establish a convincing poetical voice. In section three of this paper, her connection to both Pope and Newton will be demonstrated in her attempt to write a specific kind of poetry which her century admired. Phillis Wheatley seemed to feel no "anxiety of influence," to borrow a phrase from Harold Bloom, in her desire to emulate other "bards." It probably never occurred to her that her "seraphic fire" might be snuffed out by rank imitation. In truth, her poetry did sometimes succumb to formula and repetition, but her adoration of Pope in particular often resulted in a grace snatched beyond the reach of artificiality.

What Phillis Wheatley learned from Alexander Pope, her favorite author, was an ability to transform her real self into an imagined self, a *persona,* which functioned as a means to a precise end, rhetorical persuasion. Instead of being a liability, this imagined self became a poetic asset. Often it was used as the cornerstone of an argument which was building in a poem, and since the imagined self was based upon assumptions about race and "natural genius" which she and her age understood, the poem was convincing to people who read it. Whatever her real feelings, it was her imagined self which she showed to the world. Whatever the disadvantages, her imagined self made her eloquent in places where she might have been simply maudlin.

Let us look more closely at a poem in which Phillis Wheatley uses her imagined self for rhetorical purposes. In **"To The Right Honourable William, Earl of Dartmouth, His Majesty's Principal Secretary of State for North America,"** she congratulates Dartmouth on his new political post and pleads with him to protect and preserve the rights of Americans, vis-à-vis England, in the New World. To reinforce her point, she makes an analogy between America's situation and her own:

> I, young in life, by seeming cruel fate
> Was snatch'd from *Afric's* fancy'd happy seat:
> What pangs excruciating must molest,
> What sorrows labour in my parent's breast?
> Steel'd was that soul and by no misery mov'd
> That from a father seiz'd his babe belov'd:
> Such, such my case. And can I then but pray
> Others may never feel tyrannic sway?

These lines have been alternately praised and blamed for their sincerity or lack of sincerity. Saunders Redding specifically singles out the words "seeming cruel" and "fancy'd happy seat" to argue that Phillis Wheatley did not believe "either in the cruelty of the fate that had dragged thousands of her race into bondage in America nor in the happiness of their former freedom in Africa" [see excerpt dated 1939]. In other words, not only had Phillis Wheatley's poetic personality been enslaved by "neo-classicism," but also her political attitudes were the products of the culture which owned her.

Redding's argument is based upon a twentieth-century interpretation of the word "fancy'd." As we know from Dr. Johnson's dictionary (1755), the word "fancy" can be a synonym for "delusion," but it can also be a synonym for the "imagination" which, in Johnson's words, "forms to itself representations of things, persons, or scenes of being." In this definition, "fancy" is that part of the mind which makes images, which in turn have their origin in sense experience. An alternative reading of Phillis Wheatley's "Afric's fancy'd happy seat" might be "the happy seat" which other poets have pictured Africa to be—either from seeing it themselves or from seeing it in their imaginations. We know that Phillis Wheatley was aware of the primitivistic tradition in eighteenth-century England which often conceived of Africa as a fruitful paradise. Not only did she use this idea in her poem to Rochfort, but we also know that in her poem **"To Imagination"** she used "fancy" and "imagination" interchangeably and that both words were placed in the context of the mind's ability to perceive a truth beyond one's own immediate experience.

Thus the entire passage above might be read as follows. I, Phillis Wheatley, now a Christian slave, was once taken from my native land, Africa, which others besides myself have recognized as a Golden World. Not only did it cause my father much grief but also it has given me an understanding of the word "freedom." Fortunately for me, everything worked out for the best, for now I am a Christian (the "fate" is only "seeming cruel"), but others like myself, the Americans of these Colonies, are being threatened by political tyranny.

In this poem, Phillis Wheatley has artfully used the pathos of her own past to persuade Dartmouth to assuage the wrongs done to the Americans by the British. This is neither the poetry of self-expression nor the poetry of cold elegance; rather it is the poetry of argument. As such, it is reminiscent—not in excellence but in intention—of some of the great poems of the Restoration and eighteenth century: "Absalom and Achitophel," "An Essay on Man," and "An Epistle to Dr. Arbuthnot."

"To the University of Cambridge, in New England" also illustrates Phillis Wheatley's ability to manipulate an imagined self for the sake of argument. This poem is addressed to the students at Harvard who are urged by this young black slave to mend their profligate ways. To underscore her didactic theme, Phillis Wheatley describes the world from which she came:

> 'Twas not long since I left my native shore
> The land of errors, and *Egyptian* gloom:
> Father of mercy, 'twas thy gracious hand
> Brought me in safety from those dark abodes.

This is a different picture of Africa from one of carefree primitives; it is an Africa without Christianity and without civilization. Although this portrait is not flattering to her native land, it is rhetorically useful; it creates an ironic contrast between her lot and that of the

Harvard students. The latter are Christians by birth, and because they have the privileges of class, they are offered a knowledge of the highest civilization which man has attained. Yet they are abusing this god-given gift—a gift which has been denied to members of Phillis Wheatley's race. A lowly African must remind them that they too, like all men, may be destroyed by sin:

> Ye blooming plants of human race divine,
> An *Ethiop* tells you 'tis your greatest foe;
> Its transient sweetness turns to endless pain,
> And in immense perdition sinks the soul.

The situation here is archetypal. Phillis Wheatley is like the Roman slave in antiquity who stands behind the general marching triumphantly into Rome and who whispers into his ear that he is mortal. In this situation, the simple savage *knows* more than the sophisticated Harvard students.

In another well-known poem, **"On Being Brought From Africa to America,"** we see a similar rhetorical strategy. Phillis Wheatley begins by celebrating God's mercy in bringing her from her *"Pagan* land" to the New World: "Once I redemption neither sought nor knew." Nevertheless, she is aware that some Christians in America "view our sable race with scornful eye." These Americans see the Negro's color as "diabolic" and thus Phillis reminds them in the last two lines of the poem:

> Remember, *Christians, Negroes,* black as *Cain,*
> May be refin'd, and join th' angelic train.

As Phillis Wheatley said in one of her letters, God "was no respecter of Persons." Although the Negro appears to be Cain to white Americans, he is not Cain in Christ's eyes. The italicized words not only emphasize the falsehood of the analogy but they also serve as a reminder that all human beings—including whites—need to be "refined" before they "join th' angelic train."

The quiet irony of these last two lines seem to echo Pope's "lo, the poor indian" passage in "An Essay on Man." In Pope's poem, civilized man thinks himself superior to the naive savage whose conception of the afterlife is unimaginative. For the "poor indian," Heaven is simply a place where "No fiends torment, no Christians thirst for Gold." Yet it is this very simplicity which serves as a satiric comment upon the actual behavior of those people who call themselves "Christians." By placing her imagined self in ironic juxtaposition to the "Christians" who would view her as "diabolic," Phillis Wheatley is making the same satiric point.

Pope was not her only tutor in the use of a *persona* to rhetorical advantage. One poem recently discovered in manuscript indicates that Phillis Wheatley was probably aware of John Dryden's poetry. **"To Deism"** is similar to "Religio Laici" in both theme and technique; both authors use the *persona* of the "layman" to attack the web-spinning sophistry of Deism. Phillis Wheatley appears in the poem as an unlettered African who nevertheless knows the fundamental truths of Christian-

ity. Her antagonist, a Deist, is out to disprove the doctrines of revelation and the trinity at the risk of losing his own soul to win an argument. Like John Dryden, Phillis Wheatley cannot hide her indignation for such folly:

> Must Ethiopians be imploy'd for you
> [I] greatly rejoice if any good I do
> I ask O unbeliever satan's child
> Has not thy saviour been to [o] meek [and]
>   mild. . .

(pp. 284-88)

Phillis Wheatley's mastery of poetic technique, such as her ability to shape a *persona* for rhetorical purposes, shows her to be a more artful poet than we have previously recognized. If, at time, her elegies seem only a cut above "The Ode to Stephen Dowling Bots" in *Huckleberry Finn,* at other times she eloquently wrote in the "sublime" mode which so fascinated her age. As a religious poet, she found the "sublime" a perfect vehicle for expressing transcendent emotions. As an artist, she responded to the secular theories of the "sublime," a kind of poetry which tried to be grandiloquent rather than clear, astonishing in its effects rather than logical. In this verse, whether sacred or profane, Milton and the Old Testament were influences upon her but so was Alexander Pope.

Phillis Wheatley's critics have had difficulty in explaining her indebtedness to Pope, and thus they tend to bury him under the generalizations which they make about "neo-classicism." Actually, we are told by Margaretta Odell that Phillis Wheatley specifically admired "Pope's Homer." This fact is significant, for Pope's preface to *The Iliad* and translation of it helped to create the critical opinion in the eighteenth century that Homer was the master of "sublimity."

The "sublime" reached the zenith of its popularity around the same time that Phillis Wheatley began writing poetry. A rash of essays on the subject appeared in the 1750s and 60s (the most famous being Edmund Burke's essay on *The Sublime and the Beautiful* in 1757), and Edward Young's final version of *Night Thoughts* (1746) and James Thomson's revised *Seasons* (1744) became models for poets hoping to write in this exciting poetic style. Mark Akenside, Thomas Gray, William Collins, Thomas and Joseph Warton, James Macpherson and others all wrote their poetry between 1740 and 1773, and if Phillis Wheatley was reading the best English writers, as she and Margaretta Odell say she was, then she was probably also aware of the writings of her contemporaries.

One essay dealing indirectly with the "sublime" has a special relevance to our subject. In 1756, Joseph Warton wrote "An Essay on the Genius and Writings of Pope," in which he argued that whereas Pope excels in the poetry of wit, he is nevertheless not one of our greatest poets because "he does not . . . ravish and transport his reader." Warton insists that "The Sublime and the

Pathetic are the two chief nerves of all genuine poesy." And he asks, "What is there transcendently sublime or pathetic in Pope?"

Phillis Wheatley could have answered this question, because she saw another facet of Pope's poetry besides the familiar one of social satire. In **"To Maecenas,"** she describes herself as a humble poet who wishes to soar in exalted flight. Homer, she says, is her model, but she laments that she cannot "paint" with his power. Homer makes lightning "blaze across the vaulted skies," and causes the thunder to shake "the heavenly plains," and as she reads his lines: "A deep-felt horror thrills through my veins." She too would fly like both Homer and Virgil but complains:

> . . . here I sit, and mourn a grov'ling mind,
> That fain would mount, and ride upon the wind.

Not only is there an oblique reference to the Old Testament in the last line, but she is also remembering two lines from Pope's "An Essay on Man":

> Nor God alone in the still Calm we find;
> He mounts the Storm, and *walks upon the wind.*

Phillis Wheatley identifies herself with Pope, because as the translator of Homer and as the author of "An Essay on Man," Pope is a poet who has already excelled in the "sublime" mode; in these two works, he has, as it were, mounted "the storm" and walked "upon the wind." To the pious young slave poet, for instance, "An Essay on Man" would be an example of the highest kind of "sublimity," for Pope's poem contains passages which grandly describe the vast, mysterious, awe-inspiring universe of God's creation.

The "sublime" takes various forms in Phillis Wheatley's poetry. In **"Goliath of Gath,"** she is consciously creating an epic character who terrifies us through our inability to imagine him as finite. In **"On Imagination,"** she celebrates the imagination's capacity to seize upon what our senses cannot hold, the vast immensity of the universe. In **"Ode to Neptune"** and **"To A Lady on Her Remarkable Preservation in an Hurricane in North Carolina,"** she is concerned with the "natural sublime," the fact that some objects in nature such as storms and hurricanes fill us with terror because of their uncontrollable power. In **"Niobe In Distress For Her Children Slain By Apollo,"** Phillis Wheatley is domesticating a mythological personage by treating her as a distressed mother. Not only is the poet's portrait contemporary in that this figure is a favorite one in the "Age of Sensibility," but Phillis Wheatley is also illustrating an aesthetic commonplace of the period: pathos is a branch of the "sublime."

If we examine two of her "sublime" poems, we shall see just how thoroughly Phillis Wheatley knew the taste of her age. In **"Goliath of Gath,"** for instance, she illustrates Edmund Burke's famous dictum in *The Sublime and the Beautiful* that "to make anything very terrible, obscurity seems in general to be necessary." Burke's

point is that if a character is going to affect our imaginations with ideas of terror and power, the artist must not draw him too precisely. Hence, Phillis Wheatley describes Goliath as a "monster" stalking "the terror of the field" as he comes forth to meet the Hebrews. She mentions his "fierce deportment" and "gigantic frame," but never descends to particulars when she refers to his physical characteristics. Rather, she obliquely depicts Goliath by focusing upon his armor and weapons:

> A brazen helmet on his head was plac'd,
> A coat of mail his form terrific grac'd,
> The greaves his legs, the targe his shoulders prest:
> Dreadful in arms high-tow'ring o'er the rest
> A spear he proudly wav'd, whose iron head,
> Strange to relate, six hundred shekels weigh'd;
> He strode along, and shook the ample field,
> While *Phoebus* blaz'd refulgent on his shield:
> Through *Jacob's* race a chilling horror ran. . . .

Like Achilles in Book 22 of *The Iliad* and Satan in Book 1 of *Paradise Lost,* Goliath is terrifying because our sensory perceptions fail to contain him. If she had not read Edmund Burke, she at least knew about his psychological theory of the "sublime."

Goliath is meant to frighten us (like storms and hurricanes in nature), but the imagination in **"To Imagination"** is meant to bring us to an emotional state of religious awe. Following Mark Akenside's lead ("The Pleasures of the Imagination"—1744), Phillis Wheatley sees the infinite soul of man as a microcosm of God's infinite universe; only the imagination can capture a sense of that infinity:

> *Imagination!* who can sing thy force?
> Or who describe the swiftness of thy course?
> Soaring through air to find the bright abode,
> Th' empyreal palace of the thund'ring God,
> We on thy pinions can surpass the wind,
> And leave the rolling universe behind:
> From star to star the mental optics rove,
> Measure the skies, and range the realms above.
> There in one view we grasp the mighty whole,
> Or with new worlds amaze th' unbounded soul.

The imagination is a kind of mental eyesight ("optics") which allows us to penetrate the finite world and discover, to use Majorie Nicolson's phrase, "the aesthetics of the infinite." In this context, it is no wonder that Phillis Wheatley referred to Sir Isaac Newton as one of the greatest "bards" of the age, for Newton's theories about the universe expanded God's world at the same time that they explained it.

Although eighteenth-century England saw Phillis Wheatley as a "natural genius," she had larger plans for herself. She aspired to be an artist in the manner of Homer, Milton, and Pope. If we still complain that she failed as a poet because she did not express, with sufficient vehemence, her suffering black self, then we might do well to listen to Ralph Ellison, a contemporary black writer, who has argued [in *Shadow and Act,* 1953] against "unrelieved suffering" as the only basis of Afro-American art

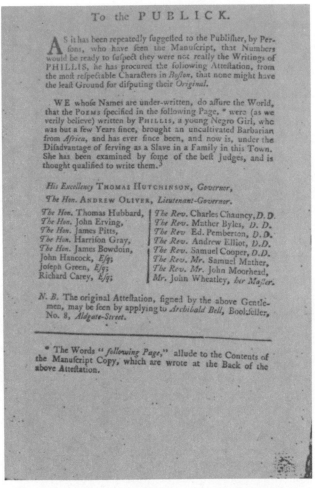

To the PUBLICK.

AS it has been repeatedly suggested to the Publisher, by Persons, who have seen the Manuscript, that Numbers would be ready to suspect they were not really the Writings of PHILLIS, he has procured the following Attestation, from the most respectable Characters in *Boston*, that none might have the least Ground for disputing their *Original.*

WE whose Names are under-written, do assure the World, that the POEMS specified in the following Page,* were (as we verily believe) written by PHILLIS, a young Negro Girl, who was but a few Years since, brought an uncultivated Barbarian from *Africa,* and has ever since been, and now is, under the Disadvantage of serving as a Slave in a Family in this Town. She has been examined by some of the best Judges, and is thought qualified to write them.

His Excellency THOMAS HUTCHINSON, *Governor,*

The Hon. ANDREW OLIVER, *Lieutenant-Governor.*

The Hon. Thomas Hubbard,	*The Rev.* Charles Chauncy, *D. D.*
The Hon. John Erving,	*The Rev.* Mather Byles, *D. D.*
The Hon. James Pitts,	*The Rev.* Ed. Pemberton, *D. D.*
The Hon. Harrison Gray,	*The Rev.* Andrew Elliot, *D. D.*
The Hon. James Bowdoin,	*The Rev.* Samuel Cooper, *D. D.*
John Hancock, *Esq;*	*The Rev. Mr.* Samuel Mather,
Joseph Green, *Esq;*	*The Rev. Mr.* John Moorhead,
Richard Carey, *Esq;*	*Mr.* John Wheatley, *her Master.*

N. B. The original Attestation, signed by the above Gentlemen, may be seen by applying to *Archibald Bell,* Bookseller, No. 8, *Aldgate-Street.*

---

* The Words " *following Page,*" allude to the Contents of the Manuscript Copy, which are wrote at the Back of the above Attestation.

This attestation to the authenticity of Wheatley's writings was first published in a 1773 edition of Poems on Various Subjects.

. . . there is also an American Negro tradition which teaches one . . . to master and contain pain. It is a tradition which abhors as obscene any trading on one's own anguish for gain and sympathy; which springs not from a desire to deny the harshness of existence but from a will to deal with it as men at their best have always done. It takes fortitude to be a man and no less to be an artist. Perhaps it takes even more if the black man would be an artist.

Phillis Wheatley could be called the founding mother of this tradition which Ellison describes, for the eighteenth century provided her with the tools to transmute her pain into art. She saw herself as a *poeta,* a maker of poems, and not as a suffering black slave who happened to be a poet. She may not have been a great poet, or even a good one, but she did write some good poems, and they were written because she had mastered the best which her century had to offer. (pp. 288-92)

> *Charles Scruggs, "Phillis Wheatley and the Poetical Legacy of Eighteenth-Century England," in* Studies in Eighteenth-Century Culture, *Vol. 10, 1981, pp. 279-95.*

June Jordan (essay date 1986)

[Jordan is an American poet, essayist, and editor whose writings reveal her strong commitment to feminist and civil rights issues. The following excerpt is a tribute to Wheatley's life and work.]

It was not natural. And she was the first. Come from a country of many tongues tortured by rupture, by theft, by travel like mismatched clothing packed down into the cargo hold of evil ships sailing, irreversibly, into slavery; come to a country where, to be docile and dumb, to be big and breeding, easily, to be turkey/horse/cow to be cook/carpenter/plow to be 5'6" 140 lbs. in good condition and answering to the name of Tom or Mary; to be bed bait; to be legally spread legs for rape by the master/the master's son/the master's overseer/the master's visiting nephew; to be nothing human nothing family nothing from nowhere nothing that screams nothing that weeps nothing that dreams nothing that keeps anything/anyone deep in your heart; to live forcibly illiterate forcibly itinerant; to live eyes lowered head bowed; to be worked without rest to be worked without pay to be worked without thanks to be worked day up to nightfall; to be 3/5ths of a human being at best: to be this valuable, this hated thing among strangers who purchased your life and then cursed it unceasingly: to be a slave: to be a slave: come to this country a slave and how should you sing? After the flogging the lynch rope the general terror and weariness what should you know of a lyrical life? How could you, belonging to no one, but property to those despising the smiles of your soul, how could you dare to create yourself: A poet?

A poet can read. A poet can write.

A poet is African in Africa, or Irish in Ireland, or French on the Left Bank of Paris, or white in Wisconsin. A Poet writes in her own language. A poet writes of her own people, her own history, her own vision, her own room, her own house where she sits at her own table quietly placing one word after another word until she builds a line and a movement and an image and a meaning that somersaults all of these into the singing, the absolutely individual voice of the poet: At liberty. A poet is somebody free. A poet is someone at home.

How should there be Black poets in America? (p. 252)

It was not natural. And she was the first: Phillis Miracle: Phillis Miracle Wheatley: The first Black human being to be published in America. She was the second female to be published in America.

And the miracle begins in Africa. It was there that a bitterly anonymous man and a woman conjoined to create this genius, this lost child of such prodigious aptitude and such beguiling attributes that she very soon interposed the reality of her particular, dear life between the Wheatley's notions about slaves and the predictable outcome of such usual blasphemies against Black human beings.

Seven-year-old Phillis changed the slaveholding Wheatleys. She altered their minds. She entered their hearts. She made them see her and when they truly saw her, Phillis, darkly amazing them with the sweetness of her spirit and the alacrity of her forbidden, strange intelligence, they, in their own way, loved her as a prodigy, as a girl mysterious but godly.

Sixteen months after her entry into the Wheatley household Phillis was talking the language of her owners. Phillis was fluently reading The Scriptures. At eight and a half years of age, this Black child, or "Afric's Muse," as she would later describe herself, was fully literate in the language of this slaveholding land. She was competent and eargerly asking for more: more books, more and more information. And Suzannah Wheatley loved this child of her whimsical good luck. It pleased her to teach and to train and to tutor this Black girl, this Black darling of God. And so Phillis delved into kitchen studies commensurate, finally, to a classical education available to young white men at Harvard.

She was nine years old.

What did she read? What did she memorize? What did the Wheatleys give to this African child? Of course, it was white, all of it: White. It was English, most of it, from England. It was written, all of it, by white men taking their pleasure, their walks, their pipes, their pens and their paper, rather seriously, while somebody else cleaned the house, washed the clothes, cooked the food, watched the children: Probably not slaves, but possibly a servant, or, commonly, a wife: It was written, this white man's literature of England, while somebody else did the other things that have to be done. And that was the literature absorbed by the slave, Phillis Wheatley. That was the writing, the thoughts, the nostalgia, the lust, the conceits, the ambitions, the mannerisms, the games, the illusions, the discoveries, the filth and the flowers that filled up the mind of the African child.

At fourteen, Phillis published her first poem, **"To the University of Cambridge":** Not a brief limerick or desultory, teenager's verse, but 32 lines of blank verse telling those fellows what for and whereas, according to their own strict Christian codes of behavior. It is in that poem that Phillis describes the miracle of her own Black poetry in America:

> While an intrinsic ardor bids me write
> the muse doth promise to assist my pen

She says that her poetry results from "an intrinsic ardor," not to dismiss the extraordinary kindness of the Wheatleys, and not to diminish the wealth of white men's literature with which she found herself quite saturated, but it was none of these extrinsic factors that compelled the labors of her poetry. It was she who created herself a poet, notwithstanding and in despite of everything around her.

Two years later, Phillis Wheatley, at the age of sixteen, had composed three additional, noteworthy poems. This is one of them, **"On Being Brought from Africa to America":**

> Twas mercy brought me from my Pagan land,
> Taught my benighted soul to understand
> That there's a God, that there's a Saviour too:
> Once I redemption neither sought nor knew
> Some view our sable race with scornful eye,
> "Their color is a diabolic die."
> Remember, *Christians,* Negroes, black as Cain,
> May be refin'd, and join the angelic train.

Where did Phillis get these ideas?

It's simple enough to track the nonsense about herself "benighted:": *benighted* means surrounded and preyed upon by darkness. That clearly reverses what had happened to that African child, surrounded by and captured by the greed of white men. Nor should we find puzzling her depiction of Africa as "Pagan" versus somewhere "refined." Even her bizarre interpretation of slavery's theft of Black life as a merciful rescue should not bewilder anyone. These are regular kinds of iniquitous nonsense found in white literature, the literature that Phillis Wheatley assimilated, with no choice in the matter.

But here, in this surprising poem, this first Black poet presents us with something wholly her own, something entirely new: It is her matter-of-fact assertion that "once I redemption neither sought nor knew," as in: Once I existed beyond and without these terms under consideration. *Once I existed on other than your terms.* And, she says, *but* since we are talking with your talk about good and evil/redemption and damnation, let me tell you something you had better understand. I am Black as Cain *and* I may very well be an angel of the Lord: Take care not to offend the Lord!

Where did that thought come to Phillis Wheatley?

Was it a nice day?

Does it matter?

Following her "intrinsic ardor," and attuned to the core of her own person, this girl, the first Black poet in America, had dared to redefine herself from house slave to, possibly, an angel of the Almighty.

And she was making herself at home.

And, depending on whether you estimated that nearly naked Black girl on the auction block to be seven or eight years old, in 1761, by the time she was eighteen or nineteen, she had published her first book of poetry, ***Poems on Various Subjects Religious and Moral.*** It was published in London, in 1773, and the American edition appeared, years later, in 1786. Here are some examples from the poems of Phillis Wheatley:

from **"On the Death of Rev. Dr. Sewell":**

> Come let us all behold with wishful eyes
> The saint ascending to his native skies.

from **"On the Death of the Rev. Mr. George Whitefield"**:

> Take him, ye Africans, he longs for you,
> *Impartial Savior* is his title due,
> Washed in the fountain of redeeming blood
> You shall be sons and kings, and priest to God.

Here is an especially graceful and musical couplet:

> But, see the softly stealing tears apace,
> Pursue each other down the mourner's face;

This is an especially awful, virtually absurd set of lines by Ms. Wheatley:

> Go, Thebons! great nations will obey,
> And pious tribute to her altars pay:
> With rights divine, the goddess be implor'd,
> Nor be her sacred offspring nor ador'd.
> Thus Manto spoke. The Thebon maids obey,
> And pious tribute to the goddess pay.

Awful, yes. Virtually absurd, well, yes, except, consider what it took for that young African to undertake such a persona, such values, and mythologies a million million miles remote from her own ancestry, and her own darkly formulating race! Consider what might meet her laborings, as a poet, should she, instead, invent a vernacular precise to Senegal, precise to slavery, and therefore, accurate to the secret wishings of her lost and secret heart?

If she, this genius teenager, should, instead of writing verse to comfort a white man upon the death of his wife, or a white woman upon the death of her husband, or verse commemorating weirdly fabled white characters bereft of children diabolically dispersed, if she, instead, composed a poetry to speak her pain, to say her grief, to find her parents, or to stir her people into insurrection, what would we now know about God's darling girl, that Phillis?

Who would publish that poetry, then?

But Phillis Miracle, she managed, nonetheless, to write, sometimes, towards the personal truth of her experience.

For example, we find in a monumental poem entitled **"Thoughts on The Works of Providence,"** these five provocative lines, confirming every suspicion that most of the published Phillis Wheatley represents a meager portion of her concerns and inclinations:

> As reason's pow'rs by day our God disclose,
> So we may trace him in the night's repose.
> Say what is sleep? and dreams how passing
>   strange!
> When action ceases, and ideas range
> Licentious and unbounded o'er the plains.

And, concluding this long work, there are these lines:

> Infinite *love* whene'er we turn our eyes
> Appears: this ev'ry creature's wants supplies,
> This most is heard in Nature's constant voice,

> This makes the morn, and this the eve rejoice,
> This bids the fost'ring rains and dews descend
> To nourish all, to serve on gen'ral end,
> The good of man: Yet man ungrateful pays
> But little homage, and but little praise.

Now and again and again these surviving works of the genius Phillis Wheatley veer, incisive and unmistakable, completely away from the verse of good girl Phillis ever compassionate upon the death of someone else's beloved, pious Phillis modestly enraptured by the glorious trials of virtue on the road to Christ, arcane Phillis intent upon an **"Ode to Neptune,"** or patriotic Phillis penning an encomium to General George Washington ("Thee, first in peace and honor"). Then do we find that "Ethiop" as she once called herself, that "Africa's muse," knowledgeable, but succinct, on "dreams how passing strange! When action ceases, ideas range/licentious and unbounded o'er the plains."

Phillis Licentious Wheatley?

Phillis Miracle Wheatley in contemplation of love and want of love?

Was it a nice day?

It was not natural. And she was the first.

Repeatedly singing for liberty, singing against the tyrannical, repeatedly avid in her trusting support of the American Revolution (how could men want freedom enough to die for it but then want slavery enough to die for that), repeatedly lifting witness to the righteous and the kindly factors of her days, she was no ordinary teenage poet, male or female, Black or white. Indeed, the insistently concrete content of her tribute to the revolutionaries who would forge America, an independent nation state, indeed the specific daily substance of her poetry establishes Phillis Wheatley as the first decidedly American poet on this continent, Black or white, male or female.

Nor did she only love the ones who purchased her, a slave, those ones who loved her, yes, but with astonishment. Her lifelong friend was a young Black woman, Obour Tanner, who lived in Newport, Rhode Island, and one of her few poems dedicated to a living person, but neither morbid nor ethereal, was written to the young Black visual artist, Sapio Moorhead, himself a slave. It is he who crafted the portrait of Phillis that serves as her frontispiece profile in her book of poems. Here are the opening lines from her poem, **"To S. M., A Young African Painter, On Seeing His Works"**:

> To show the lab'ring bosom's deep intent,
> And thought in living characters to paint.
> When first thy pencil did those beauties give,
> And breathing figures learnt from thee to live,
> How did those prospects give my soul delight,
> A new creation rushing on my sight?
> Still, wondrous youth! each noble path pursue,
> On deathless glories fix thine ardent view:
> Still may the painter's and the poet's fire
> To aid thy pencil, and thy verse conspire!

And many the charms of each seraphic theme
Conduct thy footsteps to immortal fame!

Remember that the poet so generously addressing the "wondrous youth" is certainly no older than eighteen, herself! And this, years before the American Revolution, and how many years before the 1960's! This is the first Black poet of America addressing her Brother Artist not as so-and-so's Boy, but as "Sapio Moorhead, A Young African Painter."

Where did Phillis Miracle acquire this consciousness?

Was it a nice day?

It was not natural. And she was the first.

But did she, we may persevere, critical from the ease of the 1980's, did she love, did she Need, freedom?

In a poem typically titled at such length and in such deferential rectitude as to discourage most readers from scanning the poem that follows, in the poem titled, **"To the Right Honorable William, Earl of Dartmouth, His Majesty's Principal Secretary of State for North America,"** Phillis Miracle has written these irresistible, authentic, felt lines:

> No more America in mournful strain
> Of wrongs, and grievance unredress'd complain,
> No longer shalt Thou dread the iron chain,
> Which wanton tyranny with lawless head
> Had made, and with it meant t' enslave the land
> Should you, my Lord, while you peruse my song,
> Wonder from whence my love of Freedom
>   sprung,
> Whence flow these wishes for the common food,
> By feeling hearts alone best understood,
> I, young in life, by seeming cruel fate
> Was snatch'd from Afric's fancy'd happy seat.
> What pangs excruciating most molest,
> What sorrows labour in my parent's breast?
> Steel'd was that soul and by no misery mov'd
> That from a father seiz'd his babe belov'd
> Such, such my case. And can I then but pray
> Others may never feel tyrannic sway?

So did the darling girl of God compose her thoughts, prior to 1772.

And then.

And then her poetry, these poems, were published in London.

And then, during her twenty-first year, Suzannah Wheatley, the white woman slaveholder who had been changed into the white mother, the white mentor, the white protectorate of Phillis, died.

Without that white indulgence, that white love, without that white sponsorship, what happened to the young African daughter, the young African poet?

No one knows for sure.

With the death of Mrs. Wheatley, Phillis came of age, a Black slave in America.

Where did she live?

How did she eat?

No one knows for sure.

But four years later she met and married a Black man, John Peters. Mr. Peters apparently thought well of himself, and of his people. He comported himself with dignity, studied law, argued for the liberation of Black people, and earned the everyday dislike of whitefolks. His wife bore him three children; all of them died.

His wife continued to be Phillis Miracle.

His wife continued to obey the "intrinsic ardor" of her calling and she never ceased the practise of her poetry.

She hoped, in fact, to publish a second volume of her verse.

This would be the poetry of Phillis the lover of John, Phillis the woman, Phillis the wife of a Black man pragmatically premature in his defiant self-respect, Phillis giving birth to three children, Phillis the mother, who must bury the three children she delivered into American life.

None of these poems was ever published.

This would have been the poetry of someone who has chosen herself, free, and brave to be free in a land of slavery.

When she was thirty-one years old, in 1784, Phillis Wheatley, the first Black poet in America, she died.

Her husband, John Peters, advertised and begged that the manuscript of her poems she had given to someone, please be returned.

But no one returned them.

And I believe we would not have seen them, anyway. I believe no one would have published the poetry of Black Phillis Wheatley, that grown woman who stayed with her chosen Black man. I believe that the death of Suzannah Wheatley, coincident with the African poet's twenty-first birthday, signalled, decisively, the end of her status as a child, as a dependent. From there we would hear from an independent Black woman poet in America.

Can you imagine that, in 1775?

Can you imagine that, today?

America has long been tolerant of Black children, compared to its reception of independent Black men and Black women.

She died in 1784.

Was it a nice day?

It was not natural. And she was the first. (pp. 254-60)

> June Jordan, "The Difficult Miracle of Black
> Poetry in America or Something Like a
> Sonnet for Phillis Wheatley," in The Massa-
> chusetts Review, Vol. XXVII, No. 2, Sum-
> mer, 1986, pp. 252-62.

Henry Louis Gates, Jr. (essay date 1987)

[*Gates, a noted American authority on African-American literature, is the author of* Figures in Black:
Words, Signs, and the 'Racial' Self *(1987) and* The
Signifying Monkey: Towards a Theory of Afro-American Literary Criticism *(1988). He has also edited
numerous distinguished volumes, including* The Classical Slave Narratives *(1987) and the thirty-volume*
Schomburg Library of Nineteenth-Century Black
Women Writers *(1988). In the following excerpt from
his* Figures in Black, *he examines the critical reception of Wheatley by her contemporaries.*]

For reasons as various as they are complex, it would
appear that, had Phillis Wheatley not published, another African slave's poetry would have served equally well
as a refutation of certain commonly repeated assumptions about the nature of the Negro. Although the word
would reappear in the reviews of Wheatley's *Poems,*
"genius" was not her province to occupy. The formal
gap between Milton, Pope, Gray, Addison, Watts, and
Wheatley would appear to be profound, although she
rather self-consciously assumed these as her models.

Although viewers seem to have found much in her work
that is genuinely "poetic," her verse, criticized rarely,
seems to have been read primarily in nonliterary terms
and for other than literary purposes. The nature of the
function Wheatley served between 1773 and 1831 can
be described usefully but analogously by two tropes.
Wheatley and her poems bore a relation of metaphor
and metonymy in the language of the criticism her verse
elicited. Metaphors of her blackness—a blackness both
spiritual and physical—punctuate her critics' essays as
they do her own poetry, as in **"To Maecenas,"** for
example, and in **"On Being Brought from Africa to
America."** When Bernard Romans, writing [in his *A
Concise Natural History of East and West Florida*, 1775]
about the "capacity" of Africans to be other than slaves,
terms Wheatley a mere exception, the figure he utilizes
to characterize her is that of "a Phoenix of her race,"
which bears a certain resonance to Wheatley's own lines
on the mutability of blackness:

> 'Twas mercy brought me from my *Pagan* land,
> Taught my benighted soul to understand
> That there's a God, that there's a Saviour too:
> Once I redemption neither sought nor knew,
> Some view our race with scornful eye,
> "Their Colour is a diabolic die."
> Remember, *Christians, Negroes* black as *Cain,*
> May be refin'd, and join th' Angelic train.

After 1831, however, the metaphorical functions Wheatley is made to serve shift somewhat.

Metonymically, however, her relation to the potential of
other black people to assume "cultivation" remained
consistent in critical writings well into the twentieth
century, in part because of Jefferson's use of her as the
written record of the sum total of the African's potential
for "civilization," followed by the manifestly felt need
of blacks and their sympathizers to refute Jefferson's
claims. Metonymically, Wheatley bears a relation to
Africa and to the mental capacity of all other African
people in a manner remarkably similar to that which
Aristotle and Alexander, Milton, and Newton bear to
the white race in the tropes frequently repeated in the
practical criticism of her work, and in numerous disquisitions on the nature of the Negro. It would not be
incorrect to characterize the relation of Phillis Wheatley
to the black race and the relation of her *Poems* to "black
art" as a relation of synecdoche. Because the history of
the criticism of the poetry of slaves and ex-slaves
published in English between 1773 and 1831 is in large
part the history of the critical reception of Phillis
Wheatley, a short reading of her poetry could be of
sufficient relevance to sustain a digression from an
explication of her critics' judgments.

That Wheatley's verse could become cited so frequently
as "the" example of the mental and aesthetic capacity of
the African slave can be explained somewhat by the
curious circumstances of her enslavement in Africa as
well as by the condition of her servitude to Mr. and Mrs.
John Wheatley of Boston. Perhaps because of the
extensive citations of her achievement and her poetry by
both ardent supporters and opponents of racial slavery,
the Wheatley scholarship is rather extensive, although
her biographical facts are more highly refined than is the
criticism of her verse.

After 1770, Wheatley's own history, except for accounts
of her trip to London in 1773, her tragic marriage to
John Peters in 1778, and her untimely death in 1784,
has been the history of her publications, a history as
curious as her biography. In 1770, she published a
broadside in Boston called **"An Elegiac Poem, on the
Death of that Celebrated Divine, and eminent Servant of
Jesus Christ, the late Reverend, and pious George
Whitefield, Chaplain to the Right Honourable the Countess of Huntingdon."** The poem was published in the
Massachusetts Spy on October 11, 1770, and was
republished in 1770—once in Newport, four times again
in Boston, once in New York, and once in Philadelphia.
Wheatley's broadside was appended the following year
to Ebenezer Pemberton's *Heaven the Residence of
Saints.* As Julian Mason rightly concludes, the **"Elegiac
Poem"**'s "several reprintings gave Phillis her first fame
as a poet."

A recurrent suggestion has been that Wheatley remained
aloof from matters that were in any sense racial or, more
correctly, "positively" racial. Although much of the
misreading of Wheatley must certainly arise from a

blatant unfamiliarity with the conventions of neoclassical verse as well as with the various forms of the elegy she used, there is another reason why Wheatley's verse has suffered sophisticated critical neglect. As William H. Robinson demonstrates rather passionately, there exists no edition of her complete works; further, "until 1935 perhaps no more than 12 or 14 of Phillis's poems had been anthologized in excerpted and complete version," a remarkable statistic considering the extensive amount of criticism devoted to Wheatley since 1773. Although variants of her *Poems* have been reprinted frequently, they remain incomplete and inconsistent, as in the reprinting of her signature piece, **"On the Death of the Rev. Mr. George Whitefield,"** in the 1770 Boston broadside and in the 1773 American edition of the *Poems*. The 1770 broadside contains sixty-two lines. Another broadside version, likely published in London in 1771, contains sixty-four lines, including the otherwise deleted word "free" in reference to the relationships between the "Impartial Saviour" and "ye Africans":

> Take him, ye Wretched, for your only Good;
> Take him, ye hungry Souls, to be your Food;
> Take him, ye Thristy, for your cooling Stream;
> Ye Preachers, take him for your joyful Theme;
> Take him, my dear *Americans,* he said,
> Be your Complaints in his kind Bosom laid;
> Take him, ye Africans, he longs for you,
> Impartial Saviour is his Title due.
> If you will walk in Grace's heavenly Road,
> He'll make you free, and Kings, and Priests to
>   God.

In addition to errors of this sort, in the sixty published poems and twenty-two extant letters there exist a number of apparently overlooked poems and letters in which Wheatley discusses the horrors of racial slavery and reveals, to a surprising degree, the quality of concern she felt for Africans, which certainly cannot be said to be diminished by her affiliation to the idea of Christian beneficence and, always for Wheatley, its concomitant "way of true felicity." These poems include **"To the University of Cambridge, in New England"** (1767), **"America"** (1768-70), and especially **"To Maecenas,"** the first title in her *Poems*. Here Wheatley queries the Muse about the relation of the poet and poetry to "Afric's sable race":

> Not you, my Friend, these plaintive strains be-
>   come,
> Not you, whose bosom is the *Muses* home;
> When they from Tow'ring *Helicon* retire,
> They fan in you the bright immortal fire,
> But less happy, cannot raise the song,
> The fault-ring music dies upon my tongue.
> The happier Terence all the *choir* inspir'd,
> His soul replenished, and his bosom fir'd;
> But say, ye Muses, why this partial grace,
> To one alone of *Afric's* sable race;
> From age to age transmitting thus his name
> With the first glory in the rolls of fame?

Similarly, her **"Reply"** to an anonymous response ("The Answer") to Wheatley's poem, **"To a Gentleman in the Navy,"** demonstrates an uncommon amount of emotion in her "Afric's blissful plain":

> In fair description are thy powers displayed
> In artless grottos, and the sylvan shade;
> Charm'd with thy painting, how my bosom burns!
> And pleasing Gambia on my soul returns,
> With native grace in spring's luxuriant reign,
> Smiles the gay mead, and Eden blooms again,
> The various bower, the tuneful flowing stream,
> The soft retreats, the lovers golden dream,
> Her soil spontaneous, yields exhaustless stores;
> For phoebus revels on her verdent shores.
> Whose flowery births, a fragrant train appears,
> And crown the youth throughout the smiling year,
>   There, as in Britain's favour'd isle, behold
> The bending harvest ripen into gold!
> Just are thy views of Afric's blissful plain,
> On the warm limits of the land and main.
>   Pleas'd with the theme, see sportive fancy play,
> In realms devoted to the God of day!

Phillis Wheatley shared her antislavery sentiment in a compelling letter to Samuel Occom, the famous Mohegan Indian Presbyterian preacher, who that same year published *A Choice Collection of Hymns and Spiritual Songs*. The letter was written to Occom in Boston on February 11, 1774, and published in *The Massachusetts Spy* on March 24, 1774; the *Boston Post Boy* on March 21, 1774; and the *Connecticut Journal* on April 1, 1774. A headnote from the editors attests that they "are desired to insert [the letter] as a Specimen of her Ingenuity." The letter is a subtle and controlled but passionate and eloquent address on the sheer evil of racial slavery:

> I have this day received your obliging kind Epistle, and am greatly satisfied with your Reasons respecting the Negroes, and think highly reasonable what you offer in Vindication of their Natural Rights: Those that invade them cannot be insensible that the divine Light is chasing away the thick Darkness which broods over the Land of Africa; and the Chaos which has reign'd so long, is converting into beautiful Order, and reveals more and more clearly, the glorious Dispensation of civil and religious Liberty, which are so inseparably united, that there is little or no Enjoyment of one without the other: Otherwise, perhaps the Israelites had been less solicitous for their Freedom from Egyptian Slavery; I don't say they would have been contented without it, by no means, for in every human Breast God has implanted a Principle, which we call the love of Freedom; it is impatient of Oppression, and pants for Deliverance; and by the Leave of our modern Egyptians I will assert that the same principle lives in us. God grant Deliverance in his own Way and Time, and get him honor upon all those whose Avarice impels them in countenance and help forward the Calamities of their fellow Creatures. This I desire not for their Hurt, but to convince them of the strange Absurdity of their Conduct whose Words and Actions are so diametrically opposite. How well the cry for Liberty, and the reverse Disposition for the exercise of oppressive Power over others agree,—I humbly think it does not require the Penetration of a Philosopher to determine.

For what reasonable being, Wheatley asks, could hold in mind any doubt that slavery is evil incarnate: the matter is as simple as that.

The letter to Occom and a few others, when considered with the poems in which Wheatley does address Africa or Africans, suggest strongly that the nature of Wheatley's poetry remains to be ascertained, as does her role in Afro-American literary history, and even her nonrole as a poet of "racial sentiment."

Imitating Pope in rhythm and meter, Wheatley wrote in deca-syllabic lines of closed heroic couplets. There is much use of invocation, hyperbole, and inflated ornamentation, and an overemphasis of personification, all of which characterize neoclassical poetry.

Seventeen, or one-third, of her extant poems are elegies, fourteen of which appeared in the first edition of *Poems on Various Subjects, Religious and Moral* and five of which have been revised from earlier published elegies. In one of the few close readings of Wheatley's verse, Gregory Rigsby demonstrates conclusively that her elegies are a creative variation of the "English Elegy" and the "Puritan Elegy." Wheatley's elegies are threnodic after the fashion of the "Renaissance Elegy," in that they are meant "to praise the subject, to lament the death, and to comfort the bereaved." Yet they are "Medieval" rather than "Elizabethan" insofar as they prefer a sublime resignation to an unrestrained death force, and seem to avoid the protest against it. The medieval resignation toward death, the function of the "Renaissance Elegy," and the form of the threnody as it developed in Elizabethan poetry were fused together in the "Puritan Funeral Elegy," a form peculiar to colonial America.

The Puritan funeral elegy, in turn, derived its specific shape and tone from the early American funeral sermon, based as it was on energetic exhortation. But, as Rigsby argues, Wheatley utilized the triple function of the Renaissance elegy within "her own elegiac structure and established more elaborate conventions." Rigsby then identifies these elements to be the underlying "structure of a Wheatley elegy": (1) the deceased in Heaven, (2) the deceased "winging" his way to Heaven, (3) an appreciation of the deceased's work on earth, (4) seraphic strains of heavenly bliss, (5) consolation of the living, (6) exhortation. The identification of the conventions of her elegies indicates that Wheatley was an imaginative artist to a degree largely unrecognized in critical literature. Although her remaining occasional verse lacks the irony, the contrast, and the balance of Pope's poetry, which she cited as her conscious model, her critical reception since the eighteenth century has failed in a remarkably consistent way to read her verse in comparison with the various literary traditions that she so obviously attempted to imitate and by which she just as obviously sought to measure herself. Curiously, all of her extant poems, except five, utilize the heroic couplet. Vernon Loggins traces, albeit vaguely, the influence of Milton in her hymns to morning and evening, as well as

in her poem to General Lee, as he does Gray's influence on her elegy to Whitefield and Addison and Watt's presence in **"Ode to Neptune"** and **"Hymn to Humanity"** [see excerpt dated 1931]. But these, again, are suggestions of influence rather than practical criticism.

As William Cairns recognized as early as 1912, the criticism of Wheatley's poetry has been a matter centered primarily around exactly what the existence of the poeisis faculty signifies about a far more problematical inquiry. Phillis Wheatley's verses, Cairns writes,

> are good conventional work in the forms then popular, devoid of originality, but really remarkable considering the history of the author. That they have been remembered is partly due, however, to the fact that in the days of the abolitionists they were often cited to prove the intellectual capability of the negro.

The peculiar history of Wheatley's reception by critics has, ironically enough, largely determined the theory of the criticism of the creative writings of Afro-Americans from the eighteenth century to the present time. (pp. 72-9)

> *Henry Louis Gates, Jr., "Phillis Wheatley and the Nature of the Negro," in* Figures in Black: Words, Signs, and the 'Racial' Self, *Oxford University Press, Inc., 1987, pp. 61-79.*

FURTHER READING

Bell, Bernard W. "African-American Writers." In *American Literature: The Revolutionary Years, 1764-1789,* edited by Everett Emerson, pp. 171-93. Madison: University of Wisconsin Press, 1977.

   Historical overview in which Bell attempts to delineate the social and political conditions that shaped Wheatley's life and works.

"Phillis Wheatley, the Negro Poetess." *The Catholic World* XXXIX, No. 232 (July 1884): 484-98.

   Biographical and critical overview.

Davis, Arthur P. "Personal Elements in the Poetry of Phillis Wheatley." *PHYLON* XIV, No. 2 (June 1953): 191-98.

   Counters arguments that Wheatley displayed no racial consciousness or personal sentiment in her poetry.

Koike, Sekio. "Phillis Wheatley: Her Place in American Slave Literature." *Kyushu American Literature,* No. 18 (October 1977): 33-9.

   Considers Wheatley a Christian of meek temperament who regarded freedom from sin and from slavery as one and the same.

Mason, Julian D., Jr. Introduction to *The Poems of Phillis Wheatley,* edited by Julian D. Mason, Jr., rev. ed., pp. 1-22. Chapel Hill: University of North Carolina Press, 1989.

Detailed overview of Wheatley's life and career.

Odell, Margaretta Matilda. *Memoir and Poems of Phillis Wheatley: A Native African and a Slave.* 3d ed. Boston: Issac Knapp, 1838, 155 p.
The earliest book-length study of Wheatley.

O'Neale, Sondra. "A Slave's Subtle War: Phillis Wheatley's Use of Biblical Myth and Symbol." *Early American Literature* XXI, No. 2 (Fall 1986): 144-65.
Explores Wheatley's use of biblical parables and symbols in her poems.

Rawley, James A. "The World of Phillis Wheatley." *The New England Quarterly* L, No. 4 (December 1977): 666-77.
Studies correspondence between Wheatley and her literary benefactors.

Richmond, M. A. "The Critics." In his *Bid the Vassal Soar: Interpretive Essays on the Life and Poetry of Phillis Wheatley (ca. 1753-1784) and George Moses Horton (ca. 1797-1883),* pp. 53-66. Washington, D.C.: Howard University Press, 1974.
Examines the style and vision of Wheatley's poetry and attacks the effect of slavery upon the poet's artistic development.

Rigsby, Gregory. "Form and Content in Phillis Wheatley's Elegies." *CLA Journal* XIX, No. 2 (December 1975): 248-57.
Asserts that Wheatley's elegies are distinctive from others of the same period. Rigsby notes that while Wheatley employed conventional elements in her poetry, her original usage gives her works "a stamp all her own."

Robinson, William H. *Phillis Wheatley in the Black American Beginnings.* Detroit: Broadside Press, 1975, 95 p.
Assessment of Wheatley's verse in terms of race, politics, and religion. In discussing Wheatley's life and works, Robinson attempts to dispel long-standing critical arguments that her poetry falls short as literature and that she lacked self-awareness as an African-American woman.

————, ed. *Critical Essays on Phillis Wheatley.* Boston: G. K. Hall and Co., 1982, 236 p.
Includes essays about Wheatley's life and career by such early and modern writers as Benjamin Franklin, Voltaire, and Henry Louis Gates, Jr.

Walter White

1893-1955

(Full name Walter Francis White) American essayist, novelist, nonfiction writer, and autobiographer.

As a novelist during the Harlem Renaissance, White has been credited with expanding the thematic boundaries open to black writers in the early twentieth century. His novels *The Fire in The Flint* (1924) and *Flight* (1926) provided revolutionary depictions of middle-class black Americans and the effects of racism on their lives. A distinguished and influential civil rights activist, White gained national attention during the 1920s as an investigator of lynching for the National Association for the Advancement of Colored People (NAACP). His knowledge of mob violence in the South and his recorded interviews with witnesses and participants form the basis of his 1929 study *Rope and Faggot: A Biography of Judge Lynch,* in which he analyzed the underlying causes of lynching. He also wrote numerous essays that document the successes and failures of the American civil rights movement over a thirty-five year period, from the early 1920s through the mid-1950s. Primarily of historical significance today, White's works stirred the social conscience of America in their time.

White was one of seven children born to an Atlanta, Georgia, letter carrier and his wife, a former school teacher. The blond, blue-eyed son of light-complected black parents, he observed early that the type of reception he received from strangers often depended on whether his racial identity was known. In 1906, when he was thirteen years old, Atlanta was the scene of week-long racial violence that White later identified as the single most important influence on his decision to fight for racial justice and equality. Instigated by rumors of white women attacked by black men, roaming mobs beat, tortured, and murdered black citizens at random. White witnessed several acts of violence first hand while accompanying his father on his mail route. When his family was threatened, White and his father stood ready with firearms, but the rioters were scattered by gunfire from another house moments before they would have rampaged into the Whites' front yard.

After graduating from Atlanta Preparatory School, White attended Atlanta University, where he began working with the newly organized local chapter of the NAACP. In 1918 he was offered the job of assistant to the secretary at the association's national headquarters in New York. White accepted the position and was almost immediately chosen to investigate mob violence in the South, where his fair skin and youthful zeal made his impersonation of a Northern newspaper reporter believable. Most of the participants in and witnesses to mob violence whom White interviewed were eager to recount the crimes in vivid detail. Among those interviewed were public officials and community leaders

who openly confessed their participation without fear of legal redress. White himself was deputized in Tulsa, Oklahoma, and told that he could kill any black person he chose. His essays on these investigations established a notoriety for White that soon made it impossible for his undercover activities to continue. However, his reputation as a champion of civil rights persisted as victims and concerned citizens from around the country sent pleas for help to the NAACP.

In 1929 White published *Rope and Faggot,* the result of two years of work in France on a Guggenheim Fellowship. This rigorous history of lynching in America was embellished with statistical tables correlating racial crimes to locale, population, religion, economy, and other factors. While most critics acknowledge the value of this study, many of the methods and conclusions have been questioned. Specifically, the sections that link racial violence to religious beliefs and the chapter "Nordicism, Science and Religion," which discusses and refutes many old and previously exploded pseudoscientific theories of racial superiority and inferiority, have been charged with threatening the credibility of *Rope and Faggot* as a work of serious research. Such commentators as H. L. Mencken and Clarence Darrow, however, cited these correlations as crucial to understanding and resolving the problem of mob rule. Notable in the criticism of *Rope and Faggot* are the critics' personal confessions of guilt and shame over the American people's acquiescence to lynching.

After the publication of *Rope and Faggot* and his return from France, White continued to work with the NAACP, and in 1931 he was elected to succeed James Weldon Johnson as the organization's national secretary. The same year White's father was struck by a car and later died in an Atlanta hospital, where he had been removed from the emergency room to the understaffed and poorly equipped section for black patients. Years later White admitted that this was the one experience of his life that inspired lasting bitterness. By now an influential lobbyist in Washington, he stepped up efforts to secure passage of federal anti-lynching legislation and fought for equality in housing, education, and other areas. White's influence reached the White House, where he worked directly with presidents Franklin Roosevelt and Harry Truman. White was instrumental in bringing about the passage of the Gavagan anti-lynching bill and in blocking the appointment of segregationist John J. Parker to the United States Supreme Court during the 1930s. In 1939, after noted contralto Marion Anderson was denied permission by the Daughters of the American Revolution to perform in the 4,000-seat Constitution Hall in Washington, White arranged an open-air concert for her at the Lincoln Memorial—an event that attracted an audience of 75,000. White also worked hard on behalf of young writers, using his personal connections to bring the work of Nella Larsen, Countee Cullen, Langston Hughes, and others to the attention of publishers and editors.

During World War II White traveled in Europe as a reporter for the *New York Post*. While oversees he witnessed the officially sanctioned racism of the American armed forces as well as the European reaction to American racist myths. This experience led to the collection *A Rising Wind: A Report on the Negro Soldier in the European Theater of War* (1945), essays that examine the worldwide implications of such policies. Critics generally regard the work as painfully enlightening and consider the parallel drawn between American racism and imperialist domination throughout the Third World intriguing, especially in light of White's suggestion that communism might prove an attractive alternative to the present political system for black Americans. White's work in this area, along with his struggle to bring about the deployment of black soldiers in combat areas, led to experimental integration in the armed forces. His final works, *A Man Called White: The Autobiography of Walter White* (1948) and *How Far the Promised Land?* (1955) provide a record of his work with the NAACP and the organization's overall influence on racial policies in America during the first half of the twentieth century. Contemporary critics regarded the optimistic tone of the works, in the face of the facts they contain, as a remarkable statement about White himself, who modestly downplayed his role in effecting the changes he recorded. Shortly before *How Far the Promised Land?* was published, White died in New York of a heart attack at the age of sixty-one.

In addition to his nonfiction, White published two novels. The first, *The Fire in the Flint,* reflects White's extensive research into lynching. The protagonist of this story, Dr. Kenneth Harper, is a Northern-educated black Atlantan who returns home to practice medicine and attempts to rise above prejudice through an optimistic faith in the power of reason. Gradually he is forced to abandon his nonconfrontational attitude and face the brutal realities of blind racism, and in the end he is lynched by a bloodthirsty mob after saving the life of a white child. The story, told from a middle-class black man's point of view, is a deliberate attempt to counter the romantic depictions of white Southerners made popular in the early decades of the twentieth century. Although the characterizations and prose style of *The Fire in the Flint* came under attack as stilted, archaic, and marred by clichés that detract from the overall reality of the story, the novel is considered an accurate presentation of lynching and its attendant horrors. Infused with White's personal knowledge of the subject, the work nonetheless avoids dwelling on lurid details, unlike much of the socially conscious fiction written by American realists during the 1920s. Instead, graphic realism is achieved through a detailed examination of the physical, psychological, and economic effects of racism on whites and blacks alike. For example, aristocratic landowners who perpetuate racial antagonism in order to maintain the status quo are contrasted with liberal, white Southerners who legitimately fear opposing the majority. The South's double-standard of justice, portrayed throughout the novel, is illustrated most effectively by the novel's pessimistic ending, in which a quotation from a newspaper report dismisses Harper as a common hoodlum slain during the commission of a crime. This was one of the strongest indictments of Southern justice and morality in American fiction to that time. Most critics agree that despite the novel's heavy-handed propaganda, *The Fire in the Flint* is a compelling tragedy.

White's second novel, *Flight,* addresses the phenomenon of light-complected blacks "passing" as Caucasians. The story follows the life of Mimi, a New Orleans-born Creole who crosses the invisible racial boundary into mainstream white America. However, the novel breaks from the tradition of previous novels about passing, most of which depict a mulatto, envious of white society, attempting to blend in with that world. Rather, Mimi's decision to pass results from the sense of shame and disgrace she feels among black people who know about her illegitimate son. Many critics argued that White failed to achieve his major intention in the novel: to show the differences between black and white society. Other critics contended that White ignored an opportunity to divulge the unique psychological depths of Mimi and the other black characters in the novel. Only the early sections of the book, in which social stratification and prejudice among blacks in New Orleans and Atlanta come under scrutiny, are considered realistic and informative. Summing up the work's balance of success and failure, one critic noted that while everything that happens to Mimi rings true, she never comes to life as a character, and White's thesis—though based in fact—is not believably rendered.

Although his novels are little known today, White is remembered for his work as a political activist during some of the NAACP's most powerful years. One of the few black men in America of his time who had the ear of publishers, politicians, and world leaders alike, he used these associations to advance equality for blacks in the United States and throughout the world.

(For further information about White's life and works, see *Black Writers; Contemporary Authors,* Vols. 115, 124; *Dictionary of Literary Biography,* Vol. 51: *Afro-American Writers from the Harlem Renaissance to 1940;* and *Twentieth-Century Literary Criticism,* Vol. 15.)

PRINCIPAL WORKS

The Fire in the Flint (novel) 1924
Flight (novel) 1926
Rope and Faggot: A Biography of Judge Lynch (nonfiction) 1929
What Caused the Detroit Riot? [with Thurgood Marshall] (essay) 1943
A Rising Wind: A Report on the Negro Soldier in the European Theater of War (nonfiction) 1945
A Man Called White: The Autobiography of Walter White (autobiography) 1948
How Far the Promised Land? (nonfiction) 1955

Freda Kirchwey (essay date 1924)

[*In the following excerpt, Kirchwey praises the realism of* The Fire in the Flint, *arguing that the book is "warped by neither sentiment nor venom."*]

Other novels have been written about race relations in the South—novels overflowing with bitter venom and prejudice, sentimental novels, novels attempting an honest picture of a tangled, sordid scene. Novels better than [*The Fire in the Flint*] if you are looking for grace or subtlety, or depth or fire. And yet this novel is worth more than the best of the others I have read. Quite simply, in prosaic, often commonplace, phrasing, without lift or loveliness or sharp individuality, it manages to make a civilization live.

Walter F. White, Georgian and negro by birth, investigator and writer by profession, has put upon paper a problem that is in his own bone and fiber. He has taken back to a small Georgia town a young man who might have been himself, tolerant, educated, civilized and wise beyond his colored neighbors, and far beyond the majority of the white population. Kenneth Harper is a physician, and a good one. He is intelligent enough to feel superior to white intolerance, and to the growing resentment among his colored fellow-townsmen; he is intelligent enough to understand and smile and try to make life swing his way by the exercise of ability and good will.

And it does not work. To the uttermost limits of hate and blood and flame and torture, it wholly fails. Kenneth himself, almost fails. He finds himself pulled down by the horror of his sister's rape and his brother's death to a raging lust for vengeance. But he struggles up—up to a love of self-control and skill, on which he saves the life of a white girl, only to lose his own in the end at the hands of the same laughing, blood-crazy mob that killed his brother. His doctrine of amicable philosophic tolerance ends in a bewildering give and take of death.

The story is painful to a degree, and it is painful not primarily because it is tragic or bloody, but because Walter White knows so well what he is talking about. No one reading the book with any detachment could find it in him to doubt this picture of the economic and spiritual rottenness in the State of Georgia—where the negro farm worker is cheated of his poor earnings by the "land croppers" and the negro town dweller is driven to a state of sullen, dangerous resentment, and the ignorant white man through his Klan and his sheriffs and his courts, dominates the life of both races. The author does full justice to the plight of the intelligent white man, who wants to be "decent," as he does to that of the self-respecting negro who wants to be "good." Neither one is free to act; both are held by the solid mold of the life around them to helpless misery or futile opposition.

When white intolerance and ignorance and blood-lust finally come face to face with their natural offspring of black resentment and ignorance and pugnacity—what will be the end? Mr. White does not attempt to prophesy. The only reason for hope seems to lie in the steady migration northward of the more vigorous and ambitious negroes, who, like all oppressed peoples, seek a place to live and bring up their children in security and freedom . . . .

This note of hope is struck lightly. It is evident that no clear way out has shown itself to this writer. He is solidly, reasonably pessimistic. If a solution for the negro were to be found in hate and violent resistance, Kenneth's brother might have lived after avenging, so swiftly and terribly, the assault upon his sister. If friendly, self-respecting modesty on the part of the negro were to be his salvation, certainly Kenneth need not have been lynched. Both methods were tried with equal unsuccess by persons in the story, and, we may suppose they would equally fail if applied on a large and real scale....

Walter White has written a book that lives and breathes by the terrible truth and reality of its substance. He has not made his way to the inner soul of his characters; he is not even their intimate friend. Nor has he painted the surface of their lives with the rich detail needed to make its straggling pattern clear before our eyes. He does not make ideas flame into drama; he achieves clarity rather than vision. But he writes from complete knowledge of a subject that is itself so full of force and feeling that it tells its own story. It hardly needs the helping hand of art or propaganda; it demands only direct and honest handling. A subject like this can properly be left to do its own exploding, work its own havoc. For the first time it has been allowed to stand out sharply, warped by neither sentiment nor venom, and declares its significance to the world.

> Freda Kirchwey, "What Is the Solution?," in
> New York Herald Tribune Books, *September 28, 1924, p. 5*

W. E. B. Du Bois (essay date 1924)

[*Du Bois was at the vanguard of the civil rights movement in America. He was a founder of the National Association for the Advancement of Colored People (NAACP) and edited that organization's periodical the* Crisis *from 1910 to 1934. Considered the "dean" of the authors whose works initiated the Harlem Renaissance in the 1920s, he deplored the movement in black literature toward exploiting sordid aspects of black American culture, believing that the duty of the black writer was to depict exemplary characters who would counterbalance past stereotypes. In the following excerpt from a review that originally appeared in the* Crisis *in 1924, he notes that despite serious artistic problems,* The Fire in the Flint *is a compelling work.*]

Walter White has written in **The Fire in the Flint** a good, stirring story and a strong bit of propaganda against the white Klansman and the black pussyfoot. White knows his Georgia from A to Z. There is not a single incident or a single character in the book which has not its prototype in real life today. All Mr. White's white people are not villains nor are all his Negroes saints, but one gets a thrilling sense of the devilish tangle that involves good and evil in the southern South.

Perhaps most significant however is the fact that a book like this can at last be printed. For years a flood of filth about the Negro has poured out of the South while no northern firm would consider a book telling even temperately the well-known and widely proven facts concerning the Negro. Subtly and slowly the change has come and Mr. White has been among the first to sense it and to persist courageously and doggedly in having his say.

Of course one can criticise any book and particularly a first one. Perhaps on the economic side Mr. White succumbs too easily to the common mistake of piling the blame of southern wickedness on the "poor whites" and absolving the aristocrats and former slave holders. This is, of course, based on the propaganda which the sons and daughters of slave-barons have spread, but it is far from true. On the human and artistic side, with the possible exception of the younger brother, Mr. White's characters do not live and breathe and compel our sympathy. They are more like labeled figures on a chess board. But despite all this, this story goes and the reader goes with it and that is the first business of a story. (pp. 71-2)

> W. E. B. Du Bois, in a review of "The Fire in
> the Flint," in his Collected Published Works
> of W. E. B. Du Bois: Book Reviews, *edited
> by Herbert Aptheker, KTO Press, 1977, pp.
> 71-2.*

Carl Van Vechten (essay date 1926)

[*Van Vechten was one of the first white authors to take a serious and active role in studying and promoting the works of black writers, musicians, and artists. His most famous work is* Nigger Heaven *(1926), a novel set in Harlem. Praised by critics as realistic and exotic, the work helped spark interest in black culture among many white Americans. The black press, however, considered the work offensive and derogatory. W. E. B. Du Bois, notable among the novel's detractors, charged Van Vechten with insinuating himself into Harlem for exploitive purposes and with presenting a one-sided picture of the community. White had introduced Van Vechten to Harlem society and had used his influence to secure advertising space for Van Vechten in initially reluctant black publications. In the following excerpt, Van Vechten commends White for presenting a believable black heroine in* Flight *and compares Mimi to the protagonists in Ellen Glasgow's works.*]

Mr. White's first novel, **The Fire in the Flint,**...was immediately and widely hailed as a work of grim power. Dealing as it does with peonage, rape and lynching in Georgia, certain of its scenes are executed with a force sufficiently elemental to efface the memory of some amateurish writing in other passages.

It is a pleasure to be able to state that Mr. White's second novel [**Flight**] is much better than his first. It is written with a calm detachment of which **The Fire in the Flint** contains no hint. Furthermore, in Mimi Daquin, a Negro Creole girl with ivory skin and hair of reddish gold, the author has drawn a character entirely new to Afro-American fiction. Instead of the persecuted figure with which books on this general subject have made us so familiar, we are presented with a heroine who is mistress of her own fate, a woman whose ultimate acts are governed by her will. Mimi does not long permit herself to be hampered by the restrictions of Negro life and she is equally independent in her relations with the two men who play important parts in her career. She refuses to marry the father of her child; later, she leaves her white husband to return to the heart of her own race.

The subject of passing (i.e., passing for white) has infrequently been utilized by Negro authors. Charles W. Chesnutt dwelt on its tragic aspects in *The House Behind the Cedars* (1902) and James Weldon Johnson contributed a more suave study of the theme in that human document, *The Autobiography of an ex-Colored Man* (1912)....

This, then, is the distinguishing merit of this novel, that it focuses attention upon a Negro character who is not materially hindered in her career by white prejudice. It is the simple chronicle of a beautiful, intelligent, dignified, self-supporting Negro girl. There is, indeed, a curious resemblance between Mimi and the self-reliant heroines of Miss Ellen Glasgow....

Mr. White approaches the subject from a new and sufficiently sensational point of view. Mimi Daquin does not leave the colored world because she has been insulted or humiliated by white people; she leaves it because of her momentary dissatisfaction with Negroes....

The incidental Negro characters are in nowise depicted as paragons of propriety and good taste. In fact, occasionally the author deals with them even a little cruelly. The petty gossip, the small meannesses, the color snobbery of Negro society... are fully described, but Mr. White makes it plain that in these respects there is little to choose between the two worlds.

In short, an excellent novel which should be read with increasing wonder by those who are unfamiliar with the less sordid circles of Negro life, and which others may read simply as a story without thought of propaganda. Indeed, with this second book Mr. White takes on quite a new stature.

> *Carl Van Vechten, "A Triumphant Negro Heroine," in* New York Herald Tribune Books, *April 11, 1926, p. 3.*

H. L. Mencken (essay date 1929)

[*Mencken was one of the most influential figures in twentieth-century American letters. His strongly individualistic, irreverent outlook on life and vigorous, invective-charged writing style helped establish the iconoclastic spirit of the Jazz Age. As a social and literary critic—the role for which he is best known—he was the scourge of evangelical Christianity, public service organizations, literary censorship, and provincialism. As the editor of the* American Mercury *magazine and through his personal friendship with publisher Alfred A. Knopf, Mencken provided a forum for young black writers, whose works he critiqued with the same uncondescending standards by which he judged all literature. Black writers from James Weldon Johnson to Richard Wright have acknowledged*

Mencken's influence on the development of their personal literary standards. In the following excerpt, Mencken appraises White's study Rope and Faggot, *describing the purported relationship between religious practices and racial violence in the rural South.*]

It pleases Mr. White, who is a man of somewhat bitter humor, to call himself an Aframerican; he is actually almost as albino as his name, with sandy hair and china blue eyes.... [The] National Association for the Advancement of Colored People has sent him into the South to investigate lynchings.... The result of his vast experience in the Bible country, born of this unique equipment, is that he knows more about lynching than anyone else in America. He has inquired into all sorts of communal butcheries, from the simple hanging of a village bad man to the appallingly barbarous disemboweling, torture and burning of a woman with child, and at the same time he has made shrewd examination of the social background and mental equipment of the lynchers. His book [*Rope & Faggot*], in consequence, is a mine of valuable information, set forth plausibly and without too much indignation. There are unspeakable horrors in it, but he does not dwell upon them unduly. His main business is not to describe lynching, but to describe lynchers.

It will surprise no one who knows the South, I take it, to hear from him that the incidence of lynching runs in almost direct proportion to the percentage of Methodists and Baptists in the population. The reason is not far to seek. The two great evangelical faiths, down in that country, are little more than schemes of organized hatred. Their theology has been reduced to the simple doctrine that the other fellow is a scoundrel and will go to hell. (p. 382)

Other factors, to be sure, enter into the matter: among them, density of population and wealth *per capita*. The rich and heavily populated States, such as North Carolina, tend to abandon lynching. They have relatively efficient police, and their more numerous towns give them something of the city point of view....

The automobile, bringing in better roads, has also brought in a kind of civilization. Movie shows take the peasants away from the village store, and its political and theological disputations. Some of them, putting in radios, begin to defy the pastors by dancing. The revival business is not what it used to be. But in the backwaters, despite these signs of change, religion remains the chief concern of the hinds, and it is religion of a peculiarly unenlightened and degrading kind.... So long as it dominates the minds of the Southern poor whites they will remain barbarians, and so long as they are barbarians they will turn out ever and anon to butcher and barbecue a hapless darkey. The civilized Southerners waste their time combating, not the underlying disease, but superficial symptoms. If they would release the South from its bondage to ignorance and superstition, they must first destroy the simian theocracy that keeps it shackled. There is no other way out. (p. 383)

H. L. Mencken, "Sport in the Bible Country," in American Mercury, Vol. XVII, No. 67, July, 1929, pp. 382-83.

Francis Hackett (essay date 1945)

[*In the following excerpt from a review first published in 1945, Hackett positively appraises* A Rising Wind.]

A short book on an inescapable theme is often the best, and Walter White has served his cause by being terse in *A Rising Wind.* The second half of it, partly a high and glowing account of Eboué, the Negro Frenchman who saved Chad for the United Nations, branches away from the main theme, but the first half of it probes directly and tellingly into dark places. It makes the book important, not simply because Mr. White speaks as secretary of the National Association for the Advancement of Colored People, but because he is possessed by one of those mastering passions to which no wise American can refuse heed and no good citizen refuse sympathy. (p. 186)

Mr. White went overseas to look into the war and to see how the Negro soldier was getting on, but he could not have supposed that an English family would be providing cushions for Negro visitors, having heard from white soldiers that Negro tails were awkward. Mr. White tells of this. He also tells of a town in England that was led to believe that Negroes could bark but not talk. At first the Negro soldiers resented the legend, but their good humor got the better of them. They began by barking softly. The English caught on. They were soon barking back, and the joke was on the white men who started it.

These are gargoyles of race hatred. Mr. White found it had also been given official sanction, not at the top but through the Army. There were "off limits" rules on the basis of race. Red Cross segregation in clubs, not in hospitals, aroused Mr. White's scorn. He quotes a fantastic document telling the British about Negro infantility, issued by a Southern commanding officer. Then there were false charges of rape and specific injustices. And in Italy there were malignant circulars and posters.

It is impossible to read *A Rising Wind* without being moved to indignation. Mr. White does it by exhibiting these blind ignorances, these humiliating examples of prejudice off the limits. Much worse is it to hear of Negro combat troops willfully deprived of combat service. Knowing how white fliers felt about their Negro fellows who won proud laurels in combat, it seems atrocious that American citizens should, because of color, have "to fight for the right to fight." (pp. 186-87)

[Grimness] is not disguised; Mr. White does not hesitate to close his book with a menace, and the menace is Russia. Unless the western powers revolutionize their racial concepts and practices, he says, a World War III must be prepared for, and the colored peoples every-

where may "move into the Russian orbit as the lesser of two dangers." (p. 187)

A Rising Wind is a manifesto of this, and much that Mr. White saw of the Negro's status in World War II supports him. "World War II," he says, "has immeasurably magnified the Negro's awareness of the disparity between the American profession and practice of democracy." . . .

[One] telling though small instance of American idealism came in Devon when Mrs. Leonard Elmhirst (Dorothy Whitney) refused to comply with white officers who demanded that guests' cards be rescinded from Negro trainees invited to a dance. In specific instances, too, General Eisenhower impartially reviewed and corrected injustices. (p. 188)

A Rising Wind is based on substantial reality. In this war there are six times as many Negro officers as in the last, but there are only six thousand. The barriers to military service have only been slightly lifted. Granted that woman suffrage had to fight deep prejudice quite recently, as Mr. White knows, he still has a powerful case, and he presents it honestly and unflinchingly. Without a World War III, the pride of the Negro can be respected on American lines, but Mr. White does well to tell America that Russian race ideology is in the world to stay. Russia guarantees race status. That is a new factor. It is just as big and broad and inescapable as the Mississippi. (pp. 188-89)

Francis Hackett, "Affairs in General: Race Idealogy, U.S.A.," in his On Judging Books: In General and in Particular, *The John Day Company,* 1947, pp. 186-89.

Hugh M. Gloster (essay date 1948)

[*In the following excerpt from his* Negro Voices in American Fiction, *Gloster examines a selection of White's best-known works.*]

Jessie Fauset, Walter White, and Nella Larsen present well-bred, educated, aspiring Negroes who belong mainly to the professional class of the urban North. Among these people economic security and high social standing are in evidence; and within their group, except for minor variations caused by color, they live very much like other respectable middle-class Americans. Attention is focused principally upon attractive and personable mulatto heroines who yearn to "drink life to the lees" but find it difficult to do so because of racial restrictions. When fair enough in color, these women sometimes seek happiness through escape into the white world; but, after the initial thrills of passing are over, they usually long for colored society and come to believe that Negro life, though circumscribed by prejudice and persecution, is not altogether without spiritual and cultural compensations. This point of view, by the way, stands in bold contrast to that expressed in such novels as Vara Caspary's *White Girl* (1929) and Geoffrey

Barnes's *Dark Lustre* (1932), in which passing heroines, whose refinement is attributed to Nordic and whose animalism to African extraction, cross the color line because of admiration for white and abhorrence for black people but experience misery because of the "taint" of Negro blood. (p. 131)

In addition to treating the problem of passing in the urban North, Walter White's *Flight* . . . provides a study of the colored bourgeoisie of Atlanta, Georgia. (p. 139)

Flight affords a vivid commentary on Babbittry and life among Negroes of Atlanta. Through Robertson, Mimi's stepgrandparent, White satirizes Negroes who are preoccupied with the acquisition of wealth. Atlanta's social elite—placing emphasis on light pigmentation and outspoken in their dislike for Catholics, Jews, and black Negroes—are described as "victims of a system which made colour and hair texture and race a fetish." Gossip, slander, bickerings, jealousies, and sartorial competition are listed as the chief activities of bourgeois colored women. The author finds solid worth and genuine strength, however, among poor Negroes who, though deprived and mistreated, can nevertheless sing, laugh, have faith, and find enjoyment in an industrial civilization which often makes the dominant white man unhappy, morbid, and depressed. . . . [The] power to resist and endure is attributed largely to Negroes' "rare gift of lifting themselves emotionally and spiritually far, far above their material lives and selves." (pp. 139-40)

Between 1918 and 1928 White . . . probed forty-one lynchings and eight race riots. In 1924 he produced *The Fire in the Flint,* one of the most successful exposés of lynching in American fiction; and in 1929, assisted by a Guggenheim fellowship, he wrote *Rope and Faggot: A Biography of Judge Lynch,* a penetrating analysis of the causes, functioning, and cures of mob violence.

The Fire in the Flint, in which White uses fiction as the medium for his attack on lynching and the Southern small town, is chiefly the story of Kenneth Harper, a young Negro physician trained in the best universities of America and France. After World War I, Harper returns to Central City, Georgia, where his family resides, to practise medicine . . . . (pp. 147-48)

White's description of Central City is an authentic portrait of a half-rural, half-urban Georgia town. The various sections of the place—the dusty trading district, the respectable residential area, the squalid and filthy Negro ghetto, and the equally dingy and unsanitary cotton mill vicinity in which tubercular and cadaverous poor whites dwell—are convincingly pictured. In this warped environment learning and culture are decadent and effete, but the noxious growth of race prejudice thrives and prospers. Selfish, hypocritical demagogues separate Negroes and poor whites by keeping alive in the latter group a confidence in their own natural superiority and a belief that their safety rests in the subjugation of black people. In every possible way Negroes are made to feel that they are predestined to a subordinate status. They have neither legal redress nor police protection. In business dealings they are the victims of thievery and chicanery. They accept dilapidated schools and underpaid teachers and tolerate the abduction of their women and the lynching of their men. To survive in this Jim-Crow environment they practise dissimulation, evasion, and secretiveness and seek an outlet for their pent-up feelings in emotional religion. Ready to terrorize and punish the black population for infractions of the Southern code, the Ku Klux Klan, having members from all classes of white society, stands dedicated to the maintenance of Nordic supremacy and the perpetuation of the *status quo* . . . . The author describes liberal and sympathetic white Southerners as men "hemmed in, oppressed, afraid to call their souls their own, creatures of the Frankenstein monster their own people had created which seemed about to rise up and destroy its creators." (pp. 148-49)

In training, experience, and racial philosophy Kenneth Harper is similar to his probable archetype, Dr. William Miller of Chesnutt's *The Marrow of Tradition* (1901). Both are products of the best Northern and European schools, both turn their backs on practising above the Mason-Dixon Line in order to devote their efforts to the improvement of the health of the colored people of the South, and both—in spite of all evidence and counsel to the contrary—are optimistic regarding a peaceful settlement of racial difficulties. Much like Miller's are Harper's conciliatory and accommodating views on the Negro's plight . . . . Just as Miller, after the slaying of his son in a riot, ministers to the pressing needs of a sick white boy, so Harper, after the loss of his sister and brother, comes to the rescue of a very ill white girl and thus sets the stage for his own destruction. Before his death, however, he reaches the same bitter and rebellious position which Miller finally attains.

Standing in bold contrast to his philosophical and phlegmatic brother, Bob Harper represents Negro combativeness at its zenith. Sensitive and perspicacious, he broods over prejudice and is easily stirred to resentment and anger. (pp. 149-50)

More than any other novel of the Negro Renascence, *Fire in the Flint* probes the precarious position of Negroes in a small Southern town. As a living argument against prejudice and brutality, the author presents a refined, intelligent, and prosperous family that suffers insults, injuries, and deaths because of superficial distinctions based on color and caste. The difficulties of the Negro professional man are set forth, and attention is called to his troubles with dominant whites as well as with Negroes whose slavery-conditioned minds make them reluctant to trust trained members of their own race. Also revealed is the success of the Southern ruling class in pitting poor whites against Negroes by nurturing concepts of Nordic superiority. (pp. 150-51)

> *Hugh M. Gloster, "Fiction of the Negro Renascence," in his* Negro Voices in American Fiction, *The University of North Carolina Press, 1948, pp. 116-95.*

Ralph J. Bunche (essay date 1955)

[*Bunche was a distinguished American educator and diplomat who won international renown for his work as the United Nations Mediator in Palestine during the late 1940s. For his role in negotiating the 1949 Arab-Israeli truce he was awarded the Spingarn Medal by the NAACP and the Nobel Peace Prize. In the following excerpt from his foreword to White's* How Far the Promised Land? *he offers high praise for White's character and for his work in the field of interracial reconciliation.*]

I was privileged over a long period to enjoy Walter White's friendship. I admired him highly and developed a deep affection for him. One so seldom meets a truly dedicated person, and when such a one is also keenly intelligent, vibrant, engaging, and warmly human—and this was Walter White—his going leaves a sorrowful void.

In this book [*How Far the Promised Land?*] are his last thoughts and written words on the progress of the Negro toward full equality in the American society. They are straightforward words which are vital and commanding for everyone who believes in democracy and freedom and the dignity of the individual man. They are the words of a man whose life, in fuller measure than that of any I have known, was devoted to making American democracy a complete and equal reality for the black as well as the white citizen. And, characteristically, they are words of utter frankness and full integrity, and also of hope.

He gave to this book a title in the form of a question: *How Far the Promised Land?*—how far off is the day when the American citizen of Negro descent will walk beside his white fellow citizen in full equality? Thanks to Walter White's vision, his leadership, and his un-flinching devotion for more than three decades, the answer today comes unmistakably clear: "It cannot be far." For he brought the Negro close to the border of that land—perhaps even closer than he himself realized. Moreover, the good fight led by him will be carried on relentlessly by his surviving associates in the National Association for the Advancement of Colored People, which continues to grow in strength and prestige throughout the country, due to a steadily expanding body of sympathizers and supporters of all races and creeds who realize that democracy to be true must be color-blind. The basic element in Walter's faith in our country, in the American way of life, and in the inevitable achievement of full citizenship by the Negro was the conviction—and I believe it was soundly based—that the vast majority of Americans really believe in that democracy whose principles we profess and can therefore be arrayed against practices of racial injustice. His task it was—and he performed it well through the NAACP and the media of mass communication—to arouse the American conscience to the crude and costly injustice in the treatment of its minority-group citizens, and to mobilize sentiment behind the elimination of all undemocratic practices and attitudes. (pp. ix-x)

This is dynamic history written by a man who was one of the most dynamic figures of our times. We do not go backward, we do not stand still, he said; American democracy moves forward. There is an ever-stronger current of democracy which eventually will carry *all* Americans into the "Promised Land." He left behind him the reasoned hope that Lincoln's work of emancipation, in its major aspects, can actually be completed by 1963—the centennial of Lincoln's signing of the Emancipation Proclamation. (p. xi)

> *Ralph J. Bunche, in a foreward to* How Far the Promised Land? *by Walter White, The Viking Press, 1955, pp. ix-xii.*

Robert Bone (essay date 1965)

[*Bone is best known for two critical histories of black American literature:* The Negro in America *(1958; rev. ed., 1965) and* Down Home: A History of Afro-American Short Fiction from Its Beginning to the End of the Harlem Renaissance *(1975). In the following excerpt from the first-named work, he examines the relationship of White's novels to the Harlem Renaissance.*]

The storm of controversy which greeted the Harlem School in the mid-1920's marks the beginning of a growing breach between the Negro writer and the Negro middle class. The early Negro novelist, insulated from the impact of modern literature by a culture lag, was firmly integrated into the social class which produced him. With the advent of the Harlem school, however, the Negro novelist begins to develop that sense of alienation from bourgeois society which is the mark of the modern artist. (p. 96)

A distinguishing characteristic of this school is its fondness for the novel of "passing." Walter White's *Flight* . . . , Jessie Fauset's *Plum Bun* (1928), and Nella Larsen's *Passing* (1929), all deal in a similar vein with this exotic theme. Emphasis is placed on the problems which confront the person who passes: the fear of discovery, the anxious prospect of marriage, with its fear of throwback, and so forth. The invariable outcome, in fiction if not in fact, is disillusionment with life on the other side of the line, a new appreciation of racial values, and an irresistible longing to return to the Negro community. (p. 98)

At the present time it is no longer required of a Negro author that he enter political life, nor of a Negro political leader that he write novels. There was a time, however, before the present age of specialization, when a Negro intellectual of national stature was expected to double in brass. Only a few men of rare versatility such as James Weldon Johnson were equal to the challenge. Others, like Walter White and W.E.B. DuBois, were sometimes tempted into waters beyond their depth. Able political leaders and competent writers of expository prose, these men lacked the creative imagination which is the *sine qua non* of good fiction.

Walter White's first novel, *The Fire in the Flint* . . . , is an antilynching tract of melodramatic proportions. It was written in twelve days, according to White, and the novel itself provides no grounds for doubting his word. It is essentially a series of essays, strung on an unconvincing plot, involving the misfortunes of a colored doctor and his family in a small Southern town. White's second novel, *Flight* . . . , is an undistinguished treatment of passing, perhaps more susceptible to the influence of the Harlem School than most novels of the Rear Guard. Taken together, Walter White's novels comprise an object lesson in what Blyden Jackson has called "Faith without Works in Negro Literature." (pp. 99-100)

> *Robert Bone, "The Rear Guard," in his* The Negro Novel in America, *revised edition, Yale University Press, 1965, pp. 95-108.*

Edward E. Waldron (essay date 1978)

[*In the following excerpt from his critical study* Walter White and the Harlem Renaissance, *Waldron surveys White's career as a novelist.*]

In his autobiography White stated that his decision to write a novel about the true racial conditions in the South was a response to a challenge by H. L. Mencken. (p. 42)

The plot of *The Fire in the Flint* is relatively simple. Kenneth Harper, after being educated at Atlanta University and a "Northern medical school" and after serving in France during World War I, returns to his home town of Central City, Georgia, intent on becoming the best surgeon in southern Georgia; he even dreams of eventually opening a clinic "something like the Mayo Brothers up in Rochester, Minnesota." On his return he finds his younger brother Bob extremely pessimistic about the possibility of any cooperation from the whites. Kenneth believes, however, that if he leaves the white folks alone, they will leave him alone. In fact, at the beginning of the novel he voices his belief

White's parents, Madeline and George White.

that black people have to make it on their own individual initiative . . . . *Fire,* then, becomes a study of Kenneth Harper's gradual awakening to the realities of racism and the demands imposed upon the individual by an oppressed people.

Robert Bone's analysis of the novel as "a series of essays, strung on an unconvincing plot . . . " [see excerpt dated 1965] is perhaps too severe a judgment. True, the novel is episodic and melodramatic and frequently ranges into exposition, but there is a change in the central character, however belabored, and there is occasional insight into human nature. The Reverend Mr. Wilson, a black preacher, for example, startles Kenneth when his ordinarily crude speech becomes refined in private conversation. Chuckling, the older man explains a fact of southern black life to his young and racially naive neighbor:

> There's a reason—in fact there are two reasons why I talk like that [i.e., crudely]. The first is because of my own folks. Outside of you and your folks . . . and one or two more, all of my congregation is made up of folks with little or no education. They've all got good hard common sense . . . . But they don't want a preacher that's too far above them—they'll feel that they can't come to him with their troubles if he's too highfalutin. I try to get right down to my folks, feel as they feel, suffer when they suffer, laugh with them when they laugh, and talk with them in language they can understand . . . . And then there's the other reason . . . . The white folks here are mighty suspicious of any Negro who has too much learning, according to their standards. They figure he'll be stirring up the Negroes to fight back when any trouble arises . . . .

Here, in a character many white writers would present as a Bible-banging buffoon, White gives us an insight into the workings of the mind of a man who decided to mask his true capabilities in order to serve his people. And Kenneth Harper soon learns that the Reverend Mr. Wilson's statement about the suspicions white folks have of educated Negroes is accurate. (pp. 43-4)

[His] sister is raped by a gang of white toughs, and then Bob, after he succeeds in killing two of the boys who raped his sister, is hunted down and finally kills himself to prevent being taken by the mob . . . . When [Kenneth] . . . discovers what has happened, he goes into a tirade of hate against the white world which has all but destroyed his family . . . . (p. 44)

Mrs. Ewing, a white woman whose daughter Kenneth had saved earlier, calls . . . to ask Kenneth's help . . . . His first impulse is to tell her that "if by raising one finger I could save the whole white race from destruction, and by not raising it send them all straight to hell, I'd die before I raised it!" Eventually, though, his training as a doctor and Mrs. Ewing's revelation that her husband has gone to Atlanta to warn Kenneth not to return outweigh his bitterness, and he goes to the Ewings. Meanwhile, some Klansmen (including Sheriff Parker), who have been following Harper's every move, see him enter the house . . . . When Kenneth leaves, the men grab him and, after a fierce struggle, shoot him. The next day a news

dispatch headed "ANOTHER NEGRO LYNCHED IN GEORGIA" presents the "official" version of the incident . . . . Deciding to end the novel with [a] callous and obviously falsified news release was probably the most artistic stroke White accomplished in *The Fire in the Flint.* It serves as its own comment on the climactic events of the novel, and avoids the didacticism which is so characteristic of the rest of the novel.

In addition to the dominant protest against the evils of lynching, White also incorporated other minor themes of protest in *Fire.* A significant subplot is developed concerning the efforts of Kenneth Harper and some of the farmers to form a co-op from which the sharecroppers could buy their supplies at reasonable prices, instead of being gouged by the stores from which they are forced to buy . . . . Although the idea of a farmer's cooperative being used to alleviate the suffering of sharecroppers in what has been aptly termed "legalized slavery" is not new in White's novel, the merging of the protest motif with the larger antilynching theme underscores the economic factor in racial oppression that White felt was central to the problem.

The real strength of *The Fire in the Flint* lies, finally, in what it says, not in how well it says it. There are flaws in the story and, as Bone points out, there is too much exposition for narrative fiction. White's treatment of the love story involving Kenneth Harper and Jane Phillips is incredibly naive and more fitting a sentimental novel than a novel of protest. And the characters, with a few exceptions, are flatly drawn types. The Reverend Mr. Wilson is given some depth, but only after a rather stereotyped caricature of him as a "pompous, bulbous-eyed" and vain man, "exceedingly fond of long words, especially of Latin derivation." It is almost as if White changed his mind about the good Reverend in the process of writing the story. The treatment of white characters in *Fire* is even more sparse; there are few admirable white representatives in it. Judge Stevenson is one exception, and Roy Ewing is another, although Ewing at first wants nothing to do with the "nigger doctor" who operates on his daughter. Sheriff Parker and the rest of the white townspeople are presented as ignorant, bovine creatures who mull over murder as other men debate the necessity of removing crabgrass.

But we must keep in mind that this is 1924, a time when people were still being lynched with some regularity and when most white Americans' concept of Negroes was based upon the caricatures of the minstrel shows and the beasts haunting the pages of Thomas Dixon and his compatriots. *Fire* not only presented a sympathetic examination of the trials confronting an educated black man in a society geared to grind him into submission or a grave, it also presented a look at some of the foibles of that society as seen from a black perspective. For example, at the beginning of the novel Roy Ewing comes to Kenneth Harper for treatment of a "social disease" contracted during a night of abandon in Macon. As White says: "That was Kenneth's introduction to one part of the work of a colored physician in the South.

Many phases of life that he as a youth had never known about . . . he now had brought to his attention." Harper was also appalled by the whorehouses thriving in Central City, especially the ones in "Darktown": "Here were coloured women who seemed never to have to work. Here was seldom seen a coloured man. And the children around these houses were usually lighter in colour than in other parts of 'Darktown'." . . . White makes good use of his naive hero in these passages. A seasoned cynic would hardly remark the obvious discrepancies of what the whites preached about segregation and what they practiced; he would simply accept it as a matter of course. Through the eyes of the innocent Kenneth Harper, though, White can let his white reader see a world through eyes that are just as unused to the light as his own. Judging from the reactions of people who wrote White after reading the novel, this is exactly the effect the book had, at least in some quarters. (pp. 45-7)

Clearly, White was hoping his second novel would be an improvement over his first effort; he sought to overcome the propaganda label and to treat his characters more realistically. While he achieved his first goal, whether he achieved the second became the subject of some critical debate.

Flight centers on the life of Mimi Daquin (Annette Angela Daquin) as she experiences the pressures of Negro life, in the South and in the North, and the further pressures she faces when she decides to pass. (p. 83)

Walter White's style did not improve much in his second effort. In *Flight,* as in *The Fire in the Flint,* White depended heavily on melodramatic clichés in phrasing and in plot. Whenever Mimi leaves one life situation for another, inevitably she feels as if she were "opening a new book" or closing an old one. The . . . description of Jimmie Forrester after he has pined for months for Mimi is an almost classic stereotype of the rejected suitor. . . . On many occasions White's use of figurative language is awkward and, at the very least, questionable. He used this simile, for example, in describing the Atlanta gossips: "Like a great orchestra beginning *pianissimo* upon a symphony, the tongues started clacking in soft and cryptic whisperings." . . . (pp. 86-7)

There are, however, moments of some beauty or impact in *Flight,* especially centering around Jean's love of New Orleans or Mimi's fascination with Harlem. . . . In addition to the descriptions of Harlem . . . , White also offered this observation by Mimi on the Kaleidoscope of colors within the black community. Mimi is attending a dance at the Manhattan Casino when she observes

> faces of all colours, peeping from gowns of all shades. . . . There were faces of a mahogany brownness which shaded into the blackness of crisply curled hair. There were some of a blackness that shone like rich bits of velvet. There were others whose skins seemed as though made of expertly tanned leather with the creaminess of old vellum, topped by shining hair, blacker than "a thousand

> midnights, down in a cypress swamp." And there were those with ivory-white complexions, rare old ivory that time had mellowed with a gentle touch. To Mimi the most alluring of all were the women who were neither dark nor light, as many of them were, but those of that indefinable blend of brown and red, giving a richness that was reminiscent of the Creoles of her own New Orleans. . . .

In moments like these White is closer to the Harlem school of Hughes and McKay than to the "rear guard" of Du Bois and Fauset.

Perhaps the best description in the novel comes at the climactic scene in Carnegie Hall when Mimi is transported by the singer into a fantastic world of vision. Here White develops the impressions the spirituals create within Mimi:

> A vast impenetrable tangle of huge trees appeared, their pithy bulk rising in ebon beauty to prodigious heights. As she gazed, half afraid of the wild stillness, the trees became less and less blackly solid, shading off into ever lighter grays. Then the trees were white, then there were none at all. In their stead an immense circular clearing in which moved at first slowly, then with increasing speed, a ring of graceful, rounded, lithe women and stalward, magnificently muscled men, all with skins of midnight blackness. To music of barbaric sweetness and rhythm they danced with sinuous grace and abandon. . . .

From this vision Mimi enters another, where "weird creatures" burst upon the scene; with their "black reeds which spurted lead and flame," these invaders overpowered the dancers and took them across the ocean:

> . . . she saw a ship wallowing in the trough of immense waves. Aboard there strode up and down unshaven, deep-eyed, fierce-looking sailors who sought with oath and blow and kick to still the clamorous outcries of their black passengers. These were close packed in ill-smelling, inadequate quarters where each day stalked the specter whose visit meant one less mouth to feed. . . .

From that point the vision proceeds naturally to the plantations and fields of the new land, "a world of motion and labour . . . caught up and held immobile in the tenuous, reluctant notes" of the singer. In these passages White transcends the rather laborious prose of most of the novel and reaches a level of description that suggests both the strikingly stark work of Aaron Douglas and the rounded fullness of Hale Woodruff's paintings. Moments like these, unfortunately, are much the exception in White's novels.

As in *The Fire in the Flint,* thematic ideas are much more important in *Flight* than matters of art and style. While the themes of White's second novel are not as dramatically arresting as the dominant lynching theme of his first work, White does consider in *Flight* some essential issues facing the black community. The first of these is the idea of passing, and the forces which operate to drive one to pass out of her race into another. For Mimi the dominant forces which serve to drive her out center on pressures from within the race, specifically color consciousness, religious prejudice, and the petty jealousies of foolish gossips. In New Orleans it is Mimi's stepmother Mary who is confronted by prejudices of the "mellow old families, militantly proud of their Creole and Negro ancestry." In addition to being "an outsider," Mary has skin of "deep brown, in sharp contrast to the ivory tint of Jean and Mimi."... In Atlanta color is not so much a factor, at least for the Daquins, as religion. As Catholics, Jean and Mimi are totally out of step with the black community there. But it is the petty gossiping that finally drives Mimi into passing. The Fleur-de-Lis Club's gossip about Mrs. Adam's attempts to pass and the jealous "coloured person" who "turned her in" provide one sample of that gossip; the "story" Mrs. Plummer gives the Harlem gossip rag, the *Blabber,* is another, and the one which finally drives Mimi out.... With a great deal of sadness Mimi concludes that "her passing from the race seemed... persecution greater than any white people had ever visited upon her—the very intolerance of her own people had driven her from them."

In her new "white" life Mimi becomes terribly conscious of the distinctions between the two lifestyles, the white and the black. There is a quality to the latter which is completely missing in the former.... The contrast White draws between white folks and black folks hinges mostly on those two qualities: the lively, graceful spirit of the black community versus the somber, mechanical life of the white world.

Along with this concept of a difference between the two races goes the idea of racism, a topic which, as White himself suggested, no black writer could really ignore. In *Flight* White makes use of his own experience in the Atlanta riot of 1906 and recreates that riot in the novel, involving Jean and Mimi in some of the experiences he had faced as a young boy. In setting the stage for his fictionalized riot, White establishes the same causes he discussed in *A Man Called White* as the prime factors for the 1906 explosion: a long hot summer which frayed nerves and sharpened tempers "to razor-blade keenness"; a period of unemployment which caused "a marked loafing of whites and Negroes followed by a long series of petty crimes"; a "bitter political campaign,... its central issue the disenfranchisement of Negroes and 'Negro domination'"; a presentation of *The Clansman;* and an irresponsible, sensation-seeking press.... Just as Walter White and his father had been caught out in the midst of the riot, Jean and Mimi are likewise witness to several brutal scenes. (pp. 87-90)

For Mimi, as for Walter White, this riot acts as an agent for racial identity; it solidifies the racial ties...[After] the riot had quieted, White states: "Mimi dated thereafter her consciousness of being coloured from September, nineteen hundred and six. For her the old order had passed, she was now definitely of a race set apart."... This sounds very close to White's comment in *A Man Called White*.... (pp. 90-1)

Mimi's race identity and rare pride are other important elements in the novel. Whether in Atlanta, Harlem, or white New York, Mimi constantly senses the influences that draw her to her people. When they first arrive in Atlanta, Mimi and her father listen to an unfamiliar sound in a blues exchange between a man and a woman outside their window. They strain "to catch every note of this barbaric, melancholy wail as it [dies] in the distance, a strange thrill filling them."... Later Mimi watches a Negro convict gang at work and is fascinated by their work song.... While White's conception of the effect of a work song on the men working is terribly romanticized, at least he has his character in contact with the basic musical elements that make up her heritage as a black American. In fact, within a few pages White covers the work song, the spiritual, and jazz, and the effect each has on Mimi's developing race consciousness. Her reaction to the spiritual "Were You There When They Crucified My Lord?" in this section anticipates the effect of the Carnegie Hall concert at the end of the novel.... At a dance attended by Mimi and Mrs. Rodgers, Mimi marvels at the "easy grace," the variety of color, and the spontaneity that mark the people of Harlem as something special. After she passes over into the white world, she becomes increasingly aware of an emptiness within her, and her trip to Harlem with Bert Bellamy and her experience at Carnegie Hall convince her that she can never be whole, can never be completely satisfied until she rejoins her people and submerges herself once more in the soothing world she left behind.

The emptiness Mimi feels during her life in the white world stems, in large part, from the mechanization of that world. The role of the machine in the (white) Western world is the last of the thematic concerns of *Flight,* and one which puts it in tune with much of the literature of White's contemporaries.... [We] see White playing on an important theme of early twentieth-century literature: the real possibility that man might become subordinate to his mechanical creations, and ultimately become the servant rather than the served.

Echoing another set of sentiments of the time, White offers American Negroes as a group of people who have managed to escape the trap of mechanization and who are all the better for having escaped. After listening to the black chain gang, Mimi considers with admiration the strength shown by those men in the face of terrible adversity.... (pp. 90-3)

Perhaps White's most noticeable improvement in *Flight* was in the area of characterization, at least in terms of fairer treatment of whites and blacks. While there are still more stereotypes than real people in the novel, there are some "bad" black characters and some "good" white ones. The almost perfect Jean and Mimi are balanced by the gossipy Mrs. Plummer and her cohorts, and the myopic Jimmie Forrester, who spouts his disgust at blacks, Jews, "Chinks," and all other people who do not share his color and beliefs, is balanced by the sympathetic Francine and Sylvia Smith.

White's greatest pride, however, was the creation of Mimi; in her, he felt, he had created what F. E. DeFrantz called "a magnificent character."...[An] intensely personal view of his heroine made White particularly vulnerable to criticism of his character. Most of the critics found Mimi's motivation completely undeveloped....As in *The Fire in the Flint,* White demonstrated in *Flight* a flair for incident, although frequently strained and contrived, but he could not create "real" characters or go beyond the stereotyped patterns of the sentimental novel. (pp. 93-4)

The two novels that Walter White produced were not to survive as models of excellence from the Harlem Renaissance. *The Fire in the Flint,* as we have noted, did serve as a "trial balloon" in the earlier years of the period, however, and it was a minor sensation for a brief time. While *Flight* did not have as big an impact as the first novel, it was an improvement in some areas of style and control, and it did precede Nella Larsen's *Passing* by three years. And in Mimi's flight from and return to her people, we are given, as White himself stated, an insight into some of the emotional and psychological problems to be confronted by those people light enough to pass for white, people like Walter White. The most important contribution White was to make to the Harlem Renaissance, however, was not his writing, but his aid to artists who were at the core of that movement: Claude McKay, Rudolph Fisher, Langston Hughes, and Countee Cullen. (p. 112)

> *Edward E. Waldron, in his* Walter White and the Harlem Renaissance, *Kennikat Press, 1978, 185 p.*

FURTHER READING

Broun, Heywood. "It Seems to Heywood Broun." *The Nation* CXXX, No. 3385 (21 May 1930): 591.
Praises White for his role in blocking the appointment of segretationist John J. Parker to the United States Supreme Court.

Cannon, Poppy. *A Gentle Knight: My Husband, Walter White.* New York: Rinehart & Co., 1958, 309 p.
Observations of White in public and private life. White's widow discusses the people and events that shaped the American civil rights movement during the 1940s and 1950s, as well as White's national and international influence on public opinion.

Cooney, Charles F. "Walter White and the Harlem Renaissance." *The Journal of Negro History* LVII, No. 3 (July 1972): 231-40.
Discusses White's efforts to promote the literary careers of young, unestablished black writers.

Cournos, John. Review of *A Man Called White,* by Walter White. *Commonweal* XLIX, No. 4 (November 1948): 98-100.
Labels White's autobiography "a record of man's inhumanity to man and of courageous efforts to combat it."

Darrow, Clarence. "The Shame of America." *New York Herald Tribune Books* (21 April 1929): 3.
Favorable appraisal of *Rope and Faggot,* focusing on the chapter entitled "Nordicism, Science, and Lynching."

Desmond, John. "Reporting on Our Negro Troops Overseas." *The New York Times Book Review* (4 March 1945): 3.
Examines White's findings in *A Rising Wind.*

Du Bois, W.E.B. Review of *Rope and Faggot: A Biography of Judge Lynch,* by Walter F. White. In his *Collected Published Works of W.E.B. Du Bois: Book Reviews,* edited by Herbert Aptheker, pp. 133-34. Millwood, N.Y.: KTO Press, 1977.
Favorable review of *Rope and Faggot,* labelling the book "an excellent and painstaking work. It had to be done. It ought to be read, but it is not pleasant reading."

Embree, Edwin R. "Little David." In his *13 Against the Odds,* pp. 71-95. New York: Viking Press, 1944.
Biographical sketch, centering on White's work with the NAACP. Embree also discusses those who variously characterized White as either dedicated or opportunistic.

Fraser, Allison. *Walter White, Civil Right Leader.* Black Americans of Achievement. New York: Chelsea House, 1991, 112 p.
Biography of White intended for young readers.

Goodman, Anne L. "Blockade Runner." *The New Republic* 119, No. 16 (18 October 1948): 23-4.
Praises *A Man Called White* for its vivid insight into the problem of racial oppression in the United States.

Gruening, Ernest. "Going White." *The Saturday Review of Literature* II, No. 50 (10 July 1926): 918.
Discussion of *Flight.* Gruening locates artistic and thematic flaws in the work but concludes that *Flight* treats a significant subject in a sometimes moving manner.

Herskovits, Melville J. "Lynching: An American Pastime." *The Nation* CXXVIII, No. 3332 (15 May 1929): 588.
Argues that the restrained analytical approach used by White in *Rope and Faggot* is inappropriate to the passionate subject of the work.

Johnson, Gerald W. "An American Testament." *The New York Times Book Review* (6 November 1955): 46.
Extols *How Far the Promised Land?* as the crowning achievement of White's career.

Kahn, E. J., Jr. "The Frontal Attack: I and II." *The New Yorker* XXIV, Nos. 28, 29 (4 September 1948; 11 September 1948): 28-38, 38-50.

Biographical tribute that recounts many little-known anecdotes about White's life and career.

"Black and White." *The New York Times Book Review* (11 April 1926): 9.
Maintains that despite an objective thesis and realistic plot, *Flight* fails artistically because the protagonist's characterization never attains believability.

Overstreet, H. A. "Our Sins of Commission and Omission." *The Saturday Review of Literature* XXXI, No. 40 (2 October 1948): 9-10.
Laudatory appraisal of *A Man Called White.* Overstreet notes the hopeful tone in a work that documents horrors that are blindly accepted as a part of American life.

Scruggs, Charles W. "Alain Locke and Walter White: Their Struggle for Control of the Harlem Renaissance." *Black American Literature Forum* 14, No. 3 (Fall 1980): 91-9.

Examines the "uneasy tension" that existed between White and author Alain Locke during the 1920s.

"A Novel by a Negro." *Survey* LIII, No. 3 (1 November 1924): 160-62.
Review of *The Fire in the Flint,* arguing that the work "isn't a good enough novel to penetrate as literature."

"Lynch Law." *The Times Literary Supplement,* No. 1446 (17 October 1929): 806.
Positive review of *Rope and Faggot,* focusing on White's discussion of lynching and religion.

Wilkins, Roy. "Walter White." In *Rising Above Color,* edited by Philip Henry Lotz, pp. 105-12. New York: Association Press, 1946.
Studies White's work with the NAACP.

John Edgar Wideman

1941-

American novelist, short story writer, nonfiction writer, and critic.

Wideman is best known for novels and short stories that trace the lives of several generations of families in and around Homewood, the black ghetto district of Pittsburgh where he was raised. Although he deemphasized specifically black issues early in his career, his later works evidence his interest in "bringing to the fore black cultural material, history, archetypes, myths, the language itself, ... and trying to connect that with the so-called mainstream." His major interest is the individual's quest for self-discovery amidst the memory of both a personal past and a black heritage. Kermit Frazier commented: "The characters in Wideman's fiction can escape neither collective nor personal history and memory, so they are forced to deal with them in some way—be it successfully or ineffectually."

Wideman attended the University of Pennsylvania on a basketball scholarship before being selected as the first black Rhodes scholar since Alain Locke in 1905. In England, Wideman studied eighteenth-century European literature and the early development of the novel form. His first two novels, *A Glance Away* (1967) and *Hurry Home* (1969), reflect this formal training as well as his own experiments with narrative technique. These works, which involve a search for self by protagonists who are confused and controlled by their pasts, emphasize the theme of isolation and the importance of friendship in achieving self-awareness. In *A Glance Away*, a rehabilitated drug addict returns to his home, where he renews family and social ties while trying to avoid readdiction; in *Hurry Home*, a black law school graduate seeks cultural communion with white society by traveling to Europe, then reaffirms his black heritage in Africa. These characters find hope for the future only by confronting their personal and collective pasts. In *The Lynchers* (1973), a black activist group that plans to kill a white policeman in hopes of sparking widespread racial conflict is defeated by internal distrust and dissension.

Wideman has attributed the shift toward black-oriented themes and increased use of myth and dialect in his later novels to his growing awareness of such prominent black authors as Richard Wright and Jean Toomer. In *The Homewood Trilogy*, which comprises the short story collection *Damballah* (1981) and the novels *Hiding Place* (1981) and *Sent for You Yesterday* (1983), Wideman used deviating time frames, black dialect, and rhythmic language to transform Homewood into what Alan Cheuse described as "a magical location infused with poetry and pathos." The interrelated stories of *Damballah* concern the descendants of Wideman's maternal great-great-great grandmother, Sybela Owens,

and feature several characters who reappear in the novels. *Hiding Place,* published simultaneously with *Damballah,* is about a boy's strong ties to his family and his involvement in a petty robbery that results in an accidental killing. With *Sent for You Yesterday,* Wideman won the 1984 PEN/Faulkner Award for fiction. Through the characters of Doot, the primary narrator, and Albert Wilkes, an outspoken blues pianist, Wideman asserted that creativity and imagination are important means to transcend despair and strengthen the common bonds of race, culture, and class.

The eponymous narrator of Wideman's next novel, *Reuben* (1987), is an ambiguous and enigmatic figure who provides inexpensive legal aid to residents of Homewood. Among his clients are Kwansa, a young black woman whose brutal ex-husband, a recovering drug addict, kidnaps and seeks legal custody of their illegitimate child as revenge against her, and Wally, an assistant basketball coach at a local university who comes to Reuben because he fears he will be blamed for the illegal recruiting practices of his department. Wally, who may have actually murdered a white man, is possessed by an ingrained hatred of white society that leads him to fantasize about committing violence against middle-aged white males. Madison Smartt Bell commented: "[*Reuben*] is perhaps most importantly a detailed and sensitive portrait of the inner life of its characters, here rendered credibly and frighteningly as a kind of endless nightmare. Aside from, and along with that, it seems to be saying something new about the old vexed question of race relations in America. The question is not whether 'hate's bad for you,' but why."

In the novel *Philadelphia Fire* (1990), Wideman combined fact and fiction to elaborate on an actual incident involving MOVE, a militant, heavily armed black commune that refused police orders to vacate a Philadelphia slum house in 1985. With the approval of W. Wilson Goode, the city's black mayor, police bombed the house from a helicopter, killing eleven commune members—including five children—and creating a fire that razed over fifty houses. The book's narrator, Cudjoe, a writer and former Rhodes scholar living in self-imposed exile on a Greek island, returns to his native city upon hearing about the incident to search for a young boy who was seen fleeing the house following the bombing. This fictionalized narrative is juxtaposed with Wideman's address to his own son, who was sentenced to life in prison at eighteen years of age for killing another boy while on a camping trip.

Many reviewers concur that Wideman's blending of European and black literary traditions constitutes a distinctive voice in American literature. His unique combination of fact, fiction, myth, and history has allied him with the modernist tradition and solidified his reputation as a leading American author. Novelist Charles Johnson called him "easily the most acclaimed black male writer of the last decade," and the renowned critic Robert Bone, author of *The Negro Novel in America*, designated Wideman as "perhaps the most gifted black novelist of his generation."

(For further information about Wideman's life and works, see *Black Writers; Contemporary Authors,* Vols. 85-88; *Contemporary Authors New Revision Series,* Vol. 14; *Contemporary Literary Criticism,* Vols. 5, 34, 36, 67; and *Dictionary of Literary Biography,* Vol. 33: *Afro-American Fiction Writers after 1955.*)

PRINCIPAL WORKS

A Glance Away (novel) 1967
Hurry Home (novel) 1969
The Lynchers (novel) 1973
*Damballah (short stories) 1981
*Hiding Place (novel) 1981
*Sent for You Yesterday (novel) 1983
Brothers and Keepers (nonfiction) 1984
Fever: Twelve Stores (short stories) 1989
Reuben (novel) 1987
Philadelphia Fire (novel) 1990

*These works were reissued in a collected paperback edition as *The Homewood Trilogy* (1985).

Mel Watkins (essay date 1982)

[*In the following excerpt, Watkins explores the literary technique of* Damballah *and* Hiding Place.]

[In *Damballah* and *Hiding Place*] the high regard for language and craft demonstrated in [Wideman's] previous books is again evident. While *Hiding Place* is a novel set in present-day Pittsburgh, *Damballah* is a collection of interrelated stories that begins in Africa and traces the fortunes of one black family in the United States through slavery, escape and settlement in the North.... To invoke [the African deity Damballah], according to Maya Daren's *Divine Horsemen: The Voodoo Gods of Haiti,* is to "stretch one's hand back...to gather up all history into a solid, contemporary ground beneath one's feet"—to "gather up the family." And that is precisely the intent of Mr. Wideman in this collection of stories. This is something of a departure for him, and in freeing his voice from the confines of the novel form, he has written what is possibly his most impressive work.

The central character in the introductory story [of *Damballah*], which is set mainly in the antebellum South, is Ryan, a slave who is labeled a "crazy nigger" because of his refusal to abandon the customs of his African ancestors. His intransigence leads to his torture-murder at the hands of his master. From this point the book jumps in time to the late 1800's where in **"Daddy Garbage"**—the story of two men who find a dead baby in a garbage heap—we are in Homewood, the black section of Pittsburgh that is the setting for the remaining stories....

In **"Lizabeth: The Caterpillar Story,"** Lizabeth muses about the time her father, John French..., finds that she had eaten part of a caterpillar and eats the rest himself: "I got the most of it then," he says. "And if I don't die, she ain't gonna die neither." **"The Songs of Reba Love Jackson"** achieves a satiric edge through the confrontation between Reba, a devote, God-fearing gospel singer and the glib, irreverent radio announcer who interviews her. The last of these stories introduces the characters who are central to the plot of the simultaneously published novel *Hiding Place.*

But each story moves far beyond the primary event on which it is focused. The prose is labyrinthine—events and details merge and overlap. (p. 6)

It is not mere coincidence that in one story Mr. Wideman quotes Jean Tommer's description of white faces as "petals of dusk." *Damballah,* with its loosely connected sketches and stories, is indebted structurally to Toomer's *Cane* (1923), and in turn to Sherwood

Anderson's *Winesburg, Ohio*. But the kinship with *Cane* is much more direct. Like Toomer, Mr. Wideman has used a narrative laced with myth, superstition and dream sequences to create an elaborate poetic portrait of the lives of ordinary black people. And also like Toomer, he has written tales that can stand on their own, but that assume much greater impact collectively. The individual "parts" or stories, as disparate as they may initially seem, work together as a remarkably vivid and coherent montage of black life over a period of five generations.

Mr. Wideman employs the same narrative technique in *Hiding Place,* but not nearly so effectively. The novel depicts the events of a few days during which Tommy, grandson of John French, hides in the squalid shack in which his great-grandmother's sister Bess has isolated herself. Essentially this is a tale of two lost souls. "Crazy, evil" Bess, who, because of the death of her husband and son, has severed all family ties to live a reclusive life in a ramshackle house atop a hill overlooking Pittsburgh; and Tommy, who is on the run after a scheme to rob a ghetto hoodlum ends in murder. Through extended interior monologue we learn of the events that precipitated both characters' estrangement and led them to their rendezvous. But despite some arresting passages in which Mr. Wideman displays his command of the language and of the voices of his characters, this is a static novel.

After the evocative richness of *Damballah, Hiding Place* is something of a disappointment; the novel's minutely focused view of the relationship between Bess and Tommy simply does not mesh well with its ornate style. Still, taken together, these books once again demonstrate that John Wideman is one of America's premier writers of fiction. That they were published originally in paperback perhaps suggests that he is also one of our most underrated writers. (pp. 6, 21)

> Mel Watkins, "Black Fortunes," in The New York Times Book Review, *April 11, 1982, pp. 6, 21.*

Wilfred D. Samuels (essay date 1982)

[*In the excerpt below, Samuels examines major themes in* Damballah *and* Hiding Place.]

Hiding Place and *Damballah* are set for the most part in Wideman's boyhood community, Homewood, which is located in the eastern edge of Pittsburgh, Pennsylvania. His family, including Sybela Owens, his maternal great, great, great grandmother, were among its first settlers. Amidst Homewood's rich landscape and cityscape, Wideman weaves his tale around the fascinating progeny of Sybela Owens, most notably Mother Bess and Aunt May, two matriarchs who serve as griots of the family's history.

Hiding Place focuses primarily on the relationship that develops between Mother Bess and Tommy, Sybela's

great, great, great grandson, who commits a robbery during the course of which a man is killed. Though innocent of the actual shooting, Tommy flees Homewood.... When boredom drives him to return to Homewood, however, Tommy is discovered and chased. Although he returns to Bess's home while in flight, as far as Bess can tell from the shooting and sirens which assault her sleep, Tommy is killed before she can offer him a hiding place. Because she believes Tommy has been killed, Bess resolves to ... return to Homewood to tell his story.

Wideman's concern with history, salience of family, and culture seem to merge in *Hiding Place,* where they are powerfully presented through Mother Bess. In her role as griot, she knows and recites the family's history, telling Tommy his lineage. Throughout the novel, Mother Bess exudes a will and strength which allow her to take her place in the canon of Afro-American literature next to Miss Jane Pittman of Ernest Gaines's *The Autobiography of Miss Jane Pittman* and Eva Peace of Toni Morrison's *Sula.*

Damballah, too, examines the importance of family and culture. Published in concert with *Hiding Place ...,* Damballah presents Wideman's use of the short story to explore the individual experiences of Sybela's offspring: Elizabeth, Geraldine, Carl, Martha, etc. In **"Solitary,"** for example, he explores Elizabeth's story. In the family, she is known as the baby that survived a near tragic birth when Aunt May thrust her naked body in the snow.... Elizabeth is now the mother of five children; she spends her weeks visiting her imprisoned son Tommy. The emotion-ridden experience causes her to lose, for a brief moment, her faith in God.... By the end of the story, however, her faith is restored rather than destroyed.

More powerfully drawn, through, are the stories narrated by Aunt May, for through her Wideman brings mythology (folklore) and facts together, and he imbues her with the flair and dramatic abilities of the African storyteller. (p. 12)

With *Hiding Place* and *Damballah,* Wideman reaches the zenith of his concern with the themes that have been fundamental to his work since the appearance of *A Glance Away.* He continues his interest in experimenting with form, as is evident in his use of stream of consciousness and interior monologue, especially in *Hiding Place.* Critics will undoubtedly find similarities between Wideman's work and Faulkner's, especially *The Sound and the Fury* and *As I Lay Dying.* Wideman's Clement in *Hiding Place* demonstrates that the inarticulate's world is more complex than it appears on the surface to be, much in the same way that Faulkner's Benjy does. His Homewood community, with its history, place and people, is not unlike Yoknapatawpha County, which Faulkner based on fact.

By going home to Homewood, Wideman has found a voice for his work and consequently a means of celebrating Afro-American culture and further validating the Afro-American experience in literature. (pp. 12-13)

Wilfred D. Samuels, in a review of "'Hiding Place' and 'Damballah'," in The American Book Review, *Vol. 4, No. 5, July-August, 1982, pp. 12-13.*

Alan Cheuse (essay date 1983)

[*In the following excerpt, Cheuse discusses imagery, tone, and characterization in* Sent for You Yesterday.]

In this hypnotic and deeply lyrical novel [**Sent for You Yesterday**], Mr. Wideman again returns to the ghetto where he was raised and transforms it into a magical location infused with poetry and pathos.

The book's title announces both the tone and the action. "Sent for you yesterday, and here you come today." The elegiac outcry of this old Jimmy Rushing blues suggests the urgent need, apparent loss and ironic recovery that characterizes the novel's beautiful first-person narrative. The narrator, his speech laden with news and the blues, is a character who has appeared in Mr. Wideman's fiction before. His is the voice in **"Across the Wide Missouri,"** one of the stories in **Damballah.** Like Mr. Wideman, he is a young black writer who has moved to Wyoming and spends only vacation time in his native Pittsburgh; but he has returned to Homewood to take on the roles of both son and father in mind and feelings. The narration here makes it clear that both as a molder of language and a builder of plots, Mr. Wideman has come into his full powers. He is a literary artist with whom any reader who admires ambitious fiction must sooner or later reckon.

As his last two books demonstrated, he has the gift of making "ordinary" folks memorable. And many of the engaging characters from **Damballah** and **Hiding Place** tumble onstage to assist in the recreation of Homewood's communal life from the wild and vital 1920's through the drugged and debilitated 70's. (p. 13)

The man who affects the destinies of [the book's many characters], . . . the daring, dangerous but gifted Albert Wilkes, arrives early in a swirl of piano blues and departs early in a storm of police bullets. His music evokes "a moody correspondence between what his fingers shape and what happens to the sky, the stars, the moon." Through Wilkes's presence, Mr. Wideman establishes a mythological and symbolic link between character and landscape, language and plot, that in the hands of a less visionary writer might be little more than stale sociology. At one point in the novel, Albert Wilkes's ghost apparently inspires Brother Tate's otherwise unsupple hands to play at the Homewood Elks hall. The narrator, although he has a great deal of talent to begin with, appears to be equally inspired throughout the book.

Doot Brother Tate dubs him when he is only a boy, employing one of the sounds of scat singing—the only sounds that Brother makes after his son's death. The nickname seems appropriate, since Doot continually turns the barest descriptive passages into his own form of verbal music.

He can take what the normal eye might perceive as an ordinary scene . . . and spin out images over a page or more as part of a moving evocation of ghetto dreaming. He can show us rows of "wooden shanties built to hold the flood of black immigrants up from the South" and transmute them into "islands, arks, life teeming but enclosed or surrounded or exiled to arbitrary boundaries." And he can reveal the city beyond these bounded streets as he has his grandfather, John French, perceive it, with its steel mills along the river belching clouds of smoke. "If you didn't know the smoke could kill you, if you didn't think of it as an iron cloud pressing the breath out your body, the dirt and the soot and gas coloring the sky made a beautiful sight."

That is the view from Homewood—a place that, thanks to John Edgar Wideman, we have now lived and died in. (pp. 13, 41)

Alan Cheuse, "Homecoming in Homewood," in The New York Times Book Review, *May 15, 1983, pp. 13, 41.*

Garrett Epps (essay date 1983)

[*In the excerpt below, Epps compares the Homewood ghetto district in* Sent for You Yesterday *with William Faulkner's fictional Yoknapatawpha County.*]

I've never been to Pittsburgh, and I've never seen Homewood, the gallant black neighborhood which is the setting of **Sent for You Yesterday.** But Homewood is a part of my world now, like Faulkner's Yoknapatawpha County . . . .

I compare John Edgar Wideman's fictional territory with Yoknapatawpha by design: Wideman has a fluent command of the American language, written and spoken, and a fierce, loving vision of the people he writes about. Like Faulkner's, Wideman's prose fiction is vivid and demanding—shuttling unpredictably between places, narrators and times, dwelling for a paragraph on the surface of things, then sneaking a key event into a clause that springs on the reader like a booby trap . . . . [**Sent for you Yesterday** is] Wideman's story of the Frenches and the Tates and a half-century of their lives in Homewood. (p. 1)

As Wideman tells us, this story does not begin and end; it unfolds and refolds, like "one of those tissue paper and stick-fans from Murphy's Five and Dime all folded so you can't see what's inside, but you roll off the gumband and spread the sticks and it's sunsets and rainbows and peacock tails."

In fact, as in Faulkner's *Absalom, Absalom,* much of *Sent for You Yesterday* is told by narrators who did not see the events they are describing. "I am not born yet," Doot, Carl's nephew, tells us as he retells a scene from his uncle's early life. Like Faulkner, Wideman focuses not on the events themselves but on their effects on those who come after, the burden and liberation they impart to future generations, who must remember and retell them and seek in them the meaning of their own lives and the keys to their futures. (pp. 1-2)

In fact, these past lives are the only salvation for the people of Homewood, hemmed in by poverty and the impersonal malice of white society. Homewood fights back with music and with memories. An Albert Wilkes or a Brother Tate, who can play the blues "so fine you said Thank Jesus a day early," appears once a generation, fights and loses; but each new generation rises to fight again. "The old Homewood people taught me you don't have to give up," says Lucy Tate; she passes this message on to Doot, who is a young man in the 1970s when the story ends, "on my own feet.... Learning to stand, to walk, learning to dance." ...

Wideman writes the way Albert Wilkes played; *Sent for You Yesterday* is a book to be savored, read slowly and read again. (p. 2)

> Garrett Epps, "Singing the Homewood Blues," in Book World—The Washington Post, *July 3, 1983, pp. 1-2.*

James Marcus (essay date 1986)

[*In the following essay, Marcus comments on the mixing of literary traditions in Wideman's works.*]

At the conclusion of John Edgar Wideman's *Sent For You Yesterday,* a character muses over a piano performance she heard years before, a

> song so familiar because everything she's ever heard is in it ... but everything is new and fresh because [the] music joined things, blended them so you could follow one note and then it splits and shimmers and spills the thousand things it took to make the note whole, the silences within the note, the voices and songs.

This description applies equally well to Wideman's achievement in *The Homewood Trilogy,* a group of interconnected novels set in the Pittsburgh ghetto where his family has lived since the middle of the nineteenth century. The trilogy fits the bill not only because of its inclusiveness, but also because of its cadenced, highly textured music—this is prose that needs to be read out loud. There's no other way to savor its ornery swing and lilt, its stop-time rhythms as the narrative passes from voice to voice. Wideman's multiple narrators produce an effect like that of Kansas City swing, where a string of soloists egg each other on over the bedrock of a ticking rhythm section. He draws his intricate and artful music straight from speech: his work, like that of Gabriel

García Márquez or Giovanni Verga, offers a magical transcription of family stories, gossip and nuggets of local history, all brilliantly orchestrated.

The trilogy also answers a question that dogged and defeated much of Wideman's earlier work: What kind of fiction does a black man write from the predominantly white groves of academe? Wideman has spoken of the "tension of multiple traditions, European and Afro-American, the Academy and the Street," that animate his work. As an Ivy League graduate, recipient of the second Rhodes Scholarship ever awarded to a black American and later a graduate of the Iowa Writers' Workshop, Wideman must have felt an especially strong pull from the academy. And indeed his earlier novels, written between 1967 and 1973, struggle with this tension without ever quite resolving it.

A Glance Away, for example, interweaves two stories: a young black man named Eddie Lawson returns to his hometown after a year in the South kicking a drug addiction; at the same time, a middle-aged white college professor named Robert Thurley tries to face up to his homosexuality, a failed marriage and alcoholism. The book opens with an impressionistic prologue, all speed and biblical tone:

> On an April day insouciant after the fashion of spring insouciance the warm secret of life was shared with another. Bawling milk hungry mammal dropped in pain from flanks of a she. Him.
>
> Fine, healthy boy, eight pounds seven ounces.
>
> Mystery repeats itself to boredom. And he shall be called Eugene. In the name of the grandfather who balding, high on dago red, waited news in a cloud of garbage smelling smoke at the foot of steep, ringing marble stairs of Allegheny General Hospital.

But once the seventeen-page prologue has shown us the birth of Eddie's older brother, then Eddie and his grandfather's attendance at a holiness church service and finally the grandfather's funeral, the novel settles down to its alternating stories. Here the twin pulls of the academy and the street make their mark. Thurley stands unambiguously for the former. A literature professor and aesthete, he moves through the novel wrapped in a dense cloud of cognition; his monologues, festooned with literary allusion (in one two-page passage Joyce, Stendhal, Flaubert and Eliot all flit by), are often the source of unintended melodrama. When Thurley's Drama 101 class refuses to listen to his lecture on *Oedipus,* a small scene of martyrdom swims into his mind: "Thurley thought of the sea. Of a beautiful young sailor who had robbed and beaten him. It was a beatitude. A scene for Raphael to paint in his reds and blues." A beatitude? The self-pity is overdone to the point where Thurley's dilemma becomes uninteresting to us. For the most part, he resembles nothing more than an aging Stephen Dedalus who emigrated to America rather than Paris, found a university teaching post and lapsed into boozy depression.

Eddie, on the other hand, has no time for aesthetics. The details of his return home after a year kicking junk are truthfully and painfully managed, and unlike most literary prodigal sons, he doesn't find much of a welcome upon his arrival. Still, there's a sensation that he is part of a schematic, even sentimental, division of experience. In the house on Dumferline Street his embittered mother has crushed the life out of Eddie's sister, Bette, and broods over her own life without any of Thurley's cushioning aesthetic agony:

> Something told her all these momentary feelings must lead to a complete and final resolution which she by suffering could deserve to understand. But each time she waited, what came, if anything at all did, was never enough. No flash of light, no deep, settled contentment or despair, only the tickled nerve end dance leading her on and on . . . .

> Perhaps someday she would be vomited up suddenly in paradise.

Before the day is done, the old woman has toppled down a stairway and died, and Eddie has stumbled off to buy some dope at Harry's Place. There he meets Thurley, and thus begins the confrontation and attempted reconciliation of these opposites.

As a go-between Wideman introduces a character who will reappear, with only minor modifications, in his trilogy: the albino Brother Small, with his "horsy features, the pink irises of his albino eyes, the pimples, the lisp as he formed his words [which] doubled and trebled their ugliness." Brother is a welcome violation of the overly schematic yin and yang of his two companions. The three end up in a clearing in the Bum's Forest, surrounded by broken bottles and slumbering winos. While Thurley and Eddie sit on a rock and brood, Brother builds a fire, foraging for twigs and dreaming of a chocolate bar. His ruminations, which end the novel, strike a note more poignant than the poeticized murmurings of the other two:

> I wonder what it feels like to burn if it always hurts once your hand is in it deep and if it pops and sparks like wood and if the color is the same and if it hurts and where does it go if you keep it in smoke rises through the trees to the sky towards the black roof where the sun will come if the sun comes tomorrow.

Fortunately, the vitality of Wideman's prose continually bursts the boundaries of his schematic designs. And although he fails to make its polarity really work, *A Glance Away* does engage an issue that's always on Wideman's mind: the way in which time cuts its notches into whatever survives it. Eddie returns home expecting to find an unchanged world, "as if"—glossing the title—"time were never more than the space between a glance away and back." The foolishness of this hope is the novel's lesson, one Thurley learns as painfully as Eddie does.

Wideman's next novel, *Hurry Home*, just as plainly addresses the tension between academy and street. This time, though, the novelist has taken a more economical approach, combining both strains in a single character, Cecil Braithwaite. Cecil is a black man who's slogged through years of law school, subsidized by the woman he promises to marry come graduation day:

> Lawyer Braithwaite, third of his race to be admitted and second to finish the university law school aided and abetted throughout by the unflagging efforts of Esther Brown, true avatar of that selfless, sore-kneed mother every night scrubbing the halls bright . . . . Esther on all fours, the solid rock on which I stood *cum laude.*

But Cecil's effort don't win him a three-piece suit, an associate's salary and a deskful of litigation. His fellow students barely tolerate him as "a piece of their education, something to be coped with, to come to terms with, a measure of their powers of self-control." And in his own neighborhood, "the Magistrate" draws resentment: "The way he talked when he talked. A book caught in his throat or a spoon shoved up his ass he dropped each word like an egg that hurt him to lose . . . . He did keep a clean shirt." The tension of containing both worlds fragments him. Or sends him into a daze, a dreamlike state punctuated by what Mallarmé calls (in the novel's epigraph) *ce mal d'être deux*—the pain of being two.

On his wedding night, this pain propels Cecil—possessor of a brand-new law degree and a brand-new wife—out the door and into a journey that will last three years. His divided self keeps subdividing, crowding each vision with another, until time itself seems out of whack, stretched into illegibility. Geographically, Cecil's journey takes him to Spain and Africa, and then back to America, where he begins work at Constance Beauty's straightening parlor. It's a painfully appropriate job for Cecil, applying lye and relaxant to kinky hair. But the lack of resolution here gives an odd, impenetrable density to Cecil's story; the incoherence of his personality is echoed all too accurately by the incoherence of the novel.

Wideman produced one more novel during the 1970s—*The Lynchers,* a bareknuckles survey of the vigilante mind—but it wasn't until the first volume of *The Homewood Trilogy,* in 1981, that he found some of the answers to the questions posed in the earlier books. In his introduction to the trilogy, he describes a trip home for his grandmother's funeral in 1973 as "the beginning of these three books. As we sat late, late into the night, fueled by drink, food, talk, by sadness and bitter loss, by the healing presence of others who shared our grief, our history, the stories of Homewood's beginnings, were told."

The trilogy resolves the old tension between different traditions by embracing a mode of storytelling that transcends them. In these books Wideman lays aside the ornaments of modernism. In doing so, he sacrifices a certain brilliance of texture but gains the jolt of speech, of words that issue not from typewriters but from mouths. As one character notes, "It takes someone's voice to make things real." And instead of the author as demiurge, the trilogy casts the narrator (named, coincidentally, John) as a sort of curator or custodian, preserving a community of voices, refining them even as they refine him.

The three novels of the trilogy are thoroughly interlinked: for all intents and purposes, it's a single, unified work. But this extended quilt of stories contains a remarkable variety of tone and form. *Damballah* gathers a collection of family histories and apocrypha, ranging from the slave days (**"Damballah," "The Beginning of Homewood"**), through the turn of the century (**"Daddy Garbage," "The Caterpillar Story"**), all the way to contemporary events (**"Tommy," "Solitary"**). Voice and perspective keep shifting, even within a single story: **"The Caterpillar Story"** tells and retells old John French's exploits in the words of his wife and his daughter, and through the voices of the two conversing. *Hiding Place* is a less variegated book, narrowing its focus to two voices—ancient Mother Bess in her shack on Bruston Hill, and Tommy, the narrator's brother who's fled up to the hill after participating in a bungled stickup.

By the time he finished *Sent For You Yesterday,* in 1983, Wideman had completely mastered his storytelling techniques. The voices of John, his Uncle Carl, the albino Brother Tate and Carl's lover, Lucy, flow in and around each other with effortless fluency, forming and formed by the story of Albert Wilkes, a piano player who returns to Homewood seven years after he's killed a white policeman in a quarrel. Here Wideman affirms that his writing is an instrument of survival: "Past lives live in us," he says, and "Each of us harbors the spirits of people who walked the earth before we did, and those spirits depend on us for continuing existence, just as we depend on their presence to live our lives to the fullest." It's the affirmation sought by his grandmother Freeda French:

> To believe who she is Freeda must go backward, must retreat, her voice slowly unwinding, slowly dismantling itself, her voice going backward with her, alone with her as the inevitable silence envelops. Talking to herself. Telling stories. Telling herself.

Telling herself. This was the triumphant resolution Wideman finally found, telling himself through a chorus of voices and, in the process, telling us ourselves, too. (pp. 321-22)

> *James Marcus, "The Pain of Being Two," in* The Nation, *New York, Vol. 243, No. 10, October 4, 1986, pp. 321-22.*

Noel Perrin (essay date 1987)

[*In the following review, Perrin praises the musicality of* Reuben *and asserts that Wideman's works are less novels than "myths of the biracial society."*]

As everyone admits, John Edgar Wideman is one of the half-dozen leading black novelist alive today. There's just one problem with that description. He doesn't write novels. He certainly writes books *called* novels, and they contain fictional characters in fictional situations. But what they really are is myths—generally myths of the biracial society. And a good thing, too. Because if Wideman were a novelist, he would be a seriously flawed one.

Take his new book, **Reuben.** Listen to a brief account of it, and you'll see what I mean. Let's start with the title character.

Reuben is an old black lawyer, in Pittsburgh—a tiny man with a pointed gray beard and a misshapen body. When he was young, he served as janitor and occasional pimp in a white-boy fraternity at what seems to be the University of Pennsylvania.

One Sunday the frat boys chip in and buy *him* a session with Flora, the beautiful, possibly part-black madam of the bordello. It's a trap. Once Reuben and Flora start making love, the boys rush in. First they flog Reuben (his back is a mass of scars to this day) and tie Flora spread-eagled to her bed. Their amusing plan is to rape her en masse and then mash her face in. "Such a fetching piece of real estate, but when we finish with it . . . no one will want her," laughs one of the boys, no doubt a future land developer.

The plan is not completed, because just as the mass rape is about to commence, flames come leaping up the stairs. Dudley, the black piano player, has set the building on fire. Flora, tied to the bed, dies a painful death; the brave frat boys jump out the window. No one is ever caught or punished.

Now consider Wally. Wally is younger and better-looking. He's an assistant basketball coach at a mostly white university, but fantasy life is what really interests him. One of his favorites is to imagine himself armed with a baseball bat striding down an endless row of posts. Each post is topped with the head of a middle-aged white male. Wally smashes each one as he passes, and does he enjoy it! Never gets tired, never gets bored. Once (the book is deliberately ambiguous here) Wally seems to have enacted his fantasy, killing a white man picked at random in Chicago. That killing, if it really occurred, is one of the two reasons he's consulting Reuben, the other being the imminent exposure of illegal recruiting practices at his university. As junior coach, Wally will be the official sacrifice.

Then there's Kwansa (born Lily). She's a young black prostitute. Five years ago she had an illegitimate child, a son whom she named Cudjoe and whom she adores. She does not farm him out to an aunt; she raises him herself.

Now the boy's father, not having lifted a finger for five years, has decided he wants his son, and steals him. Kwansa counts on lawyer Reuben to get him back. That's not how it works out, though. Kwansa's new lover, a woman named Toodles, retrieves the kid. She uses a very basic approach. She cuts the father's throat with a razor, so that he dies "spouting blood like a fountain." No more custody fights with *him*.

In short, if *Reuben* were a novel, it would be total and shameless melodrama. But it doesn't read that way at all. It reads like the myth it is. A melodrama has a plot, and lots of suspense; the tension builds. *Reuben* has no real plot—just events, told discontinuously—and it has almost no enacted scenes. Mostly you have the voice of John Edgar Wideman, narrating as a tribal storyteller might. Mesmerizing his audience. Building sound, not story. Speaking in many tongues, from black English in Wally's thoughts and Kwansa's speech to the most whitely formal of poetic styles, as in the passage beginning "Night gnaws the city."

This is a book to be read aloud. One chapter that I thought I disliked for being too pretentious in its language—that chapter I happened to read aloud to a friend, and discovered that I liked it after all. There is true magic in the language, and if you let it crash over you like waves, you may cease to care that there is no enacted story. You may even be able to cease minding that the words "nigger" (for blacks) and "cracker" (for whites) are used as conscious obscenities, meant to shock. In the end one sees that all the shocks—the murders, the fantasies, burnings, strong words—all of them amount to a kind of metaphor for the psychic damage that human beings do to each other and that is no less hurtful than spread-eagled beating, just less visible to the outer eye.

> Noel Perrin, "*John Edgar Wideman's Urban Inferno*," in Book World—The Washington Post, *November 15, 1987, p. 7.*

Bernard W. Bell (essay date 1987)

[*Bell is an authority on African-American literature. In the following excerpt, he offers an overview of Wideman's literary career.*]

The lower frequencies of an Afro-American tradition, oral and literary, were significantly muted in the life and work of John Wideman before the black power movement. Neither in largely black Washington, D.C., where he was born on June 14, 1941, nor at white Oxford University, where as a Rhodes Scholar he was formally trained in English literature, did he read Richard Wright and other black writers. His education in black literature came after his graduation in 1963 from the University of Pennsylvania, where he was awarded both a Ben Franklin Fellowship and a Thouron Fellowship for Creative Writing, and after his acceptance in 1966 of a Kent Fellowship for Creative Writing at the University of Iowa. With this formal academic background, it is not surprising that the early influences on Wideman's craftsmanship were James Joyce and T. S. Eliot, whom he first read in high school, and Henry Fielding and Laurence Sterne, whom he studied at New College, Oxford. It was not until 1967, after the publication of his first novel, *A Glance Away,* and after he started

teaching black literature courses at the University of Pennsylvania, that he began to read slave narratives, black folklore, the novels of Wright and Ellison as well as Toomer's *Cane.* The vision and experimentation of these writers, he states in an interview, were important in the development of his Afrocentric aesthetic, for it awakened in him "a different sense of self-image and the whole notion of a third world." He also says: "If there is any single book I learned a hell of a lot from, it's *Tristram Shandy*....I hope that I have learned from the nonrepresentational school about fantasy and playing around with different forms. The novel started out with these two tendencies—realism and fantasy."

In part because of the conflict between his ethnic background and his formal training in literature, Wideman's five novels (*A Glance Away* [1967], *Hurry Home* [1970], *The Lynchers* [1973], *Hiding Place* [1981], and *Sent for You Yesterday* [1983]) and his collection of stories (*Damballah* [1981]) reveal a tension between realistic material and experimentation with form and style, especially stream-of-consciousness techniques and black speech. In *A Glance Away,* Wideman says, "I am going to school to various other writers, using other's techniques, but also trying out some things that I hope are original." Eliot's Eurocentric influence is apparent in the mood, style, and characterization of this first novel, which is a quasi-parable on the resurrection of Edward Lawson, the thirty-year-old black protagonist who returns to Philadelphia on Easter Sunday, April 20, from a drug rehabilitation center in the South only to suffer the pain and guilt of his mother's death. The person driven by his own painful memories to get him through the night is Robert Thurley, a fictionalized J. Alfred Prufrock, a middle-aged white homosexual professor of comparative literature who pursues black lovers and for whom "Eliot was...the poet of weariness, of old age." Although Eliot's specter hangs over most of the book, in the final ten pages Wideman displaces dialogue with the alternating inner thoughts of Eddie, Robert, and Brother Small, their albino friend, as they sit in spiritual communion around a small fire in a hobo camp.

Equally Prufrockian in characterization but more non-representational and experimental in time structure and point of view is *Hurry Home.* Whereas Thurley, the ineffectual, suffering intellectual in *A Glance Away,* wanders through the streets and after-hours clubs of Philadelphia, Charles Webb, the guilt-ridden white writer and intellectual of *Hurry Home,* wanders through the museums, cafés, and beaches of Spain in a vain search for redemption from the black son he has never seen because he had abandoned his black mistress not knowing she was pregnant. Using interior monologue, letters, journal entries, rapid shifts in time and point of view, surreal vignettes, mythic associations, linguistic puns, and frequent allusions to writers and painters, especially Hieronymus Bosch and his triptych of "The Adoration of the Magi," Wideman is concerned in his second novel with the thin line between reality and fantasy, "between individual and collective experience which permits one to flow into the other." Going to get a haircut for his graduation, Cecil Otis Braithwaite, the protagonist who, aided by the sacrifices of his girlfriend Esther and his scrub-woman mother, is only the second of his race to graduate from the university law school, is symbolically rejected by the black community as a "Humbug magistraitassed uppitty nigger." He, in turn, deserts Esther on their wedding night to go to Spain and Africa, seeking to understand his double-consciousness and to accommodate both the gospels and the Easter song, the "St. John Passion," of Heinrich Schultz. The question that Cecil asks throughout the book is, Why did you do that? As he actually and imaginatively travels back in the past for answers, his personal experience is conflated into the collective history of his race. But after three years of wandering through the corridors of time and foreign countries, reconstructing and reliving the journey of his race from Africa to America, he hurries home in the spring to work in a hair straightening parlor, to rejoin his wife, and to dream. "To go back into one's past," Wideman states, "is in fact dreaming. What is history except people's imaginary recreation." Thus Cecil's actual past and his dream past, like his personal and racial identities, become merged in the course of the novel.

Although the ambiguities of the imagination and of the relationship between blacks and whites in America are common themes in Wideman's first three novels, **The Lynchers** is the most intriguing blend of realism and surrealism. Its primary theme is that the historical social realities of race relations in America are driving blacks and whites to apocalyptic attitudes and actions. At the center of the novel is the destruction of the black Wilkerson family—Orin "Sweetman" and Bernice, the parents, and Thomas, their son—and a plan conceived by Willis "Littleman" Hall to lynch a white cop in order to release black people from a fear of death at the hands of whites and to assert a new vision of reality. Introduced by twenty pages of quotations from documents that immerse the reader in the historical record of the use of lynching as a ritual of brutal racial power, the novel proper is divided into three major parts whose chronological time span is less than a month but whose psychological span is years.

Set in the 1960s on the South Side of Philadelphia, Part 1 plunges the reader into a sea of internal and external events that reveal the debris of Orin's and Bernice's lives and the distress that drives Thomas to risk participating in the lynch plan. In Part 2 Wideman continues to experiment with a wide range of techniques—dream fragments, interior monologue, flashbacks, black vernacular, rapid shifts from third- to first-person narration, and overlapping time frames—to introduce us to the details of the plan, the experiences that led Littleman to conceive it, and the mixture of black history and revolutionary rhetoric he uses to recruit his three irresolute, mutually distrustful accomplices. The plan is to kill a pimping white cop's black whore and to have the community publicly lynch him for her death, symbolically liberating the community

from oppression and defining themselves in the process "as fighters, free, violent men who will determine the nature of the reality in which they exist." The "plan's as simple as death," says Littleman. "When one man kills it's murder. When a nation kills murder is called war. If we lynch the cop we will be declaring ourselves a nation." The climax of the external events occurs in Part 2 when Littleman, while making an inflammatory speech on the steps of a black junior high school, is severely beaten by the police, but the internal climax does not come until Part 3 when Wilkerson's consciousness merges with the daughter of the lynchers' intended first victim. Part 3 also reveals how the lynch plan is completely aborted after Wilkerson's father is arrested for killing his best friend; how the protagonist himself is shot in a desperate assertion of independence by Rice, an accomplice; and how Littleman dies in the hospital after a futile effort to recruit a young black hospital orderly, Alonzo, whose confusion and blind rage represent the revolutionary potential of the next generation. More important than the failure of the lynch plan, then, are the social realities that impinge on the consciousness of the characters and influence their existential choices, which are, in a sense, parodies of the revolutionary identities forged in political struggle that Frantz Fanon so brilliantly outlines in *The Wretched of the Earth*.

Wideman, in other words, is primarily concerned with delineating the reciprocal influence of reality on the imagination and the imagination on the reality of his characters. The past and present flow together in the bitter-sweet memories of Wilkerson's parents as they sit across from each other in the kitchen:

> Pocked walls breathing sourly, patient mirrors of everything and if peeled layer by layer paint to paper to paper to paint to paint you would see old lives crowded as saints in the catacombs. Their children's hand prints crawling up the wall. The low border when it was a third leg to hold them up, the grease streaks from the boys' slicked down heads as they leaned back cockily on spindly legged chairs sneaking smokes and trading lies around the kitchen table, up near crease of ceiling and wall, splash of roach where she told Thomas not to squash them even if he could reach that high. Once blue, once yellow, hopelessly white, blue again, now the rosette paper meant for somebody's living room .... She realized how easily it could all disappear. Everywhere in the neighborhood buildings were being torn down.

Of the four avenging angels—Graham Rice, a neurotic, spineless janitor; Leonard Saunders, a street-hardened post office worker; Thomas Wilkerson, an ineffectual dreamer and junior high school teacher; and Littleman, the crippled, silver-tongued messenger of historical truth and the mastermind of the lynching plan—Wilkerson and Littleman are Wideman's symbols of the modern intellectual man. In contrast to Wilkerson, Littleman has strong convictions and faith in his plan to change reality. "'Are you still so unconvinced?'" he asks Wilkerson. "'Why is it so much easier for you to doubt than believe?'" But both, as Wideman illustrates by juxtaposing the political and psychological significance of the lynch rope in America, are men of ideas rather than action. Whereas Littleman needs Wilkerson as an intellectual and revolutionary disciple, Wilkerson needs Littleman as a surrogate for the father he loves and hates because his life seemed so accidental and shapeless.

As the omniscient narrator glides in and out of third- and first-person points of view, Wideman compels us to become intimately involved with the characters, their frustrations and their existential choices. Internal and external events merge in Sweetman's mind in the opening domestic scene:

> He would call her but if it is morning she may be asleep and perhaps she slept right through and I can tell her any lie, choose the decent hour I came in just too tired so went to sleep downstairs on the couch. Even as he forms a probable fiction he knows she will be sitting in the kitchen, aware of everything. And she is and she asks why did he bother to come home for the hour he did. He wants more from her. He wants her calling him out of his name, calling him *Sweetman,* treating him like he's still in the street or like she wants him gone.

Wideman then quickly shifts to Bernice's thoughts and feelings about the emptiness in her kitchen and her life, about her husband drinking himself to death, ashamed to face her, and her getting "older, tireder and poorer." Next we see and hear Sweetman on his way before sunup to wrestle garbage cans and chase rats, rapping with other sanitation engineers, including his best friend Childress.

Later, Wideman encourages our sympathy for his protagonist, who is reflecting over the pages of his appointment book:

> Were there only two choices? Either cage time in the red lines that marched across the page or like his father in his lost weekends abandon any illusion of control. Littleman believed all men were trapped. No choice existed except to reverse or destroy the particular historical process which at a given time determines the life of individual men. He would see my father and me as equally unredeemable. Perhaps he is right. I believe in his plan. It may free men for an instant, create a limbo between prisons. But can the instant be extended? Can it support life and a society? I don't think Littleman cares. I don't think my father cared when he felt the need to escape.

By the end of the novel the reader's sympathies have shifted several times among the characters. And though he sympathizes with Littleman's historical imperatives and existential choices, Wideman, as the tragic denouement illustrates, identifies more closely with his protagonist's internal changes, especially his moral and political decision to sabotage the plan.

The Homewood trilogy marks the culmination of Wideman's move from a Eurocentric to a fundamentally Afrocentric tradition, his coming home as it were in the form and style of an extended mediation on history: oral and literary, personal and social. *Damballah,* the collection of twelve stories that the author calls long overdue

letters to his imprisoned younger brother, Robby, invokes the ancestral gods of Africa in the New World, especially Damballah Wedo, the venerable serpent god of paternity, as the spirit guides for his mythic ancestral journey. To invoke these gods, says Wideman, is "to stretch one's hand back to that time and to gather up all history into a solid contemporary ground beneath one's feet." From the prefacing texts—letter to Robby, brief note on Damballah, and Begat Chart—and the opening legend of the passing on of the spirit of Damballah to Afro-Americans, the generic distinctions between history and fiction, novel and romance, orality and literariness collapse as Wideman blends epistle, legend, myth, fable, biography, and autobiography in a series of interdependent fictive constructs. The book concludes cyclically without closure with **"The Beginning of Homewood,"** another letter to his brother. This letter is metafictional in that it is about the creative act of writing. Wideman explains that it began as a literary retelling of the family legend about how the family tree was planted on Bruston Hill in Homewood, the black community of Pittsburgh, Pennsylvania, with the arrival of Sybela Owens, their great-great-great-grandmother, who ran away from slavery with her white master's son, Charles Bell: "her lover, her liberator, her children's father...." "This woman, this Sybela Owens, our ancestor," Wideman writes reflectively and ambivalently, "bore the surname of her first owner and the Christian name Sybela, which was probably a corruption of Sybil, a priestess pledged to Apollo.... On the plantation Sybela Owens was called Belle. Called that by some because it was customary for slaves to disregard the cumbersome, ironic names bestowed by whites, and rechristen one another in a secret, second language, a language whose forms and words gave substance to the captives' need to see themselves as human beings." The story, passed on orally by the women in the family, of her legendary urge for freedom as a runaway slave, her crime, corresponds in the author-narrator's consciousness to that of his imprisoned brother and fosters anxiety and ambivalence about his own freedom and success. Why not me, he asks: "Ask myself if I would have committed the crime of running away or if I would have stayed and tried to make the best of a hopeless situation. Ask if you really had any choice, if anything had changed in the years between her crime and yours."

The two novels, *Hiding Place* and *Sent for You Yesterday,* continue Wideman's mediation on the history of his family, home, and people. Its title borrowed from the black spiritual "There's No Hiding Place Down There," *Hiding Place* expands **"Tommy,"** the imaginative rewriting of the story in *Damballah* that foregrounds Robert Wideman's actual involvement in a robbery attempt and murder, and reweaves it with the story of Mother Bess, the granddaughter of Mother Sybela and the oldest living family member. Through the interweaving of memory, reverie, and interior monologues as well as by the manipulation of black speech, music, and religion, Wideman reveals the sociopsychological process by which the gnarled old roots and wayward young branches of the Owens/Bell family tree strengthen and renew themselves together. Mother Bess, who is hiding from the world in the dilapidated ancestral home on Bruston Hill because of the loss of her only son and blues-singing husband, reluctantly shares her hiding place and spiritual wisdom with her great-grandson Tommy, who is running away from the police because he was an accomplice in a robbery attempt that resulted in murder. Reconciling their mutual ambivalence at the end of the novel, both find the resolve in themselves and each other to come out of hiding and return to confront the blueslike reality of Homewood and the world.

Its title borrowed from the blues song that Jimmy Rushing made popular, and its time structure influenced by Laurence Sterne's *Tristram Shandy*, **Sent for You Yesterday** is the long, sad song of Homewood and the contemporary inheritors of its blues legacy. Dividing the novel into three major sections ("The Return of Albert Wilkes," "The Courting of Lucy Tate," and "Brother"), Wideman, who is emotionally, psychologically, and morally close to the surnameless narrator, dances back and forth in time through dreams, memo-

Wideman playing basketball in his driveway in 1985 with his sons Jake (left), then age 14, and Danny, age 16.

ries, and reveries. He artfully yet ambivalently employs the rhythms of black speech and music, especially train symbolism, to reconstruct the blues legacy of Homewood to present and future generations of the French, Tate, and Lawson families. Spanning the years from 1941 to 1970, the novel begins in 1970 with the first-person narrator, christened "Doot" by his Uncle Carl French's best friend Brother Tate, looking back, like Tristram Shandy, to events before he was born. He remembers and affirms through stories he has heard over the years in Homewood that he is "linked to Brother Tate by stories, by his memories of a dead son, by my own memories of a silent scat-singing albino man who was my uncle's best friend." Just as the untrained Brother Tate mysteriously embodies the blues spirit and piano-playing talent of Albert Wilkes, whose return after seven years to a rapidly declining Homewood results in the police blowing his brains out in the Tate home, the narrator, "In Brother's eyes .... grew up living not only my own life, but the one snatched from Junebug," Brother's son of the same age who died in a fire in 1941.

Brother Tate's sixteen-year silence in mourning for his son, his youthful ritual of playing chicken with oncoming trains, and his recurring dreams of trains, as well as Lucy Tate's storytelling quilt and the bone fragment from Albert Wilkes's skull that she saves signify, along with the blues, the keep-on-keeping-on lessons that the old Homewood people taught their young by example. As Lucy tells her lover and the narrator's uncle, Carl French, in the closing pages of the book:

> "They made Homewood. Walking around, doing the things they had to do. Homewood wasn't bricks and boards. Homewood was them singing and loving and getting where they needed to get. They made these streets. That's why Homewood was real once. Cause they were real. And we gave it all up. Us middle people. You and me, Carl. We got scared and gave up too easy and now it's gone. Just sad songs left. And whimpering. Nothing left to give the ones we supposed to be saving Homewood for. Nothing but empty hands and sad stories."

Nevertheless, Wideman closes the novel with a ray of hope as his principal narrator, Doot, begins responding to Smokey Robinson's "Tracks of My Tears" on the radio and fantasizing that Brother Tate was signaling to Albert Wilkes to begin playing the piano. Finally, Doot was "learning to stand, to walk, learning to dance."

The major underlying theme, then, in Wideman's novels is that what we think we are is at least as important as what we are. "From the very beginning," he says, "Western civilization has an idea of what black men are, and that idea has come down to us generation after generation, has distorted and made impossible some kinds of very human and basic interaction. The mechanics of that are both very frightening and very fascinating." To explore the interior landscapes of his characters and the conflict between their ascribed and achieved identities as black men, Wideman, who also believes that racial memories exist in the imagination, draws on a wide variety of sources in his shift from a Eurocentric to a basically Afrocentric tradition. As in Demby's *Catacombs,* his innovative use of legend, myth, music, and painting in *A Glance Away, Hurry Home,* and *The Lynchers* gives resonance to the theme of double-consciousness in the tradition of the Afro-American novel. At the same time his use in the Homewood trilogy of Afrocentric terms for order to counterbalance the anxiety of Eurocentric influences in his experiment with time structure and point of view is paradigmatic of black postmodernists' double vision of contemporary black American experiences of reality. (pp. 307-15)

> *Bernard W. Bell, "The Contemporary Afro-American Novel, 2: Modernism and Postmodernism," in his* The Afro-American Novel and Its Tradition, *The University of Massachusetts Press, 1987, pp. 281-338.*

Madison Smartt Bell (essay date 1988)

[*Bell is an American novelist. In the essay below, he explores the theme of abstract racial hatred in* Reuben.]

[The] titular hero of John Edgar Wideman's new novel [*Reuben*] is lawyer to the poor, outcast and dispossessed black citizenry of the Homewood district made legendary by Wideman's earlier work. At a glance he appears to be the sort of lawyer one would more likely find in a rural place or some small town, a tireless laborer on behalf of the legally unlucky, paid in pig's feet and promises more often than anything else. Because of his considerable age, his reticence, and some dwarfish physical peculiarities, he is a figure of great mystery in the community, a queer cross between a respected and envied member of the professional classes and some new kind of witch doctor. Ingeniously, Wideman lets a sort of communal mutter introduce him:

> *Booker, you better get your behind over to see Reuben. Hey, I heard Hazel's in a trick even Reuben can't fix. Reuben's a dog. Least Reuben do for you when none of the others will. Reuben got piles of money. Just too crazy to spend it. Reuben's crazy like a fox. Like a rat, you mean.*

Reuben is also the needle's eye through which the threads of the book's plot are drawn, and in aggregate, the stories of his clients, disclosed like his own by means of interior monologue, compose the whole story of the novel. His average client is somebody like Tucker, an old craftsman who accepts a job tearing down empty buildings, without knowing that the people who hired him are strip-and-run thieves. Typically, Reuben handles not the case of mistaken identity but the case of mistaken behavior.

Of such cases the most important is that of Kwansa Parker, who comes to us straight from the welfare system's blotter: an unwed mother, not too bright, she has known a lot of sex and precious little love. She's not a prostitute, but she brings men home and lets them give her money, and because of that she is in danger of losing her son Cudjoe to his father, now established in a comparatively stable marriage.

Kwansa looks like a textbook case of an unfit mother, but we're not allowed to think that separation from her child would be much help to either one of them:

> Her son had saved her. He was her mirror, she could find herself in his eyes, laugh because he laughed, cry when he cried. Touching him, touch lived again. When he slept, she could dream."

Wideman has pulled no punches with this characterization; Kwansa is as disorganized and hapless as they come, just smart enough to see how she is contributing to the spoliation of her own life without being strong enough to stop.

> The hardest thing of all to believe was the dream she'd carried of a better Kwansa, the Kwansa she'd find one day and throw her arms around and they'd cry and laugh like long-lost sisters, like fools in the middle of Homewood Avenue don't care who's watching, don't care what anybody got to say.

Reuben's bread-and-butter work is to pilot people like Kwansa through the maze of a social and legal bureaucracy which (more through ineptitude than malice, one hopes) tends to grind down their hope and their sense of self-worth. His relationship with another client, Wally, is considerably more complex. Wally is a retired basketball player who now works as a university athletic recruiter, and he comes to Reuben because he fears he is likely to be scape-goated in an investigation of expense account fiddling, but their conversation is mostly of other matters.

Scrap by scrap, Reuben tells Wally much of his own history: how he worked as valet, janitor, and occasional pimp for a white fraternity in Philadelphia, how the white boys tricked him into a situation where they could rape the woman he loved before his eyes, how in the aftermath of this ugly affair they caused her death, how he resolved to survive the episode, to persevere until he had learned the law, as if that learning would be the means to his revenge. Wally responds with a tale of his own: how on one of his recruiting trips he encountered a middle-class white stranger in some anonymous public restroom, and apparently for no reason (no more than is given for many lynchings, etc.) knocked him cold and drowned him in a toilet. It is never clear if Wally has actually done the murder or fantasized it or been told about [it] by someone else; what seems to matter is that the thought of it attracts or at least compels him.

A blurb on the back jacket of *Reuben* gives Wideman much credit "for placing white readers deep in black heads." In the case of *Reuben,* it must be said, this is not a very pleasant place for white readers to find themselves. A clear message is given that the fundamental atrocity committed by whites on blacks, a version of which Reuben recalls, can never be forgiven or forgotten. As it's expressed in Wally's recollections:

> Abstract hate means you don't got nothing against
> any particular person. You may even like or respect a
> particular person, but at the same time there's
> something about that person, "the white part," you
> can't ever forgive, never forget.

The notion that this abstract hate is an elemental part of
the mental make-up of all or most black people is bound
to be uncomfortable for white readers, though none of
us can say for sure it isn't so. Moreover, the novel seems
to imply that not only is there nothing we can do about
it, it really isn't any of our business.

Reviewed from the standpoint of "abstract hate," the
social system against which Reuben seeks to protect his
clientele seems not merely inept but actively inimical,
controlled as it is by racial enemies. So it becomes
possible to think that every person Reuben is able to
safely steer through the bureaucratic labyrinth counts as
a kind of revenge for his own insults and injuries. Still,
one also comes to feel that, although his humiliations
persist through the end of the novel, he has somehow got
past the idea of revenge.

> Trouble is that hate's bad for you. Takes something
> away. Fucks with your insides. Spoils whatever you
> try to do, how you feel about what you've done.
> Whether you're dealing with white people or yourself
> in the mirror.

Like most of Wideman's works of fiction, this one is
perhaps most importantly a detailed and sensitive
portrait of the inner life of its characters, here rendered
credibly and frighteningly as a kind of endless nightmare. Aside from, or along with that, it seems to be
saying something new about the old vexed question of
race relations in America. The question is not whether
"hate's bad for you," but why. If black people do need to
get around their hatred, it's not so as to accommodate to
whites but to accommodate to themselves. That is what
Reuben himself seems to have accomplished finally, in
the sort of moral victory that has force to save the soul.

"Revenge," Wally says to him at one point. "So you did
try to get back at them."

"In my fashion," Reuben says. "With love and
hate...yes...it's complicated."

Well, so it is. (pp. 60-1)

> *Madison Smartt Bell, "Somehow Past Re-*
> *venge," in* The North American Review,
> *Vol. 273, No. 2, June, 1988, pp. 60-1.*

Charles Johnson (essay date 1990)

[*Johnson, an American novelist and short story writer,
has won critical acclaim for erudite fiction that
incorporates elements of fantasy, parable, folklore,
slave narrative, and Eastern and Western philosophies. In the following review, he expresses disappointment with Wideman's novel* Philadelphia Fire.]

Novelist John Edgar Wideman is easily the most
critically acclaimed black male writer of the last decade.
The author of 10 books, he received the PEN/Faulkner
Award for his 1984 novel, **Sent for You Yesterday,** and
extensive praise for **Brothers and Keepers,** his memoir of
his brother Robert's imprisonment for armed robbery
and felony murder. Each new work, such as his recent
story collection **Fever,** is regularly featured on the front
pages of the nation's various book review sections. A
new, ambitious work of fiction by a writer as prolific
and artistically uncompromising as Wideman is, therefore, a reason for celebration.

However, Wideman fans, of which I'm one, may be
disappointed, if not downright confused, by **Philadelphia Fire,** his latest novel, which purportedly is about
the May 13, 1985, assault by the City of Philadelphia on
members of a black organization called MOVE. Eleven
people who defied a police eviction order were killed in
this widely covered incident, but Wideman's book is
only tangentially about the event. It is less journalism
than an impressionistic hymn to the dead in West
Philly, not so much fictionalized history (or even a
story) as a lyric, angry brooding on the excesses of white
power, and in this sense brings to mind James Baldwin's
use of the Atlanta child-murder case as a springboard
for his own sociological reflections in *The Evidence of
Things Not Seen.*

Divided into three parts, **Philadelphia Fire** opens with
Cudjoe, a former teacher and writer (and Wideman's
alter ego), learning of the MOVE disaster while in self-
exile on the island of Mykonos. A drifter now, he feels
himself to be "a half-black someone, a half-man who
couldn't be depended upon" because "he'd married a
white woman and fathered half-white kids" whom he
believes he's failed. Cudjoe feels driven to find a lost
boy named Simmie, "the only survivor of the holocaust
on Osage Avenue." He returns to Philadelphia and
begins his quest for the boy by interviewing Margaret
Jones, a former member of the MOVE family.

MOVE's leader, says Jones,

> taught us about the holy Tree of Life. How we all
> born part of it. How we all one family. Showed us
> how the rotten system of this society is about
> chopping down a Tree. Society hates health. Society
> don't want strong people. It wants people weak and
> sick so it can use them up...He taught us to love
> and respect ourselves...He said that every day. We
> must protect Life and pass it on so the Tree never
> dies.

As it turns out, this is as close as Cudjoe ever gets to
unraveling the philosophy and history of MOVE, or to
Simmie, who Jones says "just disappeared." A dinner
with his erstwhile running buddy Timbro, a "class
dude" now working as cultural attaché for the city's
black mayor, reveals only that Philadelphia's officials
regarded the MOVE people as "embarrassing," cultists
who had to be removed because they,

didn't want no kind of city, no kind of government. Wanted to live like people live in the woods. Now how's that sound?... Mayor breaking his butt to haul the city into the twenty-first century and them fools on Osage want their block to the jungle.

In part two, the thin line that separates Wideman from Cudjoe ("Why this Cudjoe, then?" he asks. "Why am I him when I tell certain parts? Why am I hiding from myself?") disappears completely as this section opens with the author and his wife watching the MOVE fire on CNN. Wideman receives a call from his recently imprisoned son, broods on "the unmitigated cruelty of the legal system," and in a moving passage wonders,

> Will I ever try to write my son's story? Not dealing with it may be causing the forgetfulness I'm experiencing... I do feel my narrative faculty weakening... What I'm doing or saying or intending engages me only on a superficial level. I commit only minimal attention, barely enough to get me through the drill I'm required to perform.

But mostly Part Two concerns Cudjoe's failed attempt to stage a production of *The Tempest,* using black kids as performers, in a West Philly park in the late 1960s. This play is, Wideman writes, "figure within a figure, play within a play, it is the bounty and hub of all else written about the fire." Wideman's "authentically revised version of Willy's con" is, at bottom, the now familiar interpretation of Prospero as a white imperialist and Caliban as the colonized, and he invites us to see the MOVE tragedy as a "lesson... about colonization, imperialism, recidivism, the royal [expletive] over of the weak by the strong, colored by white, many by few..."

The final section, briefer than the others, focuses on a black derelict named J.B., a beggar who witnesses a white businessman jump to his death from the 19th floor of the Penn Mutual Savings and Loan building, takes the dead man's briefcase, and is himself set on fire by white hooligans. Then it shifts back to Cudjoe attending a memorial service for the dead of Osage Avenue. "Hey fellas. It's about youall," he thinks.

> If they offed them people on Osage yesterday just might be you today. Or tomorrow... because that day in May the Man wasn't playing. Huh uh. Taking no names. No prisoners... And here you are again making no connections, taking out no insurance.

And there you have it: a novel in which we learn nothing new about the MOVE incident, a book brimming over with brutal, emotional honesty and moments of beautiful prose lyricism (no one can sing the spiritual side of playing basketball better than Wideman), but by no means a page-turner. In a recent interview the author, who remains one of our most important fiction writers, said he chose to write about MOVE because, "My goal is not to let it disappear into the collective amnesia." In this noble intention, at least, *Philadelphia Fire* is not unsuccessful. (pp. 6, 12)

> *Charles Johnson, "The Fire That Time," in* Book World—The Washington Post, *October 7, 1990, pp. 6, 12.*

Mark Hummel (essay date 1991)

[*In the following review of* Philadelphia Fire, *Hummel praises Wideman's versatility, characterizing the book as a surreal work of survival.*]

Dream time. *Philadelphia Fire,* as readers of John Edgar Wideman's work have come to expect, seems to be written in dream time, that funky, hazy slipping in and out of sleep, of nightmares so real they could only mean their occupant must be awake—the everyday time of being Black in America. Wideman freely mixes fiction and nonfiction, past and present, street rap and Shakespeare, which, carried to the reader through multiple narrators, conjure a novel of layered depth. As characters surface, then disappear, each connected to the decaying cityscape of Philadelphia, they lament the loss of their children and of themselves.

The characters of this novel unite in the realization that on a Monday in May 1985, the city-sponsored destruction of the MOVE house on Osage Avenue took with it pieces of their lives, and that, in their Blackness, their common heritage will be scooped up among the ashes of eleven dead men, women, and children. This factual event, the police bombing and subsequent rush of fire which destroyed fifty-three homes, sparks the fiction. *Philadelphia Fire* is the story of intersecting lives; the MOVE fire is common ground for a series of middle-aged, educated Black men who all have, in one form or another, been living behind exteriors hiding lives of pain and isolation.

We meet Cudjoe, a writer returning to his West Philly roots from a self-imposed, invisible exile on the Greek island of Mykonos. Cudjoe, feeling a connection he cannot articulate, returns in search of a naked child reported fleeing the burning house on Osage. In returning home he must face the losses that sent him running away years before—his failed marriage and severance from his sons, his abandoned students (Black youngsters he had dreamed could stage a revised *Tempest*), his hope of a world capable of change. The child for whom he searches, Simba, is never found. Instead Cudjoe finds painful memories and shattered lives. He even finds an underground war waged by children, their apparent freedom anthems touching familiar rhythms but their words unintelligible; only graffiti messages shouting "money, power, things" are clear. We recognize the urban-renewed streets as familiar homes to our children, fighting for survival in a world of drugs, poverty, and crime, searching for identity and hope.

Those familiar with Wideman's work are accustomed to the sometimes slim divisions between fiction and nonfiction, and in the midst of this novel we encounter Wideman himself interrupting Cudjoe's story, drawn by the passing TV images of the fire in Philadelphia on the very street where he had lived years before. Like Cudjoe, he cannot distance himself from the burning, and through narrative, quotations, and letters, he finds the connections between past and present, between him and Cudjoe and the dead residents of the MOVE house.

He writes to and of a son lost to a jail cell and a split self—his own lost child. The clarity with which Wideman writes through his own pain is one of the strengths of this book; stronger still is his ability to see the connection of his experience to others.

One of those others is J.B., college-educated, perhaps once idealistic, but now living on the streets of Philadelphia, an abandoned skeleton of promise, living almost entirely in dream time. J.B. brings the novel to its climax in Independence Square, where living a daytime nightmare, he is convinced little White boys have doused his sleeping body with kerosene and ignited him. Desperate to extinguish the flames, he flails in a dry fountain. Cudjoe is there in the square, too, attending a memorial for the victims of Osage Avenue. Unaware of J.B., he shares something of J.B.'s real paranoia, questioning what may come next in a world stranger than fiction, left only with the heavy weight of words.

The potent words of *Philadelphia Fire* form a multilayered story mourning the loss of a generation—a generation of promise—and the subsequent loss of their children. This is a sad and painful book. Yet it is a book that is vital to an honest reading of contemporary America. In it Wideman shows his versatility, shifting with ease from the sweaty, out-of-breath reality of a basketball court to the dreamy ambiguity that comes with trying to make sense of a world where sons and brothers live their lives in jail, where vital teachers are furloughed, where police drop bombs from helicopters. Some of the novel's most important moments occur within the dreams of its characters, like Cudjoe's nightmare of being sprawled on a basketball court, legs amputated, while simultaneously floating above his own screaming body, witness to a child lynched from the basketball rim. He realizes the child is

> me and every black boy I've ever seen running up and down playing ball and I'm screaming for help and frozen in my tracks and can't believe it, can't believe he's dangling there and the dumb thing I'm also thinking in this dream or whatever it is, is if they'd just waited a little longer his legs would have grown, his feet would have reached the ground and he'd be OK.

This lynched boy haunts Cudjoe, as Simba has, for the loss they represent surrounds him in memory and in reality.

It is important that Simba is never found, for his absence is stronger than his presence, a symbol for the lost children everywhere. He represents a world where our children are being consumed by fire. "A child lost cancels the natural order, the circle is broken." Wideman, knowing that to break the circle of generations affects all, is willing to step forward and shoulder part of the burden. Though he purposely questions the generation who came of age in the idealism and faded hope of the 1960s, this burden is one we all must share.

The dream time depths of this novel prove difficult but immensely important and always eloquent. Despite the tough questions and the deep-rooted pain, the novel is about survival. While hope is distant, Wideman asks us to hold on. And while his own words seem—to him—heavy, even cumbersome, all he has left, they bring meaning to events apparently beyond meaning.

> *Mark Hummel, "Mourning the Loss of a Generation," in* The Bloomsbury Review, *Vol. 11, No. 2, March, 1991, p. 1.*

FURTHER READING

Bennion, John. "The Shape of Memory in John Edgar Wideman's *Sent for You Yesterday*." *Black American Literature Forum* 20, Nos. 1-2 (Spring-Summer 1986): 143-50.

> Examination based on Bennion's assertion that "the reader's struggle to apprehend the familiar and foreign elements of [*Sent for You Yesterday*] approximates the characters' struggle to apprehend their own world through perception, memory, and metaphorical reconstruction of perception and memory."

Berben, Jacqueline. "Beyond Discourse: The Unspoken versus Words in the Fiction of John Edgar Wideman." *Callaloo* 8, No. 3 (Fall 1985): 525-34.

> Analysis of Wideman's use of interior monologue and dialogue in *Hiding Place* to juxtapose the bleak reality of his characters' environments with their escape into comforting worlds of dream and fantasy.

Coleman, James W. "Going Back Home: The Literary Development of John Edgar Wideman." *CLA Journal* XXVIII, No. 3 (March 1985): 326-43.

> Overview of Wideman's novels up to and including *The Homewood Trilogy,* focusing on Wideman's treatment of family, community, and the black experience.

O'Brien, John, ed. "John Wideman." In his *Interviews with Black Writers,* pp. 213-23. New York: Liveright, 1973.

> Interview with Wideman in which he discusses such topics as the genesis of his first three novels, use of experimental forms, and treatment of race and history.

Wideman, John Edgar. "The Language of Home." *New York Times Book Review* (13 January 1985): 1, 35-6.

> Wideman comments on why he has frequently returned to his childhood neighborhood of Homewood in his fiction.

John A. Williams
1925-

(Full name John Alfred Williams; has also written as J. Dennis Gregory) American novelist, journalist, essayist, dramatist, short story writer, biographer, poet, critic, and editor.

A contemporary American novelist, Williams is best known for *The Man Who Cried I Am* (1967). "Williams, arguably the finest Afro-American novelist of his generation," James L. de Jongh asserted, "is certainly among the most prolific." He has produced a book almost every year for the past twenty years. Focusing on black Americans, his work examines the effects of racism on individual identity and pride.

"I grew up in Syracuse, New York, 'apple-knocker country,' where summers are splendid and winters war against the psyche," Williams stated in *Contemporary Authors Autobiography Series*. As a child he played with children from a variety of backgrounds and, at the time, thought nothing of it: "About forty or fifty of us went to the schools together and over the years played ball and drank together. . . . [But then] the beneficent neighbors turn[ed] watchful over their Greek, Irish, Jewish, Italian, and down-at-the-heels WASP daughters." At age seventeen, he joined the United States Navy. Upon discharge three years later, he returned to school and earned a B. A. in journalism and English from Syracuse University. He worked briefly in radio and television but entered the publishing industry after moving to New York City. While working at Comet Press Books in 1955, he completed his first novel, "One for New York," later published as *The Angry Ones* (1960). He has since published ten more novels and has taught at various colleges around the country. His most recent work is a biography of Richard Pryor, *If I Stop I'll Die: Comedy and Tragedy of Richard Pryor* (1991).

Williams's first three novels trace the problems facing blacks in a white society. *The Angry Ones, Night Song* (1961), and *Sissie* (1963) focus on black men and women who try to come to terms with a nation that discriminates against them. In *The Angry Ones,* for instance, the protagonist, Steve Hill, "struggles with various kinds of racial prejudice in housing and employment, but the focus [of the novel] is on his growing realization of the way his employers at Rocket Press destroy the dreams of would-be authors," according to Jeffrey Helterman. *The Man Who Cried I Am,* the novel that brought Williams international recognition, further explores the exploitation of blacks by white society. The protagonist, Max Reddick, is a black writer living in Europe who is dying of colon cancer. His chief literary rival and mentor is Harry Ames, a fellow black author but one who "packages racial anger and sells it in his books," Helterman stated. While in Paris to attend Harry's funeral, Max learns that Harry was murdered

because he uncovered a plot by the Western nations to prevent the unification of black Africa. Max himself unearths another conspiracy: America's genocidal solution to the race problem—code-named "King Alfred." The King Alfred Plan calls for the "handling [of] 22 million black Americans in case they become unruly." The Plan further decrees: "In the event of widespread and continuing and coordinated racial disturbances in the United States, King Alfred, at the discretion of the President, is to be put into action immediately. In case of emergency, minority members will be evacuated from the cities by federalized national guard units . . . and detained in nearby military installations until a further course of action has been decided." When Max discovers this plan, he is put to death. "What purpose does the King Alfred portion of the novel serve?" asked Robert E. Fleming in *Contemporary Literature*. "In one sense, black people have been systematically killed off in the United States since their first introduction to its shores. Malnutrition, disease, poverty, psychological conditioning, and spiritual starvation have been the tools, rather than military operations and gas chambers, but the result has often been the same. King Alfred is not only a prophetic warning of what might happen here but a fictional metaphor for what has been happening and is happening still."

Like *The Man Who Cried I Am*, *!Click Song* (1982) details the careers of two writers. Paul Cummings, a Jewish novelist, writes about the reaffirmation of Jewishness, while Cato Caldwell Douglass, a black author, aims to overcome racism in the publishing industry. "*!Click Song* is at least the equal of Williams's other masterpiece, *The Man Who Cried I Am*," stated de Jongh. "The emotional power, the fluid structuring of time, the resonant synthesis of fiction and history are similar. But the novelist's mastery is greater, for Williams's technique here is seamless and invisible." Similarly, Seymour Krim noted: "Unlike a James Baldwin or an Amiri Baraka, Williams is primarily a storyteller, which is what makes the reality of Black Rage become something other than a polemic in his hands . . . . Before [Cato's] odyssey is ended, we know in our bones what it is like to be a gifted black survivor in America today; we change skins as we read, so to speak, and the journey of living inside another is so intense that no white reader will ever again be able to plead ignorance."

Among Williams's nonfiction work are *Africa: Her History, Lands, and People* (1962), *This Is My Country Too* (1965), *The King God Didn't Save: Reflections on the Life and Death of Martin Luther King, Jr.* (1970), *The Most Native of Sons: A Biography of Richard Wright* (1970), and *Minorities in the City* (1975). "I like to switch-hit from fiction to nonfiction, and to have projects ready to go as soon as one is finished," Williams revealed. "I'm not sure I could ever get used to having more space between works than I now have. . . . There are times when I am writing a novel and it feels like walking against a great wind, since my estimation of much of the long fiction that is around is not high at all. As a society we are not great readers. Good writing demands mental exertion and exertion generally is not in much demand, despite all the exercising going on. . . . Writing novels—always with an eye to doing something new with each one—most satisfies whatever is within me that demands such satisfaction."

(For further information about Williams's life and works, see *Black Writers*; *Contemporary Authors*, Vols. 53-56; *Contemporary Authors Autobiography Series*, Vol. 3; *Contemporary Authors New Revision Series*, Vols. 6, 26; *Contemporary Literary Criticism*, Vols. 5, 13; and *Dictionary of Literary Biography*, Vols. 2, 33.)

PRINCIPAL WORKS

The Angry Ones (novel) 1960; also published as *One for New York*, 1975
Night Song (novel) 1961
Africa: Her History, Lands, and People (nonfiction) 1962
The Angry Black [editor] (anthology) 1962; also published as *Beyond the Angry Black*, 1966
Sissie (novel) 1963; also published as *Journey Out of Anger*, 1965
The Protectors: The Heroic Story of the Narcotics Agents, Citizens and Officials in Their Unending, Unsung Battles against Organized Crime in America and Abroad [as J. Dennis Gregory with Harry J. Anslinger] (nonfiction) 1964
This Is My Country Too (nonfiction) 1965
The Man Who Cried I Am (novel) 1967
Sweet Love, Bitter (screenplay) 1967
Sons of Darkness, Sons of Light: A Novel of Some Probability (novel) 1969
The King God Didn't Save: Reflections on the Life and Death of Martin Luther King, Jr. (nonfiction) 1970
The Most Native of Sons: A Biography of Richard Wright [with Dorothy Sterling] (biography) 1970
Captain Blackman (novel) 1972
Flashbacks: A Twenty-Year Diary of Article Writing (nonfiction) 1973
Minorities in the City (nonfiction) 1975
Mothersill and the Foxes (novel) 1975
The Junior Bachelor Society (novel) 1976
Last Flight from Ambo Ber (drama) 1981
!Click Song (novel) 1982
The Berhama Account (novel) 1985
Jacob's Ladder (novel) 1987
If I Stop I'll Die: Comedy and Tragedy of Richard Pryor (biography) 1991

David Henderson (essay date 1969)

[*In the essay below, Henderson summarizes* The Man Who Cried I Am, *contending that "a plan for the extermination of American Blacks" is a reality outside the novel.*]

Since we all are acquainted with the elaborate plans that the United States government has to destroy Russia and/or China in the event of an emergency vis-à-vis such "cold war" suppositions as *Fail-Safe, Doctor Strangelove* or most recently *The President's Plane Is Missing*, it should not surprise us if our government also has a plan to exterminate or detentionize black persons in America in the event that the yearly racial riots all over America (would) suddenly burst into a race war.

Since a strafing or napalm or atomic bomb has never fallen on an American city, nor a strafing and napalm mission ever performed, it would be difficult for us to imagine such a scene. Only Japan was A-bombed. But we do not speak the language. We have only the science-fiction movie monster fantasies to prepare us, and Japan is the exporter and Joseph E. Levine, the impressario of a great many of them such as *Godzilla, Rodan,* and *The Monster That Devoured Cleveland.* Whereas, the horror the Jews experienced in Nazi Germany is closer to the imagination and dream pysche of Americans.

It is not difficult for black people to recall how they were brought to America. Nor can they easily forget the usurpation of black civil rights during the post-Reconstruction era, and most recently the special treatment

Adam Clayton Powell was afforded by the House of Representatives. The so-called conscience of the nation was aroused when TV showed the police of Birmingham, Alabama, brutally suppressing black civil rights marchers. The gargantuan police use of "fire-power" (bullets) in the Harlem riots of 1964, the Newark and Detroit riots of 1967, shows that the law enforcement authorities of the land will go to great lengths to protect the stores and properties. A plan for the extermination of American Blacks would not be contrary to American History.

Such a plan, as the climax of the twenty-year saga of a black writer, which spans three continents in interracial jet-set romances and is chock full of black existential artists, spies, and counter-spies, makes *The Man Who Cried I Am* picaresque best-seller material.

The Man Who Cried I Am is the dying vision of a black writer, Max Reddick. As the book opens, we meet Max in a Dutch cafe waiting for his former Dutch wife. He is "without chick or child," forty-three, and dying from progressed cancer of the anus. Frequent doses of morphine are necessary to quell the pain. Frequent shots of liquor are also necessary to quell a different sort of pain—the pain that began twenty years ago, when he decided to be a serious writer.

America has never been kind to her writers, least of all the ones who happen to be black. Max began to die, in a way, when he became a writer. As a young writer in the early forty's, Max met and became fast friends with Harry Ames (the most vivid portrayal of Richard Wright to date) who in turn was not so kind to America either. Max regarded Ames as his mentor, as Ames was indeed "The Father of the Black writers." From the twenty-year starting line Max and Harry Ames dash through life: through women and books, parties, joy, and misery; Ames to self-exile in France where he was sure he would be treated as a man and an artist; Max Reddick from novelist to top-notch journalist, who is awarded the African desk of *Events* (a *Newsweek*-type magazine) and who becomes as well a speech writer and advisor to the President of the United States. Max, too, had wanted to be treated as an artist. Somewhere along the way he becomes aware of the fact that the publishing houses thought it sufficient to have only one black writer in the house, one boy. By the same token the monotheism that caps the spirituality of America carries over to the treatment of black writers. Therefore Ames could be the only god, the Father, and hence, his death was eagerly awaited by the younger black writers. As Marion Dawes (James Baldwin) put it to Ames: "It is the duty of the son to destroy the father." This flabbergasted Ames, but Max who was with him noticed that he was secretly pleased. The scenes depicting the black artists' expatriate scene in Europe and America are the best in the book. There is little known or written about the black artist underground and Williams in his role as novelist-documentarian has provided us with some well chosen insights. Many of Williams' characters and events parallel real-life-figures and occurrences.

Williams has been known to do this before. His second novel, *Nightsong,* for all its shortcomings, provided a powerful characterization of another famous black artist: Charlie "Yardbird" Parker, the master jazz saxophonist.

"Yardbird" is a "live" character in *Nightsong,* but ironically it is the death of Harry Ames that causes the story of *The Man Who Cried I Am* to be told. Max has traveled from his African desk to Europe to attend the surprise funeral of Harry Ames. His legal dope addiction and the alcohol combine with the funeral to swing him into a heightened state of reverie about this man who has had such a profound impact upon his life and about whom he has ambivalent feelings. Soon his reveries are fueled by the strange legacy Harry Ames has left him, in the form of a prefacing letter and a briefcase containing a top-secret United States government document called "The King Alfred Plan."

In the letter, written as it seems from the grave, Harry Ames gives a history of the international politics behind The King Alfred Plan and also tells how it got into his hands. Harry Ames starts off with the chilling remark: "knowing may kill you, just as knowing killed me and a few other people you'll met in this letter." Ames goes on to say that in the late fifties Africa threw a scare into its European masters when it seemed to be heading toward a United States of Africa. "Couldn't Africa become another giant, like China, with even more hatred for the white West?" The West acted quickly. "Representatives from France, Great Britain, Belgium, Portugal, Australia, Spain, Brazil, South Africa and the United States of America met along with white observers from most of the African countries that appeared to be on their way to independence." The meetings, called The Alliance Blanc, were held in absolute secrecy and moved from country to country. Meetings in America were held "around Saranac Lake—Dreiser's setting for *An American Tragedy.* . . ." The disclosure of America's membership in The Alliance Blanc would have touched off a racial cataclysm—but America went far beyond the evils the Alliance was perpetuating. The Europeans had recovered from their initial panic when they realized that they could control Africa's destiny economically. But "America sitting on a bubbling black cauldron felt that it had to map its own contingency plans for handling 22 million black Americans in case they became unruly . . . ," thus King Alfred:

> In the event of widespread and continuing and coordinated racial disturbances in the United States, King Alfred, at the discretion of the President, is to be put into action immediately.

Participating Federal Agencies in the plan include the FBI, CIA, National Security Council, Departments of Defense, Justice, and Interior.

> In case of emergency, minority members will be evacuated from the cities by federalized national guard units, local and state police and, if necessary, by units of the Regular Armed Forces, using public and military transportation, and detained in nearby

military installations until a further course of action has been decided.

The areas having the largest populations of black people are designated on a map by numbered priority areas. Leaders of all "minority rights" organizations are to be rounded up at once and detained. "Minority members of Congress will be unseated at once. This move is not without precedent in American History." (As indeed it is not from the post-Reconstruction era up to the unseating of Adam Clayton Powell.)

Harry Ames received the King Alfred Plan from an African ambassador named Jaja Enzkwu who had stumbled upon an Alliance Blanc meeting while vacationing in Spain, and had subsequently gathered the rest of the material. Inasmuch as the plan was top secret, concealing the report was the priority assignment of the National Security Council and the Central Intelligence Agency. They naturally came after Enzkwu when they learned he had the report. As Ames says: "Then Jaja started to deal. He'd give over the papers and keep his mouth shut, if the Americans gave him Nigeria." Nevertheless Jaja was killed, but he made sure another brother—Harry Ames—got King Alfred.

Harry Ames' letter continues:

> The material fascinated me. I'd spent so much of my life writing about the evil machinations of Mr. Charlie without really *knowing* the truth, as this material made me know it. It was spread out before me, people, places and things. I became mired in them, and I *knew* now that the way black men live on this earth was no accident. . . . I gripped the material, I hugged it to my chest, for now I would know; if they killed me, I would know that this great evil did exist, indeed thrive. And Dr. Faustus came to my mind.

Max had always wanted to provide America with a vision of her existence. He wanted black people to know the ugly truth, the ugly plot, behind their existence. He wanted white people to know that the black people "would tear up the country" rather then absorb any more lies. He spent most of his life trying—perhaps only as an artist would—to change or at least to alter the destiny of America. He rose about as high as a journalist could rise: an advisor to the President, a top man with *Events,* an important magazine. But he discovered he had no power, no say. He screamed long and hard trying to direct the President's (a caricature of Kennedy) attention away from the Russian-American space competition and the problems of Cuba to the duress of the black man in America. Max thought his bitter words warning the administration that the black man "would tear up this country," went unheeded. But indeed they could well have been taken to heart and might have contributed handsomely to the gloomy anticipation of race war that brought about the King Alfred Plan. A high-ranking civil rights activist once said that much of the data compiled by war-on-poverty agencies and other progressive government agencies for the ostensible betterment of the black race, have been classified by the government as counterinsurgency information.

The death of Harry Ames strikes a strange chord in the swan song of Max's existence. The legacy Ames left him gives Max his last chance for redemption. But *Events* magazine would never print it. They would call it a hoax. Max also begins to see from the closing lines of the letter that Ames had found out that Max had once slept with his blond wife, Charlotte. It all becomes clear. This is the *coup de grâce,* the legacy of death that the "father of the black writers" has passed on to his heir. It is nullified, though, by the fact that Max is dying anyway. But what does one do with a portable Pandora's box? Max calls up Minister Q in New York (Malcolm X?) to read off King Alfred into the minister's perpetually running tape recorder. He prefaces his reading with the remark: "Hello, you are a dead man. Maybe?"

Having passed on the truth to another brother, Max prepares to meet his fate. He loads his pistol and holds it in his lap as he drives back to Holland. As the sergeant in an all-black company during World War II leading poorly trained men who were the objects of intense hatred from both the German soldiers and the American bigoted military men, Max saw his platoon suffer great casualties. Max instructs a new platoon on survival: "You want to live, you shoot first and ask questions later. All you got to tell me is that you saw a white face. Don't tell me what the white face was wearing because I don't want to know."

But Max is in for a surprise. Death, for him, shows up in the guise of two black CIA agents (Coffin Ed Johnson and Grave Digger Jones). To boot, they had both hung around the black artist expatriate scene, posing as writers. Max's prior preoccupation with guns comes in handy. He shoots Roger "the lover" in the groin, before he dies by way of a pellet that has only to contact his skin to cause a heart eruption. So Max dies from a more modern American disease than cancer. And a hero as well, in the James Bond tradition of Her Majesty's Secret Service.

It seems one cannot rely on shooting only white faces anymore. The only black men on TV to hold down full-time jobs are law enforcement officers or military men. The medium is the message. And Bill Cosby is the swingingest spy you would ever want to meet.

Max Reddick had participated in the American power structure more than most black men, most men, get to. Perhaps the fruit of his participation is the cancer that eats away at his anus. (Even while the pain wracks away at him, he remembers that he had never had a red head.) There are those who believe that because the black mass has not participated in the mainstream of American life, due to segregation, enforced poverty and ghetto substandard living, the black man has remained free from many of the syndromes (luxury emphasis, competitiveness, imprecise) that poison much of the American way of life. But young black men such as Stokely and Rap are calling for black power, a share of the spoils—since black people are in it too, even by default, whether they want it or not. Black Power is a piece of the action. And a piece of the action will be, by agreement, not only of the good parts of society but the bad as well.

Harry Ames thought that he had found the truth in King Alfred. That truth was death. Perhaps the truth of the black masses' existence in America is destined to be death. Doctor Faustus wanted to know everything. He made a deal with the devil (Elijah-jargon for the white man) and then tried to get out of it.

In the United States six sites have already been chosen for the detention of Americans who would contribute or might contribute to what would appear to be a sabotage or insurrection. Although part one of the McCarran Act of 1950, dealing with communist registration, has been declared unconstitutional by the Supreme Court, part 2 of the National Security Act is still on the books as a protection against an emergency in the eyes of the President, involving internal security. Part 2 calls for the detention camps which are located in Florida, Tulip Lake, California, Reno, Oklahoma, Allenwood, Pa., and one other site. These camps are set up ready and waiting. (pp. 365-71)

> David Henderson, "The Man Who Cried I Am: A Critique," in Black Expression: Essays by and about Black Americans in the Creative Arts, *edited by Addison Gayle, Jr., Weybright and Talley, 1969, pp. 365-72.*

John A. Williams with John O'Brien (interview date 1971-72)

[*In the following interview, Williams and O'Brien discuss critical response to* Sissie, The Man Who Cried I Am, *and* Sons of Darkness, Sons of Light: A Novel of Some Probability. *In a preface to the interview, O'Brien notes: "The interview was conducted on a bright chilly day in early November of 1971. We talked continuously for about two hours. Williams was cordial but reserved. As his remarks in the interview make clear, he approaches critics with caution. He speaks in a low, subdued voice, letting the words carry the weight of his meaning. The following February he expanded a few of his original answers and responded to several new questions."*]

[O'Brien]: *You said in an article that appeared in* The Saturday Review *that you wished for once that you could read a review of a novel by a black writer in which it wasn't compared only to novels by other black writers. Does such treatment of black writers have its roots in racism?*

[Williams]: I think it's racism and I think it's something that black writers dealt with, with accommodating behavior, for several years, and we still do. The fact is that when you can point out the elements of racism in the business as I did in that article, it doesn't make a goddamn bit of difference. They still do it. On the soft cover of **The Man Who Cried I Am,** it says, "The best novel about blacks since Ralph Ellison." That is defining the territory where black writers are allowed to

roam. But you know, I'm a contemporary of Styron, Mailer, and Bruce J. Friedman. Chester Himes and Richard Wright were contemporaries of Hemingway, toward his later years. And Ellison. But we never somehow get into the area where we're compared with white contemporaries. It's always with black contemporaries. What else can you say, except that it is racism?

The point of the article then was that comparisons should be made along literary rather than racial lines?

Well, yes, sure . . . I'd like for somebody to begin stacking up *Native Son* with some of Frank Norris' stuff, and I'd like to see Chester Himes stacked up to some of these detective story writers and some of the fiction writers who are still writing fiction from his generation. I'd like to see how I'd stack up against Styron and others who are my contemporaries. Now this doesn't mean that I'm seeking to divest myself of my identity. But I think that one of the reasons why these comparisons are not made in many cases is that black writers would come out better. It's sort of like with Jack Johnson, the heavyweight champion. You can't have those black guys winning at everything, or even looking as though they could possibly win. That's bad business. Things begin to happen to the economic structure of the literary world.

Do you think that black writers are doing things to the form of the American novel which simply are not understood by readers and critics?

In terms of form itself, the novel is changing. I think that black writers are initiating—if not forcing—a kind of change from the "straight ahead" American novel, vis-à-vis, Hemingway and Fitzgerald. There's an inclination to do to the novel what Charlie Parker did to jazz. I don't know whether you remember this period in jazz music that is called "Bop," where the method was to take . . . well, you could take any tune that was standard, say "Stardust," for example. They would go through it once and then would come through again with all their improvisations, so that it was only recognizable in part. You knew where the players were at certain points in the music, and only by virtue of touching on those old standard parts in the second passage through did you realize that it was really "Stardust." That's the way it works. And I think that's what's happening to the novel. You see it in William Melvin Kelley's last book, *Dunford's Travels Everywheres,* which is not only an exercise in form but also an exercise in language. Ishmael Reed's books. George Lamming has a book which just came out called *Natives of My Person* which is an allegory about seventeenth-century English slave trade. I read novels like these and it's incredible. You're reading English but it comes through in such a way that it doesn't seem like English; it comes through like Spanish, French . . . anything else than what you're familiar with.

Is the difference between what these writers are doing and what white writers are doing mainly a literary one, or is there something else too?

I think that there is a difference in approach to "consciousness" between black and white writers. I don't think white writers have ever had to consciously or subconsciously concern themselves about real problems of life and survival. You can take Salinger's Holden Caulfield. The mentality that issues forth from books like that is that the evil is not within us. It's an outside thing, which perhaps has to be combated. But it's going to be combated on white horses by white knights in white suits of armor. There's no question about it. There's no concern expressed for the world that's not white. The difference with black writers is that their concern has been made extremely conscious, not only by their position in the literary world—the editors and critics—but also by virtue of their awareness of what the situation is.

Then the black writer has been forced to be more concerned with social and political issues just because of his position in society?

I think "forced" is the right word. There are many, many black writers today, and in the Renaissance, and even prior to that, who would have been happy to have had acceptance on the terms of being a writer. I think it's the critics who have made the decision for us. By boxing us into an area where our books have been labeled "protest." A very narrow pigeonhole. And I think it sort of deprived us of the ability to mirror through our work all of humanity. So "forced" is a good word, forced in terms of our area being well defined, well drawn for us.

Do you think of yourself as belonging to a realistic tradition in fiction? Have you purposely avoided experimentation?

I suppose I am a realistic writer. I've been called a melodramatic writer, but I think that's only because I think the ending of a novel should be at the ending of the book. Not on page sixty-two or page twenty-five. In terms of experimenting, I think that I've done some very radical things with form in **The Man Who Cried I Am** and in **Captain Blackman,** which had to be an experimental novel in order to hold the theme of the novel. What I try to do with novels is to deal in forms that are not standard, to improvise as jazz musicians do with their music, so that a standard theme comes out looking brand new. This is all I try to do with a novel and, like those musicians, I am trying to do things with form that are not always immediately perceptible to most people.

Do you recall your first attempts at serious writing? How old were you? What kind of things were you writing?

I started writing when I was overseas in the Navy during the War, and it wasn't very good. It was mostly what one would call "free verse" poetry. I always had a feeling that I was capable of being a writer. I never felt that I was deluding myself by trying to be a writer. The problem with writing, for me personally, lay outside writing itself. It was considered an illness to be involved in the arts since in the black community there were not artists to speak of. One did not earn one's keep by writing poetry or novels. That was out there in never never never land. What I really wanted to do was get a good job, work from nine to five, or ten to four, and live in that fashion. But it became clear to me after several years that even so simple a thing as that was subject to stresses because of discrimination. It was only then that I turned to writing fulltime. Pretty much for the same reason James Baldwin did, to remain sane, to feel that one was really in touch with oneself, that you were not a ghost, but a functioning person capable of thinking and perceiving and feeling.

Have you gone through periods where you felt that you had said everything there was to say, or periods where you felt that your writing was not accomplishing what you wanted it to?

I don't go through periods now when I think that I won't be able to write again because of some mental block. But I do feel occasionally that I've said just about all I wanted to say. But after a few days that passes. I've also had the feeling that writing has not moved things as much as I wanted things to be moved and perhaps there might be something else I could do that would get things done. To this extent I've considered quitting writing simply because it hasn't, for myself, produced the things I want to see produced, the things I feel must be produced within my lifetime. But you get past that feeling with the passage of time.

Have you observed any pattern in how ideas for novels come to you? Must you experience most of the things you write about?

No, I haven't observed any pattern. I've had some ideas for novels for several years without putting down a line, and every time I think of these ideas I add something more. I don't believe in outlines, at least they've never worked for me. When I finally sit down to write, I'm off and running because I've had the material stored up for so long. I would prefer to experience certain things myself, but I know that's not absolutely necessary. I can project on the basis of my own experiences, the experiences of others, and the testimony of still other people.

Is any one part of a novel more difficult to write than another? Do you hit any lags, perhaps after you get the basic action down? Is there a kind of crisis point after which,—if you get past—you know that everything else will fall into place?

For me the first fifty pages of a novel are the hardest. This may be a psychological thing. After I hit fifty pages I know that I've got a novel. It's not that the conception of the novel is difficult for me. But by the end of the first fifty pages I've smoothed out the form and I've got the structure licked. Then I'm off from that point.

Could you describe your work habits? Where do you write? How much each day?

I work every day. The time can vary from three to five hours, with many, many breaks in between. If it's going well I'll work at night as well, up to maybe nine o'clock or so. I no longer feel that I have to have a certain kind of atmosphere. In fact I never felt that way. I've always prided myself on being able to write anywhere, and I guess I still can. I have no ritual to go through in order to prepare myself for writing. I sit down and I write, although I have had periods when I have the urge to sharpen about two dozen pencils or polish shoes. It's not a ritual as much as it is giving myself time to think about being consciously aware of thinking of what I am going to deal with that morning, where I have to go back over the work I had done the day before, what it is I am going to repair or change or heighten.

Can you recall the circumstances in which you began working on **The Angry Ones?** *Did you have any difficulty in finding a publisher for your first novel?*

It was in some ways a very autobiographical novel. I felt very intensely about that book and about things that were happening to me at the time. I once rewrote the whole damn book in a day and a half at one sitting because there seemed to be the possibility of it being published by New American Library. The preliminary reports had been good but after that day and a half of rewriting that book, it was turned down. It had been turned down by a number of publishers. What made me sit down and write the book in the first place was that I didn't have anything else to do. It was a question of holding on to my sanity, a question of writing down some of the things that had happened to me. Seeing those situations in print made me rather determined

Williams with his wife Lori, 1983.

never to forget them. That gave me a new grip on life, feeling that there was a lot out there that I had to do.

Are you conscious of having been influenced by other writers?

Nobody has really influenced me. This is because I read without discrimination when I was a great deal younger. In terms of form, my single influence has been Malcolm Lowry in *Under the Volcano.* I tried to emulate him in **Sissie** and improve on what he did with the telescoping of time. But I think I did it much better in **The Man Who Cried I Am.**

What nonliterary influences have there been on your work?

I don't really know. I've read an awful lot of history. A great deal of it pre-ancient history. I sometimes get very depressed because I know that all of this business is quite temporary. We become too self-important about our society, our crafts and skills, our families, and so on. I believe, with some other people, that human life on this planet goes in cycles. We're here for maybe ten, twenty, thirty thousand years. And then something happens, a cataclysm, and the poles start sliding around, and it's all gone. Then you start evolving again. I suppose I'm one of the rare guys you'll talk to who believes this. Nonetheless, I'm here, and I'm sort of constrained to act in patterns that are normal for the time I live in. And I suppose that happens so that you'll have some assurance of life existing even after a cataclysm. I don't know what you would call all this. I'm pessimistic about the progress that humans are going to make with each other within the timespan that we have, how many hundreds or thousands of years that may be.

Do you think that music has influenced you?

I've always liked jazz and some classical music. If I had been from a well-to-do family when I was a child I would have been a trumpeter. But when the time came to move on to a trumpet we simply could not afford it. I haven't been too much for music lately. I don't know why, whether or not it has to do with work. . . . You're too busy playing the baby's records. But I like music, and I always say, "we ought to play a stack of records on Saturday or Sunday." But we never do. Somehow I wind up watching football games, just like any other piece of stone on Sunday afternoon.

Have you felt the influence of Albert Camus?

Maybe, I don't really know. I just don't know. These are things I think about. I can't say I consciously move about as a devotee of any particular philosophy.

Which of your novels are you most pleased with?

Well, I guess that I keep changing novels because I do different things with each one. Out of two previously published novels my preference was for **Sissie.** That was before I wrote **The Man Who Cried I Am.** I felt that in that novel I said things better and with a vehicle that had infinitely more horsepower. In the novel coming out in May, I think something different is taking place and I think that I brought that off well. So, I liked that too. Maybe when I am sixty or seventy years old I can look back and really see the differences and see which one I like. But now, things keep changing. I liked *Sons of Light, Sons of Darkness* least of all.

Why is that?

It's a potboiler. I just feel that it came too easily. It was one of those novels that I don't like very much, that I call a "straight ahead" novel. You start at A and wind up at Z and then you get off the train.

*Has **The Man Who Cried I Am** had the most critical acclaim?*

That is what I keep hearing. But I think I hear it for the wrong reasons. People keep talking about "King Alfred." There were many other things in that novel besides "King Alfred" but all they talk about is "King Alfred." I can't say that that pleases me too much, although I believe there exists such a plan as this. The acclaim has been political. I wouldn't mind so much if it was both political and literary. But the literary acclaim has been missing.

*It's been suggested that some of the characters in **The Man Who Cried I Am** are paralleled by real life figures, that Richard Wright is represented by one of the characters and yourself by another.*

I think that there are elements that could be taken as the character of Richard Wright. Actually the character that everyone thinks is me, is only me partially. I had Chester Himes in mind.

Max and Harry in that novel are two authors who are forced into becoming politically conscious and active.

I think "political" is a big word, but I think I know what you mean. And you're right. They have been forced into this kind of political role. And when I say political role, what I'm talking about is a larger humanistic role. It's outside the scope of just putting books together. The thrust may be political, per se, involving what your government is doing, but it is also an involvement in what other people are doing. It's being concerned about people, somehow relating to them, even with all their personal problems. I like to think that important writers are without flaws in terms of how they deal with other people. I feel this and sometimes say to myself that this is very childish. I think that a man who is a writer, who is good with words, should have an obligation to be a good man in his day-to-day life. It would be nice if the writer did have the responsibility to be more humane with people. Unfortunately we know that this isn't true. You can talk of Faulkner, or you can talk about Dostoevsky, bigots both.

Do you see certain similarities between the heroes in all your novels? Is it essentially the same hero?

Some people say that it's the same character in each book, that he goes through all the books. I think to a large extent they're different characters. If you wanted to be strict about it, you could say that literally they're the same character. If you wanted to be most strict about it, you could say that they are the same two characters. Steve's confidant is Obie. In *Night Song* the characters are Keel and Eagle. In *Sissie*, it's Ralph and his sister. In *The Man Who Cried I Am* it's Max and Harry. In *Sons of Darkness* the two actually are Hod and his girl. In my new novel, *Captain Blackman,* the protagonist runs throughout the story. He's one man. He is the person around whom the whole story revolves, but there are other people who are pulled into the story as the story progresses. And they flush it out from a point of view that Captain Blackman could not possibly see it from. With two characters you can more fully develop a situation than you could with only one who would have to be babbling off at the mouth all the time, or thinking all of the time for the reader to get the complete story. I've always felt that I need two people to handle the dialogue, to move it, two people who know each other well. I find that too much narrative becomes a pain in the ass. You get on a roller coaster and start breaking out the flags. Dialogue is always better.

Do you see a progression in your heroes? In your first novel the hero is in search of a good job; in your most recent novel the hero starts a revolution.

Wait till you read the next one (laughing).

Is there a difference between what Steve thinks is necessary to be human and what Eugene does?

I think so. Browning thinks in revolutionary terms out of the boredom and frustration of middle-class existence. And Steve, who hasn't had that, is thinking of getting where Browning is. He's not thinking about a revolution: he's thinking about three squares and a nine-to-five routine.

Most of your characters have a need for and are in search of love. If they find it, they are saved.

I believe in love. Which means that I live in a society. I also believe that all things, revolutions included, begin with individuals and individual choices.

Then love is looked to as a kind of ultimate solution?

I don't see that anything else has worked. Not even money. And I think that love grows out of some kind of respect. Most people just don't understand it or the processes of it. It's the only thing that can work.

There seems to be a progression from the first novel, where money is thought to be a final solution, to the second novel, where love seems to take that place.

Well, yes, but that's in the realm of books. I think economically things were better in the second novel. Not much, but better. When you get to *Sissie,* of course, ostensibly, things are even better. You've got Ralph running around Europe . . . and—it's not necessarily true—but it seems that anybody running around Europe must have the money to get back. He has some kind of economic status, however small. And as my own economic condition has improved, I think this has been matched by the conditions of the characters in my books. One of the books I'm working on now deals with a guy who has worked in a foundry for twenty-five years, but even so he owns a house in a fairly exclusive neighborhood. He's probably the only guy on the block who works with his hands. I spend a great deal of time in the opening chapter describing his kitchen, and the car which he loves (a big four-hundred-horsepower job). You've got a black man who appears to be economically solvent and perhaps he is. But he's still black and what that really means is that he's never really secure.

The theme of racial assimilation was important in your first novel and perhaps not as important in some of the later ones. Did your views change?

I tell everybody that regardless of whatever "revolutionary movement" is now current, I think we've got assimilation and there is probably more of it, in spite of a necessary period of separatism. There's got to be integration. People are deluding themselves by saying that we won't have it. This particular neighborhood is sort of a post-Village neighborhood and interracial couples are fairly frequent. If you had time to walk around on a nicer day you'd see it. It's pretty incredible. And there's more of it now than there was ten or fifteen years ago. I think that there is a lot of talk going on about how little there is and how many people are opposed to it. And I'm sure that certain so-called militants really mean it when they say they're opposed to it. But I've seen changes in the philosophy of Nicki Giovanni who lives two blocks away from here. I've been over to her place a few times, and you know she was vigorously opposed to any kind of interracial marriage. I don't know what brought about the change, certainly not us [Williams and his wife] because we're not that close. But I see changes taking place. I had a run-in with Don Lee over this situation. In his review of **The Man Who Cried I Am,** he brought in my marriage on the tail end of it . . . I told him I thought it was out of order. We almost came to pretty good blows there. We've since made peace.

Are you conscious of your usual treatment of white liberals in your novels? Without exception, I think, they wind up exploiting blacks.

I guess I'm pretty conscious of it. And I think that's pretty much the way things are. I can say this with some assurance since I do a lot of work in the white world, my editors are all very white, my agents have all been white. There are only a couple of black agents around, but I've never felt that I could go to an agent just because he was black. I'm not that crazy. An agent is an agent, just like a publisher is a publisher. It's a money-making proposition. But I've been, over a period of years, depressed about some of my white friends. I know white liberals

very well. I've known white liberals, friends, who showed me the guns they brought in from Colorado or New Mexico. And I say, "What do you want that for?" "Well, just in case." "In case of what?" "Well, you know . . ." Everybody's worried about black people getting guns but if they ever had a shakedown in some of the middle-class apartments around this city, it would be incredible. Absolutely. I don't want to be misleading here. I have many white friends whom I don't categorize as being liberal, conservative, or anything else. I try to deal with them as people and I feel that they deal with me as a person. I don't think there is more that can be asked of a relationship across the races except mutual respect.

Racial guilt, which you discuss in your introduction to **Sissie,** *is a recurring theme in your novels. Do you consider this one of your major themes?*

It could very well be, and I have personally felt some of this, though to a lesser degree now. When you are the first one in your family in seven or eight generations to go to college at a great sacrifice to yourself and your family, there has to be some degree of guilt. But my older kid is now in graduate school and he's teaching and he's married. And number two is a junior at Cornell. So the pattern is started. Nobody is going to have to feel guilty about going to college, as silly as that was.

How can your characters escape from the enormous guilt they feel?

Well, I suppose if they are going to be my characters in my books, they relate to the idea that with time one feels less and less. I would imagine that . . . well, for example, the book I'm working on now. The foundry worker has a son who is at Columbia. And there's no sense of guilt there. All the guys his age have kids away at school. That's the thing to do now. I would suppose that the longer I live and the more I write, the less I feel personally. And this will be reflected in my characters.

Must your characters—I think here especially of the characters in **Sissie***—come to some understanding of themselves and their situation before they can be relieved of the guilt?*

Yes, I think coming to an understanding of what happened gives the release. And understanding often comes with time. If you're dealing with a novel, you're restricted by time and space. So, you've got to set up certain things to make this happen.

You suggest in the preface to **Sissie** *that the matriarchal system in America is a myth. Who invented the myth?*

I think I would say that the white man did.

As a way of releasing himself from responsibility?

Well, I don't know whether it would be that or that it would be something more simple. That is, it put the black male outside the activity in the scheme of things.

In **Sons of Darkness** *Dr. Jessup represented a certain kind of radicalism in the novel. Is the thrust of the novel away from Jessup's ideas for social change and toward Eugene Browning's?*

Yes, because he's the kind of guy who's around today. It's sort of like Marcus Garvey whose "back-to-Africa movement" was very much applauded by Southerners, the KKK guys. He could send his scouts to the South in cities where a strange black guy usually disappeared overnight. But Garvey didn't lose anybody. That's because he was working hand-in-hand with the KKK, not hand-in-hand but at least they knew what he was doing and approved of it. Now Jessup is one of those guys who believes that he can make deals with the devil and come away unscorched. And Browning just never had that spirit. Browning is the kind of activist-nonactivist that all of us would like to be; so that we can press a button and set things in motion without paying the consequences. And in this sense, his thing is really a big daydream.

Browning thinks he can do this without incurring any guilt?

He would like to.

Is he becoming aware at the end of the novel of those consequences?

Of course. Yes.

Have your thinking or ideas changed since you first began writing fifteen years ago? Are you surprised when you look back to see that you were thinking one thing or another?

No, I'm not. I didn't know how things would change, but I always expect things to change. What I was writing about then was what I wanted to write about. What I write about now is what I want to write about now. I think that there have been moments when I have, perhaps with **Sons of Darkness, Sons of Light,** given under to the pressures around me and done a book on revolution. But I'm not sorry I did it. In the process of working it out I came to see pretty much the kind of things that would have to happen for any revolution to become a success and also the things that couldn't happen. In that book I was dealing with nine tunnels and bridges leading into Manhattan. Well, hell, since last spring when the bridge-and-tunnel workers had a strike, I discovered that there were something like thirty-four bridge-tunnel approaches to Manhattan. A hell of a revolutionary I'd make! . . . if I thought I could seal off Manhattan at nine points, leaving twenty-five more wide open.

What have been some of the reactions to your book on Martin Luther King? Do you think that the book was misunderstood?

I don't read reviews of a book until they're out for a year. Once in a while my wife will insist that I read a particularly good or bad one. With the King book I was glad that I had made that rule. I read some of the reviews just this September. They were pretty bad. I think that the misunderstanding was wilfull. A lot of people wanted to misunderstand, wanted to accuse me of being a traitor, a panderer for the FBI. A lot of people jumped on me, a lot of people in the black community. I got beat pretty badly. I think that over the past fourteen months or so there's been a better reaction to the book than when it first came out. Again, time, you know. But I really took a beating on that. It wasn't that I didn't expect to. I just didn't anticipate the degree of ferocity . . . . There were a lot of people running around saying, "Well, he's finished as a writer. He'll never write again." You start asking yourself, "Is that really true? Am I finished as a writer?"

Why did you write the book?

I thought that it would be a good thing for the black community to understand how much we're at the mercy of the system. And, of course, nobody wanted to believe that we were that badly off. Or that we could be that easily used. That's really the answer to it. Not in 1971. (pp. 227-43)

John A. Williams and John O'Brien, in an interview in Interviews with Black Writers, *edited by John O'Brien, Liveright, 1973, pp. 225-43.*

Jerry H. Bryant (essay date 1975)

[*In the following essay, Bryant examines the political nature of Williams's novels, focusing on* The Man Who Cried I Am.]

John A. Williams may not be an incarnation of the "black writer" of the 1960's, but he stands pretty much at the center of the black fiction of that decade. Not only a writer, he has become a monitor of black writing in general, working hard for its propagation and improvement. He is not the overt activist that Amiri Baraka has become, not a militant pusher of "black aesthetic." He is concerned with a revolution, and just as the beginning of his writing career coincides with the early activist phase of the Civil Rights Movement (his first novel, **The Angry Ones,** was published in 1960), so all of his work has a distinctly political focus.

His subject is race, and his themes reflect the most advertised concerns of the revolution: the economic and psychological emasculation of the black man by the white, the struggle of the black man to preserve his manhood, the black will to survive and the enduring strength that brings victory. He is not the kind of political novelist Irving Howe speaks of, whose main challenge is "to make ideas or ideologies come to life, to endow them with the capacity for stirring characters into passionate gestures and sacrifices." Instead, he seeks to convince the reader that his picture of society, with its black ideological tilt, is accurate, bringing home to white Americans the extent of their crime and demonstrating to blacks the means by which they might triumph over white discrimination. He has picked up the baton from Richard Wright and set out to use his art to help his people, to embody the socio-political concerns of black Americans in fictional form. Like Wright, he has made writing his profession, producing a considerable body of work in the last decade and one half. Besides six novels, he has written a history of Africa, reflections upon the life and death of Martin Luther King, a biography of Wright, and an autobiographical count of his tour through America. His articles have appeared in a wide variety of magazines, from *Holiday* to *Saturday Review* to *Partisan Review;* and he has been one of the editors of the part-literary, part-political review, *Amistad.*

Williams's novels are consistent in reflecting his ideological bias, but artistically they are quite uneven. *The Angry Ones,* dealing with discrimination against blacks who try to get specialized employment, and *Night Song* (1961), an excursion into the world of black jazz, indicate that from the beginning Williams knew how to put a novel together, but that he had not developed the emotional restraint or insight to put a *good* novel together. *Sissie* (1963), about the changing black family and the emergence of a new generation, is a great improvement. Williams, having learned much about himself and his subject, found a way to capture the complexities of both. *The Man Who Cried I Am* (1967) rises to art, as if the three earlier novels were exercises of preparation. Its story of two black novelists makes one of the best novels of the 1960's. But *Sons of Darkness, Sons of Light* (1969) and *Captain Blackman* (1972) show a sharp falling off. The former, about the use of Mafia techniques in a "possible" future, and the latter, about the role of the black soldier in America's military history, are both thin and theme-ridden.

That he has not been more frequently successful is largely explained by the fact that he has expended his talents more on politics than on art. Perhaps more important, the course upon which his political and racial loyalties have guided him is not completely the course of his natural bent. The arena in which he is most comfortable is the world of the black intellectual. His prototypical character is the man of thought whose creativity is sapped by racism. The strength of the character and his interest for the reader lie in his powers of self-analysis and understanding. The influence of William's own personality and background on his writing can best be seen by comparing them with Richard Wright's. Wright traces his influences back to the South, with its dusty black sections and Jim Crow cities, and to the North, especially Chicago's cold pavements and its decaying ghetto buildings. His reaction to the life he lived in those places is mainly rage, which he expresses in the violent details of his stories. Williams, who admires Wright perhaps more than any other writer, on the other hand, grew up in Syracuse: his family was poor, and he dropped out of school to work, without the ubiquitous oppressiveness of the South or the Northern ghettos weighing on his every moment.

Indeed, he says in *This Is My Country Too* (1965) that his first notions of America were innocent of racial anger. He had white playmates, and he thought he was the same as they, with the same privileges and the same promise of a good future. He did not discover his mistake until he was a teenager, when he underwent no sudden or explosive transformation into a rebel determined to get revenge—"the dream of America" simply began to "taste sour." The striking thing about his description is the emphasis on self-observation, on what happens to one's own emotions and thoughts, rather than on the unfairness of discrimination.

Such a temperament finds significance and drama in the struggle of the mind to know itself rather than in ideologically motivated action. Its energies go to the observation of ambiguous states of feeling and representative thought rather than unequivocal commitment to a single idea. The main strength of *The Man Who Cried I Am* and *Sissie* is that they trace the growth of their protagonist's awareness and depict his radical ambivalence toward his world. In both novels, Williams does what he is most capable of, what he has the surest instinct for. Like any novelist, he had to discover his main talent by making one or two false starts, The distressing thing is that after finding his talent, he should lose hold of it again so soon. In *Sons of Darkness, Sons of Light,* for example, he takes an intellectual, a Ph. D., and puts him to thinking about the failure of non-violent black organizations to achieve any real progress toward racial equality. White policemen are still shooting down defenseless black youths with impunity, and white Southerners are still bombing black churches and schools. Legal gradualism clearly is not the answer. Outright guerrilla warfare does not seem to be, either. The whites have too much firepower. What if, thinks mild-tempered Gene Browning, the policeman who killed the black youngster were to be "hit" by a secret gunman, in a Mafia-style execution? The white world would be put on notice that blacks will no longer tolerate indiscriminate murder of blacks. The novel, however, is less about the pain that such thought brings than about the implementation of the thought. Browning acts; he commissions a hit. The whites recognize its significance, and police invade the black ghettos around the country: a civil war begins as the novel ends. Browning's action has inaugurated the catharsis the country needs.

Williams calls it "a novel of possibility," but it is too melodramatic and contrived to seem plausible. Furthermore, not only does it do what novels are not designed to do—advocate some specific social or military strategy—it contains a character who attempts to transform reflection and interpretation into action. Williams does not have total enough insight into such a character to make him the center of an effective narrative. We can see what happened: by the end of the 1960's the pace of the black revolution had speeded up considerably. Violence was being considered as a theoretical possibility by the Movement; some groups were using it already. The pressure on black intellectuals, furthermore, became almost irresistable. They were called on to put away their ambiguities and take a stand, and this Williams sought to do. He attempted to use *Sons of Darkness* in 1969 to justify the growing confidence among some black revolutionaries in the viability of violent retaliation, and to warn white Americans that they had better listen. He was not, however, bullied into a new position against his better judgment: events, the changing ideological milieu, and his original loyalties convinced him of the urgent need to give such position priority. In following the course, he violated the natural talent he had found with *The Man Who Cried I Am,* one which charts the currents of a man's awareness rather than rationalizes the correctness of a particular line of action.

Not that *Sons of Darkness* is without interest: Williams understands and uses the novel form very well. The old Italian ex-Mafia Don, through whom Browning hires his executioner, is a good character. He also parallels the black American, for he too was forced by a WASP society into criminal behavior and the construction of a whole sub-culture to substitute for the one from which he was excluded as an immigrant Sicilian. The parallel is reinforced by another in the character of the hit man, a Jew who had been expelled from Israel for Zionist activities. His expulsion was hypocritical, for while he had endangered his life in guerrilla terrorism to gain independence and freedom for his country, the politicians who expelled him retired safely behind a shield of professed law and order, waiting for the Zionists to succeed.

So for all its contrived melodrama and overt politics, *Sons of Darkness* is imaginatively conceived and intelligently ordered. So is *Captain Blackman*. Its title character is the collective black soldier, and Williams follows him through all the wars America has fought, from the Revolution to Vietnam. We see how the white man exploited the black soldier and how the soldier overcame odds to fight valorously for a country that did not want him. Both novels are too obviously put to the service of politics. In *Captain Blackman* Williams seems too rushed in executing his idea to do it justice, as if his duties as an editor and his responsibilities as a Black Writer put demands upon his time that he could meet only by robbing from *Captain Blackman*. The result is a half-formulated novel.

Williams's case, of course, is not unique. Any novelist, no matter what the shade of his politics, who lets his bias control the degree to which he *shows* his approval or disapproval of his characters is working with the tract rather than the novel. The problem emerges with special clarity in Williams's work because he is a man of such obvious talents and intelligence who has obviously chosen to be political. He can write first-rate fiction; the irony is that his first-rate fiction, which is less loaded with doctrinal intentions than his second-rate, seems more effectively to do the job as he sets out to do. Honest politics—good politics—is much better served by good art that is not overtly or designedly political than by bad art that is. In fact, the politics that calls on its artists to falsify their vision and slant the findings of their personal observation cannot be good politics and cannot produce good art. How, then did Williams grow into *The Man Who Cried I Am,* and how does that novel fuse good art with politics so that it also turns out to be good politics? The best places to see the growth of Williams as an artist are his second and third novels, *Night Song* and *Sissie*. In them, he changes from a youthful romantic naif, who too obviously plays favorites among his characters, to a more mature observer of human behavior who realizes that characters must not be idealized or sentimentalized.

Night Song, as suggested above, is a true novel: the dialogue is authentic; the problems of its characters and the conflicts between them are well-developed; and the world of the black musician it depicts commands our belief. Williams chooses that world not because it has an inherent interest nor tells us something about the way we feel or act, but because it is a vehicle for making whites realize their guilt and for convincing blacks that they have the strength and courage to survive and triumph. Because he sees his subject from the single point of view of the doctrinaire ideologue, his imaginative world becomes one-dimensional. He approached it with a ponderous sophomoric seriousness, endowing obvious relationships with insinuated depth and implying that their profundity is perceivable only by the black man. He makes his favorite black characters tremendous sufferers, admirable stoics, tortured geniuses. Even their weaknesses turn out to reflect vast strengths. The tone is self-congratulatory and the air is full of injured innocence and outraged grievance. His two main black characters are egregiously sentimentalized: Richie Stokes, one of the many fictional characters modeled after Charlie Parker (Richie is the "Eagle" rather than the "Bird"), is a sensitive human being who has been made cynical and whose musical genius has been exploited and debased by a racist society. Deprived of freedom of expression, Richie is driven to self-destruction through liquor and heroin. Even in 1961 such a character had lost its freshness, even then more the product of the idealizing tendencies of the popular press than of direct observation. Moreover, Richie is portrayed as a sacrificial Christ, who dies at the hands of the oppressors so that others may be saved—a tradition, too, that had run its effective course. Keel, the man Richie saves, is perhaps even more stereotyped than Richie. He has been more directly emasculated by white society than Richie, and the novel is largely an account of his struggle to recover his manhood, which Williams identifies with his ability to make love to his white mistress. Williams belabors the point that Keel has every reason to give up. Heroically, he fights his oppressors and his own weakness and, through Richie's sacrifice, returns to health. When we last see him, he is riding toward his apartment with his mistress, confident of his renewed potency.

Williams also creates an obvious white foil to show how strong and courageous blacks are and how weak and pusillanimous whites are. David Hillary, who is likeable enough as whites go, is also, as whites go, insensitive and, though a college professor, poorly educated in the realities of life. Even though Richie helps him recover from a self-pitying six-month drunk and return to his undeserved teaching position, he cannot throw off his whiteness. Not only does he not go to Richie's assistance when the black musician is being gratuitously beaten by a white policeman, he realizes he enjoys seeing Richie's blood. Not only does he resent Keel's hold on a white woman, he makes a play for her himself. Williams makes Hillary realize his guilt as well as his inferiority—realize that he and all whites are to blame for Richie's death; when we last see him, he is riding a bus and disappearing, symbolically, into a tunnel, still unwilling to fully understand, still benighted.

The pattern speaks for itself: it is derivative, literary, and ineptly political; its characters and events are stereotyped; it also contains a paradox that Williams either refuses to face or fails to deal with, a paradox that arises in nearly every black novel that sentimentalizes the suffering black man as inherently heroic. On the one hand, Williams hopes, by displaying the real worth of his black protagonists, to help wipe out racism and to help strengthen blacks. On the other, the trait he finds most admirable in his sentimentized hero derives from the very condition he seeks to destroy. His black heroism needs white racism to be itself. What would either Richie or Keel have been had they not been subjected to discrimination? Williams, like any black novelist, could find authentic heroism to dramatize; when he does, he must face the irony of his position. Milton dramatized what some scholars name "the doctrine of the fortunate fall," in which Adam's sin provides the occasion for the display of God's generosity. In Williams the paradox might be termed "the doctrine of fortunate oppression." In *Night Song,* however, the paradox creates no emotional or intellectual tension; it seems to lie unrecognized and unexploited, as if it were an extension of the unresolved conflict between Williams's political and artistic inclinations.

In *Sissie* he goes a long way toward reaching a resolution. Gone is the self-pity and the youthful ideology, the easy indictment of the white man and the one-dimensional celebration of the black. In its place Williams puts a more recognizable set of human beings, marred by an unhealthy family relationship, frustrated by conditions that arise from racism but not completely explained by it. In *Sissie* victory is incomplete, rebellion defective. Loneliness and isolation are relieved by love, but even love has flaws. No sets of opposing character stereotypes are designed to demonstrate the superiority of one class at the expense of another. *Sissie* shows that Williams can be an exceptionally good novelist, working to explain the confused rhythms of everyday reality rather than contriving rhythms to prove one-sided preconceptions.

Sissie owes a debt to *Go Tell It on the Mountain.* Baldwin's novel is about a young black boy undergoing a change of mind and feeling toward his family and his past. *Sissie* is about a brother and a sister who struggle to escape their tie with their strong-willed and unloving mother. Sissie Joplin is far from the stereotype of the matriarchal martyr whose warm strength binds the poverty-stricken family into affectionate solidarity. She contrives to send her son to an orphanage and her husband to jail, seeks further to revenge herself upon the latter by hinting that her daughter, Iris, is not his, ridicules her children by constantly claiming they will never amount to anything, and displays a life-long jealousy of their youth and future. One of Williams's achievements is that he makes Sissie both plausible and attractive in a perverse way, even sympathetic. He does so, further more, not by insisting that she is the product of white atrocities, but by showing her caught in circumstances at least partly of her own making, that derive from her peculiar temperament. She is also representative: through her we see the quality of life that was the only choice for many black people in the 1920's. Her parents lived in poverty, exploited by whites and weighted down by children. When she marries Big Ralph Joplin, she enters that same cycle. Her stormy character, however, prevents her from accepting her lot stoically. We experience with her the utter futility of her rebellion against a chronic lack of money and a system in which only the woman has any permanent access to employment. What strikes home with impact is that she directs her rage not at the abstract white man but at the more immediate drags upon her, her husband and her children. We sense that is exactly what a woman of her education and character would do, and because of its rightness, we, rather than Williams, accuse that white society that bound her to such futility.

Through the family dominated by Sissie, her son Ralph and her daughter Iris catch the black disease. At thirty-five Ralph, a would-be playwright, has had no plays performed and has been given no decent job. He feels he is a failure and is paralyzed. Iris achieves considerable fame as a singer in Europe, but she cannot accept the love she is offered by the one real man in her life. With

Williams (far left) with his Navy buddies in 1945.

Sissie's ridicule ringing in her ears, she devotes all her time and energy to gaining still greater success. Williams, however, is writing in the 1960's, a decade after *Go Tell It on the Mountain,* and he sees a new generation emerging in Ralph and Iris, reflecting an important change in the traditional pattern. In his recognition of that change lie both his instinct to discern general trends and his wish to employ that instinct for political purposes. Ralph points out to Iris that Sissie's move from the South to the North and her marriage to Big Ralph were only leaps from one kind of poverty to another, a perpetuation of the old conditions. The leap made by Iris, and eventually by Ralph, has been "from pissy beds to perfumed satin ones; from one pair of run-over, paper-padded shoes to a closetful of hundred-dollar shoes; from rat-ridden rooms to penthouses and the modern castles of the Riviera; from roller skates to Citroens," all accomplished in "only three decades."

The change is too rapid. The generation to which Ralph and Iris belonged has had no time to prepare for the shift and so is more vulnerable to its psychological dislocations than Sissie and her generation were to their difficulties. They are, therefore, more dependent upon the past they remember only with pain, for, as Ralph says, Sissie was "stronger than any of us will ever be." Even while Iris and Ralph strive to escape from Sissie, they yearn for her and the life she represents, constantly returning to them like a sore tooth. With such compelling ambiguities Williams, an introspective intellectual, deals most expertly. They admit of no rational or political solution, but they tell black people a great deal about themselves and whites a great deal about blacks. They also show that blacks are driven by forces other than the ones named by most doctrainaire revolutionaries.

More explicitly than *Go Tell It on the Mountain, Sissie* is an allegory of the passing of the old world, Sissie's world, of frustrated rage, of penury, of absolute futility. Ralph, too, finally achieves artistic success, and he marries a woman he can love and who can love him. In the end, Sissie dies, freeing both Iris and Ralph of her and their past, after a fashion. They still bear some of the wounds and scars of the racial and family trauma, but they are better off than Sissie was at their age. Ralph and Iris represent special circumstances in the black life of the 1960's; they have broken from the ghetto, have made it into the economic middle class. But for just that black does Williams speak here, trying to articulate the unique experience of those who have surmounted the simplest kinds of racism and failure. What Williams makes us feel is not so much the exhilaration of successful change as the spiritual agony that such change brings, the pain of self-discovery, the recognition of the worst sides of human nature, the exposure of the weaknesses of blacks, and their dependence upon a past they hate. Williams says in *Sissie* that escape from the familiar problems of the black man opens up new problems that require new strengths. The new black cannot be born without travail, and the cost is nothing less than the death of the past.

For Ralph, and for most of Williams's intellectuals, the goal is to understand, an achievement of the mind which for Williams is sometimes satisfying in itself. Its importance for him is illustrated by the structure of *Sissie* and *The Man Who Cried I Am,* both made up of movement toward understanding. By "understanding," Williams means a clear perception by the black protagonist of his relationship to the realities of the world he lives in. Ralph comes to such perception by going to a psychiatrist when he feels paralyzed by his sense of failure. The psychiatrist tries to formulate the problem in terms of Freudian personality theory—that is, by claiming an internal dysfunction of Ralph's psyche—but Ralph finally realizes that Freudian psychology was designed for conditions other than his own. The fear of emasculation that emerges in his sense of failure is neither merely symbolic nor pathological—it is a rational reaction to reality, to his status as a black man in white America. He has actually been kept from decent housing and has actually been excluded from jobs commensurate with his abilities and education. His discovery is a highpoint in his mental development and in his fight to free himself from Sissie and the past. Not that he has found anything new. The connection between his sense of failure and the black experience reduces to a truism. What Williams says is that each man must come to a realization of that connection on his own, feel it in his own bones. When he does, it has the quality of fresh revelation. The implication is that the artist searches for those moments of revelation, clothes them in metaphors that effectively convey the discoverer's feelings, and creates an imaginative world that draws the reader into the same discovery.

What is important for Williams in his political avatar is how this "understanding" can be used for the revolution. His metaphors are political; the "understanding" they purvey is resurrection, the achievement of a new strength with which to engage the conditions of black life. Reaching "understanding" is what the artist is uniquely equipped to do; it is his contribution to the struggle. He does not formulate plans for action, draw up lists of legal actions to take, or decide that the new strategy is going to be violent retaliation through guerrilla action. He clarifies the psychological stance toward his world, catches the deep emotional barriers to change, and notes the spaces of the mind where the contradiction lies between ideological commitment and the hidden powers of feelings. When Ralph discovers that his blackness actually does limit his possibilities, he realizes that the American dream of equality is not for him to live at this time. With that realization, he washes himself clean of his hampering delusions and becomes better fit to deal with reality. Full "revolutionary" understanding is not quite so clear-cut, however. Ralph's new perspective is also made up of the ambiguity of values and the state of mind in which those values exist. Thus, though his new knowledge frees him of the failure syndrome he inherited from the past and fits him to succeed in his profession and in marriage, he deeply feels the loss of Sissie, too. Part of the delusion, in other words, is that a simple answer exists to his—and many black's—problems. Ironically, true illumination comes from a tired cliche: "that everything good was balanced inexorably with something bad."

The Man Who Cried I Am gives such awareness of ambiguities its best expression and, consequently, seems Williams's most personal novel. It deals with the discoveries and the truths and the understandings that Williams finds crucial to the life and creative energy of the black writer. The story is of his own intellectual life, put together from his intimate knowledge of the main black writers on the scene from 1940 to 1966. He builds his characters from the personalities and experiences of men like Wright, Baldwin, Chester Himes, perhaps even himself. Their lives reflect that period's history, and Williams attempts to explain the nature and significance of that history in his novel. He traces the black writer's gradually improving status, from the days when only a black newspaper would hire him to the time when the President of the United States invites him to join his staff of speech writers. He traces the development of black consciousness through the awakening of the African nations in the 1950's to the growing activism in America. The novel is, then, his most political; more than any other, it deals with the sweeping issues of the time—the 1954 Supreme Court decision, the first effective boycott in a fictional Montgomery, led by a fictional Martin Luther King, the use of police dogs and cattle prods in the South, and the emergence of some of the militant leaders in the North. Furthermore, his narrative demonstrates the political conclusion that any improvement of black life in America is only on the outside. The President's black speech writer has no influence nor independence, and the increase in black activism simply elicits an escalation of white resistance. Finally, his protagonist, Max Reddick, whose story it is, concludes with the most revolutionary black politicians that violence is the only feasible alternative to continued suppression.

Williams never loses his characters to stereotype nor his narrative to mere theme. Always the personal world of his characters has priority. Always the contradictions and ambiguities of their thoughts and feelings make up the texture of the novel, so that we see through individual eyes the history and the doctrine of the period. His African leaders are sometimes marred by arrogance and an irresistable taste for white women. His American leaders are often combinations of dedicated and self-sacrificing workers in the cause and of self-serving hypocrites not above chasing women and raiding their organizations' treasuries. His writers often feel petty jealousy and make attacks upon each other. Some blacks work with sincere loyalty for the white man; some expatriate themselves in bitterness. All of them have personal appetites to serve that undermine any inclination Williams might have to idealize them. Permeating all is a kind of amber sense of a man's life, Max Reddick's as viewed from the present, giving the novel a mood of dense nostalgia, a sense of loss, a sense of sadness at the unnecessary waste of black lives.

These are the most important qualities of the novel, the ones that mean the most to us as we read and that stay with us after we put the book down. More detailed analysis explains why we feel as we do and reinforces our initial sense of the novel's depth and complexity, the intelligence and validity of its conception, and the effectiveness of its structure. Its central motif, as already mentioned, is the importance of "understanding" to the black man, where understanding depends upon the discovery of the truth. To convey the truth—that is, the "truth" about America—with exactness, Williams invents the "King Alfred Plan," developed for use "in the event of widespread and continuing co-ordinated racial disturbances." It calls for national, state, and local military and police agencies to imprison all black leaders, detain all black people, and contain any black military force that might emerge. The plan is a condensed version of the white's treatment of blacks in America, a symbol of the historical and systematized control of blacks since the country's beginnings. The lives of the characters in the novel are continual reminders that such a plan has always existed in one form or another, and that now, in the novel's present, it has been codified. It is part of a larger plan, the Alliance Blanc, organized by white western Europe in the face of an increasingly militant Africa to preserve white world hegemony over the peoples of color.

If Williams does not believe in an Alliance Blanc and a King Alfred Plan (by those names and organized specifically in those forms), he does maintain that they are truthful representations of a reality outside the novel. The movement inside the novel is toward discovery of the specific truths that symbolize the more general ones outside. In the hours before he is doomed to be killed, ironically, by two black CIA agents, novelist Max Reddick reads a long letter from his fellow novelist, Harry Ames, a Richard Wright figure. Harry's letter documents the existence of the Alliance Blanc and the King Alfred Plan. As he reads, Max relives his own life in America. Both the reader and Max move back and forth from the present to the past. As the letter unfolds the information about the King Alfred Plan, flashbacks unfold the information about Max's life, and the life of the black in white America. Thus, the evidence against America accumulates on two parallel tracks, the past and the present, and reflect each other. In the end, Max reads the letter straight through. By then, with a knowledge of the past in his mind, the reader—and Max—realize that the King Alfred Plan is a logical extension of historical American policy. The letter carries with it that sudden and vivid illumination of the familiar that Williams first formulates in *Sissie:* as Harry writes to Max, "I'd spent so much of my life writing about the evil machinations of Mr. Charlie without really *knowing* the truth, as this material made me know it." That Williams puts this knowledge into the hands of two novelists indicates his conviction about the role of the black writer. *The Man Who Cried I Am,* as a novel, does what its characters do in the story that makes it up.

Once the truth is discovered, the final crucial step is revelation. Discovery requires insight and doggedness; revelation requires courage. Again, Harry's letter and his and Max's novels are acts of revelation. In the world of *The Man Who Cried I Am,* to perform such acts is dangerous. Every statesman or artist who exposes the truth about the institutionalization of the white man's crimes is killed, either literally or figuratively. In the end, both Harry and Max are assassinated. One of the ironies of the plot is that Max, dying of cancer, arrives in Europe for a last meeting with Harry. Instead of a reunion, he attends Harry's funeral, and between the funeral and his own death Max reads the revelations about the King Alfred Plan. If we have melodrama and some obvious contrivance, they work to serve the novel's main political contention that the black who discovers and reveals the truth is a dead man.

Two instances especially illustrate Williams's effectiveness in handling this theme. In the first, Max is, as a young reporter before the War, assigned to do a series of articles on Moses Boatwright, who has been arrested, convicted, and is eventually put to death for the crime of murder and cannibalism. Boatwright, a brilliant young black with a master's degree in philosophy from Harvard, has been perverted by white America, which has no place for a black with his education. He kills a white man and eats his heart and genitals, the two organs whose symbolic qualities America has deprived the black man. The crime is crude and disgusting, and Max reacts to it with "horror and disgust." It has, however, a certain poetry in it, for Boatwright's is a purely symbolic version of the act of discovery and revelation. Disgusting as it is, the crime is appropriate to its times, when the Germans are barbarously invading Poland, the Stalinists are killing Trotsky in Mexico, and the white Americans are continuing their destruction of the black spirit. Boatwright has no other recourse.

The Boatwright episode has another meaning, too, in its analogy to the writing and publication of *Native Son.* Williams does not mention the novel by name, but he makes much out of the year in which the fictional crime was committed, 1939, and the year after. *Native Son* was published in 1940, and through Boatwright, Williams attempts to explain why *Native Son* is like it is and why such a novel had to be published at that time. The grotesque crime of a black against a white in *Native Son* elicited "horror and disgust" from many quarters, both black and white. That Wright and Boat*wright* have to resort to such crude atrocities illustrates what black novelists—and black people—were up against in those days. Both appeared at a time when only the crude and the barbarous could shock people into readiness for the truth.

These acts, moreover, have a profound influence on other writers. After the Boatwright affair, Max says, he could no longer "sing golden arias." Boatwright showed him that no black writer could legitimately disregard the atrocities of white America against black. Whatever his inclination before, Max now would have to enlist his writing in the struggle. By analogy, after *Native Son,* no black writer could legitimately disregard Wright's interpretation of the race problem and the form in which he cast that interpretation.

The other instance of William's skillful handling of the theme of discovery and revelation is Max's rectal cancer. It begins as hemorrhoids, some irritating discomfort, a bloody stool or two. It develops slowly, until Max arrives in Europe and reads Harry's letter with only a little time to live. The cancer is the growth of Max's knowledge and "understanding" of America, the thing that at first makes his life merely uncomfortable, and then in the bloom of its completeness, agonizing and fatal. It suggests that, ironically, as the black person rises toward the high goal of his existence, understanding, he also moves toward death. The cancer is also the terminal illness of being black in America. This aspect of the symbol has a jazzy bathos, reducing to a gutter cliche: America gives Max "a pain in the ass," a pain which underlies nearly every moment of the narrative. Max moves through his last hours in a cloud of agony, only able to cut it in the classical way that black people have always cut their cancerous suffering—through liquor and drugs.

Implicit again is the "doctrine of fortunate oppression." Max's cancer confirms that he *is.* When he is bored with the hypocrisy of America's "New Deals and Square Deals and New Frontiers and Great Societies" and is "suspicious of the future, untrusting of the past," how can he be sure that he exists at all? "The pain in his ass told him so." The logical conclusion that might be drawn from the metaphor is that if the black were free of the cancer of white oppression or blissful in his ignorance of it, he would live a less vivid life. In *The Man Who Cried I Am,* Williams sees the irony of the paradox and treats it with sardonic humor. Max feels no self-pity—nor does Williams sentimentalize his condition. The pain of it is no fun, and certainly it is not redeemed by any romantic heroism. It is a bad joke played on the black man by an indifferent cosmos as well as a malicious white man. Max laughs, but bitterly.

Bitter humor, indeed, pervades the whole process of discovery and revelation and contributes to the depth of *The Man Who Cried I Am.* The process, furthermore, works at the personal and political levels simultaneously. Max Reddick, novelist, is the man who cries "I am," and that cry is both an assertion of his individual existence and a sign that he is determined to act. Action here, though, is not picking up a gun and shooting someone, or even organizing non-violent resistance. It is modifying one's perceptions, a forerunner to causing change in society. Max knows that publication of the King Alfred Plan will begin a civil war, but he sees no other recourse. He becomes the Moses Boatwright of the 1960's and reluctantly decides to "loose those beasts, black and white." His decision is made in the context of the historical resourcefulness of the black person in finding reasons for not acting, for not moving out of the old circuits of feeling and thought. The voice of those reasons is "Saminone," Max's other side, who appears to him, like the devil to Ivan Karamazov, at critical times in his life. Saminone, perhaps a composite Black Sambo, is all the Uncle Toms and cynical hipsters wrapped into one. To Max's desperate "I am!" Saminone counters, "You am whut, you piece of crap? Turd." Max's assertion defies the white man's negation of the black. Saminone finds in that defiance a contemptibleness that causes him to laugh bitterly, as well as a little nervously. You are only a black man, he says to Max in effect, what do you expect to do? Saminone is the fatalistic strain in the black character, the strain that Max struggles to defeat—and does. His decision to reveal Harry's information is another way of saying "I am." The enlistment of discovery and revelation in the revolution is to assert one's black existence—more, identity—and may mean death for Max and others. Not to make that revelation, not to fight to the end, is to place no value on his life, to allow the white world to make him what it will: a Saminone who has internalized a paralyzing fear and pessimism. To fight, to accept death as a consequence of that fight, is to put the ultimate value upon life, to affirm quality rather than quantity of existence. Thus, the deaths, real and symbolic, suffered by blacks who come to understand and reveal what they understand, are really life. "What looks like death," says Max, reaching deep into Christianity, "is life and what for so long looked like life is death."

The Man Who Cried I Am is Williams's adaptation of the rhetoric of black power to his own needs as a novelist. It is a gloss on a sentence in *This Is My Country Too:* "Today the strength of the contemporary Negro is in being ready to die." But the novel also expresses a feeling about the implications of prototypical black militancy no other novel has. It does not end with a flourish of trumpets and a martyred death of a black victim who triumphs even in defeat; it ends on a note of sadness and uncertainty, of lament for the necessary metamorphosis of the new black into a revolutionary ready to die. Melancholy pervades the novel, not heroic anger or righteous wrath. The violent ending cannot erase the sorrow that dominates every scene, sorrow over the tarnishing of America's bright dream. After the political implications in the failure of the American Creed comes yet another discovery that makes the politics of the novel so complex and effective: men, black and white, can be petty and self-serving; women can be grasping and self-centered. Every relationship carries with it warm human promise, and every promise gradually dissipates in the air of human frailty and the deficiency of conditions. No motive is pure, no act is untinged with bias. Blacks as well as whites display greed, jealousy, duplicity, opportunism. Even the authenticity of Max's decision to risk death by exposing the King Alfred Plan is undercut by the fact that he is already dying of cancer.

The Man Who Cried I Am is in a sense Williams's *Huckleberry Finn.* It reflects his deep skepticism over the capacity of America to live up to its professed ideals, and a development of deep pessimism about whites in particular and man in general. The intensity of its melancholy demonstrates the strength of Williams's emotional attachment to America. The gloom that the novel conveys is the result of seeing that one's most optimistic convictions are laid in sand, and that the building of the pure ideal was doomed from the start.

Yet, what seems most pessimistic turns out also to be the foundation of a tenacious hope. Max refuses to do nothing not because he wants revenge upon American, but because he still considers America worth saving. His successor, Gene Browning in *Sons of Darkness, Sons of Light,* operates on the same premise. Each concludes only with the utmost reluctance that violent confrontation is necessary. They have exhausted every other recourse and want desperately to make their country healthy. They accept violence with the same sadness that one accepts electric shock treatments for a loved one. That it *is* their country is a conviction that Williams never wavers from. For him the problems of the black in America can be solved only in America. He believes that being American rivals his being black in the things important to him. The central question of the black person in America, says Ralph Joplin in *Sissie,* is "Who in hell are we and just where do we belong?" Leave America and the answer grows dim. "To live here," says Ralph, "is not only to know who you are but what you are." There may be pain in that light, but it is better than blindness.

Similarly, the black writer can have no subject but America and Americans, as Harry Ames tells Max. The artist cannot abandon to the politicians the issues of the race question; they are too important to be subjected to political oversimplification. Furthermore, they constitute the truly valid material the artist has to work with. Thus, the question for Williams is not whether the novelist shall be political, but how shall he be so? His answer is that the black novelist uses his art to transform America and the black person through understanding. He cannot afford to forget the danger, fear, and hate in America nor can he afford to forget, as he says in *This Is My Country Too,* "much love" and "goodwill." Williams's last three novels suggest that he has modified the optimism of that statement, made in 1964. Williams continues writing novels trying to warn whites and encourage blacks, appealing to reason and goodwill, sometimes fear and nationalism. That in itself is an act of faith in the potential of white Americans eventually to implement their Creed and of black Americans to help them do it. Williams suggests that the black novelist has a greater stake in this effort than the white. As a descendent of those original slaves who survived at all costs, he "is committed to the search, the hope, the challenge, whether I want to be or not, for America has yet to sing its greatest song."

In *The Man Who Cried I Am,* Williams fuses the pessimism and the optimism that divide his own mind and feelings and makes good fiction and good politics. By recognizing men's moral, mental, and physical limitations, he delivers to politics a vision that is both more realistic and more human than the conventional political rhetoric gives us. He frees politics of its exaggerations and posturing and helps the reader avoid the danger of believing in the oversimplified version of the struggle that reduces all contention to the conflict between hero and villain. Though Williams resolves the paradox of "fortunate oppression" in **The Man Who Cried I Am,** he has perhaps gone too far on the road to polemics to turn back. He has chosen, more often than not, to use his art for the narrow rather than the larger political purpose, and it has led him into implausible exaggeration and offensive sentimentality. Unless a change in the times frees him of his deep sense of obligation to the narrower purpose, he will probably never write another novel as good as **Sissie** or **The Man Who Cried I Am.** (pp. 81-100)

> *Jerry H. Bryant, "John A. Williams: The Political Use of the Novel," in* Critique: Studies in Modern Fiction, *Vol. XVI, No. 3, 1975, pp. 81-100.*

FURTHER READING

Cowan, Paul. "The Diary of a Writer." *The New York Times Book Review* (6 May 1973): 34-35.
> Reviews *Flashbacks: A Twenty-Year Diary of Article Writing,* noting: "I have been a fan of John Williams ever since I read his brave, underrated *The Man Who Cried I Am. Flashback,* his most recent collection of essays, is not nearly so impressive a book."

Motola, Gabriel. "Knowing When to Struggle and When to Wait." *The Bloomsbury Review* 8, No. 1 (January-February 1988): 10.
> Favorable review of *Jacob's Ladder.*

Nadel, Alan. "My Country Too: Time, Place and Afro-American Identity in the Work of John Williams." *Obsidian II* 2, No. 3 (Winter 1987): 25-41.
> Examines narrative structure in *Sissie, The Man Who Cried I Am, Mothersill and the Foxes, Captain Blackman,* and *!Click Song.*

Reilly, John M. "Thinking History in *The Man Who Cried I Am.*" *Black American Literature Forum* 21, Nos. 1-2 (Spring/Summer 1987): 25-42.
> Describes *The Man Who Cried I Am* as "one of the milestones of recent Black American literary history." The critic concludes of the work: "This bleak and remarkable novel shows us that, to escape becoming victims of history, we must neither leave history unquestioned nor relate it as inevitable."

Sale, Roger. "Williams, Weesner, Drabble." In his *On Not Being Good Enough: Writings of a Working Critic,* pp. 42-53. New York: Oxford University Press, 1979.
> Discusses Theodore Weesner's *The Car Thief,* Margaret Drabble's *The Needle's Eye,* and Williams's *Captain Blackman,* concluding of the last-named work: "So if Williams's fictional device is clumsy, and many of his attempts to flesh out history are vulgar, the central vision is one worth reading."

Walcott, Ronald. "*The Man Who Cried I Am*: Crying in the Dark." *Studies in Black Literature* 3, No.1 (Spring 1972): 24-32.
> Summary and review of *The Man Who Cried I Am.*

Sherley Anne Williams
1944-

(Also Shirley Williams) American poet, short story writer, novelist, critic, and educator.

Best known for *Dessa Rose* (1986), her fictional account of the life of an escaped slave, Williams addresses the African-American experience in her poetry, fiction, and criticism. Wrote critic Michele Wallace: "*Dessa Rose* reveals both the uniformities and the idiosyncracies of 'woman's place,' while making imaginative and unprecedented use of its male characters as well. Sherley Anne Williams's accomplishment is that she takes the reader someplace we're not accustomed to going, someplace historical scholarship may never take us—into the world that black and white women shared in the antebellum South. But what excites me the most, finally, about this novel is its definition of friendship as the collective struggle that ultimately transcends the stumbling-blocks of race and class."

As a girl, Williams lived in a Fresno, California housing project and worked with her parents in fruit and cotton fields. Her father died of tuberculosis before her eighth birthday, and her mother, a practical woman from rural Texas who had tried to discourage Williams's early interest in reading, died when Williams was sixteen. "My friends were what you would call juvenile delinquents. Most of them didn't finish school," she stated. Williams herself never dreamed of a future as a writer. But a series of events, including guidance from a science teacher and the discovery of Richard Wright's *Black Boy*, Eartha Kitt's *Thursday's Child*, and other books by black authors, stimulated her to write. "It was largely through these autobiographies I was able to take heart in my life," she told Mona Gable in an interview. Williams studied at Fresno State, Fisk, Howard, and Brown universities before deciding to become a writer and to support herself by teaching. She is now a professor of African-American literature at the University of California, San Diego.

The publication of *Give Birth to Brightness: A Thematic Study in Neo-Black Literature* in 1972 marked Williams's debut as a writer. The essays are, she wrote in the book's dedication, "a public statement of how I feel about and treasure one small aspect of Blackness in America." The author's aim, according to Lillie P. Howard, "is to recreate 'a new tradition built on a synthesis of black oral traditions [such as the blues] and Western literate forms'." Reviewers found some fault with *Give Birth to Brightness*, but it was generally well received.

The Peacock Poems (1975), her second published book, also earned praise from critics. A collection of autobiographical poems, some about her early family life and the balance about her feelings as a single mother, it drew

a National Book Award nomination in 1976. Of the work, Williams noted: "I wanted specifically to write about lower-income black women . . . . We were missing these stories of black women's struggles and their real triumphs . . . . I wanted to write about them because they had in a very real sense educated me and given me what it was going to take to get me through the world."

Two economically disadvantaged women tell their stories in Williams's first novel and most highly acclaimed work, *Dessa Rose*. The book begins with the memories of its title character, a whip-scarred, pregnant slave woman in jail for committing violent crimes against white men. Dessa recalls her life on the plantation with her lover, a life that ended for her when he was killed by their master. In turn, Dessa kills the master and is arrested and chained to other slaves in a coffle. She escapes by killing her white captors. Tracked down and sentenced to die after the birth of her child, who would be valuable property to the whites, Dessa is interviewed by Adam Nehemiah, a white author who expects to become famous when he publishes the analysis of her crimes. When asked why she kills white men, Dessa replies evenly, "Cause I can." After Dessa escapes again, Rufel Sutton, a poor white woman, provides refuge for her and other runaway slaves. Taking pity, Rufel breastfeeds Dessa's newborn infant. "As a result of this extraordinary bond, the two women achieve one of the most intricate and ambivalent relationships in contemporary fiction," Elaine Kendall remarked. In a scam designed by the runaways, Rufel earns money by selling the runaways as slaves, waiting for them to escape, and then by re-selling them. All goes well until the end, when Dessa is arrested by the enraged Nehemiah, but the two women elude capture with the help of a female officer.

Williams told Gable that she hoped *Dessa Rose* would "heal some wounds" made by racism left in the wake of slavery. In her view, she explained, fiction is one way to conceive of "the impossible... and putting these women together, I could come to understand something not only about their experience of slavery but about them as women, and imagine the basis for some kind of honest rapprochement between black and white women."

(For further information about Williams's life and works, see *Black Writers; Contemporary Authors,* Vols. 73-76; *Contemporary Authors New Revision Series,* Vol. 25; and *Dictionary of Literary Biography,* Vol. 41: *Afro-American Poets since 1955.*)

PRINCIPAL WORKS

Give Birth to Brightness: A Thematic Study in Neo-Black Literature (criticism) 1972
The Peacock Poems (poetry) 1975
Some One Sweet Angel Chile (poetry) 1982
Dessa Rose (novel) 1986

Mel Watkins (essay date 1972)

[*Watkins is an American editor, journalist, and children's book writer. In the following excerpt, he reviews* Give Birth to Brightness: A Thematic Study in Neo-Black Literature.]

During the last few years' questions concerning the pertinence of black literature to the black community have been hotly debated, along with the possibility of establishing a viable criterion for judging literature. Various writers and critics have suggested theories of a "black esthetic," but generally these theories have eschewed aspects of form and have focused on the themes and subject matter treated by black authors. Consequently, rather than providing strictly esthetic guidelines, they have usually offered what might more properly be termed a theory of black sensibility—a significant accomplishment in itself. As it is further refined, this theory may obviate discussion of a separate

esthetic dealing with form. Sherley Anne Williams's *Give Birth to Brightness* is a book that should give more impetus to that development.

It is a survey of black fiction from the 19th century to the present, but it focuses on those contemporary works that the author labels "neo-black" writing. According to Miss Williams, neo-black writing is characterized by its debunking of art-for-arts-sake; by its authors' insistence upon addressing themselves to a black readership, and by their attempt to "define themselves and their people in images which grow out of their individual quests and group explorations." Selected works of Imamu Amiri Baraka (LeRoi Jones), James Baldwin and Ernest J. Gaines are analyzed in depth as Miss Williams lays the foundation for her theory.

Neo-black writing (which she depicts as part of a continuum growing out of the poetry of Phillis Wheatley, the slave narratives, and the novels of the 19th-century writers such as William Wells Brown) provides the author with examples of the variegated roles and images of the black hero. In examining specific works of Baraka, Baldwin and Gaines, she illuminates similarities in their perceptions of some archetypal figures in black life (the rebel or streetman and the musician) and she compares how these figures in fiction struggle to wrest some sense of manhood from their interaction with the white world and particularly the white woman. Despite some overgeneralizations, Miss Williams persuasively demonstrates the commonality of viewpoint that she asserts characterizes neo-black fiction. Moreover, she evokes a real sense of what the street life is about.

But while the book's analytical foundation is convincing, the final theoretical edifice has its cracks. The streetman may function as rebel and black hero in literature, as Miss Williams points out; by flouting the mainstream (white) society's values and laws he provides visible symbolic resistance to its oppressive forces and counteracts the image of docility associated with slavery and segregation. Still, to lionize the streetmen (hustlers, pimps, pushers) and suggest, as the author does, that they are *actual* heroes in the black community because of their potential for "rechanneling their driving strength into [less destructive] direction" is dangerous and highly romantic. Glaring exceptions such as Malcolm X aside, most hustlers don't undergo the revelation that transforms them from parasites into prophets and Prometheans. They usually remain as predatory in black communities as the establishment itself does. And, outside of the misguided youths who are both their prey and protégés—and some intellectuals—it would be difficult to locate the groundswell of sympathy that the author suggests exists in the black community. Too many blacks have been their victims for the community to maintain that romanticism.

Criticisms such as this notwithstanding, Miss Williams has written a readable and informative survey of black literature. In using both her knowledge of Western literature and her understanding of black life, she provides insights into the sadly neglected area of reversed values that plays such a significant role in much black literature.

Mel Watkins, "Some Art for Blacks' Sake,"
in The New York Times, *July 8, 1972, p. 23.*

Sherley Anne Williams with Claudia Tate (interview date 1983)

[*Tate is an American editor, critic, and short story writer. In the interview excerpted below, she questions Williams about her ideas on blues music and on her own writing.*]

[Tate]: *How does being black and female constitute a particular perspective in your work?*

[Williams]: I don't think I keep my being black and female self-consciously in mind. I just assume that whatever I write comes from that perspective. Whether it's there in an overt manner or not doesn't really change that source. What I do think about self-consciously is that I am a writer. That assumes, of course, that I must also be a person; and that, in turn, assumes that I must have some racial background and gender; I just go on from that starting point.

I feel that a writer ought to transcend his or her background to some extent. Background ought not to be the only source of creativity. On the other hand, I do know the reason I was first inspired to do a story was because I wanted specifically to write about lower-income black women. I didn't see them as dominant forces in any of the literature I had read; they were always incidental to a larger story. I felt that they had significance, that something could be learned from them. We were missing these stories of black women's struggles and their real triumphs. I wanted to see them in stories, and I felt that I was capable of writing them. That is the basis of the first writing I did. I didn't want to write about myself, a young, black, female college student. I wanted to write about them because they had in a very real sense educated me and given me what it was going to take to get me through the world.

My interest in black women writers grew out of my discovery of writers, not necessarily women writers, but writers who wrote about people and things I knew about from my own experience. It didn't matter that I was in Fresno, California, and Zora Neale Hurston, for instance, was in Eatonville, Florida. It was a deeper experience reading her work than that by Langston Hughes or Sterling Brown, though they are great writers. Zora Neale focused in on a situation in a very different way from them. Hughes wrote about the north, and Sterling is writing about farmers and sharecroppers. Zora Neale's society sits in between, which is precisely what my background is.

The blues perspective dominates your work. You are quoted in The Black Scholar *in reference to the sexist*

debate as saying, "But until we know the blues intimately and analytically, we will not know ourselves."

What I really believe is that we as a people must be consciously aware that we must perpetuate ourselves and some idea of ourselves. Western, white people do this through literature, but we black people don't have that: we don't emanate from a literate tradition. We do not have a literature in which we see ourselves perpetuated. What we learn from most literature concerns white people; but where we do, in fact, perpetuate ourselves is in the blues.

I use blues to refer to a body of continuous expression that encompasses popular Afro-American music, so that at any given time whatever is popular among black people can be found in that mass of songs and instrumentation. In blues there is some kind of philosophy, a way of looking at the world. When the black-consciousness people came along, they disavowed the blues expression, and put down whatever was popular at that time because of ideology, because it was supposedly "slavery time"; this disavowal made a rupture in the continuity of our preserved history in this art form. We, as writers, are not revealing what the philosophy is. The people who perform the songs do this. The blues records of each decade explain something about the philosophical basis of our lives as black people. If we don't understand that as so-called intellectuals, then we don't really understand anything about ourselves. Blues is a basis of historical continuity for black people. It is a ritualized way of talking about ourselves and passing it on. This was true until the sixties. (pp. 207-08)

How do you fit writing into your life?

I fit writing in any way I can. Before my years in administration, I never really had to think about fitting writing into my schedule. I would write anytime and anywhere. I could write in a room full of people; I could write on a train. I don't know if that was out of necessity, but I think it says I was comfortable enough to write anywhere. I could be at a party and would pull out my little sheet of paper and start writing. I could work with the TV on, with kids running around. I was happy I could do this. Prior to being an administrator I don't think I had any real consciousness of needing any special time to write; but now that I do, you can be sure I'm going to be really greedy.

Would you describe your writing process? How do you select your topics?

My topics select me. Then I just go ahead and try to work with them. I really try not to push things. If it's going to come, it'll come. I've always had enough projects going, so that if one was not going well at one point, I could just go on to something else. I've never been on a schedule, and I don't want to get on one. I don't think that's the most fruitful way for me to work.

What is your responsibility as a writer?

Basically, to be as good as I can be and to say as much of the truth as I can see at any given time. It's just as simple as that.

Is there a transition between your critical and the creative postures?

When I wrote **Give Birth to Brightness,** Toni Morrison said that the book was very masculine. I had never thought about that. It was a book of criticism about a given body of literature, and the fact that I was a woman looking at how the hero was characterized never bothered me. I was a critic, and I was looking at those writers. The fact that the works were by black men didn't concern me. If I had found women who fit my subject—a certain kind of heroic black character—I would have dealt with that, too. My approach wasn't divided up according to gender.

How I work with the language constitutes the difference between critical and creative writing. I have read a few books of criticism, though, which I consider to be in and of themselves like works of art. There is a kind of leap the writer takes that not only illuminates the particular subject he or she is writing about, but shows the reader how to get from A to Z in ways that weren't possible before. That kind of illumination is not any different for me than the kind you want to have happen in a poem, a story or any imaginative piece.

For whom do you write?

I think writing is really a process of communication. I bore everybody to death when I'm writing—"I want you to read this; I changed a word since yesterday. Read it, see what you think." It's the process of reading to people and getting their feedback that's important to me. It's the sense of being in contact with people who are part of a particular audience that really makes a difference to me in writing. I don't think there's anything I've ever published that has not been seen by a lot of people, whether they gave me feedback, whether I acted upon it or not. Writing for me is really a process of saying, "Here, read this." It reinforces the fact that I'm in touch with somebody other than my own mind.

What determines your interest as a writer?

It has to do with what is out there, where the gaps are, and do I have the wherewithal to fill in some of those gaps that ought not to be there. The imaginative work is wide open—whatever comes to mind and whatever I think is going to be fruitful in terms of showing people something about themselves and their relationship to the world. I really believe writing has a purpose: to teach and to delight.

Have you written stories from the male perspective?

I've done a couple of stories from that perspective, neither of which has been published. I think one ought to be able to do this as a writer; writers ought to be able to project themselves into another voice and from another point of view. In a very real way that's not very different from what I have to do when I create anyway. If I achieve that initial projection, then the character assumes a life of his or her own. At the time I wrote these stories, my approach wasn't, "Now I'm going to write a story about a man." It was, "Now I'm going to write a story that has to do with these things," and those things came with characters who happen to be male or female.

Does your work attempt to show the cohesion and meaning in life?

For me writing is a process of ordering the world. It is a process of bringing insight, playing around with possibilities, solutions, in a way I could never play around with actual life. Just think of the difference between the "order" of a poem and a novel and the chaos of life. That can give you some insight in knowing that if the chaos cannot be ordered, at least it can be dealt with in a constructive way. It's this that I'm after.

Do you write from experience?

For me that is not a meaningful question because whatever I'm writing about, whether it's drawn directly from my own experience or something imaginative, if the incident doesn't move beyond the initial observation, the initial imagination, then it doesn't work. No matter how close to autobiography any one piece happens to be, if all I can see is that this happened to the writer, then the writer has failed. The autobiographical thread must represent something else.

Do you have any advice for young, black, women writers?

I think that we writers should get out there, even if we are wrong 99 percent of the time. That 1 percent would be enough to give us some insight, but it takes a lot to get out there. Somebody has to be first to take all the flak. We have to stop being afraid. I have to stop being afraid of being wrong; I can't wait until everything is perfect before the work comes out. I don't have that kind of time. That's not to say that the poem has not been attended to, that it's not gotten to be the best it can. The poem or the story or the play doesn't just jump out there; it has been attended to; it's gotten to be the best it can. (pp. 209-12)

Sherley Anne Williams, in an interview with Claudia Tate, in Black Women Writers at Work, *edited by Claudia Tate, Continuum, 1983, pp. 205-13.*

David Bradley (essay date 1986)

[*Bradley is an American educator. In the following excerpt, he reviews* Dessa Rose.]

Two things can happen when poets venture into fiction. They can approach the business with the arrogant (or naive) assumption that they already understand the purposes and problems of fiction, and end up producing books which, while sometimes pyrotechnic in terms of poetry, are duds in terms of prose. This, alas, is the usual case. Sometimes, however, a gifted poet comes to the novel with a humble determination to do what fiction has to do: tell a story worth telling. The product in this case is not only good fiction, but fiction enlivened by symbolic connections and daring imagery—elements that those who write only prose often neglect. It must have been with such a desire that Sherley Anne Williams, whose *Peacock Poems* was nominated for the 1976 National Book Award, began her first novel, *Dessa Rose.* For what she has written is an absorbing fusion that is both elegant poetry and powerful fiction.

The plot of *Dessa Rose* was born of two accounts from the antebellum South. The first concerns a pregnant black woman who reportedly led an uprising among a group of slaves being herded to market. She was caught and sentenced to death, but her hanging was delayed until after the birth of her child. (It was, after all, valuable property.) In the other account, a lone white woman struggling for survival on an isolated North Carolina farm was said to have given illegal sanctuary to a permanent colony of fugitive slaves. Ms. Williams has fused these two unconnected, obscure incidents, after reshaping them as the stories of Odessa Rose (called Dessa), a young pregnant slave woman, and Ruth Elizabeth (called Rufel), a privileged Charleston bride.

The two women meet at a time of stress for both. Dessa has been captured after rebelling while being transported to market and killing a white slave driver in the process. In a departure from the historical record, Dessa has been rescued before she is hanged and has been brought to Rufel's plantation. There an old slave woman, Rufel's Mammy, has organized an underground community of runaways. Despite the apparent safety, however, Dessa is debilitated by her past incarceration, confused by her surroundings and weakened by the birth of her child.

Rufel too is in a weakened state. She has just discovered, too late, that her dashing groom is really a riverboat gambler, and an unlucky one at that. His back-country plantation has neither good land nor slaves, and the mansion comprises a single room and a grand stairway to a nonexistent second story. Worse, she has been abandoned by him. (Officially, he has departed on a trip to raise money.) She has also been abandoned by her distant family, who are angry about her husband's gold-digging, and even by Mammy, who died after organizing the slave community, leaving Rufel only vaguely aware of the arrangement. Trained from birth to follow the orders of men, the dictates of family and the guidance of slave women, Rufel is as confused as Dessa.

The heart of the story is the growth of a relationship between the two women, a relationship that allows them both to escape the roles and concepts of race and gender that antebellum society forced on them. The success of that escape is symbolized by a con game. The two women sell the fugitive slaves, have them run away

again, and then use the money to finance a final escape for them all. Besides having delightful irony, the caper is described in a way that gives it all the rousing entertainment value of "The Sting."

In this episode and others Ms. Williams shows that she has both a sense of scene and a feel for the way historical context can make the most ordinary actions significant. In one sequence, Rufel nurses Dessa's baby. This interracial intimacy of course reverses the usual pattern; that it shocks even runaway slaves, upsets Dessa and makes Rufel feel oddly defensive, reveals the inhuman illogic of Dessa and Rufel's world.

But while Ms. Williams shows that she can write a novel better than a lot of novelists, nowhere does she cut herself off from her poetic roots: the language of *Dessa Rose* is everywhere infused with rhythm and image. For example, here is Dessa, in jail, recalling her lover, Kaine, killed by a master's whim:

> Kaine, his voice high, and clear as running water over a settled stream bed, swooping to her, through her. ... He walked the lane between the indifferently rowed cabins like he owned them, striding from shade into half-light as if he could halt the setting sun ... Talk as beautiful as his touch. Shivering, she pulled at his shirt. This was love, her hand at his back, his mouth ...
>
> Desire flowered briefly, fled in dry spasm, gone as suddenly as the dream had come, so lifelike she had felt herself with him ... And woke. She closed her eyes. Chains rasped, rubbed hatefully at her ankles and wrists. Coarse ticking scratched at her skin; corn husks whispered dryly beneath her at each move. Kaine's eyes had been the color of lemon tea and honey. Even now against closed eyelids, she could see them.

Dessa Rose is of course not without flaw. Like many writers whose experience is with shorter forms, Ms. Williams occasionally underdramatizes and at times commits errors in pacing, rushing crucial scenes and making the book shorter than it needs or ought to be. And though she shows herself capable of finding elegant solutions to problems of narration, she has an unfortunate tendency to keep *on* finding solutions, rather than extending the original ones. Also, some plot elements, exciting, useful and strongly realized in the beginning of the novel—are allowed to wither or languish, which causes problems at the end.

The most obvious example of this last flaw is likely to cause Ms. Williams other sorts of problems, by inspiring the kind of literary-political controversy that is silly, unfortunate ... and delicious fun. In a prefatory author's note she admits to having been "outraged by a certain, critically acclaimed novel of the early seventies that travestied the as-told-to memoir of slave revolt leader Nat Turner." This reference to William Styron's *Confessions of Nat Turner* (which is a bit inaccurate; the novel was published in 1967) is echoed in the first part of the novel proper, where Ms. Williams portrays the details of Dessa's revolt through the narrative of a character called Nehemiah. Author of *The Masters' Complete Guide to Dealing With Slaves and Other Dependents,* Nehemiah is researching "a book on slave uprisings, [which] touching as it must upon the secret fears of non-slave holder and slave holder alike, should be an immediate success, easily surpassing the heart- (and pocket-) warming sales of the *Guide*...The book would establish Nehemiah as an important southern author."

In terms of both fictional technique and historical accuracy, Ms. Williams makes better and fairer use of Dessa's "confession" than Mr. Styron did with Nat Turner's. Although Nehemiah is a minor character, Ms. Williams handles him with such skill that we are able to see that he falls in love with Dessa in the course of their interviews, despite the fact that he could never admit to himself what is happening. His love becomes a bizarre obsession and, following Dessa's escape, he becomes determined to track her down, which leads to the novel's final confrontation. The details of the pursuit, however, are absent from the novel, as Ms. Williams, herself a bit obsessed with the story of Dessa and Rufel, loses track of Nehemiah. His reappearance therefore seems a bit contrived.

These flaws however do not destroy the novel. *Dessa Rose* remains a powerful story and as such will cause much favorable comment even among those who do not share Ms. Williams's outrage at Mr. Styron's *Confessions.* For this is a book that almost demands comparison—to Mr. Styron's *Confessions,* to Jean Toomer's *Cane,* to Grace Paley's *Enormous Changes at the Last Minute.* And, because Ms. Williams is a black woman, originally a poet, writing about a liberating relationship between two women, some readers may expect *Dessa Rose* to be a second *Color Purple.* While that comparison is somewhat superficial, it is not wholly inappropriate. For, like Alice Walker, Sherley Anne Williams has written a novel that is artistically brilliant, emotionally affecting and totally unforgettable.

> David Bradley, "On the Lam from Race and Gender," in *The New York Times Book Review, August 3, 1986, p. 7.*

Doris Davenport (essay date 1986)

[*In the following essay, Davenport examines how* Dessa Rose *"fits into, yet subtly alters, several Afro-American literary traditions."*]

Recently there have been panels, papers, anthologies, and fights devoted to revising, updating, and enlarging the "canon" of literature. Some professors, most feminist critics, and other enlightened people want to make the literature we read and teach more representative and inclusive of different classes (not just the middle), races (not just white), and at least two sexes. From the Society for the Study of Multi-Ethnic Literature (MELUS) to individual spokespersons, the concern has been growing stronger since the late sixties. Sherley Anne Williams's

novel *Dessa Rose* provides each of us another opportunity to alter that "canon." We need only read and teach the book.

For those of us who are knowledgeable and concerned about the "canon" and traditions of Afro-American literature, *Dessa Rose* is doubly significant. The novel fits into, yet subtly alters, several Afro-American literary traditions, playing against and with them as a tight jazz combo does (or used to). For example, the book is a "contemporary" slave narrative, which draws on the history of slave insurrections in America. Dessa is a heroine in her own times, much as Sojourner Truth was in hers. The book contains many indirect allusions to Afro-American novels and poems, including Hurston's *Their Eyes Were Watching God* and Robert Hayden's "Runagate Runagate." Additionally, many of the favored or repeated motifs, themes, and "mascons" of black culture appear and reappear, from rootworking to the north star. What this novel is depends, partly, on the reader's context(s) or reading strategies.

Dessa Rose is the triumphant story of a heroic, young, ex-slave woman in Marengo County, Alabama, in 1847. It is also the story of a "working-class" black woman (a field hand, as opposed to a "house nigger") who eventually tells her own story. Because of the multifaceted aspects of the novel, it could easily fit into a course in literary realism or in women's, feminist, or "Southern" literature—even a history, psychology, or self-assertiveness training course. Additionally, it is "controversial" and thought-provoking enough to generate at *least* as much discussion as Walker's *The Color Purple* has.

Dessa Rose, a continuation of Williams's 1980 short story **"Meditations on History,"** collected in Mary Helen Washington's *Midnight Birds,* has been in progress for at least four years. According to the "Author's Note" in *Dessa Rose,* the story grew from two "historical incidents": a pregnant black woman who helped lead an uprising on a coffle (and was hanged after her baby's birth) and a white woman who helped runaway slaves. Williams writes, "How sad...that these two women never met"—then introduces them to each other in her novel. Another motive for the novel was Williams's need to "reclaim" Afro-American history and literature: "I admit also to being outraged by a certain, critically acclaimed novel of the early seventies that travestied the as-told-to memoir of slave revolt leader Nat Turner. Afro-Americans, having survived by word of mouth—and made of that process a high art—remain at the mercy of literature and writing; often, these have betrayed us." If literature and writing, particularly that by some whites about black folk, have sometimes betrayed us, then Williams's *Dessa Rose* is partly literary revenge for that betrayal. It is also a celebration of Afro-American folk-cultural traditions. Dessa, an illiterate yet astute *black* black woman, is the focus of both the celebration and the revenge.

The novel's structure, content, and style emphasize both revenge and reclamation/celebration. It has three main parts, with a prologue and epilogue by Dessa. The first two sections present the erroneous perspectives of Dessa's two white antagonists, while an omniscient narrator provides Dessa's countering perspectives and reality. The first section, "The Darky," is about Adam Nehemiah, a young white male; the second, "The Wench," is mainly about Ruth Elizabeth or "Rufel," the white woman who takes in runaway slaves. The third section, "The Negress," is presented totally from Dessa's perspective. Each section advances the action of the whole, which is told in a circuitous, spiral manner. Dessa's tale, appropriately, concludes the action; she has the last word, her own story, her own history, as well as her own book.

"The Darky" begins with what could be considered a parody of the travestied as-told-to memoir. Ambitious nineteenth-century yuppie Nehemiah callously interviews Dessa, who is chained in a cellar and eight months pregnant. He intends to write a book—and make his fame and fortune—on the "origins of uprisings among slaves," which will tell slaveowners how to predict and forestall any insurrections or rebellions among their slaves. However Dessa turns the tables on Nehemiah, just as Williams turns the tables on all such interviewers. In the next section, Rufel is initially revealed as Nehemiah's female counterpart—just as arrogant, but ultimately more "human."

As Dessa tells her own story, and even as she is seen through the distorting eyes of the two white antagonists, Williams skillfully uses various aspects of Afro-American culture and history, as she does in her poetry. First, Williams carefully reinforces the concept of a well-knit, loving slave community. Unity and culture repeatedly save Dessa, as she talks to Nehemiah, tolerates Rufel, and eventually makes her way to California and true freedom. Initially, the single strongest reason for her strength and determination is her murdered husband Kaine and their baby, whom she carries. The memory of the couple's love and her fierce desire to be free sustain her. The prologue, in fact, consists of a dream of Dessa's about Kaine: his laughter, his banjo music and singing, and his eyes, "the color of lemon tea and honey." (Kaine is a more sophisticated, more intelligent, more cynical Teacake.) As Nehemiah questions Dessa about her escape from the coffle, she constantly thwarts him by talking of Kaine—their love, their life, the fact that Kaine "chosed" her, and of how "Masa" killed Kaine. Her love for Kaine and the others of her family sustains her; she exists on a level which is incomprehensible to Nehemiah, and almost equally off limits to Rufel.

While Nehemiah is condescending, arrogant, and—in his mind—quite superior to any "darky," Dessa's perceptions reveal him to be a pretentious buffoon. Nehemiah, a white man of his times, thinks of all black folks as being akin to animals; Dessa, to him, is merely something to be used. However, he is repeatedly frustrated in his attempts to use her, and driven to the point of rage. As he observes, "I must constantly remind myself that she is but a darky and a female at that."

Among other things, their two modes of being and talking reveal a total "culture conflict," a juxtaposition of two value systems. Nehemiah's language is cold, "intellectual," sterile, and, of course, "proper," whereas Dessa's language is warm, lively, colorful, and black. At one point, Dessa asks him, "'You a *real* white man?... You don't talk like one. Sometime, I don't even be knowing what you be saying. You don't talk like Masa and he a real uppity white man...'" As Dessa ridicules and laughs at Nehemiah, he arrogantly informs her that he teaches men like her master how to talk. Dessa responds, "'Was a teacher man on the coffle.... He teached hisself to read from the Bible, then he preach. But course, that only be to niggas, and he be all right till he want teach other niggas to read the Good Word. That be what he call it, the Good Word; and when his masa find out what he be doing, he be sold south same's if he teaching a bad word.... Onliest freedom he be knowing is what he call the righteous freedom. That what the Lawd be giving him or what the masa be giving him and he was the first one the patterrollers killed.'" Dessa is truly signifying; she is unimpressed with either the preacher's or Nehemiah's "knowledge."

Dessa's reality repeatedly surfaces to undermine Nehemiah's, who grows increasingly to appreciate, and even lust after, her. Dessa, on the other hand, is repelled by Nehemiah. When she first sees his eyes up close, she recoils, "thinking in that first instance of seeing that his eyes were covered by some film, milky and blank. His eyes were 'blue,' she saw in the next moment.... That's why we not supposed to look in white folks' eyes, she thought with a shiver. There was only emptiness in them; the unwary would fall into the well of their eyes and drown." Dessa is equally repelled by Rufel when, in the book's second section, she comes out of her postpartum delirium and illness to see a white woman.

In an ironic, somewhat hilarious fashion, Dessa retreats from that horror and threat to the world of dreams, attempting, while dreaming, to ask her mother what it means to *dream* of a white woman. Finally facing the fact that Rufel is no dream, she confronts the thing—a white woman—that she most hates and fears. (Her mistress, after all, sold her south; was the reason she was on the coffle.) Even more so than with Nehemiah, Dessa has a problem with Rufel. A lonely, self-deluded young white woman with two children, one of whom is still at her breast, Rufel has been deserted in an isolated part of Alabama, in a half-built house, by her gambler husband. She consoles herself by thinking out loud of her "glorious" days in Charleston and of her "wedding present"—a black "Mammy," recently dead, named Dorcas. In fact, Rufel thinks of all black folk as being like her "Mammy": always accessible to her needs, always available to soothe, take care of, and love her. Although Rufel used Mammy—for everything from a hairdresser to an overseer—, she also "loved" her. Because of Mammy, Rufel is enamored of black skin and is a closet Negrophile. She is full of contradictions and, like Scarlet O'Hara, puts off thinking not just until another day, but almost forever.

For instance, since Dessa is ill and cannot nurse her baby, Rufel nurses him, rationalizing that he is, after all, only a baby. (Here, Williams obviously does a deliberate role reversal on the thousands of black women who were forced to nurse white babies.) Meanwhile, she feels "wonder" at the baby and "liked to watch the baby as he nursed, . . . the contrast between his mulberry-colored mouth and the pink areola surrounding her nipple, between his caramel-colored fist and the rosy cream of her breast." Eventually, Dessa wakes up and asks where her baby "at." When Rufel shows the baby at her breast, Dessa freaks out. When Dessa reawakens, we learn that "she almost suffocated in her terror for she knew the white woman held her and they were together in the big feather bed." Rightfully terrified, Dessa "scoots" to the edge of the bed, holding her baby, and tries to move to the slave quarters the next day.

Fortunately for Dessa, there are several other ex-slaves at Rufel's—the three black men who helped her escape the second time, and Ada and her daughter—who take care of Dessa while she's sick. They help her maintain her sanity, especially Ada, who calls Rufel "Miss Ruint." Yet, Rufel is as oblivious to the realities of these non-slaves as she is of how to plant her land. All of the black folk, including Dessa, see that Rufel is a bit "odd." But whereas Dessa plays Nehemiah off, she is finally forced to speak out, passionately and at length, to Rufel.

One day Rufel, who has a habit of talking to herself, speaks of "Mammy," and as she rambles (or babbles), Dessa listens and thinks of *her* mammy, her own mother. The juxtaposition continues until Dessa finally shouts, "'Mammy ain't made you nothing!'" and then, "'You don't even know mammy.'" From that point until the end of the exchange, Dessa overrides Rufel. "'"Mammy" ain't nobody name,'" says Dessa, "'not they real one.'" Then Dessa chants an oral, passed-down litany of her mother's name, *Rose:* where she lived, and how each of Rose's ten children lived, died, or was sold—on up to herself, "'Dessa, Dessa Rose, the baby girl.'" That "conversation" is a major turning point in their relationship. Just as Dessa let Nehemiah know that he did *not* know her, she lets Rufel know. Relatedly, Williams lets types like these two whites know, again and again, that *they* do not know. Dessa drives Nehemiah into an obsession which borders on insanity; she indirectly drives Rufel into the arms—the blue-black black arms—of Nathan.

The first two sections of the novel contain a story of "power" reclaimed. At one level, Dessa is totally powerless compared to these two whites, yet this "Devil Woman" radically alters and reshapes their realities. Section three, "The Negress," begins with Dessa's telling her own story to an avid listener, a continuation of the main narrative from a point in time soon after Rufel "meets" Nathan. Rufel is necessary for the "plan" of the black folk to make it to California, an idea which Dessa at first rejects, then reluctantly accepts. In time, and with numerous adventures, Rufel and Dessa in-

creasingly learn from and respect each other. Rufel comes to see black folk as people and to abhor slavery; Dessa reluctantly concedes that a white woman could be her friend, especially after Rufel saves her, a second time, from the rabid grasp of Nehemiah.

Dessa's section is the structural, stylistic, and political climax of the novel. An old woman, whose fingers are almost too stiff to braid the hair of the listening woman-child seated between her legs, Dessa speaks in vivid detail of her past. She concludes her story in the epilogue with these words: *"I hopes I live for my people like they do for me, so sharp sometime I can't believe it's all in my mind. And my mind wanders. This why I have wrote it down, why I has that child say it back. I never will forget Nemi trying to read me, knowing I had put myself in his hands. Well,* this *the childrens have heard from our own lips . . ."* Not only have the "childrens" heard the story "from our own lips," the readers of the novel have also heard the story in and from Williams's own style and perspective.

This story, like almost all of Williams's poetry and fiction, is rooted in a black-female reality. The novel has a few minor flaws, most notably the "plan" which gets the black folk to California. Yet it is told in an inimitable style: a style which draws on call and response, the blues, and jazz riffs; draws on Afro-American history and culture; and plays off a knowledge of Afro-American literature and language. The story of Dessa Rose is conveyed in a thoroughly loved, researched, and "worked" style which only Sherley Anne Williams has. (pp. 335-40)

> Doris Davenport, in a review of "Dessa Rose," in Black American Literature Forum, Vol. 20, No. 3, Fall, 1986, pp. 335-40.

Elizabeth Schultz (essay date 1988)

[*In the following essay, Schultz examines the title character's increasing self-understanding in* Dessa Rose.]

The facts of slavery, historical and experiential, form the substructure for most Afro-American novels, yet only a few—Arna Bontemp's *Black Thunder* (1936), Margaret Walker's *Jubilee* (1966), Ernest Gaines's *The Autobiography of Miss Jane Pittman* (1971), Ishmael Reed's *Flight to Canada* (1976), Toni Morrison's *Beloved* (1987), and Sherley Anne Williams's **Dessa Rose** (1986)—have focused explicitly on the time of slavery. With the publication of her critical work, **Give Birth to Brightness** (1972), Sherley Anne Williams dedicated herself to an examination and interpretation of the continuity of traditions and culture in Afro-American literature, arguing that the goal of the contemporary Afro-American writer is "to reveal the beauty and pain, the ugliness and the joy of four hundred years of living in the New World, what this has done to Black people, and, most importantly, what it can and does mean to them." **Dessa Rose** in its recreation of the complex lives of the ancestors of contemporary black Americans and in its illumination of the struggle of one black woman to know herself and her community and, thereby, to free herself and her community from slavery, fulfills Williams's self-prescribed goal. From the pain and ugliness of bondage, Dessa Rose, Williams's title character, comes to create beauty and joy; her story of this creative process is her legacy to the children—the future, a time we might hope, beyond slavery.

Knowledge precedes liberation, and in *Dessa Rose* Williams makes both personal and communal knowledge of history fundamental. Recognizing in the "Author's Note," with which her novel opens, the importance of historical accounts of her own developing knowledge of her people, Williams explains that Americans have been at the mercy of the written word which has often betrayed them. It thus seems that she attempts in her novel the conscious and imaginative re-writing of history so as to reflect the goal Henry James could acknowledge as being valid for the novel; it should project "the felt life." In *Dessa Rose* Williams deliberately recreates and merges three historical accounts according to the "Author's Note": the account of a black woman who led a revolt from a slave coffle, that of a white woman who harbored escaped slaves on her plantation, and that of a white man, who, like the interviewer who first recorded Nat Turner's story following his rebellion and like William Styron later, distorted Afro-American experience linguistically. For each of these accounts, Williams generates a particular voice, a particular character, with a particular name. The language characterizing each of these voices, in turn, reveals the degree to which not only each is enslaved through lack of knowledge, but also the degree to which each subsequently becomes liberated with the acquisition of knowledge. Thus, throughout her novel, Williams repeatedly demonstrates that, historically, language, the process of naming, as it reflects and projects either a distorted, limited vision or a clear, full vision, is a primary means of institutionalizing injustice as well as for discovering consciousness and salvation. As other Afro-American writers have recognized, an individual's name may become a metaphor for bondage or for liberation, thus the white man—Adam Nehemiah—never realizes the personal and communal history implied by his name, whereas both the black woman, Dessa Rose, and the white woman, Ruth Elizabeth, neither of whose names is associated with the surname of a man, do.

Nehemiah's voice commands Part I of *Dessa Rose* entitled "The Darky." Williams convinces us that his is the voice of a particular individual—insecure, conscious of his short stature, eager to rise from his lower class background to associate with the powerful plantation owners and their beautiful wives—as well as the general voice of white paternalism and racism, masculine patriarchy and sexism, American self-reliance and capitalism. He is also the representative voice of the intellect, separated from the heart, the soul, the psyche, and committed to rationalizing, through rhetoric, the systems of racism, sexism, and capitalism. As Williams describes Nehemiah's attempt to elicit the story of Dessa's revolt from her, she makes apparent both the nature of his exploitation and the failure of that exploitation through his language. While writing a book on *The Roots of Rebellion in the Slave Population and Some Means of Eradicating Them,* Nehemiah interviews the lashed and shackled pregnant Dessa with the expectation that her revelations will provide him with information that will make his fortune as a best-selling author and give him an entry into the best Southern homes. In recording "the facts" of Dessa's story, however, he is accurate with regard to time—1847—and place—Alabama, but otherwise, he manages not only to reinforce his own limited vision of black people and the black community, but also, because of his personal desires for commercial success, to perpetuate the distorted views of the slave-holding class at large—his potential audience. Repeatedly referring to Dessa as "the darky," he degrades her race, her mind, her humanity, her individuality; his other terms for her, such as "girl," "slut," "devil woman," "sly bitch," "treacherous nigger bitch," degrade her gender as well: both demonstrate his use of words to control. That he should tell Dessa that is he writing his book "'in the hope of helping others to be happy in the life that has been sent them to live'" is the cruellest irony.

By juxtaposing Nehemiah's words with Dessa's words, reflections, and memories (designated by italics), Williams creates a prolonged pang of irony and reveals the white man's incomprehension of his own humanity, of the dehumanizing circumstances of slavery, and of the emotions and motivations of this complex black woman who because she didn't want her baby "slaved," was compelled to attack both her slave owners and the slave-trader to whom she was subsequently sold. For Dessa, there "Wasn't no darky to it"; her beloved Kaine, whose child she was bearing and who had been beaten to death by their Master, "was the color of the cane syrup taffy they pulled and stretched to a glistening golden brown in winter." In antiphony with Nehemiah's speculative and biased analysis of her life, Dessa's memories are rendered lyrically, evoking the beauty and the songs and the love which characterized her relationship with Kaine and with her friends and family. Kaine had helped her to become articulate in the language of imagination, emotion, and clarity. With him, *"Talk [was] as beautiful as . . . touch";* he has told her that it *"'Don't take much, Dess—if you got the right word. And you know when it come to eating beef, I steal the right word if it ain't hiding somewhere round my own self's tongue.'"* In Williams's description of Dessa's thought processes, such language becomes the basis for her understanding of herself and her circumstances and for her liberation. Thus as Nehemiah questions her for his own purposes, she starts "seeing as she spoke the power of Master as absolute and evil." She consequently comes to give verbal form to concepts of freedom and selfhood, saying to her uncomprehending white male interlocutor, "'Onliest mind I be knowing is mines.'" Williams implies the depth of Nehemiah's failure to comprehend Dessa through his commentary on her language. Describing the songs by which Dessa remembers her communal past and by which she continues to communicate with the black community beyond the bars of her prison merely as "monotonous melodies," he ignores their revolutionary role, and in protesting that Dessa "answers questions in a random manner, a loquacious, roundabout fashion," he rejects the validity of the oral tradition, of much of women's writing, of "the careful disorderliness" which Herman Melville sees as often being the only "true method." Nehemiah may see "the facts of the darky's history" as the basis for "some kind of fantastical fiction," but Williams is transforming historical facts into imaginative fiction which illuminates our road behind and ahead.

In Part II of **Dessa Rose,** "The Wench," events are registered through the consciousness of both Ruth and Dessa. Alone with her two children on a backwater Alabama plantation and abandoned by her gambler husband, Ruth is completely dependent upon the escaped slaves who have found refuge on her property; yet Williams makes it clear that the blacks are also dependent upon Ruth to project a business-as-usual facade behind which they will be able to create a secure communal life. In addition, Ruth needs the black women on the plantation to assist her with her children even as Dessa needs Ruth to nurse her new-born babe. (Reversing stereotypes, Williams not only creates the first white "Mammy," but also implies that "mammying," a woman's suckling a child not biologically her own, may have nothing to do with race and everything to do with nurturing.) Williams continues to demonstrate in the second section of her novel the distortions of perception caused by racism and capitalism, but she does so within a framework of interdependency which eliminates sexist distortions and becomes the means for subsequently eliminating racist and capitalist distortions. Ruth, unlike Nehemiah, speaks with the same lilting syntax as the blacks in the novel; yet her words can reflect as did his the fact that racism limits consciousness. Before she can be free to reject her ne'er-do-well husband who had restricted her to the stereotype of the Southern belle, be free to love the good black man who loved her, and be free to discover her own womanhood, she must come to recognize the dignity and complexity of black womanhood. Williams reveals Ruth's growth through changes in her speech. Thus Ruth comes to realize that to call her beloved black friend and surrogate mother "Mammy," when her given name was "Dorcas," was to degrade her. She comes, too, to reflect upon the tragic irony that Dorcas, deprived of nurturing her own children, who could not escape being "slaved," had come to nurture her. Contemplating Dorcas's suffering, Ruth begins to understand Dessa's suffering, her bravery, her love; Ruth can no longer simply classify her as "the wench." Thus in the second section of her novel, Williams shows the accuracy of Franz Fanon's statement that the oppressed may be the first to become oppressors, for Ruth, stereotyped herself, stereotypes other women. In her description of the white woman, Williams, however, transcends stereo-

types; neither the evil white Mistress, the pathetic Southern belle, nor the goody-goody Lady Bountiful, Ruth is represented as struggling to see herself and those with whom she has come to live—a courageous community of blacks—with clarity and with caring.

In the third section of **Dessa Rose,** "The Negress," Williams lets Dessa tell her own story. Viewed in the two previous sections of the novel in part through the lenses of whites, Dessa—determined to create a life of dignity and love and driven to remember her losses and to revolt against inequity—seems staggeringly, perhaps even incredibly, heroic. Here as she becomes the "Negress," learning the words from the black man who becomes her lover and learning that it means "black woman" and comes from "some islands way out to sea, somewheres out from there, where black peoples had made theyselfs free," here as she becomes herself, "Dessa Rose," rather than "darky" or "wench," Dessa becomes a more credible, complex human being. Williams connects Ruth's emerging vision of her humanity with Dessa's, thereby confirming the correlation between knowledge and liberation, on the one hand, and between knowledge and love, on the other. Through this correlation Williams also asserts the interdependence between black and white women and proposes the possibility of their friendship; she thus joins Alice Walker and Toni Morrison, who in *Meridian* (1976) and *Tar Baby* (1981) have described the difficult process by which black and white women realize their common victimization by the white patriarchy as well as their common concerns as women, human beings, and individuals.

If Ruth debased Dessa by referring to her as "wench," Dessa, we read at the beginning of the novel's last section, has distanced herself from Ruth by classifying her as "white woman," "Miz Lady," "Mis'ess," "Miz Rufel," and "Miz Ruint." These first anonymous terms confine Ruth to a race and a class; "Mis Rufel," an ellipsis of "Ruth Elizabeth," is the name assigned to her by Dorcas in retribution for being called "Mammy." With "Miz Ruint" or simply "Ruint," however, Dessa reveals her anger and utter antipathy toward white women in general: "White woman was everything I feared and hated." She rages against Ruth in particular for making her feel beholden and for making love to a black man, the one being in the world who should have been reserved for the black woman. The name, "Ruint," Dessa believes "did fit her. Way she was living up there in them two rooms like they was a mansion, making out like we was all her slaves. For all the world like we didn't know *who* we was or how *poor* she was." But Ruth gradually becomes fully conscious of her financial impoverishment as well as of her great good fortune in knowing the blacks with whom her life has become involved, and Dessa becomes cognizant of Ruth's growing consciousness. Not only does she apologize for calling her out of her name, but she also realizes that "The white woman was subject to the same ravishment [from men] as me." As it becomes imperative that the free white woman and the escaped black slaves link their destinies and embark on a mutually dangerous plan of flight, Dessa comes to feel:

> Sometimes, there in the darkness, I'd catch myself about to tell her, oh, some little thing, like I would Carrie or Martha; and I wondered at her, her peoples, how she come to be like she was . . . . But I wouldn't talk about Kaine, about the loss of my peoples; these was still a wound to me and remembrance of that coffle hurt only a little bit less . . . . Still, I think me and Miz Lady was in a fair way to getting along with each other.

Yet with Dessa's continued reference to Ruth as "Miz Lady," Williams suggests that the process of vision is slow and anguished; not until the conclusion when Ruth assists Dessa in the final escape from Nehemiah, can she trust the white woman. Only then does she have the knowledge that guarantees freedom and love. Only then are both women able to call each other by their proper given names, to acknowledge each other neither in terms of race or class, but in terms of friendship. Their disagreements at the end of the novel's third section are testimony to their mutual respect rather than to institutionalized perceptions. They speak a shared language, and their merged laughter rings off the page in the last paragraph.

In the "Epilogue," Dessa reports that she and Ruth separate as she and the other blacks head West: the traditional goal for Americans questing for spiritual and physical freedom. In a reversal of Huck and Jim's situation at the end of *Adventures of Huckleberry Finn,* the black leaves the white to light out for the Territory, but Dessa, unlike Huck, explicitly yearns for Ruth: *"Miss her in and out of trouble— . . . And who can you friend with, love like that?"* Williams also makes it clear that in her search for freedom, Dessa is never separated from others, either in her memories of those whom she loved and lost to slavery or in her awareness of those whom she loves in freedom.

In her "Epilogue" for *Dessa Rose* as in the novel's third section, Williams projects the illusion that Dessa addresses her story to the "children" and for the "children"; no longer bound by slavery's shackles or by Nehemiah's words, she can speak in her own voice and have her words recorded by her kin:

> I hopes I live for my people like they do for me, so sharp sometimes I can't believe it's all in my mind. And my mind wanders. This why I have it wrote down, why I has the child say it back. I never will forget [Nehemiah] trying to read me, knowing I had put myself in his hands. Well, this the childrens have heard from our own lips.

Thus Williams concludes her novel in the tradition of the Afro-American slave narrative in which Dessa, like other former slaves, liberates herself through the articulation of her own particular life and attempts to liberate her descendants through the creation of a narrative in which she figures as a representative of their history. From the beginning of her novel, Williams has attempted to generate the illusion through Dessa's italicized

memories that one becomes what one remembers. Thus as Dessa speaks her memories, her self becomes fulfilled, and her story will keep her descendants from being "slaved." No longer at the mercy of words, Dessa and her descendants articulate their own history.

Endorsing Alice Walker's "womanist" reading of Afro-American literature, Williams has written a novel which supports "the survival and wholeness of entire peoples, female *and* male, as well as a valorization of women's works in all their varieties and multitudes." She has written a novel, much like other great works by contemporary Afro-American women writers, which is committed to reconciling antitheses of "the beauty and pain, the ugliness and the joy." As Dessa comments in the "Epilogue," using a distinctly "womanist" image, *"anytime something go wrong, . . . I get to braiding hair. It do give me pleasure. Simple as it sound, just the doing of it, the weaving of one strand with the other, have seen me through some pretty terrible days,"* in her novel Williams allows Dessa to braid together the strands of her story and our common history. In showing us how language weaves our sense of reality and how knowledge weaves our ability to love and to be free, Williams's novel does give us pleasure and should see us through some terrible days. This is the book Nehemiah and other white men could not write; this is a book which may truly help us to be happy in the life that has been sent us to live. (pp. 371-76)

> *Elizabeth Schultz, "And the Children May Know Their Names," in* Callaloo, *Vol. 11, No. 2, Spring, 1988, pp. 371-77.*

FURTHER READING

Davis, Mary Kemp. "Everybody Knows Her Name: The Recovery of the Past in Sherley Anne Williams's *Dessa Rose." Callaloo* 12, No. 3 (Summer 1989): 544-58.
  Examines how Williams handles names in *Dessa Rose.*

Greene, Cheryl Y. "A Conversation with Sherley Anne Williams, about the Impact of Her New Novel, *Dessa Rose." Essence* 17, No. 8 (December 1986): 34.
  Interview with Williams, who discusses why she wrote *Dessa Rose* and comments on male-female and white-black relationships in the novel.

Henderson, Mae G. "(W)riting *The Work* and Working the Rites." *Black American Literature Forum* 23, No. 4 (Winter 1989): 631-60.
  Argues that "Meditations on History," the short story that Williams expanded to *Dessa Rose,* is "a critical parody."

Inscoe, John C. "Slave Rebellion in the First Person: The Literary 'Confessions' of Nat Turner and Dessa Rose." *The Virginia Magazine of History and Biography* 97, No. 4 (October 1989): 419-36.

Examines the portrayal of slavery in works of fiction, comparing *Dessa Rose* to William Styron's *Confessions of Nat Turner.*

McDowell, Deborah E. "Negotiating between Tenses: Witnessing Slavery after Freedom—*Dessa Rose.*" In *Slav-ery and the Literary Imagination: Selected Papers from the English Institute,* edited by Deborah E. McDowell and Arnold Rampersad, pp. 144-63. Baltimore: The Johns Hopkins University Press, 1989.
Examines the slave experience in *Dessa Rose.*

August Wilson
1945-

American dramatist.

Wilson emerged in the 1980s as a major new voice in American theater. His dramas, for which he has variously received such coveted prizes as the Tony Award, the New York Drama Critics Circle Award, and the Pulitzer Prize, are part of a planned play-cycle about black American experience in the twentieth century. "I'm taking each decade and looking at one of the most important questions that blacks confronted in that decade and writing a play about it," Wilson explained. "Put them all together and you have a history." The leisurely pace and familial settings of his dramas have evoked comparisons to the works of Eugene O'Neill. Praised for their vivid characterizations, Wilson's plays often center upon conflicts between blacks who embrace their African past and those who deny it. He commented: "I've tried to fuse my artistic consciousness and my political consciousness. I may be saying there's an illness here, but I don't know what the prescription is. I don't consider myself a suffering writer. I don't create my art out of the suffering and pain of the human condition, I create it out of the zestful part of life." Wilson's rich yet somber explorations of black history prompted Samuel G. Freedman to describe the playwright as "one part Dylan Thomas and one part Malcolm X, a lyric poet fired in the kiln of black nationalism."

Wilson grew up in a Pittsburgh, Pennsylvania, ghetto called the Hill, the son of a white father and a black mother. He gained an early pride in his heritage through his mother, who worked as a cleaning woman to support her six children after their father abandoned them. Wilson often proudly recalls the time his mother won a brand-new washing machine in a radio contest, only to be offered a secondhand washer instead when the contest suppliers discovered the winner was black. Wilson's mother refused the prize, continuing to scrub her children's laundry by hand rather than compromise her principles. Wilson himself experienced rampant racism in many of the schools he attended; finally, frustrated by a teacher's false accusation of plagiarism, he dropped out in the ninth grade, thereafter getting his education from neighborhood experiences and at the local library. "I didn't think this at the time, but in retrospect it was one of the best things that could have happened," Wilson noted. "Suddenly I had the freedom to explore and develop my mind. I went to the library to read things I didn't know anything about. I read anything I wanted to." In a collection of books marked "Negro," he discovered works of Harlem Renaissance and other African-American writers. After reading works by Ralph Ellison, Langston Hughes, and Arna Bontemps, Wilson realized that blacks could be successful in artistic endeavors without compromising their

traditions. In his early writings, he was so strongly inspired by other styles that he found it difficult to establish his own voice. More recently, in a 1990 lecture, he cited the "four B's" as the main influences of his works: the collagist painter Romare Bearden, writers Amiri Baraka and Jorge Luis Borges, and blues music. In 1968, inspired by the civil rights movement, Wilson cofounded Black Horizon on the Hill, a community theater aimed at raising black consciousness in the area. The playhouse became a forum for his first dramas, in which Wilson purposely avoided the study of other artists in order to develop his own medium of expression.

Wilson's first professional breakthrough occurred in 1978 when he was invited to write plays for a black theater founded by Claude Purdy, a former Pittsburgh director, in St. Paul, Minnesota. In this new milieu, removed from his native Pittsburgh, Wilson began to recognize poetic qualities in the language of his hometown. While his first two dramas garnered little notice, his third, *Ma Rainey's Black Bottom* (1984), was accepted by the National Playwrights Conference, where it drew the attention of Lloyd Richards, the artistic director of the Yale Repertory Theater. Upon reading the script, Richards recalled, "I recognized it as a new voice. A very important one. It brought back my youth. My neighborhood. Experiences I had." He directed *Ma Rainey* at the Yale Theater and later took the play to Broadway. Since then, with Richards in the role of mentor and director, all of Wilson's plays have had their first staged readings at the Playwrights Conference, followed by runs at the Yale Repertory Theater and regional theaters before opening on Broadway. During the run of *Ma Rainey,* Richards praised Wilson's abilities: "Some of the oldest and most wonderful traditions in theater exist in storytelling. What a playwright needs is wit and wisdom and great respect for life. These qualities cannot be taught. August Wilson has them."

Ma Rainey, set in the 1920s, is an exploration of racism. The play is based on an imaginary episode in the life of legendary black singer Gertrude Ma Rainey, regarded by some artists as the mother of the blues. The action takes place in a recording studio and involves four musicians who are waiting for Ma's arrival. As the details of the musicians' lives unfold, the audience becomes aware of the racism that these successful black performers have had to face throughout their careers. "White folks don't understand the blues," Ma later says. "They hear it come out, but they don't know how it got there. They don't understand that's life's way of talking. You don't sing to feel better. You sing 'cause that's a way of understanding life." The attitudes of the group's white manager and the owner of the studio reveal continuing exploitation of Ma and her band, and the play climaxes when one of the musicians, Levee, vents his frustrations on the others. Critics praised Wilson for the vitality of *Ma Rainey,* as well as for the authentic, lively dialogue. In *Fences* (1985), which won Wilson his first Pulitzer Prize, the playwright again examined the destructive and far-reaching consequences of racial injustice. Set in the late 1950s, on the eve of the civil rights movement, *Fences* revolves around Troy Maxson, an outstanding high school athlete who was ignored by major league baseball because of his color. Struggling through middle age as a garbage man, Troy's bitterness results in family conflicts: his son, who also aspires to an athletic career, must battle his father's fear and envy of him, and Troy's wife is humiliated by his adultery. Describing the two plays, Wilson commented: "My concern was the idea of missed possibilities. Music and sports were the traditional inroads for blacks, and in both *Ma Rainey* and *Fences,* with both Levee and Troy, even those inroads fail."

A new play by Wilson, *Joe Turner's Come and Gone* (1986), debuted while *Fences* was still running on Broadway, an unprecedented accomplishment for a black playwright in the New York theater. *Joe Turner,* which is generally regarded as more mystical than Wilson's other works, is about the struggles of migrants in the post-Civil War North. The play takes place in 1911 in the Pittsburgh boardinghouse owned by Seth and Bertha Holly. Following seven years of illegal bondage, Herald Loomis, a black freedman, travels to Pennsylvania in search of his wife who fled north during his enslavement. The critical issue of white oppression is symbolized in Herald's haunted memories of Joe Turner, the infamous Southern bounty hunter who captured him. Herald's sojourn ends at the Holly boardinghouse, where the black residents there are also searching for wholeness in their lives. Partially assimilated into white America, they nevertheless embrace the African traditions of their past. At the play's end, the boarders sing and dance a *juba,* an African celebration of the spirit. Their shared joy represents an achievement of unity—evidence that they have come to terms with the trauma of slavery and the harsh reality of white persecution. Herald, however, is unable to accept these truths and does not join in the *juba. Joe Turner* was an immensely popular and critical success—Wilson himself cited it as his personal favorite play—and reviewers lauded Wilson's metaphorical language and tragicomic tone.

The Piano Lesson (1987) won a Pulitzer Prize before appearing on Broadway. A piano is the major focus of this play, which is set in 1936 in Doaker Charles's Pittsburgh home. Decades earlier, the white owner of the Charles family traded Doaker's father and grandmother for the piano, and the grief-stricken grandfather carved African totems of his wife and son in the piano's legs. Later, Doaker's older brother was killed in a successful conspiracy to steal the piano, which now sits, untouched and revered, in Doaker's living room. Conflict arises when Boy Willie, the son of the man who stole the piano, wants to sell it to purchase the land on which his ancestors were slaves. Frank Rich asserted: "What ever happens to the piano,... the playwright makes it clear that the music in *The Piano Lesson* is not up for sale. That haunting music belongs to the people who have lived it, and it has once again found miraculous voice in a play that August Wilson has given to the American stage." In *Two Trains Running* (1990), Wilson again illuminated the inevitability of life, death, and change. The drama takes place in a Pittsburgh restaurant on a single day in 1969, four years after the assassination of Malcolm X, and concerns the burial preparations occurring across the street at a funeral parlor.

In an interview, Nick Flournoy, a companion of Wilson's for over twenty-five years, deftly summed up his friend's career: "August Wilson is on a trek. He's saying who you are and what you are are all right. It's all right to be an angry nigger. It's all right to be whatever you are. It's what the great Irish writers did. They took that narrow world and they said, 'Here it is.' Here it is and its meaning is universal."

(For further information about Wilson's life and works, see *Black Writers; Contemporary Authors,* Vols. 115,

122; and *Contemporary Literary Criticism,* Vols. 39, 50, 63.)

PRINCIPAL WORKS

Black Bart and the Sacred Hills (drama) 1981
Jitney (drama) 1982
Ma Rainey's Black Bottom (drama) 1984
Fences (drama) 1985
Joe Turner's Come and Gone (drama) 1986
The Piano Lesson (drama) 1987
Two Trains Running (drama) 1990

Samuel G. Freedman (essay date 1987)

[*In the excerpt below, Freedman traces Wilson's life from early childhood to the present, illuminating aspects that helped determine the form and content of his plays.*]

During the early 1960's, as August Wilson was reaching manhood, the church of St. Benedict the Moor took up a collection for a statue atop its steeple. The church straddled the border between the Hill, the black Pittsburgh slum where Wilson grew up, and the city's downtown district. And when the statue was unveiled, Wilson remembers, Saint Benedict was opening his arms to the skyscrapers and department stores, and turning his back on the Hill.

A generation later, as August Wilson walks its streets on a visit home, the Hill looks godforsaken indeed. Gone are Lutz's Meat Market, the Hilltop Club and Pope's Restaurant. The New Granada Theater is closed. An abandoned truck rusts in a weeded lot and a junkie lurches up the street, hawking a stolen television set. Beyond the decay, past the plywood and charred bricks, rise the new glass towers of Pittsburgh, glistening like shafts of crystal.

"Hey, professor," a man in a worn overcoat says to Wilson, extending a calloused hand for a soul shake.

"Hey, man," Wilson says, meeting his grip.

This passing moment is the ultimate compliment, for if August Wilson has wanted anything in his career as a playwright it is to be recognized by the people of the ghetto as their voice, their bard. Wilson gives words to trumpeters and trash men, cabbies and conjurers, boarders and landladies, all joined by a heritage of slavery. Their patois is his poetry, their dreams are his dramas. And while Wilson's inspiration is contained—a few sloping blocks in Pittsburgh—his aspiration seems boundless. He intends to write a play about black Americans in every decade of this century, and he has already completed six of the projected 10.

Fences, a drama set in the 1950's, is the second of the cycle to reach Broadway. It was preceded by *Ma Rainey's Black Bottom,* which won the New York Drama Critics Circle Award as the best play of the 1984-85 season and, as Frank Rich, chief drama critic for *The New York Times,* wrote, it established Wilson as "a major find for the American theater," a writer of "compassion, raucous humor and penetrating wisdom." (p. 36)

Fences may prove the most accessible of Wilson's plays, faster-moving than *Ma Rainey* and less mystical than *Joe Turner's Come and Gone.* Several critics have likened this family drama to Arthur Miller's *Death of a Salesman,* centering as it does on a proud, embittered patriarch, Troy Maxson, and his teen-age son, Cory. Their immediate conflict is kindled when Cory is recruited to play college football and Troy, once a baseball star barred from the segregated big leagues, demands he turn down the scholarship because he cannot believe times have truly changed. Behind the narrative looms Wilson's concern with legacy. As Cory Maxson almost grudgingly discovers the value in his father's flawed life, he accepts his part in a continuum that runs from Pittsburgh to the antebellum South and finally to Mother Africa.

For Wilson, at the age of 42, that journey is not only historical, but personal. His father was a white man who all but abandoned him. The playwright dismisses the subject of his parentage in a temperate tone more unsettling than any anger, and one can only speculate how Wilson's origins fueled the pursuit of blackness, his own and his people's. Troy Maxson of *Fences,* then, embodies not only the black stepfather Wilson found in his teens, but something rather more metaphysical.

"I think it was Amiri Baraka who said that when you look in the mirror you should see your God," Wilson says.

> All over the world, nobody has a God who doesn't resemble them. Except black Americans. They can't even see they're worshipping someone else's God, because they want so badly to assimilate, to get the fruits of society. The message of America is 'Leave your Africanness outside the door.' My message is 'Claim what is yours.'

Last April, when *Joe Turner's Come and Gone* was in rehearsal at the Yale Repertory Theater, a Jewish friend invited Wilson to a seder, the ritual Passover meal. *Joe Turner* is the story of Herald Loomis, a black freedman pressed into illegal bondage—decades after the Emancipation Proclamation—by the Tennessee bounty hunter of the play's title. Freed after seven years, he makes his way to Pittsburgh, looking for the wife who had fled north during his enslavement. He is in many ways a crippled man, driven to his knees by visions of slavery, of "bones walking on top of the water," and it takes the powers of an African healer named Bynum to raise him upright again. Set against *Joe Turner,* the seder was a powerful coincidence.

"The first words of the ceremony were, 'We were slaves in Egypt,'" Wilson recalls.

> And these were Yale students, Yale professors, in 1986, in New Haven, talking about something that happened thousands of years ago. Then it struck me that Passover is not just happening in this house in New Haven, it's happening in Jewish homes all over the world. And the concluding line—'Next year in Jerusalem'—they've been saying that for thousands of years. And that is the source of Jewish power and Jewish pride.
>
> I thought this is something we should do. Blacks in America want to forget about slavery—the stigma, the shame. That's the wrong move. If you can't be who you are, who can you be? How can you know what to do? He have our history. We have our book, which is the blues. And we forget it all.

If Wilson's mission is memory, his method is more artistic than archival. He is one part Dylan Thomas and one part Malcolm X, a lyric poet fired in the kiln of black nationalism. The highly polemical black theater of the 1960's made the play the vehicle for the message, but Wilson encountered literature before ideology, and he still abides by that order. He is a storyteller, and his story is the African diaspora—not because it suits a political agenda but because everything in his life conspired to make it so.

Most of Wilson's plays concern the conflict between those who embrace their African past and those who deny it. "You don't see me running around in no jungle with no bone between my nose," boasts one character in *Ma Rainey*. Wilson's answer is that Africa remains a pervasive force, a kind of psychic balm available to 20th-century blacks through blues songs, communal dances, tall tales. Wilson the mythologist coexists with Wilson the social realist. There is a broad historical truth to his characters—to Levee, the jazz musician who naïvely sells off his compositions to a white record-company executive; to Troy Maxson, whose job prospects go no further than becoming the first black truck driver in the Pittsburgh Sanitation Department.

Wilson makes these lives ring with dignity. "I do the best I can do," Troy tells his wife, Rose, in *Fences*.

> I come in here every Friday. I carry a sack of potatoes and a bucket of lard. You all line up at the door with your hands out. I give you the lint from my pockets. I give you my sweat and blood. I ain't got no tears. I done spent them. We go upstairs in that room at night and I fall down on you and try to blast a hole into forever. I get up Monday morning, find my lunch on the table. I go out. Make my way. Find my strength to carry me through to the next Friday.

There is an extraordinary acuity to Wilson's ear, a quality that has a black audience murmuring "That's right" or "Tell it" during his plays, as they might during a Jesse Jackson speech or a B. B. King concert. Wilson's virtuosity with the vernacular can lull an audience into laughter, too. Early in *Fences,* Troy Maxson's best friend needles him about flirting outside his marriage. "It's all right to buy her one drink," he says. "That's what you call being polite. But when you wanna be buying two or three—that's what you call eyeing her."

By evening's end, it is apparent that Troy has done more than eye her, and the kidding has assumed a prophetic power—a prime characteristic of Wilson's work. With one set and a half-dozen major roles, a Wilson play can seem talky and static, but if wordiness is a weakness at times, it is also a masterly way of deceiving the audience into amused complacency. By the end of his first acts, Wilson characteristically begins to detonate his dramatic bombshells, and at the final explosion—a murder, a madman's howl or a self-inflicted stabbing—a shudder ripples through the audience.

Wilson writes of the particulars of black life, elevating his anger to a more universal plane. As a thinker, if not a stylist, Wilson descends less from the Richard Wright tradition of social protest than from the ontological one of Ralph Ellison. Ellison's *The Invisible Man*, like Wilson's characters, confronts blackness not as a function of pigment but as a condition of the soul. The white man in Wilson's plays can be finessed, ignored, intimidated; it is the Almighty against whom his characters rail. After a musician in *Ma Rainey* hears of a white mob forcing a black reverend to dance, he shouts to the rafters, "Where the hell was God when all of this was going on?" (pp. 36, 40)

Wilson received a positive racial identity from his mother, who died in 1983. Living on welfare and, later, on the wages of a janitorial job, Daisy Wilson kept her children healthy, fed and educated. She would stretch eggs with flour to make breakfast go seven ways. She would wait until Christmas Eve for the $1 tree she could afford. She would get second-hand Nancy Drew mysteries and other books for the daily reading she required of her children. Wilson's favorite story about her, and her gifts, involves a radio contest:

> Morton Salt in the 1950's had come out with their slogan, 'When it rains, it pours.' When the announcer said the words, the first caller to identify it as the Morton slogan won a Speed Queen washer. My mother was still doing the wash with a rub board. One night, we're listening to the station and the contest comes on. We didn't have a telephone, so Mommy sends my sister right out with a dime to call in and say, 'Morton Salt.' When they found out she was black, they wanted to give her a certificate to go to the Salvation Army for a used washing machine. And she told them where they could put their certificate. I remember her girlfriends' telling her, 'Daisy, get the used washer.' But she'd rather go on scrubbing.

As a writer, Wilson has honored his mother and imagined the father he might have had. "I know there are not strong black images in literature and film," he says, "so I thought, why not create them? Herald Loomis is responsible. Troy Maxson is responsible. Those images are important. Every black man did not just make a baby and run off."

Fences in rehearsal at the Yale Repertory Theater. Wilson and director Lloyd Richards are at the far right.

But unlike the more politicized black writers of the 1960's—or, at the other end of the spectrum, the mass-market creators of television's *Julia* and *The Cosby Show*—Wilson has created fallible humans, not simplistic paragons. Troy Maxson can turn gales of rage on the son who adores him, but he also feeds him, clothes him, teaches him. Troy can sneak around on the wife who loves him, fathering a baby out of wedlock. But when the child is born, Troy brings it home and Rose, however hurt, agrees to raise it as her own.

It is not surprising that Wilson's fictive families form bulwarks against a hostile world, for his own encounters with white Pittsburgh offered the racist commonplaces of America—bricks through the window when the family tried moving into mostly white Hazelwood; "Nigger, go home" notes on his desk at an overwhelmingly white parochial high school; accusations of cheating when a term paper on Napoleon seems a bit too good to have been done by a black boy. Hounded out of one school, frustrated by another, Wilson dropped out in the ninth grade. At the age of 15, his formal education had come to an end.

He split his days between the street and the library, where he chanced upon a section marked "Negro." There were about 30 books, and he read them all—Arna Bontemps, Ralph Ellison, Richard Wright and Langston Hughes. He remembers especially a sociology text that spoke of "the Negro's power of hard work" because it was the first time anything ever suggested to him that a Negro could have any power in America. "I was just beginning to discover racism, and I think I was looking for something," Wilson recalls. "Those books were a comfort. Just the idea black people would write books. I wanted my book up there, too. I used to dream about being part of the Harlem Renaissance."

Supporting himself as a short-order cook and stock clerk, Wilson began to write: stories, poetry—even a college term paper on Carl Sandburg and Robert Frost for [his sister] Freda. She got an A, he made $20, and it bought a used Royal typewriter, the first he had owned. "The first thing I typed was my name," he would recall years later. "I wanted to see how it looked in print. Then I began to type my poems."

Around the neighborhood, Wilson kept his eyes and ears open: How Miss Sarah sprinkled salt and lined up pennies across her threshold. He listened to the men talk at Pat's Place, a cigar store and pool room, and if someone said, "Joe Foy's funeral's today," he would find out who Joe Foy was. Most of all, Wilson saw in the Hill a pageant of violence. One night, he watched a black man walk into a bar with a white woman. Another black man, passing the first, said to him, "Say, Phil, I see you got your white whore." Phil drew his knife and began slashing the man across the chest, slashing to the cadence of his cry, "That's my wife! That's my wife! That's my wife!" His rage spent, he got into his car with his wife and drove off.

One part of Wilson understood the futility of the violence, the self-destruction, and he summons it in his plays as the ultimate, diabolical triumph of white bigotry: turning blacks against themselves. *Ma Rainey's Black Bottom,* for instance, ends with Levee stabbing not the white man who has appropriated his music but the bandmate who accidentally steps on his shoe. *Fences* brings Cory to the brink of attacking Troy with a baseball bat, symbol of the father's manhood.

Yet another part of Wilson admired the Hill's criminals. His own family lived near the bottom of the Hill's social scale, which roughly conformed to its topography, and he grew up with a hot hate for the affluent blacks up in Sugar Top, the doctors and lawyers who would send their children to a Saturday movie downtown with the admonition "Don't show your color." In Wilson's plays, the black middle-class exists only as an object of contempt; if he had written *A Raisin in the Sun,* the Younger family would not have moved to the suburbs, it would have joined either the Blackstone Rangers street gang or the Nation of Islam. Wilson's characters are almost all the kind of street blacks for whom his longtime friend Rob Penny invented the term "stomp-down bloods."

"For a long time, I thought the most valuable blacks were those in the penitentiary," Wilson says, recalling his teens and 20's.

> They were the people with the warrior spirit. How they chose to battle may have been wrong, but you need people who will battle. You need someone who says, 'I won't shine shoes for $40 a week. I have a woman and two kids, and I will put a gun in my hand and *take,* and my kids will have Christmas presents.' Just like there were people who didn't accept slavery. There were Nat Turners. And that's the spirit that Levee has, and Troy has, and Herald Loomis has.

In 1969, when Wilson was 24, his stepfather, David Bedford, died. The two had not been close for almost a decade, since Wilson quit his high school football team against Bedford's wishes, and the late 1960's was a time when young black men like Wilson often disparaged their fathers as a generation of compromisers. Then Wilson heard a story about Bedford that changed his life.

Bedford, it turned out, had been a high school football star in the 1930's, and had hoped a sports scholarship would lead to a career in medicine. But no Pittsburgh college would give a black player a grant and Bedford was too poor to pay his own way. To get the money, he decided to rob a store, and during the theft he killed a man. For the 23 years before he met Wilson's mother, Bedford had been in prison. By the time he was free, only a job in the city Sewer Department beckoned.

"I found myself trying to figure out the intent of these lives around me," Wilson says. "Trying to uncover the nobility and the dignity that I might not have seen. I was ignorant of their contributions. Part of the reason I wrote *Fences* was to illuminate that generation, which shielded its children from all of the indignities they went through."

Wilson's personal discoveries coincided with the rise of the black nationalist movement, which was based in large part on venerating the Afro-American past. Wilson and Rob Penny, a playwright and professor, founded a theater called the Black Horizon on the Hill, and it produced Wilson's earliest plays. Poetry readings, jazz concerts and art galleries all flourished. Wilson and Penny also belonged to a group of Pittsburgh's black artists and intellectuals who studied and discussed the writings of Ed Bullins, Richard Wesley, Ron Milner, Ishmael Reed, Maulana Karenga and, most importantly, Amiri Baraka and Malcolm X.

In some ways, though, Wilson didn't quite fit in. His sympathies resided with black nationalism, but as a writer he could not produce convincing agitprop. Nor had he yet found the true dramatic voice of the Hill. His development as a writer shared less with black American authors than with black Africans like novelist Chinua Achebe, who fell under the sway of white writers while studying abroad and only later returned home to adapt those influences to their indigenous oral tradition and tribal lore.

The self-educated Wilson counts among his strongest early influences Dylan Thomas, for the theatricality of his verse, and John Berryman, for the process of condensing language that the poet called "psychic shorthand." Wilson also admired the jazzy rhythms and street sensibility of Baraka's poetry and plays . . . . (pp. 40, 49)

Between performance and publication royalties and grants—including Guggenheim and Rockfeller fellowships—Wilson has been able since 1982 to devote himself wholly to writing. Now, the posters, awards, programs and reviews from Wilson's first six shows line the long hallway of his St. Paul apartment. But, the playwright adds, there is plenty of wall space left to cover.

"You have to be willing to open yourself up," Wilson says of his approach to writing. "It's like walking down the road. It's the landscape of the self, and you have to be willing to confront whatever you find there." (p. 70)

Samuel G. Freedman, "A Voice from the Streets," in The New York Times Magazine, March 15, 1987, pp. 36, 40, 49, 70.

Jack Kroll (essay date 1988)

[*In the following excerpt, Kroll reviews* Joe Turner's Come and Gone, *calling it "Wilson's best play to date and a profoundly American one."*]

With the resounding arrival of *Joe Turner's Come and Gone,* and the continuing run of *Fences,* last year's Pulitzer Prize winner, August Wilson, 42, now has two plays running on Broadway, an unprecedented feat for a black playwright. And these two plays, along with the earlier *Ma Rainey's Black Bottom,* make up a sustained and developing synthesis of black history and sensibility.

Joe Turner is Wilson's best play to date and a profoundly American one. Like all of his plays it resonates far beyond its explicit details. Wilson takes the homeliest of locales, a black boardinghouse in 1911 Pittsburgh, and makes it a way station for the destiny of blacks still marked by the trauma of slavery and the haunting presence of their African heritage. The house, run by Seth Holly and his wife, Bertha, is a repository of dreams deferred. The simplest dream is Seth's: a craftsman, he'd like to have his own little shop where he could turn out his pots and pans. The most mystical dream is that of the chief boarder, Bynum Walker, a voodoo conjurer who's looking for the "shiny man" that he once encountered in a vision of transcendence. In the stream of men and women who come to the house on various quests a disturbing force enters in the black-clad Herald Loomis with his 11-year-old daughter, Zonia. Loomis, a storm cloud of a man, is searching for the wife who had left him in Tennessee while he was held in forced labor by the notorious plantation owner Joe Turner.

The dreams, quests, hopes and fears of all the characters interweave in a web of black fatality. It's the mysterious Loomis who finally rips the web apart, leaving everyone freer to pursue their personal variations on the theme of freedom. That freedom becomes visible in a shared *juba* dance, a signal that these blacks will never be free until they accept and build on their African heritage. Wilson is a generous artist; he provides 11 compelling characters, an irresistible story and a power of language that lends a vivid music to a myriad of emotions. Rare for a male playwright, he even includes four strongly imagined women: the earthy, common-sensical Bertha; Mattie Campbell, whose dream is simply to find a man who won't disappear; the cynical Molly Cunningham, who understands on which side her biscuit is buttered, and Martha Pentecost, Loomis's wife, who is the final strand in the play's web of destiny....

Wilson's gift of verbal music reflects his love of the blues. He got his basic idea while listening to a recording of W. C. Handy singing about Joe Turner, who enslaved black workers and got away with it because he was the

Wilson on the banks of the Mississippi River in St. Paul, Minnesota.

brother of the governor of Tennessee. Wilson's sense of history tempers his own anger about racism. At Central Catholic High School in Pittsburgh he was the only black: "Every day I'd find a note on my desk saying, 'Go home, nigger'."

His father was white, a German baker who "came and went." But culturally and psychologically, Wilson's self-definition is entirely black. After more racist incidents he dropped out of school at 15. "I spent the next five years in the library," he says. "It was actually liberating." At 20, he got a job, saved some money and left his mother's house. In the Hill district, Pittsburgh's black ghetto, he met a group of writers and artists, "the people who shaped my life and ultimately provided it with its meaning." Wilson was writing poetry and short stories but he had not seen any theater. Then the *Tulane Drama Review* published an issue on the black theater movement and Wilson promptly sat down to write a play.

But, he found, "I couldn't make the people talk." He asked his friend writer-teacher Rob Penny, "How do you make them talk?" Penny replied: "You don't. You listen to them." "I wasn't sure what he meant," says Wilson. It wasn't until he had moved to St. Paul, Minn., that it hit him. "Being removed was what enabled me to hear. All those black voices came back in a rush. I sat down to write a play called *Jitney* and the characters just talked to me. In fact they were talking so fast that I couldn't get it all down."

He sent *Jitney* to the Eugene O'Neill Theater Center in Waterford, Conn., which rejected it. After five rejections, they accepted *Ma Rainey's Black Bottom,* his play about jazz musicians in the '20s. It was the beginning of the unique collaboration between Wilson and the O'Neill's director, Lloyd Richards, who has introduced all of Wilson's plays at his Yale Repertory Theatre. Wilson is working on the next in his cycle of plays about the black experience, this one set in the '60s.... For Wilson the voices are stronger than ever. When he was writing the climactic scene in *Joe Turner,* in which Loomis slashes himself across the chest, "I had no idea where it was going. When Loomis cut himself it was a surprise to me. I looked down at the page and said, 'Where did that come from?' I was drained. I was limp. But I felt good. I knew I had something." So has the American theater.

> *Jack Kroll, "August Wilson's Come to Stay,"*
> *in* Newsweek, *Vol. CXI, No. 15, April 11,*
> *1988, p. 82.*

Margaret E. Glover (essay date 1988)

[*In the excerpt below, Glover examines the role of blues music in Wilson's plays.*]

A black man walks into a bar. The words "for whites only" do not hang over the neon sign in the window, but as he enters he senses that the bartender and his patrons wish he were not there. He is thirsty and does not know the city well enough to look for another bar where he would be welcome. He takes a seat at the bar and orders a drink. The bartender serves him; the next song begins to play on the juke box. He recognizes the music as the same music he would hear coming out of a juke box on the other side of town. He begins to breathe more deeply; he stops trying to make himself invisible; he rests his arms firmly on the bar; he moves the beer bottle to the right, his glass to the left and marks out his space at the bar. "If they are playing my music, this is where I belong."

The man is August Wilson. The year is 1987. The voices of his characters come back to him. Ma Rainey in Sturdyvant's Chicago recording studio. "Wanna take my voice and trap it in them fancy boxes with all them buttons and dials...and then too cheap to buy me a coca-cola." Bynum to Jeremy in Seth Holly's boarding house [in *Joe Turner's Come and Gone*]. "You ought to take your guitar and go down to Seefus...That's where the music at...The people down there making music and enjoying themselves. Some things is worth taking the chance going to jail about." And Wining Boy at one of the stops along his road [in *The Piano Lesson*].

> You look up one day and you hate the whiskey, you
> hate the women, and you hate the piano. But that's
> all you got. You can't do nothing else. So all you

know is how to play that piano. Now, who am I? Am I me...or am I the piano player? Sometimes it seem like the only thing to do is shoot the piano player 'cause he's the cause of all the trouble I'm having.

This is the dilemma. His music gave the black man a place in the white man's world, but at the cost of losing his right to that music and the part of himself he put in it. Ma Rainey knows that once Sturdyvant and Irvin have gotten what they want from her music, "then it's just like I'd been some whore and they roll over and put their pants on." But the same music she sold to make a name for herself was the blues that "help you get out of bed in the morning. You get up knowing you ain't alone. There's something else in the world...You get up knowing whatever your troubles is you can get a grip on them 'cause the blues done give you an understanding of life." Ma Rainey chooses to believe that the blues from which she took the melodies for her own songs will always be there, just as the blues has always been there waiting for the people to find their own songs in its fullness.

But does that music remain whole and free when strains of it are sold to the white man? Berneice and Boy Willie struggle to resolve a similar question in *The Piano Lesson.* Berneice argues that to sell the piano for a stake in a new life is to sell one's soul. Boy Willie counters that to guard the piano as a shrine to those who died for it is to bind him to the slavery and homelessness of the past.

The underlying agony is between the personal freedom that the music and its songs provide and the fact that just singing the music for one's self is not enough to live free in the white man's world. It is through music that Levee seeks a way to tell the stories that gnaw at him [in *Ma Rainey's Black Bottom*], but he is denied the right to tell people how to play it. Where is the law preventing him from leaving his mark on the world by playing his own music? Others have left their mark on him while exercising what they called their "Freedom." For Levee, as for the other marked men in August Wilson's plays, personal freedom is not enough.

In *Joe Turner's Come and Gone* Bynum tells the story of how he found his Binding Song as a lesson to Loomis. "All you got to do is sing it. Then you'll be free." But Joe Turner took Loomis' song to fill his own emptiness, and Herald Loomis may never get it back. In *The Piano Lesson* Wining Boy calls his music an albatross. It has become a way for others to name him without knowing him. He looks at the piano and sees something the white man gives him to play on. (pp. 69-70)

Others hear what they want to, but do not really listen to what the words, the rhythms and the melodies of Levee's songs of the city or Wining Boy's and Doaker's songs of the road tell them about the souls of these men.

There is something frightening in this music "that breathes and touches. That connects. That is in itself a way of being, separate and distinct from any other."

(August Wilson) It frightens the white man because it is something the characters in August Wilson's plays are not only willing to go to jail for but to fight each other for. It frightens the singers because they know they can neither control nor contain it. To find their songs they must open themselves to be consumed by this music.

> Its warmth and redress, its braggadocio and roughly poignant comments, its vision and prayer . . . instruct and allow them to reconnect, to reassemble and gird up for the next battle to which they could claim both victim and ten thousand slain.

(p. 70)

Margaret E. Glover, "Two Notes on August Wilson: The Songs of A Marked Man," in Theater, *Vol. XIX, No. 3, Summer-Fall, 1988, pp. 69-70.*

Mei-Ling Ching (essay date 1988)

[*In the following excerpt, Ching explores myth and superstition in Wilson's works.*]

Every culture generates its own myths and superstitions, taboos and rituals of exorcism. To secure a glorious after-life, early Egyptians embalmed their deceased rulers. Ancient Greeks went to Delphi to worship divine wisdom and to learn about their fates. Most Chinese people still follow elaborate burial rites which commemorate the dead for 49 days with chants and incantation. Being a black American, August Wilson's heritage goes back to African traditions which are based on similar pantheistic views of celestial order ruling both the living and the dead. From *Joe Turner's Come and Gone,* through *Fences* to his present work *The Piano Lesson,* a seamless blend of Christianity with the inherent African cosmology defines the spiritual landscape within which the characters suffer and rejoice.

Set in small-scaled domestic environments, the three plays are immersed in a sense of mystery that transgresses the confinements of rigid realism. Wilson's central characters are all marvelous story-tellers. In their fantastic tales, daily life takes on a subliminal cloak, transforming mundane facts into allegorical rituals. Their magic words mold their own and other characters' consciousness as Seth Holly molds the metal sheets into pots and pans.

Religious rituals, however different, share one common goal: to delve into the power of the unknown in order to deal with the supernatural. The semi-prophets in Wilson's plays assume the same role as the magus figure in a religious ceremony. Bynum in *Joe Turner's Come and Gone* is virtually "a bone man," a clairvoyant who inherits all his skills from his shaman father. He recognizes Herald Loomis' dark secret (his "song") hidden in the depth of his suppressed memory; he partly conducts and observes the reunion of Loomis and his wife; he perceives Loomis' mental elevation the moment Loomis has undergone a private purging ritual.

The source of Herald Loomis' struggle lies in the past; he has to disown the burden of the past in order to gain strength for his new start in life. Troy Maxson's problem lies in the future, in his inevitable fate of being mortal. In *Fences,* Troy's personal ritual presents itself as a frenzied nightmare of his battle with death. Death, in Troy's feverish vision, is personified as a figure dressed in white with a sickle in his hand. Having survived pneumonia, Troy invents a story of his triumph over Death in a grueling wrestling match that lasted for three days and nights, boasting of his vigilance and strength. Through his intentional mockery of death, he cleanses himself of his deepest fear and reaffirms his claim to life.

Troy's imaginary battle described in *Fences* becomes a concrete event in *The Piano Lesson.* Unlike Troy, Boy Willie's struggle has more to do with his origin than with his ending; similar to Loomis, Boy Willie confronts a mysterious something coming from the past, a menace beyond human comprehension. Both fights, however, symbolize the tremendous efforts spent in overcoming one's destiny and the difficulty, if not impossibility, of doing so.

Troy tries not to succumb to his mortality, as Boy Willie tries to recover from the scars of slavery passed on to him through his ancestors. Troy's combat represents a universal theme repeatedly enacted in life's drama. Boy Willie's contest is one against history, against the burden of being black in 1936 as a man who had just arrived in Pittsburgh from Mississippi. The past has never really passed; history literally haunts the present. The atrocious nature of Boy Willie's battle recalls the ordeal of 200 years' slavery. It further reflects the ongoing struggle against racism in a changing society.

In *The Piano Lesson,* the characters' reactions against the shadow of the past reveal their different perceptions of heritage, which determine their attitudes toward the piano. The piano is a relic of their common past, an icon of their inheritance. The ominous quality attached to the piano still lingers and affects their present life. In fact, the conflict arises between Boy Willie and Berneice for the piano constitutes the play's major action.

Berneice wants the piano to be a sacred reminder of her parents' sacrifice, a symbol of sadness that her hands can no longer bear to touch. Boy Willie wants the piano to be the collateral for his homestead, a foundation on which to stake his territorial claim. For Berneice, the piano is both a legacy and a taboo. For Boy Willie, the piano is an antique souvenir with only a neutral spiritual value, hence, a profitable object. To sell the piano is not to betray their family identity but to make it productive. After all, the luxury of keeping a museum piece at home belongs to those who need not struggle for life.

As a spiritual journey craving for its completion, the conflict between brother and sister moves toward its resolution in the face of an external crisis imposed from the past.

A ritual of exorcism is performed against the obsessions of the past, challenging nature's demoniac potential. Through a process of ceremonial evocation, the psychic shaman/priest becomes possessed by the spirit of Messianic stature. In a state of trance, he engages himself in a ritualistic battle against the Devil, accompanied by the music of the people who have gathered in support of this healing process. In their joint effort to exorcise the past, Berneice and Boy Willie are finally spiritually reconciled. (pp. 70-1)

> Mei-Ling Ching, "Wrestling Against History," in Theater, Vol. XIX, No. 3, Summer-Fall, 1988, pp. 70-1.

Robert Brustein (essay date 1990)

[*In the following excerpt, Brustein claims that Wilson's artistic vision is limited to the black experience and that he should "develop the radical poetic strain that now lies dormant in his art."*]

There are reasons why I didn't review the three previous August Wilson productions that moved from the Yale Repertory to Broadway. Lloyd Richards, who directed them all and guided their passage through a variety of resident theaters to New York, succeeded me as Yale's dean and artistic director eleven years ago, and protocol required that I hold my tongue about the progress of my successor. I broke my resolve in an article for *The New York Times* about the role of Yale and other resident theaters in what I viewed as the homogenization of the non-profit stage. I called this process "McTheater"—the use of sequential non-profit institutions as launching pads and tryout franchises for the development of Broadway products and the enrichment of artistic personnel. Since the universally acclaimed Broadway production of *The Piano Lesson* brings this process to some kind of crazy culmination—and raises so many troubling cultural questions—I'm going to break my silence once again.

First, let's take a look at the Wilson phenomenon. *The Piano Lesson* is an overwritten exercise in a conventional style—to my mind, the most poorly composed of Wilson's four produced works. None of the previous plays was major, but they each had occasional firepower, even some poetry lying dormant under the surface of their kitchen-sink productions. I don't find much power or poetry at all in *The Piano Lesson,* though the play has earned Wilson his second Pulitzer Prize and inspired comparisons with O'Neill. (One critic likened him to Shakespeare!) In one sense, the comparison is apt. Like O'Neill, Wilson has epic ambitions, handicapped by repetitiousness, crude plotting, and clumsy structure. But where O'Neill wrote about the human experience in forms that were daring and exploratory, Wilson has thus far limited himself to the black experience in a relatively literalistic style.

Before his death, O'Neill determined to compose a nine-play cycle about the progressive degeneration of the American spirit. (Only *A Touch of the Poet* was completed to his satisfaction.) Wilson's four plays also have a historical plan: each attempts to demonstrate how the acid of racism has eaten away at black aspirations in the various decades of the twentieth century. *Ma Rainey's Black Bottom,* set in the 1920s, shows how black musicians were prevented from entering the mainstream of the American recording industry. *Fences,* set in the 1950s, shows how black athletes were prevented from participating in major league baseball. *Joe Turner's Come and Gone,* set in 1911, shows how blacks were reduced to poverty and desperation by the chain-gang system. And *The Piano Lesson,* set in the 1930s, shows how black ideals were corroded by slavery. Presumably Wilson is preparing to cover at least five more theatrical decades of white culpability and black martyrdom. This single-minded documentation of American racism is a worthy if familiar social agenda, and no enlightened person would deny its premise, but as an ongoing artistic program it is monotonous, limited, locked in a perception of victimization.

In comparison with the raging polemics of Ed Bullins or Amiri Baraka, Wilson's indictments are relatively mild. His characters usually sit on the edge of the middle class, wearing good suits, inhabiting clean homes. Securely shuttered behind realism's fourth wall, they never come on like menacing street people screaming obscenities or bombarding the audience with such phrases as "black power's gonna get your mama"—which may further explain Wilson's astounding reception. It is comforting to find a black playwright working the mainstream American realist tradition of Clifford Odets, Lillian Hellman, and the early Arthur Miller, a dignified protest writer capable of discussing the black experience without intimidating the readers of the Home section. Still, enough radical vapor floats over the bourgeois bolsters and upholstered couches to stimulate the guilt glands of liberal white audiences. Unable to reform the past, we sometimes pay for the sins of history and our society through artistic reparations in a cultural equivalent of affirmative action.

On its three-year road to Broadway, *The Piano Lesson* could have benefited from some more honest criticism; in its present form, it represents a step backward. A family drama, like *Fences,* it lacks the interior tension of that work . . . , and at three hours it's about an hour and a half too long for its subject matter. Buried inside much tedious exposition is a single conflict between Boy Willie and his sister, Berniece, over a carved piano. Boy Willie wants to sell the piano and buy some farmland down South. Berniece wants to keep it as a token of the family heritage (their mother polished it every day for seventeen years). A repetitive series of confrontations between the two adds little about the conflict but a lot more about the symbolic history of the piano. It belonged to Sutter, a slave owner, who sold members of their family in order to buy the piano for his wife as an anniversary present. Eventually, their father stole it back from Sutter and was later killed in a boxcar fire, while Sutter fell, or was pushed, down a well.

Wilson pounds this symbolic piano a little heavyhand-edly. Like Chekhov's cherry orchard, it is intended to reflect the contrasting values of its characters—Berniece finds it a symbol of the past while Boy Willie sees only its material value. But Chekhov's people are a lot more complicated than their attitudes; and because Wilson's images fail to resonate, the play seems like much ado about a piano, extended by superfluous filler from peripheral characters. Frying real food on a real stove, turning on real faucets with real hot-and-cold running water, ironing real shirts on real ironing boards, and flushing real toilets . . . , these amiable supernumeraries natter incessantly on a variety of irrelevant subjects, occasionally breaking into song and dance. These super-fluous riffs are partly intended as comic relief, and *The Piano Lesson* has been praised for its humor. But the domesticated jokes, most of them about watermelons, are about at the level of *The Jeffersons*—even the audience's laughter seemed canned. As for Wilson's highly lauded dialogue, his language here lacks music (except for one potentially strong speech by Boy Willie about his Daddy's hands), usually alternating between the prosaic and the proverbial: "God don' ask what you done. God asks what you gonna do."

What ultimately makes this piano unplayable, however, is the ending, which tacks a supernatural resolution onto an essentially naturalistic anecdote. Sutter's ghost is (inexplicably) a resident in this house, his presence signified from time to time by a lighting special on the stairs. In the final scene, Boy Willie, after numerous efforts to remove the piano (after three hours I was prepared to run on stage and give him a hand), is blown off his feet by a tumultuous blast. He rushes upstairs to do battle with the ghost, now represented through a scrim by flowing, glowing window curtains. Returning, Boy Willie renounces his desire to take the piano from the house, while the supernumeraries laugh and cry, and Berniece praises the Lord. Willie adds: "If you and Maretha don't keep playin' on that piano, me and Sutter both likely to be back." Curtain.

This ending is considerably more forced, though argu-ably less ludicrous, than the version I saw three years ago at one of the play's numerous station stops. There Willie rushed upstairs as the curtain fell on the illumi-nated portraits of his slave ancestors in the attic. Either way, the supernatural element is a contrived intrusion. When ghosts begin resolving realistic plots, you can be sure the playwright has failed to master his material . . . . (pp. 28-9)

August Wilson is still a relatively young man with a genuine, if not yet fully developed, talent. O'Neill's early plays were just as highly praised, though he wrote nothing truly great until the end of his life. Premature acclaim was actually one of the obstacles to his develop-ment; only by facing the demons in his heart at the end of his days, a sick, lonely man in a shuttered room, was he able to write with total honesty about his true subject. To judge from *The Piano Lesson,* Wilson is reaching a dead end in his examination of American racism,

though another play on the subject (appropriately titled *Two Trains Running*) is now gathering steam at Yale on its way through the regional railroad depots to its final Broadway destination. It will probably be greeted with the same hallelujah chorus as all his other work. But if Wilson wishes to be a truly major playwright, he would be wise to move on from safe, popular sociology and develop the radical poetic strain that now lies dormant in his art. It is not easy to forsake the rewards of society for the rewards of posterity, but the genuine artist accepts no standards lower than the exacting ones he applies to himself. (pp. 29-30)

> Robert Brustein, "The Lesson of 'The Piano Lesson'," in The New Republic, *Vol. 202, No. 21, May 21, 1990, pp. 28-30.*

August Wilson (essay date 1991)

[*The following essay was adapted from a talk given by Wilson in 1991 at Manhattan's Poetry Center. Here, he discusses his personal writing techniques.*]

When I discovered the word breakfast, and I discovered that it was two words, I think then I decided I wanted to be a writer. I've been writing since April 1, 1965, the day I bought my first typewriter, for $20. That's, I don't know, 26 years now. And so, behind each one of the plays are all those thousands of poems and stories and things I wrote many, many years ago. I had begun writing then as a 20-year-old poet. And I don't care what anybody says, as a 20-year-old poet you cannot sit at home and write poetry, because you don't know any-thing about life. So you have to go out and engage the world.

My friends at the time were painters. I was not envious of them, because they were always trying to get money for paint and get money for canvas. I felt that my tools were very simple. I could borrow a pencil and write on a napkin or get a piece of paper from anyone. So I began to write out in bars and restaurants little snatches of things.

I still do it that way. I start—generally I have an idea of something I want to say—but I start with a line of dialogue. I have no idea half the time who's speaking or what they're saying. I'll start with the line, and the more dialogue I write, the better I get to know the characters. For instance, in writing the play *The Piano Lesson,* one of the characters, Berniece, says something to Boy Willie, her brother, and he talks about how "Sutter fell in the well." Well, this is a surprise to *me.* I didn't know that.

Then I say, "Well, who is Sutter?" You see, if you have a character in a play, the character who knows everything, then you won't have any problem. Whenever you get stuck you ask them a question. I have learned that if you trust them and simply do not even think about what they're saying, it doesn't matter. They say things like, "Sutter fell in the well." You just write it down and make it all make sense later. So I use those characters a lot. Anything you want to know you ask the characters.

Part of my process is that I assemble all these things and later try to make sense out of them and sort of plug them in to what is my larger artistic agenda. That agenda is answering James Baldwin when he called for "a profound articulation of the black tradition," which he defined as "that field of manners and ritual of intercourse that will sustain a man once he's left his father's house."

So I say, O.K., that field of manners and ritual of intercourse is what I'm trying to put on stage. And I best learn about that through the blues. I discovered everything there. So I have an agenda. Someone asked the painter Romare Bearden about his work and he said, "I try to explore, in terms of the life I know best, those things which are common to all cultures."

So I say, O.K., culture and the commonalities of culture.

Using those two things and having the larger agenda, I take all this material, no matter what it is, and later, I sit down and assemble it. And I discovered—and I admire Romare Bearden a lot; he's a collagist, he pieces things together—I discovered that that's part of my process, what I do. I piece it all together, and, hopefully, have it make sense, the way a collage would.

As for the characters, they are all invented. At the same time they are all made up out of myself. So they're all me, different aspects of my personality, I guess. But I don't say, "Oh, I know a guy like this. I'm going to write Joe." Some people do that. I can't do that. So I write different parts of myself and I try to invent or discover some other parts.

I approach poetry and plays differently. For me, if there is such a thing as public art and private art, then the poems are private. They are a record, a private journey, if you will. I count them as moments of privilege. I count them as gifts.

In terms of influence on my work, I have what I call my four B's: Romare Bearden; Imamu Amiri Baraka, the writer; Jorge Luis Borges, the Argentine short-story writer; and the biggest B of all: the blues. I don't play an instrument. I don't know any musical terms. And I don't know anything about music. But I have a very good ear and I'm a good listener. And I listen mostly to the blues. I have been variously influenced by them and also by the 2,000 or some poets I have read. I have not been, per se, influenced by playwrights or any writers other than that. Some of the black writers I read. For instance, I read Ralph Ellison's *Invisible Man* when I was 14. I guess I've been influenced by him. I've certainly been inspired by examples like that.

In my own work, what I hope to do is to "place" the tradition of black American culture, to demonstrate its ability to sustain us. We have a ground that is specific, that is peculiarly ours, that we can stand on, which gives us a world view, to look at the world and to comment on it. I'm just trying to place the world of that culture on stage and to demonstrate its existence and maybe also indicate some directions toward which we as a people might possibly move.

For instance, in the play *Two Trains Running,* there are so many references to death. The undertaker in the black community is the richest man. It's still true today. In the midst of all that, though, in the midst of all this death, you have that which doesn't die—the character of Aunt Esther, which is the tradition. And when the people, the characters in the play, go to see Aunt Esther, the main thing she tells them, each in a different way, is that if you drop the ball you have to go back and pick it up. If you continue running, if you reach the end zone, it's not going to be a touchdown. You have to have the ball.

And I think that we as black Americans need to go back and make the connection that we allowed to be severed when we moved from the South to the North, the great migration starting in 1915. For the most part, the culture that was growing and developing in the Southern part of the United States for 200 and some years, we more or less abandoned. And we have a situation where in 1991 kids do not know who they are because they cannot make the connection with their grandparents—and therefore the connection with their political history in America.

In *The Piano Lesson,* where you have a brother and sister arguing over a piano that is a family heirloom, and each with different ideas of ways to use it, the ending was a very difficult thing because I didn't want to choose sides.

We had about five different endings to the play. But it was always the same ending: I wanted Boy Willie to demonstrate a willingness to battle with Sutter's ghost, the ghost of the white man—that lingering idea of him as the master of slaves—which is still in black Americans' lives and needs to be exorcised. I wasn't so much concerned with who ended up with the piano, as with Boy Willie's willingness to do battle.

In staging it, there were also the ghosts of the guys in the play who had burned up in the boxcar. Ideally, I had wanted Boy Willie to fight it out himself. But then we thought, well, maybe we'll have those ghosts come in and they'll help him with this battle with Sutter. At the same time, Berniece must break her taboo about playing the piano and call up the ghost of her mother and her grandmother and all of her ancestors, whom she has been rejecting. And she does that, and it's a very powerful force. And Sutter's ghost leaves the house. And that's as clear as I can put it. (pp. 5, 17)

August Wilson, "How to Write a Play Like August Wilson," in The New York Times, *Section 2, March 10, 1991, pp. 5, 17.*

FURTHER READING

Brown, Chip. "The Light in August." *Esquire* III, No. 4 (April 1989): 116, 118, 120, 122-27.
> Detailed article tracing Wilson's literary career through events in his personal life.

Christiansen, Richard. "Artist of the Year: August Wilson's Plays Reveal What It Means to be Black in This Century." *Chicago Tribune* (27 December 1987): 4-5.
> Biographical essay concentrating on Wilson's success after the premier of *Fences.*

Davies, Hilary. "August Wilson—A New Voice for Black American Theater." *Christian Science Monitor* 76, No. 226 (16 October 1984): 29-30.
> Interview in which Davies explores the origins of Wilson's plays and the author's strong involvement with black history.

Hunter-Gault, Charlayne. "On Broadway: Everybody's America." *Vogue* 178, No. 7 (August 1988): 200, 204.
> Interview. Hunter-Gault and Wilson discuss the latter's cyclical treatment of black American history.

O'Neill, Michael. "August Wilson." In *American Playwrights Since 1945: A Guide to Scholarship, Criticism, and Performance,* edited by Philip C. Kolin, pp. 518-27. Westport, Conn.: Greenwood Press, 1989.
> Bibliography of Wilson's plays and criticism of his works.

Poinsett, Alex. "August Wilson: Hottest New Playwright." *Ebony* XLIII, No. 1 (November 1987): 68, 70, 72, 74.
> Biographical article focusing on Wilson's career and the impact of cultural heritage on his writing.

Smith, Philip E., II. "*Ma Rainey's Black Bottom*: Playing the Blues as Equipment for Living." In *Within the Dramatic Spectrum,* edited by Karelisa V. Hartigan, pp. 177-86. Lanham, Md.: University Press of America, 1986.
> Explores Wilson's portrayal of the black American instinct for survival.

Staples, Brent. "August Wilson." *Essence* 18, No. 4 (August 1987): 51, 111, 113.
> Examines blues music and oral tradition in Wilson's plays.

Harriet Wilson

1827?-?

(Full name Harriet E. Adams Wilson; wrote under pseudonym "Our Nig") American novelist.

Author of *Our Nig; or, Sketches from the Life of a Free Black in a Two-Story White House, North. Showing that Slavery's Shadows Fall Even There* (1859), Wilson is believed to be the first black American woman to have published a novel in English. Until recently, however, she was virtually unknown among literary scholars. Henry Louis Gates, Jr.—while browsing at a Manhattan bookstore in 1981—came upon *Our Nig* and reintroduced the work to the public. By pure literary standards, *Our Nig* is not considered a great work; rather, its importance lies in its historical contribution. "In many ways [*Our Nig*] is an indictment," Francis Browne summarized, "not alone of oppression, but of the hypocritical liberalism that held sway in the North during the middle years of the nineteenth century when all eyes were focused on the heinous legalized servitude in the South.... Harriet E. Wilson ... gives us, through her novel, a different perception of what lay behind the horrible paradox of being free and black in Northern states...." *Our Nig* also broke ground in the African-American literary tradition: "*Our Nig*," Gates explained,"is a major example of generic fusion in which a woman writer appropriated black male (the slave narrative) and white female (the sentimental novel) forms and revised these into a synthesis at once peculiarly black and female. For Harriet Wilson is not only the first black woman novelist in the tradition, she is also the first major innovator of fictional narrative form."

Not much is known about Wilson, but what little is available indicates a life marked by tragedy and pathos. She is believed to have been born in 1827 or 1828 in Milford, New Hampshire. Public documents show that in 1850 she was working for the family of Samuel Boyles—a white carpenter—as a free black indentured servant. Like the heroine in *Our Nig*, she was treated harshly by her mistress. She moved to Massachusetts for a short time—taken there by "an itinerant colored lecturer"—and started working for Mrs. Walker as a hatmaker. In 1851 she married Thomas Wilson, a fugitive slave and former house servant, and returned to New Hampshire. When Wilson was pregnant, her husband deserted her. Strapped for money and having no place to go, she sought shelter at the "County House," where he son, George Mason Wilson, was born. As suddenly as he had disappeared, Thomas Wilson returned and retrieved his wife and son from the Hillsborough County Farm, only to disappear again, this time for good. Once again, unable to support herself and her son, Wilson entrusted George to a white foster couple. She hoped to earn enough money to get her son back, so she moved to Boston in 1855, where she worked as a dressmaker and wrote *Our Nig*. She wrote in the preface to the novel: "In offering to the public the following pages, the writer confesses her inability to minister to the refined and cultivated, the pleasure supplied by abler pens. It is not for such these crude narrations appear. Deserted by kindred, disabled by failing health, I am forced to some experiment which shall aid me in maintaining myself and child without extinguishing this feeble life. . . . I sincerely appeal to my colored brethren universally for patronage, hoping that they will not condemn this attempt of their sister to be erudite, but rally around me a faithful band of supporters and defenders." George died six months after the publication of *Our Nig*. A few years later, Wilson disappeared, and no further information about her is available. Her death date is unknown.

Various claims have been advanced for *Our Nig*. Most commonly, the work is considered the first novel in English published by a black American woman. Although works were published prior to 1859 by black American women—at least two such are known: *The Life and Religious Experiences of Jarena Lee, A Coloured Lady* (1836) and *A Narrative of the Life and Travels of Mrs. Nancy Prince* (1853)—*Our Nig* is considered the first "fictional third person autobiography" of its kind, according to Gates. *Our Nig* combines fact and fiction; Alfrado—the protagonist in the work—resembles and follows closely the true life of Wilson. Born the daughter of a white woman and a black man, Frado is an indentured servant to the Bellmonts, a middle-class white family living in a "large, old-fashioned, two-story white house." The mistress of the house treats Frado cruelly, often beating and whipping her without cause. Frado endures and survives. At age eighteen she is freed from her contract and finds work as a hatmaker for a kind white woman. She meets and marries Samuel, a fugitive slave and traveling lecturer. When she is pregnant, he deserts her and later dies of yellow fever in New Orleans. Frado's health fails and the novel ends "with a hurried and abbreviated account of Frado's adventures in New Hampshire and Massachusetts.... The text ends in Harriet Wilson's own voice, in a direct appeal to her readers to purchase her book so that she might retrieve her son," Gates summarized.

Almost no early criticism exists on *Our Nig*; it appears that soon after its publication in 1859, *Our Nig* was promptly forgotten. As Gates has noted, there were brief mentions of the novel in Herbert Ross Brown's 1940 work *The Sentimental Novel in America* and James Joseph Kinney's 1972 thesis "The Theme of Miscegenation in the American Novel to World War II," but serious consideration of the work did not appear until 1983. Reviewing *Our Nig* in the *Nation*, Margo Jefferson wrote: "*Our Nig* is part drama, part declaration and part documentary. Wilson sometimes tells her tale baldly; sometimes hurries it along, issuing stage directions and inserting exposition; sometimes crafts it with crisp scores and dialogue shrewdly attuned to the rhythms and phrasings of class and character." Francis Browne, in a 1987 review of *Our Nig,* conceded that the novel "hardly ranks with the masterpieces of the genre." He continued, however: "Wilson's art might indeed be defective but her imaginative effort, lately revealed, has proven itself worthy and signally prophetic. In the final analysis . . . the comparisons between this single work and those of her better-known American contemporaries . . . may eventually reveal that Wilson's lonely effort may show itself more valuable and worthy as the forerunner of the Afro-American literary tradition."

Since its rediscovery in 1981, interest in *Our Nig* has abated somewhat. In 1983 the book was reissued by Random House, with an informative introduction by Gates. How significant *Our Nig* is as a *literary* document remains debatable. William L. Andrews, editor of *Three Classic African-American Novels* (1990), viewed *Our Nig* as a "classic" and ranked it as the equal of Frederick Douglass's *Heroic Slâve* and William Wells Brown's *Clotel; or, The President's Daughter: A Narrative of Slave Life in the United States.* Other critics seem hesitant to pronounce such a favorable judgment. Regardless of its literary merit, however, *Our Nig* is considered a seminal work: "[*Our Nig* offers] new forms, new modes, new styles to our rigid definition of literature," Frances Smith Foster concluded. "[It adds] contours and color to our picture of American, the proper study of which will enrich our concepts of our history, our literature, and ourselves."

(For further information about Wilson's life and work, see *Dictionary of Literary Biography,* Vol 50: *Afro-American Writers before the Harlem Renaissance.*)

PRINCIPAL WORK

Our Nig; or, Sketches from the Life of a Free Black, in a Two-Story White House, North. Showing that Slavery's Shadows Fall Even There [as "Our Nig"] (novel) 1859.

Margo Jefferson (essay date 1983)

[*In the following excerpt, Jefferson admires Wilson's style and technique in* Our Nig, *describing the work as "part drama, part declaration and part documentary."*]

Poor Harriet Wilson. Neither religion, love, freedom, domesticity nor motherhood could match the power of poverty, mistreatment and ill health. Her life was obscure, the date of her death uncertain. The novel she

wrote about her circumstances earned her a second death—124 years of literary oblivion.

Our Nig was published in Boston at Wilson's expense. It appeared in 1859, two years before the Civil War, a time marked by antislavery agitation, fugitive slave laws and a group of extraordinary activists that included Sojourner Truth, Frederick Douglass, John Brown, the Grimké sisters, Harriet Tubman, Harriet Beecher Stowe, William Wells Brown and William Lloyd Garrison. Wilson was all too aware that, with New England's moral attention turned to enslaved blacks down South, a tale of a black female indentured servant up North was ill timed. "I do not pretend to divulge every transaction in my own life, which the unprejudiced would declare unfavorable in comparison with treatment of legal bondmen," she declared in a preface designed to ease advanced minds and frail egos. "I have purposely omitted what would most provoke shame in our good anti-slavery friends at home . . . . I sincerely appeal to my colored brethren universally for patronage, hoping that they will not condemn this attempt of their sister to be erudite, but rally around me a faithful band of supporters and defenders." Alas, 'twas not to be. Even the durable feminine plea that publication would not have been attempted "but that I am forced to some experiment which shall aid me in maintaining myself and child" failed.

Only the most fragmentary records of Wilson's work and life exist. Henry Louis Gates Jr., a professor of Afro-American studies and English at Yale, came upon the novel in a Manhattan bookshop last year; through painstaking research he set about retrieving what little biographical information could be gleaned from public documents. In a thorough and excellent introduction, he analyzes the books' social and literary history, its link to contemporary slave narratives and, particularly, its use and revision of the conventions of women's sentimental fiction. From all indications, *Our Nig* was the first novel published by a black in the United States, and the first published by a black woman in English.

At the time it appeared, the question of what authority a black author's voice carried was crucial; so was the literary struggle over whether fiction or nonfiction was more effective in portraying black life. *Our Nig* is at the heart of this struggle. It contains, as slave narratives invariably did, an appendix with letters from white friends verifying the tale's truth and the teller's decency. But in choosing fiction over autobiography, Wilson not only chose a form dominated by her sex; she chose one ultimately not dependent on testimonies from members of another race, and so managed to present, if not settle, those issues in a fresh way.

The book's full title is ***Our Nig; or, Sketches from the Life of a Free Black, in a Two-Story White House, North. Showing That Slavery's Shadows Fall Even There.*** Note how the tone shifts with each clause—from crude to genteel to factual to melodramatic. That progress is emphasized in the facsimile edition; each clause is given a different script. The author's line, *by "Our Nig,"* is the final coup: it's both a curt reminder of the politics of slave names and epithets and a wicked parody of the common feminine practice of publishing under coyly domestic pseudonyms like "Aunt Kitty" or "Cousin Alice."

"It is the complex interaction of race-*and*-class relationships . . . which **Our Nig** critiques for the first time in American fiction," writes Gates, and the complex interaction of race, class and sex is present from the startling opening chapters. There we meet "lonely Mag Smith," a white New Englander seduced and abandoned by a gentleman above her station—hence an outcast in her village—befriended only by Jim, a "kind-hearted African" who delivers the coal. Stirred by love, pity and dreams of marital upward mobility, Jim proposes ("she'd be as much of a prize to me as she'd fall short of coming up to the mark with white folks"). Acknowledging that "I can but do two things . . . beg my living or get it from you," Mag accepts.

Having proved a kind and dutiful husband, Jim dies, leaving behind "two pretty mulattos." Expelled from the white community, Mag takes up with Jim's business partner, who soon persuades her that they had best give the children away and seek a living elsewhere. Six-year-old Alfrado—the well-read Wilson understood the charm a Mediterranean-sounding name could bestow upon a black girl forced into servitude—is left with the white middle-class Bellmonts.

Wilson builds her broad characterizations upon well-observed foundations: the kindness or cruelty of the Bellmonts is linked with the way they view their social and economic needs and privileges. Frado's chief tormentor, Mrs. B., is a vicious social climber renowned for her brutality with servants; an indentured black enlarges her domestic and sadistic horizons. One daughter, Mary, is a gleeful follower; the other, Jane, is an invalid whose kind instincts are thwarted by her dependence. Mr. B. is good-hearted but prefers domestic quiet to upholding principles and justifies his reticence by claiming he is henpecked. His sister, Aunt Abby, has a measure of financial and marital independence, and so can sometimes risk standing by her beliefs in decency and religious equality. Brothers Jack and James, the twin pillars of good in Frado's grim world, are adored and indulged by all: Jack is a manly protector, James a spiritual mentor whose concern for her is made sexually benign by being linked to religion and illness.

With Frado, an artful creation, Wilson revises one of *Uncle Tom's Cabin's* most riveting and repellent dualities. Like Topsy, she is clever and spirited, but shorn of pickaninny pranks and grotesqueries. Like Little Eva, she is the measure of adult salvation and damnation, but without the aid of Christianity. Despite the earnest efforts of Aunt Abby and James, Frado decides no heaven that could countenance Mrs. B. is worth the price of admission, and learns that defiance can win her a freedom that submission never will. (I wish Wilson

had shown Frado's spirit more and attested to it less; perhaps her determination to avoid creating a little black dervish made her overly cautious. One craves more scenes like the one in which, ordered to eat from Mr. B.'s dirty plate, Frado has the dog lick it clean first.)

Our Nig is part drama, part declaration and part documentary. Wilson sometimes tells her tale baldly; sometimes hurries it along, issuing stage directions and inserting exposition; sometimes crafts it with crisp scenes and dialogue shrewdly attuned to the rhythms and phrasings of class and character. Her tone changes continually—the result, I think, of the haste and pain with which she wrote, the mixed audience she anticipated with dread and the conflict between her gift for biting realism and her taste for genteel lyricism. She will be brusque, then fastidious; she will shift from melancholy to outrage and sarcasm.

A number of strategic touches intrigued me: how Frado is subtly paired with worthy whites because of her character rather than her mixed parentage (Wilson dwelt less than was customary on her fair skin and glossy curls), and how, like some Puck or Ariel, she sets familial and marital discord right. When, at 18, her term of servitude is over, she goes out into the world with one decent dress, a Bible, hard-won literacy and a privilege hitherto conceded only to white ladies of means in fact or fiction—a constitution too frail for housework. She learns the craft of making straw hats from a poor white woman "who could see merit beneath a dark skin"; in return, she teaches the woman "the value of useful books."

Into this fragile peace comes Samuel, a professed fugitive slave: "a fine straight negro, whose back showed no marks of the lash, erect as if it never crouched beneath a burden. . . . She opened her heart to the presence of love—that arbitrary and inexorable tyrant." Reader, she marries him and lives to regret it—Samuel deserts her, "with the disclosure that he had never seen the South and that his illiterate harangues were humbugs for hungry abolitionists." (Let us remember that between 1847 and 1859 William Lloyd Garrison's newspaper carried sixteen exposés of blacks posing as fugitive slaves, an interesting commentary on the limited employment opportunities for free blacks in the North. Let us also remember that Frederick Douglass was criticized by more than one abolitionist for not sounding illiterate enough to be a convincing former slave.) Samuel dies of yellow fever in New Orleans; Frado, unhappily pregnant, gives birth and goes back into the world to earn her keep.

The final chapters are poignant and dissonant. As Frado drags herself from destitution to subsistence and from town to town, "watched by kidnappers, maltreated by professed abolitionists, who didn't want slaves at the South, nor niggers in their own houses, North," the narrator's voice seems about to disappear beneath the weight of its burden. But Wilson draws herself up and abruptly presents a combined autobiographical and fictional ending.

Frado prevails: "Nothing turns her from her steadfast purpose of elevating herself." And, we are told in a tone that fuses a lady's claim to modesty with a free woman's right to privacy, she merits our help—"Enough has been unrolled to demand your sympathy and aid." The closing history of the Bellmonts is briskly supplied. Frado has outlived all but Jane and her husband, who perhaps signify her hopes for a better marriage. Then, in a sweeping Old Testament image, Wilson reduces even them to minor functionaries and elevates Frado to the stature of a chosen prophet and ruler.

I'm glad that in her final imaginative vision Wilson associates herself with personal power and the salvation of a people, for, in real life, *Our Nig*'s publication brought no change in her circumstances. If, as she wrote, she had hoped it would provide for her son, it did not; he died within six months of the book's publication. If she had hoped it would provide access to the world of free blacks who traveled, wrote, preached and lectured on the major racial and sexual issues of her day (and ours), she was disappointed. That we do not know the date of Harriet Wilson's death says a great deal about the remainder of her life. (pp. 675-77)

Margo Jefferson, "Down & Out & Black in Boston," in The Nation, *New York, Vol. 236, No. 21, May 28, 1983, pp. 675-77.*

Francis Browne (essay date 1987)

[*In the excerpt below, Browne examines* Our Nig *as a literary mirror of what it meant to be "free and black in the North."*]

The words that begin the novel [*Our Nig*] are themselves neither profound nor imaginative. Indeed, they are as sentimentally commonplace as can be found in melodrama:

> Lonely Mag Smith! See her as she walks with downcast eyes and heavy heart. It was not always. She *had* a loving, trusting heart. Early deprived of parental guardianship, far removed from relatives, she was left to guide her tiny boat over life's surges alone and inexperienced. (*Author's italics*).

With these words, the author introduces an apologia for the mother who abandoned her child, and who, as an immigrant, faces circumstances of a vague wretchedness more hinted at than shown. But from these words of pity the framework for the heroine's unfortunate life is established and initiates the subsequent shame and regret. The opening apologia portends a work significant not so much for its imaginative portrayal, as for its historical importance with respect to the development of an Afro-American perspective in a popular medium. This seminal work was, it appears, the first published novel in English in the United States by a black American, male or female.

According to Henry Louis Gates, Jr., the indefatigable scholar and researcher behind the re-discovery of this novel, little is know about Harriet E. Wilson: "While there remains no questions as to her race or her authorship of *Our Nig*, we have been able to account for her existence only from 1850 to 1860. Even her birth-date and date of death are unknown."

Of course Wilson was not the first black to publish a novel, but evidently she was the first to do so in the United States, and at a time when the abolitionist movement was at its peak. While well acquainted with the Bible, the primary source for most people in any acceptable walk of life during this era, Wilson was also familiar with the Romantic poets of England (noted in the chapter headings of her book). Additionally, she may have had some reading experience with popular romantic fiction of the period, which probably encouraged her to pursue this medium as a means to earn money to support her child and herself. The parochial world in which she lived and the constricting circumstances of her experiences were all the ingredients needed to undertake the task of writing her novel.

The novel itself? It hardly ranks with the masterpieces of the genre. Nor, from what her editor indicates, was it meant to. In many ways the novel is an indictment, not alone of oppression, but of the hypocritical liberalism that held sway in the North during the middle years of the nineteenth century when all eyes were focused on the heinous legalized servitude in the South. The irony resonates when one recognizes that the locales of the novel, New Hampshire and Massachusetts, were hotbeds of abolition, where escaping blacks sought refuge from bondage in the South on the train of Freedom by means of the Underground Railroad. (Perhaps, this novel gives some insight as to why so many escaping slaves were dutifully hustled into Canada. De facto servitude in the North was as great a danger to free blacks as was the possibility of their capture and return to the cradle of slavocracy in the South.) But this irony of place may have as much to do with the novel's neglect as its lack of promotion. The fact is that Harriet E. Wilson was *not* a slave, technically; her experiences as an uncertified bondswoman would not promote the cause of abolition in the trendy appropriation of legitimate slave narratives of the period; she did not speak out directly against the oppressive system; and, finally, this daughter of a black laborer and an outcast white woman was not the kind of spokesperson liberal whites of the time were quite ready to endorse. In these respects, *Our Nig* stands as a disturbing counterbalance to the plethora of anti-slavery propaganda that held sway among all the prominent protesters of mid-nineteenth century America.

It may be mentioned here, as a digression, that Frances E. W. Harper and Frederick Douglass, among others, were aware of the hypocrisy evidenced in the North toward escaped or freed blacks, and their writings and lectures ably ring out against the contradictory status that prevailed among this maligned group, in reference

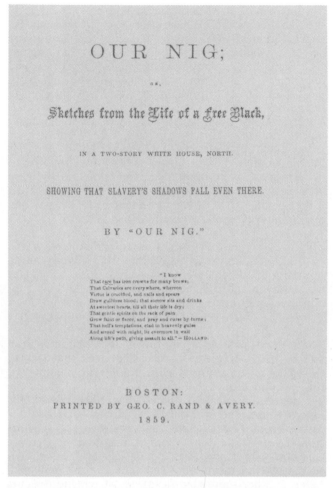

Title page of Wilson's 1859 work, considered the first novel written by a black American woman.

to their white counterparts. But these distinguished black voices had as their support (although strained, at times) dominant anti-slave personalities, such as Wendell Philips, Harriet Beecher Stowe and William Lloyd Garrison, to shield them from possible reaction to the hypocritical stance of Northern liberals. After all, the "real" issue was slavery *by law*. It was the institution of authorized slavery that had to be dismantled.

Our Nig is not a strange tale or much different from stories of its kind told by many others during this horrendous era. In our time, there are sufficient reminders to acquaint and re-acquaint present-day Americans, black and white, with how portentous Wilson's narrative is. One hundred twenty-five years later, incredibly, there are those who claim not to know of injustices here or elsewhere (whatever their contexts); there are those who want to forget such things ever happened here or elsewhere, those who apologize and excuse what happened here and elsewhere, and there are those who can't *believe* such things happened at all!

Books, movies and lectures recount varying degrees of oppression that haunt the United States; while blacks by no means hold the patent on being victims of racism in the United States, they surely bear the stigma, as is evident in their various complexions. The fascination, sense of guilt, horror, indignation and, yes, even romance that accompanied such television mini-series as "Roots," "The Autobiography of Miss Jane Pittman," and the more recent dramatization of the pre-Civil War novel, "North and South," are often looked upon with ambivalent eyes, as the fictively opportunistic efforts of authors out to capitalize on what is timely. Viewers, if black, talk about these depictions relative to black experiences as times gone "forever"; publically, they speak of them as if they were happenings from Herodotus and the Persian wars; privately, they laugh away their pain. If white, there is silence, lowered voices, embarrassment, or they avoid the problem altogether; is it little wonder then that Wilson's plea (presupposing, of course, that the book had some form of advertising) for "my colored brethren universally for patronage" went unheeded? It is not so bewildering that we, in our time, cannot recognize the possibility of a similar dilemma. What cannot be laughed at in private, or cried over in public, is perhaps best received in embarrassed silence and neglect.

Turning more directly to the novel, the reader's sympathy is gained by the plight of the protagonist, Frado, the offshoot of the mixed relationship. She invites from us a different—if not altogether new—perspective on the black experience in American literature of the period.

In her simple but dignified preface Wilson remarks on the condition of her fellows by stating that she intends not to "palliate slavery at the South, by disclosures of its appurtenances North," even though her cruel and brutal mistress was "wholly imbued with *Southern* principles" (author's italics). And so, as if aware of her story's divergence from the common pale of fugitive slave narratives of the period, she "purposely omitted what would most provoke shame in our good anti-slavery friends at home"; presumably, she meant in the North. Here then is the crux of her indictment in which she has the good taste not to condemn (to her own detriment) the hypocritical stance of those who made strong avowals of freedom for enslaved blacks in the South while never addressing the treatment of indigenous, suffering "free" blacks in their own backyards.

Again, one is not surprised at this kind of hypocrisy. Its prevalence carried well into our era, as most realize from the riots in the North, the lynchings, the discriminatory practices only recently proscribed from the many statutes at various levels of government. From the National Association for the Advancement of Colored People, the Urban League, the movement spawned by Marcus Garvey in the 1920s, the Muslim reactions and Civil Rights struggles of the 1960s, to the Black Power voices of the 1970s, I must repeat: *One is not surprised at the kind of hypocrisy Wilson depicts in her novel.* Where is the horror? That such groups and movements existed? Or, that they *had* to be? It is to Wilson's credit that she demonstrated the courage and insight to depict a condition little shown by abolitionists or others who rightly condemned the human bondage of the South, but wrongly closed their eyes to the *de facto* (and often *de jure* in discriminatory practices) human bondage in the North. Her work is, as it were, an *insider's report* of how deeply inbred white hatred was toward blacks. Northern whites might never have professed to being slave masters, but they nevertheless looked upon blacks as intelligent animals fit by some to be abused and castigated, or by others to be "good" and to "stay out of trouble and they wouldn't be whipped."

On another level, the depiction in the novel of a black female's abuse at the hands of white females detracts from the sympathy of feminism where the deprivation and mistreatment of women by men have historical precedence. It seems that the kindness of white males toward Frado in her sufferings is offset by their ineffectuality to counter the cruelty of the two major female antagonists, Mrs. Bellmont and her daughter Mary. For Frado, the captive black heroine, the dehumanization process she undergoes is all but lethal.

To begin with, Frado is abandoned by her white mother soon after the death of her mother's black husband. She is left at the home of the Bellmonts as a child of six years. From that period to the age of eighteen years, she endures the hardships and difficulties of a bondswoman. When occasional relief comes from the kind words of an intrusive aunt and sister of the Bellmont males, she ultimately is powerless to alleviate the child's abuse. Frado's attempt at running away is thwarted by having no place to go. As the only black among the family, and neither knowing nor seeing any others like herself in the surrounding area, her isolation is worse than her legally enslaved brothers and sisters. Even her pet dog, Fido, is sold by her mistress in order to deny her the slightest companionship. Through her husband's urging, Mrs. Bellmont reluctantly permits the child the luxury of three years schooling, enough to gain the rudiments of "grammar, arithmetic and writing." Beyond these basics, the stolen moments of intellectual improvement come from the occasional glimpses of the Bible as interpreted for her by the spinster sister of Mr. Bellmont, Aunt Abby, who herself is treated as an interloper.

When the male presence of the household extends itself in Frado's behalf, it is not so much to protect her from the cruel treatment of her mistress, as to chasten her to accept her lot. James, the elder brother and son, steeped in the Christianity of his time, shows the most benevolence toward Frado. She develops a kind of "love" for him. But he is not always available, visiting the house from his home in another state only on rare occasions. His death however, is the greatest blow to the bereft young black woman, for while Aunt Abby and Mr. Bellmont try to lessen her deprivation by tolerance of her position in the household, rarely do they interfere with Mrs. Bellmont's tyranny. It is, nevertheless, James

who instructs her in deportment and how, as a black, she should behave. When after a particularly bitter attack on her by her mistress, the child asks who made her to be "kicked and whipped," James tells her that God made her, even as he made every one else. The reluctance—or ignorant acceptance—by the seemingly most humane of the Bellmont family to grasp the indignities perpetrated against Frado mocks the occasional kindness extended toward her. Throughout the novel, the same attitude prevails, and if the author seems unwittingly clever in her defense of the kindlier Bellmonts, then the horror of Frado's condemnation to her living hell is compounded. The issue and the case are clearly put, regardless of her legal status: Because she is black, she is not fit for treatment beyond what one might show toward an intelligent monkey.

This is how the book works as an indictment of the "liberal"-minded, as portrayed by the Bible-spouting members of the Bellmont household. Surely, it might have proven more significant if Wilson had had an opportunity to read a tract or two from the hand of John Brown.

The series of indignities continues and, while rebellion seethes in Frado, only on occasion does she dare to trump her mistress. Once, while dining with members of this peculiar family, her mistress enters and finds the girl sharing a meal at their table. Shocked at this impertinence, she commands Frado to eat from her mistress's unwashed plate. The girl, feigning submission, coyly has her dog, Fido, first lick it clean, then she eats from it, to show her disdain. Her mistress, mortified, feels the insult and demands she be punished. Later, another more significant act of rebellion occurs soon after the death of James, her champion. When ordered to retrieve some wood, Mrs. Bellmont, for unstated reasons, attempts to beat her while she carries the wood. Frado, much older now, challenges her mistress directly by refusing to work for her ever again should she strike her. Repulsed, Mrs. Bellmont relents. This represents the first truly independent act Frado has demonstrated, and it becomes an initial step toward her eventual manumission.

Finally, in her eighteenth year, Frado is "released" by Mrs. Bellmont, with a "present of a silver half dollar," and a litany of recriminations. She leaves the house after years of involuntary servitude, physically ruined by degradation, with a wardrobe consisting of "one decent dress" and a Bible. Having become lame during her last year at the Bellmont residence, she must fend for herself—although in "delicate health" and "so wearied out . . . by her mistress, she felt disposed to flee from any and every one having her similitude of name and feature."

It doesn't matter much that Frado's life after having left the Bellmonts is tragic; nor does it matter that she meets and marries a charlatan black who deserts her after fathering her child. Nor does it matter that the novel's ending is inconclusive and unsatisfactory. What matters is that Harriet E. Wilson, attempting to find some reputable means to support herself and her child, gives us, through her novel, a different perception of what lay behind the horrible paradox of being free and black in Northern states, where "there were thousands upon thousands who favored the elevation of her race, disapproving of oppression in all its forms; that she was not unpitied, friendless, and utterly despised; that she might hope for better things in the future."

Wilson's art might indeed be defective, but her imaginative effort, lately revealed, has proven itself worthy and signally prophetic. In the final analysis, and upon further readings and study, the comparisons between this single work and those of her better-known American contemporaries whose melodramatic voices were among the "thousands upon thousands . . . disapproving of oppression in all its forms" may eventually reveal that Wilson's lonely effort may show itself more valuable and worthy as the forerunner of the Afro-American literary tradition. The last word, then, is best related by her editor: Wilson's "legacy is an attestation of the will to power as the will to write. The transformation of the *black-as-object* into *black-as-subject*" (italics mine). (pp. 149-54)

> *Francis Browne, in a review of "Our Nig," in* fiction international, *No. 17:2, 1987, pp. 149-54.*

Henry Louis Gates, Jr. (essay date 1987)

[*In the following excerpt, Gates—an American critic and educator—recounts his discovery of* Our Nig *at a bookshop and discusses how he established Wilson's race and authorship.*]

I picked up a copy of *Our Nig* while browsing at the University Place Bookshop in Manhattan in May 1981. I was curious about the book's title. I am an avid collector of images of blacks in Western literature and art, and I had not before encountered the use of the word *nigger* in a title published before the end of the Civil War. I assumed that *Our Nig* was a book full of happy, shiny darkies, strumming banjos out in the field. Since I did not especially relish the notion of entering this fabricated never-neverland of racial fantasy, I put *Our Nig* on the shelf where it sat for about a year.

In May 1982, I finally read it. Immediately, I was convinced that *Our Nig* was the creation of a black novelist. There were several reasons for this, which I have outlined in my introduction to the second edition of *Our Nig,* published in March 1983 by Random House. No reason was of more importance to my hypothesis, however, than the most obvious one: Mrs. H. E. Wilson *claimed* to be black. There was little to be gained by "passing" for black in 1859, either within the publishing world or without it. *Claim,* perhaps, is too strong a term, for the author of *Our Nig* does not make a case for her racial identity; rather, she presumes its self-evidence and treats the matter accordingly.

While some white authors such as Mattie Griffiths, who in 1857 published *The Autobiography of a Female Slave,* has adopted a black persona in their novels, few had pretended to be black. No black author became wealthy from writing a book, although Frederick Douglas, among others, did well as a writer. Harriet Beecher Stowe's artistic success was not hindered at all by her race. Presenting her race as black and not bothering to demonstrate or establish it, H.E. Wilson, it seemed to me, was quite probably a black woman. An interracial marriage, rendered with balance and a depiction of a dishonest black "fugitive slave" also were remarkably uncommon aspects of the received conventions of the sentimental novel, suggesting a curious rupture in this text's relation to that tradition, of which it so obviously was part but from which its structure departed dramatically. But how could I establish Mrs. H. E. Wilson's race and authorship? This essay recounts that curious tale, the resolution of which turned in large part upon the juxtaposition of two parallel discursive universes: the plot structure of a text claiming to be a "fiction" and the seemingly antithetical biographical documents published as the text's "Appendix," which claim to demonstrate that this fiction is indeed fact—"an Autobiography," as one dares to assert.

On the eighteenth day of August 1859, Mrs. Harriet E. Wilson entered at the clerk's office of the district court of Massachusetts the copyright of her novel, a fictional third-person autobiography, which she entitled *Our Nig; or, Sketches from the Life of a Free Black, in a Two Story White House, North. Showing That Slavery's Shadows Fall Even There.* The novel, printed for the author by the George C. Rand and Avery Company, was published by Wilson on September 5, 1859, under the pseudonym "By 'Our Nig,'" the designation that forms the final line of the book's title. Wilson, in a disarmingly open preface to *Our Nig,* states her purpose for publishing her novel, a novel addressing a theme that, she confesses, could be misread:

> In offering to the public the following pages, the writer confesses her inability to minister to the refined and cultivated, the pleasure supplied by abler pens. It is not for such these crude narrations appear. Deserted by kindred, disabled by failing health, I am forced to some experiment which shall aid me in maintaining myself and child without extinguishing this feeble life.

Wilson explains that only an urgent need to support herself and her child has compelled her to publish this book, a book that takes as its central theme the nature of northern white racism as experienced by a free black indentured servant. We can begin to understand how controversial such a subject was if we remember that John Brown launched his aborted raid on Harper's Ferry in October 1859, just one month after Wilson published *Our Nig.* Despite the potential controversy, however, Harriet E. Adams Wilson asked her "colored brethren" to "rally around me a faithful band of supporters and defenders" and to purchase her book so that she might support herself and her child.

Just five months and twenty-four days later, the Amherst, New Hampshire, *Farmer's Cabinet* of February 29, 1860, included in its list of deaths the following item: "In Milford, 13th inst[ant], George Mason, only son of H. E. Wilson, aged 7 yrs. and 8 mos." George Mason Wilson, according to his death certificate, succumbed to "Fever" on February 15, 1860. The child quite probably received his name in honor of George Mason, the prominent Revolutionary era Virginia planter and statesman who opposed the institution of slavery. More relevant to our search for Harriet E. Wilson, however, George Mason Wilson, according to his death certificate, was the son of Thomas and Harriet E. Wilson. The "color" of the child is listed as "Black." This document alone confirms that "Mrs. H. S. Wilson," a designation echoed by the *Farmer's Cabinet* death notice, was a black woman, apparently the first to publish a novel in English.

The irony of George Mason Wilson's untimely death is that it confirms the racial identification of Harriet E. Wilson, his mother, who had published her first novel to raise funds to retrieve her son less than six months before. Had it not been for George's death and his death certificate, it would have proved remarkably difficult to confirm my strong suspicion that his mother was an Afro-American. His mother's concern for her only child's welfare is responsible for her retrieval from literary oblivion. The irony is profound.

George's death certificate made possible the confirmation of a number of details about Wilson, which parallel rather closely statements about her by three of her friends and printed as an "Appendix" to *Our Nig*. George's death serves as a convenient emblem of the tragic irony of his mother's life and subsequent literary reputation. His mother wrote a sentimental novel, of all things, so that she might become self-sufficient and regain the right to care for her only son; six months later, her son died of that standard disease of fever; the record of this death alone proved sufficient to demonstrate his mother's racial identity and authorship of *Our Nig*. These curious historical events could easily have formed part of a plot in sentimental fiction itself, if any author had been bold enough to venture into that shadowy realm of the highly improbable. Nevertheless, these are the facts, as unlikely as they may seem. That Wilson dared to name her text with the most feared and hated epithet under which the very humanity of black people had been demeaned both adds to the list of ironies in her endeavor and attests to an intelligence that turned racist epithet into irony, subverting a received definition by inverting its common usage.

With this audacious act of titling, Wilson became most probably the fifth Afro-American to publish fiction in English (after Frederick Douglass, William Wells Brown, Frank J. Webb, and Martin R. Delany), the third Afro-American to publish a novel, and (along with Maria F. dos Reis, who published a novel called *Ursula* in Brazil in 1859) one of the first two black women to publish a novel in any language. Despite these profound claims to a central place in the Afro-American literary tradition, however, Wilson and her text—reasons as curious and as puzzling as they are elusive, reasons about which we can venture rather little more than informed speculation—seem to have been ignored or overlooked both by her "colored brethren universally" and by even the most scrupulous scholars during the next hundred and twenty-three years. (pp. 125-29)

Until the publication of the second edition of *Our Nig* in 1983, there existed almost no critical commentary on this novel, except for a brief mention by Herbert Ross Brown in *The Sentimental Novel in America* (1940), who marvels at Wilson's relatively balanced depiction of an interracial marriage. James Joseph Kinney's superb dissertation, "The Theme of Miscegenation in the American Novel to World War II" (1972), also analyzes the novel according to this theme, asserting along the way that the fiction is autobiographical.

The fullest contemporary reference to the novel is perhaps to be found in a letter that Lydia Maria Child sent on July 9, 1878, to Sarah Shaw. The relevant passage reads as follows:

> . . . Poor Mag! She was one of that host of forlorn beings, who go through life with souls gasping and perishing, for want of somebody to love them, and somebody to love. It is so hard to tell what to *do* with characters so blighted by neglect, and hardened by harshness! Every kind person is willing to make efforts to redeem them; but where to place them, after the process of redemption is begun,—that is the puzzling question. Compassion is not enough for them; they need the consciousness of being loved by somebody and of being essential to the comfort of some one. Dear Bessie Green's rule never to separate a mother from her illegitimate child was a wise provision for this craving of human nature. How to find a *home* for such outcasts as poor Mag is a very difficult problem. Public institutions are generally anything but healing to their wounded souls, and it is rare to find a family *all* the members of which are disposed to help them forget the past. In three cases, I tried the experiment of taking a cast-a-way into my own room for several months. While they were with me, all went well; but every case proved a failure after they went out into the world to earn their living; one after a probation of a few months, the other two after a term of years. I confess that if I had known human nature as well as I now know it, I never should have had courage to try such experiments. But is it not strange that some way cannot be discovered by which the elements of human society can be so harmonized as to prevent such frightful discords? Oh, Sarah, my heart is very weary striving to solve this strange problem of human life. If men only *could* be convinced that selfishness is very short-sighted *policy!* If they only *would* realize that to save another soul is the only way to save their own!

It seems likely that Child here refers to "lonely Mag Smith." Child is struck by Mag's seduction and subsequent abandonment, and the desperate behavior that this abandonment engenders. It seems curious that Mag Smith's condition assumes a precedent over Frado's, until we recall that the action of the plot is set in motion by Mag's unmarried pregnancy.

What does *Our Nig* teach us about the Afro-American tradition, beyond allowing us to chart beginnings of the black woman's tradition of the novel? As Martin Price argues, *Our Nig* recalls other sentimental novels, such as those of Defoe or Scott. It was not written in the first person, as Defoe's novels were, as the slave narratives were, but it cultivates a remarkable documentary authority—not least in that final appeal to the reader which can be read as an assertion of the tale's authentic subjectivity, of its "authenticity." But what recalls Defoe, apart from the strict attention to narrative, without description and evocation, is the openness of motives of various kinds. Frado acts out her dreams of independence or superiority, however unguardedly and humorously. She is not shorn of all aggression or self-esteem as is generally the case in the sentimental novel. The reader is drawn to her all the more because of this trait, and finds her more impressive as an individual for her capacity to resent, and especially to hate. Harriet Wilson's characterization of her protagonist in this way recalls the sort of complexity and abstention from moralistic simplification that makes a book such as *Moll Flanders* so attractive, and which is not to be found in any other black novel published before the turn of the century. Had Wilson lived, had she possessed, as Alice Walker has written of her, "a body of her own, a room of her own, and a love of her own," it is difficult to imagine the degree of artistic attainment that the black novel might have realized before the examples of Dunbar and Chesnutt. We can cogently argue, however, without strain that Wilson is the most accomplished and subtle black novelist of the nineteenth century. (pp. 142-43)

> *Henry Louis Gates, Jr., "Parallel Discursive Universes: Fictions of the Self in Harriet E. Wilson's 'Our Nig',"* in his *Figures in Black: Words, Signs, and the "Racial" Self, Oxford University Press, Inc., 1987, pp. 125-63.*

FURTHER READING

Foster, Frances Smith. "Adding Color and Contour to Early American Self-Portraitures: Autobiographical Writings of Afro-American Women." In *Conjuring: Black Women, Fiction, and Literary Tradition,* edited by Marjorie Pryse and Hortense J. Spillers, pp. 25-38. Bloomington: Indiana University Press, 1985.
    Examines *Our Nig* as one of three works by free black American women of the early nineteenth century.

Review of *Our Nig,* by Harriet Wilson. *New Yorker* LIX, No. 18 (20 June 1983): 101-2.
    Briefly reviews *Our Nig,* stating: "Mrs. Wilson's recollections of her heartless mistress, her kindly master, and their mixed bag of children and in-laws are always vivid and convincing. . . ."

Charles Wright

1932-

(Full name Charles Stevenson Wright) American novelist, essayist, and journalist.

Wright is known as a "black black humorist" whose fiction focuses on the difficulties black men face in their quest for the American dream. Unlike many other black writers who have dealt with similar themes, however, Wright uses humor, sarcasm, and surrealism to depict his protagonists' struggles against an unjust society. Jerome Klinkowitz remarked: "Wright's 'blackness' is closer to the hue of Nathaniel Hawthorne, Franz Kafka, and the other great artists who looked past the reality of our lives toward what was really going on. His novels and essays try all aspects of that reality, from the Great Society ambitions to the dead end of the last, drug-spent frontier."

Wright was born in New Franklin, Missouri, in 1932. When he was four years old his mother died and he went to live with his grandparents. He attended public schools in New Franklin and Sedalia and began writing in high school. "[I wrote] little pieces called 'So Long, Buddy'," Wright revealed in an interview. "When I read it in class everyone would start, and one of the students said that I had copied it out of *Reader's Digest*. I was furious because even back then *Reader's Digest* was not a magazine I would have read. At the same time, I was flattered. The story was about a soldier with a limp." He left high school in his junior year and "sort of hung around" before joining the army. Of his military experience, he fondly recalled: "After I learned to survive I had a marvelous time." During the late 1950s, Wright moved to New York City and tried writing for a living. Loosely based on his experiences in the city, his first book, *The Messenger,* was published in 1963. Charles Stevenson, the title character and narrator of the work, views New York City as both a land of boundless opportunity and as a sordid underworld replete with drugs, violence, and sexual aberration. Charles is equally fascinated and repulsed by the two sides of New York yet is unable to find a place in either existence. William Barrett commented: "As a novel, [*The Messenger*] is very slight, but manages nevertheless to carve out a pretty large slice of New York life; and it is all done with an economy of means that would be admirable in an older writer but is little short of amazing in a first novel."

Wright turned to satire in his second novel, *The Wig: A Mirror Image* (1966), which several critics interpreted as a denunciation of racial self-hatred. In this work, Wright recounted Lester Jefferson's chaotic attempts to assimilate into mainstream society. Taking the advice of a disreputable Harlem pharmacist, Lester, a fair-skinned black man, chemically straightens and bleaches his hair "silky smooth" blond in order to become more socially

acceptable. Naively confident with his new hairstyle, or "wig," he embarks on a picaresque journey through Manhattan in search of wealth and power. During his adventures, Lester's faith in his wig subsides and his fortunes turn sour, resulting in his disillusionment and, ultimately, physical mutilation. While Conrad Knickerbocker hailed *The Wig* as "a brutal, exciting, and necessary book," most reviewers found its satire unconvincing. Since the novel's recent critical reevaluation, however, Wright has been acknowledged as one of the first contemporary black writers to use humor and farce to delineate racial injustice.

As in his previous works, Wright wove his own experiences into the fabric of his next novel, *Absolutely Nothing to Get Alarmed About* (1973). Remarked David Freeman in the *New York Times Book Review:* "one of the pleasures of this book . . . is that one is never certain what is fact and what is fiction." The work is a "journal-novel, an act of self-definition [which] appears at first to be more an act of the will than of the imagination,"

Freeman continued. "But at its best, the two worlds—private imagination and harsh reality—merge and hover between gentle evocation of the sad eccentricity of street life and canny social and political views." "There is plenty to get alarmed about in Charles Wright's literary world," noted Joel Weixlmann. "On the one hand, it records, in excruciating detail, the result of deferred and destroyed black dreams. On the other hand, it warns of the consequences that await the destroyers." *Absolutely Nothing to Get Alarmed About* is more pessimistic than Wright's first two novels, relating as it does all the disillusionment and none of the hope that Wright's previous characters had for the "Great Society." Freeman stated of the work: "[It] feels like the rough draft of a suicide note." In assessing Wright's work, however, Clarence Major emphasized its quality rather than its content: "[Wright's] language has the power to suddenly illuminate the dullest moment.... He has worked out a language and a landscape that is a kaleidoscope of mystery and simplicity, filled with miracles and puzzles."

Since publishing *Absolutely Nothing to Get Alarmed About,* Wright has not written any new novels, although he is reported to be working on a book based on the life of Jean Rhys. "Yet if Wright's critical reputation were to rest on his output to date," Weixlmann asserted, "he would be remembered."

(For further information about Wright's life and works, see *Black Writers*; *Contemporary Authors*, Vols. 9-12; *Contemporary Literary Criticism*, Vol. 49; and *Dictionary of Literary Biography*, Vol. 33: *Afro-American Fiction Writers after 1955*.)

PRINCIPAL WORKS

The Messenger (novel) 1963
The Wig: A Mirror Image (novel) 1966
Absolutely Nothing to Get Alarmed About (essays) 1973

Nat Hentoff (essay date 1963)

[*In the following excerpt, Hentoff presents an overview of* The Messenger, *praising Wright's "deceptively simple style."*]

Following the decline of Jack Kerouac and his genre of misty disaffiliation, there has been less talk recently about the Beats. Still among us, however, are those who reject the "square" world. They prefer to subsist on the periphery of society rather than commit themselves to full-time upward mobility, with—by their criteria—its debatable rewards and chronic compromises.

In his first novel [*The Messenger*], Charles Wright speaks for one such outsider. His protagonist, Charles Stevenson, is apparently not greatly different in background and attitude from the author himself. Stevenson is a messenger only in order to eat and pay his rent. For the rest of the time, he wanders—more as an observer than as a participant—through intersecting demi-mondes. Most of his acquaintances are homosexuals, prostitutes, and con men. The messenger has writing aspirations; but in his twenty-ninth year, he is a transient in New York with no specific goal except to move on somewhere else. He stands, as he puts it, "at a distance from life."

Unlike Kerouac and his boyish emulators, Wright views the microcosms of the disaffiliated with a total lack of sentimentality. The fact that the messenger and his associates scorn middle-class values has brought them few positive satisfactions. The messenger himself is acutely lonely....

Hardly anyone he knows, in bleak fact, is really honest, and that realization is the cold core of *The Messenger.* He admits this condition, common to both squares and hipsters, without self-pity or self-righteousness. His defensive stance is ironic, but he can be surprised into acknowledging his own vulnerability. There is, for example, a spare, painfully direct description of a Puerto Rican woman whose drunken husband has smashed their month-old son against the wall. The messenger cannot help but respond with compassion, but then he walks away; there is nothing he can do for her.

The messenger is a Negro; and inevitably he has to confront dimensions of hypocrisy and guilt that white drifters are spared. Yet the messenger's color is only part of the reason for his detachment. Looking at a crowd of office workers, he sees "my people too, like dark dots in a white field"; and he recognizes that "I could become one of the horde, despite the fact that I am Negro." But his conception of meaningful living calls for more than getting "a soft, white-collar job, save the coins, marry, and all in the name of middle-class sanctity."

The messenger does not yet know, however, what it is he *does* want. He tries to force himself into a posture of not allowing himself to care what becomes of him.... Nonetheless, there is enough hope in Stevenson-Wright to have produced a book and to drive the messenger at its end to get a bus ticket to Mexico.

Charles Wright may not yet have "found" himself, but he has an advantage over the more self-adulatory Beats in that he knows who he is not. As a writer, he has developed a deceptively simple style that is clearly the result of honest distillation of experience and hard-won craftsmanship. And in this discipline itself there is a kind of commitment.

Nat Hentoff, "Neo-Beat," in The Reporter, *Vol. 29, No. 1, July, 1963, p. 40.*

Conrad Knickerbocker (essay date 1966)

[*In the following excerpt, Knickerbocker reviews* The Wig, *calling the novel "a brutal, exciting, and necessary book." Wright stated of this essay: "[This is] the best review of [*The Wig*]. When I was a messenger I used to think, if I ever published a novel, I would like [Knickerbocker] to review it. And it so happened that he understood [*The Wig*] so well that . . . it was uncomfortable."*]

Charles Wright's Negro world explodes with the crazy laughter of a man past caring. In *The Wig,* he strops his razor on white men's intentions and then lunges for the jugular vein, but one cannot be sure it is our neck he is after, or his own. He joins James Baldwin to testify that the worst burden the Negro must bear is not racial discrimination, but self-loathing.

The Wig saves its deepest contempt for the Negroes who accept at face value the roles the white world imposes on them. Malevolent, bitter, glittering, the book calls a plague on both houses and thumbs its nose at everything in between.

Like *The Messenger,* Mr. Wright's excellent first novel, *The Wig* is a comic portrait of the loser as a young man. Its narrator, Lester Jefferson, hungry as a Greek mountain dog, sequestered in the racial outhouse, wants his share of the Great Society—pretty girls, credit cards, and fine shoes. He has already tried being a Negro, which means masquerading as an Arab waiter in a Greenwich Village coffee house and tap dancing in front of the Empire State Building for $1.27 a week. Nor can he make it as a Spaniard, American Indian, or Jew. His social security card is silent on the point of whether or not he is human. It is time for a miracle. . . .

Silky Smooth turns Lester's wig into a rich reddish-golden cascade. He sets forth to make his fortune, filled with dreams of being able to leap from the ocean and shake the water triumphantly from his hair like any white boy. At last, he has "a dog's sense of security."

But Silky Smooth is not divine grace, and Lester's sub-basement world contains no doors leading upward. His new wig, like every other gimmick foisted off the Negro, merely gives him false hope. In the weird carnival of people Lester encounters, Mr. Wright categorizes the disguises the Negro assumes in order to survive. Most of these roles are escapist in nature; some are fraudulent; a few are evil. And all, according to him, are as funny, quite literally, as hell.

Mr. Wright's Harlem is almost as nightmarish as the real thing. Human hair rugs, clipped from "live Negro traitors," are on sale in a department store. A shop window advertises coats of arms done on "rat proof antique paper." The police wear Brooks Brothers shirts, and their night sticks are trimmed with lilies of the valley. A group of Black Muslims sells chances on a special armored tank guaranteed to go from New York to Georgia and back on a gallon of gas. . . .

Mr. Wright's style, as mean and vicious a weapon as a rusty hacksaw, is the perfect vehicle for his zany pessimism. On Lester's visit to Fifth Avenue, "gouty, snobbish mongrel dogs howled discontentedly. Infected infants sat in Rolls-Royce baby carriages guarded by gaunt nursemaids. Good Humor men equipped with transistor laughing machines hawked extrasensory and paranoiac ice-cream bars. The unemployed formed a sad sea in front of their apartment buildings . . . while merry apartment wives peered from plate-glass windows, hiding smiles behind Fascisti silk fans."

In Mr. Wright's view, the whole gamut of Negro behavior—even drugs and sex—involves one form or another of "Tomming it:" being like Uncle Tom. Like all good satirists, he sees no hope. His jibes confirm the wound no Great Society will ever salve, and his laughter has no healing powers. *The Wig* is a brutal, exciting, and necessary book.

> Conrad Knickerbocker, "Laughing on the Outside," in The New York Times, *March 5, 1966, p. 25.*

Frances S. Foster (essay date 1971)

[*In the excerpt below, Foster examines* The Wig *as the work of a "black black humorist."*]

When the Black protagonist of *The Wig,* Lester Jefferson, discovered his hair had turned "a burnished red gold," he said, "At least I was the first . . . . a minority within a minority." These words could have been spoken just as well by Charles Stevenson Wright when certain white critics began to agree with Victor Navasky's judgment that Wright as author of *The Wig* is "the first certified Negro black humorist." Disregarding the ideas of whether he actually is the first and of what *certified* actually implies, the fact that he is so proclaimed places him as a "minority within a minority." Like any other Black Humorist, he is isolated from the American literary mainstream by his constant concern with a realization of new perspectives on all aspects of reality: one which includes a search for new artistic means of presenting contemporary experience as well as a question of the established ideas concerning the reality of this experience. However, like any other Black author, he is because of his race generally isolated from even the Black Humor tributary of American literature. Yet being a Black Humorist, he represents a deviation from what is considered the usual course of the Black writer. Nevertheless, Charles Stevenson Wright does fit the criteria of Black Humor. He shares the same slightly-raised-eyebrow attitude about the same concerns as the other authors included in that casually coined term of Black Humor. (p. 44)

In general Black Humorists are among those who have concluded that traditional Western literature ultimately fails in its primary aim: that of exploring and explaining the meaning and relationship of man to himself, his society, and the universe, or, in other words, to life.

They are concerned that traditional Western literature has through its usual means of selecting and ordering somehow missed the essence of the reality of (at least) contemporary existence. Rather than considering life as literature usually shows it as an orderly progression of events, they have discovered that life is simultaneously comic, tragic, humane, inhumane, unpredictable and seemingly illogical. In short, it is absurd. Unlike most existentialists who in traditionally structured and polished literary works argue the absurdity of life, the Black Humorists maintain that a literature which arbitrarily selects its topics, incidents and events and which adheres to an equally arbitrary literary structure is not only misleading, it is fraudulent. Thus they seek alternatives to Aristotle and Henry James. They seek to discuss what has heretofore been ignored and they seek new forms which can be integrated with these new subjects in an effort to present alternative concepts of reality. In short, they are characterized by dispassionate attempts to exhaust the varieties of possible experience in an effort to challenge the traditional concepts of temporal, spatial, and causal order, while searching for the Reality(ies) of existence.... Charles Wright like other Black Humorists does not theorize, he presents his novel and through its form and content we see his suggested reality.

One way in which he differs from tradition is through his development of plot. (pp. 44-5)

In *The Wig* there is a plot or sequence of events that make up a story. Lester Jefferson is attempting to join the Great Society. He says, "Everyone seemed to jet toward the goal of The Great Society, while I remained in the outhouse, penniless, without 'connections'.... I had to make it." Therefore, he Silky Smooths his hair, attempts to attain the dream of overnight success and then to succeed in the Horatio Alger tradition. He ends up as a chicken man wearing a suit of electrified feathers and crawling on his hands and knees ten hours a day, five and a half days a week for ninety dollars a week. He also masquerades as a Swede, uses credit cards, and collects rat pelts in an effort to win his "All-American Girl," The Deb. All efforts fail. Deciding that his "impersonation had caused the death of a bright dream," he visits Madame X, but rejects her offer of ritual, marijuana, and money as the realities with which to replace the American Dream. Then he discovers his wig has turned red-gold. He is picked up by a mysterious woman who offers him money to become her lover. He finally runs into Mr. Fishback who, following another concept of reality, shaves his head and renders him impotent.

The book, however, contains many episodes which have little or nothing to do with this plot. The false labor of Nonnie's false pregnancy is one example of the extraneous incidents. There is also an extended description of a walk through Harlem where "Everything's still the same...But it's different now." There is the meeting with the mother who kills her son because he doesn't want to attend a segregated school. There is the appearance and disappearance of Little Jimmie Wishbone which does not form a sub-plot or double plot but which simply enters Lester's life, parallels the action for a while then exits. There is the episode of the rat fight. Finally, the marijuana session with The Duke is still another of the numerous examples of incidents unrelated to the main action.

Not only is much of the action unrelated, but it is also unmotivated. There is no foreshadowing nor reason given for Nonnie's imaginary pregnancy, for Miss Sandra Hanover's decision to go to Europe, for Mrs. Tucker's death, or even for Lester's decision to leave the mysterious woman and to acquiesce to Mr. Fishback's solution.

Although Mr. Fishback seems to have connections with several of the characters, the exact relationship to these persons and the degree of his responsibility for any one incident is always obscure. Thus coincidence or chance appears to bring about most of the climactic incidents. Lester accidentally meets The Deb. His hair accidentally turns red. He accidentally meets the mysterious lady in Central Park. He also just happens to meet Mr. Fishback who tells him The Deb is dead and who provides a solution to his dilemma.

Unmotivated action, chance, and coincidence are vital to the novel. This is contrary to the tradition that novels must make order from chaos and that fiction must be less strange than fact. Instead, their emphasis supports an idea of irrationality in life. This is not the same as merely copying chaos, nor is it simply a rebellious "anti-novel" technique. It is an attempt to examine, in other ways, other views of life. It is an exploration of reality by adapting, improvising, or in some cases, abandoning techniques in a studied attempt to discover what life is, not by picking examples to illustrate an ideal, but by observing experiences to form conclusions. By ignoring the usual constraints concerning plot, Wright presents an alternative and possibly more realistic method of giving artistic expression to the twentieth century experience.

His use of character is another example of a varied literary technique. M. H. Abrams says, "Whether he remains stable or changes, we require 'consistency' in a character—he should not suddenly break off and act in a way not plausibly grounded in his temperament as we already have come to know it."

Charles Wright disregards these requirements. His characters' motivations are vague. Their actions seem arbitrary. They are neither convincing nor lifelike, rather they are grotesque. They have no specific past nor future but exist only in their particular episodes, then disappear. Their purpose is not so much to advance the plot or to "show human nature in all its complexity and multiplicity" in order to know or understand people as [Laurence] Perrine demands, but to suggest alternative views of human nature. By choosing a protagonist whose real self is unknown to him, his society, and ultimately to the reader, and by refusing to present any character who is clearly motivated, consistent, and plausible, Wright raises questions concerning the possibility of any reality other than the assumed masks of his characters and thereby questions the idea that man is a complex but rational being and not simply at any given moment a variation of one (or all) types presented here. In *The Wig,* a wide variety of characters exist only to support the statement of "Miss Sandra Hanover, ex-Miss Rosie Lamont, ex-Mrs. Roger Wilson, nee Alvin Brown" that "Everybody's got something working for them." Miss Hanover is a black man who believes he is a white Southern lady, "does" people, and plays the roles of leading ladies in old movies. Miss Nonnie Swift maintains she is a "Creole from New Orleans" who lives in Harlem so that her unborn child of a two-year pregnancy will know all the good and bad things in the world. Mr. Sunflower Ashley-Smith appears to be "a thoroughbred American Negro" whose life is devoted to plotting the future of his "golden-voiced colored brethren." Tom Lacy portrays an Uncle Tom who beneath a placid mask has the face of a natural killer and who spends his time counting the deaths of whites. Even the central character, Lester Jefferson, is known only by the roles he plays.... Not one character stands out as having a sure grasp of reality. The author presents his characters as harmless humorless examples of modern man's loss of individuality in an attempt to fit into life as they have been conditioned to see it. Each of the characters is trying to maintain a masquerade, to acquire a gimmick in order to fit a pre-established and thus more desirable mode. Not one is trying to comprehend or to assert his own individuality. Max Schultz in "Pop, Op, and Black Humor" describes this kind of activity as a character's search "to realize the authenticity of his self through his identity with its commonplaces" and warns that this leads not only to submission to "a code of behavior more determinedly abstract than that of the Waverly hero," but that this also results in an inability to relate to any other person "because of the reduction of his being to a contrived ratio which renders the extremes of personality nonexistent." This behavior is seen in *The Wig* in so far as the characters are not only anxious, frustrated, and imitative social misfits but also are preoccupied with appearances.

The first indication of this interest is the novel's subtitle, *A Mirror Image.* It is with this clue that The Wig emerges as a multi-dimensional symbol. The author explains in a prefatory note that *wig* is a slang word for hair. The idea that changing one's hair, or one's appearance in general, makes one a new person connotes an identity which is based entirely upon appearance. It brings to mind the mentality of a nation that seriously considers, if not believes, the version of reality symbolized by the question, "Is it true that blondes have more fun?" An example of this is when The Deb says, "When I get my hair fixed tomorrow I will be like you. Almost, anyway. And pretty soon us colored people will be as white as Americans." *Wig* also carries the connotation of masquerade. Clarence Major sheds more light upon the possibilities of this term in his *Dictionary of Afro-American Slang* when he reveals that *wig* means "a

man's or woman's natural hair that has been processed or straightened; one's mentality, brain, skull, thoughts." Thus, the word *wig* becomes a symbol for the idea of reality and illusion on several levels.

Exploration of the idea of illusion and reality begins on page one. The narrator, "a desperate man," is finding it "hard to maintain a smile." He is desperate because everyone but he "seemed" to be part of the Great Society. The illusion motif is strengthened by the purchase of Silky Smooth, a hair relaxer, with its Faustian promise, "With this you may become what ever you desire." Les' adaption of The Wig represents a new attempt to achieve what he considers Reality, for we are told that before this, he had "masqueraded as a silent Arab waiter in an authentic North African coffeehouse in Greenwich Village" where he'd been successful in "tempting dreamers of Gide, Ivy League derelicts, and hungry pseudo-virgins" until "unmasked by two old-maid sisters." He now says, "I realize people have to have a little make believe.... Sooner or later though, you have to step into the spotlight of reality. You've got to do your bit for yourself and society. I was trying to do something real, concrete, with my Wig." Like the other characters in the book, he recognizes the illusory worlds of others. Furthermore, he seems to be able to recognize specific instances when he has been mistaken, but in seeking to replace an illusion with reality, he inevitably chooses another illusion.

The point of view used in *The Wig* is primarily first person narration, a method which usually increases a reader's sense of immediacy and reality. Wright uses it for a slightly different purpose. Because the narrator has revealed himself as shallow, gullible, vacillating, and often intoxicated, the reality of the view presented is always questionable. Thus Wright can present incidents which pass from realistic to plausible to fantastic with no clue as to how or when the boundaries were crossed. An example of this is Les' tale that the fifth floor of The Duke's mansion had fallen into the street killing three ricket-ridden children, raising the ire of the Sanitation Department, and causing a joyous Welfare Department to send The Duke a twenty-five-year-old quart of Scotch and to officially ax the children from their list.... Wright's use of a narrator who blurs reality and fantasy presents the idea that reality being a mental construct exists on multiple levels anyhow. This preoccupation with reality and illusion is Wright's most outstanding Black Humor characteristic and constitutes the central concern of the novel.

Though the characters are Black and the setting is Harlem, *The Wig* is not a story of Black people only. Charles Wright seems to agree with Richard Wright's idea that "The Negro is America's metaphor," for his characters are actually reflections of American society. Les' values are those of the American dream. He completely accepts the Horatio Alger legend. He believes he has no limitations and needs only an "acquisitional gimmick," i.e. education, connections, or The Wig, to succeed. His resolve is fortified by a slogan he'd heard, "You are not defeated, until you are defeated," and he exhibits the famed optimism of the American people. At one point he says, "No, I like drama. I had to be someone else. I had such a celestial picture of being someone else, and a part of that picture was that my luck would change. But had he? . . . Oh, well, tomorrow's Monday." The closest he comes to recognizing his illusions is when he says, " . . . I had progressed to the front door of hell when all I had actually been striving for was a quiet purgatory," but then he sees a girl. Unsure whether she was "a trick of nature or a goddam trick of my eyes" he follows her anyway. Even when The Wig is clipped and that dream has ended, he says, "I smiled at my bald-headed reflection. 'It's over, I can always do it again'." Les is an incurable role player, a nutty-putty creation who can assume as many identities as desired and who may be easily flattened, but destroyed only with difficulty. The conclusion of the novel is not the end. Lester is still determined to make it. Furthermore, there is no proof that this incident is not another of a series for Black Humor is less concerned with the fate of a protagonist than with the multiplicity of experience possible. The story of Lester Jefferson's struggle to enter the Great Society is, then, exemplary. It is a catalogue of some forms of illusion and reality accepted by contemporary man. When viewed from this perspective, the previously discussed extraneous incidents become an integral part of the novel because they represent alternative visions of reality. Like Bruce Jay Friedman, Thomas Berger, and other Black Humorists, Wright peoples his books with anonymous, undistinguished persons. His protagonist is the reluctant hero— the convention any / everyman trying to make it in contemporary society. (pp. 46-52)

Frances S. Foster, "Charles Wright: Black Black Humorist," in CLA Journal, *Vol. XV, No. 1, September, 1971, pp. 44-53.*

Charles Wright with John O'Brien (interview date 1971-72)

[*In the following interview, Wright contrasts* The Messenger *and* The Wig *and reveals his reasons for leaving New York City, the setting of the two novels. In a preface to the interview, O'Brien stated: "The interview was done in two parts. I met with Mr. Wright in New York City in October of 1971. He appeared for the interview in matching and faded blue denim pants, jacket, and fisherman's hat, and was ill at ease for most of the session. He talked very quickly and rarely directed his remarks to the questions asked. In the summer of 1972 we talked long distance while he was staying in Veracruz, Mexico. The change of locale seems to have rescued him from the terror of New York. His answers on the second occasion were lucid and detailed. Frequently he would return to previous answers to clarify or expand on them. He is presently working on short fiction and plans to begin a third novel."*]

[O'Brien]: *This question may call forth too obvious an answer, because when we met last year in New York you talked about wanting to leave the City and both of your novels concern characters who are trying to escape there, but why did you go to Veracruz?*

[Wright]: Years ago Katherine Anne Porter was here in Veracruz. When I was younger I was sort of hung up on Katherine Anne's work and I decided to come here. But, of course, things have changed for me after nine years. It's no longer a Graham Greene setting as it was then. I don't know whether you have read too much of Katherine Anne's work, but one gets the impression that she was not totally happy in this particular city. The same can be said for me also.

Now that you are in Veracruz are you going to keep writing about New York City?

It seems at present that I am writing about things that happen down here, but I plan to continue writing the things I do for *The Village Voice.* The short stories I've done here . . . although the setting is Mexico, the charac-

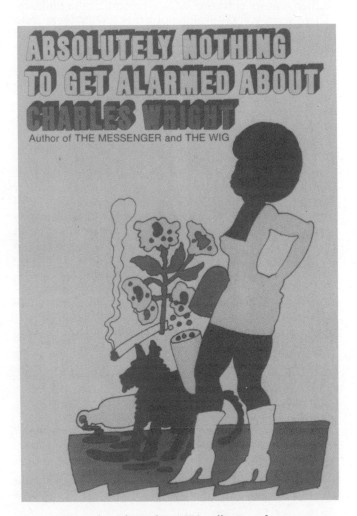

Dust jacket of Wright's 1973 collection of essays.

ters are mostly American. If I do the novel I want to, I will call it *The Gulf of Oz.*

Do you find it easier to write about American things down in Mexico because you have a certain distance?

It doesn't seem so. There may be superficial changes in America, but I think if you have the country clear in your mind then everything is fine. All I have to do is look through the August issue of *Harpers.* There's a photograph in black-and-white on page seventy-eight of an Italian woman and her daughter standing on their porch in Newark, and there's a statue of what appears to be a Madonna covered in plastic. Now below that are flowers, and I will bet my life that those flowers are plastic. When I was delivering circulars in the Bronx I knew neighborhoods like that. So, if nothing else, I have good old *Time* magazine to get a realistic picture of what's going on in America by just looking at the photographs. But I don't even think that I would really need the photographs because everything seems to be very, very clear in my mind.

Did you feel that you had to get away from New York?

Either that or crack-up or else commit some violence. There were several disappointments for me there from which I still haven't recovered. *The Wig* was one of them. That's my retarded child. I had to get away.

It's not clear at the end of **The Messenger** *whether Charles will be able to escape New York. Do you think he will?*

Well, I certainly hope he does.

Do you have any plans for returning to New York?

Yes, I'll probably go back in a couple of months. If I get set up on the novel I might stay here until December or January. Who knows? I'm very impulsive. Like when I returned to Mexico this time I decided on a Thursday night that I was leaving the following day. And I left. But even here I sometimes think, "Oh, God, let me get out of this place." I know this place so well; it's a small city and no one stays here. Even the natives don't stay here. If they are shrewd enough they make a connection so that they can leave. The tourists never stay longer than three or four days. There's really nothing here.

But it is an alternative to New York, I remember in **The Messenger** *that Charles looks out at the city one morning and describes it as "surrealistic." Does that term characterize his whole experience there?*

Yes, yes, indeed.

The surrealism in your stories is so prevalent that it becomes almost ordinary, it seems to have worked its way into everyone's life.

(Laughing) I agree with you one hundred percent. But there are a great many people out there, who live in New

York City, who don't believe this. For example, I received a letter from a young man, a Puerto Rican who lives in New York. It said, "Dear Mr. Wright, I read you in *The Village Voice* but ninety percent of the things you write about I don't believe really happen."

When Eli Bolton in Clarence Major's novel All-Night Visitors *encounters the same kind of experiences he finally feels that "nothing seemed real." Did your experiences in New York seem unreal, and did you then attempt to create something in the imagination that did appear real?*

They seemed quite real. But I suppose Clarence Major creates a fictional world in order to make something real. I think perhaps that is what I do because I know that the world out there is very real, or at least a part of me knows that it is very real. But it's also terrible and so frightening. And although sometimes the things I write about are frightening, it seems so much more comfortable in this fictional world where I would like to remain. Say, "No, no, no," and not go out there. I have to go downtown today and mail a story to my editor because I want her to get it soon. I don't want to get on the bus here at the corner. I would much prefer to remain in my room, but I can't.

What I am wondering about is that both of the novels **The Messenger** *and* **The Wig** *seem to be trying to find some meaning, to put all the parts together. But the parts don't want to seem to come together so you go to fantasy instead. Do you see art—writing a novel—as a superior way of putting things together because people try to put things together in their lives and sometimes they're successful and sometimes they're not. What advantages do you see in going to fantasy?*

You take these things and put them together and, of course, you somehow have a plan.

Is fantasy better than realistic fiction?

I don't think it is. I don't think that one is better than the other. It's whatever suits your purpose. I could have written *The Wig* as a realistic novel . . . but, oh God! Before the Black Panthers appeared on the scene, I started a short action-type novel in the Hemingway style about a group of blacks like the Panthers, except that they didn't have black berets and black leather jackets. But who knows, if I would have continued the novel perhaps they would have even had those. I sent a few sample chapters to my agent and she said, "Oh, God, Charles. We can't publish this!" And a few years later the Panthers were there. That frightened me. So I decided to write it as a fantasy because I wanted to see if I could do it in both ways.

Does the fantasy come easier now that you are removed from New York?

I don't know. I haven't even thought about that and I don't want to think about it because I'm living a fantasy (laughing). Here it is and it's unbelievable.

Do you see The Messenger *and* The Wig *as being very different novels?*

Yes.

What are the differences as far as you're concerned? I see basic differences, especially in style, but there are also several similarities.

Different and at the same time they're the same? Is that what you said? I think that Graham Greene a few weeks ago said that there's only one novel you have to tell, and that you (laughing) write it over and over again. As you know *The Messenger* was a first novel with almost nothing going for it and almost no advertising campaign. Yet, it took off on its own, found its own audience, and was well received by the critics. I realized that they were waiting for me to write a sequel to *The Messenger* or another novel like that. I said I'll be damned if I'll do what is expected of me. Of course, I didn't have any idea that I was going to write anything like *The Wig.* However, in spite of the fantasy in *The Wig* and the realism in *The Messenger,* the novels are similar. At least, physically the heroes are the same.

Do you like comparisons to be made between the two?

The strange thing that I don't understand—or understand only in a sense—is that the readers and critics felt very sympathetically toward Charles of *The Messenger.* He may be going through a bad time but eventually he will be all right. It's what the ordinary person goes through . . . well, maybe not the *ordinary* person (laughing). At the same time, I think that Lester of *The Wig* is tragic. My God, if anyone needs understanding and sympathy, it's him. He will eventually go mad, kill himself, or kill a dozen other people.

What's the real difference between the two?

I think that the "slice-of-life" things that happen to Charles are quite typical. He goes through life, sensitive and aware, but really quite ordinary. The things that happen around him do not have a cancer. Hemingway said something like, "Nothing can hurt you or affect you if you don't want it to . . . if you don't let it get next to you." That's what kept Charles going. At times it does get next to him and it takes a terrible toll, both mentally and physically. But he doesn't let it get him down. It's a survival technique. Lester, who could easily be his brother, is really different because he takes a long-range view of things. What happens to him is that he sees it as a part of a larger design. This could be a sickness, but he feels this. The things that happen to him cut into him, not like a razor blade, but like a dagger. Because of that these emotions build up in his mind.

Are you conscious of any stylistic influences upon The Wig*?*

No. I suppose somewhere in the back of my mind I was thinking about James Joyce. Someone has said that it reminded him of Nathanael West because *The Wig* is not a plotted novel; it's in episodes and you might think of it in relation to vaudeville. I avoided reading other contemporary writers because I didn't want to be influenced. They might come along and say somebody else did a thing like that. I was totally at work on my own and I didn't know what the hell I thought I was doing. . . . I take it back—I knew exactly what I was doing. The first draft was in the third person and then I changed it into the first person. I rewrote *The Wig* in twenty-nine days in New York City. Twenty-nine days, that was the happiest period of my life (laughing). I never felt so happy in my whole life. One of the interesting things about the novel is that all of it was pure imagination, yet they came to pass—the slang, the see-through plastic dresses, abortions, vibrators.

Have you felt the influence of writers who are not your contemporaries?

The only one I would say is Hemingway. There's nobody else. I've learned many things, including from Uncle Norman [Mailer], who I think is as sweet as sugar. But I'd say no one else.

What interested you about Katherine Anne Porter's fiction?

I suppose it was her style, something offbeat that I could identify with. In the *Paris Review* interview Katherine Anne said that when she was ten years old, someone asked her what she wanted to be when she grew up. She said that she didn't know, but she shouted, "I want glory." And that's what I am trying for.

When did you first start writing?

That was in high school, little pieces called "So Long, Buddy." When I read it in class everyone would start, and one of the students said that I had copied it out of *Reader's Digest.* I was furious because even back then *Reader's Digest* was not a magazine I would have read (laughing). At the same time, I was flattered. The story was about a soldier with a limp. I was reading Hemingway at the time and I remember being very impressed with "Indian Camp."

What did you do when you finished high school? You didn't go to college, did you?

No, no. What did I do when I got out of high school? Well, in those days they didn't have draft dodgers (laughing), so I went into the army. That wasn't out of high school directly, though. I just sort of hung around, as they say.

What kind of experiences did you have in the army?

I would say that mine were really good. After I learned to survive I had a marvelous time.

How long were you in the army?

Two years. One year in the United States and one year in Korea. The first two days were really something else. On the third day a soldier told me that if you stay in the army you learn what you have to do and what you can get away with. You have to be a politician. I always remembered that. The army was a fantastic experience and I don't regret it at all. I didn't see any fighting because when I got there all the fighting was over. All the fighting that occurred took place in the company that I was in. I was always that strange one, the one that was different; that created problems for me, but I always won. It was a game of wits. I was not only a loner but I looked much younger than I was, and I was black and little and skinny. There was no one to protect me but myself—no black buddies, no white buddies. No one. Just me.

Will you ever try writing about your army experiences?

I've thought of it, yes. Doing a comic novel (laughing). One of my friends suggested that's what I should do. Maybe one of these days I will.

Did you ever try writing straight realistic fiction?

(Laughing) I think perhaps once upon a time. That was only natural, and it was very bad. That was when I was at a writer's colony with James Jones. It was a Korean War novel that Putnam's was interested in. But they were also interested in getting Jim. If they could have latched on to Jim, they would have published my novel. Mine was a James-Jones-type novel, except for certain set pieces of poetic stuff that I do. It was just a straight, hard-hitting war novel.

I wonder whether you ever worry that your innovations might cause some people to get lost?

Most of them were lost. Most of them, the few readers who read **The Wig,** are still lost. But I thought it was perfect and I thought that I was communicating. The most shocking thing was when I was out at the University of California—Irvine branch, I thought that the young black ones would be aware, that they would understand it. Oh, no. When Lester gets castrated at the end? They said, "How dare you end it that way." But since then I occasionally receive a letter from someone who understood it. The best review of it was by the late Conrad Knickerbocker in the *New York Times* [see excerpt dated 1966]. He was a man I admired for many years. When I was a messenger I used to think, if I ever publish a novel, I would like him to review it. And it so happened that he understood it so well that . . . (laughing) it was uncomfortable.

What has been the reaction of other black writers to your work?

Among the younger black writers like Ishmael Reed and Cecil Brown—that's one thing that makes me very happy—they like it. That makes me feel good.

Have you received any criticism from critics who say that such fiction will not aid in a revolution?

No, not from critics. But quite often, from young blacks in colleges where I might be lecturing. How juvenile they are. A young man once told me that he wanted to be a playwright and start a theater in the streets. He wasn't even going to use professional actors. Beautiful. But he regretted that he couldn't continue with the classes in playwrighting with William Inge, of all people. Can you imagine? How tragic that is. To tell me about your revolutionary theater in the streets and then to regret this!

Do you see any black writers emerging as true cultural figureheads; such as, perhaps, LeRoi Jones?

Well . . . oh, oh, LeRoi, what is there to say? I think he's a good man. And I think he's a very good playwright, and he's very concerned. He's doing marvelous things up in Newark. But he's the only one: look at the thing with Eldridge Cleaver and George Jackson who just died. There's so much infighting. But it's all only for the moment. Next year it may be Cold Dog Eskimo.

What kind of writing habits do you have?

(Laughing) I have the worst . . . well, not the worst, but I place among the top ten. It depends upon how I feel, number one. I may screw around all night long until about midnight. Then when I start to work, I work. I'll build and design houses for maybe two days. And then for ten days I'll do nothing but write.

Your next book will be a collection of pieces from The Village Voice?

The Village Voice is the only thing that has kept me going. Without it I don't know what would happen to me. **Absolutely Nothing to Get Alarmed About** is a collection of old *Village Voice* pieces. Some of them I've changed. It reads exactly like **The Messenger.** It was originally called *Black Studies* but the salesmen thought that it would get put on the wrong bookshclvcs.

What exactly is the difference between your journalism and your fiction?

It's a very thin line. I intend to break every cocksucking heart in America with **Absolutely Nothing to Get Alarmed About.** And I think I'm slowly but surely succeeding.

My last question: what is a "paranoid ice cream bar"? It appears in The Wig *if you remember.*

What is a "paranoid ice cream bar"? I don't know (laughing). Well, ah . . . . What's a paranoid ice cream bar? There's no paranoid ice cream bars. But maybe there are. If Good Humor doesn't have them, maybe they will. Especially if they've read **The Wig.** I don't know; it's like when everybody is getting *on* a train, I'm going the opposite way. (pp. 247-57)

> *Charles Wright and John O'Brien, in an interview in* Interviews with Black Writers, *edited by John O'Brien, Liveright, 1973, pp. 245-58.*

Anatole Broyard (essay date 1973)

[*In the following excerpt, Broyard negatively reviews* Absolutely Nothing to Get Alarmed About *and wonders: "Why do many black writers deal only in*

*extreme experiences? . . . Don't any blacks lead bour-
geois or even ordinary working-class lives?"*]

Somewhere under all these affectations there's a promising black author named Charles Wright. He says he's
about 40, which means he's pretty old to be promising.
You would think with two highly praised books already
to his credit, he would be further along in the evolution
of his style. He should have outgrown for example lines
like "pierced with cut crystal sensitivity"; "the uric
sperm of those years has flooded my mind"; "hoarded
prejudices beget slaves who impale their masters on the
arrow of time"; "mankind prepares not to scale the
summit but to take the downward path into the great
valley of the void"; "life's eyedropper is being sterilized
with ant [urine]." . . .

When is the last time anybody speaking his own
language ever talked about scaling summits? Has any
black man outside of politics or the church used the
word scale in that sense in the last 50 years? What is
life's eyedropper, anyway, and why is it being sterilized
with ant urine? . . .

Sonny Liston had better lines, on the average, than
you'll find in *Absolutely Nothing to Get Alarmed About.*
As an uneducated prize fighter like Liston proved, there
is a rich black idiom, but so few black writers use it.
Here and there, Mr. Wright shows that he has a good ear
for genuine speech rhythms, but he keeps falling instead
into a forced, amphetamine splutter or a drone of
Cadillac oratory. In the middle of a nice blues-like scene
with an ironic obbligato, he'll remember that he has
read Faulkner—but it will probably be Faulkner crossed
with a Lower East Side social worker.

When he's relaxed and moving naturally, Mr. Wright
can bring life—sad, bleak, painful, embarrassing or
funny life—to the drug, wino, East Village and Bowery
scenes that are his territory. (Much of this book appeared as separate essays in *The Village Voice.*) Sometimes he's so good-humored in these unpropitious
environments that he makes it sound as if being black
was a form of entertainment. And perhaps it is, under
certain circumstances. Perhaps the human comedy is
even funnier when your laughter has a touch of hysteria
in it. At other times, though, Mr. Wright sounds all
smug and buttoned up. Although he rarely *is* alone, he's
always telling us how much he *wants* to be alone, how
sufficient unto himself he is, how far beyond the
blandishments of poor, deluded humanity. He pontifi-
cates as if meditation was his thing, yet he's always
popping dexies or drinking enough for half a dozen
Madison Avenue executives.

As you read on in *Absolutely Nothing to Get Alarmed
About,* a question is likely to arise in your mind. Why do
many black writers deal only in extreme experiences?
It's too easy: the drama is already there, and all too often
it is the *same* drama. Don't any blacks lead bourgeois, or
even ordinary working-class lives? Mr. Wright's cards
are so stacked that, even when we know the elements of

the scene are real, we feel that the characters are self-
consciously posing too. The first to protest against
stereotyping, many black writers seem determined to
create one of their own.

The day has come, also, to reconsider one of their
fundamental propositions: that "whitey" will never let
you forget you're black. In Mr. Wright's case, the patent
leather shoe is on the other foot. A further assumption
that needs re-examination is the notion that a life
thrown away constitutes a tragedy, a "horror," as the
author would say. If a man shoots heroin into his arm,
or a woman takes up prostitution, it is still possible that
he or she, individually, is responsible and not "society."
They are not always "forced" into it. If we take that line,
who shall we blame for forcing the forcers into *their*
special brands of unhappiness? Are we seriously to
suppose that all American society is a hierarchy of
imposed unhappiness with President Nixon at the top, a
primum mobile?

Mr. Wright is at his best in his throw-away lines, like the
time he described two junkies trying to sell him a pair of
ice-skates. When he sums up a particular kind of white
girl as having "a ban-the-bomb-air," we feel that, yes,
we've met her. We're even willing to forgive him his
dangling clauses when he goes down to the Chelsea
health center to show up a busy surrealist day at the
V.D. clinic. We want to like him—he's appealing in his
cranky way—but he keeps fading out of focus on us. He
insists on blowing both hot and cool, and the two don't
jive.

At one point in his hot phase, he says that blacks have
nothing to lose but their lives—and it ain't necessarily
so. Mr. Wright, for example, can lose his audience, his
talent, his dignity, his sense of humor—oh, any number
of things.

> *Anatole Broyard, "It Ain't Necessarily So,"
> in* The New York Times, *April 9, 1973, p.
> 35.*

FURTHER READING

Schulz, Max F. "The Aesthetics of Anxiety; and, The
Conformist Heroes of Bruce Jay Friedman and Charles
Wright." In his *Black Humor Fiction of the Sixties: A
Pluralistic Definition of Man and His World,* pp. 91-123.
Athens, Ohio: Ohio University Press, 1973.
      Compares the protagonist in Friedman's *Stern* with
      Lester Jefferson in Wright's *The Wig.*

Sedlack, Robert P. "Jousting with Rats: Charles Wright's
The Wig." *Satire Newsletter* 7, No. 1 (Fall 1969): 37-9.
      Contends that the purpose of *The Wig* is "to reveal the
      futility of a black man's attempt to succeed in the
      white world."

Richard Wright

1908-1960

American novelist, autobiographer, short story writer, nonfiction writer, essayist, scriptwriter, dramatist, poet, and editor.

A seminal figure in black literature, Wright has been called one of the most powerful and influential writers of twentieth-century America. He was one of the first writers to portray—often in graphic, brutal accounts—the dehumanizing effects of racism on blacks. His stories usually center on alienated and impoverished black men who, denied freedom and personal identity, lash out against society. Scholars have hailed *Native Son* (1940) and *Black Boy: A Record of Childhood and Youth* (1945) as Wright's most accomplished works. Critic Irving Howe declared: "The day *Native Son* appeared, American culture was changed forever." Of *Black Boy,* another reviewer simply announced: "[This] is a masterpiece." Although some critics fault the works as too violent and unabashedly propagandistic, such prominent writers as James Baldwin and Ralph Ellison consider them essential works of black literature. "Wright's stories of helpless or long-suffering blacks victimized by societal and individual white brutality mark the beginning of a new era in black fiction," William Peden observed, "and even his least important pieces contain unforgettable scenes and characters that burn their way into the reader's consciousness."

Wright's childhood was harsh and filled with fear. He was born on a plantation near Natchez, Mississippi, in 1908. His mother was a former schoolteacher and his father a sharecropper who drank heavily. When Wright was six years old, his father abandoned the family, forcing his mother to work low-paying, menial jobs. Life in the South was difficult, and Wright and his younger brother Leon frequently went without food. In his autobiography, *Black Boy,* Wright recalled a familiar childhood event: "I would feel hunger nudging my ribs, twisting my empty guts until they ached. I would grow dizzy and my vision would dim." Wright's first indelible encounter with racial hatred and violence occurred during the family's brief stay with an uncle, who was murdered by a group of white men trying to seize his property. Fearing for their own lives, the Wrights fled to West Helena, Arkansas; young Wright was about eight or nine years old. They eventually returned to Mississippi, but Wright went to live with his grandmother when his mother became ill. Grandmother Wilson was a religious Seventh-Day Adventist, and she forced Wright to pray and attend church so that his soul may be saved. He was resentful of her religious fervor and would later deride Christianity in his work.

Wright was largely self-educated. His formal schooling, frequently interrupted as he moved from town to town, ended when he was fifteen. Thereafter, he read widely, beginning with H. L. Mencken, whose books he obtained from a "whites only" public library by forging a note: "Dear Madam: Will you please let this nigger boy have some books by H. L. Mencken?" Wright was strongly affected by Mencken, whose trenchant language and outspoken critical opinions awakened him to the possibility of social protest through writing. He also read the fiction of Fedor Dostoevski, Sinclair Lewis, Sherwood Anderson, and Theodore Dreiser. In 1927 Wright left the South for Chicago. He worked at various menial jobs, all the while reading and writing extensively. During the Depression he joined the WPA Writers' Project and became active in the Communist Party, contributing articles, poems, and short stories to various communist newspapers. Several years later, however, Wright found himself repelled by the narrowness and rigidity of his fellow communists, whose minds he found "sealed against new ideas, new facts, new feelings, new attitudes, new hints at ways to live. They denounced books they could never understand, and doctrines they could not pronounce." In 1944, after witnessing the trial of a party member for ideological "deviationism," Wright resigned from the party.

Until 1938, Wright's work appeared only in left-wing publications such as *New Masses* and *Left Front*. In that year, *Story* magazine offered a $500 prize for the best book-length manuscript by a writer connected with the Federal Writers' Project. Wright's collection of four long stories inspired by the life of a black communist he had known in Chicago won the contest and was published as *Uncle Tom's Children: Four Novellas* (1938). Malcolm Cowley found the book "heartening, as evidence of a vigorous new talent, and terrifying as the expression of a racial hatred that has never ceased to grow and gets no chance to die." All of the stories (a fifth, "Bright and Morning Star," was added to subsequent editions) deal with the oppression of black people in the South, of the violence of whites against blacks, and the violence to which the black characters are driven by their victimization. Some critics found the stories in *Uncle Tom's Children* too melodramatic and marred by the infusion of Communist ideology. But Houston A. Baker, in his *Black Literature in America,* wrote: "Wright showed a mastery of style and a dramatic sense far superior to that of most of his black contemporaries and predecessors and on a par with that of his most talented white contemporaries. The violence and the terrible effects of prejudice are perhaps nowhere more skillfully set forth."

Although *Uncle Tom's Children* was well received, Wright was dissatisfied with the public's response. He realized, he wrote later, "that I had written a book which even bankers' daughters could read and weep over and feel good. I swore to myself that if I ever wrote another book, no one would weep over it; that it would be so hard and deep that they would have to face it without the consolation of tears." The book he wrote next was *Native Son,* the story of Bigger Thomas, a young black man in Chicago who accidentally murders a white woman and is condemned to death. To depict the dehumanization of blacks in the "hard and deep" manner he wished, Wright avoided making his protagonist a sympathetic character. As reviewer Margaret Marshall wrote in the *Nation*: "Mr. Wright has chosen for his 'hero,' not a sophisticated Negro who at least understands his predicament and can adapt himself to it, but a 'bad nigger,' a 'black ape,' who is only dimly aware of his extra-human status and therefore completely at the mercy of the impulses it generates.... Mr. Wright has laid bare, with a ruthlessness that spares neither race, the lower depths of the human and social relationship of blacks and whites.... It is not pleasant to feel at the end that one is an accessory to the crimes of Bigger Thomas; but that feeling is impressive evidence of the power of Mr. Wright's indictment with its cutting and accurate title of 'Native Son.'"

Bigger Thomas is a young, petty thief who is hired as a chauffeur by a rich white man. He drives his employer's daughter, Mary, to a political lecture. He meets Mary's friend Jan, a white communist who insists on treating Bigger as an equal. Bigger interprets Jan's "kindness" as mockery: "Were they making fun of him? What was it that they wanted? . . . He was very conscious of his black skin and there was in him a prodding conviction that Jan and men like him had made it so that he would be conscious of that black skin. Did not white people despise black skin? Then why was Jan doing this?" Bigger drives Mary and Jan, at their insistence, to Ernie's Kitchen Shack, "one of those places where colored people eat." At the restaurant, Mary gets drunk; Bigger takes her home and carries her to her room. When Mary's blind mother enters the bedroom, Bigger accidentally smothers Mary while trying to keep her from revealing his presence. He burns Mary's body in a furnace, then conceives a scheme to extort money from her parents by pretending to have kidnapped her. When Mary's charred bones are discovered, Bigger kills his girlfriend, Bessie, who was his accomplice in the kidnap plot. He is captured by the police and, despite an eloquent defense by his communist lawyer, convicted and condemned. The lawyer argues that Bigger cannot be held responsible for his crimes, that the greater guilt lies with the society that would not accept him as a full human being and so drove him to his brutal acts. Bigger feels that he has at last found a measure of freedom in the act of murder: for the first time in his life, he feels truly alive and unafraid.

James Baldwin, who began his writing career as Wright's protégé, called *Native Son* "the most powerful and celebrated statement we have yet had of what it means to be a Negro in America." But he also criticized Wright for stereotyping Bigger Thomas and for failing to convey a sense of "group reality" in *Native Son*: "Bigger has no discernible relationship to himself, to his own life, to his own people, nor to any other people.... It is remarkable that, though we follow him step by step from the tenement room to the death cells, we know as little about him when this journey is ended as we did when it began.... What is missing in this situation and in the representation of his psychology... is any revelatory apprehension of Bigger as one of the Negro's realities or as one of the Negro's roles. This failure is part of the... failure to convey any sense of Negro life as a continuing and complex group reality." Darryl Pinckney, in the *Village Voice,* argued otherwise: "*Native Son* is unmatched in its power. The rage, the human misery, seizes the mind and there is no relief. It is not true, as Baldwin claims, that Bigger Thomas, the doomed, frustrated black boy, is just another stereotype.... Baldwin criticizes Wright for not giving us black life, black community, the sense of shared experience.... It is wrong to read this novel as a matter of group reality, a matter of race. Bigger had no real relations with other blacks. Everyone was an enemy.... [Wright] claimed he valued the 'state of abandonment, aloneness.' In this he was, finally, a true product of Western culture.... In *Native Son* he gave us a lasting record of the howl of modern man."

As popular and acclaimed as *Native Son* is, it is *Black Boy* that has garnered critics' highest praise. *Black Boy* has been called a masterpiece. A work structured in many ways like a novel, the book recounts Wright's experiences as a youth in the South. "In scene after scene," noted Morris Dickstein in Gates of Eden, "Wright represents his younger self as a rebellious misfit.... He makes an intense effort of self-restraint, but try as he will there is always a provocative hint of pride and self-respect, a touch of the uppity nigger about him. A latecomer to the white world, he is unable to quite master the shuffling, degraded, but apparently contented manner that will tell whites he not only knows his place but loves it." Ralph Ellison described Black Boy thus: "Imagine Bigger Thomas projecting his own life in lucid prose, guided, say, by the insights of Marx and Freud, and you have an idea of this autobiography." In this work, Wright attacks both white oppression and the predatory nature of members of his own race. He rebukes his strict religious upbringing and reprimands blacks for their servile response to racial subjugation. While some reviewers contended that Black Boy offered a bleak, one-sided view of black life in the South, Raymond Kennedy argued: "This, with few exceptions, is precisely how race relations are in the Southern States: clean-cut black and white. The Negroes must either surrender and allow themselves to be spiritually stunted and deformed, or they must get out of the South."

After the commercial success of Native Son and Black Boy, Wright moved with his second wife and daughter to Paris, France, in 1947. Here, he found refuge from the racial tensions of the United States and became friends with several noted intellectuals, including Simone de Beauvoir, Jean-Paul Sartre, and Albert Camus. Wright's literary output during this period, including the novels The Outsider (1953), Savage Holiday (1954), and The Long Dream (1958), is generally considered inferior to his earlier achievements. Many critics attribute Wright's creative decline to his newfound interest in existentialism, which they believe stripped his work of its urgency and power. Gloria Bramwell declared: "Wright, an emotional writer, could paint a stunning picture of the Negro's plight but when he attempted to intellectualize it he embraced it from the wrong angle, from the inside out rather than in terms of his own characters." The Outsider, the first novel Wright produced after leaving the United States, is one of the first existentialist novels written by an American author. Avoiding racial issues in this work, Wright recounted the story of a man who joins the Communist Party and kills several of its members in his search for identity and meaning. Critics generally dismiss The Outsider as an ambitious but unsuccessful work. Wright's next novel, Savage Holiday, is a psychological thriller about a white insurance salesman who becomes a symbol for modern alienated humanity. Few critics reviewed this book, and those who did deemed it Wright's least effective work. Wright followed Savage Holiday with The Long Dream, a novel that returns to his early thematic concerns. Set in Mississippi, this work depicts the psychological growth of Fishbelly, a middle-class black youth who must come to terms with his father's amoral business practices and the racial conflicts ravaging the South.

After serving a prison sentence for a crime he did not commit, Fishbelly leaves for France, fleeing the violence and oppression of his past. Like Wright's other expatriate novels, The Long Dream received unfavorable notices from reviewers, many of whom argued that Wright had lost touch with the black American experience. Eight Men (1961), a posthumously published collection of short stories, contains "The Man Who Lived Underground," which is often regarded as Wright's most important fictional work of the 1950s. Reminiscent of Fedor Dostoevski's Notes from the Underground, this story concerns a black man who attempts to escape punishment for a crime of which he is innocent by hiding in the city sewer system.

In addition to his novels and short stories, Wright produced several nonfiction works: 12 Million Black Voices: A Folk History of the Negro in the United States (1941), a textual and photographic history of racial prejudice in the United States; Black Power: A Record of Reactions in a Land of Pathos (1954), a work that recalls Wright's visit to Takoradi, a British colony in Africa where a black man had been appointed prime minister; and The Color Curtain: A Report on the Bandung Conference (1956), Wright's reflections on a conference held in Indonesia by the free nations of the Third World. Pagan Spain (1957) recounts Wright's bitterness over the poverty and corruption he observed while traveling in Spain, and White Man, Listen! (1957) contains four lectures by Wright on race relations. Wright died in Paris at the age of fifty-two on November 28, 1960.

Wright's reputation ebbed during the 1950s as younger black writers such as James Baldwin and Ralph Ellison gained in popularity. But in the 1960s, with the growth of the militant black consciousness movement, there was a resurgence of interest in Wright's work. Wright's place in American literature remains controversial: some contend that his writing is of sociological and historical, rather than literary, interest. In the judgment of many critics, however, Wright remains the most influential black protest writer in America. According to Ellison, Wright "converted the American Negro impulse toward self-annihilation and 'going-underground' into a will to confront the world, to evaluate his experience honestly and throw his findings unashamedly into the guilty conscience of America."

(For further information about Wright's life and works, see Black Writers; Contemporary Authors, Vol. 108; Contemporary Literary Criticism, Vols. 1, 3, 4, 9, 14, 21, 48; Dictionary of Literary Biography Documentary Series, Vol. 2; and Short Story Criticism, Vol. 2.)

PRINCIPAL WORKS

Uncle Tom's Children: Four Novellas (short stories) 1938; also published as Uncle Tom's Children: Five Long Stories [enlarged edition], 1940
*Native Son (novel) 1940

"How Bigger Was Born" (essay) 1940; published in
    periodical *The Saturday Review of Literature*
*12 Million Black Voices: A Folk History of the Negro in
    the United States* (nonfiction) 1941
Black Boy: A Record of Childhood and Youth (autobiog-
    raphy) 1945
The Outsider (novel) 1953
Black Power: A Record of Reactions in a Land of Pathos
    (nonfiction) 1954
Savage Holiday (novel) 1954
The Color Curtain: A Report on the Bandung Conference
    (nonfiction) 1956
Pagan Spain (nonfiction) 1957
White Man, Listen! (lectures) 1957
The Long Dream (novel) 1958
†*Eight Men* (short stories) 1961
Lawd Today (novel) 1963
Daddy Goodness [with Louis Sapin] (drama) 1968
American Hunger (autobiography) 1977
The Richard Wright Reader (essays, novel excerpts,
    letters, and poetry) 1978
‡*Richard Wright: Works.* 2 vols. [edited by Arnold
    Rampersad] (novels, essays, and autobiography)
    1991

*This work was adapted for the stage in 1941 and made into a
  movie in 1951 and again in 1986.
†This work contains "The Man Who Lived Underground,"
  Wright's most acclaimed short story.
‡Vols. 55 and 56 of "Library of America." Includes restored
  texts of *Native Son, Lawd Today,* and *The Outsider,*
  incorporating passages deleted or altered at time of first
  publication.

Richard Wright (letter date 1938)

[*The following letter was written by Wright in 1938 to
his literary agent, Paul Revere Reynolds, in New York
City. Here, Wright discusses contract negotiations for*
Native Son.]

My dear Mr. Reynolds:

A faulty phone connection no doubt made it difficult for
us to hear each other Saturday, so I'm sketching the
facts about the novel in a letter.

As I said, the first draft of the book is done, amounting
to now some 576 pages. When it is finished, it will be
somewhat less. I took this first draft to Mr. Whit Burnett
of Story Press (you remember that my book is being
printed under the double imprint of Harper' and Story
Press?). Mr. Burnett read it and passed it on to Harper's.
When I submitted the script I told them that it was not
finished. My main object in letting them see it in its
present condition was to ask for an advance. Both Story
Press and Harper's seem to like the book, and Mr.
Edward Aswell, the editor at Harper's said that he would
be willing to sign a contract for it. As for an advance, he

suggested $250 and asked me if I thought that ample. I
did not give him any definite answer, but told him I
would let you talk to him about it.

I have reason to believe that they like what I'm doing, so
I think that perhaps a little more than $250 can be
gotten. If, however, they balk, I'm willing to take
whatever you can get as an advance from them.

I have found no satisfactory title for the book as yet. The
title at present is **Native Son.** I'm going to try to find a
more colorful one before the book is published. Meanwhile, Story Press will try to find an appropriate one
also.

I shall keep in mind the idea of making at least three
copies of the book, so that you may have one to send to
the movie people and to England.

Mr. Aswell wants the book for spring publication. I'm
going to try as hard as possible to have it ready by then.
He understands, however, that if I cannot have it ready
by spring, I'll have it ready for early fall.

I hope that this is enough information for you in your
dealings with Harper's. If not, if you drop me a line at
the above address, I shall be more than glad to come in
and discuss it further.

                          Sincerely yours,
                          Richard Wright

*Richard Wright, in a letter to Paul Revere
Reynolds on October 23, 1938, in* Dictionary
of Literary Biography Documentary Series,
Vol. 2, *edited by Margaret A. Van Antwerp,
Gale Research Company, 1982, p. 401.*

Richard Wright (essay date 1940)

[*The following excerpt is from an essay that originally
appeared in* The Saturday Review of Literature *in
1940. Here, Wright reveals his inspiration for Bigger
Thomas and discusses his initial reluctance and fear
in publishing* Native Son.]

I am not so pretentious as to imagine that it is possible
for me to account completely for my own book, **Native
Son.** But I am going to try to account for as much of it as
I can, the sources of it, the material that went into it,
and my own years' long changing attitude toward that
material. (p. vii)

The birth of Bigger Thomas goes back to my childhood,
and there was not just one Bigger, but many of them,
more than I could count and more than you suspect. But
let me start with the first Bigger, whom I shall call Bigger
No. 1.

When I was a bareheaded, barefoot kid in Jackson,
Mississippi, there was a boy who terrorized me and all
of the boys I played with. If we were playing games, he
would saunter up and snatch from us our balls, bats,

spinning tops, and marbles. We would stand around pouting, sniffling, trying to keep back our tears, begging for our playthings. But Bigger would refuse. We never demanded that he give them back; we were afraid, and Bigger was bad. We had seen him clout boys when he was angry and we did not want to run that risk. We never recovered our toys unless we flattered him and made him feel that he was superior to us. Then, perhaps, if he felt like it, he condescended, threw them at us and then gave each of us a swift kick in the bargain, just to make us feel his utter contempt.

That was the way Bigger No. 1 lived. His life was a continuous challenge to others. At all times he *took* his way, right or wrong, and those who contradicted him had him to fight. And never was he happier than when he had someone cornered and at his mercy; it seemed that the deepest meaning of his squalid life was in him at such times.

I don't know what the fate of Bigger No. 1 was .... But I suspect that his end was violent. Anyway, he left a marked impression upon me; maybe it was because I longed secretly to be like him and was afraid. I don't know.

If I had known only one Bigger I would not have written **Native Son.** Let me call the next one Bigger No. 2; he was about seventeen and tougher than the first Bigger. Since I, too, had grown older, I was a little less afraid of him. And the hardness of this Bigger No. 2 was not directed toward me or the other Negroes, but toward the whites who ruled the South. He bought clothes and food on credit and would not pay for them. He lived in the dingy shacks of the white landlords and refused to pay rent. Of course, he had no money, but neither did we. We did without the necessities of life and starved ourselves, but he never would. When we asked him why he acted as he did, he would tell us (as though we were little children in a kindergarten) that the white folks had everything and he had nothing. Further, he would tell us that we were fools not to get what we wanted while we were alive in this world. We would listen and silently agree. We longed to believe and act as he did, but we were afraid .... Bigger No. 2 wanted to live and he did; he was in prison the last time I heard from him.

There was Bigger No. 3, whom the white folks called a "bad nigger." He carried his life in his hands in a literal fashion. I once worked as a ticket-taker in a Negro movie house ... and many times Bigger No. 3 came to the door and gave my arm a hard pinch and walked into the theater. Resentfully and silently, I'd nurse my bruised arm. Presently, the proprietor would come over and ask how things were going. I'd point into the darkened theater and say: "Bigger's in there." "Did he pay?" the proprietor would ask. "No, sir," I'd answer. The proprietor would pull down the corners of his lips and speak through his teeth: "We'll kill that goddamn nigger one of these days." And the episode would end right there. But later on Bigger No. 3 was killed during

the days of Prohibition: while delivering liquor to a customer he was shot through the back by a white cop.

And then there was Bigger No. 4, whose only law was death. The Jim Crow laws of the South were not for him. But as he laughed and cursed and broke them, he knew that some day he'd have to pay for his freedom. His rebellious spirit made him violate all the taboos and consequently he always oscillated between moods of intense elation and depression.... He had no job, for he regarded digging ditches for fifty cents a day as slavery. "I can't live on that," he would say. Ofttimes I'd find him reading a book; he would stop and in a joking, wistful, and cynical manner ape the antics of the white folks. Generally, he'd end his mimicry in a depressed state and say: "The white folks won't let us do nothing." Bigger No. 4 was sent to the asylum for the insane.

Then there was Bigger No. 5, who always rode the Jim Crow streetcars without paying and sat wherever he pleased. I remember one morning his getting into a streetcar ... and sitting in the white section. The conductor went to him and said: "Come on, nigger. Move over where you belong. Can't you read?" Bigger answered: "Naw, I can't read." The conductor flared up: "Get out of that seat!" Bigger took out his knife, opened it, held it nonchalantly in his hand, and replied: "Make me." The conductor turned red, blinked, clenched his fists, and walked away, stammering: "The goddamn scum of the earth!" A small angry conference of white men took place in the front of the car and the Negroes sitting in the Jim Crow section overheard: "That's that Bigger Thomas nigger and you'd better leave 'im alone." The Negroes experienced an intense flash of pride and the streetcar moved on its journey without incident. I don't know what happened to Bigger No. 5. But I can guess.

The Bigger Thomases were the only Negroes I know of who consistently violated the Jim Crow laws of the South and got away with it, at least for a sweet brief spell. Eventually, the whites who restricted their lives made them pay a terrible price. They were shot, hanged, maimed, lynched, and generally hounded until they were either dead or their spirits broken. (pp. viii-xi)

[Why] did Bigger revolt? No explanation based upon a hard and fast rule of conduct can be given. But there were always two factors psychologically dominant in his personality. First, through some quirk of circumstance, he had become estranged from the religion and the folk culture of his race. Second, he was trying to react to and answer the call of the dominant civilization whose glitter came to him through the newspapers, magazines, radios, movies, and the mere imposing sight and sound of daily American life. In many respects his emergence as a distinct type was inevitable.

As I grew older, I became familiar with the Bigger Thomas conditioning and its numerous shadings no matter where I saw it in Negro life. It was not, as I have already said, as blatant or extreme as in the originals;

but it was there, nevertheless, like an undeveloped negative.

Sometimes, in areas far removed from Mississippi, I'd hear a Negro say: "I wish I didn't have to live this way. I feel like I want to burst." Then the anger would pass; he would go back to his job and try to eke out a few pennies to support his wife and children.

Sometimes I'd hear a Negro say: "God, I wish I had a flag and a country of my own." But that mood would soon vanish and he would go his way placidly enough.

Sometimes I'd hear a Negro ex-soldier say: "What in hell did I fight in the war for? They segregated me even when I was offering my life for my country." But he, too, like the others, would soon forget, would become caught up in the tense grind of struggling for bread. (pp. xiii-xiv)

It was not until I went to live in Chicago that I first thought seriously of writing of Bigger Thomas. Two items of my experience combined to make me aware of Bigger as a meaningful and prophetic symbol. First, being free of the daily pressure of the Dixie environment, I was able to come into possession of my own feelings. Second, my contact with the labor movement and its ideology made me see Bigger clearly and feel what he meant.

I made the discovery that Bigger Thomas was not black all the time; he was white, too, and there were literally millions of him, everywhere. The extension of my sense of the personality of Bigger was the pivot of my life; it altered the complexion of my existence. I became conscious, at first dimly, and then later on with increasing clarity and conviction, of a vast, muddied pool of human life in America. It was as though I had put on a pair of spectacles whose power was that of an x-ray enabling me to see deeper into the lives of men. Whenever I picked up a newspaper, I'd no longer feel that I was reading of the doings of whites alone (Negroes are rarely mentioned in the press unless they've committed some crime!), but of a complex struggle for life going on in my country, a struggle in which I was involved. I sensed, too, that the Southern scheme of oppression was but an appendage of a far vaster and in many respects more ruthless and impersonal commodity-profit machinc. (pp. xiv-xv)

As my mind extended in this general and abstract manner, it was fed with even more vivid and concrete examples of the lives of Bigger Thomas. The urban environment of Chicago, affording a more stimulating life, made the Negro Bigger Thomases react more violently than even in the South. More than ever I began to see and understand the environmental factors which made for this extreme conduct. It was not that Chicago segregated Negroes more than the South, but that Chicago had more to offer, that Chicago's physical aspect—noisy, crowded, filled with the sense of power and fulfillment—did so much more to dazzle the mind with a taunting sense of possible achievement that the segregation it did impose brought forth from Bigger a reaction more obstreperous than in the South. (p. xv)

There is in me a memory of reading an interesting pamphlet telling of the friendship of Gorky and Lenin in exile. The booklet told of how Lenin and Gorky were walking down a London street. Lenin turned to Gorky and, pointing, said: "Here is *their* Big Ben." "There is *their* Westminister Abbey." "There is *their* library." And at once, while reading that passage, my mind stopped, teased, challenged with the effort to remember, to associate widely disparate but meaningful experiences in my life. For a moment nothing would come, but I remained convinced that I had heard the meaning of those words sometime, somewhere before. Then, with a sudden glow of satisfaction of having gained a little more knowledge about the world in which I lived, I'd end up by saying: "That's Bigger. That's the Bigger Thomas reaction."

In both instances the deep sense of exclusion was identical. The feeling of looking at things with a painful and unwarrantable nakedness was an experience, I learned, that transcended national and racial boundaries. It was this intolerable sense of feeling and understanding so much, and yet living on a plane of social reality where the look of a world which one did not make or own struck one with a blinding objectivity and tangibility, that made me grasp the revolutionary impulse in my life and the lives of those about me and far away.

I remember reading a passage in a book dealing with old Russia which said: "We must be ready to make endless sacrifices if we are to be able to overthrow the Czar." And again I'd say to myself: "I've heard that somewhere, sometime before." And again I'd hear Bigger Thomas, far away and long ago, telling some white man who was trying to impose upon him: "I'll kill you and go to hell and pay for it." While living in America I heard from far away Russia the bitter accents of tragic calculation of how much human life and suffering it would cost a man to live as a man in a world that denied him the right to live with dignity. Actions and feelings of men ten thousand miles from home helped me to understand the moods and impulses of those walking the streets of Chicago and Dixie.

I am not saying that I heard any talk of revolution in the South when I was a kid there. But I did hear the lispings, the whispers, the mutters which some day, under one stimulus or another, will surely grow into open revolt unless the conditions which produce Bigger Thomases are changed. (pp. xvii-xviii)

All Bigger Thomases, white and black, felt tense, afraid, nervous, hysterical, and restless. From far away Nazi Germany and old Russia had come to me items of knowledge that told me that certain modern experiences were creating types of personalities whose existence ignored racial and national lines of demarcation, that these personalities carried with them a more universal drama-element than anything I'd ever encountered before; that these personalities were mainly imposed upon men and women living in a world whose fundamental assumptions could no longer be taken for granted: a world ridden with national and class strife; a world whose metaphysical meanings had vanished; a world in which God no longer existed as a daily focal point of men's lives; a world in which men could no longer retain their faith in an ultimate hereafter. It was a highly geared world whose nature was conflict and action, a world whose limited area and vision imperiously urged men to satisfy their organisms, a world that existed on a plane of animal sensation alone. (p. xix)

From these items I drew my first political conclusions about Bigger: I felt that Bigger, an American product, a native son of this land, carried within him the potentialities of either Communism or Fascism. I don't mean to say that the Negro boy I depicted in *Native Son* is either a Communist or a Fascist. He is not either. But he is product of a dislocated society; he is a dispossessed and disinherited man; he is all of this, and he lives amid the greatest possible plenty on earth and he is looking and feeling for a way out. Whether he'll follow some gaudy, hysterical leader who'll promise rashly to fill the void in him, or whether he'll come to an understanding with the millions of his kindred fellow workers under trade-union or revolutionary guidance depends upon the future drift of events in America. But, granting the emotional state, the tensity, the fear, the hate, the impatience, the sense of exclusion, the ache for violent action, the emotional and cultural hunger, Bigger Thomas, conditioned as his organism is, will not become an ardent, or even a lukewarm, supporter of the *status quo.*

The difference between Bigger's tensity and the German variety is that Bigger's, due to America's educational restrictions on the bulk of her Negro population, is in a nascent state, not yet articulate. And the difference between Bigger's longing for self-identification and the Russian principle of self-determination is that Bigger's, due to the effects of American oppression, which has not allowed for the forming of deep ideas of solidarity among Negroes, is still in a state of individual anger and hatred. Here, I felt, was *drama!* Who will be the first to touch off these Bigger Thomases in America, white and black?

For a long time I toyed with the idea of writing a novel in which a Negro Bigger Thomas would loom as a symbolic figure of American life, a figure who would hold within him the prophecy of our future. I felt strongly that he held within him, in a measure which perhaps no other contemporary type did, the outlines of action and feeling which we would encounter on a vast scale in the days to come. Just as one sees when one walks into a medical research laboratory jars of alcohol containing abnormally large or distorted portions of the human body, just so did I see and feel that the conditions of life under which Negroes are forced to live in America contain the embryonic emotional prefigura-

Wright (left) with his younger brother Leon, 1916.

tions of how a large part of the body politic would react under stress. (pp. xx-xxi)

But several things militated against my starting to work. Like Bigger himself, I felt a mental censor—product of the fears which a Negro feels from living in America—standing over me, draped in white, warning me not to write. This censor's warnings were translated into my own thought processes thus: "What will white people think if I draw the pictures of such a Negro boy? Will they not at once say: 'See, didn't we tell you all along that niggers are like that? Now, look, one of their own kind has come along and drawn the picture for us!'" I felt that if I drew the picture of Bigger truthfully, there would be many reactionary whites who would try to make of him something I did not intend. And yet, and this was what made it difficult, I knew that I could not write of Bigger convincingly if I did not depict him as he *was*: that is, resentful toward whites, sullen, angry, ignorant, emotionally unstable, depressed and unaccountably elated at times, and unable even, because of his own lack of inner organization which American oppression has fostered in him, to unite with the members of his own race. And would not whites misread Bigger and, doubting his authenticity, say: "This man is preaching hate against the whole white race"?

The more I thought of it the more I became convinced that if I did not write of Bigger as I saw and felt him, if I did not try to make him a living personality and at the same time a symbol of all the larger things I felt and saw in him, I'd be reacting as Bigger himself reacted: that is, I'd be acting out of *fear* if I let what I thought whites would say constrict and paralyze me. (pp. xxi-xxii)

Another thought kept me from writing. What would my own white and black comrades in the Communist party say? This thought was the most bewildering of all.... How could I create such complex and wide schemes of associational thought and feeling, such filigreed webs of dreams and politics, without being mistaken for a "smuggler of reaction," "an ideological confusionist," or "an individualistic and dangerous element"? Though my heart is with the collectivist and proletarian ideal, I solved this problem by assuring myself that honest politics and honest feeling in imaginative representation ought to be able to meet on common healthy ground without fear, suspicion, and quarreling. Further, and more importantly, I steeled myself by coming to the conclusion that whether politicians accepted or rejected Bigger did not really matter; my task, as I felt it, was to free myself of this burden of impressions and feelings, recast them into the image of Bigger and make him *true*. (p. xxii)

There was another constricting thought that kept me from work. It deals with my own race.... I knew from long and painful experience that the Negro middle and professional classes were the people of my own race who were more than others ashamed of Bigger and what he meant. Having narrowly escaped the Bigger Thomas reaction pattern themselves—indeed, still retaining traces of it within the confines of their own timid personalities—they would not relish being publicly reminded of the lowly, shameful depths of life above which they enjoyed their bourgeois lives. Never did they want people, especially *white* people, to think that their lives were so much touched by anything so dark and brutal as Bigger. (pp. xxii-xxiii)

But Bigger won over all these claims; he won because I felt that I was hunting on the trail of more exciting and thrilling game. What Bigger meant had claimed me because I felt with all of my being that he was more important than what any person, white or black, would say or try to make of him, more important than any political analysis designed to explain or deny him, more important, even, than my own sense of fear, shame, and diffidence. (p. xxiii)

I don't know if **Native Son** is a good book or a bad book. And I don't know if the book I'm working on now will be a good book or a bad book. And I really don't care. The mere writing of it will be more fun and a deeper satisfaction than any praise or blame from anybody.

I feel that I'm lucky to be alive to write novels today, when the whole world is caught in the pangs of war and change. Early American writers, Henry James and Nathaniel Hawthorne, complained bitterly about the bleakness and flatness of the American scene. But I think that if they were alive, they'd feel at home in modern America. True, we have no great church in America; our national traditions are still of such a sort that we are not wont to brag of them; and we have no army that's above the level of mercenary fighters; we have no group acceptable to the whole of our country upholding certain humane values; we have no rich symbols, no colorful rituals. We have only a money-grubbing, industrial civilization. But we do have in the Negro the embodiment of a past tragic enough to appease the spiritual hunger of even a James; and we have in the oppression of the Negro a shadow athwart our national life dense and heavy enough to satisfy even the gloomy broodings of a Hawthorne. And if Poe were alive, he would not have to invent horror; horror would invent him. (p. xxxiv)

> *Richard Wright, "How 'Bigger' Was Born,"*
> *in his* Native Son, *Harper and Row, Publishers, 1966, pp. vii-xxiv.*

W. E. Burghardt Du Bois (essay date 1945)

[*Du Bois was an American educator, poet, novelist, historian, and sociologist who helped spark interest in black writers and black writing in America. Biographer Herbert Aptheker said of Du Bois: "[He] was more a history-maker than an historian." Du Bois's best-known work,* The Souls of Black Folk *(1903), is considered a landmark in the history of black self-awareness. In the following excerpt, he offers one of the earliest reviews of* Black Boy, *criticizing Wright's "misjudgment of black folk" and the unconvincing nature of the work.*]

[**Black Boy**] tells a harsh and forbidding story and makes one wonder just exactly what its relation to truth is. The [subtitle], *A Record of Childhood and Youth*, makes one at first think that the story is autobiographical. It probably is, at least in part. But mainly it is probably intended to be fiction or fictionalized biography. At any rate the reader must regard it as creative writing rather than simply a record of life....

Not only is there [a] misjudgment of black folk and the difficult repulsive characters among them that he is thrown with, but the same thing takes place with white folk. There is not a single broad-minded, open-hearted white person in his book....

One rises from the reading of such a book with mixed thoughts. Richard Wright uses vigorous and straightforward English; often there is real beauty in his words even when they are mingled with sadism....

Yet at the result one is baffled. Evidently if this is an actual record, bad as the world is, such concentrated meanness, filth and despair never completely filled it or any particular part of it. But if the book is meant to be a creative picture and a warning, even then, it misses its possible effectiveness because it is as a work of art so patently and terribly overdrawn.

Nothing that Richard Wright says is in itself unbeliev-able or impossible; it is the total picture that is not convincing.

> W. E. Burghardt Du Bois, "Richard Wright Looks Back," in New York Herald Tribune Weekly Book Review, *March 4, 1945, p. 2.*

Ralph Ellison (essay date 1945)

[*Ellison, one of the most accomplished American authors of the twentieth century, is best known for his highly acclaimed novel* Invisible Man *(1952). In the excerpt below from an essay that first appeared in* The Antioch Review *in 1945, he favorably reviews* Black Boy, *suggesting that the work is a sophisticated version of* Native Son.]

Richard Wright has outlined for himself a dual role: To discover and depict the meaning of Negro experience; and to reveal to both Negroes and whites those prob-lems of a psychological and emotional nature which arise between them when they strive for mutual under-standing.

Now in *Black Boy,* he has used his own life to probe what qualities of will, imagination, and intellect are required of a Southern Negro in order to possess the meaning of his life in the United States. Wright is an important writer, perhaps the most articulate Negro American, and what he has to say is highly perceptive. Imagine Bigger Thomas [in *Native Son*] projecting his own life in lucid prose, guided, say, by the insights of Marx and Freud, and you have an idea of this autobiog-raphy. (p. 77)

As a nonwhite intellectual's statement of his relation-ship to western culture, *Black Boy* recalls the conflicting pattern of identification and rejection found in Nehru's *Toward Freedom.* In its use of fictional techniques, its concern with criminality (sin) and the artistic sensibili-ty, and in its author's judgment and rejection of the narrow world of his origin, it recalls Joyce's rejection of Dublin in *A Portrait of the Artist.* And as a psychological document of life under oppressive conditions, it recalls *The House of the Dead,* Dostoievski's profound study of the humanity of Russian criminals. (p. 78)

[Along] with the themes, equivalent descriptions of milieu and the perspectives to be found in Joyce, Nehru, Dostoievski, George Moore and Rousseau, *Black Boy* is filled with blues-tempered echoes of railroad trains, the names of Southern towns and cities, estrangements, fights and flights, deaths and disappointments, charged with physical and spiritual hungers and pain. And like a blues sung by such an artist as Bessie Smith, its lyrical prose evokes the paradoxical, almost surreal image of a black boy singing lustily as he probes his own grievous wound. (p. 79)

[The] prerequisites to the writing of *Black Boy* were, on the one hand, the microscopic degree of cultural free-dom which Wright found in the South's stony injustice,

and, on the other, the existence of a personality agitated to a state of almost manic restlessness. There were, of course, other factors, chiefly ideological; but these came later. (pp. 79-80)

Born on a Mississippi plantation, he was subjected to all those blasting pressures which, in a scant eighty years, have sent the Negro people hurtling, without clearly defined trajectory, from slavery to emancipation, from log cabin to city tenement, from the white folks' fields and kitchens to factory assembly lines; and which, between two wars, have shattered the wholeness of its folk consciousness into a thousand writhing pieces.

Black Boy describes this process in the personal terms of *one* Negro childhood. Nevertheless, several critics have complained that it does not "explain" Richard Wright. Which, aside from the notion of art involved, serves to remind us that the prevailing mood of American criticism has so thoroughly excluded the Negro that it fails to recognize some of the most basic tenets of western democratic thought when encountering them in a black skin. They forget that human life possesses an innate dignity and mankind an innate sense of nobility; that all men possess the tendency to dream and the compulsion to make their dreams reality; that the need to be ever dissatisfied and the urge ever to seek satisfaction is implicit in the human organism; and that all men are the victims and the beneficiaries of the goading, tormenting, commanding, and informing activ-ity of that imperious process known as the Mind.... (pp. 80-1)

[While] it is true that *Black Boy* presents an almost unrelieved picture of a personality corrupted by brutal environment, it also presents those fresh, human re-sponses brought to its world by the sensitive child.... (p. 81)

There were also those white men—the one who allowed Wright to use his library privileges and the other who advised him to leave the South, and still others whose offers of friendship he was too frightened to accept.

Wright assumed that the nucleus of plastic sensibility is a human heritage—the right and the opportunity to dilate, deepen, and enrich sensibility—democracy. Thus the drama of *Black Boy* lies in its depiction of what occurs when Negro sensibility attempts to fulfill itself in the undemocratic South. Here it is not the individual that is the immediate focus, as in Joyce's *Stephen Hero,* but that upon which his sensibility was nourished.

Those critics who complain that Wright has omitted the development of his own sensibility hold that the work thus fails as art. Others, because it presents too little of what they consider attractive in Negro life, charge that it distorts reality. Both groups miss a very obvious point: That whatever else the environment contained, it has as little chance of prevailing against the overwhelming weight of the child's unpleasant experiences as Beetho-ven's Quartets would have of destroying the stench of a Nazi prison. (p. 82)

Wright saw his destiny—that combination of forces before which man feels powerless—in terms of a quick and casual violence inflicted upon him by both family and community. His response was likewise violent, and it has been his need to give that violence significance which has shaped his writings. (p. 83)

Ralph Ellison, "Richard Wright's Blues," in his Shadow and Act, *Random House, 1964, pp. 77-94.*

Irving Howe (essay date 1963)

[*Written in 1963, the following excerpt is one of the most important and controversial reviews of* Native Son. *Here, Howe declares* Native Son *a literary tour de force but points out "grave faults" in the work. For Ralph Ellison's rebuttal to this essay, see Further Reading.*]

The day *Native Son* appeared, American culture was changed forever. No matter how much qualifying the book might later need, it made impossible a repetition of the old lies. In all its crudeness, melodrama and claustrophobia of vision, Richard Wright's novel brought out into the open, as no one ever had before, the hatred, fear and violence that have crippled and may yet destroy our culture.

A blow at the white man, the novel forced him to recognize himself as an oppressor. A blow at the black man, the novel forced him to recognize the cost of his submission. *Native Son* assaulted the most cherished of American vanities: the hope that the accumulated injustice of the past would bring with it no lasting penalties, the fantasy that in his humiliation the Negro somehow retained a sexual potency—or was it a child-like good-nature?—that made it necessary to envy and still more to suppress him. Speaking from the black wrath of retribution, Wright insisted that history can be a punishment. He told us the one thing even the most liberal whites preferred not to hear: that Negroes were far from patient or forgiving, that they were scarred by fear, that they hated every moment of their suppression even when seeming most acquiescent, and that often enough they hated *us,* the decent and cultivated white men who from complicity or neglect shared in the responsibility for their plight. (pp. 100-01)

At first *Native Son* seems still another naturalistic novel. . . . Behind the book one senses the molding influence of Theodore Dreiser, especially the Dreiser of *An American Tragedy* who knows there are situations so oppressive that only violence can provide their victims with the hope of dignity. Like Dreiser, Wright wished to pummel his readers into awareness; like Dreiser, to overpower them with the sense of society as an enclosing force. Yet the comparison is finally of limited value, and for the disconcerting reason that Dreiser had a white skin and Wright a black one.

The usual naturalistic novel is written with detachment, as if by a scientist surveying a field of operations; it is a novel in which the writer withdraws from a detested world and coldly piles up the evidence for detesting it. *Native Son,* though preserving some of the devices of the naturalistic novel, deviates sharply from its characteristic tone: a tone Wright could not possibly have maintained and which, it may be, no Negro novelist can really hold for long. *Native Son* is a work of assault rather than withdrawal; the author yields himself in part to a vision of nightmare. Bigger's cowering perception of the world becomes the most vivid and authentic component of the book. Naturalism pushed to an extreme turns here into something other than itself, a kind of expressionist outburst, no longer a replica of the familiar social world but a self-contained realm of grotesque emblems.

That *Native Son* has grave faults anyone can see. The language is often coarse, flat in rhythm, syntactically overburdened, heavy with journalistic slag. Apart from Bigger, who seems more a brute energy than a particularized figure, the characters have little reality, the Negroes being mere stock accessories and the whites either "agit-prop" villains or heroic Communists whom Wright finds it easier to admire from a distance than establish from the inside. (pp. 103-04)

The main literary problem that troubled Wright in recent years was that of rendering his naturalism a more terse and supple instrument. I think he went astray whenever he abandoned naturalism entirely. . . . Wright needed the accumulated material of circumstance which naturalistic detail provided his fiction; it was as essential to his ultimate effect of shock and bruise as dialogue to Hemingway's ultimate effect of irony and loss. But Wright was correct in thinking that the problem of detail is the most vexing technical problem the naturalist writer must face, since the accumulation that makes for depth and solidity can also create a pall of tedium. (pp. 117-18)

Irving Howe, "Black Boys and Native Sons," in his A World More Attractive: A View of Modern Literature and Politics, *Horizon, 1963, pp. 98-122.*

Ronald Sanders (essay date 1968)

[*In the following excerpt, Sanders evaluates Wright's novels.*]

[In] *Native Son* Wright almost succeeds in achieving the imaginative liberation he sought by writing it. The book eventually runs aground in the author's own intellectuality, a quality which, for the novel's sake, he had succeeded in suppressing both too well and not well enough.

The first two-thirds of *Native Son* constitute one of the most exciting stretches of melodrama in American literature. (p. 33)

From [the moment of Mary Dalton's death] until Bigger's capture by the police on a snow-covered tenement rooftop some two hundred pages later the novel is pure movement, the kind of overwhelming narrative torrent that Wright had already made into a trademark in a story like **"Down By the Riverside."** In *Native Son* this narrative flow serves the additional function of showing what has happened to Bigger's existence. Every one of his acts now, in contrast with the torpor that had prevailed in the descriptions of his life prior to the murder of Mary Dalton, is swift, vigorous and meaningful, another element in a headlong process of self-definition.

Wright spares no horror in this unfolding of the hidden meaning of his protagonist's existence; Bigger's ultimate and most completely unforgivable act of violent self-assertion is his murder of his mistress Bessie, with whom he has shared his secret and whose life has therefore become intolerable to him. According to Constance Webb, Wright wanted to include this episode in the novel so that there would be no mistaking Bigger's stark responsibility for his acts, no catering to the sensibilities of bankers' daughters. In retrospect, it seems also to be another of the novel's prophetic glimpses of the ghetto revolt of the sixties, ultimately turning against itself and burning down homes with black women and children inside. This, then, is the culminating act of Bigger's self-emancipating revolt, his one unequivocally wilful act of annihilation—performed upon a poor black working-girl. Did Wright mean for the irony to read this way? Is it an intended qualification to his vision of a black revolutionary apocalypse, or an inadvertent prophecy? Miss Webb does not tell us, but this much must be said: if this is ultimately the outcome of Bigger's revolt, then it is not so likely to disturb the sensibilities of bankers' daughters after all.

The last third of the novel, dealing with Bigger's imprisonment and trial, is Wright's final bout with the Communist worldview, and the narrative moves slowly and indecisively again.... He seems to want to give what he can back to the Communists after the heresy he has committed in the first two-thirds of the book; it is only they, for example, who show compassion and some understanding towards Bigger, and he is deeply appreciative of this despite his refusal to be categorized by them as a mere phenomenon of the oppressed part of mankind.... The old lawyer Max tries to defend Bigger from the death sentence in a long courtroom summation indicting society's injustices. Max is even able to see, beneath the blanket of Communist myth, the more unruly revolutionary force that Bigger represents.... But ultimately it is Max who comes forth, not only in the courtroom but within Wright's internal moral dialectic, as the last defender of the old vision of a coalition of the oppressed.... (pp. 34-5)

The spirit of Max, partly consumed in a European nostalgia shared by every American Jewish intellectual, was never completely exorcised by Wright. He had absorbed this nostalgia as part of his education, and his vision of black revolt was as blurred by it as his pursuit of the vision was spurred by a passion to shake it off. This is the meaning of Bigger's final but somehow inconclusive show of defiance before Max in his death cell, ending with "a faint, wry, bitter smile" through the bars as the lawyer walks down the corridor. Here is the way Wright's revolt ends, not with a bang but a smirk....

In his search after a certain notion of the primitive, Wright had come dangerously close to creating a character who was a mere vehicle for ideas. Bigger still works despite the ambiguity, but Wright's growing preoccupation with the metaphysics of blackness turned many of the characters he subsequently created into hardly more than metaphors.... ["**The Man Who Lived Underground**"] is an interesting attempt to use blackness as a metaphor for the condition known in Jewish literature as that of "one who sees but is not seen"; but the idea—originally inspired by a reading of Dostoyevsky—is more appealing than the realization is unsuccessful.... (p. 36)

[*Black Boy*] is his masterpiece, and yet it would seem, from Miss Webb's narrative, that it was written almost inadvertently, after Wright's agent surprised him by suggesting that he try an autobiography. Persuaded to drop the mantle of a writer of fiction for a moment (although he uses the techniques of the novel here most effectively), Wright has recourse in this book to "telling it like it is" without drawing upon his arsenal of symbolism and melodramatic plot-making. A simple and powerful account of his boyhood and young manhood in the South, it is his one book-length narrative that does not border on solipsism but contains a whole array of real characterizations. Even the whites that appear, almost all of them as persecutors, are more real and hence human than such caricatures as Dalton or the private detective in *Native Son.* Focusing more resolutely on real experience than he had ever done before, Wright had lighted upon conventions that were, for the first time, entirely his own. Evoking, as Ellison says, "the paradoxical, almost surreal image of a black boy singing [the blues] lustily as he probes his own grievous wound" [see excerpt dated 1945], the book suggests possibilities for a whole genre of Negro writing, signs of which we are now beginning to see today.

But in Wright's own life and work, *Black Boy* proved to be the swan song of his struggle to achieve his own identity as a writer and a man in America. In the latter half of 1946 he visited France as the guest of its government, and in the summer of the following year he brought his wife and five-year-old daughter to Paris to settle there for good.... By merely trading in the lilt with which he once had sung the blues, Wright became eligible to put on the French-made mantle of Negritude, whose graceful and classic lines obscured the homely contours of Mississippi and Chicago. In other words, his color became in France what he had always sought to make it: a kind of metaphor.

This transmutation is reflected in Wright's next book, *The Outsider*.... It is a novel laden with language and concepts borrowed from French existentialism.... Cross Damon, a new variant of Bigger Thomas perceived through the French philosophical sensibility, commits a series of murders that read like ritual metaphors for the series of rejections Wright had made in his own life.... In the end it is not the law but the Communists who destroy him, shooting him down in the street.

The thrust of Wright's work had now brought him to a point of extreme alienation. His next novel, *Savage Holiday*... is a suspense thriller about a retired white insurance executive who, stepping out of the shower to pick up his newspaper in the hallway one Sunday morning, finds himself trapped there naked when his door accidentally slams shut. Caught naked in the hallway—this is what had become of Wright's creative metaphor, of his very inner identity!

During the next few years, Wright made strenuous efforts to recover roots for a theme that had now become, in literary terms, a mere abstraction.... [*Pagan Spain*] was a recapitulation of his old quest for a primitive reality behind the mask of Communist myth. Pagan Spain, whose border with France marks "the termination of Europe and the beginning of Africa," was the dark truth that had reposed beneath the right-left conventions of the Spanish Civil War era. So also, at the Bandung Conference, did Wright perceive an underlying reality—formed out of race and religion—that was "beyond left and right." He was thus moving in the direction of what was in fact another left-wing myth— that of the Third World—which was being generated in France during this period. It was a possible outcome of

the logic of his own development: in a sense, Bigger Thomas could be viewed retrospectively as a representative of Frantz Fanon's theories about the self-realization of the colonized through violent revolt. But this, in the end, would tend to make Bigger as much a creature of Jean-Paul Sartre's universe as the lawyer Max had wanted to make him of the universe of American Communism in the nineteen-thirties.

Wright did not seem content with this resolution, either; he had been very keenly aware, for example, of the gulf between himself and the black man of Africa during his trip there. The short time that now remained of his life was filled with what seems to have been a frantic struggle to recover his themes, as he thrashed about through possibilities both old and new. He tried writing again about the Negro in the American South, but the resulting novel, *The Long Dream,* published in 1958, was severely criticized for its manifest remoteness from reality; it was far more popular in France than in the United States. His short stories, mere fanciful creations, were better because they were able to bear up somehow under the weight of being intellectual constructs. A story published in 1957, **"Big Black Good Man,"** suggests the possibility that the course of Wright's sensibility was seeking to come full circle.... Does the similarity of name to those of Big Boy and Bigger suggest what Wright was trying to do? It is one of his few stories displaying some of the sunniness and humor for which he was apparently well known in person. Was he making his peace at last, and if so, where was it to take him? No one will ever know, for he was dead three years later, in the fall of 1960. (pp. 36-9)

Ticket for a dinner featuring Wright and Paul Robeson. At the benefit, Wright discussed his novel Native Son.

Ronald Sanders, "Richard Wright and the Sixties," in Midstream, Vol. XIV, No. 7, August-September, 1968, pp. 28-40.

Edward Margolies (essay date 1969)

[*In the following excerpt from his* The Art of Richard Wright, *Margolies discusses Wright's development as a writer, focusing on the thematic progression of Wright's fiction.*]

Wright at his best was master of a taut psychological suspense narrative. Even more important, however, are the ways Wright wove his themes of human fear, alienation, guilt, and dread into the overall texture of his work. Some critics may still today stubbornly cling to the notion that Wright was nothing more than a proletarian writer, but it was to these themes that a postwar generation of French writers responded, and not to Wright's Communism—and it is to these themes that future critics must turn primarily if they wish to re-evaluate Wright's work. (p. 3)

Wright not only wrote well but also he paved the way for a new and vigorous generation of Negro authors to deal with subjects that had hitherto been regarded as taboo. [His] portraits of oppressed Negroes have made a deep impression on readers the world over. (p. 4)

Wright's existentialism as it was to be called by a later generation of French authors, was not an intellectually "learned" process (although he had been reading Dostoevsky and Kierkegaard in the thirties) but rather the lived experiences of his growing years. The alienation, the dread, the fear, and the view that one must construct oneself out of the chaos of existence—all elements of his fiction—were for him means of survival. There were, of course, externals he grasped for as well. (p. 6)

In general, Wright's nonfiction takes one of two directions. The first concerns itself with the devastating emotional impact of centuries of exploitation on its individual victims. The second is the overall cultural characteristics of oppressed peoples. The first is largely psychological; the second socio-anthropological. Obviously no such absolute division obtains since it is impossible to discuss one without making reference to the other, but for purposes of analysis it may be said that Wright lays greater or lesser stress on one or the other of these issues in each of his works of nonfiction. *Black Boy* (1945), Wright's autobiography of his Southern years, serves perhaps as the best point of reference from which to make an examination of his ideas, since, as we have seen, Wright generalizes from his own experiences certain conclusions about the problems of minorities everywhere. (p. 15)

Possibly the problems presented by *Black Boy* are insoluble since the environment in which *Black Boy* operates is so alien to the average reader that it is almost essential for Wright to hammer home in little digressive essays the mores of the caste system so that *Black Boy*'s

psychology and behavior may be better understood. As a result, its authority as autobiography is reduced—Wright frequently appears to stand aside and analyze himself rather than allow the reader to make inferences about his character and emotions from his actions—and its strength as sociology seems somewhat adulterated by the incursions of the narrative. Yet, despite these failures—or possibly because of them—the impact of the book is considerable and this perhaps is Wright's artistic triumph. (p. 16)

Wright's theme is freedom and he skillfully arranges and selects his scenes in such a way that he is constantly made to appear the innocent victim of the tyranny of his family or the outrages of the white community. Nowhere in the book are Wright's actions and thoughts reprehensible. The characteristics he attributes to himself are in marked contrast to those of other characters in the book. He is "realistic," "creative," "passionate," "courageous," and maladjusted because he refuses to conform. Insofar as the reader identifies Wright's cause with the cause of Negro freedom, it is because Wright is a Negro—but a careful reading of the book indicates that Wright expressly divorces himself from other Negroes. Indeed rarely in the book does Wright reveal concern for Negroes as a group. Hence Wright traps the reader in a stereotyped response—the same stereotyped response that Wright is fighting throughout the book: that is, that all Negroes are alike and react alike. (p. 18)

[It] is in [*Uncle Tom's Children*] that the reader may find the theme, the structure, the plot, and the ideational content of all his later fictional work. Although Wright, when he wrote these stories, was a convinced Communist, it is revealing how related they are to the later phases of intellectual and political development. Here, for example, one finds Wright's incipient Negro nationalism as each of his protagonists rises to strike out violently at white oppressors who would deny him his humanity. More significantly his Negro characters imagine whites as "blurs," "bogs," "mountains," "fire," "ice," and "marble." In none of these stories do his heroes act out of a sense of consciously arrived at ideology (most of them, as a matter of fact, are ignorant of Marxism), but rather out of an innate, repressed longing for freedom—or sometimes merely as an instinctive means of self-survival. Often the act of violence carries along with it a sudden revelatory sense of self-awareness—an immediate knowledge that the world in which the protagonist dwells is chaotic, meaningless, purposeless, and that he, as a Negro, is "outside" this world and must therefore discover his own life by his lonely individual thoughts and acts. We find thus in these first short stories a kind of black nationalism wedded to what has been called Wright's existentialism—the principal characteristics of Wright's last phase of political and philosophical thinking.

Paradoxically, Wright's Marxism seldom intrudes in an explicit didactic sense. . . . To be sure, Communists are viewed in a kindly light in the last two of Wright's stories, but they are only remotely instrumental in effecting his heroes' discovery of themselves and their world. Oddly enough, in three of the stories ("**Down by the Riverside,**" "**Fire and Cloud,**" and "**Bright and Morning Star**"), Wright's simple Negro peasants arrive at their sense of self-realization by applying basic Christian principles to the situations in which they find themselves. In only one ("**Bright and Morning Star**"), does a character convert to Communism—and then only when she discovers Communism is the modern translation of the primitive Christian values she has always lived. There is a constant identification in these stories with the fleeing Hebrew children of the Old Testament and the persecuted Christ—and mood, atmosphere, and settings abound in biblical nuances. Wright's characters die like martyrs, stoic and unyielding, in their new-found truth about themselves and their vision of a freer, fuller world for their posterity.... The spare, stark accounts of actions and their resolution are reminiscent in their simplicity and their cadences of Biblical narrations. The floods, the songs, the sermons, the hymns reinforce the Biblical analogies and serve, ironically, to highlight the uselessness and inadequacy of Christianity as a means of coping with the depression-ridden, racist South. Even the reverse imagery of white-evil, black-good is suggestive in its simple organization of the forces which divide the world in Old Testament accounts of the Hebrews' struggle for survival. (pp. 57-9)

There is a thematic progression in these stories, each of which deals with the Negro's struggle for survival and freedom. In the first story ["**Big Boy Leaves Home**"] flight is described—and here Wright is at his artistic best, fashioning his taut, spare prose to the movements and thoughts of the fugitive. (p. 61)

Although "**Big Boy**" is a relatively long story, the rhythm of events is swift, and the time consumed from beginning to end is less than twenty-four hours. The prose is correspondingly fashioned to meet the pace of the plot. The story is divided into five parts, each of which constitutes a critical episode in Big Boy's progress from idyll, through violence, to misery, terror, and escape. As the tension mounts, Wright employs more and more of a terse and taut declaratory prose, fraught with overtones and meanings unspoken—reminiscent vaguely of the early [Ernest] Hemingway. (pp. 62-3)

"**Down by the Riverside,**" the next story in the collection, is not nearly so successful. If flight (as represented by "**Big Boy Leaves Home**") is one aspect of the Negro's struggle for survival in the South, Christian humility, forbearance, courage, and stoic endurance are the themes of Wright's second piece. But here the plot becomes too contrived; coincidence is piled upon coincidence, and the inevitability of his protagonist's doom does not ring quite as true. (p. 63)

Yet, there is a certain epic quality to the piece—man steadily pursuing his course against a malevolent nature, only to be cut down later by the ingratitude of his fellow men—that is suggestive of [Mark] Twain or [William] Faulkner. And Mann's long-suffering perseverance and stubborn will to survive endow him with a rare mythic Biblical quality. Wright even structures his story like a Biblical chronicle, in five brief episodes, each displaying in its way Mann's humble courage against his fate. But if Mann's simple Christian virtues failed to save him, it was in part because the ground had not yet been laid on which these virtues might flourish. The recognition that the bourgeois ethic is incapable of providing men with the possibility of fulfilling themselves is an element of Wright's next story ["**Long Black Song**"]. (p. 65)

The success of the story, perhaps Wright's best, lies in the successful integration of plot, imagery, and character which echo the tragic theme of Silas's doomed awareness of himself and the inadequacy of the bourgeois values by which he has been attempting to live. Silas's recognition is his death knell, but he achieves a dignity in death that he had never known in life. (pp. 65-6)

It is Sarah, though, who is the most memorable portrayal in the story. The narrative unfolds from her point of view—and she becomes, at the end, a kind of deep mother earth character, registering her primal instincts and reactions to the violence and senselessness she sees all about her. But for all that, she remains beautifully human—her speech patterns and thoughts responding to an inner rhythm, somehow out of touch with the foolish strivings of men, yet caught up in her own melancholy memories and desires.... Wright conveys her mood and memories and vagaries of character in sensuous color imagery—while certain cadences suggest perhaps Gertrude Stein whom Wright regarded as one of his chief influences. (pp. 66-7)

Sarah is Wright's most lyrical achievement, and Silas, her husband, Wright's most convincing figure of redemption. (p. 67)

Wright's militant Negroes, despite their protestations to the contrary, often sound more like black nationalists than Communist internationalists. It was perhaps this facet of Wright's work, in addition to the obvious, extreme, and frequent isolated individualism of his heroes that [began] to disturb Communist Party officials. Yet regardless of whether Wright had been at heart a Communist, an outsider, or a nationalist when he wrote these pieces, there can be little doubt that they draw a good deal of their dramatic strength from the black and white world Wright saw. There is little the reader can do but sympathize with Wright's Negroes and loathe and despise the whites. There are no shadings, ambiguities, few psychological complexities. But there are of course the weaknesses of the stories as well.

How then account for their overall success? First of all, they *are* stories. Wright is a story teller and his plots are replete with conflict, incident, and suspense. Secondly, Wright is a stylist. He has an unerring "feel" for dialogue, his narrations are controlled in terse, tense rhythms, and he manages to communicate mood, atmosphere, and character in finely worked passages of lyric intensity. But above all they are stories whose sweep and magnitude are suffused with their author's impassioned convictions about the dignity of man, and a profound pity for the degraded, the poor and oppressed who, in the face of casual brutality, cling obstinately to their humanity. (pp. 72-3)

Unlike the pieces in **Uncle Tom's Children,** [the stories in the posthumously published **Eight Men**] are not arranged along any progressively thematic lines; instead the order in which they are assembled indicates that Wright was more concerned with showing a variety of styles, settings and points of view. To be sure, they all deal in one way or another with Negro oppression, but they do not point, as Wright's previous collection of stories did, to any specific social conclusion. (p. 73)

The only significant work of fiction Wright produced in the decade of the forties was his long story, **"The Man Who Lived Underground."** (p. 76)

Here Wright is at his storytelling best, dealing with subject matter he handles best—the terrified fugitive in flight from his pursuers. Like Wright's other fugitives, Fred Daniels exercises a kind of instinct for survival that he perhaps never knew he possessed. But what makes him different from the others is that he is not merely a victim of a racist society, but that he has become by the very nature of his experiences a symbol of all men in that society—the pursuers and the pursued. For what the underground man has learned in his sewer is that all men carry about in their hearts an underground man who determines their behavior and attitudes in the aboveground world. The underground man is the essential nature of all men—and is composed of dread, terror, and guilt. Here then lies the essential difference between Wright's Communist and post-Communist period. Heretofore dread, terror, and guilt had been the lot of the Negro in a world that had thrust upon him the role of a despised inferior. Now they are the attributes of all mankind. (pp. 78-9)

Fred Daniels is then Everyman, and his story is very nearly a perfect modern allegory. The Negro who lives in the underground of the city amidst its sewage and slime is not unlike the creature who dwells amidst the sewage of the human heart. And Fred Daniels knows that all of the ways men attempt to persuade themselves that their lives are meaningful and rational are delusions.... But paradoxically despite Fred's new found knowledge of the savagery of the human heart and the meaninglessness of the aboveground world, he recognizes its instinctive appeal as well, and he must absurdly rise to the surface once more. (pp. 79-80)

The dread, the terror, the guilt, the nausea had always been basic thematic elements in Wright's fiction—and now in **"The Man Who Lived Underground,"** they are made the explicit components of the human personality. Like Wright's heroes, the characters of existentialist authors move about in a world devoid of principles, God, and purpose—and suffer horror at their awesome godlike powers as they create their own personalities and values out of the chaos of existence. But in some respects Wright's heroes are different. They are alien-

ated often enough not from any intellectually reasoned position (at this stage in Wright's career), but by chance happenings in their lives or an accident of birth—race, for example. (In Fred Daniels' case, for instance, he is a Negro who quite by chance happened to be near the scene of a crime.) They arrive then accidentally at their insights, and as a result of having discovered themselves outside the rules of conventional social behavior recognize that they are free to shape (and are therefore responsible for) their own lives. But this is not primarily why they suffer guilt. Wright seems to prefer a Freudian explanation; guilt is instinctively connected with the trauma of birth. Hence, for Wright, a man's freedom is circumscribed by his very humanity. In ways he cannot possibly control, his nature or "essence" precedes his existence. But however different the routes French existentialist authors and Wright may have taken, they meet on common ground in regard to their thrilled horror at man's rootlessness—at the heroism of his absurd striving.

"The Man Who Lived Underground" undoubtedly owes something in the way of plot and theme to [Victor Hugo's] *Les Miserables,* and to what Camus called the "Dostoevskian experience of the condemned man"—but, above all, Fred Daniels' adventures suggest something of Wright's own emotions after ten years in the Communist underground. The air of bitterness, the almost strident militancy are gone—momentarily at least—and in their place a compassion and despair—compassion for man trapped in his underground nature and despair that he will ever be able to set himself free. (pp. 80-1)

The fifties saw Wright experimenting with new subject matter and new forms. Problems of race remain the central issue, but are now dealt with from changing perspectives. For the first time there are two stories with non-American settings, and race neurosis is treated more as the white man's dilemma than as the black man's burden. This shift in emphasis from black to white is accompanied by corresponding shifts in social viewpoint. Racial antagonisms do not appear to be immediately—or for that matter remotely—traceable to compelling class interests. It is clear that Wright was trying to broaden the range and scope of his fiction—that he was trying to move away somewhat from the psyche of the oppressed Negro peasant or proletariat toward characters of varying social and ethnic backgrounds. The three novels Wright produced in this ten year period bear out this conclusion. In the first, **The Outsider** (1953), he wrote of his hero that though a Negro "he could have been of any race." **Savage Holiday,** written the following year, contains no Negro characters and deals with the misfortunes of a white, "respectable" middle-aged retired insurance executive. **The Long Dream** (1957) is written from the point of view of an adolescent, middle-class Negro boy. Wright was apparently reaching for a universality he felt he had not yet achieved—but his craft was not quite equal to the tasks he had set for himself. Too often, as before, his whites appear as stereotypes, and his Negroes are a bit too noble or innocent. In the 1930's Wright's social vision lent his stories an air of conviction, a momentum all their own; in the 1950's Wright's quieter catholicity, his wider intellectuality, perhaps removed his stories from this kind of cumulative dread tension, the sense of urgency, that made his earlier works so immediately gripping.

Nonetheless it cannot be said that Wright's new stories do not possess their own narrative qualities.... What these stories sorely lack are the charged, vibrant rhythms and vivid lyric imagery that so rounded out character and theme in his earlier works. Perhaps Wright wanted to pare his prose down to what he regarded as bare essentials—just as he may have fancied his idol, Gertrude Stein, had done. Whatever the reasons, the results are only occasionally successful. (pp. 82-3)

Native Son possesses many of the characteristic failings of proletarian literature. First, the novel is transparently propagandistic—arguing for a humane, socialist society where such crimes as Bigger committed could not conceivably take place. Secondly, Wright builds up rather extensive documentation to prove that Bigger's actions, behavior, values, attitudes, and fate have already been determined by his status and place in American life. Bigger's immediate Negro environment is depicted as being unrelentingly bleak and vacuous—while the white world that stands just beyond his reach remains cruelly indifferent or hostile to his needs. Thirdly, with the possible exception of Bigger, none of the characters is portrayed in any depth—and most of them are depicted as representative "types" of the social class to which they belong. Fourthly, despite his brutally conditioned psychology, there are moments in the novel when Bigger, like the heroes of other proletarian fiction, appears to be on the verge of responding to the stereotyped Communist version of black and white workers marching together in the sunlight of fraternal friendship. Finally, Wright succumbs too often to the occupational disease of proletarian authors by hammering home sociological points in didactic expository prose when they could just as clearly be understood in terms of the organic development of the novel.

Yet if *Native Son* may be said to illustrate some of the more flagrant conventions of proletarian fiction, there are aspects of this novel that reveal Wright exploring problems of character portrayal, prose style, and theme.... [There] is first of all the sympathetic presentation of perhaps one of the most disagreeable characters in fiction. That Wright had to a large degree achieved this may be attested to as much by the loud protests of his critics as by the plaudits of his admirers. Second, although *Native Son* makes its obvious sociological points, one should bear in mind that for well over two thirds of the novel Wright dwells on the peculiar states of mind of his protagonist, Bigger, which exist somehow outside the realm of social classes or racial issues.... Hence if categorizing terms are to be used, *Native Son* is as much a psychological novel as it is

sociological, with Wright dwelling on various intensities of shame, fear, and hate.... To require of his readers that they identify themselves with the violent emotions and behavior of an illiterate Negro boy is no mean feat—but Wright's success goes beyond the shock of reader recognition with its subsequent implications of shared guilt and social responsibility. A rereading of Wright's novel some twenty-five odd years after its publication suggests that Wright was probing larger issues than racial injustice and social inequality. He was asking questions regarding the ultimate nature of man. What indeed are man's responsibilities in a world devoid of meaning and purpose? ... The contradiction is never resolved, and it is precisely for this reason that the novel fails to fulfill itself. For the plot, the structure, even the portrayal of Bigger himself are often at odds with Wright's official determinism—but when on occasion the novel transcends its Marxist and proletarian limitations the reading becomes magnificent. (pp. 104-07)

The entire action described in Book I totals fewer than seventy-seven pages. Bigger's character and circumstances are related in a few quick almost impressionistic episodes—but the real plot movement does not actually commence until Bigger confronts the Daltons. Yet Wright has forecast Bigger's doom from the very start. Bigger knows deep in his heart that he is destined to bear endless days of dreary poverty, abject humiliation, and tormenting frustration, for this is what being a Negro means. Yet should he admit these things to himself, he may well commit an act of unconscionable violence.... Hence, Bigger's principal fear is self-knowledge—and this, of course, is the theme and title of Book I. The other kinds of fear that constitute Bigger's life are by-products of this basic error. (pp. 108-09)

[Bigger opts for] the identity of a murderer. In an absurd, hostile world that denies his humanity and dichotomizes his personality, Bigger has made a choice that has integrated his being; "never had he felt [such] a sense of wholeness." Ironically, Bigger has assumed the definition the white world has thrust upon the Negro in order to justify his oppression. If the Negro is a beast at heart who must be caged in order to protect the purity of the white race, Bigger will gladly accept the definition. It is at least an identity—preferable to that of someone obsequious, passive, and happily acquiescent to his exploitation. Bigger's choices are moral and metaphysical—not political or racial. He might have chosen love or submission, instead he has elected violence and death as a sign of his being, and by rebelling against established authority—despite the impossibility of success—he acquires a measure of freedom. None of the above is intended to deny that oppressive environmental factors do not limit the modes of Bigger's actions; nonetheless, environment by itself does not explain Bigger. (pp. 110-11)

The chief philosophical weakness of *Native Son* is not that Bigger does not surrender his freedom to Max's determinism, or that Bigger's Zarathustrian principles do not jibe with Max's socialist visions; it is that Wright himself does not seem to be able to make up his mind. There is an inconsistency of tone in the novel—particularly in Book III, "Fate," where the reader feels that Wright, although intellectually committed to Max's views, is more emotionally akin to Bigger's. Somehow Bigger's impassioned hatred comes across more vividly than Max's eloquent reasoning. (p. 113)

The failures of *Native Son* do not then reside in the proletarian or naturalistic framework in which Wright chose to compose his novel. Any great artist can after all transcend the limitations of form—if he so wishes. In any event if Wright had stuck closer to an organic naturalistic development, his novel might have achieved more consistent artistic results. The basic problems of *Native Son* lie elsewhere. There is an inconsistency of ideologies, an irresolution of philosophical attitudes which prevent Bigger and the other characters from developing properly, which adulterate the structure of the novel, and which occasionally cloud up an otherwise lucid prose style. There are three kinds of revolutionism in *Native Son*—and none of them altogether engages the reader as representing Wright's point of view. Max's Communism is of course what Wright presumes his novel is expressing—yet this kind of revolutionism is, . . . more imposed from without than an integral element of Bigger's being. . . .

A second kind of revolutionism is of a Negro nationalist variety—and this is far more in keeping with Bigger's character. (p. 115)

But Bigger's nationalism, whatever its components, is nothing compared to what Camus has subsequently described as metaphysical revolution. "Human rebellion ends in metaphysical revolution," Camus writes in *The Rebel*—and it is in the role of the metaphysical revolutionary that Bigger looms most significantly for modern readers. The metaphysical revolutionary challenges the very conditions of being—the needless suffering, the absurd contrast between his inborn sense of justice and the amorality and injustice of the external world. He tries to bring the external world more in accord with his sense of justice, but if this fails he will attempt to match in himself the injustice or chaos of the external world. (p. 116)

Bigger's crimes then signify something beyond their therapeutic value. In a world without God, without rules, without order, purpose, or meaning, each man becomes his own god and creates his own world in order to exist. Bigger acts violently in order to exist and it is perhaps this fact, rather than his continued undying hatred of whites, that so terrifies Max at the close of the novel. It is possible that Max senses that as a Communist he too has worked hard to dispense with the old social order—but the metaphysical vacuum that has been created does not necessarily lead men like Bigger to Communism, but may just as easily lead to the most murderous kind of nihilism. (pp. 116-17)

James Baldwin writing of *Native Son* says every Negro carries about within him a Bigger Thomas—but that the characterization by itself is unfair in that there are complexities, depths to the Negro psychology and life that Wright has left unexplored. To depict Bigger exclusively in terms of unsullied rage and hatred is to do the Negro a disservice. In Baldwin's view Bigger is a "monster." This, of course, is precisely the point Wright wishes to make—and herein lies its most terrible truth for the reader. Wright is obviously not describing the "representative" Negro—although he makes clear that what has happened to Bigger can more easily befall Negroes than whites. He is describing a person so alienated from traditional values, restraints, and civilized modes of behavior, that he feels free to construct his own ethics—that for him an act of murder is an act of creation. . . . But do such "monsters" as Baldwin calls them exist? Our tabloids could not exist without them. But even supposing they do not commit murder, their sense of isolation and alienation is growing in the face of an increasingly impersonal, industrialized mass society. And in mass, the isolated, the alienated, are capable of consent or indifference to nuclear holocaust or extermination camps. It is perhaps in this respect that *Native Son* is so much more disturbing a novel today than when it was first published. It is not that Bigger Thomas is so different from us; it is that he is so much like us. (pp. 119-20)

> *Edward Margolies, in his* The Art of Richard Wright, *Southern Illinois University Press, 1969, 180 p.*

Stanley Edgar Hyman (essay date 1970)

[*In the following excerpt, Hyman describes three phases of Wright's career, maintaining that "The Man Who Lived Underground" is the author's most notable work.*]

[It is] possible to see that Wright's literary career divided sharply into three phases. The first was the early flawed work of the 1930s, melodramatic and tractarian. (p. 127)

Principally, it includes his early short fiction, of which the five examples he preferred were reprinted in *Uncle Tom's Children*, along with an essay, **"The Ethics of Living Jim Crow."** The first three of these are medleys of racial violence in the South. The first of them, **"Black Boy Leaves Home,"** is typical: Black Boy shoots to death a white man who has just killed two of his friends and is about to kill him, and spends the night hiding out, in a pit in the dirt, from a lynch mob, watching them burn (with rather unconvincing details) his surviving friend, beating to death a rattlesnake with "long white fangs" to start the night, and throttling to death a dog belonging to a member of the mob to end it.

The other two stories are Stalinist tracts and caricatures. In one of them, **"Fire and Cloud,"** a moderate Negro preacher in the South is brutalized into becoming a militant leader (it is a kind of "Waiting for Blackie"). The other, **"Bright and Morning Star,"** is based on an anecdote that Wright heard in his childhood and retells in **Black Boy,** about a Negro woman whose husband was lynched by a mob, and who came to lay out her husband's body for burial with a sheet in which she had concealed a loaded shotgun, and managed to kill four members of the mob before they got her. ("I did not know if the story was factually true or not, but it was emotionally true," Wright observes in **Black Boy,** adding, "I resolved that I would emulate the black woman if I were ever faced with a white mob.") The story is that symbolic emulation, within a frame of heroic Communist martyrdom, which very much weakens and worsens the original anecdote.

Wright's second phase was the period of his important writing, from **Native Son** in 1940 to **Black Boy** in 1945, and it includes what I believe to be his masterwork, a novella, **"The Man Who Lived Underground"** (it seems to have been an uncompleted novel). The mark of this period is Wright's break with the convention of realism. (pp. 127-28)

"The Man Who Lived Underground" is a radically symbolist and fantasist work, finding the perfect metaphor for Negro identity in life under the streets in a sewer that is the foundation of *ecclesia supra cloacam,* with passageways to other institutions of our culture. Brignano quotes the anonymous protagonist as saying, "Yes, if the world as men had made it was right, then anything else was right, any act a man took to satisfy himself, murder, theft, torture" [see Further Reading]. Brignano identifies this idea as an extension of Nietzsche, but it is more obviously Ivan Karamazov's ethic for a world without God, and the novella seems primarily indebted to the Dostoevsky of *Notes from The Underground* and *The Brothers Karamazov....*

The last fifteen years of Wright's work, from the publication of **Black Boy** until his death in France in 1960, were as flawed as his early writing, now by a mild megalomania which combined with increasingly blurred memories of the United States to make his later work not symbolist or fantasist, but just unconvincing. (p. 128)

James Baldwin, in the days before his voice had become shrill and hysterical, wrote in *Notes of a Native Son:* "There is . . . no Negro living in America who has not felt, briefly or for long periods, with anguish sharp or dull . . . simple, naked and unanswerable hatred; who has not wanted to smash any white face he may encounter" [see Further Reading]; Baldwin's own recent fiction has as its one authentic motif this intense bitterness and race hate. Those whites with a commitment to integration and interracial fraternity, who find the open hostility of present-day black militants so distressing, can be cheered (or at least reconciled) by the realization that if one grants the universality of that hatred—and, if not its legitimacy, at least its inevitability—it is probably healthier for everyone concerned to

have it openly expressed than to have it bottled up and seething.

What Wright did with this hatred and inner violence in the period of his important work was what every serious writer must do, which is to find what Eliot called an "objective correlative" for his emotions. (pp. 128, 130)

If Wright never attained the classic control of [other artists'] works, his best books show comparable objective correlatives; the terror-inspired muscle tension that unwittingly smothers Mary Dalton in **Native Son**; the dirt floor of the sewer cavern studded with useless diamonds (Burke would call this a "perspective by incongruity") in **"The Man Who Lived Underground"**; Shorty allowing himself to be kicked sprawling by whites for a quarter in **Black Boy**; and so on. For this brief period of four or five years, Wright had an aesthetic mastery over his passions. Earlier, he had not yet attained that control, and later he lost it. If a Negro writer never strives for this sort of control, or rejects it as not worth having, he may end as an artless racist demagogue on the order of LeRoi Jones; if he overcontains his emotions, he becomes a white Negro writer, in the long gray line from Phillis Wheatley to Frank Yerby.

The second problem that Wright faced, and briefly resolved, was the development beyond the confines of realism and naturalism. Here it is important to see **Native Son** as deliberately modeled on *An American Tragedy.* The account of young Wright's first reading of Dreiser in Memphis in his late teens given in **Black Boy** is quite revealing: from reading Dreiser, Wright says, he derived "nothing less than a sense of life itself. All my life had shaped me for the realism, the naturalism of the modern novel." **"The Man Who Lived Underground"** is a pioneering work in going beyond the realism and naturalism to symbolism and fantasy, and is thus perhaps the single most revolutionary work in American Negro literature. . . .

The final problem that Wright confronted, and inadvertently solved for at least a brief period, was how to be a novelist in a post-Freudian world. Wright attempted to make deliberate fictional use of the unconscious imagery charted by Freud, to add an unconscious dimension to the power of his effects, from at least the stories in **Uncle Tom's Children** in 1938, which deliberately utilize castration imagery in the lynching scenes and elsewhere, to the contrived Freudian dream in **Savage Holiday** in 1954. This worked, but not in the simple fashion that Wright anticipated. As Freud pointed out, when the lairs of the unconscious are known, the unconscious simply goes elsewhere. What happened in Wright's case, I believe, is that the tensions and guilts connected with sexuality, openly recognized and deliberately manipulated in the fiction, fled into the color imagery, and gave it a sexual resonance and ambiguity *not* consciously contrived, which powerfully reflected the racial undercurrents of American life and *did* increase the power of Wright's work. We can see it in Sarah's nightmare of "a wide black hole" in the aptly titled **"Long Black Song"** in *Uncle Tom's Children*; in the white cat which perches on Bigger's shoulder in *Native Son*; in the imagery of school as white chalk on a black board in *Black Boy*; in Cross's image in *The Outsider* of Eva looking "into the black depths of his heart." (p. 130)

In a final evaluation of Richard Wright, we would have to say that however ill-written, flawed, and limited his work is, at least that part of it from *Native Son* to *Black Boy*, particularly **"The Man Who Lived Underground,"** seems likely to survive. The wintry cage-pacing of his best writing speaks to our condition; as Baldwin says, "Wright's unrelentingly bleak landscape was not merely that of the Deep South, or of Chicago, but that of the World, of the human heart." (p. 132)

> *Stanley Edgar Hyman, "Richard Wright Reappraised," in* The Atlantic Monthly, *Vol. 225, No. 3, March, 1970, pp. 127-32.*

Martha Stephens (essay date 1971)

[*In the following excerpt, Stephens argues that Wright's best work was written before* Native Son.]

The most obvious mistake in past attempts to sum up Wright's achievement has hardly begun to be rectified: I'm speaking of the mistaken assumption that Wright as artist must stand or fall with *Native Son*. It is hard to see how anyone who reads through, in the order it was written, the seven volumes of Wright's fiction could fail to conclude that his best work was in fact already done when he began *Native Son* in New York in 1938. I'm referring to the slender body of work completed during his remarkable first decade in the North—the decade in Chicago, 1927-37. This work consists of the five long stories of *Uncle Tom's Children,* a few additional short stories, and the novel which remained unpublished for nearly three decades, *Lawd Today.* (p. 451)

What is particularly frustrating, of course, about this exclusive concentration on *Native Son* is that the stock charges constantly brought against Wright are almost wholly inapplicable to his other books. Consider, for instance, the conventional view of Wright as race propagandist and dogmatic Marxist. Wright's *The Outsider* is a fierce attack on American Communists and on socialist thought in general, and though its central figure is a Negro, it eschews the race issue almost altogether. (p. 452)

Neither does this view of Wright seem any more reasonable when it is based on *Uncle Tom's Children* and *Lawd Today.* Yet Ellison wrote: "How awful that Wright found the facile answers of Marxism [early in the Chicago period] before he learned to use literature as a means for discovering the forms of American Negro humanity. I could not and cannot question their existence, I can only seek again and again to project that humanity as I see it and feel it" [see Further Reading]. To say that in such stories as **"Big Boy Leaves Homes"** and **"Down by the Riverside,"** which are surely two of

the finest long stories in our literature (they were originally termed novellas and both run to some sixty pages in the original *Uncle Tom's Children*), Wright was not discovering "the forms of Negro humanity" is hardly forgivable. There is not a single line in either of these stories of racial or political argument—no authorial interpretation, no message, nothing whatever of that kind attached or even tucked in. *Of course* in a sense they are protest literature—perhaps, had Wright only realized it, the most effective pieces of protest he ever wrote; in the sense, that is, that each one constitutes, among other things, an indictment of the Southern caste system such as one can hardly find words to describe. But **"Big Boy Leaves Home"** is also simply the lynching story to beat all lynching stories (a tale nearly all black writers have tried at once); and **"Down by the River-side,"** the story of a black man trapped with his family in a flood, trapped as well in the infinitely more terrible trap of the white supremacy world, is a story of such terror and beauty as to make comparable tales about poor Southern blacks look almost like trifles. (And I do not except the Trueblood story in *Invisible Man*.)

Yet Ellison and Baldwin [see Further Reading] insist that Wright could not write about *real* Negroes. Ellison makes much of Wright's confessions in *Black Boy* that he could not find among his own people evidence of the tenderness, nobility, and devotion to family that races who have been able to maintain a culture of their own have always developed. There were moods, certainly, in which Wright did feel these traits to be lacking in Negro life (and unlike Ellison, he had certainly found them lacking in his own childhood), but in fact he knew, instinctively, better. To get a balanced view of Wright's feelings about the effect on blacks of living in a caste system, one has to consider, not just the spiritually stunted figure of Bigger Thomas, but also the heroic and deeply emotional people of *Uncle Tom's Children.*

In these earliest stories the passional communal and family life of the black peasants of the South is always in view and sometimes given lyrical expression. There is, for instance, in **"Big Boy Leaves Home"** the intense, almost idyllic camaraderie of the four gamboling boys as we see them in the opening scene (within the hour the crack of doom will sound over their innocent lives and three of them will die). And after the white woman's stupid hysteria on finding the boys naked in the swimming hole, her husband's shooting of two of them, and Big Boy's frantic and half-accidental shooting of the husband, we see, as Big Boy reaches home and the news is spread, the black community instinctively forming its solid front against the dread white invader, rallying to the family in trouble, the deepest trouble that black people in the South can know—trouble with "the white folks." Then as Big Boy runs through the darkening fields to his appointed hiding place in the hillside kiln, we share, first, his anguished hope that Bobo will be able to get to the hill to join him and then his terror as he is forced to watch from the kiln Bobo's capture and death by burning at the hands of the mob.

Wright on a Long Island beach, ca. 1946.

In **"Bright and Morning Star"** there is Aunt Sue's fanatical devotion to her two sons and her dogged loyalty to the revolution in which they have taught her to believe. When the sheriff and his men come to Aunt Sue's in search of Johnny Boy, Aunt Sue is beaten for refusing to tell them where he is, and in an almost religious ecstasy she discovers in herself at last the strength to defy the powers that have ruled her life. (pp. 452-54)

In **"Fire and Cloud"** Preacher Taylor discovers, when he himself is whipped almost to death by white men ("his whole back a living sheet of fire"), the historical agony of his race. He sees his beating as a sign from God for him to assume at last the real leadership of his people. "Ah know whut yo life is! Ah done felt it! Its fire! Its like the fire that burned me last night!" Completing the Biblical metaphor, Wright shows us, at the end of the story, Taylor marching before the people, who are "moving under the sun like a pregnant cloud."

When you consider the kinds of characters I've been describing, it seems strange, to say the least, that Ralph Ellison should have insisted over and over again that Wright could not appreciate the positive qualities of the American Negro, that he could see them only as a people morally and emotionally destroyed by the long history of their oppression. Ellison insists that his own view of black people is quite different from Wright's—that he, Ellison, sees a people made strong and wise by their suffering; but in fact it is Wright, it seems to me, and not Ellison who has given us the classic portrait of the heroic and morally invincible Negro in Mann of **"Down by the Riverside."**

What seems largely to account for the emotional power of this narrative is the skillful metaphorical use of the flood itself, which is both the immediate source of and the symbol for the desperate confusion in Mann's tormented mind. Making his amazing night-time journey by rowboat into the town from his shack in the outlying countryside, Mann again and again loses his way as he struggles to interpret the shifting and veering landmarks of the submerged landscape. At one point the boat is hurled suddenly against an unseen object, and in the pitch dark Mann reaches forth and catches hold of what seem to be bars of round smooth wood; he suddenly realizes that what he is holding is the railing around the country store and that he has been rowing down the main road of the district. The reader, sharing the feeling of complete disorientation of the flood-trapped people, realize half-consciously—the analogy is felt throughout the story but never stated—that it is just this sense of terrifying disorientation (the sense that at any moment the unexpected may happen, that one's life is at the mercy of some awesome unpredictable force) that has been the daily lot of the black man throughout his history under white rule. (pp. 455-56)

[In the conclusion of **"Down by the Riverside,"**] the master race triumphs again over the life of a tormented black man, but here the *moral* victory is clearly Mann's. On the fact that he chooses, in effect, to die (rather than to abandon his family or, later, to murder the Heartfields [who witnessed the murder that he committed in self-defense]) the author has no comment nor does he endow Mann himself with a sense of his own heroism. (p. 460)

Wright's fiction has reminded many readers of Theodore Dreiser's; thus many of the complaints against him are the tiresomely familiar ones commonly made against Dreiser. Wright's characters are said to be mere inert victims, society the villain and real protagonist. Wright, we are given to understand, is no writer; he is artistically an innocent, an interesting and sincere primitive. His prose is crude and careless; he could not attend to details. Or so it is said. (p. 466)

Wright's stories may appear to be simple in technique, but they are not so simple as they seem. Like many fine stories of the highly dramatic type, they give the impression of being effortlessly written, hardly "written" at all—so engrossed does one become in the story and so oblivious of an author behind it carefully arranging his effects. Wright's forte, it seems to me, is the rendering of states of intense emotional suffering, and his best pieces are, as we have seen, relatively short...and describe a brief critical period in one individual's life, often no more than a few hours. Mann's story, for instance, begins in the afternoon, with the water rising past the windows of his shack, as he realizes he must get his family out of the flood and his wife to a doctor; it ends the next morning, some twelve tortured hours later, with his wife dead in child-birth and he himself, now the murderer of a white man, dying at the edge of the flooding river. Big Boy's story encompasses one terrible afternoon and evening, in which we see Big Boy's transformation from a lazy, smart-alecky kid into a hunted man riding out of the county at dawn hidden in the bed of a truck. (pp. 466-67)

As for Wright's narrative mode, it is the mode in which much of our best modern fiction has been written. The point of view is third-person limited, where everything is seen through the eyes of the major character. This is the narrative mode of his first published story, **"The Man Who Was Almos' a Man,"** and from which he was never thereafter to deviate. It may seem strange that a writer of Wright's intensity should never have written a first-person narrative, but of course for writers writing about primitive peoples, first-person narration does present a serious problem—perhaps for black writers even more than others since the last thing with which they want their work associated is the Negro dialect story popularized by such humorists and romanticists as Joel Chandler Harris, Charles Chesnutt, and Paul Laurence Dunbar. Third-person narration, as Wright used it, did, in any case, effect a powerful intimacy between reader and character. This is partly because much of a Wright story is generally "told" in effect by the protagonist, as his thoughts, often coming to us in his own voice, are skillfully interwoven with the narration of the hidden author; and also because the character's immediate sensory and emotional experience is the object of such fierce, uninterrupted concentration. Minor characters are hardly ever assumed to have a story of their own, even in the novels, though they often come into very sharp focus as we see them through the heightened awareness of the embattled central character. (pp. 467-68)

One cannot hope to make a wholly persuasive case for Wright's fiction in one essay, but at least one can entreat further historians not to take Wright at Ellison's and Baldwin's—or their critics'—assessment of him, which it seems to me many commentators have, in fact, done. Ellison's and Baldwin's views on the race issue, formed as they were in a different period, do seem on the whole more balanced than Wright's, at times even more intelligent; but their strategy as novelists, though *different* from his (and from each other's of course, as well), is not necessarily superior. (pp. 468-69)

Martha Stephens, "Richard Wright's Fiction: A Reassessment," in The Georgia Review, *Vol. XXV, No. 4, Winter, 1971, pp. 450-70.*

James R. Giles (essay date 1973)

[*In the following excerpt, Giles studies* Uncle Tom's Children, *viewing the stories in the collection as precursors of* Native Son.]

[Only] two years after its publication, Wright dismissed *Uncle Tom's Children* as an overly sentimental, naive book. The evaluation seems to have remained unchal-

lenged ever since. Yet it seems, *pace* the author, as shortsighted as the criticism that the book lacks unity.

[The thematic progression in both] *Uncle Tom's Children* and *Native Son* is the same—from a spontaneous, fear-motivated reaction by a black character against "the white mountain" of racial hatred to a realization of the necessity for concentrated Marxist organization of the poor. Also developed in both works are the ideas that sexual taboos between the races confuse and confound the black man's struggle for justice and that nature herself often seems to join with the white man to oppress the Negro (Bigger, fleeing from the police through the hostile, unrelenting Chicago snowstorm) permeate both books. Similarly, such images as "the white mountain" or "the white fog" to refer to the crushing weight of white society on the individual black man appear in both *Uncle Tom's Children* and *Native Son.* It is contended here that *Uncle Tom's Children* not only possesses unity and makes an unsentimental artistic statement about the position of the black man in the South, but that it employs several of the central images and themes of *Native Son* in an aesthetically more sophisticated manner than does the later and more famous work.

The first edition of *Uncle Tom's Children* contained only the four stories, **"Big Boy Leaves Home," "Down by the Riverside," "Long Black Song,"** and **"Fire and Cloud."** Subsequent editions added the introductory essay, **"The Ethics of Living Jim Crow,"** and the concluding story, **"Bright and Morning Star."** Both these additions significantly contributed to the aesthetic integrity of the work. In fact, their absence in the first edition probably explains to a large degree that initial critical reaction to the book which so dismayed Wright; in fact, neither Wright nor his critics seem ever to have realized how much these two additions contributed, both to the aesthetic unity and to the thematic militancy of the volume. At any rate, they are invaluable additions in both regards. The essay, **"The Ethics of Living Jim Crow,"** is a much abbreviated version of the racial outrages described in Wright's autobiography, *Black Boy* .... The essay ends with Wright quoting a Memphis elevator operator he had known: "Lawd, man! If it wuzn't fer them polices 'n' them o'lynch-mobs, there wouldn't be nothin' but uproar down here!'" **"Ethics"** is an aesthetically valid introduction to the stories which follow, both because of its concentrated description of the brutality endured by Wright himself in the South and because of the warning contained in this closing quotation. The five stories are all concerned with similar instances of degradation and the final message of the book is an answer to "them polices 'n' them ol'lynch mobs." As will be seen later, the addition of **"Bright and Morning Star"** brings this answer much more sharply into focus than it was initially.

One must note here that four of the five stories depict a brutal death suffered by a black man at the hands of white sadists and the other (**"Fire and Cloud"**) describes a flogging. However, beginning with the third and climactic story **"Long Black Song,"** there is a marked shift in the manner in which the black victims meet the white brutality. It is as if the viewpoint most dramatically stated in Claude McKay's famous 1919 poem, "If We Must Die" becomes the central theme of the last half of the book. In **"Long Black Song,"** the character, Silas, dramatically enacts McKay's message of courage and defiance. In contrast, the main characters in the first two stories, **"Big Boy Leaves Home"** and **"Down by the Riverside,"** react to white intimidation in a definitely non-militant way.

"Big Boy Leaves Home" describes the tragic events which occur after four young black boys decide to go swimming in a pond on the property of a notorious local white racist. While splashing about joyously in the nude, they are horrified when they look up and see a white woman standing by their clothes, transfixed in apparent horror (and fascination?) as she watches them. Big Boy, the "leader" of the gang, forces the inevitable tragedy to a swift culmination by climbing out of the pond, approaching the woman, and begging her to leave their clothes so that they can dress and go. The woman simply remains by the clothes and begins to scream.... Now terrified, the other three boys climb out of the pond and rush for their clothes. Instantly, a young white soldier (who is later revealed as the woman's fiance and the son of the notorious racist) rushes up with a rifle. The predictable results are that two of the black boys are shot, and Big Boy has to shoot the white soldier in order to save himself and his remaining friend Bobo. The woman stands terrified but unharmed throughout the scene—that she is a more fortunate forerunner of Mary Dalton, the white woman of *Native Son* who also causes tragedy by more or less unconsciously stumbling against the American racial-sexual taboo, is obvious.

After a brief respite at home, during which his mother gives him some corn bread, Big Boy goes to hide out in some deep kilns he and his friends had dug. The kilns are close to a highway, and a plan is laid for Big Boy and Bobo to wait in them overnight before catching a ride in a truck which a friend will drive to Chicago the next morning. As he is about to crawl into the first hole, Big Boy is met by a huge rattlesnake which he must kill. With the snake, Wright calls attention both to the sexual overtones of the beginning of the tragedy and to the theme, mentioned earlier, of a hostile nature.

Big Boy does spend the night hiding in a kiln—a night during which he sees his remaining friend, Bobo, caught and burned alive by a white mob just a few feet away from him. Also, just as it begins to rain, filling the kiln with freezing water, a bloodhound discovers Big Boy and the terrified youth has to grab the animal and choke it to death; again, the rain and the hound are elements of a nature which seems in league with white society to persecute the individual black man.

In the morning, the truck arrives on time and Big Boy does make his escape to Chicago:

The truck swerved. He blinked his eyes. The blades of daylight had turned brightly golden. The sun had risen.

The truck sped over the asphalt miles, sped northward, jolting him, shaking out of his bosom the crumbs of corn bread symbolic of the rejected South, making them dance with the splinters and sawdust in the golden blades of sunshine.

He turned on his side and slept.

Despite the symbolic overtones of rebirth in this passage, the rest of the book and certainly all of *Native Son* assert that fleeing to Chicago is not the answer to the Southern black man's oppression. It is merely a form of sleeping. Big Boy is, in fact, a younger Bigger Thomas in several ways—like Bigger, he is the leader of a gang, which he dominates physically, and he stumbles inadvertently into violence because of a white woman and then seeks refuge in "Flight" (the title of part two of *Native Son*). Also, Big Boy's reflexes are every bit as controlled by "Fear" (part one of *Native Son*) as are Bigger's. The conclusion, then, that Chicago will prove to be no more of an answer for Big Boy than it is for Bigger Thomas seems inevitable. (pp. 256-59)

The next story in the book, **"Down by the Riverside,"** repeats the basic ingredients of **"Big Boy"**—a helpless black individual, Mann, is forced by white bigotry into an act of violence and is forced by white oppression to flee from the inevitable consequences. But unlike Big Boy, Mann is killed trying to escape. The symbolism of the main character's name is quite important here; Big Boy and Bobo are youths, but the adult "Mann" dies pathetically while trying to flee. Thus, Wright reemphasizes the main point of the volume's first story: flight is no answer. **"Down by the Riverside"** also occurs during a flood, which represents a structural transition from Big Boy's water-filled ditch and reinforces the hostile nature theme. (p. 259)

The next story, **"Long Black Song,"** contains a significant change in mood. It is the character Silas who personifies this change. He dies, as [Claude McKay's poem "If We Must Die"] advocates, dealing the "one death-blow." But the reasons for his action lie as much within the character of his wife Sarah as within himself; and the story focuses on her at length. She is associated with all the forces—white oppression, the animosity of nature, and the violation of sexual taboos—which have destroyed Bobo and Mann and forced Big Boy to flee. Sarah, a primitive earth-mother figure, allows herself to be seduced by a young white traveling salesman of graphophones (a combination clock-gramophone) while Silas is away buying farm supplies. "I offer you time and music rolled into one," brags the salesman, unaware that Sarah has no use for time and is the soul of music. Sarah's contempt for such an abstract concept as time is emphasized at the beginning of the story when she gives her baby a clock to beat on.... (p. 260)

When he hears the full truth, Silas drives Sarah out of the house with their baby in her arms and awaits the return of the white salesman. The description of Sarah running away through the fields grasping the child and not really comprehending what she has done, emphasizes beautifully the earth mother motif. Like [William] Faulkner's Lena Grove, she is as incapable of controlling the animalistic side of her self as she is of comprehending an abstract concept like time.

In the morning, the salesman does return, and Silas shoots him. Knowing that a lynch mob is inevitably coming for him, Silas still refuses to flee, even after Sarah returns with the baby to beg him to do so. His speech to her is the turning point of **Uncle Tom's Children:**

> "The white folks ain never gimme a chance. They ain never give no black man a chance! There ain nothing in yo whole life yuh kin keep from 'em! They take yo lan! They take yo freedom! They take yo women! N then they take yo life! ... N then Ah gets stabbed in the back by mah own blood! When mah eyes is on the white folks to keep em from killin' me, mah own blood trips me up! ... Ahm gonna be hard like they is! So hep me, Gawd. Ah'm gonna be *hard!* When

Dust jacket of Wright's first nonfiction work, an illustrated "folk history of Negro Americans."

> they git me outta here theys gonna *know* Ahm gone!
> Ef Gawd lets me live Ahm gonna make em *feel* it!"

Silas is true to his word. When the mob comes, he opens fire and kills several of them. The whites set fire to his house, hoping to drive Silas out; but they fail. Silas chooses to die in the fire fighting back as long as he can. (pp. 261-62)

It is interesting to note the parallels between Silas' death and that of Jean Toomer's Tom Burwell in *Cane.* Both men die in flames, without giving their white oppressors the pleasure of a single scream of pain, and both die defending the honor of a black woman, even though it has already been defiled by a white man. But as heroic as it is, Silas' death is not yet the complete answer. Since it is an individual act with no specific political overtones—the theme of Marxist unity has yet to be introduced. The remaining stories, **"Fire and Cloud"** and **"Bright and Morning Star,"** introduce that theme, while **Long Black Song"** serves as a transition story between the negative flight of the first two stories and the positive Marxist defiance of the last two. It is significant that the titles of the last two stories come from spirituals, but are not used ironically as in the case of **"Down by the Riverside."**

"Fire and Cloud" depicts Minister Taylor's initiation into real leadership of his people. Taylor has been a "black leader" in the past mainly because of the largesse of the town's white power structure. However, when a depression strikes his people and threatens them with starvation, Taylor rebels. At the instigation of two Communists (one white and one black—Wright's symbolic propaganda here is evident), Taylor encourages a protest march, but will not let his name be used in the leaflets promoting the demonstration. On the other hand, he also refuses to stop the planned march: to the mayor, the chief of police, and another white leader, he simply says over and over that his people are "jus plain hongry!" ... Taylor is truly between two worlds: his religious orthodoxy and fear of the white establishment will not allow him to align himself openly with the Marxists, but his conscience will not allow him to stop the march. In contrast, there is his son Jimmy, a big boy with the courage of Silas, who wants to organize his band of black youths for open, pitched racial warfare.

Taylor's initiation into true leadership comes when his compromising only serves to bring out the bestiality of the white society. He is kidnapped and flogged, and a large number of his congregation are also brutally beaten. After the beating, Taylor has to struggle home through a white neighborhood, feeling that he is enclosed in a "white fog." Upon learning of his father's ordeal, Jimmy wants to rush out immediately and organize his band of black youths for revenge; but Taylor stops him.... (pp. 262-63)

Taylor has transcended even Silas and has learned, as it were, the lesson of McKay's "If We Must Die." He may not be ready to endorse Marxism in name—he still is a Christian minister—but he is ready to practice its doctrine (God is the people). Taylor does organize the march personally, and it is such a success that the starving poor whites join in, the combined forces bringing the white power structure to its knees. Taylor has become a real leader of his people, much in the way that Toomer suggests that Kabnis will do at the end of *Cane.*

The transition into **"Bright and Morning Star"** is one of the most aesthetically satisfying achievements of *Uncle Tom's Children.* This last story opens with the main character, an elderly black mother named Sue, remembering her conversion from Christianity to Communism because of the inspiration of her two Marxist sons. (Taylor, of course, has undergone a nearly identical transformation with similar inspiration.) The story also does a beautiful job of tying together all the ingredients of the preceding stories: It takes place during a driving rainstorm (again, hostile nature); at one point, Sue taunts a white sheriff into brutally beating her so that she can prove to herself that her faith in her new "religion" is as strong as was her belief in the old (this incident shows white oppression, of course, plus another example of the admirable, but finally futile, kind of courage earlier exemplified by Silas and Jimmy); Sue's hatred of white society is so intense that she is plagued by visions of "white mountains" and "white fog" (the latter, the most frequently used image in this book, as well as in *Native Son)*; and, finally, there is a white girl, Reva, who is in love with Sue's son, Johnny-Boy (the racial-sexual motif again). In Reva, though, one sees the distance covered in this book between **"Big Boy," "Long Black Song,"** and **"Bright and Morning Star."** Reva's love for Johnny-Boy is love, not just sexual fascination. Moreover, Reva exemplifies a sensitivity and sincerity which are infinitely superior to that possessed by Jan and Mary Dalton, the sympathetic white Communists of *Native Son.*

Sue herself personifies the final thematic element in the book. Just as Taylor's understanding of the need for group unity represents a thematic progression from Silas' individualistic heroism (which is itself an improvement over Big Boy's and Mann's attempts at flight), so Sue's belief in Marxism extends the characterization and depth of the kind of person Taylor is and Sue has been. Not only is she willing—unlike Taylor—to endorse Marxism openly and by name, but she accepts it with a religious fervor, much like Taylor's old feelings for the church, but with significant and promising social differences. Sue's faith in her new religion is in fact so strong that it nearly causes her to betray her party. (pp. 263-64)

[When her son is being tortured by a white mob, Sue tries to shoot him to relieve his suffering. Before she can], the gun is taken away from her. However, the sheriff simply takes the gun and shoots first Johnny-Boy and then Sue. Her death is still a triumph, however . . . . For the first time in the book, nature, as represented by a rain, is not a hostile force—Sue has, by fording the stream, conquered its treachery. Her death, by negating her unintended betrayal of the party and thus preserving Marxist unity, has prevented white oppression from destroying the potential power of the people (that God which Taylor in the preceding story had come to worship). In addition, Reva, a white woman who honestly loved a heroic black man, is safe in Sue's bed. Finally, the "white mountain" which has so intimidated all the black characters in the book has been obliterated in the killing of "the Judas" Booker.

"Bright and Morning Star" (the title comes from a spiritual describing Jesus, making the point that Sue and Johnny-Boy are the martyred saviors of the new "religion" of Marxism) effectively unites all the major elements of the book on a positive note. Certainly, then, the importance of the inclusion of this story after the first edition cannot be overstated. In fact, it adds so much to the overall work that its initial exclusion does undoubtedly explain the feeling of incompleteness on the part of the initial reviewers. That Wright himself sensed this incompleteness is proved by the beautiful transition between this and the preceding story; incomprehensibly, however, he apparently *never* grasped the degree to which **"Bright and Morning Star"** had improved his book. At any rate, the thematic progression of the book is now obvious—there is Big Boy the youth who runs, then Mann the adult who runs, then Silas who meets a heroic but lonely death, then Taylor the minister who will not openly endorse Marxism but who acts out its implications, and finally there is Sue who dies a martyred convert to Communism and thus triumphs over all the forces which have limited the characters in the first four stories.

Obviously, then, *Uncle Tom's Children* in its final form cannot be dismissed as a collection of unrelated stories, and Wright's own low opinion of his work represents an excess of self-criticism. The book makes the same progression in theme as *Native Son* (Bigger Thomas initially out of fear, runs, and finally comprehends the necessity of the unity of the masses) and achieves this progression symbolically, without a long editorial appendage to the reader by a Marxist lawyer. Moreover, such characters as Silas, Sarah, and Sue come much more vibrantly alive than does anyone in *Native Son.* Certainly Reva is nowhere near so offensive, intentionally or otherwise, as Jan and Mary Dalton, the "good" white characters of Bigger's story. In fact, it seems much more likely that "bankers' daughters" would have "wept" over *Native Son* than over *Uncle Tom's Children,* an idea which the relative sales at least of the two books, at the time of their publication, would seem to confirm. (pp. 265-66)

James R. Giles, "Richard Wright's Successful Failure: A New Look at 'Uncle Tom's Children'," in PHYLON: The Atlanta University Review of Race and Culture, Vol. XXXIV, No. 3, third quarter (September, 1973), pp. 256-66.

David Bradley (essay date 1986)

[*Bradley is the author of the award-winning novel* The Chaneysville Incident *(1981). In the following excerpt, he recounts his reactions to* Native Son, *confessing that at first he hated the work "with a passion," but now he finds it to be "a valuable document."*]

I first began Richard Wright's *Native Son* in the winter of 1971, when, as an undergraduate at the University of Pennsylvania, I was taking a course called "Readings in Black Literature." (p. 68)

Although I had never read *Native Son,* I had long been aware of it.... And I had occasionally run across references to *Native Son.* I knew, for example, of Irving Howe's declaration that "the day *Native Son* appeared, American culture was changed forever" [see excerpt dated 1963], and I had seen the contents page of David Littlejohn's *Black on White: A Critical Survey of Writing by American Negroes,* which had sections headed "Before *Native Son*: The Dark Ages" and "Before *Native Son*: The Renaissance and After." Also, since I wanted to be a writer, I was acutely aware that *Native Son* was the first book published in America to make a black author a lot of money. I therefore opened it with great expectations. Like Dickens's Pip, I was terribly disappointed.

Put simply, I hated *Native Son.* Put more accurately, I hated it with a passion. Hated it because it violated most of the principles of novelistic construction I was struggling to master. The plot was improbable, the narrative voice intrusive, the language often stilted and the characters—especially that silly little rich white tease Mary Dalton and her stupid, gigolo Communist boyfriend, Jan—were stereotypical beyond belief. At first I tried to rationalize these flaws as precisely the "ineptitude" and "unfitness" that James T. Stewart had written about. But I couldn't get around what I hated with a passion: Bigger Thomas.

It wasn't that Bigger failed as a character, exactly. I had read Wright's essay **"How Bigger Was Born"** [see excerpt dated 1940], and therefore knew that Wright had set out to write a book "no one would weep over." In this, for me, Wright succeeded. I shed no tears for Bigger. I wanted him dead, by legal means if possible, by lynching if necessary. (The only difference between me and the mob that pursued him was that I hated him not because he had accidentally killed Mary—I *understood* that and would have preferred it to have been intentional—but because he had intentionally murdered Bessie, a woman who loved him and would have done almost anything for him.) But I knew, too, that Wright had intended Bigger to be a flat character, so he could serve as a "meaningful and prophetic symbol" of the black masses. In this, for me, Wright failed. I did not see Bigger Thomas as a symbol of any kind of black man. To me he was a sociopath, pure and simple, beyond sympathy or understanding. The truth is, my first reading of *Native Son* ended at the passage in which Bigger, after practically raping Bessie, bashing in her face with a brick and tossing her body down an airshaft, thought that "he was living, truly and deeply." This, I thought, is sick.

I said so in class.... I silently endured my classmates' charge that I had been so brainwashed by the dominant culture that I was "not black enough" to appreciate *Native Son.* I did not even protest (though I thought about it) that it was the dominant culture which had declared *Native Son* a work of brilliance. (pp. 68, 70)

[James] Baldwin expressed eloquently the things I had tried to express in class. In "Everybody's Protest Novel" [see Further Reading], he charged that the works belonging to the sub-genre known as the protest novel, such as Harriet Beecher Stowe's *Uncle Tom's Cabin* and Wright's *Native Son* were unreasonably forgiven "whatever violence they do to language, whatever excessive demands they make of credibility. It is, indeed, considered the sign of a frivolity so intense as to approach decadence to suggest that these books are badly written and wildly improbable." In "Many Thousands Gone," Baldwin criticized *Native Son* in particular. "A necessary dimension," he wrote, "has been cut away; this dimension being the relationship that Negroes bear to one another.... It is this which had led us all to believe that in Negro life there exists no tradition, no field of manners, no possibility of ritual or intercourse...." Aha! I thought triumphantly. Who is going to tell James Baldwin *he* isn't black enough?

But Baldwin did something more significant than rescue my claim to racial identity in arguing that the flaws in *Native Son* were common to novels distinguished not by the race of the author but by the form of the work. Baldwin, in effect, was challenging the black esthetic. This made me realize that although a course in black literature had made it possible for me to read works by black authors which were otherwise absent from the curriculum, the assumptions behind the course had made it impossible for me to see those works as part of an American, as opposed to Afro-American, literary tradition. I wondered if I would have a different reaction to *Native Son* if I considered it in a new context. So I went in search of a copy.

My reaction was indeed different. Put simply, *Native Son* infuriated me. Put sequentially, it bemused, astonished, horrified and then infuriated me. And then it frightened me out of my wits. (p. 70)

[The] original edition of *Native Son* ... included an introduction by Dorothy Canfield. It seemed curious that a contemporary novel would require an introduction at all. But especially *that* introduction. For, while Canfield said things you would expect an introducer to say, testifying that "the author shows genuine literary skill in the construction of his novel," and comparing him to Dostoyevsky, she also said things you would expect an introducer *not* to say—for example, that she "did not at all mean to imply that *Native Son* as literature is comparable to the masterpieces of Dostoyevsky...." What was horrifying was what she thought Wright's novel *was* comparable to.

"How to produce neuroses in sheep and psychopathic upsets in rats and other animals has been known to research scientists for so long that accounts of these experiments have filtered out to the general public," she began, and went on that "our society puts Negro youth in the situation of the animal in the psychological laboratory in which a neurosis is to be caused." *Native Son,* she said, was "the first report in fiction we have had from those who succumb to these distracting crosscurrents of contradictory nerve impulses, from those whose behavior patterns give evidence of the same bewildered, senseless tangle of abnormal nerve reactions studied in animals by psychologists in laboratory experiments."

Suddenly I realized that many readers of *Native Son had* seen Bigger Thomas as a symbol in 1940 when *Native Son* hit the shelves, they, like Mary Dalton, had probably never come into enough contact with blacks to know better. God, I thought, they think we're all Biggers.

I found myself wondering how many of the attitudes of 1940's whites toward blacks may have been confirmed, influenced, if not totally shaped by such a tremendously popular "report." Had *Native Son* contributed to the fact that in 1947 less than half of all white Americans approved of integrated transportation facilities, and that only about one in three approved of integrated schools or neighborhoods? And, if they believed *Native Son* was an accurate "report," who could blame them for those attitudes? I myself did not want a nut like Bigger Thomas sitting next to me on a bus or in a schoolroom and certainly I did not want him moving in next door.

Still, I thought, while Canfield's characterization may have seemed credible to the general public, it seemed incredible to me that literary critics would have accepted it. So I sought out Irving Howe's essay, "Black Boys and Native Sons," from which the "changed the world" quote had come [see excerpt dated 1963]. In Howe, I thought, I'd surely find someone who knew that a novel is not a report.

But Howe was just as bad. True, he praised *Native Son* for having changed our culture, but he also wrote of

> all its crudeness, melodrama and claustrophobia of vision.... The language if often coarse, flat in rhythm, syntactically overburdened, heavy with journalistic slag.

> *Native Son,* though preserving some of the devices of the naturalistic novel, deviates sharply from its characteristic tone: a tone Wright could not possibly have maintained and which, it may be, no Negro novelist can really hold for long.

At that moment, I saw how *Native Son* could be a classic according to the black esthetic and still be loved by white critics: the whites did not view it as literature, except in the sense that scientific journals or polemical pamphlets are literature. (pp. 70, 72)

My second full reading of *Native Son* filled me with a terrible sorrow. Not for Bigger Thomas—I still did not give a damn about him—but for Richard Wright himself. For when I read the passage in which Mary Dalton tells Bigger how she had long wanted to enter a ghetto house "and just see how your people live," I heard the echo of Dorothy Canfield's introduction. And in the passage in which Jan tells Bigger that it was really O.K. that Bigger had killed the woman he, Jan, loved, because "You believed enough to kill. You thought you were settling something, or you wouldn't've killed." I heard Irving Howe's blithe waiver of the esthetic standards that he, as a critic, had to hold dear. And when Bigger, at the end of his life, reiterates that piece of dialectic insanity, I saw Richard Wright letting somebody tell him where his life logically ended.

And I realized that previously I had done *Native Son* the injustice of trying to fit it into my America.... Richard Wright's America was a very different place, a place where a black who hoped to survive needed a sense of humility more than a sense of dignity, and where Bigger Thomas's story was no more melodramatic, crude or claustrophobic than the times themselves.

In Richard Wright's America, a novelist could—as Wright did—base descriptions of lynch mobs in the streets of Chicago on reports taken directly from newspapers. In Richard Wright's America, a best-selling, financially independent novelist—if he was a Negro— could not lunch with his agent in a midtown Manhattan restaurant, could not buy a house in Greenwich Village and could only rent an apartment there if he found a landlord willing to defy half the neighborhood. In Richard Wright's America, a critically acclaimed, Guggenheim Fellowship-winning Negro novelist would hesitate to use the surnames of his agent and his editor in the dedication of a book because he was not sure they would want to be so closely associated with a black. In Richard Wright's America, they didn't have black literature courses: a black boy who wanted to be a writer could remain tragically unaware of the writing of black people, and could say, while explaining the origins of his characters, that "association with white writers was the life preserver of my hope to depict Negro life in fiction, for my race possessed no fictional works...no novels that went with a deep and fearless will down to the dark roots of life."

And so I came to realize that *Native Son* was not as inaccurate as I had thought, and that, in a sense, Dorothy Canfield was not entirely wrong. Not that there was great validity in Wright's use of Bigger Thomas as a type. Nor is there any validity in reading any piece of fiction as "a report" of general social conditions. But fiction is a report of specific conditions, that is its value. *Native Son,* I realized, shows the vision one black man held of his people, his country, and, ultimately, himself. And I thought, Dear God, how horrible for a man to have to write this. And, Please, God, let no one ever have to write this again.

It is the autumn of 1986. I have just finished reading *Native Son* for the fourth time. I have been invited to write an introduction to a new edition. Put simply—and frighteningly, to me—I have been asked to step into the role of Dorothy Canfield, and dared to do a better job.

I am not sure I can do a better job. For while what Canfield wrote still infuriates me, she was a part of her time, as I am a part of mine. Still, I have had the opportunity—as she did not—to read *Native Son* over a span of years. And I find that I can be kinder toward *Native Son* than I have been in the past.

Not that I think *Native Son* has suddenly become artistically brilliant. But I have realized, belatedly, that *Native Son* is a first novel. Its flaws are typical of first novels, no more severe than those found in most. And now I can see beneath the shroud of politics and accept that *Native Son* is, in fact, a valuable document—not of sociology, but of history. It reminds us of a time in this land of freedom when a man could have this bleak and frightening vision of his people, and when we had so little contact with one another that that vision could be accepted as fact.

But despite that, I find that Wright, after all these years, has failed in an ironic way. He wanted *Native Son* to be a book "no one would weep over." With me, he once succeeded. He no longer does. *Native Son* is an ineffably sad expression of what once were the realities of this nation. We have not come as far as we ought. But I hope we have come far enough by now to read *Native Son* and weep. (pp. 74, 78-9)

> *David Bradley, "On Rereading 'Native Son'," in* The New York Times Magazine, *December 7, 1986, pp. 68-79.*

FURTHER READING

Baldwin, James. *Notes of a Native Son.* Boston: Beacon Press, 1955, 175 p.
   Includes three of Baldwin's best-known essays on Wright's work: "Everybody's Protest Novel," "Many Thousands Gone," and "Notes of a Native Son."

————. "Alas, Poor Richard: *Eight Men.*" In his *Nobody Knows My Name: More Notes of a Native Son,* pp. 181-89. New York: Dial Press, 1961.
   Reconsiders Wright's work. Here, Baldwin perceives a "new depth" in Wright's later short stories.

Blau, Eleanor. "The Works of Richard Wright, This Time Published as Written." *The New York Times* (28 August 1991): B1, B2.
   Discusses the discovery of hitherto overlooked galleys of original passages that were deleted from *Native Son, Lawd Today,* and *The Outsider* at time of publication. Restored texts of these and other works appear in *Richard Wright: Works* (1991), edited by Arnold Rampersad and published as Vols. 55 and 56 of "Library of America."

Bloom, Harold, ed. *Modern Critical Views: Richard Wright.* New York: Chelsea House Publishers, 1987, 246 p.
   Ten critical essays on various aspects of Wright's writing, including works by Edward Margolies, Michel Fabre, and Houston A. Baker, Jr.

Bone, Robert. *The Negro Novel in America.* New Haven: Yale University Press, 1965, 289 p.
   Details the evolution of the black novel in America from 1890 to 1952, specifically examining the influence of Wright and the protest novels of the 1930s and 1940s.

Bramwell, Gloria. "Articulated Nightmare." *Midstream* VII, No. 2 (Spring 1961): 110-12.
   Briefly surveys Wright's career, offering critical commentary on "The Man Who Went to Chicago" and "The Man Who Lived Underground."

Brignano, Russell Carl. *Richard Wright: An Introduction to the Man and His Works.* Pittsburgh: University of Pittsburgh Press, 1970, 202 p.
   Biographical and critical study that examines the ideological bases of Wright's works.

Brown, Cecil. "Richard Wright's Complexes and Black Writing Today." *Negro Digest* XVIII, No. 2 (December 1968): 45-50, 78-82.
   Contends that Wright's consistent portrayal of blacks as violent and ignorant propagates stereotypes and constitutes negative rather than positive protest fiction.

Cowley, Malcolm. "Long Black Song." *The New Republic* LXXXIV, No. 1218 (6 April 1938): 280.
   Review of *Uncle Tom's Children,* commenting on the communist ideals in "Fire and Cloud" and on Wright's skillful portrayal of racial hatred.

Delmar, P. Jay. "Tragic Patterns in Richard Wright's *Uncle Tom's Children.*" *Negro American Literature Forum* 10, No. 1 (Spring 1976): 3-12.
   Outlines the tragic patterns in each of the five stories in *Uncle Tom's Children,* focusing on the dilemmas and fatal personality flaws that doom Wright's protagonists.

Ellison, Ralph. "The World and the Jug." In his *Shadow and Act,* pp. 107-43. New York: Random House, 1964.
   Responds to Irving Howe's essay "Black Boys and Native Sons" [see excerpt dated 1963], arguing that Howe's assessment of Wright and Baldwin is false and merely reflects his own "northern white liberal" attitudes.

Embree, Edwin R. "Native Son." In his *13 Against the Odds,* pp. 25-46. New York: Viking Press, 1944.

Biographical and critical study covering Wright's life up to the publication of *Native Son.*

Everette, Mildred W. "The Death of Richard Wright's American Dream." *CLA Journal* XVII, No. 3 (March 1974): 318-26.
Describes "The Man Who Lived Underground" as a portrait in utter despair. Everette explores the theme of death and darkness in the work, stating that the mood of the story reflects Wright's own bleak perspective at the time he wrote it.

Fabre, Michel. *The Unfinished Quest of Richard Wright.* Translated by Isabel Barzun. New York: William Morrow, 1973, 652 p.
Biographical and critical study.

————. *The World of Richard Wright.* Jackson: University Press of Mississippi, 1985, 268 p.
Collection of reprinted essays from the 1970s and early 1980s on Wright's work.

Felgar, Robert. *Richard Wright.* Boston: Twayne Publishers, 1980, 189 p.
Critical overview that examines the short stories in *Eight Men,* including a commentary on Wright's two comic radio plays "Man, God Ain't Like That..." and "Man of All Work."

Hakutani, Yoshinobu, ed. *Critical Essays on Richard Wright.* Boston: G. K. Hall & Co., 305 p.
Anthology of criticism of Wright's work. Contributors include Irving Howe, Lewis Leary, Michel Fabre, and Ralph Ellison.

Hurston, Zora Neale. "Stories of Conflict." *The Saturday Review of Literature* XVII, No. 23 (2 April 1938): 32.
Review of *Uncle Tom's Children.* Hurston objects to the extreme hatred and despair in the stories, declaring its communist standpoint simplistic.

Jackson, Blyden. "Richard Wright in a Moment of Truth." *Southern Literary Journal* III, No. 2 (Spring 1971): 3-17.
Biographical reading of "Big Boy Leaves Home," focusing on the significance of Wright's upbringing in the South.

————. "Two Mississippi Writers: Wright and Faulkner." *The University of Mississippi Studies in English* 15 (1978): 49-59.
Explores similarities and differences in the fiction of William Faulkner and Wright, stressing the authors' common Mississippi background.

Joyce, Joyce Ann. *Richard Wright's Art of Tragedy.* Iowa City: University of Iowa Press, 1986, 129 p.
Study of Wright's use of tragedy in his works.

Negro Digest XVIII, No. 2 (December 1968).
Issue devoted to Wright that includes articles on his work, life, and influence on black literature.

Ray, David, and Farnsworth, Robert M., eds. *Richard Wright: Impressions and Perspectives.* Ann Arbor: University of Michigan Press, 1973, 207 p.
Collection of essays, letters, and miscellaneous observations about Wright and his works. The pieces are arranged chronologically according to the periods of Wright's career and include several articles on Wright's early years in Memphis and Chicago.

Reilly, John M. "Self-Portraits by Richard Wright." *Colorado Quarterly* XX, No. 1 (Summer 1971): 31-45.
Compares the 1942 and 1944 versions of "The Man Who Lived Underground."

————. "Richard Wright: An Essay in Bibliography." *Resources for American Literary Study* 1, No. 2 (Autumn 1971): 131-80.
Reviews bibliographical studies and articles on Wright and his writings.

————. "Richard Wright's Apprenticeship." *Journal of Black Studies* 2, No. 4 (June 1972): 439-60.
Provides biographical information on Wright, focusing on his involvement with the Communist Party.

Studies in Black Literature 1, No. 3 (Fall 1970).
Entire issue devoted to Wright. Included are an interview with Simone de Beauvoir and a letter from Dorothy Padmore as well as reviews of Wright's poetry and novels.

Sullivan, Richard. "Lives of More Than Quiet Desperation." *New York Times Book Review* (22 January 1961): 5.
Reviews Wright's *Eight Men,* praising the author's realism and technical mastery.

Timmerman, John. "Trust and Mistrust: The Role of the Black Woman in Three Works by Richard Wright." *Studies in the Twentieth Century,* No. 10 (Fall 1972): 33-45.
Compares the passivity of Sarah in "Long Black Song" to the determination of Sue in "Bright and Morning Star," arguing that the latter character utilizes her inner strength to shape her circumstances.

Webb, Constance. *Richard Wright: A Biography.* New York: G. P. Putnam's Sons, 1968, 443 p.
Biographical and critical study.

Weigel, Henrietta. "Personal Impressions." *New Letters* 38, No. 2 (Winter 1971): 17-20.
Recounts several of Weigel's personal encounters with Wright.

Frank Yerby

1916-

(Full name Frank Garvin Yerby) American novelist, poet, and short story writer.

A prolific novelist who has published over thirty tales of adventure, Yerby has sold over fifty-five million hardback and paperback books in the last forty years. While many of these novels have been best-sellers, their popularity has had little effect on Yerby's critical stature. Since the appearance of his first novel, *The Foxes of Harrow*, in 1946, the author has been routinely—and some say unfairly—slighted by critics. Early in his career, for instance, when Yerby was producing mainstream fiction, black reviewers attacked him for abandoning his race. Those who knew his work, but not his color, accused him of squandering his writing talent on cardboard characters and hackneyed plots. Still others objected to his "over-blown" prose and the way he sensationalized his material. Writing in *The Negro Novel in America*, Robert A. Bone dubbed him "the prince of the pulpsters."

Yerby, the second of four children of a racially mixed couple, was born in Augusta, Georgia, in 1916. He attended Haines Institute in Augusta, a private primary and secondary school for blacks, and received a B. A. degree in English from Paine College in 1937 and an M. A. in English from Fisk University in 1938. A year later he began doctoral work at the University of Chicago but was forced to give up his studies after nine months because of financial problems. In Chicago he worked with the Federal Writers' Project and met authors William Attaway, Arna Bontemps, Margaret Walker, and Richard Wright. After leaving Chicago, Yerby taught at Florida A&M University in Tallahassee and at Southern University in Baton Rouge, Louisiana. Dissatisfied with what he regarded as the "stifling" atmosphere of these "Uncle Tom factories," he gave up teaching in 1941 and moved with his wife, Flora Claire Williams, to Dearborn, Michigan, where he worked in a defense plant. During this period he published poems and short stories in *Challenge, Shard, Arts Quarterly*, and other periodicals. An early work of fiction, which earned him an O. Henry Memorial Award in 1944, is a bitter story of racial injustice called "Health Card." It was the last time Yerby would directly address a racial theme in his fiction for almost thirty years. In 1946, with the publication of the blockbuster best-seller *The Foxes of Harrow*, Yerby became famous almost overnight. Since the early 1950s he has lived abroad, mostly in France and Spain. Currently, he lives in Madrid.

Yerby's novels are characterized by colorful language, complex plot lines, and a multiplicity of characters. Hugh M. Gloster called Yerby's formula "the recipe of Southern historical romance," listing the following ingredients: "a bold, handsome, rakish, but withal

somewhat honorable hero; a frigid, respectable wife; a torrid unrespectable mistress; and usually a crafty, fiendish villain." *Time* magazine summed up his writing as "a crude, shrewd combination of sex, violence, sadism, costuming and cliche." Gloster, commenting on Yerby's treatment of racial issues—especially his use of Anglo-Saxon protagonists—added: "[Yerby] gained his laurels by focusing upon white rather than Negro characters. Performance—and not pigmentation—has been the basis of his success." Yerby has staunchly defended his focus, explaining that "the novelist hasn't any right to inflict on the public his private ideas on politics, religion or race. If he wants to preach he should go on the pulpit." He also stated: "My mother was Scotch-Irish, a grandparent was an Indian; I've far more Irish blood than Negro. I simply insist on remaining a member of the human race. I don't think a writer's output should be dictated by a biological accident. It happens there are many things I know far better than the race problem."

The Foxes of Harrow is a lush southern romance that traces the fortunes of the dashing young Stephen Fox in his rise from poverty to great wealth. While acknowledging Yerby's ability to hold the reader captive with his fast-paced plotting and vivid prose, many critics dismissed the book as insignificant melodrama. Edmund Wilson, for instance, noted that Yerby "has packed everything in—passion, politics, creole society, sex, the clash of races, and war—but he never captures the faintest flutter of the breath of life." In recent years, Yerby himself has belittled the work, telling *People* magazine that *The Foxes of Harrow* comprises "every romantic cliche in history." The novel's literary shortcomings, however, had no effect on its enormous popularity. With sales in the millions, it was one of the hottest titles of the decade. It was translated into at least twelve languages, reprinted in several national magazines, and made into a movie starring Rex Harrison and Maureen O'Hara.

Though Yerby despised the film adaptation, he was pleased with his novel's popular acceptance, and he continued to work the vein of historical fiction in future books. His next novel, *The Vixens* (1947), utilized research material he had not been able to use in his first book. He followed *The Vixens* with a string of other southern romances, set for the most part in the nineteenth century. With *The Golden Hawk*, in 1948, Yerby turned to picaresque adventure in other lands and earlier centuries. And his research, which had been careless in his first novels, became meticulous.

While Yerby's novels of the 1950s and 1960s qualify as popular fiction, they also reflect serious concerns. Wrote Darwin T. Turner: "Ideas—bitter ironies, caustic debunkings, painful gropings for meaning—writhe behind the soap-facade of his fiction." In 1971, after protesting his indifference to racial issues for many years, Yerby addressed the matter directly in *The Dahomean*, his novel of Black Africa. Set in the nineteenth century, *The Dahomean* traces the life of Nyasanu/Hwesu as he advances in position from a chief's son to governor of an entire province, only to be sold into American slavery by two jealous relatives. In a prefatory note to the novel, Yerby explained that part of his reason for writing the book was "to correct, so far as possible, the Anglo-Saxon reader's historical perspective" on black history. By portraying the Dahomean culture in all its rich complexity, Yerby aimed to dispel the myth of a totally primitive Africa, even hinting at times that the tribal cultures "sometimes surpassed in their subtlety, their complexity, their dignity the ones to which the slaves were brought," according to a reviewer in *Best Sellers*. But in depicting the cruelties that certain tribesmen perpetrated on other blacks, including selling them into slavery, Yerby also shattered the illusion that blacks are inherently superior morally. What Yerby seems to be suggesting, Turner maintained, is that "the differences between people do not stem from a difference of blood, but from a difference of opportunity and power."

Yerby has postulated that critical reaction to his books reflects reviewers' biases: "Those who confuse literature with sexual morality damn them; those wise enough, emotionally mature enough to realize that the two things have practically nothing to do with each other, generally like them very much indeed." Since the publication of *The Dahomean*, Yerby noted, "two things have been of considerable comfort to me. First is the fact that I am no longer accused of colorful, purplish overwriting. And the second is the dawning realization that fifty-five million readers in eighty-two countries and twenty-three languages (who have bought and paid for my novels) are not necessarily all idiots. Strangely enough (or perhaps not so strangely after all) the degree of appreciation for a novel of mine is directly increased by the degree of knowledge the reader has of the subject. In other words, people who know the themes I've written about either by reason of having lived through them, or deeply and professionally studied them, find no fault with my novels. I am praised by experts, attacked by—well, let's be kind and call them amateurs."

(For further information about Yerby's life and works, see *Black Writers*; *Contemporary Authors*, Vols. 9-12; *Contemporary Authors New Revision Series*, Vol. 16; *Contemporary Literary Criticism*, Vols. 1, 7, 22; *Dictionary of Literary Biography*, Vol. 76: *Afro-American Writers, 1940-1955*; and *Major 20th-Century Writers*.)

PRINCIPAL WORKS

The Foxes of Harrow (novel) 1946
The Vixens (novel) 1947
The Golden Hawk (novel) 1948
Pride's Castle (novel) 1949
Floodtide (novel) 1950
A Woman Called Fancy (novel) 1951
The Saracen Blade (novel) 1952
The Devil's Laughter (novel) 1953
Benton's Row (novel) 1954
Bride of Liberty (novel) 1954
The Treasure of Pleasant Valley (novel) 1955
Captain Rebel (novel) 1956
Fairoaks (novel) 1957
The Serpent and the Staff (novel) 1958
Jarrett's Jade (novel) 1959
Gillian (novel) 1960
The Garfield Honor (novel) 1961
Griffin's Way (novel) 1962
The Old God's Laugh: A Modern Romance (novel) 1964
An Odor of Sanctity: A Novel of Medieval Moorish Spain (novel) 1965
Goat Song: A Novel of Ancient Greece (novel) 1968
Judas My Brother: The Story of the Thirteenth Disciple (novel) 1968
Speak Now: A Modern Novel (novel) 1969
The Dahomean: An Historical Novel (novel) 1971
The Girl from Storyville: A Victorian Novel (novel) 1972
The Voyage Unplanned (novel) 1974
Tobias and the Angel (novel) 1975
A Rose for Ana Maria (novel) 1976
Hail the Conquering Hero (novel) 1977

A Darkness at Ingraham's Crest: A Tale of the Slaveholding South (novel) 1979
Western: A Saga of the Great Plains (novel) 1982
Devilseed (novel) 1984
McKenzie's Hundred (novel) 1985

Hugh M. Gloster (essay date 1948)

[*In the excerpt below, Gloster reviews* The Foxes of Harrow *and* The Vixens.]

As a novelist Yerby has gained laurels by focusing upon white rather than Negro characters. Performance—and not pigmentation—has been the basis of his success . . . .

The recipe for Yerby's achievement in fiction is not new. It is an old one used many times before but still sufficiently toothsome to please the literary appetites of American readers. It is the recipe of Southern romance: a bold, handsome, rakish, but withal somewhat honorable hero; a frigid, respectable wife; a torrid, unrespectable mistress; and usually a crafty, fiendish villain. These characters, with their conflicting passions, are brought together in the land of mansions and magnolias during a period replete with social, political, and racial strife. The result is sufficient to satisfy any reader who likes bloody fights and sexy romance. (p. 12)

The Foxes of Harrow reflects painstaking study of the Louisiana milieu and its history. Steamboat races, lavish social affairs, duels, yellow fever epidemics, secession, and war are depicted on the broad canvas of the novel. The institution of slavery is described, and events leading to the Civil War are woven into the story. Convincing portraiture is done of Inch, Etienne's upstanding Negro servant who rises from bondage to become an influential figure in Reconstruction government. In the delineation of Inch and several other Negro characters Yerby makes noteworthy departures from the handkerchief-head stereotypes who conventionally appear in Southern historical fiction . . . .

Like **The Foxes of Harrow**, **The Vixens** gives a good picture of its historical setting. The economic and social foundations of feudal Louisiana are in ruins as a result of four years of war. Negroes are casting the ballot, holding office, and seeking to gain a foothold as citizens. Die-hard Dixie aristocrats, operating through the Knights of the White Camellia and the Ku Klux Klan, are straining to wrest power from Carpetbaggers, Scalawags, and Negro freedmen. In portraying these varied characters of Reconstruction Louisiana, Yerby neither condemns nor glorifies, but lets the reader draw his own conclusions.

Despite their popular appeal, **The Foxes of Harrow** and **The Vixens** do not establish Yerby as a first-rate novelist. The use of secondhand materials . . . causes the reader to think that the young writer knows more about libraries than about life. Furthermore, the author's seeming lack of ideological conviction is somewhat unexpected in fiction treating the cross-currents of life and thought in nineteenth-century Louisiana. Yerby also has a flair for melodrama . . . . While the assignment of Yerby's first novel to this category is highly debatable, the criticism does point to an inclination which assumes sizable proportions in **The Vixens**. Another questionable practice in Yerby's work is a delight in over-embellished diction . . . . This relish for melodrama and flamboyant phrases suggests a lack of restraint.

Nevertheless, Yerby has assets as a writer. He shows intimate knowledge, gained through study and research, of his locale and its history. He exercises balance in handling inflammatory, controversial subjects. He has faculty in the use of words, especially pictorial and passionate ones, and the power to maintain interest from the beginning of a tale to its close. His chief contribution, however, has been to shake himself free of the shackles of race and to use the treasure-trove of American experience—rather than restrictively Negro experience—as his literary province. (p. 13)

> *Hugh M. Gloster, "The Significance of Frank Yerby," in* The Crisis, *Vol. 55, No. 1, January, 1948, pp. 12-13.*

Frank Yerby (essay date 1959)

[*In the following essay, "How and Why I Write the Costume Novel," Yerby explains his approach to writing popular literature.*]

Editors, writers, and students sometimes ask me how to write "best-selling novels" but I am always forced to disappoint them. If I knew how, I should most certainly turn one out every year. The fact is I try and sometimes—rarely—I succeed; more often, I come reasonably close; occasionally I fail.

However, I can discuss something I know and can do: a certain genre of light, pleasant fiction, which, in the interest of accuracy, I call the costume novel. The word "historical" won't do at all. I have repeatedly loaded them with history, only to have ninety-nine and ninety-nine one-hundredths of said history land on the Dial Press cutting-room floor. Which is not a complaint. That is exactly where it belongs. For, at bottom, the novelist's job is to entertain. If he aspires to instruct, or to preach, he has chosen his profession unwisely.

I believe I can write the costume novel with a fair average of success. I have made a rather serious study of the elements that go to make up a novel of wide appeal. In fact, I made this study immediately prior to writing **The Foxes of Harrow**, in order to eliminate as far as was humanly possible, the chances of its failing.

My reasons for doing so may or may not be of interest. I had been writing all my life; my first ludicrously immature verses, mostly sonnets in rather sweet sickly imitation of Millay—with an occasional *lointain* bow in the direction of Shakespeare—were published in the little, arty magazines when I was seventeen years old. But, as I grew older, the conviction that an unpublished writer, or even one published but unread, is no writer at all began insidiously to impress itself upon me. The idea dawned that to continue to follow the route I had mapped out for myself was roughly analogous to shouting one's head off in Mammoth Cave. Rather unsatisfactory things, echoes of one's own feeble voice. I made for, and to, myself the usual excuses: I was just too intelligent, too *avant-garde* for the average mind, and so on.

But I am cursed with a rather painful sense of honesty; once past my teens, this nonsense began to have an increasingly hollow ring. University courses in English and American literature showed me one thing very surely: real talent is seldom, if ever, neglected in the world of letters—even during the lifetime of the writer. Offhand, I can think of but three exceptions: Nathaniel Hawthorne, Walt Whitman, and Herman Melville. They managed to be really *avant-garde* for their times, which, in our basically imitative profession, is no mean feat. A wise teacher pointed out to me another fact: the classics of today are very nearly always the best sellers of the past. Thackeray, Dickens, Defoe, Byron, Pope, Fielding —the list is endless—enjoyed fabulous popularity in their day. And, crossing the channel, what can one say of Balzac, Hugo, Maupassant, Dumas?

Once having been forced to admit that unpalatable truth: a writer is unread only because he fails to communicate, has not really mastered his craft, I was faced with a greater problem: how the blazes does one get published—and, more important, read? It took me years to stumble upon the solution, which I found, oddly enough in a magazine devoted to ancient automobiles! I was thumbing through this magazine when my eye was caught by a photo of a car with no less than *eight* wheels. The caption stated, in effect, that this vehicle had failed to capture the imagination of the public, because the designer had insisted upon giving the buyers more wheels than they wanted. Other models illustrated had three wheels. They likewise failed, presumably because the automotive public found that number too few. No one, it seems, had heard of consumer research in those days.

So—neither three wheels nor eight, then. But how many wheels does the public want? The analogy was plain. One of the basic elements of the writer's temperament is a certain species of megalomania; when one thinks of it, the unmitigated gall it takes to believe steadfastly that one's mere words set down upon paper about imaginary people in imaginary situations could possibly be of interest to anyone is nothing short of stupendous. Yet, we carry our delusions of grandeur to even greater lengths: we, most of us, insist upon writing what *we* want to write, and then have the naïveté to be surprised and hurt when the readers stay away from the bookstores in droves. How long would a doctor survive if he insisted upon removing the tonsils of a man with an inflamed appendix because *he* prefers tonsillectomies? Or a man who builds cars with eight wheels when four are jolly well enough?

Therefore, having collected a houseful of rejection slips for works about ill-treated factory workers, or people who suffered because of their religions or the color of their skins, I arrived at the awesome conclusion that the reader cares not a snap about such questions; that, moreover, they are none of the novelist's business. Sociologists, reformers, and ministers of the Gospel have been handling those matters rather well over the years; why not, then, let them continue? The writer is, or should be, concerned with individuals. They may be workers, Negroes, Jews, if you will; but they must be living people, with recognizably individual problems, and confronted with individual, personified opposition, not Prejudice, Bigotry, and what-have-you in capital letters. Those problems exist; but they are awfully hard to pin down in interesting fashion. The reader will believe in Tobias Skinflint, the hard-hearted banker; he balks when the antagonist is "The Bank."

From there on, my primary venture into consumer research was easy. I set myself two criteria: the novels I selected for study must be those which have passed a double test: *i.e.*, they must have been successful when published, and must have continued to be successful over the years. I reread then *Tom Jones, Vanity Fair, Moll Flanders, Wuthering Heights, Jane Eyre, Joseph Andrews* among others. I read no contemporary novels, not out of prejudice against my fellows, but because I was searching for those elements of the novelist's art which have weathered the test of time.

All of these books, I already knew, met both qualifications: they were read then; they are being read, now. What I wanted to find out was why. The whys soon became obvious: they are all good, rousing tales, and fun to read. They all end—except *Wuthering Heights*— more or less happily; and their characters, carefully studied, were a revelation. The cardinal point about Tom Jones, Joseph Andrews, Becky Sharp, Moll, Heathcliff, Rochester, *et al*, is that they are not at all like the man who lives next door. They may or may not be realistic; only their contemporaries would have been qualified to discuss the point. I suspect that they aren't. One needs only to read Terence, Plautus, or Seneca to realize how little human nature has changed in two thousand years. (If it has changed at all, which I doubt.) What they are is interesting, even exciting. All these authors—Fielding, the Brontës, Defoe, Thackeray— have achieved the novelist's highest attainment: not the still life of literal representation of people and events— which would be a thumping bore—but a magistral suspension of the reader's sense of disbelief.

From them I drew certain basic rules which I have subsequently ignored only at grave peril. These rules are my own. They very probably would not work for anyone else. But, for whatever they may be worth, here they are:

The protagonist must be picaresque. In other words, he must be a charming scoundrel, preferably with a dark secret in his past. His anti-social tendencies must be motivated by specific reasons—an unfortunate childhood, injustices heaped upon himself or upon his loved ones, physical and moral sufferings which incline the reader to sympathize with his delinquency. He must be a doer, never resignedly submitting to the blows of fate; but initiating the action of the plot himself.

Curiously enough, he must be a dominant male. I think this quality appeals most of all to American women readers. For, after having had their mothers and grandmothers convert the United States into a matriarchy with their ardent femininism, and reduce the bearded patriarch that grandfather was into the pink and paunchy Caspar Milquetoast of today, the average American female reader subconsciously enjoys reading about a male who can get up on his hind legs and roar. They will deny this statement, hotly. Nevertheless, it is so.

Physically, he can be of almost any type except short, bald, and bearded. These taboos, since women make up a large part of the costume novel's readers, are absolute. He should not be too good-looking, or the more sophisticated will doubt him. But exciting to look upon, he must be. And "romantic"—a curious word meaning all things to all people. From my point of view, it means that in his emotional relationships he should not be too bright—something, perhaps, that I should not state so baldly. But again and again the action of the costume novel's plot is carried forward by our hero's failure to realize that in any man's life there are literally dozens, if not hundreds, of women who will do just as well; that he won't die if he doesn't win fair Susan's dainty hand; and that very probably he will catch a most uninteresting variety of hell if he does win it. Which, come to think of it, is not unrealistic: emotional maturity is one of the rarest qualities in life.

All of the above applies also to the heroine, or, preferably heroines, since my conviction that the male of the species is incurably polygamous remains unshaken. The little dears should, of course, be a trifle less picaresque, except when, as in the case of Moll Flanders or Becky Sharp, they are the protagonists. They can, in the costume novel, approach real loveliness; for feminine readers tend to identify themselves with their fictional heroines and so can accept female beauty. And they must be even more emotionally immature, that is romantic, than the protagonist. The reader will accept the portrait of the at-first unloved, but ever so much finer, little creature's waiting for years until the opportunity presents itself to win our Jonathan; which, in life, happens about as frequently as being struck by lightning. I never cease to marvel at the reader's willingness to catch John Donne's falling star, and to attempt that impossibly intimate feat with his mandrake root. These aspects of the costume novel sometimes distress me; but, there they are.

The heroine must have an aura of sex about her. When I reach this point, I must admit that I am writing about a thing of which I am entirely unsure. I have held, at different times, quite opposite points of view about literary sex. I once believed it essential to popular success; then, later, I believed it fatal to that success. Now, I just don't know. I find writing about sex childish, boring, and distressing; but I find a too careful avoidance of the subject artificial. After all, with the exception of some individuals held back by religious scruples, most people do have a regular sex life. I am inclined to think now that the way of handling the subject is all important. If it can be done with enough delicacy, tact, indirection, implication, understatement, it can help a novel. If not, better let it alone. I have often longed for our Victorian forebears' delightfully contrived phrase: "Let us now draw the curtain of charity over the ensuing scene."

To illustrate, *Foxes of Harrow* has very little sex in it. And that little occurs behind Victorian curtains, carefully drawn. But, in my next work, a novel entitled *Ignoble Victory* (far better written, I stubbornly insist upon believing, than anything I have ever done before or since) I ran into difficulties. It was, in a way, literary. I was solemnly assured that it would lose me the public I had gained. One of my editors kept writing me pithy memos: "More sex, Frank! For goodness sake, more sex!" So I went overboard. *Ignoble Victory* was downgraded into *The Vixens*, a book I have never since been able to read. I can get as far as the point where Denise appears with her violet eyes, miraculous figure, and untamed libido. Then my stomach revolts. Perhaps I am wrong. *The Vixens* had impressive sales. I think, however, that it was bought by readers of *The Foxes*, hoping for more of the same. To them, my humblest apologies. It should have been banned, or burned.

I hotly insisted that it wasn't its overcharged sexiness that made it sell. Then the letters began to come in. They were better than 90 per cent pro-sex. Later, I made an interesting discovery: the many, many readers whose good taste must have been offended, almost surely didn't write. Because those approving letters were so alike as almost to have been written by one hand. They made me sorrowfully remember the remark of a healthily profane, if somewhat ungrammatical friend: "God help them as has to *read* about it."

So I toned sex down again. In some books, such as *A Woman Called Fancy* and *The Treasure of Pleasant Valley* I all but eliminated it. *Fancy* sold. *Treasure* didn't. Conclusion: sex neither helps nor hurts a book; it all depends upon whether the novel, itself, is interesting. But, as I said before, even of this conclusion I am not sure. I think that, depending upon how it is handled, it may do either.

The third essential of the costume novel is a strong, exteriorized conflict, personified in a continuing, formidable antagonist or antagonists. The phrase comes from my publisher, the late George Joel. I have an unfortunate habit of underplaying the villain. In the first place, to the twentieth-century mind, wickedness is equivalent to sickness, and sickness is dull. In the second, I find it impossible to believe that two people can keep up a quarrel, however vital, for four hundred pages. But no good costume novel can move unless the conflict is there. I know I am wrong, professionally, about my point of view; but it costs me great effort to keep my boys banging away at each other. I find myself wanting to say: "Why don't you idiots shake hands, have a quiet drink together, and forget it?" But, if they do, what becomes of my novel? Now I do believe in interior conflicts: man warring with himself. I have seen them go on lifelong. But these are not the stuff of the costume novel.

Once the characters, and the supporting, minor players have been assembled, they, themselves, with some slight assisting impetus from the histories, make the plot. If they don't assume life, take the bit between their teeth, and start galloping all over the landscape, they were stillborn in the first place, and it is much better to let them lie.

The plot should be lean, economical, stripped down. Life is meandering, often pointless; but a novel is not life, but a deliberate distortion of it, solely designed to give pleasure to a reader. Therefore, hewing to the line of the plot is essential; there must be no wandering for so much as a single paragraph from the point. Anything that can be cut, should be. One superfluous word is too

Yerby, circa 1950.

much. Go on with your windy flights, and friend reader puts the book down and turns on the TV set. If he hasn't it on already. The trick is to make him forget that vast, moronic eye is there.

The plot should be dramatic. The reader must be snatched out of his reclining chair and set down as a participating witness in the midst of it. Therefore nothing should be told which can be shown; nothing shown which can be implied. Suggestion is always more powerful than statement, because it assures the reader's participation by forcing his imagination to supply the details that the novelist left out. And he will supply them. Doubled. And in spades.

There must, finally, be a *theme* to the novel: our characters must rise above themselves and their origins and contribute—toward the end, in one or two brief scenes—something ennobling to life. This is delicate. If Tom Jones, having been more or less a gigolo, starts acting like a scoutmaster, the results will be pretty dreary. The reader likes to believe he is going to reform, but doesn't want to hang around to witness that distressing spectacle. For these, and many other reasons, theme is the most difficult part of the costume novel. More than in any other type of novel, the writer of costume entertainments must be concerned with the problems of individual men and women. While these problems can turn upon such themes as religion, race, politics, and economics, it is far better that they do not. Such themes by their very nature, tend to transform the novel into a propagandist's tract basket; and few novelists have the will power to prevent them from so doing. Worse, using them, most novelists succumb to the temptation to put their own burning opinions into the mouths of their characters, thus reducing them out of life into puppets dancing on very visible strings. I cannot repeat often enough that the novelist's concern is not what interests himself, but what interests his readers. Negatively, therefore, he should avoid themes about which he has fixed opinions. He cannot do them justice. He is very likely mistaken, and attendant circumstances modify the rightness or wrongness of a thing totally. Even murder can be an entirely moral action under special circumstances of absolute necessity.

I have mentioned that in my early days, I, too, employed the themes I now avoid like the plague, in one or two so-called proletarian novels so typical of the depression epoch. Like all the young in body or in mind, I then believed that all problems can be solved; and that it was my duty to help solve them through my sterling prose. But I grew up in the late thirties, a period that went out of its way to educate a man. I rapidly arrived at the conviction I have held ever since: that many, if not most of life's problems cannot be solved at all. Build a dam on the Nile, and the staring fellaheen, better fed from the increased productivity of their newly irrigated land, grow strong enough to produce an explosion in the birthrate, so that the next generation has half as much to eat as their fathers had before the dam. I no longer believe that all peoples should be Christian or live under a democracy. I find the fact deplorable that an over-whelming majority of mankind, including, I am sure, very many so-called liberals, instinctively dislike people with different colored skins, oddly—to them—textured hair, and eyes aslant. But they always have. And they always will. The best we can do is to make the cost of acting upon their prejudices legally prohibitive. The prejudices themselves are immune to legislation, reason, or Christian charity.

What then, are we shouting about? Life is too short for wasted motions in writing as in all else. Besides, pragmatically, if we serve up, lightly browned, themes which run counter to the way the reader really feels, though he may be too civilized or too prudent to admit it, we are again offering him for his hard-earned money that eight-wheeled car. In proof of which, one needs but read Cozzens' masterfully crafted *By Love Possessed*. One of the reasons for its success was, I submit, that Cozzens managed to make the unfortunate American tendency toward anti-Semitism and anti-Catholicism very nearly intellectually respectable. People want their prejudices, and their beliefs, however unethical, con-firmed, not attacked. To confirm them is, of course, as nearly immoral as anything is in this world. But one can hold one's tongue. And with dignity. (pp. 145-49)

What, then, are the good and useful themes? Even, often, the great themes? First, I should list the unsolv-able problem of evil. MacLeish has tackled it, I under-stand, wonderfully in *J. B.* Second, man against himself, which is, *au fond*, the root of all problems: the mature, the emotionally secure, the psychologically healthy don't need the compensatory behavior mechanisms of prejudice and hate. Third, man's relationship with God, which is but a projection of his relationship with himself, greatly idealized. Fourth, the eternal warfare of the sexes, with its fitful, biologically imposed truces. Beyond these four, I decline to proceed; because all the lesser, though still important themes, are actually mat-ters of taste. As an afterthought, I might except the theme of man faced with death, measuring up, or failing to, to the fact that he is finite, trying to face the termination of all his hopes, beliefs, dreams with dignity and pride, or groveling abjectly in terror before the inevitability of his fate. That is a true theme, and hardly a matter of taste. But all the rest are. There is an apt saying here in Spain: *"Sobre gustos, no hay nada escrito."* ("Of tastes, there is nothing written.")

I have nibbled at the edges of all these themes. They are, admittedly, too big for my slim talent. Perhaps they are beyond any writer's skill, but they should be tried. As Faulkner says, "We shall be judged by the splendor of our failures." I have, I think, been somewhat successful with Theme Four. Like most men in their forties, I have marched, and retreated, in the ranks. With the other three, I have failed; but, I like to think, not utterly. And as far as Theme One, the problem of evil, is concerned, I have accepted failure from the outset. One always fails with that question, splendidly or not. It is not a defeat to

be ashamed of; the greatest intelligences of all times have come a cropper on that one, too.

Inescapably, the costume belongs to what has been called escape literature. I have often wondered, with weary patience, why that term is used by critics as a dirty word. Considered coldly, what kind of fiction is not escapist? The route indicated by the novelist may differ markedly; but the destination is still the never-never land of the spirit, of imagination; and all the arrows point away from the here and now. Your writer guide may take you through the South Side of Chicago, down Los Angeles' Skid Row, rub your refined nostrils in the raw odors of realism; but you know, and he knows, that you don't read his opus if you live on the South Side, Skid Row, or the Bowery—or even if you happen to be a *clochard* sleeping in the cold and wet under one of the bridges of the Seine.

If he is honest, as he so seldom is, the novelist will admit that at best he is aiming for a carefully contrived, hypnotic suspension of his reader's sense of disbelief—not ever for a real slice of life. Because, in life, people think of the proper response two hours, or two days, too late; things go wrong, not upon the respectable scale of tragedy, but on the slow, bumbling, painfully embarrass-ing, minuscule dimensions of inept, amateur farce. In life, conversation is an endless series of *non sequiturs*, of windy nonsense, or of just plain dull nonsense. And no realist would ever dare pinpoint on paper the most realistic of all life's attributes: the thundering, crashing boredom of the life of the average man.

The point of all this is, I suppose, that novels written with the deliberate intention to amuse and entertain have—or should have—a very real place in contempo-rary literature. It seems to me that people have the right to escape occasionally and temporarily from life's sprawling messiness, satisfy their hunger for neat pat-terns, retreat into a dreamlife where boy gets girl and it all comes out right in the end always. They need such escapes to help them endure the shapelessness of modern existence. It is only when they try to escape permanently that the trip out to Kansas and Karl Menninger's becomes indicated. I honestly believe that thumbing through an occasional detective yarn, science-fiction tale, or costume novel, is rather better preventive therapy than tranquilizers, for instance.

It has been some time since I checked, but I don't think our constitutional right to the pursuit of happiness has been repealed. (pp. 149-50)

> *Frank Yerby, "How and Why I Write the Costume Novel," in* Harper's Magazine, *Vol. 219, No. 1313, October, 1959, pp. 145-50.*

Darwin T. Turner (essay date 1970)

[*In the excerpt below, Turner explores theme and plot in Yerby's works.*]

Yerby's plot construction reveals artistic weakness. Despite his skillful tangling and untangling of exciting narratives which mesmerize even many sophisticated readers, Yerby too often depends on contrived endings. Even more dangerously for a spinner of thrillers, he frequently snarls his plots with digressive essays on customs, language, philosophy, and history.

Such strengths and weaknesses are the trademark of an entertainer.... Surprisingly, however, Yerby's costume novels exhibit another dimension, disregarded by the readers who lament his failure to write an historical novel and by the others who condemn his refusal to write an overtly polemical treatise on the plight of the American Negro. Ideas—bitter ironies, caustic debunkings, painful gropings for meaning—writhe behind the soap-opera facade of his fiction.

Significantly, Frank Yerby, a Georgia-born Negro exile from America, has concentrated on the theme of the outcast who, as in existentialist literature, pits his will against a hostile universe. By intelligence and courage, he proves himself superior to a society which rejects him because of his alien, inferior, or illegitimate birth. (pp. 64-5)

But Yerby discounts the possible amalgamation of certain groups. Regardless of talent, beauty, or wealth, the quadroons of Louisiana remain outcasts.... If, apparently, Frank Yerby sees intermarriage and amalgamation as the ultimate solution to all animosities, but recognizes that some societies prohibit that solution, there is little reason to wonder why he taints his tales with the somber hint that man's life is a joke played by a merciless and senile deity.

Furthermore, despite his avowed respect for his reader's prejudices, Yerby repeatedly has violated his own dictum that a writer should neither preach nor instruct. Driven by emotions which inspired him to write fiction of social protest in his early years, Frank Yerby now writes anti-romantic, existentialist melodrama which is frequently as satirical as Voltaire's *Candide*. (p. 65)

Yerby inflicts such severe physical and mental tortures upon his protagonists that a thoughtful reader searches for a reason. Although Yerby may have wished merely to gratify his American readers' avidity for sadism or to imitate the bloody, tragic incidents abundant in the dramas of Shakespeare, whom he admired and frequently quoted, another possibility must be considered—that Frank Yerby, who now admits that discrimination compelled his exile, has avenged himself vicariously by punishing his American protagonists who, unrestricted by skin color, can attain the status denied to him. (p. 66)

In addition to maintaining his own disbelief by creating anti-romantic stories, Frank Yerby teaches more than a careless reader would suspect.... [He] has debunked historical myths relentlessly. Perhaps this crusade eventually will be considered Yerby's major contribution to American culture....

Chiefly, of course, he has attacked America, in particular the South. Until recent years this section of America has received literary glorification as a region of culture and gentility. The males reputedly were aristocratic, cultured, brave, and honorable. The females were gentle and chaste. Savagely, Yerby has ridiculed these myths.

The South, he has pointed out, was founded by adventurers, outcasts, and failures who migrated to America because they had nothing to lose; the actual aristocrats, having nothing to gain by emigration, remained on the continent....

Second-generation Americans, Yerby has shown, did not resemble the idealized stereotypes of the myth. (p. 67)

Yerby has charged that even the houses and towns have been idealized in the myth....

Unlike a typical propagandist, however, Yerby has not restricted his attack to one group. He has also castigated Americans above the Mason-Dixon line. (p. 68)

Relentlessly condemning the senselessness of war, Yerby has exploded many myths which glorify heroes and causes. (p. 69)

Yerby is no misanthrope; he has heroes: Thomas Jefferson, who freed his slaves; George Washington, who led American revolutionists heroically despite his incompetence as a military tactician; Henri Christophe, who helped free Haiti from French authority. Moreover, Yerby has struggled to evolve a positive philosophy. Significantly, he has repudiated the patient goodness frequently held before Negroes as a desirable standard. Yerby persists in showing that men succeed and are extolled because they are smarter, stronger, bolder, and braver than other men. Sometimes, they act morally and honorably; more often they do not. But neither their contemporaries not their descendants evaluate the morality of the successful, the heroes. The minority groups in Yerby's stories suffer because they are ignorant, weak, and cowardly. Foolishly, they beg for help from a deity, which, according to Yerby, if it exists, views mankind hostilely, indifferently, or contemptuously. Life has meaning only when man—frail and insignificant—sparkles as brightly as possible in his instant of eternity. (p. 70)

[Yerby] has not yet demonstrated, however, that he can make a significant theme emerge credibly from the interaction of characters. Unless he does this, the philosophy will stand out as incongruously and as absurdly as a candle on a fallen cake.

It is to be hoped that, questing for the Grail of significance, Yerby will not tarnish his golden luster as an entertaining debunker of historical myths. (p. 71)

Darwin T. Turner, "Frank Yerby as Debunker," in The Black Novelist, *edited by Robert Hemenway, Charles E. Merrill, 1970, pp. 62-71.*

Jack B. Moore (essay date 1975)

[*Moore is an American educator, editor, and short story writer. In the following excerpt, he addresses Yerby's treatment of black characters in his works.*]

[After writing successful fiction with some racial implications, Yerby] published *The Foxes of Harrow* which was not concerned with racial problems; and it sold over 2 million copies and was translated into at least twelve other languages; and he followed that book with over twenty others that his publishers tell us have sold 25 million copies. 25,000,000.

How did Yerby suddenly become such a bad writer?—he must be bad [critics] feel because he is a very popular writer. And how could he betray his race to become a best seller with a big reputation...? Even Saunders Redding in "The Negro Writer and American Literature" (in *Anger and Beyond*, 1966), places Yerby in the tradition of Alice Dunbar, who totally "ignored her racial and social heritage." Redding suggests that Yerby's allegedly white writing exhibits "pathological overtones."

Yet Yerby does not write pure escape fiction, because many of his white novels deal at least secondarily with the race issue. Generally, in his earliest novels, the racial problems are employed peripherally, almost perfunctorily, and occupy little space or overt interest in the novel. None the less Yerby's racial attitudes pervade these early novels of the South, sometimes in obvious and sometimes in disguised fashion.

A surprising number of white males in Yerby's books are paralyzed from the waist down.... Very few white children are in evidence in his books, while there are scores of Negro infants and even more yard children, the product of miscegenation between white males and Negro females. Negro males, incidentally, never are sexually attracted to white females (until his recent novel, *Speak Now*, 1969) as they often are in the works of white writers such as Thomas Dixon (*The Leopard's Spots*), William Styron (*The Confessions of Nat Turner*), and Tennessee Williams (*The Seven Descents of Myrtle*). Several Negro women are raped by whites, and the sexual superiority of the Negro female is emphasized even by white women. (pp. 747-48)

But another submerged racial element in Yerby's books is black self-betrayal.... In the instance of betrayal, Yerby may have been unconsciously impelled by what seemed to so many and perhaps himself, his own betrayal.

I have been offering perhaps latent, perhaps unconscious employment of racial attitudes in Yerby's faction. But his books often clearly and consciously use the white-black problem as well. Generally his thrust has been toward greater and more organic, that is artistically relevant, emphasis on race issues. (p. 748)

Griffin's Way [was] published in 1962, some sixteen years after *The Foxes of Harrow*, by which time Yerby was financially secure as a writer. And of course the book appeared eight years after the Supreme Court's historic decision on school integration. *Griffin's Way* is possibly Yerby's first Negro novel. That is, the white novel within it is quite unimportant, and the book focuses clearly and directly on the Negro's predicament in Mississippi in the 1870's. (p. 751)

In 1969 Yerby published his twenty-third book, *Speak Now*. Though the novel is Yerby's most open, extended portrait of racial conditions, it is an ambivalent book.

Yerby's hero is clearly black to his soul's bones. His skin is black and his awareness is black.... He is a classic example of the black artist who found in his music an honest and creative mode of black self-expression and further one that he could practice openly (and be rewarded for) while living in alien white territory, for the music becomes a coded black self-assertion and white denial. (p. 753)

Harry is truly a marginal man, pained by knowing that wherever he goes he is an American, and yet knowing that he cannot live in America. Further, he is black and yet cannot take total pride in his color. Though his attitude toward radicalism shifts slightly, I cannot see that his response to his own race moves from that stated in his diatribe declaring "the guilt of the victim." He is totally hostile to white American life, and ashamed of his own race's history as he sees it. How close is he to Frank Yerby, who still writes realistically about the American experience, obsessively about the black experience, and still for all that I can see lives in Madrid, Spain?

Yerby in no way turned his back upon his race after he published *The Foxes of Harrow*. Instead, he used his popularity to write frequently about blackness in works that were widely disseminated in America. In his fiction Yerby indicates every lousy, crippling, murderous pressure that the white man applied to the black. But he also reveals a not so latent contempt for the resistance the black man put up (or did not put up). Furthermore, in a number of books, such as *Griffin's Way* and *Speak Now*, he suggests a kind of assumed inferiority that he claims black history reveals. At least characters within these books state a strong case against black history that is never successfully refuted. Yerby appears to have adopted a posture similar to that of Harry Forbes in *Speak Now*. He hates white American society for what it has done to him and his people, and he cannot live in that society. Yet he respects the accomplishments of the white world, does not feel a part of the African experience, and feels some shame at being part of a race that has allowed itself to be victimized for so long—that indeed in Africa and America was complicit in its own victimization. I would suggest this is another reason why Yerby left America and straight protest fiction. Perhaps he could not whole-heartedly attack the enemy—white America—feeling out of touch with the (he would claim) voluntary victims.

Many of my remarks on Yerby's assumptions about race are conjectural, based upon interpreting the books from my angle of vision. I may very well be incorrect or my vision out of focus. But what is not out of focus, what is not conjectural, is the fact that from the very early poems and stories on through the best sellers, Yerby has ... almost systematically written of all the chief elements of the black experience .... (p. 755)

> *Jack B. Moore, "The Guilt of the Victim: Racial Themes in Some Frank Yerby Novels," in* Journal of Popular Culture, *Vol. VIII, No. 4, Spring, 1975, pp. 747-56.*

FURTHER READING

Klotman, Phyllis R. "A Harrowing Experience: Frank Yerby's First Novel to Film." *CLA Journal* XXXI, No. 2 (December 1987): 210-22.
    Examines racial issues in the film version of *The Foxes of Harrow*.

Al Young

1939-

American novelist, poet, short story writer, screenwriter, and editor.

A popular and influential figure in black letters, Young is known for his contemplative and humorous fiction and poetry. In his writings he explores the inner complexities of his characters, giving them highly personal, unorthodox philosophies and unique mannerisms of speech rooted in black vernacular. Music and dance often figure heavily in Young's work: his study of music resulted in three volumes of what Young calls "musical memoirs," a hybrid genre combining elements of autobiography, criticism, mysticism, and poetry.

Born in Ocean Springs, Mississippi, Young spent his boyhood in rural areas of the state and in an urban community in Detroit, Michigan. In the first volume of the musical memoirs, *Bodies & Soul* (1981), he noted that his earliest memories are of the 78 r.p.m. phonograph records of his father, an auto worker and amateur musician. As an undergraduate majoring in Spanish at the University of Michigan, Young seriously considered a musical career before ultimately dedicating himself to literature. In 1961 he moved to San Francisco, where he worked as a disc jockey and writing instructor. His first volume of poetry, *Dancing,* was published in 1969 and received enthusiastic notices; Louis L. Martz remarked on "his use of the everyday past, his ear for colloquial language, his talent for personal introspection, and his outward glance toward his fellowship in the human race." *Snakes,* Young's first novel, was published the following year. Incited by what he perceived as limited publishing opportunities for writers of various ethnic backgrounds, he cofounded and coedited with Ishmael Reed *Yardbird Reader,* a magazine that operated from 1972 until 1976, searching out and publishing the works of new talent. His involvement with "little" magazines continued with *Quilt,* a similar project begun in 1981.

Young's work shows his ability to capture the language of the ghetto as well as his metaphysical attachment to the details of everyday life. One of his most admired poems is "Dance for Militant Dilettantes," a gentle satire of black rights advocates included in *Dancing. Geography of the Near Past,* a 1976 poetry collection, introduced a fictive "alter-ego" named O. O. Gabugah, who also appears in *Things Ain't What They Used to Be* (1987), the third of the musical memoirs. Although Young avoids overtly political messages in his fiction, critics have commented that by creating vivid characters and unique first-person narrators, he counteracts racial stereotypes. *Snakes* is told by MC, an aspiring adolescent musician with an oddball assortment of friends including Shakes, a young black man who speaks in Shakesperean English. In *Sitting Pretty* (1976), Sidney J. Prettymon relates how he became a local celebrity by

calling up a radio talkshow and airing his quirky views. Mamie Franklin, the narrator of the 1989 novel *Seduction by Light,* travels the astral plane communing with her dead husband and Benjamin Franklin. Young has been praised for his ability to imagine the thoughts of characters very different from himself; the protagonists of *Who Is Angelina?* (1975) and *Seduction by Light,* for example, are females. In an interview, Young explained: "People simply can't grasp that you can create believable characters, settings, situations, believable writing without having gone through all of the details personally. What do they think creative means?"

(For further information about Young's life and works, see *Black Writers; Contemporary Authors,* Vols. 29-32; *Contemporary Authors New Revision Series,* Vol. 26; *Contemporary Literary Criticism,* Vol. 19; and *Dictionary of Literary Biography,* Vol. 33: *Afro-American Fiction Writers after 1955.*)

PRINCIPAL WORKS

Dancing (poetry) 1969
Snakes (novel) 1970
The Song Turning Back into Itself (poetry) 1971
Who Is Angelina? (novel) 1975
Geography of the Near Past (poetry) 1976
Sitting Pretty (novel) 1976
Ask Me Now (novel) 1980
Bodies & Soul: Musical Memoirs (prose) 1981
The Blues Don't Change: New and Selected Poems
     (poetry) 1982
Kinds of Blue: Musical Memoirs (prose) 1984
Things Ain't What They Used to Be: Musical Memoirs
     (prose) 1987
Mingus/Mingus: Two Memoirs [with Janet Coleman]
     (memoirs) 1989
Seduction by Light (novel) 1989

Mel Watkins (essay date 1976)

[*In the following review, Watkins praises Young's
characterization of Sidney J. Prettymon in* Sitting
Pretty.]

It's a pleasure, occasionally, to get away from the
mayhem, violence and mania that are so vividly depicted in much of today's fiction; and Al Young's *Sitting
Pretty* provides just such an opportunity. In this novel,
Young introduces Sidney J. Prettymon, a.k.a., Sitting
Pretty or just Sit—one of the most charming and
engaging characters I've encountered in some time.

Sitting Pretty is a 50-year-old black man—father, lover,
philosopher and just plain old observer of life. Having
left his wife, after assuring that his two children
graduated from college, he is ensconced in the Blue Jay,
a S.R.O. hotel in Palo Alto. There, he is, well, just taking
it easy and mulling things over: "I left a good job and a
good family, lookin for that something else. It was gettin
to the point where I felt like I couldnt breathe, and yet I
still feel horrible for doin what I figgered was best for all
concerned.... I still keep takin long looks at different
parts of myself. Dont nobody feel the same way bout
everything every day, so I keep on hopin it's still some
hope for me."

There is almost no plot, to speak of, in this tale. Young's
first-person narrative just rolls easily along, and the
feeling is that the story could have begun or ended
almost anywhere. What happens is that one simply
listens and watches as Sit moves through the normal
routine of his life: conversations with his friends at the
Blue Jay; an incident where he is arrested for nonpay-
ment of some old parking tickets and has to call his son,
a lawyer, to bail him out; visits to the homes of his
children and of his former wife and her husband;
helping a small child fly her kite on the beach; hanging
out in the North Beach section of San Francisco.

Sit's one exceptional talent is his gift for gab and,
besides his friends, the major outlet for it is a local radio
talk show, which he calls regularly. Having gained a
small following among the show's listeners, he is asked
to do a few TV ads to promote the show. Because of his
naturalness, the ads are instantly successful, and he
becomes something of a local celebrity. He takes it all in
stride, however, maintaining his room at the Blue Jay
and changing very little about his life. "Say you do get
hold to a few things," Sit says, "a good education
(somethin I always wish I'd got), prestige, a taste of
power.... So what happen? You get old, that's what
happen. You get old and, same as everything else, you
crumble on away and turn to dust."

This is a thoroughly enjoyable book. In Sitting Pretty, Al
Young presents a character who in many ways reminds
one of Jesse B. Semple, Langston Hughes's unforgettable
creation, except that Sit is less a caricature and a more
richly depicted human being. He is the natural man,
with no pretenses, just trying to live with as little chaos
as possible and to enjoy the simple pleasures of growing
old. And his tale is told with grace and dignity. There
are no literary fireworks, no gimmicks here, and *Sitting
Pretty* is obviously not a novel that is going to rock the
literary world in any way. But it is a novel that can be
read and enjoyed by everyone (Sit's color, after you've
begun this book, will be no more important than your
mother's), for its humor, its warmth and its revelations
about the commonplace aspects of living that are too
often ignored in fiction. "Sometime it do good to tell
what you know real slow to yourself so you can get it
fixed in your own mind good."

> Mel Watkins, "Lookin for That Something
> Else," in The New York Times Book Re-
> view, *May 23, 1976, p. 44.*

Alan Cheuse (essay date 1980)

[*In the following review, Cheuse describes* Ask Me
Now *as a "triumph of psychological insight and subtle
narrative tones."*]

Like Durwood "Woody" Knight, the tall, brown bean-
pole of a basketball player who serves as the main
character of *Ask Me Now,* Al Young's fiction has always
stood out in a crowd. His earlier novels presented a
broad and entertaining variety of (mostly) Afro-American characters and voices. Among them was the elderly
but vigorous lay philosopher Sidney J. Prettymon, a.k.a.
"Sitting Pretty," who still jogs in my memory through
the streets of Palo Alto—testimony to Mr. Young's
unpretentious but substantial talent for making average
Americans memorable in his prose.

Ask Me Now is another triumph of psychological insight
and subtle narrative tones. For this story of how a 39-
year-old professional ballplayer turns his retirement
from the game into a victory over adversity both real
and imagined, Mr. Young borrows his title from a tune
by jazzman Thelonius Monk. When we first encounter

"Woody" Knight he appears to be suffering from an appropriate kind of blues, a man unable to catch the rhythm and spirit of what he senses to be "plain old ordinary everyday life." We follow him from Thanksgiving to Christmas in his home base of San Francisco (where for years he has played dependably though unspectacularly as guard for the "Bay Area Beanstalks"); his days seem measured out in fouls for which he cannot go to the line. While he's shopping for the holiday turkey, someone steals his station wagon. When he finally reaches home (a four-bedroom semi-Victorian house in the Upper Mission district), his rain-soaked shopping bags bottom out around his ankles.

Home presents as much trouble as the street. His 15-year-old daughter Celia has become more of a stranger to him than he is to himself, now that he's no longer playing basketball. She wants to be a songwriter, and her usual accompanist is a flute-playing teenager named Moby, whom Knight fears may be her accomplice in more than music. His jazz musician son Leon, the product of his first, short-lived marriage, instructs him in the baffling art of Zen. His younger daughter Nissa is a brainy nuisance with a runny nose. And the exasperating Dixie, whom he married soon after he began playing professional ball, is someone the rangy, sensitive athlete both loves and would like to throw out the window.

Knight soon makes the ironic discovery that he needs as much "elbow room" at home as he had during the lonely years when he was on the road with the team. While worrying "about money and bills and growing old and the future" and Celia's virginity and Nissa's problems and Dixie's attitude and Leon's love and the prospects for the retail record business he's about to launch with Beanstalk trainer Brewster Day (the company is to be called "Knight and Day"), the embattled ex-ballplayer fights constantly for possession of his new self.

He enjoys, of course, some pleasures in the midst of his dilemma of adjustment: the music in which he douses his soul; the company of friends and former colleagues from the world of professional sport, including Wilt Chamberlain, who appears in the novel; the familiar but savory love-making of his wife of nearly two decades. Many times, however, Knight finds himself watching Betamax replays of his old games or thinking back to extraordinary moments on the court when "he would feel himself and all the players around him—teammates and opposition—heating up while, at the same time, his perceptions would be cooling to the point where it seemed that he was both watching and acting in a slow-motion movie. . . . Every pass, fake, and turn would feel predetermined, orchestrated like a musical score, counterpointed, with every note and beat and nuance in place, right there where and when it was supposed to happen."

When Celia mysteriously disappears, apparently abducted by the same people who stole the family station wagon, the metaphors of sport and music, which ent-

wine so neatly in Knight's memory, assume new meaning for his everyday existence. The crime is resolved, although I shouldn't say how, except that it involves a mounted policeman who is a Woody Knight fan, a pistol-packing woman with nearly albino complexion and long, snowy-white hair, and a quarter of a million dollars worth of cocaine. By the time it's all settled, Knight has taken charge of his life with the same resolve he displayed on the basketball court.

It takes much less time for this extremely appealing and yet thoroughly unsentimental novel to take charge of the reader. In unspectacular but appropriate language, Mr. Young dramatizes the difficulties of family life and fatherhood, the uneasy distinctions between youth and middle-age and, as Knight himself puts it in an informal interview toward the end of the novel, how "you learn everything there is to know about life no matter what line of endeavor you take up." Like Knight's dream game, his story is beautifully orchestrated, with every note and beat and nuance in place, right there where and when it is supposed to happen. (pp. 9, 20-1)

> Alan Cheuse, "Woody's Comeback," in The New York Times Book Review, *July 6, 1980, pp. 9, 20-1.*

Al Young with William J. Harris (interview date 1981)

[*In the following interview—"recorded in late November 1981 on a rainy day in Seattle, Washington"—Young discusses his literary and philosophical interests and explains his goals as a writer.*]

[Harris]: *In* Snakes *you have Champ initiate MC into music. Was there somebody who initiated you into writing?*

[Young]: No one initiated me into writing. I've always loved to read and watch what happens inside my head as scenes, feelings, and people and ideas are brought to life. It would be fun, I thought from early on, to do this myself. As a child I read Mark Twain, *The Adventures of Huckleberry Finn* and *The Adventures of Tom Sawyer.* I was fascinated by Ben Franklin's career as a writer and printer. Don't ask me why. The idea of working with type and with print and with paper and with ink and with writing utensils—that has always been exciting, very powerful. Kenneth Patchen was a writer that I read . . . oh, I suppose from junior high, along with Li Po, the T'ang dynasty Chinese poet. Patchen was probably highly influential on me during those turbulent, pubescent years. I was particularly attracted to his extended prose works, such as *The Journal of Albion Moonlight* and *Memoirs of a Shy Pornographer.* These were the writers whose books became well-thumbed items in my modest library. You might say I initiated myself into literature, but who knows how that works? I remember first picking up *Studs Lonigan*—I must have been in 9th grade—somewhere in there—and just being astounded that somebody was writing about the working class and the kinds of people that I knew something about, even though James T. Farrell was writing about the Irish scene and I knew more about the Negro or Afro-American scene. It was an exciting moment, that "shock of recognition" as Edmund Wilson called it.

You talk about having a mystical experience. Has this influenced your writing? Angelina seems quite sensitive to the mystical, for example.

Obviously man did not create this world or the universe. And ever since I was three-years-old, despite my being surrounded by Christian this and that and Islam and later Buddhism and all the formalized and codified religions, I've always regarded myself as a religious person who does not fit into the orthodox scheme of things. I think that in defining man you have to keep in mind that, whatever else he might be about, he is a religious person. This religion might take the form of Maoism or of an overwhelming desire to become a tycoon or a desire to land a best-seller or whatever, but it is a religious impulse that sparks all of this. For me the purpose of life has always been to find out who or what created life and how does man fit into the scheme of things. Art and science are not separate; they both fundamentally proceed from intuitive processes; it's our perversely pragmatic society that separates them. I have been delighted lately reading such books as *The Dancing Wu Li Masters: An Overview of the New Physics* by Gary Zukav and *The Origins of Consciousness in the Breakdown of the Bicameral Mind* by Julian Jaynes. These are fascinating books because they do reinforce a concept I have held all my life which is that in the search for truth the creative faculty flowers. Some of these concerns come into play in my second novel, *Who Is Angelina?,* which is indeed a religious novel with a contemporary setting but it might not be looked upon as such by most people and to me that's good.

I know this is difficult but it seems important. Do you think that your father's death has had an impact on your writing? It seems to be a source of the father-daughter relationship in **Angelina.**

My father's death is profoundly significant, quite naturally in my life but *Who Is Angelina?* was written before his passing. Both my mother and father played important roles in shaping me; I was separated from my father at an early age, although I kept in touch with him. And, of course, as it is with most people—and certainly with most artists—there was the father I had and the father I never had and both doubtless emerge in my fiction—sometimes fused as one. Angelina's father is an example of the kind of responsible black father who rarely gets represented in American literature, black or white, and the truth of the matter is there are so many of these men who are unsung heroes in our midst. That the myth persists of the derelict or irresponsible or absent black father astonishes me in its acceptance and proliferation.

Do you think writing for Hollywood has influenced your writing? In **Ask Me Now** *the action writing seems from a movie.*

Yes, Hollywood influenced my sense of story and dramatic strategy considerably. *Ask Me Now,* for example is an action novel but it is not without its reflective and even poetic concerns which I think have become the trademark of my work. Character for me is plot—a marvelous and seemingly inexplicable thing. I'm fond of exploring. Too many so-called literary or academically trained writers are contemptuously ignorant of the fundamentals of sound dramatic structure or motivation—to say nothing of developing engaging, believable characters. In script-writing you've got to be in command of these elements or your story, no matter how beautifully or artistically conceived as it might be, falls apart. Shakespeare, whatever else he might have been attempting, was trying to keep the Globe Theatre out of the red. I don't find it at all surprising that he had something for everybody in his plays from the coarse drunks who'd plunked down good money to see his plays to the elegant and refined. In that regard, nothing has changed since Shakespeare's time. The entertainment value in a work of art is superbly important. My experience in Hollywood simply sharpened my sense of dramatic values, story values. Writers in some circles regard such an experience as being necessarily cheapening but, far from being cheapening, I think it was truly important to my development as a novelist.

Which is worse for you as an artist, writing for Hollywood or teaching?

That's a deceptive question because what you are really asking is "What would I rather do?" Well, I'm a writer—the real thing—as distinct from someone who merely desires to achieve a reputation as a writer. Universities and colleges pay you to teach, not to write, which means your time is tied up and your creative energies are directed toward getting students to better their own imaginative work. On the other hand, Hollywood studios pay you to *write* but there is always the problem of having to deal with people who figure they could do what you do if they had a few spare weekends. Writers are pariah in Hollywood, there are so many of them and yet nothing happens to protect the money invested in a film until some poor man or woman with an idea and some imagination sits down in a room with a typewriter or a pen and gets something concrete and workable or at least discussable down on paper. Teaching is draining . . . if you take the job seriously as I tend to do. But to teach occasionally sharpens a writer's critical faculties. I think that Hollywood still offers limited opportunities for a black writer such as myself, but as the old song says: "It's nice work if you can get it." Script-writing pays well and it also buys you some soul space, as I call it—some writing time.

Can you think of other biographical happenings which have influenced your writing? It is interesting how the personal is transformed into art.

Well, perhaps I should cite the American painter, Stuart Davis, who always said that he was influenced by absolutely everything: air travel, television, jazz music—all those things. In my own case, for my own life, I could say that everything has had an effect on me. My interests and my attention are diffuse as you probably know from having been around me—I'm interested in all kinds of things. Moreover, I have been involved with the issues of my time. I travel quite a bit; I'm given to reflection. I see myself as having been born in a transitional era, with one foot in the old era and one foot in the new one. I think that people born around 1939, 1940—all the way up to, say, '45 probably have that sense. We were young enough to have seen something of . . . if we can make an arbitrary dividing line, the pre-atomic world, and they are old enough to have fused their earlier experiences with later nuclear realities. I found that learning to metamorphose is the secret of perpetuating growth as an artist; that is, by taking what you have personally experienced and transforming it. I get very upset now when someone will ask me about a novel of mine: "Did you personally go through that?" After *Sitting Pretty* came out, I remember several readers asking me: "Did you actually go to one of those walk-up transient hotels and stay there for a while to get your research?" These kinds of questions annoy me because they indicate how the imagination is held in such flagrant disregard today. People simply can't grasp that you can create believable characters, settings, situations, believable writing without having gone through all of the details personally. What do they think creative means?

One of the wonderful things about your books is the joy you have in recording the contemporary world. Do you think that is one reason you are a realist novelist instead of being a more experimental writer?

Yes, experiment is wonderful and I have always engaged in it but it's results that interests me, not process alone as such. Where does the joy come from? Well, it comes like humor from having a cosmic view of creation, if you will, but it also comes from bearing in mind how amazing and miraculous it is that we're here together in this world that is disappearing as we know it by the hour.

In Angelina *you wrote in—or through—the persona of a woman. Was that difficult for you? Do you think of Angelina as a sort of contemporary Janie Crawford coming to terms with herself? They are both women fighting for their personal freedom.*

As for Angelina's point of view, I had a ball writing that book. That's one of those instances where people have come up and said, "Hmm, there must be something about you we don't know. You write very convincingly through the eyes of a woman." Oh, it makes you furious! Dickens and the older, earlier—I should say—novelists could presume to be anyone; I mean someone like Charles Dickens thought nothing of getting inside the heads of rich people, poor people, powerful people, people of seemingly little social significance—children, old people, middle-aged people. Early novelists sometimes assuming an imperious authorial stance didn't

hesitate to depict any character they felt like. We have grown down since then. Our trivialized sense of reality is often laughable. All you have to do is keep a journal to see that reality is very illusive phenomenon. But getting back to *Angelina,* I had a lot of fun writing that, and I believe that with a bit of empathy you can really get down inside characters who are quite different from you. For me creativity always proceeds from joyousness or fun. I hadn't thought about it before now, but Angelina could very well be a contemporary Janie Crawford—the charming protagonist of Zora Neale Hurston's classic, *Their Eyes Were Watching God.* In this age that seems to favor disaffection, alienation, and despair, my personal hero as distinct from the prevailing existential hero, is the man or woman who is spiritually adventurous and can see around corners and through barriers, so to speak, in their quest for ultimate truth. I'm an idealist but that's o.k.; I'm also very realistic. In other words, I keep my eyes open, and yet I know that spirit is real, realer than matter. Eventually we'll discover that this is true and proveable.

Let's talk about your protagonists in general for a moment. It seems to me that even though they are very different, they do share certain traits: they all seem like questers; they're un-together; they have small but honorable successes; they are all marginal people. What do you think of my characterization of your protagonists? do you have any general statements to make about your main characters?

My main characters aren't marginal people—marginal people, no. They're today's human beings as we have been rendered by inhumane business and technical practices. You have to get beyond mass media images of who you truly are or should be in order to face and reckon with your true human origins. Joy, sorrow, tears, laughter, the need to belong and be part of a meaningful whole—that's all I have ever written about, from the worlds of MC in *Snakes,* Angelina Green in *Who Is Angelina?,* Sidney J. Prettymon in *Sitting Pretty,* to Durwood Knight in *Ask Me Now* and Mamie Franklin, who is the protagonist and narrator in the novel I'm working on now, called *Seduction by Light.* In each of these works that's all I'm saying—that's what I am writing about; each of these major characters is displaced in some way; perhaps you can say they are all displaced people clinging to intuitive notions of how they really are and pursuing those notions in their lives. It's an ancient and currently neglected theme of self-realization.

You seem to write about what we can loosely call the black middle class. Is this a conscious decision on your part? Are you trying to react against stereotypes of blacks?

Curious question and you aren't the first one to pose it, but I see myself fundamentally as a working-class writer geared to a blues esthetic. The black middle class is marginal, to use your term, in the broader American middle-class contexts they're not only middle class they are also black and because blacks are still what I call sub-Americans, black middle-class people are sub-American middle-class people. I won't keep playing with language this way. I'll simply say that blacks are apt to know what it has taken to achieve dubious middle-class respectability in the United States. There were people in my family working two jobs, husband and wife, each of them working two jobs, trying to get a house, get that car, acquire all those nice things that will make their lives "normal" like Ozzie's and Harriet's on television. Stereotypes are one thing and truth quite another. In examining the kind of verisimilitude imaginatively explored in much black fiction or poetry, you find a one-sidedness that I feel it has been my destiny in part to balance. It is explicitly because most whites still refuse to see black people as people that racism prevails. Blacks turn around and do the same thing to whites, that is, not regard them as human beings, then we turn around and do the same thing to ourselves. We tend to write about one narrow little aspect of the "black experience," clouding the truth about the richness and range of characters and of personality diversity that exists among Afro-Americans. So I simply try to write stories about people who are, for the most part, black, and how their lives are affected by what's going on around them, or some goal they set out to achieve.

Do you feel any kinship with John Updike? The working class aside, you both have the guts to celebrate the middle class.

Updike is just fine and true to his experience—that's all you can ask of any good imaginative writer. I will say this about the middle class, however: the rich are customarily very busy protecting their holdings, protecting their profits, their power. Poor people are apt to be just as busy trying to get a hold of something, trying to survive. There has traditionally been a lot of vitality in the middle class which produces scientists, writers, artists, innovative people, people who don't necessarily have it made but who aren't struggling so much that they don't have time to think about something else, something higher. Of course, today's middle class is being sold down the river by greedy corporate interests. Frankly, I never gave any thought to my affinity with Updike until this was pointed out recently, I think, in one of the reviews of **Ask Me Now**—the unpromoted novel I wrote last year about a newly retired basketball player. McGraw-Hill has not made it very available. Some reviewer compared me with Updike. He seemed a little shocked that a black writer had written what he thought was a bourgeois novel. My emotional response, of course, was that I must have stepped on some esthetic toes. (Laughter.)

I think the only novel of yours which has a totally black cast is **Snakes.** *And the other novels are set in California. Do you think living in California has made you multi-cultural? If it has, could you talk about it in your own work and your multi-cultural publishing projects like* Yardbird *and* Quilt?

No, I don't think living in California has made me multi-cultural, although that setting might have stimulated some of my natural interests in multi-cultural modes of expression. Growing up in the midwest and in the south—and there were some stops in between Mississippi and Michigan that I won't go into here—but always, so to speak, being the new kid on the block because we did move around quite a bit and I always had to establish for myself a place in the social pecking order, as I found it, I probably took more interest in the ways in which people from different cultural backgrounds expressed themselves and conducted themselves than most people would. (pp. 4-12)

Do you see yourself having a particular function as a writer?

My function as a writer as I have come to see it is to share my gift and my insights, however meager, with the world. I have always thought that my writing could be tremendously commercial if it were marketed properly. Moreover, I still think that books do get into the hands of the people whom they were intended to reach and I know you will draw mystical conclusions from that statement, but ultimately I have to fall back on that and I don't think I have any choice but to continue in my struggling way to produce.

Do you think that Spanish has influenced your work? As an artist you seem to be interested in world literature. Can you account for this? Did this have something to do with the time you spent in Europe? Or how did a black boy from Detroit end up majoring in Spanish?

The Spanish connection. I have always loved language. My interest in Spanish has proceeded from a love of language. At a more mundane level it proceeded from a desire to avoid teaching English and creative writing. Since I knew early on that writing was going to be my chosen burden—my own form of volunteer slavery. The irony is I have never taught Spanish. I was trained at the University of Michigan and at the University of California to teach Spanish, but I have never taught it. I have learned quite a bit from translating, literally and meta-phorically. Translating has taught me how culture functions. There is a gentleman name Luciano Federighi who is my Italian translator; he has rendered **Who Is Angelina?** into Italian and he came over here to talk with me. He had pages of questions and he would ask these very funny questions—funny to me at that time. "Here on page such and such," he asked, "you have a character saying: "You come in here with your ass up on your shoulders." Luciano would look at me and say: "Now, what does that mean?" and I would laugh because I would realize the ultimate impossibility of rendering such an idiom into Italian. I got a big kick out of that because what you do when you translate really is you make . . . you create possibilities, comparative possibilities for understanding something from another culture. Well, at any rate, I got very involved with Spanish and at various points with Russian and Japanese and French. I've been interested in language all my life.

Who are your most important literary influences?

I am the kind of person who will answer this differently on different days but on this rainy, sleety, cold day in the Pacific Northwest at the very end of November 1981, I would say that early storytelling has been my major influence. I mean the kind of stories that the people in my family told sitting around the fire wood stove at night—my grandfather and grandmother and others. They told me stories sitting in swings on the front porch in the south. You can call it folklore if you wish, but I think true storytelling really has to fall back to that level at some point in order to have meaning. The printing press is limited in what it can convey. There were oral storytellers before there were literary storytellers. But early storytelling around the house has had a tremendous influence on me, obviously. From there I would venture to folklore, biblical lore, to writers such as Blaise Cendrars, the Swiss writer who is generally thought of as being French; Kenneth Patchen, John Steinbeck, Langston Hughes, Richard Wright, Mark Twain, William Saroyan, Céline; oral histories such as Alan Lomax's *Mister Jelly Roll,* Jelly Roll Morton being the subject of that book; Chester Himes, Jack Kerouac, Nelson Algren, Eudora Welty, Nathanael West, Maxim Gorki, the Cuban Poet, Nicolás Guillén; Lorca, Sherwood Anderson, James T. Farrell, Mayakovsky, Dickens, Amos Tutuola, the African writer; Shakespeare; the black writer from the then Belgian Congo, René Maran (I have never forgotten the thrill of finding his book, *Batoula,* back when I was around 15 years old in a bookstore in Detroit); Rimbaud, Carl Sandburg, Chaucer, the French writer Georges Simenon; the religious writer, Saint Theresa, Djuna Barnes, Selden Rodman, the William Faulkner of *Light in August,* Kenneth Rexroth, the poet; Juan Ramón Jiménez; Ralph Ellison, Li Po, the Chinese poet of centuries back; Dylan Thomas; and then I would have to switch to musicians, such as Louis Armstrong, and Charlie Parker. I probably left some important writers out but that should be enough for now. I was influenced by these people—I have read from an early age.

Do you think of your work growing out of the black tradition?

There are many black traditions. I would say yes, the black tradition of oral storytelling and versifying and also the black musical tradition with the many facets that entails: different musical idioms—gospel, blues, jazz, pop song and also the idea of additive rhythm and the spirit of improvisation. Improvisation I think is very misunderstood: people think you are simply making things up on the spot. Well, perhaps you are but in the same spirit that the old Zen painters would study a tree for years before attempting to execute a drawing of it in a single stroke. The improvising artist in any field pays a lot more dues than the person who simply tries to reproduce some effect that has been well learned. I like for my writing to have the feeling of spontaneity, even though it might have taken me a *long* time to achieve that effect. It's like what Thelonious Monk said: "A song

should sound as if you just found it in the street—like it's always been there—it's always existed." I think a story or novel or poem should have the same quality. It should appear as if its form were simply unalterable and inevitable. But of course the art is buried somewhere back there. Art is never in as good shape as when it is not suspected of being art.

Sometimes do you feel trapped as a black writer—do you feel pigeonholed?

Well, yes and no. In the marketplace I know that widespread interest in black writers is at best cyclical. Every 30 years or so white readers and black readers get interested in black writing. Now, if you happen to be around when the wave washes in, then you will get a ride for awhile. I think it is unfortunate that people will pick up books of mine and if there is a photograph of me or if it says anything about race in the jacket copy, the reader—black or white—is apt to form a predisposition. I'm immediately cubbyholed. They figure, "Oh, I've read a lot of these books about ghettos and rats and black-white conflict and all that." And that is very telling and very unfortunate. So in that respect sometimes I do feel trapped as a black writer. On the other hand, being black can be marvelous if you're a novelist or a fiction writer because you see things differently. I'm not just talking about the obvious things such as oppression and inequality and psychological and physical violence. There is another angle from which you see things based upon how you actually experience the world. (pp. 14-17)

> *Al Young and William J. Harris, in an interview in* The Greenfield Review, *Vol. 10, Nos. 1 & 2, 1982, pp. 1-19.*

Elizabeth Schultz (essay date 1982)

[*In the following excerpt, Schultz discusses freedom and identity in* Who Is Angelina?]

As students of Afro-American literature have frequently observed, one of the literature's dominant themes has always been the search for freedom, what poet Robert Hayden calls, "the beautiful, necessary thing." From William Wells Brown's *Clotelle* (1864) to Ernest Gaines' *The Autobiography of Miss Jane Pittman* (1971), the individual black American's attempt to achieve liberation has been associated with the liberation of the Afro-American people as a group. Ralph Ellison's narrator in *Invisible Man* (1952) however, expresses a conviction that underscores the personal, existential nature of the Afro-American's yearning to be free: "When I discover who I am, I'll be free." The struggle to achieve self-knowledge and hence personal freedom characterizes the lives of several of Afro-American literature's most memorable characters: Kabnis of Jean Toomer's *Cane* (1923), Janie Woods of Zora Neale Hurston's *Their Eyes Were Watching God* (1937), Bigger Thomas of Richard Wright's *Native Son,* (1941), John Grimes of James Baldwin's *Go Tell It on the Mountain* (1953), and

Sula Peace of Toni Morrison's *Sula* (1973). The heroine of Al Young's ***Who Is Angelina?*** (1975), by contrast with other black protagonists is startingly free at the beginning of the novel; yet her story is also her struggle to understand herself and the meaning of her freedom.

In ***Who Is Angelina?*** Young has written his *Portrait of a Lady,* with the center of consciousness being Angelina Green, who, like Isabel Archer, begins her travels into life alone and independent. Unlike the protagonists of other Afro-American novels, Angelina is not enslaved because of her race. Her color has not barred her from acting according to her will, from obtaining the jobs she wishes, from traveling as she wishes; nor has her color caused her to view either herself or her people as other than complex human beings. In this, as in other respects, Angelina resembles the three, all male, protagonists of Young's other novels: MC of ***Snakes*** (1970), Sidney J. Prettymon of ***Sitting Pretty*** (1976), and Durwood Knight of ***Ask Me Now*** (1980). As others readily acknowledge Isabel's beauty, so do they Angelina's, and hence, like James' heroine, like Gaines' Miss Jane, Morrison's Sula, Paule Marshall's Merle Kinbona of *The Chosen Place, The Timeless People* (1969), Corregidora of Gayl Jones' *Corregidora* (1975), or Cora Green of Alice Childress' *A Short Walk* (1979), Angelina never evaluates her appearance. Although Angelina does not become an heiress as does Isabel—indeed in the novel's third chapter, she is robbed of all her worldly possessions—she has friends who provide, unpredictably and extravagantly. She is not, consequently, enslaved by either toil or poverty. Discussing his heroine and his novel in an interview, Young has said, "I tried to make Angelina anything but a stereotype of any kind. That book is really about . . . Uprootedness, in general." Angelina's "uprootedness," her very freedom, however, prevents her from discovering her identity and answering the questions which haunt her from the beginning of the novel: "Who am I? Who is Angelina?"

In the course of *The Portrait of a Lady,* Isabel learns the limits of her freedom; in the course of ***Who Is Angelina?,*** Angelina learns to recognize both the limitations and the possibilities of freedom. She progresses from a terrifying state of independence to an exhilarating state of independence, from a condition of "uprootedness" to a condition in which she is deeply and firmly rooted in herself. Initially adrift in the chaos of the present time and the chaos of shifting relationships, she is, finally, able to convert chaos to opportunity and to find her place, her "soul space," in the continuity of time and the continuity of evolving relationships. Initially vulnerable to unpredictable, chance circumstances, she is, finally, able to make conscious choices. Both James and Young bring their heroines to knowledge of self as they come to define themselves in relation to others and to circumstances and limitations beyond their control and as they learn to make their choices in terms of these conditions. To follow the process by which Angelina discovers the joys of being herself, a free Afro-American woman, a free soul, we must examine the "changes" she goes through—Young's frequently used, Afro-American idi-

om for describing any series of experiences an individual may encounter in the course of time.

Young's carefully structured novel is divided into four books. In Books I and II, Angelina travels from California to Mexico and on to Michigan; changes happen to her. In Books III and IV, she travels from Michigan back to California; here she makes the changes happen. Thus Young brings his heroine full cycle geographically. Her journeying also forces her to time-travel—to look backward into her past and to dream ahead into the future; her cycle becomes a spiral, and she learns to play the changes on it. With audacious and delightful simplicity, Young lays out the plot of his novel in the second chapter when Angelina visits a fortune teller who spells out her character as well as her past, present, and future for her. Quite predictable the gypsy predicts that Angelina will meet "'a man—very tall, very dark . . . And very handsome'" and that she is going to take a trip. She is also told, however, that her journeying will be along

> " . . . a special path, call it what you will—the path of righteousness, the spiritual path. In your heart you like adventure. You want to know the truth about yourself, the real truth, because by finding that you feel that then you'll know all there is to know about everything under the sun . . . It's nothing to be afraid of. We all got to go down secret paths sooner or later."

In her traveling, Angelina becomes associated with the theme which Morrison has identified as that usually characteristic of male characters in Afro-American literature:

> The big scene is the traveling Ulysses scene, for black men. They are moving . . . And, boy, you know, they spread their seed all over the world. They are really moving! Perhaps it's because they don't have dominion. You can trace that historically, and one never knows what would have been the case if we'd never been tampered with at all. But that looking out and over and beyond and changing and so on—that, it seems to me, is one of the monumental themes in black literature about men. That's what they do. It is the Ulysses theme, the leaving home . . . Curiosity, what's around the corner, what's across the hill, what's in the valley, what's down the track. Go find out what that is, you know! And in the process of finding, they are also making themselves.

With Morrison's own Sula and Pilate Dead of *Song of Solomon* (1977), Young's heroine seems an anomaly among Afro-American women characters, for she is a true Ulysses, making a cyclical journey in time and space and making herself "strong in will / To strive, to seek, to find, and not to yield."

In discussing ***Who Is Angelina?,*** Young indicates that his novel emphatically reflects a particular period in our recent history: " . . . during that particular period I guess a lot of things were newly crystallizing that I felt a need to get out. That book was written in the early 70s." Angelina's existence in Books I and II of the novel exemplify this period of the late sixties and early seventies; in her actions and her associations, her life epitomizes the excesses, the vagaries, the irresponsibilities of that time, especially as Young saw them flourishing in California. Later, in Book III, Angelina is able to observe about this time and place:

> "It's kind of crazy, I mean, it's more than kind of crazy. You've got all these people and all that mild weather and no seasons really and your brain operates funny. You go around trying to figure out where you fit in and come to find out there're all these other people wandering around trying to figure out where *they* fit in."

In the same book, she further comments on the pretentiousness of the time and place: "'Berkeley's a state of mind, an attitude, a pose, a style, a way of dealing with the real world by not dealing with it.'"

In the first chapter of the novel, Young describes Angelina's life as "crazy" indeed; it has no center. For five nights she has been partying, ending up each night in bed with a different man; she pictures herself in different worlds—a quiet gallery in New York or "in Paris with talented Africans . . . or at sea in Barcelona." She is without a job, a lover, a purpose or a direction; she has recently attempted suicide. She is alone, and unconnected to place, time, people, or plan, she is unconnected to herself; she claims to be "sick of time and the world." But she is free, terrifyingly so.

When she is robbed of her household possessions in the novel's third chapter, her loss frees her further. Young, however, unlike William Faulkner and Morrison, whose Ike McCaslin and Milkman Dead must relinquish their material possessions in order to gain the wilderness and themselves, does not suggest that, paradoxically, loss equals gain. Angelina's robbery, the first of several which occur or are referred to in the course of the novel, contributes to her sense of purposelessness and helplessness; in losing her possessions, she exercises no choice of her own. Although Angelina's gypsy had told her, "'You see, we all have a certain amount of control over our lives. We have free will. We're born with that—the freedom to choose between this and that'," Angelina, not knowing herself and hence not knowing how to exercise her free will, is at the mercy of arbitrary, external circumstances. Her friend, Margo Tanaka, decides how Angelina should act in this instance; she pays for Angelina to fly to Mexico. Unlike Bigger Thomas, who yearned to fly, unlike the other caged birds of Afro-American literature for whom flight was synonymous with freedom, Young's heroine flies, not because of her own choice, with no plans and with exhilarating ease: "Suspended this way, between heaven and earth, she felt happy to be free and uncommitted for the time being, at least until the plane set down again." Although Morrison in *Song of Solomon*, a novel which makes flight its central image, recognizes that plane travel may be the equivalent of escape, Young's description of Angelina's condition at the beginning of *Who Is Angelina?* and his description of her flight to Mexico represent a unique expression in Afro-American litera-

ture of a character's sense of absolute freedom. Angelina neither yearns nor struggles for freedom; it is a given in her life, and as such, Young insists that she must understand its value; she must, therefore, learn to exercise her free will, choosing carefully and consciously between this and that.

In Mexico, away from the chaos of California, Angelina begins to work through the gypsy's predictions. She begins her journeying, and she meets that tall, dark, and handsome stranger. Although she does not direct the changes and the choices during her Mexican sojourn, and although, consequently, her identity remains obscure to her, in this section of the novel, Young reveals the qualities in her character which prove to be the basis for her choices and her identity. These qualities, which she shares with the protagonists of Young's other novels, reflect his constant values. Like MC, Sitting Pretty, Woody, Angelina grows, and her growth is the product of a questing, questioning mind; yet she, like them, is also characterized by certain constant traits: an appreciation of Afro-American style, especially as it is expressed in language and music; an abhorrence of all forms of hypocrisy and a corresponding concern for honesty in all matters; a delight in the diversity of human beings and a corresponding delight in the integrity and independence of one's self; an ease with sex; and a devotion to the members of one's family.

In defining the time in which he had set *Who Is Angelina?,* Young comments that

> . . . during that time I was affected deeply by a lot of the phony Black literature that was getting attention in America. I've always felt that a writer should project his or her visions from where they happen to find themselves, and if other people disapprove of it that's all well and good but you've at least tried your shot. So I might have been trying in [*Who Is Angelina?*] to compensate, subconsciously, for things that weren't being said and types of people that weren't being written about.

Who Is Angelina? seems the fulfillment of a statement Young had made in 1972 in which he aligned himself with other writers,

> . . . original men and women striving to express and give shape to the unthinkable variety of feeling and thought in the black communities we weren't allowed to share in the 1960s say, when Black Anger was all the rage and media made a killing.

Thus we find in *Who Is Angelina?* that Young creates a black woman who represents the unrepresented black community, in particular those who are middle-class, educated, and free, in particular those who, uprooted as they may be, know their "roots" and accept their blackness unself-consciously, naturally, and jubilantly. "Everybody nowadays is busy digging for roots. Well, I know my roots," explains Angelina. "I know them well and it doesn't make a damn bit of difference when it comes to making sense of who I am and why I make the kinds of mistakes I do." Angelina's search is neither to understand nor to accept her race; steeped in its ways, she both appreciates and revels in them. (pp. 263-69)

Book III is the pivotal section of *Who Is Angelina?*. In Books I and II, we see Angelina committed to defining herself as an individual, a woman, an Afro-American, a human being against the shifting trends, systems, ideologies, and events of her particular time. However, she struggles to do so, unable either to control or to accept the changes which happen to her. Book II concludes with Angelina's receiving word of her beloved father's hospitalization and with her reluctant departure from Mexico and Watusi for Detroit. Book III begins with her learning that her father, like herself, had been robbed, but had barely escaped death in defending himself and the sanctity of his home. The circumstances of the "particular period," which Young initially associates with California and Berkeley, thus come to seem ubiquitous. In the course of her Detroit sojourn, Angelina verifies her Aunt Jujie's description of her hometown:

> "It's a whole lotsa thievin *and* killin go on round this Detroit now. It aint never been no Garden of Eden, you wanna know the truth, but it's done got so here lately where you cant even walk down the street in broad daylight without worryin bout whether some dope fiend gon snatch your purse or knock you in the head."

She sees the physical deterioration of her neighborhood and hears stories of the moral deterioration of black people into "crazy niggers"; she is saddened by "'a respectable ex-soldier colored man,'" who accosts her selling stolen produce; depressed by guards and bars and signs threatening thieves; outraged by the orgy of drugs and sex in which her wealthy white friends engage. Young implies, however, that both the ubiquity and the intensity of external changes, of the elements of chaos, cause Angelina to determine to make her own changes. In Detroit, she recognizes the essential contribution of three factors—time, solitude, and her own free will—to the making of herself and her "soul space."

Coming back to Detroit, Angelina returns to the past. In Mexico, she had said to Watusi, "'Never look back,'" and he had reinforced her imperative, "'Never look back—somethin might be gainin on you. That's my philosophy . . . I try to live every day like it might be the last.'" But Angelina must look back, not to understand her roots, but to understand herself. Her initial response on returning was that "For the first time in years she felt connection to something real again, to something from the past that had more than immediate meaning." Yet Young also indicates from the outset of this stage of her journey that she cannot retreat into the past. She cannot linger over the pleasures of childhood:

> What happy times she remembered from those days! Why do people have to grow up and spoil everything? It'd been so nice being a child and feeling that adults knew what they were doing and what the world was all about. Now that she was one of them, the truth was out, and the truth was breaking her heart by the hour.

Nor can she any longer sentimentalize with self-pity upon her attempted suicide. Nor can she become mired in the guilt generated by having struck for independence from her family.

Separated by death from her mother, she constantly seeks her approval for her liberated ways. Separated geographically from her father, she thinks lovingly about him. Watusi instantly reminds her of him, in appearance and in wit, and on the night they first make love, he plays music her father had taught her to appreciate and describes her father to her as if he had known him. As they make love, the past seems recreated as if

> Suddenly it was raining moments, moments that stretched into soft, fleshy years. Some ancient tune was sweetening the silence inside her head, some song that conveyed without words just how her mother might have felt the instant her father's seed entered her womb and—

Young's description here prompts not a snap Freudian judgment, but rather a recognition of his conviction that an individual, to be fulfilled, must be able to reconcile the past with the present. For a moment, Angelina is able to do this in Mexico.

With her father during the days of his recuperation in Detroit, she ponders her present identity, however, by examining the familiar, taunting questions through the medium of the past:

> Daddy, what was the weather like the day I was born? Why did you and Mama have me? What was it that first attracted you to Mama? Why did you give up playing music? What possessed you to move from Georgia to Michigan and why that little racist town Milan and all that farming stuff? Why'd you pick the post office to work at for the rest of your life? Was I strange as a little girl? Do you love me as much as Mama did? Do you still love Mama? Do you still love me now that Ive been away for so long? Why'd you name me what you did? Did my name have any special significance to you and Mama? What was it? Who is Angelina?

In her long talks and walks with her father, he reveals himself to her and implicitly herself to herself. He speaks to her of his enduring love for her mother, who he watched over while she was dying of cancer even as Angelina is watching over him; he speaks to her of his subsequent belief:

> " . . . in a high power, some kinda God or spirit or whatever you wanna call it that's bigger and more beautiful than anything we know in this world . . . Going to church is a style the same as just eating vegetables or not wearing a hat. Later for that! I'm for the real thing which is being for real, if you get me, like, religion is for real—you can feel it from the minute you wake up till the minute you lie down at night and all through your dreams if youre living right— . . . That secret little thing that gives you the power to go on living when everything else says 'Forget it and die!'—that's what I'm talking about."

His statement of belief becomes his legacy to Angelina. It releases her from the tormented past, from "the dusty corner of herself that was nothing but guilt and shadow" through her knowledge that her father will be able to continue to live a full and vigorous life; it also releases her into the present and the future, into the continuity of time, far bigger than herself, but her own "secret little thing," her secret path the gypsy had predicted she would find.

In Detroit, face-to-face with her past, with the presence of her father and memories of her mother, with her old high school friends and memories of their days together, she realizes that "Time was her drug really":

> All her life she'd been rummaging around in time looking for some version of this bliss she'd heard and read so much about . . . Call it whatever you wanted. She called it ecstasy—a joyous feeling of total release. She wanted to rise up out of herself and go zooming above the stupid-ass world like some giggly old saint who knew that nothing short of ecstasy mattered anyway. Was this what she sought in a man? Was this the kind of freedom she was looking for when she drifted away from this very town to become a wanderer like so many of her old friends had done?

"The beautiful thing about time, she was coming to believe, was that it never stands still." In Mexico, there were brief moments when, as it were, she had time, when she felt at one with the peasants moving slowly across the land as her ancestors might have done, when she reenacted her parents' experience as she made love to Watusi, when she found a day for "unscheduled and imaginative loafing [such as] she never seemd to have time for in the States anymore . . . Most of all she loved being on top of time as it flowed on and passed by and simply slipped away." To lose time, as she does taking drugs with Renee is, for Angelina, to lose contact with life's possibilities. Young seems to suggest that to be unaware of time's flow or to be unable to accept is is to be trapped by time. Thus Angelina's time in Detroit, by forcing her to confront the past, frees her to accept certain changes which time brings: in particular, her father's near death and his recovery. She writes to Curtis, again defining herself in a letter, "Time's the biggest problem (or asset) I've got. What used to take months to make itself clear now only takes weeks. I feel older than old, and if the world ended tonight I'd feel that I died a merciful death."

Angelina's ability to accept the changes which time brings coincides with her study of meditation and her realization of her need for solitude. She recognizes the anomaly of the fact that her interest should have flowered in Detroit rather than in San Francisco: "It amused her that she'd avoided mystical literature . . . the whole time she'd been in California, and now, stranded in hardbop do-or-die Detroit, she found herself gobbling up yoga, Zen and occult books as if by doctor's prescription." "In hardbop do-or-die Detroit," however, Angelina is alone. In the house where she had been raised, with the memories of the past surrounding her, she finds that there is wonder in silence and solitude. The fear that solitude might sour into loneliness, the fear that she realizes has been partially responsible for

her dependence on men, is absolved. As she learns how to meditate, time flows through her, bringing images of past, present and future, but gradually, she seems to transcend her own personal involvement with time to make contact with time eternal: "For the first time in her life, she felt the windows of her loneliness opening wide to the world. There was nothing she wanted to leave unframed."

Young's description of Angelina's success with meditation—the achievement of "peace of mind . . . all you can really count on . . . what the gypsy was trying to tell me"—seems almost too good to be true. Her's and her father's experiences however, seem based on Young's own "remarkable and continuing series of (non-drug induced) mystical experiences that I consider, thus far, to be the high points of my life";

> . . . since the mid-sixties, I have been nourished by these intense and blissful interludes and, hence, have drawn much of my inspiration to write . . . from what could be termed religious sources. I am not, of course, referring to church religion. Sometimes there is a vastness I feel growing within me that I could explore and delight in forever. No mere church could contain it. I cannot help but believe that all men have sensed this beautiful endlessness about themselves at one time or another. It is what I call soul.

Angelina's success is also credible because we realize that she has mastered not an absolute state of mind, but a technique for achieving that state of mind; although her questions continue, Young demonstrates that his heroine can, of her own free will, temporarily dispel them. The chapter describing her success with meditation is entitled "Getting Over," and we are led to believe that Angelina has learned how to use meditation in order to get over. The final chapter in Book III suggests that she has learned to join the freedom which meditation gives her with the freedom of choice, to join the infinity of time with the finite nature of self, to create from the feeling of total release her own "soul space." Disgusted with the good times contrived by banalities of conversation and pretentious posturing between strangers, by sex and drugs, at Renee's New Year's party, Angelina leaves, choosing to welcome in a new year—and a renewed commitment to life—by meditating in silence.

Angelina's choice to leave the party, a choice she would have been unable to make at the beginning of the novel, points to the third factor of which her sojourn in Detroit has made her conscious: her own free will. Although the gypsy had reminded her of its importance, in Books I and II, Angelina had passively let those changes happen to her whereas in Book III, she is able to distinguish between those changes which, being beyond her control, she must accept and those which she can both judge and control. In a letter to Curtis she once again reflects upon herself, this time setting forth her determination to create her own life, to make conscious choices:

> I love [my father] and yet at the same time I can't wait to get back to Berkeley to pick up my raggedy

life where I left it hanging, flapping like some tattered garment hung out on a clothesline. I feel I'm at some kind of crossroads. I can go either this way or that. I can keep on being passive and taking whatever shit the world's dealing out and continue to get messed around at every turn, or I can do a turn-around and do a little dishing out myself . . . I plan to start exercising a bit of my own free will . . . you know that old blues lyric that goes: "Cried last night / and I cried the night before / I'm gonna change my way of living / so I won't have to cry no more?"

Exercising a bit of her own free will, she does change her way of living; no longer passive, she chooses and she acts. At the conclusion of Book III, she not only identifies the pretentious intellectualizing of white Renee and the pretentious attitudinizing of black Ernest, but she also leaves Renee's party and leaves Detroit. Her departure from Berkeley and from Mexico had been determined for her by circumstances and by the generosity of friends; her departure from Detroit and from her beloved father is the result of a difficult decision, but one made with knowledge of the continuity of time, the sanctity of solitude, and the necessity of her own "soul space."

In Book IV of *Who Is Angelina?,* Young brings Angelina full cycle. For his heroine as well as for the hero of *Invisible Man,* "the end is in the beginning." Angelina's life is a spiraling rather than a stagnant circle; in returning to pick up her "raggedy life" where she left it hanging in Berkeley, she tests her newly acquired sense of time and self in the context of her recent past and her former acquaintances. To the extremes of terror and ecstasy, which freedom had brought before, she adds responsibility.

In the opening episode of Book IV, Young reveals the strength of his heroine's self, of her independence and integrity, as she chooses and acts in the familiar social context of a busy street corner in Berkeley. Witness to the robbery of a white acquaintance's purse, Angelina does not stand by passively. Reminded of previous robberies—her own apartment, her father's home, her aunt's purse—she determines to pursue, to catch, and to prosecute the thief. Her action above all suggests that she no longer will be victimized by circumstances, nor allow others to be victimized by them if she can choose. Her outrage . . . at being identified as an "'Uncle Tom collaborationist'" reflects her conviction that her decisions and actions can benefit humanity. In Young's novels, the protagonists are not ennobled by profound suffering or poverty, by desperate flights or murders, but rather by making what appear to be simple choices to defend simple principles of right and wrong. Thus if Angelina's pursuit of the thief, which involves her brandishing her umbrella like a samurai sword and her being assisted by a comic bulldog, is mock-heroic, it is also poignantly human.

In the course of Book IV, Angelina must make other choices. She applies for a job, recognizing the possibility of ther potential employer's humility as well as of her arrogance; she helps Margo, recognizing the necessity of adjusting her needs to Margo's. However, Young most clearly demonstrates Angelina's triumphant ability to retain her "soul space" as he describes her relationships with men. Not a self-conscious feminist, Angelina implicitly embodies an explicit feminist principle in these relationships; she knows that neither her sense of life's possibilities nor her sense of herself is dependent upon either sex or a man. In Mexico she had succumbed to Watusi; in Detroit, she had cared for her father; back in Berkeley, she is confronted by the memories of her former lover; the pressure and presence of Curtis, her epistolary lover; and the return of Watusi. She is troubled by her jealousy over her former lover; she yearns not to "get involved and all excited and lose this hard-earned spiritual high . . . [not] to go through all those changes again. It took too much out of her to be tempted that way." She is able to put to rest her feelings about this man by realizing that "'Cant no one person cause you to suffer if you make up your mind you dont want em to'"; she is able to put to rest her feelings for Curtis by insisting that they can be "soul mates," by insisting that they can enjoy good food and the rain, music and the ocean together without having to have sex; she puts to rest her feelings about Watusi by determining to pay back the money he has given her and by recognizing that she can love him without being wedded to him:

> "That's the way I used to think . . . either you do or you dont [love someone]. But it isnt always that easy. Most of the time it's someplace in between. It's taken me all my life to learn that. You can love somebody and not love em. You can hate somebody and not hate em. I love you . . . but . . . I mean, you have to understand how I mean that."

Watusi understands; he leaves, but with appreciation for her and a promise of future meetings. Thus Angelina, by choosing to continue to define herself through her own mind and through multiple experiences rather than through the mind of another and a single relationship, continues to increase her sense of possibilities, the dimensions of her "soul space."

Coming to terms with the past in Detroit and in Berkeley, Angelina is at ease with the on-going present. Meditation had provided the means of attaining peace with time, and although it continues to do so, Angelina perceives that it is a means rather than an end. To meditate or not to meditate? Angelina chooses to meditate when it helps her—"Later for a movement! She loved being moved all alone this way; ablutions performed, meditation attended to, stomach empty, her entire body tingling with energy in the familiar seclusion of a newly cleaned cottage." But she will choose not to meditate if it becomes as constricting as a movement: "Maybe she was being too uptight about meditation and the pursuit of serenity. The last thing she wanted to become was dull and inflexible like most people she saw around her lately—dreary, cheerless hippies and straights, whites and off-whites, blacks and browns, oldsters and youngsters."

To her distraught friend, Margo, Angelina explains that while meditation has helped her, it has not resolved all her difficulties: "'I still have hassles to work out. I still get headaches. I still get fed up with everybody and wanna go hide someplace. I'm saying that the change Ive been going through makes things a lot more interesting probably because I myself feel more in control and on top of stuff.'"

But even as she talks with Margo, an elderly neighbor dies. The event illuminates Young's conviction that the individual may choose his or her options and thus control the changes in his or her life within a framework of inevitable limitations which prohibit absolute free will or control. Although Angelina may, through meditation, believe she can transcend time, she must and does also realize that time passes, moving one closer to the last, inevitable change: death. In the novel's final chapter—"Time on Fire"—Young suggests that her heroine is aware of time's possibilities and its limitations; acknowledge the moment's passing: "Would [time] ever catch up with her? . . . [she went] for a head-clearing walk and let time continue to do what time does as it burns itself up with each moment."

In the novel's penultimate chapter, Angelina makes two seemingly contradictory comments about freedom. When her neighbor dies, Angelina says, "'Mama Lou is free.'" Thus death can be seen to represent both the final limitation and the ultimate liberation, a liberation from the restrictions of time and self into the eternity of time and selflessness. Mama Lou's death intrudes upon Angelina's pondering whether Margo longed "to be free, free of herself, free of being Margo." We are reminded that Angelina had herself earlier longed for death, longed to be rid of "the stifling little cocoon of . . . Self." The Angelina of the novel's conclusion, however, says emphatically, "'I just wanna be me.'" Finally for Young, it seems therefore, as with Ellison, that liberation lies with self-knowledge, with the simultaneous acceptance of the limitations and responsibilities of time and self on the one hand and of choices and possibilities of time and self on the other hand. Explaining the title of his second book of poetry, *The Song Turning Back Into Itself* (1971), Young expresses his belief that "In essence you're never anyone but yourself. You go through all these changes but in a sense you're always turning back into what you really are." Thus in the conclusion of *Who Is Angelina?,* Angelina turns back into herself to discover "Possibilities . . . beginning to trouble her again. choices, decisions! That was all her life had been." Knowing herself, knowing at last who Angelina is, she knows, however, that she can choose and that in her choices lie both her freedom and her bondage. In the novel's final words, Young sets forth a range of possibilities for her life, possibilities which express choice and limitation, which in their openendedness express the full dimensions of her "soul space" and the continuation of her travels:

> Soon it would be time to either get up and get dressed and go to meditation, or lie in bed and feel guilty about skipping. This was order enough for her for now. There was tomorrow's drive down to Big Sur with Curtis. There would always be papers to correct.

With Angelina, Young seeks to create a character who represents an individual, an Afro-American woman, at a particular moment in time—"I really was trying to write about a young woman and options in the 1970s in America. Just what was out there? But because she was Black that was something I wanted to deal with"; [this was] "my primary purpose in writing the book." If he has succeeded in these ends, he has also succeeded in creating a heroine who can be identified with the heroines of classic American literature—Hester Prynne and Isabel Archer, who come to know themselves, their possibilities and limitations, through the choices they make—as well as certain heroines of Afro-American literature, created by Afro-American women writers. Mary Helen Washington describes these heroines— Paule Marshall's Reena of the story by that name (1962), Alice Walker's Sarah Davis of "A Sudden Trip Home in the Spring" (1971), and Nella Larsen's Clare Kendry of *Passing* (1929) and Helga Crane of *Quicksand* (1928)—as anticipating the educated, middle-class black woman who has emerged as a force in American life in recent decades:

> As black women move further into areas that were once the private reserve of whites, those few of us— those fortunate few whose lives are not stunted and dreamless—are finding ourselves facing the tensions that Nella Larsen knew, and it is for us to do something about them, to take what she started further than she was able to go . . . we are condemned to a new freedom.

Al Young's Angelina Green finds, ultimately, triumph in being condemned to the dimensions of this "new freedom." She finds "soul space." (pp. 277-87)

> *Elizabeth Schultz, "Search for 'Soul Space': A Study of Al Young's 'Who Is Angelina?' (1975) and the Dimensions of Freedom," in* The Afro-American Novel Since 1960, *edited by Peter Bruck and Wolfgang Karrer, B. R. Grüner Publishing Co., 1982, pp. 263-87.*

Francis Davis (essay date 1988)

[*Davis is a jazz critic and essayist. In the following review of* Things Ain't What They Used to Be, *he discusses how music activates Young's poetic imagination.*]

Perhaps the best way to explain what the poet and novelist Al Young has been up to in *Bodies and Soul, Kind of Blue* and now *Things Ain't What They Used to Be* is to yield him the floor. This is a lyrical rush from **"Nostalgia in Times Square,"** named after a Charles Mingus blues:

> One night we were walking to her place through Times Square—back before genitals and orifices were being packaged—and she turned to me and, letting go of my hand, shaped her lips to say

something I sensed was going to be urgent and deep, but changed her mind.

It is this remembered silence of hers that has hovered for decades in a secret part of me that would come out sounding—were it ever orchestrated—like Mingus' subway-grounded, wounded slash-and-burn landscape of love.

Music jolts Mr. Young's memory, and his essays on jazz, pop and rhythm-and-blues amount to piecemeal autobiography. Harold Arlen and Johnny Mercer's "Accentchu-ate the Positive" is the springboard for vivid ruminations on his childhood in rural Mississippi, his futile attempts to win a word of approval from his gruff maternal grandfather and his grandmother's fortitude in standing by a contrary husband. Woody Herman's classic 1947 recording of Ralph Burns's "Summer Sequence," with a supernal tenor saxophone solo by Stan Getz, makes Mr. Young long for the "virtually freezer-like" air-conditioning of his Detroit adolescence, which "wasn't muted or subtle or energy-saving the way air-conditioning later became." And any number of songs, including "As Time Goes By," remind him of the breathtaking vistas, changeable climate and cultural diversity of San Francisco, where he has lived most of his adult life.

Mr. Young avoids the kind of literary scat song too many other writers lapse into when attempting to evoke the thrill of jazz—he's too rational a thinker for that, despite a stubborn mystical streak, and too rigorous a craftsman, despite a sentimental attachment to Jack Kerouac's spontaneous bop prosody (the song "Marta," a hit for Arthur Tracy in 1931 and again for Tony Martin in 1952, triggers a fantasy about a love affair with a Mexican woman that reads like an affectionate parody of Kerouac's "Tristessa").

Besides, Mr. Young has too much of his own to say for him to spend his hours at the typewriter mimicking his favorite saxophonists and singers. He has no standard approach. His prose turns lavishly purple in eulogies for Ben Webster and Otis Redding. But his is wickedly funny and matter-of-fact when recounting a brush he and his wife had with scam artists pushing a vacation-home time-sharing scheme (in a piece titled **"Stormy,"** after the 1968 hit by the Classics IV that was playing over the Muzak as the Youngs prepared to face "Mr. Hard Sell"). And he spins a perfect little fiction about an estranged couple forced into renewed contact by a stuck copy of Billy Joel's "Just the Way You Are."

Some of the pieces in *Things Ain't What They Used to Be* are journalistic in nature. The best is a profile of the cartoonist Gary Larson, the shy creator of "The Far Side," who shares Mr. Young's passion for the jazz guitarist Django Reinhardt. Primarily a jazz fan, Mr. Young also finds inspiration in pop songs, although he is almost embarrassed to admit they mean much to him. To discuss Motown and Hugh Masekela, he brings in his alter ego O. O. Gabugah, a contemporary variation on Langston Hughes's Simple who thinks of Mr. Young as inhibited and somewhat pedantic.

In **"Moody's Mood for Love,"** named after King Pleasure's vocal twist on a James Moody saxophone solo, Mr. Young remembers that "what we liked to do at Hutchins Intermediate School in Detroit was get together—a whole gang of us, say, half a dozen to ten kids—and either walk through the halls or hang out by the grocery store over there off Woodrow Wilson, or step through streets singing 'Moody's Mood for Love' in loud unison with a vengeance calculated to blow grown people and other squares clean away; keep them right there were we wanted them—at a distance and out of our business." *Things Ain't What They Used to Be* is about the bonds that music can form among the young. But it's also about finding oneself in middle age, alone with one's record collection and one's thoughts. Mr. Young's triumph is in convincing us that this isn't such a bad place to be.

Francis Davis, "O. O. Gabugah Interviews Himself," in The New York Times Book Review, *January 24, 1988, p. 10.*

Charles Johnson (essay date 1988)

[*Johnson, an American novelist, short story writer, and essayist, is best known for* Middle Passage, *the winner of the 1990 National Book Award for fiction. In the following excerpt, he surveys Young's career, describing the author's humor and optimism as valuable qualities in a black writer.*]

[Al Young is a writer strong in comic yet serious entertainment.] He is distinguished by the emphasis in his large body of work on a gentle vision of black American life that is, at bottom, harmonious and spiritual. Young is a philosophically interesting writer, as readers will come to see in his forthcoming novel, *Seduction by Light;* he has, like Toomer, exposed himself to the universe of Eastern metaphysics, specifically to the meditation methods of Yogananda and the large, distinguished body of work by Eknath Easwaran, who is, in my opinion, our most trustworthy interpreter of Oriental thought. In short, nothing of importance in the universe of global culture and consciousness is lost on Al Young. As poet Richard Shelton described him in his introduction of Young at a 1986 meeting for the Associated Writing Programs, he is beyond all doubt a "man of letters." In contrast to the Angry School of black writing in the 1960s, which Young has criticized in his poem **"A Dance for Militant Dilettantes,"** he provides a refreshing difference. His heart, if this doesn't sound corny to say, is with the "common folk," as was Langston Hughes's, with black people whose lives display endurance, folk wisdom, and the sort of humor Sterling Brown might appreciate. In his novels such as *Snakes* (1970), chronicling the life of a young musician, and *Sitting Pretty* (1976), a comic and vivid character sketch of an aging black man who becomes a radio talk show celebrity, Young shows just how well he can handle authentic black dialect that nails down the music of rural and urban black voices, and also demonstrates a talent for stories that sometimes disarm a reader with their substitution of quiet insights and maturity for the bristling rage of the Black Nationalists. In his **"Statement on Aesthetics, Poetics, Kinetics"** in *New Black Voices* (1972), he expresses himself as a writer primarily concerned with the communal spirit underlying artistic activity, which he sees as a moral, humanizing activity, especially today in a postindustrial society where individuals are so easily lost in the crowd, an activity that comes down hard on the idea of black life (all life) as a process. In his work the individual is in movement, a process of continual change; "dancing" seems to be his favorite metaphor, so that no one is trapped in a situation, good or bad, for very long. In other words, Young emphasizes hope but adds that to complete his or her *telos* each individual must surrender completely to feeling and faith. Like that of many writers to emerge from the 1960s, his interest in black music (**Bodies and Souls** [1981], **Snakes**) stems from a belief that music, as a creative act, expresses not only feeling and becoming but community as well.

No question that we've seen this before in the Black Arts Movement. But in Young's novels, at the heart of his fictional process, there is no hatred. Only a weariness with the more extreme political postures of the late 1960s and early 1970s. There is also a wisdom that comes with age, from having observed a great deal of human behavior, which leads to both faint disenchantment and great compassion, and from these emerges a noble yet slightly nervous belief that there is, and perhaps always has been, a basic harmony to Being that cannot be broken. An author must *will* himself, I suspect, to write as Young does; he must will positive, time-honored values, as he conceives them—faith, love, a belief in family life—against the staggering evidence at his elbow for despair and disintegration, his intention being to balance the darker moments so easy to dramatize with other experiences that soften the terror, the pain of dislocation, the horrors of black history, and to leave us in the end—as in many of Young's books and better poems—with a feeling of thanksgiving, which is damned hard to dramatize. It is *easy,* as one of my students puts it, to be "despairingly effective" in fiction. And nearly impossible to deliver convincingly a portrait of black life that is, to use one of John Gardner's phrases, "life-affirmative." Al Young tries. And in **Sitting Pretty**—a crowd pleaser when he reads it aloud to large audiences—he succeeds in delivering characters whose humanity transcends stereotypes. In this fact alone, Young provides a necessary transition from the hysterical, race-baiting black fiction of an earlier decade. (pp. 69-71)

Charles Johnson, "The Men," in his Being & Race: Black Writing Since 1970, *Indiana University Press, 1988, pp. 57-93.*

Robert Ward (essay date 1989)

[*In the following review, Ward praises the narrative voice in* Seduction by Light.]

Al Young's **Seduction by Light** is a sneaky, beautiful novel. Like some shape-shifter out of primitive mythology, the book keeps changing form, upsetting the reader's expectations. Just when you feel you've got it figured, the novel veers crazily toward higher poetic ground.

The story is told in the folksy, warm voice of one Mamie Franklin, a middle-aged black woman who works as a maid and lives with her paralyzed husband, Burley Cole, in Santa Monica, Calif. She talks of her life (a son, Benjie; a promising singing career ended by racism) in the tired voice of a good woman who is struggling to make do in glitzy L.A.:

> "Well, sense is still pretty much the only thing I ever had plenty of. It might not be common sense, but it's sense all the same. And it's what helped me start slowin down, straightenin up, and tryna put my own little fallin-down house in order."

But order is not easy to come by. Mamie's ramshackle life is filled with comic chaos. In the first pages of the novel, she is almost robbed by two young thugs but dispatches them with a tear-gas gun. A day later, she goes off to work for Carlton T. Chrysler, a motion picture and television producer, and runs into a typically weird Hollywood scene: Mr. Chrysler is entertaining a nude actress while his wife is away. And by page 58 likeable, funny Burley has died from a heart attack and Mamie is thrust into a world of grief. All of this is well written, but seems like familiar territory. One begins to think that one is in for another earnest book about the hard times of a good woman in an uncaring, hostile world—a book we have all read too many times.

But happily, the novelist, essayist and poet Al Young is too imaginative a writer to fall into that trap. Soon good old Burley is back again, as a ghost. Indeed, he seems energized by death, altogether happier and more lively. He is able to move about, to check out his stepson Benjie as well as his own son, Kendall. He once again lies in bed with Mamie and reassures her about the hereafter. (His spectral scope does have some limitations, however; he can't touch her.)

Once Burley reappears, the novel takes on a fantastic quality that works to its advantage. At one point, Mamie has to confront her ex-lover, the white producer Harry Silvertone. She wants the movie mogul to tell their son Benjie that he is indeed the boy's father and to give him a break as a scriptwriter. This could be a melodramatic bit out of *Mildred Pierce,* but Burley Cole's ghostlike presence gives the scene a devil-may-care lunacy that makes the whole thing float.

Indeed, the entire book "floats" in a spacey, comic way. Of course, there is a story, a good one; and yes, black life in Los Angeles is something we haven't read much about before. But the real power of the novel, the likable strangeness of it, has more to do with its voice and tone than with either the characters or the plot.

In a charming comic moment, Mamie falls for a handsome young waiter named Theo. After thinking it over, she takes him to her house and has terrific sex with him; just as they fall off to sleep, the entire city of Los Angeles is hit by a major earthquake. Mamie awakes Theo and tells him what happened.

"'An earthquake?' he said, 'Is that what this is?'

"'What'd you think it was?'

"'I don't know. I was having such a strange dream, I thought maybe this was merely an extension of it, or something.'

"'Well, it doesnt matter if we're in a dream or not. We better get our butts someplace else before the roof caves in on us!'"

This is precisely the effect the earthquake sequence has on the reader as well. Comical disaster scenes float by, as if seen from behind some affable scrim; the sound of Mamie Franklin's ironic, funky voice gives us the feeling that anything at all might happen.

This would not do in most novels, but works surprisingly well here, because Mamie is a bit of a philosopher and seer. She has a kind of distanced flakiness indigenous to actors (black *or* white—actor flakiness transcends race). Thus, when Mamie faints in a case of postquake nerves, flies to heaven with Burley in an out-of-body experience and meets her idol, Benjamin Franklin, we find ourselves smiling and accepting it: Well, old Ben, of course; why not?

At the book's end, Mamie has learned a few things from her ghostly encounter, and so has the reader—about life and love and making the time we have on this earth count.

Frankly, I felt myself *wanting* to resist Al Young's jazzy, baggy novel. Ordinarily, I'm not much on either ghosts or the highly advertised L.A. state of mind (of which this book is, in its own imaginative way, a superior example). But Mamie Franklin is so charming, her voice so human, that I was quickly won over. Al Young is a poet, a gentle philosopher and a man of real sensibility. **Seduction by Light** is brilliant, funny and sweet. (pp. 11-12)

> *Robert Ward, "Burley Cole Is Dead and Well in L.A.," in* The New York Times Book Review, *February 5, 1989, pp. 11-12.*

FURTHER READING

Bolling, Douglass. "Artistry and Theme in Al Young's *Snakes*." *Negro American Literature Forum* 8, No. 2 (Summer 1974): 223-25.
> Laudatory review of *Snakes*. Bolling writes: "Young reaffirms the great tradition of the novel as a form which explores the dialectic of spirit in loving war with itself."

Flower, Dean. "Fiction Chronicle: *Sitting Pretty*." *The Hudson Review* XXIX, No. 2 (Summer 1976): 270-82.
> Comments favorably on the vernacular captured by Young in creating the character Sidney J. Prettymon.

Martz, Louis L. "Recent Poetry: Established Idiom." *The Yale Review* LIX, No. 4 (June 1970): 551-69.
> Review of *Dancing*. Martz claims: "The power of Young's poetry comes from his refusal to allow himself to be segregated from this world."

O'Brien, John, ed. "Al Young." In his *Interviews with Black Writers*, pp. 259-69. New York: Liveright, 1973.
> Interview in which Young explains some of the recurring themes in his works and discusses literature's social obligation: "Poets should alert people that they have imaginations. There's something else down beneath that flesh and blood and grey matter. And that's the only thing that's going to change the direction we're moving in."

Sissman, L. E. "Growing Up Black." *The New Yorker* XLVI, No. 21 (11 July 1970): 77-9.
> Praises the restraint and vividness of the prose in *Snakes*.

Young, Al. "Prelude." In his *Things Ain't What They Used to Be*, pp. xiii-xvii. Berkeley, Calif.: Creative Arts Book Co., 1987.
> Describes the idea of "musical memoirs" and how it developed over the course of the three volumes in the series. Young writes: "It has taken some time for me to realized how flexible and unpredictable a so-called musical memoir can be. There's no defining it, just as there's no way to define poetry or the blues, which are, by nature of the indomitable life-spirit that feeds them, unruly and wild."

INDEXES

BLC Author Index

This index lists all author entries in *Black Literature Criticism* and includes cross-references to other series published by Gale Research Inc. Authors who have used pseudonyms professionally are listed under their real names, with suitable cross-references. References in the index are identified as follows:

AAYA	*Authors & Artists for Young Adults,* Volumes 1-6
BW:	*Black Writers*
CA:	*Contemporary Authors* (original series), Volumes 1-133
CAAS:	*Contemporary Authors Autobiography Series,* Volumes 1-13
CABS:	*Contemporary Authors Bibliographical Series,* Volumes 1-3
CANR:	*Contemporary Authors New Revision Series,* Volumes 1-33
CAP:	*Contemporary Authors Permanent Series,* Volumes 1-2
CA-R:	*Contemporary Authors* (first revision), Volumes 1-44
CDALB:	*Concise Dictionary of American Literary Biography*
CLC:	*Contemporary Literary Criticism,* Volumes 1-65
CLR:	*Children's Literature Review,* Volumes 1-24
DC:	*Drama Criticism,* Volume 1
DLB:	*Dictionary of Literary Biography,* Volumes 1-107
DLB-DS:	*Dictionary of Literary Biography Documentary Series,* Volumes 1-8
DLB-Y:	*Dictionary of Literary Biography Yearbook,* Volumes 1980-1989
LC:	*Literature Criticism from 1400 to 1800,* Volumes 1-16
MTCW:	*Major 20th-Century Writers*
NCLC:	*Nineteenth-Century Literature Criticism,* Volumes 1-31
PC:	*Poetry Criticism,* Volumes 1-2
SAAS:	*Something about the Author Autobiography Series,* Volumes 1-12
SATA:	*Something about the Author,* Volumes 1-65
SSC:	*Short Story Criticism,* Volumes 1-7
TCLC:	*Twentieth-Century Literary Criticism,* Volumes 1-41

Achebe, Chinua
1930- 1:1-15
See also BW; CA 1-4R; CANR 6, 26; CLC 1, 3, 5, 7, 11, 26, 51; CLR 20; MTCW; SATA 38, 40

Afton, Effie
See Harper, Francis Ellen Watkins

Al-Amin, Jamil Abdullah (H. Rap Brown)
1943- 1:16-24
See also BW; CA 112, 125

Alexander, Margaret Abigail Walker
See Walker, Margaret

Allen, Sarah A.
See Hopkins, Pauline Elizabeth

Angelou, Maya
1928- 1:25-39
See also BW; CA 65-68; CANR 19; CLC 12, 35, 64; DLB 38; MTCW; SATA 49

Armah, Ayi Kwei
1939- 1:40-55
See also BW; CA 61-64; CANR 21; CLC 5, 33; MTCW

Attaway, William
1911?-1986....................... 1:56-74
See also DLB 76

Baldwin, James
1924-1987...................... 1:75-107
See also AAYA 4; BW; CA 1-4R; obituary CA 124; CABS 1; CANR 3, 24; CDALB 1941-1968; CLC 1, 2, 3, 4, 5, 8, 13, 15, 17, 42, 50; DC 1; DLB 2, 7, 33; DLBY 87; MTCW; SATA 9, 54

Bambara, Toni Cade
1939- 1:108-20
See also AAYA; BW; CA 29-32R; CANR 24; CLC 19; DLB 38; MTCW

Baraka, Amiri (LeRoi Jones)
1934- 1:121-51
See also BW; CA 21-22R; CABS 3; CANR 27; CDLB 1941-1968; CLC 1, 2, 3, 5, 10, 14, 33; DLB 5, 7, 16, 38; DLB-DS 8; MTCW

Bass, Kingsley B.
See Bullins, Ed

Beckham, Barry
1944- 1:152-71
See also CA 29-32R; CANR 26; DLB 33

Bell, James Madison
1826-1902...................... 1:172-79
See also BW; CA 122, 124; DLB 50

Bennett, Louise
1919- 1:180-88
See also CLC 28

Beti, Mongo (Alexandre Biyidi)
1932- 1:189-206
See also CLC 27

Biyidi, Alexandre
See Beti, Mongo

Bontemps, Arna
1902-1973...................... 1:207-25
See also BW; CA 1-4R; obituary CA 41-44R; CANR 4; CLC 1, 18; CLR 6; DLB 48, 51; MTCW; SATA 2, 44; obituary SATA 24

Boto, Eza
See Beti, Mongo

Bradley, David
1950- 1:226-37
See also BW; CA 104; CANR 26; CLC 23; DLB 33

Braithwaite, William Stanley
1878-1962...................... 1:238-46
See also BW; CA 125; DLB 50, 54

Brooks, Gwendolyn
  1917- **1**:247-69
  See also BW; CA 1-4R; CANR 1, 27;
    CDALB 1941-1968; CLC 1, 2, 4, 5,
    15, 49; DLB 5, 76; MTCW; SATA 6

Brown, Claude
  1937- **1**:270-80
  See also BW; CA 73-76; CLC 30

Brown, H. Rap
  See Al-Amin, Jamil Abdullah

Brown, Hubert Gerold
  See Al-Amin, Jamil Abdullah

Brown, Sterling
  1901-1989 ....**1**:281-91
  See also BW; CA 85-88; obituary CA
    127; CANR 26; CLC 1, 23, 59; DLB
    48, 51, 63; MTCW

Brown, William Wells
  1816?-1884......................**1**:292-306
  See also DC 1; DLB 3, 50; NCLC 2

Bruin, John
  See Brutus, Dennis

Brutus, Dennis
  1924- **1**:307-20
  See also BW; CA 49-52; CANR 2, 27;
    CLC 43

Bullins, Ed
  1935- **1**:321-42
  See also BW; CA 49-52; CANR 24;
    CLC 1, 5, 7; DLB 7, 38; MTCW

Cade, Toni
  See Bambara, Toni Cade

Casely-Hayford, J. E.
  1866-1930......................**1**:343-54
  See also CA 123; TCLC 24

Casey, Patrick
  See Thurman, Wallace

Césaire, Aimé
  1913- **1**:355-73
  See also BW; CA 65-68; CANR 24;
    CLC 19, 32; MTCW

Chesnutt, Charles W.
  1858-1932......................**1**:374-400
  See also BW; CA 106, 125; DLB 12,
    50, 78; MTCW; SSC 7; TCLC 5, 39

Childress, Alice
  1920- **1**:401-13
  See also BW; CA 45-48; CANR 3, 27;
    CLC 12, 15; CLR 14; DLB 7, 38;
    MTCW; SATA 7, 48

Clark, Al C.
  See Goines, Donald

Clark, John Pepper
  1935- **1**:414-29
  See also BW; CA 65-68; CANR 16;
    CLC 38

Clarke, Austin
  1934- **1**:430-44
  See also BW; CA 25-28R; CANR 14;
    CLC 8, 53; DLB 53

Cleaver, Eldridge
  1935- **1**:445-57
  See also BW; CA 21-24R; CANR 16;
    CLC 30

Clifton, Lucille
  1936- **1**:458-69
  See also BW; CA 49-52; CANR 2, 24;
    CLC 19; CLR 5; DLB 5, 41;
    MTCW; SATA 20

Coleman, Emmett
  See Reed, Ishmael

Cotter, Joseph Seamon, Sr.
  1861-1949......................**1**:470-84
  See also BW; CA 124; DLB 50; TCLC
    28

Cullen, Countee
  1903-1946......................**1**:485-515
  See also BW; CA 108, 124; CDLB
    1917-1929; DLB 4, 48, 51; MTCW;
    SATA 18; TCLC 4, 37

Davis, Frank Marshall
  1905-1987......................**1**:516-25
  See also BW; CA 123, 125; DLB 51

Delaney, Samuel R.
  1942- **1**:526-40
  See also BW; CA 81-84; CANR 27;
    CLC 8, 14, 38; DLB 8, 33; MTCW

Demby, William
  1922- **1**:541-59
  See also BW; CA 81-84; CLC 53; DLB
    33

Diamano, Silmang
  See Senghor, Léopold Sédar

Dodson, Owen
  1914-1983......................**1**:560-73
  See also BW; CA 65-68; obituary CA
    110; CANR 24; DLB 76

Domini, Rey
  See Lorde, Audre

Douglass, Frederick
  1817?-1895......................**1**:574-96
  See also CDLAB 1640-1865; DLB 1,
    43, 50, 79; NCLC 7; SATA 29

Du Bois, W. E. B.
  1868-1963......................**1**:597-621
  See also BW; CA 85-88; CDALB 1865-
    1917; CLC 1, 2, 13, 64; DLB 47, 50,
    91; MTCW; SATA 42

Dunbar, Paul Laurence
  1872-1906......................**1**:622-42
  See also BW; CA 104, 124; CDALB
    1865-1917; DLB 50, 54, 78; SATA
    34; TCLC 2, 12

Edwards, Eli
  See McKay, Claude

Ekwensi, Cyprian
  1921- **1**:643-60
  See also BW; CA 29-32R; CANR 18;
    CLC 4; MTCW

Elder, Lonne, III
  1931- **1**:661-72
  See also BW; CA 81-84; CANR 25;
    DLB 7, 38, 44

Ellison, Ralph
  1914- **1**:673-706
  See also BW; CA 9-12R; CANR 24;
    CDALB 1914-1968; CLC 1, 3, 11,
    54; DLB 2, 76; MTCW

El-Shabazz, El-Hajj Malik
  See Malcolm X

Emecheta, Buchi
  1944- **2**:707-18
  See also BW; CA 81-84; CANR 27;
    CLC 14, 48; MTCW

Equiano, Olaudah
  1745?-1797......................**2**:719-39
  See also DLB 37, 50; LC 16

Eseki, Bruno
  See Mphahlele, Ezekiel

Fanon, Frantz
  1925-1961......................**2**:740-56
  See also BW; CA 116; obituary CA 89-
    92

Farah, Nuruddin
  1945- **2**:757-70
  See also CA 106; CLC 53

Fauset, Jessie Redmon
  1882-1961......................**2**:771-88
  See also BW; CA 109; CLC 19, 54;
    DLB 51

Fisher, Rudolph
  1897-1934......................**2**:789-806
  See also BW; CA 107, 124; DLB 51;
    TCLC 11

Forten, Charlotte L.
  1837?-1914......................**2**:807-23
  See also DLB 50; TCLC 16

Fuller, Charles
  1939- **2**:824-40
  See also BW; CA 108, 112; CLC 25;
    DC 1; DLB 38; MTCW

Gaines, Ernest
  1933- **2**:841-63
  See also BW; CA 9-12R; CANR 6, 24,
    CDALB 1968-1988; CLC 3, 11, 18;
    DLB 2, 33; DLBY 80; MTCW

Garvey, Marcus
  1887-1940......................**2**:864-80
  See also BW; CA 120, 124; TCLC 41

Giovanni, Nikki
  1943- **2**:881-99
  See also BW; CAAS 6; CA 29-32R,
    CANR 18; CLC 2, 4, 19, 64; CLR 6;
    DLB 5, 41; MTCW; SATA 24

Goines, Donald
  1937?-1974......................**2**:900-909
  See also BW; CA 124; obituary CA
    114; DLB 33

Gregory, J. Dennis
  See Williams, John A.

Grimké, Charlotte L. Forten
  See Forten, Charlotte L.

Guillén, Nicolás
  1902-1989......................**2**:910-26
  See also BW; CA 116, 125; obituary
    CA 129; CLC 48

Guillén y Batista, Nicolás Cristobal
  See Guillén, Nicolás

Haley, Alex
  1921- **2**:927-42
  See also BW; CA 77-80; CLC 8, 12;
    DLB 38; MTCW

Hammon, Jupiter
  1711?-1800?......................**2**:943-49
  See also DLB 31, 50; NCLC 5

Hansberry, Lorraine
1930-1965.......................2:950-74
See also BW; CA 109; obituary CA 25-
28R; CABS 3; CDALB 1941-1968;
CLC 17, 62; DLB 7, 38; MTCW

Harper, Frances Ellen Watkins
1825-1911.......................2:975-85
See also BW; CA 111, 125; DLB 50;
TCLC 14

Hayden, Robert
1913-1980.......................2:986-94
See also BW; CA 69-72; obituary CA
97-100; CABS 2; CANR 24; CDALB
1941-1968; CLC 5, 9, 14, 37; DLB 5,
76; MTCW; SATA 19; obituary
SATA 26

Head, Bessie
1937-1986...................2:995-1003
See also BW; CA 29-32R; obituary CA
119; CANR 25; CLC 25; MTCW

Himes, Chester
1909-1984......................2:1004-22
See also BW; CA 25-28R; obituary CA
114; CANR 22; CLC 2, 4, 7, 18, 58;
DLB 2, 76; MTCW

Hopkins, Pauline Elizabeth
1859-1930.....................2:1023-37
See also DLB 50; TCLC 28

Hughes, Langston
1902-1967......................2:1038-67
See also BW; CA 1-4R, obituary CA
25-28R; CANR 1; CDALB 1929-
1941; CLC 1, 5, 10, 15, 35, 44; CLR
17; DLB 4, 7, 48, 51, 86; MTCW;
PC 1; SATA 4, 33; SSC 6

Hurston, Zora Neale
1901?-1960.....................2:1068-89
See also BW; CA 85-88; CLC 7, 30,
61; DLB 51, 86; MTCW; SSC 4

Johnson, Charles
1948-..........................2:1090-1103
See also BW; CA 116; CLC 7, 51, 65;
DLB 33

Johnson, Fenton
1888-1958......................2:1104-14
See also BW; CA 118, 124; DLB 45,
50

Johnson, James Weldon
1871-1938......................2:1115-37
See also BW; CA 104, 125; CDALB
1917-1929; DLB 51; MTCW; SATA
31; TCLC 3, 19

Jones, Gayl
1949-..........................2:1138-48
See also BW; CA 77-80; CANR 27;
CLC 6, 9; DLB 33; MTCW

Jones, LeRoi
See Baraka, Amiri

Kaymor, Patrice Maguilene
See Senghor, Léopold Sédar

Kennedy, Adrienne
1931-..........................2:1149-63
See also BW; CA 103; CABS 3; CANR
26; DLB 38

Kincaid, Jamaica
1949-..........................2:1164-78
See also BW; CA 125; CLC 43

King, Martin Luther, Jr.
1929-1968..................2:1179-1209
See also BW; CA 25-28; CANR 27;
CAP 2; MTCW; SATA 14

Knight, Etheridge
1931-1991.....................2:1210-23
See also BW; CA 21-24R; CANR 23;
CLC 40; DLB 41

Lamming, George
1927-..........................2:1224-39
See also BW; CA 85-88; CANR 26;
CLC 2, 4; MTCW

Larsen, Nella
1891-1964.....................2:1240-50
See also BW; CA 125; CLC 37; DLB
51

Laye, Camara
1928-1980.....................2:1251-60
See also BW; CA 85-88; obituary CA
97-100; CANR 25; CLC 4, 38;
MTCW

Lee, Andrea
1953-..........................2:1261-68
See also BW; CA 125; CLC 36

Lee, Don L.
See Madhubuti, Haki R.

Lee, George Washington
1894-1976.....................2:1269-74
See also BW; CA 125; CLC 52; DLB
51

Little, Malcolm
See Malcolm X

Lorde, Audre
1934-..........................2:1275-89
See also BW; CA 25-28R; CANR 16,
26; CLC 18; DLB 41; MTCW

Machado de Assis, Joaquim Maria
1839-1908..................2:1290-1305
See also CA 107; TCLC 10

Madhubuti, Haki R. (Don L. Lee)
1942-..........................2:1306-22
See also BW; CA 73-76; CANR 24;
CLC 6; DLB 5, 41; DLB-DS 8

Major, Clarence
1936-..........................2:1323-39
See also BW; CAAS 6; CA 21-24R;
CANR 13, 25; CLC 3, 19, 48; DLB
33

**Malcolm X (Malcolm Little; El-Hajj
Malik El-Shabazz)**
1925-1965.....................2:1340-62
See also BW; CA 125; obituary CA
125; MTCW

Mandrake, Ethel Belle
See Thurman, Wallace

Marshall, Paule
1929-..........................3:1363-74
See also BW; CA 77-80; CANR 25;
CLC 27; DLB 33; MTCW; SSC 3

McKay, Claude
1889-1948..................3:1375-1401
See also BW; CA 104, 124; DLB 4, 45,
51; MTCW; PC 2; TCLC 7, 41

McKay, Festus Claudius
See McKay, Claude

Milner, Ron
1938-..........................3:1402-09
See also BW; CA 73-76; CANR 24;
CLC 56; DLB 38; MTCW

Mofolo, Thomas
1876-1948.....................3:1410-21
See also CA 121; TCLC 22

Morrison, Toni
1931-..........................3:1422-45
See also AAYA 1; BW; CA 29-32R;
CANR 27; CDALB 1968-1988; CLC
4, 10, 22, 55; DLB 6, 33; DLBY 81;
MTCW; SATA 57

Mphahlele, Ezekiel
1919-..........................3:1446-58
See also BW; CA 81-81; CANR 26;
CLC 25

Mphahlele, Ez'kia
See Mphahlele, Ezekiel

Mqhayi, S. E. K.
1875-1945.....................3:1459-68
See also TCLC 25

Myers, Walter Dean
1937-..........................3:1469-81
See also AAYA 4; BW; CA 33-36R;
CANR 20; CLC 35; CLR 4, 16; DLB
33; SAAS 2; SATA 27, 41

Myers, Walter M.
See Myers, Walter Dean

Naylor, Gloria
1950-..........................3:1482-94
See also AAYA 6; BW; CA 107; CANR
27; CLC 28, 52; MTCW

Ngugi, James Thiong'o
See Ngugi wa Thiong'o

Ngugi wa Thiong'o
1938-..........................3:1495-1514
See also BW; CA 81-84; CANR 27;
CLC 3, 7, 13, 36; MTCW

Nkosi, Lewis
1936-..........................3:1515-21
See also BW; CA 65-68; CANR 27;
CLC 45

Okigbo, Christopher
1932-1967.....................3:1522-30
See also BW; CA 77-80; CLC 25;
MTCW

Ousmane, Sembène
1923-..........................3:1531-50
See also BW; CA 117, 125; MTCW

Parks, Gordon
1912-..........................3:1551-58
See also BW; CA 41-44R; CANR 26;
CLC 1, 16; DLB 33; SATA 8

p'Bitek, Okot
1931-1982.....................3:1559-80
See also BW; CA 124; obituary CA
124; MTCW

Powell, Adam Clayton, Jr.
1908-1972.....................3:1581-91
See also BW; CA 102; obituary CA 102

Randall, Dudley
1914-..........................3:1592-1607
See also BW; CA 25-28R; CANR 23;
CLC 1; DLB 41

Reed, Ishmael
1938-............................**3**:1608-26
See also BW; CA 21-24R; CANR 25;
CLC 2, 3, 5, 6, 13, 32, 60; DLB 2,
5, 33; DLB-DS 8; MTCW

Roumain, Jacques
1907-1944......................**3**:1627-46
See also BW; CA 117, 125; TCLC 19

Sanchez, Sonia
1934-..........................**3**:1647-1670
See also BW; CA 33-36R; CANR 24;
CLC 5; CLR 18; DLB 41; DLB-DS
8; MTCW; SATA 22

Sembène, Ousmane
See Ousmane, Sembène

Senghor, Léopold Sédar
1906-...........................**3**:1671-87
See also BW; CA 116, 125; CLC 54;
MTCW

Shange, Ntozake
1948-..........................**3**:1688-1702
See also BW; CA 85-88; CABS 3;
CANR 27; CLC 8, 25, 38; DLB 38;
MTCW

Soyinka, Wole
1934-..........................**3**:1703-1724
See also BW; CA 13-16R; CANR 27;
CLC 3, 5, 14, 36, 44; DLBY 86;
MTCW

Thurman, Wallace
1902-1934......................**3**:1725-33
See also BW; CA 104, 124; DLB 51;
TCLC 6

Tolson, Melvin B.
1898?-1966......................**3**:1734-47
See also BW; CA 124; obituary CA 89-
92; CLC 36; DLB 48, 76

Toomer, Jean
1894-1967......................**3**:1748-68
See also BW; CA 85-88; CDALB 1917-
1929; CLC 1, 4, 13, 22; DLB 45, 51;
MTCW; SSC 1

Tutu, Desmond
1931-...........................**3**:1769-75
See also BW; CA 125

Tutuola, Amos
1920-..........................**3**:1776-89
See also BW; CA 9-12R; CANR 27;
CLC 5, 14, 29; MTCW

Vassa, Gustavus
See Equiano, Olaudah

Walcott, Derek
1930-..........................**3**:1790-1807
See also BW; CA 89-92; CANR 26;
CLC 2, 4, 9, 14, 25, 42; DLBY 81;
MTCW

Walker, Alice
1944-..........................**3**:1808-29
See also AAYA 3; BW; CA 37-40R;
CANR 9, 27; CDALB 1968-1988;
CLC 5, 6, 9, 19, 27, 46, 58; DLB 6,
33; MTCW; SATA 31; SSC 5

Walker, Margaret
1915-..........................**3**:1830-50
See also BW; CA 73-76; CANR 26;
CLC 1, 6; DLB 76; MTCW

Washington, Booker T.
1856-1915......................**3**:1851-78
See also BW; CA 114, 125; SATA 28;
TCLC 10

Wheatley, Phillis
1753?-1784.................**3**:1879-1902
See also CDALB 1640-1865; DLB 31,
50; LC 3

White, Walter
1893-1955......................**3**:1903-16
See also CA 115, 124; DLB 51; TCLC
15

Wideman, John Edgar
1941-.........................**3**:1917-31
See also BW; CA 85-88; CANR 14;
CLC 5, 34, 36; DLB 33

Williams, John A.
1925-..........................**3**:1932-49
See also BW; CA 53-56; CAAS 3;
CANR 6, 26; CLC 5, 13; DLB 2, 33

Williams, Sherley Anne
1944-..........................**3**:1950-61
See also BW; CA 73-76; CANR 25;
DLB 41

Williams, Shirley
See Williams, Sherley Anne

Wilson, August
1945-..........................**3**:1962-74
See also BW; CA 115, 122; CLC 39,
50, 63; MTCW

Wilson, Harriet
1827?-?.......................**3**:1975-83
See also DLB 50

Wright, Charles
1932-..........................**3**:1984-93
See also BW; CA 9-12R; CANR 26;
CLC 49; DLB 33

Wright, Richard
1908-1960...................**3**:1994-2021
See also AAYA 5; BW; CA 108;
CDALB 1929-1941; CLC 1, 3, 4, 9,
14, 21, 48; DLB 76; DLB-DS 2;
MTCW; SSC 2

Yerby, Frank
1916-..........................**3**:2022-31
See also BW; CA 9-12R; CANR 16;
CLC 1, 7, 22; DLB 76, MTCW

Young, Al
1939-..........................**3**:2032-47
See also BW; CA 29-32R; CANR 26;
CLC 19; DLB 33

BLC Nationality Index

AMERICAN

Al-Amin, Jamil Abdullah   1:16-24
Angelou, Maya   1:25-39
Attaway, William   1:56-74
Baldwin, James   1:75-107
Bambara, Toni Cade   1:108-20
Baraka, Amiri   1:121-51
Beckham, Barry   1:152-71
Bell, James Madison   1:172-79
Bontemps, Arna   1:207-25
Bradley, David   1:226-37
Braithwaite, William Stanley   1:238-46
Brooks, Gwendolyn   1:247-69
Brown, Claude   1:270-80
Brown, Sterling   1:281-91
Brown, William Wells   1:292-306
Bullins, Ed   1:321-42
Chesnutt, Charles W.   1:374-400
Childress, Alice   1:401-13
Cleaver, Eldridge   1:445-57
Clifton, Lucille   1:458-69
Cotter, Joseph Seamon, Sr.   1:470-84
Cullen, Countee   1:485-515
Davis, Frank Marshall   1:516-25
Delany, Samuel R.   1:526-40
Demby, William   1:541-59
Dodson, Owen   1:560-73
Douglass, Frederick   1:574-96
Du Bois, W. E. B.   1:597-621
Dunbar, Paul Laurence   1:622-42
Elder, Lonne III   1:661-72
Ellison, Ralph   1:673-706
Equiano, Olaudah   2:719-39
Fauset, Jessie Redmon   2:771-88
Fisher, Rudolph   2:789-806
Forten, Charlotte L.   2:807-23
Fuller, Charles   2:824-40

Gaines, Ernest   2:841-63
Giovanni, Nikki   2:881-99
Goines, Donald   2:900-909
Haley, Alex   2:927-42
Hammon, Jupiter   2:943-49
Hansberry, Lorraine   2:950-74
Harper, Frances Ellen Watkins   2:975-85
Hayden, Robert   2:986-94
Himes, Chester   2:1004-22
Hopkins, Pauline Elizabeth   2:1023-37
Hughes, Langston   2:1038-67
Hurston, Zora Neale   2:1068-89
Johnson, Charles   2:1090-1103
Johnson, Fenton   2:1104-14
Johnson, James Weldon   2:1115-37
Jones, Gayl   2:1138-48
Kennedy, Adrienne   2:1149-63
Kincaid, Jamaica   2:1164-78
King, Martin Luther, Jr.   2:1179-1209
Knight, Etheridge   2:1210-23
Larsen, Nella   2:1240-50
Lee, Andrea   2:1261-68
Lee, George Washington   2:1269-74
Lorde, Audre   2:1275-89
Madhubuti, Haki R.   2:1306-22
Major, Clarence   2:1323-39
Malcolm X   2:1340-62
Marshall, Paule   3:1363-74
McKay, Claude   3:1375-1401
Milner, Ron   3:1402-09
Morrison, Toni   3:1422-45
Myers, Walter Dean   3:1469-81
Naylor, Gloria   3:1482-94
Parks, Gordon   3:1551-58

Powell, Adam Clayton, Jr.   3:1581-91
Randall, Dudley   3:1592-1607
Reed, Ishmael   3:1608-26
Sanchez, Sonia   3:1647-70
Shange, Ntozake   3:1688-1702
Thurman, Wallace   3:1725-33
Tolson, Melvin B.   3:1734-47
Toomer, Jean   3:1748-68
Walker, Alice   3:1808-29
Walker, Margaret   3:1830-50
Washington, Booker T.   3:1851-78
Wheatley, Phillis   3:1879-1902
White, Walter   3:1903-16
Wideman, John Edgar   3:1917-31
Williams, John A.   3:1932-49
Williams, Sherley Anne   3:1950-61
Wilson, August   3:1962-74
Wilson, Harriet   3:1975-83
Wright, Charles   3:1984-93
Wright, Richard   3:1994-2021
Yerby, Frank   3:2022-31
Young, Al   3:2032-47

ANGLO-AFRICAN

Equiano, Olaudah   2:719-39

ANTIGUAN

Kincaid, Jamaica   2:1164-78

BARBADIAN

Clarke, Austin   1:430-44
Lamming, George   2:1224-39

BENINESE

Equiano, Olaudah   2:719-39

BOTSWANAN

Head, Bessie   2:995-1003

BRAZILIAN
Machado de Assis, Joaquim
Maria   2:1290-1305
CAMEROONIAN
Beti, Mongo   1:189-206
CANADIAN
Clarke, Austin   1:430-44
CUBAN
Guillén, Nicolás   2:910-26
ENGLISH
Emecheta, Buchi   2:707-18
Equiano, Olaudah   2:719-39
GHANAIAN
Armah, Ayi Kwei   1:40-55
Casely-Hayford, J. E.   1:343-54
GUINEAN
Laye, Camara   2:1251-60
HAITIAN
Roumain, Jacques   3:1627-46

JAMAICAN
Bennett, Louise   1:180-88
Garvey, Marcus   2:864-80
McKay, Claude   3:1375-1401
KENYAN
Ngugi wa Thiong'o   3:1495-1514
LESOTHAN
Mofolo, Thomas   3:1410-21
NIGERIAN
Achebe, Chinua   1:1-15
Clark, John Pepper   1:414-29
Ekwensi, Cyprian   1:643-60
Emecheta, Buchi   2:707-18
Equiano, Olaudah   2:719-39
Okigbo, Christopher   3:1522-30
Soyinka, Wole   3:1703-24
Tutuola, Amos   3:1776-89
RHODESIAN
Brutus, Dennis   1:307-20
SENEGALESE
Ousmane, Sembène   3:1531-50

Senghor, Léopold Sédar   3:1671-87
SOMALI
Farah, Nuruddin   2:757-70
SOUTH AFRICAN
Brutus, Dennis   1:307-20
Head, Bessie   2:995-1003
Mphahlele, Ezekiel   3:1446-58
Mqhayi, S. E. K.   3:1459-68
Nkosi, Lewis   3:1515-21
Tutu, Desmond   3:1769-75
UGANDAN
p'Bitek, Okot   3:1559-80
WEST INDIAN
Césaire, Aimé   1:355-73
Fanon, Frantz   2:740-56
Kincaid, Jamaica   2:1164-78
Walcott, Derek   3:1790-1807
ZIMBABWEAN
Brutus, Dennis   1:307-20

BLC Title Index

"A l'appel de la race de Saba"
(Senghor)   3:1686
*A propos de la campagne
'antisuperstitieuse'* (Roumain)   3:1640
"Aa! Silimela!" (Mqhayi)   3:1467
"Abiku" (Clark)   1:426
"Abiku" (Soyinka)   3:1719, 1721
"abortion cycle #1" (Shange)   3:1694
"Absence" (Roumain)   3:1643
"L'Absente" (Senghor)   3:1683
Absolutely Nothing to Get Alarmed About
(Wright)   3:1992-93
"Abu" (Randall)   3:1597
"Aburi and After" (Clark)   1:421
"Acana" (Guillén)   2:917
"Accountability" (Dunbar)   1:629
"Across the Wide Missouri"
(Wideman)   3:1920
Adam by Adam (Powell)   3:1589-90
An Address to Miss Phillis Wheatly
(Hammon)   2:945
*Address to the Negroes in the State of
New-York* (Hammon)   2:945, 948
"Adivinanzas" (Guillén)   2:922
"Admonition" (Bell)   1:177
"Adulthood" (Giovanni)   2:886
"Advice to a Beauty" (Cullen)   1:504
"Advice to Youth" (Cullen)   1:507
Une affaire de viol (*A Case of Rape*)
(Himes)   3:1013-14
"Africa and the Francophone Dream"
(Armah)   1:53
The African Child (Laye)
   See *L'Enfant noir*
"African Morning" (Hughes)   2:1048
African Nights (Johnson)   2:1109, 1111
African Night's Entertainment
(Ekwensi)   1:645, 652

African Religions in Western Scholarship
(p'Bitek)   3:1562
"African Suite" (Randall)   3:1605
Africa's Cultural Revolution
(p'Bitek)   3:1562
"After a Visit" (Dunbar)   1:626, 629
"After a Visit (At Padraic Colum's Where
There Were Irish Poets)"
(Cullen)   1:512
"after Kent State" (Clifton)   1:461
"After the Killing" (Randall)   3:1605
After the Killing (Randall)   3:1598,
1600, 1605
"After the Winter" (McKay)   3:1398
"After Winter" (Brown)   1:291
"Afterimages" (Lorde)   2:1286
"Agbor Dancer" (Clark)   1:426-27
"The Agricultural Show"
(McKay)   3:1395
"AIDS: The Purposeful Destruction of the
Black World" (Madhubuti)   2:1321
"Aim" (Randall)   3:1605
"Air" (Toomer)   3:1763
Ajaiyi and His Inherited Poverty
(Tutuola)   3:1787-88
Aké (Soyinka)   3:1715-17, 1720, 1722
"Alethia" (Johnson)   2:1098
"Algernon Charles Swinburne"
(Cotter)   1:477
All God's Children Need Traveling Shoes
(Angelou)   1:35-36
"all i gotta do" (Giovanni)   2:888-89
All is mine (Guillén)
   See *Tengo*
All-Night Visitors (Major)   2:1326, 1330
All Shot Up (Himes)   2:1009, 1016,
1020-21
"All This Review" (Dodson)   1:571

All Us Come Cross the Water
(Clifton)   1:461
Aloneness (Brooks)   1:264, 266
*Along This Way: The Autobiography of
James Weldon Johnson*
(Johnson)   2:1124, 1135
"Alpha" (Tolson)   3:1742, 1746
The Amen Corner (Baldwin)   1:89
"America" (McKay)   3:1385
America, Their America (Clark)   1:422
*The American Fugitive in Europe:
Sketches of Places and People Abroad*
(Brown)
   See *Three Years in Europe; or, Places
   I Have Seen and People I Have Met*
"American Journal" (Hayden)   2:991
Amongst Thistles and Thorns
(Clarke)   1:431, 433, 438
"Amos (Postscript 1968)"
(Walker)   3:1838
"Amos-1963" (Walker)   3:1838
"Amy Son" (Bennett)   1:185
L'an V de la révolution algérienne (*Year
Five of the Algerian Revolution*)
(Fanon)   2:746
"Ancestors" (Randall)   3:1597, 1605
"And Another Thing"
(Giovanni)   2:885
"And I am driftwood" (Brutus)   1:318
"And Pass" (Toomer)   3:1762
And Still I Rise (Angelou)   1:31
"And the Other Immigrant"
(Soyinka)   3:1721
"Andrew Johnson Swinging Around the
Circle" (Bell)   1:174
"The Angel's Visit" (Forten)   2:814,
817
The Angry Ones (Williams)   3:1938,
1941-42

"Anner Lizer's Stumblin' Block"
(Dunbar)   1:636, 641
"The Anniad" (Brooks)   1:250-52
Annie Allen (Brooks)   1:250, 252, 254-
55, 261, 264
Annie John (Kincaid)   2:1166-67, 1172-
75, 1177
"Anniversary Words" (Randall)   3:1605
Another Country (Baldwin)   1:81-86, 88,
90-92, 100, 105
"Another Life" (Walcott)   3:1792
Another Life (Walcott)   3:1796-97,
1799, 1801-02
"Another Poem for Me–after Recovering
from an O.D." (Knight)   2:1216
"Answer to Dunbar's 'After a Visit'"
(Cotter)   1:477
"An Answer to Some Questions on How
I Write" (Giovanni)   2:898
Anthills of the Savannah (Achebe)   1:13
*Anthologie de la nouvelle poésie nègre et
malgache de langue française*
(Senghor)   3:1679
The Anthology of Magazine Verse
(Braithwaite)   1:241-42, 244
"Antigone, This Is It" (Reed)   3:1623
"Antigua Crossings" (Kincaid)   2:1168,
1170
"Anxiety" (Roumain)   3:1643
"Any Human to Another"
(Cullen)   1:512
"El apellido" ("The surname")
(Guillén)   2:917
"Apology for Apostasy?"
(Knight)   2:1215
"An Appeal from Marcus Garvey"
(Garvey)   2:868
"An Appeal to My Countrywomen"
(Harper)   2:984
"An Appeal to the American People"
(Harper)   2:980, 982-83
"Appel" (Roumain)   3:1637, 1644
"Appendix to the Anniad"
(Brooks)   1:251, 255
"The Apple Woman's Complaint"
(McKay)   3:1383
"The Apprentice" (Bambara)   1:118
"Apres-midi" (Roumain)   3:1642
"Are You the Right Size?"
(Powell)   3:1587
Are Your Teeth White? Then Laugh!
(p'Bitek)
   See *Lak tar miyo kinyero wi lobo*
The Arkansas Testament
(Walcott)   3:1802-06
Les Armes Miraculeuses (*Miraculous
Weapons*) (Césaire)   1:368, 370
"Around Us Dawning"
(Soyinka)   3:1721
"Arrival" (Guillén)   2:920, 922
Arrow of God (Achebe)   1:3, 6-7, 9
"As the Manatees go to Drink at the
Source" (Senghor)   3:1684
"As You Leave Me" (Knight)   2:1216
"The Ascent" (Randall)   3:1597, 1604
"Ash-Cake Hannah and Her Ben"
(Dunbar)   1:637
Ask Me Now (Young)   3:2033, 2035,
2037, 2039
Ask Your Mama: 12 Moods for Jazz
(Hughes)   2:1050, 1056, 1062, 1066

"An Aspect of Love, Alive in the Ice
Fire" (Brooks)   1:257
"At a funeral" (Brutus)   1:311
"at creation" (Clifton)   1:468
"at gettysburg" (Clifton)   1:468
"At Last" (Kincaid)   2:1172
"At Odd Moments" (Brutus)   1:319
"At Sea" (Toomer)   3:1765
"At Shaft II" (Dunbar)   1:626, 628,
630
"At the Bottom of the River"
(Kincaid)   2:1174-76
At the Bottom of the River
(Kincaid)   2:1170-77
"At the Lincoln Monument in
Washington, August 28, 1963"
(Walker)   3:1836, 1838
"At the Wailing Wall in Jerusalem"
(Cullen)   1:510
Atlanta Offering: Poems (Harper)   2:982
"Atlantic City Waiter" (Cullen)   1:486,
497, 506-07
"Attente" (Roumain)   3:1637
"Augury for an Infant"
(Randall)   3:1603
"Aunt Hanna Jackson"
(Johnson)   2:1109
"Aunt Jane Allen" (Johnson)   2:1112-
13
"Aunt Lucy's Search" (Chesnutt)   1:388
"Aunt Mandy's Investment"
(Dunbar)   1:636
"Aunt Tempy's Revenge"
(Dunbar)   1:637
"Aunt Tempy's Triumph"
(Dunbar)   1:637
The Autobiography of an Ex-Colored Man
(Johnson)   2:1123-29, 1133
The Autobiography of LeRoi Jones
(Baraka)   1:141-42
The Autobiography of Malcolm X
(Haley)   2:928, 936-37
The Autobiography of Malcolm X
(Malcolm X)   2:1342, 1347-48, 1350,
1352-54, 1356-61
The Autobiography of Miss Jane Pittman
(*Miss Jane Pittman*) (Gaines)   2:843-
44, 847, 850-54
The Autobiography of W. E. B. Du Bois
(Du Bois)   1:603
"The Averted Strike" (Chesnutt)   1:387
"Avey" (Toomer)   3:1752, 1759
"Ay negra, si tu supiera" ("Aye, black
lover, if you only knew")
(Guillén)   2:915
"Aye, black lover, if you only knew"
(Guillén)
   See "Ay negra, si tu supiera"
"Ayer me dijeron negro" ("Yesterday I
was called nigger") (Guillén)   2:915
Babel-17 (Delany)   1:530-31, 536-37
"Baby Sister" (Himes)   2:1014
The Bacchae of Euripides
(Soyinka)   3:1713
"Back Again, Home"
(Madhubuti)   2:1311
"Back to Africa" (Bennett)   1:182, 185
"The Backlash Blues" (Hughes)   2:1054
"The Backslider" (Fisher)   2:794, 800-
01, 803, 805
"Bad Man" (Hughes)   2:1065

"Balada de los dos abuelos" ("Ballad of
the two grandfathers")
(Guillén)   2:917
"Ballad for a Brown Girl"
(Cullen)   1:493
"The Ballad of Birmingham"
(Randall)   3:1594, 1600-01, 1603
"The Ballad of Chocolate Mabbie"
(Brooks)   1:260
"Ballad of Pearl May Lee"
(Brooks)   1:260
"Ballad of Simón Caraballo"
(Guillén)   2:919, 922
Ballad of the Brown Girl
(Cullen)   1:499-500, 508, 510
"Ballad of the Free" (Walker)   3:1836,
1844
"Ballad of the Rattlesnake"
(Tolson)   3:1740
"Ballad of the two grandfathers" (Guillén)
   See "Balada de los dos abuelos"
Banana Bottom (McKay)   3:1391-97
"Banishment of Man from the Garden of
the Lord" (Bell)   1:175
Banjo (McKay)   3:1389-94
"The Banjo-Player" (Johnson)   2:1109,
1112-13
"Banking Coal" (Toomer)   3:1762
"Banquet in Honor" (Hughes)   2:1048
"Bans O'Killing" (Bennett)   1:185
The Baptism (Baraka)   1:126, 139, 145
"Barbados" (Marshall)   3:1366, 1370
"Barren Summer" (Gaines)   2:857
"The Barrier" (McKay)   3:1385
"De Bathsuit And De Cow"
(Bennett)   1:182
"Beale Street Love" (Hughes)   2:1065
Beale Street: Where the Blues Began
(Lee)   2:1270-72
"The Bean Eaters" (Brooks)   1:252
The Bean Eaters (Brooks)   1:255, 261,
264-65
"The Beast" (Clark)   1:420
"A Beast in the South" (Clark)   1:428
A Beast Story (Kennedy)   2:1154-55
"Beating that Boy" (Ellison)   1:695
"Beautiful Black Men (with compliments
and apologies to all not mentioned by
name)" (Giovanni)   2:886, 888
Beautiful Feathers (Ekwensi)   1:646-48,
652, 656, 658-59
"The beauty of this single tree"
(Brutus)   1:319
The Beautyful Ones Are Not Yet Born
(Armah)   1:42-43, 45, 49-50
Beckonings (Brooks)   1:258, 264-67
"Becky" (Toomer)   3:1751, 1755, 1759
"Bed Time" (Hughes)   2:1052
"Beehive" (Toomer)   3:1763-64
Beetlecreek (Demby)   1:542-46, 550-54,
556-58
"The Beginning Is Zero"
(Giovanni)   2:884
"The Beginning of Homewood"
(Wideman)   3:1923, 1926
*Being and Race: Black Writing Since
1970* (Johnson)   2:1098-99
"Belitis Sings (From the French of Pierre
Louys)" (Cullen)   1:512
"Belle Isle" (Randall)   3:1594
"Belly Song" (Knight)   2:1218

Belly Song and Other Poems
(Knight)   2:1215
Beloved (Morrison)   3:1434, 1440, 1444
"Berry" (Hughes)   2:1047
"Beta" (Tolson)   3:1736
Betsey Brown (Shange)   3:1696
"Beverly Hills, Chicago"
(Brooks)   1:255
Beware the Bight of Benin
(Ekwensi)   1:645
"Beyond the Peacock: The Reconstruction
of Flannery O'Connor"
(Walker)   3:1816
"The Bible Defense of Slavery"
(Harper)   2:980
"Big Bessie Throws Her Son into the
Street" (Brooks)   1:256
"Big Black Good Man"
(Wright)   3:2005
"Big Boy Leaves Home"
(Wright)   3:2007, 2010, 2012, 2014-
15, 2017
The Big Gold Dream (Himes)   2:1009,
1015
"Big Momma" (Madhubuti)   2:1309,
1318
The Big Sea (Hughes)   2:1060, 1062
The Bigger Light (Clarke)   1:434, 438,
440
"The Bilal's Fourth Wife"
(Ousmane)   3:1545-46, 1549
Billy Bud (Fuller)   2:831
"Biography" (Baraka)   1:149-50
"Birds of Prey" (McKay)   3:1385
"Birmingham" (Walker)   3:1843
"the birth in a narrow room"
(Brooks)   1:254
"Black Ars Poetica" (Baraka)   1:148
"Black Art" (Baraka)   1:148
Black Art (Baraka)   1:144, 147-50
The Black BC's (Clifton)   1:460
Black Boy (Wright)   3:2001-02, 2004,
2006, 2011-12
"The Black Boy Looks at the White Boy"
(Baldwin)   1:93, 105
"The Black Christ" (Cullen)   1:488,
491, 493, 495-96, 501, 508, 511
"The Black Christ"
(Madhubuti)   2:1313-14
The Black Christ and Other Poems
(Cullen)   1:503-04, 510-13
"Black Dada Nihilismus"
(Baraka)   1:125, 144-45
Black Feeling, Black Talk
(Giovanni)   2:882, 886-87, 889, 891,
893, 895, 898
*Black Fire: An Anthology of Afro-
American Writings* (Baraka)   1:142
Black Folk: Then and Now (Du
Bois)   1:604, 606
Black Gangster (Goines)   2:903, 905,
909
Black Girl Lost (Goines)   2:903, 905
Black Judgement (Giovanni)   2:882,
886-87, 889, 893, 895, 898
"Black Love" (Madhubuti)   2:1316
"Black Magdalens" (Cullen)   1:501, 508
"Black magic" (Randall)   3:1603
"Black Magic" (Sanchez)   3:1661-62
*Black Magic: Sabotage, Target Study,
Black Art; Collected Poetry, 1961-1967*
(Baraka)   1:147, 150

"The Black Mammy" (Johnson)   2:1121
*The Black Man: His Antecedents, His
Genius, and His Achievements*
(Brown)   1:294-96
"A Black Man Talks of Reaping"
(Bontemps)   1:224
Black Manhattan (Johnson)   2:1124-25
"Black Manhood: Toward a Definition"
(Madhubuti)   2:1321
Black Man's Verse (Davis)   1:517-21,
524
"The Black Man's Wrongs"
(Bell)   1:177
A Black Mass (Baraka)   1:145
*Black Men: Obsolete, Single, Dangerous?
(The Afrikan American Family in
Transition)* (Madhubuti)   2:1321
Black Moods: New and Collected Poems
(Davis)   1:525
"Black Mother Praying"
(Dodson)   1:568-69
"Black Mother Woman"
(Lorde)   2:1286
Black Music (Baraka)   1:143
Black on Black (Himes)   2:1014
The Black Pearl and the Ghost
(Myers)   3:1478-79
"Black People!" (Baraka)   1:148
"Black Poems, Poseurs and Power"
(Giovanni)   2:884
"Black Poet, White Critic"
(Randall)   3:1595
Black Poetry (Randall)   3:1600, 1603
The Black Poets (Randall)   3:1602
Black Pride (Madhubuti)   2:1310, 1312-
14, 1320-21
Black Reconstruction (Du Bois)   1:603-
06, 608-09
"The Black Sampson of Brandywine"
(Dunbar)   1:626
"Black Sketches" (Madhubuti)   2:1310
Black Skin, White Masks (Fanon)
See *Peau noire, masques blancs*
Black Thunder (Bontemps)   1:210, 215-
16, 218-19, 222-23, 225
The Black Unicorn (Lorde)   2:1278-79,
1282-83
Black Wafers (Senghor)
See *Hosties Noires*
"A Black Wedding Song"
(Brooks)   1:266
The Blacker the Berry
(Thurman)   3:1727-32
"Blackgirl Learning"
(Madhubuti)   2:1319
"Blackman/an unfinished history"
(Madhubuti)   2:1318
"Blackness" (Kincaid)   2:1172-73, 1176
"Blackstudies" (Lorde)   2:1278
"Blades of Steel" (Fisher)   2:792, 794,
797,799, 804
Les Blancs (Hansberry)   2:965-66
"Bleecker Street, Summer"
(Walcott)   3:1795
"Blessed Assurance" (Hughes)   2:1049
"A Blessed Deceit" (Dunbar)   1:637
Blind Man with a Pistol
(Himes)   2:1010, 1016, 1019-21
"blk/chant" (Sanchez)   3:1650
"Blood-Burning Moon"
(Toomer)   3:1752, 1758
"Blood of the Beast" (Cleaver)   1:447

Blood on the Forge (Attaway)   1:58-61,
64, 66, 68-69, 71-72
"Blood River Day" (Brutus)   1:312-13,
318
"Bloodbirth" (Lorde)   2:1278
"Bloodline" (Gaines)   2:846, 857
Bloodline (Gaines)   2:843-44, 846-47,
853
"Bloodsmiles" (Madhubuti)   2:1311
"The Blue Meridian"
(Toomer)   3:1765-66
The Blue Meridian and Other Poems
(Toomer)   3:1766
"Blues" (Walcott)   3:1801
*A Blues Book for Blue Black Magical
Women* (Sanchez)   3:1652-54, 1657,
1663-64
Blues for Mister Charlie
(Baldwin)   1:79-80
"The Blues I'm Playing"
(Hughes)   2:1047, 1049, 1059-62
*Blues People: Negro Music in White
America* (Baraka)   1:132, 139, 143
The Bluest Eye (Morrison)   3:1426-29,
1431-34
Bodies and Soul (Young)   3:2044, 2046
"Bois d'ébène" (Roumain)   3:1645
Bois d'ébène (Ebony Wood)
(Roumain)   3:1629, 1631-32, 1636,
1645-46
"Bona and Paul" (Toomer)   3:1753,
1757, 1760, 1763
"The Bones of My Father"
(Knight)   2:1216
"Bong song" (Guillén)
See "Canción del bongó"
Boogie Woogie Landscapes
(Shange)   3:1697, 1702
The Book of American Negro Poetry
(Johnson)   2:1118-19
"Booker T. and W. E. B."
(Randall)   3:1594, 1603
"The Books' Creed" (Cotter)   1:471
Born of a Woman (Knight)   2:1214-15,
1217-18
Borom Sarret (Ousmane)   3:1533
"Bound No'th Blues" (Hughes)   2:1052
"The Bouquet" (Chesnutt)   1:376
*Les bouts de bois de Dieu (God's Bits of
Wood)* (Ousmane)   3:1532 1536,
1543, 1548
"Box Seat" (Toomer)   3:1753, 1759-60,
1763
"The Boy and the Bayonet"
(Dunbar)   1:637
Boy at the Window (Dodson)   1:564,
566, 568
"The Boy Died in My Alley"
(Brooks)   1:265, 267
"Boy in the Double Breasted Suit"
(Gaines)   2:857
"Boys, Black" (Brooks)   1:258, 266
Brainstorm (Myers)   3:1478
A Branch of the Blue Nile
(Walcott)   3:1802
"Brass Spittoons" (Hughes)   2:1058
The Brave African Huntress
(Tutuola)   3:1779, 1785
"Brazil" (Marshall)   3:1366, 1370
"Bread and Wine" (Cullen)   1:508
The Bride Price (Emecheta)   2:709-13,
718

"The Brief Cure of Aunt Fanny"
(Dunbar)   1:637
"Bright and Morning Star"
(Wright)   3:2007, 2011, 2013-14,
2017
"Brindis" ("Cheers!") (Guillén)   2:917
"British Guiana" (Marshall)   3:1366,
1370
"Broken Field Running"
(Bambara)   1:118
The Bronx is Next (Sanchez)   3:1666
"A Bronzeville Mother Loiters in
Mississippi. Meanwhile a Mississippi
Mother Burns Bacon"
(Brooks)   1:251, 253, 255, 265
"Bronzeville Woman in a Red Hat"
(Brooks)   1:252
"Brooklyn" (Marshall)   3:1366-67,
1370-71
"Brother Alvin" (Lorde)   2:1287
"Brothers" (Johnson)   2:1120-21, 1124
Brothers and Keepers
(Wideman)   3:1929
"Brown Boy to Brown Girl"
(Cullen)   1:500, 506
Brown Girl, Brownstones
(Marshall)   3:1365-69, 1372-73
"A Brown Girl Dead" (Cullen)   1:504,
506
The Brownsville Raid (Fuller)   2:825,
829-31, 834
"Bubba" (Myers)   3:1478
"The Burden in Boxes" (Clark)   1:421
"Burial" (Walker)   3:1816
Burning Grass (Ekwensi)   1:645, 647,
650, 657-59
"Bury Me In a Free Land"
(Harper)   2:977, 979-80, 982
"Búscate plata" ("Go and look for
bread") (Guillén)   2:915
"But He Was Cool or: he even stopped
for green lights"
(Madhubuti)   2:1309, 1315
"The Butterfly" (Giovanni)   2:888
"By an Inland Lake"
(Braithwaite)   1:243
"By Little Loving" (Soyinka)   3:1721
Cabaret (Davis)   1:518
"De Cabin" (Johnson)   2:1112
"Cables to Rage" (Lorde)   2:1278
Cahier d'un retour au pays natal (*Return
to My Native Land*) (Césaire)   1:360,
364-66, 368-70
"Cahoots" (Dunbar)   1:637
Caitaani Mutharaba-ini (*Devil on the
Cross*) (Ngugi)   3:1503, 1505-07,
1511, 1514
"Caleb" (Cotter)   1:478
Caleb, the Degenerate (Cotter)   1:471-
79, 483
"Calling Jesus" (Toomer)   3:1752
"The Calling of Names"
(Angelou)   1:31
"Calme" (Roumain)   3:1637, 1643
"Caminando" (Guillén)   2:916
"Caña" (Guillén)   2:918
The Cancer Journals (Lorde)   2:1285,
1288
"Canción del bongó" ("Bong song")
(Guillén)   2:917, 924-25
"Candy Seller" (Bennett)   1:181

Cane (Toomer)   3:1750-55, 1757-59,
1761-64
Cantos para soldados y sones para turistas
(*Songs for Soldiers and Sones for
Tourists; Songs for Soldiers and Tunes
for Tourists*) (Guillén)   2:913-14, 917,
919
"Canzones" (Okigbo)   3:1526
"Caprice" (Cullen)   1:508
Captain Blackman (Williams)   3:1937,
1939, 1942-43
"The Caribbean" (Guillén)   2:914
"Carma" (Toomer)   3:1759
Caroling Dusk (Cullen)   1:489, 503,
505
"The Case of 'Ca'line"
(Dunbar)   1:630, 636
A Case of Rape (Himes)
See *Une affaire de viol*
Cast the First Stone (Himes)   2:1012
The Castaway and Other Poems
(Walcott)   3:1800, 1803
"The Casualties" (Clark)   1:421
Casualties: Poems (Clark)   1:421-23,
425-26
"The Cat" (Cullen)   1:513
The Catacombs (Demby)   1:542, 544,
546-52, 554-58
"Categories" (Giovanni)   2:887-88
Catherine Carmier (Gaines)   2:843-46,
850, 852-53, 856-57
"Cats" (Cullen)   1:513
"The Caucasian Storms Harlem"
(Fisher)   2:799
"A Causa Secreta" ("The Secret Cause")
(Machado de Assis)   2:1299
Caviar and Cabbage (Tolson)   3:1739,
1744
"Cell Song" (Knight)   2:1213
"Cent mètres" (Roumain)   3:1630,
1637, 1643
Cerebro y corazón (Guillén)   2:912, 920
Ceremonies in Dark Old Men
(Elder)   1:663-68, 670-71
"Chain" (Lorde)   2:1279
Chaka (Mofolo)   3:1411-13, 1415,
1417-18, 1420-21
"Chaka" (Senghor)   3:1675, 1686
The Chaneysville Incident
(Bradley)   1:228, 230, 232-34
"Le chant de l'homme"
(Roumain)   3:1644
"A Chant for Young/Brothas and Sistuhs"
(Sanchez)   3:1656
Chants d'Ombre (Senghor)   3:1674,
1676, 1682
Chants pour Naëtt (*Songs for Naëtt*)
(Senghor)   3:1675, 1683
Chants pour Signare (Senghor)   3:1675
"The Chase" (Toomer)   3:1766-67
Checkmates (Milner)   3:1408
"Cheers!" (Guillén)
See "Brindis"
"chemotherapy" (Clifton)   1:468
"Chévere" (Guillén)   2:916, 918
"The Chicago 'Defender' Sends a Man to
Little Rock" (Brooks)   1:265
"The Chicago Picasso" (Brooks)   1:256
"Chicago's Congo (Sonata for an
Orchestra)" (Davis)   1:517-18, 522,
524

"The Child Who Favored Daughter"
(Walker)   3:1811, 1815, 1818
"Childhood" (Walker)   3:1835, 1837
The Children of Ham (Brown)   1:271,
275-77
"Children of the Mississippi"
(Brown)   1:290
"Children of the Sun"
(Johnson)   2:1112
"China" (Johnson)   2:1098
The Chinaberry Tree (Fauset)   2:773-74,
778, 780, 782, 787
"Chippo Simon" (Gaines)   2:857
A Choice of Weapons (Parks)   3:1554-
55
"Chorus" (Lorde)   2:1288
The Chosen Place (Marshall)   3:1365-
68, 1371-73
Chosen Poems, Old and New
(Lorde)   2:1286
"Christ in Alabama" (Hughes)   2:1058
"Christ Is a Dixie Nigger"
(Davis)   1:519
"Christmas Eve at Johnson's Drugs N
Goods" (Bambara)   1:109, 118
"De Chu'ch" (Johnson)   2:1112
"Church Building" (Harper)   2:984
"Cicle One" (Dodson)   1:571
"Circle Two" (Dodson)   1:571
Cities Burning (Randall)   3:1595, 1597-
98, 1601-02
Cities in Bezique (Kennedy)   2:1154,
1156-57
"The City of Refuge" (Fisher)   2:792,
795, 797-98, 800-02, 805
"A City's Death by Fire"
(Walcott)   3:1799
Clara's Ole Man (Bullins)   1:326, 331-
32, 335
Close Sesame (Farah)   2:765-67, 69
*Clotel; or, The President's Daughter: A
Narrative of Slave Life in the United
States* (*Miralda; or, The Beautiful
Quadroon; Clotelle: A Tale of the
Southern States; Clotelle; or, The
Colored Heroine*) (Brown)   1:294-95,
297, 302-03, 305-06
Clotelle: A Tale of the Southern States
(Brown)
See *Clotel; or, The President's
Daughter: A Narrative of Slave Life in
the United States*
Clotelle; or, The Colored Heroine (Brown)
See *Clotel; or, The President's
Daughter: A Narrative of Slave Life in
the United States*
"Cloud" (Toomer)   3:1766-67
"The Cockerel in the Tale"
(Clark)   1:420
"Codicil" (Walcott)   3:1803
"Coleman A. Young: Detroit
Renaissance" (Randall)   3:1598
Collected Poems 1948-1984
(Walcott)   3:1794, 1796
Collector of Treasures (Head)   2:1001
"The Colonel's Awakening"
(Dunbar)   1:626, 636
The Colonel's Dream (Chesnutt)   1:387,
396-97, 399
"Colonisation in Reverse"
(Bennett)   1:184

Color (Cullen) **1**:486-87, 494-96, 498-99, 503-05, 507-08, 511

Color and Democracy: Colonies and Peace (Du Bois) **1**:606

The Color Purple (Walker) **3**:1813-14, 1816-20, 1822, 1824, 1826-27

"The Colored Band" (Dunbar) **1**:626

"Colored Blues Singer" (Cullen) **1**:492

"The Colored Soldiers" (Dunbar) **1**:629, 631

"Colors" (Cullen) **1**:499

"Colour Bar" (Bennett) **1**:185

"The Comeback" (Gaines) **2**:857

Comedy: American Style (Fauset) **2**:773, 779, 781, 787

"Common Meter" (Fisher) **2**:793-97, 799, 804

"communication in whi te" (Madhubuti) **2**:1314

"Confession" (Cullen) **1**:509

"A Confidence" (Dunbar) **1**:629

"Coniagui Woman" (Lorde) **2**:1288

Conjure (Reed) **3**:1612

The Conjure Man Dies (Fisher) **2**:792-93, 800, 802

The Conjure Woman and Other Stories (Chesnutt) **1**:375-78, 380-87, 389-96

"The Conjurer's Revenge" (Chesnutt) **1**:380, 383, 385-86, 388, 395

"The Conjuring Contest" (Dunbar) **1**:633, 637

"Conscience raciale" (Roumain) **3**:1641

Constab Ballads (McKay) **3**:1381, 1383, 1388, 1393, 1396

Contending Forces (Hopkins) **2**:1024, 1026-30, 1032-33, 1035-36

"A Contract" (Baraka) **1**:126

"Conversation" (Giovanni) **2**:885

"Conversation on V" (Dodson) **1**:572

"Conversation with Langston Hughes" (Guillén) **2**:923

"A Conversation with Myself" (Knight) **2**:1215

"Conversations at Accra" (Clark) **1**:421

"Conversion" (Toomer) **3**:1763-64

"Cop-Out Session" (Knight) **2**:1218

Copper Sun (Cullen) **1**:495, 499, 503-04, 509-11

"A Coquette Conquered" (Dunbar) **1**:629

"Cor Codium" (Cullen) **1**:509

"Cora Unashamed" (Hughes) **2**:1047, 1049

"Coral Atoll" (Randall) **3**:1604

"Cordelia the Crude" (Thurman) **3**:1732

The Corner (Bullins) **1**:336

Corregidora (Jones) **2**:1144-45

"Corrida" (Roumain) **3**:1640, 1644

"Cotton Candy" (Giovanni) **2**:897

Cotton Candy on a Rainy Day (Giovanni) **2**:889, 893-95, 897-98

The Cotton Club: New Poems (Major) **2**:1325

Cotton Comes to Harlem (Himes) **2**:1010, 1015, 1017, 1019-20

"Cotton Song" (Toomer) **3**:1763

"A Council of State" (Dunbar) **1**:633, 636, 639

Counselor for Ayres' Memorial (Machado de Assis)
   See *Memorial de Ayres*

"Countee Cullen" (Dodson) **1**:571

"Counter Mood" (Cullen) **1**:504, 511

"Counterpoint" (Dodson) **1**:571

The Crazy Kill (Himes) **2**:1009, 1015-17, 1020

"Crazy Mary" (McKay) **3**:1395

"The Creation" (Johnson) **2**:1117-18, 1124

"Creation Light" (Bell) **1**:175, 177

"Creole" (Roumain) **3**:1644

Crime Partners (Goines) **2**:904-05

"Cross" (Hughes) **2**:1056, 1058

"Crowing-Hen Blues" (Hughes) **2**:1053

"The Crucifixion" (Johnson) **2**:1124

"Crusoe's Island" (Walcott) **3**:1800

Cry Revenge! (Goines) **2**:905

Crying in the Wilderness (Tutu) **3**:1771

Crystal (Myers) **3**:1476-77, 1480

"Cuba Libre" (Baraka) **1**:144

"Cul De Sac Valley" (Walcott) **3**:1803

"Cuss-Cuss" (Bennett) **1**:185

Daddy (Bullins) **1**:341

Daddy Cool (Goines) **2**:901, 904-05, 907

"Daddy Garbage" (Wideman) **3**:1918, 1923

Daggers and Javelins: Essays (Baraka) **1**:147

"Dahomey" (Lorde) **2**:1278

"The Daily Grind" (Johnson) **2**:1112-13

The Daily Grind: 41 WPA Poems (Johnson) **2**:1112

"Dakar Hieroglyphs" (Armah) **1**:52

"Damballah" (Wideman) **3**:1923

Damballah (Wideman) **3**:1918-20, 1923-24, 1926

Les damnés de la terre (*The Wretched of the Earth*) (Fanon) **2**:741-44, 750-55

"A Dance for Militant Dilettantes" (Young) **3**:2045

A Dance of the Forests (Soyinka) **3**:1708-13

The Dancers (Myers) **3**:1471, 1479

"Dancing Gal" (Davis) **1**:521

"Dandy Jim's Conjur Scare" (Dunbar) **1**:633, 637

"DANDY, or Astride the Funky Finger of Lust" (Bullins) **1**:336

"La danse du poète-clown" (Roumain) **3**:1643-44

Dante (Baraka)
   See *The Eighth Ditch*

The Dark and Feeling: Black American Writers and Their Work (Major) **2**:1331

"Dark Blood" (Walker) **3**:1841-42

The Dark Child (Laye)
   See *L'Enfant noir*

"Dark O' the Moon" (Brown) **1**:283

"The Dark Side of the Moon" (Myers) **3**:1478

"Dark Symphony" (Tolson) **3**:1740, 1742, 1744-45

"Darkness" (Roumain) **3**:1643

"Darkness and Light" (Clark) **1**:422, 424

Darkwater (Du Bois) **1**:601-02

A Daughter's Geography (Shange) **3**:1696

"Dave's Neckliss" (Chesnutt) **1**:392-93, 395

"Dawn" (Soyinka) **3**:1719

"The Dawn of Freedom" (Bell) **1**:173, 177

"Dawn of Liberty" (Bell) **1**:175

The Day and the War (Bell) **1**:176-77, 179

"Daybreak" (Hughes) **2**:1052

"Daydream" (Walker)
   See "I Want to Write"

The Dead Lecturer (Baraka) **1**:125, 141, 144, 147

"Dear God" (Brutus) **1**:319

"Dear Mama" (Sanchez) **3**:1669

Death (Davis) **1**:518

Death and the King's Horseman (Soyinka) **3**:1717-18

"death in the afternoon" (Brooks) **1**:267

"Death in the Dawn" (Soyinka) **3**:1709, 1719, 1721

Death List (Bullins) **1**:331

Death List (Goines) **2**:901, 904-05

"Death of a Weaver Bird" (Clark) **1**:421

"The Death of Lincoln" (Bell) **1**:177

"The Death of Malcolm X" (Baraka) **1**:147

"The Death of Samora Machel" (Clark) **1**:428

"Débris" (Césaire) **1**:367

"Debtor's Lane" (Okigbo) **3**:1525-26

A Decade of Tongues: Selected Poems 1958-1968 (Clark) **1**:422

"December of My Springs" (Giovanni) **2**:893

"Declaration of Rights of the Negro Peoples of the World" (Garvey) **2**:871

"The Decline of the Black Muslims" (Cleaver) **1**:452

Decolonising the Mind (Ngugi) **3**:1509, 1514

"Dedication" (Soyinka) **3**:1719-21

"A Deep Sleeper" (Chesnutt) **1**:387-88, 392, 394

"The Defection of Mary Ann Gibbs" (Dunbar) **1**:637

"A Defender of the Faith" (Dunbar) **1**:637

"Definition" (Dodson) **1**:572

"The Deliberation of Mr. Dunkin" (Dunbar) **1**:633, 636

"The Deliverance" (Harper) **2**:983-84

"Delta" (Walker) **3**:1834, 1837, 1841-42

"Descriptive Voyage from New York to Aspinwall" (Bell) **1**:177

"The Deserted Plantation" (Dunbar) **1**:625, 629

"Desire" (Toomer) **3**:1766

Dessa Rose (Williams) **3**:1954-55, 1957-60

Detained (Ngugi) **3**:1506, 1508-12

"Detroit Conference of Unity and Art" (Giovanni) **2**:896

The Devil Catchers (Bullins) **1**:341

The Devil Finds Work (Baldwin) **1**:93-94, 96

Devil on the Cross (Ngugi)
See *Caitaani Mutharaba-ini*
Dhalgren (Delany)   1:528-35, 537
Dialect Determinism (Bullins)   1:341
Die Nigger Die! (Al-Amin)   1:19, 21-24
"Died of Starvation" (Harper)   2:980
"A Different Image" (Randall)   3:1596
"The Dilemma (My poems are not
sufficiently obscure? To please the
critics–Ray Durem)"
(Randall)   3:1597, 1605
"Dinner at Eight" ("We'll Have Dinner
at Eight") (Mphahlele)   3:1451, 1453
Directionscore: Selected and New Poems
(Madhubuti)   2:1310, 1321
"Dirge" (Clark)   1:421
"Dirty Negroes" (Roumain)
See "Sales nègres"
*The Disabilities of the Black Folk and
Their Treatment, with an Appeal to the
Labour Party* (Casely-Hayford)   1:346
Discours sur le colonialisme (*Discourse on
Colonialism*) (Césaire)   1:360, 364
Discourse on Colonialism (Césaire)
See *Discours sur le colonialisme*
"Discovered" (Dunbar)   1:629
"The Dismissal of Tyng"
(Harper)   2:980
"Distances" (Okigbo)   3:1525
Distances (Okigbo)   3:1527-28
Divine Comedy (Dodson)   1:563, 570-
71
"Dizzy-Headed Dick" (Dunbar)   1:637
"Do" (Tolson)   3:1745-46
Le docker noir (Ousmane)   3:1532
"Dr. Booker T. Washington to the
National Negro Business League"
(Cotter)   1:476, 478
"A Dog Named Trilby"
(Hughes)   2:1048
Dom Casmurro (Machado de
Assis)   2:1292, 1296-97, 1299, 1303
"The Domain of the Ndlambe People"
(Mqhayi)
See "Izwe IakwaNdlambe"
"The Don't Care Negro"
(Cotter)   1:476
"Don't Cry, Scream"
(Madhubuti)   2:1309
Don't Cry, Scream
(Madhubuti)   2:1310, 1314-19, 1321-
22
Don't Get God Started (Milner)   3:1408
"Don't Have a Baby Till You Read
This" (Giovanni)   2:883
"Don't You Want to Be Free?"
(Hughes)   2:1055
Dopefiend: The Story of a Black Junkie
(Goines)   2:901-03, 905
"The Double Standard"
(Harper)   2:977, 980, 983-84
Double Yoke (Emecheta)   2:714
The Dove of Popular Flight (Guillén)
See *La paloma de vuelo popular:
Elegiás*
"Down By the Riverside"
(Wright)   3:2004, 2007, 2012-16
Down Second Avenue
(Mphahlele)   3:1447-49, 1452, 1454,
1457
The Dragon Takes a Wife
(Myers)   3:1471-72, 1479

Dramouss (*A Dream of Africa*)
(Laye)   2:1253, 1255-59
A Dream Awake (Dodson)   1:565
A Dream of Africa (Laye)
See *Dramouss*
Dream on Monkey Mountain
(Walcott)   3:1800
"The Dreamer" (Soyinka)   3:1720
"Dreams" (Giovanni)   2:886
"Drenched in Light" (Hurston)   2:1071-
72
"Dressed All in Pink"
(Randall)   3:1601, 1603
Driftglass (Delany)   1:537
The Drinking Gourd (Hansberry)   2:966
Drummer Boy (Ekwensi)   1:645, 652
Drums and Voices (Ekwensi)   1:645
Drums at Dusk (Bontemps)   1:225
"The Drunkard's Child"
(Harper)   2:980
"Dry Foot Bwoy" (Bennett)   1:186
"The Dumb Witness"
(Chesnutt)   1:387-88
"Duncan Spoke of a Process"
(Baraka)   1:125
*The Duplex: A Black Love Fable in Four
Movements* (Bullins)   1:331-36, 38,
340
"Dust" (Fisher)   2:799, 804
Dust Tracks on a Road
(Hurston)   2:1070, 1078, 1080-82,
1084-85
Dutchman (Baraka)   1:125-29, 131, 137,
139, 140-41, 145
"Duties of a Black Revolutionary Artist"
(Walker)   3:1826
"The Dying Bondman"
(Harper)   2:977, 979
"The Eagles" (Guillén)   2:914
"Earth" (Toomer)   3:1763
"Easter" (Soyinka)   3:1720
"Easter 1976" (Clark)   1:425
"An Easter Carol" (Clarke)   1:442
"The Easter Wedding" (Dunbar)   1:637
"Ebano real" ("Royal ebony")
(Guillén)   2:917
"Ebony under Granite" (Davis)   1:520-
21
Ebony Wood (Roumain)
See *Bois d'ébène*
"The Education of Mingo"
(Johnson)   2:1097-98
"Eena Wales" (Bennett)   1:185
"Ego Tripping" (Giovanni)   2:897
Eight Men (Wright)   3:2008
The Eighth Ditch (*Dante*)
(Baraka)   1:139
The Einstein Intersection
(Delany)   1:529, 531, 536-37
Eldorado Red (Goines)   2:905
*Eldridge Cleaver: Post-Prison Writings and
Speeches* (Cleaver)   1:452
"Electrical Storm" (Hayden)   2:989
The Electronic Nigger (Bullins)   1:326,
331

"Elegiac Poem" (Wheatley)
See "An Elegiac Poem, on the Death
of that Celebrated Divine, and
eminent Servant of Jesus Christ, the
late Reverend, and pious George
Whitefield, Chaplain to the Right
Honourable the Countess of
Huntingdon"
"An Elegiac Poem, on the Death of that
Celebrated Divine, and eminent Servant
of Jesus Christ, the late Reverend, and
pious George Whitefield, Chaplain to
the Right Honourable the Countess of
Huntingdon" ("On the Death of the
Rev. Mr. George Whitefield"; "Elegiac
Poem") (Wheatley)   3:1897, 1899,
1900
Elegiás (*Elegies*) (Guillén)   2:913
"Elégie des circoncis" ("Elegy of the
Circumcised") (Senghor)   3:1676,
1686
Elegies (Guillén)
See *Elegiás*
"Elegy" (Walker)   3:1838
"Elegy for Alto" (Okigbo)   3:1528
"Elegy in a Rainbow" (Brooks)   1:265,
267
"Elegy of Midnight" (Senghor)   3:1676
"Elegy of the Circumcised" (Senghor)
See "Elégie des circoncis"
"Elegy of the Waters"
(Senghor)   3:1676
"Elegy to Emmett Till"
(Guillén)   2:919
"Elethia" (Walker)   3:1816
"Eliza Harris" (Harper)   2:980, 982
"Elsewhere" (Walcott)   3:1804
"Emancipation" (Bell)   1:173
Emergency Exit (Major)   2:1328-30
The Emigrants (Lamming)   2:1227-29,
1232, 1236-37
Empire Star (Delany)   1:528, 530-31,
538
"Encher Tempo" (Machado de
Assis)   2:1294
Enemies: The Clash of Races
(Madhubuti)   2:1321
L'Enfant noir (*The African Child*; *The
Dark Child*) (Laye)   2:1252-59
The Entire Son (Guillén)
See *El son entero*
"Epilogue" (Cullen)   1:503
"Epilogue to 'Casualties'"
(Clark)   1:422
"Epitaph for a Negro Woman"
(Dodson)   1:568-69
Epitaph for the Young: XII cantos
(Walcott)   3:1799
"Epitaphs" (Cullen)   1:486, 493
"Epîtres à la Princesse"
(Senghor)   3:1675, 1687
"Equal in Paris" (Baldwin)   1:93
"Ere Sleep Comes Down to Soothe the
Weary Eyes" (Dunbar)   1:628
"Erosion: Transkei" (Brutus)   1:312
"The Erotic Poetry of Sir Isaac Newton"
(Randall)   3:1606
Esaú and Jacob (Machado de Assis)
See *Esaù e Jacó*
Esaù e Jacó (*Esaú and Jacob*) (Machado
de Assis)   2:1297

*The Escape; or, A Leap for Freedom,
Drama in Five Acts* (Brown)   **1**:295,
297-302, 304
*España: Poema en cuatro angustias y una
esperanza (Spain: A Poem in Four
Anguishes and a Hope)*
(Guillén)   **2**:913
"Ester" (Toomer)   **3**:1752
Et les chiens se taisaient: Tragédie
(Césaire)   **1**:360-61
"Eta" (Tolson)   **3**:1746
"The Eternal Self" (Braithwaite)   **1**:243
"The Ethics of Living Jim Crow"
(Wright)   **3**:2010, 2014
"Ethiopia" (Harper)   **2**:980
"Ethiopia" (Johnson)   **2**:1110, 1112
Ethiopia Unbound (Casely-
Hayford)   **1**:344-53
Ethiopiques (Senghor)   **3**:1675, 1683,
1687
"Eulogy for Alvin Frost"
(Lorde)   **2**:1279, 1287
Eva's Man (Jones)   **2**:1141, 1144
"Evening" (Wheatley)   **3**:1885
*An Evening Thought: Salvation by Christ,
with Penetential Cries*
(Hammon)   **2**:945, 948
"An Evening Thought: Salvation by
Christ with Penitential Cries"
(Hammon)   **2**:945-47
An Evening with Dead Essex
(Kennedy)   **2**:1162
An Evening's Improvement (Hammon)
See *An Evening's Improvement:
Shewing the Necessity of Beholding
the Lamb of God*
*An Evening's Improvement: Shewing the
Necessity of Beholding the Lamb of God
(An Evening's Improvement)*
(Hammon)   **2**:945
"Every Lover" (Cullen)   **1**:512
"Everybody's Protest Novel"
(Baldwin)   **1**:86, 98, 103
"Everyday Use" (Walker)   **3**:1818
The Evidence of Things Not Seen
(Baldwin)   **1**:93-97, 105
"Evolutionary Poem No. 1"
(Knight)   **2**:1215
"Evolutionary Poem No. 2"
(Knight)   **2**:1215
"Ex-Judge at the Bar" (Tolson)   **3**:1740
"The Exception" (Chesnutt)   **1**:388
"Exchange Value" (Johnson)   **2**:1097-98
"Exodus" (Clark)   **1**:421
*Experience, or How to Give a Northern
Man a Backbone* (Brown)   **1**:299
Experimental Death Unit #1
(Baraka)   **1**:145
"An Extravagance of Laughter"
(Ellison)   **1**:700
"Ezekiel" (Fisher)   **2**:799
"Ezekiel Learns" (Fisher)   **2**:800
The Fabulous Miss Marie
(Bullins)   **1**:336, 340
"Face" (Toomer)   **3**:1759, 1763-64
"Faces" (Randall)   **3**:1603
Failure (Davis)   **1**:518
"A Fairer Hope, A Brighter Morn"
(Harper)   **2**:980
Faith and the Good Thing
(Johnson)   **2**:1091-92, 1095-97

"The Faith Cure Man"
(Dunbar)   **1**:636
The Fall of the Towers (Delany)   **1**:531
Fallen Angels (Myers)   **3**:1478, 1480
"The Fallen Soldier" (Clark)   **1**:424
"A Family Feud" (Dunbar)   **1**:626, 636
Family Pictures (Brooks)   **1**:251, 257-
58, 261, 264, 266
The Fanatics (Dunbar)   **1**:628, 630-35,
640
Les fantoches (Roumain)   **3**:1629, 1636,
1638, 1640-42
"A Far Cry from Africa"
(Walcott)   **3**:1794, 1796, 1800
Fast Sam, Cool Clyde and Stuff
(Myers)   **3**:1473, 1477
"Father and Daughter"
(Sanchez)   **3**:1658, 1662-64
"Father and Son" (Hughes)   **2**:1047-48
"Father Son, and Holy Ghost"
(Lorde)   **2**:1286
Feather Woman of the Jungle
(Tutuola)   **3**:1779
"Feeling Fucked Up" (Knight)   **2**:1216,
1218
Fences (Wilson)   **3**:1964-65, 1967-68,
1970-71
"Fern" (Toomer)   **3**:1759-60
Fever (Wideman)   **3**:1929
"Fiddlah Ike" (Johnson)   **2**:1112
Fields of Wonder (Hughes)   **2**:1062
"Fifty Years" (Johnson)   **2**:1117, 1134-
35
Fifty Years and Other Poems
(Johnson)   **2**:1117, 1120-21, 1134
"the final solution" (Sanchez)   **3**:1649,
1662
"The Finding of Martha"
(Dunbar)   **1**:637
"The Finding of Zach"
(Dunbar)   **1**:628, 636
Fine Clothes to the Jew
(Hughes)   **2**:1051-53, 1055, 1062-66
"The Finish of Patsy Barnes"
(Dunbar)   **1**:636
"Fire" (Toomer)   **3**:1763
"Fire and Cloud" (Wright)   **3**:2007,
2010, 2013-14, 2016
"Fire by Night" (Fisher)   **2**:794, 797,
799, 803-04
The Fire in the Flint (White)   **3**:1905-
06, 1909, 1911-13, 1915
"The Fire Next Time"
(Baldwin)   **1**:100
The Fire Next Time (Baldwin)   **1**:79,
83, 88, 93-94, 96, 103-05
The First Cities (Lorde)   **2**:1282
"The Five Most Often Used Excuses
Black Men Give Black Women"
(Madhubuti)   **2**:1321
Five Plays of Langston Hughes
(Hughes)   **2**:1044
"Five Vignettes" (Toomer)   **3**:1762
"Flame-Heart" (McKay)   **3**:1396-98
Flavio (Parks)   **3**:1556
Flight (White)   **3**:1906, 1909-11, 1913-
15
Flight to Canada (Reed)   **3**:1617, 1624
Florence (Childress)   **1**:403-04, 406-07
"Flowers for my land"
(Soyinka)   **3**:1721
Fly, Jimmy, Fly (Myers)   **3**:1479

Folks from Dixie (Dunbar)   **1**:626-28,
634, 636, 638
"Footnote To A Pretentious Book"
(Baraka)   **1**:125
"For a Dead African" (Brutus)   **1**:316
"For a Lady I Know" (Cullen)   **1**:504,
507
"For a Lovely Lady" (Cullen)   **1**:486
"For a Mouthy Woman"
(Cullen)   **1**:493
"For a Poet" (Cullen)   **1**:508
For a Role of Parchment
(Ekwensi)   **1**:645
"For a Virgin" (Cullen)   **1**:507
"For Adrian" (Walcott)   **3**:1804
"For All Common People"
(Davis)   **1**:520
"For an Atheist" (Cullen)   **1**:507
"For Andy Goodman, Michael Schwerner,
and James Chaney" (Walker)   **3**:1837
"For Black People"
(Madhubuti)   **2**:1320
"For Black Poets Who Think of Suicide"
(Knight)   **2**:1215
*for colored girls who have considered
suicide/ when the rainbow is enuf*
(Shange)   **3**:1691-92, 1694, 1696-99,
1700-02
"For Daughters of Magdalen"
(Cullen)   **1**:508
"For Freckle-Faced Gerald"
(Knight)   **2**:1216
"For Gwendolyn Brooks, Teacher"
(Randall)   **3**:1605
"For John Keats, Apostle of Beauty"
(Cullen)   **1**:500
"For Koras and Balafong"
(Senghor)   **3**:1674
For Love of Imabelle (A Rage in Harlem)
(Himes)   **2**:1016-17, 1020-21
For Malcolm X (Randall)   **3**:1594-95,
1601, 1603
"For Margaret Danner/ In Establishing
Boone House" (Randall)   **3**:1594
"For My Grandmother" (Cullen)   **1**:507
"For My People" (Walker)   **3**:1834,
1839-40, 1842
For My People (Walker)   **3**:1833, 1835,
1839, 1842-43, 1846
"For My Sister Molly Who in the
Fifties" (Walker)   **3**:1811
"For Paul Laurence Dunbar"
(Cullen)   **1**:507
"For Pharish Pinckney, Bindle Stiff
During the Depression"
(Randall)   **3**:1604
"For Saundra" (Giovanni)   **2**:883, 895-
96
For the Highest Good
(Johnson)   **2**:1108, 1112
"For Unborn Malcolms"
(Sanchez)   **3**:1656-57, 1661
"For Vivian" (Randall)   **3**:1605
"Forced Retirement" (Giovanni)   **2**:894
Forest Leaves (Harper)   **2**:976
"Formula or Freedom" (Major)   **2**:1331
The Fortunate Traveller
(Walcott)   **3**:1797-98, 1802-03, 1805
"47th Street" (Davis)   **1**:520, 522
47th Street (Davis)   **1**:519-20
"The Fount of Tears" (Dunbar)   **1**:626

Four Black Revolutionary Plays: All Praises to the Black Man (Baraka)   1:142

Four Canzones (Okigbo)   3:1525-26

"4 daughters" (Clifton)   1:468

"Four Glimpses of Night" (Davis)   1:524

"Four Introductions" (Giovanni)   2:898

The Foxes of Harrow (Yerby)   3:2024, 2026, 2030

"fragment 3" (Sanchez)   3:1669

"Fragment d'une confession" (Roumain)   3:1637

"Fragments out of the Deluge" (Okigbo)   3:1527-28

"Frederick Douglass" (Dunbar)   1:629

"Frederick Douglass" (Hayden)   2:990

The Free-Lance Pallbearers (Reed)   3:1610-11, 1620-21

"Frescoes of the New World II" (Walcott)   3:1801

"Friends" (Clark)   1:424-25

From a Crooked Rib (Farah)   2:758, 760-62

"From the Crowd" (Braithwaite)   1:243

"From the Dark Tower" (Cullen)   1:503, 508

"From the House of Yemanjá" (Lorde)   2:1278

"Fruit of the Flower" (Cullen)   1:486-87

"The Fruitful Sleeping of the Rev. Elisha Edwards" (Dunbar)   1:636

"The Fugitive's Wife" (Harper)   2:978, 982

"Fugue in Gardenia" (Braithwaite)   1:246

"Fulani Cattle" (Clark)   1:422, 427

Funnyhouse of a Negro (Kennedy)   2:1154, 1157-61

"The Furlough" (Tolson)   3:1745

The Future of the American Negro (Washington)   3:1856

"Gaily teetering on the bath's edge" (Brutus)   1:311

A Gallery of Harlem Portraits (Tolson)   3:1738-39, 1741, 1743-44, 1746

"Games" (Randall)   3:1606

Garden of Time (Dodson)   1:562

Gather Together in My Name (Angelou)   1:28-30, 33, 37

A Gathering of Old Men (Gaines)   2:852-53, 860

"Gaugin" (Walcott)   3:1803

"Gay Chaps at the Bar" (Brooks)   1:251, 265

"Gay Paree" (Bennett)   1:182, 185

"Gemini–A Prolonged Autobiographical Statement on Why" (Giovanni)   2:884

Gemini: An Extended Autobiographical Statement on My First Twenty-five Years of Being a Poet (Giovanni)   2:883-86, 888, 890, 893-95

Generations (Clifton)   1:459-61, 466

The Gentleman Caller (Bullins)   1:331, 341

"George" (Randall)   3:1600, 1603

"Georgia Dusk" (Toomer. Jean)   3:1763-64

"Georgia's Atlanta" (Davis)   1:517-18

"Georgie Grimes" (Brown)   1:289

"Ghosts" (Cullen)   1:511

The Gift of Black Folk (Du Bois)   1:602

The Gift of Laughter (Fauset)   2:782

"The Gilded Six-Bits" (Hurston)   2:1070, 1072

Gingertown (McKay)   3:1393-96

Giovanni's Room (Baldwin)   1:81, 83-84, 87, 89-90, 98, 105

"Girl" (Kincaid)   2:1172

"A Girl's Story" (Bambara)   1:118

Give Birth to Brightness (Williams)   3:1951, 1953, 1957

A Glance Away (Wideman)   3:1919, 1921-22, 1924, 1928

"Glimpses of New England" (Forten)   2:814

"Glittering City" (Ekwensi)   1:657

Glittering City (Ekwensi)   1:645

"The Glory Trumpeter" (Walcott)   3:1795-96

"Go and look for bread" (Guillén)   See "Búscate plata"

"Go, Down Death" (Johnson)   2:1118

Go Tell It on the Mountain (Baldwin)   1:78, 80, 83-84, 88-89, 91-93, 99, 105

"Goats and Monkeys" (Walcott)   3:1792, 1795

"God Be With You" (Johnson)   2:1106

God Sends Sunday (Bontemps)   1:209, 215, 224

"Gods" (Cullen)   1:503

"The Gods Are Here" (Toomer)   3:1765

God's Bits of Wood (Ousmane)   See *Les bouts de bois de Dieu*

God's Trombones: Seven Negro Sermons in Verse (Johnson)   2:1117-22, 1124

Goin' a Buffalo (Bullins)   1:326, 328, 331-34, 336

"The Going On" (Myers)   3:1478

Going to the Territory (Ellison)   1:700

Gold Coast Land Tenure and the Forest Bill (Casely-Hayford)   1:346

Gold Coast Native Institutions (Casely-Hayford)   1:346-49, 351

The Golden Serpent (Myers)   3:1479

Golden Slippers (Fisher)   2:801

"Golgotha Is a Mountain" (Bontemps)   1:224

"Goliath of Gath" (Wheatley)   3:1884-85, 1894

A Good Girl Is Hard to Find (Baraka)   1:139

"A Good Job Gone" (Hughes)   2:1047, 1049

"Good Morning Revolution" (Hughes)   2:1063

Good News About the Earth (Clifton)   1:461

"Good Night, Willie Lee, I'll See You in the Morning" (Walker)   3:1828

Good Times (Clifton)   1:460-61, 463

"Goodbye Christ" (Hughes)   2:1063

Goodnight Willie Lee (Walker)   3:1816

"The Goophered Grapevine" (Chesnutt)   1:378-80, 383, 385-86, 390, 394

Gorilla, My Love: Short Stories (Bambara)   1:109-10, 113, 117-19

Gouverneurs de la rosée (*Masters of the Dew*) (Roumain)   3:1629-32, 1636

"Graduation nite" (Shange)   3:1694

"A Grain of Sand" (Harper)   2:979

A Grain of Wheat (Ngugi)   3:1502-03, 1506-07, 1509, 1511-12

El gran zoo (*Patria o muerte! The Great Zoo and Other Poems by Nicolás Guillén*) (Guillén)   2:911, 914

"The Gray Wolf's Ha'nt" (Chesnutt)   1:380, 383, 386, 395

Great Goodness of Life (*A Coon Show*) (Baraka)   1:145

"Green Lantern's Solo" (Baraka)   1:125

Griffin's Way (Yerby)   3:2030

"Gros Islet" (Walcott)   3:1803

Growing Up Stupid under the Union Jack: A Memoir (Clarke)   1:432-33, 439-42

"Guadalcanal" (Randall)   3:1604

"Guadeloupe, W.I." (Guillén)   2:913, 922

"Guardian of the Law" (Fisher)   2:797, 800, 804

The Guardian of the World (Laye)   See *Le Maître de la parole: Kuoma Lafolo Kuoma*

"Guinea" (Roumain)   3:1635

"Guitar" (Dodson)   1:568

"The Gulf" (Walcott)   3:1796

The Gulf (Walcott)   3:1800-01

Gullah (Childress)   1:411-12

"Gulliver" (Soyinka)   3:1720

"Gum" (Toomer)   3:1762

"Gums" (Myers)   3:1478

"Gypsy Man" (Hughes)   2:1065

"Habits" (Giovanni)   2:898

"Halfway to Nirvana" (Armah)   1:54

"Halmaherra" (Randall)   3:1604

"Hamlet" (Soyinka)   3:1720

"The Hammer Man" (Bambara)   1:119

The Hand and the Glove (Machado de Assis)   See *A mão e a luva*

"Hands of a Brown Woman" (Davis)   1:519, 521

"Hanging Fire" (Lorde)   2:1288

"Hard Daddy" (Hughes)   2:1065

Hard Facts: Excerpts (Baraka)   1:138

"Hard Luck" (Hughes)   2:1053, 1064

"Hard Rock" (Knight)   2:1216

"Hard Times" (McKay)   3:1382

Harlem (Thurman)   3:1726-28, 1730, 1732

"Harlem" (Tolson)   3:1744

The Harlem Book of the Dead (Dodson)   1:567

"The Harlem Dancer" (McKay)   3:1377, 1386

Harlem Gallery: Book I, The Curator (Tolson)   3:1735-39, 1741-46

"The Harlem Ghetto" (Baldwin)   1:95-96

"The Harlem Group of Negro Writers" (Tolson)   3:1743

Harlem: Negro Metropolis (McKay)   3:1393, 1396

"Harlem Shadows" (McKay)   3:1386, 1397

Harlem Shadows (McKay)   3:1377, 1379-80, 1386-87, 1393

L'harmattan (Ousmane)   3:1533
"Harriet" (Lorde)   2:1283
"Harsh World That Lashest Me"
    (Cullen)   1:501, 504
"Harvest Song" (Toomer)   3:1763-64
"The Haunted Oak" (Dunbar)   1:626,
    639
"He and the Cat" (Mphahlele)   3:1453
"He Knew" (Himes)   2:1015
"He Sees Through Stone"
    (Knight)   2:1214, 1216
The Healers (Armah)   1:44-45, 52, 54
The Heart of a Woman
    (Angelou)   1:32, 37
The Heart of Happy Hollow
    (Dunbar)   1:627-28, 634, 636-37
The Heat's On (Himes)   2:1010, 1016-
    17, 1019-20
Heavensgate (Okigbo)   3:1523-28
"Helmeted Boy" (Randall)   3:1604
The Helper (Bullins)   1:341
"Henri Christophe" (Walcott)   3:1800
Her Blue Body Everything We Know
    (Walker)   3:1828
"Her Lips Are Copper Wire"
    (Toomer)   3:1762
"Her Sweet Jerome" (Walker)   3:1815
"Her Three Days" (Ousmane)   3:1547-
    48
"Her Virginia Mammy"
    (Chesnutt)   1:388
"Here and Elsewhere"
    (Walcott)   3:1802
"Here Be Dragons" (Baldwin)   1:98
"here is another bone to pick with you"
    (Clifton)   1:468
"Heritage" (Cullen)   1:486, 491-93,
    495, 497-98, 501-06
The Heritage of Quincas Borba (Machado
    de Assis)
    See *Quincas Borba*
A Hero Ain't Nothin' But a Sandwich
    (Childress)   1:402, 410-11
The Heroic Slave (Douglass)   1:585-88,
    592-94
"Hey!" (Hughes)   2:1065
"Hidden Name, Complex Fate"
    (Ellison)   1:695
Hiding Place (Wideman)   3:1918-20,
    1923-24, 1926
"High Yaller" (Fisher)   2:793-94, 798,
    801-02, 804-05
Hintsa the Great (Mqhayi)
    See *U-Mhlekazi u-Hintsa*
"A Historical Footnote to Consider Only
    When All Else Fails"
    (Giovanni)   2:893
"Holly Berry and Mistletoe"
    (Braithwaite)   1:243
"Homage to Duke Ellington on His
    Birthday" (Ellison)   1:701
"Home" (Hughes)   2:1047-49
Home and Exile (Nkosi)   3:1516
"The Home-Coming of 'Rastus Smith"
    (Dunbar)   1:637, 640
Home: Social Essays (Baraka)   1:127,
    141, 145, 147
"Home-Thoughts" (McKay)   3:1396,
    1398
Home to Harlem (McKay)   3:1378-80,
    1389-91, 1393-94
"Homecoming" (Sanchez)   3:1660-61

"Homecoming" (Sanchez)   3:1650, 1655,
    1657, 1659-60, 1662, 1665
Homegirls and Hand Grenades
    (Sanchez)   3:1669
"Homesickness" (Bennett)   1:182
The Homewood Trilogy
    (Wideman)   3:1921-22
Hoops (Myers)   3:1473, 1480
Hope and Suffering (Tutu)   3:1771-73
Hopes and Impediments (Achebe)   1:14-
    15
"Horizontal Cameos" (Davis)   1:525
Horn of My Love (p'Bitek)   3:1573,
    1577
"Horses Graze" (Brooks)   1:265
*Horses Make a Landscape Look More
    Beautiful* (Walker)   3:1825
"Hosea" (Walker)   3:1838
Hosties Noires (*Black Wafers*)
    (Senghor)   3:1674, 1676, 1682-83,
    1686-87
"Hot-Foot Hannibal" (Chesnutt)   1:380,
    383, 385, 387-88, 392, 394-95
"Hotel Normandie Pool"
    (Walcott)   3:1802
The House Behind the Cedars
    (Chesnutt)   1:387, 390, 397
*The House of Falling Leaves with Other
    Poems* (Braithwaite)   1:243
"House O'Law" (Bennett)   1:185
"How Bigger Was Born"
    (Wright)   3:2018
"How Brother Parker Fell from Grace"
    (Dunbar)   1:637
How Do You Do (Bullins)   1:341
How Far the Promised Land?
    (White)   3:1910
"How It Feels to Be Colored"
    (Hurston)   2:1074
"How Long Is Forever"
    (Myers)   3:1478
"How Poems Are Made/ A Discredited
    View" (Walker)   3:1825
"Hunchback Girl. . ." (Brooks)   1:254
"Hunger" (Cullen)   1:510
The Hungered One: Early Writings
    (Bullins)   1:327-28, 336
"Hunt of the Stone" (Soyinka)   3:1719
Hurry Home (Wideman)   3:1922, 1924,
    1928
"Hymn" (Randall)   3:1605
"Hymn to Evening" (Wheatley)   3:1887
"Hymn to Lanie Poo" (Baraka)   1:125
I Am Lucy Terry (Bullins)   1:341
I Am the American Negro
    (Davis)   1:519-20
"I Break the Sky" (Dodson)   1:571
"I Declare Myself an Impure Man"
    (Guillén)   2:914
"I don't love you" (Baraka)   1:144
"I Have a Dream" (King)   2:1203-1207
"I Have a Rendezvous with Life"
    (Cullen)   1:487
I Know Why the Caged Bird Sings
    (Angelou)   1:27-30, 33-35, 37-38
I, Laminarian (Césaire)
    See *Moi, Laminaire*
"I love those little booths at Benvenuti's"
    (Brooks)   1:252
"I Loved You Once" (Randall)   3:1605
I-nzuzo (*Reward*) (Mqhayi)   3:1465,
    1467

"I See the Promised Land"
    (King)   2:1205
"I Substitute For The Dead Lecturer"
    (Baraka)   1:125
"I think it Rains" (Soyinka)   3:1706
"i useta live in the world"
    (Shange)   3:1694
"I Want to Sing" (Giovanni)   2:893
"I Want to Write" ("Daydream")
    (Walker)   3:1845
I Will Marry When I Want (Ngugi)
    See *Ngaahika Ndeenda*
I Wonder As I Wander
    (Hughes)   2:1049
"Ibadan" (Clark)   1:418, 422, 427
"Ibadan Dawn–After Pied Beauty"
    (Clark)   1:425
"Idanre" (Soyinka)   3:1706, 1719-20
Idanre and Other Poems
    (Soyinka)   3:1706, 1708, 1719-20,
    1722
"Iddo Bridge" (Clark)   1:424
"The Idea of Ancestry"
    (Knight)   2:1212, 1214, 1217
"The Idiot" (Randall)   3:1596
If Beale Street Could Talk
    (Baldwin)   1:86, 88, 91-92
If He Hollers (Himes)   2:1006
"If Into Love The Image Burdens"
    (Baraka)   1:125
"If We Must Die" (McKay)   3:1379-80,
    1384, 1397-98
"If You Should Go" (Cullen)   1:501,
    507
Ignoble Victory (Yerby)   3:2026
"Ikeja, Friday, Four O'Clock"
    (Soyinka)   3:1720
Ikolo the Wrestler and Other Ibo Tales
    (Ekwensi)   1:659
"Ilu, the Talking Drum"
    (Knight)   2:1217-18
"Imagination" (Wheatley)   3:1883,
    1885, 1887, 1892, 1894
Imihobe nemibongo (*Songs of Joy and
    Lullabies*) (Mqhayi)   3:1464
"The Immigrant" (Soyinka)   3:1721
"Impasse" (Hughes)   2:1055
"In a Grave Yard" (Braithwaite)   1:243
In a Green Night: Poems 1948-1960
    (Walcott)   3:1799
"In a Troubled Key" (Hughes)   2:1051-
    52
"In de Beulahlan" (Johnson)   2:1112
"In Memoriam" (Senghor)   3:1682
"In Memory of Col. Charles Young"
    (Cullen)   1:508
"In Memory of Segun Awolowo"
    (Soyinka)   3:1706, 1719
"In Montgomery" (Brooks)   1:257
In My Father's House (Gaines)   2:856,
    859, 862
In New England Winter
    (Bullins)   1:331-38, 341
In Old Plantation Days
    (Dunbar)   1:627, 632, 634, 636-37
In Search of Our Mother's Gardens
    (Walker)   3:1826
"In Spite of Death" (Cullen)   1:503,
    509
"In Taba kaNdoda" (Mqhayi)   3:1462
"In the Beginning" (Lamming)   2:1236

In the Castle of My Skin
   (Lamming)   2:1225, 1227-29, 1231-
   32, 1236-37
"In the Closet of the Soul"
   (Walker)   3:1824
In the Ditch (Emecheta)   2:709-10, 712-
   15
"In the greyness of isolated time"
   (Brutus)   1:312-14
"In the Mecca" (Brooks)   1:256
In the Mecca (Brooks)   1:251, 255-56,
   258, 261, 264-67
"In the Night" (Kincaid)   2:1172
"In the night, in the mind"
   (Brutus)   1:312-13
"In the Wine Time" (Bullins)   1:336
In the Wine Time (Bullins)   1:326, 328,
   333-36, 341
"incantation" (Clifton)   1:468
"Incident" (Baraka)   1:149
"Incident" (Cullen)   1:498, 501, 505,
   507
"Independence" (Bennett)   1:182, 184
"Indianapolis/Summer/1969/Poem"
   (Sanchez)   3:1662
Infants of the Spring
   (Thurman)   3:1728-32
"Informer" (Randall)   3:1597
"The Ingrate" (Dunbar)   1:630, 636-37
"The inherent impulse to good"
   (Brutus)   1:313
Inner City Hoodlum (Goines)   2:905
"Insomnie" (Roumain)   3:1631, 1637,
   1643
*The Interesting Narrative of the Life of
   Olaudah Equiano, or Gustavas Vassa,
   the African* (*Narrative*; *The Life of
   Olaudah Equiano*) (Equiano)   2:721-
   38
"The Interference of Patsy Ann"
   (Dunbar)   1:637
"The Intervention of Peter"
   (Dunbar)   1:636
"Interview" (Randall)   3:1597, 1605
introducing a new loa (Reed)   3:1610
"Introspection" (Giovanni)   2:894
Invisible Man (Ellison)   1:676-77, 679-
   81, 683, 687-88, 691-93, 695-96, 698-
   701, 704
Iola Leroy; or Shadows Uplifted
   (Harper)   2:976-78, 982
"Iota" (Tolson)   3:1737
"Iphigenia" (Dodson)   1:572
"Isaiah" (Walker)   3:1838
"ISandlwana" (Mqhayi)   3:1462
Isarà (Soyinka)   3:1722-23
"I'se Jes'er Little Nigger"
   (Cotter)   1:476
Iska (Ekwensi)   1:651, 657
"Islands" (Walcott)   3:1805
It Ain't All for Nothin' (Myers)   3:1477,
   1480
It Bees Dat Way (Bullins)   1:331
It Has No Choice (Bullins)   1:327, 336-
   37, 341
"It Was a Funky Deal"
   (Knight)   2:1218
"It's a Long Way" (Braithwaite)   1:243
Ityala lamwawele (*The Lawsuit of the
   Twins*) (Mqhayi)   3:1460-61, 1463-64,
   1466-67
Ivbie (Clark)   1:425-26

I've Been a Woman (Sanchez)   3:1655,
   1657-59, 1664-65
"The Ivory Dancer" (Ekwensi)   1:657
"Izwe IakwaNdlambe" ("The Domain of
   the Ndlambe People")
   (Mqhayi)   3:1466
J-E-L-L-O (Baraka)   1:145
"Jackson, Mississippi" (Walker)   3:1843
Jagua Nana (Ekwensi)   1:645-46, 648,
   651, 653-56, 658
"Jailhouse Blues" (Randall)   3:1604
"Jamaica Elevate" (Bennett)   1:184
Jamaica Labrish (Bennett)   1:184, 186
"Jazz Band" (Davis)   1:517
Jazz-set (Milner)   3:1407
"Jazzonia" (Hughes)   2:1055
"Jeremiah" (Walker)   3:1838
The Jewels of Aptor (Delany)   1:531
Jim Crow's Last Stand
   (Hughes)   2:1050
"Jim's Probation" (Dunbar)   1:636
"Jim's Romance" (Chesnutt)   1:388
"Jimsella" (Dunbar)   1:628, 636
Jitney (Wilson)   3:1969
Jo Anne (Bullins)   1:341
Joe Turner's Come and Gone
   (Wilson)   3:1964, 1968-71
"Joel" (Walker)   3:1838
"John Archer's Nose" (Fisher)   2:800
John Brown (Du Bois)   1:604
"John Crossed the Island on His Knees"
   (Johnson)   2:1106
"John Redding Goes to Sea"
   (Hurston)   2:1070-72
"Johnny Thomas" (Brown)   1:283
"Johnsonham, Jr." (Dunbar)   1:640
The Joker of Seville (Walcott)   3:1801
Jonah's Gourd Vine (Hurston)   2:1078,
   1082-83, 1085
"Jonathan's Song" (Dodson)   1:572
"Joseph" (Soyinka)   3:1720
Journal (Forten)
   See *The Journal of Charlotte L.
   Forten: A Free Negro in the Slave
   Era*
*The Journal of Charlotte L. Forten: A
   Free Negro in the Slave Era* (*Journal*)
   (Forten)   2:809-22
"Journey" (Soyinka)   3:1720-21
The Joys of Motherhood
   (Emecheta)   2:709-13, 718
Jubilee (Walker)   3:1832, 1839, 1846-47
"Juby" (Myers)   3:1478
"Judas Iscariot" (Cullen)   1:508
"Judgment Day" (Johnson)   2:1118,
   1124
"A Judgment of Paris" (Dunbar)   1:637
Juju Rock (Ekwensi)   1:649, 652
"July" (Sanchez)   3:1657
"July Wake" (Clark)   1:421
"Junta" (Walcott)   3:1801
Just Above My Head (Baldwin)   1:86-
   88, 92
*Just Give me a Cool Drink of Water 'fore
   I Die* (Angelou)   1:31
"Just Like a Tree" (Gaines)   2:843-44,
   846, 850
"Ka 'Ba" (Baraka)   1:150
"Kabnis" (Toomer)   3:1753-54, 1760-
   61, 1763
"Karintha" (Toomer)   3:1758-59, 1763
"Kas-Kas" (Bennett)   1:185

Keep the Faith, Baby! (Powell)   3:1586-
   87
Kenyatta's Escape (Goines)   2:904-05
Kenyatta's Last Hit (Goines)   2:904-05
"Kin" (Clark)   1:424
"The Kind Master and Dutiful Servant"
   (Hammon)   2:945, 948
Kind of Blue (Young)   3:2044
King Lazarus (Beti)
   See *Le roi miraculé: Chronique des
   Essazam*
"The Kiss" (Chesnutt)   1:388
"KKK" (Guillén)   2:914
"Kneeling before you in a gesture"
   (Brutus)   1:312
"Knocking Donkey Fleas off a Poet from
   the Southside of Chi"
   (Madhubuti)   2:1319
"Koko Oloro" (Soyinka)   3:1719, 1721
Kongi's Harvest (Soyinka)   3:1711-13
"Kwa Mamu Zetu Waliotuzaa"
   (Sanchez)   3:1658, 1665
"A Lady Slipper" (Dunbar)   1:637
laiá Garcia (*Yayá Garcia*) (Machado de
   Assis)   2:1294
Lak tar miyo kinyero wi lobo (*Are Your
   Teeth White? Then Laugh!*)
   (p'Bitek)   3:1562, 1573
"Lament" (Dodson)   1:568
Lament for an African Pol (Beti)
   See *La ruine presque cocasse d'un
   polichinelle: Remember Ruben deux*
"Lament of the Flutes"
   (Okigbo)   3:1526
"Lament of the Lavender Mist"
   (Okigbo)   3:1526
"The Land Question and Black
   Liberation" (Cleaver)   1:452
"Landscape of my young world"
   (Brutus)   1:312-14
"Langston Hughes" (Randall)   3:1605
"Langston Hughes" (Roumain)   3:1631,
   1644
The Langston Hughes Reader
   (Hughes)   2:1048-49
The Last Days of Louisiana Red
   (Reed)   3:1617, 1623
"The Last Fiddling of Mordaunt's Jim"
   (Dunbar)   1:637
"The Last Quatrain of the Ballad of
   Emmett Till" (Brooks)   1:265
"The Last Ride of Wild Bill"
   (Brown)   1:290
"Laughing I left the earth./ Flaming
   returned" (Randall)   3:1604
Laughing to Keep from Crying
   (Hughes)   2:1047-48
"Laughters" (Hughes)   2:1065
"Laventille" (Walcott)   3:1795-96, 1800
Lawd Today (Wright)   3:2012
The Lawsuit of the Twins (Mqhayi)
   See *Ityala lamwawele*
Lazarus: A Novel (Beti)
   See *Le roi miraculé: Chronique des
   Essazam*
"The Lazy School of Literary Criticism"
   (Armah)   1:53
Leadbelly (Parks)   3:1557
"Leader of the Hunt" (Clark)   1:421
"A Leader of the People (for Roy
   Wilkins)" (Randall)   3:1599
The Learning Tree (Parks)   3:1553-56

"Leaves Falling" (Clark)　1:428
"Legacies" (Giovanni)　2:887
The Legend of Tarik (Myers)　3:1472, 1477, 1480
The Leopard's Claw (Ekwensi)　1:645, 649, 652
"The Lesson" (Bambara)　1:119
A Lesson in a Dead Language (Kennedy)　2:1161
"Let America Be America Again" (Hughes)　2:1050
"Let Koras and Balafong Accompany Me" (Senghor)
　See "Que m'accompagnent Kôras et Balafong"
Let Me Breathe Thunder (Attaway)　1:57, 59-60, 64, 66, 68
"Let My People Go" (Johnson)　2:1124
"Let not this plunder be misconstrued" (Brutus)　1:312
"Letter for Jan" (Lorde)　2:1282
"Letter from a Region in My Mind" (Baldwin)　1:93
Letter from Birmingham Jail (King)　2:1189-91, 1193-97, 1199-1208
"A Letter from Brooklyn" (Walcott)　3:1795
"A Letter from Phillis Wheatley" (Hayden)　2:991
"The Letter Home" (Kincaid)　2:1172, 1175
"Letter to a Bourgeois Friend Whom Once I Loved (and Maybe Still Do If Love Is Valid)" (Giovanni)　2:896
"Letter to a Poet" (Senghor)　3:1682
"A Letter to Oliver Tambo" (Clark)　1:428
"Letters from France" (Ousmane)　3:1549
"Letters from Prison" (Cleaver)　1:448
Letters to Martha and Other Poems from a South African Prison (Brutus)　1:314-15, 317
"Lettres de l'Hivernage" (Senghor)　3:1684
"leukemia as white rabbit" (Clifton)　1:468
"The Liar" (Baraka)　1:125
"Liberty and Peace" (Wheatley)　3:1884
Libretto for the Republic of Liberia (Tolson)　3:1736, 1739, 1741, 1744-46
"Lif' Up de Spade" (Johnson)　2:1106
"Life" (Dunbar)　1:631
"Life" (Head)　2:1001
Life and Times of Frederick Douglass (Douglass)　1:581-82, 585
"The Life I Led" (Giovanni)　2:893
Life of J. K. Bokwe (Mqhayi)
　See *U-bomi bom-fundisi uJohn Knox Bokwe*
"The Life of Lincoln West" (Brooks)　1:257, 265-66
The Life of Olaudah Equiano (Equiano)
　See *The Interesting Narrative of the Life of Olaudah Equiano, or Gustavas Vassa, the African*
"Life on the Sea Islands" (Forten)　2:815, 819
"Life's Tragedy" (Dunbar)　1:626

Light beyond the Darkness (Harper)　2:982
"The Light of the World" (Walcott)　3:1802-03, 1805-06
"The Lighthouse" (Walcott)　3:1803
"The Limb of Satan" (Chesnutt)　1:387
Limits (Okigbo)　3:1524, 1527-28
"Lincoln" (Bell)　1:173
"Lincoln" (Dunbar)　1:626
Linden Hills (Naylor)　3:1487-89, 1491-92
"The Line-Up" (Randall)　3:1597, 1604
"Lineage" (Walker)　3:1840
"Lines" (Harper)　2:980
The Lion and the Jewel (Soyinka)　3:1709-13
"Listen Here Blues" (Hughes)　2:1065
"The Litany for Survival" (Lorde)　2:1283, 1288
"A Litany of Atlanta" (Du Bois)　1:601
"A Litany of Friends" (Randall)　3:1606
A Litany of Friends (Randall)　3:1598, 1600, 1602, 1604, 1606
"Litany of the Dark People" (Cullen)　1:493, 503, 509
"A Little Child Shall Lead Them" (Harper)　2:977
"Little Dog" (Hughes)　2:1047, 1049
A Little Dreaming (Johnson)　2:1106, 1108-10, 1112-13
Little Ham (Hughes)　2:1044
"Little Rock" (Guillén)　2:919
"Little Sheik" (McKay)　3:1395
"A Little Song" (Braithwaite)　1:243
"The Living and Dead" (Mphahlele)　3:1453-54
The Living and Dead (Mphahlele)　3:1453
Living by the Word (Walker)　3:1824, 1826-27
"Living Earth" (Toomer)　3:1765
"Lizabeth: The Caterpillar Story" (Wideman)　3:1918, 1923
"Llegada" (Guillén)　2:922
"The Loafing Negro" (Cotter)　1:476
Lokotown and Other Stories (Ekwensi)　1:657
Lonely Crusade (Himes)　2:1012
"The Lonely Mother" (Johnson)　2:1106
"Lonesome" (Dunbar)　1:626
"Lonesome Ben" (Chesnutt)　1:392
"Long Black Song" (Wright)　3:2007, 2011, 2014-17
"A Long Day in November" (Gaines)　2:846, 857
"Long de Cool O'Night" (Johnson)　2:1112
The Long Dream (Wright)　3:2005, 2008
"Long Gone" (Brown)　1:282, 287
"Long Track Blues" (Brown)　1:290
A Long Way from Home (McKay)　3:1393, 1396-97, 1399
"Longing" (Brutus)　1:312
"The Lost Dancer" (Toomer)　3:1765
The Lost Zoo (Cullen)　1:490, 493, 504
"Love and Sorrow" (Dunbar)　1:626
"Love: Is a Human Condition" (Giovanni)　2:894
"Love Letta" (Bennett)　1:185

The Love of Landry (Dunbar)　1:627, 630-31, 634-35
Love Poems (Sanchez)　3:1655, 1657-58, 1662-64
"Love Song for Seven Little Boys Called Sam" (Fuller)　2:829-30
"Love Song to Idi Amin" (Knight)　2:1215
Love Story Black (Demby)　1:552, 556-58
"The Love Tree" (Cullen)　1:504, 509
Love You (Randall)　3:1596, 1598, 1601, 1603
"A Lovely Love" (Brooks)　1:250, 255
"Lover's Tangle" (Cotter)　1:477
Lucy (Kincaid)　2:1177
"Lullaby (Melody for a 'Cello)" (Davis)　1:517
"Luo Plains" (Soyinka)　3:1721
"Lustra" (Okigbo)　3:1526
"Lynch" (Guillén)　2:914
"Lynched (Symphonic Interlude for Twenty-one Selected Instruments)" (Davis)　1:517
The Lynchers (Wideman)　3:1922, 1924-25, 1928
"The Lynching" (McKay)　3:1385
"The Lynching of Jube Benson" (Dunbar)　1:628, 637, 639
Lyrics of Life and Love (Braithwaite)　1:243
Lyrics of Love and Laughter (Dunbar)　1:629, 639
Lyrics of Lowly Life (Dunbar)　1:628-29
Lyrics of Sunshine and Shadow (Dunbar)　1:629
Lyrics of the Heartside (Dunbar)　1:629
"Ma Man" (Hughes)　2:1065
"Ma Rainey" (Brown)　1:287, 290
Ma Rainey's Black Bottom (Wilson)　3:1964-65, 1967-69, 1971
"Madman of the Uncharmed Debris of the South Side" (Major)　2:1325
"Madrigal" (Guillén)　2:912
"Magnets" (Cullen)　1:512
"Magnolia Flowers" (Hurston)　2:1070
"Maiden, Open" (Randall)　3:1599, 1606
Main basse sur le Cameroun: Autopsie d'une décolonisation (Beti)　1:202
"Mainly By the Music" (Randall)　3:1597
Le Maître de la parole: Kuoma Lafolo Kuoma (The Guardian of the World) (Laye)　2:1257-59
Maitu Njugira (Ngugi)　3:1509
Majors and Minors (Dunbar)　1:625, 628, 630, 638
"Malcolm" (Walker)　3:1837
"Malcolm Spoke/Who listened?" (Madhubuti)　2:1315
Malcolm X: Selected Speeches and Statements (Malcolm X)　2:1347
"Malediction" (Soyinka)　3:1719
Mama Day (Naylor)　3:1488-89, 1491-92
"Mammy Peggy's Pride" (Dunbar)　1:636
A Man Called White (White)　3:1914
Man Must Live (Mphahlele)　3:1448, 1450-51

A Man of the People (Achebe)   1:3-4, 6-7, 9-10, 13
The Man Who Cried I Am (Williams)   3:1934, 1936-40, 1943, 1945-49
"The Man Who Lived Underground" (Wright)   3:2004, 2008, 2011-12
"The Man Who Was Almos' a Man" (Wright)   3:2014
Manchild in the Promised Land (Brown)   1:272-77
Mandabi (Ousmane)   3:1534-35
Mandela and Other Poems (Clark)   1:428
Mandela's Earth (Soyinka)   3:1722
A mão e a luva (*The Hand and the Glove*) (Machado de Assis)   2:1294
Maps (Farah)   2:764, 769
Marching Blacks (Powell)   3:1583-84
"The Marked Tree" (Chesnutt)   1:388
The Marrow of Tradition (Chesnutt)   1:387, 397
"Mars Jeems's Nightmare" (Chesnutt)   1:381-83, 386, 388, 394-95
"Martha Graham" (Dodson)   1:572
"The Martyr of Alabama" (Harper)   2:980, 982
Maru (Head)   2:996-99, 1000, 1002
"Mary at the Feet of Christ" (Harper)   2:980
"Mary Louise" (Gaines)   2:857
"Mash Flat" (Bennett)   1:185
"Masks and Marx: The Marxist Ethos vis-à-vis African Revolutionary Theory and Praxis" (Armah)   1:53
The Masquerade (Clark)   1:415-16, 419
"Mass Man" (Walcott)   3:1801
"Massacre October '66" (Soyinka)   3:1721-22
"The Master of Doornvlei" (Mphahlele)   3:1453
Masters of the Dew (Roumain)
   See *Gouverneurs de la rosée*
Matigari ma Njiruungi (Ngugi)   3:1514
Mating Birds (Nkosi)   3:1517-21
"A Matter of Doctrine" (Dunbar)   1:637
"A Matter of Principle" (Chesnutt)   1:388
Maud Martha (Brooks)   1:257
"Maumee Ruth" (Brown)   1:283, 289
"May and December: A Song" (Randall)   3:1606
"Me Bredda" (Bennett)   1:185-86
Me, Mop, and the Moondance Kid (Myers)   3:1476, 1479
"Medea" (Cullen)   1:491
The Medea and Some Poems (Cullen)   1:490, 495, 502, 504, 511-12
"Meditations on History" (Williams)   3:1955
"Mediterranean" (Senghor)   3:1676
"Medley" (Bambara)   1:110, 118
The Meeting Point (Clarke)   1:431-32, 438-41
Melinda (Elder)   1:668
"The Melting Pot" (Randall)   3:1596
Memorial de Ayres (*Counselor for Ayres' Memorial*) (Machado de Assis)   2:1293

"Memorial Wreath" (Randall)   3:1594
Memórias póstumas de Bras Cubas (*Posthumos Reminiscences of Braz Cubas*) (Machado de Assis)   2:1292, 1294-96, 1299, 1301, 1303-04
"Memory" (Walker)   3:1842
"The Memory of Martha" (Dunbar)   1:633, 637
"Memphis Blues" (Brown)   1:282-83, 289
"Men" (Toomer)   3:1765
Men of Color, to Arms! (Douglass)   1:583
"Menagerie, a Child's Fable" (Johnson)   2:1097
Meridian (Walker)   3:1813-15, 1817, 1825
"Merle" (Marshall)   3:1371
"A Mess of Pottage" (Dunbar)   1:636, 638
"A Message All Blackpeople Can Dig" (Madhubuti)   2:1315
"Message to a Black Soldier" (Madhubuti)   2:1313
"The Messenger" (Bullins)   1:336
The Messenger (Wright)   3:1985-86, 1990-92
"Metamorphoses, I/ Moon" (Walcott)   3:1792
"Micah" (Walker)   3:1838
Michael (Bullins)   1:341
"Middle Passage" (Hayden)   2:990, 992-93
Middle Passage (Johnson)   2:1099-1102
"Midi" (Roumain)   3:1642
"Midnight Chippie's Lament" (Hughes)   2:1052
Midsummer (Walcott)   3:1802-03
"militant Black, Poet" (Randall)   3:1597
"Mill Mountain" (Brown)   1:289
"The Mini Skirt" (Randall)   3:1606
"The Minister" (Johnson)   2:1109, 1111-12
"Minutely Hurt" (Cullen)   1:511
"A Miracle Demanded" (Cullen)   1:511
Miraculous Weapons (Césaire)
   See *Les Armes Miraculeuses*
"Mirage" (Roumain)   3:1643
Miralda; or, The Beautiful Quadroon (Brown)
   See *Clotel; or, The President's Daughter: A Narrative of Slave Life in the United States*
"The Mirror" (Machado de Assis)
   See "O Espelho"
"Mirror Sermon" (Brutus)   1:312
"Mirrors" (Giovanni)   2:894
Miscellaneous Poems (Harper)
   See *Poems on Miscellaneous Subjects*
"Misery" (Hughes)   2:1065
"Miss Cynthie" (Fisher)   2:792-93, 795, 797, 800-05
Miss Jane Pittman (Gaines)
   See *The Autobiography of Miss Jane Pittman*
Mission Accomplished (Beti)
   See *Mission terminé*
"The Mission of Mr. Scatters" (Dunbar)   1:637

Mission terminé (*Mission Accomplished*; *Mission to Kala*) (Beti)   1:191-96, 201
Mission to Kala (Beti)
   See *Mission terminé*
"Mississippi Levee" (Hughes)   2:1053
"Mr. Cornelius Johnson, Office Seeker" (Dunbar)   1:636
"Mr. Groby's Slippery Gift" (Dunbar)   1:637
Mr. Monkey and the Gotcha Bird (Myers)   3:1478-79
"Mr. Samuel and Sam" (Brown)   1:283
"Mrs. Plum" (Mphahlele)   3:1454
"Mrs. Small" (Brooks)   1:251
"The Mob" (Brutus)   1:312
"Modern Man–The Superman (A Song of Praise for Hearst, Hitler, Mussolini and the Munitions Makers)" (Davis)   1:520
"Modern Moses" (Bell)   1:174
"Modern Moses, or 'My Policy' Man" (Bell)   1:177, 179
Moeti oa bochabela (*The Pilgrim of the East*; *The Traveller to the East*) (Mofolo)   3:1413-17
Moi, Laminaire (*I, Laminarian*) (Césaire)   1:368
Mojo: A Black Love Story (Childress)   1:404, 407
Mojo and the Russians (Myers)   3:1477-78, 1480
"Mojo Mike's Beer Garden" (Davis)   1:521
"Monet's Waterlilies" (Hayden)   2:990
The Money-Order; with White Genesis (Ousmane)
   See *Véhi-Ciosane; ou, Blanche-Genèse, suivi du Mandat*
Montage of a Dream Deferred (Hughes)   2:1050, 1055-56, 1058, 1062, 1066
La montagne ensorcelée (Roumain)   3:1630, 1642
"Mood" (Cullen)   1:504
"Moody's Mood for Love" (Young)   3:2045
More to Remember (Randall)   3:1596-98, 1600-01, 1604-06
"More Un-noticed to be Noticed: A Nationhood Poem" (Madhubuti)   2:1320
"Morning" (Wheatley)   3:1885
"Morning After" (Hughes)   2:1053
"morning mirror" (Clifton)   1:468
Moses: A Story of the Nile (Harper)   2:976-84
Moses: Man of the Mountain (Hurston)   2:1077-78, 1082
"The Mother" (Ousmane)   3:1547
"A Mother's Story" (Clark)   1:428
"Motion and Rest" (Toomer)   3:1766-67
The Motion of History (Baraka)   1:131, 134, 137
Motivos de son (Guillén)   2:912, 915, 918, 920-24
Motown and Didi (Myers)   3:1476
"Moving Pictures" (Johnson)   2:1097-98
Mqhayi of the Mountain of Beauty (Mqhayi)
   See *U-Mqhayi Wase-Ntab'ozuko*

"Mt. Pisgah's Christmas Possum" (Dunbar)   **1:**632, 636, 641

"Mu" (Tolson)   **3:**1736, 1746

"Mujer nueva" (Guillén)   **2:**922

"Mulata" (Guillén)   **2:**915

Mulatto (Hughes)   **2:**1044, 1056, 1058, 1065

"The Mulatto's Song" (Johnson)   **2:**1109

"De Mule" (Johnson)   **2:**1112

Mules and Men (Hurston)   **2:**1073, 1081

Mumbo Jumbo (Reed)   **3:**1610, 1612-14, 1616-20, 1623

"The Muse of History" (Walcott)   **3:**1795

"Muttsy" (Hurston)   **2:**1070, 1072

"Mwilu/or Poem for the Living" (Madhubuti)   **2:**1321

My Amputations: A Novel (Major)   **2:**1329

My Bondage and My Freedom (Douglass)   **1:**581, 588

My Brother Fine with Me (Clifton)   **1:**460

"My Dream" (Bennett)   **1:**186

"my dream about the cows" (Clifton)   **1:**468

"My Dungeon Shook" (Baldwin)   **1:**93

"My Father and Stokely Carmichael" (Cleaver)   **1:**452

"My Grandma and the Haint" (Gaines)   **2:**857

"My House" (Giovanni)   **2:**888, 897

My House (Giovanni)   **2:**885-88, 895-96

My Larger Education (Washington)   **3:**1864

"My Last Name" (Guillén)   **2:**913

My Life in the Bush of Ghosts (Tutuola)   **3:**1778-79, 1781, 1785-87

My Life of Absurdity (Himes)   **2:**1014

My Lives and How I Lost Them (Cullen)   **1:**504

My Main Mother (Beckham)   **1:**153-54, 159

"My Mother" (Kincaid)   **2:**1175

"My Muse" (Randall)   **3:**1599

"My Name is Red Hot. Yo Name Ain Doodley Squat" (Brooks)   **1:**265, 267

"My Native Land (Rodina)" (Randall)   **3:**1606

"My Next-Door Neighbor" (Soyinka)   **3:**1721

"My People" (Hughes)   **2:**1065

"My Poem" (Giovanni)   **2:**882, 887

"My Soul and I" (Tolson)   **3:**1745

My Southern Home; or, The South and Its People (Brown)   **1:**294-97

"My Students" (Randall)   **3:**1606

The Mystery of Phillis Wheatley (Bullins)   **1:**341

A Naked Needle (Farah)   **2:**758, 761, 763

Nappy Edges (Shange)   **3:**1696

Narrative (Equiano)
     See *The Interesting Narrative of the Life of Olaudah Equiano, or Gustavas Vassa, the African*

Narrative of the Life of Frederick Douglass, an American Slave, Written by Himself (Douglass)   **1:**576-58, 581, 583-85, 588

Narrative of William W. Brown, a Fugitive Slave, Written by Himself (Brown)   **1:**294-95, 297, 305

Natalie Mann (Toomer)   **3:**1760

Native Son (Wright)   **3:**1997, 1999, 2000-04, 2009-12, 2014-15, 2017-19

Natives of My Person (Lamming)   **2:**1232-34, 1236-37

"Nature for Nature's sake" (Mqhayi)   **3:**1462

"Near White" (Cullen)   **1:**506

"Ned's Psalm of Life for the Negro" (Cotter)   **1:**476

The Negro (Du Bois)   **1.**606, 615

"Negro Artist and the Racial Mountain" (Hughes)   **2:**1059-60, 1064-65

"Negro Bembón" ("Thick-lipped Nigger") (Guillén)   **2:**916

"The Negro, Communism, Trade Unionism and His (?) Friend" (Garvey)   **2:**874

"The Negro Hero" (Brooks)   **1:**252

The Negro in the American Rebellion: His Heroism and His Fidelity (Brown)   **1:**294, 296-97

"The Negro in the Drawing Room" (Hughes)   **2:**1047-48

"Negro Love Song" (Cotter)   **1:**476

"A Negro Peddler's Song" (Johnson)   **2:**1112

"A Negro Saw the Jewish Pageant, 'We Will Never Die'" (Dodson)   **1:**572

"A Negro Speaks of Rivers" (Hughes)   **2:**1056, 1063

Negro Tales (Cotter)   **1:**479

"The Negro Woman" (Cotter)   **1:**476

"The Negro Writer and His World" (Lamming)   **2:**1235

"Negroes are anti-Semitic because they are anti-White" (Baldwin)   **1:**96

"The Negro's Educational Creed" (Cotter)   **1:**476

"The Negro's Ten Commandments" (Cotter)   **1:**474

"Nelse Hatton's Vengeance" (Dunbar)   **1:**632, 636

"Neo-HooDoo Manifesto" (Reed)   **3:**1625

Never Die Alone (Goines)   **2:**905

"The New Day" (Johnson)   **2:**1112

"New England Winter" (Bullins)   **1:**336

The New Nationalism (Baraka)   **1:**146

"The New Negro in Literature, 1925-1955" (Brown)   **1:**286

A New Song (Hughes)   **2:**1050-51, 1062

"The New Woman" (Guillén)   **2:**912, 920

"The New Woman" (Randall)   **3:**1606

"New World" (Madhubuti)   **2:**1321

"New York" (Senghor)   **3:**1683

The New York Head Shop and Museum (Lorde)   **2:**1282

"Newcomer" (Okigbo)   **3:**1526

"News from Ethiopia and the Sudan" (Clark)   **1:**428

Next (Clifton)   **1:**467

Ngaahika Ndeenda (I Will Marry When I Want) (Ngugi)   **3:**1507

Niaye (Ousmane)   **3:**1533-34

The Nicholas Factor (Myers)   **3:**1473, 1480

"Nigerian Unity/or little niggers killing little niggers" (Madhubuti)   **2:**1315-16

"Nigger" (Sanchez)   **3:**1661

"Nigger Lover" (McKay)   **3:**1395

The Night Blooming Cereus (Hayden)   **2:**988

Night of the Beast (Bullins)   **1:**331-32, 334-35

"Night Rain" (Clark)   **1:**418, 422, 426-28

"Night Song" (Clark)   **1:**421

Nightsong (Williams)   **3:**1934, 1939, 1942-44

"Nightsong: City" (Brutus)   **1:**311-13, 315, 317

"Nightsong: Country" (Brutus)   **1:**310

"Nikki-Rosa" (Giovanni)   **2:**893

Nine Men Who Laughed (Clarke)   **1:**443

"Nineteen Fifty-Five" (Walker)   **3:**1817

19 Necromancers (Reed)   **3:**1611

"Niobe In Distress For Her Children Slain By Apollo" (Wheatley)   **3:**1894

Njamba Nene and the Flying Bus (Ngugi)   **3:**1508

No. 1 with a Bullet (Elder)   **1:**668

"no assistance" (Shange)   **3:**1694

No Hidin Place (Brown)   **1:**287

No Longer at Ease (Achebe)   **1:**3, 5, 10-11

"no more love poems" (Shange)   **3:**1694-95

"No More Marching" (Madhubuti)   **2:**1313

No Name in the Street (Baldwin)   **1:**93-94, 96

"Noah Built the Ark" (Johnson)   **2:**1122, 1124

Nobody Knows My Name: More Notes of a Native Son (Baldwin)   **1:**84-85, 93, 104

"Noche de negros junto a la catedral" (Guillén)   **2:**920

Nocturnes (Senghor)   **3:**1675, 1677, 1683, 1686

"Noh Lickle Twang" (Bennett)   **1:**185-86

La noire de. . . (Ousmane)   **3:**1534

"North" (Walcott)   **3:**1802

"North and South" (McKay)   **3:**1380

"North and South" (Walcott)   **3:**1798

"Nostalgia in Times Square" (Young)   **3:**2044

"Not Sacco and Vanzetti" (Cullen)   **1:**513

Not Without Laughter (Hughes)   **2:**1045-46, 1050, 1055, 1058

"Notes of a Native Son" (Baldwin)   **1:**93, 98

Notes of a Native Son (Baldwin)   **1:**78, 85, 89, 93, 103

"Notes on a Native Son" (Cleaver)   **1:**447

"Nothing and Something" (Harper)   **2:**977, 980

Nothing Personal (Baldwin)   **1:**93

"Noturne at Bethesda" (Bontemps)   **1:**224

"Nouveau sermon nègre" (Roumain)   **3:**1631, 1635, 1645

Nova (Delany)   **1:**530-31, 536-37

"November Cotton Flower"
(Toomer)   3:1759, 1763
"Now" (Walker)   3:1835
"now I love somebody more than"
(Shange)   3:1694
"Nuit de Sine" (Senghor)   3:1674
"Nullo" (Toomer)   3:1763-64
"Nympholepsy" (Braithwaite)   1:243
O Babylon (Walcott)   3:1801
"O Casa da Vara" (Machado de
Assis)   2:1294
"O Espelho" ("The Mirror") (Machado
de Assis)   2:1299
O Pays, mon beau peuple!
(Ousmane)   3:1532
"O, Roots!" (Soyinka)   3:1719, 1721
Oak and Ivy (Dunbar)   1:628, 630
"Obeah Win de War" (Bennett)   1:185
"obituary for a living lady"
(Brooks)   1:261
Obra poética (Guillén)   2:917
"The Occasion for Speaking"
(Lamming)   2:1231
"October Journey" (Walker)   3:1843
October Journey (Walker)   3:1843, 1846
"Ode to Ethiopia" (Dunbar)   1:629
"Ode to Neptune" (Wheatley)   3:1894,
1897, 1901
"Odes" (Senghor)   3:1676
"Odyssey of Big Boy" (Brown)   1:282,
287, 291
Oeuvres choisies (Roumain)   3:1629
Of Age and Innocence
(Lamming)   2:1226-27, 1229-32, 1236
"Of Liberation" (Giovanni)   2:882-83
"Of Love and Dust" (Gaines)   2:843-
46, 849-50, 853
"Of Men and Cities" (Tolson)   3:1740
Of One Blood, or The Hidden Self
(Hopkins)   2:1029-30, 1032
"Of the Coming of John" (Du
Bois)   1:619
"Of the Faith of the Fathers" (Du
Bois)   1:619
"Of the Passing of the First-Born" (Du
Bois)   1:613
"Of the Sorrow Songs" (Du
Bois)   1:613
"Of the Wings of Atalanta" (Du
Bois)   1:613
"Off The Campus: Wits"
(Brutus)   1:312
"Off the New England Coast"
(Braithwaite)   1:246
Ogun Abibimañ (Soyinka)   3:1719-22
"Oh, For a Little While Be Kind"
(Cullen)   1:507
*Oh Pray My Wings are Gonna Fit Me
Well* (Angelou)   1:31
"De Ol' Home" (Johnson)   2:1112
Ol' Man Forest (Ekwensi)   1:645
"Old Abe's Conversation"
(Dunbar)   1:637
"The Old Front Gate" (Dunbar)   1:626
"Old Man Buzzard" (Brown)   1:289
"old marrieds" (Brooks)   1:260
"The Old-Marrieds" (Brooks)   1:253
"The Old Repair Man"
(Johnson)   2:1112
"An Old Time Christmas"
(Dunbar)   1:636
"Old Words" (Sanchez)   3:1663

"Olokun" (Clark)   1:426
"Omega" (Tolson)   3:1747
Omeros (Walcott)   3:1804-06
"On a Name for Black Americans"
(Randall)   3:1597
"On a Saturday afternoon in summer"
(Brutus)   1:312-13, 316
"On Becoming a Catholic"
(McKay)   3:1396
"On Being Asked What It's Like to Be
Black" (Giovanni)   2:883
"On Being Brought from Africa"
(Wheatley)   3:1885, 1887-88, 1893,
1896, 1899
"On Being Female, Black, and Free"
(Walker)   3:1844
"On Getting a Natural (For Gwendolyn
Brooks)" (Randall)   3:1597, 1605
"On Hearing James W. Riley Read
(From a Kentucky Standpoint)"
(Cotter)   1:477
"On Liberty and Peace"
(Wheatley)   3:1889
"On Seeing Diana go Madddddddd"
(Madhubuti)   2:1319
"On the Birth of a Black/Baby/Boy"
(Knight)   2:1216
"On the Birth of Bomani"
(Clifton)   1:465
"On the Death of Rev. Dr. Sewell"
(Wheatley)   3:1896
"On the Death of the Rev. Mr. George
Whitefield" (Wheatley)
    See "An Elegiac Poem, on the Death
    of that Celebrated Divine, and
    eminent Servant of Jesus Christ, the
    late Reverend, and pious George
    Whitefield, Chaplain to the Right
    Honourable the Countess of
    Huntingdon"
"On the Road" (Brutus)   1:312, 313
"On the Road" (Hughes)   2:1048
"On the Way Home" (Hughes)   2:1047,
1049
On These I Stand (Cullen)   1:493, 499,
502
"On Universalism" (Knight)   2:1211
Once (Walker)   3:1816
"one" (Shange)   3:1694
"One Christmas at Shiloh"
(Dunbar)   1:637
"One Friday Morning"
(Hughes)   2:1047
"125th Street and Abomey"
(Lorde)   2:1278
"One Man's Fortune" (Dunbar)   1:628,
630, 636, 641
One Way Ticket (Hughes)   2:1055,
1062
One Way to Heaven (Cullen)   1:488,
511, 513-14
"One Writer's Education"
(Armah)   1:53
"Only a Few Left"
(Madhubuti)   2:1314
"Open Letter" (Dodson)   1:572
Opera Wonyosi (Soyinka)   3:1713-14
"Orage" (Roumain)   3:1642
"The Ordeal at Mt. Hope"
(Dunbar)   1:626, 628, 636
An Ordinary Woman (Clifton)   1:459,
461, 463-65

"The Organizer's Wife"
(Bambara)   1:118
"Orient and Immortal Wheat"
(Walcott)   3:1795
"Others" (Johnson)   2:1111
"Our aims our dreams our destinations"
(Brutus)   1:312, 314
"Our Duty to Dependent Races"
(Harper)   2:983
"Our Greatest Want" (Harper)   2:984
"Our Language Problem"
(Armah)   1:52
"Our Need" (Walker)   3:1842
*Our Nig; or, Sketches from the Life of a
Free Black, in a Two-Story White
House, North. Showing that Slavery's
Shadows Fall Even There*
(Wilson)   3:1976-83
"Out of the Hospital and Under the Bar"
(Ellison)   1:693-94
"Out of the Tower (For Derry for his
Festschrift)" (Clark)   1:426-28
"Outcast" (McKay)   3:1386
"Outside Gethsemane" (Clark)   1:424
The Outside Shot (Myers)   3:1473
The Outsider (Wright)   3:2005, 2008,
2012
The Owl Answers (Kennedy)   2:1154-55,
1157
Oxherding Tale (Johnson)   2:1092-93,
1097
"The Oxygen of Translation"
(Armah)   1:52-53
"Pacific Epitaphs" (Randall)   3:1600,
1604, 1606
"Pagan Prayer" (Cullen)   1:503, 506-07
Pagan Spain (Wright)   3:2005
"Palabras en el trópico"
(Guillén)   2:922
The Palm-Wine Drinkard
(Tutuola)   3:1777-84, 1788-89
La paloma de vuelo popular: Elegiás (*The
Dove of Popular Flight*)
(Guillén)   2:913, 919
The Panther and the Lash
(Hughes)   2:1054, 1062
Pantomime (Walcott)   3:1801-02
"Parades Parades" (Walcott)   3:1801
"the parents: people like our marriage,
Maxie and Andrew" (Brooks)   1:254
"Parting" (Bennett)   1:182
"Parting Hymn" (Forten)   2:814
"The Partners" (Chesnutt)   1:387-88
"The Party" (Dunbar)   1:629
"Pass Fe White" (Bennett)   1:185
"Passage" (Okigbo)   3:1526
Passing (Larsen)   2:1242-45
"Passion is a Fuel" (Clark)   1:426
Passport of Mallam Ilia
(Ekwensi)   1:645, 649
"Past" (Sanchez)   3:1657, 1664
"The Past, Present and Future"
(Tolson)   3:1743
"Patent Leather" (Brooks)   1:254
"Path of Thunder" (Okigbo)   3:1525
Path of Thunder (Okigbo)   3:1528-29
*Patria o muerte! The Great Zoo and
Other Poems by Nicolás Guillén*
(Guillén)
    See *El gran zoo*
"Paul Laurence Dunbar"
(Hayden)   2:991

"Paul's Letter to American Christians" (King)   2:1195

Le Pauvre Christ de Bomba (The Poor Christ of Bomba) (Beti)   1:192-94, 200-01, 203-05

"Payday" (Hughes)   2:1052

Peacock Poems (Williams)   3:1954

Peau noire, masques blancs (Black Skin, White Masks) (Fanon)   2:746-47, 750, 752

"Pedestrian Crosses" (Bennett)   1:182-84

"Peers" (Toomer)   3:1765

"People" (Toomer)   3:1765

People of the City (Ekwensi)   1:645-48, 651, 653-56, 658-59

"People of Unrest" (Walker)   3:1842

"Pequeña oda a un negro boxeador cubano" ("Small Ode to a Cuban Boxer") (Guillén)   2:918

Perpetua and the Habit of Unhappiness (Beti)
   See Perpétue et l'habitude du malheur

Perpétue et l'habitude du malheur (Perpetua and the Habit of Unhappiness) (Beti)   1:201-02

"Perplex" (Bennett)   1:184

"Personal and Sexual Freedom" (Major)   2:1325

"Personal Letter No. 2" (Sanchez)   3:1662

"Personal Letter No. 3" (Sanchez)   3:1662

"Personal Recollections of Whittier" (Forten)   2:815

Personals (Bontemps)   1:223-24

Petals of Blood (Ngugi)   3:1503-11, 1513

Philadelphia Fire (Wideman)   3:1929-31

The Philadelphia Negro (Du Bois)   1:602, 610, 615

Philosopher or Dog? (Machado de Assis)
   See Quincas Borba

"Philosophy" (Dunbar)   1:626

Philosophy and Opinions (Garvey)   2:873

A Photograph: Lovers in Motion (Shange)   3:1697

The Piano Lesson (Wilson)   3:1969-73

The Pig Pen (Bullins)   1:331-34, 336

The Pilgrim of the East (Mofolo)
   See Moeti oa bochabela

Pitseng (Mofolo)   3:1413, 1415, 1417

"Pity the Deep in Love" (Cullen)   1:509

"The Plaint of the Factory Child" (Johnson)   2:1109, 1112

A Play of Giants (Soyinka)   3:1717

"The Playwright and the Colonels" (Clark)   1:422

The Pleasures of Exile (Lamming)   2:1227, 1231, 1235-36

"Pluie" (Roumain)   3:1642

Plum Bun (Fauset)   2:773, 775, 778, 780, 782, 787-88

"Po' Boy Blues" (Hughes)   2:1051, 1065

"Po' Sammy" (Bennett)   1:185

"Po' Sandy" (Chesnutt)   1:379-81, 383-84, 388, 394-95

"Po' Ting" (Bennett)   1:182

"A Poem" (Bell)   1:176

"Poem at Thirty" (Sanchez)   3:1659, 1662-63

Poem Counterpoem (Randall)   3:1594, 1597-98, 1601-03

"A Poem for 3rd World Brothers" (Knight)   2:1215

"Poem for a Poet" (Lorde)   2:1287

"A Poem for a Poet" (Madhubuti)   2:1319

"A Poem for Children with Thoughts on Death" (Hammon)   2:945, 948

A Poem for Farish Street (Walker)   3:1846

"A Poem for My Father" (Sanchez)   3:1658, 1665

"A Poem for Myself" (Knight)   2:1219

"Poem No. 2" (Sanchez)   3:1658

"Poem No. 4" (Sanchez)   3:1663

"Poem (No Name No. 3)" (Giovanni)   2:882

"Poème liminaire" (Senghor)   3:1687

Poems (Harper)   2:977-79, 981-82

Poems (Walcott)   3:1799-1800

Poems 1962 (Clark)   1:418, 422

"Poems for Aretha" (Giovanni)   2:887

Poems from Prison (Knight)   2:1212, 1214-15

Poems on Miscellaneous Subjects (Miscellaneous Poems) (Harper)   2:976-78, 981-82

Poems on Various Subjects (Wheatley)   3:1890-91, 1896, 1899, 1900-01

"The Poet" (Cullen)   1:509

"The Poet" (Randall)   3:1597

"A Poet Is Not a Jukebox" (Randall)   3:1599, 1606

Poetic Equation (Giovanni)   2:894

The Poetic Year for 1916: A Critical Anthology (Braithwaite)   1:245

The Poetical Works of James Madison Bell (Bell)   1:175-77, 179

Poetry for the Advanced (Baraka)   1:147

"The Politics of Rich Painters" (Baraka)   1:126, 144

The Poor Christ of Bomba (Beti)
   See Le Pauvre Christ de Bomba

"Poor Dumb Butch" (Randall)   3:1606

"Poor Gum" (Bennett)   1:185

"Poor Little Black Fellow" (Hughes)   2:1047-48, 1059

Popo and Fifina, Children of Haiti (Bontemps)   1:217

"Popper's Disease" (Johnson)   2:1097

"Portrait in Georgia" (Toomer)   3:1763-64

"Portrait of a Lover" (Cullen)   1:509

"Positives for Sterling Plumpp" (Madhubuti)   2:1321

Posthumos Reminiscences of Braz Cubas (Machado de Assis)
   See Memórias póstumas de Bras Cubas

"Pour Khalam" (Senghor)   3:1683

"Powder-White Faces" (Hughes)   2:1048

"Power" (Lorde)   2:1283, 1286

Powerful Long Ladder (Dodson)   1:563, 568, 571

Praisesong for the Widow (Marshall)   3:1368-69, 1371, 1374

"Prayer for Peace" (Senghor)   3:1683

"Prayers" (Toomer. Jean)   3:1763-64

"The Precedent" (Dodson)   1:572

"Préface à la vie d'une bureaucrate" (Roumain)   3:1637-40, 1642

Preface to a Twenty Volume Suicide Note (Baraka)   1:125, 143, 147

"Prelude" (Johnson)   2:1112

"Prelude" (Walcott)   3:1794

"Prelude to Love–Three Letters" (Cleaver)   1:448

"Present" (Sanchez)   3:1657, 1664

"The Present Age" (Harper)   2:979, 983

The Price of the Ticket: Collected Nonfiction (Baldwin)   1:93-95, 97

"Prière de paix" (Senghor)   3:1687

The Prime Minister (Clarke)   1:434, 436, 438, 442

Primer for Blacks (Brooks)   1:258

The Primitive (Himes)   2:1011-12, 1014

"Primitives" (Randall)   3:1603

Prince (Fuller)   2:838

"Princes and Powers" (Baldwin)   1:103, 105

"The Prisoner" (Nkosi)   3:1517

"Prisoner" (Soyinka)   3:1721

"Problems of Underdevelopment" (Guillén)   2:914

"Professor" (Hughes)   2:1048

"The Profile on the Pillow" (Randall)   3:1596, 1603-04

The Progress of Liberty (Bell)   1:176-77, 179

"The Progress of the Gold Coast Native" (Casely-Hayford)   1:346

La proie et l'ombre (Roumain)   3:1629, 1636-39, 1641-42

"The Promised Land" (Fisher)   2:795, 798, 801-02, 804-05

"The Promoter" (Dunbar)   1:637

"Prophets" (Walker)   3:1837

Prophets for a New Day (Walker)   3:1835, 1837-38, 1843-44, 1846

"Propos sans suite" (Roumain)   3:1638

"Propositions on the Death of Ana" (Guillén)   2:914

"The Proud Heart" (Cullen)   1:504

"Proverbs" (Bennett)   1:185

"Psi" (Tolson)   3:1738, 1747

The Psychic Pretenders (Bullins)   1:341

"Pub Song" (Clark)   1:426

"Puerto Rican Song" (Guillén)   2:913

"Les Pur-Sang" (Césaire)   1:367

"Purgatory" (Soyinka)   3:1721

"Put Your Muzzle Where Your Mouth Is (or shut up)" (Randall)   3:1597

"pyramid" (Shange)   3:1694

The Quality of Hurt (Himes)   2:1006, 1013-14

"Quand bat le tam-tam" ("When the Tom-Tom Beats") (Roumain)   3:1629, 1644

"Qué color" (Guillén)   2:917, 920

"Que m'accompagnent Kôras et Balafong" ("Let Koras and Balafong Accompany Me") (Senghor)   3:1683, 1685-87

"Que tue es grossier!" (Brooks)   1:267

A Question of Power (Head)   2:996-1000, 1002

Quicksand (Larsen)   2:1241-42, 1245-47

Title Index

Quincas Borba (Philosopher or Dog?; The Heritage of Quincas Borba) (Machado de Assis)   2:1292, 1298
"The Race Question" (Dunbar)   1:637
"The Race Welcomes Dr. W. E. B. Du Bois as Its Leader" (Cotter)   1:476
The Radiance of the King (Laye)
   See *Le Regard du roi*
The Raft (Clark)   1:415, 417, 419
A Rage in Harlem (Himes)
   See *For Love of Imabelle*
"The Ragged Stocking" (Harper)   2:980
"Rain" (Davis)   1:524
Raise, Race, Rays, Raze: Essays since 1965 (Baraka)   1:142, 147
A Raisin in the Sun (Hansberry)   2:952-53, 955, 957-60, 963-70, 973
A Rat's Moss (Kennedy)   2:1157, 1161
"Raymond's Run" (Bambara)   1:109
"Re-Act for Action" (Madhubuti)   2:1312
The Real Cool Killers (Himes)   2:1017-20
"The Real Me" (Bullins)   1:327
"Really, Doesn't Crime Pay" (Walker)   3:1815
"Reapers" (Toomer)   3:1759, 1763
"Rebirth" (Sanchez)   3:1664
Reckless Eyeballing (Reed)   3:1624
"Recollection" (Wheatley)   3:1885, 1887
"Records" (Giovanni)   2:893
Re:Creation (Giovanni)   2:887, 889, 895, 898
"The Red Girl" (Kincaid)   2.1172
"Red-Headed Baby" (Hughes)   2:1047, 1049
"Red Silk Stockings" (Hughes)   2:1065
A Reed in the Tide (Clark)   1:422
"Reena" (Marshall)   3:1366, 1371
Reena, and Other Stories (Marshall)   3:1370-71
"The Refiner's Gold" (Harper)   2:979
"Reflections of an Earth-Being" (Toomer)   3:1767
"Reflections on My Profession" (Giovanni)   2:898
Reflex and Bone Structure (Major)   2:1325, 1327-28, 1330-31
Le Regard du roi (The Radiance of the King) (Laye)   2:1252-57
"The Reign of the Crocodiles" (Clark)   1:421
"Relief" (Soyinka)   3:1720
Religion of the Central Luo (p'Bitek)   3:1562
Reliquas de casa velha (Machado de Assis)   2:1294
The Reluctant Rapist (Bullins)   1:328, 336, 340
Remember Ruben (Beti)   1:201-03
"Remembering Richard Wright" (Ellison)   1:701
Remembrance (Walcott)   3:1801
"Rendezvous with America" (Tolson)   3:1740
Rendezvous with America (Tolson)   3:1739-42, 1744-46
"Renewal of Strength" (Harper)   2:979
"Répliques au Révérrend Père Foiset" (Roumain)   3:1640

"Reply" (Wheatley)   3:1900
Report from Part One (Brooks)   1:252
"Requiescam" (Cullen)   1:504
Ressurreição (Resurrection) (Machado de Assis)   2:1294, 1296-97
Resurrection (Machado de Assis)
   See *Ressurreição*
"The Resurrection of Jesus" (Harper)   2:979
"Le retour de l'enfant prodigue" ("The Return of the Prodigal Son") (Senghor)   3:1681, 1686
"Retribution" (Harper)   2:980, 983
"Return" (Bontemps)   1:224
"Return Home" (Clark)   1:421
"The Return of the Prodigal Son" (Senghor)
   See "Le retour de l'enfant prodigue"
"Return to D'Ennery: Rain" (Walcott)   3:1795
Return to My Native Land (Césaire)
   See *Cahier d'un retour au pays natal*
Reuben (Wideman)   3:1923-24, 1928
"The Reunion" (Dodson)   1:571
"The Revenge of Hannah Kemhuff" (Walker)   3:1818
"Revolutionary Dreams" (Giovanni)   2:887
"Revolutionary Music" (Giovanni)   2:886
Revolutionary Petunias (Walker)   3:1814
"Revolutionary Tale" (Giovanni)   2:884
"The Revolutionary Theatre" (Baraka)   1:145
Reward (Mqhayi)
   See *I-nzuzo*
"Rho" (Tolson)   3:1737, 1747
"Rhobert" (Toomer)   3:1752
"Rhythm and Blues" (Baraka)   1:125-26
The Rhythm of Violence (Nkosi)   3:1517
Richard Wright: A Daemonic Genius (Walker)   3:1845
"Riddles" (Guillén)   2:913
"Riders to the Blood-red Wrath" (Brooks)   1:253, 266
"Ringtail" (Fisher)   2:794, 797-98, 802-04, 806
"Riot" (Brooks)   1:256
Riot (Brooks)   1:256, 261, 264, 266-67
"The Rising of the Storm" (Dunbar)   1:629
The Rising Son; or, The Antecedents and Advancements of the Colored Race (Brown)   1:294, 296-97
A Rising Wind (White)   3:1908
"The Rite" (Randall)   3:1595
"The Rites for Cousin Vit" (Brooks)   1:255
The River Between (Ngugi)   3P:1497-99, 1500, 1503, 1507, 1509
River George (Lee)   2:1273
"Riverbank Blues" (Brown)   1:287
"Rizpah, the Daughter of Ai" (Harper)   2:980
The Road (Soyinka)   3:1705, 1709-10, 1712-13
"Roas Turkey" (Bennett)   1:184
"A Rock Thrown into the Water Does Not Fear the Cold" (Lorde)   2:1288
"Rodney" (Cotter)   1:475

Le roi miraculé: Chronique des Essazam (King Lazarus; Lazarus: A Novel) (Beti)   1:192-94, 200
Roots (Haley)   2:929-35, 938-39, 941
Rope and Faggot: A Biography of Judge Lynch (White)   3:1907, 1909
"The Rose Bush" (Giovanni)   2:894
"Roselily" (Walker)   3:1818
"Roses and Revolutions" (Randall)   3:1595, 1602
"The rosy aureole of your affection" (Brutus)   1:310, 314
"Royal ebony" (Guillén)
   See "Ebano real"
La rueda dentada (The Serrated Wheel) (Guillén)   2:914, 920
"The Rugged Way" (Dunbar)   1:626
La ruine presque cocasse d'un polichinelle: Remember Ruben deux (Lament for an African Pol) (Beti)   1:202
"Ruins of a Great House" (Walcott)   3:1800
"Rulers" (Johnson)   2:1112-13
"Rumba" (Guillén)   2:918
"Ruminations of Luke Johnson" (Brown)   1:284
Run Man Run (Himes)   2:1009
Runner Mack (Beckham)   1:154-56, 158-62, 164, 166-70
Russian Journal (Lee)   2:1262-65
"Ruth and Naomi" (Harper)   2:980
S-1 (Baraka)   1:140
"S-Trinity of Parnassus" (Tolson)   3:1738
"Sabás" (Guillén)   2:913, 916
Sabotage (Baraka)   1:144, 147
"Sacrament" (Cullen)   1:508
Sacred Cows and Other Edibles (Giovanni)   2:898-99
"Sadie and Maude" (Brooks)   1:261
"Sailor Ashore" (Hughes)   2:1048
St. Domingo: Its Revolutions and Its Patriots (Brown)   1:294-95, 297
"Saint Joey" (Demby)   1:552
"St. Peter Relates an Incident of the Ressurection Day" (Johnson)   2:1121, 1124
St. Peter Relates an Incident: Selected Poems (Johnson)   2:1121
Une saison au Congo (A Season in the Congo) (Césaire)   1:360, 362, 363, 372
"Sales nègres" ("Dirty Negroes") (Roumain)   3:1631, 1636, 1645
Sally (Fuller)   2:838
"Salsa" (Walcott)   3:1804
The Salt Eaters (Bambara)   1:110, 113, 117-19
"Sam Smiley" (Brown)   283, 289-90
The Sanctified Church (Hurston)   2:1082
"Sanctuary" (Larsen)   2:1245
"Sanctuary" (Randall)   3:1604
"Sandy Star and Willie" (Braithwaite)   1:243, 245-46
Sarah Phillips (Lee)   2:1265-67
Sardines (Farah)   2:758, 761-63, 765-67
Sassafrass, Cypress & Indiago (Shange)   3:1691, 1696
"Saturday's Child" (Cullen)   1:487, 506
Savage Holiday (Wright)   3:2005, 2008, 2011

"Saved by Faith" (Harper) 2:979
"Saved from the Dogs"
 (Hughes) 2:1047
"The Scapegoat" (Dunbar) 1:637
"The Scarlet Woman"
 (Johnson) 2:1109, 1111-13
"The Schooner Flight"
 (Walcott) 3:1797-99, 1801-02
"Schwalliger's Philosophy"
 (Dunbar) 1:637
Scorpions (Myers) 3:1478
"Scottsboro, Too, Is Worth Its Song (a
 poem to American poets)"
 (Cullen) 1:504, 513
*The Sea Birds Are Still Alive: Collected
 Stories* (Bambara) 1:109-10, 117-118
"A Sea-Chantey" (Walcott) 3:1799
Sea Grapes (Walcott) 3:1801
Sea Island Song (Childress) 1:412
"Season" (Soyinka) 3:1706
"Season at Omens" (Clark) 1:421
A Season in the Congo (Césaire)
 See *Une saison au Congo*
Season of Adventure
 (Lamming) 2:1227, 1231-32, 1237
"The Season of Phantasmal Peace"
 (Walcott) 3:1797-98
"sechita" (Shange) 3:1694
Second Class Citizen (Emecheta) 2:709-
 10, 712-18
"The Second Sermon on the Warpland"
 (Brooks) 1:253
"A Secret Ally" (Chesnutt) 1:388
"The Secret Cause" (Machado de Assis)
 See "A Causa Secreta"
"Secuestro de la mujer de Antonio"
 (Guillén) 2:918
"Seduction" (Giovanni) 2:887-88, 896-
 97
Seduction by Light (Young) 3:2036,
 2045-47
"Seed" (Soyinka) 3:1720
"Seeking a Job" (Bennett) 1:185
*Selected Plays and Prose of Amiri
 Baraka/LeRoi Jones* (Baraka) 1:145
Selected Poems (Bennett) 1:186
Selected Poems (Brooks) 1:255-56, 264
Selected Poems (McKay) 3:1380-81,
 1397
Selected Poems (Walcott) 3:1795
"Self Criticism" (Cullen) 1:504, 511
"The Self Hatred of Don L. Lee"
 (Madhubuti) 2:1310-11
"Self-Interview" (Reed) 3:1624
Sent for You Yesterday
 (Wideman) 3:1920-21, 1923-24,
 1926-27, 1929
"Sequel to the Pied Piper of Hamelin"
 (Cotter) 1:472, 477
"Sequelae" (Lorde) 2:1283
"Sequences" (Sanchez) 3:1663
Seraph on the Suwanee
 (Hurston) 2:1077-78
Serowe: Village of the Rain Wind
 (Head) 2:1002
The Serrated Wheel (Guillén)
 See *La rueda dentada*
"Seventh Street" (Toomer) 3:1759
Shadow and Act (Ellison) 1:691, 700,
 702
Shaft (Elder) 1:668
Shaft (Parks) 3:1557

Shaft's Big Score (Parks) 3:1557
Shakespeare in Harlem
 (Hughes) 2:1051-53, 1062, 1066
"A Shakespearean Sonnet: To a Woman
 Liberationist" (Knight) 2:1218
"Shape of the Invisible"
 (Randall) 3:1604
"The Sheriff's Children"
 (Chesnutt) 1:387-88
"Shoot-out in Oakland"
 (Cleaver) 1:453
"Short Poem" (Sanchez) 3:1661
"Shout, My Brother, Shout"
 (Johnson) 2:1106
"The Shroud of Color" (Cullen) 1:486-
 87, 498, 501, 503-05
Shrovetide in Old New Orleans
 (Reed) 3:1624
A Shuttle in the Crypt
 (Soyinka) 3:1719-22
"Sigma" (Tolson) 3:1737
The Sign in Sidney Brustein's Window
 (Hansberry) 2:956-59, 965
"The Signifying Darkness"
 (Dodson) 1:568
"Signing the Pledge" (Harper) 2:980
"Signs of the Times" (Dunbar) 1:629
"Silas Jackson" (Dunbar) 1:630, 636
"Silences" (Okigbo) 3:1525
"Silent Samuel" (Dunbar) 1:637
Simbi and the Satyr of the Dark Jungle
 (Tutuola) 3:1779, 1782, 1788
"Simon the Cyrenian Speaks"
 (Cullen) 1:499, 501, 508
*A Simple Lust: Selected Poems Including
 'Sirens, Knuckles, Boots,' 'Letters to
 Martha,' Poems from Algiers,' 'Thoughts
 Abroad'* (Brutus) 1:315-17, 319
Simple Speaks His Mind
 (Hughes) 2:1041
Simple Takes a Wife (Hughes) 2:1041
"The Simple Truth" (Cullen) 1:511
Simply Heavenly (Hughes) 2:1044-45
"Since 1619" (Walker) 3:1835, 1842-
 43
*Singin' and Swingin' and Gettin' Merry
 Like Christmas* (Angelou) 1:28, 30
"Siren Limits" (Okigbo) 3:1527-28
Sirens, Knuckles, Boots (Brutus) 1:308,
 315, 317
"Sis' Becky's Pickaninny"
 (Chesnutt) 1:380, 383, 385-86, 388,
 395
Sissie (Williams) 3:1938-40, 1942-46,
 1949
"Sister Lou" (Brown) 1:287
Sister Son/ji (Sanchez) 3:1653, 1666
"Sit-Ins" (Walker) 3:1835-36
Sitting Pretty (Young) 3:2033, 2036,
 2039, 2045-46
"The Six" (Randall) 3:1606
"Six-Bit Blues" (Hughes) 2:1053
Sketches of Southern Life
 (Harper) 2:977-83
"The Sky is Gray" (Gaines) 2:846,
 856
The Slave (Baraka) 1:125-26, 128-30,
 137, 139-40, 145
"The Slave (For a Bass Viol)"
 (Davis) 1:517, 521
"The Slave Auction" (Harper) 2:980,
 982

The Slave Girl (Emecheta) 2:709-12,
 718
"The Slave-Girl's Prayer"
 (Forten) 2:814, 817
"The Slave Mother" (Harper) 2:978,
 982
"Slave on the Block" (Hughes) 2:1047-
 48, 1059
Slave Ship: A Historical Pageant
 (Baraka) 1:140, 145
"The Sleeper Wakes" (Fauset) 2:784-
 85, 787
"Slim Greer" (Brown) 1:283, 290
"Slim in Atlanta" (Brown) 1:289
"Small Comment" (Sanchez) 3:1661
"Small Ode to a Cuban Boxer" (Guillén)
 See "Pequeña oda a un negro
 boxeador cubano"
A Small Place (Kincaid) 2:1172
"The Smell" (Clarke) 1:443
"Snake Eyes" (Baraka) 1:125
Snakes (Young) 3:2034, 2036-37, 2039,
 2045-46
"The Snow Fairy" (McKay) 3:1396-97
"So, for the moment, Sweet, is peace"
 (Brutus) 1:311
Social Welfare (Myers) 3:1478
"Soldiers in Abyssinia" (Guillén) 2:913
A Soldier's Play (Fuller) 2:826-27, 829-
 32, 834, 837
"Solitary" (Wideman) 3:1919, 1923
"Solja Work" (Bennett) 1:185
"somebody almost walked off wid alla
 my stuff" (Shange) 3:1695
"Someday We're Gonna Tear Them
 Pillars Down" (Dodson) 1:569-70
"Somehow we survive" (Brutus) 1:310
Something in Common
 (Hughes) 2:1048-49
"Something to Be Said for Silence"
 (Giovanni) 2:893
A Son, Come Home (Bullins) 1:331,
 333, 335-36, 341
El son entero (The Entire Son)
 (Guillén) 2:913, 917, 919, 924
"Son No.6" (Guillén)
 See "Son número 6"
"Son número 6" ("Son No.6")
 (Guillén) 2:917
"Son venezolano" (Guillén) 2:919
"Song" (Clark) 1:425-26, 428
"Song for Myself" (Tolson) 3:1740,
 1745
"Song for the First of August"
 (Bell) 1:179
"Song in Spite of Myself"
 (Cullen) 1:504
Song of a Goat (Clark) 1:415-17, 419
Song of Lawino (p'Bitek) 3:1560-63,
 1565-74, 1576-77
"A Song of Living"
 (Braithwaite) 1:243
Song of Malaya (p'Bitek) 3:1562,
 1567, 1574, 1576, 1578
Song of Ocol (p'Bitek) 3:1561-62,
 1565-66, 1568, 1570-72, 1576
"Song of Praise" (Cullen) 1:486, 496-
 97, 500
Song of Prisoner (p'Bitek) 3:1562,
 1566-68, 1571-74, 1576-78
Song of Solomon (Morrison) 3:1427-28,
 1432, 1434, 1436-37, 1439

"Song of the Forest" (Okigbo)   3:1525
"Song of the Son" (Toomer)   3:1759,
1763-64
"A Song of the Soul of Central"
(Hughes)   2:1063
"Song, Skulls and Cups" (Clark)   1:421
The Song Turning Back Into Itself
(Young)   3:2044
Sóngoro consongo: Poemas mulatos
(Guillén)   2:912, 915-16, 918, 922,
924
Songs for Naëtt (Senghor)
See Chants pour Naëtt
Songs for Soldiers and Sones for Tourists
(Guillén)
See Cantos para soldados y sones para
turistas
Songs for Soldiers and Tunes for Tourists
(Guillén)
See Cantos para soldados y sones para
turistas
"Songs for the People" (Harper)   2:979,
981
Songs of Jamaica (McKay)   3:1381-83,
1388, 1393, 1396
Songs of Joy and Lullabies (Mqhayi)
See Imihobe nemibongo
"The Songs of Reba Love Jackson"
(Wideman)   3:1918
Songs of the Soil (Johnson)   2:1106,
1108, 1110, 1112-13
"Sonnet: Some for a Little While Do
Love" (Cullen)   1:512
Sons of Darkness, Sons of Light
(Williams)   3:1939, 1941-43, 1948
Soon One Morning (Dodson)   1:564
"The Sorcerer's Apprentice"
(Johnson)   2:1098
The Sorcerer's Apprentice
(Johnson)   2:1097-98
"Sorrow Home" (Walker)   3:1840,
1842, 1850
"Sorrow Is The Only Faithful One"
(Dodson)   1:568, 570
"Sort of Preface" (Bambara)   1:113
"SOS" (Baraka)   1:148
Soul Clap Hands and Sing
(Marshall)   3:1365-66, 1369-70
Soul Gone Home (Hughes)   2:1044
Soul on Fire (Cleaver)   1:456
Soul on Ice (Cleaver)   1:446-48, 452-53,
455-56
"A Soulless Corporation"
(Chesnutt)   1:388
Souls of Black Folk (Du Bois)   1:599-
602, 610, 613, 615-19
Sounder (Elder)   1:667-68
"The sounds begin again"
(Brutus)   1:311, 315, 317
"South" (Walcott)   3:1802
"The South in Literature"
(Toomer)   3:1758
"The South Lingers On" ("Vestiges")
(Fisher)   2:792, 797-98, 801-02
"South Parade Pedlar" (Bennett)   1:182
South Street (Bradley)   1:227-28, 232,
234
"South: The Name of Home"
(Walker)   3:1816
"Southeast corner" (Brooks)   1:254
"Southern Cop" (Brown)   1:289
"Southern Mansion" (Bontemps)   1:224

"Southern Road" (Brown)   1:282, 289-
90
Southern Road (Brown)   1:283, 285-89
"The Southern Road" (Randall)   3:1602
"Southern Song" (Walker)   3:1840,
1842, 1850
"Space" (Soyinka)   3:1720
Spain: A Poem in Four Anguishes and a
Hope (Guillén)
See España: Poema en cuatro
angustias y una esperanza
"The Spanish Needle"
(McKay)   3:1396, 1398
"The Sparrow's Fall" (Harper)   2:979,
982
Speak Now (Yerby)   3:2030
"Speakin o' Christmas"
(Dunbar)   1:626
spell #7 (Shange)   3:1696-97, 1699-
1700, 1702
"The Spellin' Bee" (Dunbar)   1:626,
629
"Spiritual View of Lena Horne"
(Giovanni)   2:883
"The Spoiler's Return"
(Walcott)   3:1802
"The Spoiler's Revenge"
(Walcott)   3:1798
"Sport" (Hughes)   2:1065
The Sport of the Gods (Dunbar)   1:628,
630-31, 634-36, 639-40
"Sporting Beasley" (Brown)   1:282-83
"Sports" (Guillén)   2:919
"Spring in New Hampshire"
(McKay)   3:1396-97
Spring in New Hampshire
(McKay)   3:1386, 1397
"Spring Reminiscence" (Cullen)   1:508
"Spunk" (Hurston)   2:1070-71
"The Stanton Coachman"
(Dunbar)   1:637
"The Star-Apple Kingdom"
(Walcott)   3:1797
The Star-Apple Kingdom
(Walcott)   3:1801, 1803
State of the Union (Clark)   1:422, 428
"Statement on Aesthetics, Poetics,
Kinetics" (Young)   3:2046
"Steam Song" (Brooks)   1:267; 1:265,
267
"Still a Song Shall Rise"
(Clark)   1:422-23
"Storm Ending" (Toomer)   3:1762
Storm of Fortune (Clarke)   1:438-41
"Stormy" (Young)   3:2045
"Story Books on a Kitchen Table"
(Lorde)   2:1288
The Story of a Strong Man
(Achebe)   1:7
The Story of My Life and Work
(Washington)   3:1868-69, 1871
"Straight Talk from a Patriot"
(Randall)   3:1606
"The Strange Burial of Sue"
(McKay)   3:1395
"Strange Legacies" (Brown)   1:289
A Stranger from Lagos (Ekwensi)   1:645
"Stranger in the Village"
(Baldwin)   1:93, 103
"Streamside Exchange" (Clark)   1:418
"Street Boy" (Bennett)   1:182, 185

A Street in Bronzeville (Brooks)   1:250,
252-54, 259-61, 264
Street Players (Goines)   2:901, 903, 905
"The Strength of Gideon"
(Dunbar)   1:630, 638-39
The Strength of Gideon
(Dunbar)   1:627-28, 632, 634, 636
Stride Toward Freedom: The Montgomery
Story (King)   2:1184, 1186
The Strong Breed (Soyinka)   3:1713
"Strong Men, Riding Horses"
(Brooks)   1:250
"A Strong New Voice Pointing the Way"
(Madhubuti)   2:1321
"Stryker's Waterloo" (Chesnutt)   1:388
"Stubborn Hope" (Brutus)   1:319
Stubborn Hope: New Poems and Selections
from 'China Poems' and 'Strains'
(Brutus)   1:316, 319
"A Sudden Trip Home in the Spring"
(Walker)   3:1811, 1815
"Sudor y látigo" ("Sweat and the Whip";
"Sweat and the Lash")
(Guillén)   2:913, 917, 919
"Sugarcane" (Guillén)   2:912
"Suicide" (Hughes)   2:1052
"Suicide Chant" (Cullen)   1:504
"The Suitcase" (Mphahlele)   3:1451,
1453
Sula (Morrison)   3:1427-28, 1430-31
"Summary" (Sanchez)   3:1660-61, 1663,
1666
"Summer Words of a Sistuh Addict"
(Sanchez)   3:1663
"Sunday" (Hughes)   2:1052
"The Sundays of Satin-Legs Smith"
(Brooks)   1:250-51, 253-54
The Supercops (Parks)   3:1557
"Superstitions and Folk-Lore of the
South" (Chesnutt)   1:390
"A Supper by Proxy" (Dunbar)   1:637,
640
"Supper Time" (Hughes)   2:1052
The Suppression of the African Slave
Trade (Du Bois)   1:602, 610
"Sur le chemin de Guinée"
(Roumain)   3:1631, 1644
"The surname" (Guillén)
See "El apellido"
Survive the Peace (Ekwensi)   1:658-59
"The Survivor" (Bambara)   1:117, 119
The Survivors of the Crossing
(Clarke)   1:431-33, 438
Swallow the Lake (Major)   2:1325
The Swamp Dwellers (Soyinka)   3:1710
Swamp Man (Goines)   2:901, 903, 905
"The Sway-Backed House"
(Chesnutt)   1:388
"Sweat" (Hurston)   2:1070-72
"Sweat and the Lash" (Guillén)
See "Sudor y látigo"
"Sweat and the Whip" (Guillén)
See "Sudor y látigo"
Sweet and Sour Milk (Farah)   2:758-59,
761-63, 765-67
The Sweet Flypaper of Life
(Hughes)   2:1046
Sweet Illusions (Myers)   3:1480
Symptoms and Madness
(Major)   2:1325
The Syncopated Cake Walk
(Major)   2:1325-26

The System of Dante's Hell
  (Baraka)   1:124-26, 136, 141, 145
"Tableau" (Cullen)   1:505, 512
"Tain't So" (Hughes)   2:1047
"takin a solo/ a poetic possibility/ a
  poetic imperative" (Shange)   3:1696
The Taking of Miss Janie
  (Bullins)   1:329-31
Tales (Baraka)   1:136, 142, 145
Tales and Stories for Black Folk
  (Bambara)   1:109
Tales of Darkest America
  (Johnson)   2:1108, 1112-13
"Tales of the Islands"
  (Walcott)   3:1795-96, 1799, 1802
"Talking in the Woods with Karl
  Amorelli" (Knight)   2:1216
"talking to my grandmother who died
  poor (while hearing Richard Nixon
  declare 'I am not a crook')"
  (Walker)   3:1816
Tambourines to Glory (Hughes)   2:1044-
  45, 1055
"Tapestries of Time" (Tolson)   3:1740,
  1745
Tar Baby (Morrison)   3:1424-29, 1433-
  34
Target Study (Baraka)   1:144, 147
Tasks and Masks (Nkosi)   3:1516-17,
  1521
"Tau" (Tolson)   3:1737
Tauw (Ousmane)   3:1535
"Telephone Conversation"
  (Soyinka)   3:1708, 1721
"Television" (Bennett)   1:182
"Tell Me" (Toomer)   3:1764
Tell Me How Long the Train's Been Gone
  (Baldwin)   1:85-86, 88, 90-91, 105
Tell My Horse (*Voodoo Gods: An Inquiry
  into Native Myths and Magic in
  Jamaica and Haiti*)
  (Hurston)   2:1074, 1082
"Telling Fortunes" (Brown)   1:289
*A Tempest: After 'The Tempest' by
  Shakespeare, Adaptation for the Negro
  Theatre* (Césaire)
    See *Une tempête: d'après 'La tempête'
    de Shakespeare, Adaptation pour un
    théâtre nègre*
*Une tempête: d'après 'La tempête' de
  Shakespeare, Adaptation pour un théâtre
  nègre* (*A Tempest: After 'The Tempest'
  by Shakespeare, Adaptation for the
  Negro Theatre*) (Césaire)   1:360, 362
The Temple of My Familiar
  (Walker)   3:1827
"The Temptation of Modernity"
  (Powell)   3:1586
"A Tender Man" (Bambara)   1:110,
  118
Tengo (*All is mine*) (Guillén)   2:914,
  919, 922
"The Tennessee Hero" (Harper)   2:979,
  982
The Terrible Threes (Reed)   3:1624
The Terrible Twos (Reed)   3:1624
"That Blessed Hope" (Harper)   2:979
"That Bright Chimeric Beast"
  (Cullen)   1:510
"That Star" (Dodson)   1:571

*The Anti-Slavery Harp: A Collection of
  Songs for Anti-Slavery Meetings*
  (Brown)   1:303
"Theater" (Toomer)   3:1752, 1756,
  1760, 1763
"Their Behaviour" (Brutus)   1:318
Their Eyes Were Watching God
  (Hurston)   2:1073, 1075, 1077-88
"there" (Clifton)   1:467
"There Are Blk/Puritans"
  (Sanchez)   3:1656
There is Confusion (Fauset)   2:773-75,
  780, 786-87
"These Are My People"
  (Johnson)   2:1108
"These Bad New Negroes: A Critique on
  Critics" (Hughes)   2:1066
"They Are Not Missed"
  (Toomer)   3:1766
"They Are Not Ready"
  (Madhubuti)   2:1312
"They have outposts" (Baraka)   1:148
"Thick-lipped Nigger" (Guillén)
    See "Negro Bembón"
Thickening the Plot (Delany)   1:529
Things Ain't What They Used to Be
  (Young)   3:2044-45
Things Fall Apart (Achebe)   1:3-11, 13
Think Black! (Madhubuti)   2:1310-12,
  1314, 1316, 1320
The Third Generation (Himes)   2:1011
The Third Life of Grange Copeland
  (Walker)   3:1812, 1815, 1817, 1824
"The Third World Hoax"
  (Armah)   1:53
This Is My Century (Walker)   3:1846
This Is My Country Too
  (Williams)   3:1942, 1948
"A Thorn Forever in the Breast"
  (Cullen)   1:511
Those Who Ride the Night Winds
  (Giovanni)   2:894
"Those Winter Sundays"
  (Hayden)   2:990
"Thoughts on His Excellency Major
  General Lee" (Wheatley)   3:1884-85
"Thoughts on the African Novel"
  (Achebe)   1:14
"Thoughts on the Works of Providence"
  (Wheatley)   3:1881, 1887, 1889, 1897
"Three Men" (Gaines)   2:846, 856
*Three Years in Europe; or, Places I Have
  Seen and People I Have Met* (*The
  American Fugitive in Europe: Sketches
  of Places and People Abroad*)
  (Brown)   1:294-95, 297, 305
"Threnody for a Brown Girl"
  (Cullen)   1:509
Ti-Jean and his Brothers
  (Walcott)   3:1800
Tides of Lust (Delany)   1:531
"Timber Merchant" (Ekwensi)   1:657
The Timeless People (Marshall)   3:1365,
  1368, 1371-73
"Timid Lover" (Cullen)   1:509
"Tin Roof Blues" (Brown)   1:287
"Tired" (Johnson)   2:1108-09, 1111-13
"To a Brown Boy" (Cullen)   1:506
"To a Brown Girl" (Cullen)   1:486,
  506
"To a Gentleman in the Navy"
  (Wheatley)   3:1900

"To a Jealous Cat" (Sanchez)   3:1661
"To a Lady on Her Remarkable
  Preservation in an Hurricane in North
  Carolina" (Wheatley)   3:1894
"To A Learned Lady" (Clark)   1:424,
  426
"To a Man" (Angelou)   1:32-33
"To a Winter Squirrel" (Brooks)   1:256
"To a Young Girl Leaving the Hill
  Country" (Bontemps)   1:224
"To All Sisters" (Sanchez)   3:1666
"To America" (Johnson)   2:1135
"To an Old Man" (Randall)   3:1606
"To an Unknown Poet" (Cullen)   1:511
"To Be in Love" (Brooks)   1:256-57
"To Be Quicker" (Madhubuti)   2:1321
To Be Young, Gifted and Black
  (Hansberry)   2:957
"To Blk/Record/Buyers"
  (Sanchez)   3:1655
"To Certain Critics" (Cullen)   1:504,
  512
"To Chuck" (Sanchez)   3:1662
"To Da-duh, In Memoriam"
  (Marshall)   3:1371
"To Dante Gabriel Rossetti"
  (Braithwaite)   1:244
"To Deism" (Wheatley)   3:1893
To Disembark (Brooks)   1:258
"To Don at Salaam" (Brooks)   1:258
"To Endymion" (Cullen)   1:509
"To France" (Cullen)   1:511-12
"To Gurdjieff Dying"
  (Toomer)   3:1766-67
"To Hell with Dying" (Walker)   3:1826
"To His Excellency General Washington"
  (Wheatley)   3:1883, 1889
"To John Keats, the Poet at Spring
  Time" (Cullen)   1:493, 508
"To Kentucky" (Cotter)   1:478
"To Keorapetse Kgositsile (Willie)"
  (Brooks)   1:258
"To Lovers of Earth: Fair Warning"
  (Cullen)   1:509
"To Maecenas" (Wheatley)   3:1894,
  1899-1900
"To Ms. Ann" (Clifton)   1:461
"To My Daughter the Junkie on a Train"
  (Lorde)   2:1278
"To One Not There" (Cullen)   1:512
"To One Who Said Me Nay"
  (Cullen)   1:507
To Raise, Destroy and Create
  (Baraka)   1:145
"To S. M., A Young African Painter, on
  Seeing His Works"
  (Wheatley)   3:1897
To Smile in Autumn (Parks)   3:1555-56
"To the Diaspora" (Brooks)   1:258
"To the Memory of Joseph S. Cotter,
  Jr." (Cotter)   1:477
"To the Mercy Killers"
  (Randall)   3:1598, 1605
"To the New South" (Dunbar)   1:639
"To the Rev. Mr. Pitkin on The Death
  of His Lady" (Wheatley)   3:1884
"To the Right Honorable William, Earl
  of Dartmouth" (Wheatley)   3:1883,
  1887, 1889, 1892, 1898
"To the Three for Whom the Book"
  (Cullen)   1:510

"To the Union Savers of Cleveland" (Harper) 2:980
"To the University of Cambridge, in New England" (Wheatley) 3:1883, 1885, 1888, 1892, 1896, 1900
"To the White Fiends" (McKay) 3:1385, 1389
"To Those Who Sing America" (Davis) 1:521
"To You" (Davis) 1:524
"To You Who Read My Book" (Cullen) 1:505, 508
"Today" (Walker) 3:1842
The Toilet (Baraka) 1:126-27, 129, 139, 145-46
"Tommy" (Wideman) 3:1923, 1926
"Tomorrow, Tomorrow" (Walcott) 3:1804
"Tongue-tied" (Cullen) 1:511
"Tonton-Macoute" (Guillén) 2:914
"Tornado Blues" (Brown) 1:290
"Touris" (Bennett) 1:182
"toussaint" (Shange) 3:1694
La Tragédie du roi Christophe (*The Tragedy of King Christophe*) (Césaire) 1:360-61, 364, 370-72
"The Tragedy at Three Corners" (Dunbar) 1:628
The Tragedy of King Christophe (Césaire)
  See *La Tragédie du roi Christophe*
"The Tragedy of Pete" (Cotter) 1:477
"The Tragedy of Three Forks" (Dunbar) 1:637, 639
Transatlantic (Toomer. Jean) 3:1758
"Translation from Chopin" (Randall) 3:1606
"Travel from Home" (Bullins) 1:336
The Traveller to the East (Mofolo)
  See *Moeti oa bochabela*
The Treasure of Pleasant Valley (Yerby) 3:2026
The Trial of Dedan Kimathi (Ngugi) 3:1507, 1509
"The Trial Sermon on Bull-Skin" (Dunbar) 1:632, 636, 641
The Trials of Brother Jero (Soyinka) 3:1710, 1712
Tribal Scars (Ousmane)
  See *Voltaïque*
Triton (Delany) 1:528, 537
Triumph of Liberty (Bell) 1:175-78
"Triumphs of the Free" (Bell) 1:177
"The Tropics in New York" (McKay) 3:1396, 1398
"The Trouble about Sophiny" (Dunbar) 1:637
Trouble in Mind (Childress) 1:404, 406-07
"The Trouble with Intellectuals" (Randall) 3:1597, 1605
"Trouble with the Angels" (Hughes) 2:1048
"The Trousers" (Dunbar) 1:637
"Truant" (McKay) 3:1394-95
"The True Import of Present Dialogue, Black vs. Negro" (Giovanni) 2:882, 885, 889, 893, 895-96
"The True Negro" (Cotter) 1:476
"The Trustfulness of Polly" (Dunbar) 1:630, 636
"Truth" (Harper) 2:979
"Truth" (McKay) 3:1388

The Truth About the West African Land Question (Casely-Hayford) 1:346
"The Truth of Fiction" (Achebe) 1:14
"The Turncoat" (Baraka) 1:125
"turning" (Clifton) 1:463
"The Turtles" (Gaines) 2:857
"Tuskegee" (Cotter) 1:476
25 Poems (Walcott) 3:1799
"Twilight Reverie" (Hughes) 2:1052
"Two-an'-Six" (McKay) 3:1382
"Two seedlings" (Clark) 1:425
Two Songs: Song of Prisoner and Song of Malaya (p'Bitek) 3:1562, 1567
"Two Thoughts on Death" (Cullen) 1:504
Two Thousand Seasons (Armah) 1:44-45
Two Trains Running (Wilson) 3:1972-73
"Two Views of Marilyn Monroe" (Clark) 1:426
"The Two Voices" (Forten) 2:814, 817
"Two Who Crossed a Line (He Crosses)" (Cullen) 1:508
U-bomi bom-fundisi uJohn Knox Bokwe (*Life of J. K. Bokwe*) (Mqhayi) 3:1464
U-Don Jadu (Mqhayi) 3:1460-61, 1464, 1467
U-Mhlekazi u-Hintsa (*Hintsa the Great*) (Mqhayi) 3:1465
U-Mqhayi Wase-Ntab'ozuko (*Mqhayi of the Mountain of Beauty*) (Mqhayi) 3:1465, 1467
U-Samson (Mqhayi) 3:1463, 1466-67
"Ugly Honkies, or The Election Game and How to Win It" (Giovanni) 2:883
Uh Huh; But How Do It Free Us? (Sanchez) 3:1667-68
"Ulysses" (Soyinka) 3:1721-22
"UmHlekazi uHintsa" (Mqhayi) 3:1461, 1467
"Umkhosi WemiDaka" (Mqhayi) 3:1467
"umKhosi wemiDaka" (Mqhayi) 3:1462
The Uncalled (Dunbar) 1:627-28, 630, 633-34, 640
"Uncle Isham Lies A-Dyin" (Johnson) 2:1112
"Uncle Jim" (Cullen) 1:499
"Uncle Peter's House" (Chesnutt) 1:387
"Uncle Simon's Sunday Out" (Dunbar) 1:636
Uncle Tom's Children (Wright) 3:2006, 2008, 2010-12, 2014, 2016-17
"Uncle Wellington's Wives" (Chesnutt) 1:376
Under a Soprano Sky (Sanchez) 3:1669-70
"Under House Arrest" (Brutus) 1:314
"Understanding but not Forgetting" (Madhubuti) 2:1310, 1314
United West Africa (Casely-Hayford) 1:346
"The Unsung Heroes" (Dunbar) 1:626
"Unsuspecting" (Toomer) 3:1765
"UNtsikane" (Mqhayi) 3:1466
Up from Slavery (Washington) 3:1857, 1864, 1867-71, 1873, 1875-77

"Upsilon" (Tolson) 3:1737
"Uriah Preach" (Bennett) 1:185
"The Usurers" (Guillén) 2:914
"The Usurpation" (Clark) 1:421
"Valedictory on Leaving San Francisco" (Bell) 1:173
"The Valley Between" (Marshall) 3:1371
"Variations on Hopkins on the Theme of Child Wonder" (Clark) 1:425
Variations on the Theme of an African Dictatorship (Farah) 2:764, 767, 769
"Vashti" (Harper) 2:979, 980, 983
"Vault centre" (Soyinka) 3:1721
Véhi-Ciosane; ou, Blanche-Genèse, suivi du Mandat (*The Money-Order; with White Genesis*) (Ousmane) 3:1533, 1536-41, 1543-44
"Velorio de Papá Montero" ("Wake for Papa Montero") (Guillén) 2:916, 918
"Verandah" (Walcott) 3:1800
"The Verdict" (Dodson) 1:571
"Verse Forms" (Randall) 3:1606
"La veste" (Roumain) 3:1637
"Vestiges" (Fisher)
  See "The South Lingers On"
"Vesuvius" (Tolson) 3:1740
"A Veteran Falls" (Hughes) 2:1048
The Vici Kid (Fisher) 2:801
"The Vicious Negro" (Cotter) 1:476
"A Victim of Heredity" (Chesnutt) 1:394
"The View from PEN International" (Armah) 1:53
The Village Witch Doctor and Other Stories (Tutuola) 3:1789
"Viney's Free Papers" (Dunbar) 1:633, 636
"The Violent Space (or when your sister sleeps around for money)" (Knight) 2:1212, 1214, 1217
"Virginia Portrait" (Brown) 1:287
"Virtue" (Wheatley) 3:1885
"The Vision of Felipe" (Myers) 3:1478
"The Vision of Lazarus" (Johnson) 2:1108-09
Visions of Dusk (Johnson) 2:1106, 1110, 1112-13
"The Visitor" (Dunbar) 1:626
The Vixens (Yerby) 3:2024, 2026
Voices in the Mirror (Parks) 3:1557
Voltaïque (*Tribal Scars*) (Ousmane) 3:1533, 1545
Voodoo Gods: An Inquiry into Native Myths and Magic in Jamaica and Haiti (Hurston)
  See *Tell My Horse*
"Vulture's Choice" (Clark) 1:421
"Wake for Papa Montero" (Guillén)
  See "Velorio de Papá Montero"
"Wake-Up Niggers" (Madhubuti) 2:1312
"Wakeupworld" (Cullen) 1:493
"Walking Our Boundaries" (Lorde) 2:1282, 1287
"The Wall" (Brooks) 1:256, 267
"The Walls of Jericho" (Dunbar) 1:637, 641
The Walls of Jericho (Fisher) 2:791, 793, 799, 801
"Walter Knox's Record" (Chesnutt) 1:388

The Wanderers (Mphahlele)   3:1447-49,
   1451, 1454-57
"War Poems" (Bell)   1:173
"Washin' Day" (Johnson)   2:1112
"A WASP Woman Visits a Black Junkie
   in Prison" (Knight)   2:1216
"Watchbird" (Bambara)   1:109, 118
"The Watchers" (Braithwaite)   1:244
"The Watching" (Dodson)   1:572
"Water" (Toomer)   3:1763
Water with Berries (Lamming)   2:1232-
   34, 1236-38
"Watermaid" (Okigbo)   3:1526
"The Way of a Woman"
   (Dunbar)   1:637
"De Way Tings Come"
   (Dunbar)   1:626
The Ways of White Folks
   (Hughes)   2:1046-49, 1059, 1062
We (Fuller)   2:838
We a BaddDDD People
   (Sanchez)   3:1650, 1655-58, 1660,
   1662, 1665
"We Free Singers Be" (Knight)   2:1218
"We Have Been Believers"
   (Walker)   3:1834, 1843
"We Real Cool" (Brooks)   1:250, 252
We Walk the Way of the New World
   (Madhubuti)   2:1310, 1317-21
"We Wear the Mask" (Dunbar)   1:631
"The Weary Blues" (Hughes)   2:1055,
   1058, 1064
The Weary Blues (Hughes)   2:1050,
   1054-56, 1062-65
"The Web of Circumstance"
   (Chesnutt)   1:376, 387
*Wedding Band: A Love/Hate Story in
   Black and White* (Childress)   1:408-
   09
Weep Not, Child (Ngugi)   3:1497-99,
   1503, 1507, 1509, 1511
"Welcome Back, Mr. Knight: Love of My
   Life" (Knight)   2:1218
"We'll Have Dinner at Eight"
   (Mphahlele)
      See "Dinner at Eight"
"Weltschmertz" (Dunbar)   1:626, 633
West African Leadership (Casely-
   Hayford)   1:346
West Indies, Ltd.: Poemas
   (Guillén)   2:912-13, 916-18, 922, 924
"What Do You Want America"
   (Davis)   1:520
"What I Have Been Doing Lately"
   (Kincaid)   2:1172
"What Mistah Robin Sais"
   (Johnson)   2:1112
"What the Squirrel Said"
   (Clark)   1:420
What the Wine Sellers Buy
   (Milner)   3:1404-08
What Use Are Flowers?
   (Hansberry)   2:965-66
*What Was the Relationship of the Lone
   Ranger to the Means of Production?: A
   Play in One Act* (Baraka)   1:146
"What's a Daddy? Fathering and
   Marriage" (Madhubuti)   2:1321
"When April Comes" (Johnson)   2:1113
"When de Co'n Pone's Hot"
   (Dunbar)   1:626, 629

*When He Was Free and Young and He
   Used to Wear Silks* (Clarke)   1:441,
   443
"When I Am Dead" (Dodson)   1:571
"When I Die" (Giovanni)   2:893
"When I Nap" (Giovanni)   2:888
"When I Pounded the Pavement"
   (McKay)   3:1395
"When last I ranged and revelled"
   (Brutus)   1:311
When Love Whispers (Ekwensi)   1:645,
   650-51, 659
"When Malindy Sings" (Dunbar)   1:629
When Rain Clouds Gather
   (Head)   2:996-1000
"When the Saints Go Ma'chin Home"
   (Brown)   1:284, 287
"When the Tom-Tom Beats" (Roumain)
      See "Quand bat le tam-tam"
Where Does the Day Go?
   (Myers)   3:1471, 1474, 1479
"White Arrow" (Toomer)   3:1765
"The White City" (McKay)   3:1384
"The White House" (McKay)   3:1399
"White Magic" (Walcott)   3:1803
White Man's Justice, Black Man's Grief
   (Goines)   2:901, 903, 905
"White Pickney" (Bennett)   1:185
"The White Race and Its Heroes"
   (Cleaver)   1:447
"The White Slave" (Johnson)   2:1107
"White Weeds" (Chesnutt)   1:388
"The White Witch" (Johnson)   2:1121
"Who and What is a Negro"
   (Garvey)   2:871
"Who Has Seen The Wind"
   (Dodson)   1:570
Who Is Angelina? (Young)   3:2035-37,
   2039-41, 2043-44
"Who Knows" (Dunbar)   1:631
"Who Said It Was Simple"
   (Lorde)   2:1287
"Who Stand for the Gods"
   (Dunbar)   1:637
Whoreson: The Story of a Ghetto Pimp
   (Goines)   2:902-03, 905
Who's Got His Own (Milner)   3:1403-
   04
Why Are We So Blest? (Armah)   1:43,
   46
"Why It Is Right to Write"
   (Beckham)   1:161
"Why should I Rage" (Clark)   1:424
"Why, Soldier, does it seem to you . . ."
   (Guillén)   2:913
"The Wife of his Youth"
   (Chesnutt)   1:375
*The Wife of his Youth, and Other Stories
   of the Color Line* (Chesnutt)   1:375-
   76, 396
The Wig (Wright)   3:1986-88, 1990-92
*The Wild Hunter in the Bush of the
   Ghosts* (Tutuola)   3:1788-89
"William Lloyd Garrison"
   (Cotter)   1:476
"The Wind among the Poplars"
   (Forten)   2:814, 817
"The Winds of Orisha" (Lorde)   2:1286
"Wine and Water" (Chesnutt)   1:388
Wine in the Wilderness: A Comdey-Drama
   (Childress)   1:404, 407
"Wingless" (Kincaid)   2:1174

"winnie song" (Clifton)   1:467
Winona (Hopkins)   2:1028-29
"Winter" (Giovanni)   2:897
A Winter Piece (Hammon)   2:945, 948
"Wisdom Cometh with the Years"
   (Cullen)   1:486
"The Wisdom of Silence"
   (Dunbar)   1:633, 637, 639-40
"The Wise" (Cullen)   1:504
"A Wish" (Cullen)   1:504, 511
"Witch Doctor" (Hayden)   2:990
The Witch-Herbalist of the Remote Town
   (Tutuola)   3:1787-88
"With All Deliberate Speed"
   (Madhubuti)   2:1321
"The Woman" (Giovanni)   2:893-94
A Woman Called Fancy
   (Yerby)   3:2026
"A Woman of Good Cheer"
   (Johnson)   2:1112
"The Woman Thing" (Lorde)   2:1278
"Women" (Randall)   3:1606
"The Women" (Walker)   3:1816
The Women and the Men
   (Giovanni)   2:889-90, 893, 895
The Women of Brewster Place
   (Naylor)   3:1483-85, 1487-88, 1491-92
"The Wonder Woman"
   (Giovanni)   2:886, 888
Won't Know Till I Get There
   (Myers)   3:1480
"A Word for Me . . . Also"
   (Giovanni)   2:894
"Words for the Hour" (Harper)   2:980,
   982
Words in the Mourning Time
   (Hayden)   2:989-90
"Words to My Love" (Cullen)   1:509
"Words Words Words"
   (Randall)   3:1598
"Wordsworth" (Forten)   2:820
Working with the Hands
   (Washington)   3:1863-64
The World and Africa (Du Bois)   1:606
"The World is a Mighty Ogre"
   (Johnson)   2:1112
The World of Work (Myers)   3:1478
"The Wreck of the Titanic"
   (Tolson)   3:1742
The Wretched of the Earth (Fanon)
      See *Les damnés de la terre*
"Writers as Professionals"
   (Armah)   1:53
Xala (Ousmane)   3:1535, 1540, 1542-
   43, 1545
Yaba Roundabout Murder
   (Ekwensi)   1:645, 651
"Yalluh Hammer" (Walker)   3:1835
Yayá Garcia (Machado de Assis)
      See *Iaiá Garcia*
Year Five of the Algerian Revolution
   (Fanon)
      See *L'an V de la révolution algérienne*
"The Year's first Rain" (Clark)   1:425
Yellow Back Radio Broke-Down
   (Reed)   3:1610-12, 1614-15, 1617,
   1621
"Yesterday I was called nigger" (Guillén)
      See "Ayer me dijeron negro"
"Yet Do I Marvel" (Cullen)   1:493,
   498, 506

You Can't Keep a Good Woman Down
(Walker) **3**:1817-18
"You Had to Go to Funerals"
(Walker) **3**:1814
The Young Landlords (Myers) **3**:1472,
1480

"The Young Men Run"
(Brooks) **1**:267
"The Young Wife" (Walcott) **3**:1804
"Yule-Song: A Memory"
(Braithwaite) **1**:243

Zami: A New Spelling of My Name
(Lorde) **2**:1285
"Zeta" (Tolson) **3**:1736, 1746
"Zeus over Redeye" (Hayden) **2**:989
Zooman and the Sign (Fuller) **2**:830,
834